Pennsylvania Architecture

Pennsylvania Architecture

The Historic American Buildings Survey with catalog entries 1933-1990

Deborah Stephens Burns and Richard J. Webster
with Candace Reed Stern

Foreword by Charles E. Peterson, FAIA

Boyertown Community Library
29 E. Philadelphia Avenue
Boyertown, PA 19512
610/369-0496

Commonwealth of Pennsylvania
Pennsylvania Historical and Museum Commission
Harrisburg, 2000

COMMONWEALTH OF PENNSYLVANIA

Tom Ridge, *Governor*

THE PENNSYLVANIA HISTORICAL AND MUSEUM COMMISSION

Janet S. Klein, *Chairman*
William A. Cornell Sr., *Vice Chairman*
James M. Adovasio
Thomas C. Corrigan, *Representative*
Andrea F. Fitting
Edwin G. Holl, *Senator*
Nancy D. Kolb
John W. Lawrence, M.D.
Stephen R. Maitland, *Representative*
Brian C. Mitchell
LeRoy Patrick
Allyson Y. Schwartz, *Senator*
Allen M. Wenger

Eugene W. Hickok, *Secretary of Education*
ex officio

Cover photos by Nicholas Traub
Front cover: Frontispiece, Isaac Meason House, Mount Braddock, Fayette County
Back cover: Entrance elevation, Isaac Meason House

The activity that is the subject of this publication has been financed in part with Federal funds from the Notional Park Service, U.S. Department of the Interior. However, the contents and opinions do not necessarily reflect the views or policies of the Department of the Interior.

Copyright © 2000 Commonwealth of Pennsylvania

ISBN 0-89271-086-1 cloth
ISBN 0-89271-088-8 soft cover

Contents

Foreword vii
  Charles E. Peterson, FAIA

Preface xi

Acknowledgements xiii

The Historic American Building Survey in Pennsylvania 1933-1990 1
  Deborah Stephens Burns
  Candace Reed Stern

Architecture of Pennsylvania 27
  Richard J. Webster

Region I: Great Valley and Piedmont 203
  Adams, Berks, Bucks, Chester, Cumberland, Dauphin, Delaware, Franklin, Lancaster, Lebanon, Lehigh, Montgomery, Northampton, and York Counties

Region II: Philadelphia 331
  Philadelphia County

Region III: Ridge and Valley 393
  Bedford, Blair, Centre, Clinton, Columbia, Fulton, Huntingdon, Juniata, Lycoming, Mifflin, Montour, Northumberland, Perry, Snyder, and Union Counties

Region IV: Southwestern 419
  Allegheny, Armstrong, Beaver, Butler, Cambria, Fayette, Greene, Indiana, Lawrence, Somerset, Washington, and Westmoreland Counties

Region V: Anthracite and Poconos 473
  Carbon, Lackawanna, Luzerne, Monroe, Pike, Schuylkill and Wayne Counties

Region VI: Allegheny Plateau 523
  Bradford, Cameron, Clarion, Clearfield, Crawford, Elk, Erie, Forest, Jefferson, and Wyoming Counties

Appendix 1: Historic American Buildings Survey Inventory Forms 569

Appendix 2: Photogrametric Plates 573

Appendix 3: Historic American Engineering Record in Pennsylvania 575

Bibliography 581

Index 595

Foreword

It is a privilege and pleasure to join with the Pennsylvania Historical and Museum Commission in recognition of the publication of this record of the Historic American Buildings Survey (HABS) work done in the Keystone state from 1933 to 1990. For the opportunity I thank Janet S. Klein, chairman of the Commission and Brent Glass, executive director.

This book includes the catalog of the records for buildings and building groups scattered across Pennsylvania. It should be pointed out that no state catalog for HABS will ever be complete, because the total product is always increasing in size before the publisher's ink is dry. That attests to the vitality of the survey, which really will never be complete. For Americans are making architectural history faster than it can be recorded.

In total, it took years to create and assemble the vast collection of architectural records now in Washington where the Library of Congress makes them affordable and encourages their publication.

Although it was not colonized early, Pennsylvania has been a leader in several historical fields. Swedish author Peter Kalm, as early as 1749, noticed that Philadelphia was already preserving an old house as a souvenir of its early days.

The beginnings of HABS have often been related. In brief, it was launched by the undersigned in Washington in November of 1933 at the very bottom of the Great Depression. President Franklin D. Roosevelt had just been elected and he set about creating huge projects to help those out of work. They included the professional communities, architects among them.

To keep a short story short, I was then an architect in the National Park Service, recently arrived in Washington. I had seen at close range the architectural staff of the Williamsburg restoration working to familiarize themselves with the eighteenth-century tidewater Virginia buildings. They recognized the importance of making good authentic measured drawings as a method of study. That procedure has been called "descriptive analysis." Many of the young staff were scouring the countryside with the ambition of discovering new examples and writing books about them.

With that background, I proposed a nationwide program to employ architects to make measured drawings of selected historic structures. This got a quick approval at the highest political levels and work began almost at once. The procedure was to recruit talented draftsmen with the enthusiastic help of the American Institute of Architects. The drawings were to be deposited in the fine arts division of the Library of Congress. There Dr. Leicester B. Holland, FAIA was ready. All this was speedily arranged and an impressive exhibition of fine drawings was opened in January of 1934 at the Smithsonian Institution's National Museum in Washington. Examples from Pennsylvania were included.

There had been earlier programs for the unemployed like that by the Royal Institute of British Architects. Philadelphia had considered such work a bit earlier. In 1920 Miss Frances A. Wister, with a modest grant by Mrs. Cyrus H. K. Curtis, began a movement that eventuated some years later as "The Old Philadelphia Survey." Architect Sydney E. Martin supervised the work, and by October 1931 fifty-seven draftsmen had produced 407 excellent measured drawings and 125 photographs had been taken. The collection was then deposited in the art department of the Free Library.

That campaign may have encouraged Pittsburgh architects at the other end of the state. The Western Pennsylvania Architectural Survey grew out of the Committee for the Preservation of Historic Monuments of the Pittsburgh Chapter of the American Institute of Architects, Charles M. Stotz, chairman. In October 1932, a modest grant by the Buhl Foundation set the committee into action. A book of record, *The Early Architecture of Western Pennsylvania*, published in 1936, is a masterpiece of text, measured drawings, and photographs. The eminent architectural historian Fiske Kimball, invited to write an introduction, said of the Stotz campaign: "In all the flood of recent books on the architecture of different states none surpass this one in comprehensive, scholarly thoroughness and wealth of new material." The Western Pennsylvania Survey under Stotz joined with HABS in due course and continued to make quality drawings.

The overwhelming demands of World War II brought HABS to a near standstill. Later, postwar prosperity pretty well employed the whole of the architectural profession. But the need for measured drawings on which to base restoration plans forced the National Park Service to find new sources of talent. It was proposed to recruit talented students from architectural schools around the country to form measuring teams during their summer recess. It was soon demonstrated at Philadelphia that—under competent direction—quality drawings could be produced. When funds were appropriated by Congress for the "Mission 66" program in the national parks, HABS was again activated all across the country. To increase the coverage, more emphasis was placed on photography. "Photo-Data books" were prepared for important buildings where measuring teams were unavailable.

How to quickly expand to get national coverage was a problem. In 1958 the Chester County Historical Society at West Chester carried out a test under the direction of Bart Anderson. It built up substantial dossiers on selected historical structures. A contract was then made with that society to write up one hundred representative structures, and the National Park Service provided an architectural photographer. This project was completed on time with success, and celebrated at a formal dinner.

Then it could be roughly calculated that—there being 3,000 counties in the United States—it might take 300,000 individual projects to cover the whole country. That seemed to put a stop to loose talk then current about "completing HABS."

The earliest records of the HABS were everywhere limited to the bigger cities where the architects lived. But the campaign spread quickly across Pennsylvania. A 1934 catalog listed 8 localities represented, 17 in 1935, and 104 in 1938. At the latter they had managed to make sixty sheets of drawings of the unique early medieval wooden Kloster [Ephrata Cloister] group northeast of Lancaster.

As the size of the national product grew, certain states proposed to publish their own catalogs. By 1976, ten states had published.

In the beginning, only buildings built before 1860 were considered for recording. That was because few architectural historians had studied structures built after the Civil War. I remember when Joseph Downs of New York published a study of the Lyceum in Alexandria, Virginia, a venture into the Greek Revival temple. And Howard Major's 1926 book *The Domestic Architecture of the Early American Republic: The Greek Revival* on that period was unique. All that has now changed. In recent years Victorian architecture has finally come into its own, and historians have even ventured into the late twentieth century! I have often joked that nowadays, anything with ten feet of jigsaw is eligible for consideration as a national monument.

The techniques of measuring structures have advanced in recent years. Starting with the use of photogrammetry by Professor Perry Borchers of Ohio State University in 1958, technology has developed many novel procedures. But they should never completely supersede hands-on work. The old-fashioned use of rules and tapes by HABS has introduced a large percentage of the historic preservation leaders working today.

Charles E. Peterson FAIA

Society Hill
Philadelphia
August, 1998

Preface

This volume surveys Pennsylvania's three hundred years of architecture, describes geographical and cultural influences on development patterns within the Commonwealth's major geo-cultural regions, and catalogs the Historic American Buildings Survey (HABS) holdings for each of those regions up to 1990.

For ongoing collections such as HABS, any published catalog is unavoidably dated; architectural documentation is always being added to the HABS collection. Not included here, for example, are some seventy-five buildings in Montgomery County recorded in 1994, or the loss of such buildings as the Presbyterian Church, Pittsfield, Warren County, and the Humphrey-Rockwell House, Union City, Erie County.

The historical essays would have benefited from a number of articles as well as several books published in the early 1990s, after this manuscript was completed. The four most significant books are *The Progressive Architecture of Frederick G. Scheibler, Jr.*, by Martin Aurand (Pittsburgh: University of Pittsburgh Press, 1994); *Louis I. Kahn: In the Realm of Architecture* by David B. Brownlee (New York: Rizzoli, 1991); *Architecture after Richardson: Regionalism before Modernism–Longfellow, Alden, and Harlow in Boston and Pittsburgh* by Margaret Henderson Floyd (Chicago: University of Chicago Press, 1994); *Oley Valley Heritage: The Colonial Years, 1700-1775* by Philip E. Pendleton (Birdsboro, Pa.: Pennsylvania German Society), 1994. To compensate for the articles' absence from the text and notes, the bibliography has been brought up to date through 1995.

Pennsylvania's architecture has not attracted scholars' attention to the degree that buildings of the early South and New England have. Consequently there is no great body of publication to consult for a statewide survey such as this. Also, because the limited literature is skewed toward early high-style buildings in the

Philadelphia region and because HABS surveys in Pennsylvania have not been comprehensive, this book should be viewed as a ground-breaking work on Pennsylvania's architectural heritage. It serves more appropriately as a review of available scholarship and a suggestion of needs and opportunities for study. It is a starting point. The direction of recent scholarship is suggested by the bibliographical entries of the late 1980s and the 1990s: short works published in *Perspectives in Vernacular Architecture* and the HABS/HAER publications produced in cooperation with the Southwestern Pennsylvania Heritage Preservation Commission.

Deborah Stephens Burns is an architectural historian, formerly with the Historic American Buildings Survey. While employed there, she co-authored the HABS catalog, *Shaker Built*. She received a bachelor's degree in art and architectural history from American University and a master's degree in American studies and historic preservation from George Washington University. Ms. Burns is currently the executive director of The American Institute of Architects Northern Virginia Chapter and lives in Alexandria, Virginia.

Richard J. Webster is chairman of the Department of History at West Chester University. A native of Towanda, Dr. Webster received his bachelor's degree in American Civilization at Lafayette College, was a Fellow in the University of Delaware Winterthur Program in Early American Culture, and received his Ph.D. in American Civilization from the University of Pennsylvania. Dr. Webster is the author of *Philadelphia Preserved: Catalog of the Historic American Buildings Survey*, which he prepared at the Philadelphia Historical Commission.

Candace Reed Stern earned a bachelor's degree in political science at Columbia University. A fascination with historic architecture led her to earn her master's degree in American Studies and Historic Preservation at George Washington University. Between 1976 and 1985 Ms. Stern worked as a consulting architectural historian for the Historic American Buildings Survey, the National Trust for Historic Preservation, and the Pennsylvania Avenue Development Corporation. Although architectural history is no longer her vocation, it remains a lifelong source of interest and study.

Acknowledgments

This book has been made possible by the Pennsylvania Historical and Museum Commission, Brent D. Glass, executive director, and its Bureau for Historic Preservation (BHP), Brenda Barrett, director. It was the bureau's initiative to see that the state with the largest number of HABS documented sites have its own state catalog. We would especially like to thank Dan G. Deibler and P. Gregory Ramsey of the BHP's Division of Preservation Services. In his capacity as contract manager, Dan offered valuable guidance and a thorough review of all our work during both its writing and editing. Greg Ramsey assisted us with an earlier version of the catalog manuscript. We also thank Tobi Gilson, who skillfully made the many revisions of this text. The Division of Publications provided copyediting and production management for the book, and Kathleen Alsvary designed the cover and text pages.

The Historic American Buildings Survey was very generous in its support of this project and offered all its resources to help us complete a Pennsylvania catalog. The HABS staff was always willing and able to help with our many requests and questions. We would like to express special gratitude to Dr. Robert Kapsch, former chief of HABS, for his steady support and encouragement. James C. Massey, the first chief of HABS, generously supplied valuable information on HABS's work in Pennsylvania from the 1950s on. Paul Dolinsky, the current chief of HABS, provided invaluable assistance.

The Library of Congress Prints and Photographs Division allowed us access to all its records, and we extend special thanks to Mary M. Ison, C. Ford Peatross, and Joyce Nalewajk for their suggestions and help.

Charles E. Peterson, the originator of HABS and a Philadelphian, has been an advocate for the publication of a HABS Pennsylvania catalog for years. He offered us unlimited support, a generous amount of time, valuable suggestions, and his extensive knowledge of people and events that shaped the survey's work in Pennsylvania.

Thanks also to Bernard L. Herman, Walter C. Kidney, Michael J. Lewis, Elizabeth R. Marsh, E. Lynn Miller, and Mary Elizabeth Pennypacker, who wrote regional essays for the earlier catalog manuscript. While the essays are not part of this volume, the authors contributed valuable information for each region, supplied sources for the bibliography, and thoroughly reviewed the entries for their regions, supplying corrections, updates, and additional information. Their knowledge and assistance is greatly appreciated.

We must also acknowledge the countless people throughout Pennsylvania, members of historical societies, planning commissions, local architects and historians, local and federal government employees and officials, owners of historic buildings, etc., who answered our many questions and whose valuable information contributed greatly to the accuracy of this catalog. Special thanks to the late Alice Kent Schooler, who supplied much helpful information and suggestions on buildings in the Great Valley and Piedmont Region. We are also grateful for Mary Sweeney's prompt and pleasant service in obtaining scores of books and articles through interlibrary loan at West Chester University's Francis Harvey Green Library, Professor Harry Schalck of West Chester University for his generous help on Berks County history and buildings, Professor Norbert Soldon, of the same institution, for his suggestions on the Anthracite Region, and Thomas L. Jennings for his help with some Wysox and Towanda buildings. Also helpful was Rick Meyer, architectural historian; John Milner Associates in West Chester; Helen Landmesser, former museum receptionist of the Bradford County Historical Society; Rosemary Philips, former librarian of the Chester County Historical Society; Laurie Refini, Chester County archivist; Robert Ilisevich, former archivist of the Crawford County Historical Society; Robert Currin, president of the Potter County Historical Society; Mary Ruth Kelly, former librarian of the Wyoming Historical and Geological Society; Bryan Van Sweden, formerly of Historic York, Inc.; Richard Tyler, historic preservation officer, Philadelphia Historical Commission; and Tony Wrenn, former archivist of the American Institute of Architects.

Special thanks are due to John A. Burns, a Pennsylvanian and HABS architect, who reviewed much of the manuscript, assisted in the selection of illustrations, drew the maps for the catalog, and offered helpful advice along the way.

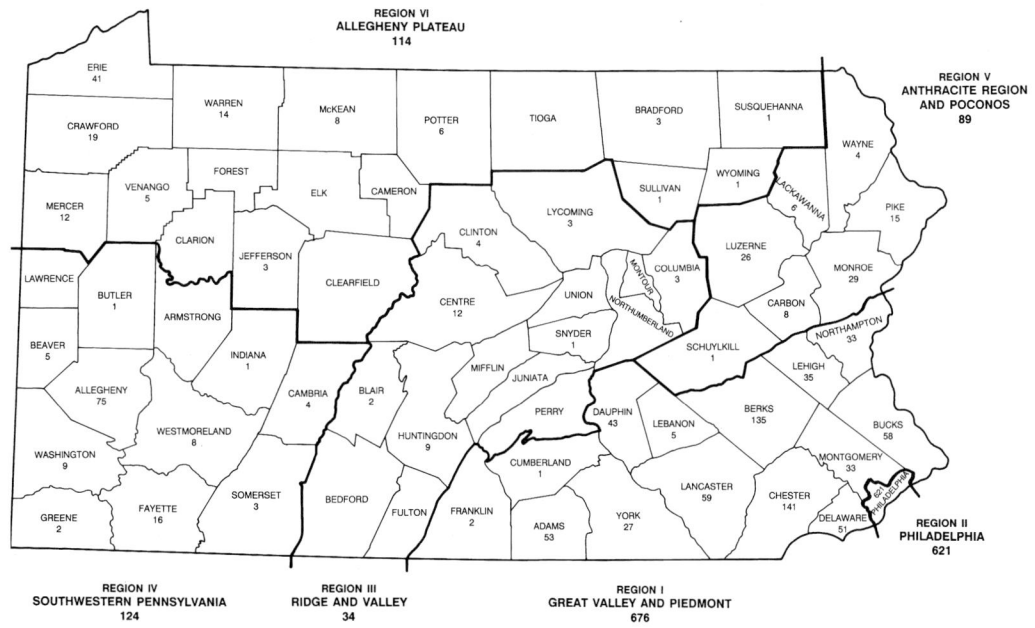

DISTRIBUTION OF HABS DOCUMENTATION BY REGION

Number of HABS recorded sites are shown by county and region. John A. Burns, delineator, 1990

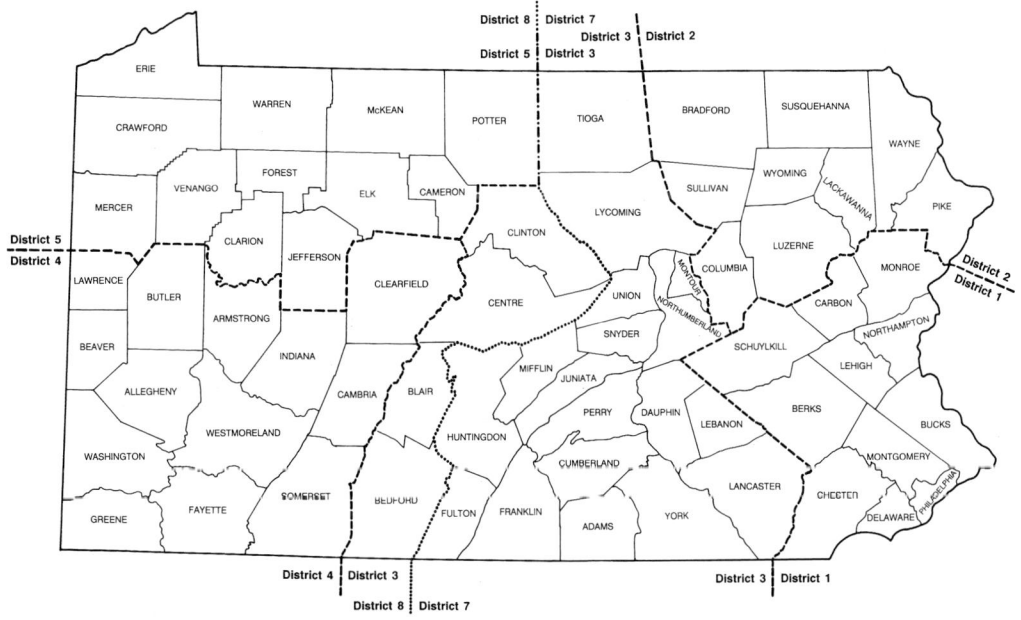

ORIGINAL HABS DISTRICTS IN PENNSYLVANIA

1933 NATIONAL DISTRICTS ··········
1934 STATE DISTRICTS ------

Districts were based on American Institute of Architects local chapters. John A. Burns, delineator, 1990

The Historic American Buildings Survey in Pennsylvania 1933-1990

*Deborah Stephens Burns and
Candace Reed Stern*

THE PURPOSE OF THE HISTORIC AMERICAN BUILDINGS SURVEY

The Historic American Buildings Survey (HABS), part of the National Park Service within the United States Department of the Interior, is an ongoing program to document American structures of architectural and historical interest. HABS was the first comprehensive federal program to survey and document American architecture. Since it began in 1933, HABS has recorded over 23,000 historic structures throughout the United States, the Virgin Islands, Puerto Rico, and the Panama Canal Zone. HABS documentation consists of measured drawings, photographs, and written data spanning four centuries of construction and covering all types and styles of structures from log cabins to state capitols, covered bridges to skyscrapers, and smokehouses to factories. There are over 47,000 sheets of drawings, 129,000 photographs, and 72,000 pages of written data. The Commonwealth of Pennsylvania has the distinction of having the greatest number of sites, over 1,600, recorded up to 1990 by HABS. HABS materials are archived in the Prints and Photographs Division of the Library of Congress in Washington, D.C. The HABS collection is one of the most extensively used collections at the Library of Congress. Professionals and laymen use its documentary materials for research, publication, and restoration purposes.

The historical forces which led William Penn and his followers to settle in Pennsylvania brought wave upon wave of immigrants to North America. The diversity of these immigrant groups produced the complex legacy of Pennsylvania history. American architecture, the buildings built as shelters and for industry, commerce, and public use, embody this history. The study of American architecture as an artifact of our nation's history helps us to understand our nation's past, but many of these artifacts are vanishing. In the nearly sixty years since HABS began its documentation of the built environment, approximately one-third of all documented sites have been demolished for urban expansion or better roads and highways, or have been lost through neglect. It is not always worthwhile or even possible to transform historic structures into museums. These endangered buildings can, however, be "preserved" by the documentation process.

The following pages tell the history of HABS, especially in Pennsylvania. Although the essay examines the entire state, it is generally light on details concerning Philadelphia, so thoroughly covered by Charles E. Peterson in his essay in *Philadelphia Preserved*, the HABS catalog for Philadelphia authored by Richard J. Webster and published in 1976. For more information on the Philadelphia catalog, books and articles on the history of HABS, and other HABS state catalogs, the reader is directed to the bibliography at the end of this book.

The Depression Era: 1933-1941

1933—The Great Depression—foreclosures—soup kitchens—breadlines—shantytowns—twelve million Americans unemployed. Franklin Delano Roosevelt was inaugurated the thirty-second President of the United States on March 4. In the first "Hundred Days" of his administration a series of far-ranging legislative initiatives was enacted. Among these was the Federal Emergency Relief Act (FERA), which appropriated $500 million for direct relief to the states, counties, cities, and towns of America. Roosevelt appointed Harry Hopkins, a brilliant and dedicated social worker, to administer the FERA program. Hopkins insisted that America's unemployed wanted jobs, not government handouts. By November 1933, Hopkins had realized that the FERA program could not move quickly enough to create jobs for the unemployed. He therefore persuaded Roosevelt to create the Civil Works Administration (CWA) as a temporary organization to speed employment. Immediately, the CWA requested recommendations for potential public projects, and within a month over four million people were put to work for the federal government on projects of benefit to the public. In less than five months Hopkins had spent $1 billion. The CWA's work relief program proved to be one of the most effective morale boosters of the New Deal.

It was at this point that Charles E. Peterson, an architect and chief of the Eastern Division, Branch of Plans and Design, of the National Park Service (NPS), developed the concept of a national architectural survey. In a November 13, 1933 memorandum to the director of the Park Service, he proposed a national architectural survey that would offer employment to the many unemployed architects and draftsmen, who would document what was known to be a quickly vanishing stock of significant early American structures. Within two weeks the CWA had committed $442,000 to the creation of the Historic American Buildings Survey, "a ten weeks unemployment relief program for one thousand architects and architectural draftsmen."[1] Work began immediately.

A national office was organized in Washington, D.C., to administer the program with the assistance of a national advisory committee. The country was divided into thirty-nine districts, each administered by a district office and advised by its own advisory committee. Local chapters of the American Institute of Architects (AIA) were called upon to nominate district officers. The national office set standards and developed guidelines for documentation, but the selection of sites to be recorded, the choice of unemployed architects to hire, and the actual supervision and approval of work rested with the district officer. The CWA funded HABS until May 1, 1934. During these first months the Survey employed 772 architects and draftsmen and produced documentation on 880 structures nationwide.

Pennsylvania was divided into two districts. District Seven, eastern Pennsylvania, comprised the counties east of and including Tioga, Lycoming, Union, Mifflin, Huntingdon, and Fulton Counties. E. Perot Bissell was appointed district officer, located in Philadelphia.[2] District Seven was authorized to hire as many as forty-two employees. Western Pennsylvania—the counties west of those named above—was organized as District Eight. Charles M. Stotz, Pittsburgh, was the district officer.[3] His personnel limit was set at forty-one.

As soon as the district officers were assigned and work was begun, the central office in Washington, D.C., headed by architect John P. O'Neill, began to publish a series of bulletins that provided guidelines and directions for the Survey. These bulletins covered everything from documentation standards and instructions for measuring buildings to directions for completing travel vouchers and applying for leave time.[4]

The volume of documentary materials grew during the early months of the Survey, and it soon became necessary to find a suitable place to archive them. As there was yet no National Archives, the national office arranged with Leicester Holland, chief of the Division of Fine Arts at the Library of Congress, to house the collection at the library in the Pictorial Archives of Early American Architecture.[5] The library was especially suited to maintain the HABS collection and to make its reproducible materials available to the public. In order to publicize the material, a list of the records was prepared in the spring of 1934 and an exhibition of selected drawings and photographs was mounted by the Smithsonian Institution's National Museum in Washington, D.C.

In May 1934 CWA funding for the HABS program ended. Continued federal funding for HABS projects was uncertain and difficult to obtain. The Public Works Administration (PWA) had some money available which kept HABS going at a reduced rate until July 1934, when the Federal Emergency Relief Administration (FERA) became operational with funds available for state relief projects. District offices in twelve states, including Pennsylvania, were able to continue the Survey using funds from FERA during 1934 and 1935. While the Survey could be funded at the state level by FERA, several small grants from the WPA funded the national HABS office in Washington, D.C.

When the future of HABS seemed in doubt, the three principal organizations backing HABS, the National Park Service, the American Institute of Architects, and the Library of Congress, joined to produce an agreement to support HABS and to promote its establishment as a permanent organization. While offering no funds to sustain the program, they formalized their commitment to the continuation of a national architectural survey program on July 13, 1934 by signing the Tripartite Agreement. The National Park Service was to administer the program, the American Institute of Architects was to nominate district officers and advise, and the Library of Congress was to house and maintain the collection. The organization of HABS is still based on this agreement. HABS is operated by the National Park Service, the records are archived in the Prints and Photographs Division of the Library of Congress, where they are made available to the public, and the American Institute of Architects provides technical advice and assistance through its Committee on Historic Resources.

The three signatories of the Tripartite Agreement made further plans to continue the documentation begun by HABS, with or without government funding. They decided to continue gathering graphic records of historic buildings from local architects, educational institutions, and governmental agencies. In late 1934, under the Tripartite Agreement, the original thirty-nine districts were divided into sixty-seven to conform with the local chapters of the American Institute of Architects. Pennsylvania was now divided into five districts.[6] Local AIA chapter members were authorized to select a district officer to oversee the continuing HABS work and to gather appropriate records. The national advisory committee was continued. The National Park Service agreed to supply the standard sheets on which drawings would be delineated and to maintain the quality of the documentation. The Library of Congress agreed to continue to house the collection. In this manner the Survey could continue its work with or without a federally funded HABS office in Washington, D.C. By the end of January 1935, seventy-six people were employed by HABS in the five Pennsylvania districts. All were engaged in projects funded by the FERA.[7]

In 1935 the Supreme Court struck down Title I of the National Industrial Recovery Act. Title II, the Works Projects Administration (WPA), however, was allowed to stand. Administered by Harry Hopkins, the WPA had set up numerous projects to employ artists, musicians, writers, and other "white collar" workers. By April 30, 1935, most of the state-supported FERA projects were closed or winding down.[8] HABS applied for and received funding from the WPA, which enabled the Survey once again to operate at a national level. A HABS office within the National Park Service was established with John P. O'Neill as director and four experienced district officers were selected to act as division chiefs under the WPA program. Hiring began early in 1936 and once again district officers received a salary.[9] WPA funding was available until June 30, 1937, when HABS was forced once again to rely on state-distributed funds, with the small central office financed by WPA money. By 1939 the national office had to close. Some local HABS work was carried on into 1940 and catalogs of all the sites recorded were published in 1938 and 1941. The outbreak of World War II effectively shut down HABS and most other non-military programs—as funds were directed toward defense—and all available manpower was pressed into military service. During the 1940s, the HABS collection at the Library of Congress grew by donations only.

A vast amount of recording was completed during the Depression years of the Survey. Despite the uncertainties of the times and the vagaries of federal funding, HABS architects and draftsmen proved to be a dedicated and determined group. In Pennsylvania, a tremendous amount of work was accomplished. Each of the five districts produced substantial documentary materials. District One (with eleven counties) concentrated heavily on Philadelphia, but also worked in Delaware, Bucks, Montgomery, and Northampton Counties. District Two (with nine counties) managed to document something in every one of its counties, although the work was heavily centered in Luzerne County, where twenty-five structures were documented.

District Three (with the largest number of counties, twenty-two) concentrated its efforts in Centre, Dauphin, Lancaster, and Adams Counties. They documented the Ephrata Cloister in Lancaster County with sixty sheets of drawings and 107 photographs. District Four (with thirteen counties) worked in Allegheny, Fayette, Somerset, Westmoreland, and Butler Counties. One great contribution of this district was the documentation of the U.S. Allegheny Arsenal, whose buildings were based on designs by Benjamin Latrobe, but are now almost entirely gone. Finally, District Five (with twelve counties) recorded a large number of properties in Erie, Crawford, Mercer, Venango, Warren, and McKean Counties, capturing many fine examples of rural Greek Revival architecture.

Post World War II: 1954-1966

In 1954 the National Park Service (NPS) established its Eastern Office of Design and Construction in Philadelphia. Charles E. Peterson was named Supervising Architect for Historic Structures of the NPS with primary responsibility for the restoration of Independence National Historical Park. Peterson was able to direct some HABS work—primarily restoration plans for NPS properties—from his Philadelphia office, but this was a modest effort compared to that during the Depression.

It was not until the NPS implemented a program called Mission 66, a ten-year plan to upgrade the national park system by 1966, that HABS received funding. Beginning July 1, 1957, HABS began to function as a federal program out of Peterson's Philadelphia office. As this was a national program not limited to NPS properties, there was a second office established in San Francisco and two smaller offices in Washington, D.C., and Chicago. It was during the time of Mission 66 that HABS became a permanently funded part of the National Park Service.

One of the primary goals of the Survey during the Depression was to provide jobs for unemployed architects using a highly labor-intensive form of recording. At that time, the professional architects available used a recording technique which emphasized detailed, measured drawings. By the late 1950s, there was no longer a pool of unemployed professional architects to draw from. A new approach to conducting a national architectural survey was needed. Based on the work performed by architecture students at Independence National Historical Park, HABS decided to employ student architects to produce the documentation formerly prepared by professional architects. Students were organized into summer recording teams and supervised by a professor of architecture at the site and by personnel from the HABS office. While teams of architecture students produced measured drawings to HABS standards, they learned about historical architecture. HABS trained many students who later were to become leaders in the fields of architectural restoration and historic preservation. James C. Massey, the first to hold the title "Chief" of HABS, began as a student architect from the University of Pennsylvania in 1953, and was assigned to work full-time for HABS under Peterson in 1957.

The practice of using summer teams of student architects to produce measured drawings, and student historians and architectural historians to prepare written data under professional supervision, with a professional photographer to produce photographs, is still employed by HABS today.

The success of HABS summer recording teams and the value of their documentation as an aid to planning, preservation, and restoration programs were soon recognized. Local governments, historical societies, educational institutions, and even private owners realized the benefits of having their structures recorded by HABS. In order to meet the rising demand for summer recording teams despite limited federal funding, HABS began cooperative recording projects in which local sponsors contributed part of the cost of bringing a team to their community. This practice is carried on today.

Pennsylvania had many valuable recording projects in the 1950s and 1960s. One of the first summer-student projects was conducted at Gettysburg National Military Park in Adams County in 1957 and 1958. Drawings, photographs, and written data were produced to aid the Park Service's restoration of structures associated with the Battle of Gettysburg.[10] HABS then returned to Gettysburg for four more summers, between 1984 and 1987, to record additional farm complexes associated with the battle. This cooperative effort involved HABS, the Mid-Atlantic Regional Office of the NPS, and the Gettysburg National Military Park. During the 1950s and 1960s, to aid another NPS restoration, HABS drawings were prepared of Hopewell Village National Historic Site in Chester and Berks Counties.[11]

Local groups also worked with HABS in cooperative recording projects. In Delaware County, HABS joined with the Radnor Historical Society to document buildings in Radnor Township threatened by demolition with photographs and written data.[12] Two similar projects were completed in Lancaster and York Counties in the 1960s.

The Survey has often worked closely with colleges and universities, as in the Schuylkill Valley Survey. In this 1958 project the University of Pennsylvania School of Fine Arts, under contract to the NPS, recorded numerous examples of Pennsylvania-German architecture in the Oley Valley of Berks County.[13] Working with both a college and a local group, HABS assigned a summer recording team in 1968 to document the Moravian buildings in Bethlehem in cooperation with Historic Bethlehem, Inc. and Moravian College. The project was undertaken as part of the restoration of local Moravian buildings.[14]

The largest group of measured drawings prepared for Pennsylvania during the 1960s came from the Carnegie Institute of Technology, Department of Architecture, in Pittsburgh. As part of a course taught by Professor John Pekruhn, students measured and drew structures according to HABS standards and on HABS sheets. These drawings were then donated to the HABS collection. One of their most ambitious projects was the Allegheny County Courthouse and Jail in Pittsburgh, designed by Henry H. Richardson. While most of their work was centered in Allegheny County, buildings in adjacent counties were also documented.

During this period of recording activity, there was talk of "completing" HABS by documenting all the historic structures in the country. One way suggested to achieve this ambitious plan was to undertake a national, county-by-county HABS survey. In order to test this approach, Chester County, Pennsylvania, was selected as a sample county. Chester County was selected for its wide range of historic structures, its proximity to the HABS office in Philadelphia, and because its local historical society was willing to participate in the project. Working with the Chester County Historical Society, one hundred buildings were chosen in 1958 to be documented with photographs and written data.[15] When the Chester County project was completed, it was clear that this type of project was too ambitious to carry out in all 3,000 counties across the nation. The Chester County Survey convinced HABS that the Survey should be an open-ended archives, constantly striving to add to its collection.

Recent History of HABS: 1966-1989

Mission 66, the ten-year program initiated by the National Park Service to update the nation's national park system by 1966, institutionalized the HABS program within the NPS by the allocation of federal funds to the Survey. The documentation and survey work done by HABS during the 1950s engaged the federal government, in a limited fashion, in the tasks of historic preservation. However, it soon became evident that there was a great need for a consolidated national historic preservation program. The National Historic Preservation Act of 1966 created the Office of Archeology and Historic Preservation (OAHP) within the NPS and gave legislative authority to a national preservation program. This office consolidated HABS with the National Landmarks Program (begun in 1935), the newly created National Register of Historic Places, Technical Preservation Services, Interagency Archeological Services, and the Grants-in-Aid Program. HABS closed its San Francisco and Chicago offices and moved its Philadelphia office to Washington, D.C. James Massey moved from Philadelphia to Washington to serve as the first Chief of HABS. As part of the Office of Archeology and Historic Preservation, HABS was no longer an isolated federal preservation program.

In 1969 the Historic American Engineering Record (HAER) was created. While HABS had always recorded engineering and industrial sites such as mills, bridges, iron furnaces, and factories, HAER was established to concentrate exclusively on industrial sites and to provide expertise in industrial technology. The decision to create a program to document historical engineering and industrial sites was in part a product of the growing interest in the nation's industrial heritage and in part a response to the rapid acceleration in technological development and consequent loss of older technologies. Although HABS and HAER have always cooperated, today they are administratively joined as the HABS/HAER Division.

Over its nearly seven decades of existence, the HABS program has been administered by several people. Charles E. Peterson, founder of HABS, served as its first administrative head in the 1950s. Those who have been designated "Chief of HABS" were James C. Massey, John C. Poppeliers, and Kenneth L. Anderson. The first chief of the combined HABS/HAER Division (1980) was Robert J. Kapsch.

The 1970s and 1980s witnessed numerous administrative changes, but the basic functions of HABS and its fellow preservation offices continued intact.[16] Today the HABS/HAER Division is part of the Cultural Resources Programs of the National Park Service, under the Department of the Interior. Preservation programs have been established in five of the Park Service's regional offices. The Mid-Atlantic Regional Office, located in Philadelphia, serves the Northeast. The HABS Washington office works closely with the regional offices and the Mid-Atlantic Region is a strong supporter of HABS programs.

Some major changes in HABS recording responsibilities occurred in the 1970s and 1980s because of Presidential Executive Order 11593, signed in 1971. This Executive Order, which was later codified and expanded in the National Historic Preservation Act Amendments of 1980, mandated that a historic building adversely affected by a federally funded project must be documented according to HABS/HAER standards. This documentation was expected to mitigate the loss of significant historic structures. The regulations further required federal agencies to inventory historic structures under their control and to nominate appropriate structures to the National Register of Historic Places. HABS and HAER have frequently acted as consultants to federal agencies complying with these regulations. To facilitate the federal process, HABS and HAER have established and maintained uniform standards for documenting historically and architecturally significant sites subject to the federally mandated documentation process. These standards were published in 1983 in *The Secretary of the Interior's Standards and Guidelines for Architectural and Engineering Documentation*. There have been numerous Pennsylvania recording projects as a result of the federally mandated program of mitigative documentation. One project was the Tulpehocken Creek Survey, a one-year recording project undertaken in 1976 in Berks County. HABS and HAER, in cooperation with the U.S. Army Corps of Engineers, recorded structures to be moved or demolished with the construction of Blue Marsh Lake.[17] The Pennsylvania-German farms recorded by this project were well-planned units which revealed some unusual log construction once the siding was removed.

A similar recording project was undertaken prior to the 1971 Executive Order. Although not yet required by law to produce mitigative documentation, the U.S. Army Corps of Engineers funded several HABS summer teams in the Delaware Water Gap National Recreation Area between 1967 and 1971.[18] As the border between New Jersey and Pennsylvania, the Water Gap area affects sections of Monroe, Pike, and Northampton Counties in Pennsylvania as well as several counties in New Jersey. The project evolved in response to plans prepared by the Corps for the proposed Tocks Island Reservoir, which called for the demolition of many farmsteads in the Water Gap area. In cooperation with the National Recreation Area, HABS teams prepared mitigative documentation for dozens of farmhouses and their outbuildings. Both the Delaware Water Gap and the Tulpehocken Creek surveys produced an extensive collection of drawings, photographs, and written data which illustrate the cultural systems of two river valleys and some interesting Pennsylvania farm complexes, now mostly gone.

Recently, two extensive urban mitigative projects were completed. In 1984 and 1985 eight structures in the Penn-Liberty area of Pittsburgh were documented for HABS prior to their demolition as part of a project by Allegheny International Corporation to develop the area as a corporate and cultural center. Then, in 1985, numerous two- and three-story row houses in the Allison Hill area of Harrisburg were documented by HABS before their demolition as part of the city's Community Development Block Grant Program. There have been numerous smaller projects across the state.

In 1983 HABS joined The Athenaeum of Philadelphia and the American Institute of Architects to establish the Charles E. Peterson Prize. The prize is an annual cash award given for the best set of measured drawings of a historic structure produced by students and donated to HABS. The prize honors Charles E. Peterson, FAIA, founder of HABS. While numerous structures across the country have been documented for the Peterson Prize, to date only one Pennsylvania site has been the subject of prize drawings—McBurney Manor and McAlevys Fort General Store in Huntingdon County, recorded by students from Pennsylvania State University in 1981. These drawings also have the distinction of being the first set of Pennsylvania HABS drawings done on a computer.

HABS also acquires documentation through donations from such sources as architects, historical societies, other federal agencies, and owners of historic structures. One of the largest collections donated, involving structures in Pennsylvania, was a series of photographs taken by Charles H. Dornbusch, AIA. During the summer of 1941 Dornbusch, a Chicago architect, conducted a photographic survey of approximately 150 southeastern Pennsylvania barns. This survey, known as the Pennsylvania German Barn Recording Project, was sponsored by a Langely Fellowship from the American Institute of Architects. A traveling exhibit of the barn photos was circulated nationally in 1943 and Dornbusch published a book in 1956 based on his survey, *Pennsylvania German Barns*.[19] Dornbusch donated his negatives and photographs to HABS and they were recently incorporated into the Survey's collection.

The National Park Service initiated a multi-year project in 1986 to promote "preservation, tourism, and economic development in a nine-county region of southwestern Pennsylvania."[20] The focus of America's Industrial Heritage Project (AIHP) is on Pennsylvania sites associated with iron and steel making, coal, and transportation. As part of this project, HABS and HAER are involved in surveying and documenting historic, industrial, engineering, and architectural works.

As part of the AIHP, HABS/HAER summer teams have surveyed entire towns and neighborhoods and documented numerous individual structures, such as the coal company towns of Star Junction in Fayette County, Windber in Somerset County, and Colver in Cambria County; industrial sites recorded by HAER in Blair and Cambria Counties; Pennsylvania Canal towns of Alexandria in Huntingdon County and Saltsburg in Indiana County; and four historic neighborhoods and several individual structures in Johnstown. Nine publications concerning these projects were published between 1989 and 1991 and further volumes are planned.[21] This project has produced considerable documentation on the industrial and architectural heritage of this region.[22]

Types of Sites Documented by HABS

The December 20, 1933 bulletin published a list of building types suitable for documentation which is as valid today as it was then.[23] The Survey proposed to document not only houses, churches, and public buildings, but also bridges, barns, shops, rural outbuildings, log houses, and mining settlements. If the concept of documenting the more mundane structures of the American landscape was farsighted, the scope of the Survey was strictly limited to buildings constructed before 1860. This terminus date was selected to insure the inclusion of Greek Revival structures and effectively excluded all the Victorian styles, which were then considered unworthy of documentation.

In 1957 the new HABS program advanced the original terminus date from 1860 to 1900. In 1966 HABS again adjusted the age limit of buildings to be consistent with the fifty-year guideline which had been developed as part of the criteria for eligibility in the National Register of Historic Places. The post-World War II building boom, urban renewal, the interstate highway system, and other advances in transportation threatened many historic structures. Buildings became obsolete more quickly. At the same time, more building types from different periods were recognized as significant. The effect was to substantially increase the number of buildings eligible for HABS documentation. With each passing year, this number increases.

While the Survey does record structures of great architectural and historical significance, it is not limited to buildings with pure style or connections with famous persons. A variety of building types, styles, and associations are documented. The selection of what to document at any given time depends on many things, such as significance, rarity, threat of demolition, planned restoration, cooperative project, federal ownership, and of course funding. Sites documented for mitigative reasons, mandated by law when federal funds are involved, are not always the most important sites in a community since priority is given to those sites threatened by demolition.

Currently, the HABS/HAER office is concentrating its limited resources on documenting nationally significant structures. Project planning and funding can often take much time. It took two years of planning to develop the cooperative recording project of the Asa Packer Mansion in Jim Thorpe, Pennsylvania. Asa Packer (1805-1879) built the Lehigh Valley Railroad, founded Lehigh University, served as U.S. Congressman, and was an unsuccessful Pennsylvania gubernatorial candidate. HABS has documented with measured drawings the Asa Packer Mansion, a well-preserved, mid-nineteenth-century Italianate villa which still contains its original furniture and fixtures. This cooperative effort has engaged the work of HABS architects, the Mid-Atlantic Regional Office of the National Park Service, the Asa Packer Mansion, and the Pennsylvania Historical and Museum Commission.

Types of HABS Documentation

The graphic records produced by HABS include measured drawings, large-format photographs, and written data pages. When HABS originated as a Depression-era relief program to employ architects, its purpose was to document historic structures primarily by means of measured drawings. Photographs were taken and written data were compiled, but these materials were considered to be supplemental to the drawings. While measured drawings continue to be produced by HABS, photographs and data have become equally important.

HABS architectural measured drawings are carefully executed and accurately scaled. They provide valuable, detailed information by illustrating a structure's site plan, plans, elevations, sections, and details. These archival drawings are produced on standardized sheets in two sizes—19"x24" and 24"x36".

In the early years of HABS, the photographs were of irregular quality. The January 8, 1934 bulletin was devoted to the subject of photographic documentation and requested two photographs for each building.[24] The bulletin stipulated that photographs should be large-format, preferably 5"x7". Practically speaking, if a photographer had been employed, one of the measuring team's members would have been eliminated since photographers were included in the total personnel allotment. A member of the team could take the photographs, but he had to supply the large-format camera himself. Fortunately, in Pennsylvania many of the architects also had considerable expertise with a camera.

With the increased number of structures eligible for documentation and the high cost of producing measured drawings in the 1950s, photographs became increasingly more important in the recording process. It became both necessary and possible to record some buildings solely with photographs and written data. This was not only more economical, but also more expedient as photographs are a faster means of recording a structure than hand measuring. In 1959, HABS hired its first staff photographer, Jack E. Boucher, who has been responsible for much of the HABS photographic documentation since that time.

HABS has developed high standards for its documentary photographs. The photographs are taken professionally and are of publication quality. Large-format cameras are used to produce perspective-corrected 4"x5" or 5"x7" black-and-white negatives. The negatives are considered to be an integral part of the collection to insure high-quality reproductions for researchers. Often copy negatives of historic views or old drawings are produced and included in the documentary materials.

When the Survey began, it was believed that "only the briefest résumé of the facts" would be necessary to provide background historical data for each documented building.[25] The circular specifically warned against "long accounts of genealogical matter and sentimental mythology," and recommended that historical documentation be collected through local and state organizations and historical societies. By 1934 a format for organizing historical information had been developed and there was a greater commitment to lengthier and more-detailed written data sheets.[26] Yet in the early years of HABS, usually no more than two pages of written data were provided for each measured structure.

Beginning in the 1950s, historians and architectural historians were hired and assigned to the summer recording teams. Their task was to prepare extensive written data following newly established HABS guidelines. This written architectural and historical information provides valuable background on surveyed structures. The data include facts derived from deed searches, local papers, municipal, county, and state records, and published histories, as well as a written description of the structure. Architectural style and historical events and persons connected with the structure are discussed as well. Many of these reports also include bibliographies to assist in further research.

Several factors distinguish HABS from other surveys. The scope of the HABS program is nationwide. From the outset, HABS developed standards for the three types of documentation employed in its survey work. Measured drawings are prepared on standard-size sheets. Photographs are taken professionally using large-format cameras and the negatives are part of the collection, as they are used for photographic reproductions. The historical documentation is prepared according to a standard format. Since one of the Survey's original purposes was to produce high-quality records for research and publication, all HABS documentation is archival and reproducible. All of these documentary materials are part of the public domain and are readily accessible to the public.

In addition to standard HABS documentation, there are other HABS records which are not formally parts of the collection, but which are available to researchers at the Library of Congress. These materials include field records, HABS Inventory (HABSI) forms, stereopairs, and large-format color transparencies.

Field records contain drawings, measurements, and photographs taken in the field in preparation for formal documentation. These records are not archival, but often contain additional details, especially the dimensions for the measured drawings. They are available at the Library of Congress for research.

Historic American Buildings Survey Inventory (HABSI) forms condense onto a single page basic information on a structure. They were intended to be preliminary data on structures considered for future documentation. These forms are no longer prepared, but existing HABSI forms are archived at the Library of Congress and a list of Pennsylvania HABSI forms is included in the appendix.

Stereopairs are glass-plate photographs taken from two or three slightly different camera positions to form a stereo image that can be measured in three dimensions. Highly accurate, measured drawings can be produced using this recording process. HABS was one of the early advocates of this technique of architectural photogrammetry, starting in the 1950s. It is used primarily to record large or complex structures too difficult to hand measure. Recently, film copy negatives have been made of all stereopair images and the copies have been incorporated into the formal HABS collection. The copy negatives have been included in the appropriate catalog entries and a list of Pennsylvania stereopairs may be found in the appendix.

In recent years, Survey photographers have begun to use color transparency film in certain instances to supplement their traditional black-and-white photographic documentation. Since color photographs are not considered archival they are not part of the formal collection.

HABS Publications and Related Materials

HABS publications are of two kinds: guidelines for producing documentation and catalogs or guides to the documentary materials. From the beginning, the HABS office produced circulars, bulletins, specifications, field instructions, and procedures manuals which set the standards for HABS documentation. As the Survey grew more active it became necessary to provide reference volumes of documentation standards. The first of these HABS manuals was completed in 1961, but it was prepared solely for office use. In 1968, Professor Harley J. McKee of Syracuse University worked with HABS architect James C. Massey to develop a comprehensive procedures manual entitled, "A Manual of the Historic American Buildings Survey." This was released in an offset edition in 1968. In 1970, when Massey became chief of HABS, the Government Printing Office published this manual for wider distribution as *Recording Historic Buildings*. It provided standards of documentation and field instructions as well as guidelines for historical documentation, both written and photographic, of Survey structures. It served as the principal reference for nearly twenty years.

In 1989 McKee's book was no longer in print. HABS released a new manual, *Recording Historic Structures*, edited by John A. Burns, principal architect of HABS/HAER. This updated and expanded manual outlines the current documentation formats and standards of HABS/HAER and includes sections on surveys, historical data, photography, measured drawings, and case studies. The Burns book is the standard text used by all HABS/HAER summer recording teams, students, professionals, government agencies, and anyone interested in recording historic sites and structures.

As a result of the National Historic Preservation Act amendments of 1980, federal agencies are required to mitigate, through documentation, any federal action that would adversely affect an historic structure. This documentation must conform to HABS/HAER standards and be accepted by HABS/HAER for their collections. In order to assist federal agencies with this task, HABS/HAER standards were published as *The Secretary of the Interior's Standards for Architectural and Engineering Documenta-*

tion in 1983. Drawing upon the experience of both offices in the documentation process, this document outlines the principal requirements and procedures.

In order to make the HABS records accessible to the public, a series of catalogs has been issued over the years to guide researchers to the collection. In 1938 HABS published its first national catalog. This publication, printed in letter-press and illustrated by drawings and photographs, announced the start of the HABS collection. Three years later, in 1941, an enlarged edition was published. Under Mission 66, the National Park Service published a 1959 supplement to the 1941 HABS catalog which listed all structures recorded since 1941. In 1983 *Historic America* was published. This book contains a comprehensive computerized checklist of HABS and HAER records up to that date—the first such comprehensive list published since the 1941 catalog.

In the 1960s, as the collection increased in size, a series of state catalogs began to appear. These catalogs were intended as guides to the HABS material for particular states, but they also usually included descriptive entries of the recorded structures, an essay on the history of architecture in the state, and numerous illustrations selected from the HABS records. This Pennsylvania catalog is part of that series as is *Philadelphia Preserved*.

The Survey has prepared a variety of publications, and HABS material is often used to illustrate other architecture and history publications. A comprehensive bibliography of books, articles, catalogs, etc., featuring HABS and HAER material was completed in 1990. The bibliography in this book specifically includes HABS publications containing material on Pennsylvania.

Using the HABS Collection and Ordering Materials

At the Library of Congress, Washington, D.C., researchers may use the HABS Pennsylvania materials in the reading room of the Prints and Photographs Division or they may write and request copies of the documentary materials they need.[27] These requests should be addressed to: The Prints and Photographs Division, Library of Congress, Washington, D.C. 20540-4730. The library's photoduplication service can provide copies of photographs, measured drawings, and data pages in the collection.

The HABS collection is also available to the public through microfilm and microfiche. In 1974 all the HABS drawings at the Library of Congress were microfilmed. A complete set of the microfilm is available at Pennsylvania State University,

University Park, Pennsylvania, or it may be ordered from the photoduplication service at the Library of Congress. In 1979, all the photographs and written data pages at the Library were microfiched. These materials are available at Pennsylvania State University—Harrisburg, the Philadelphia Free Library, and the State Archives of the Pennsylvania Historical and Museum Commission, Harrisburg, or may be ordered from the publisher, Chadwyck-Healey, Inc., 1101 King Street, suite 380, Alexandria, Virginia 22314.

For additional information on the materials and activities of HABS, write to:
Historic American Buildings Survey/Historic American Engineering Record
U.S. Department of the Interior
National Park Service
PO Box 37127
Washington, D.C. 20013-7127
www.cr.nps.gov/habshaer

Guide to Using the HABS Pennsylvania Catalog

The catalog contained in this book is a guide to the more than 1,600 structures surveyed and documented by HABS in Pennsylvania from 1933 through 1989. It is not a definitive list of the state's historic structures. The survey is an ongoing program and the collection grows constantly. Currently, much HABS/HAER recording activity is centered in Pennsylvania and the available documentation will continue to increase.

An architectural and historical overview essay on Pennsylvania as a whole is included to provide background and context for the structures included in the catalog. The catalog divides the state into six regions that correspond to the Commonwealth's historic preservation planning regions. A regional map is included to identify the counties in each region. Each regional section begins with an essay discussing the area's architecture and the historical, geographical, and cultural forces that influenced it. The essays often cite HABS examples, but are not limited to recorded structures. The HABS examples are evident by the HABS survey number included after the structure's name.

Descriptive entries for individual structures located within each region follow the regional essay. Entries are alphabetically arranged by (a) county, (b) municipality or vicinity, and (c) building name. Of the more than 1,600 structures surveyed by HABS in Pennsylvania, more than one-third are located in the city of Philadelphia. In 1976 a separate HABS catalog for the city of Philadelphia was published; therefore, the Philadelphia section of this catalog has abbreviated entries. The reader may refer to *Philadelphia Preserved* by Richard J. Webster for more information.

How to Read Catalog Entries Each entry follows the standard HABS format: historic or primary name (secondary names are given in parentheses); HABS Pennsylvania number (example: PA-123); street address or location; description of exterior and interior features; architectural style; date of construction; name of architects or builders; additions or alterations; historical information; itemized and dated list of documentary materials including sheets of measured drawings, photographs, and data pages; Library of Congress shelf code (example: LC code: PA,15-SCON.V,1); notation if structure is listed on the National Register of Historic Places (NR), or is a National Historic Landmark (NHL), and is also recorded by the Historic American Engineering Record (HAER).

Historic Name The historic name of a structure is considered to be its primary name. Secondary names are given parenthetically and are cross-referenced. The historic name is usually the name of the original owner or the name used by the original owner. In the case of a public or commercial building, the original use or name of the structure is the historic name. Secondary names may be common names, the name of a recent owner, or any name once used by HABS in its records, or published elsewhere, even if in error. In the case of a complex of buildings, the entries for individual structures follow the complex name. Example: Ephrata Cloister (PA-320), Academy (PA-320A), Almonry (PA-320B), and so on.

Street Address or Location In the case of buildings located in cities or towns, street addresses are given. However, structures located in rural areas require more descriptive siting. A building may be located by its distance in tenths of a mile from the nearest city or town, intersection, or geographic landmark. Additionally, the structure's position is given with respect to an adjacent road. Example: N side of Bull Rd. (LR66102), 1.2 mi. NW of U.S. Rte. 30.

Physical Description The physical description begins with large features and then progresses to smaller features, and it works from the exterior to the interior. The exterior description begins with construction materials, the overall dimensions and number of bays, the number of stories, shape of the roof, and concludes with notable exterior features. The interior description includes plan type and notable interior features. The building is then categorized, if appropriate, by architectural style.

Date of Construction The date of construction is given as precisely as possible. In some cases, the beginning and completion dates are given. In cases where the date is uncertain, estimates are based on style, design, or construction. The same pattern is followed in the case of alterations and additions.

Architects or Builders, and Significance The names of the architect, designer, builder, or craftsman are given whenever this information is known. A statement on the structure's historical or architectural interest is included when appropriate, noting it as an outstanding or unusual example of an architectural style, the place of an important historical event, or its association with a particular person.

Itemization of Documentary Materials HABS documentary materials are of three kinds: measured drawings, photographs, and written data pages. The itemization of these materials follows a particular sequence in each entry.

Measured Drawings The number of sheets of measured drawings is given, followed parenthetically by the date the drawings were delineated and the type of drawings available—site plans, plans, elevations, sections, isometrics, and details.

Photographs The number of interior and exterior photographs and the date they were taken are given. The number of copy photographs made from historic photographs, drawings, or prints and other visual documentation follows with the date of the original material given in parentheses. In more-recent documentation there is a separate Index to Photos page which supplies information on each photograph, including captions, photographer, and date photograph was taken.

Data Pages The number of data pages and the date they were written.

Library of Congress Shelf Code This number identifies the file location of HABS documentary materials to facilitate their speedy recovery. This number should be given to the staff at the Library of Congress when requesting information on any HABS materials.

Appendices Lists of the sites recorded by the Historic American Engineering Record, the Historic American Buildings Survey Inventory (HABSI) forms, and stereopairs available for Pennsylvania are included in the appendix.

Abbreviations Throughout this catalog certain abbreviations have been routinely used. A list of abbreviations with their full meaning appears on the following page.

ABBREVIATIONS

AIA	American Institute of Architects
approx	approximately
Ave./Aves.	Avenue/Avenues
c.	century
ca.	circa
dimensions	front elevation, then side (unless noted)
Dr.	Drive
E/W/N/S	East/West/North/South
ext.	exterior
GNMP	Gettysburg National Military Park
HABS	Historic American Buildings Survey
HAER	Historic American Engineering Record
int.	interior
LR	Legislative Route, followed by road number
LC	Library of Congress
mi.	mile
n.d.	no date
NHL	National Historic Landmark
NHP	National Historic Park
NHS	National Historic Site
NPS	National Park Service
NR	National Register of Historic Places
PA	Pennsylvania
Rd.	Road
Rte.	Route
St./Sts.	Street/Streets
T	Township road, followed by road number
U.S. Rte.	United States Route, followed by route number

Notes

[1] HABS Circular Number 1, December 12, 1933.

[2] Bissell, a graduate of the University of Pennsylvania and partner in the firm of Bissell & Sinkler, was a Philadelphia architect active in historic preservation. He was a member of the Committee for the Preservation of Historic Monuments and was involved with the restoration planning for Independence Square in Philadelphia.

[3] Stotz was a prominent Pennsylvania architect with a particular interest in historic buildings. He is the author of *The Early Architecture of Western Pennsylvania*, published in 1936.

[4] Staff architect Thomas T. Waterman, author of *The Domestic Colonial Architecture of Tidewater Virginia*, published in 1932 with John A. Barrows, and author of several subsequent books and articles, was responsible for devising HABS's first architectural standards.

[5] Holland started the Pictorial Archives in 1929 and served as chairman of the AIA's Committee on Preservation of Historic Buildings and as chairman of the HABS National Advisory Committee.

[6] Pennsylvania Districts as of December 3, 1934, HABS Bulletin Number 35. District One: (11 counties) Delaware, Chester, Philadelphia, Montgomery, Bucks, Northampton, Berks, Lehigh, Schuylkill, Carbon, and Monroe. District Two: (9 counties) Sullivan, Bradford, Luzerne, Susquehanna, Pike, Lackawanna, Wayne, Wyoming, and Columbia. District Three: (22 counties) Tioga, Lycoming, Clinton, Centre, Union, Northumberland, Snyder, Montour, Huntingdon, Mifflin, Juniata, Perry, Dauphin, Lebanon, Lancaster, York, Cumberland, Adams, Fulton, Franklin, Blair, and Bedford. District Four: (13 counties) Clearfield, Lawrence, Butler, Armstrong, Beaver, Allegheny, Indiana, Cambria, Westmoreland, Washington, Somerset, Fayette, and Greene. District Five: (12 counties) Erie, Crawford, Mercer, Elk, Venango, Warren, Forest, Clarion, McKean, Cameron, Jefferson, and Potter.

[7] The January 30, 1935 *Bulletin* (Number 39) described the projects:

> District One: Two projects, one in Philadelphia and the other in Monroe County. Each was funded by the county FERA office. Sponsors were the University of Pennsylvania and the State Department of Public Instruction. Project directors were the HABS District Officer E. Perot Bissell and the Deputy District Officer Harold T. Pinker. Three people,

including the district officer, were paid full-time while the others hired were part-time. No funds were available for travel or photography.

District Two: One project, Luzerne County. This project was sponsored by the State Department of Public Instruction and a local committee. The HABS district officer and the FERA project director was Thomas Atherton and he worked with both full-time and part-time staff. Provision was made for some photography, but for no other expenses.

District Three: Three projects, Centre, Lancaster, and Dauphin Counties. These projects were jointly sponsored by the county FERA offices and the State Department of Public Instruction. Supervision was provided by HABS District Officer Julian Millard and the Deputy District Officer Dean E. Kennedy. All workers except the supervisors worked part-time and no money was available for travel or photography.

District Four: One project, Allegheny County. This project was sponsored by the State Department of Public Instruction through the county school superintendent. The FERA supervisor was HABS District Officer Charles M. Stotz, the only full-time employee.

District Five: One project, Erie County. This project was directed by HABS District Officer Karl E. Morrison. All personnel worked full-time and there were funds for photography.

[8]In District One, Monroe County work was suspended April 4 while in Philadelphia, the work was temporarily halted, then resumed with three people working. District Two still had seven people working in Luzerne County. The Centre County and Lancaster County projects were both closed in District Three, but Dauphin County was still operating with five people. Districts Four and Five had ended their projects.

[9]Some of the original district officers were unable to accept a temporary government appointment due to other commitments. When this occurred, they nominated the deputy district officer to supervise the WPA projects, delegating the full powers of the district officer to the deputy during the WPA program. Afterwards, the title and responsibilities of the district officer reverted to the original person. The April 15, 1936, *Bulletin* (Number 50) listed the names of the Pennsylvania district officers: District One—Joseph P. Sims in Philadelphia was both the district officer and WPA supervisor. District Two—Thomas H. Atherton in Wilkes Barre was the district officer, but Ralph W. Lear, the deputy district officer, was the WPA supervisor. District Three—Julian Millard in Harrisburg was the district officer, but Edmund G. Good, Jr., the deputy district officer, was the WPA supervisor. District Four—Charles M. Stotz in Pittsburgh was the district officer, but Lamont H. Butler, the deputy district officer, was the WPA supervisor. District Five—Karl E. Morrison in Erie was both the district officer and WPA supervisor.

[10] Agnes Gilchrist, an architectural historian for the National Park Service in Philadelphia, compiled some of the data as did Frederick Tilberg, senior historian of Gettysburg National Military Park, who also took most of the photographs.

[11] Architect Norman M. Souder was involved with much of this work.

[12] The Secretary of the Society, Francis James Dallett, prepared detailed data.

[13] Drury B. Alexander, an architect at the University of Texas, was the project supervisor; Osmund R. Overby, an architectural historian with the National Park Service and later president of the Philadelphia-based Society of Architectural Historians, worked on the histories; photographs were taken by Cervin Robinson, his first of many HABS assignments.

[14] John D. Milner, who had worked in the HABS Philadelphia office as a student architect, was project supervisor. In addition to the many drawings produced by this summer team, Jack Boucher provided the photographic documentation in 1969.

[15] Ned Goode took many photographs for this project and Bart Anderson of the Chester County Historical Society prepared the data.

[16] The Carter Administration acted to decentralize the preservation program under a broader reorganization plan for the Department of the Interior, which separated the National Park Service from its traditional preservation responsibilities. The Heritage Conservation and Recreation Service (HCRS) was created as the umbrella agency to administer all preservation activities within the Department of the Interior. HCRS also incorporated the activities of the Bureau of Outdoor Recreation (BOR). Under this plan, all preservation programs were regionalized and began operation out of the existing regional offices of the former BOR. The Washington office of HABS remained, although much reduced in size. It was at this time that the HABS National Advisory Board was discontinued. The Reagan Administration acted quickly to reverse this policy of decentralization. One of Secretary of the Interior James Watt's first decisions was to abolish HCRS and to return the Office of Archeology and Historic Preservation to the NPS.

[17] Perry Benson of the University of Pennsylvania was the HABS project supervisor.

[18] Project supervisors were: Robert C. Giebner in 1967 and Kenneth N. Clark in 1968, both from the University of Arizona; Roy C. Pledger in 1969 and Melvin M. Rotsch in 1970, both from Texas A&M University; and John M. MacRae of the University of Florida in 1971. Photographs were taken by George Eisenman and Jack Boucher.

[19] Published by the Pennsylvania German Folklore Society, Volume 21, 1956, copyright 1958, Allentown, Pennsylvania.

[20] The nine counties are: Bedford, Blair, Cambria, Fayette, Fulton, Huntingdon, Indiana, Somerset, and Westmoreland.

[21] The three volumes published thus far are *A Legacy of Coal: The Coal Company Towns of Southwestern Pennsylvania*, by Margaret M. Mulrooney; *Two Historic Pennsylvania Canal*

Towns: Alexandria and Saltsburg, edited by Sara Amy Leach; *The Character of a Small Mill City: Four Historic Neighborhoods of Johnstown, Pennsylvania,* edited by Kim E. Wallace. All three were published as part of America's Industrial Heritage Project by the National Park Service, HABS/HAER, in 1989.

[22] The documentary material from the past three summers is in the HABS/HAER office undergoing editorial review, therefore it has yet to be cataloged. Since the records are not in their final form, complete catalog entries could not be prepared in time for this catalog. However, under each appropriate location there is an entry titled America's Industrial Heritage Project which lists the sites documented thus far for that area.

[23] *Bulletin* (Number 3).

[24] *Bulletin* (Number 11).

[25] Circular Number 1, December 12, 1933.

[26] *Bulletin* (Number 16), March 19, 1934.

[27] Related collections in the Prints and Photographs Division include the Pictorial Archives of Early American Architecture, the Joseph S. Allen Collection, Pictorial Iconography of Pittsburgh, the Detroit Publishing Company, the Sachse Collection, the Seagram County Courthouse Archives, and the geographic files.

Architecture of Pennsylvania

Richard J. Webster

When William Penn arrived near what is now Chester, Pennsylvania, in late 1682, he encountered approximately two hundred Swedes and Finns, some Lenape Indians, and possibly a smattering of Dutch. Within days he presented the "Laws agreed upon in England by the Governour and Divers of all Free-Men of Pennsilvania" six months earlier. Among the laws was one assuring that all persons "shall in no way be molested or prejudiced for the Religious Persuasion or Practice in matters of Faith or Worship."[1] This early and sincere proclamation of religious tolerance, plus Penn's aggressive promotion of Pennsylvania's economic potential, soon contributed to an unusual ethnic and religious diversity in Pennsylvania. This cultural heterogeneity, in turn, affected the built environment of most of Pennsylvania and ultimately influenced the shape and plan of ordinary buildings over a great part of America.[2]

Penn's recruiting of diligent European farmers was successful from the outset. Germans and Dutch, both Quakers and Mennonites, responded early to Penn's assurances and by 1683 had established Germantown in Philadelphia County. They were the start of a trickle that became a wave of persecuted sects escaping the effects of war and economic depression in the German Rhineland Palatinate. By the 1720s, from the same general region came another wave, mostly Lutherans and Reformed but also Anabaptists—the Mennonites and the Amish—who flowed into the lowlands east of the Appalachians. Among the Germans were such minor sects as the Schwenkfelders, an Anabaptist-like sect that located in the region of Pennsburg, Montgomery County, in 1734, and the Seventh-Day Baptists, who in 1735 established their mystical communal order in Ephrata, Lancaster County. At about the same time, the Scotch-Irish turned their backs on Ireland and hard times for the promise of Pennsylvania.[3]

The English, Welsh, and Germans established strong ethnic communities in which common religious tradition, business relationships, family intermarriage, and common language all served to insulate them from each other.[4] On the other hand, Britains and Germans shared the virtues of thrift, diligence, and plain living, and on the whole had the same aspirations. Without geographical barriers to maintain physical isolation or strengthen cultural cohesion, the groups mixed rather freely after a generation or two in the new land.[5]

During the first and second generations, however, settlers were relatively free to practice inherited customs. Since the construction of ordinary houses is a material manifestation of a folk culture, the ethnic groups that first settled Pennsylvania built their own distinctive dwellings.[6] Later builders, born and raised in a world of increasing diversity, tended to build differently from their predecessors. And well they might have, for they had been reared in a culture more syncretic than their ancestors. Yet while some eighteenth-century house builders were third- or fourth-generation Pennsylvanians, others were newcomers from abroad. From 1730 on, a mixture of vernacular dwellings, some reflecting acculturation, others retaining Old World forms were filling the countryside.

Log construction is a good example of an Old World building form that more than one national group brought to Pennsylvania and other groups adopted and altered. Swedes, who, with accompanying Finns, established in 1638 the first European settlement in Pennsylvania—Delaware County—introduced log construction to Pennsylvania.[7] Professor Terry Jordan argues that although their numbers were small and their tenure of power short, Swedes have had a long-term influence on vernacular architecture both locally and across a large part of eastern North America. Log construction is their significant contribution to American culture. By occupying both sides of the Delaware, the "main street" for nearly all early newcomers to Pennsylvania, the Swedes were in an excellent position to exhibit a construction technique developed and time-tested on the Swedish and Finnish frontiers. Their own acculturation and early movement into the North American frontier helped to popularize their particular type of construction deep into the American midland.[8]

Finnish and Swedish log houses are not the same. The Finnish is cruder, with such simple building techniques as chink construction, round logs, and two-sided hewing, all well suited to frontier conditions and easily learned. It is represented by the so-called Lower and Upper Swedish Log Cabins (PA-135 and 136) near Clifton Heights, Delaware County, which have characteristic V-notching and chink construction (i.e., the logs are not flush and interstices are filled with plaster, giving the

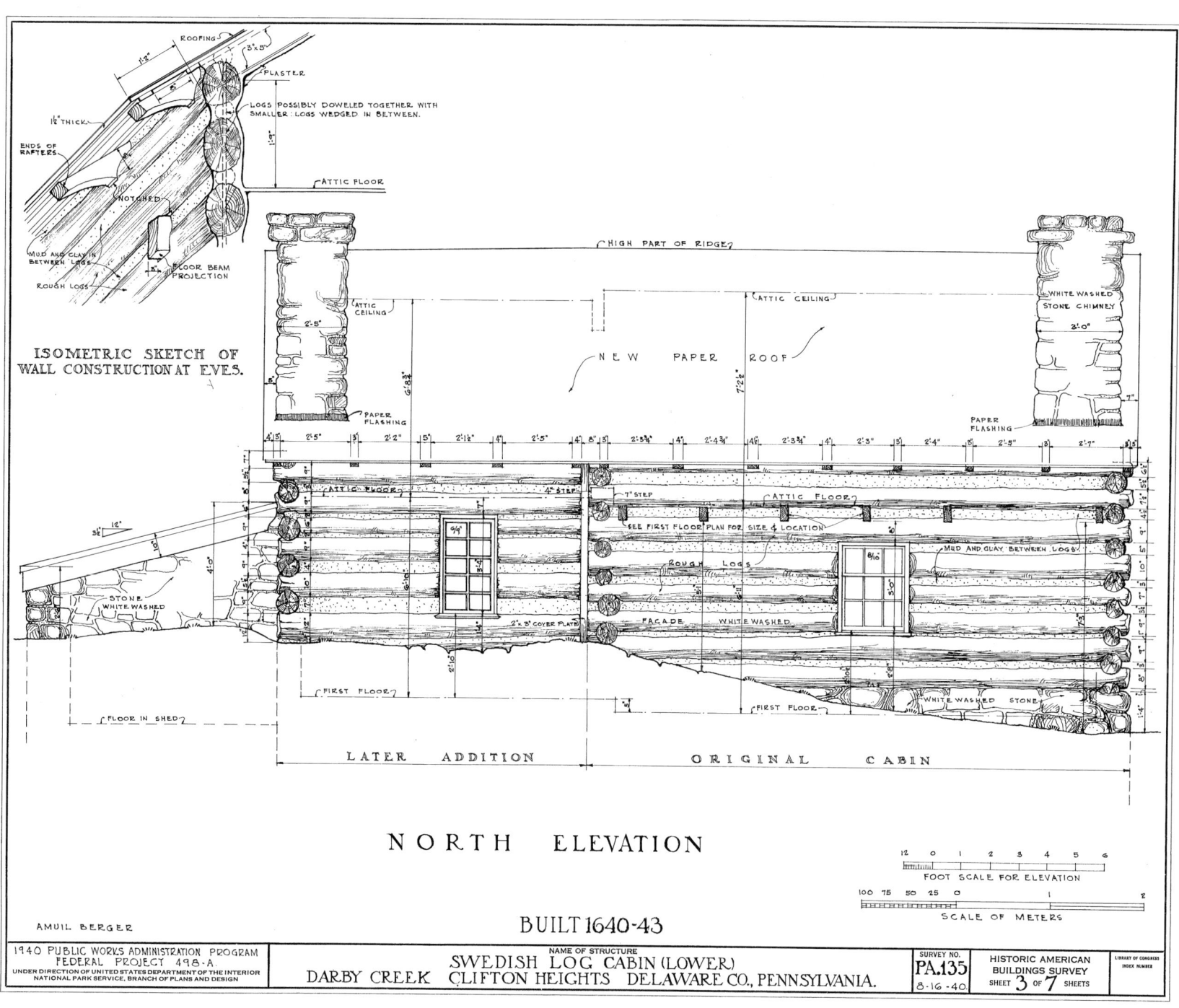

Lower Swedish Log Cabin (PA-135) Clifton Heights vicinity (Upper Darby Township), Delaware County. North elevation with construction details (Amuil Berger, delineator, 1940) PA,23-DARB.V,2.

facade a zebra- or prison-stripe effect). The Swedish log house, on the other hand, is characterized by tightly fitted timbers hewn on all four sides with dovetailed or square-notched corners, such as those of the square-notched Morton Homestead, built in Prospect Park, Delaware County, near the turn of the eighteenth century.[9]

Because many Germans were also familiar with log construction, scholars disagree over which group most influenced log construction in the United States. Professors Kniffen and Glassie contend that Germans had the lasting impact on log construction, that early Swedish influence never spread beyond New Sweden along the lower Delaware River. They argue that early Swedes had little contact with their English neighbors, and at least in their religious structures, rather quickly abandoned log construction for brick and stone.[10] Nevertheless, although some Germanic groups, such as the Schwenkfelders from Lower Silesia (now southwestern Poland) and Saxony and others from the Alpine-Alemannic region, came from log-building regions, they introduced few techniques to the Swedish-Finnish tradition that had not already been in place for nearly a century before their arrival.[11] The Schwenkfelders arrived too late (the mid-1730s) and remained too isolated to have an influence outside of Montgomery County. Similarly the Alpine house was too big, too complex, and too conspicuously ornate to be transplanted in a rural area where a German minority sought acceptance. The Germans did introduce some new techniques, such as corner posting, in which the ends of logs are tenoned into corner posts. Corner-posting was rare in colonial America, perhaps because it is a transitional stage between log construction and half-timbering, which itself was uncommon.[12] Significantly, a good example of the corner-post technique, the Golden Plough Tavern (PA-5169) in York, York County, employs corner-posting on the ground floor and half-timbering with brick in-fill on the second story. The important point is that the Germans reinforced many of the techniques already introduced and practiced for decades by the Swedes.

There is no disagreement that the English, Welsh, and Scotch-Irish, for whom log building was an alien practice,[13] quickly adopted log construction. Because so few log structures have survived the ravages of time and cultural change, it is easy to forget that they once were common to the rural landscape. One old Chester Countian, for example, reminisced that on a trip from West Chester, Chester County, to Wilmington, Delaware, in 1797, he encountered only five stone or brick houses; all the others were log.[14] Similarly, all but five of York's one hundred and eighty finished dwellings in 1754 were log. Also, in her study of the early borough of Huntingdon, Huntingdon County,

Golden Plow Tavern (PA-5169) York, York County. Interior partition showing wattle and daub construction (Paul Galbreath, photographer, 1962) PA,67-YORK,12-6.

Nancy Shedd has established that in 1798 the town had only three brick dwellings, two each of stone and timber frame, and at least fifty of log. As late as 1822, there were only eleven brick buildings, including the courthouse, in town.[15]

Swedes also have been credited as the source for the three-room dwellings that some historians have called the Quaker-plan house. It has been argued that William Penn learned of it from Swedish colonists and became convinced of its utility,[16] but recent scholarship indicates that these three-room houses were products of an ancient English wood-building tradition.[17] It was recommended that on their arrival settlers should promptly build one-story, gable-roof, clapboarded timber frame houses approximately thirty by eighteen feet. The interior was to be partitioned into three rooms with dirt floors.[18] In spite of this advice, house construction was so time-consuming in the face of essential land-clearing that many settlers spent their first winters in "caves."[19]

Many first-period houses were timber frame. Based on evidence from the small number of extant examples, it appears that early Pennsylvania timber-frame houses' framing elements, like those in the Chesapeake region, were smaller and lighter than those in seventeenth-century New England.[20] This is probably because English builders of early-eighteenth-century Pennsylvania houses, such as the one (PA-174) that originally stood in Concordville, Delaware County, adopted such labor-saving steps as reducing the number of diagonal braces and using uniformly sized elements that had been taken in the South a few decades earlier.[21] Built circa 1730 and locally known as the Mendenhall House because of its apparent associations with that prominent Quaker family, the Concordville house has twice been dismantled and moved, giving architects and historians ample opportunity to observe its framing members. Its corner fireplace, once thought to be a Swedish characteristic, is now known to have been common in England. Because the early-eighteenth-century Parke House (PA-1211) in Caln Township, Chester County, has been allowed to decay, its timber frame can be seen through the collapsing hewn-board walls, and here too the timbers are relatively light.

In seventeenth-century New England and some early-eighteenth-century Pennsylvania Germanic houses the spaces between the framing elements were filled with wattle and daub (woven twigs covered with mud) or similar materials. Its omission from the so-called Mendenhall House and the Parke House was apparently another labor-saving step taken by Pennsylvania builders. In this respect the timber-frame construction of the east addition to Joseph Gilpin's 1745 house (PA-1116) in Birmingham Township, Delaware County, is more traditional. The frame is in-filled with sun-dried bricks and covered with weatherboards. Built circa 1720, this small story-and-a-half house may have served as a first-period dwelling before being moved and attached to the larger stone house in the second quarter of the nineteenth century.[22] Nearly all of these small timber-frame houses are gone and we are left, at most, only with such tantalizing descriptions as "a cabin with yellow poplar planks."[23]

Joseph Gilpin House (PA-1116) Chadds Ford (Birmingham Township), Delaware County. Interior of southeast room toward entrance (Ned Goode, photographer, 1958) PA,23-CHAF.V,1-8.

As the Parke House indicates, time has not been kind to the rare survivors; fire and neglect have been lethal enemies.

Although never as abundant as timber-frame houses, half-timber houses were probably more common in eighteenth-century Pennsylvania than surviving stock suggests. Half-timbering was the primary mode of construction in medieval England and Europe and remained popular well into the seventeenth century. Englishmen in outlying towns built half-timber houses even after laws forbade them in London following the great fire of 1666.[24] Coming from a world in which half-timbering was prevalent, immigrants to Pennsylvania used it here as well, in cities, towns, and countryside. Where clay for brick-making was available, the half-timbering had exposed brick nogging, as in the mid-eighteenth-century Howard Avenue House (PA-1355) in Lancaster.[25] Other houses, such as the Mears-Heaton House (PA-1070) in Philadelphia, were brick with half-timber-frame back buildings. Although this two-story shed-roof back building was probably built between 1740 and 1765, it had characteristics of a pre-fire London house. It had a second-floor overhang, for example, and between the timbers oversize handmade bricks were laid on edge and then parged to make their surface flush with the frame.[26]

Although Englishmen almost certainly built these two Lancaster and Philadelphia half-timber houses, Germans also had long mastered the technique, which they called Fachwerk. In northern Europe construction of half-timber buildings declined in the seventeenth century but seems to have never completely died out. In fact, half-timber houses remain so prevalent in northern Germany that half-timber-revival buildings today are being built so new construction will meld with towns' older fabric.[27] An extant Pennsylvania example of Fachwerk, York's Golden Plough Tavern (PA-5169), was built between 1741 and 1745 for, and possibly by, Martin Eichelberger, who migrated to Pennsylvania at the age of twelve from Ittlingen in Germany's Rhineland.[28] The tavern's second story has a distinctively German pattern of diagonal timbers with brick nogging.[29] Germans in Pennsylvania, however, abandoned half-timber construction and adopted less complex English building methods rather quickly. Native-born Pennsylvanians of both German and British ancestry spurned half-timber dwellings because they were going out of fashion in the Old World, where wood supplies were dwindling, and because the English and European practice of exposing timbers as a form of conspicuous consumption was irrelevant in a land of thick forests.[30]

Barnes-Brinton House (PA-173) Chadds Ford vicinity (Pennsbury Township), Chester County. View showing brick pattern in gable end (Copy photo of circa 1905 photograph in Chester County Historical Society, photographer unknown) PA,15-CHAFO.V,1-18.

Many permanent houses are constructed of either brick or stone, usually depending on where they stand in relation to the Wertenbaker line. Historian Thomas Jefferson Wertenbaker delineated this imaginary line extending from Princeton, New Jersey, to Wilmington, Delaware, more than a half-century ago to mark the areas of brick and stone buildings in the southeastern Pennsylvania region.[31] Brick houses generally lie south and east of the line; stone houses are north and west of it. Early brick houses were usually constructed of Flemish bond, sometimes mixed with English bond, a stronger but more expensive method of laying a brick wall. American bond, which is essentially stretcher bond with every fifth or seventh course laid with headers, did not become common until the early nineteenth century.

Some early brick buildings retained medieval traditions,[32] such as the gable-end diaperwork of the Barnes-Brinton House (PA-173) near Chadds Ford, Chester County, or the brick lozenges (diamonds) flanking the entrance to Gloria Dei (PA-120) in Philadelphia's Southwark. It also was not uncommon for builders to emblazon gables with glazed-header dates and initials. As in the case of the 1762 Willis House (PA-5170) in York, they often included the owner's initials and the construction date in the gable peak. A fascinating example of one generation following the example of another is the Miller House (PA-5173) in Avondale, Chester County. The date of original construction, 1730, is laid in black brick across the front at the second story, and above it, also in black brick, is the date of the 1771 third-story addition.[33]

The earliest-known Pennsylvania houses, such as Caleb Pusey's house (PA-1079), were essentially medieval in plan and construction.[34] Pusey was forty-one in 1682 when he came to Chester Creek to what is now Upland, Delaware County, where he served as manager and agent for the colony's first official Proprietary saw and gristmill. Richard Turner, an experienced miller and builder, brought the milling works and framing from England and erected the mill and possibly Pusey's house as well.[35] Regardless, Pusey had to spend his first winter in a "dug-out" before moving into his one-room story-and-a-half rubble dwelling with a steep gable roof.[36] Except for its material (stone rather than timber frame) it was the same kind of shelter that English Separatists and Puritan settlers built in Plymouth and Salem, Massachusetts, approximately sixty years earlier, and represents the kind of dwelling most Pennsylvanians probably occupied until about 1700. In the countryside, where scarce money was used for seed, livestock, and tools rather than household goods, these first houses were sparsely furnished.[37] Time and money were also invested in enlarging homes. About 1695 Pusey extended his house one room to the west, which left his chimney near the center of the house and brought under roof the family's great iron kettle and stone-lined well, which he probably had dug shortly after arriving there. During the province's first half-century, perhaps two-thirds of Pennsylvania's citizens lived in similar two- and three-room dwellings. Although Pusey had enlarged his house to two rooms, it remained medieval in concept.[38]

As the Pusey House demonstrates, families of means added to their first houses rather quickly. Although Thomas Massey arrived in Pennsylvania an indentured servant, he married well; his wife, Phoebe Taylor, was the daughter of one of Marple Township's (in present Delaware County) largest landholders. In 1696 Massey added

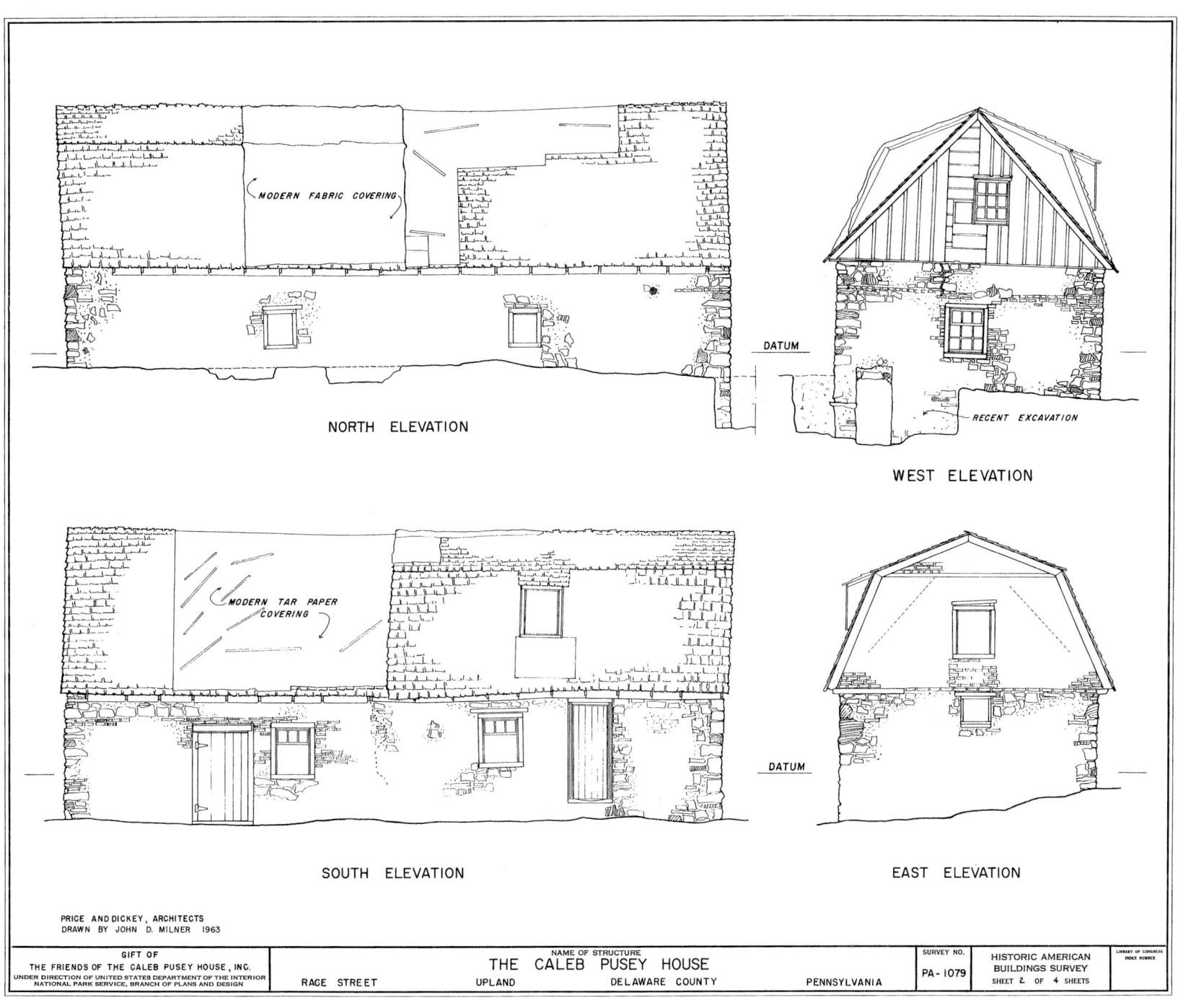

Caleb Pusey House (PA-1079) Upland Borough, Delaware County. Elevations (John D. Milner, delineator) PA,23-UPLA,1.

a two-story brick parlor block (PA-1257) to his log house, which served as the productive part of the house, where food was cooked and agricultural products processed. The brick section had no staircase and only one door, which led into the log house. Circa 1730, Massey's eldest son, Mordecai, replaced the log house with a two-and-a-half-story coursed fieldstone block, giving his family at least four living spaces, which only about one-fifth of Pennsylvanians enjoyed at the time.[39]

Houses with two-room plans were built in Philadelphia apparently from its beginning, and since Philadelphia houses generally had two or three stories, city houses usually had more rooms than their countryside counterparts. John Fanning Watson's description of the demolition of Budd's Row, which was built circa 1691, suggests that these early houses were two rooms deep.[40] Although no scientific survey has been conducted, HABS records strongly suggest that the two-room plan was predominant among the city's eighteenth-century dwellings. In Philadelphia this two-room plan is called the London house plan, because it was common in late-seventeenth- and early-eighteenth-century London.[41] It is well illustrated by the three-and-a-half-story brick Nathaniel Irish House (PA-1013), which was built in the city's Southwark section between 1762 and 1769, and resembles post-fire London houses both inside and out. Each of the three-bay brick house's three stories is clearly demarcated: a pent roof [42] above the ground story, a brick string course above the second story, and a denticulated cornice at the top, with a gable dormer providing light for the garret. An arched passage adjacent to the plain entrance leads to the rear yard and the cellar's light well. Inside the Irish House an entry hall runs along one party wall and leads to the stairs between the front and rear rooms. Because of the hallway, the front room is narrower than the rear parlor, which extends the full width of the house. As customary, fireplaces stand against the party wall opposite the hallway, and the kitchen is in the cellar.[43] Variations of this plan were built well into the nineteenth century.[44]

Also prevalent is the tradesman's house plan, which is a village variation of the two- or three-room plan.[45] Like the London house plan, it probably appeared in Philadelphia at a very early date, at least as early as 1715, when the so-called Letitia Street House (PA-184) was finished near the waterfront in a court that was later opened as Letitia Street.[46] Unlike most later houses, the Letitia Street House has its entrance in the center of its three-bay brick facade beneath a hood with boldly Baroque consoles. Its plaster cove cornice is another indication of its relatively early

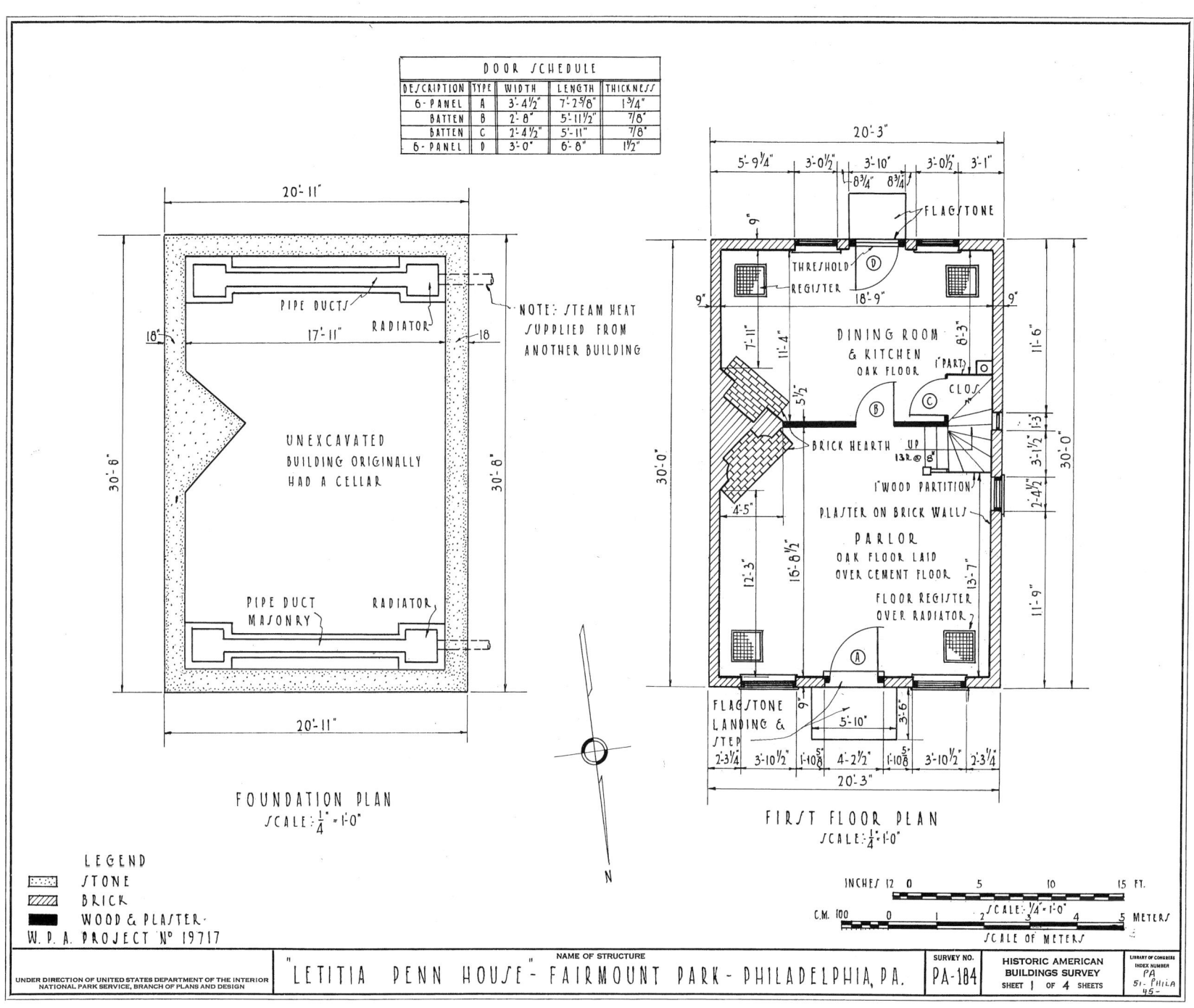

Letitia Street House (PA-184) Philadelphia. Floor plans (delineator unknown, 1931) PA,51-PHILA,45.

date. The tradesman's house plan has its roots in English villages where shopkeepers or craftsmen kept their shops in the front room and had family quarters in the back room and upper chambers. Consequently there was a need for both front and rear entry doors, stairs generally placed in the rear family area. Usually along the partition wall sat back-to-back corner fireplaces, which were more quickly and cheaply erected than separate fireplaces and chimneys. Upstairs the front chamber was usually a "lodging room," furnished for sitting and sleeping; the other chambers and the attic provided additional sleeping and storage space.

Philadelphia's cultural hegemony resulted in rural folk expressions of what Alan Gowans calls the Philadelphia house type.[47] The two-and-a-half-story Arnold-Temple House (PA-1109), for example, was built circa 1720 in West Bradford Township, Chester County, with a symmetrical two-bay front and pent roof, which resemble colonial Philadelphia house facades. Also, since Thomas Arnold operated a fulling mill and dealt with customers in his house, it has a tradesman's house plan.[48] Its coursed rubble walls, massive cooking fireplace, and plank-walled and beamed chambers, however, are clearly rural. Similarly the 1727 Joseph Collins House (PA-1114) in West Goshen Township, Chester County, has a pent roof between the two stories on its symmetrical ashlar front and pedimented gable end that mark off the floors and form classical proportions like those of Philadelphia houses. Yet the Collins House also would not have been mistaken for a city house. Initially the house had a traditionally rural three-room plan, the most common room arrangement in seventeenth-century rural England and the plan recommended by the colony's promotional literature. A later owner removed the room partitions, leaving the house with a single large room until circa 1760, when a stone-rubble kitchen was added to the rear.[49] Also, the original section is built of dressed green serpentine, a stone indigenous to Chester County,[50] with serpentine rubble sides and rear, and conspicuously centered above the center entrance is a datestone with a heart and stylized flowers. Such datestones were naively frank folk statements and were extremely rare in city houses. Furthermore, at a time when fashionable urban houses had had sash windows for a generation, the Collins House featured casement windows,[51] thus retaining a medieval element on a fundamentally Renaissance facade.

Also common among rural houses, such as the 1704 William Brinton House (PA-1258) in Birmingham Township, Delaware County, were two-room, or hall-and-parlor, plans, which by 1700 had become common in England, Wales, and

Joseph Collins House (PA-1114) West Chester vicinity (West Goshen Township), Chester County. South and west elevations (Ned Goode, photographer, 1958) PA,15-WCHES.V,2-1.

the Chesapeake area. When built, the Brinton House was a large house. Although the majority of Pennsylvania's large houses were based on this plan, in the first thirty-five years of the eighteenth century only about a third of them had the four or more rooms that the Brintons enjoyed. In these houses the hall was the family's multi-purpose room, and the parlor usually contained the family's principal bed and its best furniture. The parlor's furnishings, especially after about 1720, suggest a movement toward a private and formal space while at the same time continuing the British rural practice of sleeping on the ground floor.[52] The early date and ample dimensions of the Brinton House (nearly twice the length of the Collins House) illustrate that the date of construction was not the determining factor in the size or plan of these early

William Brinton House, 1704 (PA-1258) Dilworthtown (Birmingham Township), Delaware County. North elevation (Ned Goode, photographer, 1958) PA,23-DIL.V,1-4.

houses. The Brinton House's early date, however, probably did account for its steep gable roof, long shed dormers, and widely spaced casement windows, which contribute to a decidedly medieval feeling. Nevertheless, Renaissance influence, though weak, is apparent in the well-ordered facade with its pent roof and water table.[53] Symmetrical facades, in fact, were increasingly an assumed aspect of these houses, even where clearly medieval details like stepped moldings appear on such houses as the Richard Woodward House (PA-1192) in Thornbury Township, Chester County. Rather than detracting from the symmetry of the Woodward House's coursed-rubble front, the stepped gable serves as a string course on the three-bay, two-story facade, where a pedimented hood marks the center entrance.

Most of these houses are single-pile houses, that is, only one room deep.[54] Characterized by narrow gable ends, one-room depth, and usually a length of at least two rooms and a height of two stories, the single-pile house was an English medieval form that was common in colonial America.[55] It became the archetypical farmhouse as inland settlers carried this house westward and southward out of the Chesapeake and Middle Atlantic regions.[56] Single-pile houses were constructed of all materials. The aforementioned brick houses—the Abiah Taylor, Barnes-Brinton, and William Miller houses, and the first section of the Thomas Massey House—are all single-pile houses, as are the stone Joseph Collins, William Brinton, and Richard Woodward houses. Because the length of the logs determines the length of a log house's wall, log houses were usually single pile as well. Single-pile houses were built from the late seventeenth century through the nineteenth century, and although perceived as predominantly rural houses, they could be found in both colonial cities and small nineteenth-century towns. Because of the limitations of their one-room depth, later lateral additions and rear wings were not uncommon.[57]

Pennsylvania's Germanic people also built single-pile dwellings, but the distinctive appearance and arrangement of their houses set them apart from Anglo-American examples. Eighteenth-century Germanic immigrants came primarily from Bohemia, Moravia, and the Rhineland as far south as present-day Switzerland, and moved as directly as they could into the farming region west of Philadelphia, where they erected log and stone houses with plans like those of their homeland.[58] The Bertolet-Herbein Cabin (PA-1047), built circa 1737 in Oley Township, Berks County, is a V-notched log example of a dominant Germanic house form in America, the *Flurküchenhaus*, or hall-kitchen house. Like the classic *Flurküchenhaus*, the story-and-a-half Bertolet-Herbein Cabin has three rooms clustered about its large off-center chimney. Front and rear doors open onto the kitchen (*Küche*), which runs the depth of the house and once served the same functions as the hall in rural Anglo-American houses.[59] The larger space on the opposite side of the fireplace was partitioned into a rear chamber (*Kammer*) for sleeping or storage and a front parlor (*Stube*), which in many *Flurküchenhausen* was heated by a five-plate iron stove extending from the rear of the kitchen's fireplace.[60] There is no evidence of stairs in the Bertolet-Herbein Cabin; occupants evidently used a ladder for access to the loft. Most stone Germanic houses had enclosed stairs in the kitchen and occasionally a second set in the ground-floor chamber (*Kammer*).

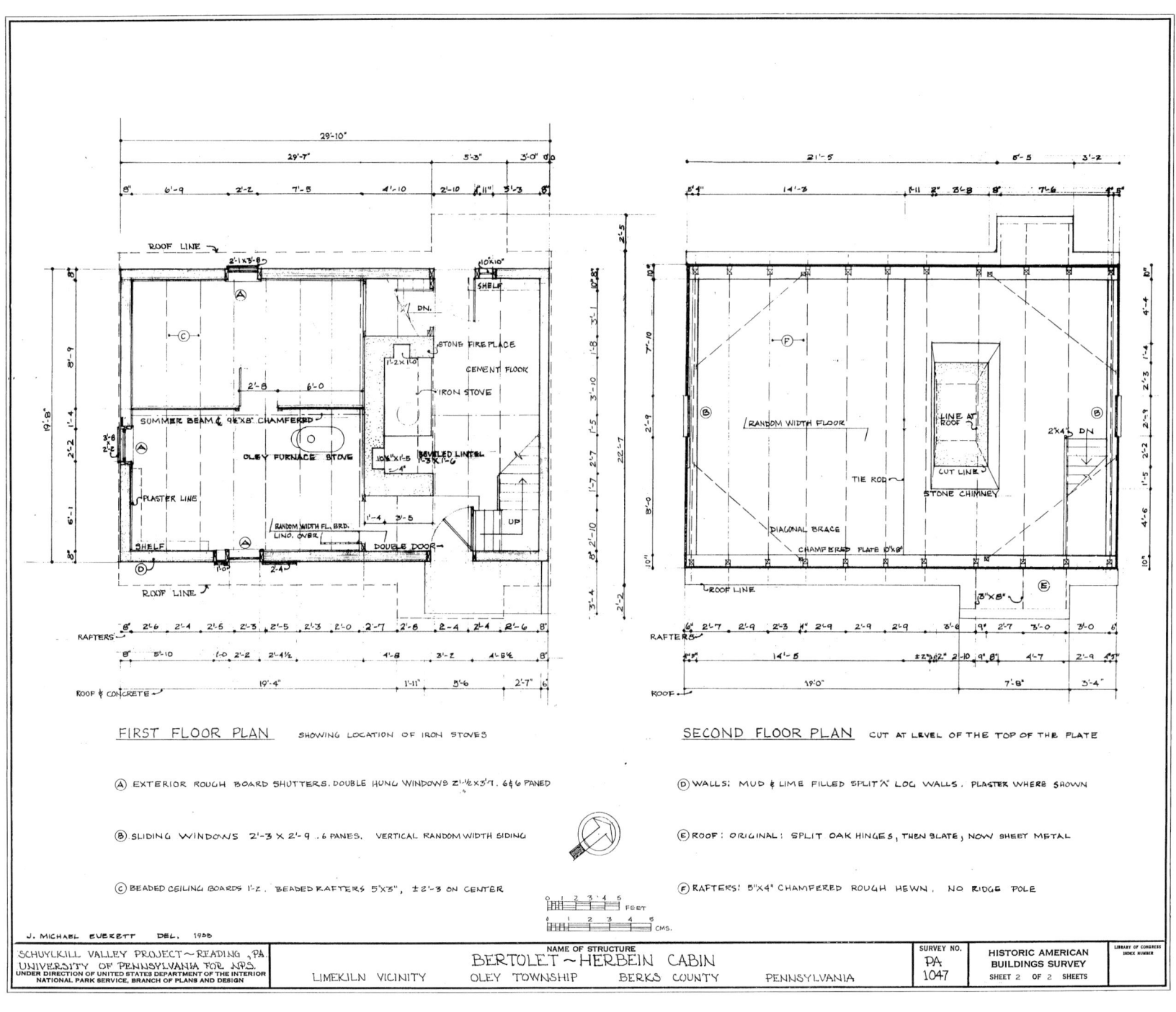

Bertolet Herbein Cabin (PA-1047) Limekiln vicinity (Oley Township), Berks County. First and second floor plans (J. Michael Everett, delineator, 1958) PA,6-LIMKI.V,5.

Pennsylvania Germans did not restrict the *Flurküchenhaus* plan to only modest dwellings but used it in such commodious residences as the 1752 Mueller House (PA-151) in Millbach, Lebanon County. Dressed quoins and brick segmental window arches offset the Mueller House's rubble walls, which rise two full stories plus two attics, which, in turn, are demarcated by pent eaves. Crowning it all is a Germanic "bell-cast" gambrel roof, with its distinctive flare at the eaves and an overlapping of the upper slope. Initially, front and back "Dutch" doors led to a large *Küche* with its large central fireplace, corner flat-balustraded stairs, and doorways to the unheated *Kammer* and the *Stube* with its five-plate stove.[61]

Variants on this pattern include the *Kreuzhaus* (cross house), which has four rooms, rather than three, arranged around the off-center chimney, as in the rubble Hans Herr House (PA-371) in West Lampeter Township, Lancaster County. The fourth room is a pantry or workroom that is partitioned off at the rear of the kitchen. The *Kreuzhaus*'s kitchen (*Küche*) is smaller than that in the *Flurküchenhaus*, but the other rooms correspond in size, location, and function to those of the three-room plan. Small houses, such as the Keim Stone Cabin (PA-1041) in Pike Township, Berks County, usually have only one room on either side of the off-center fireplace. This two-room plan is the most common room arrangement in middle and southern Germany, the homeland of most Pennsylvania Germans, and may have been more widespread in eastern Pennsylvania than surviving evidence suggests.[62] Regardless of plan, these houses invariably had cellars, either barrel-vaulted or with beam ceilings filled with mud-and-straw insulation. Often accessible only from the outside, these cellars were used for storing perishables that in the nineteenth century were kept in detached spring houses.[63] Some cellars were essentially spring houses above which the dwellings were erected.[64]

Although different in details and plans, Hans Herr's and Heinrich Zeller's houses are archetypical Pennsylvania Germanic houses. Swiss-born Christian Herr erected the Herr House in 1719 with a ground story, root cellar, and two attics. He built it near Lancaster County's Pequea Creek for his father Hans, the religious leader of local Mennonites, who, oral tradition says, worshipped here before they had a separate meetinghouse. Herr constructed the house of rubble on exposed limestone bedrock, placing the cellar entrance under the northeast gable, where the bedrock slopes down from the house. He inscribed the house's date and his initials on the lintel of the house's only door, which opens about seven feet from the house's southeast

Hans Herr House (PA-371) Willow Street vicinity (West Lampeter Township), Lancaster County. General view (George Eisenman, photographer, 1971) PA,36-WILST.V,1-1.

corner onto the kitchen and next to the enclosed stairs to the lower attic. The stairs rising along the same gable-end wall from the lower attic to the upper attic are composed of individual hewn logs set flat side up within hewn timbers. Herr probably used the upper attic for storage of grain, but upper attics also often served as smoke chambers for curing meats.[65]

Heinrich Zeller built his story-and-a-half house a quarter-century later, in 1745, along Mill Creek in Lebanon County. Like the Herr House, the Zeller House is constructed of stone, stuccoed in this case, with an off-center chimney, small stone-framed casement windows, and an asymmetrical front. Zeller also inscribed his

Keim Stone Cabin (PA-1041) Lobachsville vicinity (Pike Township), Berks County. General view (Charles H. Dornbusch, photographer, 1941) PA,6-LOBA.V,2A-5.

name and the house's construction date on a dressed stone next to the front door rather than on its limestone lintel, where he crudely carved the Swiss coat-of-arms. Zeller's front door, which he also placed near the house's southeast corner, opens onto the kitchen where in the corner enclosed stairs rise to the upper floor and, originally another set continued to the attic. The boards of the two-part "Dutch" front door and the arched cellar door are set in distinctively Germanic chevron patterns. The Zeller House, however, differs from the Herr House in a few respects. Along its front eaves, for example, four outriggers support a kick to the steep gable roof, allowing it to extend about four feet and provide protection from the elements. The Zeller House also has vertical boards in its gable peaks, a rear door to its kitchen, and a spring running through its insulated post-and-beam cellar.[66]

Although the Zeller House has traditionally been called Fort Zeller, there is no evidence that it was built to serve as a frontier fortress or blockhouse. Perhaps nineteenth-century romantics concluded that its cellar spring was designed to help its occupants withstand an Indian attack or siege. This is illogical, however, because the only access to the cellar is on the house's exterior, fully exposed to any enemy. Nevertheless, oral tradition insists that during the French and Indian War Zeller's twelve-year-old daughter survived an Indian attack in this spring-fed cellar by luring three Indians into the cellar through the spring's exit and killing each intruder with an axe as he entered the dark refuge.[67] True, false, or exaggerated, the story helps to explain the Zeller House's misnomer. Nevertheless, it does not explain the use of "Fort" as a prefix for many of the Germanic houses in Virginia's Shenandoah Valley.[68] All of these appellations, in both Pennsylvania and Virginia, probably were applied in the nineteenth century, when such squat, thick-walled stone houses, dating from Indian times, were no longer being built. When compared with the form and proportions of nineteenth century farmhouses, these eighteenth-century houses could appear fortress-like to local citizens seeking an explanation for their unconventional form and construction.[69]

When these plans were applied to bank houses, room functions generally changed because the large cooking fireplace was often placed at the lower level, built into the bank. The log Wertz-Lashee House (PA-5183), which was built circa 1765 along Conewago Creek in Washington Township, York County, and the 1767 stone John DeTurk House (PA-1023) along Manatawney Creek in Oley Township, Berks County, demonstrate the Germanic bank house in its simplest form. The log house

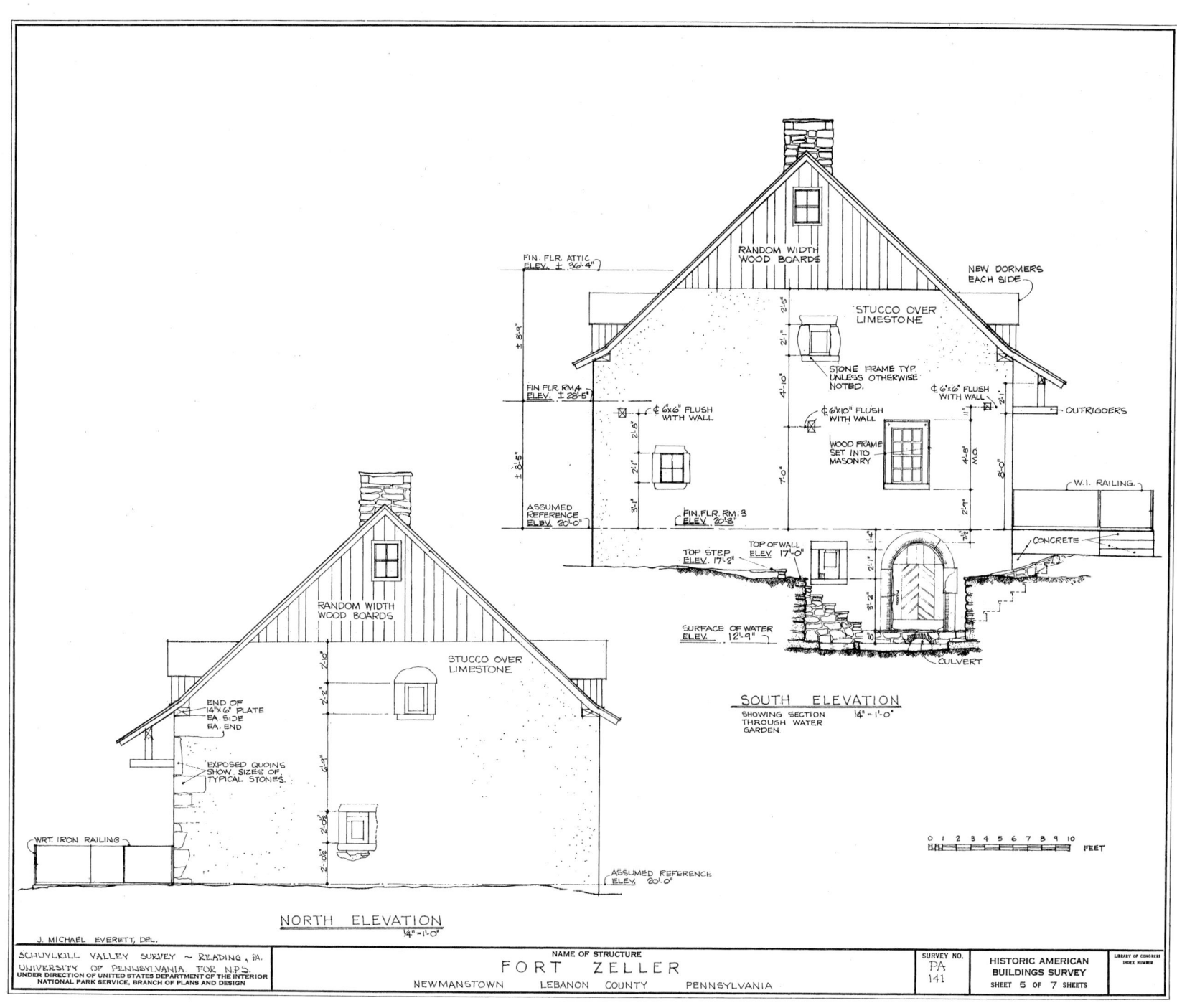

Heinrich Zeller House (Fort Zeller) (PA-141) Newmanstown vicinity (Millcreek Township), Lebanon County. North and south elevations (J. Michael Everett, delineator, 1958) PA,38-NEWM.V,1.

Architecture of Pennsylvania • 49

John DeTurk House (PA-1023) Oley vicinity (Oley Township), Berks County. General view (Charles H. Dornbusch, 1941) PA,6-OLEY,1-6.

has one room on each of its levels with the large cooking fireplace in the stone cellar. The DeTurk cellar has two rooms, one set deeply into the bank, where foodstuffs were stored and the other, opening at the house's rear, where the large fireplace stands. On the upper level of both houses a smaller fireplace shares the large chimney with the cellar fireplace. A pent roof across the front of both houses provided family members some protection while they did chores and processing activities in fresh air and sunlight. DeTurk's attic, accessible by stairs inside the upper level and through an exterior door with a hoisting beam over the upper-level entrance, was equipped for both storage and sleeping.[70]

In bank houses with traditional three-room plans, the room that customarily served as the kitchen (*Küche*) in the *Flurküchenhaus* remains the room of entry but serves as either a living room or bed chamber since the kitchen is in the cellar. Similarly in the four-room *Kreuzhaus* the upper-level room of entry is not the kitchen but a short hall. Robert C. Bucher has identified some of these bank dwellings as Swiss *Weinbauern* (wine farmers or winemakers) houses.[71] They are characterized by a vaulted cellar dug into the bank, a large working fireplace on the two-story gable wall opposite the bank, and a spring flowing through both rooms. The cellar in the stone 1736 Alexander Schaeffer House in Schaefferstown, Lebanon County, for example, once had two stills attached at the rear of its large arched central fireplace. Exterior steps lead from the cellar's work area to the upper level's living area, where under the overhanging gable roof another set of exterior stone steps reach the attic. The rubble mid-eighteenth-century Almonry (PA-320B) at Ephrata Cloister in Lancaster County is built and organized in a similar fashion, except that its lower level has two adjoining beehive ovens for baking bread instead of stills for distilling liquor.[72]

English colonists also built bank houses, but usually with the gable-to-gable axis parallel with the bank, not perpendicular to it, like most Germanic examples. Also, the English organized their interior space differently. William Harvey immigrated from Worcestershire, England, in 1712, and approximately three years later he built his rubble dwelling (PA-1204) into a bank near Brandywine Creek in Pennsbury Township, Chester County. Like German colonists, Harvey used the cellar's inner room for dark storage, and in the outer room he placed the kitchen with a corner fireplace on the western gable wall, not in the center of the room. On the upper level a short entry passage led to the hall and parlor, whose corner fireplaces used the same chimney as the cellar kitchen fireplace.[73]

Another Pennsylvania-German house type, the *Durchganigenhaus* (passage-hall house) has a center passage that separates the kitchen and chamber sides. Less common than the other Germanic house types, the *Durchganigenhaus* was invariably a large house, such as the Widows' House (PA-1155) in the Moravian complex at Bethlehem, Northampton County.[74] Planned in 1760 as a large (seventy-eight by forty-four feet) three-story building for Moravian missionaries' widows, it was built in

1767-68 with only two stories and the planned cellar and two attics. In supervising the house's construction, Carl Schulze, a member of the Moravian Church, gave it the coursed rock-faced limestone walls and brick segmental arches over its windows and doors that characterize Bethlehem's other stone Moravian buildings. A coved plaster cornice extends across its front to provide transition from the facade to the gable roof with the kick at the front eaves, another characteristic of Bethlehem's Moravian buildings. Schulze's specifications included a cedar-shingled jerkin-head roof, with an upper register of shed dormers and a lower register of gable dormers, which remained undisturbed when the roof was later altered to the present gable roof. As erected, the plan had a central entrance and stairhall, an essential aspect of the *Durchganigenhaus*. Rooms evidently were heated by stoves set into the backs of fireplaces in the lateral hall. A structural feature of this house is the brick chimneys, which rise separately to the lower attic where they vault to unite as one large mass that forges through the roof's peak as two chimneys connected by a brick screen.[75]

The contemporaneous Moravian community in Bethlehem and the Ephrata Cloister in Ephrata are outstanding concentrations of eighteenth-century Germanic architecture.[76] One is predominantly stone architecture and the other half-timber and log. Except for the clapboarded log Gemeinhaus (community house) (PA-1142), the eighteenth-century Moravian buildings are built of limestone ashlar with either gambrel or steep gable roofs.[77] Large clapboarded timber-frame structures dominate in the Ephrata Cloister. For its first twenty-one years the Moravian Community in Bethlehem operated as a communal venture. In 1762 it changed to a closed community in which families were expected to support themselves independently, yet the group's religious mission remained strong and family ties were de-emphasized by separating unmarried males and females at about the age of twelve into separate buildings, the Single Brethren's House (PA-1141) and the Single Sisters' House (PA-1153). Eventually economic pressures forced them to open the town to outsiders, and in 1844 the first non-Moravians purchased property in Bethlehem.[78]

Because of its founder, the German Pietist Conrad Beissel, the faith practiced at Ephrata Cloister was considerably more mystical than that at Bethlehem. Members of this commune led monastic lives of work and prayer guided by divine revelation and human fellowship.[79-81] As in Bethlehem, unmarried men and women lived in separate buildings, the 1742-43 weatherboarded log Saron (PA-320K) for celibate women and the circa-1746 weatherboarded half-timber Bethania (PA-320D) for celi-

Bethlehem Moravian Community, Gemeinhaus (PA-1142) Bethlehem, Northampton County. West elevation (Jack E. Boucher, photographer, 1969) PA,48-BETH,3A-4.

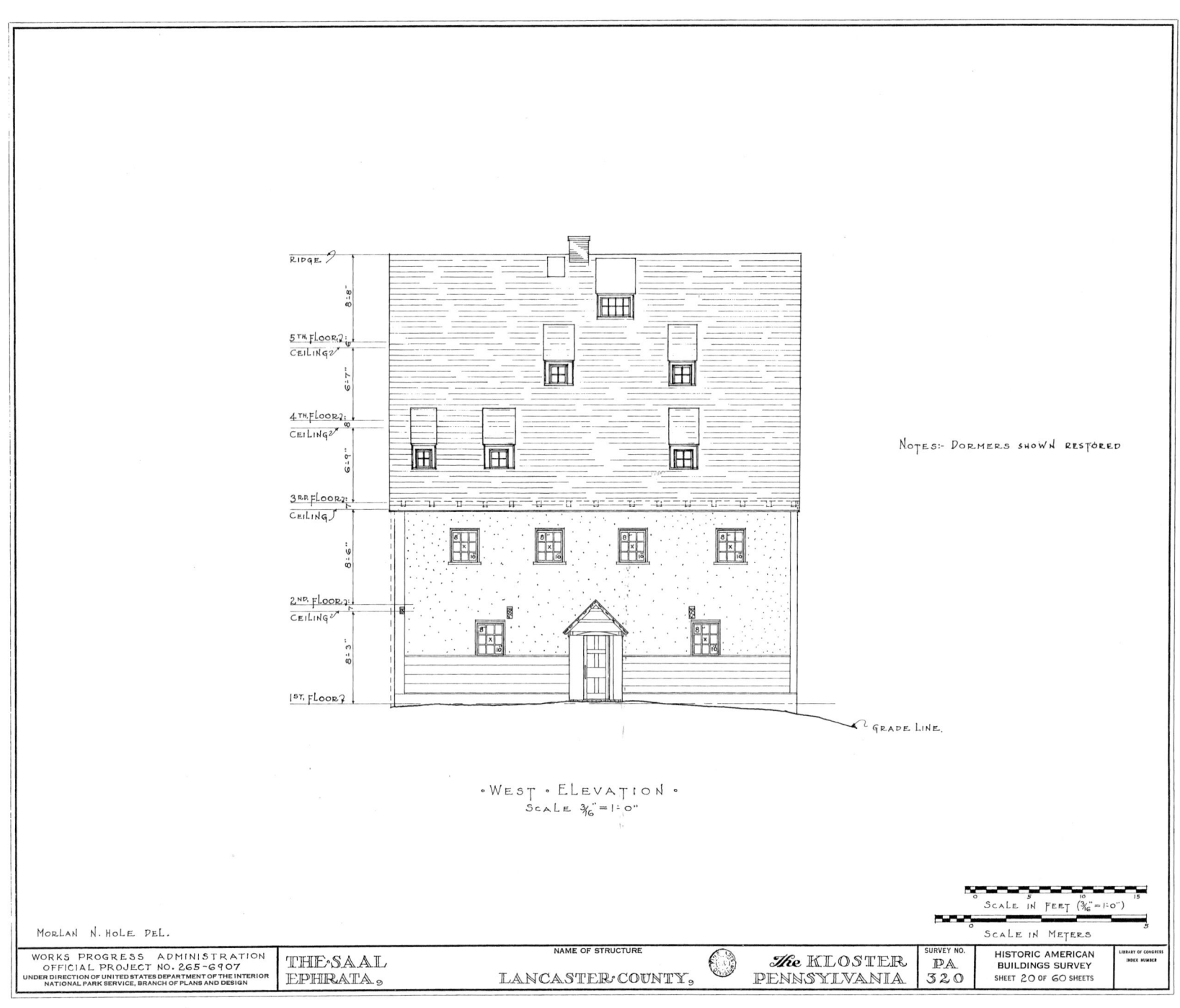

Ephrata Cloister, Saal (PA-320J) Ephrata vicinity (Ephrata Township), Lancaster County. West elevation (Morlan N. Hole, delineator, 1936-37) PA,36-EPH,1.

bate men. Married couples lived in small story-and-a-half weatherboarded timber-frame *Flurküchenhausen*. The rough weatherboarding, asymmetrical fenestration, and steep flared gable roofs with shed dormers give the large buildings a decidedly medieval Germanic appearance. The 1740-41 half-timber Saal (hall) (PA-320J), for example, with its weatherboarded walls and three registers of shed dormers on its long gable roof resembles in form and detail, if not material, southern German guildhalls. Especially similar to the Saal is the 1522 Zeughaus (textile house) in Ulm, Germany, and its 1598 extension with a triple attic and three registers of shed dormers. The Saal, however, embodies mystical and symbolic aspects that would have been extremely unusual for German public buildings at that time. Its builders used theosophic and Rosicrucian principles to orient the Saal at a mystical angle to an earlier (and now-gone) meetinghouse and built it as a forty-foot cube, then considered a mystically perfect form. Similarly inside the Saal, a massive chamfered post, perhaps symbolic of the Tree of Life in the Garden of Eden, rises the double-height of the meeting room to four beams that divide the ceiling into four equal panels and may represent the rivers that flow to the four corners of the earth.[80]

Another German utopian community is Old Economy Village (PA-1176) in Ambridge, Beaver County. This is the third and final site for this German Pietist commune. In 1805 George Rapp established the Harmony Society at Harmony, near Zelienople, Butler County, but in 1815 the group disposed of its holdings and moved to New Harmony, Indiana. After a decade there the Harmonists sold their property to Robert Owen, the English social utopian, and returned to Pennsylvania, where they purchased three thousand acres along the Ohio River for their community called Economy.[81] They laid out a grid plan that did not incorporate into the design the public square that dominated their earlier plans for Harmony and New Harmony but rather laid out a formal public garden with a reflecting pool. Also, they planned no exclusively residential blocks; stores and mills, evidence of their proud economy, were distributed throughout the town in each of the blocks.[82]

Because the Harmonists built Economy's main structures in the second quarter of the nineteenth century (between 1826 and 1831), after two decades of exposure to American culture, the society's buildings exhibit many American Georgian high-style features, such as symmetrical fenestration, pedimented frontispieces, and fanlights (particularly on the Feast Hall [PA-612] and Great House), and the Meeting House's (PA-627) entrance tower and octagonal belfry. More significant, however, is

Economy Feast Hall (PA-612) Ambridge Borough, Beaver County. East and west elevations (Carl G. Baker, delineator, 1965) PA,4-AMB,1A.

the buildings' strong medieval character, their similarity in massing and details to Germanic buildings in Bethlehem and Ephrata, in short, the persistence of the vernacular tradition. The brick Great House, for example, has a double attic and flared gable roof not unlike those of the Moravians' Gemeinhaus or the 1773 addition to their Single Sisters' House. Similarly the Meeting House's cove cornice duplicates that of the Widows' House in Bethlehem. Also, except for its greater size, the Tailor Shop's (PA-613) vaulted wine cellar is similar to those in many *Flurküchenhausen* and *Kreuzhausen,* and the exposed half-timbering of Economy's granary has rubble infill like that in Ephrata's Saal.[83] Economy slowly declined after the Civil War until its last three members dissolved the Harmony Society in 1905. The town had already lost its identity in 1902, when the society sold one hundred and five acres to the American Bridge Company, which built the world's largest structural steel fabrication plant in what they now called Ambridge, a shortened version of the company's name. The Commonwealth acquired one-and-a-half blocks of the old town in 1916 and gradually restored the buildings and gardens for their present use as a museum.[84]

German-speaking people in early America had roots in an extensive area of Europe, ranging from Poland's Silesia and Czechoslovakia's Moravia in the east to Switzerland and eastern France in the west. Consequently their architecture differed. Sometimes a building such as the 1743 Augustus Lutheran Church (PA-175) in Trappe, Montgomery County, could be Germanic yet unique. Its Germanic character is expressed in both imposing exterior features and understated interior details, ranging from the gambrel roof with its hipped octagonal end to the mortising of the stair treads to the solid stringers. Yet the Trappe church is one of a kind; no distinctively German Lutheran or Reformed church architecture developed in its wake.[85]

Scotch-Irish Presbyterian churches, on the other hand, assumed an early form that was repeated for nearly a century. Built of rubble masonry with arched openings and, usually, gable roofs, these simple one-story buildings were erected along Pennsylvania's moving frontier, beginning at the turn of the eighteenth century with the Presbyterian church that still stands in Norriton, Montgomery County. The austere appearance of these churches, in particular the 1740 Paxton Presbyterian Church (PA-31) in Paxtang, Dauphin County, reflects the sternness of the faith once practiced within their stone walls.[86] Many of these churches are combinations of common vernacular details and unique structural elements. The Guinston Presbyterian Church (PA-5187) in Chanceford Township, York County, for example, includes

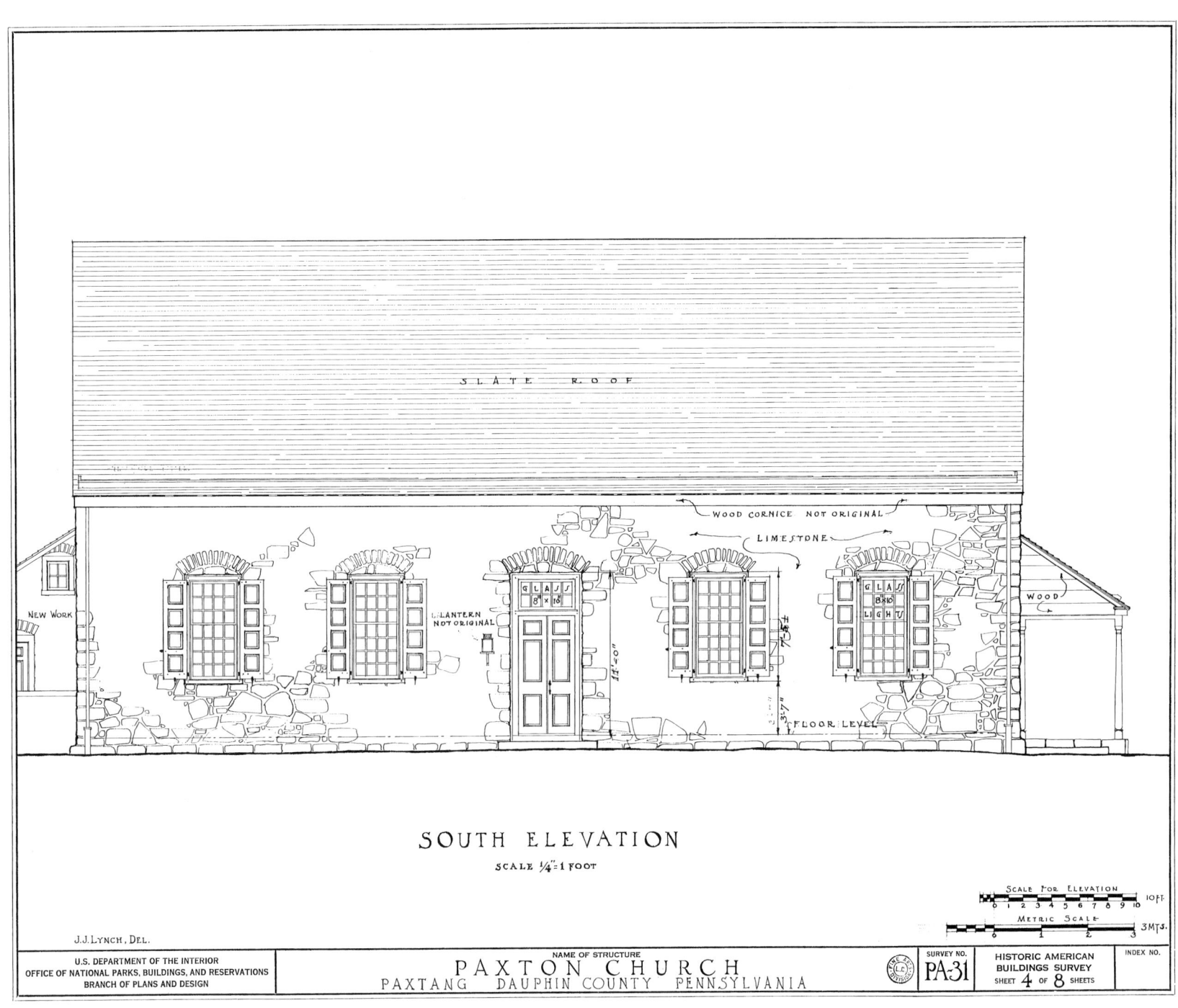

Paxtang Presbyterian Church (PA-31) Paxtang Borough, Dauphin County. South elevation (J. J. Lynch, delineator, 1935) PA,22-PAX,1.

pent eaves at its gable ends and attenuated squared posts, which appear ornamental on each side of the front and rear entrances but are actually tied into large interior beams. By the last quarter of the eighteenth century, local builders were incorporating refined architectural details into their traditional designs for these rural houses of worship. The large well-proportioned fanlight over the double-leaf entrance door of the Great Conewago Presbyterian Church (PA-345) in Hunterstown, Adams County, for example, complements the round-arch windows. Because of the building's greater scale, however, the rubble gable end, relieved only by a circular 1787 datestone, leaves the church awkwardly top-heavy.[87]

Despite the common form of these Scotch-Irish Presbyterian churches, the architecture of Pennsylvania's Scotch-Irish "is not a distinct style," according to Alan Gowans, "but a general influence, a tendency to build in rugged stone that appears wherever Scotch masons and quarries existed together."[88] Henry Glassie, who prefers to call this ethnic group Irish, explains that its "contribution is difficult to distinguish because it was integral to the formation of the American whole." The frontier farmer "meshed Irish, English and German traditions into something new."[89] Even turning to Old World roots offers limited help. The internal organization of the vernacular houses in northern and western Ireland into a large heated room with entry doors and a smaller unheated room grew out of an ancient Celtic tradition that was prevalent throughout the British Isles and in Germanic Europe.[90] The difficulty of isolating an American Scotch-Irish material culture is demonstrated by the early Scotch-Irish adoption of others' log-building techniques, by which their own distinctive building practices are intermingled with those of other groups. Historians attribute to them the rectangular-plan single-pen log house (a one-room unit with an exterior gable-end chimney), such as the late-eighteenth-century Robert Neal Cabin (PA-46) in Pittsburgh's Schenley Park,[91] but at this point they have documented little about Scotch-Irish architectural contributions. Clearly this is another aspect of Pennsylvania architecture that needs more research and field work.

In their simplicity these Scotch-Irish Presbyterian churches resemble meetinghouses, yet the Presbyterians did not build their houses of worship with the consistent and philosophical simplicity of the Quakers. Plain and simple to the extreme, early Quaker meetinghouses are domestic, rather than ecclesiastical, in both form and scale. In fact, Pennsylvania's first Quaker meetings occurred in private homes in Philadelphia. The earliest meetinghouse, on Philadelphia's Front Street, was timber

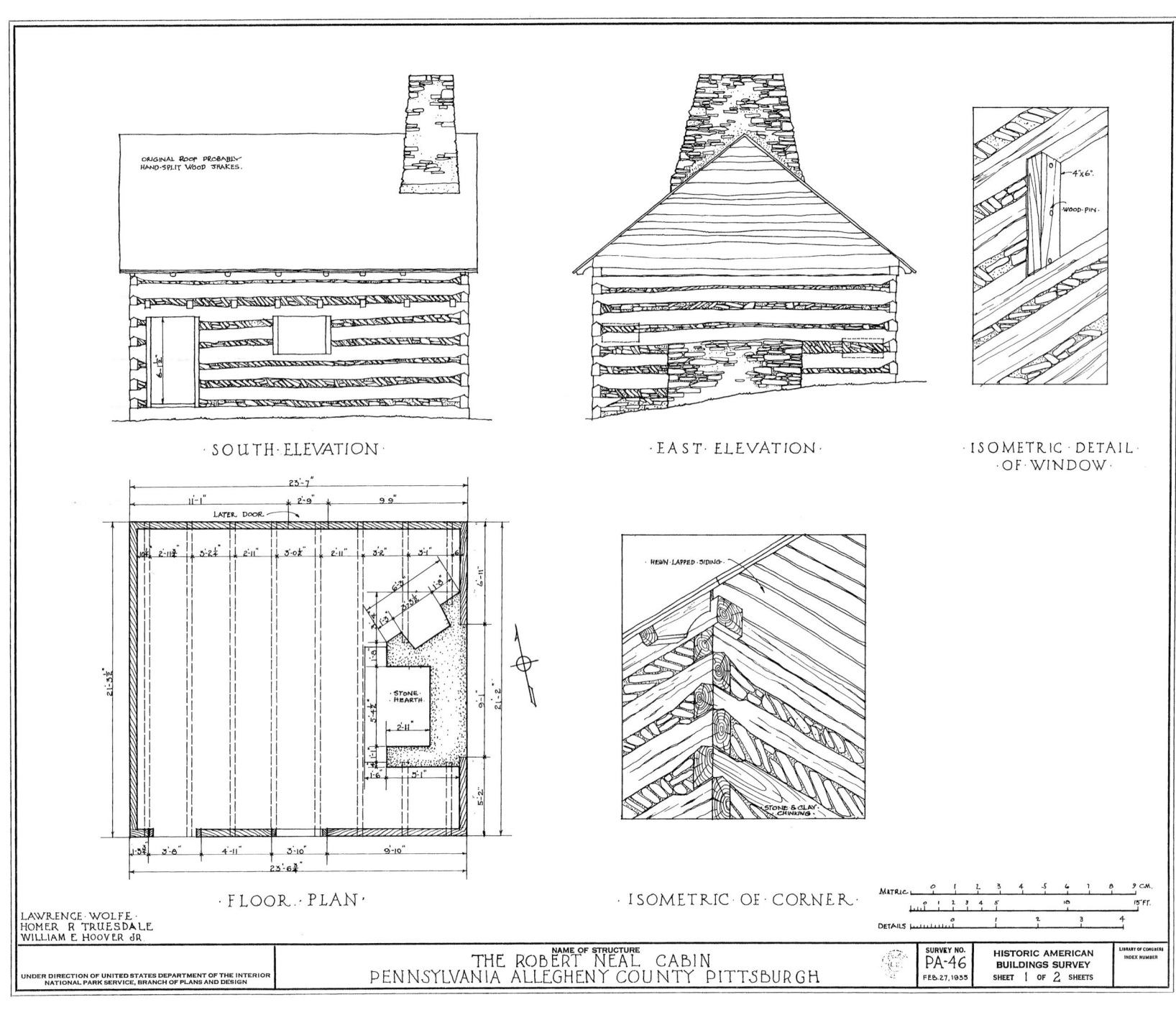

Robert Neal Cabin (PA-46) Pittsburgh, Allegheny County. Plan elevations and details (Lawrence Wolfe, Homer R. Truesdale, and William E. Hoover Jr., delineators, 1935) PA,2-PITBU,12.

Birmingham Friends Meetinghouse (PA-1193) Birmingham (Birmingham Township), Chester County. South and west elevations (Ned Goode, photographer, 1958) PA,15-BIRM,1-1.

frame, but the city's Quakers quickly turned to brick for their short-lived meetinghouse on Center Square and all subsequent meetinghouses.[92] West of the Wertenbaker line they built in stone, and in one case, in Frankford, Philadelphia County, which straddles the Wertenbaker line, local Quakers in 1775 built their meetinghouse partly of brick and partly of stone masonry.[93] The 1700 Haverford Meetinghouse (PA-179) in Haverford Township, Delaware County, is representative of the many eighteenth- and early-nineteenth-century Quaker meetinghouses throughout the southeastern part of the state: a rubble, gable-roofed, one-and-a-half-story, domestic-scaled building devoid of architectural ornament but with two doors indicating the gender-separation of the worship. The Haverford Meetinghouse has two stories, but most Quaker meetinghouses are one or one-and-a-half stories. Quakers permitted functional embellishments on their meetinghouses, such as the paneled shutters or the pedimented hoods on the 1763 Birmingham Friends Meetinghouse (PA-1193) in Birmingham Township, Chester County. Interiors are as plain as the exteriors, characterized by rows of benches without even a pulpit, for there are no ordained ministers in Quaker congregations. Because men and women worship on separate sides of the meetinghouse, many meetinghouses, such as the Birmingham example and the 1758 Exeter Friends Meetinghouse (PA-1021) near Stonersville, Berks County, have sliding partitions along the middle of the room, and some have an even more unusual feature, sliding partitions perpendicular to the long sliding partition. The log Quaker Meetinghouse (PA-212) built in Catawissa, Columbia County, in 1774-76 goes a step further and has two permanently partitioned rooms, one for women and the other for men.[94]

Where congregations remained small, nineteenth-century meetinghouses, such as the 1846 brick Friends Meetinghouse (PA-218) in Millville, Columbia County, differ little from such colonial examples as the brick 1765 York Friends Meetinghouse.[95] In Philadelphia, however, the Arch Street Friends Meeting (PA-1388), the site of the Philadelphia Yearly Meeting, had to be built on such a large scale that in 1803 its architect, Owen Biddle, gave the brick building an architectural composition that is rare for Quaker meetinghouses. He designed a main entrance with a gable roof and traditional pent eaves and a hipped-roof east wing, marking the double-leaf entrance doors with Tuscan-columned porches. Seven years later the congregation added a hipped-roof west wing, leaving the gable-roof section the visual center of the facade. Except for the attenuated Tuscan columns, the sole acknowledgment of the then-fashionable late Georgian style, the meetinghouse remains loyal to the plain style on the interior and exterior.[96]

Unrestrained by theological aversions to architectural splendors, English Anglicans quickly asserted leadership in high-style ecclesiastical architecture. The zenith of colonial Pennsylvania church design is Philadelphia's Christ Church (PA-1071), a brick Anglican church building with an aisle-and-nave plan and galleries. Evidently designed by John Kearsley, a gentleman physician with an interest in architecture, Christ Church was seventeen years in the making. Although the church wardens declared the building complete in April 1747, in November of that year, they installed a London-made chandelier in the center of the church, and between 1750 and 1754 they oversaw the erection of the church's steeple.[97] Christ Church's details were drawn from a number of English design books and two London churches in particular, St. Andrew-by-the-Wardrobe and James Gibbs's St. Martin-in-the-Fields. The correct display of those English Baroque details (molded brick, pilasters, entablatures, urns, spiral scrolls, and a great Palladian window topped with a keystone and

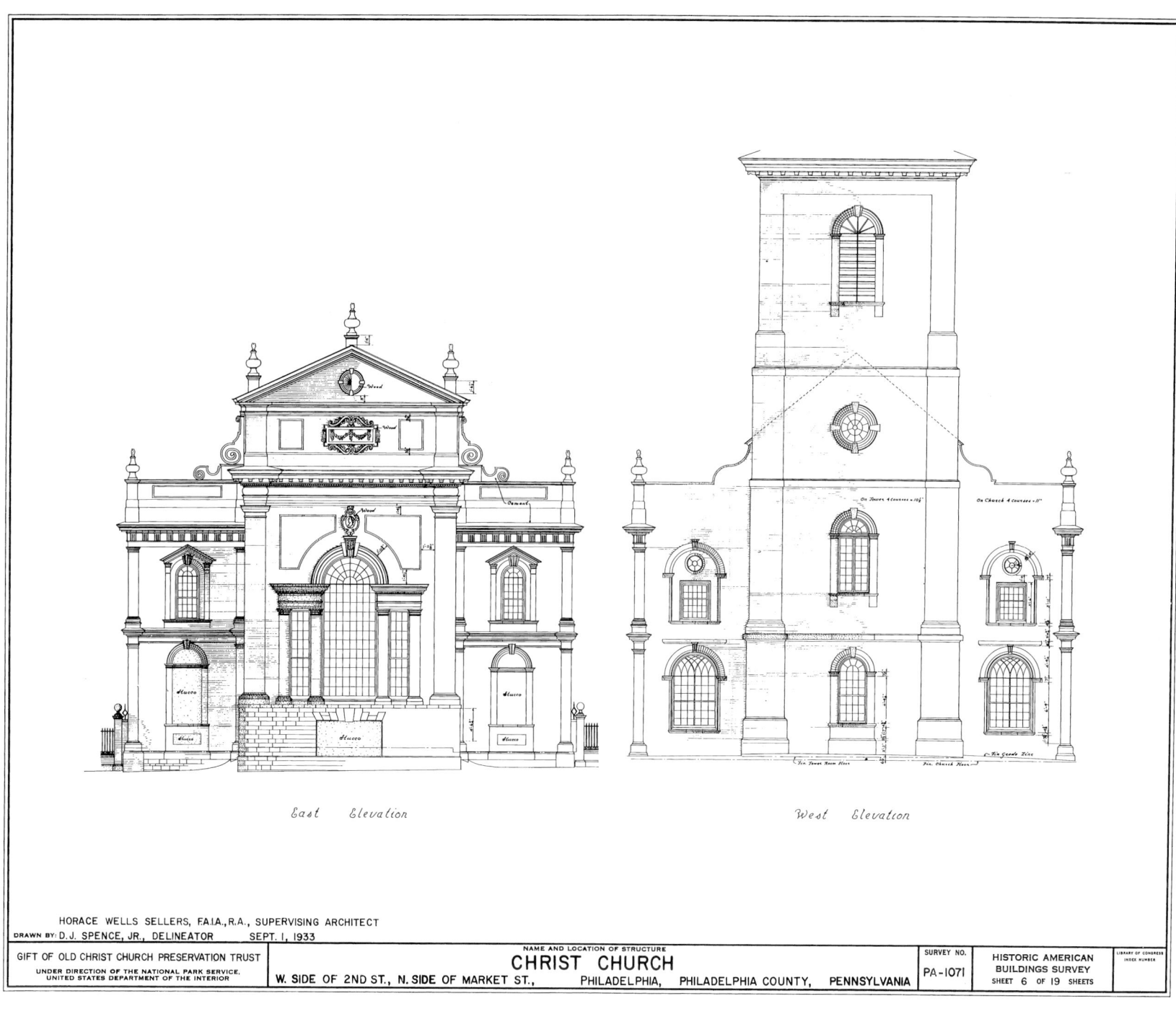

Christ Church (PA-1071) Philadelphia. East and west elevations (D.J. Spence Jr., delineator, 1933) PA,51-PHILA,7.

medallion) made it "the most ornate of Georgian churches in the colonies."[98]

Although Christ Church stood without peer in the province, there were other well-designed Georgian churches. Christ Church's "chapel of ease," St. Peter's Church (PA-1118) in Philadelphia's Society Hill, is the best of this lot. Robert Smith, the master builder who was most responsible for Christ Church's steeple, and John Kearsley, Christ Church's probable "architect," designed this marble-trimmed brick church in 1758 for Christ Church parishioners who wanted to worship closer to their Society Hill homes. Smith and Kearsley evidently based their design on Christ Church in Surrey, England, which was engraved in a 1756 book on London architecture.[99] A large Palladian window, not unlike the one in Philadelphia's Christ Church, dominates the east end. Quoins, a modillion cornice, and two stories of round-arch windows with surrounds all have their counterparts in the English church. On the inside the three aisles, high-backed box pews, galleries, and a well-crafted organ case are well-preserved elements of English Georgian church architecture. The steeple at the western end is not Smith's work; William Strickland designed it in 1842 to replace the original cupola. In 1766 Smith also designed in Philadelphia the Zion Lutheran Church, a large brick edifice with a Palladian window and urns that was demolished in 1869, and the Third Presbyterian Church (Pine Street Presbyterian Church) (PA-1374), which has since gone through many remodelings.[100]

Generally, colonial church architecture outside of Philadelphia was less sophisticated. Lancaster, however, Pennsylvania's largest inland center by the 1760s, developed the wealth and worldliness that allowed it to emulate the Provincial capital's architectural standard. Lutherans, for example, erected between 1761 and 1766 the Lutheran Church of the Holy Trinity (PA-575). Subsequent alterations in 1785 and 1792 resulted in a building that is comparable to Philadelphia's Georgian churches. With its two tiers of round-arch windows, modillion cornice, and roof urns at the corners and on the rear ridge, Holy Trinity emulates Philadelphia's Christ Church, although initially entry was through a pedimented doorway centered on the long western side, and the pulpit stood against the opposite wall with galleries on the other three walls. Between 1792 and 1794 two Philadelphia builders, William and Abraham Colliday, erected the spire (modeled after Philadelphia's Christ Church spire) atop the brick tower that George Lotman, a local mason, had built in 1785-86. Statues of the Evangelists—Matthew, Mark, Luke, and John—carved from solid pine and placed at the corners of the tower,[101] are too diminutive for the scale and height

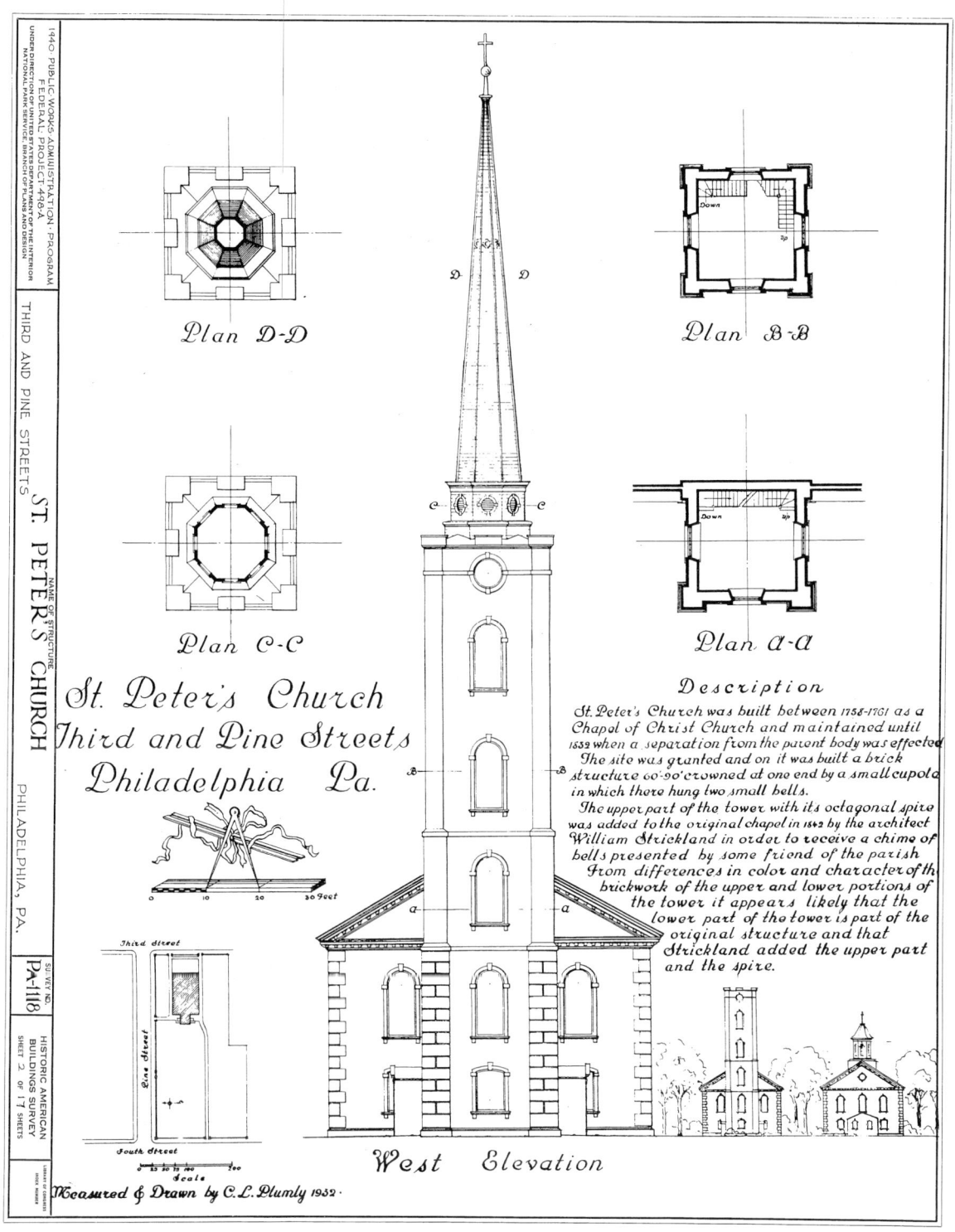

Saint Peter's Protestant Episcopal Church (PA-1118) Philadelphia. West elevation (C.L. Plumly, delineator, 1932) PA,51-PHILA,108.

of the steeple above and behind them, but they help to make the church "the most elegant surviving Georgian public building in Lancaster."[102] Most Georgian churches in Pennsylvania's small towns were considerably more modest in scale and embellishments than Holy Trinity. The 1806 St. Michael's Church in Strasburg, Lancaster County, for example, is a simple three-story rectangular brick building without a bell tower or steeple. Its five bays of round-arch windows with marble keystones and archivolts are suggestive of Holy Trinity's original fenestration, but the brick piers framing each bay are more reminiscent of Philadelphia's Zion Lutheran Church.[103] The two-story St. Gabriel's Church (PA-1038), built in 1801 in Douglassville, Berks County, possesses fundamental Georgian proportions and symmetry. Yet it retains traditional pent eaves, albeit thinner and more delicately proportioned pent eaves than those of the early and mid-eighteenth century. Except for the flat arches with projecting keystones over its openings, the church's embellishment is its striking stonemasonry: the vague herringbone pattern of the diagonally laid squared rubble, the oversized dark quoins, and the dark ashlar of its water table.

Pennsylvania's outstanding Georgian public building is its Provincial state house, better known as Independence Hall (PA-1430). Begun in 1732, Independence Hall was built over a sixteen-year period that was fraught with delays from political disputes, work obstructions, and shortage of funds. Construction was far from finished when the General Assembly convened within its walls in October 1736. Another twelve years passed before the Provincial government declared the building complete, and the distinctive tower and steeple, a separate project, were not finished until 1753. In less than thirty years the steeple decayed so badly that it was removed in 1781; the present steeple is an 1828 reconstruction designed by William Strickland.[104] As chairman of the building committee and overseer of the works, attorney Andrew Hamilton was probably Independence Hall's designer. He apparently based his design on Buckingham House in London's St. James Park. Colin Campbell had an engraving of the house in his 1715 *Vitruvius Britannicus*, a greatly touted work that was available to Hamilton.[105] With its side dependencies and connecting arcades, Independence Hall was the colonies' largest and most sophisticated public building. While the handling of the details on the northern facade has been criticized,[106] the bluestone quoins, string courses, and inset blank panels, and the balustrade along the decked gable roof highlight and frame the smooth brick walls in a manner advocated by English tastemakers of the day. The tower, which dominates the southern facade

Saint Gabriel's Church (PA-1038) Douglassville (Amity Township), Berks County. Southeast elevation (Cervin Robinson, photographer, 1958) PA,6-DOUG,2-1.

and contains the stairway, and the simple plan and large-scaled interior are appropriate for a Provincial state house that through well-known circumstances has become one of the country's most recognizable buildings.[107]

No other public building in colonial Pennsylvania could command the funds to be as monumental and well finished as Independence Hall, but within the means of their patrons, other public buildings could be well designed. York County's mid-twentieth-century replica of its 1756 two-story brick courthouse reflects the original building's relatively early date and inland location. Although its builder achieved symmetry on the facades, the windows were too widely spaced and the roof was too steeply pitched for a correctly proportioned Georgian design. Lancaster's brick City Hall (PA-1343), built forty years later (1795-97) in a more populous center, exhibited a more sophisticated design and such Georgian details as a marble string course, flat arches with keystones over its windows, a pedimented frontispiece, and a cupola. The timber-frame Luzerne County Courthouse was built a decade later (1801-1804)

Architecture of Pennsylvania • 67

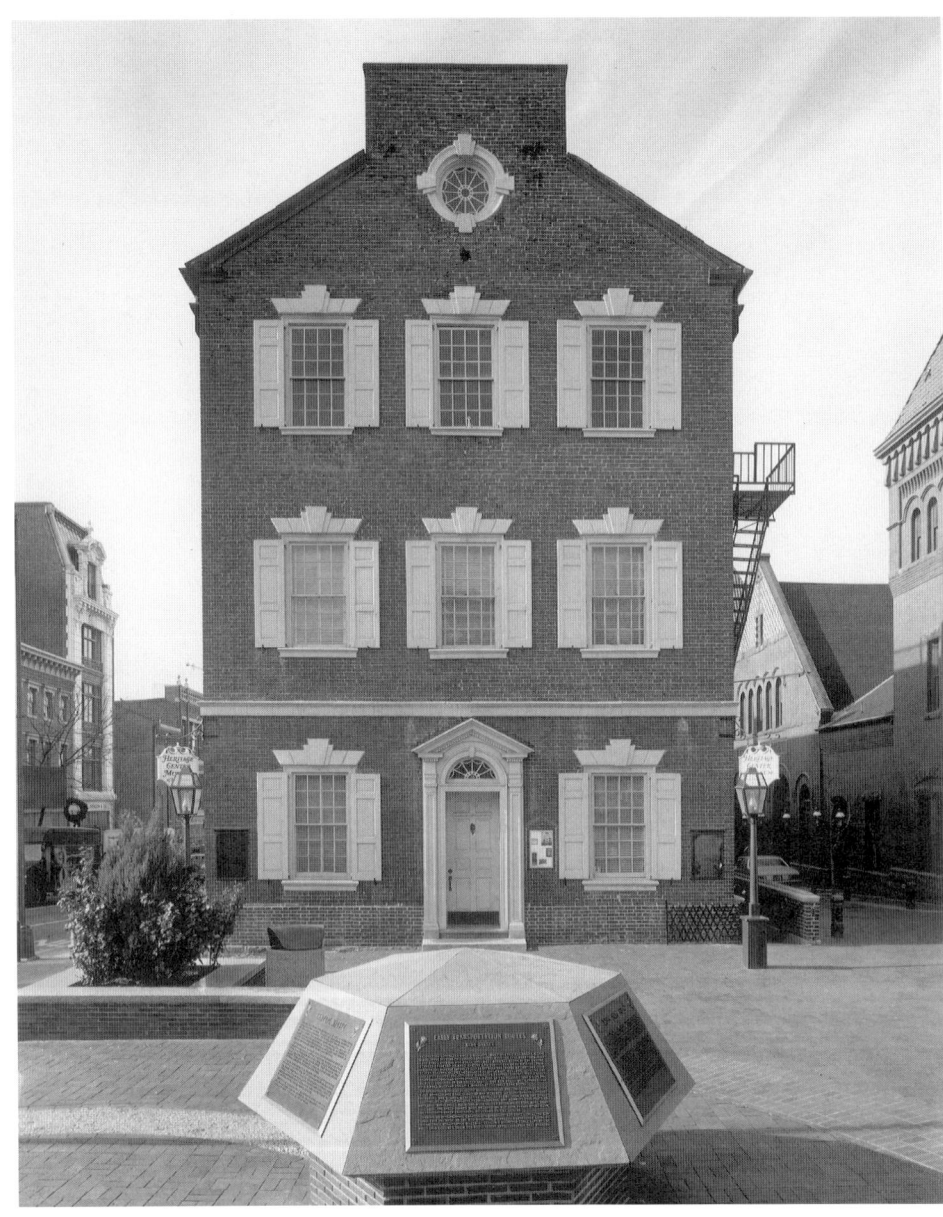

City Hall (PA-1343) Lancaster, Lancaster County. East elevation (Dan Eisenhart, photographer, 1981) PA,36-LANC,2-4.

in Wilkes-Barre. Its builder incorporated some of the same details (flat window arches with keystones, pedimented frontispieces, and quoins) and sheathed its two-story exterior with boards grooved to resemble rusticated ashlar.[108] None, however, was as sophisticated as Philadelphia's Carpenters' Hall (PA-1398), the home of America's oldest builders' organization. It served as a quasi public building from its beginning in 1774 when the First Continental Congress met here. In 1770 Robert Smith designed this two-story brick building with a cruciform plan that Beatrice Garvan ties to both Andrea Palladio's Villa Rotunda and Scottish town halls in Smith's native Scotland.[109]

By the middle of the eighteenth century, urban dwellings also reflected the Georgian style. Balanced facades, often with no more than brick string courses and architrave-framed doors characterized most of Philadelphia's modest dwellings with London house plans. The brick house (PA-1324) that James Davis built in Society Hill circa 1758 is one of many that fits this pattern. Davis built it with two stories; Major David Lenox was responsible for raising it a story and a half in 1784. Townhouses, however, displayed the Georgian style more splendidly. Wide enough to accommodate an entry and stairhall and two back-to-back ground-floor rooms in the front building, townhouses had a stair tower, or piazza, and a rear ell, or backbuilding, for the kitchen, pantry, and often dining room. Few were as well finished as the 1765 Powel House (PA-1359). From its frontispiece of engaged Roman Doric columns and Ionic entablature to its carved ballroom chimney breast, the Powel House is among the best examples of Georgian taste and craftsmanship in the state, and fortunately is open to the public as a historic house museum. In rare instances urban houses are so large that they occupy a double lot, as does the 1786 Reynolds-Morris House (PA-1107) in Philadelphia.[110]

The country house is probably the greatest and most widely distributed expression of the Georgian style in Pennsylvania. It was dependent on two significant early-eighteenth-century developments that would greatly affect Pennsylvania's architecture for at least a century. One was the arrival of the double-pile house, which had developed in England in the seventeenth century, and the other was the increasing availability, after about 1750, of English architectural pattern books.[111] The former provided the high-style framework and the latter illustrated the ways that framework could be ornamented and organized. The eighteenth-century double-pile house, called the four-over-four by cultural geographers,[112] has a double file of rooms separated by a central hall, which serves as a passageway that divides the ground floor into a number of functional units and often contains the stairs leading to the upper chambers. In many respects the double-pile house marked the triumph of Renaissance principles and the rapid fading of medieval traditions. Its central passage afforded a centralized system of circulation, which, in turn, allowed an unprecedented degree of privacy.[113]

It is not clear whether some early double-pile houses were expansions of the side-hall plan (in which the plan was duplicated, back to back)[114] or were variations of the high-style Georgian double-pile mansions. The 1768 Taylor-Parke House (PA-205) in East Bradford Township, Chester County, with its pent eaves, pent roof on all four facades, and datestone centered on the symmetrical ashlar front, is an interesting folk expression of the Georgian double-pile house. When Abiah Taylor II, a Quaker farmer, miller, and land speculator, built the two-story house in 1768, he was probably behaving less as a Quaker than as a local farmer familiar with, but not fully knowledgeable about, the new ways of organizing a "mansion house," as early deeds describe the house.[115] Its Georgian character includes what is called a Georgian gable[116] and a roof with a forty-five-degree pitch. The front, however, has four bays, not five, putting the entrance off-center and leaving the interior without a hallway. Instead, entry is into the larger of the two front rooms. The closed-string staircase, which rises steeply a few feet from the front door, has a chamfered newel post and a plain handrail without balusters. An arched passage beneath the staircase originally led to the cellar stairs and connected the two front rooms, each with traditional corner fireplaces.[117] Primitive Hall (PA-167), built in West Marlborough Township, Chester County, exactly thirty years earlier than the Taylor-Parke House, also has four bays and an off-center entrance. The asymmetrical spacing of Primitive Hall's windows, its blank brick end wall, and such traditional details as the pent roof, cove cornice, and corner fireplaces suggest that its builder (working before English design books could have reasonably reached rural Chester County) was thinking in terms of building a large dwelling according to traditional forms, which in this case may have been the combination of two large-scale, back-to-back, hall-and-parlor plans.[118]

The Georgian double-pile country house with a central passage hall evidently did not appear in Pennsylvania until near the middle of the eighteenth century. James Logan, William Penn's secretary and agent, for example, built Stenton (PA-1714) in Philadelphia's Germantown between 1728 and 1734. It is an early

Taylor-Parke House (PA-205) Copesville Vicinity (East Bradford Township), Chester County. South elevation (Ned Goode, photographer, 1960) PA,15-COPES.V,1-1

Primitive Hall (PA-167) Clonmell vicinity (West Marlborough Township), Chester County. South and east elevations (Ned Goode, photographer, 1959) PA,15-CLON.V,1-1.

two-story brick double-pile country house, but it is more appropriately "Queen Anne" than Georgian.[119] Symmetrical fenestration is restricted to only the front, where segmental arches crown the first-story windows, and the entrance doorway is capped with a rectangular transom and flanked by narrow side lights. Stenton's builder handled Georgian details with a tentativeness and sense of incompleteness that offset Georgian horizontality. The brick strips marking the front's corners and two central bays crudely emulate pilasters and interrupt the brick string course to give the facade an inappropriate verticality. Also, the builder laid out the interior with a front salon and rear stairhall rather than a through passage which is not unexpected, since Stenton's date precedes the general availability of English design books.[120]

It is presently impossible to identify with certainty Pennsylvania's earliest Georgian double-pile country house with a central passage. Nevertheless, Waynesborough (PA-208) in Easttown Township, Chester County, ranks among the earliest. As the home and possible birthplace of Revolutionary General "Mad" Anthony Wayne, the two-and-a-half-story hipped-roof house is better known for its historical associations than its architectural significance. The present house has a two-story west wing that may have been built in the 1720s and a two-and-a-half-story east wing dating from 1792. Isaac Wayne, the Revolutionary hero's father, built the main block some time between 1745 and 1763. The rubble walls with segmental-arch first-floor openings and pent eaves suggest its rural site while its denticulated cornice and classically proportioned pedimented door hood illustrate the builder's familiarity with Renaissance details. The interior flat arch spanning the central hall visually suggests the salon and rear stairhall of Stenton and earlier English double-pile country houses, while the hall's cornice and flanking pilasters introduced classical orders to a colonial Pennsylvania interior.[121]

The finest double-pile country houses were built for Philadelphians in the city's adjacent townships. By the middle of the eighteenth century Philadelphia had the wealthy patrons and skilled craftsmen who were able to commission, design, and build these monuments to Georgian taste. None is more ornate or pretentious than Mount Pleasant (PA-1130), which now stands as a historic house museum in the city's Fairmount Park. Robert Smith, the Scottish master builder who was responsible for Christ Church's steeple and St. Peter's Church, probably designed Mount Pleasant as well. Built in 1761 for the Scottish-born privateer John Macpherson, Mount Pleasant is a two-and-a-half-story hipped-roof stuccoed-stone house that evidently is

Stenton (PA-1714) Philadelphia. Southwest elevation (Jack E. Boucher, photographer, 1960) PA,51-PHILA,8-1.

Waynesborough (PA-208) Paoli vicinity (Easttown Township), Chester County. South elevation in 1853 (Copy photo of 1853 daguerreotype from the Chester County Historical Society) PA,15-PAOL.V,1-3.

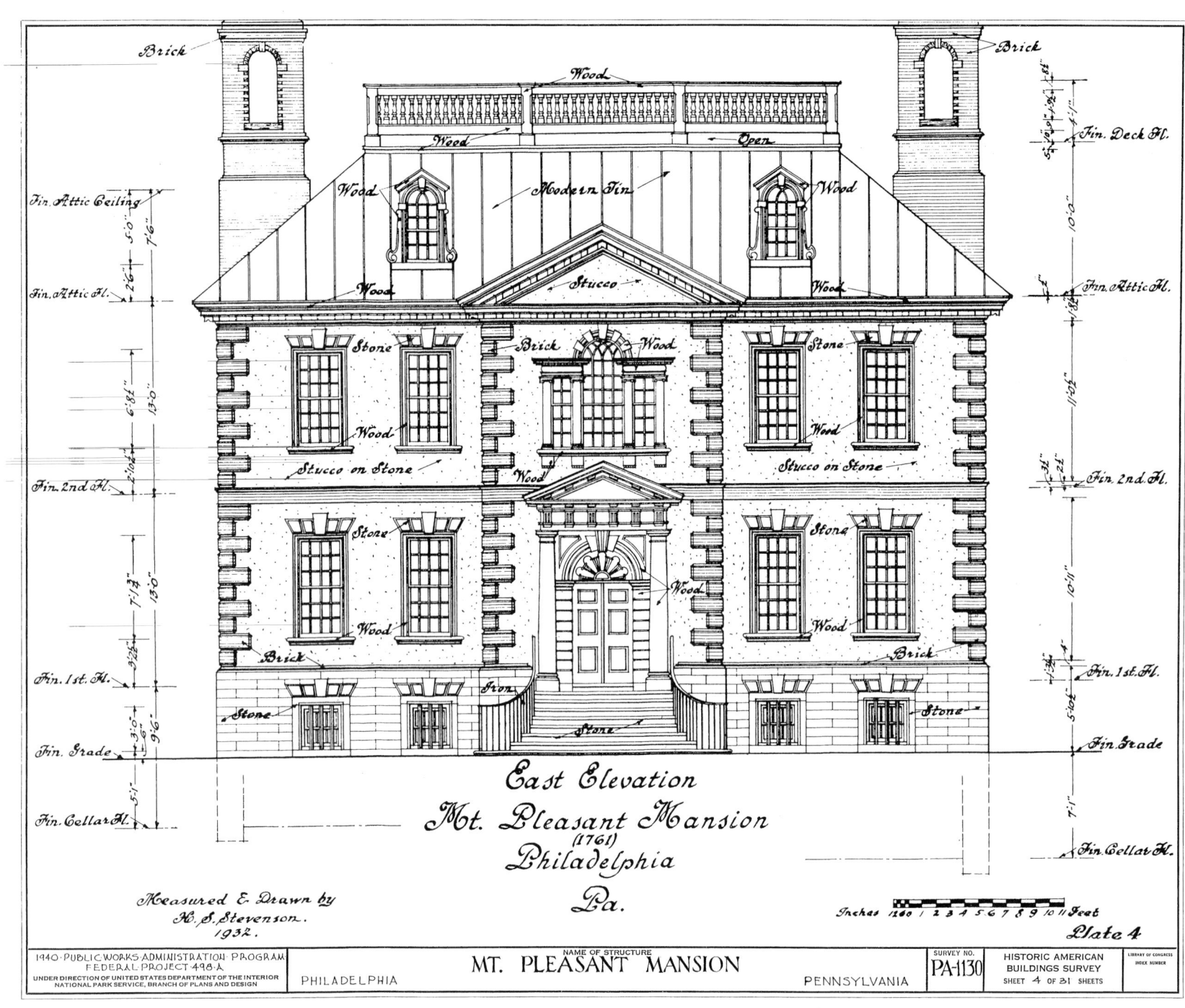

Mount Pleasant (PA-1130) Philadelphia. East elevation (H. S. Stevenson, delineator, 1932)
PA,51-PHILA,15.

based on the country houses in the Scottish lowlands around Edinburgh.[122] Two identical outbuildings flank the house, making Mount Pleasant the middle colonies' only surviving Palladian three-unit composition. Exacting symmetry and colorful detailing are its most outstanding features. Except for variances in their boldly pedimented frontispieces, front and rear facades, with their projecting central pavilions and second-story Palladian windows, are identical, as are the blank end walls. The attention to symmetry continues on the interior, where blind doors are placed against the parlor's blank wall in order to balance the two doorways at the opposite side of the room leading into the central passage hall, which runs the depth of the house on both floors. With the stairs set perpendicular to the hall, it does not contain even a visual residue of salon and stairhall, which is evident in Waynesborough. The contrasting red-brick quoins and string-course and cream-colored stuccoed walls are the more striking, because they reverse the usual order of marble trim on red brick.[123]

Mount Pleasant is but one of Philadelphia's many Georgian country houses. Woodford (PA-1307), built of brick in two stages (the first story circa 1756 and the second story circa 1772) and graced with a splendid parlor chimney breast, also stands in Fairmount Park. Cliveden (PA-1184), the Germantown fieldstone mansion that Jacob Knor built between 1763 and 1767 for Pennsylvania Chief Justice Benjamin Chew, is widely regarded as one of the colonies' finest Georgian dwellings, noted especially for its monumental entrance hall.[124] Some, such as the 1753 Cliffs (PA-185) in Fairmount Park, fell to fire.[125] Others, such as the 1761 Port Royal (PA-111) and the 1776 Chalkley Hall (PA-110) were demolished, but some of their important architectural elements were salvaged. Many exterior and interior details of Port Royal, including its entrance hall, parlor, and dining room woodwork have been installed in the H. F. duPont Winterthur Museum in Delaware; Chalkley Hall's entrance door is installed in the American Wing of New York's Metropolitan Museum of Art, and interior elements are at The State Museum of Pennsylvania in Harrisburg.[126]

Because Georgian double-pile houses were the dwellings of the elite and generally required their patrons to have a knowledge of English taste and manners, their number was limited during the eighteenth century. When they were built they occasionally retained earlier folk elements, such as the pent eaves and segmental-arch first-story windows of William Moore's mid-eighteenth-century house (PA-1135) in Schuylkill Township, Chester County.[127] It would not be until the turn of the nine-

George Ege House (PA-1026) Robesonia Borough, Berks County. North elevation (Cervin Robinson, photographer, 1958) PA,6-ROBSO,1-2.

teenth century, after Georgian forms and details had been used in Pennsylvania for about a half-century, that inland Pennsylvanians would begin to build sophisticated Georgian double-pile houses. Two of the best stand in Berks County, the 1801 Fisher House (PA-1027) in Oley Township and the 1807 Ege House (PA-1026) in Robesonia. Yet in spite of their incorporation of such obvious Georgian details as keystones on flat-arch window lintels, pedimented frontispieces, and elaborate woodwork, the builder of each house retained some traditional forms and materials or used fashionable details awkwardly. Either Ege or his builder was responsible for putting up rubble walls and emblazoning the house's date on the second-story center lintel, missing the correct date by two years.[128] Symmetrical fenestration and classical proportions prevail on its front, but on the rear elevation the off-center door and small Palladian stairhall window and the lunette abutting the cornice undermine both Georgian symmetry and proportions. Although the Fisher House is more finely rendered with its ashlar front and carefully carved details, including the bracketed cornice, its builder carried that cornice across the gable ends as pent eaves and squeezed over-sized medallions beneath the peaks. While the woodwork in both houses is well done, with hints of German gougework and appliqué in the Fisher House, it has been suggested that the basic woodwork may have been brought from Philadelphia.[129]

To have built these essentially English country houses, George Ege and Henry Fisher had to have become "anglicized." Most Pennsylvania Germans, however, seem to have been slower to give up old ways. Yet the urban Georgian taste was too strong to ignore, and as Germans melded the new Georgian fashion with old Germanic forms they developed a new house type, the Pennsylvania farmhouse.[130] Almost always with Georgian gables, usually with four bays, sometimes with datestones, dating from near the end of the colonial period through the nineteenth century, these Pennsylvania farmhouses abound in southeastern Pennsylvania. Their distinguishing exterior characteristic is two front doors, often side by side. These farmhouses were built of all materials. The 1832 John Conrad House (PA-259) in Penn Township, Berks County, was log, and the nearby Eliza Stamm House (PA-113), dating about 1865, was brick. In both houses the two front doors opened onto the kitchen and parlor of the traditional three-room *Flurküchenhaus* plan.[131] With their symmetrical facades, Pennsylvania Germans outwardly appeared to be conforming to popular taste, but behind closed doors they continued traditional ways.[132]

In rare cases a man of means in the countryside imported craftsmen to design and build a highly sophisticated country seat. The 1802 Meason House (PA-5475) is one of those cases. Isaac Meason, a Virginia-born ironmaster, brought Adam Wilson, a skilled stone mason and carpenter, from England to plan and construct his mansion near Uniontown, Fayette County. Because of its location in the bituminous coal region of southwestern Pennsylvania, architectural historians have overlooked this two-story gable-roof house, "which deserves a place in the first rank of early American architecture."[133] From its classically proportioned and balanced coursed-sandstone facade to its five-part composition with flanking outbuildings, the Meason House reflects Adam Wilson's firm grasp of the English Georgian style's subtleties. Wilson centered a pedimented frontispiece with engaged Ionic columns and a fanlight on the five-bay front with its pedimented three-bay pavilion. The double-leaf door opens onto a through-passage stairhall flanked by four symmetrical rooms; hyphens connect the main block with a kitchen at the north end and an office at the south end. Wilson ornamented the front with deftly carved details, ranging from con-

Eliza Stamm House (PA-113) Mount Pleasant vicinity, (Penn Township), Berks County. East elevation (Perry Benson, delineator, 1976) PA,6-MTPLES.V,2.

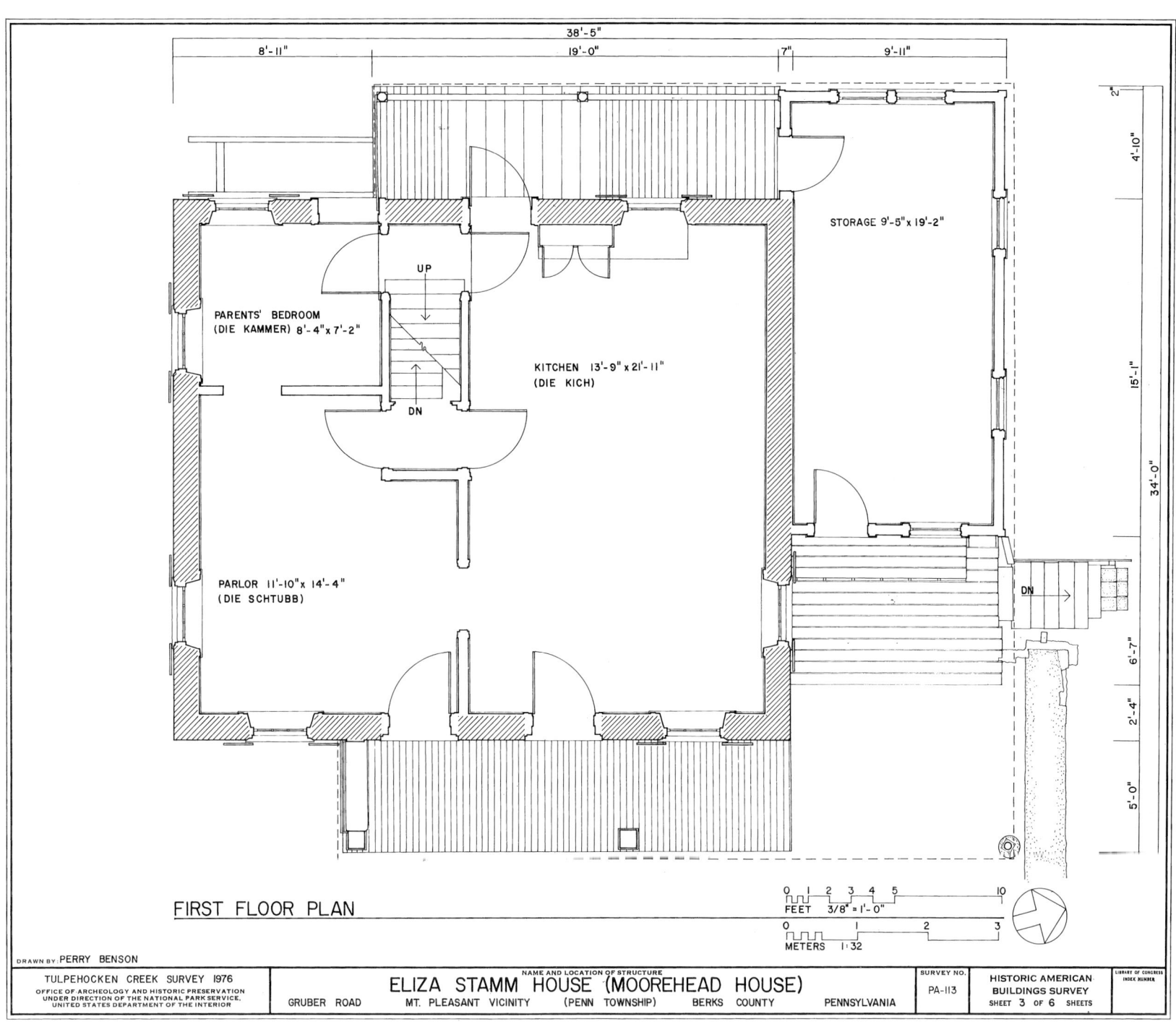

Eliza Stamm House (PA-113) Mount Pleasant vicinity, (Penn Township), Berks County. First floor plan (Perry Benson, delineator, 1976) PA,6-MTPLES.V,2.

Isaac Meason House (PA-5475) Mount Braddock (Dunbar Township), Fayette County. Northwest elevation (Jet Lowe, photographer, 1989) PA,26-DUBA,1.

soles supporting the pavilion's thin cornice to superimposed keystones on the windows' flat-arch lintels, but the most exquisite are the rinceau, bell flowers, and urn arranged around the pediment's lunette.

Many Georgian double-pile houses were built after Meason's mansion, but none exceeded this masterpiece in sophistication of design. The coursed-rubble residence (PA-38) that Archibald McAllister built circa 1814 near the Susquehanna River in Fort Hunter, Dauphin County, is a fine Georgian double-pile house, yet in facade composition and interior organization it does not measure up to Wilson's masterpiece for Isaac Meason. A central entrance with large fanlight and side lights open onto its central passage stairhall. Above the central entrance a second-story Palladian window graces the flat five-bay front of this two-and-a-half-story hipped-roof house. Flanking the center hall are two eastern rooms with corner fireplaces sharing a common chimney (a traditional pre-Georgian practice) and a large western parlor, making that half of the house functionally single pile.

Fort Hunter Mansion (PA-38) Fort Hunter, (Susquehanna Township), Dauphin County. Elevations (S. K. Wilson and T. M. Kelker, delineators, 1935) PA,22-FOHUN,1.

Georgian taste remained so strong that well into the nineteenth century many rural dwellers added lateral bays to their more modest houses to give them central halls and more nearly symmetrical five-bay facades. As late as 1862, the Deery family added two bays to the stuccoed-stone house (PA-1196) that Job Harvey had built in the middle of the eighteenth century in Charlestown Township, Chester County, to give it a five-bay facade, making the former side passage a central hall.[134] Impressive and commodious as these enlarged houses were, however, their thick stone masonry walls made it virtually impossible for these afterthought double-pile center-hall houses to convey the architectural sophistication of a house with a designed symmetrical entrance facade.

Although the term "Georgian double-pile house" implies a five-bay front with a center entrance and passage, there are also double-pile houses with Georgian proportions and features but which have three rather than five bays. An example is the three-bay double-pile house with two back-to-back rooms on one side of the passage hall. Henry Glassie calls this plan the Two-thirds Georgian House Type, because it is the result of a "subtractive step yielding two-thirds of a complete idea,"[135] assuming, of course, that the builder worked with the Georgian idea in mind. Popular throughout the Philadelphia region, this double-pile side hall plan appeared before the middle of the eighteenth century, was built for more than a century, and was particularly useful for urban or dense development, although it was used in rural areas for detached houses, often with the trappings of historical academic styles.[136] A famous example is the coursed-ashlar and rubble masonry two-and-a-half-story house (PA-1171) that Isaac Potts built circa 1772 in Upper Merion Township, Montgomery County. It is better known today as Washington's Headquarters at Valley Forge National Historical Park.[137] A variant of this type is the two-bay double-pile house. Although found in rural areas, usually with side wings, the two-bay double-pile plan was particularly popular for houses and shops on narrow town lots.[138] The circa 1835 building (PA-244) at 136 East Gay Street, West Chester, is a good example of this type.[139]

Not all dwellings conformed to these perceived house types, of course. Sometimes individuals built unique houses. The noted botanist and amateur astronomer Humphry Marshall, for example, was more interested in interior function than exterior symmetry in 1773 when he built his ashlar house (PA-203) in West Bradford Township, Chester County.[140] He introduced a host of unique elements, ranging from

136 East Bay Street (Bakery) (PA-244) West Chester Borough, Chester County. North elevation (Ned Goode, photographer, 1960) PA,15-WCHES,2-1.

a wooden observatory on the exterior to a tall clock recess and a heated greenhouse on the interior. Marshall's house originally featured a rear passage behind the stairs to form a corner passage plan;[141] the stairs today are placed in a rear corner of the central parlor.

While many of these post-Revolutionary houses were being built, a new style was being introduced in the new state's urban centers. Hints of it are seen in the delicate detailing of the Ege House's cornice and the finely carved elements in the Meason House's pediment. The roots of this new neoclassical style rest in Europe, but Americans fed more directly from the English branch that was nourished more than by anyone else by Robert Adam.[142] Adam's British work is characterized by a new lightness and delicacy of classical elements as he stripped walls of paneling and chair rails, and replaced rococo plasterwork with delicate classical details, such as swags of bellflowers, anthemion friezes, and Wedgwood panels.[143] Sometimes called the Adamesque-Federal style in America, in order to indicate both its English source and American historical period, this style can also be called late Georgian, because its sources are still Palladian and it is essentially a sophisticated refinement of the forms used in the colonies before the Revolution.[144]

Beginning in the 1780s in Philadelphia, and continuing into the 1820s, classical lightness and horizontality were exaggerated at the expense of an earlier robust three-dimensionality. The easiest way to accomplish this was to stucco the walls and lower the roof, as Michael Musser did for his Lancaster house (PA-373) about 1790 and as was done about nine years later for Philadelphia's Lemon Hill (PA-1010). Similarly, by placing string courses and window frames flush with the walls and increasing the scale, the facade's apparent one-dimensionality suggests lightness, as in the case of the 1786 Hill-Physick House (PA-1334) in Philadelphia. Here, to intensify the sense of lightness, the builder, instead of placing a three-dimensional Georgian frontispiece on the facade, recessed the entrance with a large delicate fanlight and side lights into the brick wall.[145] When frontispieces were used in the post-Revolutionary period (and they were used a great deal), pilasters replaced the engaged columns and tabernacle frames of the colonial period, and the pilasters, in turn, were attenuated and decorated with shallowly carved capitals and fluting. The frontispiece of the circa 1815 Hopewell Academy (PA-1311) in Chester County's East Nottingham Township is but one of the many excellent neoclassical examples to be found across the state. Another practice was to discard the shutters of the colonial

Hill-Physick House (PA-1334) Philadelphia. West entrance (Jack E. Boucher, photographer, 1972) PA,51-PHILA,36-3.

Hopewell Academy (PA-1311) Hopewell (East Nottingham Township), Chester County. Door on south elevation (Ned Goode, photographer, 1962) PA,15-HOPE,1-2.

era and use windows of wider proportions with larger panes of glass, such as the six-over-six sash windows in the Ege and Meason houses, rather than the nine-over-nine or twelve-over-twelve sashes that were common in the colonial period and still being used in the 1801 Fisher House. A variation was to employ particularly large panes. Those on Bishop William White's 1786 brick Philadelphia town house (PA-1490) were so large that his fire insurer cited them separately.[146]

William Hamilton's architect incorporated many of these devices into Hamilton's great West Philadelphia country house, the Woodlands (PA-1125). On his return from England in 1788, Hamilton, apparently armed with English plans, extensively remodeled an earlier stone double-pile house into Pennsylvania's—and America's—earliest and perhaps its best domestic expression of the Adamesque-Federal style. From its shaped rooms to its two-story portico, the Woodlands introduced to the new republic new spaces and details, ranging from its *chambres a l'alcove* to pilaster-and-architrave door frames. In fact, Richard J. Betts, who has thoroughly studied the building, suggests that American builders and craftsmen "may have learned as much from the Woodlands as from the English architectural books that are usually considered to have been the genesis of the federal style."[147] Particularly innovative for its time was its variety of room shapes, including square, oblong, elliptical, and oblong with semicircular apses. The interior's geometrical diversity protruded as rounded bays that contributed to the exterior's lightness and variety. Apparently few Pennsylvania builders outside of Philadelphia could master such subtlety of design, because diverse room shapes are uncommon in other parts of the state. Stephen Hills, however, an English-born architect who would later design capitols for both Pennsylvania and Missouri, could incorporate a variety of forms into his plans, and in 1804 did—for William Montgomery of Lancaster. Montgomery's three-and-a-half-story brick house (PA-1061) had the only known oval drawing room in Lancaster County. A rounded bay, swelling across two-thirds of the house's rear, still graces the top two floors and the spiral staircase with its groin-vaulted ceiling rises on the interior.[148]

Institutions and churches quickly adopted the new style, some with more success than others. Philadelphia's First Presbyterian Church rebuilt its edifice on Market Street in 1793-94 with a wooden Roman Corinthian tetrastyle portico, the state's second two-story portico. Three years later the newly chartered Bank of the United States (PA-1417) followed with its Corinthian portico, its six columns executed in mar-

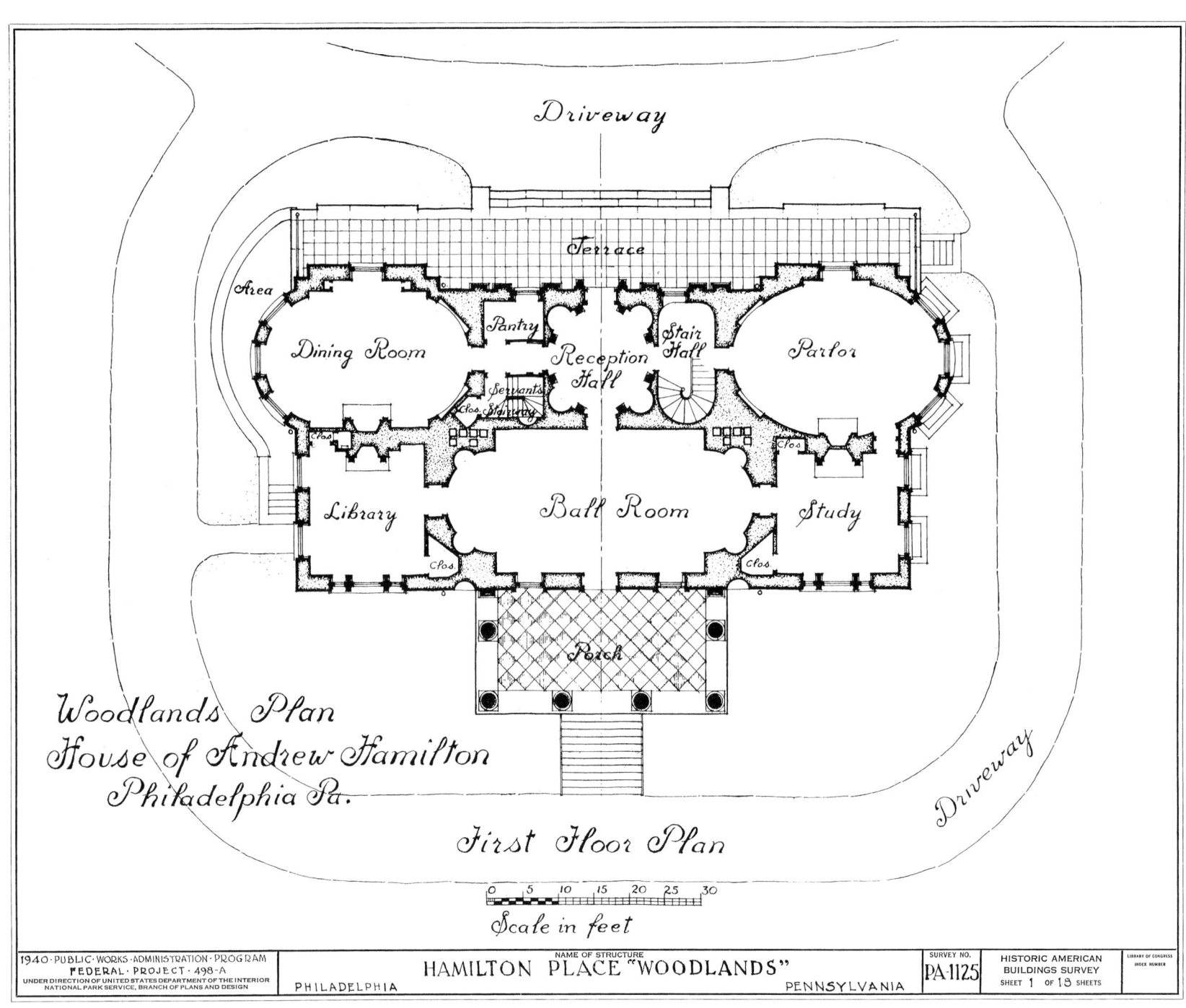

Woodlands (PA-1125) Philadelphia. First floor plan (delineator unkown, 1940) PA,51-PHILA,29.

William Montgomery House (PA-1061) Lancaster, Lancaster County. Rear facade with curved bay (Jack E. Boucher, photographer, 1965) PA,36-LANC,5-2.

ble.[149] The center building of Philadelphia's Pennsylvania Hospital (PA-1123), on the other hand, ranks with the Woodlands as one of America's finest examples of the Adamesque style. Master builder Samuel Rhoads designed a three-unit plan in 1754, but the hospital built only the east wing before the Revolution. In the 1790s the hospital put David Evans Sr., in charge of completing the project, and he and his son, David Jr., quickly demonstrated their indebtedness to Robert Adam, or at least to William Thornton, the designer of the 1790 Library Hall.[150] They finished the west wing in 1796 and the center building in 1805. The center pavilion is "characterized by elegant lightness of scale, refinement of detail, and sophisticated invention."[151] Rising from the dressed marble first story with arched windows recessed within two layers of arches, the two brick upper stories are tied together by marble Corinthian pilasters that, like the cornice, hug the wall to become nearly flat bands. From such small details as the entrance's lacy fanlight and the pediment's oval window to such

Pennsylvania Hospital (PA-1123) Philadelphia. South elevation, central block, and portion of west wing (Jack E. Boucher, photographer, 1974) PA,51-PHILA,39-5.

dominant features as the circular balustrade for the surgical amphitheater's skylight, the building is a showcase for Adamesque design.[152]

Most of Pennsylvania's Federal-style buildings fell far short of the standard set by Pennsylvania Hospital's central pavilion. It was not always because the architect was ill-equipped for the task. Often the client's funds limited the project. Benjamin Henry Latrobe was one of the most prominent architects in the United States at the beginning of the nineteenth century, but Dickinson College was an educational venture near the frontier in Carlisle, Cumberland County, when Latrobe designed the institution's West College in 1803. From its entrance's large-scale fanlight and side lights to its domed cupola behind the central pavilion, the three-story coursed limestone-rubble building is subtly designed but not equal to the better-financed Pennsylvania Hospital.[153] Yet "Old West" is clearly a more sophisticated design than Allegheny College's Bentley Hall (PA-525) in Meadville, Crawford County. Designed by an amateur, Reverend Timothy Alden, the college's first president, Bentley Hall was fifteen years in the making because of a shortage of funds. College officials and townspeople laid the cornerstone with great ceremony in 1820, but after local builders roofed in the three-story brick building in 1824, construction ceased for nearly a decade while the college sought funds from both the legislature and sympathetic friends. Today the long period of construction is less obvious than the relative awkwardness of the building's design. What Bentley Hall lacks in finesse, however, it compensates with verve, an indication of Alden's passionate determination to see the building completed and the struggling school blossom, as it indeed has.[154]

Bentley Hall's late date illustrates the enduring popularity of the Federal style. In 1828, when fashionable tastemakers were endorsing the Greek Revival, William Jenkins, a Lancaster attorney, chose the Federal style for his brick two-and-a-half-story house in Lancaster Township, Lancaster County. It has been known as Wheatland (PA-1265) since 1848, when James Buchanan acquired it, eight years before his election to the presidency of the United States. There is nothing extravagant about the house; a period newspaper considered it in "perfect accord with the strictest republican simplicity."[155] Characterized by bilateral symmetry with recessed three-bay wings flanking its five-bay main block, Wheatland's architectural style rests less in its proportions than in its details: its attenuated Doric porch, the rosettes in the windows' corner blocks, the segmental-arch dormers, and the elliptical staircase. This is the pattern that most houses of the period follow. Occasionally Federal-style houses incorporate details from the late colonial period. About 1810, for example, Moravian brewer John Sebastian Goundie built his two-and-a-half-story brick house (PA-1145) in Bethlehem, Northampton County, with a fanlight over his entrance and a bead-and-reel cornice across the front, yet incorporated Georgian Gothic sashes into his gable dormers, which, with their superimposed and thin fluted pilasters, were Adamesque in other respects. Many houses restricted Federal details to the entrance, such as the arched doorway and fanlight of the coursed rubble Samuel Lemon House (PA-1236) that was built circa 1832 in Cresson Township, Cambria County, or the pedimented frontispiece and fanlight of the 1810 rubble masonry Benner-Walker House (PA-8-5) in Bellefonte, Centre County.

Contemporaries of the Benner-Walker House range in time and place from Wallingford's 1785 Leiper House (PA-1244) in Delaware County near the state's southeastern corner to Girard's 1830 Hutchinson House (PA-59) in Erie County,

Pennsylvania's northwestern corner. All are examples of the traditional phase of American neoclassicism. Their builders chose to refine and embellish earlier Georgian forms rather than break away from them, merging familiar Palladian and fresh neoclassical elements.[156]

A later and clearly more romantic, if not radical, stage was the national phase, or the Greek Revival.[157] The first American borrowing from ancient Greece occurred in 1798 when Benjamin Henry Latrobe turned to Stuart and Revett's *The Antiquities of Athens* for the Greek Ionic order on the portico of the Bank of Pennsylvania in Philadelphia. It was not a Greek Revival building, however. Its plain surfaces and arched windows were Federal features, and the suppressed dome, invisible from the exterior, was Roman.[158] Classical Revival is a more accurate stylistic identification for such hybrid buildings. As two weatherboarded timber-frame Erie County houses illustrate, builders and carpenters in areas remote from the Commonwealth's cultural center also merged styles, but without Latrobe's subtlety and sophistication. The 1844 Dickson-Stevenson House (PA-55) in Springfield Township is a double-pile house with a central stair passage built onto an earlier dwelling that became its rear wing. Its plan is Georgian, its wide entablature and paneled frieze are Greek Revival, and the entrance's semielliptical fanlight and side lights merge Greek and Federal details. Similarly, the weatherboarded timber-frame main section of the 1820 Amos Judson House (PA-522) in Waterford combines a wide Greek Revival entablature and a Roman Revival pediment lunette.[159]

Architectural historians generally credit the Second Bank of the United States (PA-137) in Philadelphia for establishing the viability of the Greek Revival style in the United States. William Strickland won the 1818 competition for the building, edging out his mentor, Benjamin Henry Latrobe. Both men copied from *The Antiquities of Athens* the Parthenon's pedimented end for the bank's street facade. Latrobe's overall design, however, was another expert exercise in neoclassicism's rational phase, in which he excelled.[160] Strickland, on the other hand, plowed new ground. His bank assumes a temple form, without the squarish block that extrudes through the roof above Labtrobe's banking room. Strickland's bank, completed in 1824, is Greek in form, proportions, and materials; it is built of marble, albeit Pennsylvania marble. Obviously the Second Bank is not a duplication of an ancient Greek temple. Columns grace only the two ends; windows, some of them Georgian in proportion and detail, are placed on all four sides; and the interior, with a Roman

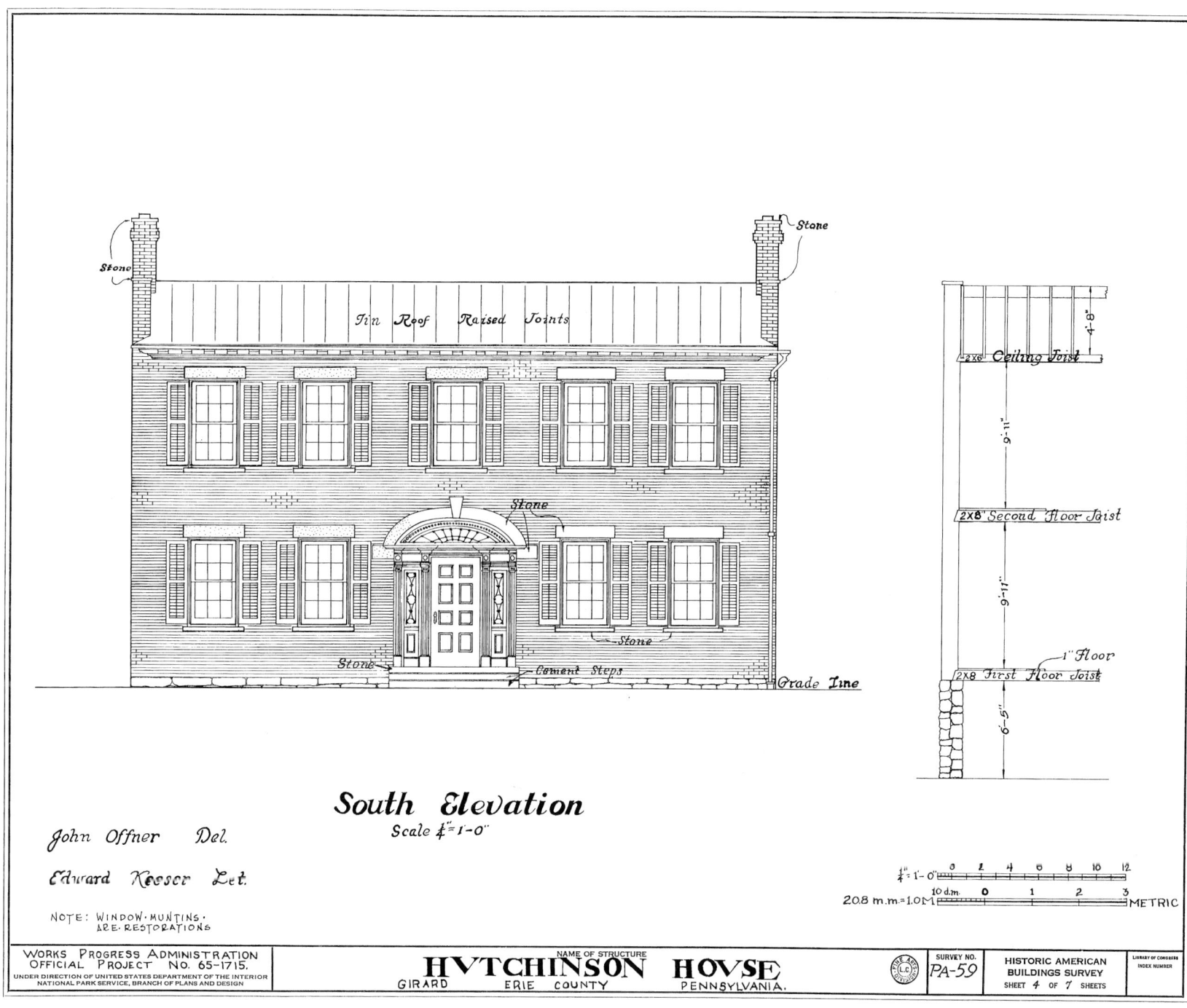

Hutchinson House (PA-59) Girard Borough, Erie County. South elevation (John Offner, delineator, 1936) PA,25-GIRA,1.

organization of space, was designed for nineteenth-century banking purposes.[161]

The Second Bank's significance rests in its Greek model and Strickland's use of it for intellectual purposes. It was about this time that architects and tastemakers, propelled by the discovery of history, found romance and inspiration in the contemplation of past civilizations. Architects began to abandon the tradition of building according to Renaissance principles and proportions and instead selected historical styles for the intellectual and emotional responses that they would conjure up in the mind of the literate beholder.[162] Intellectual responses included both evaluations of form and knowledge of historical sources. James Fenimore Cooper, for example, could not recall a single building in Europe "in which simplicity, exquisite proportion, and material unite to produce so fine a whole."[163] Others might recognize the bank's venerable model, whose permanence could be accepted as architectural advertisement for an institution seeking investors' funds during an era of periodic bank failures. In this case it proved to be false advertising, because the building served as a bank for less than twenty years. President Andrew Jackson vetoed the renewal of the Second Bank's charter in the famous 1832 Bank War, and the state bank that continued within the marble walls failed in 1841.[164] Emotional responses, although invariably grounded in historical knowledge, could give free rein to creative imaginations. When Charles Dickens gazed upon the Second Bank a year after its closing, he was struck by this "tomb of many fortunes, the Great Catacomb of investment . . . a handsome building of white marble, which had a mournful, ghost-like aspect, dreary to behold."[165]

The Second Bank established the Greek Revival as the unofficial style for not only branch banks of the Bank of the United States but also state-chartered banks, which ranged from Philadelphia's granite ashlar Mechanics Bank (PA-1443), designed by William Strickland in 1837, to Erie's 1839 United States Bank of Pennsylvania (PA-53). The latter was the Erie branch of the doomed state-chartered successor to the Second Bank of the United States. Built of Vermont marble from William Kelly's designs,[166] the former United States Bank is modest in size—about half that of its mother institution, the former Second Bank in Philadelphia. The Erie bank, however, is an exceptionally well-designed building, "one of the most successful Greek temple adaptations in America."[167] Its pedimented hexastyle Greek Doric portico with full entablature is soberer in appearance and more loyal to ancient Greek proportions than the Mechanics Bank's pedimented Corinthian distyle portico in antis.

"The popular idea that to design a building in Grecian taste is nothing more than to copy a Grecian building is altogether erroneous," insisted Thomas U. Walter. Even the Greeks themselves never made two buildings alike."[168] At the time of his statement in 1841, Walter was superintending construction of his Greek Revival masterpiece, Founder's Hall of Girard College (PA-1731). Walter learned his art under the tutelage of William Strickland, and in 1833 won the design competition for Founder's Hall, his first significant commission. In spite of Walter's claim that Greek Revival architecture was more than copies of Greek buildings, Founder's Hall comes the closest to representing the form and function of an ancient Greek temple. Built of Pennsylvania marble on a colossal scale, it is a Corinthian peristyle temple-form building honoring Stephen Girard, the eccentric millionaire who founded this school for fatherless boys. As ancient Greek temples held statues of designated deities, Founder's Hall houses both Girard's statue and his sarcophagus.[169]

Because the Greeks were known for their cultivation of arts and philosophy, the Greek Revival was an especially appropriate style for halls of learning, most of which demonstrate Walter's thesis better than Founder's Hall. Pennsylvania Hall (PA-360) of Gettysburg College (known as Pennsylvania College until 1921), for example, is a three-story brick building that Philadelphia architect John C. Trautwine designed for the new and financially strapped school in 1835.[170] Aware of the college's sparse funds, Trautwine gave the plans committee an impressive design at a modest cost. He stripped the exterior of excessive details until he considered "the front the cheapest that can be devised," and then consulted his former mentor, the renowned Strickland, who, Trautwine twice pointed out to the committee, "approves entirely of the plans, and facade of the building."[171] Trautwine agreed to nearly all of the committee's suggestions for reducing costs, including a white-painted finish in place of his recommended roughcasting, but opposed using smaller timbers or thinner walls than those specified. Yet when it opened in November 1837, Pennsylvania Hall, with its pedimented Greek Doric portico and circular cupola ornamented with fluted pilasters and swags, transformed the fledgling institution into a visually progressive, up-to-date center of learning.[172]

It was in their dwellings, however, that Americans especially found expression for the Greek Revival style. Nicholas Biddle, the Philadelphia tastemaker and banker who was responsible for the selection of the Greek Revival style for the trend-setting Second Bank of the United States and for twisting Stephen Girard's modest intentions into the majestic Founder's Hall, set a personal example and high

Girard College, Founder's Hall (PA-1731) Philadelphia. South elevation (Jack E. Boucher, photographer, 1973) PA,51-PHILA,459A-3.

standard for domestic architecture as well. In 1834 he commissioned Thomas U. Walter to transform a 1798 brick farmhouse in Bensalem Township, Bucks County, into a model of the Temple of Theseus. Andalusia (PA-1248), a "tour de force in archaeological revivalism,"[173] sits atop a knoll overlooking the Delaware River. Its Doric columns, which wrap around three of its stuccoed brick walls, and the two-story recessed wings flanking the main block help to make this country seat one of Pennsylvania's earliest and best-designed Greek Revival houses, deserving of its status as a National Historic Landmark.

Andalusia stands at the forefront of Pennsylvania's motley collection of Grecian-inspired houses. Some, such as Mayfield (PA-1104) in West Chester, Chester County, were boldly and expertly designed. Built for Pittsburgh industrialist William Ebbs about 1851, Mayfield is a two-story whitewashed brick country mansion whose projecting tetrastyle Ionic portico gives the house an imposing presence, which is enhanced by its transom-and-side-light entrance with architrave and scroll brackets. An urban contemporary of Mayfield and perhaps "the highest point of the Greek type in Pennsylvania"[175] is General Charles M. Reed's 1849 house (PA-57) in Erie. Reed's architect, E. F. Barger, abandoned the conventional temple form and projected the tetrastyle Ionic portico from the house's long side. He produced a sober grandeur by stuccoing the brick walls and applying an unusually wide entablature and Doric pilasters on all four walls, and by indenting approximately one foot the three center bays of each short side. Architects and builders also adapted the high style to modest but sophisticated urban dwellings, retaining a Grecian sense without the aid of porticoes or temple forms. William Winder of Philadelphia, for example, built three brick row houses (PA-1384) in that city in 1843-44. By deeply grooving the horizontal joints of the ground-story marble, gracing the wide entrances with marble Ionic frontispieces, and extending the broad second-story windows down to the wrought-iron balconies, his builder created an elegant Grecian ambiance. In Erie, William Kelly accomplished a similar though more modest effect when he stuccoed the brick walls of the Cashier's House (PA-56) of the United States Bank of Pennsylvania and framed its entry with Doric pilasters and a heavy entablature.[176] In small cities and towns, builders brought the familiar five-bay double-pile house up to date by applying Greek Revival elements, most commonly a broad frieze with frieze windows (often with grilles) and flat-roof columned porches. Two good examples are William Lyon's 1833 house in Bedford, Bedford County, and C. B. Grubb's 1845 house in Lancaster, Lancaster County; both have frieze windows and a four-column Doric porch marking their central entrances.[177]

    More imaginative were the many rural small-town expressions of the Greek Revival. As temples for the cult of the common man, these dwellings illustrate the pervasive popularity of the style and its adoption by people of limited means and sophistication. Usually weatherboarded timber-frame houses, their entrances are often framed by pilasters and plain entablatures on the house's gable end. Three clapboarded timber-frame Crawford County houses indicate the variety of these vernacular expressions. The Titus Ridgway House (PA-543), built circa 1850 in Hydetown, has a transom and side lights about its entrance; a wide frieze runs the length of the house but ends in cornice-and-frieze returns at the gable-end front where they meet thin corner pilasters. In nearby Townville, the builder of the circa-1846 Stevens House (PA-5126) stressed symmetry rather than Grecian details. The

Mayfield (PA-1104) West Chester Borough, Chester County. South elevation (Ned Goode, photographer, 1958) PA,15-WCHES,19-1.

Reed Mansion (PA-57) Erie, Erie County. General view (Fran Skotnicki, photographer, 1935) PA,25-ERI,4-2.

United States Bank of Pennsylvania, Erie Branch, Cashier's House (Woodruff House) (PA-56) Erie, Erie County. West elevation (William H. Page, delineator, 1935) PA,25-ERI,3.

Stevens House (PA-5126) Townville Borough, Crawford County. Front elevation (William J. Bulger, photographer, 1936) PA,20-TOWNV,1-1.

one-and-a-half-story three-bay central block, with its center entrance is flanked by recessed one-story wings with square-section pillars supporting the overhanging gable roofs. Although Greek Revival details are restricted to the wide, plain frieze along the main block's sides and the pedimented gables of the side wings, the house's composition communicates the builder's Grecian intentions. The most exuberant, if naive, of these rural Greek Revival houses is the circa-1850 Henry Hendryx House (PA-520) in Riceville. A two-story house with a side wing, it also has a wide frieze along the sides, ending with cornice-and-frieze returns on the gable-end front, whereas on the Ridgway House they are supported by corner pilasters. The house's exuberance rests in its jigsaw anthemions, which are inverted on the corner and entry pilasters but stand erect above the entry's entablature, which rises between the second-story windows.[178]

The rage for the Grecian style included nearly every building type. As Aristabulus Bragg proclaimed in James Fenimore Cooper's *Home as Found* (1828): "We build little besides temples for our churches, our banks, our taverns, our court houses, and our dwellings. A friend of mine has just built a brewery on the model of the Temple of the Winds."[179] In Philadelphia adept architects, such as English-trained John Haviland, designed high-style Greek Revival churches with historically correct porticoes. Two of Haviland's best Philadelphia church designs, both with Ionic hexastyle porticoes and stuccoed-brick walls, are the 1822 First Presbyterian Church (PA-1117), which was demolished in 1939, and St. Andrew's (Protestant Episcopal) Church (PA-1362), which was finished in 1823 and is now St. George's Greek Orthodox Cathedral.[180] Congregations far removed from the sophisticated city shared Philadelphians' enthusiasm for this new national style, but designers with Haviland's expertise were uncommon. Consequently, people employed the best they could find. In Meadville, Crawford County, the best was apparently Captain George W. Cullum, who in 1836 designed the brick Independent Congregational Church (PA-524). He spaced the church's Greek Doric columns so widely across the portico that in the frieze two triglyphs, rather than the customary one, fall between the columns, and he failed to carry the frieze along the building's sides.[181] Despite the fact that "the Greeks themselves," as Walter noted, "never made two buildings alike," they did accept some basic rules that followed from their early construction with wood. Cullum violated those rules, yet he produced a chaste and well-received building.

Most Pennsylvanians cared more about architectural effect than about architectural rules. Pilasters and a pedimented gable end with a plain frieze could suggest a portico, as they do on such weatherboarded frame churches as the 1848 Free Methodist Church (PA-531) in Pleasantville, Venango County, and the 1859 First Baptist Church (PA-513) in North East, Erie County. Other churches enjoyed even fewer allusions to Greek temples. The weatherboarded timber-frame former Presbyterian Church (PA-529) in Coudersport, Potter County, was built in 1848-52 with a plain entablature along the sides but with only cornice returns and Doric corner pilasters at the gable end where a Doric entablature and pilasters frame the double-leaf door.[182]

The rage for the Greek Revival defied reason. Ancient Greeks were pagans, and their temples did not reasonably serve as appropriate models for Christian churches. Congregations often sensed this contradiction, but apparently could not resist the temptation of this well-ordered, easily erected national style. Meadville's Unitarians, in fact, debated whether to choose a Greek or Gothic design for their independent church.[183] Architects were equipped to do either. William Strickland, also designed Philadelphia's Gothic Revival St. Stephen's Protestant Episcopal Church (PA-1576) in 1822.[184]

Much of the Gothic's romantic appeal rested in its allusions to spirituality. In comparing Greek and Gothic architecture, Mrs. Nathaniel Hawthorne concluded that a Gothic "cathedral is really an image of the whole soul of man; and a Greek temple of his understanding only."[185] Such feelings complemented growing concerns in the 1830s and 1840s about creeping secularism in England and America and the conviction that a civilization's architecture reflected its virtues and vices and, in turn, could affect the character of those who experienced it. Episcopalians and Roman Catholics in particular saw the Gothic as the only appropriate style for ecclesiastical buildings. Since nineteenth-century Americans associated the Gothic style with the Middle Ages, when European Christianity was monolithic and votaries were supposedly more devout, it formed the best environment for contemporary worshippers.[186] Philadelphia's Church of St. James the Less (PA-1725) embodies these ideas to the fullest. Built of random granite ashlar between 1846 and 1850, St. James the Less is the first American church copied detail by detail from a medieval model, the early-thirteenth-century St. Michael's Church in Long Stanton, Cambridgeshire. The affluent High Church Episcopal congregation of St. James the Less acquired the plans of this rural parish church from the Ecclesiological Society, which Anglican reformers organized as the Camden Cambridge Society in 1839 to fight secularism by restoring medieval ritual and architecture to the Church of England.[187]

It was not necessary to re-create a medieval church in order to meet the ecclesiologists' fundamental standards. John Notman, for example, designed St. Mark's (Protestant Episcopal) Church (PA-1093) for a Philadelphia High Church congregation in 1848. The Ecclesiological Society endorsed St. Mark's, because it considered the church Gothic in both design and construction. Its exposed random brown freestone walls are exposed on the interior as well as on the exterior and the timbering is structural, not ornamental. Even its means of construction followed ecclesiologists' dictates; workmen were to remain reverent in their labor, refraining from whistling, singing, or eating within the church's walls during construction.[188] Roman Catholics' British authority on medievalism was Augustus Welby Northmore Pugin, a convert to the faith who passionately proselytized for medievalism as the only logical and proper way of life.[189] St. Peter's (Roman Catholic) Church in Brownsville, Fayette County, was built on Pugin's principles in 1854; in fact, it appears to have been patterned after a plate in Pugin's *True Principles of Pointed or Christian Architecture* (1841). A small and simple church, St. Peter's coursed ashlar walls, buttresses, pointed-arch windows with hood-moldings, and three-stage tower and spire combine to produce an academically approved Gothic Revival church.[190]

Saint Stephen's Protestant Episcopal Church (PA-1576) Philadelphia. General view from southwest. (Jack E. Boucher, photographer, 1972) PA,51-PHILA,673-1.

Church of Saint James the Less (Protestant Episcopal) (PA-1725) Philadelphia. General view (Jack E. Boucher, photographer, 1972) PA,51-PHILA,318-1.

Few Americans cared to subscribe to the intense arguments of the English ecclesiologists, but many saw that the Gothic style possessed both architectural and symbolic attributes. Architects did not have to be medievalists in order to design religious buildings that clearly expressed their function. By careful use of exterior massing and sensitive handling of interior details, they could please both clients and critics. The vestry of Pittsburgh's overcrowded Trinity Church, for example, was High Church, and the genteel congregation wanted a historically accurate expression of the newly fashionable Gothic style for a new church to be called St. Peter's (PA-48). In 1851 the vestry solicited plans from John Notman, who had earned his reputation as a Gothic revivalist for his design of Philadelphia's St. Mark's. Notman gave them a coursed-sandstone ashlar "Decorated" Gothic church similar to St. Mark's but with less attention paid to such ecclesiological concerns as siting.[191] St. Peter's shows that a church did not have to pass English ecclesiological muster in order to be reasonably archaeologically correct in scholars' eyes and handsome and appropriate to lay people.

Before the arrival of English books on the Gothic style in the 1840s, a more naive version of the Gothic Revival prevailed in Pennsylvania. Medieval materials, construction, or proportions—those factors that contributed to a Gothic Revival building's integrity after approximately 1845—were rarely considered by architects, builders, or clients. For churches, builders usually employed the pointed arch, the minimal detail for determining the Gothic style, and often added as well a tower, capped with either crenellations or a spire. St. John's Lutheran Church (PA-269), a nineteenth-century brick church in Germany Township, Adams County, for example, has a crenelated three-story tower and stained glass in its pointed-arch windows. Although its builder spurned stone, the customary medieval building material, and did not attempt a medieval "integrity" in its construction, the public recognized from St. John's Gothic Revival details that it was an up-to-date Christian house of worship. In some cases, the simplest allusion to the Gothic Revival style was sufficient for many congregations and their carpenters. The 1833 Union Reformed and Lutheran Church (PA-219) in Wapwallopen, Luzerne County, for example, is a rectangular two-story weatherboarded timber-frame building with only a single exterior detail suggesting its ecclesiastical purpose—a small rose window in the west gable, that was repeated on the panels of its gallery railing.[192]

While rose windows and pointed arches could signify churches and the spirituality associated with them, battlemented octagonal and round towers suggested fortresses. Nineteenth-century American cities did not need fortresses to keep out threatening enemies, but by turning the idea of fortresses inside out, they could be used to hold enemies of civilized society while their environment helped to reform those enemies into socialized citizens. Consequently medieval fortress architecture became the most popular model for American prisons, especially after John Haviland set the example with Eastern State Penitentiary (PA-1729), which the state erected between 1822 and 1836 just north of what was then Philadelphia's city limits. Battlemented octagonal turrets at the corners of the blank granite ashlar walls and massive squarish battlemented towers flanking the central entrance gate with its portcullis form a bleak and forbidding presence, which is made more oppressive by its expanse over an entire city square. Fortresses were known not only for their defensive ramparts but also for their dreary dungeons, allowing the architecture of prisons such as Eastern State to express both function and warning. Eastern State's gloomy public face was deliberate, a result of directive and design. Prison commissioners directed

Union Reformed and Lutheran Church (PA-219) Wapwallopen vicinity (Conyngham Township), Luzerne County. Detail of balcony rail (Stanley Jones, photographer, 1936) PA,40-WAP,1-5.

that it should "convey to the mind a cheerless blank indicative of the misery that awaits the unhappy being who enters within its walls."[193] Haviland complied by turning to his native Britain for models and fitted them into his characteristic bilateral reciprocity, dividing the front wall into three roughly equal parts and imparting it a grim stability that suggests the immutability of law.[194]

Eastern State's significance also lay in its radial plan in which seven cell blocks radiated from a central surveillance tower. Each cell block held a series of eight-by-ten-foot cells which opened onto the central corridor and a private exercise yard. This plan was the physical expression of the Pennsylvania System, a penal reform that stressed rehabilitation through solitary confinement. The effect of the prison's lugubrious architecture and solitary cells was intensified by the treatment of entering prisoners. Charles Dickens visited the prison in 1842, and although he disapproved of its system, he was captivated by its operation. "Over the head and face of every prisoner who comes into this melancholy house, a black hood is drawn," Dickens observes, "and in this dark shroud, an emblem of the curtain dropped

Eastern State Penitentiary (PA-1729) Philadelphia. View of Fairmount Avenue entrance (Cortlandt V. D. Hubbard, photographer, 1967) PA,51-PHILA,354-2.

between him and the living world, he is led to the cell from which he never again comes forth, until his whole term of imprisonment has expired. . . . He is a man buried alive; to be dug out in the slow round of years; and in the meantime dead to everything but torturing anxieties and horrible despair."[195] Dickens' rhetoric is probably more extreme than was the prisoners' isolation. Yet their initially traumatic treatment reinforced the rehabilitative purpose of the prison's architecture. As the Boston Prison Discipline Society contended in 1829, "there is such a thing as architecture adapted to morals; . . . improvement in morals depends in some degree upon the construction of buildings."[196] Regardless of what it did to or for its inmates, Eastern State Penitentiary had at least three architectural consequences. It established Haviland as a prison architect, and in Pennsylvania alone he designed similar county houses of incarceration in Pittsburgh, Harrisburg, Lancaster, and Reading. It also helped to promote the viability of the radial plan which was executed for over a hundred prisons

Philadelphia County Prison, Debtors' Wing (PA-1097A) Philadelphia. Southeast elevation (Jack E. Boucher, photographer, 1965) PA,51-PHILA,672A-1.

around the world. And it made the fortress variant of the Gothic Revival style virtually the only style for jails and prisons. In Pennsylvania counties they range from Thomas U. Walter's large granite ashlar 1835 Philadelphia County Prison (PA-1097) to the modest rock-faced granite 1870 Bradford County Jail in Towanda.[197]

Another style popular for prisons was the Egyptian Revival, which Haviland used in 1835 for New York's famous Halls of Justice and House of Detention (the "Tombs") and Walter used a year later for the Philadelphia County Prison's Debtors' Wing (PA-1097).[198] Archaeological interest in Egypt dates from the turn of the nineteenth century, when artists and scholars accompanied Napoleon on his Egyptian campaigns of 1798-99. From this military episode and three-year occupation came significant published works beginning with Vivant Denon's liberally illustrated account of French warfare there and culminating with a scholarly twenty-one-volume study of the land's geography, topography, and antiquities that was published in stages between 1809 and 1828.[199] Walter created a sense of great scale for the small brown-

Independent Order of Odd Fellows (PA-1771) Philadelphia. View of windows on south elevation (Jack E. Boucher, photographer, 1961) PA,51-PHILA,353-2.

stone ashlar Debtors' Wing by placing only three battered openings on the building's front and capping it with a cavetto cornice. The low, broad center opening with two papyrus columns in antis formed a recessed porch which led to the prison's entrance door. Such large proportions and heavy detailing gave the Egyptian Revival style the massive and forbidding qualities that made it suitable for prisons.[200] The mystery surrounding ancient Egypt and its monuments, such as the inscrutable Sphinx, allowed architects to apply the Egyptian style to fraternal lodges as well. The 1846 Odd Fellows Hall (PA-1771) in Philadelphia was one of those few examples. Although the hall's design was not archaeological, its architect applied enough Egyptian Revival details on the exterior and designated an abundance of painted Egyptian elements and Egyptian Revival furnishings for the interior to make the building's style, if not its function, obvious.[201] Slender windows with battered red-painted surrounds rose three stories above the ground floor as the only accent on the plastered brick battered walls, which were crowned with a striped polychromatic cavetto cornice. The style's ancient eastern origins also made it the logical choice for synagogues and Jewish cemetery structures. Both Strickland and Walter used this style for synagogues as did an unknown person before 1849 for the stuccoed brick Mikveh Israel Cemetery Gatehouse (PA-1602) in South Philadelphia.[202]

Because Egypt was famous for its funerary arts–its pyramids were both monuments to and tombs for the dead–some considered the Egyptian style appropriate for gentile cemetery entrances as well, as Philadelphia's 1849 Odd Fellows Cemetery Gate suggests.[203] Despite the historical logic for using the Egyptian style for cemetery structures, Pennsylvanians apparently considered it inappropriately pagan for "gateways to a glorious immortality," because they clearly favored other styles for these buildings.[204] In Philadelphia alone these other styles included Roman Doric for John Notman's 1836 stuccoed-stone Laurel Hill Cemetery Gatehouse (PA-1811) on the edge of Fairmount Park, an enriched Italian Renaissance Revival for William Johnston's 1849 marble Hood Cemetery Entrance (PA-1697) in Germantown, and an amalgam of Tudor and Romanesque for S. D. Button's 1855 brownstone Mount Moriah Cemetery Gatehouse (PA-1634) in Kingsessing.[205] Pennsylvanians, however, seem to have preferred the Gothic Revival for these structures. Some, such as the octagonal board-and-batten Hollenback Cemetery Gatehouses in Wilkes-Barre, were rustic; others, such as Reading's 1846-47 brownstone ashlar Charles Evans Cemetery Gatehouse, simulated Gothic chapels, complete with pinnacles and a pointed-arch arcade forming the interior carriageway.[206] One of the finest, a sophisticated exercise in picturesque massing, is Pittsburgh's 1847 Allegheny Cemetery Gatehouse. Designed by English-born John Chislett, this sandstone ashlar composition of English Tudor elements conveyed both the Christian sobriety and intrigue that suited a burial ground so enhanced with careful plantings and winding paths that it has served as a quasi public park for nearly one hundred and fifty years.[207]

Those romantic and Christian allusions could also be assigned to domestic architecture. As New York-based apologists were launching a domestic reform crusade in the 1830s, architectural critics, led by Andrew Jackson Downing, promoted the Gothic Revival house as a moral, aesthetic, and patriotic alternative to the Greek Revival dwelling. The Gothic style's Christian associations presumably would create a tranquil, loving, and Christian interior environment for the family and an exterior presence that would blend with nature and ennoble the neighborhood. Crosses, as both house plans and house details, appeared in architectural design books. Thomas

U. Walter, for example, co-authored a pattern book in 1846 that illustrated twenty different cross designs.[208] In spite of the critics' energetic promotion of the Gothic style, Pennsylvanians were slow to apply it to their residences and never did embrace it as frequently and imaginatively as they did the Greek Revival.

There were essentially three forms of Gothic Revival residences: the suburban villa, which was rare in Pennsylvania; the house, which gained some popularity among farmers and townspeople; and the cottage. Although architectural writers' distinctions between cottage and house could be arbitrary, cottages were generally identified as modest story-and-a-half dwellings, often board-and-batten, with details restricted to simple and functional window hoods and small porches. The Gothic Revival house is more substantial; it usually has two stories and is built of brick or stone. Irregular in outline, these houses required rustic settings.[209] Tastemakers recommended siting them among tall evergreens or near a bluff, as the builder of Heathside Cottage (PA-623) did in Pittsburgh circa 1860. Although surrounded today by later houses, when it was built on its elevated, remote site overlooking the old city of Allegheny, it met nearly every requirement for early Victorian Gothic Revival houses, including its rather inappropriate English name.[210] (Its hillside site hardly resembles the English heath.) From its irregular plan with its off-center entry vestibule to its clustered chimneys, Heathside Cottage embodies Americans' romantic notions about picturesque eclecticism in general and rural English medieval dwellings in particular. In a narrow sense, the house was a showcase for high-style Gothic Revival details: pointed-arch windows with hood molds (with diamond-paned sash on the north side), a cross-gable with tracery-like barge boards, overhanging gable roof with sawn-out trim and a pinnacle at its peak, and a parapeted bay window. Such academic attention to scale and detail was uncommon. In a broader sense, Heathside Cottage embodies most of the qualities of the picturesque aesthetic that governed nineteenth-century architectural design: its varied silhouette from the pinnacle, chimney pot, and dormer, its asymmetrical plan, and its mixture of Gothic Revival details.[211]

Few local builders had a scholar's knowledge of this picturesque style whose unfamiliar details were difficult to execute. The builder of John F. Singer's 1860s ashlar rubble house (PA-433) in Wilkinsburg, Allegheny County, for example, erected steep gable roofs and placed them over doors and windows hoods dripping with sawn quatrefoils to create a Gothic feeling, but he trimmed the house's corners with rusti-

Heathside Cottage (PA-623) Pittsburgh, Allegheny County. Side elevation (Laurence Dykes, delineator, 1968) PA,2-PITBU,33.

cated Renaissance quoins and decorated the barge boards with Italianate pendants.[212] His interior details, however, such as doorways, are more accurately Gothic Revival in style. At the opposite end of the state, in West Chester, Chester County, the Sibyla Brinton House (PA-249), a later (circa 1873), smaller, and less elaborate random serpentine ashlar dwelling, illustrates the same lack of stylistic purity. Although Brinton's builder employed the standard cross-gable with elongated brackets and trefoil barge boards, he retained Georgian proportions, rusticated Renaissance quoins, and Italianate segmental-arch windows with rusticated heads.[213] The builder used segmental-arch windows because he evidently could not execute Gothic pointed-arch windows, as indicated by the crude pointed window in the cross-gable. Such simple windows (essentially rectangles capped by triangles) are expressions of Carpenter Gothic.[214]

Unsophisticated but often highly original, Carpenter Gothic houses range from the substantial and sober Sibyla Brinton House to the exuberant Mahlon Mercur House in Towanda, Bradford County. Built between 1854 and 1869, Mercur's weatherboarded frame house boasts three steep cross-gables across the front and two on the rear wing. They are connected by boldly sawn trim that runs across the front from the one-story lateral wing, up and down the three cross-gables, along the bargeboards of the gable roof and the rear wing's two cross-gables to the rear porch. The house has a total of eleven gables. In each of the front cross-gables, the Mercur House has not one but two rectangular windows capped with extremely elongated pediments to simulate pointed arches. Mercur's builder, aware of the stylistic function of gables, sawn-out bargeboards, and pointed windows, made the house as quantitatively Gothic as he could.[215] Although high-style Gothic Revival houses never proved very popular among Pennsylvanians, vernacular expressions of the style remained in vogue in small towns and farm lands well after the Civil War. Often weatherboarded balloon-frame houses with Georgian proportions, they are identified by their cross-gables and sawn and turned detailing on bargeboards and porches.

In general, however, Pennsylvanians preferred the Italian variant of the Gothic, the various round-style designs called "the Italianate manner." Although it emerged in England at the beginning of the nineteenth century as a variant of the classical style, in America the Italianate essentially grew out of the Gothic Revival, and was introduced by Gothic enthusiasts. Americans, who were uncomfortable with the foreign and medieval character of the Gothic, could enjoy the Italianate as a vaguely historical and variably picturesque style. In fact, its great virtue was this flexibility of design and allusion.[216] American Protestants who found the Gothic too popish and the Greek too pagan, could turn to the round-arched Romanesque as did the Philadelphia Episcopalians who in 1857 commissioned John Notman to design their brownstone Church of the Holy Trinity (PA-1085).[217] Other options included the Lombard and the Norman, which invariably included spires, such as the 180-foot example on York's First Presbyterian Church or the more elaborate and taller spire on Harrisburg's Market Square Presbyterian Church.[218] During the middle decades of the nineteenth-century congregations, apparently succumbing to the age's competitive fever, built church spires higher and higher. At 227 feet, the brownstone spire of Philadelphia's First Baptist Church was among the top challengers.[219] S. D. Button of Philadelphia designed the stuccoed-brick York church in 1860 with no Gothic pointed arches, but he did include enough vaguely medieval details, such as abundant corbeling beneath the cornices of the nave and tower and pinnacles at the front corners, to identify it as a traditional church. Button's brother-in-law, Joseph C. Hoxie, designed the brick Harrisburg church in a similar fashion, with abundant corbeling, hood molds over round-arch windows, and pinnacles at one front corner and above the buttresses along the sides. Contemporaries, clearly less concerned with archaeological accuracy than with visual impressions, identified these churches' styles variously as Romanesque, Byzantine, and Norman Gothic. In appraising the First Baptist Church in Philadelphia, for example, an 1856 commentator observed, "The style . . . conveys to the mind an idea of architecture of the medieval period, so many fine specimens of which are still extant in England and Normandy."[220]

For those congregations that desired different effects, their architects could stress such features as the domes that Hoxie and Notman employed respectively on Philadelphia's 1855 West Arch Street Presbyterian Church (PA-1696) and Cathedral of SS. Peter and Paul (PA-1497). By emphasizing the Roman Corinthian Order in his blending of Roman, Baroque, and Gothic details and by bathing the monochromatic Classical Revival interior with natural light from the skylights in the coffered ceiling and dome, Hoxie gave the Presbyterians a plastered brick church that was up-to-date but still evocative of the Reformation's claimed clarity of thought.[221] The cathedral (1846-64), on the other hand, with its greater scale, more dramatic brownstone facade, stained glass round-arch windows, and coffered barrel vaults and arches on the dimly lit, decoratively painted interior is more Baroque in appearance and

Baptist Church of West Chester (PA-1191) West Chester Borough, Chester County. Lithograph by Charlie C. Taylor, circa 1860 (copy photo by Ned Goode, 1958) PA,15-WCHES,21-2.

Catholic in feeling.[222] For clients with modest budgets and tastes, architects could also strip the style to its classical basics, as Samuel Sloan and John Stewart did in 1854 for the brick Baptist Church of West Chester (PA-1191). Such details as the Baptist Church's recessed central round-arch window, Tuscan pilasters, and corbeled door hood offered an acceptably moderate visual and ecclesiological alternative to the popular but pagan Greek Revival style.[223]

    This classical variant of the Italianate testifies to its flexibility, allowing it to evoke the rich heritage of the Italian Renaissance as well as suggest the medieval past. This was important for cultural institutions, such as the Athenaeum of Philadelphia (PA-1389), a private literary society founded in 1814. The Athenaeum in 1845 awarded the commission for its new quarters to John Notman, who immodestly called his design "an excellent specimen of the Italian style of architecture."[224] In fact, it is an excellent specimen patterned after the Tuscan palazzo mode of contemporary English clubhouses in which articulated windows and bold cornices replaced columns

Architecture of Pennsylvania • 115

and pilasters.[225] The Athenaeum's three-story facade is distinguished by a rusticated sandstone ground story and dressed sandstone ashlar upper stories with quoins. Tall windows with hoods on elongated consoles rise from the second-story balustraded balcony, and at the top floor, below the heavily bracketed cornice, simply framed squarish windows rest on a stringcourse.[226] The Athenaeum's stately elegance projected the desired image of urbane enlightenment as did the bold arcades and ornate interior of the city's 1857 Academy of Music (PA-1491). Napoleon LeBrun and Gustav Runge modeled the Academy after the late-eighteenth-century La Scala in Milan and intended the sandstone base and brick upper stories to be sheathed with marble. Because of a shortage of funds, however, the directors were unable to finish the facades, which has detracted somewhat from its exterior elegance but not from its interior splendor and acoustics.[227]

The splendor of concert halls and theaters was also appropriate for government buildings. As local landmarks, city halls and county courthouses expressed as much of a community's civic pride as taxpayers and public officials allowed. By the 1850s, when architectural finish increasingly became a matter of creating historical moods rather than firm historical allusions, the Italianate was as acceptable for public buildings as the earlier classical revival styles while being more picturesque and up-to-date. These Italianate buildings could be austere or exuberant, as was Samuel Sloan's 1860 design for the now-gone Lycoming County Courthouse in Williamsport, which featured rusticated quoins contrasting with plastered walls, round-arch windows set within blind arches, and a corner tower capped by a series of bracketed cornices, setbacks, and balconies leading to a domed elongated cupola. The 1864 ashlar city hall in Allegheny City (now part of Pittsburgh), Allegheny County, on the other hand, was much more restrained. Charles Antoine Colomb Gengembre designed it as simple block with pediments centered on three of its facades where pilasters flanked tall round-arch windows.[228]

After 1840, building guidebooks became increasingly important in propagating the Italianate and other picturesque architectural styles. These books contained plans and elevations of houses and often discussed their aesthetic qualities. Andrew Jackson Downing's 1841 *Treatise on the Theory and Practice of Landscape Gardening* stimulated a flood of such design books that over the next forty years enabled local carpenters to build up-to-date dwellings for clients well-removed from such cultural centers as New York and Philadelphia.[229] As Dell Upton explains, however, these pattern books, while working with familiar forms, also strengthened the idea that new buildings must appear distinctive, if not original.[230]

An increasingly popular means by which a building could be unique yet free from pedantic scrutiny was to design it in the Italianate manner, which during the 1850s "became the closest thing to a national style the United States had had since the early days of the classical revivals."[231] It became extremely popular for residences, ranging from brownstone row houses to towered suburban mansions. The latter were especially elegant and subtle expressions of the style. In Montgomery County they included both John Notman's 1850 Alverthorpe (PA-130) in Jenkintown, with its complex massing of plastered forms, such as a squarish tower with balconies and arcades, and simpler yet picturesque houses, such as the 1852 Kennedy Mansion (PA-1959) in Port Kennedy. Essentially a plastered stone cube, the Kennedy Mansion's three-story, hipped-roof, main block is accented by a four-story center tower with a second-story cast-iron balcony resting on the cast-iron veranda.[232] Materials and compositions of these villas varied widely. The 1870 brick Reuben Baer House in Lancaster, for example, has a center tower rising between a three-bay, gable-roof projection and a recessed, flat-roof, one-bay section. The 1870 weatherboard and wood-frame Elijah Parsons House in Towanda has a squarish corner tower with exaggerated pilasters and twin arched windows offsetting the heavily bracketed pediments of the intersecting gable roofs.[233]

To be Italianate a house did not need a tower. By massing forms and using such details as corbeled window hoods, porches, and bracketed cornices, as Samuel Sloan did in 1861 on the eleven brownstone and stucco semidetached houses along Philadelphia's Woodland Terrace (PA-1647), an architect could communicate the same message at less expense.[234] Cupolas, sometimes called observatories or belvederes, such as the arched example atop the 1860 Billmeyer House (PA-5188) in York, could create a picturesque silhouette at a fraction of the cost of a tower—and a fraction of its usefulness as well. Also, through careful contrast of materials, designers could generate a sense of boldness and textural richness, as the Billmeyer House's architect did by applying sandstone quoins and shaped window and door surrounds to its red brick walls. Such Italianate houses were built throughout Pennsylvania in the middle decades of the nineteenth century. In some cases, such as the 1868 Peter Herdic House in Williamsport, architects knowledgeable of proper forms, proportions, and details designed houses with a strong sense of the picturesque. Architect

Alverthorpe (PA-130) Jenkintown vicinity (Abington Township), Montgomery County. General view (Ian McLaughlin, photographer, 1937) PA,46-JENK,1-1.

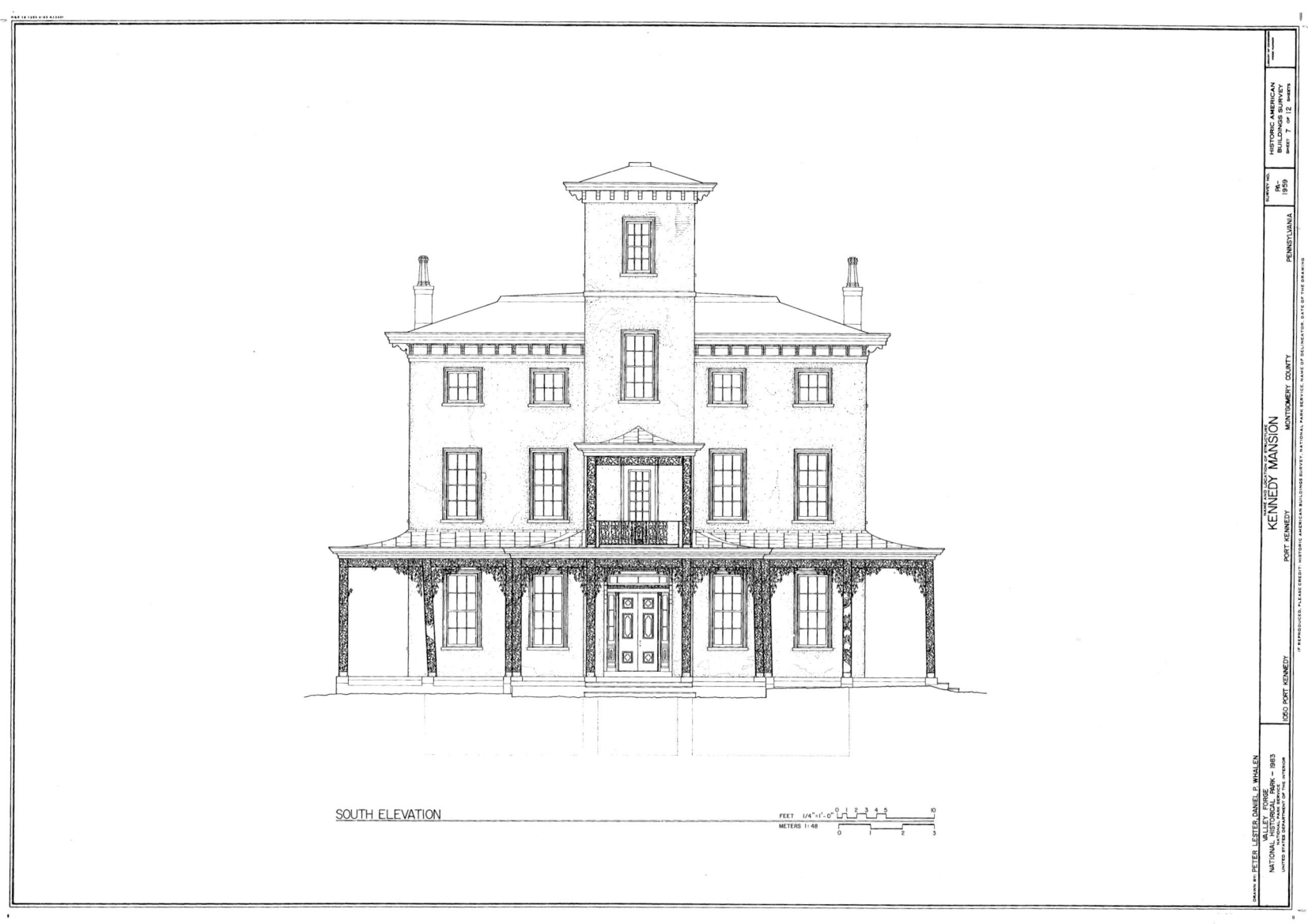

Kennedy Mansion (PA-1959) Port Kennedy (Upper Merion Township), Montgomery County.
South elevation (Peter Lester and Daniel P. Whalen, delineators, 1983) PA,46-POKEN,1.

Eber Culver accomplished this by projecting semi-hexagonal wings and porches from the house's plastered main block, placing a broad cornice with oversized brackets and coffered soffits atop the ensemble, and capping the whole with a low, flat-roof cupola.[235] In many cases new residences were essentially Georgian double-pile central-hall houses decorated with such Italianate details as bracketed eaves and hood moulds.[236] In fact, this Georgian form remained the most popular of the traditional forms in mid-century architectural design books.[237]

Nowhere did the Italianate manner prove more popular than on commercial buildings.[238] Its legacy is evident in old business districts throughout the state. Local builders applied the Italianate to stores, shops, and banks that were rarely outstanding individual buildings, but as groups of buildings they gave small-town commercial streets a distinctively urban appearance. By combining various Renaissance details, builders could cheaply erect commercial fronts that both evoked the stability and success of Venetian merchants and Florentine bankers and emulated the great avenues of metropolitan New York and Philadelphia. Many of these details, and sometimes entire facades, were cast iron, shipped from architectural iron works in such cities as Philadelphia, Pittsburgh, and Buffalo.[239] Capable of being cast as elaborately as any stone carver could cut them in stone, yet cheaper and apparently fireproof, cast iron architectural elements proved popular during the third quarter of the nineteenth century. On rare occasions even sidewalks were constructed of cast iron. An 1861 Philadelphia example (PA-1723), originally with heating pipes beneath it, survived at its original location into the late 1970s.[240]

The Italianate manner was often the picturesque medium through which mid-century architectural taste shifted from an eclecticism of taste to an eclecticism of style. In the former period, the symbolic phase of picturesque eclecticism, architects executed interiors or exteriors in a single revival style. Styles could be mixed in a building but not in the same area. Erie's Reed Mansion (PA-57), for example, has a Greek Revival exterior but contains Gothic Revival and Rococo rooms; yet the Greek and Gothic styles are not mixed in either space. After the 1850s, however, a mixture of styles became increasingly common as fascination for picturesque facades grew. Eclecticism of style liberated architects from slavishly and archaeologically following a particular past style; it meant "selecting tectonic elements from every style, and re-amalgamating them according to contemporary needs."[241] Eclecticism freed architects to pursue a synthetic picturesqueness, through either verticality, which was

Billmeyer House (PA-5188) York, York County. South and east elevations (Paul Galbreath, photographer, 1963)) PA,67-YORK,10-1.

easily accomplished with towers, imbalance from overhangs, swelling towers, or crushed tunnel-like spaces. They did this by adding picturesque elements to the familiar and flexible Italianate or through new contemporary styles.[242]

Most prominent among those new styles were the French Second Empire and the English High Victorian Gothic, both of which were contemporary rather than revival styles from an earlier era. In Pennsylvania the Second Empire mode proved more popular than the High Victorian Gothic, which tended to be associated with Anglicanism. Although the Second Empire style emerged outside of France, its spiritual home was Paris of Napoleon III. The Second Empire first appeared in the United States in the 1850s and flourished in the decade after the Civil War.[243] Characterized by the exaggerated three-dimensionality and irregular silhouettes of their mansard roofs atop end and center pavilions, Second Empire buildings were both modern and picturesque. None was richer in composition or more massive in scale than John McArthur Jr.'s Philadelphia City Hall (PA-1530). Thirty years in the making (1871-1901), it remains the country's largest municipal governmental building and the world's tallest building with masonry-bearing walls. These marble-clad brick walls are enriched with an unexcelled display of architectural and sculptural details. By becoming the zenith of the Second Empire style, City Hall rose above the style's inherent classical restraint. Its marble and iron-frame tower, unique but incongruous with the building's French sources, dominated the city's skyline for nearly a century.[244] In combination with the building's rich sculptural detailing, which ranges from deeply carved egg-and-dart frames to allegorical caryatids and free-standing figures, it "illustrates the fate of Second Empire design in America: it became florid, restless, and fragmented."[245]

Diluted and eclectic Second Empire expressions are ubiquitous throughout Pennsylvania. The key element, sometimes the only element, on these buildings is the mansard roof, which alone could make a residence or commercial building appear picturesque and up-to-date. This was especially the case when mansard roofs capped towers, which further contributed to a house's picturesque massing. Many of these houses, such as the plastered 1870 William Hartley House in Bedford or the brownstone 1876 William Weigley House in Schaefferstown, Lebanon County, are essentially Italianate villas dressed up with mansard roofs and window surrounds or hoods.[246] Because it provided usable attic space as well as a modern look, the mansard was often the most important added feature when remodeling older houses, long after

The New Public Buildings (Philadelphia City Hall) (PA-1530) Philadelphia. Elevated view of north elevation (Jack E. Boucher, photographer, 1982)) PA,51-PHILA,327-22.

the Second Empire's heyday. For example, Thomas Eakins in Philadelphia added a mansard to his mid-nineteenth-century brick row house (PA-1728) as late as 1902.[247]

Picturesqueness could also be generated from polychromatic and heavily proportioned Gothic forms, as architect Frank Furness demonstrated in a number of buildings, but especially in Philadelphia's Pennsylvania Academy of the Fine Arts (PA-1525). Furness was clearly inspired by the English High Victorian Gothic style when he designed this masterpiece in 1872, but he integrated into the polychromatic facade elements from other styles: Greek, Renaissance, Second Empire, Moorish, and what might be called industrial vernacular. Three oversized Gothic-arch windows with Ohio sandstone surrounds dominate the front facade, which is framed by rusticated, Hummelstown red sandstone Renaissance quoins. Greek metopes with medieval bas-reliefs extend across the two outer bays below the monitored mansard roofs, and along the north side exposed iron trusses frame brick diaperwork. Furness also exposed ironwork on the interior, both on the skylight above the main stair hall and in the galleries.[248] Much of the facade's eclecticism was meant to express the building's function as an art institution, but Furness executed other eclectic and picturesque—if not grotesque—designs in which he precariously balanced heavy overhanging and overscaled elements on squat columns and corbels above compressed entries. Furness, however, did not design in the High Victorian Gothic style but used the style as a springboard into his own highly individualized architectural expression. His work is synthetic picturesque eclecticism at its best. As architectural taste changed at the turn of the twentieth century, Furness's work was condemned, and as years passed was largely ignored. Since the 1960s, however, after the demise of many of his buildings, scholars have increasingly recognized him as one of the nation's most creative architects of the so-called Gilded Age.[249]

Another major architect of the synthetic picturesque eclecticism who contributed mightily to the state's architectural heritage was Henry Hobson Richardson. Richardson, Louisiana-born, French-trained, and Boston-based, had emerged as the nation's leading architect by 1884,[250] when he designed one of his last and greatest works, the Allegheny County Courthouse and Jail (PA- 610) in Pittsburgh. The county commissioners awarded Richardson the commission for this complex and monumental structure largely because of his proposal's superior lighting and ventilation schemes.[251] Richardson, well aware of Pittsburgh's reputation as the Smoky City, which dated from before the 1850s, arranged courtrooms and judges' chambers

Pennsylvania Academy of the Fine Arts (PA-1525) Philadelphia. East elevation (James C. Dillon, photographer, date unknown)) PA,51-PHILA,340-1.

around a central court so every room would receive an abundance of natural light through at least two walls. Ventilation was equally important in a coal-fueled industrial environment. Richardson employed the two hundred fifty foot tower, whose peak stood well above street-level pollution, as nostrils for a ventilation system that carried fresh air to the basement to be cleansed and warmed before being distributed throughout the building and exhausted from the twin towers behind the courtyard.[252] The public was more interested in the building's appearance, and liked what it saw, particularly in the courthouse. Working in his familiar Romanesque vein, Richardson masterfully plumbed history for forms and feelings to fabricate an outstanding example of the synthetic picturesque eclecticism. Picturesque qualities are embodied in the texture of the courthouse's rock-faced Milford granite laid in alternating wide and

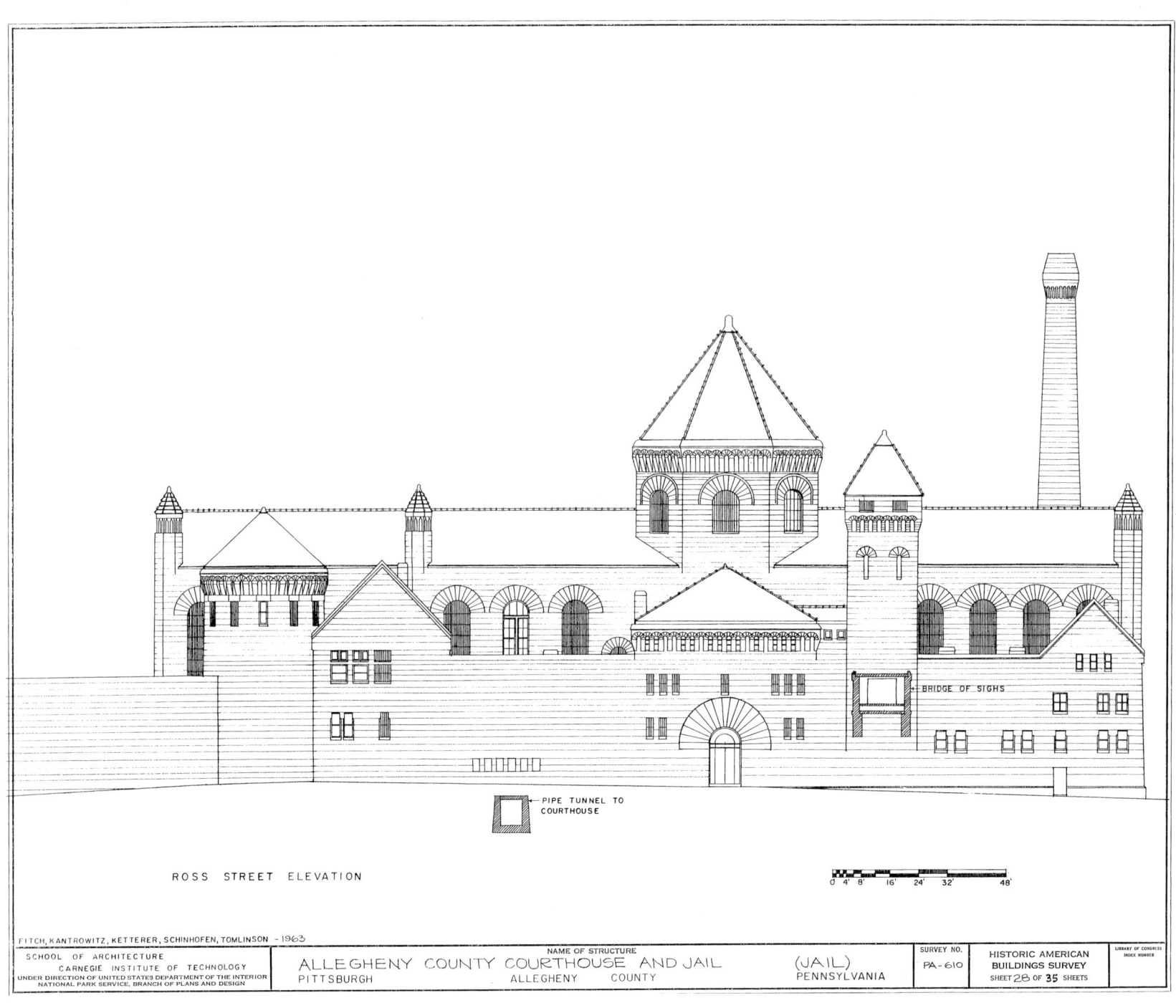

Allegheny County Courthouse and Jail (PA-610) Pittsburgh, Allegheny County. Ross Street elevation of jail (Fitch, Kantrowitz, Ketterer, Schinhofen, and Tomlinson, delineators, 1963) PA,2-PITBU,29.

narrow courses with red mortar, the variety of the squat corner pavilions and rounded side bays, and the spiky silhouette of the wall dormers and lofty tower with its corner turrets. Mariana Griswold Van Rensselaer, a Richardson contemporary, praised the courthouse's eclecticism in 1888, noting that although the courthouse's features are drawn from the southern European Romanesque, "its silhouette suggests some of the late-medieval buildings of the north of Europe, and its symmetry, its dignity and nobility of air, speak of Renaissance ideals. To combine inspirations drawn from such different sources into a novel yet organic whole while expressing a complex plan of the most modern sort—this was indeed to be original."[253] Scholars and critics today are more fascinated by the unadorned simplicity and rock-faced granite of the jail and its austere wall. "This," James O'Gorman points out, "is elemental architecture . . . a building which relies for its effect upon the basic materials and geometry of construction."[254]

Unfortunately Richardson died of Bright's disease in the spring of 1886 and never saw the courthouse completed. His influence, nevertheless, lived after him, and for a decade architects throughout the state, as well as many parts of the country, emulated the Richardsonian Romanesque style. In most cases it meant incorporating towers, large arches, and Romanesque details on rock-faced facades, but in few cases were architects able to capture the subtle sense of mass and structure typical of Richardson's best designs. In rare instances architects would all but duplicate a Richardson building, as Frederick L. Olds of State College did in 1888 when he designed a virtual copy of Richardson's famous 1885-86 Marshall Field Warehouse in Chicago for J. C. Blair's brick stationery factory in Huntingdon.[255] Plagiarism may be a form of flattery, but it does not produce fresh architecture; Olds could copy an elevation but he could not re-create a monument. By erecting a smaller building in brick, a cheaper and flatter material, rather than massively cut rock-faced stone, Olds lost the forceful character of the Chicago warehouse, and by using extremely narrow top-story windows and trabeated rather than arched windows at the next to top story, he diminished the bold gracefulness that Richardson attained in the Field building.

Olds's indebtedness to Richardson was unusual only in its degree; most of the state's architecture has always been derivative. By the last quarter of the nineteenth century, however, a flood of professional architectural periodicals, which Olds probably consulted to learn of Richardson's work, and catalogs of mail-order plans diluted, or often completely washed away, regional characteristics. A Queen Anne mansion in Dubuque differs little from one in Scranton or Washington. George Palliser, an English-born architect in Bridgeport, Connecticut, initiated the mail-order plan business in 1876, Robert W. Shoppell of New York perfected it during the 1880s, and by the 1890s a number of entrepreneurs were engaged in the enterprise, including George F. Barber of Knoxville, Tennessee, who sold not only house plans but also prefabricated dwellings.[256] Among his thousands of clients was George F. Gage, general manager of the Huntingdon and Broad Top Railroad in Huntingdon, who in 1896 purchased a set of Barber's plans for a turreted brick Queen Anne house.[257] Because of the extensiveness of the mail-order trade, the Gage house is one of probably hundreds of such residences in Pennsylvania. Identifying and documenting them is yet another need and opportunity for study.

George Gage probably considered his house architect-designed, since the person on Barber's staff responsible for the drawings probably was an architect. Gage, however, chose only his house design, not his architect. He was unable to discuss with his house's designer his wishes about the house's plan or appearance. That give-and-take process is the privilege of clients who are able to commission architects rather than select house plans. James W. Pinchot of Milford, Pike County, was one of those clients. As a young man, Pinchot left Milford and made his fortune as a paper hangings merchant in New York. In 1884, nine years after his early retirement, he decided to build a country house (PA-1400) on a hill overlooking the Delaware River and his hometown, where he held an interest in his late father's farming and lumbering holdings.[258] His architect was Richard Morris Hunt, a close family friend and one of America's leading architects, famous then—and now—as the architect for the Vanderbilts.[259] Construction was under way by the spring of 1885 and was all but complete by August 1886 when the Pinchots moved into the house they called Grey Towers.[260]

Hunt's design for Grey Towers was uniquely suited for the Pinchots. James Pinchot was proud of his French heritage, and it was logical that his architect would be Hunt, who appreciated French architecture probably more than any of his contemporary American architects and was famous for his New York and Chicago chateaux based on the Renaissance of Francois I. For Grey Towers, however, Hunt did not draw his design from the French Renaissance but from the middle ages, a rare practice for him.[261] Grey Towers' strongest source of inspiration appears to have been La Grange, Lafayette's many-towered chateau in Bleneau-en-Brie. Similarities

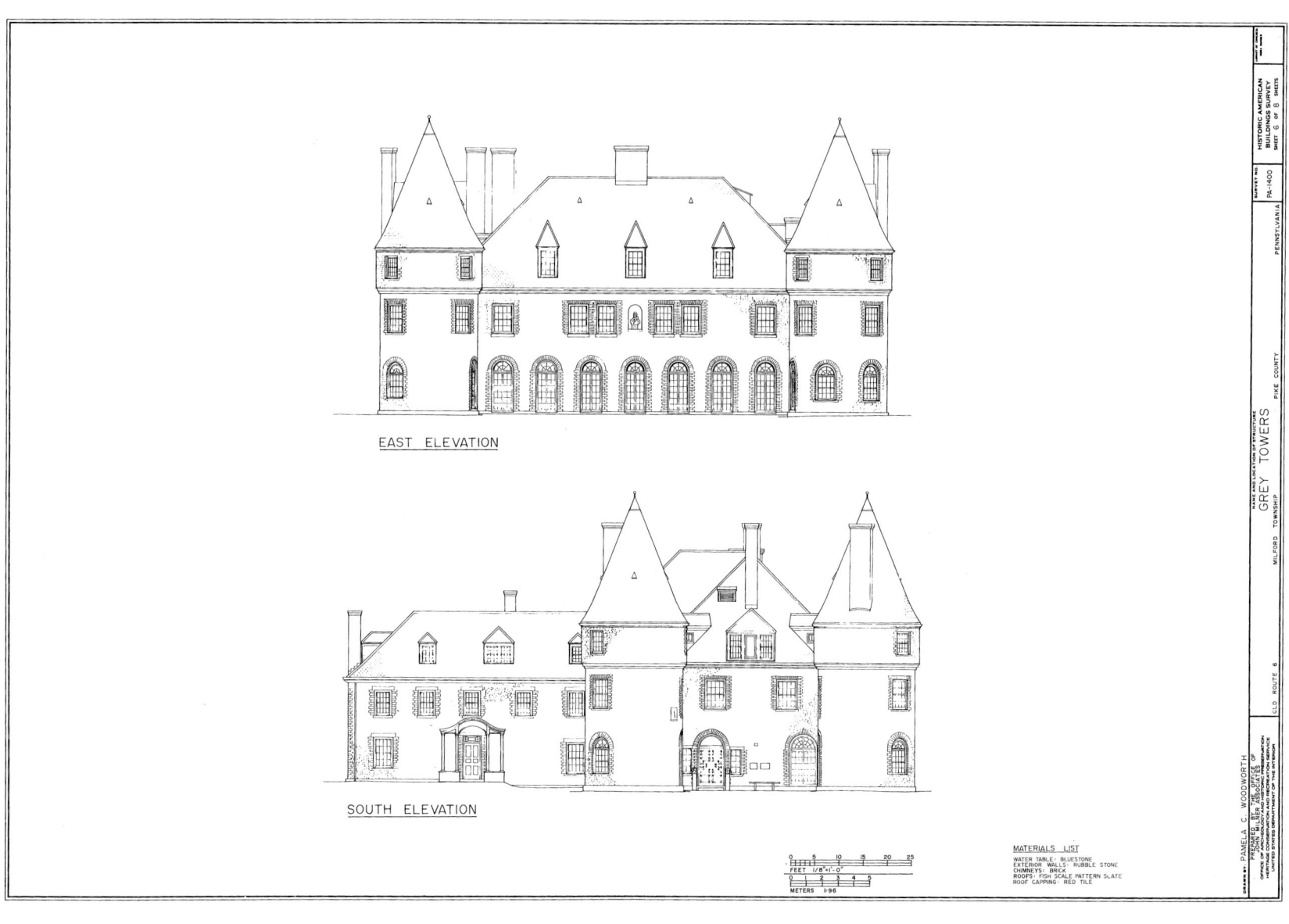

Grey Towers (PA-1400) Milford vicinity (Milford Township), Pike County. South and east elevations (Pamela C. Woodworth, delineator, 1983) PA,52-MILF,2.

between Grey Towers and La Grange include the rounded rock-faced ashlar towers with conical roofs, a hipped-roof wing, a round-arch entrance and gable dormer squeezed between two towers, and a niche housing a bust of Lafayette. (A bust of the Revolutionary War hero was apparently added to La Grange after Lafayette's death but before Grey Towers' construction.) For Hunt this was more than a case of emulating a famous monument; he developed a picturesque design to meet a client's special conditions, Pinchot's claim that his maternal grandfather had been a personal friend of the marquis. La Grange, located about fifty miles east of Paris, was a popular site for nineteenth-century Americans to visit, and during his many excursions abroad it would have been easy for Pinchot to have made a pilgrimage there. It was not necessary, however, to visit the chateau to be familiar with it; views were widely available in America.[262]

As friends, Pinchot and Hunt enjoyed a genial and productive architect-client relationship, as did Pinchot's son and daughter-in-law during the 1920s with their architect, Chester H. Aldrich of the noted New York firm, Delano and Aldrich. Gifford Pinchot inherited the Grey Towers estate in 1913 and in 1917 he and his wife began a ten-year remodeling of the mansion in addition to the erection of two significant outbuildings.[263] Although it was his parents' summer place, Gifford was evidently minimally involved in the house's architectural changes, usually only approving or vetoing final plans.[264] The person most responsible for the changes and for all consultations with the architect was his wife, Cornelia Bryce Pinchot, an energetic and progressive New York socialite with a strong social conscience, unshakable feminist convictions, and a consuming interest in every aspect of Grey Towers' transformation after World War I.[265]

On becoming the first lady of Grey Towers, Cornelia Pinchot began her first project in 1917, the four-year transformation of the billiard room and salon into a library. She oversaw every aspect of the work, from contracting with local workmen to acquiring gold-powder toning liquid for the gilded bookcases.[266] While the library was in a state of turmoil, she solicited plans from Aldrich for another major change, converting the dining and breakfast rooms to a grand dining room which could also function as a sitting room. Once she started work on the project in early 1921, she frequently consulted with Aldrich on details that ranged from rebuilding a wooden Baroque mantelpiece to her idea that "it would be a good thing to 'jazz' up the room a little bit" by painting the door frames "with lovely red pilasters." He agreed, thinking it would "kill that still too pervasive green."[267] Two projects that required even more architect-client consultation were the Bait Box (PA-1400B)[268] and the Letter Box (PA-1400C). The design of the Bait Box, a weatherboarded balloon-frame playhouse for the Pinchots' son, evolved over nearly three years of correspondence, beginning in January 1923.[269] The Letter Box, the coursed-rubble archives for Governor Pinchot's political papers, required even more deliberations. Aldrich completed his first drawings in early December 1925, and Mrs. Pinchot responded with a host of suggestions for the interior, including a circular iron staircase, which he incorporated into his final plans. They spent the spring and summer of 1926 discussing exterior details and then corresponded on flooring materials and design until the spring of 1927, when she selected a design from samples that Aldrich had sent her.[270]

Mrs. Pinchot's professional relationship with Chester H. Aldrich was warmed by a cordial friendship and mutual respect. That was not the case in all architect-client relationships, including her own with William Lawrence Bottomley, the New York architect who became a favorite house and garden designer for the east coast elite after World War I.[271] Although he worked with classical forms, he followed the picturesque tradition. "I work towards interesting silhouettes to the roof lines," he explained, "contrasting flat surfaces with projecting masses, and contrasting plain walls with interesting detail at salient points."[272] In many respects, Bottomley was the most appropriate architect for Mrs. Pinchot's imaginative project of the early 1930s, the Finger Bowl. The Finger Bowl is an outdoor dining area composed of a raised irregularly-shaped pool with a wide fieldstone ledge that is surrounded by stone-masonry posts supporting a canopy of vines. Diners sat around the pool with their plates on the ledge and balsa food dishes floating in the pool.[273] Although Mrs. Pinchot and Bottomley did not know each other before the Finger Bowl project, they were forced into a relatively close working relationship because of her strong opinions and intense involvement in any changes made at Grey Towers. Mrs. Pinchot, evidently aware that she was straining the architect's patience, apologetically wrote him in the spring of 1933 that "it's good of you not to be too indignant with such a trying client as I must be."[274] The architect and client had fundamentally different ideas on the nature of the Finger Bowl. Bottomley wanted to make it distinctive from the other garden elements by featuring decorative posts while Mrs. Pinchot sought integration, using a scale and materials similar to what was already in the garden. After protracted discussions and numerous sketches, these differences

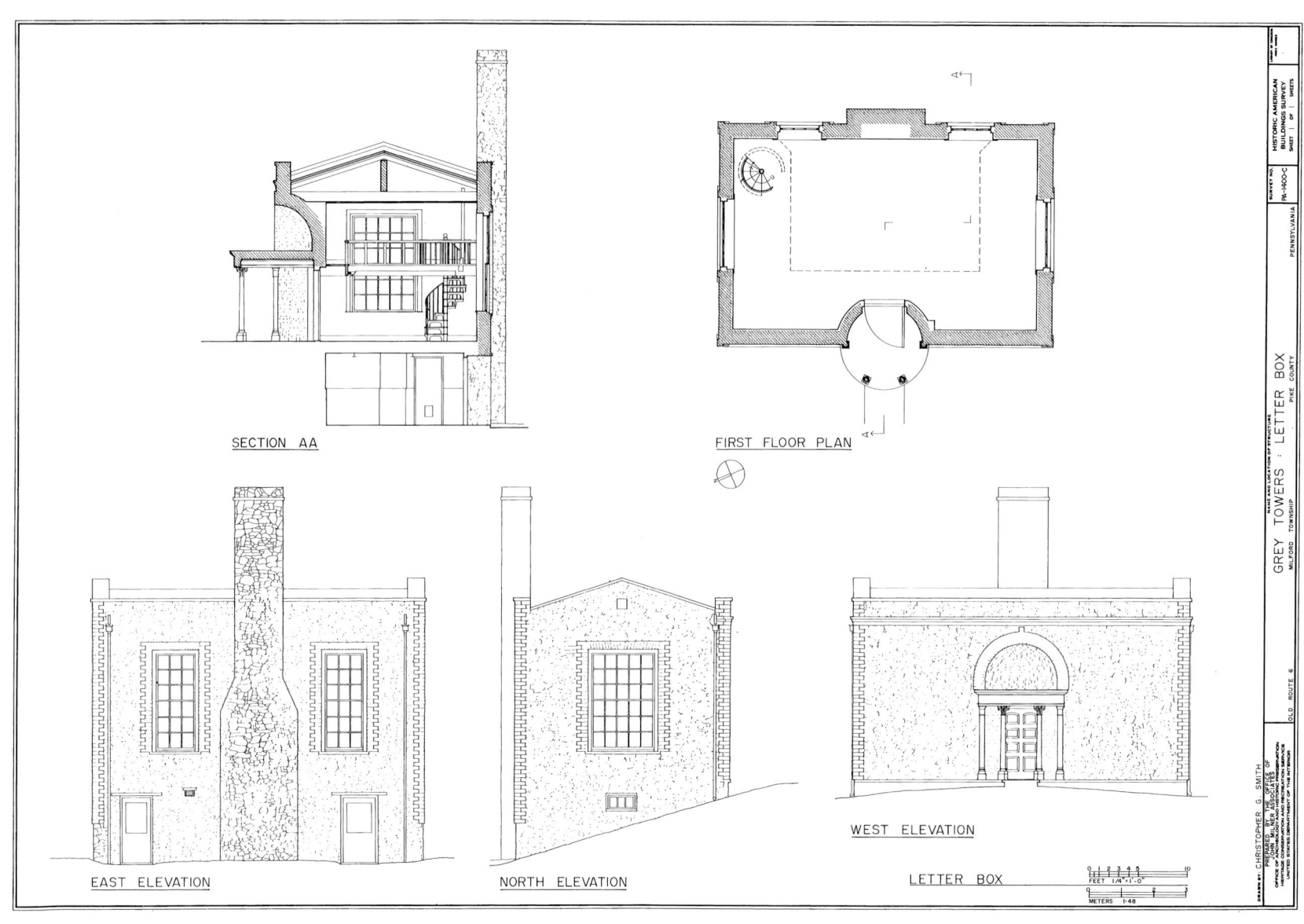

The Letter Box, Grey Towers (PA-1400) Milford vicinity (Milford Township), Pike County. South and east elevations (Christopher G. Smith, delineator, 1983) PA,52-MILF,2.

were resolved in piecemeal decisions on the nature of the canopy and the design of its supports. Bottomley prevailed on the canopy and Mrs. Pinchot on the supports. She settled on fieldstone piers, primarily because Bottomley's proposed sculptural posts proved too expensive. Construction started in July 1933.[275] In the fall of 1932 and spring of 1933, when these decisions were made, even the Pinchots were feeling the gloom and dwindling dividends of the darkest days of the Great Depression. Architect-client relations deteriorated rapidly in 1935 when Mrs. Pinchot, dissatisfied with Bottomley's fee, requested a hearing before the Professional Practice Committee of the New York Chapter of the American Institute of Architects.[276] Fee troubles notwithstanding, Mrs. Pinchot's architects served her well. They designed for her unique structures that met very special needs while expressing on a small scale the final phase of picturesque eclecticism.

The last, or creative, phase of the picturesque evolved during the 1880s and reached its maturity in the first two decades of the twentieth century. Buildings of this period are characterized by large scale, broad symbolism, and a return to eclecticism of taste, as architects creatively synthesized new designs from old sources for big buildings with archaeologically correct details and expanded functions.[277] Sometimes called the American Renaissance, it was a time when large-scale classicism was virtually de rigueur for business, institutional, and public buildings.[278] The era began with Hermann Schwarzmann's marble-faced brick and iron Memorial Hall (PA-1659), an early Beaux-Arts work for the 1876 Centennial Exhibition in Philadelphia, and faded during the Great Depression with such examples of stripped classicism as Paul Cret's marble-clad steel-frame Federal Reserve Bank of Philadelphia (PA-1506), built 1931-35.[279] After an era of rapid and rampant industrial growth, it was time to consolidate business ventures and erect buildings to house these new large-scale enterprises, and nowhere was this stage of corporate industrialism and individual enterprise better exhibited than in Pennsylvania.[280]

Metropolitan department stores, for example, were the merchandising marvels of their time; their great scale of operation demanded a comparable architecture. Consequently Philadelphia's John Wanamaker Store (PA-1692), as completed in 1910, is an overscaled twelve-story palazzo that fills an entire city block, suggesting that John Wanamaker not only was an enlightened merchant, but one who performed on a greater scale than even the most successful of his Renaissance predecessors. Daniel H. Burnham of Chicago, his architect, designed the store in 1902 with

International Exhibition of 1876, Memorial Hall (PA-1659) Philadelphia. General view from southeast (Jack E. Boucher, photographer, 1972) PA,51-PHILA,265B-1.

classically proportioned granite ashlar walls that belie its modern steel skeleton, great size, and spectacular interior spaces that range from the five-story Grand Court to an Egyptian Hall and the extensive Crystal Dining Room.[281] Burnham boasted that it was "the most monumental commercial structure ever erected anywhere in the world."[282] The dedication of such a splendid store owned by a man of Wanamaker's eminence commanded the presence of no less a person than the President of the United States; William Howard Taft opened the ceremonies, December 20, 1911, honoring both the new palace of commerce and Wanamaker's fifty years of business.[283]

Daniel H. Burnham's role as principal advisor and architect of the 1893 World's Columbian Exposition catapulted him into the top ranks of American architects, helping him to become a leading designer of tall commercial buildings. In addition to the Wanamaker Store, he also designed the Land Title Building (PA-1514) in Philadelphia. The fifteen-story first stage, built in 1897-98, is in Chicago's

John Wanamaker Store (PA-1692) Philadelphia. Interior court (Walter Smalling Jr., photographer, 1979) PA,51-PHILA,370-2.

Commercial Style with a steel skeleton and buff brick curtain walls, and the twenty-two-story steel-frame second stage, built five years later, has classical details gracing its pale granite-faced brick curtain walls.[284] Burnham's well-ordered classically detailed skyscrapers seem to have appealed to men who had amassed great wealth while bringing order to their industries. In Pittsburgh, for example, Henry Clay Frick, the coke magnate who became a partner in Andrew Carnegie's steel firm, commissioned Burnham in 1901 to design a twenty-one-story neoclassical skyscraper that he immodestly called the Frick Building.[285] In addition to being a monument to Frick's financial might and a lucrative real-estate investment, the granite-ashlar-clad steel-frame building towered over the adjacent Carnegie Building and probably was, as James Van Trump notes, "an architectural riposte in the great Frick-Carnegie battle."[286] This "edifice complex" among Pittsburgh's steelmen was so strong that it lived after them. Four years after Henry W. Oliver's 1904 death, for example, his estate commissioned Burnham to design an expanded version of the Frick Building, which it called, unsurprisingly, the Oliver Building. Although three stories taller, the steel-frame Oliver Building is in the same classical style as the Frick Building, except it is clad with terra cotta rather than granite.[287]

Perhaps no building better represents the state of Pennsylvania's high-style architecture—and its politics—at the turn of the century than its State Capitol. The 1821 Capitol (PA-37), a fusion of Federal and Classical Revival forms and details that English-born Stephen Hills had designed in 1816, burned in early February 1897.[288] Joseph M. Huston, a thirty-five-year-old Philadelphia architect active in Republican politics, won the architectural competition in late 1901, and set to work preparing working drawings for the contractor, George F. Payne Company, who began construction in January 1903.[289] The Renaissance Revival Capitol is a skillful blending in granite and Vermont limestone of elements from historical monuments. Its dome, for example, the building's most widely acclaimed feature, is clearly based on Michelangelo's dome for St. Peter's Basilica in Rome, except the Pennsylvania dome is finished in terra cotta rather than stone and is capped with Roland Hinton Perry's statue, *Commonwealth,* instead of a cross. Similarly the grand entrance lobby is drawn from Charles Garnier's 1860s Paris Opera House foyer. Huston made minor changes, such as introducing more lavish curves to the grand stairs and giving the putti above the doorway shields to carry rather than orbs, but he retained the light stands flanking the caryatid doorway and the triple-arched gallery with a second-floor marble

Land Title Bank and Trust Company (PA-1514) Philadelphia. General view (Jack E. Boucher, photographer, 1973) PA,51-PHILA,345-1.

balustrade and a third-floor iron railing. Furnished with resplendent carvings, Mercer floor tiles representing the state's natural and political history, and great murals by Edwin Austin Abbey, Violet Oakley, and William Van Ingen, the Capitol is richly endowed.[290]

On the Capitol's completion in August 1906, the press was extreme in its praise. "One of the most superb pieces of architecture, in conception and completion, ever reared on this continent," proclaimed the *Reading Herald*.[291] The Pennsylvania and Reading railroads offered reduced excursion rates to citizens eager to view this wonder of Pennsylvania. Pennsylvanians seemed most impressed by the building's size, by the seven million bricks in its dome, its length that exceeded Westminster Abbey's, its one-half-mile perimeter that was greater than that of St. Paul's in London.[292] A few found the Capitol's excess and the public's response to it offensive. "Its total lack of individuality and distinction, its great aimless bulk, its bilious, overeaten decoration, its swollen bronzes, its varicose chandeliers, expressed their [Pennsylvanians'] notion of the grand and the desirable," wrote Philadelphia author Owen Wister.[293] Wister was outraged less by the architecture than by the unfolding scandal whose scale of sin was appropriate to the grandiose building. *The New York Times* thought that there had "never been in the whole history of corrupt politics in America anything quite equal to the work of the daring thieves who built the Pennsylvania Capitol."[294] Over five million dollars were stolen from the state's taxpayers, primarily through payoffs and overcharges. A bootblack stand in the Senate men's room, for example, cost the Capitol's furniture contractor $125; he billed the state $1619.20. After the usual investigations, fourteen men were arrested, but only three were tried and two convicted, Huston and Joseph Sanderson, the furniture contractor.[295]

As the new capitol suggests, classicism was broadly interpreted. It could be the enriched Renaissance Revival style that J. G. Fulton used on his 1904 domed marble-ashlar Somerset County Courthouse in Somerset or a neoclassicism with Beaux-Arts detailing, like that of the City-County Building (PA-5193) that was built in Pittsburgh in 1915-17. As an office and court building for both Allegheny County and the City of Pittsburgh, the City-County Building is necessarily large, filling an entire city block and rising eleven stories. Palmer, Hornbostel and Jones of New York, working with Edward B. Lee of Pittsburgh, devised a bold neoclassical granite-ashlar skin with Beaux-Arts detailing for the steel skeleton. They relieved its great mass by incorporating three gigantic entrance arches and a colossal four-story colonnade on the upper stories of the principal front. They continued the theme on the interior where a forty-seven-foot-high barrel-vaulted gallery, lined with fluted bronze columns, runs the length of the building's longitudinal axis.[296]

The most popular of the period's classical styles was the Neoclassical Revival. After about 1890 Pennsylvania's banks were built in almost no other style. Whether they were small banks, such as the 1926 granite-ashlar Northumberland National Bank in Northumberland, or great institutions like Philadelphia's 1908 Girard Trust Corn Exchange Bank (PA-1510), architects designed them with a sense of monumentality. Colossal fluted Ionic columns in antis, wide Tuscan pilasters, and a high parapet give the Northumberland bank a more stately presence than its size alone would convey.[297] The marble-clad steel-frame Girard bank, on the other hand, long claimed by McKim, Mead and White, masters of the style, is modeled on the Pantheon. August, chaste, and elegant, its low form stands out among its skyscraping neighbors while inside its surprisingly spacious banking floor spreads out beneath the high dome.[298]

Architects brought back other historical styles for encores as well. Understandably, the Gothic was the style for churches. It was carried to archaeological extremes, however, in the granite-ashlar Cathedral of the Church of the New Jerusalem (Swedenborgian) in Bryn Athyn, Montgomery County, where craftsmen are still executing, in a strictly medieval fashion, details of Ralph Adams Cram's 1913 design.[299] Large-scale academic classicism and gothicism were too pompous and ecclesiastical for most dwellings. The exception was a dwindling number of new mansions, such as Fairacres (PA-607), B. F. Jones' oversized limestone-clad steel-frame Renaissance Revival palace that stood in Sewickley Heights, Allegheny County between 1915 and 1964. Passage of the federal income tax in 1913 and changing tastes in the 1920s contributed to the decline of such country seats. Instead, architects turned increasingly to America's colonial past for domestic models.

It could be argued that the colonial house never died. As noted above, the Georgian double-pile central-hall plan was the most popular layout in mid-nineteenth-century design books, and many Italianate houses are fundamentally Georgian houses with Renaissance details. Also, in the countryside carpenters continued to build traditionally, to the consternation of purveyors of mail-order house plans. George and Charles Palliser, for example, complain about the trouble caused one of

City-County Building (PA-5193) Pittsburgh, Allegheny County. Grant Street elevation (Dennis Marsico, photographer, 1981) PA,2-PITBU,34-1.

their clients by "an ignorant village carpenter" who knew only "what he had done before over and over, and he had never studied anything outside of the village in which he lived, and in which the houses are made up of white boxes with green blinds."[300] The Colonial Revival grew out of the Stick and Shingle styles in the 1870s and 1880s, and to a degree from the Queen Anne as well, as architects drew details from old American houses to enhance their picturesque designs.[301] There was even a Beaux-Arts interpretation of the Colonial Revival.[302] New York and Boston architects led the architectural profession into the American past, and are responsible for Pennsylvania's best early examples of the style, such as McKim, Mead and White's 1890-91 brick Germantown Cricket Club (PA-1693) in Philadelphia.[303] By the late 1890s, however, Pennsylvania architects, especially those with New York roots, such as Clark Wright Evans of Wilkes-Barre, were making distinctions between rustic, shingled vernacular forms and the more academic, symmetrical Georgian. In 1898, for example, Evans designed his own Wilkes-Barre house with an enlarged, stylized Palladian window in a large shingled overhanging cross-gambrel, while a few blocks away he gave L. D. Shoemaker's hipped-roof gray brick house softly swelling bays with Ionic pilasters, marble lintels with keystones, and a balustraded stone entrance porch with paired Ionic columns.[304]

Perhaps Pennsylvania's most polished early Colonial Revival architect was Wilson Eyre, a Philadelphian who in the 1890s shifted from the Queen Anne to the Colonial Revival. Over the next thirty years he designed a great variety of city and country buildings that ranged from the symmetrical brick facade and asymmetrical plan for Dr. Joseph Leidy's 1894 house and office (PA-1515) in Philadelphia to Howard Henry's 1911 rubble stone farmhouse set into a hillside in Fort Washington, Montgomery County.[305] Eyre led the way toward a distinctively regional expression of the Colonial Revival that was evident by the 1910s. Wallace Nutting found in these "Pennsylvania homesteads" "a more careful attention to the harmonizing of dwelling with country landscape" and "a quieter tone and a better taste" than in New England examples of the style.[306] Duhring, Okie and Ziegler, in particular, used Pennsylvania fieldstone and stuccoed farmhouses in the 1910s as models for new rural and suburban houses that were more vernacular than Georgian in spirit.[307] A contemporary critic thought their houses were "quite unlike most American work," finding in them "more local than borrowed precedent" and "local materials [that] are frankly expressed in terms of honest craftsmanship."[308]

The critic's comments could have been directed just as accurately toward southeastern Pennsylvania's Arts and Crafts architecture, which was visually similar to much of the Colonial Revival but with different roots. It was patterned after the English turn-of-the-century Arts and Crafts movement, when English architects, in an effort to free themselves of historical styles, focused on vernacular buildings, indigenous materials, and ornament based on nature. Free of pattern-book precedents, this style required greater understanding of local materials and building forms than any other style since the introduction of the Georgian. World War I killed the Arts and Crafts style in England, but in Pennsylvania it remained popular throughout the 1920s. Wilson Eyre was a Pennsylvania pioneer in this romantic and picturesque mode, too, as was William L. Price, founder of the Rose Valley artist colony in Delaware County. Eyre in particular had a number of disciples in the Philadelphia

Dr. Joseph Leidy Jr. House (PA-1515) Philadelphia. South elevation (Jack E. Boucher, photographer, 1972) PA,51-PHILA,498-1.

region, including the noted firm of Mellor, Meigs and Howe.[309] Like the Colonial Revival architects, Philadelphia's Arts and Crafts designers turned to regional colonial houses, studying their picturesque massing, rambling additions, the pointing of the native Wissahickon schist masonry, and the uncluttered whitewashed interiors. Also, like the colonial revivalists, they developed a uniquely regional expression of the Arts and Crafts Style. George Edgell, writing in 1928, warned that it was a mistake "to try and associate it with any historic style. It is straightforward building, and honest design, with an eye to fine proportions, picturesque composition, and the sum of the full possibilities of the material."[310]

In other parts of the state, Arts and Crafts buildings were more derivative, more frequently drawn from published English examples than from the local vernacular stock. In Pittsburgh Frederick G. Scheibler emerged early in the century as that region's leading Arts and Crafts architect.[311] One of his best known and largest works is Old Heidelberg (PA-431), a stuccoed brick apartment house in Pittsburgh that he designed in 1905. Apparently drawing on the Art Nouveau of central Europe and the Arts and Crafts of England, Scheibler considered Old Heidelberg his "declaration of artistic independence, wherein he renounced the stylistic for a rational approach to design."[312] The plan is quite simple, not unlike that of a row of houses with rear ells, but the exterior, virtually free of ornament, is striking. The large red tile roof sweeps down over the entrance pavilion where round arches and sets of squarish windows cut neatly through the stuccoed walls. Scheibler restricted his practice to mostly residential work, whose limited range in Arts and Crafts houses is illustrated by two Pittsburgh dwellings built in 1923. The Allen M. Klages House (PA-621), with its rubble stone walls, intersecting steep gable roofs, and side entrance is charming but uninspired, while in the coursed-rubble Eva Harter House (PA-622) he imitated thatch with irregularly laid blue and green shingles on the variously shaped roofs to give the house an unusually sensuous feeling.[313]

The Arts and Crafts movement helped to direct America's architecture inexorably, although not always obviously, toward twentieth-century modernism. By dealing with vernacular models, architects shunned the nineteenth-century orientation toward Europe's great works of the past, and developed designs that were less and less historical and more and more concerned with structure and space. Contributing to this break with the revivalist tradition is the Art Deco, or Modernistic, style of the 1920s and 1930s. The term Art Deco is derived from the 1925 Exposition des Arts

Decoratifs et Industriels in Paris, and is applied to the design of a wide range of daily artifacts that came under its influence. Because Art Deco's roots are many and tangled, the style defies simple analysis. Its architectural design sources sprang from the ornamental style of Art Nouveau, American jazz, industrial design and new synthetic materials, personalized expressions of such great stylists as Frank Lloyd Wright, and to a degree the Cubist and Futurist movements in painting. Self-consciously modern, Art Deco architecture is characterized by set-back forms and low-relief decoration, some of which is abstract, such as zig-zags and fluting while others come from such unusual sources as native American ornament. New York led the way in making Art Deco almost synonymous with skyscrapers during the late 1920s and 1930s,[314] but Philadelphia and Pittsburgh were not far behind.

With one exception, Pittsburgh's Art Deco skyscrapers tend to be stocky and more closely tied to historical European styles than Philadelphia's. Graham, Anderson, Probst & White, for example, trimmed the set-backs of the 1929 stone-clad steel-frame Koppers Building with pinnacles, and at the thirty-third story capped the building with a steep gothic-like roof sheathed with copper. (Pun intended?) Across the street the Gulf Building rises higher but appears stodgier. It climbs forty-four stories, but almost grudgingly, partly because its architects, Trowbridge & Livingston of New York, enclosed the blunt steel-frame tower with limestone and crowned it with a simplified version of the pyramidal Mausoleum at Halicarnassus.[315] The University of Pittsburgh's Cathedral of Learning, on the other hand, soars. Rising in breathtaking set-backs five hundred and twenty-five feet above the campus and unchallenged by any tall neighbors, its highly gothicized limestone curtain walls appear even taller than they are. Perhaps it is significant that its architect, Charles Z. Klauder, was a Philadelphian. Working closely with the university's president, John Gabbert Bowman, he designed the steel-frame building in 1926; hampered by the Great Depression, it took eleven years to construct. It contains eighteen ground-floor classrooms in different historical styles, which represent the city's ethnic pluralism, and a salvaged local landmark, the Croghan House's (PA-8-8) Greek Revival ballroom and vestibule.[316] With few exceptions, Ritter and Shay designed Philadelphia's best Art Deco skyscrapers.[317] Their 1930 Market Street National Bank Building (PA-1517), rising in setbacks twenty-four stories, is among their most dramatic in form and unusual in ornament. They wrapped the steel frame in black marble at the ground-story shopfronts, tan terra cotta offset by polychromatic Mayan ornament on

Market Street National Bank Building (PA-1517) Philadelphia. Detail of upper stories (Jack E. Boucher, photographer, 1973) PA,51-PHILA,484-2.

the tall second-story banking floor, and yellow brick on the upper office stories.[318] At the same time the building's wide piers, rising unimpeded to the terra-cotta cresting, are part of a commercial-building design aesthetic reaching back to the Philadelphia Functionalism of the 1850s,[319] and its second-story banking floor anticipates to a small degree the revolutionary changes then taking place only two blocks to the east on Market Street.

The revolution on Market Street was the erection of the Philadelphia Saving Fund Society Building (PA-1533), whose second-story banking floor is one of the few elements that it holds in common with the Market Street National Bank Building. Commonly called the PSFS Building, this thirty-two-story steel-frame structure marks the first application of the European International Style to an American commercial building, making it one of Pennsylvania's (and America's) most significant twentieth-century buildings.[320] At its centennial in 1969, the Philadelphia Chapter of the American Institute of Architects named the PSFS Building the "Building of the Century."[321] In 1929 George Howe, formerly a partner in the Mellor, Meigs and Howe firm, with whom earlier in the decade he had designed PSFS branch banks, teamed up with William Lescaze, a Swiss-trained New York architect, to design an office building for this old, fiscally and socially conservative Philadelphia institution.[322] Whereas the Art Deco style was often a romantic glorification of the technical point of view, the International style was the apotheosis of that point of view. Accordingly, the PSFS Building has no ornament and is very practical and efficient in the organization of its parts. The building seems to float above the glass-fronted ground-floor shops, which were intended to attract to the bank a middle-class clientele moving between the John Wanamaker Store and the City Hall area one to two blocks to the west and the Reading Terminal diagonally across Market Street. The projecting polished-granite second-story banking floor with its broad ribbon of steel-sash windows sweeps around the corner in a gentle curve. Above it, another three stories of limestone curtain walls provide more space for banking functions while serving as a transition to the office slab of successive brick- and limestone-clad floors cantilevered like ribs from the black brick mechanical spine. At the top, an executive suite sits next to the cooling towers of one of the nation's first central air-conditioning systems, which are masked by the twenty-seven-foot-high red-neon PSFS sign, an early and very successful example of super graphics.[323] Howe and Lescaze continued this sleek, functional design in the spacious banking room. By integrating walls of metal, glass and gray marble, curving mezzanine balconies of yellow Siena marble, indirect lighting, and chrome furniture of their own design, they produced, according to the *Architectural Review* in 1934, a "simple and impressive grandeur which is unique in modern architecture."[324] PSFS depositors seem to have liked the building as well, seeing its progressive design as reflection of the bank's good planning. Some local newspapers, however, made their displeasure clear. The *Sunday Dispatch* called it "a hideous thing . . . utterly destitute of the faintest claim to comeliness, an affront to public taste and an eyesore to the shopping community." In case the point was missed, the writer added, "It's barbaric, repellent, epically stupid."[325]

In spite of the *Sunday Dispatch's* opinion, the PSFS Building was the camel's nose beneath the tent of the Beaux-Art traditionalists. Within a year of the PSFS Building's completion, Pennsylvania set another architectural "first" in 1933 when German-born Oskar Stonorov[326] designed America's first International Style apartment building on the edge of Philadelphia's textile mill district. The American Federation of Hosiery Workers sponsored the construction of this complex, the Carl Mackley Houses (PA-1779), with a million-dollar-plus loan from the New Deal-created Public Works Administration—in fact, the first such loan.[327] Construction began on the four parallel, three-story buildings in January 1934; tenants moved in a year later. The buildings were remarkable for their time, not only for their new European design with strip windows and recessed balconies but also for their amenities, which were generous by middle-class standards and all the more remarkable for their availability to mill workers. A swimming pool, roof-top nurseries, underground garages, mechanical laundries, a library, and ample privacy were testaments to Stonorov's position that working people deserved—and one day would enjoy—a better standard of living. Buildings as innovative as these generated predictable bureaucratic and political controversy, especially over Stonorov's choice of materials and construction methods. Workers had difficulty erecting the reinforced-concrete frame and concrete-slab roof; city bureaucrats challenged the steel-frame windows and the number of fire exits; politicians railed about his use of West Virginia-made terra-cotta blocks rather than traditional Philadelphia red bricks.[328] The project's social environment was as progressive as the physical environment. A tenants' council handled grievances, and residents operated a credit union and a cooperative market.[329] "Unfortunately these concerns were lost in the evolution of public housing . . .[and] in the end, this Philadelphia project became less of a model than a yardstick by which to measure the increasing inadequacy of the movement it helped to generate."[330]

    Many multiple housing complexes have risen across Pennsylvania since the completion of the Mackley Houses. The Aluminum City Houses near New Kensington, Westmoreland County, rank among the successful ones. Walter Gropius, founder of the famed Bauhaus in Germany, and Marcel Breuer, one of his gifted instructors, designed these two-story rows in 1942 in a spacious hilly suburban setting. Flat roofs and continuous spans of glass at the second story reveal the architects' Bauhaus principles, which they softened by using vertical cedar siding on the houses' southern fronts. Perceiving the untreated wood as a cheap material, and perhaps monotonous as well, residents, aluminum industry employees, within a decade further softened the Bauhaus effects by painting the wooden fronts.[331] Among the notable failures is Oskar Stonorov's 1954 Schuylkill Falls public housing project in Philadelphia. Its design is impressive but its social flaw is the reinforced concrete apartment buildings whose fifteen stories of continuous concrete balconies form a striking hillside backdrop for the elementary school, community center, and two- and three-story rows of housing. Living in skyscrapers requires sophisticated and highly socialized behavior on the part of the residents; unfortunately the antisocial behavior of some residents threatened the welfare of others so severely that in 1978 city officials emptied the high-rise units.[332] Between the successes and failures lie many mediocre but generally adequate housing complexes. Called projects when they are publicly funded and apartment buildings when privately financed, multiple housing complexes are commonplace in the state's cities and suburbs. Beginning in the 1970s, financiers and developers introduced a variation on this theme—the condominium, a collection of attached owner-occupied housing units arranged on landscaped common grounds with abundant parking. They are essentially stylish row houses, whose recreational facilities, common grounds, and mutual investment fortunes help to form a sense of commonality, if not community, that would otherwise be difficult to generate among relatively transient suburban residents.

Although Bauhaus-influenced multiple housing complexes served the needs of Pennsylvania's masses after 1935, there were also a relatively small number of unique dwellings designed by famous architects for affluent and unconventional citizens. No house was more significant than Fallingwater (PA-5346), Edgar J. Kaufmann's weekend retreat in Stewart Township, Fayette County. The architect was Frank Lloyd Wright, who was in his late sixties and about to enter the highly productive second half of his career in 1935, when he designed this celebrated house. Oft-printed photographs highlight Fallingwater's most striking feature—the boldly cantilevered reinforced concrete terraces which seem to defy gravity by floating above the waterfalls of Bear Run. The house's design is a complex structural and visual interplay of building materials and methods: the traditional solidity and texture of stone quarried on site, the molded horizontal forms and tensile strength of modern reinforced concrete (Wright's first use of this material), and the thin membrane of glass enclosing the shelter while opening the walls to the outside. Organic in the sense that the dwelling grows out of and fits into its site and visually balances the indoor habitation and outdoor scenery, Fallingwater is also a romantic symbol in a more subtle and exciting manner than the historical literalness of American architecture a century earlier.[333] By merging the country house with its surrounding forest and encompassing stream, Wright created an adventurous and expansive environ-

Fallingwater (PA-5346) Ohiopyle (Stewart Township), Fayette County. Interior showing fireplace (Jack E. Boucher, photographer, 1985) PA,26-OHPY.V,1.

ment. An example of this sense of freedom—and its balance of elements—is the glass-enclosed living room hatch that leads to the hanging stairs suspended over the moving stream. The glass hatch opens the east end of the living room to the sky above and the water below, offsetting the fireplace's mass at the opposite end of the room and suggesting "the freedom in space which a ship signifies to the romantic imagination."[334] At the same time Wright established rootedness and security by planting the hearth, the traditional center of the home, atop a pillar of bedrock that protrudes ten inches above the living room's stone slab floor and projects nearly seven feet into the room.[335] After Kaufmann's death in 1955, his son, Edgar Kaufmann Jr., continued to use Fallingwater until 1963, when he concluded that the "house and site together form the very image of man's desire to be at one with nature, equal and wedded to nature. . . . Such a place cannot be possessed. . . . By its very intensity it is a public resource, not a private indulgence."[336] Consequently that autumn he gave the house to the public under the care of the Western Pennsylvania Conservancy. Fallingwater marked a new beginning for Wright, and he went on to design such landmark buildings as the S. C. Johnson (Wax) Administration Building in Racine, Wisconsin, in 1936, and the Guggenheim Museum in New York, which went through many changes from its 1943 inception to its 1959 completion. He also designed more buildings in Pennsylvania, including the Suntop Homes in Ardmore, Montgomery County, in 1939, the I. N. Hagen House (PA-5347) near Chalkhill, Fayette County in 1954, and the 1959 Beth Sholom Synagogue in Elkins Park, Montgomery County.[337]

After World War II young architects increasingly perceived Wright as a romantic anomaly. The International style was the new fashion for the postwar generation. Few of these architects, however, found patrons like William Stix Wasserman, who in 1932 commissioned George Howe to design his grand Whitemarsh, Montgomery County, house in the new style. Called Square Shadows, it is an interesting marriage of locally traditional fieldstone masonry and Bauhaus design principles.[338] Occasional self-consciously modern dwellings with flat roofs, stucco walls, and steel-frame windows cut into their corners appeared in Pennsylvania's towns in the postwar years, but most homeowners preferred traditional house forms, especially those that vaguely resembled colonial dwellings. Corporations, on the other hand, seeking progressive corporate images, and governments, needing cost-effective buildings, eagerly adopted the new style. Consequently Pennsylvania's best examples of the International style stand in affluent urban and suburban areas, primarily in and about Philadelphia and Pittsburgh. Wyeth Laboratories in Radnor, Delaware County, is typical of the sleek industrial buildings of the 1950s and 60s. Built in 1957 from the designs of Skidmore, Owings and Merrill, one of America's leading promoters and practitioners of the new style, the building is essentially a steel-frame rectangular box wrapped in three ribbons of stainless steel-frame windows. Four years earlier Robert W. Noble of Martin, Stewart & Noble had reduced this concept to its essentials in his design for the center city Mercantile Library of the Free Library of Philadelphia. Noble laid a flat roof over the two-story space and left the view through the building open to the rear garden by stretching tall panels of glass across the ends. As George Tatum noted shortly after its completion, "rarely has so much well-ordered space been defined by so little material."[339]

Few commercial clients, however, could afford to indulge in Noble's minimalist designs. Urban real estate values and corporate office needs fueled the ongoing demand for skyscrapers. Many suffered from unimaginative design, a particular hazard of the International style, but occasionally a building, such as Pittsburgh's Alcoa Building, stands out from the crowd. Harrison and Abramowitz of New York designed this thirty-story office building in 1949 as a standard reinforced-concrete tower, but sheathed it with prefabricated greenish-gray aluminum panels with built-in reversible windows. The faceted indentations beneath each window give the building an unconventional color and texture and transform it into an architectural billboard for the company's product.[340] Increasingly during the 1960s and 70s, architects had to be concerned with not only a skyscraper's distinctive design but also its urban context. Mitchell/Giurgola of Philadelphia faced a particularly challenging task in 1969, when Penn Mutual Life Insurance Company asked the firm to design an addition to the company's vaguely classical 1931 building, which itself was an addition to a smaller 1913 building, and to erect the addition on the site of a historic Egyptian Revival building (PA-1454) designed by John Haviland circa 1839. Compounding the problem was the addition's location on the south side of Independence Square, directly south of Independence Hall (PA-1430) and on the north-south sight line of the Hall and the site of the proposed Liberty Bell pavilion. The historic Haviland building had to be removed, but the architects reassembled the marble facade as an entrance court screen. Counterbalancing the marble screen is the concrete roof structure atop the twenty-one-story dark glass northern wall that serves as a neutral backdrop for Independence Hall.[341]

    Louis I. Kahn emerged during the 1950s as Pennsylvania's preeminent architect. By 1960 he enjoyed an international reputation and was offering an alternative to the steel and glass boxes of the postwar era. His emphasis on space-defining form, in particular walls and piers, led to forceful and imaginative expressions of buildings' functions and structural systems. The Richards Medical Research Building and Goddard Laboratories at Philadelphia's University of Pennsylvania established Kahn's reputation even before the research buildings' completion in 1961. Six blank brick towers that serve as staircases and air intake and exhaust tubes rise above the building's flat roof line to form dominating and picturesque elements, but contrary to appearance, they do not form the building's structure. The structural system is an expressed precast concrete skeleton with Vierendeel trusses that allow the glass corners to stand without support. After waiting until late middle age to break into the profession's highest ranks, Kahn was suddenly engulfed with commissions and remained so until his death in 1974.[342]

Meanwhile in the 1960s one of Kahn's protégés, Robert Venturi of Philadelphia, led the architectural profession further away from the International style and toward a new movement, postmodernism.[343] Venturi's designs for two Philadelphia buildings, the Guild House (1961-63) and his mother's house (1962-64), were radical departures from the rectangular lines, sleek historical forms, and fluid nonstructural space of the International style. Both buildings clearly reflect historical antecedents. The Guild House, a six-story apartment building for the elderly, fits into its working class neighborhood while serving the social and psychological needs of its residents. Its red brick walls and sash windows are like those of row houses; the building's name in large letters over the entrance is drawn from neighborhood commercial signs; the large granite column at the entrance recalls grand apartment house entries; the facade setbacks afford street-watching residents a number of views from their apartment windows.[344] The front of the Vanna Venturi House, on the other hand, looks much like a child's drawing of a house, a mannered classical dwelling. It has a symmetrical plan and a front elevation that includes a split gable roof and distorted classical ornament (a shoulder-high dado and an interrupted arch over the large squarish entry recess). While Venturi was clattering onto the architectural stage with these buildings that acknowledged history and symbolism, he was writing the thin but iconoclastic volume, *Complexity and Contradiction in Architecture*, which the Museum of Modern Art published in 1966.[345] In it Venturi "called for an architecture that promotes richness and ambiguity over unity and clarity, contradiction and redundancy over harmony and simplicity."[346] In 1966, at the height of the International style, his views were considered radical, but after a quarter-century of designing, writing, and teaching, Robert Venturi stands at the end of the twentieth century as one of America's most influential architects.[347]

Postmodernism with its symbolism and ornament soon spread to skyscrapers. When Philip Johnson in 1977 placed a Chippendale pediment atop the AT&T Building in New York, he seems to have set the direction of skyscraper design for the rest of the twentieth century.[348] Five years later in Pittsburgh, Johnson and John Burgee designed for Pittsburgh Plate Glass Corporation a reflective glass-sheathed steel-frame cathedral of commerce that bristles with glass pinnacles and features a massive forty-story tower. They arranged the complex's five buildings and tower around a mirrored courtyard, not unlike a cloister, in which the pleating of the curtain wall's reflective glass into sequences of facets creates a sense of medieval tracery, whose pattern changes from hour to hour, season to season. Much like the earlier Alcoa Buildings, PPG Place shamelessly but intriguingly advertises the company's primary product. At about the same time, Helmut Jahn's One Liberty Place (1985-87), a squat descendant of New York's Chrysler Building, boldly broke through Philadelphia's traditional height limit to transform the city's skyline and become its largest and most dramatic postmodern skyscraper.[349]

Because so much of postmodernism's symbolism is based on classicism, it has encouraged a climate that has fostered a return of classicism. After World War II, critics and architects considered classicism dead, but in the 1980s it was found alive and well in Harrisburg. The Capitol's East Wing, designed in 1982-83 by Thomas Celli of Pittsburgh, is probably the most extensive and expensive exercise in classicism in Pennsylvania in the second half of the twentieth century. The one-story granite and glass office building, a complex of balustrades, columns, and pediments, lies snugly against the Capitol while a semi-circular plaza with a central fountain spreads out before it. The East Wing's strength lies in its deference to the enriched Renaissance Revival Capitol and the flanking classical buildings of the 1920s and 30s. In wisely emphasizing the East Wing's deferential architectural form and low terraces, Celli promoted accessibility at the expense of monumentality. "If not a temple of democracy," it is, architecture critic Paul Goldberger suggests, "at least a mall of democracy,"[350] and in that sense relates to its clients in the democratic idiom of its day.

Despite Pennsylvania's brave gesture in behalf of traditional, low-scaled classicism, Philadelphia's Liberty Place and Pittsburgh's PPG Place express the era's dominant pattern. These office buildings make obvious a trend that has been under way since the beginning of the twentieth century—the physical, but symbolic, dominance of cities' skylines by financial and industrial interests. Until the Civil War, church steeples formed cities' spiky silhouettes, then for half a century picturesque towers of city halls and courthouses (most notably Philadelphia City Hall and the Allegheny County Courthouse) loomed above citizens' houses, stores, and workshops. At the beginning of the twentieth century, however, the skyscraper signified a growing commercial and financial dominance of the built, cultural, and economic environments. For decades Philadelphians stubbornly clung to an unofficial height limit in an effort to retain City Hall's visual dominance, but determined developers in the roaring 80s forged past that artificial barrier to dominate the skyline. Today skyscrapers often serve as images of many cities, although these buildings say less about a city's history and character than about the architectural preferences of a corporate client.

As Pennsylvania begins its fourth century, coarse developmental patterns are discernible. In the seventeenth and eighteenth centuries immigrants from Britain and Europe formed a pluralistic society that pushed inexorably westward. They initially duplicated Old World dwellings, but intermingling of subsequent generations and continuous new immigration soon produced a distinctive and complex built environment. Although approximately ninety percent of eighteenth-century Pennsylvanians tilled the land, small commercial centers developed east of the Allegheny Front. With the nineteenth-century expansion of manufacturing and commerce, older cities expanded dramatically and new boom cities rose. Some exploited their geography (Erie on the lake and Pittsburgh at the Forks of the Ohio, for example), while others grew up around an industry, such as Johnstown with its iron and steel, Scranton with its iron and coal, and Williamsport with its lumber. Agriculture remained important and became increasingly specialized. Farmers established new farmsteads and replaced worn and inadequate structures on older farms throughout the Commonwealth. European immigration supplied the burgeoning industrial work force and further diversified Pennsylvania's population. After World War I, federal legislation reduced that flood to a trickle, but the state's population continued to change as African Americans, Asian Americans and Hispanic Americans moved into urban areas. Automobile suburbs developed as Pennsylvania's dominant twentieth-century living pattern. Instead of new farmsteads being built, old farmsteads were subdivided into tract housing. Cities that had not filled their borders by World War II, completed the task in the postwar period with suburban development on their fringes rather than expansion of their downtowns. Many cities rebuilt parts of their downtowns, usually through urban renewal projects, in part to compete with the rapidly spreading suburbs. Most new construction followed highways: auto strips, shopping malls, so-called industrial and corporate parks (as if work were fun), and wave upon wave of detached single-family dwellings with garages and small grassy plots (the American Dream).

Urban renewal and suburban sprawl came at a serious cost to historic architecture. Many citizens in the last half of the twentieth century, aware of the radical transformation of Pennsylvania's landscape and the irretrievable loss of its built environment, acted to preserve what they could. Historic preservation has not dominated building activity since World War II, but it is an increasingly important concern that affects tax policies, the construction industry, and professional training; restoration architects, for example, are more numerous (and employed) than ever before in history. The preservation effort has ranged from individuals' restoring their dwellings and local groups' saving an endangered landmark to extensive government programs, such as America's Industrial Heritage Project, a cooperative state and federal survey of the industrial age's material remains. Preservation in recent decades has moved beyond historic house museums to include sophisticated legal devices, such as conservation easements, air rights, and rural land trusts.

In Pennsylvania the Pennsylvania Historical and Museum Commission's Bureau for Historic Preservation is charged with administering the state's many preservation activities. Its responsibilities include approving nominations to the National Register of Historic Places and reviewing all proposed historic building rehabilitation projects for purposes of the investment tax credit. The latter program proved especially propitious for Pennsylvanians (investors, workers, tenants, architects, and preservationists). During the program's heyday, 1982-85, Pennsylvania led the nation in the number of privately financed rehabilitation projects, money expended on these rehabilitations (over a billion dollars), number of housing units rehabilitated (6,225), and number of person-years of work created (45,025).[351] This federal program proved that preservation could be both economically lucrative and socially beneficial, as developers adapted outmoded buildings to new uses and towns and cities retained their familiar building fabric. Another federal program is the Historic American Buildings Survey (HABS), which has been playing a critical preservation role since 1933. HABS preserves through documentation. Every historic building cannot be preserved; in fact, nearly one-third of the 1,600-plus Pennsylvania sites listed in this catalog are now gone, but their images and history remain in the publicly accessible HABS files at the Library of Congress. Although the outlook for Pennsylvania's architecture at present is generally favorable, in the future some historic buildings will inevitably fall to fire, development, or neglect. When that happens, we will be grateful that HABS established a record of our built environment for future generations.

Notes

[1] Quoted in Richard S. Dunn and Mary Maples Dunn, gen. eds. *The Papers of William Penn*, 5 vols. (Philadelphia: University of Pennsylvania Press, 1981-1987), 2:225.

[2] Southeastern Pennsylvania is seen as the fountainhead for a vernacular architecture that spread southward into the Shenandoah Valley and westward as far as the Mississippi Valley. Fred Kniffen, "Folk Housing: Key to Diffusion," *Annals of the Association of American Geographers* 55 (December 1965): 555, 560-61; Henry Glassie, *Pattern in the Material Folk Culture of the Eastern United States* (Philadelphia: University of Pennsylvania Press, 1968), 36; Peirce F. Lewis, "Common House, Cultural Spoor," *Landscape* 19 (January 1975): 12.

[3] The firstcomers to Germantown evidently were Dutch Mennonites, many of whom seem to have adopted the Quaker faith; Germans soon followed them. Francis Daniel Pastorious, generally considered the founder of Germantown, wanted a "little province" for his followers, and in 1689 William Penn complied, granting the community a charter, making the settlement a borough, the first in Pennsylvania. The charter was royally approved in 1691, but after political difficulties it was nullified in 1707. Thereafter the area was a township (German Township) in Philadelphia County until it became a borough again in the middle of the nineteenth century, shortly before being incorporated into the City of Philadelphia in 1854. Stephanie Grauman Wolf, *Urban Village: Population, Community, and Family Structure in Germantown, Pennsylvania, 1683-1800* (Princeton: Princeton University Press, 1976), 12-13; Harry M. Tinkcom, Margaret B. Tinkcom, and Grant Miles Simon, *Historic Germantown: From the Founding to the Early Part of the Nineteenth Century* (Philadelphia: American Philosophical Society, 1955), 4-7; John A. Hostetler, *Amish Society* (Baltimore: Johns Hopkins Press, 1963), 23-28, 38-39, 44; Lee C. Hopple, "Germanic European Origins and Geographical History of the Southeastern Pennsylvania Schwenkfelders," *Pennsylvania Folklife* 32 (Winter 1982-83): 72-95; E. G. Alderfer, *The Ephrata Commune: An Early American Counterculture* (Pittsburgh: University of Pittsburgh Press, 1985), 8-13, 61-76; Arthur D. Graeff, "Pennsylvania, the Colonial Melting Pot," in *The Pennsylvania Germans*, ed. Ralph Wood (Princeton: Princeton University Press, 1942), 5-7; Wayland F. Dunaway, *The Scotch-Irish of Colonial Pennsylvania* (Chapel Hill: University of North Carolina Press, 1944), 28-33.

[4]Because English was the court language, Germans were greatly impeded from actively engaging in governmental affairs. The fact that a Pennsylvania German was not elected to the General Assembly until 1764 indicates the effect language had in inhibiting the Germans' direct exercise of power. Graeff, "Pennsylvania, the Colonial Melting Pot," 12; Sylvester K. Stevens, *Pennsylvania: Birthplace of a Nation* (New York: Random House, 1964), 62-64; John E. Illick, *Colonial Pennsylvania: A History* (New York: Charles Scribner's Sons, 1976), 186-87, 190.

[5]This is not to imply, however, that Germans mingled well with another English-speaking group, the Scotch-Irish. "There was inevitably a measure of necessary contact between the two peoples, but it soon became apparent that this would be held to a minimum." James G. Leyburn, *The Scotch-Irish: A Social History* (Chapel Hill: University of North Carolina Press, 1962), 190.

[6]Henry Glassie, "Eighteenth-Century Cultural Process in Delaware Valley Folk Building," *Winterthur Portfolio* 7 (1972): 29-49; Lewis, "Common Houses, Cultural Spoor," 1-22.

[7]Harold Shurtleff, *The Log Cabin Myth: A Study of the Early Dwellings of the English Colonists in North America* (Cambridge: Harvard University Press, 1939; reprint ed., Gloucester, Mass.: Peter Smith, 1967), 163-75.

[8]Terry G. Jordan, *American Log Buildings: An Old World Heritage* (Chapel Hill: University of North Carolina Press, 1985), 150-51. This is the latest and most definitive work in a long list of studies of log houses in America. Based on field studies in the United States and four overseas regions (Sweden-Norway-Finland, the Alps and southwestern Germany, the German-Slavic border area, and Great Britain-Ireland), Jordan's work argues in favor of Swedish influence in determining eighteenth and nineteenth-century American log construction. Advocates of German influence have made distinctions between the Alpine-Alemannic region and the Moravia, Bohemia, Silesia region, proposing the latter as the primary source for midland American log construction. Because of the nature of the disagreements, Jordan's thesis, well-documented and well-argued as it may be, probably will not be the last word on the subject.

[9]The Morton Homestead is composed of three units. The northern log unit was possibly built as early as 1698 as an English hall-plan house with Scandinavian-derived square-notch joinery on its northern end and double-notch joinery on its southern end. The southern log unit was built in the mid-eighteenth century as a detached parallel log ferry house with double notching on the northern end and full dovetail square-notch joinery on its southern end. Both buildings have large kitchen fireplaces and corner stairs, on the southern end of the northern unit and the northern end of the southern unit. A rubble masonry center unit, approximately twelve feet front by nineteen feet deep, was built to fill the space between the units sometime between the date of the southern unit's completion and 1798, when it appears on the glass tax list. Significantly, the northern unit was built of white cedar, a wood preferred by Scandinavians, while the later southern unit was built of white oak, which the English preferred. The house was saved and "restored," because local civic groups thought it was the

birthplace of John Morton, signer of the Declaration of Independence. There is no evidence, however, that Morton was born here, and the 1938 "restoration," criticized at the time by restoration architects and architectural historians, destroyed much of the original building fabric, including the foundations. *The Morton Homestead: A Historic Structure Report*, 2 vols. (West Chester, Pa.: Frens and Frens for Pennsylvania Historical and Museum Commission, 1989), 1:4. 13-38, 48-51, 119-84. For a description of the characteristic Swedish house with square-notched corners, see Jordan, *American Log Buildings*, 50, 54-55, 148.

[10] Henry Glassie, "The Types of the Southern Mountain Cabin," in Jan Harold Brunvand, *The Study of American Folklore: An Introduction* (New York: W.W. Norton and Company, 1968), 338-70; Fred Kniffen and Henry Glassie, "Building in Wood in the Eastern United States: A Time-Place Perspective," *Geographic Review* 56 (January 1966): 58-59.

[11] Jordan illustrates that thirteen of twenty carpentry features of American midland houses are common or occasional in Sweden, and seven of them apparently originated in Sweden. Jordan, *American Log Buildings*, 147. In at least one case, Jordan's field studies abroad have dismissed one of Kniffen's and Glassie's proposals. On the basis of local tradition, Kniffen and Glassie attributed V-notching to German Schwenkfelders. Jordan and associates, however, have found virtually every form of Pennsylvania V-notching in Scandinavia in at least a proximate form, but have located no evidence of V-notching in German-speaking Europe. Kniffen and Glassie, "Building in Wood," 59 n. 45; Terry G. Jordan, "Moravian, Schwenkfelder, and American Log Construction," *Pennsylvania Folklife* 33 (Spring 1984): 110; Terry G. Jordan, Matti Kaups, and Richard M. Lieffort, "New Evidence on the European Origin of Pennsylvania V Notching," *Pennsylvania Folklife* 36 (Autumn 1986): 20-30.

[12] Corner-posting is described, illustrated, and evaluated in Kniffen and Glassie, "Building in Wood," pp. 48-52; Terry G. Jordan, "Alpine, Alemannic, and American Log Architecture," *Annals of the Association of American Geographers* 70 (June 1980): 162-63; idem, *American Log Buildings*, 92, 94, 95. Although rare in the colonial period, corner-posting was apparently more common in the nineteenth century. Nancy S. Shedd, for example, has located many mid-nineteenth-century corner-post log houses in Huntingdon County; they probably were built by new German immigrants during a second wave of German immigration that began about 1848. Interview with Nancy S. Shedd, Huntingdon County Historical Society, Huntingdon, Pa., 12 July 1989.

[13] Of Terry Jordan's twenty carpentry features of midland American log construction, fifteen did not exist in the British Isles. Jordan, *American Log Buildings*, 148. For early-twentieth-century English acknowledgment that log construction evidently was never practiced in England, see Kniffen and Glassie, "Building in Wood," 58 n. 40.

[14] The Chester Countian was Ziba Darlington, who was seventy-nine when he shared this story with John Hill Brinton in 1867. As a reminiscence his figures cannot be assumed to be accurate, but the impression is valid. John H. Brinton's Manuscript Book No. 1, 230, Chester County Historical Society, West Chester, Pa.

[15] Of those five buildings in York that were not log, three were brick and two were stone. The study area of early Huntingdon included seven blocks. Joe Kindig III, *Architecture in York County* (York, Pa.: Historical Society of York County, 1963), 5; Nancy S. Shedd, *An Architectural Study of the Ancient Borough of Huntingdon* (Huntingdon, Pa.: John S. Rodgers Company, 1976), 15.

[16] The basis of the argument is that the three-room plan was familiar in Sweden but it was thought that it was not common in England. Thomas Tileston Waterman, *The Dwellings of Colonial America* (Chapel Hill: University of North Carolina Press, 1950), 125. The ongoing disagreement over the origins of the three-room plan is well summarized in Allen G. Noble, *Wood, Brick, and Stone: The North American Settlement Landscape*, 2 vols. (Amherst: University of Massachusetts Press, 1984), 1:45. As Noble says, the differences "will only be resolved by additional careful research on other Quaker-plan houses."

[17] Cary Carson, Norman F. Barka, William M. Kelso, Garry Wheeler Stone, Dell Upton, "Impermanent Architecture in the Southern American Colonies," *Winterthur Portfolio* 16 (Summer/Autumn 1981): 135-96, especially 138-53. A major piece of scholarship based on a synthesis of archaeological and historical evidence, this article is the authoritative source for early wooden structures in colonial Maryland and Virginia. Because of the great influx of English settlers to later seventeenth-century Pennsylvania, the monograph is an important source for understanding Pennsylvania's early impermanent architecture as well.

[18] "Information and Direction to Such Persons as Are Inclined to America, More Especially Those Related to the Province of Pennsylvania" (n.p., n.d.), 2; reprinted in *Pennsylvania Magazine of History and Biography* 4 (1880): 331-42. This circa 1684 promotional piece was attributed to William Penn in the eighteenth and nineteenth centuries, but scholars today are skeptical of this authorship. For an isometric reconstruction drawing of the house described in the pamphlet, see Carson et al., "Impermanent Architecture," 143.

[19] There is abundant documentation that some seventeenth-century Philadelphians lived in "caves" along the river banks until these dugouts were destroyed in 1701, perhaps because some had become known as places of "clandestine looseness." There is a strong oral history that early settlers in other parts of the Province followed a similar practice. Caleb Pusey, for example, is said to have lived in a "dug-out" for a winter before building his house in Upland, Delaware County, about 1683, as did yearling Chester Countians William and Ann Brinton and their son in 1684 and Joseph and Hannah Gilpin in 1695. John F. Watson, *Annals of Philadelphia and Pennsylvania in the Olden Times*, 2 vols. (Philadelphia: Whiting and Thomas, 1856), 1:171-72; J. Thomas Scharf and Thompson Westcott, *History of Philadelphia, 1609-1884*, 3 vols. (Philadelphia: L.H. Everts & Co., 1884), 1:101; Hannah Benner Roach, "The Planting of Philadelphia: A Seventeenth-Century Real Estate Development," *Pennsylvania Magazine of History and Biography* 92 (January 1968): 42; Mary Maples Dunn and Richard S. Dunn, "The Founding, 1681-1701," in Russell F. Weigley, ed., *Philadelphia: A 300-Year History* (New York: W.W. Norton and Company for Barra Foundation, 1982), 11; Peggy Robbins, "William Penn's Colony of Cave People," *Pennsylvania Heritage* 13 (Summer

1987): 4-11; J. Smith Futhey and Gilbert Cope, *History of Chester County, Pennsylvania, with Genealogical and Biographical Sketches* (Philadelphia: Louis H. Everts, 1881), 570; Josephine F. Albrecht, "A Visit to the Pusey House," Chester, Pa., n.d. (typewritten); George E. Stetson, "1704 House, Built in Chester County, Pennsylvania, by William Brinton the Younger" (M.A. thesis, University of Delaware, 1961), 24.

[20]The most complete essay on timber framing, based on both field work in Virginia and library research, is Dell Upton, "Traditional Timber Framing," in Brooke Hindle, ed., *Material Culture of the Wooden Age* (Tarrytown, N.Y.: Sleepy Hollow Press, 1981), 35-93. For his references to the various changes in American framing, including the use of smaller girts and studs, see 40-43. Upton focuses on timber framing in New England and the Chesapeake. His omission of Delaware Valley samples is another example of the unfortunate lack of recent field work and a solid body of written material on Pennsylvania architecture.

[21]Ibid., 51-60. A study needs to be done to determine if the various southern short-cuts that Professor Upton describes were adopted by builders of Pennsylvania timber frame houses.

[22]*Gideon Gilpin House and Outbuildings: A Historic Structures Report*, 2 vols. (West Chester, Pa.: Frens and Frens for Pennsylvania Historical and Museum Commission, 1988), 1:16-17, 46; Futhey and Cope, *History of Chester County*, 570.

[23]Ziba Darlington in 1845 remembered the small timber-frame house that the Brinton family occupied for nearly twenty before erecting the 1704 stone house (PA-1258) in Dilworthtown, Delaware County, as "a cabin with yellow poplar planks." John H. Brinton's Manuscript Book No. 1, 2.

[24]William J. Murtagh, "Half-Timbering in American Architecture," *Pennsylvania Folklife* 9 (Winter 1957-58): 3-5.

[25]Like so many early Lancaster houses, the Howard Avenue House is only a story and a half with a steep gable roof. Initially the house's half-timbering had exposed brick nogging, but during the first half of the nineteenth century a later owner replaced the half-timbering on the ground story of the front and sides with brick masonry, leaving the half-timber only in the gable peaks and at the house's rear, where a brick addition was attached. Such alterations of timber-frame houses apparently were not uncommon. Ibid., 4; A. Lawrence Kocher, "The Early Architecture of Pennsylvania, Part II," *The Architectural Record* 49 (January 1921): 33-35.

[26]In addition to its medieval structural features, the Mears-Heaton House's back building had relatively small windows and a door that slid on wooden tracks, because the width of the building was too small to allow the swing of a reasonably wide door. HABS discovered and recorded the building in 1954 when a local contractor began demolishing it for his parking lot. Murtagh, "Half-Timbering in American Architecture," 8-9.

[27]Celle, Germany, near Hannover, for example, has over 450 fifteenth-through seventeenth-century half-timber buildings. See Ulrich V. Witten, *Celle: Portrat einer Stadt und eines Kreises* (Berlin: Otto Meissners Verlag, 1986). Alfred Gatzke, an architect in that city, has

both restored old half-timber buildings and designed many new houses and shops with half-timber fronts.

[28]Upton, "Traditional Timber Framing," 75; Nancy J. McFall, "Preserving York's Architectural Heritage," Pennsylvania Folklife 16 (Spring 1967): 21; Kindig, Architecture in York County, 6-7.

[29]The Golden Plough Tavern is a good example of the *Frankische* style of *Fachwerk* in which diagonal timbers next to the windows and crossed members beneath the windows form a relatively intricate design against the brick nogging. Unlike the diagonal braces of English timber framing, these diagonal braces do not run from a vertical element to a horizontal element (such as from corner post to sill) but are steeply angled and run from one horizontal member to another. Another type of *Fachwerk*, the *Niedersachische* type, resembles a grid pattern. The oft-illustrated so-called Sawbuck house, which stood in Landis Valley north of Lancaster before it fell down about 1890, was a good example of this type. Its vertical timbers were placed relatively close together and its windows filled the width of the area between the two uprights. Murtagh, "Half-Timbering in American Architecture," 5, 9; G. Edwin Brumbaugh, "Colonial Architecture of the Pennsylvania Germans" Proceedings of the Pennsylvania German Society 41 (1933): 26-28, pl. 13. For classification of English timber framing, see J. T. Smith, "Timber-Framed Building in England: Its Development and Regional Differences," *Archaeological Journal* 122 (1965): 133-58.

[30]Upton, "Traditional Timber Framing," 38, 77-78, 82-84.

[31]This line apparently was meant to be slightly elliptical rather than straight. Otherwise Chester County's colonial brick houses stand as exceptions to Wertenbaker's pattern. Thomas Jefferson Wertenbaker, *The Founding of American Civilization: The Middle Colonies* (New York: Charles Scribner's Sons, 1938), 236.

[32]Although Romans built with brick in England, the first English bricks were not made until the thirteenth century. The use of brick there was limited until the beginning of the sixteenth century, after which it grew steadily. The art of forming wall patterns with colored bricks originated in mid-fifteenth-century northern France, and probably was carried across the channel to England by Flemish immigrants, who seem to have encouraged English brick building in general. The lozenge, or diamond, was the most popular pattern in Tudor times, and was used on both large buildings and farmhouses, but outside of the East Midlands its use declined after the reign of Henry VIII. Alan Gowans, however, suggests that some of these medieval carryovers, especially the exuberant zigzags on houses in southern New Jersey, are English, traceable to Anglo-Saxon times. Roger Trindell, however, wonders if it may not have been at least in part a French Huguenot contribution. R. J. Brown, *The English Country Cottage* (London: Robert Hale, 1979), 194, 201; M.W. Barley, *The English Farmhouse and Cottage* (London: Routledge and Kegan Paul, 1961), 188-91; Ian A. Melville and Ian A. Gordon, *The Repair and Maintenance of Houses* (London: Estates Gazette Limited, 1973), 154-55; Alan Gowans, *Images of American Living: Four Centuries of Architecture and Furniture as Cultural Expression* (Philadelphia: J.B. Lippincott Company, 1964), 84; Roger T. Trindell, "Building in Brick in Early America," *Geographical Review* 58 (July 1968): 486.

[33] Margaret Berwind Schiffer, *Survey of Chester County, Pennsylvania, Architecture: 17th, 18th and 19th Centuries* (Exton, Pa.: Schiffer Publishing Ltd, 1976), 24, 61; Kindig, *Architecture in York County*, 19; Richard J. Webster, *Philadelphia Preserved: Catalog of the Historic American Buildings Survey* (Philadelphia: Temple University Press, 1976), 154.

[34] Nathaniel Lloyd, *A History of the English House* (London: Architectural Press, 1975), 54; R. J. Brown, *The English Country Cottage*, 21, 28-32.

[35] Schiffer, *Survey of Chester County, Pennsylvania, Architecture*, 14.

[36] Albrecht, "A Visit to the Pusey House," 1.

[37] There is no evidence of an original staircase to a second story in Pusey's 1683 house. If there was a second floor under the steep roof, it was a loft reached by a ladder. Jack Michel, "'In a Manner and Fashion Suitable to Their Degree': A Preliminary Investigation of the Material Culture of Early Rural Pennsylvania," in Glenn Porter and William H. Mulligan, Jr., eds. *Working Papers from the Regional Economic History Research Center* 5 (1981): 33.

[38] Ibid., 31; Brown, *The English Country Cottage*, 21. Also contributing to the interpretation of the house was an archaeological excavation under the direction of Allen G. Schiek described in Josephine F. Albrecht, "Caleb Pusey House: History Hidden in the Earth," *Bulletin of the Archaeological Society of Delaware*, n.s., no. 9 (Spring 1972): 1-25. The house's plan and probably its setting were much like the widow's two-room cottage in Chaucer's Nun's Priest's Tale. The widow's cottage stood in a "yard enclosed all about with sticks, and a dry ditch." The hall was "full sooty," probably because here cottage had only a smoke hole rather than a chimney. John S. P. Tatlock and Percy MacKaye, *The Complete Poetical Works of Geoffrey Chaucer: Now First put into Modern English* (New York: Macmillan Company, 1912), 130-131.

[39] Clarissa Smith and John D. Milner, "The Thomas Massey House," *Pennsylvania Folklife* 18 (Autumn 1968): 26-35; Michel, "In a Manner and Fashion Suitable to Their Degree," 31.

[40] Michel, "'In a Manner and Fashion Suitable to Their Degree'," 33; John Fanning Watson, *Annals of Philadelphia and Pennsylvania in the Olden Times: Being a Collection of Memoirs, Anecdotes, and Incidents of the City and Its Inhabitant, enlarged and revised by Willis P. Hazard*, 3 vols. (Philadelphia: Edwin S. Stuart, 1884) 1:343; William John Murtagh, "The Philadelphia Row House," *Journal of the Society of Architectural Historians* 16 (December 1957): 8. Murtagh's article is the definitive work on Philadelphia colonial row house types; it has established the nomenclature for plan types that most architectural historians use.

[41] Murtagh, "The Philadelphia Row House," 9; A.F. Kelsall, "The London House Plan in the Later 17th Century," *Journal of Post-Medieval Archaeology* 8 (1974): 80-91; John Summerson, *Georgian London* (London: Pleiades Books, 1945; rev. ed., London: Penguin Books, 1962), 51, 66-67; Steen E. Rasmussen, *London: The Unique City* (rev. ed., London: Jonathan Cape, 1948), 224-34; Margaret B. Tinkcom, "Urban Reflections in a Trans-Atlantic Mirror," *Pennsylvania Magazine of History and Biography* 100 (July 1976): 308.

[42] Hogarth is a good contemporary source of post-fire London facades. See in particular *Morning* and *Night* in Joseph Burke and Colin Campbell, *Hogarth: The Complete Engravings* (London: Thames and Hudson, 1968), pls. 177, 180. A detail of *Morning* is illustrated in Gowans, *Images of American Living*, 83. For a discussion of the debate surrounding the origins of the pent roof, see note 14 of the Philadelphia essay.

[43] A section of the Irish House appears in Margaret B. Tinkcom, "Southwark, A River Community: Its Shape and Substance," *Proceedings of the American Philosophical Society* 114 (August 1970): 332, and Webster, *Philadelphia Preserved*, after page 190. Built on wider lots, some London houses could accommodate gracefully curving staircases, yet the houses' basic plans of two rooms to a floor with stairs near the middle of the house and a side entrance hall was the same as Philadelphia's London house plan. A plan of "a typical London house of the period after the Great Fire" is illustrated in Summerson, *Georgian London*, 51. For plans, section, and elevation of a circa 1780 house in London's Queen Anne's Gate, see Rasmussen, *London: The Unique City*, 226-27. Although the town-house plan also has two front rooms with a side hall, it also has a series of back buildings, which disqualifies it as a strictly two-room plan.

[44] The 1855 Matthew Fife House, for example, a three-story brick dwelling at 136 Race Street, Philadelphia, has a side hallway opening onto front and rear rooms and leading to a rear stair tower. Webster, *Philadelphia Preserved*, 71-72.

[45] Michel, "'In a Manner and Fashion Suitable to Their Degree,'" 33; Alice Kent Schooler, "Traditional, Popular, and Polite: Architectural History in the Lower Delaware Valley," lectures presented at Chester County Historical Society, West Chester, Pa., 11 October 1988, 18 October 1988.

[46] In the nineteenth century historians thought that this house had been built in 1682-83 for William Penn and given by him to his daughter Letitia. Consequently Philadelphians treated the house as a local shrine, and in 1883, near the city's bicentennial, city officials moved it to Fairmount Park, where it still stands near the zoo. In the 1950s researchers at the Philadelphia Historical Commission confirmed that the house was built for Thomas Chalkley between 1713 and 1715. Fiske Kimball in 1922 accepted the Penn myth and prints two old photographs of the house in *Domestic Architecture of the American Colonies and of the Early Republic* (New York: Charles Scribner's Sons, 1922; reprint ed., New York: Dover Publications, 1966), 48-49. For illustrations of the restored house in the park, see Harold Donaldson Eberlein and Cortlandt Van Dyke Hubbard, *Portrait of a Colonial City: Philadelphia, 1670-1838* (Philadelphia: J.B. Lippincott Company, 1939), 112-13; for a ground-floor plan, see Hugh Morrison, *Early American Architecture: From the First Colonial Settlements to the National Period* (New York: Oxford University Press, 1952) 516; for a circa 1828 watercolor of the house and a brief discussion of it, see George B. Tatum, *Penn's Great Town: Prints and Drawings* (Philadelphia: University of Pennsylvania Press, 1961), 24, 154, pl. 6.

[47] Alan Gowans, *Images of American Living*, 85.

[48] Futhey and Cope, *History of Chester County*, 464. Interior and exterior HABS photographs of the house by Ned Goode are illustrated in "An Album of Chester County Farmhouses," *Pennsylvania Folklife* 13 (Fall 1962): 23-24.

[49] Interview with Alice Kent Schooler, West Chester, Pa., 21 September 1989; Barley, *English Farmhouse and Cottage*, 63, 67, 71, 83, 104, 115, 141, 216-17; Michel, "'In a Manner and Fashion Suitable to Their Degree'," 30; Michel discusses the functions of these three rooms on page 42.

[50] Serpentine also is found in Delaware, Montgomery, Lancaster, and Northampton Counties, but most of it is stratified with magnesia minerals, limestone, and crystalline schists, which makes its an unsatisfactory building material. Montgomery County serpentine was used for doorsteps in late-eighteenth-century Philadelphia, but it was abandoned early in the nineteenth-century because it wore unevenly. The most durable serpentine is in Chester County and along a seventeen-mile strip in Maryland from Little Elk Creek to the Susquehanna River. Serpentine is no longer quarried. J.P. Lesley, ed., *Second Geological Survey of Pennsylvania: 4, The Geology of Chester County* (Harrisburg: Board of Commissioners of Geological Survey, 1883), 37, 86-97.

[51] Although the present windows are sliding sash, physical evidence indicates that they were originally casement. It is not known for certain when sash windows were first used in Philadelphia, but they were introduced in Boston at the turn of the eighteenth century. By the second decade of that century sash windows were no longer uncommon in Boston, and by the 1720s they were appearing in the surrounding countryside. "Joseph Collins House, West Goshen Township, Chester County, Pennsylvania, PA-1114," HABS Report (Washington, D.C.: Library of Congress, 1958), 1; Abbott Lowell Cummings, *The Framed Houses of Massachusetts Bay, 1625-1725* (Cambridge, Mass.: Belknap Press of Harvard University Press, 1979), 155; Charles F. Montgomery, "American Notes: Thomas Banister on the New Sash Windows, Boston, 1701," *Journal of the Society of Architectural Historians* 24 (May 1965): 169-70; Kenneth M. Wilson, "Window Glass in America," in Charles E. Peterson, ed., *Building Early America: Contributions toward the History of a Great Industry* (Radnor, Pa.: Chilton Book Company, 1976), 156-57.

[52] Michel, "'In a Manner and Fashion Suitable to Their Degree,'" 31, 35, 54-56.

[53] This is not to imply that medieval houses were asymmetrical in all respects. In fact, medieval houses were quite symmetrical, but about their long axis. Their entries were not part of their symmetrical organization. Peter Smith, *Houses of the Welsh Countryside: A Study in Historical Geography* (London: Her Majesty's Stationery Office, 1975), 229.

[54] The single-pile house was evidently the only house form built in Britain before the late sixteenth and early seventeenth centuries. It was dictated in part by builders' limitations in constructing roofs that could span more than a limited space. The single-pile house is so common in England, Scotland, and Wales that architectural historians, when writing about old hous-

es, usually assume the form to be single pile and make distinctions by using the term "double pile" where there are exceptions to the single-pile norm. Occasionally the two forms are discussed simultaneously, requiring use of both terms, as in Smith, *Houses of the Welsh Countryside,* 236. For a brief discussion of medieval roof construction, see Barley, *English Farmhouse and Cottage,* 21-26. Cultural geographers call the single-pile house the I house. Fred Kniffen, professor of geography at Louisiana State University, who probably has been most responsible for popularizing the term, first recognized this house type in Indiana in 1930. Because he observed so many of these houses in Indiana, Illinois, and Iowa, he adopted the term "I house" in 1936. Fred Kniffen, "Folk Housing: Key to Diffusion," 553. Architectural historians prefer the historical term "single-pile house," but the term "I house" has crept into such architectural guides as Virginia and Lee McAlester's thorough *A Field Guide to American Houses* (New York: Alfred A. Knopf, 1984), 96-97. It should be noted, however, that neither Kniffen nor the McAlesters are academic architectural historians.

[55] Outside of the city of Philadelphia with its rows of houses, the single-pile house was the dominant form in colonial Pennsylvania. The closest examination of the single-pile house in southeastern Pennsylvania has been done by Richard Pillsbury, who uses the term "I house" in "Patterns in the Folk and Vernacular House Forms of the Pennsylvania Culture Region," *Pioneer America* 9 (July 1977): 14-23.

[56] As in the case of the pent roof, disagreement surrounds the American roots of the single-pile house. Professor Kniffen at Louisiana State University and Professor Peirce Lewis at Pennsylvania State University write that the single-pile house (they use the term "I house") emanates from the Middle Atlantic region, but Henry Glassie feels that it flowed out of the Chesapeake area. They all are probably right. Kniffen, "Folk Housing: Key to Diffusion," 555; Peirce Lewis, "The Geography of Old Houses," *Earth and Mineral Sciences* 39 (February 1970): 34; Henry Glassie, *Pattern in the Material Folk Culture of the Eastern United States* (Philadelphia: University of Pennsylvania Press, 1968), 64-67, 75.

[57] The only significant variation in the American single-pile house plan came in the second quarter of the eighteenth century when a center passage hall was introduced to separate living and circulation space and give the facade a clearer Renaissance, or Georgian, symmetry. Georgian single-pile houses appeared in the Philadelphia region as early as 1730. One of the earliest known examples is Bel Air (PA-1124), a two-and-a-half-story brick country house that was built between 1714 and 1729 in Passyunk Township, now in Philadelphia's Franklin Delano Roosevelt Park. Its details—Flemish bond brick walls, steeply pitched gable roof, cove cornice across the front and rear, pent eaves at the gables, and a balcony over the center transomed entrance—indicate an early date, but not the seventeenth-century date that once was associated with the house. Most Georgian-period single-pile houses were built after mid-century, when English architectural pattern books helped to make English Georgian principles pervasive. Many architectural historians cringe at the sight of the word "Georgian." It is used here for the sake of convenience and brevity. For a good discourse on the different academic expressions of American Georgian architecture, see William H. Pierson Jr. *American Buildings and Their Architects: The Colonial and Neo-Classical Styles* (Garden City, N.Y.: Doubleday and

Company, 1970), 61-156. The Georgian Style is described in Morrison, *Early American Architecture,* 300-317. For differing dates of Bel Air, see Eberlein and Hubbard, *Portrait of a Colonial City,* 36; Herbert A. Richardson, "Bel Air," report for Department of American Civilization, University of Pennsylvania, 1964 (copy at Philadelphia Historical Commission).

[58]Germans also moved southward through the Shenandoah Valley into western Maryland, Virginia, and North Carolina, as well as westward over the Allegheny Mountains into Ohio, Indiana, and Illinois. The most complete English study of Pennsylvania German houses' Germanic sources, a significant contribution to material culture scholarship, is William Woys Weaver, "The Pennsylvania German House: European Antecedents and New World Forms," *Winterthur Portfolio* 21 (Winter 1986): 243-64. See also John D. Milner, "Germanic Architecture in the New World," *Journal of the Society of Architectural Historians* 34 (December 1975): 299; Edward A. Chappell, "Acculturation in the Shenandoah Valley: Rhenish Houses of the Massanutten Settlement," *Proceedings of the American Philosophical Society* 124 (29 February 1980): 57.

[59]The Bertolet-Herbein Cabin is illustrated in Richard S. Montgomery, "Houses of the Oley Valley," *The Dutchman* 6 (Winter 1954-55): 17, and Henry Glassie, "A Central Chimney Continental Log House," *Pennsylvania Folklife* 18 (Winter 1968-69): 39; Glassie also illustrates the house's first-floor plan. The characteristics of the *flurküchenhaus* are described by Robert C. Bucher, "The Continental Log House," *Pennsylvania Folklife* 12 (Summer 1962): 14; Glassie, "A Central Chimney Continental Log House," 38; Chappell, "Acculturation in the Shenandoah Valley," 57-60. Chappell prefers the term *ernhaus* (hall house); for his discussion, see Edward A. Chappell, "Germans and Swiss," in Dell Upton, ed., *America's Architectural Roots: Ethnic Groups That Built America* (Washington, D.C.: Preservation Press, 1986), 68-73.

[60]Weaver prefers the Pennsylvania German terms *kich* and *schtupp* for *küche* and *stube*. He notes that "Germans viewed stoves as an absolute necessity, as material proof of domesticity; . . . a room without a stove was not a Stube." Weaver, "The Pennsylvania German House," 254, 257-58. For Benjamin Franklin's description of the Germanic five-plate stove, see G. Edwin Brumbaugh, "Colonial Architecture of the Pennsylvania Germans," 28-29.

[61]Morrison, *Early American Architecture,* 542-44; Brumbaugh, "Colonial Architecture of the Pennsylvania Germans," 44, 54, pls. 51, 96.

[62]Weaver suggests that the *kreuzhaus* may have been first refined in German towns and then moved from towns to the countryside, a common pattern for folk culture. Weaver, "The Pennsylvania German House," 251-53. Robert A. Barakat, "The Herr and Zeller Houses," *Pennsylvania Folklife* 21 (Summer 1972): 9; Montgomery, "Houses of the Oley Valley," 18.

[63]Barakat, "The Herr and Zeller Houses," 10; Chappell, "Acculturation in the Shenandoah Valley," 60; Brumbaugh, "Colonial Architecture of the Pennsylvania Germans," 30.

[64]Two houses accessible to the public that have springs in their cellars are the 1749 Zeller House (PA-141) in Millcreek Township, Lebanon County, and the 1735 Daniel Boone Birthplace (PA-149) in Exeter Township, Berks County. A spring continues to flow through

the cellars of both of these stone houses, exiting at their western gable ends, which are below grade. Although frequently found in Germanic houses, including the aforementioned Keim Stone Cabin, cellar springs apparently were not exclusively Germanic. Thomas Downing, for example, was born in Devonshire, England, and in 1740 built a two-and-a-half-story coursed-rubble house (PA-171) in East Caln Township, Chester County. He used wooden pipes to carry water from a spring on the hill behind the house into a stone trough in the cellar. "The Old Downing House," 1949 (typewritten), Chester County Historical Society, West Chester, Pa.; Futhey and Cope, *History of Chester County*, 525-26; Montgomery, "Houses of the Oley Valley," 18.

[65] In Germanic farmhouses with two or three attics, the family used the lower attics for storing grain and drying fruit, and the uppermost attic was the *rauchkammer*, or smoke chamber. Smoke entered the room through a hole in the chimney stack and cured meats hanging from hooks. Weaver, "The Pennsylvania German House," 254-55. Through good sleuthing and field work, Robert Bucher has verified that many Pennsylvania German houses (and perhaps a couple of Anglo-American houses) had grain storage in the attic. It is a German practice that is still retained in Germany's agricultural villages. Barakat, "The Herr and Zeller Houses," 4, 7, 9-18; Robert C. Bucher, "Grain in the Attic," *Pennsylvania Folklife* 13 (Winter 1962-63): 7-15. For early photographs and assessment of the Herr House, see Kocher, "The Early Architecture of Pennsylvania," 32, 36, 39, 42.

[66] Barakat, "The Herr and Zeller Houses, 9-14, 18-21; Eleanor Raymond, *Early Domestic Architecture of Pennsylvania* (New York: William Helburn, 1931; reprint ed., Princeton: Pyne Press, 1973), pls. 22-25.

[67] Brumbaugh, "Colonial Architecture of the Pennsylvania Germans," 31-33.

[68] Chappell, "Acculturation in the Shenandoah Valley," 63-68, 76-92, 84-87.

[69] At least one of these houses in Virginia's Page County, Fort Rhodes, was log. Ibid., 66-68.

[70] Drury B. Alexander, "John DeTurk House, Oley Township, Berks County, Pennsylvania, PA-1023," HABS Report (Washington, D.C.: Library of Congress, 1958), 2-3.

[71] Robert C. Bucher, "The Swiss Bank House in Pennsylvania," *Pennsylvania Folklife* 18 (Winter 1968-69): 2-11.

[72] For illustrations of the Almonry and its enclosed exterior staircase and a casement window, see John L. Craft, "Ephrata Cloister, an Eighteenth-Century Religious Commune," *The Magazine Antiques* 118 (October 1980): 731-32.

[73] Oliver T. Cadbury, "The William Harvey House" ca. 1960 (typewritten), Chester County Historical Society, West Chester, Pa.; Futhey and Cope, *History of Chester County*, 522, 570, 590; Raymond, *Early Domestic Architecture of Pennsylvania*, 70.

[74] Milner, "Germanic Architecture in the New World," 299. The term *durchganigenhaus* is Pennsylvania German, not German. The German term for passage is *durchgang*.

[75] William J. Murtagh, *Moravian Architecture and Town Planning: Bethlehem, Pennsylvania and Other Eighteenth-Century American Settlements* (Chapel Hill: University of North Carolina Press, 1967), 84-86. The house's 1760 plans, sections, and elevation are illustrated on page 83.

[76] The definitive work on the architecture of Moravian Bethlehem is Murtagh's *Moravian Architecture and Town Planning*; see note 75 for its full citation. A short and dated summary is Henry J. Kauffman, "Moravian Architecture in Bethlehem," *The Dutchman* 6 (Spring 1955): 12-19. For discussion and illustrations of Moravian buildings in other Pennsylvania towns, see Vernon H. Nelson and Lothar Madeheim, "The Moravian Settlements of Pennsylvania in 1757: The Nicholas Garrison Views," *Pennsylvania Folklife* 19 (Autumn 1969): 2-13.

[77] Because the stuccoed brick Central Moravian Church (PA-1147) was built in 1803-1806 and the stuccoed log Schnitz House (PA-1154) circa 1810, they are not included among the eighteenth-century buildings.

[78] The origins of the Moravian Church are summarized in Murtagh, *Moravian Architecture and Town Planning*, 3-7. For the church's early history to circa 1760, see Edward Langton, *History of the Moravian Church: The Story of the First International Protestant Church* (London: George Allen & Unwin, 1956). An excellent study of more than a century of change in the Bethlehem group is Beverly Prior Smaby, *The Transformation of Moravian Bethlehem: From Communal Mission to Family Economy* (Philadelphia: University of Pennsylvania Press, 1988).

[79] Beissel founded the commune in 1732; after the last celibate member died in 1813, married members renamed their congregation the German Seventh Day Baptist Church. It died out in 1934. A thorough and sympathetic study of Beissel's group is Alderfer's *The Ephrata Commune*, cited in note 3.

[80] The Saron may also possess mystical qualities. Its dimensions, approximately thirty by seventy feet, contain the mystical numbers three, seven, and ten. Equally significant is how its builders were able to manipulate the vernacular *Küche* and *Stube* (large here and with more than one five-plate stove) to serve the needs of what was initially meant to be a convent for married householders who had accepted a celibate and communal life. The experiment failed within a year, and the community remodeled the building as Sisters' Hall and rededicated it in 1745. An excellent history of the Cloister buildings (and my source for their mystical and symbolic qualities) is Patrick W. O'Bannon, Keith F. Jacobs, Jeffrey C. Bourke, and George Cress, *Ephrata Cloister: A Historic Structures Report*, 2 vols. (West Chester, Pa.: John Milner Associates for Pennsylvania Historical and Museum Commission, 1988); see especially 1:20-30, 34-35; 2:6. The buildings' construction and restoration are discussed in G. Edwin Brumbaugh, "Medieval Construction at Ephrata," *The Magazine Antiques* 46 (July 1944): 18-20. For photographs of interiors and exteriors before restoration, see Raymond, *Early Domestic Architecture of Pennsylvania*, pls. 1-9; Kocher, "The Early Architecture of Pennsylvania," 39-43. Many of the restored exteriors and interiors are illustrated in Kraft, "Ephrata Cloister," 724-37. The standard biography of Conrad Beissel is Walter C. Klein, *Johann Conrad Beissel: Mystic and Martinet, 1690-1768* (Philadelphia: University of Pennsylvania, 1942).

[81] The standard history of the Harmony Society is Karl J. R. Arndt, *George Rapp's Harmony Society, 1785-1847* (Philadelphia: University of Pennsylvania, 1965) and idem, *George Rapp's Successors and Material Heirs, 1847-1916* (Rutherford, N.J.: Fairleigh Dickinson University Press, 1971). An account by the society's last member and controversial heir to its fortune is John S. Duss, *The Harmonists: A Personal History* (Harrisburg: Pennsylvania Book Service, 1943); see 14-18, 34-40, 57-62 for the selection of the society's three sites. A recent ten-volume planning study for Old Economy Village including several historical essays and individual building studies contributes new information on Harmonist art, architecture and town planning (Pennsylvania Historical and Museum Commission, *Historic Structures Report for Old Economy Village*, prepared by Clio Group Inc., and Marianna Thomas, Architects, 1989-1990, Vols. 1-10).

[82] John William Larner Jr., "'Nails and Sundrie Medicines': Town Planning and Public Health in the Harmony Society, 1805-1840," *Western Pennsylvania Historical Magazine* 45 (June 1962): 132-34.

[83] These buildings are discussed and illustrated in Charles Morse Stotz, *The Architectural Heritage of Early Western Pennsylvania: A Record of Building before 1860* (Pittsburgh: University of Pittsburgh Press, 1966), 193-213. Also see Daniel B. Reibel, *A Guide to Old Economy* (Harrisburg: Pennsylvania Historical and Museum Commission, 1972), 11-40.

[84] Arndt, *George Rapp's Successors and Material Heirs*, 319-21, 353-56, 368.

[85] Brumbaugh, "Colonial Architecture of the Pennsylvania Germans," 59, pls. 83-87; Wertenbaker, *The Founding of American Civilization*, 319; Raymond, *Early Domestic Architecture of Pennsylvania*, pls. 10-13.

[86] Arched openings probably did not appear on all of Pennsylvania's colonial Presbyterian churches, but those that today do not have arched openings have been remodeled to such a degree that the shape of their original openings cannot be determined. Gable roofs were predominant, but the Norriton church and the 1768 Tinicum Presbyterian Church in Ottsville, Bucks County, originally had hipped roofs, and the Donegal Presbyterian Church (circa 1740) in East Donegal Township, Lancaster County, has a gambrel roof. The 1757 Presbyterian church in Carlisle, Cumberland County, is one of the few colonial Presbyterian churches to have two stories. Harold Wickliffe Rose, *The Colonial Houses of Worship in America: Built in the English Colonies before the Republic, 1607-1789, and Still Standing* (New York: Hastings House, 1963), 364, 376, 389-90, 393-94; Leyburn, *The Scotch-Irish*, 288-93.

[87] The Great Conewago Presbyterian Church is illustrated in Rose, *Colonial Houses of Worship*, 393. In the mid-nineteenth century the rear and side doors were closed up, leaving the building with only its gable-end entrance.

[88] Gowans, *Images of American Living*, 91.

[89] Henry Glassie, "Irish," in Upton, ed., *America's Architectural Roots*, 75.

[90] Ibid., 76.

[91]Jordan, *American Log Buildings*, 24, 50, 73-74, 148; Waterman, *The Dwellings of Colonial America*, 124; Walter C. Kidney, *Landmark Architecture: Pittsburgh and Allegheny County* (Pittsburgh: Pittsburgh History and Landmarks Foundation, 1985), 239.

[92]Tatum, *Penn's Great Town*, 24-25.

[93]Caroline W. Smedley, "Historical Sketch of Frankford Meeting," in *Papers Read before the Historical Society of Frankford* 2 (1916): 221.

[94]The 1765 Marshallton Friends Meetinghouse (PA-1105) in Marshallton, Chester County, has sliding partitions at right angles to the sliding partition running the length of the building. These partitions are illustrated both opened and closed in Schiffer, *Survey of Chester County, Pennsylvania, Architecture*, 81.

[95]For illustrations and brief histories of Pennsylvania's colonial Quaker meetinghouses, see Rose, *Colonial Houses of Worship*, 352-55, 358-63, 368-72, 376-78, 384, 389-91.

[96]Lee Nelson and Penelope Hartshorne Batcheler, "An Architectural Study of Arch Street Meeting House," 1968 (typewritten).

[97]Robert W. Shoemaker, "Christ Church, St. Peter's, and St. Paul's," in Luther P. Eisenhart, ed., *Historic Philadelphia: From the Founding until the Early Nineteenth Century*, vol. 43, part 1 of *Transactions of the American Philosophical Society* (1953),]188-89; Tatum, *Penn's Great Town*, 28-29, 156.

[98]Morrison, *Early American Architecture*, 539.

[99]The book was William Maitland's *History of London*. Beatrice B. Garvan, "St. Peter's Church, in Darrel L. Sewell, ed., *Philadelphia: Three Centuries of American Art* (Philadelphia: Philadelphia Museum of Art, 1976), 72.

[100]Tatum, *Penn's Great Town*, 30-32, pls. 12, 13.

[101]John W. Lippold, "Early Lancaster Architecture," *Journal of the Lancaster County Historical Society* 75 (1972): 154-59; Idem, "Old Trinity Church," *Historical Papers and Addresses of the Lancaster County Historical Society*, no. 13 (1965): 127-29. Lippold attributes the statues to Philadelphia sculptor William Rush. Frederick Mann, a Lancaster carpenter, helped Lotman built the brick tower. In 1853 the entrance was moved from the west side to the tower at the south end, an apse was appended to the north end, east and west vestibules were added to the front, and the pulpit was moved to the north wall and the galleries were rebuilt. Also in the nineteenth century, the congregation replaced the many lights of clear glass in the arched windows with stained glass and replaced the churchyard's brick wall with an iron fence. In 1949 the congregation removed the original statues to the narthex and put copies in their former locations atop the tower. The original pedimented entrance door now serves as a side entrance to the western vestibule. For a print showing the church before the 1853 alterations, see page 154 of Lippold's 1972 article.

[102] John J. Snyder Jr., Lancaster Architecture, 1719-1927: A Guide to Publicly Accessible Buildings in Lancaster County (Lancaster, Pa.: Historic Preservation Trust of Lancaster County, 1979), 10.

[103] Ibid., 16.

[104] Edward M. Riley, "The Independence Hall Group," in Eisenhart, ed., *Historic Philadelphia*, 10-18, 24, 34.

[105] Beatrice B. Garvan, "The State House (Independence Hall)," in Sewell, ed., *Philadelphia: Three Centuries of American Art*, 41.

[106] Morrison, *Early American Architecture*, 534.

[107] The Liberty Bell, which annually attracts more visitors than Independence Hall, no longer rests in the building for which it was intended. The National Park Service has encased it in its own glass "box" on Independence Mall to afford it the protection and accessibility suitable for a such a national icon.

[108] William H. Shank, *York: First Capital of the United States, 1777-1778* (York, Pa.: American Canal and Transportation Center, 1985), n.p.; Snyder, *Lancaster Architecture*, 11; Oscar Jewell Harvey and Ernest Gray Smith, *A History of Wilkes-Barre, Luzerne County, Pennsylvania*, 6 vols. (Wilkes-Barre: By the author, 1927), 3:1754-55.

[109] Beatrice B. Garvan, "Carpenters' Hall," in Sewell, ed., *Philadelphia: Three Centuries of American Art*, 106-7. Smith's apparent indebtedness to Renaissance architecture is noted in Tatum, *Penn's Great Town*, 37. A succinct but thorough history of the building and biographical sketch of Robert Smith is Charles E. Peterson, "Carpenters' Hall," in Eisenhart, ed., *Historic Philadelphia*, 96-128. For a brief history of this important organization, see Roger W. Moss Jr., "The Origins of the Carpenters' Company of Philadelphia," in Charles E. Peterson, ed., *Building Early America: Contributions toward the History of a Great Industry* (Radnor, Pa.: Chilton Book Company, 1976), 35-53.

[110] Webster, *Philadelphia Preserved*, 12. Murtagh, "Philadelphia Row House," 12. Eberlein and Hubbard, *Portrait of a Colonial City*, 438-42. A superb study of the Powel House is George B. Tatum, *Philadelphia Georgian: The City House of Samuel Powel and Some of Its Eighteenth-Century Neighbors* (Middletown, Conn.: Wesleyan University Press, 1976).

[111] Early double-pile houses in Britain were just that, two single-pile houses set back to back with their long axes parallel to each other. The earliest Welsh example dates from 1582; the earliest dated English double-pile farmhouse was built in Lincolnshire in 1658. Coleshill, a 1662 English country house designed by Roger Pratt, introduced the idea of placing a front central entrance hall and a rear stairwell in the double-pile plan. Our impression of the double-pile house is derived largely from this configuration. Yet as late as the early nineteenth century small double-pile houses in the English countryside opened directly into their living rooms. Smith, *Houses of the Welsh Countryside*, 233-35, 256-59; Barley, *English Farmhouse and Cottage*, 218-19; John Summerson, *Architecture in Britain, 1530 to 1830* (Hammondsworth,

England: Penguin Books, 1952), 86-87; R.W. Brunskill, *Vernacular Architecture of the Lake Counties: A Field Handbook* (London: Faber and Faber, 1974). 62-65. For a discussion of the arrival of both the double-pile house and English architectural texts in eighteenth-century America, see Pierson, *American Buildings and Their Architects: The Colonial and Neo-Classical Styles*, 64-68, 111-14; Morrison, *Early American Architecture*, 288-91, 295-96.

[112] Richard Pillsbury and Andrew Kardos, *A Field Guide to the Folk Architecture of Northeastern United States*, Geography Publications at Dartmouth, no. 8 (Hanover, N.H.: Dartmouth College, 1970), 56.

[113] For a discussion of the many changes wrought by the double-pile layout and the coinciding switch of a house's main axis to its short axis, see Smith, *Houses of the Welsh Countryside*, 229-36.

[114] Henry Glassie discusses how the Georgian form "was not radically different from older European folk practice" in "Eighteenth-Century Cultural Process in Delaware Valley Folk Building," *Winterthur Portfolio* 7 (1972): 37.

[115] The Taylor-Parke House's kitchen wing was built before the main block and may have served for a period as a one-room-and-loft dwelling. For a study of the house and its first owner, see Arlene Horvath, "Vernacular Expression in Quaker Chester County, Pennsylvania: The Taylor-Parke House and Its Maker," in Camille Wells, ed., *Perspectives in Vernacular Architecture, II* (Columbia: University of Missouri Press, 1986), 150-60. Mrs. Horvath concludes (on page 159) that material evidence does not confirm whether Taylor built such a plain house with traditional elements "because of religious conviction, aesthetics, social and economic conservatism, available expertise, or a combination of these factors."

[116] The term "Georgian gable" here refers to gable ends with windows for each of the two rooms on both floors and two smaller windows in the gable. Glassie, "Eighteenth-Century Cultural Process in Delaware Valley Folk Building," 44.

[117] Horvath, "Vernacular Expression in Quaker Chester County," 155-59. Since no historic structure study has been done on this property, there is no information to contradict the surface visual evidence that Mrs. Horvath evaluates.

[118] Alice Kent Schooler, "The Historic American Buildings Survey in Chester County," paper presented at the second Chester County Historical Society-West Chester University Joint Conference, West Chester, Pa., 5 November 1983. Primitive Hall's plan and elevations, and interior photos, are illustrated in Schiffer, *Survey of Chester County, Pennsylvania, Architecture*, 385-87. For pre-restoration interior photos, see Raymond, *Early Domestic Architecture of Pennsylvania*, pls. 34-36.

[119] Tatum, *Penns's Great Town*, 36.

[120] Stenton's plan is illustrated in Harry M. Tinkcom, Margaret B. Tinkcom, and Grant Miles Simon, *Historic Germantown: From the Founding to the Early Part of the Nineteenth Century* (Philadelphia: American Philosophical Society, 1955), 33; Fiske Kimball, *Domestic*

Architecture of the American Colonies and of the Early Republic (New York: Charles Scribner's Sons, 1922; reprint ed., New York: Dover Publications, 1966), 74.

[121] Alice Kent Schooler, "Traditional, Popular, and Polite: Architectural History in the Lower Delaware Valley," paper presented at Chester County Historical Society, West Chester, Pa., 25 October 1988; Eberlein and Hubbard, *Portrait of a Colonial City*, 168-76.

[122] Beatrice B. Garvan, "Mount Pleasant: A Scottish Anachronism in Philadelphia," *Journal of the Society of Architectural Historians* 34 (December 1975): 304.

[123] Morrison, *Early American Architecture*, 527. See also Tatum, *Penn's Great Town*, 35; Louis C. Madeira, "Mount Pleasant," *The Magazine Antiques* 82 (November 1962): 520-24.

[124] Morrison, *Early American Architecture*, 526, 528-30; Eberlein and Hubbard, *Portrait of a Colonial City*, 313-40; Martin P. Snyder, "Woodford," *The Magazine Antiques* 82 (November 1962): 515-19; Margaret B. Tinkcom, "Cliveden: The Building of a Philadelphia Countryseat, 1763-1767," *Pennsylvania Magazine of History and Biography* 88 (January 1964): 3-36; Nancy Halverson Schless, "The Monumental Entrance and Stair Hall: Colen Campbell's Vitruvius Britannicus and Benjamin Chew's Cliveden," *Journal of the Society of Architectural Historians* 34 (December 1975): 307; Marcus Whiffen and Frederick Koeper, *American Architecture*, (Cambridge: MIT Press, 1981), 96-97.

[125] *Philadelphia Inquirer*, 25 April 1986, sec. A, 21.

[126] Webster, *Philadelphia Preserved*, 323-24, 335.

[127] Eberlein and Hubbard, *Portrait of a Colonial City*, 142-51; Schiffer, *Survey of Chester County, Pennsylvania, Architecture*, 86.

[128] There is no evidence that the builder put the date on the lintel; the owner or a later workman could have made the error. Nevertheless, such a bold dating suggests retention of a folk practice. The Fisher House is illustrated in Montgomery, "Houses of the Oley Valley," 20, and is illustrated and briefly discussed in A. Lawrence Kocher, "The Early Architecture of Pennsylvania, Part III," *Architectural Record* 49 (February 1921): 136-37.

[129] Mary Mix Foley, *The American House* (New York: Harper and Row, 1980), 65.

[130] Glassie, "Eighteenth-Century Cultural Process in Delaware Valley Folk Building," 41-43.

[131] Thomas Kneel and Deborah S. Burns, "John Conrad House," HABS Report PA-259 (Washington, D.C.: Library of Congress, 1978), 13; Thomas Kneel, "Eliza Stamm House," HABS Report PA-113 (Washington, D.C.: Library of Congress, 1976), 8.

[132] Henry J. Kauffman argues that in the early nineteenth century Pennsylvania Germans, in an effort to save time and building materials, absorbed the central hall into two front rooms, each with its own exterior door. Glassie's position, that Pennsylvania Germans retained their traditional house plans while changing facades, is more reasonable. Henry J. Kauffman, "The Riddle of Two Front Doors," *The Dutchman* 6 (Winter 1954-55): 27; idem, *The American Farmhouse* (New York: Hawthorn Books, 1975), 97-100.

[133] Stotz, *Architectural Heritage of Early Western Pennsylvania*, 19; for drawings and photos of the Meason House, see pages 60-67. The house is also illustrated in Dickson, *A Hundred Pennsylvania Buildings*, pl. 39. For Meason's biography see Evelyn Abraham, "Isaac Meason, the First Ironmonger West of the Alleghenies" *Western Pennsylvania Historical Magazine* 20 (1938): 41-49.

[134] Job Harvey built the initial three bays of the stone house circa 1740 onto an original circa 1725 log house, which was destroyed for the 1862 addition. "Job Harvey House, Charlestown Township, Chester County, Pennsylvania," HABS Report PA-1196 (Washington, D.C.: Library of Congress, 1958), 1.

[135] Glassie, "Eighteenth-Century Cultural Process in Delaware Valley Folk Building," 37. Although Noble puts Glassie's Two-thirds Georgian House Type in the same category as Waterman's three-room "Quaker-plan" house, they are not quite the same, because the hall in the Two-thirds Georgian house is a stair-passage, not a room. Noble, *Wood, Brick and Stone*, 45.

[136] An early three-bay double-pile house is the 1732 rubble Stoltzfus House (PA-159) in Valley Township, Chester County; it was expanded to a full five-bay double-pile house in 1813. A later example of the three-bay double-pile house is the 1846 timber-frame John Parke House (PA-1310) in Parkesburg, Chester County, which was demolished in 1977.

[137] The Potts House is discussed and illustrated in Dickson, *A Hundred Pennsylvania Buildings*, pl. 12.

[138] Glassie calls this plan the One-third Georgian House Type, asserting that "if the Georgian form could be reduced by one-third [to produce the Two-thirds Georgian House Type], it could be reduced by two-thirds," to yield the One-third Georgian House Type. It makes sense mathematically, but not architecturally. Yet no other terminology has been developed. Glassie, "Eighteenth-Century Cultural Process in Delaware Valley Folk Building," 38.

[139] A February 1836 sheriff's sale of this building and its adjacent neighbor referred to them as "new brick messuages." The building was erected between May 1831, when Martha Smith acquired the lot, and 1836, when she and her husband, Israel Doll, lost it in the sheriff's sale. Deed Book T4, 129, Chester County Recorder of Deeds, West Chester, Pa.; Deed Poll 4, February Term 1836, Court of Common Pleas, Chester County, West Chester, Pa.

[140] Humphry Marshall apprenticed as a mason, and he is traditionally credited with building much, if not all, of the house with his own hands. A Quaker, member of the American Philosophical Society, and cousin of the great naturalist John Bartram, Marshall in 1785 published *Arbustrum Americanum* (the American Grove), the first systematic botanical book in the United States. Futher and Cope, *History of Chester County*, 650-51; Brooke Hindle, *The Pursuit of Science in Revolutionary America, 1735-1789* (Chapel Hill: University of North Carolina Press, 1956), 303-4.

[141] The terminology, corner hall plan, is that of Professor Bernard Herman, University of Delaware. Alice Kent Schooler, comp., *The Humphry Marshall House, Marshallton, Pennsylvania: A Preliminary Architectural/Historical Study* (West Chester, Pa.: John Milner Associates for Chester County Historical Society, 1985), 26 n. 1.

[142] For a discussion of the background of neoclassicism in America and an excellent explanation of its four phases in the United States, see Pierson, *American Buildings and Their Architects: The Colonial and Neoclassical Styles*, 205-460.

[143] The latest and most thorough study of the work of Adam and his contemporaries is Damie Stillman, *English Neo-Classical Architecture*, 2 vols. (London: Zwemmer Books, 1988).

[144] Tatum, *Philadelphia Georgian*, 41-42.

[145] The history of the Hill-Physick House is related in George B. Roberts, "Dr. Physick and His House," *Pennsylvania Magazine of History and Biography* 92 (January 1968): 67-86.

[146] The panes' large size (12 1/2 inches by 22 1/2 inches) made them so expensive that, if damaged by fire, the fire insurance company would estimate their cost of replacement at the rate of panes measuring eight inches by ten inches, a more common size. Mutual Assurance Company, Policy 191, Insurance Survey, 20 November 1795. Copy at Philadelphia Historical Commission.

[147] Richard J. Betts, "The Woodlands," *Winterthur Portfolio* 14 (Autumn 1979): 229. The many aspects of Woodlands that were new to Americans are cited in Kimball, *Domestic Architecture of the American Colonies and of the Early Republic*, 100, 154, 155, 163, 174, 203, 210, 211, 217, 226, 242, 252, 253. Woodlands is also evaluated in Pierson, *American Buildings and Their Architects: The Colonial and Neoclassical Styles*, 219-21; Tatum, *Penn's Great Town*, 40-41, 51, 55; Whiffen and Koeper, *American Architecture*, 117-19.

[148] Lippold, "Early Lancaster Architecture," 171-73.

[149] The First Presbyterian Church on Market Street appears in one of Thomas and William Birch's prints, which is illustrated in Tatum, *Penn's Great Town*, pl. 23. The bank's cornice and pediment are wood; Claudius LeGrand carved the nation's coat of arms in the pediment. James O. Wettereau, "The Oldest Bank Building in the United States," and Alexander Mackie, "The Presbyterian Churches of Old Philadelphia," in Eisenhart, ed., *Historic Philadelphia*, 70-79, 217-18; Beatrice Garvan, "Bank of the United States," in Sewell, ed., *Philadelphia: Three Centuries of American Art*, 172-73; Tatum, *Penn's Great Town*, 39-40; Dickson, *A Hundred Pennsylvania Buildings*, pl. 31.

[150] Library Hall (1789-90) of the Library Company of Philadelphia was the first building designed by Dr. William Thornton, who in 1793 won the design competition for the United States Capitol (DC-38) and later was the architect of the 1800 Octagon (DC-25) and the circa 1816 Tudor Place (DC-171) in Washington, D.C. Charles E. Peterson suggests that Thornton based his facade design on a five-bay Palladian double-pile house illustrated in plate 9 in the second volume of Abraham Swan's *Collection of Designs in Architecture* (London, 1757). Library Hall stood at the northeast corner of Fifth and Library Streets, opposite Philosophical Hall. It was demolished in 1884 for the Drexel Building, which, in turn, was demolished in 1956 and replaced by the American Philosophical Society's library, whose Fifth Street facade is a reproduction of Thornton's design. Tatum, *Penn's Great Town*, 161-62, pl. 26; Charles E. Peterson, "Library Hall: Home of the Library Company of Philadelphia,

1790-1880," in Eisenhart, ed., *Historic Philadelphia*, 129-47. An 1800 Birch engraving of the building is reproduced on page 129 of Peterson's article. For an old photo of the building, see Eberlein and Hubbard, *Portrait of a Colonial City*, 419. For Thornton's Washington, D.C., work, see Nancy B. Schwartz, comp., *District of Columbia Catalog* (Charlottesville: University Press of Virginia for Columbia Historical Society, 1974), 108, 140, 141-43.

[151] Dickson, *A Hundred Pennsylvania Buildings*, pl. 34.

[152] George Tatum calls the hospital's center building "a nearly perfect example" of the style; *Penn's Great Town*, 51. For biographies of Rhoads and the two Evanses and a summary of the hospital's architectural history, see Beatrice Garvan, "Samuel Rhoads (1711-1784)," "David Evans, Sr. (1733-1817) and David Evans, Jr. (act. 1794-1806)," and "Pennsylvania Hospital" in Sewell, ed., *Philadelphia: Three Centuries of American Art*, 61-64. See also William Henry Williams, *America's First Hospital: The Pennsylvania Hospital. 1751-1841* (Wayne, Pa.: Haverford House, Publishers, 1976), 92-99; Edward B. Krumbhaar, "The Pennsylvania Hospital," in Eisenhart, ed., *Historic Philadelphia*, 237-46; Thomas G. Morton and Frank Woodbury, *The History of the Pennsylvania Hospital, 1751-1895* (Philadelphia: Times Publishing House, 1895), 37-39, 37-99.

[153] Classes assembled in the building in November 1804, but dormitory rooms were not finished until 1809. Charles Coleman Sellers, *Dickinson College: A History* (Middletown, Conn.: Wesleyan University Press, 1973), 129-30. 578; see page 128 for an elevation and basement plan of Latrobe's first proposal. For a discussion of the building's architectural merits, see Paul F. Norton, "Latrobe and Old West at Dickinson College," *Art Bulletin* 33 (June 1951): 125-30. See also Dickson, *A Hundred Pennsylvania Buildings*, pl. 43; Talbot Hamlin, *Benjamin Henry Latrobe* (New York: Oxford University Press, 1955), 192-94, 202.

[154] Dickson, *A Hundred Pennsylvania Buildings*, pl. 41; Stotz, *Architectural Heritage of Early Western Pennsylvania*, 218-21; Ernest Ashton Smith, *Allegheny–A Century of Education, 1815-1915* (Meadville, Pa.: Allegheny College History Company, 1915), 35-43.

[155] Sally Smith Cahalan, *James Buchanan and His Family at Wheatland* (Lancaster, Pa.: James Buchanan Foundation, 1988), 17.

[156] Pierson, *American Buildings and Their Architects: The Colonial and Neo-Classical Styles*, 211-12, 215-18.

[157] Pierson perceives four phases of American neoclassicism: the aforementioned traditional phase; the idealistic phase, which is best expressed by Thomas Jefferson's work; the rational phase, of which Latrobe's Baltimore Cathedral (ME-186) (circa 1804-circa 1818) and Robert Mills' 1812 Fireproof Building (SC-154) in Charleston, South Carolina, are among the best examples; and the national phase. Ibid., 210-15, 286-334, 360-94. Peter Collins discusses the sources and character of the Greek Revival in Britain and Europe in *Changing Ideals in Modern Architecture, 1750-1950* (Montreal: McGill University Press, 1965), 79-99.

[158] Completed in 1801, the bank was demolished by 1871. Pierson places it in the rational phase of neoclassicism in *American Buildings and Their Architects: The Colonial and*

Neo-Classical Styles, 348-56. The portico is copied from the Temple Erectheum in Athens, which was illustrated in James Stuart and Nicholas Revett, *Antiquities of Athens*, 3 vols. (London: John Nichols, 1762-1794; reprint ed., New York: Benjamin Blom, 1968): 2: chap. 2, pls. 4-7. See also Tatum, *Penn's Great Town*, 59, 168, pl. 42; Dickson, *A Hundred Pennsylvania Buildings*, pl. 42; Hamlin, *Benjamin Henry Latrobe*, 152-59.

[159] For photographs and elevations, plans, and details of the Judson House, see Stotz, *Architectural Heritage of Early Western Pennsylvania*, 102-3. Annie Scott Baxter, "Stevenson House, North Springfield, Erie County, Pennsylvania," HABS Report PA-55 (Washington, D.C.: Library of Congress, 1936), 2.

[160] Latrobe did not accept second place gracefully. He felt betrayed by his former student, suggested plagiarism, and left Philadelphia embittered. For an early article, sympathetic to Latrobe's claims, see Fiske Kimball, "The Bank of the United States," *Architectural Record* 58 (December 1925): 581-94. Agnes Addison (Gilchrist) sets the record straight in "Latrobe vs. Strickland," *Journal of the Society of Architectural Historians* 2 (July 1942): 26-29. Both Latrobe and Strickland based their facades on the Parthenon, which is illustrated in Stuart and Revett, *Antiquities of Athens*, 2: chap. 1, pl. 3.

[161] Agnes Addison Gilchrist, *William Strickland: Architect and Engineer, 1788-1854* (Philadelphia: University of Pennsylvania Press, 1950; reprint ed., New York: Da Capo Press, 1969), 4, 37, 53-57; Richard J. Webster, "Second Bank of the United States (Old Customs House)," in Sewell, ed., *Philadelphia: Three Centuries of American Art*, 244-45.

[162] James Early, *Romanticism and American Architecture* (New York: A.S. Barnes and Co., 1965), 29-49; Gowans, *Images of American Living*, 267-84; Tatum, *Penn's Great Town*, 53.

[163] Quoted in Lois Craig, ed., *The Federal Presence: Architecture, Politics, and Symbols in the United States Government Buildings* (Cambridge: MIT Press, 1977), 53.

[164] The standard account of the Bank War is Bray Hammond, *Banks and Politics in America: From the Revolution to the Civil War* (Princeton: Princeton University Press, 1957), 286-450. For a short history of the Second Bank, see Bray Hammond, "The Second Bank of the United States," in Eisenhart, ed., *Historic Philadelphia*, 80-85.

[165] Charles Dickens, *American Notes and Pictures from Italy* (London, 1842, 1846; reprint ed., New York: Oxford University Press, 1957), 97-98.

[166] Stotz, *Architectural Heritage of Early Western Pennsylvania*, 20, 25, 267, 271; Agnes Addison Gilchrist, "Additions to William Strickland: Architect and Engineer, 1788-1854," *Journal of the Society of Architectural Historians* 13 (October 1954): 16; Hammond, *Banks and Politics in America*, 439, 512.

[167] Stotz, *Architectural Heritage of Early Western Pennsylvania*, 20.

[168] Quoted in Craig, ed., *The Federal Presence*, 57. The quote is from a Walter lecture that was published in the January 1841 *Journal of the Franklin Institute*.

[169] Cheesman A. Herrick, *History of Girard College* (Philadelphia: Girard College, 1927), 1-39, 106-116; Talbot Hamlin, *Greek Revival Architecture in America: Being an Account of Important Trends in American Architecture and American Life prior to the War between the States* (New York: Oxford University Press, 1944), 82-88; Tatum, *Penn's Great Town*, 72, 175-76, pls. 67, 68; Richard J. Webster, "Founder's Hall, Girard College (Main Building)," in Sewell, ed., *Philadelphia: Three Centuries of American Art*, 291-92. For an account of Nicholas Biddle's role in determining the college's architectural style, see Agnes Addison Gilchrist, "Girard College: An Examination of the Layman's Influence on Architecture," *Journal of the Society of Architectural Historians* 16 (May 1957): 22-25.

[170] The college's funds consisted of $3000 in the form of local pledges and an $18,000 appropriation acquired through the efforts of Thaddeus Stevens, the newly elected state representative from Adams County and soon to be a trustee of the college, who defied his Anti-Masonic Party's position in working for state education aid. John C. Trautwine began his career in 1828, at the age of eighteen, when he entered William Strickland's office. He spent most of his career as an engineer, especially on railroad and waterway projects, many in Latin America. Trustees of Pennsylvania College (as the school was then known) chose him as the architect of Pennsylvania Hall because of his reputation as a construction engineer and an architect of large buildings. Charles H. Glatfelter, *A Salutary Influence: Gettysburg College, 1832-1985*, 2 vols. (Gettysburg, Pa.: Gettysburg College, 1987), 1:44-57; *Dictionary of American Biography*, s.v. "Trautwine, John Cresson," by F. Lynwood Garrison; Samuel Gring Hefelbower, *The History of Gettysburg College, 1832-1932* (Gettysburg, Pa.: Gettysburg College, 1932), 90-91.

[171] Quoted in Glatfelter, *A Salutary Influence*, 1:62. Even Trautwine's $100 fee, much less than 1 percent of the $15,750 construction costs, was reasonable. Ibid., 1:67.

[172] Ibid., 1:62-63, 66-67. A drawing of Trautwine's initial plans and elevation for Pennsylvania Hall is illustrated in Ibid., 1:41, and Hefelbower, *History of Gettysburg College*, on the plate facing page 90.

[173] Pierson, *American Buildings and Their Architects: The Colonial and Neo-Classical Styles*, 145. For a history of the house, see Nicholas B. Wainwright, *Andalusia: Countryseat of the Craig Family and of Nicholas Biddle and His Descendants* (Philadelphia: Historical Society of Pennsylvania, 1976).

[174] From data compiled by the house's present owners, Mr. and Mrs. W. Gerald Moore, we know that William Ebbs was born in Ireland in 1804, immigrated to Philadelphia in 1826, and by 1837 was in Pittsburgh, married, and working as a merchant. City directories in 1850 listed him as a manufacturer. In March 1851 he acquired the sixty-acre property on which has house was built. The house's architect is unknown but it may have been John Chislett, Ebbs's Pittsburgh neighbor, and the English-born architect who designed many of that city's Greek Revival buildings. For an 1856 illustration of the house, see Schiffer, *Survey of Chester County, Pennsylvania, Architecture*, 159.

[175] Hamlin, *Greek Revival Architecture*, 276.

[176] Only two of the three original houses survive; they stand at 232-34 South Third Street in Society Hill. Webster, *Philadelphia Preserved*, 35; Annie Scott Baxter, "Woodruff Residence, Erie, Erie County, Pennsylvania," HABS Report, PA-56 (Washington, D.C.: Library of Congress, 1936), 2.

[177] Dickson, *A Hundred Pennsylvania Buildings*, pl. 52; Stotz, *Architectural Heritage of Early Western Pennsylvania*, 132-34; Snyder, *Lancaster Architecture*, 20.

[178] For a plan, elevation, details, and photos of the Hendryx House, see Stotz, *Architectural Heritage of Early Western Pennsylvania*, 140-41.

[179] Quoted in Craig, ed., *The Federal Presence*, 53.

[180] Webster, *Philadelphia Preserved*, 7, 27, 73; Tatum, *Penn's Great Town*, 55, 69, 174, pl. 61; Matthew Baigell, "John Haviland in Philadelphia, 1818-1826," *Journal of the Society of Architectural Historians* 25 (October 1966): 203-4.

[181] Cullum, the son of one of the church's first members (Meadville merchant Arthur Cullum), later became a general and designed Fort Sumter in Charleston, South Carolina, where the first shots of the Civil War were fired when Confederate forces bombarded the fortress in April 1861. Earl Morse Wilbur, *A Historical Sketch of the Independent Congregational Church, Meadville, Pennsylvania, 1825-1900* (Meadville, Pa. By the author, 1903), 9, 31-34. Dickson, *A Hundred Pennsylvania Buildings*, pl. 48. For plans, elevations, and details of the church, see Stotz, *Early Architecture of Western Pennsylvania*, 234-35.

[182] Stotz, *Early Architecture of Western Pennsylvania*, 246; Annie Scott Baxter, "Free Methodist Church, Pleasantville, Venango County, Pennsylvania," HABS Report PA-531 (Washington, D.C.: Library of Congress, 1937), 1; Idem, "First Baptist Church, North East, Erie County, Pennsylvania," HABS Report PA- 513 (Washington, D.C.: Library of Congress, 1936), 1.

[183] Dickson, *A Hundred Pennsylvania Buildings*, pl. 48. Because the term "Unitarian" was new and subject to attack from older, more conservative sects, Meadville's Unitarians from their beginnings in 1825 used the more acceptable term, congregational, for their church title. Wilbur, *Historical Sketch of the Independent Congregational Church*, 9-16.

[184] Strickland's revival repertory was not restricted to only Greek and Gothic; it included Roman, Renaissance, Egyptian, Saracenic, and, if one includes his design for Independence Hall's steeple, colonial. Gilchrist, *William Strickland*, 23, 34-35. For a discussion of Strickland's design for St. Stephen's and an 1829 engraving of the church, see Tatum, *Penn's Great Town*, 82, pl. 81.

[185] Early, *Romanticism and American Architecture*, 87.

[186] Phoebe B. Stanton, *The Gothic Revival and American Church Architecture* (Baltimore: Johns Hopkins University Press, 1968), 3-29; Collins, *Changing Ideals in Modern Architecture*, 106-10.

[187] Stanton *The Gothic Revival and American Church Architecture*, 91-114; Richard J. Webster, "Church of St. James the Less," in Sewell, ed., *Philadelphia: Three Centuries of American Art*, 325-26.

[188] Stanton, *The Gothic Revival and American Church Architecture*, 115-25; Constance M. Greiff, *John Notman, Architect: 1810-1865* (Philadelphia: Athenaeum of Philadelphia, 1979), 27-28; Mrs. Greiff illustrates Notman's drawings and relates St. Mark's history on 132-42.

[189] Collins, *Changing Ideals in Modern Architecture*, 107-8.

[190] Dickson, *A Hundred Pennsylvania Buildings*, pl. 55.

[191] James D. Van Trump, "St. Peter's, Pittsburgh, by John Notman," *Journal of the Society of Architectural Historians* 15 (May 1956): 19-23; Greiff, *John Notman, Architect*, 175-76.

[192] Over the fluted pilasters on the Union Church's main (west) entrance are some hand-carved symbols of articles used in communion, but they are not architecturally Gothic. In sparsely populated communities it was not unusual for Reformed and Lutheran congregations to join in erecting a church building which they then shared, but with each congregation having its own minister. Wapwallopen overlooks the North Branch of the Susquehanna River in Conygham Township, Luzerne County; in 1833 the community was called Hellerstown after Isaac Heller, an early settler. Bettie Toal Morrissey, "Union Reformed and Lutheran Church, Wapwallopen, Luzerne County, Pennsylvania," HABS Report PA-219 (Washington, D.C.: Library of Congress, 1936), 1-2.

[193] Quoted in Negley T. Teeters and John D. Shearer, *The Prison at Philadelphia: Cherry Hill* (New York: Columbia University Press, 1957), 59.

[194] Eastern State Penitentiary's sources may have been the thirteenth-century Harlech Castle in Wales and/or the 1814 Worcester, England, prison. Richard J. Webster, "Eastern State Penitentiary (Cherry Hill)," in Sewell, ed., *Philadelphia: Three Centuries of American Art*, 258; Matthew Eli Baigell, "John Haviland" (Ph.D. dissertation, University of Pennsylvania, 1965), 36, 214-54. For illustrations of nineteenth-century aerial prints of the prison, see Theo B. White, ed., *Philadelphia Architecture in the Nineteenth Century* (Philadelphia: University of Pennsylvania Press for Philadelphia Art Alliance, 1953), 25, pl. 23; Tatum, *Penn's Great Town*, 179, pl. 77.

[195] Dickens, *American Notes and Pictures from Italy*, 100-101.

[196] Quoted in David J. Rothman, *The Discovery of the Asylum: Social Order and Disorder in the New Republic* (Boston: Little, Brown and Company, 1971), 83.

[197] Tatum, *Penn's Great Town*, 79-80; Norman B. Johnston, "John Haviland, Jailor to the World," *Journal of the Society of Architectural Historians* 23 (May 1964): 101-5.

[198] The standard work on this exotic nineteenth-century style is Richard G. Carrott, *The Egyptian Revival: Its Sources, Monuments, and Meaning, 1808-1858* (Berkeley, University of California Press, 1978). Carrott discusses Haviland's "Tombs" on pages 146-92 and Walter's Debtors' Wing on page 118.

[199]These two significant works are Vivant Denon, *Voyages dans la Basse et la Haute Egypte pendant les campagnes du general Bonaparte*, 3 vols. (Paris, 1802) and *Description de l'Egypte, ou, Recueil des observations et des recherches qui ont ete faites en Egypte pendant l'expedition de l'arme francaise, publie par les ordres de Sa Majeste l'empereur Napoleon le Grand*, 21 vols. (Paris: Commisson des monuments d'Egypte, 1809-1828). Carrott, *The Egyptian Revival*, 25, 40 (n.18), 41 (n.19).

[200]One of the country's first archaeologically based Egyptian Revival buildings, the Debtors' Wing's facade was drawn from the Temple of the Sun on Island of Elephantine, Egypt, which was illustrated in *Description de l'Egypte*, 1, pl. 35. Carrott, *The Egyptian Revival*, 118, pl. 105; idem, "The Neo-Egyptian Style in American Architecture," *The Magazine Antiques* 90 (October 1966): 483; Tatum, *Penn's Great Town*, 85, 179.

[201]Unfortunately this building burned in 1976. Its architect is unknown. Webster, *Philadelphia Preserved*, 314, 331, 379 (n.51); Carrott, *The Egyptian Revival*, 71, 110, pl. 77.

[202]Strickland designed the Mikveh Israel Synagogue on Cherry Street in 1825, and Walter designed the Synagogue Beth Israel on Crown Street in 1849. Both synagogues and the gatehouse are now gone. Gilchrist, *William Strickland*, 62-63, pl. 18B; Tatum, *Penn's Great Town*, 86; Carrott, *The Egyptian Revival*, 94, pl. 76; Webster, *Philadelphia Preserved*, 181.

[203]J. C. Hoxie and S. D. Button (working as Hoxie and Button) have been credited for the design of the brownstone Odd Fellows Cemetery Gatehouse, which was built circa 1849 in Philadelphia's northern outskirts, north of Girard College. They are cited as its architects on page 229 of *The Stranger's Guide in Philadelphia to All Public Buildings, Places of Amusement, Commercial, Benevolent, & Religious Institutions & Churches* (Philadelphia: Lindsay & Blakiston, 1860). Philadelphia architectural historian Robert Ennis, however, has seen Thomas U. Walter's drawings of the building; Hoxie and Button probably were its builders. An eighty-one-foot-high battered tower surmounted the gatehouse's center building whose recessed entrance porch with papyrus columns in antis was very similar to that of Walter's Debtors' Wing. The center building contained a chapel, offices, and the superintendent's living quarters; lateral wings served as carriage ways and pedestrian entrances. The Independent Order of Odd Fellows abandoned the cemetery in 1907, when it disinterred the bodies and removed them to its new cemetery in the city's Fox Chase section. Interview with Robert Ennis, March 30, 1990; Richard J. Webster, "Stephen D. Button: Italianate Stylist" (M.A. thesis, University of Delaware, 1963), 17, 77, 119 (n.2); Historical Society of Pennsylvania, Philadelphia, Campbell Scrapbook, vol. 19.

[204]The quoted words are those of architect James Gallier Sr., who opposed use of the Egyptian style for cemetery gatehouses in an 1836 *North American Review* article. Carrott, *The Egyptian Revival*, 83-84.

[205]Webster, *Philadelphia Preserved*, 211-12, 224, 234, 269, 368 (n.9).

[206]Carver and Hall of Philadelphia were the architects of the Charles Evans Cemetery Gatehouse. John E. Carver also executed the Ecclesiological Society's plans for Philadelphia's

Church of St. James the Less. The cemetery's original Gothic Revival chapel, designed in 1862 by John M. Gries of Philadelphia, is now gone. Charles Evans was a Reading attorney who bequeathed a small endowment and the cemetery's initial twenty-five acres in 1846; the cemetery now contains 127 acres. Morton L. Montgomery, comp., *History of Reading, Pennsylvania, and the Anniversary Proceedings of the Sesqui-Centennial, 1748-1898* (Reading, Pa.: Times Book Print, 1898), 44; Raymond W. Albright, *Two Centuries of Reading, Pa., 1748-1948: A History of the County Seat of Berks County* (Reading, Pa.: Historical Society of Berks County, 1948), 181; Harry G. Schalck, "Reading's Architecture," Philadelphia Chapter, Society of Architectural Historians, Reading Tour, 22 October 1983.

[207] Incorporated in 1844 with one hundred acres in the city's Lawrenceville section, the cemetery's acreage has since trebled. In addition to Chislett's Butler Street entrance is the 1887 Penn Avenue gateway designed by Dull & Macomb. The cemetery company acknowledges its park and sculpture-garden status and provides a map and guide for visitors. Dickson, *A Hundred Pennsylvania Buildings*, pl. 57; Kidney, *Landmark Architecture*, 218.

[208] The book, co-authored with John J. Smith, is *Two Hundred Designs for Cottages and Villas* (Philadelphia: Carey & Hart, 1846). For an excellent examination of the domestic reform movement and its effect on domestic architecture, see Clifford Edward Clark Jr., *The American Family Home, 1800-1960* (Chapel Hill: University of North Carolina Press, 1986), 3-36; idem, "Domestic Architecture as an index to Social History: The Romantic Revival and the Cult of Domesticity in America, 1840-1870," *Journal of Interdisciplinary History* 7 (Summer 1976): 33-56.

[209] Until a comprehensive examination of the Gothic Revival in the United States is written, three good but limited studies, all drawing heavily on New York and New England examples, are William H. Pierson Jr., *American Buildings and Their Architects: Technology and the Picturesque, The Corporate and the Early Gothic Styles* (Garden City, N.Y.: Doubleday & Co., 1978); Wayne Andrews, *American Gothic: Its Origins, Its Trials, Its Triumphs* (New York: Random House, 1975); Calder Loth and Julius Trousdale Sadler Jr., *The Only Proper Style: Gothic Architecture in America* (Boston: New York Graphic Society. 1975).

[210] Heathside Cottage also illustrates the arbitrary distinction between Gothic Revival cottages and houses. If size alone defines a cottage, then the story-and-a-half Heathside Cottage is indeed a cottage. If architectural simplicity defines a cottage, then Heathside Cottage, a sophisticated expression of the Gothic Revival style, is more than a cottage. Downing tends to call small, simpler dwellings cottages and larger, more sophisticated dwellings houses. See Andrew Jackson Downing, *Cottage Residences* (New York: John Wiley and Son, 1873; reprint ed., New York: Dover Publications, 1981); idem, *The Architecture of Country Houses* (New York: D. Appleton & Co., 1850; reprint ed., New York: Dover Publications, 1969). Heathside Cottage is discussed briefly and illustrated in Kidney, *Landmark Architecture*, 173, 190.

[211] The late Carroll L. V. Meeks argued that picturesque eclecticism was the unifying factor in nineteenth-century architecture. There are three phases of picturesque eclecticism: symbolic eclecticism between approximately 1790 and 1860, synthetic eclecticism between approximately 1860 and 1890, and creative eclecticism between approximately 1890 and 1914. Its

five qualities are variety, movement, irregularity, intricacy, and roughness. Alan Gowans follows the same pattern with differently named eras and slightly different dates. The Early Victorian period extends from circa 1820 to circa 1855; the High Victorian period between circa 1855 and circa 1885; the Late Victorian period between circa 1885 and circa 1920. Professor Meeks argued his case in "Picturesque Eclecticism," *The Art Bulletin* 32 (September 1950): 226-35, and *The Railroad Station: An Architectural History* (New Haven: Yale University Press, 1956), 2-25. Professor Gowans presents his thesis in *Images of American Living*, 287-418.

[212]John F. Singer's firm, Singer, Nimick and Company, manufactured all types of steel. He began building his house in 1863 and completed it in 1869, only three years before his death in 1872 at the age of fifty-six. John D. Milner, "John F. Singer House," HABS Report PA-433 (Washington, D.C.: Library of Congress, 1963), 1-5; Kidney, *Landmark Architecture*, 339; James D. Van Trump, *Life and Architecture in Pittsburgh* (Pittsburgh: Pittsburgh History & Landmarks Foundation, 1983), 258.

[213]Illustrated in Schiffer, *Survey of Chester County, Pennsylvania, Architecture*, 166.

[214]Pierson, *American Buildings and Their Builders: Technology and the Picturesque*, 416-22

[215]Mahlon Mercur's house stands at 200 Chestnut Street, Towanda. Mercur was a local entrepreneur. He was among the group of investors who acquired from the Commonwealth the North Branch Canal, which never became a technical or financial success, and built the Pennsylvania and New York Railroad along its right of way. The Lehigh Valley Railroad later made this line part of its operation. Mercur also built the short State Line and Sullivan Railroad to carry coal from his mines in Barclay, Bradford County, to Towanda. *The Daily Review* (Towanda, Pa.), 17 October 1980, 1, 3. The late Ashton Merrill wrote this article after extensively researching the history of the house and its occupants.

[216]Gowans, *Images of American Living*, 316-19. Gowans' chapter, (316-27) on the Italianate manner remains the best essay yet on this picturesque expression.

[217]Greiff, *John Notman, Architect*, 211-15.

[218]Because he corresponded with the congregation and visited the site during construction, Joseph C. Hoxie is commonly cited as the architect of York's First Presbyterian Church, but a drawing of the church's front elevation and steeple, archived in the Historical Society of York County, are signed by Button. Joe K. Kindig III correctly identifies Button as the church's architect in *Architecture in York County*, (page 25) but erroneously identifies Hoxie as John Hoxie. See also Dickson, *A Hundred Pennsylvania Buildings*, pl. 63; *The York Gazette*, 16 October 1860, 2; Joseph C. Hoxie to the Committee of the Presbyterian Congregation of the Borough of York, Pa., 26 November 1859, York County Historical Society, York, Pa.; George H. Morgan, ed., *Annals of Harrisburg* (Harrisburg: George A. Brooks, 1858), 278-85.

[219]S. D. Button was the architect of the brownstone First Baptist Church of Philadelphia. Begun in October 1853 and dedicated in May 1856, the church was demolished in 1898 after the congregation moved to Seventeenth and Sansom Streets. The United Gas Improvement

(UGI) Building now occupies the church's former site, the northwest corner of Broad and Arch Streets. Webster, "Stephen D. Button, Italianate Stylist," 79; *Public Ledger* (Philadelphia, Pa.), 7 October 1853, 2, 23 June 1898, 12.

[220] Contemporaries called the Church of the Holy Trinity "Norman, although it is sometimes called the Venetian, Romanesque, or Lombardic Style." They called the Presbyterian churches in York and Harrisburg "Romanesque," and the Baptist church in Philadelphia "Romanesque or Byzantine" and "Norman Gothic." Greiff, *John Notman, Architect*, 214; *The York Gazette*, 22 January 1861, 2; Morgan, *Annals of Harrisburg*, 280; *Ballou's Pictorial Drawing-Room Companion*, 12 January 1856, 24; Thompson Westcott, *The Official Guide Book to Philadelphia* (Philadelphia: Porter and Coates, 1875), 261. The quotation is from *Ballou's Pictorial Drawing-Room Companion*.

[221] Richard J. Webster, "West Arch Street Presbyterian Church (Arch Street Presbyterian Church)," in Sewell, ed., *Philadelphia: Three Centuries of American Art*, 338-39.

[222] It has been claimed that two priests, Fathers Mariano Maller and John B. Tornatore, designed the Cathedral's initial plan, but by 1847 newspapers were citing Napoleon LeBrun as the architect. Notman had replaced LeBrun by 1852 and seems to have been primarily responsible for the Cathedral's present appearance. The bishop reinstated LeBrun later, but the date is unknown. Greiff, *John Notman, Architect*, 31-32, 177-78; Webster, *Philadelphia Preserved*, 124; White, *Philadelphia Architecture*, 27-28, pls. 38-39.

[223] The church's entry door has been changed from its original appearance, and in 1930 West Chester architect Ralph Minich added a wooden Tuscan tetrastyle portico to the front. Alice Kent Schooler, *Livable West Chester: An Architectural Overview* (West Chester: Chester County Historical Society, 1985), 42; Bart Anderson and Marion Morton, "Baptist Church of West Chester," HABS Report PA-1191 (Washington, D.C.: Library of Congress, 1958, 1975), 1, 8; Harold N. Cooledge Jr., *Samuel Sloan, Architect of Philadelphia, 1815-1884* (Philadelphia: University of Pennsylvania Press, 1986), 193..

[224] Quoted in Robert C. Smith, *John Notman and the Athenaeum Building* (Philadelphia: Athenaeum of Philadelphia, 1951), 14.

[225] Notman modeled the Athenaeum after Sir Charles Barry's Manchester Athenaeum (1836-39), and the Travellers' Club (1829-32) and Reform Club (1839) in London. Greiff, *John Notman, Architect*, 23, 99-102; Richard J. Webster, "The Athenaeum of Philadelphia," in Sewell, ed., *Philadelphia: Three Centuries of American Art*, 322-23.

[226] The Athenaeum is illustrated in White, ed., *Philadelphia Architecture*, pls. 37-39; Dickson, *A Hundred Pennsylvania Buildings*, pl. 59; Webster, *Philadelphia Preserved*, 103.

[227] Tatum, *Penn's Great Town*, 94-95, 186. For an illustration of LeBrun's and Runge's drawing showing the marble finish, see Ibid., pl. 96. For a discussion of the building, an illustration of an original interior section, and a late-nineteenth-century photograph, see Richard J. Webster, "American Academy of Music (Academy of Music)," in Sewell, ed., *Philadelphia: Three Centuries of American Art*, 348.

[228] Both buildings are now gone. They are illustrated and briefly discussed in Dickson, *A Hundred Pennsylvania Buildings*, pl. 62; Kidney, *Landmark Architecture*, 46-47. By winning five mid-century courthouse commissions, Sloan emerged as the state's primary promoter of the Italianate as a civic style. In addition to Lycoming County's building, he designed courthouses for Delaware County in Media, 1849; Lancaster County in Lancaster, 1852-54; Westmoreland County in Greensburg, 1853-55; and Clinton County in Lock Haven, 1867-69. Either by his commissions or his writings, he influenced the design of four others: Clarion County Courthouse in Clarion, Columbia County Courthouse in Bloomsburg, Jefferson County Courthouse in Brookville, and Montour County Courthouse in Danville. Cooledge, *Samuel Sloan*, 16-18, 43, 46, 79-80, 156, 173, 187, 209, 221-22, 124-25 (n. 10).

[229] Asher Benjamin's 1797 *Country Builder's Assistant* was the first book on architecture published in America. These early works rarely provided full plans and elevations, but focused primarily on carpentry, neoclassicism and the classical revivals, and were few in number. Between 1800 and 1840, for example, twenty editions of building guide books were published. This number tripled in the next twenty years and reached fifty-eight new volumes in the 1870s. Frank J. Roos Jr., *Bibliography of Early American Architecture: Writings on Architecture Constructed before 1860 in Eastern and Central United States* (Urbana: University of Illinois Press, 1968), 11-12; Clark, "Domestic Architecture as an Index to Social History" 35.

[230] Dell Upton, "Pattern Books and Professionalism: Aspects of the Transformation of Domestic Architecture in America, 1800-1860," *Winterthur Portfolio* 19 (Autumn 1984): 149-51. This is an excellent essay on a complex subject.

[231] Gowans, *Images of American Living*, 321.

[232] Alverthorpe, the home of Philadelphia gentleman Joshua Francis Fisher, was demolished in the late 1930s. The Kennedy Mansion was the home of John Kennedy, owner of an extensive lime works in Port Kennedy. The National Park Service restored the house in the mid-1980s. Greiff, *John Notman, Architect*, 34, 164-66; Dickson, *A Hundred Pennsylvania Buildings*, pls. 60, 60A; Moses Auge, *Lives of the Eminent Dead and Biographical Notices of Prominent Citizens of Montgomery County, Pennsylvania* (Norristown, Pa.: By the author, 1879), 145.

[233] Baer's house stands at 141 East Orange Street in Lancaster, and Parsons's house is at 304 York Avenue in Towanda. Both men were in publishing, Baer as a partner in the publishing firm of John Baer's Sons, and Parsons as a publisher of the weekly *Bradford Argus*. The architects of these houses are unknown. Snyder, *Lancaster Architecture*, 25, *The Daily Review* (Towanda, Pa.), 4 May 1981, 3.

[234] Cooledge, *Samuel Sloan*, 212.

[235] Dickson, *A Hundred Pennsylvania Buildings*, pl. 61.

[236] Two Italianate-trimmed Georgian houses in the Ridge and Valley Region are the circa-1860 Iddings-Baldridge House in Milesburg, Centre County, and the 1854 Mackey House in Lock Haven, Clinton County. To each of these brick gable-roof houses with center

halls, builders added bracketed eaves, frieze windows, and boldly consoled hoods over round-arch entrances. Because of their similarity, it is possible that the same man, Henry Hipple of Lock Haven, had a role in designing both of them. Hipple is recorded as having helped L. A. Mackey design his house on Lock Haven's East Water Street. Mackey was one of that town's early leading citizens. His many roles included serving as the first secretary-treasurer of the West Branch Boom Company, president of the Bald Eagle Valley Railroad Company, and the first mayor of the City of Lock Haven. Austin C. Iddings was a Centre County land speculator and contractor. Birchenall et al., *Historic Buildings of Centre County*, 178-81; Dean R. Wagner, ed., *Historic Lock Haven: An Architectural Survey* (Lock Haven, Pa.: Clinton County Historical Society), 36.

[237] Upton, "Pattern Books and Professionalism," 131.

[238] In *The Buildings of Main Street: A Guide to American Commercial Architecture* (Washington, D.C.: Preservation Press of National Trust for Historic Preservation, 1987), Richard Longstreth categorizes commercial buildings by facade composition rather than style, but among his illustrations of the most common type, the two-part commercial block, the Italianate is the most common style for the nineteenth-century examples. See pages 24-39.

[239] For examples of architectural iron works catalogs, see Daniel D. Badger, *Badger's Illustrated Catalogue of Cast-Iron Architecture*, with an introduction by Margot Gayle (New York: Baker & Godwin, 1865; reprint ed., New York: Dover Publications, 1981); *Victorian Ironwork: A Catalogue by J. B. Wickersham*, with an introduction by Margot Gayle (Philadelphia: Athenaeum Library of Nineteenth Century America, 1977); *Buffalo Eagle Iron Works Co. Catalogue of Architectural Designs* (Buffalo: Clapp, Matthews & Co's Steam Printing House, 1859) in Diane S. Waite, ed., *Architectural Elements: The Technological Revolution* (Princeton, N.J.: Pyne Press, [ca. 1976]); *Philadelphia Architectural Iron Co. Catalog* (Philadelphia, 1972) in ibid.

[240] Because pieces of the sidewalk were being stolen, the owner had to dismantle the sidewalk in 1979. Part of it has been installed in the floor of an enclosed rear porch (conservatory) of the Ebenezer Maxwell House (PA-1098) in Philadelphia's Germantown. Webster, *Philadelphia Preserved*, 293, 358.

[241] Collins, *Changing Ideals in Modern Architecture*, 118.

[242] Meeks, *The Railroad Station*, 22-23; Gowans, *Images of American Living*, 287-88; Henry-Russell Hitchcock, *Architecture: Nineteenth and Twentieth Centuries* (Baltimore: Penguin Books, 1958), 132.

[243] The first mid-century mansarded mansions, built in 1849-51, were the T. H. Hope House in London from the designs of P. C. Dusillion, and the Hart M. Shiff House in New York from the designs of Detlef Lienau. Hitchcock, *Architecture*. 732-33.

[244] Although City Hall was not officially completed until 1901, city functionaries began to move into offices in 1881, and the tower, which underwent significant design changes from

the initial draft, was completed in the mid-1890s. The first building to rise above Alexander Calder's statue of William Penn atop City Hall's tower was One Liberty Place, a sixty-story steel-and-glass office tower from the designs of Chicago architect Helmut Jahn. One Liberty Place opened at Seventeenth and Chestnut Streets in the fall of 1987, rising 945 feet to its peak, 398 feet above City Hall. Evaluations of City Hall are in Dickson, *A Hundred Pennsylvania Buildings*, pl. 71; Tatum, *Penn's Great Town*, 109, 193-94; John Maass, "Philadelphia City Hall: Monster or Masterpiece?" *Journal of the American Institute of Architects* 43 (February 1965): 23-30; Richard J. Webster, "Philadelphia City Hall (Public Buildings of the City of Philadelphia)" in Sewell, ed., *Philadelphia: Three Centuries of American Art*, 387-88. Its sculpture is discussed in George Gurney, "The Sculpture of City Hall," and "William Penn," in Nicholas B. Wainwright, ed., *Sculpture of a City: Philadelphia's Treasures in Bronze and Stone* (New York: Walker Publishing Co., 1974), 94-103, 104-9.

[245] Whiffen and Koeper, *American Architecture*, 124.

[246] Dickson, *A Hundred Pennsylvania Buildings*, pl. 72.

[247] Webster, *Philadelphia Preserved*, 295.

[248] For brief discussions of the academy, see Dickson, *A Hundred Pennsylvania Buildings*, pls. 77, 77A; George E. Thomas, "Pennsylvania Academy of the Fine Arts," in Sewell, ed., *Philadelphia: Three Centuries of American Art*, 389-91.

[249] An exhibition of Furness' work at the Philadelphia Museum of Art in spring 1974 did much to revive his reputation, as did the accompanying volume by James F. O'Gorman, *The Architecture of Frank Furness* (Philadelphia: Philadelphia Museum of Art, 1974), which includes a catalog of selected buildings by O'Gorman and George E. Thomas.

[250] Richardson began his career in New York in 1866, and moved to Brookline in suburban Boston in 1874. By the 1880s Richardson's peers recognized his greatness. In 1885, before Richardson had finished the Allegheny County Courthouse and Jail and the more highly acclaimed Marshall Field Warehouse in Chicago, a poll of architects included five of Richardson's buildings among America's ten best buildings. Henry-Russell Hitchcock suggests that Richardson was the world's greatest architect in the early 1880s and that Richardson probably sensed it. James F. O'Gorman, *H. H. Richardson: Architectural Forms for an American Society* (Chicago: University of Chicago Press, 1987), 16, 49; Hitchcock, *The Architecture of H. H. Richardson and His Times* (Cambridge: MIT Press, 1966), 248.

[251] The commissioners reached their decision, January 31, 1884, and announced the architect of the county's third courthouse in February. The state legislature formed Allegheny County in September 1788, but its first courthouse, a small, squarish brick Georgian building with a slender cupola, was not ready for occupancy until about 1800. The county replaced it forty years later with a domed classical revival, sandstone building (1835-41) from the designs of John Chislett. It also stood approximately forty years until it burned in May 1882, necessitating the architectural competition that Richardson won. His competitors were Andrew Peeples of Pittsburgh, William W. Boyington of Chicago, Elijah E. Myers of Detroit, and John Ord of

Philadelphia. Peeples, however, missed the deadline for a final submission of drawings and was disqualified. James D. Van Trump, *Majesty of the Law: The Court Houses of Allegheny County* (Pittsburgh: Pittsburgh History & Landmarks Foundation, 1988), 3-5, 17-19, 29-30, 36-38, 59; see pages 51-55 for the architects' competition drawings.

[252]Mariana Griswold Van Rensselaer, *Henry Hobson Richardson and His Works* (Boston: Houghton Mifflin and Company, 1888; reprint ed., New York: Dover Publications, 1969), 90-91; O'Gorman, *H. H. Richardson*, 51.

[253]Van Rensselaer, *Henry Hobson Richardson*, 93.

[254]O'Gorman, *H. H. Richardson*, 52.

[255]There is no indictable evidence that Olds consciously copied Richardson's building, but to dismiss the near-duplication as coincidence severely strains one's credulity. The Blair factory stands at the southwest corner of Sixth and Penn Streets in Huntingdon. For a photograph, Olds's partial elevation, and a discussion of the building, see Shedd, *An Architectural Study of the Ancient Borough of Huntingdon*, 119-20. In the 1880s, Olds had his office in State College, where he was designing buildings for Pennsylvania State College (now University). Of his Penn State work only Old Botany, an 1887 brick and limestone building, remains without significant alteration. Sometime after designing Blair's factory, Olds moved to Wilkes-Barre and formed a partnership with F. Willard Puckey. Olds was born in Circleville, Ohio in 1851, and died in Wilkes-Barre in 1912. Birchenall et al., *Historic Buildings of Centre County*, 96-98; Vito J. Sgromo and Michael Lewis, *Wilkes-Barre Architecture: 1860 to 1890* (Wilkes-Barre, Pa.: Wyoming Historical and Geological Society, 1983), 21-22.

[256]James L. Garvin, "Mail-Order House Plans and American Victorian Architecture," *Winterthur Portfolio* 16 (Winter 1981): 309-334.

[257]Gage's house, unaltered except for a change in paint color and roofing material, stands at 317 Penn Street, Huntingdon. Shedd, *An Architectural Study of the Ancient Borough of Huntingdon*, 73.

[258]*Grey Towers: Preliminary Historic Structure Report* (Albany, N.Y.: Preservation/Design Group for U.S. Department of Agriculture, Forest Service, 1978), 1, 10. There are a number of historical monographs on architects and clients, but few on clients by clients. An interesting essay on the responsibilities of the client by one who was client but not owner of the proposed Yale Center for British Art (from the designs of Louis Kahn, 1969-74) is Jules David Prown, "On Being a Client," *Journal of the Society of Architectural Historians* 42 (March 1983): 11-14.

[259]Pinchot and Hunt shared many interests, not the least being their francophilia. Their activities often overlapped. Both were associated with the Metropolitan Museum of Art since its beginnings in 1870, Pinchot as a contributor to its fund and Hunt as a founder, advisory architect, and late in his life architect of its entrance wing. Also, Pinchot was on the executive committee that superintended the erection of the Statue of Liberty, for which Hunt

designed the base. The Pinchot and Hunt families were also close. During the 1880s, Hunt's daughter Catherine was the best friend of Pinchot's daughter Antoinette and for a period in 1885 was engaged to Pinchot's son Gifford, who in the twentieth century would twice serve as governor of Pennsylvania. Hunt's work for the Vanderbilts began in 1878, when he designed William K. Vanderbilt's tastemaking chateau on New York's Fifth Avenue. His last two great works for the family were Breakers (1892-95), the gargantuan Renaissance Revival "cottage" of Cornelius Vanderbilt II in Newport, Rhode Island, and George W. Vanderbilt's Biltmore (1889-95) in Ashville, North Carolina, where ironically Gifford Pinchot began his career as a forester. *Grey Towers*, p. 10; Paul R. Baker, *Richard Morris Hunt* (Cambridge: MIT Press, 1980), 274-86, 366-72, 415-28, 422-43; Morrison H. Heckscher, "Hunt and the Metropolitan Museum of Art," in Susan R. Stein, ed., *The Architecture of Richard Morris Hunt* (Chicago: University of Chicago Press, 1986), 173-85; *Grey Towers, Milford, Pa.: Final Historic Structure Report, Landscape Report, and Management Plan* (West Chester, Pa.: John Milner Associates for U.S. Department of Agriculture, Forest Service, 1980), 32.

[260]James and Mary Pinchot used the house only as a summer residence, spending their winters in New York. It would not be until World War II that it would be used year round, by Gifford and Cornelia Pinchot. *Grey Towers*, 11.

[261]Hunt had spent ten years in Paris studying at the Ecole des Beaux Arts and working in ateliers, had traveled extensively in France, and possessed many French architectural books. After 1880 he worked primarily in the French Renaissance style, designing only two other versions of medieval chateaux besides Grey Towers: Crumwold Hall (1889) for Archibald Rogers in Hyde Park, New York, and Joseph R. Busk's house (1891) in Newport, Rhode Island. Baker, *Richard Morris Hunt*, 24-49, 56-60. 337-41; David Chase, "Superb Privacies: The Later Domestic Commissions of Richard Morris Hunt, 1878-1895," in Stein, ed., *The Architecture of Richard Morris Hunt*, 151-71.

[262]Lafayette's wife inherited LaGrange in 1799. Four early nineteenth-century views of the house appear in Agnes Mongan, *Harvard Honors Lafayette* (Cambridge: Fogg Art Museum, 1976), 136-37. For examples of views of the country house in lithographs and on Staffordshire ware that were available in the United States after Lafayette's acclaimed visit in 1824-25, see Marian Klamkin, *The Return of Lafayette, 1824-25* (New York: Charles Scribner's Sons, 1975), 54.

[263]James W. Pinchot died in 1908 and his widow six years later. Gifford Pinchot established his legal residence at Grey Towers in 1910 to pursue his political career. Before then his legal residence had been New York City, but he concluded that New York was crowded with able and ambitious political figures and that he had more opportunities in Pennsylvania. After his mother's death, Gifford shared management of the estate with his brother Amos. The estate was not legally settled until 1922, but the brothers apparently agreed long before that that Amos and his wife would occupy the Forester's House and Gifford and his wife the main house. *Grey Towers*, 8; *Grey Towers, Milford, Pa.*, 54.

[264]Pinchot, for example, successfully resisted his wife's desire to have Allyn Cox finish the dining room ceiling with a decorative painting but evidently offered no resistance to other

changes, including the installation of large late-eighteenth-century Dutch landscape murals. He took greater interest in the library building that would house his political papers, but again let his wife consult with the architect, restricting his involvement to selecting the smaller of two proposals and asking that the doorway be given a smaller scale than initially designed. Cornelia Pinchot was responsible for all of the correspondence with Aldrich. *Grey Towers, Milford, Pa.*, 61-64, 91.

[265] As the great-granddaughter of industrialist-philanthropist Peter Cooper, granddaughter of New York mayor Edward Cooper, and daughter of Lloyd Bryce, congressman, publisher, and ambassador to the Netherlands, Cornelia Bryce Pinchot was reared in a privileged and political environment. As both a candidate (in three unsuccessful campaigns for Congress and an abortive attempt to succeed her husband as governor in 1934) and an advocate, she promoted a wide range of progressive causes, including birth control, women's trade unions, and restrictions on child labor. Her ideas were her own, not her husband's. She was thirty-three and he forty-nine when they married in 1913. John W. Furlow Jr., "Cornelia Bryce Pinchot: Feminism in the Post-Suffrage Era," *Pennsylvania History* 43 (October 1976): 329-46.

[266] Her contracting with local workmen often slowed her projects. She rejected Aldrich's recommended New York artisan for installing the library windows because his estimate was too high. It took her six months to find a local cabinetmaker, whose estimate was "most ridiculously low," but who did not complete the job for another year. *Grey Towers, Milford, Pa.*, 57-58, 112 (n. 28).

[267] Ibid., 60-61, 64.

[268] The building's name reflects both father's and son's love of fishing. The father, Gifford Pinchot, wrote a book on the subject *Just Fishing Talk* (New York: Telegraph Press, 1936), and the son Gifford Bryce Pinchot was so fascinated by fishing that the family nicknamed him "Mr. Fish." *Grey Towers: National Historic Landmark and Pinchot Institute for Conservation Studies* (U.S. Forest Service brochure, 1978), n.p.

[269] Aldrich sent Mrs. Pinchot his first set of blueprints in February 1923; they were discussing treatment of the building's forecourt as late as September 1925. *Grey Towers, Milford, Pa.*, 87-89.

[270] Cornelia Bryce Pinchot got the idea of an iron staircase from New York's Colony Club, which Delano and Aldrich designed in 1924 and of which she was a member. Aldrich recommended Stedman Naturalized Flooring, but she found it "hideous" and expensive and argued in favor of "a cement floor with some sort of big design in two or three colors, the way they have in the Italian museums." In the end they agreed on a brick and stone floor with a central stone diamond circumscribed by bricks within an elongated stone diamond filled with brick laid in a herringbone pattern. In 1964 the U.S. Forest Service replaced that floor with one of vinyl asbestos tile. Ibid., 90-93.

[271] Bottomley had prepared well for his career, having studied at the Ecole des Beaux Arts, Columbia University, and the American Academy in Rome. For contemporary and historical

discussions of his work, see Arthur Willis Colton, "The Work of William Lawrence Bottomley, Part I," *Architectural Record* 50 (November 1921): 339-57; idem, "The Work of William Lawrence Bottomley, Part II," ibid. 50 (December 1921): 418-41; William B. O'Neal and Christopher Weeks, *The Work of William Lawrence Bottomley in Richmond* (Charlottesville: University Press of Virginia, 1985), passim.

[272] Quoted in Colton, "The Work of William Lawrence Bottomley, Part I," 340.

[273] For years the concept of the Finger Bowl was thought to have been Polynesian, stemming from the Pinchots' 1929 South Seas voyage. *Grey Towers*, the 1978 brochure printed by the Forest Service, strongly implies this, noting that "this unique water table was built after the Pinchots returned from their trip to the South Seas Islands." In fact, however, Bottomley admitted that his sources were a Venetian painting of the school of Giorgione at the turn of the sixteenth century and the ornamental garden at Gamberaia. *Grey Towers, Milford, Pa.*, 130 (n. 232).

[274] Quoted in ibid., 95.

[275] Mrs. Pinchot's suggestions for a canopy ranged from apple trees at the corners of the dining area to "a regal swing of magnificent awnings—as though of emperors discussing questions of state," but nothing suggesting a "temple d'amour." She eventually adopted in late summer 1932 Bottomley's proposed planting of vines. Bottomley's initial $2,700 estimate for eight posts with carved figures shocked Mrs. Pinchot. Subsequent revisions of the schemes evidently did not sufficiently reduce the price. Ibid., 97-99.

[276] Evidently Mrs. Pinchot did not have a clearly understood contract with Bottomley. He apparently billed her for his drafting and office overhead costs plus his profit, or he charged both those fees and the customary 10 percent of the project's costs. Unfortunately Bottomley's explanation is not known and neither is the outcome of the dispute. The dispute apparently was settled quietly, and Bottomley suffered no loss of reputation among his colleagues. The American Institute of Architects elected him a Fellow in the A.I.A. in 1944. Ibid., 102; *New York Times*, 25 April 1951, sec. F, 25; Interview with Tony Wren, archivist, American Institute of Architects, 2 March 1990.

[277] Meeks, *The Railroad Station*, 14-18, 24; Gowans, *Images of American Living*, 363-86.

[278] Excellent essays on this era by Richard Guy Wilson appear in *The American Renaissance, 1876-1917* (New York: Brooklyn Museum, 1979), 11-110.

[279] For a discussion of Memorial Hall's design and architectural significance, see John Maass, *The Glorious Enterprise: The Centennial Exhibition of 1876 and Hermann H. J. Schwarzmann, Architect-in-Chief* (Watkins Glen, N.Y.: American Life Foundation for Institute for the Study of Universal History through Art and Artifacts, 1973), 32-55, 44-60. Paul Cret discusses aspects of the Federal Reserve Bank in "The New Building for the Federal Reserve Bank of Philadelphia," *The 3-C Book* 14 (September 1932): 35-36; "The New Federal Reserve Bank Building," ibid. 15 (February 1934): 168-69; "Sculptural Decoration on Our New Building," ibid. 16 (March 1935): 209-210. See also, Tatum, *Penn's Great Town*, 129, 201-2, pl. 134.

[280] Interestingly, John Wanamaker, who founded one of the country's first department stores and would soon erect one of its most tastefully ornate and consumer-oriented stores, justified building the Philadelphia Bourse in 1891 on the basis of consolidation. He compared the potential advantages of the Bourse's centralized trading to the centralized transit of the city's new rail depots, the Pennsylvania Railroad's Broad Street Station and the Reading Terminal, then under construction. *Builder, Decorator and Wood-Worker* 17 (September 1891): 1.

[281] An excellent discussion of the development and cultural significance of the department store before World War I is in Gunther Barth, *City People: The Rise of Modern City Culture in Nineteenth-Century America* (New York: Oxford University Press, 1980), 110-47. The most detailed biography of Wanamaker is Herbert Adams Gibbons, *John Wanamaker*, 2 vols. (New York: Harper & Brothers, 1926). A business autobiography that includes Wanamaker's New York store and a raft of interior and exterior photographs of the Philadelphia store is *Golden Book of Wanamaker Stores* (Philadelphia: John Wanamaker, 1911). See also "A Modern Department Store: The Construction and Equipment of the Philadelphia Wanamaker Store," *Architectural Record* 29 (March 1911): 277-88; Tatum, *Penn's Great Town*, 123, 200; Linda Kowall, "Original and Genuine, Unadulterated and Guaranteed!" *Pennsylvania Heritage* 15 (Winter 1989): 18-25.

[282] Quoted in Thomas S. Hines, *Burnham of Chicago: Architect and Planner* (New York: Oxford University Press, 1974), 303.

[283] As Postmaster General in President Benjamin Harrison's cabinet and an active reform-minded Republican, Wanamaker had more than a storekeeper's political clout. At the time, President Taft was facing a nomination battle with progressive Republicans led by former President Theodore Roosevelt, who was goaded by Gifford Pinchot of Grey Towers. This does not diminish, but instead enhances, Wanamaker's eminence as a mercantile prince and the role of the new store as his public palace. For a brief description of the dedication ceremonies, see ibid., 303-6.

[284] Webster, *Philadelphia Preserved*, 115, 132-33, 349.

[285] Coke in the late nineteenth century was known as the fuel for blast furnaces, not as a soft drink or narcotic. By 1885 Frick controlled about 80 percent of the nation's coke production, which led to his being brought into the Carnegie firm. Though once partners, Carnegie and Frick remained rivals, at least in Frick's mind, even after Carnegie had sold his interests in the Carnegie Steel Company. As a client, Frick proved to be a chronic complainer who was slow to pay his bills. Stevens, *Pennsylvania: Birthplace of a Nation*, 208, 212. The Burnham-Frick relationship is related in Hines, *Burnham of Chicago*, 298-302. The Frick Building, at Grant Street and Fifth Avenue in Pittsburgh, is discussed in Dickson, *A Hundred Pennsylvania Buildings*, pl. 83, and Kidney, *Landmark Architecture*, 166. The standard biography of Frick is George Harvey, *Henry Clay Frick, the Man* (New York: Charles Scribner's Sons, 1928).

[286] Van Trump, *Life and Architecture in Pittsburgh,* 245. In addition to its great scale and rich materials, the Frick Building's lobby has a large stained-glass window designed and executed by John LaFarge, a sculpture by Alexander P. Proctor, a protege of Augustus Saint-Gaudens,

and a bust of Frick. After blocking the Carnegie Building's natural light from the east with the Frick Building, Frick in 1906 erected the Allegheny Building to deprive Carnegie's building of light from the south as well. Franklin Toker, *Pittsburgh: An Urban Portrait* (University Park: Pennsylvania State University Press, 1986), 70-71; Hines, *Burnham of Chicago*, 298.

[287]The Oliver Building stands at Smithfield Street and Oliver Avenue in Pittsburgh; the city named Oliver Avenue in honor of Oliver after his death. Van Trump, *Life and Architecture in Pittsburgh*, 246; Kidney, *Landmark Architecture*, 156.

[288]For a review of all of Pennsylvania's capitol buildings, see John J. Snyder Jr., "Pennsylvania's Architectural Heritage: Statehouses and Capitols," *Pennsylvania Heritage* 7 (Summer 1981): 21-27. For a discussion and old photo of the Old Capitol, see Dickson, *A Hundred Pennsylvania Buildings*, pl. 44. See also, Julian Millard, "The First Capitol Buildings at Harrisburg," HABS Report PA-39 (Washington, D.C.: Library of Congress, 1936), 1-2.

[289]This was the second competition for the Capitol. The first one resulted in an incomplete building by an out-of-state architect, Henry Ives Cobb of Chicago. The second competition specified that the commission would be awarded to a Pennsylvania architect, but in other respects was so loosely defined that the Philadelphia Chapter of the American Institute of Architects notified members that participation in the competition would constitute unprofessional behavior. Yet, statewide, nine architects entered the competition. Of the competition's nine entrants, only seven are known. Four were from Philadelphia: William C. Hays, Joseph M. Huston, Addison Hutton, and Herman Miller; two were from Pittsburgh: Fred J. Osterling and Trimble & Stevens; and one, James H. Warner, was from Lancaster. Professor William R. Ware of Columbia University School of Architecture picked what he considered the four best entries, unranked, and on December 28, 1901, the Capitol Building Commission selected Huston's design as the winner. Huston, the son of an immigrant carpenter from Northern Ireland, worked in Frank Furness's office for a few years, until he graduated from Princeton University in 1892, when twenty-six. The next year he started his own architectural practice and political activity, which undoubtedly served him well in gaining the capitol commission. *The Pennsylvania Capitol: A Documentary History*, 2 vols. (Hopewell, N.J.: Heritage Studies, Inc. for Pennsylvania Capitol Preservation Committee, 1987), 1: chap. 2, 27-33, chap. 3, 60, chap. 9, 3-5; Dan G. Deibler and George E. Thomas, "Main Rotunda, Pennsylvania State Capitol," in O'Gorman et al., *Drawing toward Building*, 178-79.

[290]Ibid., 1: chap. 3. figs. 21, 29; 2: chap. 5, 13-40.

[291]Quoted in ibid., 1: chap. 3, 50.

[292]Ibid., 1: chap. 3, 49-50.

[293]Owen Wister, "The Keystone Crime: Pennsylvania's Graft-Cankered Capitol," *Everybody's Magazine* 17 (October 1907): 448.

[294]*New York Times*, 24 March 1907, sec. 3, 2.

[295] The election of William H. Berry, the Democratic mayor of Chester, as state treasurer on a fusion ticket in the fall of 1905 quickly exposed the scandal. The culprits knew the end was near; between Berry's election and his inauguration in the spring of 1906, the Capitol Building Commission approved payments to contractors totaling $3.9 million. On taking office, Berry stopped all payments and started his investigation. Ironically Berry was the last Democrat to win statewide office for over a quarter-century, until George Earle was elected governor in 1934. *The Pennsylvania Capitol*, 2: chap. 6, 1-14, 38-44.

[296] Cass Gilbert of New York supervised the architectural competition that Palmer, Hornbostel and Jones won in January 1914. After the city and county demolished fifty buildings to clear the site, contractors started their work in July 1915. In December 1917 Mayor Joseph G. Armstrong moved into his nearly empty mahogany-paneled office; the furniture, designed by the architects, had not yet arrived. Henry Hornbostel appears to have been the key figure in the architectural firm and in the City-County Building's design. Hornbostel was born in Brooklyn, New York, in 1867. He graduated from Columbia University in 1891, where he returned in 1897 as a member of the university's architectural faculty after four years at the Ecole des Beaux Arts. In 1904, a year after leaving Columbia, he won the competition for the Carnegie Institute of Technology campus, and for at least a decade he spent much time in Pittsburgh while maintaining his New York office. He eventually moved to Pittsburgh; he died in 1961. Prominent Pittsburgh buildings by him and his firms include: the 1912 Administration Building (PA-1172) and 1913 Machinery Hall Tower (PA-1174) at Carnegie Institute of Technology (now Carnegie-Mellon University), Rodef Shalom Temple (1906), Soldiers' and Sailors' Memorial (1907), Schenley Apartments (1922), and the University Club (1923). Alan B. Tinsdale, "City-County Building, 414 Grant Street, Pittsburgh, Allegheny County, Pennsylvania," HABS Report PA-5193 (Washington, D.C.: Library of Congress, 1981), 1-2; Van Trump, *Life and Architecture in Pittsburgh*, 130-34; Kidney, *Landmark Architecture*, 77, 168-69.

[297] The Northumberland National Bank stands at the northwest corner of Front Street and Wheatley Alley in Northumberland. A low one-story vault on the west side is the only significant interior and exterior change the building has experienced in the past sixty-five years. Similar banks have not been as fortunate. The 1915 Miners and Mechanics Bank (PA-5153) in Carbondale, Lackawanna County, for example, was demolished circa 1980. Its design is similar to the Northumberland bank: ashlar walls on the two street sides with a front of Roman Ionic columns in antis with wide Doric pilasters, but with a balustraded rather than a plain parapet. "Miners and Mechanics Bank, Carbondale, Pennsylvania," HABS Report PA-5153 (Washington, D.C.: Library of Congress, 1980), 1.

[298] The Girard Trust Corn Exchange Bank at the northwest corner of Broad and Chestnut Streets is now the Mellon Bank. Although McKim, Mead and White implicitly claimed the bank as their own by illustrating it with photos and drawings in *A Monograph of the Work of McKim, Mead & White, 1879-1915*, 5 vols. (New York: The Architectural Book Publishing Co. [1915]): 4, pls. 329-31, George Thomas has established Frank Furness as the bank's primary designer. Because of Furness's reputation for building what tastemakers at the turn of the

century considered grotesque buildings, the bank's directors dealt with Allen Evans, Furness's partner, who used Furness's sketches. The directors insisted that Evans work with McKim, Mead and White in the final designs, and that firm did alter the dome to its present hemisphere. The bank's design has been praised consistently since its completion. O'Gorman, *The Architecture of Frank Furness*, 66-68; George E. Thomas, *Masterpieces of Finance* (exhibit brochure, Pennsylvania Academy of the Fine Arts, 1986); "Recent Bank Buildings of the United States," *Architectural Record* 25 (January 1909): 8, 20-21; Tatum *Penn's Great Town*, 124, 200-1, pl. 132.

[299] Because John Pitcairn, a founder of Pittsburgh Plate Glass Company and prime mover of the Bryn Athyn Cathedral, and his son Raymond insisted that the cathedral be erected totally by craftsmen using only hand-wrought materials, craftsmen assumed an unusually great influence in the building's evolving design, sometimes casting aside Cram's blueprints in favor of their own ideas. Cram eventually grew so exasperated that in 1917 he withdrew from the project. The cathedral's central section is designed in fourteenth-century Gothic and the wings in twelfth-century Romanesque. The cornerstone was laid in 1914, and construction was sufficiently complete for the cathedral to be dedicated in 1919. Carol Beaver, "Bryn Athyn Cathedral: Where Man May Forget the World," *Pennsylvania Heritage* 12 (Fall 1986): 16-25; E. Bruce Glenn, *Bryn Athyn Cathedral: The Building of a Church* (New York: Fine Arts Publishers for Bryn Athyn Church, 1970), 29-31, 81-85, 109.

[300] *Palliser's Model Homes: Showing a Variety of Designs for Model Dwellings* (Bridgeport, Conn.: Palliser, Palliser & Co., 1878; reprint ed., Watkins Glen, N.Y.: American Life Foundation, [ca. 1978]), 17.

[301] William B. Rhoads, *The Colonial Revival*, 2 vols. (New York: Garland Publishing, 1977), 1:48-103.

[302] Mardges Bacon, "Toward a National Style: The Beaux-Arts Interpretation of the Colonial Revival," in Alan Axelrod, ed., *The Colonial Revival in America* (New York: W.W. Norton & Company for Henry Francis duPont Winterthur Museum, 1985), 91-121.

[303] Rhoads, *Colonial Revival*, 104, 299-301.

[304] Clark Wright Evans worked with Charles Smith and E. G. W. Dietrich in New York before coming to Wilkes-Barre in the 1890s, when he was in his mid-to late thirties. Sgromo and Lewis, *Wilkes-Barre Architecture*, 23.

[305] Eyre was born in Florence, Italy, to an old Philadelphia family with colonial roots. After studying at MIT for a year, he became a draftsman in James P. Sims's office. Edward Teitelman and Betsy Fahlman, "Wilson Eyre and the Colonial Revival in Philadelphia," in Axelrod, ed., *Colonial Revival in America*, 71-90; Betsy Fahlman and Edward Teitelman, "Wilson Eyre: The Philadelphia Domestic Ideal," *Pennsylvania Heritage* 8 (Summer 1982): 23-27; Rhoads, *Colonial Revival*, 105-7.

[306] Quoted in Teitelman and Fahlman, "Wilson Eyre and the Colonial Revival," 72.

[307] Rhoads, *Colonial Revival*, 1:109-110.

[308] Quoted in Teitelman and Fahlman, "Wilson Eyre and the Colonial Revival," 72.

[309] Edward Teitelman, "Wilson Eyre, Jr., and the Arts and Crafts in Philadelphia," *Journal of the Society of Architectural Historians* 30 (October 1971): 245-46; George E. Thomas, "William L. Price (1861-1916): Builder of Men and of Buildings" (Ph.D. dissertation, University of Pennsylvania, 1975); *A Monograph of the Works of Mellor, Meigs & Howe* (New York: The Architectural Book Publishing Co., 1923); William Ayres, *A Poor Sort of Heaven, A Good Sort of Earth: The Rose Valley Arts and Crafts Experiment* (Chadds Ford, Pa.: Brandywine River Museum, 1983),11-50.

[310] George Edgell, *The American Architecture of Today* (New York, 1928; reprint ed., New York: Arno Press, 1970), 114.

[311] Frederick Scheibler was a Pittsburgh man from beginning to end. He was born there in 1872, did nearly all of his work there, and died in the city in 1958. He learned his profession in local architectural offices before he started his own practice in 1898, working initially in the conventional historical styles of the time, until he embraced the Arts and Crafts mode in 1905. Van Trump, *Life and Architecture in Pittsburgh*, 284-85, 289.

[312] Dickson, *A Hundred Pennsylvania Buildings*, pl. 84. The building is also discussed in Kidney, *Landmark Architecture*, 270-71; Van Trump, *Life and Architecture in Pittsburgh*, 285-87.

[313] Kidney, *Landmark Architecture*, 279; Van Trump, *Life and Architecture in Pittsburgh*, 289-90.

[314] New materials incorporated into architecture of the period included formica, vitrolite (a heavy black glass), monel metal (a copper-nickel alloy), aluminum leaf, and bakelite. Cervin Robinson and Rosemarie Haag Bletter, *Skyscraper Style: Art Deco New York* (New York: Oxford University Press, 1975), 3-16, 35-73.

[315] Graham, Anderson, Probst & White of Chicago, successor to Daniel H. Burnham and Company, probably designed the Koppers Building in late 1926; construction began in 1927. Its lobby is regarded one of the best Art Deco spaces in Pittsburgh. The Koppers and Gulf buildings stand on opposite sides of Seventh Avenue at Grant Street in downtown Pittsburgh. Dickson, *A Hundred Pennsylvania Buildings*, pl. 89; Van Trump, *Life and Architecture in Pittsburgh*, 69-77; Kidney, *Landmark Architecture*, 163-64; Edgell. *American Architecture of Today*, 179-83.

[316] The Cathedral of Learning stands at Bigelow Boulevard and Fifth Avenue in the city's Oakland section. For a readable and well-illustrated account of the building's protracted planning and construction, see Robert C. Alberts, *Pitt: The Story of the University of Pittsburgh, 1787-1987* (Pittsburgh: University of Pittsburgh Press, 1986), 84-115, 121-26, 129-40, 195, 200, 202. See also Dickson, *A Hundred Pennsylvania Buildings*, pl. 50; Kidney, *Landmark Architecture*, 228. The University continues to add to the Cathedral's Nationality Rooms, as the historically styled classrooms are called. In addition to the eighteen Nationality Rooms on the first floor, five are on the third floor with more in process. Interview with E. Maxine

Bruhns, director of Nationality Rooms and Intercultural Exchange Programs, University of Pittsburgh, 14 December 1990.

[317] One of those exceptions is the N.W. Ayer & Son Building (PA-1390). It was built in 1927-29 from the designs of Ralph B. Bencker, who is probably best known for his Art Deco Horn and Hardart restaurants. Bencker carried the limestone-clad steel-frame building to fifteen stories with setbacks, integrating sculpture into the Art Deco design. "N.W. Ayer Building a Monument to 'Advertising,'" *Building* 8 ((April 1928): 15-16, 24; George E. Thomas, "Art Deco Architecture and Sculpture," in Wainwright, ed., *Sculpture of a City*, 244-45.

[318] About 1920 Howell Lewis Shay and Verus T. Ritter formed their partnership, which lasted more than a decade. Little appears to be known about Ritter. Shay, born in Alexandria, Virginia, in 1885 and raised in Seattle, Washington, graduated from the University of Pennsylvania in 1913. Before forming his partnership, he worked for McKim, Mead and White, John T. Windrim, and Horace Trumbauer. Other significant Art Deco Philadelphia buildings by Ritter and Shay include the Packard Building (1922-24) with Renaissance details, the 1928 Drake Hotel with Spanish Baroque details, and the 1933 United States Customs House with Georgian details. George Thomas, "Market Street National Bank" in Sewell, ed., *Philadelphia: Three Centuries of American Art*, 532-33; Webster, *Philadelphia Preserved*, 118, 133-34.

[319] Winston Weisman, "Philadelphia Functionalism and Sullivan," *Journal of the Society of Architectural Historians* 20 (March 1961): 3-19.

[320] Architectural historians generally consider Richard Neutra's Lovell House, built in 1927-29 in Los Angeles, America's first International style house, and William Lescaze's 1929 nursery school for Oak Lane Country Day School, just northwest of Philadelphia in Montgomery County, its first International style school building. William H. Jordy, *American Buildings and Their Architects: The Impact of European Modernism in the Mid-Twentieth Century* (Garden City, N.Y.: Doubleday & Company, 1972), 88, 103.

[321] *New York Times*, 17 June 1969, 73.

[322] It may seem incongruous for a conservative banking institution with roots dating back to 1816 to commission such a radical building. For this, James W. Willcox, president of PSFS and chairman of its building committee, was most responsible. A very reserved, autocratic leader, Willcox wanted a practical building that would remain competitive for rentals in future decades. He found it in Howe's and Lescaze's design. Furthermore, as a Philadelphian, Willcox seems to have implicitly trusted Howe as a member of his class. George Howe was born in Worcester, Massachusetts, to an old, wealthy New England family. After graduating from Harvard in 1907, he married into a well-to-do Philadelphia family, traveled in Europe, and spent five years at the Ecole des Beaux Arts before returning to the United States and making Philadelphia his home in 1913. In that year he became a partner in Furness, Evans and Company (after Furness's death), and three years later joined Walter Mellor and Arthur Meigs in an eleven-year partnership. The Howe and Lescaze partnership lasted nearly six years,

between May 1929 and March 1935. William Lescaze was born in Switzerland in 1896 and became a student of Karl Moser at the Zurich Technische Hochschule. He emigrated to the United States in 1923, and worked briefly in Cleveland before settling down in New York as a spokesman for avant-garde architecture. Howe died in 1955, Lescaze in 1969. Jordy, *American Buildings and Their Architects: The Impact of European Modernism*, 90-91; Robert A. M. Stern, *George Howe: Toward a Modern Architecture* (New Haven: Yale University Press, 1975), 3-11, 19-25, 30-33, 90-92, 158-61.

[323]The PSFS Building was only the second American skyscraper with central air-conditioning. The first was the twenty-one-story 1928 Milam Building in San Antonio, Texas. PSFS Building's other pioneering features were the acoustical ceiling tiles clipped onto a metal framework and aluminum windows. Jordy, *American Buildings and Their Architects: The Impact of European Modernism*, 91-98, 110-11; Stern, *George Howe*, 108-132.

[324]Quoted in Stern, *George Howe*, 127.

[325]Quoted in ibid., 131. Public response is based on notes that strategically placed men made of customers' comments during the bank's opening day in August 1932.

[326]Stonorov worked with Alfred Kastner on the project and W. Pope Barney served as the superintendent of construction. Because the state had not yet licensed Stonorov as an architect, Barney was cited as the architect on all forms and permits. Born in Frankfurt-am-Main, Germany, in 1905, Stonorov had studied in France, Switzerland, and Italy before emigrating to the United States in 1929. He began his Philadelphia practice in 1932 in association with Alfred Kastner, a relationship that lasted until Stonorov received his state license in 1936. Stonorov became a leader in social architecture, and was known for his housing projects around the country and his pioneer work in rehabilitating old row houses in Philadelphia. He died in a 1970 airplane crash with labor leader Walter Reuther while visiting one of his projects, a family education center for the United Auto Workers. Frederick Gutheim, "Oskar Stonorov," in Sewell, ed., *Philadelphia: Three Centuries of American Art*, 544; *New York Times*, 11 May 1979, 39; *Philadelphia Inquirer*, 11 May 1969, 1-3.

[327]The union named the complex after Carl Mackley, a twenty-two-year-old striker, who was killed by workers of the H. C. Aberle Company in March 1930. He was shot in the head while waiting in a car for a traffic light to change on Roosevelt Boulevard following an argument with nonstriking workers. The union placed plaques in the memory of Mackley and five other martyrs to unionism on the various buildings. In the 1930s the American Federation of Hosiery Workers was one of the largest unions in Philadelphia, where approximately one-quarter of the city's industrial workers labored in textile mills, which were concentrated near the Carl Mackley Houses. Webster, *Philadelphia Preserved*, 382 (n. 82); Federal Writers' Project, *Philadelphia: A Guide to the Nation's Birthplace* (Philadelphia: William Penn Association of Philadelphia for the Pennsylvania Historical Commission, 1937), 515. For a summary of the city's labor violence in the 1930s, see Philip Scranton and Walter Licht, *Work Sights: Industrial Philadelphia, 1890-1950* (Philadelphia: Temple University Press, 1986), 137-44.

[328]Frederick Gutheim, "Carl Mackley Houses (Juniata Park Project)," in Sewell, ed., *Philadelphia: Three Centuries of American Art*, 545; Eric J. Sandeen, "The Design of Public Housing in the New Deal: Oskar Stonorov and the Carl Mackley Houses," *American Quarterly* 37 (Winter 1985): 660. Sandeen's article studies the planning and construction of the Mackley Houses and Stonorov's early ideas on low-cost housing. He illustrates it with 1935 photos of the buildings, including an aerial view of the site showing hosiery mills in the background, a block of cramped semidetached houses diagonally opposite Stonorov's complex, and surrounding open spaces that would be filled after World War II. Although hosiery workers comprised less than sixty percent of the initial residents, housing reformers tried to promote Mackley Houses as a model of low-income communitarian housing reform for the city. John F. Bauman, "Public Housing in the Depression: Slum Reform in Philadelphia Neighborhoods in the 1930s," in William W. Cutler III and Howard Gillette, Jr., eds., *The Divided Metropolis: Social and Spatial Dimensions of Philadelphia, 1800-1975*, Contributions in American History, no. 85 (Westport, Conn.: Greenwood Press, 1980), 227-48. For a study that puts the buildings into the context of Depression-era housing projects, see Richard Pommer, "The Architecture of Urban Housing in the United States during the Early 1930s," *Journal of the Society of Architectural Historians* 37 (December 1978): 235-64.

[329]Gutheim, "Carl Mackley Houses," 545; *Philadelphia: A Guide to the Nation's Birthplace*, 526.

[330]Gutheim, "Carl Mackley Houses," 545. Slum clearance soon dominated Philadelphia's housing reform during the Great Depression and city officials abandoned the communitarian concerns embodied in the Mackley Houses. New housing units embodied the International style's architectural simplicity but projects, such as the Richard Allen Homes in North Philadelphia or the Tasker Homes in South Philadelphia, failed to fulfill "the spirit of the Carl Mackley Houses, that is, buildings skillfully articulated on spacious sites, replete with amenities and responsive to their residents' social and cultural needs." Bauman, "Public Housing in the Depression," in Cutler and Gillette, eds., *The Divided Metropolis*, 238. Bauman's article is a good description of how tradition, racial prejudice, federal policy, neighborhood politics, and contention between housing reform and slum clearance advocates produced a mongrelized housing program that contributed to living conditions over the next half-century that might have been worse than the bandboxes and courts that it ordered demolished. By 1990, for example, public housing was a "a public disgrace," according to state Senator Chaka Fattah, who proposed moving families out of projects such as the notorious Richard Allen Homes and relocating them in vacant houses throughout the city. *Philadelphia Inquirer*, 7 March 1990, sec. B, 1-2; 8 March 1990, sec. B, 1-2.

[331]Dickson, *A Hundred Pennsylvania Buildings*, pl. 96.

[332]John F. Bauman, *Public Housing, Race and Renewal: Urban Planning in Philadelphia, 1920-1974* (Philadelphia: Temple University Press, 1987), 111, 113; Interview with Victor Banks, Philadelphia Housing Authority, 7 March 1990.

[333]Henry-Russell Hitchcock comments on Fallingwater's dual romanticism, "the romanticism about nature, which has flourished since the eighteenth century, and the romanticism about

scientific feats of construction, often considered of quite opposite character." Henry-Russell Hitchcock, *In the Nature of Materials: The Buildings of Frank Lloyd Wright, 1887-1941* (New York: Hawthorn Books, 1942; reprint ed., New York: DaCapo Press, 1975), 90. The literature on Fallingwater is extensive. A valuable and inexpensive paperback source is Donald Hoffmann, *Frank Lloyd Wright's Fallingwater: The House and Its History*, with an introduction by Edgar Kaufmann Jr. (New York: Dover Publications, 1978). A well-illustrated book by the man who gave the house to the public is Edgar Kaufmann Jr., *Fallingwater: A Frank Lloyd Wright Country House* (New York: Abbeville Press, 1986). A succinct and illuminating assessment is Dickson, *A Hundred Pennsylvania Buildings*, pls. 95-95A.

[334]Hoffmann, *Frank Lloyd Wright's Fallingwater*, 35.

[335]Ibid., 56. In Germany, the birthplace of Kaufmann's father, the hearth, or hearthroom, was the house, the legal and taxable representation of the family household. Weaver, "Pennsylvania German House," 248.

[336]Quoted in Hoffmann, *Frank Lloyd Wright's Fallingwater*, 92.

[337]Frank Lloyd Wright, *The Natural House* (New York: Horizon Press, 1954), 106-8; Hitchcock, *In the Nature of Materials*, 89, 98-99; Frank Lloyd Wright, *Architecture: Man in Possession of His Earth*, ed. Patricia Coyle Nicholson (Garden City, N.Y.: Doubleday & Company, 1962), 103; Whiffen and Koeper, *American Architecture*, 369-70.

[338]Stern, *George Howe*, 162-69.

[339]Tatum, *Penn's Great Town*, 134. Both buildings received Awards of Merit from the American Institute of Architects (A.I.A.), the Mercantile Library in 1955 and Wyeth Laboratories in 1957. In addition, the Mercantile Library won the Bronze Medal of the Philadelphia Chapter of the A.I.A. Also receiving an Award of Merit, in 1951, was the Veterans Administration Hospital in Wilkes-Barre; Kelly & Gruzen, Isadore Rosenfield of New York were the architects. Mid-twentieth-century Pennsylvania recipients of A.I.A. First Honors Awards include Lankenau Hospital in Lower Merion Township, Montgomery County, in 1954 (Vincent G. Kling of Philadelphia, architect) and the Moore School of Electrical Engineering of the University of Pennsylvania in Philadelphia in 1960 (Geddes, Brecher, Qualls & Cunningham of Philadelphia, architects). The Moore School also received the Silver Medal from the Pennsylvania Society of Architects and the Gold Medal from the Philadelphia Chapter of the A.I.A. Ibid., 204, 206; Wolf Von Eckardt, ed., *Mid-Century Architecture in America: Honor Awards of the American Institute of Architects, 1949-1961*, with an introduction by Wolf Von Eckardt (Baltimore: Johns Hopkins Press, 1961), 89, 116. 127-28, 160, 228-32.

[340]In 1970 Alcoa erected next to its original building a near duplicate, also from the designs of Harrison and Abramowitz. "Alcoa Building, Pittsburgh," *Architectural Record* 112 (August 1952): 120-27; Kidney, *Landmark Architecture*, 100, 109-11.

[341]Each facade of the Penn Mutual Building responds to its environment. The eastern facade has large deeply set windows, the southern facade's tinted reflecting glass reduces sun glare,

and the western side fits around the setbacks of the 1931 building. Because of its relatively narrow site and the need to connect with the 1931 floor levels, the architects employed a special steel truss structure to take advantage of the high ceilings and to free the floors of structural members. Fred L. Foote, "The Architecture of Large Buildings," in Lynn S. Beedle, ed., *Second Century of the Skyscraper* (New York: Van Nostrand Reinhold Company for Council on Tall Buildings and Urban Habitat, 1988), 184; Group for Environmental Education, John Andrew Gallery, gen. ed., *Philadelphia Architecture: A Guide to the City* (Cambridge: MIT Press for Foundation for Architecture, 1984), 122; "Penn Mutual Building," *Architectural Record* 149 (April 1971): 42.

[342] Other Pennsylvania buildings by Kahn include Synagogue Ahavath Israel, Philadelphia, 1935-37; A.F. of L. Medical Service Plan Building, Philadelphia, 1954-56 (demolished 1974), Tribune Review Publishing Company Building, Greensburg, Westmoreland County, 1958-61; Mill Creek Public Housing Project II, Philadelphia, 1959-62. Vincent Scully, Jr., *Louis I. Kahn* (New York: George Braziller, 1962), 20-30; Whiffen and Koeper, *American Architecture*, 426-27; G. Holmes Perkins, "Alfred Newton Richards Medical Research Building and Goddard Laboratories, University of Pennsylvania," in O'Gorman, ed., *Drawing toward Building*, 221-22.

[343] This new movement already has its history: Heinrich Klotz, *The History of Postmodern Architecture*, Radka Donnell, trans. (Cambridge: MIT Press, 1988).

[344] Robert Venturi, *Complexity and Contradiction in Architecture*, with an introduction by Vincent Scully (New York: Museum of Modern Art in association with Graham Foundation for Advanced Studies in The Fine Arts, Chicago, 1966) 114-17; "New-Old Guild House Apartments," *Progressive Architecture* 48 (May 1967): 134-37; R. Leonard Miller, "Evaluation: Admiring Glance at a Celebrity," *AIA Journal* 69 (February 1980): 38-41.

[345] Venturi discusses his mother's house on pp. 117-21, and presents a postscript to the book in idem, "Diversity, Relevance and Representation in Historicism, of Plus Ca Change . . . " *Architectural Record* 170 (June 1982): 118-19. An early assessment of the house is "Complexities and Contradictions," *Progressive Architecture* 46 (May 1965): 168-73.

[346] Venturi, "Diversity, Relevance and Representation in Historicism," 114.

[347] Neal Levine, "Robert Venturi and 'The Return of Historicism,'" in Christopher Mead, ed., *The Architecture of Robert Venturi* (Albuquerque: University of New Mexico Press, 1989), 45.

[348] At the time, however, Johnson was reluctant to accept the mantle of postmodernism. He insisted, "I don't believe in revolution, I'm not post-anything, and I'm still a functionalist modernist." He claimed that the Chippendale top simply reflected a new pluralism that had entered American life and thought. Quoted in "Two Current Projects," *Architectural Record* 164 (July 1978): 85.

[349] Franklin K. B. S. Toker, "PJ and PPG: A Date with History," *Progressive Architecture* 60 (July 1979): 60-61; Donald Canty, "Historicist, Spired, 'City of Glass,'" *Architecture* 73 (May 1984):

242-51; Darl Rastorfer, "PPG Place, Pittsburgh, Pennsylvania," *Architectural Record* 172 (October 1984): 193-99. For references on One Liberty Place, see the Philadelphia essay, notes 47-48.

[350] *New York Times,* 8 October 1989, sec. 2, 37, 40. Construction of the East Wing began in 1984 and was completed in spring 1988 at a cost of $127 million. Thomas Celli, its architect, is a principal in Celli-Flynn Associates. H. F. Lenz Company of Pittsburgh was the engineering contractor. Interview with George McLaughlin, Construction Unit, Department of General Services, Commonwealth of Pennsylvania, Harrisburg, Pa., 9 March 1990.

[351] National Trust for Historic Preservation, "Policy Research Report: Ranking of States by Historic Rehabilitation Tax Credit Activity," Washington, D.C., 1986 (mimeographed).

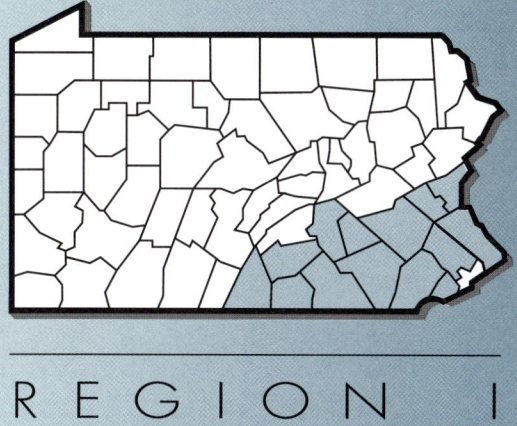

REGION I

Great Valley and Piedmont

Essay by Richard J. Webster
Catalog entries by Deborah Stephens Burns

Adams
Berks
Bucks
Chester
Cumberland
Dauphin
Delaware
Franklin
Lancaster
Lebanon
Lehigh
Montgomery
Northampton
York

Richard Woodward House (PA-1192) Westtown vicinity (Thornbury Township, Chester County. South and east elevations (Ned Goode, photographer, 1958) PA,15-WESTO.V,1-1.

PENNSYLVANIA'S earliest history unfolded in the fourteen-county Great Valley and Piedmont Region, which encompasses what scholars call the Pennsylvania Culture Region.[1] It was here in the region's southeastern quadrant that William Penn first established his Holy Experiment in 1681. Within a very few years Penn was able to establish a stable government, peace with local Native Americans, and a model of religious tolerance. Thus it was relatively easy to attract the yeomanry of Britain and northern Europe who were among the early settlers in this region of Pennsylvania.[2]

For over two hundred years immigrants entered this region along the Delaware River, the broad waterway which served as both an avenue of entry to the region, centering on Philadelphia, and the eastern political boundary of the province of Pennsylvania. Facing colonial settlers as they moved northward and westward out of Philadelphia and its environs was Blue Mountain, the first ridge of the Appalachians. Sweeping in an arc approximately fifty miles north and one hundred thirty miles west of Philadelphia, Blue Mountain stood as an effective barrier to westward movement until after the American Revolution. For decades there was no need to pass beyond that ridge, because between it and Philadelphia rest the low, undulating hills of the fertile Piedmont and the limestone and shale lowland of the Great Valley. The latter, locally known by a number of names (Lehigh Valley, Lebanon Valley, and Cumberland Valley), cuts a fifteen-mile-wide swath 150 miles across Pennsylvania from Northampton County in the north to Franklin County in the southwest. The Great Valley has been prized farmland for nearly three hundred years and in the eighteenth century served as an avenue for the transit of Pennsylvania culture into Virginia, where it is known as the Shenandoah Valley.[3] Historic American Buildings Survey records for this region are uneven. Its materials on eighteenth- and early-nineteenth-century buildings, especially vernacular buildings, are excellent, but except for some examples in Chester and Delaware Counties it has not recorded much nineteenth-century high-style architecture.

Immigrant groups who first came to Pennsylvania brought their Old World building traditions. As later generations grew up in an increasingly ethnically diverse land, however, they learned different ways to construct and organize buildings. By the 1730s, after about fifty years of both cultural interaction and fresh immigration, a myriad of vernacular buildings stood in the region. Some were virtual re-creations of Old World forms and others were combinations of different cultural traditions. Fortunately, many of these buildings survive to give the Great Valley and Piedmont Region some of the Commonwealth's most significant vernacular buildings from this early period.

British colonists arrived in the largest numbers during the earliest settlement period and their architectural forms predominated in the eastern end of the region. Depending on the time of year when they arrived, these early settlers evidently dug "caves" to shelter themselves from the harsh winters or they built traditional impermanent wood frame houses such as were typical of English charcoal burners.[4] Once these settlers were able to construct permanent housing, they preferred brick or stone single-pile dwellings with two-room hall-and-parlor-plans.[5] Many of these structures can be found in Chester and Delaware Counties adjacent to Philadelphia, where English and Welsh Quakers settled before the end of the seventeenth century. The Richard Woodward House (PA-1192) in Thornbury Township, Chester County, is a single-pile two-story hall-and-parlor plan house that was built at the turn of the eighteenth century, early enough to retain such medieval features as a steep gable roof and a stepped belt course across its front. Other early houses had one-room plans. Possibly these single-pile dwellings began as one-story cottages and were raised to two stories as time and materials became available,[6] but a more common evolution was lateral additions, to the rear or side or even the front of small two-story houses. Sometimes the original house is engulfed by a series of later accretions.[7]

Next to the British in number of settlers were Germans. Since the Pennsylvania essay deals with British building practices, this essay focuses on Pennsylvania's Germanic material culture, in particular barns and farmsteads, distinctive but not predominant features in the area. The region's Germanic people built in all materials, with logs probably more than any other material,[8] but they are more frequently identified with half-timber and stone structures that retained such medieval features as steep thatch or tiled roofs and massive rubble walls with irregular fenestration.[9] The fundamental characteristic of Germanic houses is their interior spatial organization. Most Germanic house plans are variants of the Continental plan or *Flurküchenhaus*, which is literally translated as "hallway-kitchen house."[10] It is characterized by three or four rooms clustered around a massive central chimney with an off-center entrance door opening into the kitchen.

Many examples in brick, stone, or log were built in the region as late as the mid-nineteenth century as two farmhouses in Pike Township, Berks County, indicate. The 1732 section of the Keim House (PA-1039) is a good early stone example, and the Isaac Stamm House (PA-112), built ca. 1855, is a good late brick example. During the century and a quarter that separates the erection of these two dwellings, exterior treatment changed from the Keim House's second-story door and asymmetrical windows with brick lintels set into rubble walls to the Stamm House's symmetrical brick facade. Unchanged, however, was the interior arrangement of rooms around a central chimney. The continental plan represented a comfortable and traditional means of organizing interior space, and as long as Pennsylvania Germans remained relatively culturally isolated, this plan persisted.

Settlers moved steadily across the Piedmont and into the Great Valley during the first half of the eighteenth century. Towns, however, developed rather late. Because colonial Philadelphia culturally and economically overshadowed its adjacent countryside, people in Bucks and Chester Counties gathered not in towns but in hamlets that emerged as small trading, storage, and milling centers or as clusters of houses about an inn that served travelers and farmers on their way to and from Philadelphia.[11] Many of these elements of the rural built environment have survived into the twentieth century. HABS has recorded not only the more common foci of activity, such as gristmills and blacksmith shops, but also such small manufactories as a sawmill, a currying shop, and Samuel Ankrim's multi-functional shop (PA-1194) in Mount Rocky, Chester County, that was used by a spinning wheel maker, a turner, and a shoemaker.

Farther west, however, population growth stimulated the founding of new towns. By 1729 the Penns carved Lancaster County out of Chester County and the next year they laid out the town of Lancaster, which quickly became Pennsylvania's most significant early inland town. A decade later, with Indian disputes pushed west

Samuel Ankrim Shop (PA-1194) Mount Rocky (Elk Township), Chester County. South and west elevations (Ned Goode, Photographer, 1959) PA,15-MTROC,1-1.

of the Allegheny Front, enough settlers had crossed the Susquehanna River that the Penns authorized the establishment of York in 1741. As settlement moved northward in the 1740s, Reading was laid out along the Schuylkill in 1748, Carlisle in 1749, and Easton at the forks of the Lehigh and Delaware Rivers three years later.[12] Sites for these county seats were selected on the basis of centrality in their counties, adequate (noncompetitive) distances from other county seats, and accessibility to Philadelphia. None of these five towns was closer than fifty-five miles, more than a day's return journey, to Philadelphia.[13] These towns were considerably larger than the villages within Philadelphia's cultural sphere, an area within a daylong return trip (thirty miles) of the city. Both the Penns and the towns' inhabitants expected that these towns would become trading centers, an expectation borne out in part from their strategically significant sites. Lancaster, Reading, and York had reached populations of over a thousand by the time of the American Revolution, and quickly assumed an urban compactness. As early as 1751, for example, Joseph Chambers in York built his house (PA-5189) contiguous to his Golden Plough Tavern (PA-5169), and in the nineteenth century row houses were built in these towns to a greater degree than in comparable-size towns elsewhere in the state. Offsetting the compactness was the central courthouse square, a feature that spread across nineteenth-century America. Being a county seat was important for commercial success. Only four colonial towns (Chambersburg, Gettysburg, Lebanon, and Allentown), laid out by private individuals rather than by the proprietors or the legislature, had grown to a population of five hundred before becoming county seats. Founders of such towns invariably planned around central open spaces, locally called "diamonds," that apparently served commercial purposes more than ceremonial functions.[14]

Formation of these towns and their connecting roadways and crossroads villages contributed to a regional stability that helped to make inland Pennsylvania a comfortable and secure place to live, as reflected in high-style architectural developments, in particular the Georgian double-pile house. The Pennsylvania essay contains a full discussion of this house form, as well as its rural Germanic version, the so-called Pennsylvania farmhouse.[15] Identified primarily by its two front doors, this latter house type abounds in the Piedmont and Great Valley Region.

Another distinctive Germanic feature on the southeastern Pennsylvania landscape is the Pennsylvania barn. Large, starkly utilitarian, and unique to the region, these barns possess both aesthetic and cultural significance, and have moved some to pen nostalgic odes. In 1852 Thomas Buchanan Read, a Chester County poet and painter, rhapsodized about his rural youth:[16]

> Oh, ye who daily cross the sill,
> Step lightly, for I love it still;
> And when you crowd the old barn eaves
> Then think what countless harvest sheaves
> Have passed within that scented door . . .
> There is the barn — and, as of yore,
> I smell the hay from the open door
> And see the busy swallows throng,
> And hear the peewee's mournful song . . .

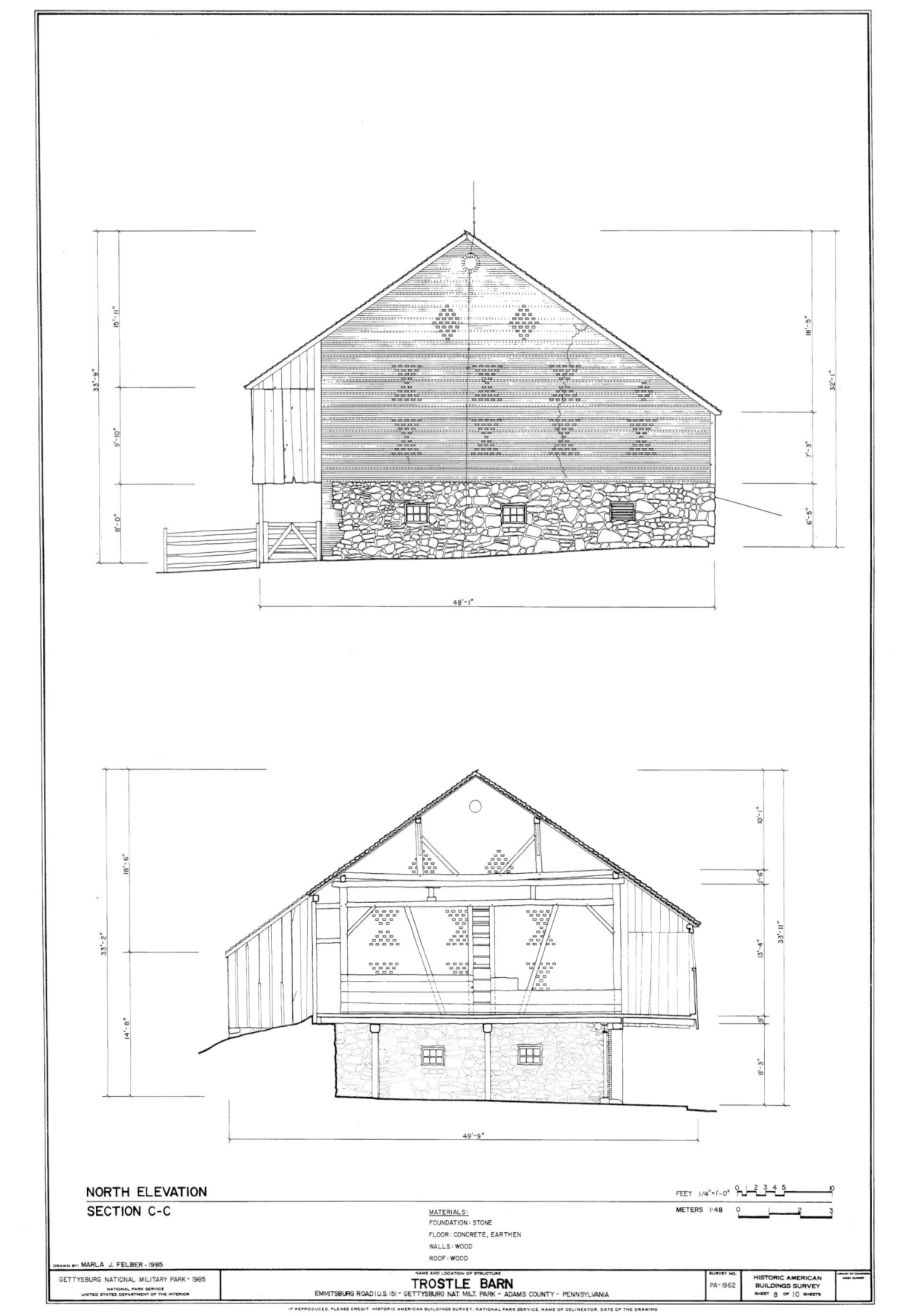

◀ *Trostle Barn (PA-1962) Gettysburg vicinity (Cumberland Township), Adams County. Elevation and section (Marla J. Felber, delineator, 1985) PA,1-GET.V,17A.*

Kaufman House, Barns (PA-1059) Oley vicinity (Oley Township), Berks County. West and south elevations (Cervin Robinson, photographer, 1958) PA,6-OLEY.V,1B-1.

Decorated Red Barn (PA-5319) Alburtis vicinity (Lower Macungie Township), Lehigh County. General view (Charles H. Dornbusch, photographer, 1941) PA,39-ALB.V,2A-1.

In our own time, two Canadian popularizers of North American barns feel that "nothing can be more rewarding than the sight of a great Pennsylvania stone barn."[17]

Although this multifunctional structure is commonly called the Pennsylvania barn, it has many alternative names including overshot barn, bank barn, hex barn, and Swisser barn.[18] The Pennsylvania barn has been classified into eleven types,[19] but its dominant characteristic is its forebay, or overhang, which is often on the barn's south side. Its three secondary features include its two levels, a banked ramp, and double-crib floor plan.[20] So-called hex signs are not a characteristic; in fact, they are not truly hex signs meant to ward off evil spirits, but only colorful folk decorations.[21]

Scholars have speculated on the Pennsylvania barn's origins for much of this century,[22] but in the past decade two geographers, investigating independently, have conclusively documented its source in Switzerland.[23] Once the Pennsylvania barn

John H. Schriner Barn (PA-5226) Lititz vicinity, Lancaster County. Detail of cantilever beams of forebay (Charles H. Dornbusch, photographer, 1941) PA,36-LIT,1A-3.

Stamm Farm (PA-266) Mount Pleasant vicinity (Penn Township), Berks County. Corn crib-wagon shed, barn, and pig barn (Anthony Bley, photographer, 1975) PA,6-MTPLES.V,11-3.

arrived in southeastern Pennsylvania,[24] it was adopted throughout the region, probably because farmers rather quickly discerned the forebay's functional advantages. As Joseph W. Glass notes, the "forebay offered protection from rain, displaced splash erosion some distance from foundation and entrances, reduced work associated with snow accumulations, blocked the more intense sunlight but harnessed lesser intensities, and facilitated the performance of daily and seasonal activities,"[25] such as throwing hay down to livestock in the winter and heaving straw from the barn during threshing. When a barn was built into a bank, it had the added benefits of affording easy access to the second-story threshing and mow floor and protecting animals on the ground floor from harsh winter winds.

The Pennsylvania barn's virtues surely traveled quickly by word of mouth, but the agricultural press probably promoted the barn more effectively. At the very beginning of the nineteenth century, the gentleman experimental farmer John Beale Bordley described the positive aspects of the Pennsylvania barn, in particular its forebay and construction into banks, recommending construction of a bridge if no bank

Stone Barn (PA-5256) Ambler vicinity (Whitpain Township), Montgomery County. Interior framing (Charles H. Dornbusch, photographer, 1941) PA,46-AMB.V,9-3.

Mountain View Dairy Farm, Barn (PA-5326) Leithsville vicinity (Lower Saucon Township), Northampton County. Detail of door hoods and round vents (Charles H. Dornbusch, photographer, 1941) PA,48-LEITH.V,1A-3.

were available.²⁶ By 1838 *The Farmer's Cabinet* was publishing both detailed building instructions for the Pennsylvania barn and farmers' testimony in support of its forebay.²⁷ Subsequent articles endorsed a number of Pennsylvania barn details, such as the Dutch door, which allowed light and air to enter the stables while keeping the animals in the barn, and southern exposure of the forebay in order to provide better light for the stables and to promote decomposition of the barnyard's manure.²⁸ Perhaps the most effective promoter of the Pennsylvania barn, however, was the United States government. In 1865 the commissioner of agriculture published plans and elevations of a large bank barn with a forebay, which he called "the Pennsylvania barn," and touted its many advantages.²⁹

HABS has the richest collection of photographs and drawings of Pennsylvania barns in the country. In addition to those included in its surveys, it possesses all of Charles Dornbusch's negatives from his survey in 1941. This great volume of illustrations indicates that barns were built of brick and log as well as stone and that Pennsylvanians built barns other than the forebay examples. In fact, the attention paid to the so-called Pennsylvania barn, largely a nineteenth-century product, creates a misleading historical impression of the scale and material of Pennsylvania barns. Many eighteenth-century barns were built on a modest scale, without forebays, and most were of log construction as were ancillary outbuildings, such as the Hause Smokehouse (PA-1206) in Marsh, Chester County.³⁰

These barns, however, were only one part, albeit often the most impressive part, of Pennsylvania German farms, which travelers through the region invariably praised for their appearance. After visiting these farmers in 1788, Dr. Benjamin Rush was impressed by "the extent of their orchards, the fertility of their fields, the luxuriance of their meadows, and a general appearance of plenty and neatness in everything that belonged to them."³¹ This apparent prosperity was credited to an adherence to traditional agricultural practices, or as one mid-nineteenth-century writer put it, "the result of old established prejudices, deeply rooted in our German population, who, resisting every modern innovation, hold fast to the time-honored principles, precepts and examples of their forefathers, and regard it as a moral and social duty to 'follow in their footsteps.'"³² In fact, all Pennsylvania farmers, regardless of national ancestry, evidently farmed in much the same way.³³

Nevertheless there was a pattern to the social and built environments of the region's eighteenth- and nineteenth-century farmsteads. As the population grew and land values increased, it became difficult for successive generations to maintain their parents' standards of living.[34] German families seem to have held on to their land and the buildings they put upon it. Architecturally, this trait is suggested by their datestones that would brand their buildings as their own for generations. It is indicated socially by farms that were run by the same family for over a century, and agriculturally by their reluctance to use fertilizers.[35]

    The Dundore Farm (PA-261), originally standing along the Union Canal, which paralleled Tulpehocken Creek in Penn Township, Berks County, was an excellent example of a Pennsylvania German farmstead. Owned by a single family, the Dundores, for five generations (141 years) and cultivated by four generations, the farm's plan developed during the late-eighteenth and mid-nineteenth centuries and remained unaltered when an HABS team surveyed it in the mid-1970s.[36] The farm's buildings were arranged to take advantage of the landscape's contours and to serve the farmer's needs. The log house sat atop a small knoll to command a view of the entire farmstead. Its back is to the canal, the primary avenue of transportation at the time of the house's construction, circa 1840, in order to face eastward toward the barn, which was built into the south side of a bank. This right-angle orientation is common in the area and gave the barn's forebay and stabling area a sunny southern exposure while leaving the barnyard, the locus of the Dundores' investment and activity, visible from the house's kitchen.[37] Similarly, the Dundores in 1842 built the story-and-a-half log springhouse into a bank to provide ground-level access on the south elevation to the living area, and at the north and east sides to the spring room. The Dundores located other mid-nineteenth-century structures in relation to the house, barn, or canal. The privy and masonry-vaulted root cellar stood at diagonally opposite corners of the farmhouse, and the log smokehouse stood a safe distance from the farmhouses, midway to the timber-frame corn crib-wagon shed. The Dundores stored their grain and perhaps neighbors' grain as well in the timber-frame granary, which they built circa 1850 on the canal's bank for easy transfer of cargo to barges. Jacob Dundore probably constructed the farm's first buildings shortly after he acquired the farm in the summer of 1771. From an inscription over a Dutch door on the barn's ground floor it is known that Jacob's son John erected the bank barn in 1788 with stone end walls and interior oak timbers. About 1840 Jacob's grandson (John Adam Dundore) built the two-story log farmhouse in a traditional (and local) Pennsylvania German fashion. Hand-hewn logs, some salvaged from an earlier build-

Dundore Farm (PA-261) Mount Pleasant vicinity, Berks County. Aerial view, PA,6-MTPLES.V,7.

ing, were tenoned into corner posts with angled knee braces to stabilize the corner; mud chinking filled the interstices; and a post stood near the center of each wall to provide further stability and allow the use of short logs. Similarly its three-room *Flurküchenhaus* plan, as well as that of the 1742 springhouse, was rooted in Pennsylvania's earliest Germanic houses. Equally significant was the survival of not only the houses' plans, virtually unchanged for nearly 130 years, but also the farmstead's outbuildings, and the absence of such twentieth-century elements as a silo or metal cattle feeding apparatus. Although the farmstead is now gone, Old Dry Road Farm, Inc., in 1976 disassembled the farmhouse, barn, and nineteenth-century outbuildings and is reassembling them as a museum near Brownsville, Lower Heidelberg Township, Berks County.[38]

By the second quarter of the nineteenth century, the industrial revolution was beginning to transform parts of the Piedmont and Great Valley Region. Underpinning this economic improvement was an expanding network of roads, canals, and railways. Canals, built in the 1820s and 30s with both public and private funds, stimulated the growth of towns along their paths. Easton, at the confluence of the Lehigh and Morris Canals and the state's Delaware Division Canal, became a significant trading and manufacturing center, as to a lesser degree did Bristol, Bucks County, at the southern end of the Delaware Division. Reading developed into a leading industrial city after 1840 in part from its early canal connections to Philadelphia and Pottsville via the Schuylkill Canal and to the Susquehanna River via the Union Canal. Harrisburg, Dauphin County, benefiting from its role as state capital and its site at the junction of the Great Valley and the Susquehanna River, joined Lancaster, Reading, and York as an important economic center in the region's western reaches.[39]

By mid-century, railroads began to cut deeply into canals' traffic volume and profit margins. The state-built Columbia and Philadelphia Railroad and the privately funded Philadelphia and Reading Railroad were the region's most important lines. The Columbia and Philadelphia Railroad opened in 1834 as a link in the state's extensive canal system, but in 1857 the state sold the line to the Philadelphia-based Pennsylvania Railroad. While its presidents systematically expanded the Pennsylvania into one of the nation's great rail systems, they extended local branches into towns like West Chester, where they built substantial high-style stations (PA-246). The Philadelphia and Reading Railroad began in 1842 as an anthracite line between those two cities, but it also carried other freight and passengers, and helped to make such boroughs as Norristown and Phoenixville manufacturing towns. The Reading Railroad also expanded during the 1850s, though more modestly than the Pennsylvania. This improved transportation and the nearby anthracite mining industry provided the fuel and distribution system that stimulated the region's iron industry after 1840. The region's iron mines yielded three-quarters of the state's iron ore, helping to make Pennsylvania the nation's top iron-mining state by 1870. These mines supplied blast furnaces and rolling mills in such towns and cities as Allentown, Bethlehem, Lebanon, and Pottstown. In addition to the region's industrial centers are the many towns that have served its fertile farms, leaving the Great Valley and Piedmont Region with the state's most highly mixed and prosperous economy and most diverse architecture.[40]

Better transportation, new industrial wealth, and a more dynamic architectural press contributed to growing disparities between ordinary and high-style architecture. There seem always to have been two class-bound worlds of gentlemen, those who shaped good taste and others who aped good taste, but in the nineteenth century architectural critics and promoters exploited social insecurities to exaggerate the interdependence of architecture, taste, and social acceptance. Philadelphia architect Samuel Sloan in 1852, for example, insisted that "a man's dwelling . . . is not only an index of his wealth, but also his character. The moment he begins to build, his tact for arrangement, his private feelings, the refinement of his tastes and the peculiarities of his judgment are all laid bare for public inspection and criticism. And the public makes free use of this prerogative.[41] As Sloan's partner for a period in the 1860s, Addison Hutton qualified as a shaper of taste. So did William Lockwood, a wealthy manufacturer of men's paper collars, who commissioned Hutton in 1865 to design his mansion (PA-181) in Glenloch, East Whiteland Township, Chester County. Its rural setting on six hundred acres[42] west of the Pennsylvania Railroad stop in Paoli was but one expression of Lockwood's knowledgeable taste, because at the time, supposedly, "the inclinations of the people, save where perverted by unwholesome education, seem decidedly in favor of a rural life."[43] The house's picturesqueness also testifies to the gentleman's and architect's good taste. Its asymmetrical massing of locally quarried ashlar, its off-center tower with a crenelated pyramidal roof, and its steep gable roofs with collar-beams and finials produce a complex and irregular exterior, and ornamented cornices and central-hall consoles add a rich finish to the interior.

Sibyla Brinton and her builder, on the other hand, lived in the world of apers among the small-town bourgeoisie and prospering farmers whose conservative tastes and modest means moderated exuberant architectural expressions. In 1873 Sibyla Brinton had a house (PA-249) built for her near the southern edge of West Chester, Chester County, using serpentine from a newly opened family quarry. Her builder combined traditional form and stylish details. He applied such Gothic Revival details as a shallow cross-gable and bargeboards to a symmetrical facade with not only Georgian proportions but also quoins and segmental-arch windows. In some respects such houses as Sibyla Brinton's represent local naiveté and social aspirations, but they also are examples of the persistence of vernacular design. Here an unschooled builder grafted a distinctive high-style detail, the cross-gable, onto a familiar form, a single-pile Georgian house. Through such selective processes, practitioners of the ver-

Loch Aerie (PA-181) Glenloch (East Whiteland Township), Chester County. South elevation showing lake (Ned Goode, photographer, 1958) PA,15-GLENL,2-3.

nacular tradition accommodated themselves to rapidly changing cultivated styles and apparently pleased their clients.[44]

High-style taste also made its mark on the new buildings of technology, especially railroad depots.[45] Since railroad stations served as gateways to towns and cities and projected a company's image wherever they stood along its line, shoddy buildings were unacceptable. Even small companies built assertive stations. Chester Valley Railroad in 1872 erected its weatherboarded wood-frame Cedar Hollow station (PA-1199) in Tredyffrin Township, Chester County with a picturesque Gothic Revival style featuring pinnacles and pendants at the peaks of its intersecting gable roofs. Because railroad stations stood in villages as well as cities, they indicate the long reach of an urban-based technology. Market houses, however, were clearly urban structures that reflected an industrially based social and economic organization. By

Sibyla Brinton House (PA-249) West Chester Borough, Chester County. North and west elevations (Ned Goode, photographer, 1960) PA,15-WCHES,1-1.

the middle of the nineteenth century, open market sheds disrupted street traffic, posed threats to public health, and no longer fit the needs of an increasingly complex food marketing system of wholesalers and retailers. City officials began to replace them with market houses[46] like the 1860 Broad Street Market House (PA-1156) in Harrisburg. Although references to Italianate or Romanesque styles are discernible in their facades, market houses generally appear more utilitarian than railway stations.

Cedar Hollow Railroad Station (PA-1199) Paoli vicinity (Tredyffrin Township), Chester County. North and west elevations (Ned Goode, photographer, 1958) PA,15-PAOL.V,4-1.

The Harrisburg market house is still used as a market house, but it is equally common for extant market houses to be rehabilitated to offices, as is the case with West Chester's 1860 Church Street Market House. The wealth and knowledge both created by and required for the industrial revolution generated a demand for cultural and educational buildings whose architectural diversity is reflected in the Romanesque Revival Chester County Horticultural Hall (PA-1121) in West Chester and Gettysburg College's Greek Revival style Pennsylvania Hall (PA-360), both designed by Philadelphia architects.[47] Churches, prominent elements in nearly every community, were often architect-designed landmarks whose appearance was determined by national stylistic trends rather than by local traditions.

By the end of the nineteenth century, there was little about the region's new architecture to distinguish it from buildings in other parts of the state. In its early-twentieth-century suburbs, Colonial Revival buildings proved especially popu-

Chester County Horticultural Hall (PA-1121) West Chester Borough, Chester County. General view circa 1870 (Copy photo, photographer unknown) PA,15-WCHES,4-4.

lar, but between the world wars some industrialists, such as the Reading candy and coughdrop manufacturer William H. Luden, preferred classically styled mansions.[48] The region's continued prosperity in the twentieth century has encouraged a great deal of new construction.[49] Developers have met the growing demand for housing by filling farmland with balloon-frame dwellings in a variety of traditional forms, most of them traceable to colonial origins, leaving architects to apply the International Style, generally in a humdrum fashion, to new industrial and office buildings.

Notes

[1] Moving in three concentric quadrants westward from Philadelphia, those fourteen counties are Bucks, Montgomery, Chester, Delaware; Northampton, Lehigh, Berks, Lebanon, Lancaster, York; Dauphin, Cumberland, Adams, and Franklin. The Pennsylvania Culture Region is identified and explained in two different contexts by Joseph W. Glass in *The Pennsylvania Culture Region: A View from the Barn* (Ann Arbor: UMI Research Press, 1986), 1-7, 21-38; and Wilbur Zelensky in "The Pennsylvania Town: An Overdue Geographical Account," *The Geographical Review* 67 (April 1977): 128-31. Henry Glassie earlier called the area the mid-Atlantic architectural region in *Pattern in Material Folk Culture of the Eastern United States* (Philadelphia: University of Pennsylvania Press, 1968), 36-64, and "Eighteenth-Century Cultural Process in Delaware Valley Folk Building," *Winterthur Portfolio* 7 (1972): 31-35. Although topographical features rarely honor political boundaries, in this case the two coincide to a remarkable degree. Except for the northern tip of Lebanon County, the northern half of Dauphin County, and the western edge of Franklin County, which push into the Ridge and Valley geographical region, and the eastern part of Delaware County, which is in the Coastal Plain, all of these counties are in the Great Valley, Piedmont and Blue Ridge geographical regions. Raymond E. Murphy and Marion Murphy, *Pennsylvania: A Regional Geography* (Harrisburg: Pennsylvania Book Service, 1937), 18, 165.

[2] Sylvester K. Stevens, *Pennsylvania: Birthplace of a Nation* (New York: Random House, 1964), pp. 32-40, 59-69; Wayland F. Dunaway, *A History of Pennsylvania* (second ed.; New York: Prentice-Hall, Inc., 1948), 28-37.

[3] Murphy and Murphy, *Pennsylvania*, 19-27, 203-42, 257-62.

[4] An isometric reconstruction drawing of the type of house most likely built by early English settlers is illustrated in Cary Carson, Norman F. Barka, William M. Kelso, Garry Wheeler Stone, Dell Upton, "Impermanent Architecture in the Southern American Colonies," *Winterthur Portfolio* 16 (Summer/Autumn 1981): 143. The "caves" cited in early settlers' accounts were probably holes dug into the ground or into banks and walled and covered with planks, probably much like the "palisaded log huts" at Pioneer Village, Salem, Massachusetts. Robert C. Bucher, "The First Shelters of Our Pioneer Ancestors," *Pioneer America* 1 (July 1969): 7-12; Stevenson Whitcomb Fletcher, *Pennsylvania Agriculture and Country Life, 1640-1840* (Harrisburg, Pa.: Pennsylvania Historical and Museum Commission, 1950), 372.

[5]The significance of the single-pile house and variations of the hall-and-parlor plan are discussed in the Pennsylvania essay.

[6]Richard Pillsbury and Andrew Kardos, *A Field Guide to the Folk Architecture of Northeastern United States*, Geography Publications at Dartmouth No. 8 (Hanover, N.H.: Dartmouth College, 1970), 53.

[7]A good example of the latter is Morriseianna in London Grove Township, Chester County. It began as a one-room house for Michael Harlan, ca. 1700, but later additions by Harlan ca. 1720 and especially by Samuel Morris in 1843 swallowed up the original house leaving it as a room off a hallway. Edgar A. Hirdler, "Morriseianna, London Grove Township, Chester County," Chester County Historical Society, 1962 (typewritten).

[8]Thomas A. Lainhoff has determined from 1798 direct tax records that 57 percent of all houses in Manheim Township, Lancaster County, were of log construction; by 1815 that had increased to 60 percent. Robert Bucher estimates that the count for Heidelberg Township, Lebanon County, may be greater than that for Manheim Township. These figures have been compiled by Professor Bernard Herman at the University of Delaware.

[9]The comprehensive study of Pennsylvania German architecture remains G. Edwin Brumbaugh, "Colonial Architecture of the Pennsylvania Germans," *Proceedings of the Pennsylvania German Society* 41 (1933). For a discussion of Pennsylvania German roof tiles, see Robert C. Bucher, "Steep Roofs and Red Tiles," *Pennsylvania Folklife* 12 (Summer 1961): 19-26.

[10]Robert C. Bucher, "The Continental Log House," *Pennsylvania Folklife* 12 (Summer 1962): 14-19; Henry Glassie, "A Central Chimney Continental Log House," *Pennsylvania Folklife* 18 (Winter 1968-69): 32-39; John D. Milner, "Germanic Architecture in the New World," *Journal of the Society of Architectural Historians* 34 (December 1975): 299.

[11]During the colonial period, no planned towns developed within a thirty-mile radius, or a day's return journey, of Philadelphia. Even county seats in Bucks and Chester counties (Newtown and Chester) suffered sluggish growth. James T. Lemon, "Urbanization and the Development of Eighteenth-Century Southeastern Pennsylvania and Adjacent Delaware," *William and Mary Quarterly* third series, 24 (October 1967): 502-3, 509-10; Zelinsky, "The Pennsylvania Town," 146. William Penn evidently planned Newtown in Bucks County as an outlying "new town," but its slow growth weakens its challenge as an exception to Zelinsky's position. When Newtown became the county seat in 1726, it consisted of only a few log houses. By the end of the eighteenth century, as the village began to take on the cultural life of a town, with an academy, library, and Masonic lodge, its growth was radically curtailed by the 1813 removal of county government to Doylestown, and Newtown did not become a borough until 1836. W. W. Davis, *The History of Bucks County, Pennsylvania* (Doylestown: Democrat Book and Job Office, 1876), 232, 238-42; George MacReynolds, *Place Names in Bucks County, Pennsylvania* (Doylestown: Bucks County Historical Society, 1942), 294.

[12]Stevens, *Pennsylvania*, 69-70.

[13]John, Thomas, and Richard Penn became Pennsylvania's proprietors on their mother's death in 1727. As the eldest son, John inherited under English law one-half of his father's proprietary interests; the other two sons shared the other half equally. On John Penn's death in 1746, his one-half share went to Thomas Penn, the next eldest son, who then owned a three-quarter interest in the colony. Thomas Penn arrived in Pennsylvania from England in 1732 and in behalf of his brothers reasserted proprietary power, including the proprietary charter right to establish towns. The Penns did not rigidly follow their criteria for site selection. In the case of Easton, they sacrificed centrality for the town's strategic location at the fork of two rivers. The county seats' fifty-five-mile minimum distance from Philadelphia is a straight line ("as the crow flies") rather than distance measured on roads of the time. Lemon, "Urbanization and the Development of Eighteenth-Century Southeastern Pennsylvania," 512-13, 539; Stevens, *Pennsylvania*, 43-44.

[14]Lemon, "Urbanization and the Development of Eighteenth-Century Southeastern Pennsylvania," 512-15, 522, 535; Stevens, *Pennsylvania*, 70; Joe K. Kindig III, *Architecture in York County* (York, Pa.: Historical Society of York County, 1963), 6-7; Zelinsky, "The Pennsylvania Town," 131-37; Edward T. Price, "The Central Courthouse Square in the American County Seat," *Geographical Review* 58 (January 1968): 39-44; Richard Pillsbury, "The Market or Public Square in Pennsylvania, 1682-1820," *Proceedings of the Pennsylvania Academy of Science* 41 (1967): 116-18.

[15]Glassie, "Delaware Valley Folk Building," 42-45.

[16]Quoted in Bernice M. Ball, *Barns of Chester County, Pennsylvania* (West Chester, Pa.: Chester County Day Committee of the Women's Auxiliary, Chester County Hospital, 1974), 97. Because this book is organized much like grandmother's attic, it is a treasure trove of such fascinating bits as Read's "The Stranger on the Sill," from which the quoted stanza is taken.

[17]Eric Arthur and Dudley Witney, *The Barn: A Vanishing Landmark in North America* (Toronto: M.F. Feheley Arts Company, 1972), 106.

[18]Glass, *Pennsylvania Culture Region*, 9. This is the most scholarly and quantified study of Pennsylvania barns to date.

[19]Charles H. Dornbusch and John K. Heyl, *Pennsylvania German Barns, The Pennsylvania German Folklore Society*, vol. 21 (1956) (Allentown, Pa.: Schlecter's, 1958). Allen G. Noble illustrates the eleven barn types in *Wood, Brick, and Stone: The North American Settlement Landscape*, 2 vols. (Amherst: University of Massachusetts Press, 1984), 2:22-35.

[20]Glass, *Pennsylvania Culture Region*, 9; Jordan, *American Log Buildings*, 99-100; Robert C. Bucher, "The Cultural Backgrounds of Our Pennsylvania Homesteads," *Bulletin of the Historical Society of Montgomery County, Pennsylvania* 15 (Fall 1966): 26; Peter O. Wacker, *The Musonetcong Valley of New Jersey* (New Brunswick: Rutgers University Press, 1968), 97.

[21]Pennsylvania Germans call these decorations "barn stars" or "barn flowers;" the most common one is the green, yellow, and white "Cocalico star." Henry Glassie points out that although these folk decorations were to beautify barns, there remained other folk elements in the barn to ward off ill fortune. "Bible verses were secreted within, and a tiny, five-pointed

star—exactly the pentangle that Sir Gawain wore on his shield when he sallied off to keep his appointment with the Green Knight—was scratched in a continuous line on beams, on trough and manger, on plow or harrow." Henry Glassie, "Folk Art," in Richard M. Dorson, ed., *Folklore and Folklife: An Introduction* (Chicago: University of Chicago, 1972), 276. Decorated barns appear principally in Berks and Lehigh Counties with a smaller concentration in Bucks and Montgomery Counties. Alfred L. Shoemaker, "Hex Signs," in Alfred L. Shoemaker, ed., *The Pennsylvania Barn*, (Kutztown, Pa.: Pennsylvania Folklife Society, [1959]), 55-68.

[22]Many people have assumed that the barn's origins are in Germany and have called it a Pennsylvania German barn. Henry Glassie suggests that its origins are a "meshing [of] the multi-level banked notion brought from both Central Europe and northwestern England with the double-crib barn idea from Central Europe." Henry Glassie, "The Double Crib Barn in South Central Pennsylvania," *Pioneer America*, 2 (July 1970): 25. In 1966, although he admitted "it may be foolhardy to do so," he sketched the barn's conjectural development. See Henry Glassie, "The Pennsylvania Barn in the South: Part II," *Pennsylvania Folklife* 15 (Summer 1966): 25. See also Glassie, "Delaware Valley Folk Building," 52. Nearly eighty years ago a University of Pennsylvania professor picked the correct country but the wrong source, claiming that the barn's forebay was "a direct survival of the projecting roof and balcony of the Swiss." M. D. Learned, "The German Barn in America," *University of Pennsylvania Lectures, 1913-1914* (Philadelphia: University of Pennsylvania, 1915), 347. Thomas Jefferson Wertenbaker was closer to the answer when he concluded that the ancestor of the Pennsylvania barn would be found "in the wooded highlands of Upper Bavaria, the southern spurs of the Black Forest mountains, in the Jura region and elsewhere in Switzerland." Thomas Jefferson Wertenbaker, *The Founding of American Civilization: The Middle Colonies* (New York: Charles Scribner's Sons, 1938), 321.

[23]The antecedents of the Pennsylvania barn, embodying all four of its major features (forebay, two levels, banked ramp, and double-crib floor plan) appear in the Alpine regions of Bavaria, central and eastern Switzerland, and Austria. Terry G. Jordan, "Some Neglected Swiss Literature on the Forebay Bank Barn," *Pennsylvania Folklife* 37 (Winter 1987-88): 75-80; idem, "Alpine, Alemannic, and American Log Architecture," *Annals of the Association of American Geographers* 70 (June 1980: 165-74; Robert F. Ensminger, "A Search for the Origin of the Pennsylvania Barn," *Pennsylvania Folklife* 30 (Winter 1980-81): 50-69.

[24]There is disagreement on whether the Pennsylvania barn evolved in America or was introduced more or less fully developed. Dornbusch and Heyl argue that the Pennsylvania barn evolved in America in response to agricultural needs. Dornbusch and Heyl, *Pennsylvania German Barns*, x. Henry Glassie also suggests that it "seems not to be a transplant from Europe, but rather an American meshing of similar traditions brought from Britain and Central Europe." Glassie, *Pattern in the Material Folk Culture*, 62. He makes more specific suggestions in "The Old Barns of Appalachia," *Mountain Life and Work* 40 (Summer 1965): 28, and "The Double Crib Barn in South Central Pennsylvania," 25. Jordan, however, writes that "it seems likely that the Pennsylvania barn was fully evolved in log and possibly also masonry-frame forms before the migrations to America occurred." Jordan, *American Log Buildings*, 101.

[25] Glass, *Pennsylvania Culture Region*, 16.

[26] John Beale Bordley, *Essays and Notes on Husbandry and Rural Affairs* (second ed.; Philadelphia: Budd & Bartram, 1801), 136-38. The owner of an estate on Wye Island in Chesapeake Bay, Bordley was an avid reader of English works on the new agriculture, experimenting with their ideas in his own fields. Unable to prod his Maryland neighbors toward his reforms, he moved to Philadelphia, where in 1785 he published his first book on agriculture and a year later helped to found the Philadelphia Society for Promoting Agriculture. Brooke Hindle, *The Pursuit of Science in Revolutionary America, 1735-1789* (Chapel Hill: University of North Carolina Press, 1956), 358, 361.

[27] "Remarks upon Agricultural Buildings," *The Farmers' Cabinet* 2 (15 February 1838): 195.

[28] "Farm Buildings," *The Farmers' Cabinet* 3 (15 September 1838): 56-58; "Barn-Yards and Manure," *The Farmers' Cabinet* 4 (15 August 1839): 17. Two-thirds of the 530 barns surveyed by Joseph W. Glass faced the quarter of the compass between southeast and southwest. As Glass points out, "most Pennsylvania farmers harnessed solar energy at an early date to ease their workaday burdens." Glass, *Pennsylvania Culture Region*, 104. Barnyard construction had been printed at least twenty-five years before the advice in *The Farmers' Cabinet*. In 1814 John Nicholson explained that barnyards should be enclosed, given clay floors, and made lower in the middle in order "to preserve the escape of much fertilizing liquor." John Nicholson, *The Farmer's Assistant* (Albany, N.Y.: H.C. Southwick, 1814), 15.

[29] Frederick Watts, "The Pennsylvania Barn," *Report of the Commissioner of Agriculture for the Year 1864* (Washington, D.C.: U.S. Government Printing Office, 1865), 269. This barn's plans and elevations are illustrated in Richard Rawson, *Old Barn Plans* (New York: Mayflower Books, Inc., 1979), 61-63. This book of illustrations is frustrating because of its author's failure to cite historical sources or provide much meaningful interpretation. Yet the compilation of so many barn illustrations indicates that the nineteenth-century agricultural press was actively discussing and illustrating barn construction and organization. Watts was a Cumberland County "mover and shaker." He was an attorney, judge, agricultural reformer, president of the Cumberland Valley Railroad, and a founder and first president of the board of trustees of Farmers' High School. (The high school became Pennsylvania State University, whose first completed building was an 1857 Watts-designed barn similar to the one illustrated in the 1864 agriculture commissioner's report; the barn burned in 1891.) Ulysses S. Grant appointed Watts U.S. commissioner of agriculture in 1871 and he served until Grant left office. He also owned a farm in Carlisle, Cumberland County, where about 1858 he built a barn extremely similar to the one illustrated in the 1864 report. An arsonist burned that barn in 1866, but Watts rebuilt it the next year. It was dismantled in late summer 1988 to make way for a truck depot's parking lot with the expectation that it will be reassembled for a residence in suburban Philadelphia. For a thorough discussion of Watts' agricultural reform ideas and his Carlisle farmstead, see Jerry Clouse and Kate Kauffman, "Watts' Folly," *Pennsylvania Heritage* 15 (Fall 1989): 12-17; see also *Dictionary of American Biography*, s.v. "Watts, Frederick," by Claribel R. Barnett.

[30] In 1798 at least 52 percent of Pennsylvania's barns were log or partially log. Jordan, American Log Buildings, 165 (n. 28). In Bucks and Chester Counties, where figures are based on the 1798 glass tax survey, 77 percent of the barns were log or partially log. The tax survey information is listed in Alfred L. Shoemaker, "The Barns of 1798," in Shoemaker, ed., *The Pennsylvania Barn*, 91-96. From these figures Glass estimates that 70 percent of Pennsylvania's barns at the turn of the nineteenth century were either log or partially log. Throughout the region wood remained a popular building material well into the twentieth century. In fact, nearly 90 percent of the 471 barns in his sample are of wood construction, either log or frame. Glass, *Pennsylvania Culture Region*, 68, 72. Log or frame smokehouses may sound improbable, because of the fire hazard they present, but they were not uncommon in the region. Amos Long Jr., "Smokehouses in the Lebanon Valley," *Pennsylvania Folklife* 13 (Fall 1962): 25-32.

[31] Quoted in Walter M. Kollmorgen, "The Pennsylvania German Farmer," in Ralph Wood, ed., *The Pennsylvania Germans* (Princeton: Princeton University Press, 1942), 30. Benjamin Rush published his views in *Columbian Magazine, or Monthly Miscellany* 3 (January 1789): 22-30. Benjamin Rush was one of the great figures of his day. He was a signer of the Declaration of Independence, served as surgeon general of the Continental Army, pioneered more humane treatment of mental illness, founded Dickinson College, and established the first American antislavery society. *Dictionary of American Biography*, s.v. "Rush, Benjamin," by Richard H. Shryock.

[32] Quoted in Glassie, *Pattern in the Material Folk Culture*, 193.

[33] James T. Lemon, "The Agricultural Practices of National Groups in Eighteenth-Century Southeastern Pennsylvania," *The Geographical Review* 56 (October 1966): 467-96.

[34] James T. Lemon, *The Best Poor Man's Country: A Geographical Study of Early Southeastern Pennsylvania* (Baltimore: Johns Hopkins University Press, 1972), 91-93.

[35] Because many Pennsylvania Germans lived in limestone soil areas, they did not need fertilizers. Others, however, lived on less fertile lands and could have benefited from lime or gypsum. Yet many actively resisted using fertilizers, perhaps because they had mishandled them in their initial attempts. Ibid., 173-74.

[36] The fifth generation, the three married daughters of Adam Ernst Dundore, acquired the farm on their father's death in 1911. They sold it the next year to George D. Fahrenbach, Berks County sheriff and owner of the adjacent John Conrad Farm (PA-259). The Union Canal operated for nearly sixty years, between 1828 and 1885. Thomas Kheel, "Dundore Farm (Hottenstein Farm)," HABS Report PA-261 (Washington, D.C.: Library of Congress, 1976), 3-6, 20; William H. Shank, *The Amazing Pennsylvania Canals* (York, Pa.: American Canal and Transportation Center, 1981), 12.

[37] Glassie calls this arrangement of farm buildings the L-shaped Variant of the Linear Mid-Atlantic Plan, as compared to the courtyard pattern found in English-dominated southern New Jersey. Glassie, "Delaware Valley Folk Building," 51-56. In Joseph Glass's study, this perpendicular relationship of house and barn was the second most popular arrangement; he

found it 30 percent of the farms studied. In the most popular plan, which Glassie calls the Linear Mid-Atlantic Plan, the house and barn share the same orientation; 42 percent of the houses and barns in Glass's study conform to this plan. In Glass's sample, 85 percent of the "farmsteads were arranged in a manner which made the barnyard visible from some part of the farmhouse." Glass, *Pennsylvania Culture Region*, 173, 176. A well-illustrated description of Pennsylvania farm buildings is Amos Long Jr., *The Pennsylvania German Family Farm: A Regional Architectural and Folk Cultural Study in an American Agricultural Community*, vol. 6 in Publications of the Pennsylvania German Society series (Breinigsville, Pa.: Pennsylvania German Society, 1972). His shorter version is *Farmsteads and Their Buildings* (Lebanon, Pa.: Applied Art Publishers, 1972).

[38] The kitchen's fireplace was not removed until 1960, when the oil furnace and baseboard radiators were evidently installed. The smokehouse was being used as late as 1972. Kheel, "Dundore Farm (Hottenstein Farm)," 1-6, 12-20. The Dundore Farm is but one of many such farms in the region. The Lauer-Gerhard Farm (PA-1954) along Spring Creek in Lower Heidelberg Township, Berks County, differed in details but not in its general pattern. Its houses were rubble rather than log and the bank barn was timber-frame rather than stone, and they were arranged in the popular Linear Mid-Atlantic Plan rather than its L-shaped variant. Yet all of the structures were integrated physically into the landscape and arranged functionally to ease daily and seasonal chores. The Gerhard family owned the farm for four generations (116 years), and when HABS surveyed it in the 1970s its plan, too, remained unaltered from its development during the early nineteenth century. Richard Tatara, "Lauer-Gerhard Farm (Reifsnyder Farm), Brownsville Vicinity, Berks County, Pennsylvania," HABS Report PA-1954 (Washington, D.C.: Library of Congress, 1981), 2-9, 15, 21. In the mid-1970s, HABS documented and recorded many such Pennsylvania-German farms near Brownsville and Mount Pleasant in Berks County as part of the Blue Marsh Lake project.

[39] The Delaware Division of the state's canal system opened in 1832 along the western bank of the Delaware River between Bristol and Easton. It had connections with the Morris Canal at Easton and the Delaware and Raritan Canal at Trenton, New Jersey. A small section of the Delaware Division remains open at New Hope, Bucks County, offering rides to the public. The Union Canal opened in 1828, but because of the porous limestone soil along its path, it faced a constant leakage problem. Also, its designers built conservatively, leaving the canal's channel too narrow for the wider freight and packet boats that became common by the late 1830s. The canal operators widened the canal in 1856, but the debt from that operation and railroad competition contributed to its closing in 1885. Shank, *The Amazing Pennsylvania Canals*, 9-19, 40-42, 54, 60-64; Murphy and Murphy, *Pennsylvania*, 119-23.

[40] James M. Swank, *Progressive Pennsylvania: A Record of the Remarkable Industrial Development of the Keystone State* (Philadelphia: J.B. Lippincott Company, 1908), 148; Jules I. Bogen, *The Anthracite Railroads: A Study in American Railroad Enterprise* (New York: Ronald Press Company, 1927), 25-27, 38-39. Murphy and Murphy, *Pennsylvania*, 142-43. The West Chester railroad station is illustrated in Alice Kent Schooler, *Livable West Chester: An Architectural Overview* (West Chester, Pa.: Chester County Historical Society, 1985), 52.

[41] Samuel Sloan, *The Model Architect*, 2 vols. (Philadelphia: E.S. Jones, 1852; reprint ed., New York: Da Capo Press, 1975), 1:10.

[42] Elizabeth Biddle Yarnall, *Addison Hutton: Quaker Architect, 1834-1916* (Philadelphia: Art Alliance Press, 1974), 39, 41-42.

[43] Henry Hudson Holly, *Holly's Country Seats: Containing Lithographic Designs for Cottages, Villas, Mansions, etc., with Their Accompanying Outbuildings* (New York: D. Appleton and Company, 1863; reprint ed., Watkins Glen, N.Y.: American Life Foundation, 1977), 21.

[44] The seminal work on the cultivated and vernacular traditions is John A. Kouwenhoven, *Made in America: The Arts in Modern Civilization* (Garden City, N.Y.: Doubleday and Company, 1948). For a discussion of vernacular builders' widespread use of the cross-gable see Henry Glassie, "Folk Art" in Richard M. Dorson, *Folklore and Folklife: An Introduction* (Chicago: University of Chicago Press, 1972), 273-74.

[45] There is no single volume that deals fully with the impact of industrialism on American architecture. Some very good works on specific building types include Carroll L. V. Meeks, *The Railroad Station: An Architectural History* (New Haven: Yale University Press, 1956) and Richard Longstreth, *The Building of Main Street: A Guide to American Commercial Architecture* (Washington, D.C.: The Preservation Press of the National Trust for Historic Preservation, 1987). William H. Pierson Jr. devotes a chapter to New England textile mills in *American Buildings and Their Architects: Technology and the Picturesque, The Corporate and the Early Gothic Styles* (Garden City, N.Y.: Doubleday & Company, 1978), 28-90.

[46] Agnes Addison Gilchrist, "Market Houses in High Street," in Luther P. Eisenhart, ed., *Historic Philadelphia: From the Founding until the Early Nineteenth Century*, Transactions of the American Philosophical Society 43, Part 1 (1953): 304.

[47] Thomas U. Walter designed Horticultural Hall in 1848; John C. Trautwine in 1835 designed Pennsylvania Hall for what was then known as Pennsylvania College.

[48] Luden's 1921-23 marble-ashlar Bon Air stands on Hill Road in Reading. Its Renaissance Revival style was popular among the east coast elite near the turn of the twentieth century. Luden, the son of an Amsterdam-born jeweler and watchmaker, was born in Reading in 1859. He started manufacturing candy behind his father's shop. His venture expanded steadily, and although his factory made all kinds of candy, his name is still associated with cough drops. Raymond W. Albright, *Two Centuries of Reading, Pa., 1748-1948: A History of the County Seat of Berks County* (Reading, Pa.: Historical Society of Berks County, 1948), 260; interview with Professor Harry G. Schalck, West Chester University, 2 February 1990.

[49] By almost any standard, the Great Valley and Piedmont Region is the most prosperous part of Pennsylvania. Ronald F. Abler, David J. Cuff, William J. Long, Edward K. Muller, and Wilbur Zelinsky, *The Atlas of Pennsylvania* (Philadelphia: Temple University Press, 1989), 182.

Catalog

Adams County

Bermudian Vicinity (Latimore Township)

Christ Evangelical Lutheran Church (PA-348), S side of LR01043, at junction with T620, approx. 3 mi. E of PA 94, approx. 2 mi. S of Bermudian. Brick, two by three bays, one story with basement, gable roof, cornice returns, belfry with corner pilasters and arched openings, brick pilasters with corbeled brick courses under cornice divide side bays, Greek Revival details. Built 1879; congregation organized 1745. 1 ext. photo (1950); 1 data page (1958). LC code: PA,1-YORSP.V,2.

Fairfield Borough

Fairfield Inn. See Miller, William, House.

Miller, William, House (Fairfield Inn) (PA-350), NW side of PA 116 (Main St.), just SW of LR01015. Built in five sections: original one-and-a-half-story stone house built ca. 1757; stone addition built to E late eighteenth century; additional story of stuccoed frame and half-timber added above two sections before 1860; separate two-and-a-half-story random-rubble house built to S ca. 1790s; three-and-a-half-story random-rubble wing added to W side of 1790s house 1832; frame wing connecting 1757 house with 1790s house built before 1860. Original 1757 house built by John Miller; acquired 1789 by son William, built 1790s house, obtained tavern license 1796, laid out streets of Fairfield (originally Millerstown), first state senator from Adams County; houses acquired by James Wilson, built 1832 section as tavern and connected all sections; still used as inn, restored. 1 ext. photo (1950, shows E gable end of 1790s house); 1 data page (1958). LC code: PA,1-FAIRF,1. NR.

Floradale Vicinity (Menallen Township)

Peters, George, House (John Peters House) (PA-362), E side of PA 34, .7 mi. N of Floradale. Brick, five-bay front, three-and-a-half stories, gable roof, bracketed cornice, three-story cast-iron porch, door with transom and side lights. Built ca. 1860; frame and brick additions to rear. Built by George Peters; purchased by Charles J. Tyson, a Gettysburg photographer. 1 ext. photo (1950); 1 data page (1958). LC code: PA,1-FLORDA.V,1.

Peters, John, House. See Peters, George, House.

Gettysburg Borough

Adams County Courthouse (PA-265), Center Square. Brick, square, four identical three-bay facades, two-and-a-half stories, cross gable roofs with pedimented gable ends with clocks on each facade, central octagonal cupola, denticulated cornice, corner pilasters, pedimented entrances. Built 1804; demolished 1859. First courthouse for Adams County, established 1800. 1 ext. copy photo of drawing (n.d.); 1 data page (1983). LC code: PA,1-GET,9.

Bushman House. See Gettysburg Vicinity (Cumberland Township), Bushman House.

Culp House (PA-354), S end of Third St., .1 mi. S of Pa. 116 (Hanover Rd.), in Gettysburg National Military Park

(NMP). Brick, L-shaped, 27'-2" (three-bay front) x 30'-1" (two bays), 19'-3" x 30'-2" rear ell, two-and-a-half stories with basement, gable roofs, paired chimneys, entrance porch and door with transom and side lights; side hall plan. Built ca. 1840s; used as park residence. Used as Confederate staging area and hospital during Battle of Gettysburg 1863. 6 sheets (1957, 1986, including plans, elevations, section, details); 2 ext. photos (1956); 1 data page (1958). LC code: PA,1-GET,3. Gettysburg NMP.

Farm and Smokehouse (PA-5379). Farm structures include ca. 1840s house, ca. 1840s bank barn, ca. 1840s springhouse, ca. 1850 smokehouse, pre-1863 woodshed, ca. 1900 wagon shed, and 1937 milk house. 1 sheet (1986-87, including site plan of farm, plan and elevations of smokehouse).

Barn (PA-5379A). Random rubble ground floor with frame upper level, bank barn, 95'-11" x 42', gable roof, ramp to upper level on N elevation, shed additions on E and W elevations. Built ca. 1840s. 6 sheets (1987, including plans, elevations, sections, framing details).

Springhouse (PA-5379B). Coursed rubble, 15'-1" x 12'-1", one story, gable roof. Built ca. 1840s. 1 sheet (1987, including plan, elevations, section).

Woodshed (PA-5379C). Frame with wooden siding, random rubble foundation, 16'-4" x 20'-3", one story, gable roof. Built pre-1863. 1 sheet (1986, including plan, elevations, section, detail).

Gettysburg College, Old Dorm. See Pennsylvania College, Pennsylvania Hall.

Lutheran Theological Seminary, Main Building (PA-359), E side of Confederate Ave., .2 mi. N of Pa. 116 (W. Middle St.). Brick, projecting center section (three-bay E elevation, five-bay W elevation) with flanking two-bay sections, approx. 100' x 40', three-and-a-half stories with elevated basement, cross gable roofs with stepped gable ends, paired chimneys, open arcaded cupola with dome, distyle Doric entrance porch with stepped pediment. Built 1832; Nicholas Pierce, architect; dormers added after 1870; "Peace Portico" (semicircular Corinthian porch with balustrade) added 1913 to mark fiftieth anniversary of Battle of Gettysburg (partially removed during restoration); cupola rebuilt after original one burned 1923; leased to Adams County Historical Society 1961; restored. Seminary was founded 1826, this was the first Lutheran theological education building in America. Used as observatory and hospital during Battle of Gettysburg 1863. 3 ext. photos (1950); 1 data page (1958). LC code: PA,1-GET,6. NR (Also in Gettysburg Battlefield Historic District).

McPherson Barn. See Gettysburg Vicinity (Cumberland Township), McPherson Barn.

Pennsylvania College, Pennsylvania Hall (Gettysburg College, Old Dorm) (PA-360), W side of N. Washington St. at intersection with Stevens St. Brick, projecting three-bay center section with flanking three-bay sections and two-bay end pavilions, approx. 150', three stories with elevated basement, gable and hip roofs, octagonal cupola, central pedimented Doric portico, Greek Revival style. Built 1835-38; John C. Trautwine, architect; Henry Winemiller and Samuel Hunter, builders; enclosed stair towers added at each end 1889; portico added on N elevation 1937; interior remodeled, restored to 1889 appearance 1969-70. Original building of Pennsylvania College (oldest Lutheran college structure in America); became dormitory and named "Pennsylvania Hall" 1898; college name changed to Gettysburg College 1921; now Gettysburg College administrative offices. Used as an observatory and field hospital during Battle of Gettysburg 1863. 1 ext. photo (1950); 1 data page (1958). LC code: PA,1-GET,7. NR (Also in Gettysburg Battlefield Historic District).

Gettysburg Vicinity (Cumberland Township)

Bender, Theodore, House (James J. Wills Farm) (PA-1964), E of Herr's Ridge Rd., W of Buford Ave., N of U.S. Rte. 30, in Gettysburg NMP. Brick, 35'-7" (five-bay front) x 32' (two bays), two-and-a-half stories with stone basement, gable roof, inside end chimneys, porch and door with transom and side lights on S (front) elevation; central hall plan. Built 1867-68; farm dates back to 1798. Outbuildings. Farm associated with Battle of Gettysburg 1863. 9 sheets (1986, including site plan, plans, elevations, sections, details). Gettysburg NMP.

Black Horse Tavern (PA-361), N side of Pa. 116, at Marsh Creek, approx. 3 mi. W of Gettysburg. Random rubble, L-shaped, two-and-a-half stories with two-story rear ell, gable roofs. Built 1812 as a tavern; residence 1958. Used as a Confederate hospital near Battle of Gettysburg 1863. 1 ext. photo (1950); 1 data page (1958). LC code: PA,1-GET.V,5. NR (Also in Gettysburg Battlefield Historic District).

Blocher House (PA-1963), E side of Tablerock Rd., at Y-intersection with Pa. 34, in Gettysburg NMP. Random rubble with concrete block and frame additions, 40'-6" (six-bay front) x 35'-7", two stories, mansard roof, paired doors and porch on S (front) elevation, shed-roof addition across N elevation. Built 1820s; raised from one-and-a-half stories to two stories with mansard roof 1882; addition of frame with asphalt shingles added on N elevation; two-bay concrete block addition built on E elevation 1944; concrete screened porch added across S elevation. House used as Confederate aid station during Battle of Gettysburg 1863. 3 sheets (1987, including site plan, plans, elevations, section). LC code: PA,1-GET.V,10. Gettysburg NMP.

Bricker Outdoor Bake Oven (Fox Outdoor Bake Oven) (PA-355), W side of Pa. 134 (Taneytown Rd.), just S of Wheatfield Rd. Brick oven and work area enclosed by frame housing with gable roof, random rubble base set on sloping site with smokehouse below oven, over-all dimensions approx. 6' x 12', squirrel tail bake oven with elaborate flue system connected to smokehouse. Built nineteenth century. Owned by Leonard Bricker during Battle of Gettysburg. Unusual combination of bake oven and smokehouse. 4 sheets (1957, including plot plan, plans, elevations, sections); 2 ext. photos (1957), 2 int. photos (1957); 1 data page (1958). LC code: PA,1-GET.V,4. NR (Gettysburg Battlefield Historic District).

Brien House. See Bryan House.

Bryan House (Brien House) (PA-342), E side of Hancock Ave., .2 mi. S of Emmitsburg Rd., in Gettysburg NMP. Frame, 24'-3" (three-bay front) x 14'-9", one-and-a-half stories, gable roof, pent roof across front elevation; two-room plan. Built early nineteenth century (before 1857); substantial alterations after 1863, roof raised to two stories, two-story frame wing and one-story shed added; restored to 1863 appearance ca. 1950s (additions removed); part of battlefield exhibit. Associated with Battle of Gettysburg 1863. 6 sheets (1936, shows altered condition, including site plan, plans, elevations, details; 1957, shows restored condition, elevations, isometric framing plan); 1 ext. photo (1957, during restoration), 3 construction detail photos (1957, during restoration); 1 data page (1958). LC code: PA,1-GET.V,2. Gettysburg NMP.

Barn (PA-342A), W side of Hancock Ave. Frame, 40' x 24', one story, gable roof. Built early nineteenth century (before 1857); part of battlefield exhibit. 2 sheets (1936, including plan, elevations, section, isometric of framing detail). LC code: PA,1-GET.V,2.

Bushman House (PA-365), .2 mi. E of Confederate Ave., just S of Emmitsburg Rd., in Gettysburg NMP. Random rubble with quoins, 27' (three-bay front) x 26'-5", two-and-a-half stories, gable roof; one-and-a-half-story brick wing added to side. Built 1808 (date stone); wing added ca. 1860; used as park residence. Used as a field hospital during Battle of Gettysburg 1863. 2 ext. photos (ca. 1935). LC code: PA,1-GET,8. Gettysburg NMP.

Barn (PA-365A). Double log barn with two frame additions, board and batten siding, random rubble foundation, 96'-5" x 31'-9', two levels, gable roof with longer W slope, two-level frame addition on N elevation, one-level shed addition on S elevation. Built ca. 1808. Used by troops during Battle of Gettysburg 1863. 12 sheets (1985, including site plan, plans, elevations, sections, details).

Cobean Farm (PA-1965), W of Pa. 34, .5 mi. N of Y-intersection of Pa. 34 and Tablerock Rd. Brick, 44'-6" (five-bay front) x 34'-2", two-and-a-half stories with coursed rubble basement, gable roof, inside end chimneys, door with fanlight flanked by pilasters on E (front) elevation, one-bay entrance porch; central hall plan; Georgian details. Built 1805; one-story frame addition on W elevation. Only Georgian style farmhouse in Gettysburg NMP and one of the oldest brick houses in Adams County. House damaged in Battle of Gettysburg 1863, used as a Confederate field hospital during battle. 4 sheets (1987, including site plan, plans, elevations, detail). NR (Gettysburg Battlefield Historic District).

Conewago Presbyterian Church. See Hunterstown (Straban Township), Great Conewago Presbyterian Church.

Culp House and Farm. See Gettysburg Borough, Culp House.

Eisenhower Farm One (PA-5372), .5 mi. W of intersection of Confederate Ave. and Emmitsburg Rd. (U.S. Rte. 15), in Gettysburg NMP. Farm purchased by President Dwight D. Eisenhower in 1951 while he was president of Columbia University. At the time the farm structures included a brick house, bank barn, and several outbuildings. Known as "The Little White House." President Eisenhower donated the farm to the National Park Service in 1967, although Mrs. Eisenhower continued to live there until her death in 1979. Farm was opened to the public in 1980. 1 sheet (1986, site plan of farm). Eisenhower NHS, NHL. LC code: PA,1-GET.V,12.

Bank Barn (PA-5372A). Coursed rubble ground level and frame with vertical siding on upper level, 95'-8" x 50'-1", two levels with lofts, gable roof with three louvered cupolas, louvered ventilator windows, windows with fanlights in gable ends, garage (formerly chicken house) on N elevation. Built post-Civil War, replaced barn used as field hospital during Battle of Gettysburg 1863. 11 sheets (1986, including plans, elevations, sections, details, axonometric of structural framing).

Eisenhower Farm Two (PA-5373), .5 mi. W of intersection of Confederate Ave. and Emmitsburg Rd. (U.S. Rte. 15), in Gettysburg NMP. President Dwight D. Eisenhower acquired Farm Two in 1954 to prevent development adjacent to his farm. He used Farm Two as a cattle farm. Farm Two dates from before the Battle of Gettysburg in 1863. 1 sheet (1986, site plans of farm). Eisenhower NHS, NHL. LC code: PA,1-GET.V,13.

Bank Barn (PA-5373A). Coursed rubble ground level, frame with vertical wooden siding and corrugated metal siding on upper level, 67'-4" x 43'-11", two levels, gable roof, shed addition and silo on NW elevation, shed addition on NE elevation, gable-roof addition on SW elevation. 7 sheets (1986, including plans, elevations, sections).

Breeding and Equipment Shed (PA-5373B). Frame with vertical wooden siding, 44'-5" x 24'-4", one level, gambrel roof of corrugated metal. 2 sheets (1986, including plan, elevations, sections, framing detail).

Showbarn (PA-5373C). Frame with horizontal wooden siding, concrete foundation, L-shaped, 144'-3" x 36'-2" barn with 80' x 24'-2" nursing barn at SE corner, gable roofs with aluminum panels and ventilators; main level of barn consists of pens, feed mixing room, washroom, and office, second-story loft. Built 1957-58; Victor Re, contractor, under direction of Robert Hartley. Showbarn was the center of President Dwight D. Eisenhower's award-winning black angus cattle operation. Maintained as a farm exhibit by the National Park Service. 6 sheets (1987, including site plan, plans, elevations, sections, details); 1 data page (1988).

Eisenhower Farms, Guard Huts (PA-5374), Back Ln. and Nevins Ln., off U.S. Rte. 15. Two frame guard huts constructed 1955 by Secret Service as part of the farms' security system to protect President Dwight D. Eisenhower. 2 sheets (1986, including site plan, plans, elevations, sections). Eisenhower NHS, NHL. LC code: PA,1-GET.V,14.

Fox Outdoor Bake Oven. See Bricker Outdoor Bake Oven.

Hummelbaugh Farm (PA-1961), N side of Pleasanton Ave., just W of Taneytown Rd. (Pa. 134), in Gettysburg NMP. Farm complex includes 1840s house, pre-Civil War smokehouse, remains of pre-Civil War summer kitchen, 1890 corn crib and chicken house, ca. 1920s cistern, barn. Jacob Hummelbaugh Farm was used by Union Army as a headquarters during Battle of Gettysburg 1863. 1 sheet (1985, including plan of farm, smokehouse drawings). Gettysburg NMP. LC code: PA,1-GET.V,15.

House (PA-1961A). Log and frame with clapboarding, 25' 1" (four bay front) x 26' (including rear lean to), two stories, gable roof, porch on E (front) elevation. Original one-story log house built 1840s; second story and rear frame lean-to added. Used by Gen. Alfred Pleasonton of the Union Army as his headquarters during Battle of Gettysburg 1863. 1 sheet (1985, including plans, elevations).

Huntingtown Presbyterian Church. See Hunterstown (Straban Township), Great Conewago Presbyterian Church.

Leister, Lydia, House (General Meade's Headquarters) (PA-341), W side of Pa. 134 (Taneytown Rd.), across from Hunt Ave., in Gettysburg NMP. Log covered with horizontal wooden siding, 24'-10" (three-bay front) x 15'-7", one-and-a-half stories, gable roof, porch across front elevation; two-room plan. Built ca. 1848; two-story wing added ca. 1870 (wing moved to new location ca. 1887 as home for Mrs. Leister when house was purchased by Gettysburg Battlefield Memorial Association); part of battlefield exhibit. Used by Gen. George Meade, Commander of the Union Army, as headquarters during the battle 1863. 9 sheets (1935, including site plan, plans, elevations, section, details); 1 ext. photo (ca. 1935). LC code: PA,1-GET.V,1. Gettysburg NMP.

Barn (PA-341A). Original log barn with frame addition to S covered with vertical wooden siding (log exposed at NE corner), 37'-8" x 24'-1", one story, gable roof, loft overhangs setback log section on E elevation. Built before 1863; later alterations. Barn served as field hospital and signal station during Battle of Gettysburg 1863. 9 sheets (1935, 1984, including site plan, plan, elevations, sections, details of framing and log construction, details).

McClean House (PA-1187), .2 mi. NE of Mummasburg Rd., approx. 1 mi. N of U.S. Rte. 30 (Chambersburg Rd.), in Gettysburg NMP. Brick house with frame and brick additions, L-shaped, brick house 25'-5" (three-bay front) x 17'-7" with frame wing on E elevation (11'-8" x 17'-7") and brick ell on N (rear) elevation (18'-1" x 22'-1"), two-and-a-half stories, gable roofs and shed roof. Original house was log built ca. 1822; present three-bay brick section added before 1863; frame wing replaced log section ca. 1870-85; brick ell added after 1895; used as park residence. Built by Moses McClean, a lawyer, who leased the property. Associated with Battle of Gettysburg 1863. 7 sheets (1968, including site plan, plans, elevations, sections). LC code: PA,1-GET.V,8. Gettysburg NMP.

McPherson Barn (PA-5139), SE corner of Chambersburg Rd. (Pa. 30) and Stone Ave, in Gettysburg NMP. Random rubble with frame forebay, 60'-6" x 22'-7" with frame shed added to rear, two-level bank barn, gable roof. Built nineteenth century. 4 sheets (1978 restoration drawings, including plot plan, plans, elevations, sections, details). LC code: PA,1-GET,10A. Gettysburg NMP.

Meade, General, Headquarters. See Leister, Lydia, House.

Patterson House (PA-580), Taneytown Rd. (Pa. 134), near Pleasonton Ave., in Gettysburg NMP. Log with later board and batten siding, 25' (three-bay front) x 18'-5", two stories, gable roof. Built ca. 1798 as one-and-a-half-story log house; raised to two stories; stone kitchen added to E elevation before 1825, replaced with frame kitchen built on original foundation. Used as headquarters by General Alfred Pleasonton during Battle of Gettysburg 1863. 5 sheets (1984, including site plan, plans, elevations, sections, construction details). Gettysburg NMP. LC code: PA,1-GET.V,16.

Rock Chapel. See Heidlersburg Vicinity (Huntington Township), Rock Chapel.

Rose Barn (PA-5348), E side of Emmitsburg Rd., .25 mi. S of Wheatfield Rd., in Gettysburg NMP. Ruinous coursed rubble barn, stone gable ends, slit ventilators. Built ca. 1812 on George Washington Rose Farm; roof destroyed 1934; deteriorated; one wall remaining when documented, later collapsed. Associated with Battle of Gettysburg 1863. 1 sheet (1985, photodrawing of S elevation, partial plan); 19 ext. photos (1985). Gettysburg NMP.

Slyder House (PA-356), .5 mi. E of Emmitsburg Rd. just N of Confederate Ave. on small road, in Gettysburg NMP. Random rubble with quoins, 30' (three-bay front) x 17'-10", one-and-a-half stories, gable roof, gabled hood over N (front) entrance; two-room plan. Built 1852 (date stone) by W.J. Slyder; one-story frame shed added on E side before 1895; part of battlefield exhibit. Associated with Battle of Gettysburg 1863. 8 sheets (1957, including site plan, plans, elevations, sections, details); 3 ext. photos (ca. 1935, 1957); 1 data page (1958). LC code: PA,1-GET,4. Gettysburg NMP.

Summer Kitchen (PA-356A). Frame, 13'-7" x 16'-3", two stories (originally one-and-a-half stories), gable roof, bake oven on E elevation (removed); attached wood shed on E elevation, frame, 13'-2" x 16'-3", one story, gable roof. Summer kitchen built ca. 1850s; roof raised to form second story and wood shed added before 1895; part of battlefield exhibit. 3 sheets (1957, including site plan, plans, elevations, sections, details). LC code: PA,1-GET,4A.

Barn (PA-356B). Double log barn with later board and batten siding, 55'-6" x 20'-1", gable roof with later metal covering; stable level, threshing floor, and lofts. Built ca. 1852; two sheds added on S elevation; forebay added on N elevation. One of four log barns still extant at Gettysburg. 5 sheets (1985, including site plan, plans, elevations, sections, details).

Spangler Barn. See Spangler Farm, *Carriage House*.

Spangler Farm (PA-1960), on farm lane, between Emmitsburg Rd. and Confederate Ave., .5 mi. N of Wheatfield Rd., in Gettysburg NMP. Farm complex includes 1820 house, early 1800s stable, 1880 summer kitchen, ca. 1880-90 smokehouse, 1890s carriage house, and ca. 1935 barn on ca. 1890 foundation. Farm used by Confederate troops during Battle of Gettysburg 1863. 1 sheet (1985, including site plan of farm, drawings of smokehouse). Gettysburg NMP. LC code: PA,1-GET, 11

House (PA-1960A). Log with later board and batten siding, stone and brick rear ell, L-shaped, 28'-10" (three-bay front) x 40'-10", two stories, gable roofs, entrance porch on front elevation. Built ca. 1820 by George Plank as a rectangular log house with separate one-story stone summer kitchen at rear, acquired by Henry Spangler 1862; 1880 brick second story added on summer kitchen and kitchen attached to house. 2 sheets (1985, including plans, elevations).

Summer Kitchen (PA-1960B). Frame with board and batten siding, 14'-5" x 20'-4", one-and-a-half stories, gable roof, fruit cellar. Built 1880 as replacement for original stone kitchen incorporated into house. 2 sheets (1985, including plans, elevation, section).

Storage House and Woodshed (PA-1960C). Frame with wooden siding, 19'-7" x 13'-1", one story, gable roof. Built late nineteenth century. 1 sheet (1985, including plan, elevations, framing elevation).

Carriage House (Spangler Barn) (PA-357). Frame with board and batten siding, 17'-9" x 20'-2" with 8' rear lean-to, two levels, gable roof. Built ca. 1890s; small additions to N elevation (removed after 1955). 2 sheets (1987, including plan, elevations, section); 1 ext. photo (1955); 1 data page (1958). LC code: PA,1-GET,5.

Trostle Barn (PA-1962), N side of United States Ave., between Emmitsburg Rd. and Sedgwick Ave., in Gettysburg NMP. Stone and brick with frame forebay on E elevation and frame shed on S elevation, 79'-1" x 48'-2", two-level bank barn, gable roof with brick gable ends, ramped wagon entrance on W elevation, patterned vents in brick end walls. Built pre-1860; part of W elevation collapsed and was replaced with frame wall; silo removed from N elevation. Farm used as headquarters by Union General Daniel Sickles during Battle of Gettysburg 1863. 10 sheets (1985, including site plan, plans, elevations, section, framing details, details). Gettysburg NMP. LC code: PA,1-GET.V,17A.

Weikert House (PA-363), SW corner of Sedgwick and United States Aves., in Gettysburg NMP. Coursed rubble with quoins, 27' (three-bay front) x 22', two-and-a-half stories, gable roof, porch across S (front) elevation; two-room plan. Built ca. 1820 (originally one-and-a-half stories, altered to two stories after 1863); used as park residence. Outbuildings. Associated with Battle of Gettysburg 1863. 2 ext. photos (1934); 1 data page (1957). LC code: PA,1-GET.V,6. Gettysburg NMP.

Barn (PA-358). Log encased in frame shell (SW section) and frame with board and batten siding, 61'-3" x 31'-4", one story, uneven gable roof, shed roof across SE elevation; double barn with center passageway. Original double log barn built late eighteenth century (pre-1798, only SW half remains), remaining log section encased in frame shell and frame section added nineteenth century; one-story frame shed added on side elevation before Civil War. Used as field hospital by Union troops during Battle of Gettysburg 1863. 8 sheets (1985, including site plan, plan, elevations, sections, framing details); 2 ext. photos (1934); 1 data page (1958). LC code: PA,1-GET.V,6B.

Summer Kitchen (PA-353). Log with random rubble fireplace wall, 16'-6" x 16', one story, gable roof, porch formed by overhang of roof across S (front) elevation (partially enclosed after 1934); one room. Built ca. 1798; frame shed added (removed after 1934). 3 ext. photos (1934, 1935); 1 data page (1958). LC code: PA,1-GET.V,6A.

Wills, James J., Farm. See Bender, Theodore, House.

Heidlersburg Vicinity (Huntington Township)

Rock Chapel (Methodist) (PA-352), SW side of LR01004, .6 mi. NW of U.S. Rte. 15 (business rte.), approx. 1.5 mi. N of Heidlersburg. Random rubble with quoins, one by three bays, one story, gable roof, belfry with louvered openings, recessed arched opening with paneled reveal on E (front) elevation. Built ca. 1775; belfry added later. First Methodist church built in county. 1 ext. photo (1950); 1 data page (1958). LC code: PA,1-HEID.V,1.

Hunterstown (Straban Township)

Conewago Presbyterian Church. See Great Conewago Presbyterian Church.

Great Conewago Presbyterian Church (Conewago Presbyterian Church, Huntingtown Presbyterian Church) (PA-345), W side of Church Rd. (LR01005), .3 mi. N of Pa. 394. Random rubble with quoins, approx. 51' (three-bay front) x 65' (six bays), one story, gable roof, cornice returns, arched openings with voussoirs and keystones, door with fanlight on E (front) elevation; arched interior ceiling. Built 1787 (date stone). Used as Confederate hospital during Gettysburg campaign of Civil War. Good example of early church built by Scotch-Irish settlers. 1 photo of doorway (1925). LC code: PA,1-HUNTO,1. NR.

Hunterstown Vicinity (Straban-Tyrone Townships)

Covered Bridge Over Conewago Creek. See Snyder's Fording Covered Bridge.

Snyder's Fording Covered Bridge (Covered Bridge Over Conewago Creek) (PA-351), over Conewago Creek, on Church Rd. (LR01005), 2.5 mi. NE of Hunterstown. Burr arch truss supported on stone abutments and piers, double span 158', single lane roadway, covered with vertical wooden siding, gable roof. Built 1868; J. M. Pittenturf and Brothers, builders; demolished and replaced with triple span bridge 1963. 1 ext. photo (1950); 1 data page (1958). LC code: PA,1-HUNTOV,1.

Indian Springs Vicinity

Stevens Furnace and Viaduct. See Iron Springs Vicinity (Hamiltonban Township), Stevens Furnace and Stevens Viaduct.

Iron Springs Vicinity (Hamiltonban Township)

Stevens Furnace (PA-346), N side of LR01021, 1.6 mi. W of Pa. 116. Remaining random rubble walls with quoins of office-house associated with Stevens Furnace; remains of furnace approx. 100 yds. to NE. Built ca. 1820; Thaddeus Stevens started extensive mining operation and iron furnaces in the area ca. 1820; ruinous condition by 1872. 1 ext. photo (1950); 1 data page (1958). LC code: PA,1-IRONSP.V,2.

Stevens Viaduct (PA-347), over Tom's Creek, one end cut by LR01021, approx. 1.5 mi. W of Iron Springs. Stone arch bridge, single span, dressed voussoirs with projecting keystones. Built ca. 1820; deteriorating. Only visible structural remains of the "Tapeworm Railroad" which served Thaddeus Stevens's iron furnaces. 1 ext. photo (1950); 1 data page (1958). LC code: PA,1-IRONSP.V,1.

Littlestown Vicinity (Germany Township)

Saint John's Lutheran Church (PA-269), W side of small road just W of borough boundary, .1 mi. N of Pa. 194 (Taneytown Rd.). Brick, cross-shaped with tower, one story with three-story crenelated tower, cross-gable roofs, corbeled brick cornice, pointed-arch openings with stained-glass windows, Gothic Revival details. Built nineteenth century. 1 ext. photo (1950). LC code: PA,1-LIT.V,1.

Christ Evangelical Lutheran Church. See Bermudian Vicinity (Latimore Township), Christ Evangelical Lutheran Church.

Berks County

Baumstown Vicinity (Exeter Township)

Bertolet-Herbein Cabin. See Limekiln Vicinity (Oley Township), Bertolet-Herbein Cabin, original location.

Boone, Daniel, Birthplace (PA-149), W side of Daniel Boone Rd., 1.2 mi. N of U.S. Rte. 422, in Daniel Boone Homestead State Park. Museum operated by Pennsylvania Historical and Museum Commission. Random rubble, approx. 52' (irregularly spaced five-bay front) x 26', two-and-a-half stories, gable roof with pent eaves, porch on S (front) elevation, pent roof surrounds house. Built in two sections; W two bays added to original log cabin 1735; log cabin replaced with E three bays 1779 (remains of cabin foundations visible in cellar); porch later addition; acquired by state 1938 and later restored. Daniel Boone was born in original log cabin in 1734 and lived here until 1750. Good example of a typical English Quaker house. 6 ext. photos (1940 before restoration, 1958); 3 data pages (1958, 1962). LC code: PA,6-BAUM.V,1. NR.

Bernville Vicinity (Jefferson Township)

Haag-Haak Log House (PA-254), NE side of Pa. 183 (Bernville Rd.), just W of Northkill Creek, approx. .5 mi. NW of Bernville. Squared logs set in corner posts partially clapboarded, two bays, one-and-a-half stories, gable roof, pent roof over entrance; one room. Built mid-nineteenth century; used as summer kitchen. 1 ext. photo (1975); 1 data page (1980). LC code: PA,6-BERN.V,2.

Haak Log House. See Haag-Haak Log House.

South Bernville Hotel (PA-257), SW corner of Bernville-Robesonia Rd. (LR06047) and Host Rd. (LR06020), just S of Northkill Creek. Brick, T-shaped, approx. 37' (five-bay front) x 36' (four bays) with rear wing (approx. 25'-6" x 32'), three-story main block with two-and-a-half-story wing, hip roof with gable roof on wing, bracketed cornice, two entrances with transoms on E (front) elevation, porch across E elevation (rebuilt in brick ca. 1950), two-story porch on each side of wing, Italianate details. Built ca. 1858; probably built by Elias Staudt; interior altered when converted to apartments ca. 1950; demolished 1977. Frame privy and storage shed. Hotel built to serve nearby Union Canal (canal active 1828-84); used as farmhouse after canal closed 1884. 6 ext. photos (1975, 1976, also shows privy and storage shed), 3 int. photos (1975); 10 data pages (1976). LC code: PA,6-BERN.V,1.

Bernville Vicinity (North Heidelberg Township)

House, Log (PA-255), on private road .2 mi. S of T507, .7 mi. S of Host Rd. (LR06020), approx. 2 mi. SW of Bernville. Squared logs, two-bay front, two-and-a-half stories, gable roof, pent roof over S (front) entrance. Built nineteenth century. 1 ext. photo (1975); 1 data page (1980). LC code: PA,6-BERN.V,3.

Birdsboro Borough

Bird, William, House (PA-1024), N side of Main St. (Pa. 724), across from Mill St. Stuccoed stone, eight-bay front (built in two sections, five-bay section and three-bay section, each with central entrance), two-and-a-half stories with basement, gable roof with gabled dormers, pent eaves. Built 1751; pedimented entrance porches added on S (front) elevation; windows and doors altered; interior altered; additions to rear; used as Y.M.C.A. and police station. Built by William Bird, ironmaster and founder of Birdsboro. 2 ext. photos (1958); 2 data pages (1958). LC code: PA,6-BIRD,1.

Brooke Manor (PA-1075), Furnace St. Brick, approx. 121' x 66' (over-all dimensions including three-bay central section with two-bay wing to each side and two additions), two-and-a-half stories, gable roof with pedimented gable end on N (front) elevation, pilasters with plain entablature, tetrastyle Doric porch, Greek Revival style; side hall plan. Built ca. 1840; large two-and-a-half-story dining wing added ca. 1865; two-story kitchen wing added ca. 1880; demolished 1961. Continuously owned by Brooke family, active in iron-making industry, owned Birdsboro, Hibernia, and Hopewell Furnaces. 3 sheets (1962, plans); 2 copy photos from ca. 1876, ca. 1920; 4 data pages (1962). LC code: PA,6-BIRD,2.

Brownsville Vicinity (Lower Heidelberg Township)

Dundore Farm. See Mount Pleasant Vicinity (Penn Township), Dundore Farm, original location.

Gerhard Farm. See Lauer-Gerhard Farm.

Lauer-Gerhard Farm(Reifsnyder Farm) (PA-1954), W side of Spring Creek, NE of Brownsville Rd. (LR06056). The farm is a good example of a Pennsylvania German family farm, planned to take advantage of the sloping site located on a creek. Earliest structures date from the late 1760s with improvements through the twentieth century. 2 sheets (1980, site plans); 3 general views (1977); 28 data pages (1981). LC code: PA,6-BROWV.V,1.

Main house (PA-1954A). Random rubble, 32' (three-bay front) x 27', two-and-a-half stories with basement, gable roof, porch added. Built late eighteenth century. 6 sheets (1980, including plans, elevations, section, details); 3 ext. photos (1977), 5 int. photos (1977). LC code: PA,6-BROWV.V,1A.

Small House (PA-1954B). Random rubble, built in two sections, overall dimensions 35'-11" (two-bay front) x 17'-3", two-and-a-half-story section with one-and-a-half-story kitchen wing, gable roofs, 6' bake house attached to kitchen wing; large cooking fireplace. Kitchen wing probably built ca. 1765-86 as original dwelling for farm; two-story addition probably built ca. 1813. 2 sheets (1980, including plans, elevation); 1 ext. photo (1977), 2 int. photos (1977). LC code: PA,6-BROWV.V,1B.

Barn (PA-1954C). Large frame bank barn built in several stages from late eighteenth century to twentieth century. 3 ext. photos (1977), 5 int. photos (1977). LC code: PA,6-BROWV.V,1C.

Wagon House (PA-1954D). Two-story frame outbuilding built mid-late nineteenth century. 1 ext. photo (1977). LC code: PA,6-BROWV.V,1D.

Garage (PA-1954E). One-story frame outbuilding built second quarter of twentieth century 1 ext. photo (1977). LC code: PA,6-BROWV.V,1E.

Reifsnyder Farm. See Lauer-Gerhard Farm.

Centerport Vicinity (Center Township)

Reber Barn (PA-5275), W of Centerport. Random rubble lower level and frame with vertical siding upper level, two-level bank barn, gable roof, forebay over stable entrances, sheds flank ramp to wagon entrance. Built ca. 1770. 3 ext. photos (1941), 1 int. photo (1941). LC code: PA,6-CENPO.V,1A.

Douglassville (Amity Township)

Jones, Mouns, House (Old Swede's House) (PA-1032), on NE bank of Schuylkill River, .2 mi. S of intersection of U.S. Rte. 422 and Pa. 662. Museum operated by Historic Preservation Trust of Berks County. Coursed rubble partially stuccoed (walls 20" thick), 34' (three-bay front) x 20', two-and-a-half stories, gable roof; two room plan. Built 1716 (date stone); ruinous condition 1958; reconstructed and restored 1970. Built by Mouns Jones, an early Swedish settler of the area, son of Jonas Nilsson who immigrated from Sweden with Governor Printz in 1642. Good example of a Swedish settler's home; considered oldest extant house in area. 1 sheet (1957, including site plan, plan, elevations); 2 ext. photos (1958); 4 data pages (1961). LC code: PA,6-DOUG,1. NR.

Old Swede's House. See Jones, Mouns, House.

Saint Gabriel's Church (PA-1038), S side of E bound lane of U.S. Rte. 422, .2 mi. W of Pa. 622 (Old Swedes Rd.). Squared rubble laid diagonally with contrasting quoins (rear elevation and gable ends random rubble), approx. 40' (three-bay front) x 35' (two bays), two stories, gable roof with pent eaves, water table framed by contrasting stones, door with transom on SE (front) elevation, flat arches with projecting keystones over openings; originally one room with gallery on three sides (changed to two stories). Built 1801; frame wing added; used as parish hall and school since larger church was built 1880-84. Interesting stone patterns. 4 ext. photos (1958); 2 data pages (1958). LC code: PA,6-DOUG,2. NR.

Friedensburg Vicinity (Oley Township) (See also Oley for Friedensburg area)

Barn (1787) (PA-5278), on old Pa. 73, approx. 2 mi. E of Friedensburg. Random rubble with frame forebay projecting over stable entrances, bank barn, gable roof, slit ventilators. Built 1787; larger barn attached to side 1839; pent roof and silo added to other side. Chamfered frame wellhead pump with iron handle next to barn. 2 ext. photos (1941). LC code: PA,6-FRIEB.V,1A.

Cricket Slope Farm Barn (PA-5276), approx. 1 mi. NW of Friedensburg. Random rubble with quoins (coursed at stable entrances), frame forebay contained within stone end walls, bank barn, gable roof, diamond-shaped brick vent in gable end. Built ca. 1795. 1 ext. photo (1941). LC code: PA,6-FRIEB.V,2A.

Farm Group (PA-5265), Pa. 73, S of Friedensburg. Farm complex with two-and-a-half-story five-bay stone house; barn with stone end walls and frame forebay and three cupolas; several stone and frame outbuildings. Built nineteenth century. 1 ext. photo (1941). LC code: PA,6-FRIEB.V,3.

Leinbach Barn (PA-5267), on dirt road, E of Pa. 73, S of Friedensburg. Random rubble with frame forebay contained within stone end walls, two-level bank barn, gable roof, stable entrances lower level, ramp leads to threshing floor entrance, decorated with four star designs on forebay. Built 1851 by Thomas and Elisabeth Leinbach (date stone). 2 ext. photos (1941). LC code: PA,6-FRIEB.V,4A.

Gabelsville (Colebrookdale Township)

Barn, Decorated (PA-5264), on old Pa. 73. Coursed and random rubble, frame forebay contained within stone end walls, bank barn, gable roof, stables lower level, threshing floor above, decorated with painted "hex signs." Built nineteenth century. Other stone Gabelsville structures visible in background. 1 ext. photo (1941). LC code: PA,6-GABEL,1.

Hopewell Village (Union Township)

Hopewell Village National Historic Site (PA-5157), W side of Pa. 345, approx. 2.5 mi. S of Geigertown Rd., in both Berks and Chester Counties. Hopewell Furnace was established by Mark Bird in 1770. Many employees lived in the company-owned town that developed around the furnace. The charcoal-fired furnace supplied much of early America's iron products, including cannon and shot for the Revolutionary Army. Hopewell Village was acquired by the National Park Service in 1938 and restored to its appearance of 1820-40. 1 data page (1984). See following entries and entries in Chester County, Hopewell Village (Warwick Township). LC code: PA,6-HOPVI,1. NHS.

Boarding House (PA-5157B). Random rubble with quoins (partially stuccoed), 34' (two-bay front) x 19'-1" with wing to E 21'-4" (two-bay front) x 19'-1", one-and-a-half stories, gable roof, random rubble shed on S elevation; originally one room plan with central fireplace, partitions and wing added. Built ca. 1806 (W two bays); wing to E and shed added ca. 1830; entrance porch added early twentieth century.; restored 1963. 6 sheets (1956-57, including site plan, plans, elevations, section, details). LC code: PA,6-HOPVI,22.

Charcoal House (PA-5157C). Random rubble with quoins and buttresses, 101'- 9" x 29', one story, gable roof, projecting frame section (22'-3" x 17'-7") with large sliding doors added on S elevation, board and batten double doors on N elevation through which charcoal was loaded into building (changed to windows connected to dormers ca. 1880); earth floor. Built ca. 1801; frame section added ca. 1880 (originally open shed, later enclosed); 1957 charcoal shed (open frame superstructure) reconstructed adjoining N elevation of charcoal house; restored 1965, replaced roof, N windows restored to doors, frame section demolished and replaced with reconstruction of connecting shed (covered passageway) which originally connected charcoal house to bridge house to furnace. Hopewell Furnace used charcoal for fuel, the charcoal shed protected the hot coal before being placed in charcoal house, where it cooled and was stored. 3 sheets (1956-58, including site plan, plan, elevations); 1 data page (1984). LC code: PA,6-HOPVI,5.

Furnace and Bridge House (PA-5157A). Separate but related structures. Remains of furnace before surrounding building was reconstructed. Bridge house, adjacent to furnace, from which raw material was fed into furnace, joined by connecting shed to charcoal house (PA-5157C). 1 photo of furnace (ca. 1950), 1 photo of bridge house (ca. 1950).

Furnace Office-Store (PA-5157D). Random rubble (later stuccoed), 28'-3" (two-bay front) x 24'-1", two stories with fully exposed basement to S (originally one-and-a-half stories), gable roof, two large doors to basement on S elevation (originally small doors); wall safe built into corner fireplace ca. 1870, stove pipe holes in some walls (heated by stoves, a product of the furnace). Built ca. 1784; frame shed added on E elevation ca. 1815-20; roof raised to form second story and most window and door openings changed ca. 1870; restored 1960-61 (roof and windows changed to original state). The Office-Store was the center of Hopewell Village, used as general office for the furnace and supplied all the needs of employees. 6 sheets (1956-58, including site plan, plans, elevations, section, details); 1 ext. photo (n.d.); 1 data page (1984). LC code: PA,6-HOPVI,7.

Tenant House #1 (PA-5157F). Stuccoed random rubble, 30'-3" (two-bay front) x 18'-3", two stories, gable roof, one-story random rubble shed on S elevation, entrance porch on E (front) elevation; two room plan, large cooking fireplace. Built between 1790 and 1810; roof raised 2' (date unknown); restored 1965. 7 sheets (1938, including plans, elevations, details); 1 data page (1984). LC code: PA,6-HOPVI,19.

Tenant House #2 (PA-5157G). Stuccoed random rubble with quoins, 24'-10" (two-bay front) x 18'-1", one-and-a-half stories, gable roof, large chimney in S gable end, one-story random rubble shed on S elevation; two room plan. Built between 1790 and 1810; fire between 1878 and 1883 left only stone walls standing; remained a ruin until 1905 reconstruction; porch across E (front) elevation and frame shed added after 1920; restored 1958 (porch and frame shed removed). Traditionally one of the oldest houses in Hopewell Village. 5 sheets (1956-58, including site plan, plans, elevations, section, details); 1 data page (1984). LC code: PA,6-HOPVI,20.

Tenant House #3 (PA-5157H). Random rubble (partially stuccoed), 32'-2" (four-bay front) x 28'-2", two-and-a-half stories, gable roof, two doors on E (front) elevation, porches across E and W elevations; built as a duplex with partition running E-W (openings in partition later). Built ca. 1845; porches later additions; restored 1958 (porches removed). 2 sheets (1956-58, including site plan, plan); 1 data page (1984). LC code: PA,6-HOPVI,21.

Ironmaster's House (PA-5162). Stuccoed random rubble, T-shaped, main section approx. 54' (five-bay front) x 24' with rear wing 22' x 36' (four bays), two-and-a-half stories, gable roofs with stepped S gable end; central hall plan. Built in three stages; N three bays (side hall plan) built ca. 1770; rear wing added before 1825; S two bays added ca. 1830; porch with brackets added across central three bays of W (front) elevation 1867, extended across front 1870; porches added in NE and SE corners (enclosed second story of NE porch is 1870 bathroom); restored 1966. 5 sheets (1957, including site plan, plans, sections); 1 ext. copy photo (n.d.), 1 int. photo (1958). LC code: PA,6-HOPVI,8.

Village Barn (PA-5166). Random rubble, 67'-11" x 28'-4" with wing to E 33'-5" x 28'-4", bank barn, two levels, gable roof, projecting frame forebay. Built ca. 1775; E addition early nineteenth century; stone and frame carriage shed added to E ca. 1850; straw shed replaced forebay ca. 1870; original barn partially demolished and rebuilt and enlarged 1926, cinder block and frame walls built over remaining original stone walls and stuccoed; 1926 additions removed to expose remaining original stone walls and barn reconstructed to ca. 1840 condition 1960 (includes main section and E wing with forebay). 3 sheets (1956-58, illustrates restored condition, including site plan, plans, elevations, section); 1 ext. photo (n.d.). LC code: PA,6-HOPVI,16.

Jacksonwald (Exeter Township)

Boyertown Road (House) (C. Hock Farmhouse) (PA-150), N side of Boyertown Rd. (Pa. 562), E of town. Random rubble with quoins, built in three sections; three-bay E section, two-and-a-half stories, gable roof, recessed door framed by pediment and pilasters, lintels with projecting keystones, belt course, side hall plan; setback two-bay center section, two-and-a-half stories, gable roof, porch across front; two-bay W section, two stories, gable roof. E section built ca. 1800; other two sections added nineteenth century; twentieth-century rear additions; demolished ca. 1942. Possibly the Althouse Tavern; later used as dwelling. 2 ext. photos (1940), 1 int. photo (1940). LC code: PA,6-JACSO,1.

Hock, C., Farmhouse. See Boyertown Road (House).

Kutztown Vicinity (Maxatawny Township)

LeVan Mill (PA-1030), SE side of Eagle Point Rd., 1.8 mi. NE of Pa. 737, approx. 2.5 mi. NE of Kutztown. Random rubble (foundations and first story) and heavy frame filled with wattle and daub and covered with wooden siding, 51'-3" x 24'-10", two-and-a-half stories and wheel well, gable roof, recessed open balcony on second story, stone arches at openings to mill race. Built 1732 (one of the earliest grist mills in area); vacant and in poor condition. Built by Jacob LeVan, a Huguenot from France; mill remained in LeVan family into twentieth century. Count Zinzendorf, a Moravian missionary, preached from the balcony 1742; as did Rev. Michael Schlatter, organizer of the Reform Church and first superintendent of public instruction in Pennsylvania 1747. 3 sheets (1958, 1961, including site plan, plans); 4 ext. photos (1958), 2 int. photos (1958); 3 data pages (1958). LC code: PA,6-KUTZ.V,1.

Lenhartsville

Konig-Speicher Farm, Log House. See Mount Pleasant Vicinity (North Heidelberg Township), Konig-Speicher Farm, Log House, original location.

Limekiln Vicinity (Exeter Township)

Barn (PA-5262), approx. 1 mi. S of Oley Turnpike, next to Daniel Boone's grandfather's farm. Random rubble, frame forebay contained within stone end walls, two-level bank barn, gable roof, decorated with painted folk designs. Built nineteenth century. 1 ext. photo (1941). LC code: PA,6-EXTO,1.

Bieber Mill. See Knabb-Bieber Mill.

Ha Penny Farm. See Knabb, Abraham, House.

Knabb, Abraham, House (Ha Penny Farm) (PA-1045), E side of Oley Line Rd., .7 mi. SW of Limekiln Rd., approx. 1 mi. S of Limekiln. Random rubble, five-bay front, two-and-a-half stories, gable roof, door with fanlight set in paneled reveal framed by pilasters and wide entablature on N (front) elevation, Georgian details; central hall plan. Built 1817 (date stone); interior remodeled. 2 ext. photos (1958); 2 data pages (1958). LC code: PA,6-LIMKI.V,3.

Barn (PA-1043). Random rubble, bank barn, two levels, steep gable roof supported by large braced timbers with mortised and tenon joints, frame forebay projects over stable entrances on S elevation, ramp leads to threshing floor entrance on N elevation, slit ventilators. Built early nineteenth century. 2 ext. photos (1958); 1 data page (1958). LC code: PA,6-LIMKI.V,3A.

Knabb-Bieber Mill (PA-1031), N side of Bieber Mill Rd., just NW of Quarry Rd. Random rubble with quoins, approx. 35' x 25', two and a half stories on sloping site fully exposing basement to SE, gable roof with pent eaves, two doors set in arched openings framed by pilasters and pediments (unusual refinement for a mill), loading doors on three levels of SW side with pedimented hood over attic door, entrance porch on NW elevation; mill machinery in working order 1958. Built 1809 for John Knabb (name and date painted on pedimented hood). 5 ext. photos (1958); 2 data pages (1958). LC code: PA,6-LIMKI.V,1

Limekiln Vicinity (Oley Township)

Bertolet-Herbein Cabin (PA-1047), NE side of Bieber Mill Rd., .9 mi. NW of Oley Turnpike to driveway entrance, adjacent to David Schneider House (PA-1044); moved to Daniel Boone Homestead State Park (PA-149), W side of Daniel Boone Rd., 1.5 mi. N of U.S. Rte. 422, Baumstown vicinity (Exeter Township). Museum operated by Pennsylvania Historical and Museum Commission. Log, 29'-10" (two-bay front) x 19'-8", one-and-a-half stories, steep gable roof with flared eaves, central chimney, roof extends to form hoods over entrances; large free-standing central fireplace with original wooden crane divides two rooms. Built ca. 1737; small belfry added at gable end; acquired by state and moved 1967. A rare example of a Huguenot pioneer structure. 2 sheets (1958, including site plan, plans); 4 ext. photos (1958), 3 int. photos (1958); 5 data pages (1960). LC code: PA,6-LIMKI.V,5. NR.

DeBenneville, George, House (PA-1029), N side of Hunter Rd., 1 mi. SE of Oley Turnpike, approx. 1.5 mi. SE of Limekiln. Stuccoed stone, six by three bays, two-and-a-half stories, gable roof with large gabled dormers, central dormer with broken scroll pediment, deep cornice. Built 1745; many alterations and additions; dormers later additions; doors and windows changed; porch added across SE (front) elevation. Numerous outbuildings. Dr. DeBenneville, French Huguenot nobleman, was a preacher and founder of Universalism in America. 2 ext. photos (1958); 2 data pages (1958). LC code: PA,6-YEL.V,4. NR (Oley Township Historic District).

Herbein Cabin. See Bertolet-Herbein Cabin.

Schneider, David, House (PA-1044), NE side of Bieber Mill Rd., .9 mi. NW of Oley Turnpike to driveway entrance, adjacent to original site of Bertolet-Herbein Cabin (PA-1047). Random rubble, L-shaped, four by two bays with kitchen wing to N (rear), two-and-a-half stories, gable roof with cornice returns, two doors on S (front) elevation (one later addition), porch across S elevation (later addition). Built 1831 (date stone); owned by David Schneider, who inherited farm from uncle, Peter Herbein, in 1828. 2 ext. photos (1958); 2 data pages (1958, 1961). LC code: PA,6-LIMKI.V,2. NR (Oley Township Historic District).

Lobachsville Vicinity (Pike Township)

Keim House (PA-1039), SE side of Keim Rd. (T500), .7 mi. E of Hoch Rd. (LR06191), .5 mi. W of Lobachsville Rd. (LR06055). Random rubble, three-bay original section with two-bay addition to NE, two-and-a-half stories, gable roof, central chimney and inside end chimney, flat and segmental brick arches over windows, pent roof across NW (rear) elevation; three rooms divided by central chimney (original section). Built 1732; two bays added ca. 1780; porches added late nineteenth century; owned by Historic Preservation Trust of Berks County. Built by Johannes Keim, an early settler from Bavaria. Good example of a Pennsylvania-German farmhouse. 3 ext. photos (1941, 1958); 2 data pages (1958). LC code: PA,6-LOBA.V,2. NR.

Keim Stone Cabin (PA-1041). Random rubble, approx. 25' x 17', one-and-a-half stories on sloping site fully exposing basement to S, steep gable roof, central chimney, segmental brick arches over windows, double Dutch doors with original hinges; two rooms divided by large fireplace. Built between 1706 and 1732; small belfry and imbricated roof shingles added nineteenth century. Good example of small Pennsylvania-German house. 4 ext. photos (1941, 1958), 1 int. photo (1958); 2 data pages (1958). LC code: PA,6-LOBA.V,2A.

Keim Barn (PA-1182). Random rubble with quoins, frame forebay contained within stone end walls, two levels with loft, gable roof, pent roof over side entrance. Built eighteenth century 2 ext. photos (1941). LC code: PA,6-LOBA.V,2B.

Yoder, Jacob, House (PA-1036), on Lobachsville Rd. (LR06055), .1 mi. NE of Keim Rd. (T500). Random rubble, five by two bays, two-and-a-half stories, gable roof, door with transom on S (front) elevation; central hall plan. Built 1829 (date stone); entrance porch added; one-and-a-half-story stone kitchen wing added on N connecting house with small one-story stone kitchen or smokehouse; dormer added on rear slope. Numerous outbuildings. 3 ext. photos (1958); 2 data pages (1958). LC code: PA,6-LOBA.V,1.

Barn (PA-1060). Random rubble, bank barn with two wings to N, two levels, gable roofs, deep frame forebay across S elevation over stable entrances, ramp to N entrance, stone wing at NW corner, frame wing at NE corner. Built early nineteenth century. 2 ext. photos (1958); 1 data page (1958). LC code: PA,6-LOBA.V,1B.

Stone Cabin (PA-1040). Random rubble, approx. 25' (two-bay front) x 15', two stories built into side of hill with entrances to each level, gable roof, deep pent roof on S (front) elevation. Built mid-eighteenth century. Good example of early settler's house. 1 ext. photo (1958); 2 data pages (1958). LC code: PA,6-LOBA.V,1A.

Maiden Creek Vicinity (Maiden Creek Township)

Barn, Decorated White (PA-5273), W of Maiden Creek. Random rubble, frame forebay contained within stone end walls, two levels, gable roof, decorated with painted "hex signs" and arches over openings on forebay. Built nineteenth century. 1 ext. photo (1941). LC code: PA,6-MAICR.V,1A.

Moselem Springs (Richmond Township)

Barn A (1779) (PA-5271A), W of Moselem Springs. Random rubble with cantilevered frame forebay, two-level bank barn, gable roof, stone arches over stable openings, slit ventilators; simple wooden trusses support roof. Built 1779 (date stone); stone wall under forebay added for extra support. LC code: PA,6-MOSP.V,2A-B.

Barn B (PA-5271B) on same farm. 2 ext. photos (1941), 2 int. photos (1941). Barn B (PA-5271B), located across road on same farm as Barn A (1779) (PA- 5271A). Random rubble, frame forebay contained within stone end walls, two-level bank barn, gable roof, decorated with painted "hex signs" and arches over openings on forebay. Built 1850; sheds added. 1 ext. photo (1941).

Barn, Decorated (1849) (PA-5270), on Rte. 122, N of Moselem Springs. Random rubble, frame forebay contained within stone end walls, two levels, gable roof, pedimented lintels over windows and doors, decorated with painted "hex signs." Built 1849; shed added on side. 1 ext. photo (1941). LC code: PA,6-MOSP.V,1A.

Barn, Decorated Red (PA-5272), on Rte. 135, W of Moselem Springs. Random rubble, frame forebay contained within stone end walls, two levels, gable roof, decorated with painted "hex signs" and arches over openings on forebay. Built nineteenth century. 1 ext. photo (1941). LC code: PA,6-MOSP.V,3A.

Mount Pleasant Vicinity (Bern Township)

Reber Farm, House (PA-256A), S side of Palisades Rd. (T499), .4 mi. E of Gruber Rd. (LR06038), approx. 2 mi. SE of Mount Pleasant. Random rubble with quoins, 40' (five-bay front) x 35' (two bays), two-and-a-half stories, gable roof; originally central hall plan. Built 1834 (date stone); interior extensively altered ca. 1965; demolished 1977. Good example of a prosperous Pennsylvania-German farm. 4 ext. photos (1975), 2 int. photos (1975), 1 copy photo of ext. (n.d.); 11 data pages (1976, including house, barn and store). LC code: PA,6-MTPLES.V,5.

Barn (PA-256B). Random rubble, 65' x 35', bank barn, two levels, gable roof, frame forebay projects over stable entrances on E elevation, slit ventilators. Built mid-nineteenth century; second level partially rebuilt after fire late nineteenth century; concrete block addition on N elevation; demolished 1977. 1 ext. photo (1976), 2 int. photos (1976), 1 photo of Union Canal stones with rope marks moved from disassembled canal lock and used as paving for barn (1976). LC code: PA,6-MTPLES.V,5B.

Canal Store (PA-256C). Random rubble with quoins, 20' (two-bay front) x 18', one-and-a-half stories, gable roof, brick chimney for large bake oven. Built ca. 1835; small stone smokehouse added ca. 1890; demolished 1977. Built as canal store on Union Canal (canal active 1828-84); converted to summer kitchen ca. 1890. 3 ext. photos (1975, 1976), 3 int. photos (1975, 1976). LC code: PA,6-MTPLES.V,5C.

Mount Pleasant Vicinity (North Heidelberg Township)

Berger Farm. See Konig-Speicher Farm.

Konig-Speicher Farm (Berger Farm) (PA-258), N side of Church Rd. (LR06048), just S of Tulpehocken Creek, .3 mi. SW of Pa. 183 (Bernville Rd.), approx. 1 mi. SW of Mount Pleasant. Typical Pennsylvania-German farm with numerous outbuildings built at various times as the farm expanded. 1 sheet (1976, site plan of farm); 3 general views of outbuildings (1975); 11 data pages (1976, including houses and outbuildings). LC code: PA,6-MTPLES.V,13.

Main House (PA-258B). Frame with clapboarding, 40' (four-bay front) x 25', two-and-a-half stories with fully exposed basement at rear, gable roof, porch across S elevation; traditional Pennsylvania-German three-room plan. Possibly built in two stages; date stone "Johann-Sarah Konig 1856" possibly refers to one section or major alterations; porch later addition; demolished 1976. 2 ext. photos (1975, 1976, also show small log house). LC code: PA,6-MTPLES.V,13B.

Log House (PA-258A). Squared logs set into corner posts with clapboarding (clapboarding removed except E elevation), 20' (two-bay front) x 16' (two bays), two-and-a-half stories with fully exposed basement at rear, gable roof; fireplace and spring in cellar. Possibly built late eighteenth century; alterations early nineteenth century; dismantled and moved by Pennsylvania Dutch Folk Culture Society 1976, moved next to their headquarters in Lenhartsville and rebuilt as one-story house. 6 ext. photos (1975, 1976, also show main house), 5 int. photos (1975). LC code: PA,6-MTPLES.V,13A.

Barn (PA-258C). Frame, 80' x 30', bank barn, two levels, gable roof with three bracketed ventilator cupolas, frame forebay projects over stable entrances. Built ca. 1850; two-and-a-half-story frame wing added at NW corner late nineteenth century; one-and-a-half-story frame shed added on N elevation late nineteenth century; demolished 1976. 3 ext. photos (1975, 1976, one during demolition, photos also show outbuildings). LC code: PA,6-MTPLES.V,13C.

Outdoor Bake Oven (PA-258D). Brick and stone oven built into embankment, protected by gable roof, central brick chimney, work area sheltered by frame superstucture in front of oven openings at E end. Possibly originally built eighteenth century, rebuilt several times, present oven ca. 1825; demolished 1976. 2 ext. photos (1975). LC code: PA,6-MTPLES.V,13D.

Smokehouse (PA-258E). Frame, octagonal, 4' each side, one story, polygonal roof, large iron strap hinges on door. Built nineteenth century; demolished 1976. 1 sheet (1976, including plan, elevation, section); 1 ext. photo (1975). LC code: PA,6-MTPLES.V,13E.

Speicher Farm. See Konig-Speicher Farm.

Mount Pleasant Vicinity (Penn Township)

Conrad, John, House (Sheidy House) (PA-259), Sheidy Rd. (T489), between Pa. 183 (Bernville Rd.) and Tulpehocken Creek, approx. 1.5 mi. NW of Mount Pleasant. Log set in corner posts (main block) and frame (rear wing) with clapboarding, L-shaped, 38'-9" (four-bay front) x 26'-11" with rear wing, two-and-a-half-story main block and one-and-a-half-story rear wing, sloping site exposes basement at rear, gable roofs, two doors and bracketed porch on NW (front) elevation; main block traditional Pennsylvania-German three-room plan, iron butcher's stove in cellar of wing, interior and exterior arched root cellars. Built ca. 1830 (main block); frame wing added ca. 1870-90; main block dismantled and moved to Kintnersville, Bucks County, placed in storage with plans to rebuild as a one-and-a-half-story house. Large nineteenth-century bank barn moved to Myerstown, Lebanon County, rebuilt as smaller barn 1976. Numerous nineteenth- and twentieth-century outbuildings demolished 1977. Good example of a well-planned Pennsylvania-German farm. 6 sheets (1976, including site plan of farm, plans, elevations); 7 ext. photos (1976), 11 int. photos (1976, including photos of butcher's stove and root cellar), 4 copy photos of general views of farm (ca. 1895, ca. 1910, ca. 1970), 2 copy photos of adjacent covered bridge (ca. 1959); 20 data pages (1976, 1978 on entire farm). LC code: PA,6-MTPLES.V,3.

Conrad, Joseph, Farm (Miller's Farm) (PA-260), N side of Bright School Rd. at Pa. 183 (Bernville Rd.), just E of Powder Mill Rd. (T524), approx. 1.5 mi. NW of Mount Pleasant. Good example of a farm combined with industrial activities. Numerous outbuildings and several mills on the farm. Farm demolished 1977. 1 sheet (1976, site plan of farm); 15 data pages (1976, including house and outbuildings). LC code: PA,6-MTPLES.V,6. Conrad's Warehouse recorded by HAER.

House (PA-260A). Random rubble, L-shaped, 45'-6" (five-bay front) with 31' W elevation and 17'-6" E elevation, two-and-a-half stories, sloping site exposes basement on S (front) elevation, gable roof (W side full gable, E side half gable with slight rear slope), entrance porch on S elevation, wooden lintels with keystones; central hall plan. Built ca. 1815; two sheds added ca. 1900; demolished 1977. 4 sheets (1976, including plans, elevations, sections); 7 ext. photos (1975, 1976), 7 int. photos (1975, 1976). LC code: PA,6-MTPLES.V,6A.

Barn (PA-260B). Frame, T-shaped, 67' x 38' with wing (28' x 16') on S elevation, bank barn, two levels, intersecting gable roofs, frame forebay projects over stable entrances, pedimented lintels over windows. Built ca. 1850; wing added ca. 1880; concrete block silo added at NW corner ca. 1930; demolished 1977. 5 sheets (1976, including plans, elevations, section); 4 ext. photos (1975, 1976), 2 int. photos (1975). LC code: PA,6-MTPLES.V,6B.

Pig Barn (PA-260C). Frame, 30' x 12', one-and-a-half stories, gable roof, pedimented lintels over windows. Built nineteenth century; demolished 1977. 2 int. photos (1975, 1976); see *Barn* photos for exterior view. LC code: PA,6-MTPLES.V,6C.

Springhouse-Root Cellar (PA-260D). Random rubble, 16'-6" x 11', one story built into embankment, shed roof, pedimented lintel over entrance; stone arched interior used as root cellar and springhouse. Built nineteenth century; demolished 1977. 1 ext. photo (1975), 1 int. photo (1975); see *House* for drawings and additional photo. LC code: PA,6-MTPLES.V,6D.

Deppen House. See Riem-Schmidt-Deppen Farm, House.

Dundore Farm (Hottenstein Farm) (PA-261), .2 mi. S of Pa. 183 (Bernville Rd.) on private road, .5 mi. NE of Church Rd. (LR06048), approx. 1 mi. W of Mount Pleasant. Good example of eighteenth- and nineteenth-century Pennsylvania-German farm with log house and numerous outbuildings, some log. House and early outbuildings moved by Old Dry Road Farm, Inc. to be operated as a museum, moved to Brownsville Vicinity (Lower Heidelberg Township), .3 mi. E of T534 on private road, .5 mi. N of Rebers Bridge Rd. (LR06056), approx. 2 mi. NE of Brownsville. 1 sheet (1976, site plan of farm); 8 general views of farm (aerial photo ca. 1953, 1975, 1976); 20 data pages (1976, including house and outbuildings). LC code: PA,6-MTPLES.V,7.

House (PA-261A). Squared logs set into corner and intermediate posts (clapboarding removed 1975), 32'-6" x 26'-6", two-and-a-half stories, gable roof, inside end chimneys (N chimney removed ca. 1960); traditional Pennsylvania-German three-room plan. Built ca. 1840 (original log house on property built mid-eighteenth century, present log house built from salvaged logs, possibly from remains of original house); porch added across E elevation mid-nineteenth century; porch added on W elevation mid nineteenth century (enclosed ca. 1950, removed 1975); moved to new location. 2 sheets (1976, including plans, elevations, also shows privy); 5 ext. photos (1975, 1976, also shows privy), 3 int. photos (1975), 1 detail of door lock (1976). LC code: PA,6-MTPLES.V,7A.

Barn (PA-261B). Frame and random rubble (first level and E end wall), 116'-5" x 37'-4", bank barn, two levels, gable roof, frame forebay projects over stable entrances, slit ventilators in E stone wall. Built 1788 (inscription over stable door); enlarged with 36'-6" extension on W end ca. 1850 (stone from original W end wall probably used for first level of extension); thatched roof removed ca. 1900; small shed added on W elevation (removed 1976); moved to new location. 4 sheets (1976, including plans, elevations, section); 8 ext. photos (1975, 1976, also show milk shed, wheat barn, pig barn), 1 int. photo (1976); see *Milk Shed* for additional photos. LC code: PA,6-MTPLES.V,7B.

Corn Crib-Wagon Shed (PA-261C). Frame with vertical wooden siding (W and E elevations) and vertical wooden slats (corn cribs on N and S elevations), 24'-6" x 30'-7", one-and-a-half stories, gable roof; central space for storage of farm equipment with flanking corn cribs. Built ca. 1840; moved to new location. 1 sheet (1976, including plan, elevations, section); 3 ext. photos (1975, 1976, also show wood shed), 1 int. photo (1976). LC code: PA,6-MTPLES.V,7C.

Granary (PA-261D). Frame and random rubble, 15' x 11'-6", one-and-a-half stories, gable roof, random rubble bridge abutment attached to W elevation (remains of a bridge over Union Canal); interior divided into five grain storage bins. Built ca. 1840; moved to new location. Built on Union Canal to store and transfer grain to canal boats. 1 sheet (1976, including plan, elevations); 5 ext. photos (1975), 1 int. photo (1975). LC code: PA,6-MTPLES.V,7D.

Milk Shed (PA-261E). Frame, 15' x 12', one story, gable roof with central metal ventilator, slightly pedimented lintels over windows, concrete cooling trough. Built early twentieth century; demolished 1976. 1 sheet (1976, including plan, elevations, section); 1 ext. photo (1976, also shows barn). LC code: PA,6-MTPLES.V,7E.

Root Cellar (PA-261F). Concrete bulkhead (probably stone under concrete) with wooden doors opens to steps to underground root cellar, stone arched root cellar with brick floor, 10' x 16'. Built ca. 1840. 1 sheet with root cellar and smokehouse (1976, including plan, elevations, sections); 1 ext. photo (1976), 2 int. photos (1975). LC code: PA,6-MTPLES.V,7F.

Smokehouse (PA-261G). Log, 9'-7" x 8", one story, gable roof, wooden ventilator cupola, door with molded frame and wrought-iron hinges and latch. Built early-nineteenth century; trim possibly salvaged from eighteenth century structure; moved to new location. 1 sheet with smokehouse and root cellar (1976, including plan, elevations, section); 4 ext. photos (1975, 1976), 1 int. photo (1975). LC code: PA,6-MTPLES.V,7G.

Springhouse (PA-261H). Squared logs set into corner posts (clapboarding removed), 28'-6" x 21', one-and-a-half stories with basement, gable roof, porch across S (front) elevation; spring in basement. Original springhouse built ca. 1775 (probably second structure on property); rebuilt 1842 (inscription on chinking), original notched corners changed to corner posts, original central fireplace removed and small addition to E built ca. 1842 possibly to accommodate new fireplace; iron butcher's stove in basement and flue and chimney in E wall added twentieth century; moved to new location. 1 sheet (1976, including plans, elevations, section); 4 ext. photos (1975, 1976), 1 int. photo (1976). LC code: PA,6-MTPLES.V,7H.

Wheat Barn (PA-261I). 1 photo taken during demolition, shows mid-nineteenth-century structural frame only (1975). LC code: PA,6-MTPLES.V,7I.

Gruber House. See Penn, William, Tavern.

Gruber, Jacob, House (Speicher House) (PA-262), N side of Mt. Pleasant Rd. (T713), just N of intersection with Pa. 183 (Bernville Rd.). Frame with novelty siding (balloon frame construction), L-shaped, 35' (four-bay front) x 26' (two bays) with rear wing (22' x 18'), two-and-a-half stories with basement, gable roof with shed roof on wing, bracketed cornice with decorative pierced frieze, two doors with carved panels and porch with turned posts on S (front) elevation, carved pediments over windows, two-story porch on wing; two-room plan with kitchen in wing. Built 1895-96; demolished 1976. Built by Franklin Gruber, founder of Gruber Wagon Works, for his son Jacob; much of the ornamental woodwork was produced in the wagon works. Good example of a late-nineteenth-century Pennsylvania-German house in plan and carved details. 5 ext. photos (1975), 1 int. photo (1975); 8 data pages (1976). LC code: PA,6-MTPLES.V,8. Gruber Wagon Works recorded by HAER.

Heck-Stamm-Unger Farm. See Stamm Farm.

Hottenstein Farm. See Dundore Farm.

Miller's Farm. See Conrad, Joseph, Farm.

Moorehead House. See Stamm, Eliza, House.

Obolds-Billman Hotel. See Penn, William, Tavern.

Octagon House. See Stoudt, George, House.

Penn, William, Tavern (Gruber House, Obolds-Billman Hotel) (PA-263), E side of Gruber Rd. (LR06038), just S of Pa. 183 (Bernville Rd.), approx. .5 mi. S of Mount Pleasant. Random rubble, 38'-9" (five-bay front) x 32'-1" (three bays), two-and-a-half stories with fully exposed basement on W (front) elevation, gable roof, porch topped with balustrade at basement level (originally two-story porch, altered several times, present porch built ca. 1930); central hall plan. Built ca. 1830; porch altered; carved gabled hoods added over doors ca. 1900; demolished 1976. Outbuildings. Probably originally built as a tavern; acquired by Gruber family 1882, Gruber Wagon Works built across road from house. William Penn Tavern sign owned by PHMC's Landis Valley Museum, Lancaster. Commonly confused with Obolds-Billman Hotel, a different structure. 5 ext. photos (1975, 1976, photos also show Gruber Wagon Works), 7 int. photos (1975), 1 copy photo of ext. (n.d.); 8 data pages (1976, including outbuildings). LC code: PA,6-MTPLES.V,9. See also Gruber Wagon Works, recorded by HAER.

Privy (PA-263A). Frame, square, one story, hip roof with central finial (finial serves as vent), scalloped cornice. Built nineteenth century; demolished 1976. 1 ext. photo (1975). LC code: PA,6-MTPLES.V,9A.

Smokehouse (PA-263B). Brick, rectangular, one story, concrete gable roof with decorative terra cotta vent. Built nineteenth century; demolished 1976. 1 ext. photo (1975). LC code: PA,6-MTPLES.V,9B.

Wash house and Butcher Shop (PA-263C). Frame with novelty siding (W front elevation) and brick (side walls), rear wall built into hillside, rectangular, five-bay front, one story, gable roof; vaulted root cellar. Built nineteenth century; demolished 1976. 1 ext. photo (1975), 2 int. photos (1975). LC code: PA,6-MTPLES.V,9C.

Querean House. See Stamm, Isaac, House.

Reifsnyder House. See Riem-Schmidt-Deppen House.

Riem-Schmidt-Deppen Farm, House (Reifsnyder House) (PA-264), S side of Pa. 183 (Bernville Rd.), just W of Church Rd. (LR06048), approx. .5 mi. W of Mount Pleasant. Random rubble with quoins, 40' (five-bay front) x 30' (two bays), two-and-a-half stories, gable roof, porch across front elevation, one-and-a-half-story rear kitchen wing (25' x 18'), one-story smokehouse (8' x 10') to rear of kitchen wing; central hall plan, fine interior woodwork. Built 1791 (date stone); demolished 1971. George Riem acquired land from Penn family 1764; 1793 passed to Philip Schmidt who used house for Catholic services; 1836 passed to son-in-law Dr. Daniel Deppen who cared for Union Canal workers stricken with "canal fever." 11 data pages (1976, including house and Deppen Barn). LC code: PA,6-MTPLES.V,10.

Deppen Barn (PA-264A). Random rubble (lower level) and frame (upper level), 100' x 45', bank barn, two levels, gable roof with three bracketed ventilator cupolas, frame forebay projects over stable entrances, windows flanked by louvered ventilators surrounded by moldings forming pointed arches over windows (Palladian motif). Built ca. 1850; rebuilt ca. 1880 after fire; demolished 1975. Built during Deppen ownership. 2 ext. photos (1975). LC code: PA,6-MTPLES.V,10A.

Schmidt House. See Riem-Schmidt-Deppen Farm, House.

Sheidy House. See Conrad, John, House.

Speicher House. See Gruber, Jacob, House.

Stamm Farm (Heck-Stamm-Unger Farm) (PA-266), E side of Gruber Rd. (LR06038), .4 mi. S of Pa. 183 (Bernville Rd.), approx. 1 mi. S of Mount Pleasant. Good example of a Pennsylvania-German log house with numerous outbuildings. Werner Stamm probably acquired land from Penn family ca. 1760. Farm demolished 1977. 4 general views of farm (1975); 12 data pages (1976, including house and outbuildings). LC code: PA,6-MTPLES.V,11.

House (PA-266A). Squared logs set into corner and intermediate posts (first story) and dovetailed (second story) with wattle and daub chinking, wooden siding (partially removed 1975), 32' (four-bay front) x 26' (two bays), two-and-a-half stories, gable roof, inside end chimneys (originally central chimney); traditional Pennsylvania-German three-room plan (unusual that kitchen runs length rather than depth of plan), fine interior door with carved panels. Possible built late eighteenth century or early nineteenth century; central fireplace removed and interior altered reusing some original woodwork mid-nineteenth century; enclosed porch on S (front) elevation added ca. 1925; demolished 1977. 3 ext. photos (1975, one photo after siding was removed; photos also show butcher shed, wash house and root cellar, and summer kitchen-smokehouse), 3 int. photos (1975, one shows carved door). LC code: PA,6-MTPLES.V,11A.

Barn (PA-266B). Frame, 50' x 30', bank barn, two levels, gable roof, frame forebay projects over stable entrances, arched windows flanked by louvered ventilators in gable ends, original hardware. Built ca. 1860; demolished 1977. 6 ext. photos (1975, one photo after siding was removed;

photos show pig barn, corn crib-wagon shed, chicken house), 1 int. photo (1975). LC code: PA,6-MTPLES.V,11B.

Chicken and Brooder Houses (PA-266C). Three separate structures: chicken house, frame, 20' x 15', one story with loft, gable roof, built nineteenth century; chicken house, frame set on concrete piles, 18' x 12', one story, shed roof, built ca. 1940; brooder house (heated structure for raising chickens), sheet metal, round, conical metal roof with metal ventilator (probably for central stove), built twentieth century, moved from nearby John Dundore Farm ca. 1942. All three structures demolished 1977. 1 ext. photo (1975, shows all three structures), 1 int. photo of older chicken house (1975); see *Barn* for additional photos. LC code: PA,6-MTPLES.V,11C.

Corn Crib-Wagon Shed (PA-266D). Frame, 15' x 25', one-and-a-half stories, gable roof, sliding door on S elevation for sheltered wagon storage, corn crib of horizontal wooden slats on W elevation. Built nineteenth century; demolished 1977. 1 ext. photo (1975), 2 int. photos (1975); see *Barn* for additional photos. LC code: PA,6-MTPLES.V,11D.

Butcher Shed, Wash House, Root Cellar (PA-266E). Structure built in two sections: root cellar, random rubble structure over arched root cellar, one story, gable roof, bulkhead to cellar on SW (front) elevation, possibly built late eighteenth century; butcher and wash house (used for processing foods) added to NW elevation of root cellar, frame, four by two bays, 30' x 18', one story, gable roof, large iron butcher's stove inside, added ca. 1920; both demolished 1977. 1 ext. photo (1975, also shows house), 2 int. photos (1975, show root cellar and butcher's stove); see *House* for additional photos. LC code: PA,6-MTPLES.V,11E.

Summer Kitchen-Smokehouse (PA-266F). Random rubble, 18' (two-bay front) x 16', one-and-a-half stories, gable roof; summer kitchen with smokehouse in attic. Built nineteenth century; demolished 1977. 1 ext. photo (1975), 1 int. photo (1975); see *House* for additional photos. LC code: PA,6-MTPLES.V,11F.

Stamm, Eliza, House (Moorehead House) (PA-113), W side Gruber Rd. (LR06038), .2 mi. S of Pa. 183 (Bernville Rd.), approx. .5 mi. S of Mount Pleasant. Brick, 28'-6" (four-bay front) x 24' (two bays), two-and-a-half stories with fully exposed rear basement, gable roof, two doors with transoms on E (front) elevation, two-bay porch on E elevation (third bay added as carport), two-story porch on W elevation; traditional Pennsylvania-German three-room plan. Built ca. 1865; one-story frame wing covered with hexagonal asphalt shingles and elevated on posts added across N elevation ca. 1925 (connects front and rear porches); demolished 1977. 6 sheets (1976, including site plan, plans, elevations); 2 ext. photos (1976); 11 data pages (1976). LC code: PA,6-MTPLES.V,2.

Stamm, Isaac, House (Querean House) (PA-112), E side of Gruber Rd. (LR06038), just S of Pa. 183 (Bernville Rd.), approx. .5 mi. S of Mount Pleasant. Brick, 24'-6" (three-bay front) x 38' (main block and rear kitchen wing), two-and-a-half stories, intersecting gable roofs, bracketed cornice with decorative pierced frieze, porch with decorative pierced brackets and cornice on W (front) elevation, two-story porch on kitchen wing (later enclosed); traditional Pennsylvania-German three-room plan. Built ca. 1855; two frame wings added on E elevation ca. 1910 and ca. 1930 (housed grocery until ca. 1950); shed dormer added to kitchen wing ca. 1925; demolished 1977. Outbuildings. 5 sheets (1976, including site plan, plans, elevations); 7 ext. photos (1976), 1 int. photo of pressed tin ceiling (1976), 1 photo of barn ruins (1976), 1 photo of stairs to root cellar (1976); 12 data pages (1976). LC code: PA,6-MTPLES.V,1.

Stoudt, George, House (Octagon House) (PA-267), N side of Eight Cornered House Rd. (T579), .6 mi. E of Gruber Rd. (LR06038), approx. 1.5 mi. SE of Mount Pleasant. Half timber with wattle and daub nogging with clapboarding, octagonal, 16' each side, two stories, polygonal roof, central chimney (parlor stove) and end chimney (kitchen fireplace), entrance porch on S (front) elevation (N originally front entrance, entrance changed to S when road direction changed ca. 1930), porch on two N sides connects house with adjacent wing; adaptation of traditional Pennsylvania-German three-room plan. Built 1865-70; separate two-story frame wing built to E ca. 1880, porch connects wing and house; interior altered when entrance changed to S elevation; demolished 1971. Stoudt purchased land 1865 with agreement to allow Lydia Dundore, widow of previous owner, to continue to live in original house (frame and stone house built 1812, enlarged 1848). 1 ext. photo (1970), 1 ext. copy photo (ca. 1930), 1 ext. copy photo of Dundore House (ca. 1930), 1 copy photo of horse and plow (ca. 1930); 11 data pages (1976). LC code: PA,6-MTPLES.V,12.

New Berlinville (Colebrookdale Township)

Barn (PA-5259), on dirt road, off Pa. 100. Stuccoed stone with brick corners with quoins, frame forebay contained within stone end walls, two levels, gable roof, frame gable ends with three-part windows, X-shaped brick ventilators, decorated with painted "hex signs." Built ca. 1850; addition to side. 2 ext. photos (1941). LC code: PA,6-NEBER,1A.

Oley Vicinity (Oley Township) (See also Friedensburg for Oley area)

DeTurk, John, House (PA-1023), N side of DeTurk Rd., .2 mi. S of Pa. 73, .6 mi. W of Pa. 662 (Old Swedes Rd.), on Manatawny Creek. Maintained by the Historic Preservation Trust of Berks County. Coursed squared rubble (S front elevation) and random rubble, 17'-10" (two-bay front) x 24'-1", one-and-a-half stories with fully exposed basement to N, steep gable roof, pent roof across S elevation (removed, reconstructed 1976), tulips and birds painted on door and shutter panels (all missing except door to basement, decoration still discernible), pedimented hood over attic window; one room plan, simple interiors. Built 1767 (date stone); vacant 1958; exterior restored 1976. Good example of Huguenot settler's house. DeTurk farm was center of Moravian activity in Oley Valley; 1742 meeting to unite the various German Protestant groups in area held in barn. 2 sheets (1958, 1961, including site plan, plans); 7 ext. photos (1941, 1958); 3 data pages (1958). LC code: PA,6-OLEY,1. NR (Oley Township Historic District).

Barn (PA-1023A). Random and coursed rubble, frame forebay contained within stone end walls, two levels, gable roof with ventilators, slit ventilators, decorated with painted panels showing farm animals (cow, donkeys, horse). Built nineteenth century; frame sheds and silo added. 2 ext. photos (1941).

Farmhouse, Stone (PA-5261), no location provided. Random rubble, two bays, one and a half stories with exposed basement, gable roof, porch across front elevation. Early house, date unknown. 1 ext. photo (1941).

Barn (PA-5261A). Random and coursed rubble, frame forebay contained within stone end walls, two-level bank barn, gable roof, louvered ventilators in end walls, decorated with painted "hex signs." Built nineteenth century. 3 ext. photos (1941).

Hoffman, Guy, Farm (PA-5266), no location provided. Typical Pennsylvania-German farm complex including two stone and frame barns, 1824 stone and brick farmhouse (date stone), earlier stone farmhouse, stone and frame outbuildings. 1 ext. photo (1941). LC code: PA,6-OLEY.V,2.

Barn (PA-5266A). Random rubble with frame forebay contained within stone end walls, two-level bank barn, gable roof, decorated with three star designs on forebay. Built nineteenth century. Adjacent stone walls, wooden fences, and newer barn. 2 ext. photos (1941).

Original Farmhouse (PA-5266B). Random rubble, two-and-a-half-story bank house, three-bay front, gable roof, shed roofs across front and side elevations. Probably built eighteenth century. Adjoins stone outbuilding at rear corner. 1 ext. photo (1941).

Shed (PA-5266C). Stone and frame, rectangular, one story, gable roof, recessed opening and door on front. 1 ext. photo (1941).

Kaufman House (PA-1042), E side of Pa. 662 (Old Swedes Rd.), 1.5 mi. S of Pa. 73. Coursed squared rubble (S front elevation) and random rubble, 55' (four-bay front) x 27', two-and-a-half stories with basement, steep gable roof with pent eaves, large central chimney, gabled hood over S entrance; two rooms divided by large central fireplace. Built ca. 1766; two-story random rubble wing added to W 1834; porch added across N elevation. Jacob Kaufman built this house, leaving the smaller house on the property which his father, David, built. The Kaufman Farm is one of the finest complete examples of a Pennsylvania-German farm group in the area. 3 ext. photos (1958), 3 int. photos (1958); 3 data pages (1958). LC code: PA,6-OLEY.V,1. NR (Oley Township Historic District).

Barns (PA-1059). Two barns of similar design, one larger than the other. Random rubble, two levels, gable roofs, projecting frame forebays contained in stone end walls over stable entrances, louvered ventilators; stables lower level, threshing floor above. Dates unknown (between 1727 and 1834). Well preserved typical Pennsylvania-German barns. 3 ext. photos (1958); 1 data page (1958). LC code: PA,6-OLEY.V,1B.

Small House (PA-1046). Random rubble, four-bay front, two-and-a-half stories on sloping site, steep gable roof, large central chimney; divided into two rooms by large central fireplace, exposed beam ceiling. Built eighteenth century (between 1727 and 1762); connected to springhouse by a stone-walled trout pond. Built by David Kaufman, who immigrated to Germantown in 1720 and settled in the Oley Valley in 1727. Excellent example of a simple Pennsylvania-German farmhouse. 2 ext. photos (1958), 2 int. photos (1958); 1 data page (1958). LC code: PA,6-OLEY.V,1A.

Pikeville (Pike Township)

Barn, Decorated Red (PA-5274), no location provided. Stone with frame forebay contained within stone end walls, two levels, gable roof, lintels with keystones over openings, decorated with painted "hex signs." Built nineteenth century. 1 ext. photo (1941). LC code: PA,6-PIKVI,1A.

Pleasantville Vicinity (Colebrookdale Township)

Barn, Stone (PA-5351), approx. 5 mi. E of Pleasantville. Random rubble with frame forebay contained within stone end walls, two levels, gable roof, small barn with two stable entrances, ventilator openings in gable ends, frame shed added to rear. Probably built eighteenth century. 2 ext. photos (1941). LC code: PA,6-PLEAS.V,6A.

Pleasantville Vicinity (Earl Township)

Barn, Decorated (PA-5260), Pa. 73, approx. 1.5 mi. E of Pleasantville. Original stone barn with frame forebay contained within stone end walls, frame additions built on both sides to extend barn, two levels, gable roof, decorated with painted "hex signs." Built 1817 (date stone "E.C. and M.C. 1817"). 2 ext. photos (1941). LC code: PA,6-PLEAS.V,2A.

Pleasantville Vicinity (Oley Township)

Barn (PA-5281), on dirt road off old Pa. 73, approx. .25 mi. E of Pleasantville. Random rubble with cantilevered frame forebay over stable entrances, bank barn, two levels with lofts, gable roof, slit ventilators. Built ca. 1750. 2 ext. photos (1941), 1 int. photo showing framing detail in loft (1941). LC code: PA,6-PLEAS.V,1A.

Lee, A. and S., Barn (PA-5277), just S of old Pa. 73, on Manatawny Creek. Random rubble with frame forebay cantilevered over stable entrances, two-level bank barn, stone wing and frame wing flank ramp entrance to threshing floor, steep gable roof, slit ventilators. Built 1797 (arched date stone in gable end); stone supporting wall added to forebay; bridge joins forebay to separate shed. 2 ext. photos (1941). LC code: PA,6-PLEAS.V,3A.

Maul Stone Barn (PA-5280), N of old Pa. 73, E of General Lesher's gravesite. Random rubble with frame additions, one level, gable roof, slit ventilators, pent roof (partially removed). Built 1791 (date stone in gable end). 2 ext. photos (1941). LC code: PA,6-PLEAS.V,4A.

Stolzfus Stone Barn (PA-5279), N of old Pa. 73, just past General Lesher's gravesite. Random rubble, two levels, gable roof, silo added next to ramp, frame addition built out from stable entrances. Date unknown. 1 ext. photo (1941). LC code: PA,6-PLEAS.V,5A.

Pricetown (Ruscombmanor Township)

Barn, Decorated (PA-5269), no location provided. Random rubble with frame forebay contained within stone end walls, two levels, gable roof, exterior access stair near stable entrances, decorated with painted folk designs. Built early nineteenth century. 1 ext. photo (1941). LC code: PA,6-PRICE,1A.

Reading

Colonial Berks Real Estate Company. See Mutual Fire Insurance Company Building.

12 North Fifth Street (commercial building) (PA-5143). Brick with stone trim, three-bay facade, three stories, store front, bay windows, modillioned cornice. Built ca. 1890s; John B. Brooks, architect; demolished. 5 ext. photos (1980); 6 data pages (1980). LC code: PA,6-READ,8.

16-20 North Fifth Street (commercial building). See Mutual Fire Insurance Company Building.

26 North Fifth Street (commercial building) (PA-5146). Brick, one by five bays, three stories, flat roof, store fronts, bay windows, pedimented hood on scroll brackets over entrance. Built ca. 1878; Cyrus G. Derr, architect; probably originally built as apartment house and store; later changed to offices; demolished. 5 ext. photos (1980); 7 data pages (1980). LC code: PA,6-READ,5.

Mutual Fire Insurance Company Building (Colonial Berks Real Estate Company) (PA-5144), 16-20 N. Fifth St. Brick, three structural bays with grouped windows, four stories, storefronts, corbeled cornice with parapet. Built ca. 1892; storefronts altered; demolished. 5 ext. photos (1980); 7 data pages (1980). LC code: PA,6-READ,7.

401 Penn Street (commercial building) (PA-5147). Two joined buildings: four-story brick commercial building with six-bay facade facing N. Fourth St. built late nineteenth century; four-story brick building with three-bay facade facing Penn St. built early twentieth century; demolished. 5 ext. photos (1980); 3 data pages (1980). LC code: PA,6-READ,4.

Philadelphia and Reading Railroad, Skew Arch Bridge. See Skew Arch Bridge.

Reading Friends Meetinghouse (PA-1048), W side of N. Sixth St., between Washington and Walnut Sts. Coursed squared rubble, three by four bays, one-and-a-half stories, gable roof with cornice returns, flat hood across E (front) elevation, double door with fanlight and plain cornice, segmental window heads and fanlight on E elevation. Built 1868. 2 ext. photos (1958); 1 data page (1958, 1962). LC code: PA,6-READ,2.

Reading News Building (Sharp Building) (PA-5145), 22-24 N. Fifth St. Brick and granite with terra cotta and limestone trim, approx. 31' (four-bay facade) x 55', three stories, low slope roof, parapet and bracketed cornice, two-story Ionic pilasters, arched storefront windows and bay window on facade, Beaux Arts details; built as fireproof building with steel girders and concrete floors. Built 1912; William A. Sharp, building contractor; demolished. 8 ext. photos (1980); 12 data pages (1980). LC code: PA,6-READ,6.

Rennas Hotel (State Store Building) (PA-5148), 403 Penn St. Brick later covered with glazed steel veneer, approx. 30' facade, three stories, shed roof, original Italianate details covered. Built 1867; Jac. C. Hoof, possible architect; probably originally built as house; storefront and glazed steel veneer added 1950s; demolished. 4 ext. photos (1980); 3 data pages (1980). LC code: PA,6-READ,1.

Sharp Building. See Reading News Building.

Skew Arch Bridge (PA-1025), N. Sixth St. at Woodward St., carries double track of Philadelphia and Reading Railroad. Coursed brownstone ashlar, triple arch bridge (central arch spans roadway 40', smaller arches to each side of main arch span sidewalks), arches laid in elliptical courses eliminating need for keystones, bridge set diagonally to street. Built 1856-57; Richard Osborne, designer; owned by Reading Railroad Company. 3 ext. photos (1958); 1 data page (1958). LC code: PA,6-READ,1. HAER, NR.

State Store Building. See Rennas Hotel.

Reading Vicinity

Barn (PA-5268), S of Reading. Random rubble with quoins, frame forebay contained within stone end walls, two levels, gable roof, slit ventilators. Date unknown. 1 ext. photo (1941). LC code: PA,6-READ.V,1A.

Robesonia Borough

Ege, George, House (PA-1026), NE side of Freeman St., E of intersection with S. Church St., .7 mi. S of U.S. Rte. 422. Random rubble, L-shaped, five-bay front, two-and-a-half stories, gable roof with dormers, bracketed cornice, lintels with keystones, pedimented entrance with fanlight on S (front) elevation, Palladian window at stair landing, two-story setback random rubble wing to E (five bays), Georgian details; central hall plan, elaborate interior woodwork. Built 1807 (date stone "1809"); porch added on W elevation; enclosed porch added on ell; frame shed connects ell to random rubble outbuilding; used as nursing home. 3 ext. photos (1958), 6 int. photos (1958); 2 data pages (1958, 1961). LC code: PA,6-ROBSO,1.

St. Peters Vicinity

Hopewell Village, Ironmaster's House and Village Barn. See Hopewell Village (Union Township), Hopewell Village National Historic Site.

Spangsville Vicinity (Oley Township)

Griesemer Mill (PA-1019), S side of T575, .3 mi. E of Covered Bridge Rd., on W bank of Manatawny Creek. Random rubble, 20' (three-bay front) x 35' (four bays), three-and-a-half stories on sloping site, gable roof, loading doors on three levels with pedimented hood on NW (front) elevation, segmental stone arch at mill race entrance. Built 1847 (date stone); one-story frame wing added on SE elevation. One of the principal mills in Oley Valley in nineteenth century. 3 ext. photos (1958); 2 data pages (1958). LC code: PA,6-YEL.V,1. NR (Oley Township Historic District).

Griesemer Mill Covered Bridge (PA-1020), Over Manatawny Creek (T579), .5 mi. N of Spangsville. Burr arch truss supported on stone abutments, single span 124', single lane roadway, partially covered with horizontal boarding, gable roof. Built 1832; new siding and roof. The oldest covered bridge extant in Berks County. 1 ext. photo (1958), 1 int. photo (1958); 1 data page (1958). LC code: PA,6-YEL.V,2. NR (Also in Oley Township Historic District).

Hunter House (PA-1034), N side of Oley Turnpike, .9 mi. E of Pa. 662 (Old Swedes Rd.). Random rubble, T-shaped, five-bay front with two-bay rear kitchen wing, two-and-a-half stories, gable roof with pent eaves, elaborate door with fanlight framed with engaged fluted columns and pediment, wooden lintels with projecting keystones over windows, Georgian details; central hall plan. Built 1803; two-story porch added on wing; one-story frame wing added on main section. 4 ext. photos (1958); 2 data pages (1958). LC code: PA,6-YEL.V,6. NR (Oley Township Historic District).

Spang House (PA-1033), on private road .1 mi. E of Covered Bridge Rd., .1 mi. N of Oley Turnpike, W side of Manatawny Creek. Random rubble with quoins, L-shaped, five-bay front with three-bay rear wing, two-and-a-half stories, gable roof with cornice returns, door with fanlight framed with pilasters and pediment with gouge work and reeding, wooden lintels with projecting keystones over windows, Georgian details; central hall plan. Built 1795 (main section); rear wing added ca. 1803; interior remodeled. 2 ext. photos (1958); 2 data pages (1958). LC code: PA,6-YEL.V,5. NR (Oley Township Historic District).

Stonersville (Exeter Township)

Blacksmith Shop (PA-148), S side of Pa. 562 (Boyertown Rd.), E end of town. Log, rectangular, one-and-a-half stories, steep gable roof, central chimney. Built late eighteenth century or early nineteenth century; demolished. 2 ext. photos (1940). LC code: PA,6-STONV,1.

Boone, Daniel, Birthplace. See Baumstown Vicinity (Exeter Township), Boone, Daniel, Birthplace.

Stonersville Vicinity (Exeter Township)

Exeter Friends Meetinghouse (PA-1021), E side of Boone Rd., .5 mi. S of Pa. 562 (Boyertown Rd.), approx. 1 mi. SE of Stonersville. Random rubble, 50'-3" (six-bay front) x 30'-1", one-and-a-half stories, gable roof, two doors on S (front) elevation (pedimented hood over main double door); one room with sliding partition, simple unpainted woodwork. Built 1758; porch (partially enclosed) added across E elevation nineteenth century. Early members included the ancestors of Abraham Lincoln and Daniel Boone. Good example of well-preserved Pennsylvania Quaker meetinghouse. 2 sheets (1958, 1960, including site plan, plan); 3 ext. photos (1958), 5 int. photos (1958); 2 data pages (1958). LC code: PA,6-STONV.V,1.

Mill Tract Farm (PA-1037), W side of Mill Rd., .7 mi. N of Pa. 562 (Boyertown Rd.). 1.3 mi. NE of Stonersville. Coursed rubble (partially stuccoed), L-shaped, over-all dimensions approx. 56' x 70' (built in many stages) including five-bay main section (W three bays built first, E two bays added later) with wing to W and wings to N, two-and-a-half and one-and-a-half stories, gable and shed roofs, pent eaves, belt course on S (front) elevation (originally pent roof); central hall plan, excellent Georgian-design paneling, much original hardware. Outbuildings. Built mid-eighteenth century through second decade of nineteenth century (chronology not known); renovated 1958. House probably built by Samuel Lee, built on Boone family property. 9 sheets (1958, including site plan, plans, elevations, details); 6 ext. photos (1958), 8 int. photos (1958); 2 data pages (1958). LC code: PA,6-STONV.V,2. NR.

Union Township

Hopewell Village National Historic Site. See Hopewell Village (Union Township), Hopewell Village National Historic Site.

Womelsdorf Vicinity (Heidelberg Township)

Lime Kilns (PA-142), N side of Pa. 419, .2 mi. S of Womelsdorf. Random rubble kilns with two triangular openings, built into slope of hill. Built early nineteenth century; poor condition. 1 ext. photo (1940). LC code: PA,6-WOM.V,2.

Womelsdorf Vicinity (Marion Township)

Brown House (PA-1049), W side of N. Mill Rd., .1 mi. N of U.S. Rte. 422, W of intersection of Pa. 419 and U.S. Rte. 422. Brick, six by two bays, two-and-a-half stories with basement, gable roof, two identical doors with fanlights and Ionic pilasters and entablature on E (front) elevation, flat stone lintels with corner rosettes; central hall plan. Built 1819 (date stone); two-story brick wing added to W elevation; restored. 2 ext. photos (1958), 2 int. photos (1958); 2 data pages (1958). LC code: PA,6-WOM.V,1. NR (Tulpehocken Creek Historic District).

Charming Forge, Iron Master's House (PA-1022), SW side of Charming Forge Rd. (LR06050), 1.3 mi. E of Pa. 419, 3.5 mi. N of Womelsdorf. Irregular coursed ashlar (SE front elevation) and random rubble, L-shaped, five-bay front, two-and-a-half stories, gable roof with dormers, lintels with keystones, pent roof forms pediment over window, Georgian details; central hall plan, elaborate woodwork; setback wing to NE, irregular coursed ashlar and random rubble, six-bay front, two-and-a-half stories, gable roof, three entrances with pent roof. Wing built ca. 1749-77; main block built 1777; porch with carved brackets forming low pointed arches added on SE elevation late nineteenth century. 4 ext. photos (1958), 5 int. photos (1958); 3 data pages (1958, 1961). LC code: PA,6-WOM.V,1. NR (Tulpehocken Creek Historic District).

Yellow House (Amity Township)

Yellow House Hotel (PA-1035), SW corner of Pa. 562 (Boyertown Rd.) and Pa. 662 (Old Swedes Rd.). Stuccoed stone, L-shaped, eight-bay front by four bays with three-bay rear wing, two-and-a-half stories, gable roof with dormers, cornice with brackets and decorative panels (probably later addition), bracketed porch across E (front) and N elevations. Built early nineteenth century; used as hotel, tavern, general store, and post office. Small hotel built by Peter Nagle Jr.; this crossroads community took its name from this yellow-painted hotel. 2 ext. photos (1958); 2 data pages (1958, 1961). LC code: PA,6-YEL,1.

Yellow House Vicinity

Barn (PA-5263), W of Pa. 100, between Yellow House and Boyertown. Random rubble with quoins, frame forebay originally contained within stone end walls (one wall replaced with frame), two levels, gable roof, stone arches over stable entrances. Built nineteenth century. 1 ext. photo (1941). LC code: PA,6-YEL.V,7A.

Yellow House Vicinity (Oley Township)

DeBenneville, George House. See Limekiln Vicinity (Oley Township), DeBenneville, George, House.

Fisher, Henry, House (PA-1027), E side of Pa. 662 (Old Swedes Rd.), 1.3 mi. N of Pa. 562 (Boyertown Rd.). Coursed squared rubble (W front elevation) and random rubble, approx. 40' (five-bay front) x 30' (two bays), two-and-a-half stories with basement, gable roof with pedimented dormers with pilasters, bracketed cornice and pent eaves, applied circular medallions in gable ends, recessed door with fanlight framed by pilasters and pediment, lintels with projecting keystones over windows, Georgian details; central hall plan, excellent interior woodwork. Built 1801; Gottlieb Drexel, carpenter; two stone additions to E built nineteenth century; still owned by Fisher family. Excellent well preserved example of Georgian design taken from builders' handbook, but enriched with details expressive of the Germanic craftsman. 5 ext. photos (1958), 12 int. photos (1958); 2 data pages (1958). LC code: PA,6-YEL.V,3. NR (Also in Oley Township Historic District).

Griesemer Mill. See Spangsville Vicinity (Oley Township), Griesemer Mill.

Griesemer Mill Covered Bridge. See Spangsville Vicinity (Oley Township), Griesemer Mill Covered Bridge.

Hunter House. See Spangsville Vicinity (Oley Township), Hunter House.

Spang House. See Spangsville Vicinity (Oley Township), Spang House.

Bucks County

Andalusia (Bensalem Township)

Andalusia (Nicholas Biddle House, John Craig House) (PA-1248), .3 mi. S of State Rd. on private road, 1.5 mi. E of Grant Ave., on N bank of Delaware River. Stuccoed brick scored to imitate ashlar, T-shaped, 120'-2" (N front, central five bays with projecting symmetrical two-bay wings) x 94'-1" with 51'-5" S (river) elevation, two-story N section and two-and-a-half-story S section, gable roofs with pedimented gable ends, two-story projecting bays on E and W elevations, door with fanlight and pedimented entrance porch on N elevation, pedimented hexastyle Doric portico with classical entablature across S elevation, Greek Revival style; central hall plan. Outbuildings. Land bought by John Craig 1795 and he erected N section 1797-98; 1807-08 side bays and small front wings added, Benjamin Henry Latrobe, architect; Nicholas Biddle married Craig's daughter and acquired house 1811; 1834 Greek Revival S section added and additions to N section covered Latrobe's design, Thomas U. Walter, architect. John Craig was a successful Philadelphia merchant. Nicholas Biddle served in the state legislature and was president of Second Bank of the United States 1823-36. Early example of Greek temple form in country. 15 sheets (1974, including site plans, plans, elevations, sections, details); 11 ext. photos (1968, 1973), 23 int. photos (1968, 1973), 2 copy photos of watercolors by Thomas U. Walter (ca. 1834), 1 copy photo of oil painting (n.d.), 1 copy photo of Nicholas Biddle portrait by Thomas Sully; 6 data pages (1974, 1983). LC code: PA,9-ANDA,1. NHL.

Billiard Room (PA-1248C). Stuccoed random rubble (first story) and frame with flush boards (second story), 24'-2" x 24'-4", two stories built on foundations of earlier building, gable roof with pedimented gable ends, recessed second story with Doric porch on three sides, door with fanlight (1976 replacement) on E elevation. Built 1815-16 (one story with covered porch on roof); remodeled 1827 (porch removed); second story added 1830 (present form). 1 sheet (1974, including plans, elevations, section); 2 ext. photos (1968, 1973); 2 data pages (1974, 1983). LC code: PA,9-ANDA,1C.

Cottage (PA-1248A). Heavy timber with brick nogging covered with asbestos shingles (original scored stucco remains on first story S elevation), built in two sections, 49'-2" (three-bay front) x 44'-10" (including rear kitchen ell) with 42' x 36' L-shaped wing added to rear, two-and-a-half stories, cross gable roofs, crenelated bays on E and W elevations, porch across S (front) elevation (originally lattice-work porch), door with transom and side lights, diamond-pane windows with label molds, Gothic Revival style; central hall plan. Built ca. 1839 (original front ell); Thomas U. Walter, architect; ca. 1853 rear ell added, both sections covered with flush boards (original section was scored stucco), original rear porch removed; ca. 1925 present front porch added; exterior covered with asbestos shingles; restored. 2 sheets (1974, including plans, elevations); 3 ext. photos (1973), 1 int. photo (1973); 2 data pages (1974, 1983). LC code: PA,9-ANDA,1A.

Graperies (PA-1248D). Random rubble complex of buildings with two walls extending 280' to S (walls originally enclosed artificially heated greenhouses), several one-story furnace houses attached to walls, one- and two-story buildings (water supply tanks, coach house and stables) with three-story rectangular tower and circular tower. Built 1835-36; Thomas U. Walter, architect; original wooden tower burned ca. 1910, replaced by stone tower, Mellon, Meigs, and Howe, architects; storm damaged greenhouses, only stone portion remains. 1 sheet (1974, isometric view); 2 data pages (1974, 1983). LC code: PA,9-ANDA,1D.

Grotto (PA-1248B). Random rubble built to simulate a gothic ruin, 17'-6" x 18'-9", one story, shed roof behind irregular stone parapet (to simulate collapsed wall), door with wooden bosses and strap hinges (to simulate iron) with urn in niche above door on W (front) elevation (urn replaced original statue), pointed-arch windows with diamond panes, pointed-arch label molds over openings; one room, diamond-patterned marble floor with central cross, interior walls stuccoed and scored to imitate ashlar (restored 1974). Built ca. 1834-36; Thomas U. Walter, architect; central marble columbarium installed 1974. 2 sheets (1974, including plan, elevations, section); 2 ext. photos (1973); 2 data pages (1974, 1983).LC code: PA,9-ANDA,1B.

Biddle, Nicholas, House. See Andalusia.

Craig, John, House. See Andalusia.

Aquetong Vicinity (Solebury Township)

Barn, Stone (PA-5298), on Aquetong Rd. (PA-09060), S of Aquetong. Random rubble, two levels, gable roof, several horizontally divided wooden doors. Possibly built ca. 1740; burned 1861 and rebuilt using original stone walls. 1 ext. photo (1941). LC code: PA,9-AQUE.V,1A.

Bensalem

Bensalem African Methodist Episcopal Church. See Bridgewater (Bensalem Township), Bensalem African Methodist Episcopal Church.

Bridgewater (Bensalem Township)

Bensalem African Methodist Episcopal Church (Little Jerusalem, Little Bethel) (PA-1721), 1200 Bridgewater Rd. Frame with shiplap siding covered with asphalt siding, one story, gable roof, central door with lancet window above. Built between 1832 and 1850; renovated ca. 1860 and ca. 1890, lancet window added then. One of the oldest Black churches in America, organized in 1820. 4 ext. photos (1982), 2 int. photos (1982); 1 data page (1982). LC code: PA,9-BRIDWA,2. NR.

Little Bethel. See Bensalem African Methodist Episcopal Church.

Little Jerusalem. See Bensalem African Methodist Episcopal Church.

Bristol Borough

Keene House. See Lenox-Keene House.

Lenox-Keene House (PA-1234), 710 Radcliffe St. Stuccoed stone, rectangular (three-bay front) with projecting bays on E and W elevations, two-and-a-half stories with basement, hip roof with dormers and central pediment, door with side lights and large fanlight, large gabled hood supported on brackets over door, Federal details. Built 1816; demolished 1964. 4 ext. photos (1963), 6 int. photos (1963); 1 data page (1983). LC code: PA,9-BRIST,1.

Buckingham (Buckingham Township)

Farm group (PA-5295), Pa. 263 (Old York Rd.). Random rubble with clapboarding added on gable end, rectangular with numerous frame sheds and additions, three-level bank barn, gable roof, pent roof over stable entrances, canted stone barnyard wall with buttresses. Date unknown. 1 ext. photo (1941). LC code: PA,9-BUCK,2.

Chalfont Vicinity (New Britain Township)

Barn, Stone (PA-5284). See Doylestown Vicinity (New Britain Township), Barn, Stone (PA-5284).

Croyden (Bristol Township)

White Hall of Bristol College (PA-5486), 701-21 Shadyside Ave. Photographic documentation underway 1990.

Curley Hill Vicinity (Plumstead Township)

Barn (PA-5286), U.S. Rte. 611, N of Curley Hill Rd. Coursed squared rubble with quoins, frame forebay, two levels, gable roof with frame in upper portion of gable ends, diamond-shaped stone laid in top courses of masonry. Built 1805; frame sheds added. 1 ext. photo of gable end (1941). LC code: PA,9-CURHI,1A.

Doylestown Borough

Bucks County Historical Society. See Mercer Museum.

Harvey House (PA-1006), 15 E. State St. Brick, three-bay front, two-and-a-half stories, gable roof with segmental dormer, door with transom and entrance porch; side hall plan. Built ca. 1820-30; two-story addition to rear. 1 ext. photo (1925); 1 data page (1941). LC code: PA,9-DOYLT,2.

Mercer Museum (Bucks County Historical Society) (PA-1007), SW corner of Pine and Ashland Sts. Museum operated by Bucks County Historical Society. Reinforced concrete, irregular rectangle, approx. 97' x 71', four-and-a-half-story center section with six-and-a-half-story N tower and seven-and-a-half-story S tower with raised basement, hip roof with dormers (both concrete), numerous chimneys with pyramidal caps, variety of window shapes and sizes; open central court surrounded by irregular circulation galleries and display rooms, exposed concrete interior walls, exterior took form from interior arrangement; eccentric design with medieval characteristics. Built 1913-16; Henry Chapman Mercer, designer; William Lab, building supervisor; attached to S of older historical society, a brick Georgian Revival building from 1904, Horace Trumbauer, architect; reinforced concrete library wing added to S of museum 1933-36, Fred Martin, architect; reinforced concrete entrance wing and stair tower added 1974, Shappell and Crothers, architects. Built by Mercer to house his large collection of preindustrial-era tools, machines and implements; willed to Bucks County Historical Society. An early and impressive example of reinforced concrete construction. See Fonthill (PA-1140) and Moravian Pottery and Tile Works (PA-1139), both Doylestown Vicinity. 5 ext. photos (ca. 1935, 1966), 11 int. photos (1966), 4 copy photos of photos taken during construction (ca. 1913, 1916), 1 copy photo of site plan (1917); 6 data pages (1965, 1984). LC code: PA,9-DOYLT,3. NR.

Doylestown Vicinity

Barn, stone (PA-5285), Pa. 113, N of Doylestown. Random rubble with frame gable ends (stonework more evenly laid on front elevation), barn with wing connected to side, open wagon shelter between barn and wing, two levels, gable roof with scalloped bargeboards, ramp to wagon entrance. Built 1827. 6 ext. photos (1941). LC code: PA,9-DOYLT.V,6A.

Barn, stone (PA-5292), Pa. 212, E of Doylestown. Coursed (front elevation) and random rubble with quoins, bank barn, gable roof, louvered ventilator windows, two-level stone and frame addition to rear. Roofed stone well at corner. Built eighteenth century 2 ext. photos (1941). LC code: PA,9-DOYLT.V,4A.

Moore, William, Barn (PA-5297), LR 09060, approx. 2 mi. N of Doylestown. Random rubble with quoins (stonework more evenly laid on front elevation), bank barn with narrow (gable) end built into slope, several levels, gable roof, slit ventilators. Built 1797; frame additions. Straw storage area with adjustable roof next to barn. Unusual type of early bank barn found primarily in Bucks County. 3 ext. photos (1941). LC code: PA,9-DOYLT.V,5A.

Doylestown Vicinity (Buckingham Township)

Fonthill (Henry Chapman Mercer House) (PA-1140), NW side of E. Court St., .1 mi. SW of Pa. 313 (Swamp Rd.). Museum operated by Bucks County Historical Society. Reinforced concrete, irregular plan, approx. 100' x 50', two-and-a-half-story and three-and-a-half-story sections and four-story tower with raised basement, steeply pitched hip, gable and pyramidal roofs of brushed concrete and tile with concrete dormers, numerous chimneys, various windows (rectangular, arched and triangular), many terraces and balconies; vaulted interior spaces, exposed concrete interior elaborately decorated with tiles from the Moravian Pottery and Tile Works, exterior took form from interior arrangement; eccentric design with medieval characteristics. Built 1907-12 (built around original farmhouse on estate); Henry Chapman Mercer, designer; willed house to public as a museum of tiles, engraving and woodcuts. Adjacent reinforced concrete garage pavilion of similar design. Home of Henry C. Mercer, noted archaeologist and anthropologist, known for his work with tiles (see Moravian Pottery and Tile Works, PA-1139) and for his extensive collection of preindustrial artifacts (see Mercer Museum, PA-1007). Pioneering example of reinforced concrete used in the construction of a residence. 6 ext. photos (1966), 16 int. photos (1966), 2 copy photos (n.d.); 4 data pages (1984). LC code: PA,9-DOYLT.V,7. NHL.

> *Farmhouse* (PA-1140B). Stuccoed stone, seven-bay front built in three sections, two-and-a-half stories, gable roofs, inside end chimneys. Built eighteenth century; moved to site and used as an arboretum. 1 ext. photo (1966). See Fonthill for data. LC code: PA,9-DOYLT.V,7B.
>
> *Garage* (PA-1140A). Design similar to house, reinforced concrete, irregular plan, two stories with tower, steeply pitched hipped roofs, dormers and chimneys designed to serve as birdhouses, concrete-railed balcony and exterior stairway. Built 1907-12; Henry Chapman Mercer, designer. 2 ext. photos (1966). See Fonthill for data. LC code: PA,9-DOYLT.V,7A.

Mercer, Henry Chapman, House. See Fonthill.

Mercer, Henry Chapman, Tile Works. See Moravian Pottery and Tile Works.

Moravian Pottery and Tile Works (Henry Chapman Mercer Tile Works) (PA-1139), SW side of Pa. 313 (Swamp Rd.), .2 mi. NW of E. Court St. Museum operated by Bucks County Department of Parks and Recreation. Reinforced concrete with concrete buttresses, U-shaped, approx. 120' x 100' with central arcaded courtyard (similar to medieval cloisters), two-and-a-half stories built in tiers with towers, gable roofs with rounded ridges of brushed concrete with stepped parapets at gable ends and concave hip roofs of tiles on towers, chimneys of various shapes and sizes of concrete, brick and tile, variety of windows, Mission Style characteristics (design based on several southern California mission churches); concrete groin and barrel-vaulted interior spaces, decorative tiles set in interior and exterior walls, five kilns. Built 1911-12; Henry C. Mercer, designer; operated until 1964; acquired by county. Founded 1898 (original works burned) by Henry C. Mercer, anthropologist, archaeologist and collector of preindustrial artifacts. Mercer was interested in Pennsylvania-German pottery, to revive the craft he began producing a small quantity of fine decorative tiles by his own processes. Pioneer use of reinforced concrete. See Fonthill (PA-1140) and Mercer Museum (PA-1007), both in Doylestown. 12 ext. photos (1966), 7 int. photos (1966), 1 copy photo of ext. (n.d.); 4 data pages (1965, 1984). LC code: PA,9-DOYLT.V,8. HAER, NHL.

Doylestown Vicinity (Doylestown Township)

Barn, Stone (PA-5191), U.S. 202, on grounds of National Farm School, W of Doylestown. Random rubble with quoins, two-level bank barn, original ramp to wagon entrance and pent roof over stable entrances removed, louvered ventilator windows. Probably built late eighteenth century. 2 ext. photos (1941). LC code: PA,9-DOYLT.V,3A.

Barn, Stone (PA-5282), S of U.S. 202 on dirt road, on grounds of National Farm School, W of Doylestown. Stuccoed fieldstone, two levels, gable roof, slit ventilators, later frame additions. Probably built mid-eighteenth century. 1 ext. photo (1941), 2 int. photos (1941). LC code: PA,9-DOYLT.V,2A.

Doylestown Vicinity (New Britain Township)

Barn, Stone (PA-5284), U.S. 202 near W county line. Random rubble (horizontal siding and stucco added to one gable end), two levels, gable roof, ramp to wagon entrance with root cellar underneath, pent roof over stable entrances, pedimented hood over upper door, paired sliding windows. Probably built late eighteenth century. 2 ext. photos (1941). LC code: PA,9-DOYLT.V,1A.

Fallsington (Falls Township)

Gambrel Roof House (Meetinghouse) (PA-5344), 3 S. Main St. Coursed rubble partially whitewashed, three by two bays, two-and-a-half stories, gambrel roof, one- and two-story frame wings added. Built 1728; enlarged 1758 (possibly date gambrel roof was added); additions. Outbuildings. Second meetinghouse in Fallsington; used as a school, then apartments; owned by Historic Fallsington, Inc. since 1969. 4 ext. photos (1985). LC code: PA,9-FALLSI,2. NR (Fallsington Historic District).

South Dependency (PA-5344A). Small outbuilding, coursed rubble with large corner stones, one story, gable roof, door of vertical boards with strap hinges, slit ventilators. Built eighteenth century. 2 ext. photos (1985). LC code: PA,9-FALLSI,2A.

West Dependency (PA-5344B). Small outbuilding, coursed rubble with large corner stones, one story, gable roof, door of vertical boards with strap hinges. Built eighteenth century. 1 ext. photo (1985). LC code: PA,9-FALLSI,2B.

Meetinghouse. See Gambrel Roof House.

Moon-Williamson House (PA-5343), Yardley Rd. Squared logs, three-bay front, one-and-a-half stories with basement, gable roof, inside end chimneys; frame addition to W, one and a half stories on raised basement, gable roof, pent roof with balcony above, shed attached to side. Built ca. 1685, possible cabin of early Swedish settlers; addition possibly an early settler's cabin moved from its original site and attached to log house; restored ca. 1971, G. Edwin Brumbaugh, restoration architect; owned by Historic Fallsington, Inc. One of the earliest log structures in the state. 6 ext. photos (1985), 7 int. photos (1985). LC code: PA,9-FALLSI,1. NR (Fallsington Historic District).

Williamson House. See Moon-Williamson House.

Kintnersville Vicinity (Durham Township)

Barn, Log (PA-5301), on dirt road, approx. 2 mi. NW of Kintnersville. Small log barn incorporated in later frame barn, squared and untrimmed round logs with log and lime chinking, logs later sheathed with wooden siding (partially removed), two levels. Built eighteenth century. 3 ext. photos (1941). LC code: PA,9-KINVI.V,2A.

Kintnersville Vicinity (Nockamixon Township)

Hoffman Barn (PA-5300), Pa. 611, approx. 1 mi. S of Kintnersville. Coursed and random rubble with quoins, frame forebay contained within stone end walls, two-level bank barn, gable roof, decorative round vents edged in brick, frame wing added to forebay, both decorated with painted star designs. Built ca. 1790. 3 ext. photos (1941). LC code: PA,9-KINVI.V,1A.

Langhorne Borough

Richardson, Joseph, House (PA-5488), Bellevue and Maple Aves. Photographic documentation underway 1990.

Langhorne Vicinity (Middletown Township)

Edgemont (PA-5489), 212 Bridgetown Pike, .25 mi. E of Pa. 413. Photographic documentation underway 1990.

Levittown (Middletown Township)

Hibbs, Hannah M., House (PA-5487), 34 Woodbourne Rd., .6 mi. S of U.S. Rte. 1. Photographic documentation underway 1990.

Morrisville Borough

Barclay, Thomas, House. See Summerseat.

Clymer, George, House. See Summerseat.

Summerseat (George Clymer House, Thomas Barclay House, Summerseat School) (PA-5345), Clymer St. and Morris Ave. Brick (E front elevation) and coursed rubble (rear elevation), stuccoed side elevations, approx. 52' (five-bay front) x 36', two-and-a-half stories with partially raised stone basement, gable roof with pedimented ends, pedimented entrance with pilasters and transom, flat and segmental arches over windows, Georgian style; central hall plan, original moldings and built-in cabinets, marble fireplaces, cast iron stove by Isaac Potts dated 1795. Built ca. 1770; restored 1931; renovated for school offices 1935. Built for Thomas Barclay; acquired 1806 by George Clymer, a signer of the Declaration of Independence. 10 ext. photos (1985), 11 int. photos (1985), 3 copy photos of ext. (n.d., ca. 1890). LC code: PA,9-MORVI,1. NHL.

>*Barn* (PA-5345B). Stone and frame, horizontal siding, two levels, gable roof, poor condition. 1 ext. copy photo (n.d.). LC code: PA,9-MORVI,1B.

>*Outbuildings* (PA-5345A). Several unidentified stone outbuildings, poor condition. 3 ext. copy photos (n.d.). LC code: PA,9-MORVI,1A.

Summerseat School. See Summerseat.

Neshaminy Vicinity

Barn A, Stone (PA-5294A), Pa. 132 (Street Rd.), between Neshaminy and Warminster. Random rubble with quoins (whitewashed), two levels with lofts, gable roof with central tin vent, louvered ventilator windows, silo and shed added on one side, attached to adjacent structure on other side. Built nineteenth century (date stone in gable end obliterated by whitewash). On same farm as *Barn B, Stone* (PA-5294B). 2 ext. photos (1941). LC code: PA,9-NESH.V,1A.

>*Barn B, Stone* (PA-5294B). On same farm as Barn A, Stone (PA-5294A). Stuccoed stone, large L-shaped barn with additions, three levels, gable roofs, louvered ventilator windows. Built nineteenth century 2 ext. photos (1941). LC code: PA,9-NESH.V,1B.

New Britain Vicinity

Barn, Stone (PA-5283), U.S. Rte. 202. Random rubble with quoins, two-level bank barn built in two sections, gable roof with stuccoed gable ends, beam ends and watertable remain from pent roof. Original barn (stone section with central door at threshing-floor level) built ca. 1790; stone wing added to side; two-story frame wing added to other side. 1 ext. photo (1941). LC code: PA,9-NEBRI.V,1A.

New Hope Vicinity (Solebury Township)

Thompson-Neeley-Pedcock Barn (Stone Barn). See Washington Crossing Vicinity (Solebury Township), Thompson-Neeley-Pedcock Barn (Stone Barn).

Newtown Vicinity (Middletown Township)

Jenks Hall (PA-1235), Woodbourne Rd., adjacent to bridge over Lake Luxembourg, approx. 2 mi. SE of Newtown. Random rubble, 56' x 20' with kitchen addition 20' x 20', two-and-a-half stories, gable roof; central hall plan. Built 1734; kitchen wing added early. Built by Thomas Jenks, a fuller; fulling mill built near house 1740, mill attacked by British in Revolutionary War; son, Thomas, born in house 1738, active in politics. 1 data page (1983); photographic documentation underway 1990. LC code: PA,9-NETO.V,1.

Miller's House (PA-5490), Tollgate Rd., in Cove Creek Park. Photographic documentation underway 1990.

Naylor House (PA-5491), Swift and Silver Lake Rds. Photographic documentation underway 1990.

Newtown Vicinity (Newtown Township)

Barn, Stone (1810) (PA-5332), Rte. 632. Random rubble, three-level bank barn, gable roof, entrance bridge to threshing floor, wooden louvered vents in gable ends, evidence of earlier stone barn on side elevation. Built 1810. 3 ext. photos (1941). LC code: PA,9-NETO.V,2A.

Pitner House (PA-5498), Pa. 332, just W of Upper Silver Lake Rd. Photographic documentation underway 1990.

Ottsville Vicinity (Tinicum Township)

Barn, Stone (circa 1815) (PA-5290), Pa. 611, S of Ottsville. Random rubble with quoins, two levels, gable roof, watertable remains from original pent roof over stable entrances, glazed windows and wooden louvered vents, hood over door on side elevation. Built ca. 1815. 2 ext. photos (1941). LC code: PA,9-OTVI.V,1A.

Peter's Corner Vicinity (Solebury Township)

Barn (PA-5291), S of Peter's Corner. Small random rubble barn with coursed rubble and frame addition at corner, two levels, gable roof, dormers on addition, wooden louvered vents. Date unknown. 1 ext. photo (1941). LC code: PA,9-PETCO.V,1.

Pleasant Valley Vicinity (Springfield Township)

Finady, W.A., Barn (1829) (PA-5287), Pa. 212, N of Pleasant Valley. Random rubble, projecting frame forebay supported on iron posts added over stable entrances, two levels, gable roof, slit ventilators, pedimented hoods over side doors. Built 1829 (date stone). 2 ext. photos (1941). LC code: PA,9-PLEVA.V,1A.

Solebury Vicinity (Solebury Township)

Paxson Barn (PA-5299), SE of Solebury. Whitewashed random rubble, two levels, gable roof, ramp to wagon entrance, slit ventilators. Probably built eighteenth century; remodeled 1837. 1 ext. photo (1941). LC code: PA,9-SOLBU.V,1A.

Springtown Vicinity (Springfield Township)

Barn, Stone (PA-5289), Pa. 212, just E of Springtown. Random rubble, two-level bank barn, gable roof, criss-cross and vertical accents on wagon entrance, decorative hoods over side entrances. Date unknown (house dated 1773). 2 ext. photos (1941). LC code: PA,9-SPRITO.V,1A.

Barn, Stone (1790) (PA-5288), Pa. 212, W of Springtown. Random rubble with frame forebay contained within stone end walls, two-level bank barn, gable roof, slit ventilators, hood over side entrance. Built 1790. 2 ext. photos (1941). LC code: PA,9-SPRITO.V,2A.

Stoopville Vicinity (Newtown Township)

Barn, Stone (PA-5334), on Stoopville Rd. Random rubble with quoins, two levels, gable roof, supports remain from pent roof over stable entrances, bridge to wagon entrance, glazed transom over wagon doors, well house at corner. Probably built eighteenth century (house built ca. 1740); wagon doors on side elevation added later. 3 ext. photos (1941). LC code: PA,9-STOVI.V,1A.

Washington Crossing Vicinity (Solebury Township)

Barn, Stone (PA-5293). See Thompson-Neeley-Pedcock Barn.

Neeley Barn. See Thompson-Neeley-Pedcock Barn.

Pedcock Barn. See Thompson-Neeley-Pedcock Barn.

Thompson-Neeley-Pedcock Barn (Stone Barn) (PA-5293), E side of River Rd. (Pa. 32), in Washington Crossing State Park, approx. 1.5 mi. S of New Hope. Administered by Pennsylvania Historical and Museum Commission. Random rubble barn and attached carriage shed, L-shaped, three sections built to conform with grade levels, one level with lofts, gable roofs with vertical wooden siding in gable ends, doors of vertical boards with wrought iron hardware, slit ventilators; central wagon passage flanked by stalls with hay mow platforms above. Built 1772. Barn for Thompson-Neeley House (built in stages 1702-1788) used by General George Washington to plan for his crossing of the Delaware to attack Trenton in 1776. House used as a museum. 5 ext. photos (1941). LC code: PA,9-WACRO.V,1A. See also HABSI on Thompson-Neeley House. NHL (Washington Crossing State Park).

Westboro Vicinity

Barn (1813) (PA-5296), Pa. 232, W of Westboro. Random rubble (one end wall stuccoed), frame forebay contained within stone end walls and supported by two tapered stone columns, two levels, gable roof with scalloped bargeboards, enclosed bridge to threshing floor entrance. Built 1813; enlarged ca. 1880. 3 ext. photos (1941). LC code: PA,9-WEBO.V,1A.

Yardley Borough

Lakeside (PA-5496), 20 N. Main St. Photographic documentation underway 1990.

Lanrick Manor (PA-5495), 137 S. River Rd., NW of Letchworth Ave. Photographic documentation underway 1990.

Yardley (Lower Makefield Township)

Hough, Richard, House (PA-5494), 20 Moyar Rd. Photographic documentation underway 1990.

Kirkbride-Palmer House (PA-5492), 559 Palmer Farm Dr. Photographic documentation underway 1990.

Patterson Farm (PA-5493), 949 Mirror Lake Rd. Photographic documentation underway 1990.

Stapler, John, House (PA-5497), 1505 Dolington Rd. Photographic documentation underway 1990.

Chester County

Anselma Vicinity (West Pikeland Township)

Barn, Stone (PA-5244), Pa. 401, between Anselma and Opperman's Corner. Random rubble with quoins, three-level bank barn, gable roof, enclosed bridge to threshing floor entrance, projecting wooden bay at threshing level. Built 1824. 2 ext. photos (1941). LC code: PA,15-ANS.V,1A.

Avondale Borough

Avondale. See Miller, William, House.

Miller, William, House (Avondale) (PA-5137), E side of Ellicott Rd., .2 mi. SW of Pa. 41 (Pennsylvania Ave.). Brick, L-shaped, 45'-3" (five-bay front) x 43'-4" including N (rear) kitchen ell, three-and-a-half stories with two-and-a-half story ell, gable roof with flared eaves, cove cornice, pent roofs (removed, belt courses remain); fine original woodwork and hardware, large bake oven in kitchen. Outbuildings. Built 1730 as two-and-a-half stories with kitchen ell (date in black bricks across facade "WM 1730"); 1771 third story added (date in black bricks across facade "WM 1771"); 1806 large addition to E (burned 1920s); brick shed added on ell; entrance porch added; restored 1959. Fine example of eighteenth-century house with interesting brick patterns and outstanding original interior woodwork. 5 ext. photos (1958), 11 int. photos (1958); 9 data pages (1958). LC code: PA,15-AVON,1.

Barn (PA-5137A). Random rubble, approx. 60' x 40', two levels, gable roof, belt course, stone arches over first-story openings. Built probably late eighteenth century; vacant and in poor condition. 1 ext. photo (1958). LC code: PA,15-AVON,1A.

Tenant House (PA-5137B). Random rubble, three by two bays, one-and-a-half stories on sloping site exposing basement, gable roof. Probably built early nineteenth century 1 ext. photo (1958). LC code: PA,15-AVON,1B.

Bacton (East Whiteland Township)

Hopper, Margaret, Log House. See Jacobs, John, House.

House (PA-174). See Delaware County, Concordville (Concord Township), House (Mendenhall House) (PA-174), original location.

Jacobs, John, House (Margaret Hopper Log House) (PA-1209), intersection of Pa. 401 (Conestoga Rd.) and Spring Valley Rd. Log, 19'-6" x 18', one-and-a-half stories, gable roof, large random rubble chimney on N elevation (not original); one room with loft (roof later raised for second-story room). Probably built late eighteenth century by John Jacobs; one-and-a-half-story frame wing (14'-4" x 15') added early nineteenth century; one-and-a-half-story board and batten wing added early twentieth century (wing originally a post office, converted to a kitchen mid-twentieth century); owned by Chester County Historical Society. 1 ext. photo (1958); 3 data pages (1958). LC code: PA,15-BACT,1. NR.

Barn (PA-1209A). Random rubble, approx. 27' square, two levels on sloping site, gable roof, frame forebay contained within stone end walls. Built mid-nineteenth century; original barn on site was probably log. 1 ext. photo (1958). LC code: PA,15-BACT,1A.

Mendenhall House. See Delaware County, Concordville (Concord Township), House (Mendenhall House) (PA-174), original location.

Bacton Vicinity (East Whiteland Township)

Barn (PA-5243), N side of Pa. 401 (Conestoga Rd.), W of Pa. 29. Random rubble, projecting frame forebay supported on braced wooden posts, two-level bank barn, gable roof, frame sheds added. Date unknown. 1 ext. photo (1941). LC code: PA,15-BACT.V,2A.

Gunkle, Michael, Spring Mill (PA-1113), E side of Moore Rd., at junction with Pa. 401 (Conestoga Rd.), approx. 1.5 mi. E of Bacton. Random rubble with large quoins, approx. 40' (three-bay front) x 36' (two bays), two-and-a-half stories with basement exposed to rear, gable roof with dormer, pent eaves across gable ends, hood over entrance. Built 1793 (date stone over entrance); interior remodeled 1863. Operated as mill for over a century. Well preserved example of prosperous Chester County mill. 3 ext. photos (1958); 5 data pages (1958). LC code: PA,15-BACT.V,1.

Berwyn Vicinity (Tredyffrin Township)

Bair, Mary A., House (Hunter-Bair House) (PA-117), Conestoga Rd. and Cassatt Ave. Random ashlar, widely spaced three-bay front, irregular L-shaped plan, two-and-a-half stories with attic and basement, gable and hip roofs with dormers and bands of imbricated shingles, cove cornice with brackets, three-story balustraded porch with dome and finial (second floor porch altered; third floor porch and dome removed), carved balustraded porch across facade (later partially enclosed), Queen Anne details; fine interior woodwork. Built 1877; addition at NW corner. 10 ext. photos (1971), 9 int. photos (1971), 1 ext. copy photo from 1909 shows original porch; 1 data page (1979). LC code: PA,15-BER.V,1.

Hunter house. See Bair, Mary A., House.

Birchrunville (West Vincent Township)

House (PA-174), on Hollow Rd., approx. .25 mi. E of Horseshoe Trail. See Delaware County, Concordville (Concord Township), House (Mendenhall House) (PA-174), original location.

Mendenhall House. See Delaware County, Concordville (Concord Township), House (Mendenhall House) (PA-174), original location.

Birmingham (Birmingham Township)

Birmingham Friends Meetinghouse (PA-1193), E side of Birmingham Rd., at intersection with Meetinghouse Rd. Random serpentine stone, 41' (three-bay front) x 38'-6" (three bays), one story, steep gable roof, pedimented hoods over entrances; sliding partition divided men's and women's sides. Built 1763; 1818 two-bay extension added to E elevation and new interior partition built; 1968 school wing added to E elevation (replaced horse sheds), Mather Lippincatt, architect. Well preserved eighteenth-century meetinghouse; served as hospital for British troops during the Revolutionary War at the Battle of Brandywine 1777. 5 sheets (1962, including site plan, plan, elevations, sections, details); 3 ext. photos (1958), 1 copy photo of 1855 Benjamin J. Losing engraving, 1 copy photo of 1881 sketch; 6 data pages (1958). LC code: PA,15-BIRM,1. NR (also Brandywine Battlefield NHL).

Birmingham Octagonal Schoolhouse (PA-5138), E side of Birmingham Rd., at intersection with Meetinghouse Rd., .4 mi. S of Pa. 926 (Street Rd.), behind Birmingham Friends Meetinghouse. Stuccoed stone, octagonal, one story, polygonal hip roof, pedimented hood over entrance; one room. Built 1819; used by Birmingham Society of Friends until 1920. 1 ext. photo (1958); see Birmingham Friends Meetinghouse (PA-1193) for data. LC code: PA,15-BIRM,2. NR (also Brandywine Battlefield NHL).

Birmingham Vicinity (Birmingham Township)

Sharpless House (Walker House) (PA-118), Birmingham Rd. (LR15087), N of Pa. 926 (Street Rd.). Coursed hexagonal serpentine ashlar (W front elevation) and coursed and random rubble, T-shaped, main section three by four bays with three-bay rear wing, two-and-a-half stories, gable roof with gable end over front elevation, gabled dormers, deep eaves, cornice returns, porch across front elevation, two-story wing on N elevation. Built in several stages, chronology unknown; earliest section may date from ca. 1700; front section built ca. 1800 (prior to 1810); additions between 1800-31; remodeled 1861 and mid-twentieth century. Birthplace of Isaac Sharpless, a Quaker leader and president of Haverford College 1887-1917. 3 ext. photos (1962); 1 data page (1979). LC code: PA,15-BIRM.V,2.

Walker House. See Sharpless House.

Birmingham Vicinity (Thornbury Township)

Darlington, Thomas, House (Spackman Corner Chimney House) (PA-1110), 228 W. Street Rd. (Pa. 926). Random dressed serpentine ashlar, 22'-1" (two-bay front) x 15'-11", one-and-a-half stories, gable roof, corner chimney; two room plan. Built ca. 1800; one-room frame kitchen shed added to S (front) elevation twentieth century (after 1931). Owned by Atwater Kent 1930-45, inventor and large radio manufacturer. 1 ext. photo (1958); 4 data pages (1958). LC code: PA,15-BIRM.V,1. In Brandywine Battlefield NHL.

Spackman Corner Chimney House. See Darlington, Thomas, House.

Bulltown (East Nantmeal Township)

Bull, Thomas, House. See Mount Pleasant.

Mount Pleasant (Thomas Bull House, Roberts' Plantation) (PA-248), E side of Bulltown Rd. (LR15144), .25 mi. N of Pa. 401 (Conestoga Pike). Random rubble with quoins, T-shaped, main section approx. 41' (three-bay front) x 22' (two bays), rear wing approx. 22' x 42' (four bays), two-and-a-half stories, gable roofs, gable end with pent eave (forming pediment) oriented over W (front) elevation, door with fanlight flanked by pilasters (fanlight removed), stone lintels with keystones, entrance porch and porch on wing (removed), beehive oven, late Georgian-early Federal features; central hall plan, fine interior woodwork. Built in three sections: E (end) two bays of wing built ca. 1715 probably by Owen Roberts; two bays added forming four-bay rear wing; main section added to wing ca. 1785 by Thomas Bull; vacant since 1942. Bull was a stone mason by trade, but served as manager of nearby Warwick Furnace; house remained in Bull family over 150 years. Fine example of eighteenth-century house with few alterations. 3 ext. photos (1959), 1 copy photo of 1919 ext. view. LC code: PA,15-BULT,1. NR.

Roberts' Plantation. See Mount Pleasant.

Chadds Ford Vicinity (Pennsbury Township)

Barnes-Brinton House (PA-173), S side of U.S. Rte. 1 (Baltimore Pike), .6 mi. E of Hickory Hill Rd., approx. 2 mi. W of Chadds Ford. Brick approx. 40' (three-bay front) x 20', two-and-a-half stories, gable roof with pent eaves, pent roof on four sides (removed), diamond pattern of burned bricks in W gable end; two room plan, fine original interior woodwork and hardware. Built ca. 1720; shed on N (rear) elevation replaced original lean-to; entrance porch added on S elevation; acquired by Chadds Ford Historical Society 1969, restored. Licensed as a tavern 1722. Fine example of eighteenth-century brick house with exceptional original interior woodwork. 5 ext. photos (1959), 12 int. photos (1959), 1 copy photo of ca. 1905 ext. photo; 5 data pages (1959). LC code: PA,15-CHAFO.V,1. NR (also Brandywine Battlefield NHL).

Brinton House. See Barnes-Brinton House.

Harvey, William, House (PA-1204), E side of Brinton Bridge Rd. (LR15199), .2 mi. N of U.S. Rte. 1 (Baltimore Pike). Random rubble, approx. 20' (two-bay front) x 30' (two bays), two-and-a-half stories with basement, steep gable roof, pent eaves across gable end (restored), pedimented hood over N (front) entrance, pent roof on S elevation (removed); two room plan with basement kitchen, corner fireplaces (removed 1957). Built ca. 1715; two-story porch added on S elevation; interior alterations; two-and-a-half-story wing added on E elevation 1957 (replaced frame addition built between 1931 and 1954). 2 ext. photos (1958), 2 int. photos (1958); 6 data pages (1958). LC code: PA,15-CHAFO.V,2. NR (also Brandywine Battlefield NHL).

Charlestown (Charlestown Township)

Charlestown Village House. See Harvey, Job, House.

Harvey, Job, House (Charlestown Village House) (PA-1196), N side of Church Rd., .2 mi. S of Charlestown Rd. Stuccoed random rubble, 52'-6" (five-bay front) x 28', two-and-a-half stories, gable roof, cornice returns, entrance porch on S (front) elevation, porch across W elevation; central hall plan, fine original interior woodwork. Built in two sections; E three bays built ca. 1740 onto original log or plank house; W two bays (20') built 1862 replacing original section. Job Harvey, a fuller, built original house ca. 1725 and then added E section; Deery family built 1862 section. Good example of mid-eighteenth-century and nineteenth-century house with original interior woodwork; probably earliest house in village. 1 ext. photo (1958), 3 int. photos (1958); 3 data pages (1958). LC code: PA,15-CHAST,1. NR (in Charlestown Village Historic District).

Charlestown Vicinity (Charlestown Township)

Barn (PA-5242), Pa. 29, S of Pickering Creek. Whitewashed stone, large projecting frame forebay supported on stone wall and tapered stone columns, two-level bank barn, gable roof with ship weathervane, forebay extends to shed on side elevation, frame shed on other side. Date unknown. 5 ext. photos (1941). LC code: PA,15-CHAST.V,1A.

Chatham (London Grove Township)

Center Chimney House. See New Half-Way House Tavern.

New Half-Way House Tavern (Center Chimney House) (PA-119), NW corner of Pa. 41 (Gap Newport Pike) and Pa. 841 (Coatesville Rd.). Stuccoed random rubble, 33'-10" (irregular three-bay front) x 30'-6", two-and-a-half stories on sloping site exposing basement on S (front) elevation, gable roof (pent eaves across gable ends removed), large central chimney, pent roof across N elevation (other removed), porch across S elevation; four rooms on each floor, original interior woodwork and hardware. Built ca. 1763; two-story wing added on E elevation. Original New Half-Way House was in Chatham, the new tavern was first licensed 1763 to Robert Baldwin, who leased property from Joseph Pennock. One of few houses with a central chimney in Chester County. 2 ext. photos (1959); 5 data pages (1959). LC code: PA,15-CHATH,1.

Chatham Vicinity (London Grove Township)

Morriseianna (PA-146), Pa. 41 (Newport-Lancaster Pike), S of London Grove Rd. Brick, eight-bay front (adjoining five-bay and three-bay facades) with wing to rear of each section, two-and-a-half stories, gable roof with dormers, paired chimneys in parapet, two doors with transoms on E elevation (one for each section), porch with Doric columns across E elevation; large cooking fireplace in kitchen. Built 1843 according to plaques on two front downspouts, but appears to have been built in several stages and may incorporate parts of earlier house (possibly ca. 1700). 2 ext. photos (1960), 5 int. photos (1960), 1 copy photo of 1857 view; 1 data page (1979). LC code: PA,15-CHATM.V,1.

Pusey House (PA-158), W side of Woodview Rd., at McCue Rd., S of London Grove Rd. Coursed rubble and brick (partially stuccoed and painted), U-shaped built in three sections, original stone center section 27'-6" (four-bay front) x 38', brick wing to E 18' (two-bay front) x 39'-6", brick wing to W 16' (two-bay front) x 35', two-and-a-half stories, gable roof, pent roof across S (front) elevation of all three sections; excellent original interior woodwork and hardware with unusual features such as a concealed sliding desk. Original stone section built 1728 by William Pusey; E wing added ca. 1740 by his son Joshua Pusey; W wing added ca. 1815. Good example of early-eighteenth-century house expanded as more space was required. 2 ext. photos (1959), 8 int. photos (1959); 7 data pages (1959). LC code: PA,15-CHATM.V,2.

Chester Springs (West Pikeland Township)

Chester Springs Hotel. See Yellow Springs Tavern.

Good News Building. See Yellow Springs Tavern.

Yellow Springs Tavern (Chester Springs Hotel, Good News Building) (PA-1131), intersection of Yellow Springs Rd. (LR15216) and Art School Rd. Stuccoed stone, W section approx. 90' (eight-bay front) x 35' with setback E section approx. 38' (five-bay front) x 25', three-and-a-half stories (E section originally two stories, third story added 1826), gable roofs, porch across S (front) elevation. Outbuildings. Originally two separate structures; E section built ca. 1810 on foundations of mid-eighteenth-century tavern; W section built 1839, Hugh Walters, architect; two sections later connected by one-bay addition; one-story addition on E elevation; Historic Yellow Springs, Inc. acquired property 1974, used as community center. One of the oldest and most successful spas in the country, medicinal qualities realized by 1722, inn established by 1750; military hospital during Revolutionary and Civil Wars; hotel used as headquarters by General George Washington 1777. 1 ext. photo (1959), 1 int. photo (1959), 1 copy photo of ca. 1845 lithograph of tavern complex; 26 data pages (1959). LC code: PA,15-CHESP,3. NR.

Bathhouse (PA-1197). Stone with scored stucco, enclosed vestibule, open-air sulfur-spring pool in courtyard surrounded by semicircular rear wall with pedimented alcoves, approx. 26' x 34', one story, gable roofs on vestibule and alcoves, pedimented hood over W (front) entrance. Built ca. 1840; attributed to Hugh Walters, architect. 1 ext. photo (1959), 1 int. photo (1959); 3 data pages (1959). LC code: PA,15-CHESP,1.

Summer House (PA-1198). Wooden gazebo with central opening for spring, octagonal, approx. 15' across, posts with carved spandrels forming arches, pierced railing with surrounding benches, polygonal hip roof with octagonal cupola. Built ca. 1840; attributed to Hugh Walters, architect. 1 ext. photo (1959); 2 data pages (1959). LC code: PA,15-CHESP,2.

Chester Springs Vicinity (West Pikeland Township)

Up-and-Down Sawmill (PA-116), on E side of Lower Pine Creek Rd. (LR15190), .1 mi. S of Yellow Springs Rd. (LR15009). Water-powered vertical saw with single blade and wooden log carriage set in heavy wooden frame, saw operated at 100-130 strokes per minute, log advanced approx. 2' per minute, frame superstructure with gable roof covers saw, superstructure on stone foundation built over millrace, wooden undershot waterwheel housed in shed on side, water supplied by adjacent stone dam. Built mid-nineteenth century; dismantled and moved to National Museum of American History, Smithsonian Institution, Washington, D.C. 2 ext. photos (1961), 4 int. photos (1961); 1 data page (1979). LC code: PA,15-CHESP.V,1.

Chrome (East Nottingham Township)

Chrome Hotel. See Cross Keys Tavern.

Cross Keys Tavern (Chrome Hotel) (PA-1200), NW corner of Pa. 272 (Christine Rd.) and Pa. 42 (Barnsley-Chrome Rd.). Random rubble (partially stuccoed), 30'-9" (three-bay front) x 30'-6", two-and-a-half stories, gable roof, pent roofs and eaves removed, unusual paneled S (front) door; fine interior paneling and original hardware. Built ca. 1720 (original center section); two-and-a-half-story random rubble wing added to E elevation before 1745; one-and-a-half-story random rubble kitchen wing added to W elevation before 1745. Fine example of early-eighteenth-century tavern with fine original woodwork. 4 ext. photos (1959), 7 int. photos (1959); 10 data pages (1959). LC code: PA,15-CHROM,1.

Clonmell Vicinity (West Marlborough Township)

Pennock, Joseph, House. See Primitive Hall.

Primitive Hall (Joseph Pennock House) (PA-167), NE side of Pa. 841 (Greenlawn-Chatham Rd.), .2 mi. SE of Pa. 842 (Clonmell-Upland Rd.), .7 mi. NW of Pa. 926 (Street Rd.). Museum. Brick, four-bay front, two-and-a-half stories, gable roof with pent eaves, deep cove cornice (reconstructed), pent roof across elevations (reconstructed), corbeled inside end chimneys, segmental arches over openings; wide central hall plan, fine original interior woodwork. Built 1738 by Joseph Pennock; porch on S elevation and one-story ell on E elevation added early nineteenth century (removed); restored 1974 as a museum and park operated by the Primitive Hall Foundation. Excellent example of a grand eighteenth-century house built in a rural area. 2 ext. photos (1959), 10 int. photos (1960), 1 copy photo of sketch on quilt from 1842; 1 data page (1979). LC code: PA,15-CLON.V,1. NR.

Coatesville

Thompson Building (PA-1955), 163-67 E. Main St. (E. Lincoln Hwy.). Brick with brownstone sills and terra cotta trim, irregular rectangle, four stories, flat roof, pressed metal cornice and pediment, corner tower (removed), terra cotta store fronts (altered). Built 1901; A.W. Dilks, architect; demolished. 6 ext. photos (1981), 2 int. photos (1981); 18 data pages (1981). LC code: PA,15-COAT,1.

Coatesville Vicinity

Romansville Friends Meetinghouse Sheds. See Romansville (West Bradford Township), Romansville Friends Meetinghouse Sheds.

Coatesville Vicinity (Caln Township)

Barn, Stone (PA-5230), U.S. Rte. 30 (Lincoln Highway), between Coatesville and Downingtown. Random rubble with quoins, large projecting frame forebay supported on beam and braced square wooden posts on concrete bases, two-level bank barn, gable roof with shed roof on forebay, ramp to threshing entrance. Built nineteenth century. 3 ext. photos (1941). LC code: PA,15-COAT.V,2A.

Coatesville Vicinity (Valley Township)

Stoltzfus House (PA-159), on private road N of U.S. Rte. 30 (Lincoln Hwy.), .5 mi. W of Rainbow Rd. Coursed and random rubble, five-bay main section with setback side wings; original house E three bays of main section, two-and-a-half stories, gable roof, transom over S (front) door; side hall plan, some original wood trim and stencil work remain. Original house built 1732; two-and-a-half-story section (two bays) added to W 1813; one-and-a-half-story wing added to E 1956; one-story wing added to W of 1813 section 1958; glazed porch added on 1956 wing; pent roof added on main block. 2 ext. photos (1960), 3 int. photos (1960); 1 data page (1979). LC code: PA,15-COAT.V,1.

Coatesville Vicinity (West Brandywine Township)

Barn (PA-5231), Pa. 82 (Manor Rd.), approx. 3 mi. N of Coatesville. Random rubble with frame forebay, frame shed projecting from forebay supported on tapered stone columns, two levels, gable roof with gabled ventilators, attached frame addition with gabled ventilator, stone retaining wall. Built nineteenth century. 1 ext. photo (1941). LC code: PA,15-COAT.V,3A.

Copesville (East Bradford Township)

Brandywine Bridge. See Cope's Bridge.

Cope's Bridge (Brandywine Bridge) (PA-206), over Brandywine Creek, Pa. 162 (Strasburg Rd.). Random rubble, three arches (wider center span), cut voussoirs, buttresses. Built 1805-08 (date stone 1807); John Lewis, engineer; Thomas Taylor and Samuel Townsend, superintendents. Original 1805 bridge date stone built into gable end of Anthony Taylor's house (a mason, worked on bridge) in 1836 on Strasburg Rd. in East Bradford Township. Fine example of early stone arched bridge. 3 ext. photos including 1 photo of each date stone (1960); 5 data pages (1963). LC code: PA,15-COPES,1. NR.

Copesville Vicinity (East Bradford Township)

Parke House. See Taylor-Parke House.

Taylor, Abiah, House (PA-204), E side of Brandywine Creek Rd. (LR15103), .1 mi. S of Strasburg Rd. (Pa. 162). Brick, approx. 30' (three-bay front) x 20' (two bays), two-and-a-half stories with basement, steep gable roof, pent roofs (removed), one-story stuccoed stone kitchen on E elevation; stone springhouse to E. Built 1724 (date stone); kitchen wing added eighteenth century; door on S elevation later addition; entrance porches added. Fine example of early eighteenth-century English Quaker house. 5 ext. photos (1958); 5 data pages (1958). LC code: PA,15-COPES.V,2.

Taylor-Parke House (PA-205), N side of Pa. 162 (Strasburg Rd.), .2 mi. E of Brandywine Creek Rd. Coursed ashlar (S front elevation) and random rubble, approx. 37' (four-bay front) x 34' (two bays) with setback kitchen wing to E (approx. 26' x 21'), two-and-a-half stories with one-and-a-half-story wing, gable roofs, pent eaves and roof, porch across S elevation; original woodwork and hardware remain. Built 1768 (date stone) for Abiah and Ann Taylor; kitchen wing original to house and possibly predates house; porch on wing added twentieth century. Excellent example of mid-eighteenth-century house with interesting masonry and many original features. 4 ext. photos (1960), 6 int. photos (1960). LC code: PA,15-COPES.V,1. NR.

Coventryville (South Coventry Township)

Coventry Forge Inn (Samuel Nutt House) (PA-1133), E side of Nantmeal Rd., .1 mi. N of Ridge Rd. (Old Pa. 23). Log (S half) and stone (N half) covered with stucco, approx. 36' square (built in three sections), original log section 36' (three-bay front) x 18', stone wing added to NE 20' x 18', second stone wing added to NW completing square, two-and-a-half stories, gable roof (roof raised when N wings were added), bracketed cornice (not original), porch across S (front) elevation (replaced by glass-enclosed porch after 1959); fine mid-eighteenth-century interior woodwork. Log section built ca. 1717; addition to NE built ca. 1750; addition to NW built ca. 1800; converted to restaurant after 1959. Built on land owned by Samuel Nutt, founder of Coventry Forge in 1717. One of few log structures in Chester County, oldest extant structure in Coventryville. 1 ext. photo (1959), 4 int. photos (1959); 6 data pages (1959, 1979). LC code: PA,15-COV,1. NR (in Coventryville Historic District).

Nutt, Samuel, House. See Coventry Forge Inn.

Devault Vicinity (Charlestown Township)

Bones, William and Rebecca, House (PA-1189), on private road .3 mi. S of White Horse Rd. (LR15134), approx. 1.5 mi. NE of Devault. Random rubble, approx. 25' (three-bay front) x 34', two-and-a-half stories sloping to three and a half stories, gable roof, porches (removed); side hall plan. Springhouse and barn. Built 1810 (date stone "W & RB AD 1810"); few alterations; vacant and in ruinous condition. 2 ext. photos (1958), 2 int. photos (1958); 6 data pages (1958, 1975). LC code: PA,15-DEV.V,2.

Springhouse (PA-1189A). Random rubble, approx. 34' (irregular three-bay front) x 14', two-and-a-half stories on sloping site, gable roof; kitchen with large cooking fireplace. Probably built early nineteenth century. 1 ext. photo (1958). LC code: PA,15-DEV.V,2A.

Williams Barn (PA-1216), E side of Mine Rd., .7 mi. N of White Horse Rd. (LR15134). Random rubble, approx. 60' x 58', bank barn, two levels (stable entrance S lower level, wagon entrance N upper level), gable roof, frame forebay supported by tapered circular piers. Built 1806 (date stone "JMW AD 1806"); Joseph Williams, builder; few changes. Well preserved example of nineteenth-century bank barn. 2 ext. photos (1958); 3 data pages (1958). LC code: PA,15-DEV.V,1.

Devault Vicinity (East Whiteland Township)

Church of Saint Peter-in-the-Great Valley (Saint Peter's Protestant Episcopal Church) (PA-1106), Saint Peters Rd., .3 mi. W of Church Rd., .4 mi. S of Yellow Springs Rd. Random rubble, 47' (three-bay front) x 28', one story, gable roof, central double door with fanlight flanked by arched windows. Built 1774; ca. 1750 interior gallery added; 1830 arched windows altered; 1856 one bay extension on E elevation and walls stuccoed; 1901 alterations, arched windows restored and parish house added to rear; restored 1940s, R. Brognard Okie, restoration architect; parish house extended 1952. Served as chapel for British army and hospital for both British and American armies during the Revolutionary War. 3 ext. photos (1958), 1 photo of 1743 gravestone (1958); 5 data pages (1958, 1967). LC code: PA,15-DEV.V,3. NR.

Saint Peter's Protestant Episcopal Curch. See Church of Saint Peter-in-the-Great Valley.

Downingtown Borough

Downingtown Public Library. See Todd, William A., House.

Hunt-Pollock Mill (PA-170), S side of Race St., off Pa. 322 (Horseshoe Pike, Manor Ave.), on Beaver Creek (branch of Brandywine Creek). Random rubble (partially stuccoed), 48' x 30'-6", two-and-a-half stories and attic on sloping site, gambrel roof. Built ca. 1752; frame shed added on N elevation 1920s; dormer added; ruinous condition. Mill continued in operation until the 1930s. Rare survival of mid-eighteenth-century mill; one of the earliest mills of Downingtown. 2 ext. photos (1959); 5 data pages (1959). LC code: PA,15-DOWT,3.

Pollock Mill. See Hunt-Pollock Mill.

Todd, William A., House (Downingtown Public Library) (PA-169), 330 E. Lancaster Ave. Random rubble with quoins, five by three bays, two-and-a-half stories, gable roof, semicircular dormers with tracery, decorative carved cornice with modillions, door with fanlight framed by columns and entablature on N (front) elevation, Federal details; central hall plan, fine interior gesso and wood details. Built 1800 for Dr. William A. Todd; became boarding school 1817; Downingtown Public Library 1912-present; enclosed entrance added on N elevation. 3 ext. photos (1962), 3 int. photos (1962). LC code: PA,15-DOWT,2.

Downingtown Vicinity (Caln Township)

Edge House. See Mendenhall-Valentine-Edge House.

Edge Mill. See Valentine-Edge Mill.

Hoopes Currying Shop (PA-1222), N side of U.S. Rte. 322 (Horseshoe Pike), at junction with Edges Mill Rd. (LR-15126), .5 mi. W of Downingtown. Random rubble, 18' (two-bay front) x 17', one-and-a-half stories with fully exposed basement on W (front) elevation, gable roof, large exterior end chimney, porch supported by protruding first-floor joists; one room on each level, no interior stairs to basement. Built ca. 1789; demolished 1961. 2 ext. photos (1958); 3 data pages (1958). LC code: PA,15-DOWT.V,4.

Mendenhall-Valentine-Edge House (PA-1201), E side of Pa. 340 (King's Hwy.), N of Edges Mill Rd. (LR15126), approx. 1.5 mi. W of Downingtown. Random rubble with quoins, 41'-6" (five-bay front) x 35'-6" with setback side wing 24'-6" (two-bay front) x 23'-9", two-and-a-half stories with one-and-a-half-story wing, gable roofs, pent roof across S (front) elevation (restored 1925); central hall plan. Built in three sections during eighteenth century; setback W wing built ca. 1721 by Aaron Mendenhall; W two bays of main section built ca. 1768 by Robert Valentine; E three bays built ca. 1790 by his son; dormers added to wing; partially restored 1925; E addition built 1945 by Jacob Edge. 2 ext. photos (1959); 5 data pages (1959). See also Valentine-Edge Mill (PA-1202). LC code: PA,15-DOWT.V,5.

Parke House (PA-1211), W side of Rock Raymond Rd. (LR15211), .2 mi. N of U.S. Rte. 322 (Horseshoe Pike). Frame with horizontal hewn boarding, 18' (three-bay front) x 14'-4", one-and-a-half stories with basement, gable roof, random rubble chimney with interior circular construction on E elevation, porch across S (front) elevation. Built early eighteenth century; occupied until 1940; few alterations except stairway to attic removed 1950s; poor condition. Early frame house on the Old Conestoga Wagon Trail, possibly oldest extant frame house in county. 2 ext. photos (1959); 3 data pages (1959). LC code: PA,15-DOWT.V,6.

Valentine-Edge House. See Mendenhall-Valentine-Edge House.

Valentine-Edge Mill (PA-1202), W side of Pa. 340 (King's Hwy.), N of Edges Mill Rd. (LR15126), approx. 1.5 mi. W of Downingtown. Random rubble, 38'-6" x 53'-6", one-and-a-half stories (W side) sloping to three-and-a-half stories (E stream side), gable roof, pent roofs (removed), over-shot waterwheel (removed). Built 1784 (date stone); ceased operation by 1918; later used as offices. James Mendenhall had mill on site as early as 1757, present mill built by Robert Valentine, Jr. 1 ext. photo (1959); 4 data pages (1959). See also Mendenhall-Valentine-Edge House (PA-1202). LC code: PA,15-DOWT.V,7.

Downingtown Vicinity (East Caln Township)

Ashbridge House. See Baldwin-Sharpless House.

Baldwin-Sharpless House (Ashbridge House) (PA-1309), N side of U.S. Rte. 30 (Lincoln Hwy.), .7 mi. E of Pa. 113, .4 mi. E of Downingtown. Random rubble, 51' (six-bay front) x 33'-6" with kitchen wing on N elevation (13'-6" x 18'-6"), two-and-a-half stories with one-story wing, gable roof with shed roof dormer (dormer is a rare early eighteenth century survival), porch on S (front) elevation, pent roof; central hall plan, fine interior woodwork and paneling from 1755 and 1810. W three bays and kitchen built early eighteenth century; E three bays added ca. 1755; ca. 1810 original house deepened and roof changed to match 1755 addition. Excellent example of prosperous Quaker family house of the eighteenth century. 4 ext. photos (1959), 9 int. photos (1959); 6 data pages (1961, 1975). LC code: PA,15-DOWT.V,8.

Belle School (PA-168), location not determined. Stuccoed octagonal schoolhouse, two stories, polygonal hip roof with octagonal louvered cupola, two-story frame entranceway. Built ca. 1818; demolished early twentieth century 1 copy photo of ext. view. LC code: PA,15-DOWT.V,3.

Downing House (PA-171), E side of Bell Tavern Rd., .3 mi. N of U.S. Rte. 30 (Lincoln Hwy.), approx. 1 mi. NE of Downingtown. Coursed rubble (S front elevation) and random rubble, E section approx. 22' (two-bay front) x 32' and W section approx. 42' (four-bay front) x 32', two-and-a-half stories, gambrel roof, two recessed doors with paneled reveals and transoms on S elevation, porch across S elevation, pent roof on N elevation, random rubble lean-to kitchen; fine stone kitchen fireplace and bake ovens. E two bays built ca. 1740; W four bays added before 1772. Fine example of mid-eighteenth-century house. 2 ext. photos (1960), 5 int. photos (1960); 1 data page (1979). LC code: PA,15-DOWT.V,9.

Sharpless House. See Baldwin-Shapless House.

Glenloch (East Whiteland Township)

Loch Aerie (William E. Lockwood House) (PA-181), S side of U.S. Rte. 30 (Lincoln Hwy.), .2 mi. E of U.S. Rte. 202. Random dressed rubble with cut quoins and window surrounds, irregular cross-shaped with asymmetrical tower, approx. 77' x 48', two-and-a-half stories with four-story tower, cross-gable roofs with dormers, wooden pinnacles and braced pendants in gable peaks, bracketed cornice, several bracketed porches, Italianate massing with Italianate and High Victorian Gothic details; elaborate interiors with plaster ornament, marble fireplaces, walnut staircase. Built 1865; Addison Hutton, architect; few changes. Fine landscaping including gardens, fountains, lake and walks; Charles P. Miller, landscape architect. Built for William E. Lockwood, who made fortune manufacturing paper collars and folding boxes. 4 ext. photos (1958), 3 int. photos (1958); 7 data pages (1958). LC code: PA,15-GLENL,2.

Lockwood, William E., House. See Loch Aerie.

Zook Barn (PA-1218), S side of King Rd. (LR15095), .5 mi. W of Pa. 352 (Sproul Rd.). Squared logs with heavy chinking, approx. 60' x 25', two levels, steep gable roof with longer N slope over rear shed; pegged floor (one of few remaining in county). Built late eighteenth century; few changes. Rare survival of eighteenth-century log barn. 1 ext. photo (1958), 5 int. photos (1958); 3 data pages (1958). LC code: PA,15-GLENL,1.

Glenmoore Vicinity (Wallace Township)

Barn, Large (PA-5232A), Old Creek Rd. (Pa. 282), between Pa. 82 and Glenmoore. Random rubble, projecting frame forebay supported on stone walls and wooden posts, board and batten siding, two levels, gable roof, several attached frame sheds with board and batten siding. Date unknown. 1 ext. photo (1941). LC code: PA,15-GLENOR,1A.

Barn, Small (PA-5232B), adjacent to Large Barn (PA-5232). Random rubble with quoins partially whitewashed, frame forebay contained within stone end walls, two levels, gable roof with weathervane, ramp to threshing floor entrance, iron strap hinges on double stable doors. Date unknown. 2 ext. photos (1941). LC code: PA,15-GLENOR,1B.

Green Lawn Vicinity (West Marlborough Township)

Marlborough Plank House. See Sharitz Road (House).

Sharitz Road (House) (Marlborough Plank House) (PA-160), N side of Sharitz Rd., .5 mi. E of Pa. 841 (Greenlawn-Springdell Rd.). Sawn horizontal boards with chinking (little chinking remains) and vertical corner posts covered with horizontal siding, two-bay front, one-and-a-half stories, sloping site exposes random rubble basement on S (front) elevation, steep gable roof, exterior chimney, porch across S elevation. Probably built early eighteenth century; small frame addition; novelty siding added on E elevation early twentieth century; ruinous condition. Unusual construction. 2 ext. photos (1960), 3 construction detail photos (1960); 1 data page (1979). LC code: PA,15-GRELA.V,1.

Grubbs Mill (East Bradford Township)

Ivy House. See Wollerton, Charles, House.

Log House. See Wollerton, Charles, House.

Wollerton, Charles, House (Ivy House, Log House) (PA-1208), isolated site approx. 3/4 mi. NE of Valley Creek Rd. (LR15093) and Sunset Hollow Rd., approx. 3 mi. SE of Downingtown. Squared logs with diagonal stone pattern in chinking (mostly covered with novelty siding), approx. 28' x 22' (including 10' extension to E), two-and-a-half stories, gable roof, central chimney, pent roof across S (front) elevation. Original section built ca. 1770s (approx. 18' x 20', one and a half stories); house enlarged and second story added before 1813; two-story wing added to N; one-story wing added to E; garage added to S. Interesting log construction. 1 ext. photo (1958), 2 details of log construction (1958); 6 data pages (1958). LC code: PA,15-GRUB,1.

Hamorton Vicinity (Pennsbury Township)

Barn, Stone (PA-5240), Pa. 52 (Kennett Pike), between Hamorton and Delaware state line. Random rubble with quoins, frame forebay contained within stone end walls, two levels, gable roof, enclosed entrance to threshing floor, entrance ramp and bridge with stone walls with coping, stone arches over windows. Date unknown. 3 ext. photos (1941). LC code: PA,15-HAMO.V,3A.

Honeybrook Vicinity (Honeybrook Township)

Barn (PA-5233), on LR15146, E of Honeybrook, near Suplee. Random rubble, projecting frame forebay extending beyond end supported by tapered stone columns, two levels, gable roof, silo and several frame additions attached to barn. Built nineteenth century 1 ext. photo (1941). LC code: PA,15-HOBRO.V,1A.

Barn (PA-5234), on LR15146, between Honeybrook and Suplee. Whitewashed stone, projecting frame forebay supported on squared wooden posts, perpendicular frame extension of forebay supported on tapered stone columns, two levels, gable roof with shed and gable roofs on forebays, pent roof over stable entrances on side. Built 1836 (date stone). 1 ext. photo (1941). LC code: PA,15-HOBRO.V,2A.

Hopewell (East Nottingham Township)

Hopewell Academy (PA-1311), N side of Hopewell Rd. (LR15005), at junction with Lower Hopewell Rd., .7 mi. W of U.S. Rte. 1. Brick, L-shaped, 50' (five-bay S facade) x 50' (similar five-bay W facade), three stories, low gable roof, identical doors on S and W facades with fanlights and carved designs and gouge work, Federal details; central hall plan, carved mantels similar to exterior carving. Built ca. 1815-20; third story added ca. 1850; two classroom wings added ca. 1850, removed ca. 1862; original ell to N remodeled ca. 1965; presently a residence. Interesting vernacular Federal-style carved details. 2 ext. photos (1962), 2 int. photos (1962); 11 data pages (1976). LC code: PA,15-HOPE,1.

Hopewell Village (Warwick Township)

Hopewell Village National Historic Site (PA-5157), W side of Pa. 345, approx. 2.5 mi. S of Geigertown Rd., in both Berks and Chester counties. See entries under Berks County, Hopewell Village (Union Township) for general entry and individual structures in Berks County and following entries for structures located in Chester County. NHS.

Bethesda Baptist Church (PA-5157J). Stuccoed random rubble, 30'-2" (three-bay front) x 35'-2" (two bays), one story with attic, gable roof, cornice returns, double paneled doors with transom on E (front) elevation. Built 1782 (pencil inscription in attic "Built 1782 by T. Lloyd," said to have been transcribed from original date stone in W elevation); S door and W window sealed before 1890; cornice and windows replaced 1911-16. 6 sheets (1956-57, including site plan, plan, elevations, section, details); 1 data page (1984). LC code: PA,15-HOPVI,3.

Employees' Quarters (Lloyd House, Lucas House) (PA-5160). Stuccoed random rubble, 42'-3" (three-bay front) x 28', two-and-a-half stories with basement, gable roof, entrance porch and door with transom on N (front) elevation, partially enclosed porch across S elevation; central hall plan, corner fireplaces with carved mantels with Federal motifs. Built ca. 1810 (E two bays, side hall plan); W bay added shortly after; stucco probably applied when W wing was built; porches later additions; rear porch reconstructed without enclosure after 1958. 9 sheets (1957, including site plan, plans, elevations, details); 4 ext. photos (1958), 8 int. photos (1958); 1 data page (1983). LC code: PA,15-HOPVI,2.

Lloyd House. See *Employees' Quarters*.

Lloyd, Harrison, House (PA-5168). Stuccoed random rubble, three adjoining sections, three-bay central section with two-bay section to W and two-bay setback section to E, two-and-a-half stories, gable roofs. Built nineteenth century; poor condition 1958. 1 ext. photo (1958), 5 int. photos (1958). LC code: PA,15-HOPVI,1.

Lucas House. See *Employees' Quarters*.

Kaolin (New Garden Township)

Barn, Eighteenth-Century (PA-5239), on Pa. 41. Random rubble bank barn, frame forebays supported by circular and square stone columns on rear and side elevations, two levels, gable roof, frame and stone additions. Built eighteenth century. British and Hessian soldiers camped here in 1777, two days before Battle of Brandywine. 2 ext. photos (1941). LC code: PA,15-KAOL,1A.

Kaolin Vicinity (Kennett Township)

Pyle, Walter C., Barn (PA-5238), on LR15037), .5 mi. E of Kaolin. Random rubble with frame forebay supported by log beams and circular stone columns, two-level bank barn, gable roof, flanking frame and stone wings attached to forebay with stone wall enclosing stable area, enclosed frame entrance to threshing floor, numerous frame additions. Built 1768. 4 ext. photos (1941). LC code: PA,15-KAOL.V,1A.

Kennett Square (East Marlborough Township)

Cedarcroft (Bayard Taylor House) (PA-172), W side of Bayard Dr., .1 mi. W of Pa. 82 (Unionville Rd.), 1 mi. N of U.S. Rte. 1 (Baltimore Pike). Brick with stone quoins, L-shaped with projecting entrance tower on E (front) elevation, five by five bays, two-and-a-half stories, hip and gable roofs, corbeled cornice, four-and-a-half-story tower with iron balcony, projecting pedimented pavilion on S elevation, bay window on W elevation, belt courses, Italianate style; central hall plan. Built 1859 (date stone); shed added on N elevation; restored. Home of Bayard Taylor (1825-78), poet, novelist and journalist, considered a significant literary figure by contemporaries; wrote many of his works here. 4 ext. photos (1960), 4 int. photos (1960), 1 copy photo of 1881 ext. view. LC code: PA,15-KENSQ.V,3. NHL.

Taylor, Bayard, House. See *Cedarcroft*.

Kimberton Vicinity (West Vincent Township)

Barn (PA-5246), Kimberton Rd., approx. 3 mi. NE of St. Matthew's, W of Kimberton. Random rubble with frame forebay, two-level bank barn, gable roof, ramp to threshing entrance, semicircular vent openings edged in brick, horse weathervane. Date unknown (date stone missing). 1 ext. photo (1941). LC code: PA,15-KIMB,1A.

Knauertown (Warwick Township)

Halley House. See *Rogers, Philip, House*.

Penn Wick. See *Rogers, Philip, House*.

Rogers, Philip, House (Penn Wick, Halley House) (PA-114), N side of Pa. 23 (Ridge Rd.), .1 mi. E of Sunrise Dr. Random rubble with contrasting quoins (N and W elevations stuccoed), five by two bays, two-and-a-half stories, sloping site fully exposes basement to W, gable roof, cornice returns (originally pent eaves across W gable end), massive inside end chimneys; central hall plan, excellent original interior woodwork. Built mid-eighteenth century (1739 date stone, probably a later addition); two-and-a-half-story random rubble kitchen wing added to E before 1825; one-story semicircular Doric portico added to S (front) elevation. Well preserved example of prosperous English Quaker house with fine original interior woodwork. 1 ext. photo (1959), 4 int. photos (1960). LC code: PA,15-KNATO,10. NR.

Barn (PA-114A), across Pa. 23 from house. Random rubble with contrasting quoins, two levels on sloping site, steep gable roof, frame forebay with tapered stone piers on S elevation, slit ventilators. Built eighteenth century; addition to E; demolished ca. 1960. 1 ext. photo (1959). LC code: PA,15-KNATO,1A.

Knauertown Vicinity (Warwick Township)

Branson, William, House. See Warrenpoint.

Templin House. See Warrenpoint.

Warrenpoint (William Branson House, Templin House) (PA-115), .2 mi. S of Pa. 23 (Ridge Rd.) on small road, approx. 1 mi. W of Knauertown. Random rubble with contrasting quoins, approx. 44' (five-bay front) x 33' with kitchen wing (20' x 17'-6") on E side, two-and-a-half stories, gable roof with pent eaves, massive inside end chimneys, small frame bell housing on roof of kitchen wing, outdoor cooking area and oven in stone enclosure (only part of enclosure remained 1960, reconstructed 1972); central hall plan, fine original interior woodwork including built-in cabinets, original hardware, Georgian details. Outbuildings. Built 1756; porch added on S (front) elevation early twentieth century; restored 1972. Branson was a leader in early iron and steel production. Excellent example of mid-eighteenth-century house with few alterations and outstanding original interior woodwork. 3 ext. photos (1960), 14 int. photos (1960), 1 copy photo of int. from ca. 1890; 4 data pages (1963). LC code: PA,15-KNATO.V,1. NR.

Landenberg Vicinity (New Garden Township)

Miller-Pusey Mill (PA-252), S side of Broad Run Rd. (LR15155), .4 mi. E of Buttonwood Rd., SE of Landenberg. Water-powered grist and saw mill, random rubble lower level with frame upper level and loft, irregular shape, 53'-9" x 29'-2" (including setback E section), gable roofs, wooden-framed openings of peg construction. Built 1769-70; John Miller, builder; mill operated until early 1920s; unaltered but in poor condition (walls and roof partially collapsed) 1964; some machinery removed to Hagley Museum, Wilmington, Delaware; mill given to Friends of the Caleb Pusey House, Inc. for restoration ca. 1964. Example of a simple, but typical, late-eighteenth-century saw and grist mill. 8 sheets (1964, including site plans, plans, elevations, sections, details). LC code: PA,15-LAND.V,1.

Pusey Mill. See Miller-Pusey Mill.

Lenape Vicinity (Pocopson Township)

Barn, Wood (PA-5235), on road S of Pa. 52 at Denton's Bridge across Pocopson Creek. Frame with vertical wooden siding on stone foundation, projecting frame forebay supported on braced posts, two-level bank barn, gable roof, frame and stone shed on side elevation, stone wall encloses stable yard. Date unknown. 1 ext. photo (1941). LC code: PA,15-LENA.V,2A.

Brinton, John, Barn. See Clark, Tom, Barn.

Clark, Tom, Barn (John Brinton Barn) (PA-5236), Pa. 52, just W of Lenape. Random rubble, frame forebay with gabled center bay supported on stone and wooden piers added across S elevation, gable roof, ramp with stone retaining walls and enclosed frame bridge to threshing entrance, flat stone arch from original entrance behind bridge, louvered ventilators with stone arches. Built mid-eighteenth century as all stone barn; later alterations and additions. Used as hospital during Battle of Brandywine 1777 during John Brinton ownership. 4 ext. photos (1941), 1 int. photo (1941). LC code: PA,15-LENA.V,3A.

Ludwigs Corner Vicinity (East Nantmeal Township)

Buckwalter, John, House (PA-1195), N side of Pa. 401 (Conestoga Pike), .8 mi. W of Pa. 100 (Pottstown Pike). Random rubble partially stuccoed, 35'-3" (four-bay front) x 31', two-and-a-half stories, gable roof, carved cornice, two doors with transoms on S (front) elevation, porch across S and E elevations; four rooms, original interior woodwork, fine mantelpiece. Built 1821 (date stone). Excellent interior and exterior carved details. 4 ext. photos (1959), 1 int. photo (1959); 3 data pages (1959). LC code: PA,15-LUDCO.V,1.

Marsh (East Nantmeal Township)

Hause Store (PA-1205), N side of Pa. 401 (Conestoga Pike), at junction with Mansion Rd. Stuccoed random rubble, 30'-2" (three-bay front) x 45'-3", one-and-a-half stories, gable roof, porch across S (front) elevation; one room. Built ca. 1815; 16' addition to N built 1879; addition (13'-4") built to E 1900; porch added on E elevation (enclosed ca. 1960); used as store until 1929; vacant. Built by John Jones, acquired by Hause family 1818 and remained in family until 1958. 1 ext. photo (1959), 2 copy photos of ca. 1905 int. views; 5 data pages (1959, 1975). LC code: PA,15-MAR,2.

Hause Smokehouse (PA-1206). Log with heavy chinking, 9'-3" x 11'-9", one story, gable roof; one room with earthen floor. Built ca. 1815; unaltered except for roof. Probably built by John Jones, acquired by Hause family 1818 and remained in family until 1958. 1 ext. photo (1959); 3 data pages (1959). LC code: PA,15-MAR,1.

Marshallton (West Bradford Township)

Bradford Friends Meetinghouse. See Marshallton Friends Meetinghouse.

Cunningham Blacksmith Shop. See Marshallton Blacksmith Shop.

Marshall, Humphry, House (PA-203), N side of Pa. 162 (Strasburg Rd.), just W of intersection with Northbrook Rd. Coursed ashlar (S front elevation) and random rubble, approx. 51' (six-bay front) x 28' with setback kitchen wing to W, two-and-a-half stories with one-story wing, gable roof (originally had pent eaves, roof and cornice replaced), pent roof across S and N elevations (replacements), originally small observatory projected from second story S elevation (removed late nineteenth century); original interior woodwork, greenhouse in main block with flue system through house to heat greenhouse. Built 1773 (date stone); Humphry Marshall, builder (apprenticed as mason); porch added on S elevation (removed); shed added on kitchen wing; frame kitchen wing added to W of original kitchen 1949; restored 1967. Surrounding land planted with botanical garden, remains of arboretum evident. Marshall was an amateur astronomer and early American botanist. 3 ext. photos (1958), 5 int. photos (1958), 1 copy photo of 1870s watercolor; 6 data pages (1958). LC code: PA,15-MARSH,1. NHL (Also in NR Marshallton Historic District).

Marshallton Blacksmith Shop (Cunningham Blacksmith Shop) (PA-1102), S side of Pa. 162 (Strasburg Rd.), .1 mi. W of N. Wawset Rd., just E of Marshallton Friends Meetinghouse (PA-1105). Stuccoed random rubble, two adjoining rectangular shops, over-all dimensions 40'-4" (six-bay front) x 30'-4", one-and-a-half-story W section and two-story E section, carriage entrance on S elevation (ramp to second story removed); one-room W section served as blacksmith shop, two-room E section served as wheelwright and carriage-making shops. Built early nineteenth century, but may incorporate parts of mid-eighteenth-century blacksmith shop. A blacksmith shop has operated on this site since mid eighteenth century, still used as a blacksmith shop in 1958. 2 ext. photos (1958); 4 data pages (1958). LC code: PA,15-MARSH,2. NR (Marshallton Historic District).

Marshallton Friends Meetinghouse (Bradford Friends Meetinghouse) (PA-1105), E side of Northbrook Rd. (LR15077), .1 mi. S of Pa. 162 (Strasburg Rd.). Random rubble, approx. 38' (three-bay front) x 45' (three bays), one-and-a-half stories, gable roof with pent eaves, door with pedimented hood on S (front) elevation (hood removed when porch was added); one room with sliding partition to divide men's and women's sides, additional set of sliding partitions at right angles to other partitions (unusual feature), original interior woodwork and hardware. Built 1765; roof replaced after two fires, 1788 and 1883; porch added late nineteenth century Fine example of eighteenth-century Friends meetinghouse with unaltered original interior details and little exterior alteration; still used as meetinghouse. 4 ext. photos (1958), 6 int. photos (1958), 1 copy photo of ca. 1850 daguerreotype; 5 data pages (1958). LC code: PA,15-MARSH,3. NR (Also in Marshallton Historic District).

Marshallton Vicinity (West Bradford Township)

Arnold-Temple House (Temple-Webster-Stoner House) (PA-1109), E side of Broad Run Rd., .1 mi. S of Pa. 162 (Telegraph Rd.), approx. 1 mi. W of Marshallton. Coursed rubble (S front elevation) and random rubble, 21'-8" (two-bay front) x 26'-6" with setback kitchen wing on W elevation (18'-6" x 17'-4"), two-and-a-half stories with one-and-a-half-story wing, steep gable roofs, massive inside end chimneys, pent roof across S elevation of main section, porch with well on S elevation of wing; excellent original interior woodwork, large cooking fireplace and bake oven in kitchen wing. Built ca. 1720 (main section); kitchen wing added ca. 1800; roof of kitchen wing raised 3' early-nineteenth century. Excellent example of well preserved early eighteenth-century house with many original exterior and interior details. 6 ext. photos (1958), 10 int. photos (1958); 4 data pages (1958). LC code: PA,15-MARSH.V,1. NR.

Stoner House. See Arnold-Temple House.

Temple House. See Arnold-Temple House.

Temple-Webster-Stoner House. See Arnold-Temple House.

Webster House. See Arnold-Temple House.

Martin's Corner (West Caln Township)

Martin's Corner House (PA-209), N side of Cedar Knoll Rd. (LR15121), .15 mi. E of Martin's Corner Rd. (LR15185). Squared logs with large random rubble chimney wall, approx. 34' (three-bay front) x 26', two-and-a-half stories, gable roof; four rooms on each floor, some exposed interior log walls and beam ceilings, original pegged floor, wooden door hinges, fine kitchen fireplace with wooden crane. Built ca. 1769; hood added over S (front) elevation; few interior or exterior changes; demolished. Rare house type for area with some unusual features such as original pegged floor, wooden door hinges and wooden fireplace crane. 1 ext. photo (1959), 4 int. photos (1959); 4 data pages (1959). LC code: PA,15-MARCO,1.

Milltown (East Goshen Township)

Hickman House (Milltown Plank House) (PA-166), S side of Pa. 3 (West Chester Pike), .1 mi. W of Westtown Way. Unusual frame of sawn vertical supports with spaced sawn horizontal planks with lath nailed to interior and exterior, exterior walls stuccoed and covered with novelty siding, approx. 25' (three-bay front) x 15', two-and-a-half stories, gable roof, brick chimney on front slope of roof, porch across E (front) elevation. Built ca. 1805; small addition on S elevation; demolished. 1 ext. photo (1960), 2 construction detail photos (1960), 2 int. photos (1960). LC code: PA,15-MILT,1.

Milltown Plank House. See Hickman House.

Mount Rocky (Elk Township)

Ankrim, Samuel, Shop (Brick Shop) (PA-1194), S side of Chrome Rd. (LR15007), .5 mi. W of Barren Rd. (LR15010). Brick, 14' (two-bay front) x 12', one story with loft, gable roof, denticulated brick cornice; one room with ladder to loft. Built ca. 1790s; few changes. Used as the shop of a spinning wheel maker, a turner, and a shoemaker. Fine example of a well preserved eighteenth-century shop. 1 ext. photo (1959); 3 data pages (1959). LC code: PA,15-MTROC,1.

Brick Shops. See Ankrim, Samuel, Shop.

Mount Rocky Methodist Church (PA-1210), intersection of Chrome Rd. (LR15007) and Chrome-New London Rd. (LR15008). Squared logs notched into upright corner posts, three-bay front, one story with loft, gable roof, central chimney for stove; one room. Built ca. 1831; collapsed 1920s; only foundations remain. Unusual construction for area. 1 ext. detail view (1959), 1 copy photo of ca. 1898 ext. view; 3 data pages (1959, 1975). LC code: PA,15-MTROC,2.

Newtown Square Vicinity

Bartram's Covered Bridge. See Whitehorse Vicinity (Willistown-Newtown Townships), Bartram's Covered Bridge.

Northbrook Vicinity (Pocopson Township)

Allen House (PA-1190), W side of Northbrook Rd. (LR15048), .5 mi. S of Corinne Rd. (formerly W. Locust Grove Rd.) (LR15175), .9 mi. S of Pa. 842. Brick, approx. 25' (four-bay front) x 14', one story with loft, sloping site fully exposes random rubble basement, gable roof, porch on wooden posts across S (front) elevation; two room plan with basement kitchen, enclosed interior stairs, original interior woodwork and hardware. Built ca. 1780; stone wing added to E elevation mid-nineteenth century; ruinous condition. Possibly original house on farm, used as tenant house by mid-nineteenth century. Fine example of a bank house, once a common building type of area. 1 ext. photo (1959), 2 int. photos (1959); 5 data pages (1959). LC code: PA,15-NORB.V,1.

Paoli Vicinity (Easttown Township)

Waynesborough (PA-208), 2049 Waynesborough Rd., .3 mi. W of Pa. 252, S of Paoli. Random rubble, central section with setback side wings, 40' (five-bay front) x 33', W wing 20' (two bays) x 18', E wing 17' (two bays) x 32', two-and-a-half stories, gable roofs with pent eaves, denticulated cornice, double doors with transom and pedimented hood on S (front) elevation, porch across N elevation; central hall plan, fine original interior woodwork; Georgian style. Built in several sections; W wing possibly built 1724 by Anthony Wayne; central section built between 1745 and 1763 by Isaac Wayne; E wing (one-and-a-half stories) built 1792 by General Anthony Wayne; additional story added on E wing 1860; two-story wing added to rear of E wing 1902; restored 1965-68. Home of General Anthony Wayne (1745-96), a brigadier general of the Continental Army during the Revolutionary War; continuously owned by Wayne family; famous visitors included Washington, Franklin, Lafayette and Alexander Hamilton. 2 ext. photos (1960), 1 copy photo of 1853 daguerreotype, 1 copy photo of 1855 Lossing engraving, 1 copy photo of ca. 1870 engraving; 6 data pages (1963, 1976). LC code: PA,15-PAOL.V,1. NHL.

Paoli Vicinity (Tredyffrin Township)

Cedar Hollow Railroad Station (PA-1199), E side of Cedar Hollow Rd. (LR15215), .5 mi. S of Swedesford Rd. (LR15132), 1.5 mi. NW of Paoli. Frame with clapboarding, T-shaped, main block with projecting center pavilion on N (track side), approx. 45' (three-bay front) x 18'-6", two stories, intersecting gable roofs with pinnacles and pendants at peaks of gables, triangular transoms of stained glass, canopy across N elevation, one-story wing (approx. 25' x 28') on S elevation, Carpenter Gothic details; freight and passenger station in main block, station master's dwelling in S wing and second floor of main block. Built 1872 for the Chester Valley Railroad; few changes. 2 ext. photos (1958), 1 int. photo (1958); 3 data pages (1958). LC code: PA,15-PAOL.V,4.

Diamond Rock Schoolhouse (PA-207), NW corner of Yellow Springs Rd. (LR15050) and Diamond Rock Hill Rd., approx. 2.5 mi. N of Paoli. Stuccoed stone, octagonal, 10' each side, one story, polygonal hip roof with central chimney, hood over S (front) entrance; one room with central stove. Built 1818; used as school until 1864; 1918 restored by Diamond Rock Old Scholars Association. 1 ext. photo (1958); 6 data pages (1958). LC code: PA,15-PAOL.V,2.

Jerman-Walker Springhouse (Wilson Springhouse) (PA-1217), on N. Valley Rd. (LR15108), approx. .5 mi. S of Swedesford Rd. (LR15132). Stuccoed random rubble, approx. 23' x 15', one story with lower spring level and loft, gable roof, large chimney (3' x 8') at NE corner, entrances at first-story and spring level on S (front) elevation; two rooms at each level. Built eighteenth century; doubled in size with early-nineteenth-century addition. Well preserved example of eighteenth-century springhouse. 2 ext. photos (1958); 3 data pages (1958). LC code: PA,15-PAOL.V,3A.

Walker Springhouse. See Jerman-Walker Springhouse.

Wilson Springhouse. See Jerman-Walker Springhouse.

Parkesburg Borough

Parke, David, House (PA-200), 40 E. Main St. Random rubble (partially stuccoed), L-shaped, five-bay front with rear ell, two-and-a-half stories, gable roofs, recessed door with transom on S (front) elevation; central hall plan, fine interior woodwork. Built late eighteenth century; rear ell added in two stages; ell connects house to outbuilding; wooden porch and two-story wrought-iron porch added; open scalloped bargeboard added in gable ends. 4 ext. photos (1960), 3 int. photos (1960); 1 data page (1979). LC code: PA,15- PARK,1.

Parke, John, House (PA-1310), 345 Main St. Frame (later covered with asbestos shingles), approx. 20' (three-bay front) x 24', two-and-a-half stories with basement fully exposed on

S (front) elevation, gable roof with dormers, two-story porch; side hall plan, notable interior wall murals by Louis Mader, now in The State Museum, Harrisburg. Decoration includes murals of American, European, and Asian scenes, trompe-d'oeil woodwork and trim including baseboards, pilasters, and marbleized dadoes. Wall paintings of this type are rare in Pennsylvania. Built ca. 1846; demolished 1977. 2 ext. photos (1964), 10 int. photos (1964); 5 data pages (1975). LC code: PA,15-PARK,2.

Parkesburg Vicinity (Sadsbury Township)

Upper Octoraro Presbyterian Church Session House (PA-201), SE corner of Pa. 10 (Octoraro Trail Rd.) and Octoraro Rd., .5 mi. N of Parkesburg. Stuccoed stone, 20'-8" (two-bay front) x 15'-2", one story, gable roof; one room, corner fireplace. Built ca. 1740-45; seldom used. Rare survival of a once common type of building used by Presbyterian Church officials for business meetings. 2 ext. photos (1960), 1 copy photo of 1877 ext. view; 1 data page (1963). LC code: PA,15-PARK.V,1.

Phoenixville Vicinity (Schuylkill Township)

Moore Hall. See Moore, William, House.

Moore, William, House (Moore Hall) (PA-1135), between Pa. 23 (Valley Forge Rd.) and Reading RR tracks, .2 mi. E of White Horse Rd., E of Phoenixville. Coursed squared rubble (S front elevation) and coursed rubble, approx. 45' (five-bay front) x 29' with offset kitchen wing to W, two-and-a-half stories, gable roof with pedimented gable end, door with transom and pedimented distyle Ionic entrance porch on S elevation (porch added after 1894, possibly 1930s); central hall plan, fine original interior woodwork; Georgian style. Built mid-eighteenth century; restored 1930s according to 1819 description, G. Edwin Brumbaugh, restoration architect. Home of Tory William Moore. 1 ext. photo (1959), 5 int. photos (1959), 1 copy photo of ca. 1890 ext. view; 14 data pages (1959). LC code: PA,15-PHOEN.V,1. NR.

Pottstown Vicinity

Nutt, Samuel, House (now Coventry Forge Inn). See Coventryville (South Coventry Township), Coventry Forge Inn.

Pughtown Vicinity (South Coventry Township)

Lundale Farm, House (Samuel Townsend House) (PA-1308), on private road .1 mi. W of Pa. 100 (Pottstown Pike), .3 mi. S of Pughtown Rd. Stuccoed random rubble with quoins, 47'-9" (five-bay front) x 32'-7", two-and-a-half stories, gable roof, door with transom on S (front) elevation; central hall plan, W room originally kitchen with large cooking fireplace and stone sink. Outbuildings. Built in two sections, E three bays (side hall plan) built ca. 1796, early-nineteenth-century two-bay kitchen wing added to W (forming central hall plan); entrance porch added on S elevation 1950; setback stuccoed frame wing with modern kitchen added to E elevation 1950. Land acquired by James Pugh in 1713, and by David Yarnall in 1753, his son-in-law Samuel Townsend, active in local politics, built original section of house. Well preserved, typical local farmhouse. 6 sheets (1975, including site plan, plan, elevations); 1 copy photo of rectified photo of rear elevation (1975); 10 data pages (1976, 1980). LC code: PA,15-PUGH.V,1. NR.

Springhouse (James Pugh Springhouse) (PA-1308A). Random rubble with quoins partially stuccoed, 18'-2" (one-bay front) x 16'-1", two-and-a-half stories on sloping site fully exposing basement to E, gable roof, large chimney in NE corner serves interior and exterior fireplaces. Built early eighteenth century by James Pugh. Pugh acquired land in 1713, this is the earliest structure on property, built as dwelling and springhouse. 1 sheet (1975, including plan, elevations); 1 data page (1985). LC code: PA,15-PUGH.V,1A.

Pugh, James, Springhouse. See Lundale Farm, *Springhouse*.

Townsend, Samuel, House. See Lundale Farm, House.

Rocky Hill Vicinity (East Goshen Township)

Barn (PA-5241), Pa. 352, just S of Rocky Hill. Random rubble with quoins (partially stuccoed), frame forebay contained within stone end walls and supported by two circular stone columns, two levels, gable roof, ramp and enclosed frame entrance to threshing floor, stone-arched entrances, frame and stone additions. Date unknown. Adjacent to Barn (PA-5333). 3 ext. photos (1941). LC code: PA,15-ROHI.V,2A.

Barn (PA-5333), Pa. 352, just S of Rocky Hill. Random rubble (partially stuccoed), frame forebay contained within stone end walls and supported by two stone columns, two levels, gable roof. Date unknown. Adjacent to Barn (PA-5241). 1 ext. photo (1941). LC code: PA,15-ROHI.V,1A.

Romansville (West Bradford Township)

1804 Barn. See Romans, John, Barn.

Romans, John, Barn (1804 Barn) (PA-165), W side of Star Gazer Rd. (LR15072), .1 mi. S of Strasburg Rd. (LR15080). Random rubble, 46'-6" x 44'-6", two levels on sloping site (stables lower level, threshing floor above), gable roof, projecting frame forebay supported on stone piers across S elevation, slit ventilators. Built 1804 (date stone). Fine example of early-nineteenth-century barn with few changes. 3 ext. photos (1959); 3 data pages (1959). LC code: PA,15-ROMAV,2A.

Romansville Friends Meetinghouse Sheds (PA-1101), SE side of Shadyside Rd. (LR15075), .1 mi. NE of Strasburg Rd. (LR15180). Frame with vertical wooden siding, 72' x 14', one story, gable roof, open front divided into eight stalls. Built 1846. Unusual survival of mid-nineteenth-century horse sheds in unaltered condition. 2 photos (1959); 3 data pages (1959). LC code: PA,15-ROMAV,1.

Saint Matthews Corner (West Vincent Township)

Barn (PA-5245), Pa. 401 (Conestoga Rd.), near St. Matthew's Church. Random rubble (whitewashed), projecting frame forebay with tapered circular stone piers, two levels, gable roof, frame and stone wing added to forebay, shed additions on side and front elevations, stone wall shelters stable area. Built 1812 (date stone); adjacent to house dated 1774. 4 ext. photos (1941). LC code: PA,15-SAMAC,1A.

Saint Peters Vicinity

Hopewell Village, Employee's Quarters and Harrison Lloyd House. See Hopewell Village (Warwick Township), Hopewell Village National Historic Site.

Sconnelltown (East Bradford Township)

Sconnelltown House (PA-202), E side of Birmingham Rd. (LR15198), between Pa. 842 (W. Miner St.) and Sconnelltown Rd. (LR10587). Random rubble (partially stuccoed), approx. 27' (three-bay front) x 20', one-and-a-half stories, steep gable roof with shed dormer (rare original eighteenth-century dormer), chimneys in gable end and corner; two rooms on each floor (partitions removed). Built mid-eighteenth century; large double doors cut in wall when house used as barn; ruinous condition. Rare example of a house type once common in area. 4 ext. photos (1958); 4 data pages (1958). LC code: PA,15-SCON,1.

Sconnelltown Vicinity (East Bradford Township)

Strode's Grist Mill (PA-251), SE corner of Pa. 52-100 (Lenape Rd.) and Birmingham Rd. (LR15087). Random rubble, approx. 58' x 30', sloping site exposes two-and-a-half stories with basement, gable roof, pent eaves across S elevation (removed 1940s), entrance porch on N elevation (removed, replaced with clapboarded addition early twentieth century), frame housing for mill wheel on W elevation (removed). Built 1721 (date stone); Carter, Scott, and Willis, builders; most original machinery present 1958; large dormer added 1960s; used as residence and gallery. Grist mill had been in almost continuous operation since its erection until the mid-twentieth century; ground grain for Washington's army at the Battle of Brandywine and Valley Forge. Excellent example of an early grist mill with few alterations. 1 ext. photo (1958), 1 copy photo of 1899 ext. view; 4 data pages (1958). LC code: PA,15-SCON.V,1. NR.

Strafford (Tredyffrin Township)

Eagle School (PA-1129), E side of Old Eagle School Rd. (Pa. 543), across from intersection with Homestead Rd. Random rubble, 19'-2" (three-bay front) x 31'-10" (four bays), one story, gable roof, recessed entrance with paneled reveal on S (front) elevation; one room. Built 1788 (date stone), original building was N three bays with entrance on W elevation; 1835 one-bay addition to S and entrance changed to S elevation; restored 1897 (stucco removed, date stone moved, cornice and chimney replaced). Possibly the oldest school building extant in Chester County. 2 ext. photos (1958), 2 copy photos of 1909 ext. photos; 7 data pages (1958). LC code: PA,15-STRAFO,1.

Strafford Railroad Station (PA-268), E side of Old Eagle School Rd., between Strafford Ave. and Penn Central Railroad tracks. Frame with vertical siding faced with vertical and diagonal boards (main floor) and board and batten siding (lower level), 28'-6" (three-bay front) x 23' with projecting bay on S (rear) elevation, two stories (main floor elevated to track level), gable roof with large gabled dormers, deep cornice with brackets, applied wooden decoration in gable ends. Built 1876 as the Centennial Catalogue Building for the 1876 Centennial in Philadelphia; bought by the Pennsylvania Railroad and erected in Wayne as a railroad station in 1885; 1887 taken down and moved to Strafford. 2 ext. photos (1958); 3 data pages (1958). LC code: PA,15-STRAFO,2. NR.

Tanguy Vicinity (Westtown Township)

Hoopes, Daniel, House (PA-161), N side of Pa. 926 (Street Rd.), .4 mi. E of Pa. 352 (Middletown Rd.). Coursed dressed serpentine stone (S front elevation) and random rubble, L-shaped built in two sections, original W section 18'-4" (two-bay front) x 20'-8", L-shaped wing to E 21'-4" (two-bay front) x 42'-11", two-and-a-half stories, gable roofs, pent roof on W section (removed); W section one room plan, E section two room plan, original interior woodwork. W section built 1723 (date stone) by Daniel and Jane Hoopes; E section added 1740 (date stone) by Joshua H. Hoopes; N roof slope of 1723 section changed to conform with 1740 roof line; twentieth-century kitchen wing added to 1740 section. Built and owned until 1908 by the Hoopes, a prominent Quaker family. Fine example of eighteenth-century house with excellent original interior woodwork and hardware. 5 ext. photos (1958), 5 int. photos (1958); 7 data pages (1958). LC code: PA,15-TANG.V,1.

Thorndale (Caln Township)

Pim Hexagonal School (Six-Sided School) (PA-5136), original location W side of N. Bailey Rd., approx. .5 mi. N of U.S. Rte. 30 (Lincoln Hwy.); moved to Caln Township Municipal Park, set back from NE corner of N. Bailey Rd. and U.S. Rte. 30. Coursed rubble with cut face, hexagonal, 9' each side, one story with attic, cellar at spring level, polygonal hip roof with hexagonal cupola with ogee-arched openings (cupola removed, now inside school), denticulated cornice; one room, spring in cellar. Built 1841; shed added on N elevation; moved 1968. Built by Richard Pim as family and neighborhood schoolhouse. 3 ext. photos (1961, 1962), 1 int. photo (1961); 3 data pages (1963). LC code: PA,15-THORN,1.

Six-sided School. See Pim Hexagonal School.

Towerville (East Fallowfield Township)

Fallowfield Octagonal House. See Pierce, Lukens, House.

Pierce, Lukens House (Fallowfield Octagonal House) (PA-1139), NE side of Wilmington Rd., .1 mi. E of Park Ave. (LR15178), .2 mi. S of Strasburg Rd. (LR15067). Stuccoed random rubble, octagonal, two stories with basement, polygonal hip roof with octagonal cupola, deep cornice with brackets, slightly pedimented lintels, entrance porch (originally had veranda, removed), original two-story wing (removed), Italianate details; four large rectangular rooms and four small triangular rooms with central circular stairway. Built 1856; kitchen addition. Built by Lukens Pierce, one of America's first nurserymen. 2 ext. photos (1961). LC code: PA,15-TOW,1. NR.

Warwick Township

Hopewell Village, Bethesda Baptist Church. See Hopewell Village (Warwick Township), Hopewell Village National Historic Site.

Wawaset (Pocopson Township)

Barn, Stone, circa 1975 (PA-5237), Pa. 842, S of Wawaset Bridge. Random rubble, three-level bank barn, gable roof, ramp with enclosed frame entrance to threshing floor, remnants of pent roof over lower level, louvered ventilators, terraced farmyard with stone walls. Built ca. 1795. 6 ext. photos (1941), 1 int. photo (1941). LC code: PA,15-WAWA,1A.

West Chester Borough

Bank of Chester County (National Bank of Chester County, Southeast National Bank) (PA-1126), 17 N. High St. Marble faced brick, 45' x 90', two stories set on podium, gable roof, pedimented Doric portico on W (front) elevation (based on Stuart and Revett's *Antiquities of Athens*, 1762), wide entablature flanked by elongated scrolls over central entrance; originally interior had large banking room with vaults flanking entrance and two levels of offices at E end. Built 1836 (date and names of architect and mason inscribed in portico); Thomas U. Walter, architect; bank lengthened to E; wing added to S; level of floor and portico lowered and N and S walls rebuilt 1928; interior redecorated 1854 and 1928. Chartered 1814, first bank in Chester County. Fine Greek Revival design by Walter. 2 ext. photos (1958), 5 copy photos of ext. views from 1836, 1840, 1849, 1856 and 1899, 2 copy photos of int. views from 1895 and ca. 1914; 8 data pages (1958). LC code: PA,15-WCHES,13. NR (Also in West Chester Downtown Historic District).

Baptist Church of West Chester (PA-1191), 221 S. High St. Brick, approx. 41' (three-bay front) x 81' (six bays), two stories, gable roof (originally with pedimented gable end), brick pilasters, wide entablature, door with heavy architrave and entablature (originally architrave on scroll brackets), arched stained-glass window above door with blind windows with pedimented hoods to either side, Classical Revival style. Built 1854-57; Samuel Sloan and John Stewart, architects; two-story brick school wing (40' x 50') added to SE elevation early twentieth century; school enlarged 1930; pedimented tetrastyle Tuscan portico added 1930 by Ralph Minick, architect; one-story addition on N elevation 1960s. 1 ext. photo (1958), 1 copy photo of ext. from ca. 1860; 10 data pages (1958, 1975). LC code: PA,15-WCHES,21. NR (West Chester Downtown Historic District).

Brinton Serpentine House. See Brinton, Sibyla, House.

Brinton, Sibyla, House (Brinton Serpentine House) (PA-249), 311 S. Church St. Irregularly coursed serpentine ashlar with quoins, T-shaped, three-bay front, two-and-a-half stories with two-story rear wing, cross gable roof with bracketed cornice and pierced bargeboards, rock-faced segmental arches over windows, entrance porch with scroll brackets, Gothic Revival style; central hall plan. Built ca. 1873. 1 ext. photo (1960). LC code: PA,15-WCHES,1.

Chester County Courthouse (PA-1119), 10 N. High St. Brick faced with Pictou stone (originally faced with mastic), 62' x 119', two stories with basement, low gable roof, polygonal clock tower, denticulated cornice, pedimented hexastyle Corinthian portico (cast-iron columns and capitals) on E (front) elevation, slightly projecting pedimented pavilion on S elevation, pilasters divide bays; central hall with offices on first floor, courtroom on second floor. Built 1846; Thomas U. Walter, architect; three-story stone wing (135' x 50') added to W elevation 1893, T. Roney Williamson, architect; addition to N elevation 1966. Fine Greek Revival design by Walter. 2 ext. photos (1958), 4 copy photos of mid-nineteenth-century print, 1881 engraving, and photos from 1885 and ca. 1900, 1 copy photo of 1846 floor plan; 22 data pages (1958). LC code: PA,15-WCHES,3. NR (Also in West Chester Downtown Historic District).

Chester County Historical Society. See Chester County Horticultural Hall.

Chester County Horticultural Hall (Chester County Historical Society) (PA-1121), 225 N. High St. Coursed serpentine stone (W front elevation) and stuccoed brick, approx. 45' (one-bay front) x 75' (four bays), one story with basement, gable roof, corner buttresses, entrance arch with splayed soffit and reveal on W elevation, door with fanlight; open exhibition space. Built 1848 (date stone); Thomas U. Walter, architect; ca. 1870 gallery added (removed ca. 1930), roof raised and one-story stage wing added to E; 1885 two-story brick entrance tower added by E.F. Bertolette (removed before 1904); 1894 first wing demolished and gambrel-roof addition built; 1942 gable-roof addition by Price and Walton replaced 1894 addition. Used as exhibition space, town meeting hall, theater, roller skating rink and historical society. Uriah Painter (owner 1873-1900), friend of Thomas Edison, introduced electric lights early, main chandelier moved to U.S. Senate 1885. 2 ext. photos (1958), 4 copy photos of ext. photos from 1870s, ca. 1885, 1899 and 1942, 2 copy photos of int. photos from 1870s and ca. 1883; 12 data pages (1958). LC code: PA,15-WCHES,4. NR (West Chester Downtown Historic District).

Chester County Hotel (Mansion House Hotel) (PA-1112), 36 W. Market St. Brick, L-shaped, 68'-6" (seven-bay front) x 96'-6", three-and-a-half stories with basement, gable roofs with dormers, modillioned cornice, paired chimneys in parapets. Built 1832 for William Everhart; William Strickland, architect; second-floor veranda added across N (front) elevation 1856 (later removed); first-story facade altered 1871; mansard roof with bays and dormers added on W section 1900; further alterations early 1960s; demolished ca. 1972. Built as a temperance house but changed to a licensed hotel soon after; continuously used as a hotel. 1 ext. photo (1958), 2 copy photos of ext. from 1856 and ca. 1902, 1 copy photo of 1842 advertisement; 4 data pages (1958). LC code: PA,15-WCHES,17.

Chester County Prison (PA-1134), 235 W. Market St. Coursed ashlar (S front elevation) and random rubble, T-shaped with surrounding wall, approx. 106' across S elevation (five-bay main section and two-bay symmetrical side wings), three-story main block and two-story wings, cross gable roof with octagonal cupola on main block, hip roofs on wings, denticulated cornice, three-bay pedimented projecting pavilion on S elevation, rusticated granite piers and columns frame entrance, slightly pedimented granite lintels, Greek Revival style; upper-level cells reached by galleries supported on iron brackets, each cell 9' x 12', corridor lit by skylights. Built 1838 (date stone); Thomas U. Walter, architect; additional cells added to N 1871; porch added to E wing (warden's quarters); demolished 1960. Excellent example of nineteenth-century prison architecture, designed by Walter. 7 ext. photos (1958, 1960), 9 int. photos (1958, 1960), 3 copy photos of watercolor from 1839, an engraving from 1856 map and engraving from 1881; 18 data pages (1958). LC code: PA,15-WCHES,5.

Ebbs, William, House. See Mayfield.

Everhart, William, Building (Highly Building) (PA-1207), 28 W. Market St. Brick, 20'-6" (three-bay front) x 39'-10", three-and-a-half stories with basement, gable roof with dormer on each slope, paired chimneys in parapet at gable end, corbeled brick cornice; side hall plan, much original interior detail. Built ca. 1834; elaborate cast-iron balcony added at second-story level 1868; storefront added later at basement level; restored. Has functioned continuously as commercial office space; once occupied by *Chester County Times*; first published biography of Abraham Lincoln which introduced him to public as potential presidential candidate printed here in 1860; balcony added for the convenience of Republican speakers during the campaign of 1868. 2 ext. photos (1958), 1 int. photo (1958); 3 data pages (1958). LC code: PA,15-WCHES,11. NR (Also in West Chester Downtown Historic District).

First Presbyterian Church (PA-1115), 130 W. Miner St. Stuccoed stone, 45' (three-bay front) x 75', one story with gallery and basement, gable roof with pedimented gable end, wide plain entablature, recessed entrance portico with two Ionic columns in antis on N (front) elevation, corner pilasters, splayed entrance with low pediment on scroll brackets, Greek Revival style. Built 1832; Thomas U. Walter, architect; ca. 1860 enlarged 25' to S and interior altered; 1874 further interior remodeling; 1892-93 large brownstone school wing added to E, T. Roney Williamson, architect; 1923 school wing partially demolished and remodeled; 1956-57 school wing completely rebuilt to blend with church, William D. Savage, architect. First building designed by Walter in West Chester, possibly his first commission. 2 ext. photos (1958), 1 copy photo from 1899; 13 data pages (1958). LC code: PA,15-WCHES,6. NR.

136 East Gay Street (Bakery) (Sorber Brick Store) (PA-244). Brick, two-bay row house, two-and-a-half stories, gable roof with dormer, denticulated cornice, fanlight over entrance, shop window; large bake oven in basement. Built early nineteenth century, before 1837. 1 ext. photo (1960), 1 photo of bake oven (1960). LC code: PA,15-WCHES,2. NR (West Chester Downtown Historic District).

Hickman Fountain (PA-247), originally located at NW corner of High and Market Sts., in front of Chester County Courthouse (PA-1119), moved to garden of Matlack-Townsend House (PA-243), 225 N. Matlack St. Marble carved to resemble rock-faced ashlar and rubble stone, 6' high, carved heads on sides, topped by a marble ball (originally a cross), one basin on sidewalk side, two basins on street side for animals. Built 1869 (date stone); Reverend John Bolton, designer; Garrett and Jones, stonemasons; commissioned by Mrs. John Hickman, whose husband was a member of U.S. Congress; moved to new location in 1960. 2 photos (1960), 1 copy photo of ca. 1869-78 view; see Chester County Courthouse (PA-1119) for data. LC code: PA,15-WCHES,7. NR (West Chester Downtown Historic District).

Highly Building. See Everhart, William, Building.

Holy Trinity Protestant Episcopal Church (PA-1223), 238 S. High St. Green serpentine stone with brick trim, 55' x 102' with 20' square entrance tower at SE corner, one story with four-stage tower (113' high), gable roof (originally polychrome with cast iron cresting on ridge, replaced 1957), buttresses, pointed-arch openings, bartizan on tower, stained-glass windows, decorative terra cotta panels, Gothic Revival style; exposed wooden trusses. Built 1868-70; John Bolton, designer and rector of church; tower built 1871-90, T. Roney Williamson, architect; school wing to N completed 1882 by Bolton; choir and covered passageway to school built 1892; dormers added and interior trusses altered ca. 1900; offices added to N of school and area W of chancel enlarged ca. 1950. 2 ext. photos (1958), 1 copy photo of ext. photo taken after 1890; 10 data pages (1958, 1975). LC code: PA,15-WCHES,18. NR (West Chester Downtown Historic District).

Mansion House Hotel. See Chester County Hotel.

Matlack-Townsend House (David Townsend House) (PA-243), 225 N. Matlack St. Brick with scored stucco, L-shaped, three-story main section approx. 28' (three-bay front) x 36' (two bays), two one-and-a-half-story adjacent wings to N, gable roof with shed roofs on wings, paired chimneys in parapet, fanlight over S (front) elevation, porch across E side; side hall plan, original mid-nineteenth-century woodwork. Built in three sections; ca. 1785 W wing built for Isaiah Matlack; 1830 two-and-a-half-story section added on S (before 1874 changed to three stories); 1849 E wing built by Thomas Bateman for David Townsend; obtained by Chester County Historical Society 1951. Townsend was a noted botanist and lawyer and active in Chester County affairs. 3 ext. photos (1958), 5 int. photos (1958); 10 data pages (1958). LC code: PA,15-WCHES,10.

Mayfield (William Ebbs House) (PA-1104), 600 N. New St. Whitewashed brick, 48' (five-bay front) x 45', two-and-a-half stories, gable roof with pedimented gable ends, denticulated cornice, wide entablature, pedimented tetrastyle Ionic portico on S (front) elevation, door with transom and side lights and architrave on scroll brackets on S elevation, conservatory on W elevation (rebuilt 1915, glass sides and roof removed 1972), two-story porch on E elevation (enclosed 1950s); central hall plan, notable interior woodwork and plaster work. Built 1848-51 for William Ebbs, Pittsburgh industrialist; kitchen wing added 1915; house now surrounded by housing development. Fine example of elaborate Greek Revival style house, locally attributed to Thomas U. Walter. 1 ext. photo (1958), 1 copy photo of drawing on a map from ca. 1856; 5 data pages (1958, 1975). LC code: PA,15-WCHES,19.

National Bank of Chester County. See Bank of Chester County.

Pennsylvania Railroad Station (PA-246), S side of Market St., between Matlack and Franklin Sts. Brick with banded brick quoins, approx. 72' (five-bay front) x 46' (three bays), two stories, flat roof behind elaborate brick parapet topped with bracketed cornice, projecting pedimented three-bay pavilion on N (front) elevation, paired arched windows, hoods supported by paired brick brackets over second-story windows (first-story windows originally had hoods with paired brackets, removed), covered passageway from entrance to street (originally two), interesting brick details, Renaissance Revival massing with High Victorian Gothic details. Built ca. 1875; brick addition to N (half of the wing demolished by 1962); station demolished 1968. 3 ext. photos (1962), 1 int. photo (1962), 2 copy photos of ext. from ca. 1930. LC code: PA,15-WCHES,8.

Sharples, Philip, House (PA-164), 400 S. Church St. Brick, L-shaped, main block approx. 33' (four-bay front) x 32' (four bays) with kitchen ell to W (approx. 45' x 15'), three-story main section with two-story wing, low gable roofs, pedimented S (front) gable end, Doric porch across S elevation and part of E elevation, Greek Revival details. Built 1838; brick and frame ell added in reentrant angle; brick addition to W of ells. 2 ext. photos (1958); 1 data page (1958). LC code: PA,15-WCHES,20.

Sorber Brick Store. See 136 East Gay Street (Bakery).

Southeast National Bank. See Bank of Chester County.

Townsend, Davil, House. See Matlack-Townsend House.

West Chester State College. See West Chester State Normal School.

West Chester State Normal School (West Chester State College, West Chester University) (PA-250), W side of S. High St., between College St. and Rosedale Ave. Random serpentine ashlar with limestone quoins, three-bay projecting center pavilion with five-bay hyphens and three-bay projecting end pavilions, three-and-a-half stories with basement, mansard roof with dormers, limestone pilasters and pediment frame entrance on E (front) elevation, limestone belt courses and lintels, Second Empire style. Built 1871; Yarnall and Cooper of Philadelphia, builders; symmetrical end pavilions added ca. 1880, Addison Hutton, architect; rear additions 1880 and later; cupola removed; used as dormitory; demolished 1971. 1 ext. photo (1960), 2 copy photos of prints, one from 1881, the other undated. LC code: PA,15-WCHES,9.

West Chester University. See West Chester State Normal School.

West Chester Young Ladies Seminary (Villa Maria Convent) (PA-1215), 300 Maple Ave. Brick, over-all dimensions approx. 130' x 45', consisting of 50' projecting central pavilion (five bays) with 40' flanking side wings (side wings consist of two-bay hyphens and two-bay projecting end pavilions), 100' parallel wings to N (six bays each), three-and-a-half-story center pavilion, three-story side wings, one-story rear wings, elevated basement, flat roofs with parapets, octagonal cupola, attic windows in plain frieze, belt course, entrance porch on S (front) elevation, Greek Revival style. Built 1838; Thomas U. Walter, architect; 1914 cupola removed and mansard roof with dormers added creating additional story; brick later stuccoed; front porch changed; 1914 large granite chapel built to W; addition to E elevation; demolished after 1958. Built as girls' seminary (1837-40), then used for several schools 1840-73 and a Roman Catholic convent 1873 until demolition. 1 ext. photo (1958), 3 copy photos from ca. 1838, ca. 1850 and ca. 1862; 5 data pages (1958). LC code: PA,15-WCHES,12.

Villa Maria Convent. See West Chester Young Ladies Seminary.

West Chester Vicinity

Arnold-Temple House. See Marshallton Vicinity (West Bradford Township), Arnold-Temple House.

Darlington, Thomas, House (Spackman Corner Chimney House). See Birmingham Vicinity (Thornbury Township), Darlington, Thomas, House.

West Chester Vicinity (West Bradford Township)

Barn, Stone (PA-5229), off U.S. Rte. 322, on Shadyside Rd. at East Branch of Brandywine Creek, approx. 4.5 mi. W of West Chester. Random rubble (small scale ledgestone), cantilevered frame forebay, two-level bank barn, gable roof, frame and stone shed additions on sides, louvered ventilator openings, stone wall encloses farmyard. Built eighteenth century; adjacent to 1760 stone house. 4 ext. photos (1941). LC code: PA,15-WCHES.V,5A.

West Chester Vicinity (West Goshen Township)

Collins, Joseph, House (PA-1114), 633 Goshen Rd. Coursed serpentine ashlar (S front elevation) and random rubble, 23' (three-bay front) x 21'-6", two-and-a-half stories, gable roof with pent eaves, pent roof with cantilevered pediment over entrance on S elevation; fine interior woodwork and hardware. Built 1727 (date stone) by Joseph Collins; random rubble kitchen wing added on N elevation 1758-60 by Nathaniel Moore; 1760 interior and exterior alterations; acquired by Chester County Historical Society and restored 1958. Excellent example of well preserved eighteenth-century house with fine stonework and interior details. 3 ext. photos (1958), 5 int. photos (1958); 5 data pages (1958). LC code: PA,15-WCHES.V,2. NR.

Hoopes House. See Rogers-Hoopes House.

Matlack, George, House (PA-1221), 409 Westtown Rd. Brick (E three bays) and stone (W two bays) covered with stucco, five-bay front, two-and-a-half stories, gable roof; central hall plan, original interior woodwork remains. Built in two sections; brick E section built ca. 1786 as addition to log house which then became kitchen; log kitchen demolished and replaced with stone W section ca. 1811 forming present central hall plan house; lean-to and entrance porch added. 1 ext. photo (1958), 2 int. photos (1958); 3 data pages (1958). LC code: PA,15-WCHES.V,3.

Rogers-Hoopes House (Mary Rogers House) (PA-1212), 1021 Fernhill Rd., approx. 1.5 mi. E of West Chester. Random rubble (dressed on S front elevation), 55'-1" (five-bay front) x 31'-10", two-and-a-half stories, gable roof, gabled dormers with dentils and pilasters, modillioned cornice, pilasters and entablature frame door with fanlight on S elevation, Federal details; central hall plan, excellent original interior woodwork, plaster work and hardware. Built in two sections; E three bays built 1807 (date stone); W two bays added ca. 1815; kitchen wing added to W. Built by William and Mary Rogers, owned by Hoopes family for almost 100 years. Fine early-nineteenth-century house with excellent exterior and interior woodwork. 3 ext. photos (1958), 5 int. photos (1958); 4 data pages (1958). LC code: PA,15-WCHES.V,4.

Rogers, Mary, House. See Rogers-Hoopes House.

Taylor, Lowndes, Barn (PA-1100), 937 Pottstown Pike. Random dressed serpentine ashlar and partially stuccoed random rubble (N elevation), 45'-4" x 34', two levels, gable roof, arched stable entrances with cut voussoirs with keystones, lintels with keystones over upper openings, original hardware remains. Built 1820; Albin Hall, mason; frame addition built 1859 (removed before 1958). Well preserved early-nineteenth-century bank barn with interesting masonry. 5 ext. photos (1958), 1 copy photo of 1833 oil painting; 4 data pages (1958). LC code: PA,15-WCHES.V,1.

Carriage House (PA-1100A). Random dressed serpentine ashlar (S half) and frame with vertical wooden siding (N half), approx. 15' (two-bay front) x 35', one-and-a-half stories with basement, gable roof with shed dormers. Built mid-nineteenth century. 1 ext. photo (1958). LC code: PA,15-WCHES.V,1A.

Smokehouse (PA-1100B). Stuccoed random rubble, 10' x 8', one story, gable roof. Built ca. 1820. 1 ext. photo (1958). LC code: PA,15-WCHES.V,1B.

West Grove Vicinity (London Grove Township)

Jackson, Joseph, House (PA-1224), N side of Old Baltimore Pike, .6 mi. NW of Baltimore Pike, W of West Grove. Brick, L-shaped, 38' (five-bay front) x 19' with ell to N 18' x 22', two-and-a-half stories with basement, gable roof, cove cornice (remains only on S front elevation), pent eaves (remain only on W gable end), pent roof removed, diaper pattern of black bricks in W gable end, date in 2' numerals of black bricks across W elevation; central hall plan, fine original interior woodwork (including some excellent graining) and hardware remain. Numerous outbuildings. Built 1742; Joseph Jackson (an English Quaker miller), builder; N ell extended 11' early nineteenth century; frame kitchen wing covered with composition shingles added to N next to ell twentieth century; porch added across S elevation ca. 1900. Fine example of mid-eighteenth-century Quaker house with interesting brick patterns and excellent interior details. 4 ext. photos (1958), 10 int. photos (1958), 1 copy photo of farm from 1881; 7 data pages (1958). LC code: PA,15-WGRO.V,1.

Westtown Vicinity (Thornbury Township)

The Beehive. See Woodward, Richard, House.

Woodward, Richard, House (The Beehive) (PA-1192), E side of Concord Rd., 1.2 mi. S of Pa. 926 (Street Rd.). Coursed rubble, 37'-8" (three-bay front) x 22', two-and-a-half stories with basement, steep gable roof, stepped belt course, pedimented hood over S (front) entrance; two room plan. Built ca. 1700; random rubble lean-to added on N elevation mid-eighteenth century; tile roof added ca. 1910; random rubble kitchen wing added to N elevation of lean-to 1938; random rubble springhouse to NE (originally not connected) possibly original building built last decade of seventeenth century, springhouse remodeled and connected to kitchen ca. 1938; interior alterations twentieth century. 2 ext. photos (1958), 2 int. photos (1958); 4 data pages (1958). LC code: PA,15-WESTO.V,1.

Whitehorse Vicinity (Willistown Township)

Hibberd House. See Yarnall-Hibberd House.

Plumsock. See Yarnall-Hibberd House.

Thomas Mill (PA-1214), W bank of Crum Creek, NW of Goshen and Boots Rds. junction. Random rubble, 23'-6" x 35'-6", two-and-a-half stories on sloping site fully exposing basement to E, gable roof, wooden-framed openings constructed with wooden pegs; quartered log stairs in interior, much original machinery remained in 1958 such as wooden water wheel and gears. Built 1774 (date stone); Isaac Thomas, builder; early 16' frame and stone addition to N (rear) elevation; in running order as late as 1940s; machinery remained but deteriorating 1958; machinery acquired by Smithsonian Institution ca. 1973; mill restored ca. 1982. 7 ext. photos (1958), 4 int. photos (1958, showing machinery); 3 data pages (1958). LC code: PA,15-WHIHO.V,2.

Vogdes, Jacob, House (PA-1219), W side of Providence Rd. (LR15107), .4 mi. S of Goshen Rd. (LR15098). Random rubble with quoins, 30' (three-bay front) x 33' with setback wing to E 15' (two-bay front) x 21', two-and-a-half stories, gable roofs, pent roof on S (front) elevation (removed); side hall plan, fine original interior woodwork. Built 1795; E wing added early nineteenth century; tetrastyle Doric porch added mid-nineteenth century. 1 ext. photo (1958), 2 int. photos (1958); 4 data pages (1958). LC code: PA,15-WHIHO.V,4.

Yarnall-Hibberd House (Plumsock) (PA-182), W side of Plumsock Rd., .2 mi. S of Goshen Rd. (LR15098). Random rubble (partially stuccoed), 15' (two-bay front) x 28' (two bays), two-and-a-half stories, gable roof, porch across N (rear) elevation; two room plan, corner fireplaces. Built early eighteenth century; two-and-a-half-story random rubble wing added to W elevation ca. 1780; wing added twentieth century; restored and new addition built 1983, John Milner Associates, architect. Original house possibly built by Francis Yarnall; owned by Hibberd family over 100 years. Well preserved example of early-eighteenth-century English Quaker house. 2 ext. photos (1958), 1 int. photo (1958); 3 data pages (1958). LC code: PA,15-WHIHO.V,1.

Whitehorse Vicinity (Willistown-Newtown Townships)

Bartram's Covered Bridge (PA-1108), over Crum Creek, S of Goshen Rd. (LR15098), approx. 2 mi. E of Whitehorse. Burr arch truss supported on stone abutments, single span 60', overall length 80', 13' roadway, partially covered with horizontal boarding, gable roof, boarding covers gable ends including eaves overhang and knee bracing. Built 1860; Ferdinand Wood, contractor; concrete bridge built 1940 and covered bridge moved short distance to S and preserved. Named for Israel Bartram, a local resident. One of the few remaining covered bridges in area. 1 ext. photo (1958), 2 int. photos (1958), 1 copy photo of 1940 photo; 5 data pages (1958). LC code: PA,15-WHIHO.V,3. NR.

Willistown Vicinity (Willistown Township)

Garrett House. See Yarnall-Garrett House.

Yarnall-Garrett House (PA-1203), S side of Pa. 3 (West Chester Pike), .5 mi. E of Pa. 926 (Street Rd.). Random rubble, rectangular with many additions, original house irregularly spaced three-bay E section, two-and-a-half stories, gable roof; two room plan, early built-in closets. Built 1727 (date stone); 1812 (date stone) two-and-a-half-story random rubble wing (two-bay front) added to W; mid-nineteenth-century one-and-a-half-story random rubble wing added to E of 1727 section (roof raised to two stories twentieth century); mid-twentieth-century one-and-a-half-story random rubble wing added to N of 1812 wing, porches added. Original house built by Amos Yarnall, an English Quaker; 1812 section built by Aaron Garrett (Yarnall's stepson). 3 ext. photos

(1958), 2 int. photos (1958); 4 data pages (1958). LC code: PA,15-WILS.V,1.

Willowdale (East Marlborough Township)

Pyle House (PA-162), NE corner of Pa. 926 (Street Rd.) and Mill Rd., 1.1 mi. W of Pa. 82 (Unionville Rd.). Brick (stuccoed W elevation), three-bay front, two-and-a-half stories, gable roof, double doors on S (front) and N elevations (one N door removed), brick arches over openings; some original interior details. Built 1734 (date in brick headers on N elevation); one-bay wing added to E elevation; shed added to wing; porch added across S elevation. 4 ext. photos (1960), 1 int. photo (1960). LC code: PA,15-WIL,1.

Wyebrooke Vicinity (West Nantmeal Township)

Isabella Furnace (PA-163), W side of Bollinger Dr. (LR15151), at T-intersection with Creek Rd. (LR15149). Large complex of stone, brick and frame buildings, including the furnace, a variety of shops, tenant houses, barns and other farm structures. Water powered (on Perkin's Run), converted to steam power ca. 1880. Furnace built 1835, established by Potts family, ceased operation 1894; poor condition 1959; partially restored. Last sizable furnace built in Chester County; last active iron furnace in county. 2 ext. photos (1959), 1 copy photo from 1892; 7 data pages (1959). LC code: PA,15-WYBRO.V,1.

Cumberland County

Newville Vicinity (Upper Mifflin Township)

Sterrett, David, House (PA-5354), State Game Lands Plot No. 169. Brick, five-bay front with original two-bay service wing on S gable end, two-and-a-half-story house with one-and-a-half-story wing, gable roofs, inside end chimneys, watertable and belt course, porch across front elevation (added or enlarged mid-late nineteenth century), bake oven attached to service wing removed; half-passage plan, original interior woodwork remains including folding partition. Built 1789-91; interior of service wing remodeled ca. 1830; frame shed added on rear elevation; vacant and owned by Pennsylvania Game Commission. One of the oldest brick houses in county with few alterations. 8 ext. photos (1985), 12 int. photos (1985); 2 data pages including first floor plan (1986). NR. LC code: PA,21-NEWVI.V,1.

Dauphin County

Fort Hunter (Susquehanna Township)

Fort Hunter Mansion (Archibald McAllister House) (PA-38), W side of U.S. Rte. 22 (River Rd.), approx. 3 mi. N of Harrisburg. Museum. Coursed rubble with quoins, T-shaped, 55'-8" (five-bay front) x 39'-4" (two bays) with rear wing (20'-1" x 36'-1"), two-and-a-half stories with basement, hip roof with dormers and gable roof on wing, door with fanlight and side lights with Palladian window above on S (front) elevation, two-story porches on wing; central hall plan. Main section built ca. 1814; wing added mid-nineteenth century; two-story frame wing added to stone wing later nineteenth century; distyle entrance porch and bracketed cornice added ca. 1850. Built near site of Fort Hunter. 9 sheets (1935, including plans, elevations, details); 8 ext photos (1935); 2 data pages (1936). LC code: PA,22-FOHUN,1. NR.

McAllister, Archibald, House. See Fort Hunter Mansion.

Harrisburg

2533-39 Agate Street (Houses). See North Sixth Street (Houses).

Allison Hill (Houses) (PA-5203), bounded on the N by State St., on the E by Seventeenth St., on the S by Berryhill St., and on the W by Crescent St. and Royal Terrace. Cohesive residential area with some neighborhood commercial development, mostly two- to three-story brick or frame rowhouses, diverse nineteenth-century architectural styles. Developed 1870-1920; named for William Allison, early area landowner; growth coincided with construction of city bridges and a rail line. 6 ext. photos showing streetscapes of Hunter St., Regina St., N. Twelfth St., and N. Sixteenth St. (1985); 7 data pages including maps of area (1985). LC code: PA,22-HARBU,11. See following entries on individual structures in Allison Hill area (PA-5203 A-W).

1618 Hunter Street (House) (PA-5203A). One side of semi-detached house, frame with brick-patterned asphalt siding, L-shaped, approx. 14' x 50', three stories, flat roof with mansard front, gabled dormer, bay windows, entrance porch with latticework. Built 1900; fire damaged and vacant. 1 ext. photo (1985); 2 data pages including floor plans (1985). LC code: PA,22-HARBU,12. See also other half of house *1620 Hunter Street* (House) (PA-5203B).

1620 Hunter Street (House) (PA-5203B). One side of semi-detached house, frame with shingles, L-shaped, approx. 14' x 50', three stories, flat roof with mansard front, gabled dormer, bay windows, entrance porch with latticework. Built 1900; fire damaged and vacant. 4 ext. photos including streetscape (1985); 2 data pages including floor plans (1985). LC code: PA,22-HARBU,13. See also other half of house *1618 Hunter Street* (House) (PA-5203A).

1152 Market Street (House) (PA-5203C). One half of brick row house, L-shaped, two two-bay sections, three stories, flat roof, bracketed cornice. Built ca. 1889-1901; vacant. 3 ext. photos (1985); 2 data pages including floor plans (1985). LC code: PA,22-HARBU,14A. See also other half of house *1152 1/2 Market Street* (House) (PA-5203D).

1152 1/2 Market Street (House) (PA-5203D). One half of brick row house, L-shaped, two two-bay sections, three stories, flat roof, bracketed cornice. Built ca. 1889-1901; vacant. 3 ext. photos including streetscapes (1985); 2 data pages including floor plans (1985). LC code: PA,22-HARBU,14B. See also other half of house *1152 Market Street* (House) (PA-5203C).

1400 Regina Street (Commercial Building/House) (PA-5203E). Frame with brick-patterned asphalt siding, three-story row house with two-story addition on W elevation, flat roofs, wooden storefront with pilasters and cornice, corner entrance. Built ca. 1880; additions and storefront added early 1900s; vacant. 6 ext. photos including streetscape (1985); 2 data pages including floor plans (1985). LC code: PA,22-HARBU,15A. See also other houses in row 1400 1/2-1408 Regina Street (Houses) (PA-5203 F-J).

1400 1/2 Regina Street (House) (PA-5203F). One half of row house, frame with brick-patterned asphalt siding, L-shaped, approx. 12' (two-bay front) x 52', three stories, flat roof with front mansard, gabled dormers, bracketed cornice, wooden pilasters and cornice surround door. Built ca. 1880; vacant. 1 ext. photo (1985); 2 data pages including floor plans (1985). LC code: PA,22-HARBU,15B. See also other houses in row 1400-8 Regina Street (Houses) (PA-5203 E-J).

1402 Regina Street (House) (PA-5203G). One half of row house, frame with brick-patterned asphalt siding, L-shaped, approx. 12'-6" (two-bay front) x 46', three stories, flat roof with front mansard, gabled dormer, bracketed cornice, wooden pilasters and cornice surround door. Built ca. 1880; vacant. 2 data pages including floor plans (1985). LC code: PA,22-HARBU,15C. See also other houses in row 1400-8 Regina Street (Houses) (PA- 5203 E-J).

1404 Regina Street (House) (PA-5203H). Frame with clapboarding, L-shaped row house, approx. 20' (three-bay front) x 63', three stories, flat roof with front mansard, pedimented dormers, bracketed cornice, wooden pilasters and cornice surround door. Built ca. 1880; vacant. 1 ext. photo (1985); 2 data pages including floor plans (1985). LC code: PA,22-HARBU,16. See also other houses in row 1400-8 Regina Street (Houses) (PA-5203 E-J).

1406 Regina Street (House) (PA-5203I). Frame with brick-patterned asphalt siding, L-shaped row house, approx. 20' (three-bay front) x 61', three stories, flat roof with front mansard, pedimented dormers, bracketed cornice, wooden pilasters and bracketed cornice surround door. Built ca. 1880; vacant. 2 ext. photos (1985); 2 data pages including floor plans (1985). LC code: PA,22-HARBU,17. See also other houses in row 1400-8 Regina Street (Houses) (PA-5203 E-J).

1408 Regina Street (House) (PA-5203J). Frame with clapboarding and brick-patterned asphalt siding, L-shaped row house, approx. 20' (three-bay front) x 56', three stories, flat roof with front mansard, pedimented dormer, bracketed cornice, wooden pilasters and cornice surround door. Built ca. 1880; vacant. 2 ext. photos (1985); 2 data pages including floor plans (1985). LC code: PA,22-HARBU,18. See also other houses in row 1400-8 Regina Street (Houses) (PA-5203 E-I).

1526 Regina Street (House) (PA-5203K). One side of semi-detached house, frame with clapboarding, L-shaped, approx. 17' x 62', three stories, flat roof with front mansard, gabled dormer, cornice with brackets and dentils, bay window, porch with columns and denticulated cornice. Built ca. 1880; vacant. 2 ext. photos (1985); 2 data pages including floor plans (1985). LC code: PA,22-HARBU,19A. See also other half of house *1528 Regina Street* (House) (PA-5203L).

1528 Regina Street (House) (PA-5203L). One side of semi-detached house, frame with asphalt siding, L-shaped, approx. 17' x 58', three stories, flat roof with front mansard, gabled dormer, cornice with brackets and dentils, bay window, porch with columns and denticulated cornice. Built ca. 1880; vacant. 3 ext. photos including streetscapes (1985); 2 data pages including floor plans (1985). LC code: PA,22-HARBU,19B. See also other half of house *1526 Regina Street* (House) (PA-5203K).

1415 Shoop Street (House) (PA-5203M). Frame with shingles, L-shaped row house, approx. 12' (two-bay front) x 48', two-and-a-half stories, gable roof with pedimented dormer. Built ca. 1889-1901; vacant. 2 ext. photos (1985); 2 data pages including floor plans (1985). LC code: PA,22-HARBU,20D. See also other houses in row 1417-21 Shoop Street (Houses) (PA- 5203 N-P).

1417 Shoop Street (House) (PA-5203N). Frame with shingles, L-shaped row house, approx. 12' (two-bay front) x 48', two-and-a-half stories, gable roof with pedimented dormer. Built ca. 1889-1901; vacant. 1 ext. photo (1985); 2 data pages including floor plans (1985). LC code: PA,22-HARBU,20C. See also other houses in row 1415-21 Shoop Street (Houses) (PA-5203 M-P).

1419 Shoop Street (House) (PA-5203O). Frame with clapboarding, L-shaped row house, approx. 12' (two-bay front) x 48', two-and-a-half stories, gable roof with pedimented dormer. Built ca. 1889-1901; vacant. 1 ext. photo (1985); 2 data pages including floor plans (1985). LC code: PA,22-HARBU,20B. See also other houses in row 1415-21 Shoop Street (Houses) (PA-5203 M-P).

1421 Shoop Street (House) (PA-5203P). Frame with brick-patterned asphalt siding, L-shaped row house, approx. 12' (two-bay front) x 48', two-and-a-half stories, gable roof with pedimented dormer. Built ca. 1889-1901; vacant. 4 ext. photos including streetscapes (1985); 2 data pages including floor plans (1985). LC code: PA,22-HARBU,20A. See also other houses in row 1415-19 Shoop Street (Houses) (PA-5203 M-O).

63 North Sixteenth Street (House) (PA-5203S). Frame with brick-patterned asphalt siding, L-shaped row house, approx. 14' (two-bay front) x 62', two-and-a-half stories, gable roof with gabled dormer, bracketed cornice, wooden porch with turned posts and brackets (little remains of porch). Built 1901; vacant. 2 ext. photos (1985); 2 data pages including floor plans (1985). LC code: PA,22-HARBU,22E. See also other houses in row 65-71 North Sixteenth Street (Houses) (PA-5203 T-W).

65 North Sixteenth Street (House) (PA-5203T). Frame with brick-patterned asphalt siding, L-shaped row house, approx. 13' (two-bay front) x 52', two-and-a-half stories, gable roof with gabled dormer, bracketed cornice, wooden porch with turned posts and brackets. Built 1901; vacant. 1 ext. photo (1985); 2 data pages including floor plans (1985). LC code: PA,22-HARBU,22D. See also other houses in row 63-71 North Sixteenth Street (Houses) (PA-5203 S-W).

67 North Sixteenth Street (House) (PA-5203U). Frame with brick-patterned asphalt siding, L-shaped row house, approx. 12'-6" (two-bay front) x 52', two-and-a-half stories, gable roof with gabled dormer, bracketed cornice, wooden porch with turned posts and brackets. Built 1901; vacant. 3 ext. photos (1985); 2 data pages including floor plans (1985). LC code: PA,22-HARBU,22C. See also other houses in row 63-71 North Sixteenth Street (Houses) (PA-5203 S-W).

69 North Sixteenth Street (House) (PA-5203V). Frame with brick-patterned asphalt siding, L-shaped row house, approx. 12'-6" (two-bay front) x 52', two-and-a-half stories, gable roof with gabled dormer, bracketed cornice, wooden porch with turned posts and brackets. Built 1901; vacant. 1 ext. photo (1985); 2 data pages including floor plans (1985). LC code: PA,22-HARBU,22B. See also other houses in row 63-71 North Sixteenth Street (Houses) (PA-5203 S-W).

71 North Sixteenth Street (House) (PA-5203W). Frame with brick-patterned asphalt siding and clapboarding, L-shaped row house, approx. 13' (two-bay front) x 50', two-and-a-half stories, gable roof with gabled dormer, bracketed cornice, wooden porch with turned posts and brackets (partially gone). Built 1901; vacant. 4 ext. photos including streetscape (1985); 2 data pages including floor plans (1985). LC code: PA,22-HARBU,22A. See also other houses in row 63-69 North Sixteenth Street (Houses) (PA-5203 S- V).

38 North Twelfth Street (House) (PA-5203Q). One side of semi-detached house, brick, approx. 16' (three-bay first story, two-bay upper stories) x 45'-6", three stories, flat roof, wooden cornice with finials and brick corbels, porch with pedimented central gable and iron supports (replaced original Ionic columns). Built 1910; vacant. 2 ext. photos (1985); 2 data pages including floor plans (1985). LC code: PA,22-HARBU,21A. See also other half of house *40 North Twelfth Street* (House) (PA-5203R).

40 North Twelfth Street (House) (PA-5203R). One side of semi-detached house, brick, approx. 16' (three-bay first story, two-bay upper stories) x 49'-6", three stories, flat roof, wooden cornice with finials and brick corbels, porch with pedimented central gable and Ionic columns. Built 1910; vacant. 2 ext. photos including streetscape (1985); 2 data pages including floor plans (1985). LC code: PA,22-HARBU,21B. See also other half of house *38 North Twelfth Street* (House) (PA-5203Q).

Broad Street Market, Frame Wing (PA-1156), Verbeke St., between Third and Sixth Sts. Frame with board and batten siding, 86'-6" x 50'-1", one-story market area with central mezzanine in roof monitor, low gable roof with central gabled monitor, series of windows and doors protected by roof overhang, clerestory windows in monitor. Built 1869 as addition to original market building; demolished 1977. Original stone market building built 1856- 60; frame wing added on E elevation 1869; separate adjacent brick building built in three sections 1874, 1877, 1886; stone and brick buildings restored 1976-77. Market has been in continuous operation since 1863, one of the oldest markets in the state. 3 sheets (1977, including site plans, plans, elevations, section); 2 ext. photos (1977), 2 int. photos (1974); 1 data page (1984). LC code: PA,22-HARBU,4A. NR.

Cathedral House. See Griffith, William R., House.

Elder, John, House (PA-32), 2426 Ellerslie St. Random rubble with frame kitchen wing, irregular L-shaped, 41'-7" (four bay front) x 31'-5" (two bays) with setback kitchen wing to side 20'-1" (two bays) x 17'-3", two-and-a-half stories with basement, gable roof with cross gable forming large dormers; central hall plan. Built 1740; porches added; frame shed attached to rear porch connects house with stone milk shed. Oldest house in Harrisburg. Stone bank barn built 1744, demolished. 7 sheets (1935, including site plan, plans, elevations, sections, details); 1 ext photo (1935), 1 copy photo (ca. 1875); 2 data pages (1936). LC code: PA,22-PAX,2.

First Capitol Buildings. See State Capitol Complex, Original.

Griffith, William R., House (Saint Stephen's Protestant Episcopal Cathedral Church, Dean's House; Cathedral House) (PA-39), 215 N. Front St. Brick, L-shaped, 28'-2" (three-bay front) x 40'-3" with kitchen ell to E (16' x 50'-2"), two-and-a-half stories with basement, low gable roof with narrow pedimented gable ends, hip roof on ell, attic windows in frieze, door with transom and side lights flanked by pilasters on W (front) elevation, arcaded porch across W elevation (original Ionic entrance porch moved to S elevation 1931, restored to W elevation 1950 when arcaded porch removed), one-story laundry wing to rear of ell; side hall plan. Built 1840-43; attributed to Stephen Hills, architect; St. Stephen's acquired house 1915; restored 1950; used for classrooms. 16 sheets (1935, including plans, elevations, details); 3 ext. photos (1935), 2 int. photos (1935); 1 data page (1936). LC code: PA, 22-HARBU,2. NR (Also in Harrisburg Historic District).

1618-20 Hunter Street (Houses). See Allison Hill (Houses).

Maclay, William, House (PA-310), 401 N. Front St. Coursed rubble, L-shaped, 48'-8" (five-bay front) x 33'-5" with rear kitchen ell (20' x 15'-9"), two-and-a-half stories with elevated basement and one-story ell, gable roof with pedimented gable ends, decorative wooden cornice; central hall plan. Built 1792; extensively altered 1909, elevated basement now main entrance with semicircular Ionic entrance porch (original door replaced with window with broken scroll pediment), dormers added, original ell replaced with two large additions; now Pennsylvania Bar Association. William Maclay was a member of the first United States Senate. 5 sheets (measured 1909 before alterations, drawn 1935, including plans, elevations, details); 1 copy photo (ca. 1870); 2 data pages (1936). LC code: PA,22-HARBU,3. NR (Harrisburg Historic District).

1152-52 1/2 Market Street (Houses). See Allison Hill (Houses).

1400-8 Regina Street (Houses). See Allison Hill (Houses).

1526-28 Regina Street (Houses). See Allison Hill (Houses).

Saint Stephen's Protestant Episcopal Cathedral Church, Dean's House. See Griffith, William R., House.

1415-21 Shoop Street (Houses). See Allison Hill (Houses).

63-71 North Sixteenth Street (Houses). See Allison Hill (Houses).

North Sixth Street (Houses) (PA-5204), bounded on the N by Radnor St., on the E by Jefferson St., on the S by Maclay St., and on the W by Bersinger Alley. Late-nineteenth- and early-twentieth-century commercial corridor along North Sixth St. with adjacent residential streets, developed as city expanded northward, city trolley line ran on North Sixth St. (formerly Ridge Rd.) and main line of the Pennsylvania Railroad was three blocks E, mostly two to three-story brick row houses, diverse late-nineteenth-century architectural styles. Developed primarily between 1880 and 1920; currently area deteriorating. 6 data pages including maps of area (1985). LC code: PA,22-HARBU,6. See following entries on individual structures (PA-5204 A-D)

2533 Agate Street (House) (PA-5204A). Brick row house, approx. 13' (two-bay front) x 49', two stories, flat roof with brick parapet, corbeled brick cornice, brick arches over openings, wooden entrance porch with turned posts and brackets, rear porch and balcony. Built ca. 1901-09; vacant. 6 ext. photos including streetscape (1985); 2 data pages including floor plan (1985). LC code: PA,22-HARBU,7. See also other houses in row 2535-39 Agate Street (Houses) (PA-5204 B-D).

2535 Agate Street (House) (PA-5204B). Brick row house, L-shaped, approx. 13' (two-bay front) x 49', two stories, flat roof with brick parapet, corbeled brick cornice, brick arches over openings, wooden entrance porch with turned posts and brackets, rear porch and balcony. Built ca. 1901-09; vacant. 1 ext. photo (1985); 2 data pages including floor plans (1985). LC code: PA,22-HARBU,8. See also other houses in row 2533-39 Agate Street (Houses) (PA-5204 A-D).

2537 Agate Street (House) (PA-5204C). Brick row house, L-shaped, approx. 13' (two-bay front) x 49', two stories, flat roof with brick parapet, corbeled brick cornice, brick arches over openings, wooden entrance porch with turned posts and brackets, rear porch and balcony. Built ca. 1901-09; vacant. 1 ext. photo (1985); 2 data pages including floor plans (1985). LC code: PA,22-HARBU,9. See also other houses in row 2533-39 Agate Street (Houses) (PA-5204 A-D).

2539 Agate Street (House) (PA-5204D). Brick row house, L-shaped, approx. 13' (two-bay front) x 49', two stories, flat roof with brick parapet, corbeled brick cornice, brick arches over openings, wooden entrance porch with turned posts and brackets, rear porch and balcony. Built ca. 1901-09; vacant. 2 ext. photos including streetscape (1985); 2 data pages including floor plans (1985). LC code: PA,22-HARBU,10. See also other houses in row 2533-37 Agate Street (Houses) (PA-5204 A-C).

State Capitol Complex, Original (PA-37), on site of present State Capitol grounds, Capitol flanked by Land Office to SE and Treasury to NW. Capitol: brick, rectangular with slightly projecting terminal pavilions and concave semicircular entrance with semicircular Ionic portico, 171' (thirteen-bay front) x 80'-9" (five bays), two stories with basement, hip roof with colonnaded drum and dome; Senate Chamber on NW side and Hall of Representatives on SE side. Built 1816-22; Stephen Hills, architect; wing added (not recorded); burned 1897. Land Office and Treasury (same design): brick, rectangular with projecting terminal pavilions, approx. 64' (five-bay front) x 40', two stories with basement, hip roofs, semicircular Ionic porticos. Built 1812-16; Stephen Hills, architect; large additions (not recorded); demolished ca. 1901. 3 sheets (1935, including plans, elevations); 4 copy photos (n.d.); 2 data pages (1936). LC code: PA,22-HARBU,1.

Telegram Building (PA-5370), 227 Walnut St. Brick with iron and wood framing, 24'-2" (three-bay front) x 91', five stories with basement, flat roof, bay windows, decorative wooden spandrels and cornice topped with broken pediment, Queen Anne style details; original elevator mechanism remains. Built 1887-88; John C. Smith and James H. Warner, architects; storefront altered 1965; demolished. Built to house Sunday newspaper, *The Telegram*. 5 ext. photos (1988), 6 int. photos (1988); 19 data pages including floor plans and historical views (1988). LC code: PA,22-HARBU,24.

38-40 North Twelfth Street (House). See Allison Hill (Houses).

United States Post Office and Courthouse (PA-1255), NW corner of Walnut and Third Sts. Coursed ashlar (rusticated first story), rectangular with projecting center pavilion, seven by three bays, three stories, hip roofs, modillioned cornice, arched doorways and windows with fanlights, large arched windows with molded archivolts and pilasters on third floor of central pavilion (courtroom), belt courses, Classical Revival style; post office on first and second stories, courtroom on third story. Built 1877-82; James G. Hill, Supervising Architect of the Treasury Department; John DeHaven, local supervisor; addition (three bays deep) built 1918 almost doubling size of the building; demolished 1965. 4 ext. photos (1964), 1 int. photo (1964), 1 copy photo (1877); 1 data page (1984). LC code: PA,22-HARBU,5.

Highspire Vicinity (Lower Swatara Township)

Burd, Colonol James, House. See Tinian.

Tinian (Colonel James Burd House) (PA-34), N side of Rosedale Ave., .4 mi. E of Lumber St., .6 mi. E of Highspire. Random rubble (stuccoed ca. 1870, stucco removed after 1936), 30'-2" (three-bay front) x 28'-2", two-and-a-half stories, gable roof, transom over W (front) door. Built ca. 1768; two-and-a-half-story frame wing (30'-2" x 20'-2") with entrance porches added to E ca. 1870 (porches removed after 1936); porch added on W elevation (changed to two-story porch after 1936); door on W elevation and porch on N elevation added after 1936. 9 sheets (1935, including plans, elevations, details); 1 ext photo (1935), 1 copy photo (ca. 1870), 1 copy photo of Colonel Burd; 5 data pages (1936). LC code: PA,22-HISPI.V,1.

Linglestown Vicinity (West Hanover Township)

Mackey, Captain James, House (PA-312), 6648 Fox Hill Rd., 1.5 mi. NE of Linglestown. Log with clapboarding, L-shaped, 28'-8" (three-bay front) x 28'-10" with 18'-2" kitchen ell to N, two-and-a-half stories with basement and one-and-a-half-story ell, gable roof with shed roof on ell, porch on S (front) elevation; side hall plan. Built ca. 1730; frame shed added to ell; covered with stucco and asphalt shingles after 1935. 13 sheets (1935, including plans, elevations, sections, details). LC code: PA,22-LING.V,1.

Middletown Borough

Saint Peter's Kierch. See Saint Peter's United Lutheran Church.

Saint Peter's United Lutheran Church (Saint Peter's Kierch) (PA-36), 31 W. High St., NW corner of W. High and N. Union Sts. Irregular coursed ashlar and random rubble, 40' (three-bay front) x 46' (three bays), one story with galleries, gable roof, semi-elliptical doorway on E (front) elevation, Georgian style; high pulpit supported on column. Built 1767 (date stone); George Lowman, stonemason; tower with cupola and spire added 1813; original windows of church on two levels joined to form long narrow windows 1850. Good example of an early German Lutheran Church.

5 sheets (1935, including site plan, plans, elevations, sections, details); 2 ext. photos (1936), 2 int. photos (1935); 1 data page (1936). LC code: PA,22-MIDTO,1. NR.

Paxtang Borough

Elder House. See Harrisburg, Elder, John, House.

Paxton Presbyterian Church (PA-31), NE corner of Paxtang Ave. (State Rte. 543) and Sharon St. Random rubble, 65'-10" (five-bay front) x 36' (three bays), one story, gable roof, transom over S (front) entrance, semi-elliptical stone arches over openings; vaulted ceiling. Built 1740; porch added across E elevation; galleries added and windows added at gallery level 1931; random rubble school wing added to W (not recorded). Oldest church in Dauphin County. 8 sheets (1935, including site plan, plans, elevations, section, details); 4 ext. photos (1935); 1 data page (1936). LC code: PA,22-PAX,1.

Paxtang Vicinity

Willow Dale Farm. See Progress (Susquehanna Township), Willow Dale Farmhouse.

Paxtang Vicinity (Swatara Township)

Rutherford Stone House, Springhouse (PA-33), W side of Paxtang Ave. (State Rte. 543), in Paxtang Park next to Spring Creek. Random rubble, 28' (three-bay front) x 20'-9", one-and-a-half stories with cellar at creek level, gable roof; two rooms. Built before 1755 (ca. 1740); poor condition 1935; restored. 4 sheets (1935, including site plan, plans, elevations, section, details); 1 ext. photo (1935); 1 data page (1936). LC code: PA,22-PAX,3.

Progress (Susquehanna Township)

Willow Dale Farmhouse (PA-35), N side of Union Deposit Rd. (State Rte. 183), .1 mi. W of S. Progress Ave. (State Rte. 543). Brick, T-shaped, 41'-9" (five-bay front) x 32'-1" (two bays), two-and-a-half stories with basement, gable roof, wooden lintels with keystones, transom over S (front) doorway; random rubble kitchen wing (18'-4" x 22'-1") connected to rear by frame wing (18'-4" x 10'); central hall plan. Built ca. 1758; carved porch and bracketed cornice added ca. 1860; demolished ca. 1970. 5 sheets (1935, including plans, elevations, details); 2 ext. photos (1935); 2 data pages (1936). LC code: PA,22-PAX.V,1.

Delaware County

Broomall Vicinity

Massey, Thomas, House. See Lawrence Park (Marple Township), Massey, Thomas, House.

Chadds Ford (Birmingham Township)

Chad, John, House (PA-1256), E side of State Rte. 100, .2 mi. N of Baltimore Pike (U.S. Rte. 1). Museum operated by Chadds Ford Historical Society. Random rubble, 28' (three-bay front) x 18', two-and-a-half stories on sloping site exposing basement, gable roof, door with transom on S (front) elevation. Built ca. 1725; possibly built by John Wyeth, Jr. (initials "J.W.Jr." carved next to second story right window on S elevation); porch added across S elevation (removed during restoration); restored 1970s, pent roof and eaves reconstructed, shed to W (removed between 1843 and 1895) reconstructed. Associated with the Battle of Brandywine. 3 ext. photos (1958), 10 int. photos (1958), 4 copy photos from 1855, ca. 1905, ca. 1930, ca. 1952; 4 data pages (1958, 1984). LC code: PA,23-CHAF,2. NR (Also Brandywine Battlefield NHL).

> *Springhouse* (PA-1256A), W side of State Rte. 100. Random rubble, one story, gable roof. Built early eighteenth century. 1 ext. photo (1958). LC code: PA,23-CHAF,2A.

Gilpin, Joseph, House (Lafayette Quarters) (PA-1116), N side of Baltimore Pike (U.S. Rte. 1), 1.1 mi. E of State Rte. 100, in Brandywine Battlefield State Park. Museum administered by Pennsylvania Historical and Museum Commission. Random rubble, 18'-2" (two-bay front) x 30'-1", two-and-a-half stories, gable roof, pent roof and pent eaves; wing on E, half-timber with clapboarding, 17'-6" (three-bay front) x 20'-2", one-and-a-half stories, steep gable roof, casement windows with diamond panes; kitchen addition to N, random rubble, 21'-9" x 19', one-and-a-half stories, gable roof, bake oven on N elevation covered with wooden superstructure. Stone house built 1745 (date stone); N addition built 1782 (date stone) replacing earlier frame wing; ca. 1820-50 half-timber wing moved from another site and added to house (possibly early house from Gilpin tract built ca. 1700); ca. 1850-90 rear wing extended with frame addition (later removed); ca. 1930 porch added across front elevation (later removed); restored ca. 1950. Good examples of early stone and half-timber houses. House used as Lafayette's headquarters during the Battle of Brandywine. 3 ext. photos (1958), 4 int. photos (1958), 1 copy photo from 1930, 1 copy photo of undated sketch; 10 data pages (1958). LC code: PA,23-CHAF.V,1. NHL (Brandywine Battlefield NHL).

Cart House (PA-1116A). Random rubble, 23' x 23', one-and-a-half stories, gable roof, S side open. Built 1798 by Isaac G. Gilpin (date stone); restored ca. 1950. 1 ext. photo (1958). LC code: PA,23-CHAF.V,1A.

Root House (PA-1116B). Random rubble, one story, gable roof, door on W elevation with small door above. Built 1809 by Joseph Gilpin's son Gideon (date stone "18GG09"); restored ca. 1950. 1 ext. photo (1958). LC code: PA,23-CHAF.V,1B.

Springhouse (PA-1116C). Random rubble, one story partially under ground level, gable roof. Built ca. 1830-50; restored ca. 1950. 1 ext. photo (1958). LC code: PA,23-CHAF.V,1C.

Lafayette Quarters. See Gilpin, Joseph, House.

Clifton Heights Vicinity (Upper Darby Township)

Lower Swedish Log Cabin (PA-135), at end of Creek Rd., on E bank of Darby Creek, 1 mi. N of Clifton Heights. Log, one story with attic, gable roof, two stone chimneys on N roof slope; two rooms of unequal size with two corner fireplaces. Possibly built ca. 1640-50 (original cabin was one room W section); shed added on S elevation at W end; screened porch added on S elevation at E end; random rubble and frame addition on E elevation; owned by Upper Darby Township, porches and sheds removed. Built by early Swedish settlers, this is one of the few remaining Swedish Colonial cabins and possibly the oldest extant log structure in country. 7 sheets (1940, including plans, elevations, section, details); 3 ext. photos (1937, 1940), 1 int. photo (1940); 1 data page (1937). LC code: PA,23-DARB.V,2. NR.

Upper Swedish Log Cabin (PA-136), Behind 3860 Dennison Ave., on bluff above Darby Creek. Log, one story with attic and cellar, gable roof with overhanging eaves, attic overhangs on SW elevation; two rooms of unequal size. Possibly built ca. 1650 (original cabin was one room SW section); altered after 1900, wing with porch added on NE elevation (porch removed), porch added on SW elevation (removed), windows and shingles added in gable ends, shed dormer added on SE roof slope; destroyed ca. 1982. Built by early Swedish settlers, this is one of the few remaining Swedish Colonial cabins and possibly one of the oldest extant log structures in country. 4 sheets (1940, including plans, elevations, section); 4 ext. photos (1937, 1940); 1 data page (1937). LC code: PA,23-DARB.V,3.

Concordville (Concord Township)

House (Mendenhall House) (PA-174), original location on dirt road .1 mi. S of U.S. Rte. 1 (Baltimore Pike), .1 mi. W of intersection with U.S. Rte 322 (Conchester Rd.). Frame with novelty siding (siding not original), three-bay front, two-and-a-half stories, gable roof with dormers, pent roof, exposed brick and stone chimney wall on W elevation; large cooking fireplace with wooden crane and bake oven. Built ca. 1720; two- and three-story frame wings added; large window cut in E elevation; donated to Chester County Historical Society, original section dismantled 1968 and placed in storage; reassembled 1970s in Bacton (East Whiteland Township), Chester County, adjacent to John Jacobs House (PA-1209); moved 1980s to Birchrunville (West Vincent Township), Chester County, on Hollow Rd., approx. .25 mi. E of Horseshoe Trail. Possibly built by the Mendenhall family, a prominent Quaker family. One of the earliest frame houses in area. 3 ext. photos (1968), 11 int. photos (1968, taken during dismantling, show frame construction). LC code: PA,23-CON,2.

Mendenhall House. See House (Mendenhall House) (PA-174).

Darby Borough

Bonsall House (PA-127), 1009 Main St. Frame with clapboarding and wooden shingles and vertical siding, three-bay front, two-and-a-half stories with basement, steep gable roof, pent roof, deep cornice. Built ca. 1745; two-story addition to rear; demolished. Was the oldest house in Darby and a notable example of pent roof construction introduced by the Rhine Valley Germans. 3 ext. photos (1940). LC code: PA,23-DARB,1.

Darby Vicinity

Lower Swedish Cabin. See Clifton Heights Vicinity (Upper Darby Township), Lower Swedish Log Cabin.

Upper Swedish Cabin. See Clifton Heights Vicinity (Upper Darby Township), Upper Swedish Log Cabin.

Dilworthtown (Birmingham Township)

Brinton 1704 House (PA-1258), E side of Oakland Rd., just W of Wilmington West Chester Pike (U.S. Rte. 202-322), .4 mi. S of Brintons Bridge Rd. Museum operated by Chester County Historical Society. Coursed rubble, 40' (three irregular bays) x 22', two-and-a-half stories, steep gable roof with shed dormers, pent eaves and roof, casement windows with diamond panes, door with transom and entrance porch on S (front) elevation. Built 1704 for William Brinton; frame wing added to E elevation nineteenth century; front porch added late 1820s; Carpenter Gothic details (front gable and porch around building) added 1870s; stone wing added to N and porch added to W 1881; restored 1954-55 (stone wing and all other nineteenth-century features removed), G. Edwin Brumbaugh, restoration architect. A large medieval type of English Quaker dwelling. 4 ext. photos (1958), 5 int. photos (1958), 1 copy photo of view from ca. 1870s, 1 copy photo of oil painting by Thomas Eakins from 1878; 12 data pages (1958). LC code: PA,23-DIL.V,1. NHL (Also in Brandywine Battlefield NHL).

Privy (PA-1258A). Stuccoed stone, approx. 10' x 8', one story, gable roof, double door of vertical boards with strap hinges. Built late eighteenth century. 1 ext. photo (1958). LC code: PA,23-DIL.V,1A.

Essington (Tinicum Township)

Lazaretto (PA-125), S side of Second Ave., opposite Wanamaker Ave. (State Rte. 420), on Delaware River. Brick, five-bay central block with nine-bay flanking wings, three-and-a-half-story main block with two-and-a-half-story wings, hip roof with dormers and balustrade with domed cupola on main block and gable roofs with dormers on wings; central hall plan. Built 1799-1800; porch added across S (front) elevation; rear addition; now a seaplane base and yacht club. Built as a quarantine hospital, eventually the complex included seven major buildings and many minor structures (main building, one block house, the physician's house, and two small outbuildings remain). 4 ext. photos (1936), 1 undated copy photo, 1 copy photo of 1895 drawing; 3 data pages (1937). LC code: PA,23-ESTO,1. NR.

Guard House (PA-125A). Stuccoed, one story, hip roof, window set in large recessed arch on S elevation. Built 1799-1800; originally there were two symmetrically placed Guard Houses on the Delaware River flanked by a balustrade (one Guard House demolished). 1 ext. photo (1936).

Outbuilding (PA-125B). Brick, one story, gable roof. Built 1799-1800; now used as a garage; deteriorating. 1 ext. photo (1936).

Stable (PA-125C). Brick, five irregular bays, two stories, gable roof. Built 1799-1800; stable is outbuilding for the physician's house; deteriorating. 1 ext. photo (1936).

Haverford Vicinity

Pont Reading House. See Havertown Vicinity (Haverford Township), Pont Reading House.

Havertown Vicinity (Haverford Township)

Flintlock (Joseph Reese House) (PA-1230), 1543 Lawrence Rd., approx. 1 mi. W of Havertown. Log covered with board and batten siding with random rubble chimney wall to W, three-bay front, two-and-a-half stories, gable roof. Built early eighteenth century; two-bay stone wing added to W 1725; frame shed added on N elevation of wing; porch added on wing; frame wing added to E elevation of original section. 2 ext. photos (1963), 3 photos of int. wall construction details (1963); 1 data page (1983). LC code: PA,23-HAVTO.V,1.

Haverford Meetinghouse (Quaker Meetinghouse) (PA-179), S side of Eagle Rd., .4 mi. W of Haverford Rd., approx. 1 mi. N of Havertown. Random rubble, one-and-a-half stories, gable roof, porch across front elevation. Built 1690, rebuilt 1700. 1 ext. photo (1926). LC code: PA,46-HAV,1.

Lawrence Cabin (PA-1238), S side of West Chester Pike (State Rte. 3), opposite Lawrence Rd., approx. 1.5 mi. SW of Havertown. Museum. Log with random rubble chimney wall on W elevation, one-and-a-half stories, gable roof; one room with loft. Built early eighteenth century; two-and-a-half-story random rubble wing (two-bay front) added to E elevation ca. 1750; dormers added; stuccoed frame summer kitchen added to log section; random rubble wing and summer kitchen demolished 1961; log section moved to Powder Mill Park, S side of Karakung Drive between Mill Rd. and Manoa Rd., in 1961 by Haverford Township Historical Society. Log cabin resembles those built by Swedish settlers in the area. 11 ext. photos (1960), 1 int. photo (1960); 1 data page (1983). LC code: PA,23-HAVTO.V,2.

Nitre Hall Powder Magazine (PA-1279), W side of Karakung Drive, between Mill Rd. and Manoa Rd., approx. 1 mi. E of Havertown, in Powder Mill Park. Random rubble, approx. 30'-1" x 39'-11", one story. Built ca. 1805-10; ca. 1905 W wall removed and rebuilt askew to make room for railroad tracks; roof destroyed; only masonry walls, one door, and some floor joists remain. The only remaining mill building of the Nitre Hall Mills, one of the leading gunpowder-producing mills until middle of nineteenth century. 2 sheets (1973, including plot plan, plan, elevation). LC code: PA,23-HAVTO.V,3A. NR.

Pont Reading House (PA-1239), 2713 Haverford Rd., approx. 1 mi. N of Havertown. T-shaped building with rear wing, construction spans three centuries: 1683 log house incorporated in two-and-a-half-story stuccoed stone center section (four bays) with curb roof built ca. 1730; one-and-a-half-story stuccoed stone kitchen wing built to rear before 1780; two-story stuccoed stone addition (three-bay front) with pedimented pavilion and distyle entrance porch built 1813; Greek Revival portico and pedimented dormers added to center section nineteenth century. 3 ext. photos (1964); 1 data page (1983). LC code: PA,23-HAFO.V,1. NR.

Quaker Meetinghouse. See Haverford Meetinghouse.

Reese, Joseph, House. See Flintlock.

Ithan

Godfrey, Lincoln, House. See Villanova Vicinity (Radnor Township), Godfrey, Lincoln, House.

Landingford Plantation

Pusey, Caleb, House. See Upland Borough, Pusey, Caleb, House.

Lawrence Park (Marple Township)

Massey, Thomas, House (PA-1257), 1696 Lawrence Rd., opposite Springhouse Ln. Museum operated by Marple-Newtown Historical Society and Marple Township. Brick, approx. 20' x 20', two-and-a-half stories, gable roof, stepped belt course, diaper brick work in E gable end. Built 1696 as addition to log house; log house replaced with two-and-a-half-story random rubble addition to W ca. 1730; gable roof on 1696 section lowered to match gable roof of 1730 section; casement windows replaced with sash windows ca. 1840; window cut in E gable end; one-and-a-half-story random rubble wing added to W of 1730 section ca. 1840; second story and attic added to 1840 section ca. 1860; porch and dormer added on 1730 section (removed 1965); cinderblock shed added to W over bake oven (replaced with clapboarded wing during restoration); roof restored to original pitch 1965; pent roofs restored on brick section and 1730 stone section; restoration completed 1973. Represents three periods of architecture; E section is one of the earliest brick houses surviving in Pennsylvania. 8 ext. photos (1964, 1968), 16 int. photos (1964, 1968); 1 data page (1983). LC code: PA,23-BROOM.V,1. NR.

Media Borough

Providence Quaker Meetinghouse (PA-180), E side of Providence Rd. (State Rte. 252), opposite E. State St. Random rubble, six-bay front, one-and-a-half stories, gable roof, two double entrances on W elevation with projecting pedimented porches. Built 1814; open shed added to S; four-bay stone addition built to N 1931; three-bay stone wing connected to N of 1931 wing by small passage; roof slope of 1814 section changed; restored. Meeting was established in 1684. 1 ext. photo (1926). LC code: PA,23-MED.V,1.

Norwood Borough

Mortonsen, Morton House (PA-1240), .1 mi. S of Winona Ave., on Darby Creek. Brick, 33'-8" (three-bay front) x 20'-6", two-and-a-half stories, gable roof, pent eaves and roofs, entrance porch with porch above on S (front) elevation, transoms over doors; wing to E, brick, 21'-7" (two-bay front) x 21', one-and-a-half stories, gambrel roof with shed dormers, initials "MM" on E elevation. Built 1730-40; heavily altered; E section only ruins; W section changed to three stories with windows altered and pent roofs and eaves missing; restored to eighteenth-century appearance ca. 1968. 7 sheets (1966, before restoration, including plans, elevations, sections, details). LC code: PA,23-NOR,1.

Radnor

Old Saint David's Protestant Episcopal Church. See Saint David's Vicinity (Newtown Township), Saint David's Protestant Episcopal Church.

Radnor (Radnor Township)

Bel Orme (PA-1001), W side of County Line Rd., opposite Meadowcroft Rd. Random rubble, two connected sections of two bays each (contains original L-shaped farmhouse), two-and-a-half stories, gable roofs, shed roof over N (original front) entrance, projecting hood over S entrance. Original L-shaped farmhouse built ca. 1806-15 by Nathan Brooke; ca. 1900 minor alterations (half-timbering and stucco applied) probably by architect George B. Shaw; 1917 additions by architect Wilson Eyre, two-story random rubble wing with jerkinhead roof added to W elevation, large two-story stuccoed wing with hip roof added to E elevation, half-timbering and stucco removed; 1938 minor alterations by Lester H. Sellers. 2 ext. photos (1958), 1 int. photo (1958); 4 data pages (1958). LC code: PA,23-RAD,3.

Bolingbroke (Saint Martin's Parish Hall) (PA-1000), W side of King of Prussia Rd., .1 mi. N of Glen Mary Rd. Random rubble, irregular ten-bay front, two-and-a-half stories, gable roof with dormers, pedimented hood over N (front) entrance, two-story porch on W elevation, two-story portico on S elevation. Numerous additions have transformed a small farmhouse into a large mansion; originally a two-and-a-half-story random rubble farmhouse built ca. 1700 (third and fourth bays from the E); 1792 (date stone with initials of owner David Brooke) two-and-a-half-story random rubble wing added to E (last two bays on E); 1901 two-and-a-half-story random rubble wing added to W (middle two bays), continuous roofline added on S side, new front entrance added; 1908 addition to S covered original rear wall, two-and-a-half-story random rubble wing added to W doubling size of house, roof on S extended to overhang and columns added to form two-story portico, W end extended to incorporate original (ca. 1748) springhouse; 1901 and 1908 additions by R. Brognard Okie, architect. 4 ext. photos (1958), 1 int. photo (1958), 1 copy photo (ca. 1897); 5 data pages (1958). LC code: PA,23-RAD,2.

Gaybrook. See Hillside.

Hillside (Gaybrook) (PA-1002), W side of King of Prussia Rd., .1 mi. S of Gulph Creek Rd. Stuccoed random rubble, five irregular bays, two stories, gable roof, pedimented hood over W door on S (front) elevation. Built before 1816 (probably eighteenth century); one-story two-bay random rubble wing with porch added to W elevation before 1830 (second story of frame added later); 1929 two-story set-back frame kitchen wing added to E elevation. A typical early Pennsylvania farmhouse of simple design which retains many original features. 2 ext. photos (1958), 1 int. photo (1958); 4 data pages (1958). LC code: PA,23-RAD,4.

Morgan Farmhouse (PA-1004), N side of Matson Ford Rd., .4 mi. E of King of Prussia Rd. Stuccoed random rubble, three-bay front, two-and-a-half stories, gable roof with dormers, pedimented hood over S (front) entrance; central hall plan. Built 1760-70; three-story stuccoed random rubble wing (three-bay front) added to W early nineteenth century; one-story stone and frame wing added on W addition; one-story frame addition on original section; deteriorating in 1958; demolished. 4 ext. photos (1958), 4 int. photos (1958); 5 data pages (1958). LC code: PA,23-RAD,5.

Barn (PA-1003). Large rectangular barn, random rubble lower level with frame above, projecting forebay on S supported by large tapered stone piers, gable roof. Built early nineteenth century; adjacent small outbuildings; deteriorating in 1958; demolished. Typical Pennsylvania barn of the early 1800s. 1 ext. photo (1958); 2 data pages (1958). LC code: PA,23-RAD,5.

Saint Martin's Church (PA-1242), NW corner of King of Prussia Rd. and Glen Mary Rd. Random rubble, three-bay front, one story with three-story entrance tower, steep gable roof, projecting crenelated entrance tower on center bay of S (front) elevation with gabled hood over doorway and buttresses at corners, pointed-arch windows; barrel vault ceiling. Built 1894; Theophilus P. Chandler, architect; two-story random rubble school wing added to W early 1900s (now church offices); nave extended to E and barrel vault ceiling removed early 1950s. 1 ext. and 1 int. copy photo taken prior to 1901; 1 data page (1983). LC code: PA,23-RAD,3.

Saint Martin's Parish Hall. See Bolingbroke.

Vanor (PA-193), W side of King of Prussia Rd., between Lancaster Pike (U.S. Rte. 30) and Matson Ford Rd. Stuccoed brick, five-bay front, three stories (originally two and a half stories, raised to three 1919), hip roof with balustrade and large central gable on S slope (balustrade and dormer added 1919), denticulated cornice, porch across S (front) elevation (replaced by semicircular porch with columns ca. 1890s-1919), projecting three-story bay added to center of N elevation, two-and-a-half-story stuccoed brick wing (three bays) to W. Built as small eighteenth-century farmhouse and enlarged to mansion in nineteenth and twentieth centuries; original house built ca. 1715 (said to be W wing, but brick not used in this area until 1800, so 1715 structure may be concealed); large E section built mid-nineteenth century; demolished 1958. 3 ext. photos (1958), 4 ext. copy photos from ca. 1880, ca. 1925; 5 data pages (1958). LC code: PA,23-RAD,2.

Radnor Vicinity

Nantmell Hall. See Saint Davids (Radnor Township), Nantmell Hall.

Saint Davids (Radnor Township)

Nantmell Hall (PA-192), NW corner of Lancaster Pike (U.S. Rte. 30) and Radnor Chester Rd. Stuccoed random rubble, three-bay front, two-and-a-half stories, gable roof; central hall plan. Built eighteenth century; large shed dormer added on S roof slope; entrance porch added on S (front) elevation; two-story frame wing added to N; farm until early twentieth century. when it became a golf club; deteriorated 1958; demolished. 2 ext. photos (1958), 1 int. photo (1958); 4 data pages (1958). LC code: PA,23-___,1.

Tenant House (PA-1066). Stuccoed random rubble, three-bay front, two-and-a-half stories, gable roof, two-story porch on S (front) elevation, pedimented hood over W entrance. Built early nineteenth century (after 1808); frame kitchen wing added to N elevation; demolished 1958. 1 ext. photo (1958), 2 int. photos (1958); 3 data pages (1958, 1961). LC code: PA,23-___,1A.

Saint Davids Vicinity (Newtown Township)

Saint David's Protestant Episcopal Church (PA-176), W side of Valley Forge Rd., .2 mi. NE of Church Rd. and Darby Paoli Rd. Random rubble, approx. 44' (three-bay front) x 27', one story, large arched windows; barrel vault ceiling. Built 1715 (date stone); interior gallery and enclosed exterior stairway to gallery added 1771; one-story random rubble vestry (third vestry on site) added on N elevation 1871; enclosed entryway added on S (front) elevation ca. 1920; nineteenth- and early-twentieth-century interior alterations. Built by Welsh settlers; oldest non-Quaker house of worship in area and one of the earliest in the state. General Anthony Wayne is buried in the graveyard. 6 ext. photos (1925,

1958), 4 copy photos from 1850s, 1862 and 1907; 6 data pages (1958). LC code: PA,23-RAD,1. NR.

Grave of General Anthony Wayne (PA-176B). Gravestone of General Anthony Wayne, Revolutionary War hero, erected 1809. 1 ext. photo (1958); 1 data page (1984). LC code: PA,23-RAD,1B.

Horse Shed (PA-176A). Open frame horse shed, L-shaped, uneven gable roof supported on braced squared posts. Built ca. 1850; enlarged 1871. 1 ext. photo (1958). LC code: PA,23-RAD,1A.

Swarthmore Vicinity (Springfield Township)

Pennock, William, House (PA-1243), N side of Swarthmore Ave., between Yale Ave. and University Ave. Log, three irregular bays, two-and-a-half stories, gable roof, large random rubble chimney on E (rear) elevation. Built ca. 1790; deteriorated 1960s; moved to Upland Borough on Race St. near Caleb Pusey House (PA-1079) and restored 1966 by the Friends of Caleb Pusey House, Inc.; one-story board and batten wing added on E (rear) elevation. 7 ext. photos (1964), 8 int. photos (1964); 1 data page (1984). LC code: PA,23-SWAM,1.

Upland Borough

Pennock, William, House. See Swarthmore Vicinity (Springfield Township), Pennock, William, House, original location.

Pusey, Caleb, House (PA-1079), 15 Race St., Landingford Plantation. Museum operated by the Friends of Caleb Pusey House, Inc. Random rubble with flush wooden siding in W gable end and brick in E gable end, approx. 46' x 18' (E and W sections), one-and-a-half stories, gable roof on W section and gambrel roof on E section (E originally gable roof, replaced with gambrel roof ca. 1752, shed dormer probably added on S slope at same time); large fireplace in central wall, stone well in W section. E section built 1683; W section built ca. 1696 (may have originally been an enclosed area without a roof); windows and doorways altered; restored 1964, shed dormer removed, windows and doors restored, bake oven on S restored. Considered the earliest surviving English-built house in Pennsylvania; based on the vernacular tradition of sixteenth- and early-seventeenth-century English models. The only know home left in America which was visited by William Penn. 4 sheets (1963, including plans, elevations, sections); 7 ext. photos (1963), 8 int. photos (1963), 4 undated copy photos, 1 copy photo of proposed int. restoration from 1963; 1 data page (1983). LC code: PA,23-UPLA,1. NR.

Villanova (Radnor Township)

Ashwood (PA-194), 208 Ashwood Rd., W of Kenilworth Rd. Stuccoed random rubble, five-bay main section with two-bay setback wing on NE elevation, two-and-a-half stories, gable roof with dormers on main section and hip roof on wing, denticulated cornice, pedimented distyle entrance porch on SE (front) elevation; central hall plan. Original farmhouse built ca. 1723; enlarged ca. 1820-83; several rear frame additions after 1883. Built by the Jarman family. 2 ext. photos (1958), 4 int. photos (1958); 5 data pages (1958). LC code: PA,23-VILLA,1.

Brick House. See Chuckswood.

Chuckswood (Brick House) (PA-195), E of S. Spring Mill Rd., SE of Sproul Rd. (State Rte. 320). Brick, three-bay front, two-and-a-half stories, gable roof, denticulated cornice extends across gable ends, entrance with semi-elliptical fanlight and side lights on N (front) elevation, oblong marble panels beneath second story windows on N elevation, Federal details; central hall plan. Built 1808 (date stone); ca. 1880 four large gabled dormers added (two on N slope removed 1946); small wing added to SW corner ca. 1902; two-story brick wing added to E 1946, Walter Durham, architect; two-story frame wing added to S of 1946 wing. 3 ext. photos (1958), 4 int. photos (1958), 1 copy photo from ca. 1860; 5 data pages (1958). LC code: PA,23-VILLA,2.

Woodstock (PA-196), N side of Vassar Circle, E of Woodstock Rd. Stuccoed random rubble, six-bay front (two three-bay sections), two-and-a-half stories, gable roofs with dormers, door with fanlight framed by pilasters and pediment on W elevation (original entrance on E elevation changed to French window when W became facade). S section built 1776 (date stone); N section added ca. 1800, Samuel Morgan, probable builder; one-story kitchen wing added on N elevation and two-story porch added on S elevation by George Bispham Page, architect, 1931. Originally owned by James Hunter, has remained in family. 3 ext. photos (1958), 3 int. photos (1958); 5 data pages (1958). LC code: PA, 23-VILLA,3.

Barn (PA-197). Random rubble and board and batten, seven-bay front, two stories with basement, gable roof, projecting frame forebay on E elevation supported by tapered stone piers, large two-story studio window on W elevation, two-story frame kitchen wing and sleeping porch on N elevation. Built 1804 (date stone "JH 1804"); Samuel Morgan, builder; converted to studio-residence for artist Thornton Oakley in 1926 by George Bispham Page, architect. 4 ext. photos (1958), 3 int. photos (1958); 4 data pages (1958). LC code: PA,23-VILLA,3A.

Villanova Vicinity (Radnor Township)

Academy of Notre Dame De Namur. See Godfrey, Lincoln, House.

Godfrey, Lincoln, House (Hillsover, Academy of Notre Dame de Namur) (PA-1241), 560 Sproul Rd. Coursed rubble, large irregular-shaped mansion, two-and-a-half stories, steep gable roofs with large dormers, arcaded porte cochere, Tudor Revival details. Built 1893-95; Theophilus Parsons Chandler, architect; extensive alterations and additions (almost doubled size of house) 1926-27, Paul Philippe Cret, architect; 1943 became Academy of Notre Dame de Namur. 1 copy photo from 1902; 1 data page (1983). LC code: PA,23-ITH,2.

Hillsover. See Godfrey, Lincoln, House.

Wallingford (Nether Providence Township)

Avondale. See Leiper, Thomas, House.

Furness, Horace Howard, Estate. See Lindenshade.

Jayne, Horace, House. See Subrosa.

Leiper, Thomas, House (Avondale) (PA-1244), 519 Avondale Rd., between Rose Valley Rd. and Chester Rd. (State Rte. 320), near Crum Creek. Museum. Random rubble with stucco scored to resemble ashlar, L-shaped, 36'-6" (three-bay front) x 30' main block with 30' x 17' kitchen ell, two-and-a-half stories with basement, gable roof with dormers, paired chimneys in parapets at gable ends, pedimented distyle entrance porch with carved frieze on E (front) elevation, door transom with Adamesque tracery, tetrastyle porch supported on sloping site by monolithic granite piers on N elevation. Built 1785 (date stone); kitchen ell built as separate building (later joined); restored. Four dependencies remain: springhouse, carriage house, privy, and vault. Important example of an eighteenth-century estate which developed around the manufacturing activities of the Leiper tobacco, snuff, and quarry business. 5 ext. photos (1962), 4 int. photos (1962); 1 data page (1983). LC code: PA,23-WALF,1. NR.

Vault (PA-1244A). Stuccoed stone, one story, low hip roof, scored stucco forms plain entablature, monolithic stones frame entrance, narrow openings. Built late eighteenth century. 2 ext. photos (1962). LC code: PA,23-WALF,1A.

Lindenshade (Horace Howard Furness Estate) (PA-1245A), at end of Furness Ln., .2 mi. E of Providence Rd. (State Rte. 252). Stucco with wooden trim, large irregular L-shaped house, two- and two-and-a-half stories with three-and-a-half-story tower, variety of roof shapes with dormers and clipped gables, several wooden porches. Originally a farmhouse; remodeled 1890s by Frank Furness, architect; demolished 1940s (library, stable, and kitchen and servants quarters remain; all remodeled as houses). Home of Horace Howard Furness, brother of architect Frank Furness and a noted Shakespeare scholar. 1 photo of entrance gate (1962), 3 undated copy photos; 1 data page (1983). LC code: PA,23-WALF,2. See Subrosa (PA-1213), located on same estate.

Kitchen and Servants Quarters (PA-1245C). Stucco with wooden trim, L-shaped, five-bay front, one-and-a-half stories, mansard roof with dormers, pedimented entrance porch. Built late nineteenth century; remodeled as house. 1 ext. photo (1962). LC code: PA,23-WALF,2B.

Library (PA-1245B). Brick, rectangular, two-bay front, two stories, hip roof; fine interior woodwork. Built 1903; Furness, Evans and Company, architects; one-story cinderblock wing added to rear ca. 1950; remodeled as house. Built to house book collection of Horace Howard Furness. 1 ext. photo (1962), 3 int. photos (1962), 1 copy photo of Furness in library. LC code: PA,23-WALF,2A.

Subrosa (Horace Jayne House) (PA-1213), W side of Turner Rd., N of Possum Hollow Rd., on Horace Howard Furness Estate. Frame with wooden shingles, large rectangular house with wing to one side, two-and-a-half stories, hip roof with large hipped dormers, large two-story porch. Built 1895-96; burned early 1940s. 1 copy photo of undated view. LC code: PA,23-WALF,3. See Lindenshade (PA-1245A), located on same estate.

Wayne

Saint David's Church. See Saint Davids Vicinity (Newtown Township), Saint David's Protestant Episcopal Church.

Wayne (Radnor Township)

Jones Farmhouse (PA-198), NW corner of Lancaster Pike (U.S. Rte. 30) and Farm Rd. Stuccoed random rubble, L-shaped, five-bay front, two-and-a-half stories, gable roof with dormers, transom over S (front) entrance, rear kitchen wing; central hall plan. Built 1775 (date stone); second story added to kitchen wing 1926; demolished after 1958. 3 ext. photos (1958), 4 int. photos (1958); 4 data pages (1958). LC code: PA,23-WAYN,1.

> *Springhouse* (PA-199). Stuccoed random rubble, small rectangle with wing to W, one story with elevated basement, gable roof with small bell cupola, pedimented hood over E entrance. Built ca. 1775; remodeled as a studio before 1958; demolished. Typical early springhouse. 1 ext. photo (1958); 2 data pages (1958). LC code: PA,23-WAYN,1A.

Franklin County

Chambersburg Borough

Brand Stable. See Fisher, Rev. Samuel R., Stable.

Fisher, Rev. Samuel R., Stable (Brand Stable) (PA-5155), 123-25 S. Main St. Brick, 24' square, two stories, gable roof. Built 1865; frame addition 1929; demolished 1980. 2 ext. photos (1980); 4 data pages (1980). LC code: PA,28-CHAMB,4A.

59 West Queen Street (House) (PA-5156). Brick, approx. 60' (five-bay main block with four-bay addition to N) x 15' (two bays), two-and-a-half stories, gable roof on main block, flat roof on addition, decorative bargeboards, porches with scroll brackets, doors with transoms, Gothic Revival details. Built ca. 1868; demolished 1980. 7 ext. photos (1980), 2 int. photos (1980), 1 photo of outbuilding (1980); 8 data pages (1980). LC code: PA,28-CHAMB,3.

Lancaster County

Bausman Vicinity (Manor-Lancaster Townships)

Stoneroads Mill Covered Bridge (PA-321), over Little Conestoga Creek, .6 mi. S of State Rte. 462 (Lincoln Hwy., old U.S. Rte. 30), .2 mi. W of School House Rd. King-post truss supported on stone abutments, single span, overall length 55', 12' wide roadway, covered with vertical wooden siding, gable roof. Built 1868; Elias McMellen, builder. Adjacent mill built 1770. 2 sheets (1936, including elevation, sections, details). LC code: PA,36-MAP.V,1.

Bird-in-Hand Vicinity (Leacock Township)

Barn (PA-5212), State Rte. 340, on creek, E of Bird-in-Hand. Random rubble with quoins, cantilevered frame forebay over stable entrances, two levels, steep gable roof with two louvered cupolas, slit and louvered ventilators, ramp to threshing level, one-story gabled wing attached to forebay. Built ca. 1770. 3 ext. photos (1941). LC code: PA,36-BIRDI.V,1A.

> *Grain Mill* (PA-5212A), on same farm as Barn (PA-5212). Random rubble with quoins, two-and-a-half stories, gable roof with small shed dormers and large gabled cupola. Built 1770. Used as Tory gaol during Revolutionary War. 1 ext. photo (1941). LC code: PA,36-BIRDI.V,1B.

Brickersville Vicinity (Elizabeth Township)

Emanuel Evangelical Lutheran Church (PA-364), S side of U.S. Rte. 322, .9 mi. E of State Rte. 501. Detail of arched window in brick wall, brick arch with stone keystones, paneled shutters with original hardware. Built 1808. 1 photo of window detail (1935). LC code: PA,36-BRICK,1.

Chickie's Creek

Johnson's Mill Covered Bridge. See Marietta Vicinity (East Donegal-Rapho Townships), Johnson's Mill Covered Bridge.

Churchtown Vicinity (Caernarvon Township)

Barn (PA-5221), .25 mi. S of Churchtown. Random rubble partially whitewashed, projecting frame forebay supported on stone walls, two levels, gable roof, louvered ventilators, two-story stone and frame wing. Date unknown. 2 ext. photos (1941). LC code: PA,36-CHUR.V,1A.

Cocalico (West Cocalico Township)

Bricker, Peter, Farm (Farm Group and Mill Pond) (PA-154), W side of Cocalico Rd. (LR36013), .6 mi. S of State Rte. 897. House with adjacent barn, bake house, outbuildings and mill pond. Coursed squared rubble house, irregular four-bay front by three bays, two-and-a-half stories, gable roof with pent eaves, porch across S (front) elevation. Built 1759 (date stone). 1 general view of farm (1940). LC code: PA,36-COCAL,1.

Barn (PA-154A). Coursed squared rubble with frame forebay, two levels, gable roof. Built mid-eighteenth century; E stone gable end collapsed and replaced with frame after 1940. 1 ext. photo (1940).

Bake House (Outdoor Cook House) (PA-155). Coursed squared rubble shelter for oven, one story, gable roof, work area sheltered by overhang of roof with door to bake house and oven opening in stone wall. Built mid-eighteenth century. 1 ext. photo (1940). LC code: PA,36-COCAL,2.

Cotton Mill. See Grist and Saw Mill.

Farm Group and Mill Pond. See Bricker, Peter, Farm.

Grist and Saw Mill (Cotton Mill) (PA-156), E side of LR36013, .7 mi. S of State Rte. 897. Random rubble and frame, two-and-a-half stories on sloping site, gable roofs. Built 1793; additions; demolished to random rubble foundation level and new frame structure built on old foundations after 1940. 2 ext. photos (1940). LC code: PA,36-COCAL,3.

Outdoor Cook House. See Bricker, Peter, Farm, *Bake House*.

Drumore Vicinity (Drumore Township)

Cider Press at Hesses' Mill (PA-367), on Fishing Creek. Cast-iron screw and screwblock (other iron work hand forged) supported by wooden frame with wooden trough below, base approx. 7' x 5', height approx. 14', press protected by gable roof. Built first half of nineteenth century. 1 sheet (1933, including plan, elevations, section, details). LC code: PA,36-DRUM.V,1A.

Ephrata Vicinity

Buck, Adam R., Barn (PA-5210), no location provided. Random rubble with red-stone quoins, frame forebay contained within stone end walls, two levels, gable roof, pent roof over entrance to threshing floor, stable doors with iron strap hinges. Built ca. 1830. 4 ext. photos (1941). LC code: PA,36-EPH.V,2A.

Ephrata vicinity (Ephrata Township)

Ephrata Cloister (PA-320), S of intersection of U.S. Rte. 322 and U.S. Rte. 272. Museum operated by Pennsylvania Historical and Museum Commission. Ephrata Cloister was one of the earliest communal religious societies established in America, founded in 1732 by Conrad Beissel, a German Pietist, when he separated from the Dunkers. The Cloister buildings, built 1735-49, are excellent examples of medieval Germanic architecture in America. The Cloister was built to house the celibate orders of Sisters and Brothers and included a congregation of married couples (Householders). These Seventh-Day German Baptists followed a strict, simple life of labor, meditation and worship. Cultural expressions, such as establishing one of the earliest printing presses in the colonies in 1745, illuminating manuscripts, composing hymns and singing, were considered a form of worship. The community of 300 was self-sufficient at its peak around 1750. Wounded soldiers were nursed at the Cloister after the Battle of Brandywine, but typhus was introduced and the hospital buildings were burned. This, along with internal quarrels, and aging and declining membership weakened the sect. In 1814 the celibate orders dissolved, but the congregation continued using the buildings until 1934. The Commonwealth of Pennsylvania acquired the property in 1941 and restored the Cloister as a museum between 1946 and 1960. 9 general views (1936, 1937). Complete records comprise 60 sheets (1936-37); 107 photos (1936, 1937, n.d.); 5 data pages (n.d.). LC code: PA,36-EPH,1. NHL.

Academy (PA-320A). Frame with clapboarding, three by two bays, two-and-a-half stories, gable roof with open octagonal belfry, double paneled door with transom and pedimented hood. Built 1837; restored. 2 ext. photos (1936). LC code: PA,36-EPH,1J.

Almonry (PA-320B). Random rubble, L-shaped, 33'-3" x 33'-2", one-and-a-half stories with basement, intersecting gable roofs, gable end projects over porch on S (front) elevation, frame and stone shed on W elevation, two adjoining beehive ovens (reconstructed ca. 1950s), wooden pump on front porch; kitchen and bakery in basement and sleeping rooms above. Built mid-eighteenth century; restored. Used to distribute alms, and to house and feed wayfarers. 9 sheets and 1 partial sheet (1936-37, including plans, elevations, details); 2 ext. photos (1937), 4 int. photos (1937). LC code: PA,36-EPH,1C.

Bake House (PA-320C). Random rubble oven partially enclosed in frame structure, 7'-5" x 12'-3", one story, gable roof, central chimney; oven opening and small work space inside. Built late eighteenth century; restored. 2 sheets (1936-37, including plan, elevations, sections, details); 1 ext. photo (1936). LC code: PA,36-EPH,1D.

Beissel's Cottage (Whitehaus) (PA-320L). Log with mud chinking covered with weatherboards, 26'-5" (two-bay front) x 20' (two bays), one-and-a-half stories, gable roof with flared eaves, chimney of wood lined with clay (reconstructed ca. 1950s); summer kitchen connected by porch to SE elevation, frame covered with wooden siding (work area) and exposed half-timber with stone nogging and random rubble (chimney end), 13'-6" x 26'-5" (including porch), one story, gable roof, adjoining beehive oven (reconstructed ca. 1950s). Built 1748; kitchen possibly original community bake house built ca. 1734; restored. Probably home of Conrad Beissel, founder of Ephrata Cloister. 3 sheets (1936-37, including plans, elevations, details); 3 ext. photos (1936, 1937). LC code: PA,36-EPH,1F.

Bethania (PA-320D). Half-timber with stone nogging covered with weatherboards, rectangular, two stories with setback third story and attic forming a clerestory, steep gable roof with flared eaves, small casement windows. Built ca. 1746; demolished ca. 1910. Housed the celibate order of Brothers. 2 copy photos of ext. (n.d.), 5 copy photos of int. (n.d.). LC code: PA,36-EPH,1H.

Cabin #3 (PA-320E). Detail of shutter hinge. 1 sheet (1936-37). LC code: PA,36-EPH,1G.

Clockmaker's Cottage. See *Print Shop*.

Graveyard (PA-320G). Contains graves of Conrad Beissel, founder of the Cloister and his successor, Peter Miller. 2 photos (1936). LC code: PA,36-EPH,1M.

Hill House (PA-320H). Half-timber with stone nogging covered with weatherboards (later partially covered with wooden shingles, weatherboarding restored ca. 1950s), two-bay front, one-and-a-half stories, gable roof with flared eaves, central chimney of wood lined with clay, one-bay entrance porch. Built mid-eighteenth century; one-and-a-half-story shed-roof board and batten wing added mid-nineteenth century, removed during restoration ca. 1950s. 2 ext. photos (1937). LC code: PA,36-EPH,1L.

Mill (PA-320I), located approx. .5 mi. from the Cloister, not owned by Commonwealth of Pennsylvania. Stuccoed random rubble, three by four bays, three stories with double attic, gable roof with decorative wooden cornice, arch with cut voussoirs spans stream, loading doors at each level of front elevation, frame sheds at each side. Built ca. 1740s, rebuilt 1784 (date stone). Built by the Brothers of Ephrata Cloister. 3 ext. photos (1937). LC code: PA,36-EPH,1K.

Print Shop (Clockmaker's Cottage) (PA-320F). Half-timber with stone nogging covered with weatherboards, 18'-5" x 14'-1", two stories, gable roof, large chimney (originally wood lined with clay); larger section added on side, frame covered with weatherboards, 19'-3" (three bays) x 16'-11", two-and-a-half stories, gable roof with pent eaves. Original half-timber section built ca. 1730s (possibly oldest building at Ephrata); frame wing added ca. 1800-10; restored. The third printing press in America was established at Ephrata in 1743; the most ambitious work was the translation and publication of *Martyrer Spiegel* in 1748, the largest book printed in the colonies. 6 sheets (1936-37, including plans, elevations, details); 2 ext. photos (1936, 1937). LC code: PA,36-EPH,1E.

Saal (PA-320J). Half-timber with stone nogging covered with weatherboards (later partially stuccoed and covered with metal sheathing, weatherboarding restored ca. 1950s), 37'-6" (three-bay front) x 40'-2" (four bays), two stories with triple attic, steep gable roof with flared eaves, three rows of shed dormers (reconstructed ca. 1950s), central chimney of wood lined with clay (reconstructed ca. 1950s), small casement windows, one-story coursed rubble kitchen wing (16' x 18'-6") on E elevation; contains chapel, meeting room and community dining room, simple interior with exposed beam ceiling and chamfered supports, walls decorated with hand-illuminated German scripts by the Sisters. Built 1740-41; kitchen wing added ca. 1780; restored. Services consisted of preaching, Scripture reading and a cappella singing; the love feast, a fellowship meal, was served here. 25 sheets and 4 partial sheets (1936-37, including plans, elevations, sections, details, furniture details); 7 ext. photos (1936, 1937), 43 int. photos (1936, 1937, including illuminations on walls). LC code: PA,36-EPH,1B.

Saron (PA-320K). Log dovetailed at corners and chinked with wooden splints and clay and covered with weatherboards (later partially covered with wooden shingles and stucco, weatherboarding restored ca. 1950s), 72' (ten-bay front) x 30'-3", two stories with double attic, steep gable roof with flared eaves, two rows of shed dormers (restored ca. 1950s), two medial chimneys of wood lined with clay (reconstructed ca. 1950s), small casement windows; austere interior of small sleeping cells furnished with wooden benches and pillows and common rooms for work and prayer, narrow hallways and low doorways to remind one of the 'straight and narrow path' and humility. Built 1742-43; porch on E elevation and cupola added (removed during restoration); restored. Built to house celibate Householders, but within a year the structure was reserved for the Sisters and the Bethania was built for the Brothers. 11 sheets and 3 partial sheets (1936-37, including plans, elevations, section, details, furniture details); 6 ext. photos (1935, 1936, 1937), 14 int. photos (1936, 1937, including furniture and weaving equipment). LC code: PA,36-EPH,1A.

Whitehaus. See *Beissel's Cottage.*

Farmersville Vicinity (West Earl Township)

Barn, Victorian (PA-5209), on Conestoga Creek, between Farmersville and Brownstown. Random rubble, frame with clapboarding on gable ends and cantilevered forebay, two-level bank barn, gable roof with three decorative ventilators, scrolled bargeboards, windows flanked by louvers with pediments, attached wagon shed. Possibly early stone barn remodeled with Victorian details. 2 ext. photos (1941). LC code: PA,36-FARM.V,1A.

Gap Vicinity (Sadsbury Township)

Barn (PA-5219), township road off State Rte. 372, S of Gap. Detail of barn showing stone corner and frame forebay with vertical siding. Date unknown. 1 ext. photo (1941). LC code: PA,36-GAP.V,1A.

Hinkletown (Ephrata Township)

Barn (PA-5220), U.S. Rte. 322 on Conestoga Creek, between Hinkletown and Ephrata. Random rubble with quoins, two-level bank barn, gable roof with three square ventilators, slit ventilators. Built late eighteenth or early nineteenth century. 1 ext. photo (1941). LC code: PA,36-HINK.V,1A.

Barn, Old Red (PA-157), N side of U.S. Rte 322, .2 mi NW of Conestoga Creek. Random rubble with frame forebay, two levels, gable roof, frame wings on each side. Built late eighteenth century or early nineteenth century. 2 ext. photos (1940). LC code: PA,36-HINK,1.

Ironville Vicinity (West Hempfield Township)

Farmhouse (PA-5214), on LR36065, between Ironville and Salunga. Random rubble (partially stuccoed), six by two bays, two-and-a-half stories, gable roof with inside end chimneys, two doors on front elevation, one-story porch across front and side elevations, shed added at rear, iron wellhead pump in front of house. Date unknown. 1 ext. photo (1941). LC code: PA,36-IRON.V,1.

> **Barn** (PA-5214A). Random rubble with cantilevered frame forebay over stable entrances, two levels, gable roof, louvered ventilators, large stone and frame wings on both sides. Built probably nineteenth century. 2 ext. photos (1941). LC code: PA,36-IRON.V,1A.

Lancaster

City Hall (Old City Hall, Heritage Center) (PA-1343), NW corner of Penn Square. Brick, five bays (original S front elevation) by three bays (present E front elevation), three-and-a-half stories with basement, gable roof with dormers, massive inside end chimneys, balustrade along roof ridge, door with fanlight framed by pilasters and pediment on E elevation, flat stone arches with double keystones over windows. Built 1795-97; third story added early nineteenth century (originally had cupola); interior remodeled several times. First City Hall of Lancaster; housed Commonwealth offices when Lancaster was capitol of Pennsylvania 1799-1812. 7 ext. photos (1965, 1981); 9 data pages (1981). LC code: PA,36-LANC,2. NR.

Ellicott House. See Sehner-Ellicott House.

Heritage Center. See City Hall.

Howard Avenue (House) (PA-1355), 125 Howard Ave. Brick (first story) and half-timber covered with asbestos shingles (second story), four-bay front, one-and-a-half stories with basement, steep gable roof with dormers. Built probably mid-eighteenth century as half-timbered structure; first half of nineteenth century front and side walls of first story replaced with brick walls (original rear half-timber wall remains as an interior wall between main house and rear addition); rear brick addition probably added early (possibly originally frame, rebuilt in brick same time as house); small frame shed added to rear; restored (original central chimney rebuilt, shingles in gable end removed exposing half-timber construction, frame shed removed). Unusual survival of half-timber construction. 3 ext. photos (1965); 1 data page (1984). LC code: PA,36-LANC,4.

Lancaster Municipal Building. See United States Post Office and Courthouse.

Lutheran Church of the Holy Trinity (PA-575), 31 S. Duke St. Brick, approx. 60' (three-bay front) x 80' (six bays), two stories, four-story brick tower with octagonal frame belfry with spire (195' high), gable roof with pedimented gable end pierced by tower, denticulated cornice, belt courses, arched openings, four carved wooden statues of the Evangelists on corners of tower (possibly by William Rush); interior galleries supported by six cast-iron columns, retains original 1771 organ case by David Tannenberg (renowned organ builder). Built 1761-66; tower added 1785-94; 1853 apse and E and W vestibules added, galleries rebuilt and pulpit installed on N wall (originally pulpit on E wall and galleries on other three); 1949 original statues moved to narthex and replaced by copies on tower. Church founded 1729, one of the oldest Lutheran congregations in the country. 5 ext. photos (1937, 1965), 12 photos of original statues (1965); 1 data page (1984). LC code: PA,36-LANC,1. NR (Lancaster Historic District).

Montgomery, William, House (PA-1061), 21 S. Queen St. Brick, rectangular (three by three bays) with semicircular bay on E (rear) elevation, three-and-a-half stories, gable roof with pedimented dormers flanked by pilasters, paired chimneys in parapet, denticulated cornice, lintels with keystone motifs, Federal details; original spiral staircase with series of groined vaults springing from decorative impost blocks above. Built 1804; Stephen Hills, architect (later architect for Pennsylvania and Missouri State Capitols); remodeled for commercial use (storefront added, interior altered, one-story rear addition). 4 ext. photos (1965), 3 int. photos (1965); 1 data page (1984). LC code: PA,36-LANC,5.

Musser-Reigart House (PA-373), 323 W. King St. Stuccoed stone scored to imitate ashlar with brick ell, L-shaped, main block five by two bays with three-bay ell, two-and-a-half stories with two-story ell, gable roofs with dormers, denticulated cornice, pedimented frontispiece with brackets and keystone motif with recessed door, molded window frames with keystone motifs; fine interior woodwork. Built ca. 1790 (E three bays); W two bays added ca. 1860 carefully matching original; kitchen ell added. Probably built by Michael Musser; Adam Reigart is thought to have entertained the Marquis de Lafayette here in 1825. 4 ext. photos (1965), 4 int. photos (1965); 1 data page (1984). LC code: PA,36-LANC,6.

Old City Hall. See City Hall.

Reigart House. See Musser-Reigart House.

Sehner-Ellicott House (PA-372), 123 N. Prince St. Brick, L-shaped, 26'-6" (three-bay front) x 69'-2" (including rear kitchen ell), two-and-a-half stories with two-story ell, gable roof with flat roof on ell, modillioned cornice, double belt course, door with shouldered architrave and pediment with scroll consoles on W (front) elevation, flat brick arches with stone keystones over windows; side hall plan, outstanding elaborate interior woodwork. Built ca. 1788-89; Gottlieb Sehner, master carpenter, built as his residence; original kitchen ell (14'x 17') widened to present size (approx. 30' x 31') mid-nineteenth century; two small brick sheds added to ell early twentieth century; acquired by Historic Preservation Trust of Lancaster County 1973 and restored. Residence of Andrew Ellicott 1801-13, first U.S. Surveyor General under George Washington, assisted L'Enfant with plan of Washington, D.C., secretary of Pennsylvania Land Office. 15 sheets (1969, 1975, including site plan, plans, framing plans, elevation, details); 5 ext. photos (1965), 8 int. photos (1965); 5 data pages (1965). LC code: PA,36-LANC,7. NR.

Smith, Judge Charles, House (PA-369), 22 S. Queen St. Brick, L-shaped, main block three by three bays with three-bay rear ell, three-and-a-half stories with two-story ell, gable roof with pedimented gable end and pedimented dormer, modillioned cornice, belt courses, flat brick arches with stone keystones over windows, Federal details; side hall plan. Built 1784-85; first story completely remodeled for commercial use (front entrance altered, storefront added, interior altered); demolished 1967. 4 ext. photos (1965), 1 int. photo (1965); 1 data page (1984). LC code: PA,36-LANC,8.

United States Post Office and Courthouse (Lancaster Municipal Building) (PA-370), 120 N. Duke St. Coursed ashlar (rusticated first story), rectangular with entrance pavilion and elaborate corner tower, two stories, intersecting hip roofs, parapets with finials, horseshoe arch openings with columns, Renaissance Revival and Moorish styles. Built 1891; James H. Windrim, Supervising Architect of the Treasury Department; C. Emlen Urban, local architect; homogeneous addition 1907-08, James Knox Taylor, architect; changed from post office to new city hall 1931. 5 ext. photos (1981), 2 int. photos (1981), 1 copy photo of ext. (ca. 1890); 4 data pages (1981). LC code: PA,36-LANC,3. NR (Lancaster Historic District).

Lancaster Vicinity

Barn (PA-5213), Rte. 280, NW of Lancaster. Frame with vertical siding and whitewashed stone, two levels, gable roof with six metal ventilators, several additions. Built nineteenth century. 1 ext. photo (1941). LC code: PA,36-LANC.V,5A

Barns (PA-5222), no location provided. Two barns. Random rubble with cantilevered frame forebay, two levels, gable roof. Frame with vertical siding, two levels, gable roof. Dates unknown. 1 ext. photo (1941). LC code: PA,36-_____,1.

Miller, Jacob and Elizabeth, Barn (PA-5228), on State Rte. 23 (New Holland Pike), E of Lancaster. Random rubble with cantilevered frame forebay over stable entrances, large six-bay barn, two levels, gable roof, two threshing floor doors with paired ramps, transoms over stable doors, slit ventilators, circular brick design around gable-end vent. Built 1804 (date stone); frame sheds added. 3 ext. photos (1941), 2 int. photos of stable area (1941). LC code: PA,36-LANC.V,6A.

Lancaster Vicinity (East Hempfield Township)

Barn (PA-5227), N of U.S. Rte. 30 (Lincoln Highway), approx. 4 mi. W of Lancaster. Detail of brick end with patterned louvers. Built nineteenth century. 1 ext. photo (1941). LC code: PA,36-LANC.V,4A.

Lancaster Vicinity (Lancaster Township)

Buchanan, James, House. See Wheatland.

Wheatland (James Buchanan House) (PA-1265), 1120 Marietta Ave. (State Rte. 340), W of President Ave. Museum operated by James Buchanan Foundation for the Preservation of Wheatland. Brick, main section approx. 46' (five-bay front) x 38' with setback wings to side, E wing approx. 25' (three-bay front) x 20', W wing approx. 30' (three-bay front) x 20', two-and-a-half stories with basement, gable roof with dormers and shed roofs with stepped ends on wings, doors with fanlights and three-part windows above, Doric entrance porch on N (front) elevation, Doric porch across S elevation; central hall plan, fine interiors with many pieces from the Buchanan family, good interior graining. Built 1828 by William Jenkins; James Buchanan purchased 1849; bought by Lancaster Junior League 1930s and foundation formed to operate house. Home of James Buchanan, fifteenth president of the U. S.(1857-61), 1849 until his death in 1868. 19 sheets (1965, including site plans, plans, elevations, details). LC code: PA,36-LANC.V,7. NHL.

Lancaster Vicinity (Manheim Township)

Landis, Christian and Fanny, Barn (PA-5223), U.S. Rte. 222, S of Landis Valley Museum. Stone partially whitewashed, cantilevered frame forebay over stable entrances, two levels, gable roof with three louvered ventilators, slit ventilators, silo at gable end, two-level wing near threshing entrance. Built 1842 (date stone under lunette in gable end). 2 ext. photos (1941). LC code: PA,36-LANC.V,3A.

Landis, Henry, Barn (PA-5224), county road, approx. 1 mi. NW of Landis Valley, across road from Jacob E. Long Barn (PA-5225). Random rubble; cantilevered frame forebay over stable entrances, two levels, steep gable roof with metal ventilators, loft dormer, silo at gable end. Built 1754 (date on frame of stable door); section with loft dormer and silo later additions; stable wall altered. According to local tradition barn site of first meeting of United Brethren in county. 2 ext. photos including date on door frame (1941), 1 int. photo showing framing (1941). LC code: PA,36-LANC.V,2A.

Long, Jacob E., Barn (PA-5225), on county road, approx. 1 mi. NW of Landis Valley, across road from Henry Landis Barn (PA-5224). Random rubble with coursed rubble at stable entrances, cantilevered frame forebay, two levels, gable roof, slit ventilators, ramp to threshing floor entrance, circular brick design around gable-end vent. Built 1803 (date stone); later addition and silos. 3 ext. photos (1941). LC code: PA,36-LANC.V,8A.

Lancaster Vicinity (West Lampeter Township)

Hand, General Edward, House. See Rock Ford.

Rock Ford (General Edward Hand House) (PA-368), on Rock Ford Rd., .3 mi. S of junction of S. Duke St. and Conestoga Creek, W of Williamson Park. Museum operated by Rock Ford Foundation. Brick, approx. 49' (five-bay front) x 39' (four bays), two-and-a-half stories with basement (original kitchen in basement), gable roof with pent eaves, double belt course, door with fanlight framed by pilasters and pediment on N (front) elevation, flat brick arches with stone keystones, porch with Doric columns on S, E and W elevations; central hall plan, fine original interior woodwork and hardware. Built 1793-94; original porches removed late nineteenth century, reconstructed during restoration; acquired by Lancaster Junior League and Rock Ford Foundation 1958; restored 1958-62. Home of General Hand 1793-1802, Adjutant General of Continental Army, member of Continental Congress and active in Federalist Party. 13 sheets (1961, 1962, including site plan, plans, elevations, details); 7 ext. photos (1964), 7 int. photos (1964); 10 data pages (1961). LC code: PA,36-LANC.V,1. NR.

> *Springhouse* (PA-368A). Stone and frame, one story with lower level to spring, gable roof; adjacent brick-arched root cellar. 1 sheet (1961, including plans, elevations, sections, details of both springhouse and root cellar). LC code: PA,36-LANC.V,1A.

Landisville (East Hempfield Township)

Bachman-Landis-Kauffman House (PA-1246), S side of Kauffman Rd., .3 mi. S of Main St. (LR36184), between T552 and Reading Railroad tracks. Random rubble, 40'-1" (five-bay front) x 33'-8", two-and-a-half stories, gable roof, cornice returns, door with transom and porch on N (front) elevation (porch not original, remains of original porch extant), one-bay porch on E elevation connected to small clapboarded wing (not original); central hall plan, original interior woodwork remains. Built ca. 1790; few alterations. Built by Michael Bachman; passed to son-in-law John Landis, who with his son laid out Landisville 1828-30; passed to Hiram G. Kauffman, a Mennonite minister. 5 sheets (1977-79, including site plan, plans, details). LC code: PA,36-LAND,1.

Kauffman House. See Bachman-Landis-Kauffman House.

Landis House. See Bachman-Landis-Kauffman House.

Lititz Vicinity

Hollinger, C.H., Barn (PA-5216), State Rte. 722, between Lititz and Manheim. Brick with stone foundation and frame forebay supported on wooden corner posts, two-level bank barn, gable roof with dormers and central cupola, metal roof ventilators, patterned brick and builder's initials form vents in gable ends, openings with low pediments, cast-iron star plates. Built ca. 1850. 3 ext. photos (1941). LC code: PA,36-LIT.V,1A.

Schriner, John H., Barn (PA-5226), Rte. 3. Random rubble with cantilevered frame forebay over stable entrances, two-level bank barn, gable roof forms protective pent over entrance to threshing floor, ramp to double threshing floor doors, slit ventilators, brick-arched opening in gable end with iron pulley above to hoist hay to loft. Built 1827 (date stone). 3 ext. photos (1941). LC code: PA,36-LIT,1A.

Manheim Vicinity (Mount Joy Township)

Barn, Pink (PA-5215), intersection of Colebrook Rd. and Sunnyburn Rd., approx. 9 mi. NW of Manheim. Coursed rubble (stable area) and frame with vertical siding, two-level bank barn, gable roof with metal ventilators, windows with low pediments. Built nineteenth century. 1 ext. photo (1941). LC code: PA,36-MAN.V,1A.

Maple Grove Vicinity

Stoneroads Mill Bridge. See Bausman Vicinity (Manor-Lancaster Townships), Stoneroads Mill Covered Bridge.

Marietta Vicinity (East Donegal-Rapho Townships)

Johnson's Mill Covered Bridge (PA-1173), over Little Chickies Creek, on T356, .1 mi. N of State Rte. 23. Burr arch truss supported on stone abutments, single span 64', overall length 80'-4", roadway width 10'-6", covered with board and batten siding, gable roof. Built 1866-67; Elias McMellen, builder. 7 sheets (1962, including site plan, plans, elevations, sections, details). LC code: PA,36-CHICK,1.

Mechanicsville Vicinity

Barn (PA-5208), State Rte. 23, between Mechanicsville and Lancaster. Random rubble with cantilevered frame forebay over stable entrances, two levels, gable roof with gabled dormers, ramp to several threshing-level entrances, slit ventilators and diamond-shaped vent in gable end. Built nineteenth century. 2 ext. photos (1941). LC code: PA,36-MECH.V,1A.

Oregon Vicinity

Bushong's Mill Covered Bridge. See Leaman Rifle Works Covered Bridge.

Oregon Vicinity (Manheim-Upper Leacock Townships)

Leaman Rifle Works Covered Bridge (Nolts Point Mill Covered Bridge, Bushong's Mill Covered Bridge) (PA-319), over Conestoga Creek, just E of mouth of Lititz Run, at end of Pinetown Rd. Burr arch truss supported by stone abutments, single span, over-all length 135'-8", covered with vertical wooden siding, gable roof. Built 1867; Elias McMellen, builder; washed off abutments 1972 in Hurricane Agnes, repaired and raised higher on abutments. 1 sheet (1936, including elevation, sections, details). LC code: PA,36-PINTO,1. NR.

Nolts Point Mill Covered Bridge. See Leaman Rifle Works Covered Bridge.

Pinetown

Leaman Rifle Works Bridge. See Oregon Vicinity (Manheim-Upper Leacock Townships), Leaman Rifle Works Covered Bridge.

Strasburg Vicinity (Paradise Township)

Barn (PA-5218), county road between U.S. Rte. 30 at Paradise and State Rte. 741. Random rubble gable wall with slit ventilators, two levels, gable roof, stone and frame wing attached. Date unknown. 1 ext. photo (1941). LC code: PA,36-STRAS.V,1A.

Strasburg Vicinity (Strasburg Township)

Barn, 1809 (PA-5217), county road between Lime Valley and Strasburg. Random rubble, cantilevered frame forebay with cross-gable center section over stable entrances, two-level bank barn, gable roof, slit ventilators, several frame wings. Built 1809. Adjacent brick house built 1740. 4 ext. photos (1941). LC code: PA,36-STRAS.V,2A.

Swartzville Vicinity (East Cocalico Township)

Barn, Decorated, circa 1910 (PA-5211), U.S. Rte. 222. Frame with vertical siding, two levels, gable roof, recessed stable area, ramp to threshing entrance, decorated with painted folk designs ("hex signs" and picture of horse), frame ells on stable and threshing sides. Built ca. 1910. 3 ext. photos (1941). LC code: PA,36-SWAR.V,1A.

Willow Street Vicinity (West Lampeter Township)

Herr, Hans, House (PA-371), E side of Hans Herr Rd., .6 mi. S of U.S. Rte. 222. Museum operated by Lancaster Mennonite Conference Historical Society. Random rubble with quoins, 37'-9" (three-bay front) x 30'-10" (two bays), one-and-a-half stories with loft, sloping site exposes vaulted cellar, steep gable roof with projecting rafter ends cut in scalloped pattern, central stone chimney, cut stone window frames, date and initials carved in lintel over S (front) door; four rooms divided by central fireplace, interior walls and ceilings of vertical posts filled with paling, stairs carved from solid logs. Built 1719 (date stone "17 CHHR 19"); ca. 1800 some interior partitions and part of stairway replaced and some windows enlarged; early nineteenth-century chimney replaced with brick chimney; restored to 1719 appearance 1972-73. Built by Christian Herr for his father, Hans Herr, a Mennonite Bishop; early Swiss Mennonite immigrants. House served as first Mennonite meetinghouse in America. Excellent example of early Germanic architecture. 2 ext. photos (1971), 1 ext. copy photo (n.d.); 1 data page (1984). LC code: PA,36-WILST.V,1. NR.

Lebanon County

Kleinfeltersville Vicinity (Heidelberg Township)

Barn, Brick End (PA-153), E side of Millbach Rd., .4 mi. N of State Rte. 897. Brick end walls and frame center section with vertical wooden siding, two levels, gable roof, frame forebay contained within brick end walls, triangular ventilators in brick walls. Built early nineteenth century; two-level frame shed added on N elevation prior to 1940; two-level frame wing added on E elevation after 1940; one-level frame shed added across W elevation after 1940; silo added on S elevation after 1940. 1 ext. photo (1940). LC code: PA,38-KLEIN,l.

Millbach (Millcreek Township)

Illigs Mill. See Miller's House and Mill.

Miller's House and Mill (Mueller House, Illigs Mill) (PA-151), E side of Millbach Rd., at road to Stricklerstown, .3 mi. S of State Rte. 419. House: random rubble with quoins, three irregular bays, two-and-a-half stories and attic with basement, gambrel roof with flared eaves, pent eaves; exposed painted summer beams and rafters. Built 1752 (date stone); pent roof removed (belt course remains); original casements replaced by double hung sash nineteenth century; porch on N elevation added late nineteenth century; interiors of two rooms removed 1926 and installed in Philadelphia Museum of Art. Mill attached to E of house: coursed rubble with quoins, three-bay front, two-and-a-half stories on sloping site, gable roof with large gabled dormer with door, pent eaves, gabled hood over N entrance. Built 1784 on foundations of earlier log structure; late-nineteenth-century porch replaced original pent roof on S elevation. Good example of Pennsylvania German architecture. A significant example of the combination of a small industry connected with the house. 8 ext. photos (1940, 1958); 2 data pages (1958). LC code: PA,38-MILB,1. NR.

Mueller House. See Miller's House and Mill.

Millbach Vicinity (Millcreek Township)

Barn, Brown Stone (PA-152), E side of Millbach Rd., 1.5 mi. S of State Rte. 419. Random rubble, bank barn, gable roof, slit ventilators. Built early nineteenth century; frame shed added on N elevation prior to 1940; concrete block milk shed added to S elevation after 1940. 1 ext. photo (1940). LC code: PA,38-SHER,1.

Newmanstown

Lime Kilns. See Berks County, Womelsdorf Vicinity (Heidelberg Township), Lime Kilns.

Newmanstown Vicinity (Millcreek Township)

Fort Zeller. See Zeller, Heinrich, House.

Zeller, Heinrich, House (Fort Zeller) (PA-141), NE side of N. Fort Zeller Rd., .4 mi. NW of State Rte. 419, W of Newmanstown. Stuccoed random rubble, approx. 35' (irregular three-bay front) x 30', one-and-a-half stories and attic with partially exposed basement at S (spring level), steep gable roof with flared eaves which overhangs approx. 4' on E (front) elevation, chevron-patterned Dutch door with stone jambs and lintel with crudely carved replica of arms of Switzerland on E, chevron-patterned door in stone arch on S at spring level, small casement windows (some replaced with double hung sash ca. 1850); fireplace divides interior into two rooms with additional partition wall of frame with wattle and daub. Built 1745 (date stone); gabled dormers added ca. 1850; porch added on E. Typical small farmhouse introduced by the Huguenots from France in the eighteenth century. Oldest existing fort in Pennsylvania, erected as refuge during Indian Wars. 7 sheets (1958, including site plan, plans, elevations, section, details); 11 ext. photos (1940), 11 int. photos (1940). LC code: PA,38-NEWM.V,1. NR.

Schaefferstown (Heidelberg Township)

Stiegel House (PA-5341), E side of State Rte. 419, just N of State Rte. 897. Half-timbered house enlarged with log wing added on N side. Original section: half-timber (braced box framing) with wattle and daub infill, whitewashed plaster finish within panels, 24'-7" (two-bay front) x 20'-1", one-and-a-half stories, gable roof, decorative carved corner posts and gable ends; three-room plan, interior chimney, molded and beaded boards and beams, decorative sponge painting. Built 1757 (inscribed corner post); late-eighteenth- or early-nineteenth-century two-room dove-tailed log wing added to side; original chimney removed nineteenth century; shed added and whole covered with composition siding early twentieth century; restoration in progress. Very rare example of eighteenth-century half-timbered Pennsylvania-German house. 7 sheets (1984, including plans, elevation, sections, details, construction details); 3 ext. photos (1983), 20 int. photos (1983); 1 data page (1986). LC code: PA,38-SCHAF,1.

Sheridan

Brown Stone Barn (PA-152). See Millbach Vicinity (Millcreek Township), Barn, Brown Stone (PA-152).

Lehigh County

Alburtis Vicinity (Lower Macungie Township)

Barn, Decorated (PA-5320), between Alburtis and Macungie. Random rubble (coursed flanking forebay and stuccoed at stable entrances), frame forebay contained within stone end walls, two levels, gable roof, frame shed added, decorated with painted folk designs ("hex signs," hearts, and trim around openings) on forebay. Built nineteenth century. 1 ext. photo (1941). LC code: PA,39-ALB.V,1A.

Barn, Decorated Red (PA-5319), between Alburtis and Macungie. Random rubble (coursed flanking forebay and stuccoed at stable entrances), frame forebay contained within stone end walls, two levels, gable roof, decorated with painted "hex signs" and scallop pattern, painted accents around openings. Built nineteenth century. 1 ext. photo (1941). LC code: PA,39-ALB.V,2A.

Allentown

Mewhorter, Thomas, House (Daniel Nunnemacher House) (PA-1271), 301 S. Lehigh St. Stuccoed random rubble scored to imitate ashlar, 28'-4" (three-bay front) x 32'-1" (two bays), two-and-a-half stories with basement, gable roof with pedimented gable ends, denticulated cornice, pedimented doorway with carved consoles and pilasters on W (front) elevation, flat lintels with keystones; side hall plan. Built ca. 1797; brick wing added to E ca. 1890 not recorded; demolished 1973. 2 sheets (1970, including plans, elevations, section, detail); 4 data pages (1970). LC code: PA,39-ALLEN,1.

Nunnemacher, Daniel, House. See Mewhorter, Thomas, House.

Rialto Theater (PA-5340), 943 Hamilton Mall. Brick with travertine facade, L-shaped, approx. 180' x 230', two stories with higher auditorium, later plain moderne facade; elaborate classical style interior, columns and pilasters, wall panels and niches, murals, polychrome plaster decoration. Built 1918-21; Chanock and Senderowitz, architects; 1946 fire damage and then substantial alterations mainly to exterior; 1979 theater closed and used for storage. 3 ext. photos (1985), 34 int. photos (1985); 1 data page (1985). LC code: PA,39-ALLEN,2.

Allentown Vicinity

Barn, Wood (PA-5324), N of Allentown. Log (untrimmed) covered with vertical wooden siding, two structural bays connected by central passage, one level, gable roof. Built mid-eighteenth century (adjacent house built by Lorentz Guth dated 1745). 1 ext. photo (1941), 1 int. photo (1941). LC code: PA,39-ALLEN.V,1A.

Bethlehem

Central Railroad Station of New Jersey: Bethlehem Station (PA-1149), S side of Lehigh St., just E of Main St. Brick, seven-bay central section with setback two-bay end sections, two stories, mansard roofs with clipped gable roof over central bay, bracketed carved bargeboard in clipped gable end, dormers with bracketed cornices, decorative cornice with paired brackets, projecting roof supported on large carved brackets with pendants between stories, central bay window on S (track side) elevation. Built 1873; restored as restaurant ca. 1974. 4 ext. photos (1969). LC code: PA,39-BETH,1. HAER, NR (Bethlehem Historic District).

Catasauqua Borough

2 Race Street (House) (PA-5448). Stone, rectangular with rear wing, two and a half stories, gable roof with dormers, bracketed cornice, decorative window trim, porch across front and side elevations. Built early nineteenth century; alterations mid-nineteenth century. By 1876 home of G. Deily, owner of adjacent coal yards on Lehigh Canal. 1 ext. photo (1979); 1 data page (1979). LC code: PA,39-CATS,2.

Catasauqua Vicinity (Hanover Township)

Combs House (PA-5447), N. Dauphin St. at Catasauqua Lake, in county park, adjacent to Lehigh Canal. Brick with random rubble foundation, approx. 27' (three-bay front) x 30', two-and-a-half stories, gable roof, denticulated brick cornice, tetrastyle porch across front elevation; several interior curved walls. Built 1850s; vacant. 1 ext. photo (1979), 1 photo of lake (1979); 1 data page (1979). LC code: PA,39-CATS,3.

Center Valley (Upper Saucon Township)

Barn, Decorated Red (PA-5321), at intersection of State Rte. 309 and State Rte. 191 (old Rte. 12). Random rubble with frame forebay contained within stone end walls, two levels, gable roof, window vent in gable end, forebay decorated with painted "hex signs" and scallop design, painted arches over openings, pedimented hood with "hex sign" over stable door in gable end, attached frame sheds. Built ca. 1840. 2 ext. photos (1941). LC code: PA,39-CENVA,1A.

East Texas Vicinity (Lower Macungie Township)

Barn A (1834) (PA-5310A), SE of East Texas. Stuccoed stone with frame forebay contained within stone end walls, two levels, gable roof with fish weathervane, diamond-shaped brick vents, "hex signs" and scallop design painted on forebay, painted arches over windows. Built 1834. Adjacent slatted corn crib and eighteenth-century barn. 1 ext. photo (1941). LC code: PA,39-MAC.V,2A. See *Barn B* (PA-5310B) for photo showing brick vents.

Barn B (PA-5310B). Random rubble with quoins, frame forebay contained within stone end walls (recessed stable area below concealed by addition of sliding wooden doors), two-level bank barn, gable roof, off-center wagon entrance, painted "hex signs" on forebay, wooden louvered vents. Built eighteenth century. 2 ext. photos (1941), 1 int. photo (1941). LC code: PA,39-MAC.V,2B.

Barn, Decorated (1857) (PA-5309), on dirt road between East Texas and Macungie. Random rubble with quoins, frame forebay contained within stone end walls, two levels, gable roof with frame gable ends, decorated with painted "hex signs" and arches over openings, additions on front elevation. Built 1857 (date on quoin); painted date 1924 over threshing floor doors indicates date of painted decorations. 3 ext. photos (1941). LC code: PA,39-ETEX.V,3A.

Barn (1853) (PA-5307), on Little Lehigh Creek. Random and coursed rubble (stuccoed at stable entrances), frame forebay contained within stone end walls, two levels, gable roof with cupola, faded painted "hex signs," painted arches over windows on forebay. Built 1853. 1 ext. photo (1941). LC code: PA,39-ETEX.V,2A.

Barn (1839) (PA-5308), SE of East Texas. Random rubble with frame forebay contained in stone end walls, two levels, gable roof, diamond-shaped vents in gable end walls, painted scallop design on forebay, additions next to ramp entrance. Built 1839 (date painted over threshing level door). 2 ext. photos (1941). LC code: PA,39-ETEX.V,1A.

Farm Groups (PA-5311), SE of East Texas. General view of several farms (1941). LC code: PA,39-MAC.V,5

Emmaus Vicinity

Barn, Decorated Red (PA-5315), State Rte. 29, N of Emmaus. Whitewashed stone (lower level) and frame with vertical siding (upper level), two levels, recessed lower level with brick piers, gable roof, transoms over doors, shallow pediments over windows, decorated with painted "hex signs" and arches over windows. Built nineteenth century. 1 ext. photo (1941). LC code: PA,39-EMMA.V,2A.

Dorfer, Abraham, Barn A (PA-5316A), no location provided. Random rubble partially stuccoed (stucco originally scored to resemble cut stone), frame forebay contained within stone end walls, two levels, gable roof, gabled hoods over stable entrances in gable end. Built 1840 (date stone). 1 ext. photo also shows *Barn B* (1941). LC code: PA,39-EMMA.V,3A.

Barn B (PA-5316B). Random and coursed rubble, frame forebay contained within stone end walls, two levels, gable roof, louvered ventilators, part of stable area open for storage, no grade-level entrance to hayloft. Built mid-eighteenth century. 1 ext. photo (1941). LC code: PA,39-EMMA.V,3B.

Emmaus Vicinity (Lower Macungie Township)

Wenner, Howard W., Barn (PA-5314A&B), off State Rte. 29, approx. 1 mi. N of Emmaus. Random rubble with quoins (stuccoed on three sides), two-level bank barn, gable roof, double barn with two threshing floors, stable entrances recessed behind arcade of five stone arches (one arch covered by sliding doors), granary doors with double-hung windows and louvered vents form symmetrical facade over arches. Built 1803; structure leaning 1941; center section collapsed in 1954 storm and entire barn demolished. Large impressive barn of a type found only in Lehigh and Montgomery Counties. 3 ext. photos (1941). LC code: PA,39-EMMA.V,4A&4B.

Emmaus Vicinity (Upper Milford Township)

Barn (PA-5306), off State Rte. 29, approx. 1 mi. S of Emmaus. Random rubble partially stuccoed, two levels, gable roof, window vent in gable end, ramp to threshing floor entrance. Date unknown. 1 ext. photo (1941). LC code: PA,39-EMMA.V,1A.

Fogelsville Vicinity

Barn, Decorated (circa 1845) (PA-5322), S of old U.S. Rte. 22, between Fogelsville and Allentown. Random rubble with quoins, frame forebay contained within stone end walls, two-level bank barn, gable roof, diamond-shaped brick vents, painted arches over openings, "hex signs" painted on forebay and gabled hood over entrance in gable end, stone and frame wing added on front elevation. Adjacent to slatted corn crib. Built ca. 1845. 2 ext. photos (1941). LC code: PA,39-FOGVI.V,2A.

Fogelsville Vicinity (Upper Macungie Township)

Barn (PA-5323), between Haase Mill and Steton School. Lower level random rubble with quoins and upper level squared logs (no chinking) covered with vertical siding, cantilevered frame forebay over stable entrances, two-level bank barn, gable roof, two-part stable doors with iron strap hinges, stone and frame addition to side. Built probably eighteenth century. 3 ext. photos including one of log construction (1941). LC code: PA,39-FOGVI.V,1A.

Limeport Vicinity (Lower Milford Township)

Barn, Decorated Red (PA-5317), between Limeport and Steinsburg. Random rubble, projecting frame forebay supported on V-topped wooden columns, two levels, gable roof with square cupola, louvered ventilators, forebay decorated with painted "hex signs," decorated hood over side entrance, frame wings added. Built nineteenth century. 1 ext. photo (1941). LC code: PA,39-LIM.V,1A.

Lyon Valley Vicinity

Barn, Red (PA-5325), between Lyon Valley and New Tripoli. Lower level whitewashed stone with upper level squared logs (no chinking) with vertical siding, frame forebay projects over stable entrances (originally cantilevered, later stone end walls added), two-level bank barn, gable roof, haysheds added. Probably built eighteenth century. 2 ext. photos (1941), 3 int. photos showing log construction (1941). LC code: PA,39-LYVA,1A.

Macungie Borough

Singmaster, John Adam, Barn (PA-5303), on State Rte. 100. Random rubble with quoins, frame forebay (added extension supported on wooden columns), two levels, gable roof with exposed eave plate, stone-arched entrance to storage area next to threshing door ramp, louvered ventilators, pair of gabled hoods with openings for birds over doors in gable end. Built mid-eighteenth century (pre-Revolutionary War); demolished. 4 ext. photos (1941). LC code: PA,39-MAC,1A.

Macungie Vicinity

Barn A (1834) and **Barn B** (PA-5310A&B). See East Texas Vicinity (Lower Macungie Township), Barn A (1834) and *Barn B* (PA-5310A&B).

Barn, Decorated Red (PA-5312), State Rte. 100. Stuccoed stone with frame forebay contained within stone end walls, two levels, gable roof, painted "hex signs" and scallop design on forebay, hood over side door. Built nineteenth century. 1 ext. photo (1941). LC code: PA,39-MAC.V,3A.

Farm Groups (PA-5311). See East Texas Vicinity (Lower Macungie Township), Farm Groups (PA-5311).

Roeder, S. and R.G., Barn (PA-5313), no location provided. Random rubble with projecting frame forebay, two levels, gable roof with square cupola, louvered ventilators, frame sheds added. Built 1820, 1886 (date stone fallen from gable end). 1 ext. photo (1941), 1 photo of date stone (1941). LC code: PA,39-MAC.V,6A.

Macungie Vicinity (Upper Milford Township)

Barn (PA-5305), on dirt road off State Rte. 100, E of Macungie. Random rubble with frame forebay contained within stone end walls, two levels, gable roof, painted single and double arches over openings in forebay, scalloped design painted along forebay edge, hood with "hex sign" over stable entrance in gable end. Built nineteenth century. 2 ext. photos (1941). LC code: PA,39-MAC.V,1A.

Barn, Stone (PA-5304), on dirt road off State Rte. 100, E of Macungie. Random rubble with quoins, frame forebay contained within stone end walls, two-level bank barn, gable roof, painted arches over windows in forebay and small door set in wagon entrance. Built nineteenth century. 2 ext. photos (1941). LC code: PA,39-MAC.V,4.

New Smithfield

Barn, Decorated Red (PA-5302). See New Smithville (Weisenberg Township), Barn, Decorated Red (PA-5302).

New Smithfield (Weisenberg Township)

Barn, Decorated Red (PA-5302), SW of U.S. Rte. 22 and New Smithville. Random rubble (stable level) and frame with vertical siding (threshing level), forebay supported on stone end walls, two levels, gable roof, painted "hex signs" on forebay and gable end, windows and doors with painted arches and folk designs (one door painted on to form symmetrical arrangement on forebay). Built nineteenth century. 1 ext. photo (1941), 1 int. photo (1941). LC code: PA,39-NESMI,1A.

Shimerville Vicinity (Upper Milford Township)

Barn, Decorated Red (PA-5318), SW of Shimerville. Whitewashed stone with cantilevered frame forebay, two levels, gable roof with shed roof over forebay, painted "hex signs" and window trim on forebay. Built nineteenth century. 1 ext. photo (1941). LC code: PA,39-SHIM.V,1A.

Slatington Borough

Slatington Houses along Main Street (PA-5453). 4 general views of Main St. (1979).

Whitehall Township

Whitehall Township General Views (PA-5450). 3 photos showing frame house, curved porch roof, and general view in North Whitehall Township (1979).

Montgomery County

Ambler Vicinity

Mather's Mill. See Whitemarsh (Whitemarsh Township), Farmar Mill.

Ambler Vicinity (Whitpain Township)

Barn, Stone (PA-5256), Mt. Pleasant Ave., at bridge over Wissahickon Creek. Random rubble, projecting frame forebay removed, two levels, gable roof, frame sheds added on front and rear, louvered ventilators. Built early nineteenth century (date stone in gable end not discernable, adjacent mill dated 1809). 2 ext. photos (1941), 1 int. photo (1941). LC code: PA,46-AMB.V,9.

Bala Cynwyd (Lower Merion Township)

Pencoyd Farm, House (Roberts Estate) (PA-1087), 355 City Line Ave. (U.S. Rte. 1). Random rubble, L-shaped, approx. 75' (eight-bay front) x 28' with extensive ell to N (rear), two-and-a-half stories with basement, gambrel roof with dormers, variety of porches; elaborate interiors. Early farmhouse built in seventeenth century with numerous additions into twentieth century; original house (W four bays) built ca. 1690; setback stone kitchen wing added to E elevation before 1827; various changes (wings, dormers, porches, interior remodeling) in nineteenth and twentieth century; 1884 two-and-a-half-story stone wing added to N elevation, Frank Furness, architect; 1913 extensive alterations and remodeling (continued S facade 34' eastward, carried E elevation back to join 1884 wing, interior extensively remodeled), Louis Carter Baker Jr., architect; 1951 N area of kitchen wing demolished; 1964 sold for demolition. Occupied by Roberts family from seventeenth century until demolition. 6 copy photos of measured drawings (1849, ca. 1914, 1962), 2 ext. photos (1963), 4 int. photos (1963), 4 copy photos of ext. (1870, 1891, ca. 1893), 21 data pages (1964). LC code: PA,46-BALA,1.

> *Barn* (PA-1090). Dressed coursed rubble and random rubble (partially stuccoed), rectangular bank barn, two levels, gable roof. Built 1791 (replaced original barn); ruinous

condition 1963; demolished ca. 1964. 1 ext. photo (1963). LC code: PA,46-BALA,1B.

Smokehouse (PA-1089). Stuccoed brick, small octagonal smokehouse, two stories, polygonal roof with small cupola, pointed-arch louvered openings. Built ca. 1840; demolished. 1 copy photo of ext. (ca. 1872). LC code: PA,46-BALA,1A.

Roberts Estate. See Pencoyd Farm.

Barren Hill (Whitemarsh Township)

Lukens Stone Barn (PA-5255), on Park Ave., at Ridge Pike. Stuccoed random rubble, two levels, gable roof, stable entrances recessed behind three stone arches, gabled hood over loft door. Built late eighteenth century. 2 ext. photos (1941). LC code: PA,46-BARRHI,1A.

Blue Bell Vicinity (Whitpain Township)

Barn, Stone (PA-5250), Walton Rd., S of Blue Bell. Random rubble with quoins, two levels, gable roof, extended by stone addition to side, stone shed added to rear, louvered ventilators, adjacent windmill and stone-walled farmyard. Built 1760; additions. 1 ext. photo (1941). LC code: PA,46-BLUEB.V,1A.

Bryn Mawr (Lower Merion Township)

Bryn Mawr Hospital Thrift Shop. See Whitehall Railroad Station.

Pennsylvania Railroad Bryn Mawr Station (PA-1081), NW corner of Bryn Mawr and Morris Aves. Random irregular ashlar with quoins and sandstone trim, irregular H-shaped, 113'-6" x 28'-3", one-and-a-half and two stories, jerkinhead roofs with gabled dormers, decorative bargeboards, chimney with paired octagonal stacks, sandstone lintels and label moldings over openings, porches with columns and brackets, Victorian Gothic style; center and E sections waiting rooms, two-story W section living quarters. Built 1869; Joseph M. Wilson, architect; alterations 1900; demolished 1963. 3 ext. photos (1963), 1 ext. copy photo (ca. 1870), 1 int. photo (1963); 5 data pages (1963- 64). LC code: PA,46-BRYN,1.

Whitehall Railroad Station (Bryn Mawr Hospital Thrift Shop) (PA-577), junction of Glenbrook Ave. and Haverford Rd. Frame with clapboarding, cross-shape, two-story center section (one bay) with gable roof flanked by one-story side wings (two bays each) with hip roofs, carved bargeboards with central pendent on center section, bracketed cornice with pendents under eaves on wings, arched windows in center section. Built 1859; large display window added; Bryn Mawr Hospital Thrift Shop 1964. This station served original Pennsylvania Railroad route; in 1868 the railroad straightened the line and built a new station (see Pennsylvania Railroad Bryn Mawr Station PA-1081). 1 ext. photo (1964); 1 data page (1983). LC code: PA,46-BRYN,2.

Center Square Vicinity (Whitpain Township)

Barn, Stone (PA-5251), on State Rte. 73, approx. 1 mi. E of U.S. Rte. 202 and Center Square. Whitewashed random rubble, built in three sections, two-level bank barn, gable roof, pent roofs over stable entrances, slit ventilators. Original barn (section with slit ventilators) built late eighteenth-early nineteenth century; more than doubled in size with addition to side dated 1844; stone addition built next to threshing floor entrance. 4 ext. photos (1941). LC code: PA,46-CENSQ.V,1A.

Conshohocken Vicinity

Andorra Inn Barn (PA-5254), corner of Ridge and Butler Pikes, N of Conshohocken. Random rubble with quoins, two-level bank barn built in two sections, projecting frame forebay with random-width clapboarding over stable entrances on one half, stable entrances recessed behind stone arcade on other half, gable roof, louvered ventilators, stone-walled farmyard. Section with frame forebay built mid-eighteenth century; arcaded section added shortly after (possibly when adjacent inn was constructed in 1756). 5 ext. photos (1941). LC code: PA,46-CONSH.V,1A.

East Greenville Vicinity (Upper Hanover Township)

Baus, Alfred B., Barn. See Mack, Abraham, Barn.

Mack, Abraham, Barn (1858) (Alfred B. Baus Barn) (PA-5257), State Rte. 29, NE of East Greenville. Brick (upper level) and stuccoed stone (lower level), frame forebay contained within end walls, two levels, gable roof, X-shaped brick vents, painted scenes on forebay, three-part windows with painted interlocking arches, gabled hood with painted star design over side stable door. Built 1858. 3 ext. photos (1941). LC code: PA,46-GRENVE.V,1A.

Fairview Village Vicinity

Barn, Stone (PA-5258), on U.S. Rte. 422 (Germantown Pike), between Fairview Village and Norriton. Random rubble, two levels, gable roof, stable entrances recessed behind arcade, three arches with larger central arch, door to threshing floor and window to hayloft above central arch (window probably originally doors for hay hoist), frame shed added to side. Built 1813 (date stone). 2 ext. photos (1941). LC code: PA,46-PROVL,3A.

Haverford

Quaker Meetinghouse. See Delaware County, Havertown Vicinity (Haverford Township), Haverford Meetinghouse.

Horsham Vicinity (Horsham Township)

Graeme Park (PA-579), E side of Keith Valley Rd., .3 mi. S of County Line Rd., .8 mi. W of State Rte. 611 (Easton Rd.). Museum operated by Pennsylvania Historical and Museum Commission. Coursed dressed rubble (walls 2' thick), approx. 60' (six-bay front) x 25' (two bays), two-and-a-half stories, high gambrel roof with shed dormers, paired clustered chimneys in center of roof; one room deep, excellent Georgian style interior woodwork. Built 1721-22; John Kirk, mason; built by Sir William Keith, Royal Governor of Pennsylvania, as a malt house, part of an industrial settlement planned by Keith; remodeled into a dwelling 1739-40 (fine interiors added at this time) by Dr. Thomas Graeme, a prominent physician; acquired by Commonwealth of Pennsylvania 1958; restored 1968-71. 3 ext. photos (1958), 2 int. photos (1958). LC code: PA,46-HORM,1. NHL.

Barn (PA-579A). Random rubble (partially stuccoed), bank barn, two levels, gable roof, projecting frame forebay supported on circular stone piers. Built eighteenth century; acquired by Commonwealth of Pennsylvania 1958; restored for use as visitors' center 1968-71. 2 ext. photos (1958). LC code: PA,46-HORM,1A.

Jenkintown Vicinity (Abington Township)

Alverthorpe (PA-130), between Meetinghouse Rd., Jenkintown Rd., Fox Chase Rd. and Forest Ave., E of Jenkintown. Stuccoed stone with quoins, irregular plan, central block with projecting pedimented end pavilions with tower to side and wing to rear, three stories with five-story tower and two-story rear wing, cross gable roofs with hip roofs on tower and wing, bracketed cornices, semicircular Doric portico on front elevation, balustraded balconies, walkway with elaborate ironwork to side, Italianate style. Built 1850-60; John Notman, architect; demolished 1937; site now Alverthorpe Park. Large greenhouse on grounds. Built for Joshua Francis Fisher. 3 ext. photos (1937), 3 int. photos (1937), 1 photo of greenhouse (1937); 3 data pages (1937). LC code: PA,46-JENK,1.

King of Prussia (Upper Merion Township)

Commercial Building (King of Prussia Antique Shop) (PA-5360), U.S. Rte. 202 (Swedesford Rd.), just W of intersection with State Rte. 23. Stuccoed stone, 22'-2" (three-bay front) x 40', two-and-a-half stories, gable roof with gable end over entrance. Built late eighteenth century; kitchen addition to rear; one-story addition on E elevation; porch added across front elevation; demolished 1986. One of last three remaining village structures from historic crossroad. 4 sheets (1986, including site plan, plans, elevations, section); 1 data page (1987). LC code: PA,46-KING,2.

King of Prussia Antique Shop. See Commercial Building.

King of Prussia Inn (PA-1009), on median strip of U.S. Rte. 202 (Dekalb Pike), opposite King of Prussia Rd., .1 mi. W of Gulph Rd. Stuccoed random rubble, 48'-2" (six-bay front) x 33'-4" (two bays), two-and-a-half stories with basement, gable roof; central hall plan. Built ca. 1719 (three W bays) by William Rees; 1769 enlarged (three E bays) by

Daniel Thompson; stuccoed random rubble shed added at NE corner nineteenth century; two-story porch added across N (front) elevation nineteenth century; one-story concrete block wing added at SE corner (removed after 1960); one-story frame shed added across S elevation (removed after 1960); unoccupied and in poor condition 1975; owned by King of Prussia Historical Society and restored. Named for Frederick the Great of Prussia, this early-eighteenth-century inn, located at a major crossroad, served as a public house for over two hundred years, Lafayette and Washington were among the patrons. 5 sheets (1959, including site plan, plans); 3 ext. photos (1960), 9 int. photos (1960), 2 ext. copy photos (ca. 1860-70, ca. 1880), 1 photo of tavern sign (1935, depicts King Frederick); 9 data pages (1959-60). LC code: PA,46-KING,1. NR.

King of Prussia Vicinity (Upper Merion Township)

Barn (PA-5247), Beidler Rd., near Valley Forge National Historical Park. Random rubble with projecting frame forebay supported on tapered stone columns, two levels, gable roof, stone buttresses on side, louvered ventilators, frame sheds added. Built ca. 1837 (date stone covered). 1 ext. photo (1941). LC code: PA,46-KING.V,1A.

Barn (PA-5248), Beidler Rd. Random rubble, frame forebay with stone end walls and tapered stone columns, two levels, gable roof with frame gable ends, shed roof over forebay, frame shed with passage at threshing-floor entrance. Date unknown. 1 ext. photo (1941). LC code: PA,46-KING.V,2A.

Barn 1790 (PA-5249), State Rte. 23 (Valley Forge Rd.). Random rubble with quoins, frame forebay inset in stone wall, two-level bank barn, gable roof, louvered ventilators, smaller random rubble barn connected to side by frame wing, stone shed added next to wagon entrance of larger barn. Larger barn built 1790 (date stone); smaller barn built by same person 1802 (date stone). 3 ext. photos (1941). LC code: PA,46-KING.V,3A.

Lower Providence Township

Barn, Stone (PA-5258). See Fairview Village Vicinity, Barn, Stone (PA-5258).

Vaux-Wetherill Stone Barn (PA-5350). See Wetherills Corner (Lower Providence Township), Vaux-Wetherill Stone Barn (PA-5350).

Merion

Wayne, General Anthony, Inn. See Narberth Vicinity (Lower Merion Township), Wayne, General Anthony, Inn.

Narberth Vicinity (Lower Merion Township)

Lower Merion Friends Meetinghouse (Merion Friends Meetinghouse) (PA-145), intersection of State Rte. 320 (Montgomery Ave.) and Meetinghouse Ln. Stuccoed random rubble scored to imitate ashlar (stuccoed 1829), T-shaped, three-bay front, one-and-a-half stories, cross gable roofs with pent eaves, semi-elliptical arches over openings, pedimented hoods over entrances. Built 1695 (date stone); addition and completed 1712. William Penn preached in this early Quaker meetinghouse; oldest house of worship in state. 3 ext. photos (1923, 1940), 1 ext. copy photo (n.d.), 1 photo of carriage sheds (1940); 1 data page (1983). LC code: PA,46-NARB.V,1.

Merion Friends Meetinghouse. See Lower Merion Friends Meetinghouse.

Wayne, General Anthony, Inn (PA-144), 625 Montgomery Ave. Stuccoed random rubble, main section five by two bays with two-bay wing to N (rear), two-and-a-half-story main section with three-story wing, gable roofs, two-story porch across S elevation (partially enclosed later). Built 1704 (original inn was eastern three bays of main section); between 1704 and 1750 two western bays added; 1750 three-story rear wing built; 1940 one-story brick wing added; interior rebuilt after 1964 fire; has continuously served as a tavern since construction by Edward Rees. Named for Major General Anthony Wayne after he dined and lodged here in 1795; Washington and Lafayette also stopped here. 1 ext. photo (1940). LC code: PA,46-MER,1. NR.

Niantic Vicinity

Barn (PA-5329), Hill Rd. (LR46012), NW of State Rte. 663. Random rubble with frame forebay contained within stone end walls, two-level bank barn, gable roof with frame gable ends, moldings around openings, pediments painted over forebay windows, three-part window with decorated vent above in gable end, pedimented hood over side stable door. Built ca. 1855. 3 ext. photos (1941). LC code: PA,46-NIANT.V,1A.

Barn, Decorated Red (PA-5349), off Hill Rd. (LR46012). Stone and frame with vertical siding, forebay supported by end walls, two levels, gable roof, painted decorations on forebay and in gable end. Built nineteenth century. 2 ext. photos (1941). LC code: PA,46-_____,1.

Niantic Vicinity (Douglass Township)

Hoffman, H. & S., Barn (1853) (PA-5252), on Hill Rd. (LR46012), NW of State Rte. 663. Stuccoed stone with frame forebay contained within stone end walls, two levels, gable roof with frame gable ends, pediments over openings, painted "hex signs," three-part windows with pediments decorated with painted hearts. Built 1856 (painted inscription). 2 ext. photos (1941). LC code: PA,46-POTTS.V,2A.

Norristown Vicinity

King of Prussia Tavern Sign. See King of Prussia (Upper Merion Township), King of Prussia Inn.

Port Kennedy (Upper Merion Township)

Kennedy Mansion (PA-1959), 1050 Port Kennedy Rd., in Valley Forge National Historical Park. Stuccoed stone, main block 46'-8" (five-bay front) x 40'-7" with three rear sections, three stories with four-story central tower, hip roof, bracketed cornice, door with transom and side lights, porch with cast-iron treillage, Italianate style; central hall plan, elaborate plaster decoration. Built 1852; additions ca. 1920 and 1950; remodeled into apartments; acquired by National Park Service 1978 and restored. 12 sheets (1983, including site plan with planting plan, plans, elevations, section, details, sheet on garage); 19 ext. photos (1982), 7 int. photos (1982), 1 photo of garage (1982). LC code: PA,46-POKEN,1. NR.

Pottstown Vicinity

Barn (PA-5329). See Niantic Vicinity, Barn (PA-5329).

Pottstown Vicinity (Douglass Township)

Hoffman, H. & S., Barn (1853) (PA-5252). See Niantic Vicinity (Douglass Township), Hoffman, H. & S., Barn (1853) (PA-5252).

Pottstown Vicinity (Upper Pottsgrove Township)

Barn, Decorated Red (1852) (PA-5253), on State Rd. (LR46002), just off State Rte. 100. Stuccoed random rubble with brick stable wall, frame forebay contained within stone end walls, two-level bank barn, gable roof with frame gable ends, brick X-shaped ventilators, pediments over openings in forebay, painted "hex signs," window flanked by louvered vents and painted stars with decorative vent above in gable end, hood over side stable entrance. Built 1852. 2 ext. photos (1941). LC code: PA,46-POTTS.V,1A.

Trappe Borough

Augustus Lutheran Church (Old Trappe Church) (PA-175), NW side of E. Seventh Ave., at U.S. Rte. 422 (Main St.). Stuccoed random rubble, rectangular with semi-hexagonal apse (E elevation), two stories, gambrel roof, enclosed projecting pedimented entrance bay with arched opening on W (front) and S elevations; hand-hewn timbers, hand-forged nails, hinges and door latches, heart-shaped cut-out gallery railing. Built 1743; built by Dr. Heinrich Melchoir Muhlenberg; restored. Oldest extant Lutheran Church in country. 7 ext. photos (1925), 3 int. photos (1925). LC code: PA,46-TRAP,1. NHL.

Old Trappe Church. See Augustus Lutheran Church.

Valley Forge Vicinity (Upper Merion Township)

Jones House (Old Superintendent's Quarters) (PA-5369), on Trace Rd., just N of State Rte. 23, in Valley Forge National Historical Park adjacent to Isaac Potts House (Washington's Headquarters) (PA-1171). Random rubble, 25' (three-bay front) x 30', two-and-a-half stories, gable roof (originally mansard roof), hood over front entrance. Built ca. 1870, Second Empire style; 1926 extensively altered to blend with surrounding colonial structures; one-story stone kitchen wing (15' x 17'-6") added ca. 1937; vacant and in poor condition. 2 data pages (1986). LC code: PA,46-VALFO,3.

Old Superintendent's Quarters. See Jones House.

Potts, Isaac, House (Washington's Headquarters) (PA-1171), on Trace Rd., .1 mi. N of State Rte. 23, just S of Schuylkill River, in Valley Forge National Historical Park. Museum. Coursed ashlar and random rubble, rectangular (three-bay front) with setback kitchen wing to N, two-and-a-half stories with two-story wing, gable roof with pent eaves, transom and pedimented hood over entrance; side hall plan. Built ca. 1772; wing originally one story with arched opening, second story added mid-nineteenth century, changed to one-and-a-half stories ca. 1887, changed to two stories and arch enclosed ca. 1926, changed to original appearance 1973-76; log shed added to N of kitchen wing ca. 1887, clapboarded shed replaced log shed ca. 1926, shed replaced with beehive oven 1973-75; restored 1887, 1926, 1933-34, 1953, 1973-76. Acquired by Centennial and Memorial Association of Valley Forge 1879; acquired by Commonwealth of Pennsylvania 1893; transferred to National Park Service 1976. General George Washington's headquarters during encampment of Continental Army at Valley Forge in winter of 1777-78. 18 copy photos of 1931 measured drawings (including plans, elevations, sections, details), 6 ext. photos (1937), 1 int. photo (1937). LC code: PA,46-VALFO,1. NHL.

Washington's Headquarters. See Potts, Isaac, House.

Wetherills Corner (Lower Providence Township)

Vaux-Wetherill Stone Barn (PA-5350), Pawling Rd. Large random rubble barn, three levels, gable roof, wooden louvered ventilators, arched window surrounded by arched louvered vent in gable end, two stone and frame additions with gable roofs built at threshing entrance, stone ramp and barnyard wall. Built 1826 by Samuel Wetherill; additions 1845 by John Wetherill, John Price, mason and Salomay Artible, carpenter. 3 ext. photos (1941), 1 int. photo showing grinding wheel (1941). LC code: PA,46-PROVL.1A.

Wetherill Stone Barn. See Vaux-Wetherill Stone Barn.

Whitemarsh (Whitemarsh Township)

Farmar Mill (Mather Mill) (PA-126), N side of Mathers Ln., .1 mi. N of junction of State Rte. 73 (Skippack Pike) and Bethlehem Pike, on E side of Wissahickon Creek. Dressed random rubble, irregular five-bay front by three bays, two-and-a-half stories with attic and basement, gable roof with dormers (gable of central dormer projects to protect crane and pulley). Built ca. 1690 by Edward Farmar; altered 1787 by Isaac Mather; one-story random rubble wing added on E elevation; functioned as mill until 1896, remained in operation over two hundred years; owned by Pennsylvania Historical and Museum Commission, restored. Built by Edward Farmar, the first settler in the area, on land given to his father, Jasper, by William Penn. Rare example of an extant late-seventeenth-century gristmill. 5 ext. photos (1936); 2 data pages (1937). LC code: PA,46-AMB.V,6. NR.

Hope Lodge. See Morris, Samuel, House.

Mather Mill. See Farmar Mill.

Morris, Samuel, House (Hope Lodge) (PA-18), .2 mi. E of Bethlehem Pike on private road, .2 mi. N of State Rte. 73 (Skippack Pike). Museum operated by Pennsylvania Historical and Museum Commission. Random rubble faced with brick on facade and stuccoed on sides and rear, L-shaped, 56' (seven-bay front) x 39'-8" with two-bay kitchen wing (25'-5") connected by porch to house, two-and-a-half stories, gabled hip roof and gable roof on wing with dormers, Georgian style; central hall plan, fine interior woodwork. Built 1723; pedimented hood added over W entrance; porch connection to kitchen glass enclosed; two-and-a-half-story wing added to E of kitchen wing. Built for Samuel Morris, a successful mill operator; served as headquarters of General Greene after Battle of Germantown. Random rubble barn. 12 sheets (1936, including plot plan, plans, elevations, sections, details); 2 ext. photos (1937), 3 int. photos (1937), 1 ext. photo of barn (1937); 2 data pages (1937). LC code: PA,46-WHIM,2. NR.

Northampton County

Belfast Vicinity (Bushkill Township)

Henry Gun Factory (PA-122), N side of LR18040, approx. .5 mi. SW of Belfast and State Rte. 115, in Jacobsburg State Park. Random rubble with quoins (first story) and clapboarded half-timber with stone and brick nogging (second story), T-shaped, 84'-6" x 32'-3" with ell on S (rear) elevation 18' x 24', two-and-a-half stories, gable roof with shed dormers, opening on first story for water wheel and mill race channel; room to either side of channel. Built 1811-12; rear ell removed before 1936; poor condition 1936; demolished soon after; archeological work done by Jacobsburg Historical Society. Built by William Henry, Jr.; supplied arms for the War of 1812; manufactured arms here until 1895; part of important eighteenth- and nineteenth-century industrial area. 11 sheets (1936, including plans, elevations, section, details); 4 ext. photos (1936), 4 ext. copy photos (ca. 1900), 1 photo of wooden flywheel (1936), 1 photo of Henry guns (1936), 2 photos of William Henry and son portraits (1936); 7 data pages (1936). LC code: PA,48-BOLT,1. Site part of NR Jacobsburg Historic District.

Henry Gun Factory, Workman's House (PA-123), N side of LR48040, approx. .5 mi. SW of Belfast and State Rte. 115, in Jacobsburg State Park. Random rubble (exposed basement) and frame with clapboarding (first story), 16'-4" (two-bay front) x 18'-2" (two bays), one-and-a-half stories on sloping site fully exposing basement to rear, cellar built into hill, gable roof, gabled hoods over entrances (later additions); living room on main floor with sleeping quarters in attic and kitchen in basement, vaulted cellar. Built 1812; restored ca. 1936. Originally occupied by workman from Henry Gun Factory. 7 sheets (1936, including plans, elevations, section, details); 2 ext. photos (1936), 1 int. photo (1936), 1 ext. copy photo (ca. 1900); 3 data pages (1936). LC code: PA,48-BOLT,2. NR (Jacobsburg Historic District).

Bethlehem

Bethlehem Moravian Community

Bethlehem was the first permanent Moravian settlement in America, founded in 1740. The Moravians, originally from Bohemia and Moravia, came to America for religious freedom and to christianize the Indians. Living communally, they developed Bethlehem as a carefully planned community built around an open square. The architecture was Germanic in character, built first of log, then of native stone with simple, symmetrical facades and the characteristic double rows of dormers. An industrial area was developed along the Monocacy Creek in 1743 to support the self-sufficient community. All structures are now included in the NR Bethlehem Historic District, and some are individually listed. Entries for the recorded structures follow:

Bell House (Moravian Seminary, Bell House) (PA-1152), 56 W. Church St. Coursed ashlar, 35' (three-bay front) x 27', two stories with double attic, gambrel roof with two rows of dormers and octagonal belfry (railing added later); central hall plan. Built 1746 as residence for married people of the Moravian community; E wing added 1748 and W wing added 1749 (both 21' long); original balcony over central door removed ca. 1766 (window above was a door opening onto balcony); central doorway on S elevation added post 1875; door on E elevation now a window. Structure housed Moravian Seminary for Girls 1749-91; still owned by the Moravians. 4 ext. photos (1935, 1937, one photo shows the adjacent Single Sisters' House, one photo shows 1751 Old Chapel which connects *Gemeinhaus* [PA-1142] with the Bell House). LC code: PA,48-BETH,3C.

Central Moravian Church (Moravian Seminary, Church) (PA-1147), 406 Main St. Stuccoed brick, H-shaped, nine by six bays, two-and-a-half stories with raised basement (end pavilions) and one story (center section), gable roof, central open belfry on octagonal clock tower, entrances on S elevation in pavilions are raised to nave level by double staircase with elaborate iron railing, large arched windows on center section of S elevation, Federal details; roof trusses supported by exterior walls to allow uninterrupted nave space. Built 1803-06 for the Moravian community; John Cunis, designer.

When constructed it was probably the largest church in Pennsylvania. 9 ext. photos (1935, 1937, 1969). LC code: PA,48-BETH,2.

Eighteenth-Century Moravian Industrial Area (PA-1151), on banks of Monocacy Creek, N of Hill-to-Hill Bridge Ramp, W of Main St. and Old York Rd. Established by the Moravians by 1741, this area eventually housed thirty-two industries which employed advanced technological methods to produce a variety of products making Bethlehem nearly self-sufficient. 1 general view (1969), including Luckenbach Grist Mill (PA-1148), Grist Miller's House (PA-1144), Tannery (PA-1143) and Waterworks (PA-1146). LC code: PA,48-BETH,7. NR.

Gemeinhaus (PA-1142), 62-66 W. Church St. Museum operated by Moravian Museum. Log, 93'-7" (ten-bay front) x 32'-7", two stories with double attic and basement, steep gable roof with flared eaves, shed dormers on S slope (N and S slope originally had two rows of shed dormers), two chevron-patterned double doors with entrance porches; two parallel central hall plans. W section built 1741, E section finished by 1743 completing original concept; small frame addition at NW corner; ashlar ell added on NE corner to connect structure to Bell House (PA-1152); covered with rough cast ca. 1800; clapboards applied 1868; restored 1965. The second structure built by the Moravians at Bethlehem (oldest existing structure) and one of the largest log structures erected in this country, *Gemeinhaus* was built as a community house for the newly founded Moravian settlement. Birthplace and home of Lewis David von Schweinitz, one of America's leading botanists. 10 sheets (1968, including site plans, plans, elevations, details); 4 ext. photos (1969), 8 int. photos (1969). LC code: PA,48-BETH,3A. NHL.

Goundie House (PA-1145), 501 Main St. Museum operated by Historic Bethlehem, Inc. Brick, 40'-9" (five-bay front) x 33'-2", two-and-a-half stories with basement, gable roof with dormers with Gothic sash, cornice with bead and reel motif, semicircular entrance with pilasters and projecting cornice on E (front) elevation, flat lintels with keystones; central hall plan. Built ca. 1810; shingled additions on W elevation; storefront on E elevation (removed during restoration); entrance to basement added on E elevation; restored 1969-75. Built by a prominent Moravian brewer, John Sebastian Goundie, this was probably the first brick building in Bethlehem. 9 sheets (1968, including plans, elevation, section, details); 9 ext. photos (n.d., 1969), 2 int. photos (1969). LC code: PA,48-BETH,12.

Grist Miller's House (PA-1144), 459 Old York Rd., in Eighteenth-Century Moravian Industrial Area. Brick, three-bay front, one-and-a-half stories on sloping site fully exposing random rubble basement, gable roof with gabled dormer, fanlight over E (front) entrance, two-story porch added. Stone portion built 1782 as home for Moravian miller and his family; enlarged ca. 1830s with brick addition; exterior partially restored 1973 by Historic Bethlehem, Inc. 5 ext. photos (1969). See Eighteenth-Century Moravian Industrial Area (PA-1151). LC code: PA,48-BETH,7D. NR.

Lester House (PA-1005), location not provided. Detail of chevron-patterned double door; built 1743. 1 photo of door (ca. 1935). LC code: PA,48-BETH,1.

Luckenbach Grist Mill (PA-1148), N side of Ohio Rd., on E bank of Monocacy Creek, in Eighteenth-Century Moravian Industrial Area. Museum operated by Historic Bethlehem, Inc. Brick, L-shaped, five-bay front, three-and-a-half stories, gambrel roof with gabled dormers and later L-shaped frame monitor, loading doors on three levels, small one-story E wing (collapsed). Built in 1869 (third mill on site) on remaining stone foundations from earlier mill; brick addition at NE corner; grain elevator of crib construction covered with shingles added at SW corner prior to 1892 and connected to mill by additional bay (removed 1973); two-story addition at NW corner behind elevator; restored. 3 ext. photos (1969). See Eighteenth-Century Moravian Industrial Area (PA-1151). LC code: PA,48-BETH,7C. HAER, NR.

Moravian Seminary, Bell House. See Bell House.

Moravian Seminary, Church. See Central Moravian Church.

Schnitz House (PA-1154), 38 W. Church St. Log covered with stucco, seven-bay front, one-and-a-half stories with basement, gable roof with shed dormer, flat brick arches over windows and doors. Built ca. 1810 by the Moravian community. Used for cutting and drying apples (schnitz). 1 ext. photo (1937). LC code: PA,48-BETH,6.

Single Brethren's House (PA-1141), 89 W. Church St. Coursed rubble, 82'-11" (ten-bay front) x 49'-10" (five bays), three stories with double attic, hipped gambrel roof with balustrade, gabled dormers on lower slope and shed dormers on upper slope, central chevron-patterned double doors on N and S elevations; central hall plan. Built 1748; windows and doors on N elevation altered ca. 1814; four-story addition to W ca. 1859; N elevation stuccoed and pedimented lintels added to windows and bargeboards added to dormers to blend with style of addition; numerous additions to S of 1859 addition; interior altered; restored. This is the largest structure in the Bethlehem Moravian community. Served as hospital for Continental Army 1776-78; occupied by Moravian brethren until 1814; Moravian Seminary for Girls until 1950s; now part of Moravian College. 21 sheets (1968, including site plans, plans, elevations, sections, details); 9 ext. photos (1969), 13 int. photos (1969). LC code: PA,48-BETH,4.

Single Sisters' House (PA-1153), 44 W. Church St. Built in three sections: coursed and random rubble, approx. 48' (five-bay front) x 30', two stories with double attic, gambrel roof hipped at W end, two rows of dormers (gable and shed dormers), brick arches over windows, central entrance with chevron-patterned door on S (front) elevation; two-story stone addition with double attic to N connects Single Sisters' House to the Bell House; large two-story stone addition with double attic to E. Original section built 1744 by the Moravians as Single Brethren's House, became Single Sisters' House 1748 when Brothers moved to new quarters (PA-1141); N connecting wing added 1752, buttresses added to wing 1755; wing to E added 1773; still owned by the Moravians. Original section was first stone building in Bethlehem and set the architectural character for later structures. 1 ext. photo (1937, shows 1773 wing only), see Bell House (PA-1152) for partial ext. view of 1752 connecting wing. LC code: PA,48-BETH,3B.

Sun Inn (PA-1150), 564 Main St. Museum operated by Sun Inn Preservation Association. Originally native limestone, 66' (seven-bay front) x 40', two-and-a-half stories with basement, jerkinhead roof with slight flare at eaves, shed dormers and central dormer with segmental arch and scroll motifs, pedimented entrance porch on S elevation; central hall plan. Built 1758-60 to house the growing number of visitors to the Moravian community; substantially altered from original appearance (sections of original inn survived within the southern portion of the remodeled structure); 1826 third story added and entire building covered with rough cast; 1850s fourth story added and covered with flat roof, four-story addition built to N, shops installed at street level; 1921 brick veneer added, interior altered and floor levels changed; restored 1982. 5 sheets (1970, showing altered and original conditions, including site plan, plans, elevations, sections). LC code: PA,48-BETH,13. NR.

Tannery (PA-1143), on E bank of Monocacy Creek, SW of Ohio Rd., in Eighteenth-Century Moravian Industrial Area. Museum operated by Historic Bethlehem, Inc. Coursed rubble, 66'-5" (five-bay front) x 36'-4", three-and-a-half stories, gable roof with flared eaves, brick segmental arches over openings. Built 1761 to replace 1743 frame tannery; most openings altered (restored); N elevation and part of E elevation stuccoed (removed); roof tiles replaced with asphalt shingles (tiles replaced); interior altered with only third floor remaining largely original (restored); restored 1968-71. Tanning was one of the first and largest industries in colonial Bethlehem; 1870s tanning operations ceased and building used as tenement then laundry until vacated 1962. 16 sheets (1968, before restoration but original elements are noted, including site plans, plans, elevations, sections, framing details); 7 ext. photos (1969, before restoration), 18 int. photos (1969, before restoration). See Eighteenth-Century Moravian Industrial Area (PA-1151). LC code: PA,48-BETH,7B. NR.

Waterworks (PA-1146), on E bank of Monocacy Creek, W of Main St., in Eighteenth-Century Moravian Industrial Area. Museum operated by Historic Bethlehem, Inc. Random rubble, rectangular, three-bay front, two-and-a-half stories, gable roof with flared eaves, central chimney, brick arches over openings. Built 1762; 1793 view shows jerkinhead roof on W elevation (removed); window replaced main entrance on S elevation (entrance restored); sliding garage door added on W elevation (restored); tile roof replaced (restored); exterior restored 1972, interior restored 1976. Bethlehem had one of the first waterworks in America to successfully use a pumped system (developed 1754); this structure built 1762 to house enlarged system. 3 ext. photos (1969), 6 int. photos (1969). See Eighteenth-Century Moravian Industrial Area (PA-1151). LC code: PA,48-BETH,7A. NHL.

Widows' House (PA-1155), 53 W. Church St. Coursed ashlar, 78' (nine-bay front) x 44', two stories with double attic, gable roof with gabled dormers on lower roof and shed dormers on upper roof, six paired chimneys, brick arches over windows; central hall plan. Built 1768 to house widows of Moravian missionaries; Carl Schulze in charge of construction; Andrew Schober and Martin Schenck, master masons; Tobias Hirte, master carpenter; W end originally had jerkinhead roof (removed); 20' section added to E 1794-95; annex (40' x 80') built to S in 1889 (connected to original structure by a wooden wing); still owned by the Moravians. 1 ext. photo (1937). LC code: PA,48-BETH,5.

Bolton

Henry Gun Factory and Workman's House. See Belfast Vicinity (Bushkill Township), Henry Gun Factory and Workman's House.

Easton

Cinruss Building. See 31 North Fourth Street (Commercial Building).

31 North Fourth Street (Commercial building) (Cinruss Building) (PA-5140). Brick, 30' (three-bay front) x 71', three stories, flat roof, bracketed cornice with paneled frieze, curved wooden window heads, storefronts. Built 1857; demolished. 3 ext. photos (1979), 2 int. photos (1979); 18 data pages (1980). LC code: PA,48-EATO,2.

33-35 North Fourth Street (Commercial building) (Patio Club Building) (PA-5141). Brick with wooden trim, 30' (four-bay front) x 72', three stories, flat roof, bracketed cornice, store front with pilasters. Built ca. 1857; rear addition; demolished. 2 ext. photos (1979), 2 int. photos (1979); 16 data pages (1980). LC code: PA,48-EATO,3.

Parson-Taylor House (PA-1008), NE corner of S. Fourth and Ferry Sts. Coursed squared rubble, 16' (two-bay front) x 26' (three bays), two and a half stories, gable roof, large chimney at N gable end, transoms over doors, pent roof on W (front) elevation, gabled hood over S door. Built 1757; 1904 purchased by George Taylor Chapter of the Daughters of the American Revolution and restored. Built by William Parsons, a surveyor sent to area by the Penns; George Taylor, a signer of the Declaration, lived here. Oldest extant house in Easton. 1 ext. photo (ca. 1925); 1 data page (1941). LC code: PA,48-EATO,1. NR.

Patio Club Building. See 33-35 North Fourth Street (Commercial Building).

520 Pine Street (House) (PA-5342). Frame row house, aluminum siding added over original wood siding, 25' (two-bay front) x 30', two-and-a-half stories, gable roof with gabled dormer. Built ca. 1874; brick addition on rear elevation built early twentieth century; fire damaged and in poor condition. 1 ext. photo (1983); 1 data page (1983). LC code: PA,48-EATO,4.

Taylor House. See Parson-Taylor House.

Glendon Borough

Glendon Hotel (PA-5445), Main St., E of Glendon Bridge. Masonry (faced with brick twentieth century), ten-bay front, three-and-a-half stories, gable roof (dormers added second half of nineteenth century), porch added along first story. Built 1740 as refuge from Indians with walls perforated with loopholes; extensively altered several times, currently used as tavern and dwelling. 1 ext. photo (1979); 1 data page (1979). LC code: PA,48-GLEN,1.

Hellertown Vicinity (Lower Saucon Township)

Barn, Decorated (PA-5327), off State Rte. 412, S of Hellertown. Random rubble with coursed rubble flanking frame forebay, two levels, gable roof, painted arches with "rising sun" motifs span openings, gabled hood with ogee curve front over side entrance, fanlights in gable ends, stone farmyard wall. Built 1850. 3 ext. photos (1941). LC code: PA,48-HELLT.V,1A.

Barn, Stone (PA-5328), Water St., W of Hellertown. Random rubble with quoins, two levels, gable roof, pent roof over stable entrances (later removed), slit ventilators (later filled in with stone), wagon storage opening next to stables filled in with stone. Built ca. 1770; large frame and stone barn attached to side. 2 ext. photos (1941), 1 int. photo (1941). LC code: PA,48-HELLT,1A.

Leithsville Vicinity (Lower Saucon Township)

Mountain View Dairy Farm, Barn (PA-5326), on State Rte. 412, near Bucks County line. Random rubble with quoins, two levels, gable roof with frame gable ends, circular brick vents, gabled hood over side entrance, decorated with painted "hex signs," painted arches over wagon entrance. Built 1845 (inscribed in gable end); projecting frame forebay supported on wooden posts added over stable entrances. 3 ext. photos (1941). LC code: PA,48-LEITH.V,1A.

Nazareth Borough

137 Main Street (Commercial building) (PA-1655). 1 sheet showing shop window (1974). LC code: PA,48-NAZ,1.

Northampton Borough

Main Street (Houses) (PA-5449). Two-and-a-half-story frame duplex housing typical of nineteenth-century company towns. 2 ext. photos (1979).

Portland Vicinity (Upper Mount Bethel Township)

Mount Minsi Farm. See Slateford House.

Munsch House. See Slateford House.

Slateford House (Munsch House, Mount Minsi Farm) (PA-1249), on private road, .4 mi. N of T707 and .7 mi. W of U.S. Rte. 611, approx. 2 mi. NW of Portland, in Delaware Water Gap National Recreation Area. Frame with clapboarding (stuccoed early twentieth century), L-shaped, 40'-4" (five-bay front) x 30'-6" (two bays) with rear shed (17'-4"x 18'-1"), two-and-a-half stories with one-story shed, gable roof (slate roof quarried on property with poured concrete ridge cover), decorative cornice; central hall plan, much original woodwork and hardware, fine carved mantels. Built first half of nineteenth century; porch added across SE (front) elevation early twentieth century. Outbuildings. 14 sheets (1969, including site plan, plans, elevations, sections, details); 5 ext. photos (1969), 11 int. photos (1968, 1969); 5 data pages (1969). LC code: PA,48-PORT.V,1.

Small Dwelling (PA-1249A). Frame with clapboarding (later covered with bark-covered slabs to simulate a log cabin), 26'-2" x 19'-6", one-and-a-half stories, gable roof (slate roof quarried on property with poured concrete ridge cover), projecting hood over door; two rooms with loft, large fireplace. Probably built early nineteenth century; small bathroom wing (8' x 7'-4") added on rear elevation. Possibly the original farm house. 3 sheets (1969, including site plan, plans, elevations, section); 4 ext. photos (1969), 1 int. photo (1969). LC code: PA,48-PORT.V,1A.

Springhouse (PA-1249B). Random rubble with quoins, 21'-2" x 14'-1", one story, gable roof (slate roof quarried on property with poured concrete ridge cover), one original door with wrought-iron strap hinges remains; two rooms, springhouse and washhouse. Built 1827 (date stone "P x T 1827"). 2 sheets (1969, including site plan, plan, elevations, section); 3 ext. photos (1969), 1 int. photo (1969). LC code: PA,48-PORT.V,1B.

Treichlers (Lehigh Township)

Treichlers Cafe (PA-5451), no address provided. Frame with clapboarding, three-bay front, two-and-a-half stories, gable roof, entrance porches. Built nineteenth century. 1 ext. photo (1979). LC code: PA,48-TREIC,2.

Walnutport Borough

Anchor Hotel (PA-5471), Main and Canal Sts. Stone, six-bay front, two-and-a-half stories, gable roof, two-story front porch. Built 1834; functions as tavern, restaurant, and inn. 1 ext. photo shows Lehigh Canal, hotel in background (1979); 1 data page (1979). LC code: PA,48-WALNPO,2.

Houses (PA-5452), on banks of Lehigh Canal. 3 general views showing mid-nineteenth-century houses and Lehigh Canal (1979). LC code: PA,48-WALNPO,3.

Wind Gap Vicinity

Ross Common Manor. See Monroe County, Saylorsburg Vicinity (Ross Township), Ross Common Manor.

York County

Dallastown Vicinity (York Township)

Beard Tavern (Valley Inn). See York Vicinity (Springettsbury Township), Beard Tavern, original location.

Davidsburg Vicinity (Washington Township)

Kleiser House. See Wertz-Lashee House.

Lashee House. See Wertz-Lashee House.

Wertz-Lashee House (Kleiser House) (PA-5183), on N bank of Conewago Creek, E side of Julius Ln. (T808), .35 mi. S of Davidsburg Rd. (LR66035). Squared log, 20' (two-bay front) x 14'-10", one-and-a-half stories on sloping site exposing basement to S (rear), steep gable roof, pent roof; one room, large cooking fireplace. Built ca. 1765; frame shed added on E elevation; few alterations; restored ca. 1958. Peter Wertz probably built house for his widowed sister, Christiana Lashee, and her children in 1765. Rare example of a once common type of early settler's dwelling; medieval German characteristics. 2 ext. photos (1962), 3 int. photos (1962); 1 data page (1984). LC code: PA,67-DAVBU.V,1.

Detters Mill (Warrington-Dover Townships)

Detters Mill Covered Bridge (PA-5184), over Conewago Creek, on Harmony Grove Rd. (LR66034), bypassed by new bridge built to N. Burr arch truss supported by stone abutments and central pier, double span, overall length 296'-11" and 21'-9" wide, covered with clapboards (most removed by vandals), gable roof. Built ca. 1815; possibly designed by Theodore Burr, based on structural not documentary evidence; poor condition 1962; collapsed 1965. One of the longest wooden bridges in state. 1 ext. photo (1962), 1 int. photo (1962); 1 data page (1984). LC code: PA,67-DETMI,1.

Dover

Barn (PA-129). See Harmony Grove (Dover Township), Barn (PA-129).

Hallam Borough

Shultz, Martin, House (PA-5185), E side of Emig St., .2 mi. S of E. Market St. (State Rte. 462). Coursed rubble, 50' (three-bay front) x 29'-9", one-and-a-half stories, steep gable roof with flared eaves, dormers added later, central doors with transoms and side lights (later additions) and entrance porches (later additions); central hall plan, large central fireplace, some interior partitions of half-timber with stone nogging, exposed beam ceilings, vaulted cellar, some original hardware. Built ca. 1736; restored 1956-57. One of the earliest extant houses in county; built by early Pennsylvania-German settlers. 2 ext. photos (1962), 5 int. photos (1962); 1 data page (1984). LC code: PA,67-HAL,1.

Harmony Grove (Dover Township)

Barn (PA-129), Chestnut Hill Rd. Squared logs (originally logs exposed first level and covered with vertical boards second level, nineteenth century entire barn sheathed), U-shaped, approx. 75' x 27', two levels, gable roof with longer N slope covering projecting end bays; central passageway with stables to each side. Built 1759-73; owned by Michael or Frederick Spahr originally; dismantled 1962-63 with plans to reconstruct at Susquehanna Memorial Gardens, not rebuilt. 2 ext. photos (1962, 1963 during dismantling), 2 int. photos (1962 showing construction details; 1 data page (1984). LC code: PA,67-DOV,1.

Laurel Vicinity (Chanceford Township)

Guinston United Presbyterian Church (PA-5187), W side of Old Forge Rd. (T645), .1 mi. S of Guinston-Laurel Rd. (LR66058), 1.6 mi. E of Laurel. Random rubble, 50'-3" (three-bay front) x 34'-3" (one bay), one story, gable roof (originally had pent eaves, removed), central bay on front and rear flanked by squared supports tied into large interior beams, arched openings; one room with gallery. Built 1773 by Scotch-Irish settlers; discontinued as church when new church built to S 1868. Congregation is the oldest United Presbyterian congregation in United States. 2 ext. photos (1962), 4 int. photos (1962), 1 int. copy photo (ca. 1900); 1 data page (1984). LC code: PA,67-LAUR.V,1. NR.

York

Billmeyer House (York House) (PA-5188), 225 E. Market St. Brick with stone trim and quoins, L-shaped, 30'-6" (three-bay front) x 36' (three bays) with ell extending 64' to N in three sections, three stories, hip roof with bracketed cupola, bracketed cornice, stone window and door surrounds with keystone motif, bay windows and two-and-a-half-story ell on E elevation, High Victorian Italianate style; side hall plan, elaborate interiors including painted parlor ceiling by L. Costagini (worked on dome of U.S. Capitol). Built 1860; wing probably built ca. 1815 with different front section; Charles Billmeyer, a manufacturer of ornate railroad coaches, built 1860 section; housed Historical Society of York County 1937-59; owned by First Presbyterian Church of York and restored. 2 ext. photos (1963), 2 int. photos (1963); 1 data page (1984). LC code: PA,67-YORK,10. NR (Also in York Historic District).

Chambers, Joseph, House (General Horatio Gates House) (PA-5189), 157 W. Market St., adjacent to Golden Plough Tavern (PA-5169). Coursed rubble and brick house built 1751 by Joseph Chambers, second owner of Golden Plough Tavern; acquired by Historical Society of York County and restored as museum 1961-64. General Horatio Gates lived in house 1777-78 while Continental Congress met in York. 1 data page (1984). LC code: PA,67-YORK,11. NR (Also in York Historic District).

Christ Lutheran Church (PA-366), 29 S. George St. Brick, rectangular, brick tower with frame octagonal belfry and spire. Built 1812-14; originally Georgian and Greek Revival details, remodeled in Gothic style 1874; changed back to 1812 appearance and cloister added 1926; vestibules and stair halls added to either side of tower. First church on the site was built 1735, for first Lutheran congregation organized west of the Susquehanna River. 2 photos of tower (1935). LC code: PA,67-YORK,1. NR (York Historic District).

Cookes House (PA-5190), originally located at 438-440 Codorus St., house moved to Martin Luther King Jr. Park. Coursed dressed rubble (E front elevation) and random rubble with quoins, approx. 33' (four-bay front) x 25', two stories, steep gable roof with slightly flared eaves, central chimney, Georgian and Germanic features; originally two-room plan. Built 1761 (date stone); built by Johannes Cookes (Guckes or Gugges); changed to duplex early twentieth century; poor condition 1963; house moved and restored 1980-81; now headquarters for Historic York, Inc. Reputed residence of Thomas Paine during 1777 session of Continental Congress in York. 3 ext. photos (1937, 1962); 6 data pages (1963). LC code: PA,67-YORK,13. NR.

439-41 South Court Street (Houses) (PA-5338). Frame with clapboarding, two two-bay row houses, two-and-a-half stories, gable roofs, bracketed cornices. Built ca. 1880; one-story frame additions to rear; vacant. 2 ext. photos (1982); 3 data pages including floor plans (1982). LC code: PA,67-YORK,8.

443 South Court Street (House) (PA-5339). Frame with clapboarding, three-bay front, two-and-a-half stories, gable roof, bracketed cornice, porch on front elevation (later addition), frame wing with asbestos siding on rear. Built ca. 1870; vacant. 2 ext. photos (1982); 1 data page (1982). LC code: PA,67-YORK,9.

Direct Hotel. See North George Street Historic District, 101-3 North George Street (Commercial Building).

428 South Duke Street (House) (PA-5335). Frame with clapboarding, L-shaped row house, three-bay front, two-and-a-half stories, gable roof with large shed dormer (dormer later addition), bracketed and denticulated cornice, second-story bay window (later addition), second-story porch on rear ell. Built ca. 1880; vacant. 2 ext. photos (1982); 3 data pages including floor plans (1982). LC code: PA,67-YORK,6.

431 South Duke Street (House) (PA-5336). Frame with asbestos siding (siding later addition), L-shaped, three-bay front (first story altered with shop window and second door), two-and-a-half stories, mansard roof with gabled dormers, shed roof on rear ell, bracketed cornice, second-story porch on rear ell. Built ca. 1880; rear shed added; vacant. 2 ext. photos (1982), 1 int. photo (1982); 4 data pages including floor plans (1982). LC code: PA,67-YORK,7.

Gates, General Horatio, House. See Chambers, Joseph, House.

North George Street Historic District (PA-573). Streetscape composed of three-story commercial building converted to a hotel and three buildings with first-floor storefronts and apartments above. All built mid-nineteenth century; demolished 1979. 4 general views (1979). LC code: PA,67-YORK,3.

101-3 North George Street (Commercial building) (Direct Hotel) (PA-569). Brick, 37' (six-bay front) x 129', three stories, flat roof, bracketed cornice, storefronts. Built mid-nineteenth century; demolished 1979. 2 ext. photos (1979); 3 data pages (1979). LC code: PA,67-YORK,3A.

105 North George Street (Commercial building) (PA-570). Brick, 19' (two-bay front) x 60', two-and-a-half stories, mansard roof, dormer with Eastlake trim, storefront. Built mid-nineteenth century; demolished 1979. 1 ext. photo (1979); 3 data pages (1979). LC code: PA,67-YORK,3B.

107 North George Street (Commercial building) (PA-571). Brick, 23' (three-bay front) x 60', two-and-a-half stories, mansard roof, two dormers with Eastlake trim, storefronts. Built mid-nineteenth century; demolished 1979. 1 ext. photo (1979); 3 data pages (1979). LC code: PA,67-YORK,3C.

109-11 North George Street (Commercial building) (PA-572). Brick, 23' (three-bay front) x 60', three stories, flat roof, storefronts. Built ca. 1850; originally two-and-a-half stories, bay window added ca. 1910; demolished 1979. 1 ext. photo (1979); 3 data pages (1979). LC code: PA,67-YORK,3D.

Golden Plough Tavern (PA-5169), 159 W. Market St., adjacent to Joseph Chambers House (General Horatio Gates House) (PA-5189). Museum operated by Historical Society of York County. Squared logs mortised into large upright corner timbers (first story) and half timber with brick nogging (second story), 34' (four-bay front) x 28'-5", two-and-a-half stories, gable roof with flared eaves, central chimney of fieldstone and framing and wattle and daub (reconstructed), casement windows (replacements), medieval German features; wattle and daub interior partitions. Built 1741 by Michael Eichelberger as a tavern; clapboarded soon after construction; nineteenth-century windows changed and storefront added; acquired by Historical Society of York County and restored to original appearance 1961-64 (much original construction remained). Public meeting place during period the Continental Congress met in York. Rare survival of combination of log and half timber construction. 1 ext. photo (1962), 1 copy photo of ca. 1830 view, 7 int. photos (1962, mainly construction details); 1 data page (1984). LC code: PA,67-YORK,12. NR (Also in York Historic District).

21-23 West Market Street (Commercial building) (PA-1313). Brick with wooden trim, 31' (four-bay front) x 66', three stories, flat roof, carved and incised cornice with paired brackets, decorative lintels with sawtooth edging over windows; two shops on first floor, residence on second and third. Built ca. 1860; modern storefronts added; demolished 1978. 4 ext. photos (1978), 2 int. photos (1978); 6 data pages (1978). LC code: PA,67-YORK,2.

339 East Prospect Street (House) (PA-5101). Frame with aluminum siding (siding later addition), approx. 22' (three-bay front) x 50', two-and-a-half stories, gable roof with gabled dormer, door with transom. Built ca. 1870-95; second-story bay window added; frame garage and brick porch added 1950s; vacant. 2 ext. photos (1982); 2 data pages including floor plans (1984). LC code: PA,67-YORK,4.

415-21 Short Way (Houses) (PA-5337). Frame row houses, four two-bay houses, one-and-a-half stories, gable roofs. Built ca. 1860; asphalt shingle siding added; rear additions; vacant. 3 ext. photos (1982); 2 data pages including floor plans (1982). LC code: PA,67-YORK,5.

Willis, William, House (PA-5170), 135 Willis Run Rd., adjacent to Prospect Hill Cemetery. Brick, 26'-9" (five-bay front) x 32', two-and-a-half stories with basement, gable roof (pent eaves originally, removed twentieth century), belt course (pent roof originally surrounded house, removed twentieth century), Georgian details; central hall plan, corner fireplaces. Built 1762 ("WW 1762" in glazed headers in W gable end); William Willis, builder; porch added on S elevation 20th c. (original N front then became rear); restored 1979 by Historic York, Inc. Fine example of rural English Georgian design, Willis was a mason by trade and probably aware of design books. 2 ext. photos (1962), 1 int. photo (1962), 1 ext. copy photo (ca. 1900); 5 data pages (1963, 1974). LC code: PA,67-YORK,14. NR.

York County Courthouse Doorway (PA-5171), 250 E. Market St. (in museum of Historical Society of York County). Pedimented doorway flanked by pilasters, arched opening with paneled reveal, semicircular fanlight, paneled door with sliding upper panel to cover glazed portion of door. Built ca. 1815; probably from 1815 remodeling of courthouse (1754-63); doorway has been moved four times since courthouse was demolished 1841; present door is not original to the frame; installed as museum exhibit ca. 1941. Members of the Continental Congress met in the York County Courthouse while the British occupied Philadelphia from September, 1777 to June, 1778. 3 photos (1963); 1 data page (1984). LC code: PA,67-YORK,15.

York House. See Billmeyer House.

York Vicinity (Manchester Township)

Wolff Barn (PA-5174), N. side of Bull Rd. (LR66102), 1.2 mi. NW of U.S. Rte. 30. Squared logs (joined by mortise and tenon into corner posts) partially sheathed with wide boards, 49'-3" (three-bay front) x 30'-4", one level with loft, gable roof, end bays overhang on SE (front) elevation; open central space with stable area to each side with lofts above. Built ca. 1750; remaining exposed logs sheathed with wide boards; frame shed added on NW elevation. One of few eighteenth-century log barns extant in county. Unusual log construction. 2 ext. photos (1962), 1 int. photo (1962); 1 data page (1984). LC code: PA,67-YORK.V,3.

York Vicinity (Springettsbury Township)

Beard Tavern (Olde York Inn, Valley Inn) (PA-5172), originally located N side of U.S. Rte. 30 (Lincoln Hwy.), 1.4 mi. E of York; moved to Susquehanna Memorial Gardens, E side of Chestnut Hill Dr. (T714), approx. 1 mi. N of Dallastown (York Township). Coursed rubble (S front elevation) and random rubble, approx. 42' (five-bay front) x 30', two-and-a-half stories, gable roof, pent roof; central hall plan. Built ca. 1750 by John Michael Beard, licensed as tavern 1754; late-eighteenth-century ell added to NE corner; nineteenth-century three-bay addition to E; nineteenth-century addition at NW corner to form rectangle 95' x 65'-9"; twentieth-century cement block addition at NE corner; dismantled 1962 and original five-bay section reconstructed at Susquehanna Memorial Gardens. 5 ext. photos (1962), 7 int. photos (1962); 1 data page (1984). LC code: PA,67-YORK.V,1.

Dietz House (Hermit's House) (PA-5173), S side of Pleasant Valley Rd. (T947), .1 mi. W of Alpine Rd. (T764), approx. 1 mi. N of U.S. Rte. 30, approx. 3 mi. NE of York. Random rubble with quoins, 40'-5" (three-bay front) x 30'-7", one-and-a-half stories with basement, gable roof, door with fluted pilasters on N (front) elevation; central hall plan. Built ca. 1810; poor condition 1962; restored 1974. 3 ext. photos (1962); 1 data page (1984). LC code: PA,67-YORK.V,2.

Hermit's House. See Dietz House.

Olde York Inn. See Beard Tavern.

Valley Inn. See Beard Tavern.

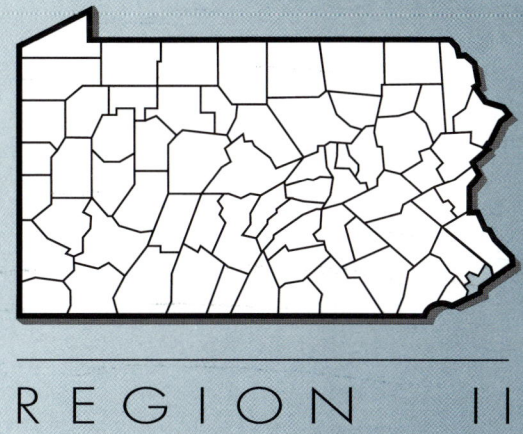

REGION II

Philadelphia

Essay by Richard J. Webster

Catalog entries by Deborah Stephens Burns

Samuel Powel House (PA-1192) Philadelphia. East elevation (Jack E. Boucher, photographer, 1972) PA,51-PHILA,25-2.

PHILADELPHIA sits astride the fall line (or zone) between the Piedmont Region and the Coastal Plain in the Commonwealth's southeast corner. Present-day neighborhoods of Manayunk, Germantown, and Chestnut Hill developed along the edge of this geographical transition where rapids and small waterfalls interrupt navigable streams to provide prime sites for early industrial facilities. Northwest of this line rises the rolling hills of the Piedmont where in the late nineteenth and early twentieth centuries farms gave way to suburban development in the city's northwestern reaches and its adjoining communities. Southeast of the line lies the Coastal Plain, the setting of the city's historic origins and early commercial activity and the geographic region in which most of the city stands. The Delaware River dominates this coastal zone, serving as both the city's eastern border and a tidal estuary. Although it stands one hundred miles inland from the Atlantic Ocean, Philadelphia, through the river's link to the Delaware Bay and the ocean beyond, developed during the eighteenth century into one of America's two largest seaports, a position it held until after World War II.[1] Along the river arrived nearly all of Pennsylvania's early settlers: the Dutch beginning in 1633, Swedes and Finns in 1634, and about 1664 the British, who came in great numbers after 1681, the year William Penn obtained the proprietary province which bears his name. Penn's plans for Philadelphia and its prime geographic location established it from its beginning as Pennsylvania's principal city, which it remains.[2] With over six hundred Philadelphia buildings and structures in its records, the Historic American Buildings Survey's holdings for the city are the most thorough and representative of any county or region in the Commonwealth.

Penn placed his city above the confluence of the Delaware and Schuylkill rivers. He extended the city's plan from river to river and bisected it with major north-south and east-west thoroughfares, Broad and High (later Market) Streets respectively.[3] Outside of the city spread the rest of the county of Philadelphia, that was organized during the eighteenth and early nineteenth centuries as various boroughs, districts, and townships. In the colonial period most of this outlying area was rural, but by the middle of the nineteenth century the city's commercial and residential districts flowed beyond its political boundaries, creating an administrative and law-enforcement nightmare. The state legislature's approval of the consolidation of the city and county as a single political unit in 1854 made the metropolitan area more governable, increased its tax base, and eased its transition into the nation's second largest city.[4]

Philadelphia's original city plan reflects the living experiences and religious principles of its founder. Penn's wish to have "a greene Country Towne, which will never be burnt, and allways be wholsome"[5] was motivated by his life on an Irish country estate and memories of plague and conflagration in London during the mid-1660s, and was embodied in the plan's grid system with open squares and large blocks to be filled with dwellings surrounded by gardens. Equally significant is what does not appear in Thomas Holme's famous plat—city walls, fortified garrisons, and dominant civic structures. As a pacifist, Penn ideologically spurned protective walls and military force, and since he expected his Holy Experiment to produce a city free of pride and factional disputes, he saw no need for conventional civic monumentality.[6]

Penn expected settlers to fill the city's lots more or less uniformly, and in 1685 he had a meetinghouse built on Center Square in preparation for its development as the hub of urban activity. Penn's vision, however, foundered on the profit motive. Within less than a decade after the city's founding, its population began to concentrate along the Delaware River, along which Penn had envisioned a public esplanade but where wharves had been under construction since 1684. By the turn of the eighteenth century, Penn's dream of "a greene Country Towne" was severely compromised. A burgeoning population was crushing into narrow subdivided lots along side streets and alleys that cut through the original large blocks and gradually pushed along the waterfront outside the city's boundaries southward into "suburban" Southwark and northward into Kensington. In 1702 the Center Square meetinghouse was dismantled and its materials were used to erect a new meetinghouse on Front Street, north of Arch.[7] It would be nearly two hundred years before Center Square would indeed become the city's center, the event the start of construction in 1871 of the present city hall (PA-1530).

By 1700 Philadelphia's fundamental social pattern for the rest of the eighteenth century had been established. Quaker merchants, many of whom were experienced West Indies traders, asserted an economic leadership in the 1690s that succeeding Quakers maintained, well into the national period.[8] Penn's energetic promotion of his province contributed to the city's and the province's steady growth and to a religious and ethnic diversity unusual for colonial American cities. As early as 1683, Dutch Quakers and Mennonites, and shortly thereafter German pietists, settled northwest of Philadelphia in German Township, later known as Germantown. They used local building materials, initially log but later the distinctive Wissahickon schist with its flecks of mica.[9] Meanwhile, the people in the developing area near the Delaware quickly abandoned the log construction they apparently had adopted in the first years and turned to brick and timber frame.[10] Even the Swedes, masters of log construction, turned to brick in 1698 to build their new church, Gloria Dei (PA-120). Its steep roof and projecting entrance pavilion's pinched proportions give the church an unusual appearance. Once thought to be Swedish, its Flemish bond brickwork, with glazed headers and lozenge diaperwork, was a standard part of seventeenth and early-eighteenth-century English bricklayers' repertoires.[11]

Because English builders were incorporating Renaissance principles into their buildings in the last half of the seventeenth century, early Philadelphia buildings conveyed few clearly medieval details.[12] As Carpenter's Mansion (PA-1397) indicates, houses in the first quarter of the eighteenth century possessed a sense of medieval bulk, which was exaggerated by jerkin-head roofs and windows that pushed in toward the facade's center and up against heavy pent roofs and deep cove cornices that often crossed gable ends.[13] The pent roof is a characteristic of Philadelphia regional architecture that slowly lost its popularity about the time of the American Revolution.[14]

By the second quarter of the eighteenth century, Philadelphia houses assumed a standard appearance, not unlike that of the Nathaniel Irish House (PA-1013), which Irish, a house carpenter, probably built between 1762 and 1769. With its gable roof and wooden cornice parallel to the street and a pent roof originally above its ground story, the Irish House emulates on a smaller scale the town houses of Restoration London.[15] Even its plan, a side hall leading to winding stairs between the front and back rooms, is called the London house plan, and its vertical ordering of interior spaces is typical of late-seventeenth- and eighteenth-century

London houses.[16] During his 1750 visit to Philadelphia, the Swedish traveler Peter Kalm was struck by this vertical exploitation of space in which "the building was so constructed that rooms for dwelling purposes extended up to the roof," including the garret, which unlike Swedish examples, was built "sometimes with dormer windows so that the servants at least could in the summer live in them comfortably." Even the stone masonry basement "was used for a cellar, pantry, wood-shed, or sometimes a kitchen, and merchants occasionally kept their goods in it."[17]

Philadelphians did not call these modest dwellings townhouses; they reserved that term for grand residences with architectural pretensions and ample dimensions, such as the brick Powel House (PA-1359). The Powel House was built in 1765 on a deep double lot, with approximately forty feet of frontage, providing space for a garden along the house's south side where customarily another house would stand. The Powel House is wide enough to have an entrance and stair hall in the house's main block with a stair tower, or piazza (as Philadelphians called it), and a series of attached back buildings behind it. The front is not trimmed with vernacular elements, such as the pent roof, but is graced with Renaissance details: stone string-courses for classical horizontality, flat-arch lintels with keystones, and a frontispiece with engaged Roman Doric columns and an Ionic entablature.[18]

These houses were not built row by row progressively across the city's open land. They were not put up speculatively but singularly, often with blank end walls in anticipation of future construction on adjoining lots. The result was streets like Elfreth's Alley (PA-1103): rows of houses rather than row houses. The city's first row, that is, houses planned and built as contiguous units, was Sansom's Row (PA-1476). About 1799, William Sansom, an early real estate promoter, employed Thomas Carstairs and Benjamin Henry Latrobe to design similar rows on Sansom and Walnut Streets between Seventh and Eighth Streets, on what was then the city's western edge. In plan and design the houses were standard Philadelphia city houses with three-bay, three-story fronts and London-house plans. The innovation was the scale of the undertaking: twenty-two houses planned as a unit on each street and erected more or less simultaneously. Sansom Row established the model that other speculative developers and builders eagerly emulated in the rapidly growing city. Outsiders so identified the city with these speculative dwellings that row houses in other east coast cities were often referred to as "Philadelphia rows."[19] Most of Philadelphia's row houses were built in the nineteenth century without benefit of architects, but when

Nathaniel Irish House (PA-1013) Philadelphia. Front elevation (Cervin Robinson, photographer, 1959) PA,51-PHILA,243-1.

William Sansom House (PA-1476) Philadelphia. General view (George Eisenman, photographer, 1958) PA,51-PHILA,602-1.

architects did design row houses, the effect is easily discernible. Robert Mills, for example, designed the ten brick dwellings of Franklin Row in 1809, of which only the Sims House (PA-1186) survives. Gone is the visual monotony inherent in row house design. It is replaced by a lightness and grace formed from arches: arched entries with fanlights, first- and second-story tripartitie windows within blind arches, and small arched dormers. A generation later, in 1831-33, Thomas U. Walter introduced even more plasticity to row house facades, by giving each of the paired entries of Portico Square (PA-1534) three-columned marble Ionic porches.[20]

After the Civil War, some row developers embellished their facades with current historical styles. Robert Kaighn, for example, used High Victorian Gothic detailing on brick and brownstone Delancey Street row houses (PA-1502) in the mid-1870s. Few developers, however, matched the success of the Page Brothers, who in 1887 commissioned Furness, Evans, and Co. to design a Diamond Street row (PA-1726) of twenty-two brick houses with rock-faced brownstone trim and uniquely Furnessian cornice decoration resembling medieval maces. By the early twentieth century developers along the elevated train line in West Philadelphia and Frankford and in parts of Germantown engaged architects to design row upon row of classically inspired brick houses with columned front porches and second-story bays. During the 1920s, architects responded to changing tastes and lifestyles by introducing some facade variety with different roof profiles or wall finishes and a degree of convenience with below-grade garages. E. Allen Wilson was the most prolific of these architects; in fact, his approximately fifteen thousand dwellings make him the most productive Philadelphia architect of all time. Row houses continue to be a major aspect of Philadelphia's architectural presence. I. M. Pei incorporated row houses into his Society Hill Towers project in the early 1960s, and as recently as 1988 Rouse Urban Housing, Inc., had erected thirty-two modular brick row houses in the city's Northern Liberties.[21]

Nineteenth-century row houses can be dated almost decade by decade as the city expanded from its origins near Front and Market streets. By 1800 the city had moved westward to Washington Square and its waterfront had developed virtually from Kensington to Southwark. Shipyards bustled at each end of the developed waterfront, and for seventy-five years the United States Navy Yard stood in Southwark until it was moved to League Island in 1876. By the time of the Civil War, Philadelphians were building villas in West Philadelphia and Germantown and mills

Diamond Street Area Study (PA-1726) Philadelphia. General view (Jack E. Boucher, photographer, 1973) PA,51-PHILA,393-1.

in Kensington, Manayunk, and parts of Germantown; and as steam power proved safe and reliable they erected factories inland as well, particularly on the west side of North Broad Street, where by 1880 the Baldwin Locomotive Works was the largest of the many manufacturing facilities there.[22]

Philadelphia became an early railroad center, beginning in 1831 with the Northern Liberties and Penn Township Railroad, which ran along Willow Street, two blocks above the city's northern border, between the Delaware River and Broad Street. A year later the Philadelphia, Germantown and Norristown Railway opened a line between Germantown and the city's northern outskirts. By the end of the nineteenth century, Pennsylvania's two major rail lines had built large terminals and train sheds in center city. The Pennsylvania Railroad built its Broad Street Station (PA-1527) in 1880-82 and enlarged it twelve years later; the Philadelphia and Reading Railroad's Terminal Station (PA-1528) went up in 1891-93. Both featured gigantic train sheds. When finished in 1894, Broad Street Station's shed had the world's largest permanent roof, but it stood for less than thirty years, burning in 1923. Reading Terminal's shed, America's only surviving single-span arched train shed, has fared better as the centerpiece of the Philadelphia Convention Center. More important to average Philadelphians, however, was the Frankford Elevated, which ranks second only to the Penn Plan in its impact on the city's living patterns. In the first two decades of the twentieth century, the thirteen-mile-long Frankford Elevated opened up the vast reaches of West Philadelphia, west to Sixty-ninth Street, and after World War I reached northeast to Frankford, greatly expanding the size of its surrounding neighborhoods. Construction of the Broad Street Subway in stages between 1928 and 1938 stimulated row house construction in North and South Philadelphia, while development of the upper parts of the northeast came during the post-World War II boom and was tied to the automobile and the construction of Roosevelt Boulevard.[23]

Philadelphia also became an early leader in architectural design. It made its mark among the colonies almost from its beginning. Sometime between 1687 and 1699, James Porteus, a Scottish-born master builder, built a commodious two-story H-plan brick dwelling for Samuel Carpenter, a merchant of means and apparent sophistication. Called the Slate Roof House because of its unusual roofing, the Carpenter House was perhaps the first large colonial building to incorporate an understanding of Renaissance principles in both plan and details. The city's architectural leadership flourished during the heyday of the so-called Georgian Style of the eighteenth century, beginning in April 1744, when the churchwardens of Christ Church (PA-1071) considered their brick house of worship "happily completed."[24] It was constructed over a seventeen-year period with a masterful blend of English Baroque details that made Christ Church "the most advanced and completely English church in America,"[25] at a time when emulation of Mother England's style and standards was the highest goal. Christ Church's counterpart in civic architecture is the Pennsylvania Statehouse, better known as Independence Hall (PA-1430). Not only is Independence Hall historically significant as the site where the Declaration of Independence and United States Constitution were drafted, it is also architecturally significant. Despite its many restorations, it remains, in the opinion of many archi-

Pennsylvania Railroad, Broad Street Station (PA-1527) Philadelphia. General view circa 1894 (Copy photo of ca. 1894 photograph by William H. Rau) PA,51-PHILA,341-7.

Philadelphia and Reading Railroad, Terminal Station (PA-1528) Philadelphia. General view circa 1893 (copy photo of 1893 photograph, photographer unknown) PA, 51-PHILA, 521-1

tectural historians, one of the country's "most authentic English buildings surviving from the eighteenth century."[26] Its initial five-part composition of a brick main block with its Georgian bluestone details flanked by brick arcades and small two-story brick buildings made it the colonies' most ambitious civic project to that date. Christ Church and Independence Hall, as well as a wide array of other buildings, demonstrate colonial Philadelphians' sophistication and the presence of a small army of builders who could transform that taste into up-to-date architecture.[27]

Philadelphia retained its architectural leadership after the American Revolution, beginning with the Woodlands (PA-1125), William Hamilton's monumental country house west of the city. In 1788-89 Hamilton extensively remodeled an earlier stone house into this early and outstanding example of the Federal style, which may have been as influential in promoting the new neoclassicism as English design books.[28] Much of Philadelphia's architectural leadership in the early republic stemmed from its position as the country's largest and wealthiest city, and during the 1790s its capital as well. These circumstances helped to attract such people as Benjamin Henry Latrobe, an English-trained architect of considerable talents. His use of the Greek Ionic Order on the 1798 Bank of Pennsylvania has led some to consider it America's first Greek Revival building.[29] Similarly Sedgeley, William Cramond's 1799 country house, has been called the country's first Gothic Revival building, because of the pointed-arch windows and Tudor label moldings that Latrobe designed for it. The city demolished the house in 1857, but its one-story rubble porter's house (PA-1665) still stands in the city's Fairmount Park. Latrobe was among the competitors for the highly coveted commission for the Second Bank of the United States (PA-137) in 1818, but he lost it to one of his former apprentices, William Strickland. In establishing the viability of the Greek Revival style, the Second Bank building became one of the style's most important models.[30]

Improved communications, a growing proliferation of architectural design books, and the rise of new cities and expansion of old ones contributed to a diffusion of architectural leadership beginning in the 1830s. Nevertheless, Philadelphia architects continued to design high-quality buildings. The Athenaeum of Philadelphia (PA-1389), for example, was not the first Italianate building in America, but it was an early and significant example of this new style. Because John Notman's Athenaeum was the winner of an 1845 architectural competition and was built of brownstone for a respectable literary and cultural society on Washington Square, a prominent downtown site, it attracted attention from its beginning and helped to promote the popularity of the Italianate.[31] No building in the city, however, drew as much attention—and controversy—in the nineteenth century as did City Hall (PA-1530). Having outgrown their modest quarters in Independence Hall, city officials in 1860 took the first steps toward building a new municipal building. After two design competitions and one appointment (all won by John McArthur), political wrangling and litigation in both Philadelphia and Harrisburg, and a referendum that

Philadelphia Athenaeum (PA-1389) Philadelphia. General view (Jack E. Boucher, photographer, 1972) PA, 51-PHILA, 116-1.

selected Center Square over Independence Square as the building's site, construction began in 1871. Its erection ended thirty years later with a building that is more than the sum of its parts. McArthur used the Second Empire Style as a medium for an exuberant exhibition of civic pride. He displayed this pride in City Hall's marble walls, opulent public spaces, mammoth size (the world's tallest building with load-bearing masonry walls), and its vertical sculpture garden by Alexander Milne Calder, which carries the Victorian fascination with complexity and irregularity to sensuous extremes.[32] It remains one of the country's great buildings of the immediate post-Civil War era.

During the late nineteenth and early twentieth centuries, when Philadelphia was the nation's leading industrial city, local clients remained conservative and chose architects close to home. Frank Furness, Philadelphia's greatest and most creatively individualistic designer at that time, designed only a handful of buildings outside of Philadelphia and its suburbs. Architects with national practices, such as Richard Morris Hunt and Henry Hobson Richardson, overshadowed Furness's significance as an imaginative designer of equal importance, and architectural historians failed to recognize Furness's architectural contribution for decades. It would not be until the 1970s that Furness' work received the recognition that it deserved.[33] The insularity of Philadelphians made Philadelphia in many respects an architecturally closed city. The High Victorian Gothic style and its variations by Furness and his contemporaries created such a strong presence in the city that the Richardsonian Romanesque, which swept across the rest of the nation, never took root in Philadelphia.[34] *The Philadelphia Real Estate Record and Builders' Guide*, the local weekly that listed architectural competitions and new and pending building contracts, generally did not mention Philadelphia works by out-of-town architects until the twentieth century.[35] This provincialism may have contributed to Philadelphia architects' forfeiting leadership in skyscraper design to Chicago and New York. In fact, Philadelphia clients sometimes chose Chicago architects to design their skyscrapers, as the Land Title Bank and Trust Company did in 1897 and 1902, when it commissioned Daniel H. Burnham & Co. for its two adjacent office buildings (PA-1514) on South Broad Street.[36]

In suburban domestic architecture, however, Philadelphia architects excelled. Although some early-twentieth-century Philadelphia entrepreneurs erected suburban mansions in the Second Renaissance Revival and Neoclassical Revival styles, there seem to have been fewer of them than in other American cities. Within the city limits, in particular in Chestnut Hill, clients preferred understated but well-designed country houses inspired by the Arts and Crafts movement and the rediscovery of Pennsylvania farmhouses. Clients' choice of style seems to have been determined by their social standing, whether they were from "old families" or enjoyed newly acquired wealth. The former considered reproductions of Versailles vulgar and rambling country houses in Philadelphia's pastoral style tasteful.[37] Wilson Eyre Jr., was the first of the local architects to cultivate this regional vernacular style. It was dependent on the Colonial Revival style, but was patterned after the English Arts and Crafts movement, in which English architects, in an effort to free themselves of historical styles, focused on vernacular buildings, indigenous materials, and ornament based on nature.[38] This synthesis of local materials, colonial forms, Arts and Crafts detailing, and, occasionally, European spaces required sophisticated design skills because it was free of pattern-book precedents and dependent on an understanding of traditional materials and forms. Mellor, Meigs, and Howe developed as one of the most adept practitioners of this distinctive regional style during the first quarter of the twentieth century. It designed rambling, crisply edged stone houses with "terraces, walled gardens, cobbled forecourts and other nostalgic Europeanized details for which the cultivated and traveled patrons . . . yearned."[39] Deliberately free of foreign and high-stylistic details and designed for families' comfort and convenience, these houses mark the zenith of upper-middle-class design and a transition to the modern era.

George Howe, a member of the Mellor, Meigs, and Howe firm between 1916 and 1927, personifies this shift from the traditional to the modern. In 1914 Howe designed the greatest of these carefully synthesized country houses (High Hollow, his Chestnut Hill home) and fifteen years later, in partnership with Swiss-born William Lescaze, designed America's first skyscraper in the International Style, the Philadelphia Saving Fund Society Building (PA-1533). Howe and Lescaze stripped the building of all ornament and expressed the building's steel skeleton and banking and office functions in its form and materials. Even before its completion in 1932, critics were hailing the PSFS Building as a true expression of the new European architecture; Philadelphia was again an architectural pace setter.[40] Within a year's time, the city could also lay claim to one of the country's earliest applications of the International Style to domestic architecture. The Carl Mackley Apartments (PA-1779) are four concrete-block apartment buildings faced with tan tile that were built as a planned community in the city's lower northeast section on the edge of the textile mill dis-

Philadelphia Saving Fund Society (PA-1533) Philadelphia. Elevated view of office floors (Jack E. Boucher, photographer, 1985) PA,51-PHILA,584-6.

trict. Designed by Oskar Stonorov, a newly arrived Swiss-trained architect, the complex was built for the American Federation of Hosiery Workers with a million-dollar loan from the Public Works Administration, making it one of the first federally aided low-rent developments in the country.[41]

World War II brought a nearly total cessation of nonmilitary construction.[42] As Philadelphia after the war embraced the International Style with one arm and urban renewal with the other, Louis I. Kahn, who during the war had worked in George Howe's and Oskar Stonorov's office, emerged as one of the nation's leading architects. With his Beaux Arts training and consequent emphasis on structure and mass, Kahn had had difficulty finding his place in a world of European modernism. He was better known for his teaching (at the University of Pennsylvania) and writings than for his buildings, until his Alfred Newton Richards Medical Research Building and Goddard Laboratories at the University of Pennsylvania, 1957-64, brought him so much notice that he was swamped with commissions.[43] His work as an architect and his influence as a teacher were so great that the editors of *Progressive Architecture* considered Kahn the center of an emerging Philadelphia school of architecture, a notion that was later corrected.[44] Robert Venturi, who considered Kahn his closest mentor, at this time moved into the vanguard of the postmodern movement with his 1962 design for his mother's house in Chestnut Hill. Like Kahn, Venturi was also a writer and teacher (at Yale and Penn) and through his architecture, writing, and students he contributed to the turbulent 60s and suggested a new direction to American architects for the 70s and 80s.[45]

In an era of urban renewal, when designs can assume a very broad scope, planners can be as important as the architects who execute their grand schemes. None drew more attention in the postwar period than Edmund N. Bacon, executive director of the Philadelphia City Planning Commission. Bacon's success could not have been possible, however, without the reform administrations of Mayors Joseph S. Clark, Jr., and Richardson Dilworth and a cooperative redevelopment authority. Demolition in 1952-53 of the Pennsylvania Railroad's Broad Street Station (PA-1527) and the infamous Chinese Wall that had carried trains to and from the station allowed the city to redevelop a multiblock area west of City Hall (PA-1530). The Penn Center complex of office buildings, the Kennedy and Dilworth Plazas, and the 1964 Municipal Services Building on Reyburn Plaza filled the short-lived void. At the same time federal and state agencies razed blocks of buildings near Independence Hall (PA-1430) to create Independence National Historical Park and Independence Mall, which the federal government and private corporations lined in the 1960s and 70s with a new mint and large office and court buildings. This activity, in turn, encouraged the preservation and restoration of eighteenth- and early-nineteenth-century houses in nearby Society Hill. The cooperative efforts of the Philadelphia City Planning Commission, the Redevelopment Authority, the Philadelphia Historical Commission, Old Philadelphia Development Corporation, and "buttoned-down" pioneers transformed this former slum into the city's most fashionable residential neighborhood. During the 1970s and 80s, while the University City Science Center, University of Pennsylvania, and Drexel University were forming an extensive and interlocking academic and research complex in West Philadelphia, the city completed its massive Market Street East Project, and worked doggedly on its slow-moving Penn's Landing project along the Delaware River waterfront and its proposed convention center north of the Reading Terminal (PA-1528).[46]

Like so many other east coast cities, Philadelphia, beginning about 1960, faced the shift from a manufacturing economy to a service economy. One result for the city's center was an increase in new office construction, which in the mid-1980s became more political than usual. In 1984 when Willard Rouse III proposed building office towers that would exceed the traditional height limit of City Hall tower, he ignited a complex public controversy in which Philadelphians grappled with aesthetic, symbolic, economic, planning, and humane issues. By imposing a deadline on the city government, however, Rouse cut off debate and carried the day. The first of the two Liberty Place towers, from the designs of Chicago architect Helmut Jahn, opened in late 1987.[47] Rising four hundred feet above City Hall's tower, One Liberty Place has radically transformed the city's skyline, shifting its focal point westward. In spite of the controversy surrounding its conception, both architectural critics and the public like the building. In fact, Philadelphians are quite proud of it, as if its height and bold design make the city a legitimately modern, if not altogether flashy, city.[48] One Liberty Place was the most spectacular but not the only one of the roaring 80s skyscrapers to transform the shape and color of the city's skyline. At least seven other office buildings rose west of City Hall to alter not only the city's silhouette but also the locus of its business activity.[49] Yet as One Liberty Place weakly mimics the Chrysler Building and the nearby Bell Atlantic Tower suggests Rockefeller Center, Philadelphia appears to be backing toward the new century by emulating another

Lit Brothers Store (PA-1438) Philadelphia. General view (Jack E. Boucher, photographer, 1972) PA,51-PHILA,519-2.

city's jazzy past. Such romantic allusions do not constitute architectural leadership or regional distinctiveness, but perhaps it is no longer possible for a city to retain a distinctive regional architecture in a world of international investors, national architects, and transient power elites.

While attention was focused on such sleek and spectacular new construction, much of the city's housing stock suffered from deferred maintenance, vandalism, and abandonment. Government programs fashioned to save and put to new uses old commercial buildings succeeded in refurbishing from the inside out the familiar fabric of declining commercial and industrial districts, but did little for aging row house neighborhoods where disposable income was scarce. During the 1980s, developers, motivated by generous federal investment tax credits, found it more profitable to rehabilitate historic commercial buildings than to replace them. Between 1981 and 1986, those tax credits totaled an investment of nearly a billion dollars in Philadelphia construction, nearly half of which was rehabilitation of old buildings.[50] Projects have ranged from lush hotels (the conversion of Joseph C. Hoxie's 1856 Elliott Building in the Old City section to a business travelers' inn) to low-income housing (the rehabilitation of the Rensselaer Lee and Hamilton Disston houses in North Philadelphia to apartments for low-income families).[51] Two of the most extensive ventures were the eighty-six-acre Frankford Arsenal complex in Bridesburg and Lit Brothers Store (PA-1438), an abandoned department store filling an entire block in center city.[52] Large or small, such projects allowed parts of the city with its great stock of old buildings to be revitalized and yet retain some of its distinctive appearance.

Notes

[1] Raymond E. Murphy and Marion Murphy, *Pennsylvania: A Regional Geography* (Harrisburg: Pennsylvania Book Service, 1937), 18-20, 165-66, 188-91.

[2] The standard histories of early Dutch and Swedish settlement of the Delaware Valley are C. A. Weslager, *Dutch Explorers, Traders, and Settlers in the Delaware Valley, 1609-1664* (Philadelphia: University of Pennsylvania Press, 1961) and Amandus Johnson, *The Swedish Settlements on the Delaware*, 2 vols. (Philadelphia: University of Pennsylvania Press, 1911). See also C. A. Weslager, *The English on the Delaware: 1610-1682* (New Brunswick: Rutgers University Press, 1967). The founding of Philadelphia and its English settlement is well chronicled. The three major histories of the city are: J. Thomas Scharf and Thompson Westcott, *History of Philadelphia, 1609-1884*, 3 vols. (Philadelphia: L. H. Everts & Co., 1884), Ellis Paxson Oberholtzer, *Philadelphia: A History of the City and Its People*, 2 vols. (Philadelphia: S.J. Clarke Publishing Co., 1911), and Russell F. Weigley, ed., *Philadelphia: A Three-Hundred-Year History* (New York: W.W. Norton & Company for Barra Foundation, 1982).

[3] The east-west streets north of High (Market) Street were called Mulberry (now Arch), Sassafrass (now Race), and Vine; those south of High Street were called Chestnut, Walnut, Spruce, Pine, and Cedar (now South). In 1839 the north-south streets were numbered consecutively from Front Street along the Delaware River to the Schuylkill River. Front Street takes the place of a first street and what would be Fourteenth Street is Broad Street.

[4] At the time of the city's consolidation with the county, there were six boroughs, nine districts, and thirteen townships surrounding the city. The area near the city was so built up that it was a part of the city in every sense but political, but in the outlying regions there remained about 1,500 farms with about 10,000 cattle. Elizabeth M. Geffen, "Industrial Development and Social Crisis, 1841-1854," in Weigley, ed., *Philadelphia*, 359-60; Russell F. Weigley, "The Border City in the Civil War, 1854-1865," in ibid., 363; Howard Gillette, Jr., "The Emergence of the Modern Metropolis: Philadelphia in the Age of Its Consolidation," in William W. Cutler, III, and Howard Gillette, Jr., eds., *The Divided Metropolis: Social and Spatial Dimensions of Philadelphia, 1800-1975*, Contributions in American History, no. 85 (Westport, Conn.: Greenwood Press, 1980), 3-25.

[5] Quoted in Richard S. Dunn and Mary Maples Dunn, gen. eds., *The Papers of William Penn*, 5 vols. (Philadelphia: University of Pennsylvania Press, 1981-1987), 2:121. See also Mary Maples Dunn and Richard S. Dunn, gen. eds., *William Penn and the Founding of Pennsylvania, 1680-1684: A Documentary History*, ed. Jean R. Soderlund (Philadelphia: University of Pennsylvania, 1983), 85. Penn briefly explained his concept of Philadelphia's plan in his September 1681 instructions to three commissioners responsible for acquiring land for his capital city.

[6] For more extensive discussions of Penn's plan, see Mary Maples Dunn and Richard S. Dunn, "The Founding, 1681-1701," in Weigley, ed., *Philadelphia*, 1-10; Hannah Benner Roach, "The Planting of Philadelphia: A Seventeenth-Century Real Estate Development," *Pennsylvania Magazine of History and Biography* 92 (January 1968): 3-47, (April 1968): 143-94; Anthony N. B. Garvan, "Proprietary Philadelphia as Artifact," in Oscar Handlin and John Burchard, eds., *The Historian and the City* (Cambridge, Mass.: MIT Press for the Joint Center for Urban Studies, 1963), 177-201.

[7] Dunn and Dunn, "The Founding," 14-16.

[8] Penn had expected that economic leadership would come from the Free Society of Traders in Pennsylvania, a joint-stock company that he had incorporated in 1682 and granted a strip of city land now called Society Hill. For many reasons, not the least being an absence of cooperation from Pennsylvanians who suspected the company of monopolistic designs, the company was essentially defunct within four years. It did not sell its property and formally disband, however, until 1723. The merchants who filled the void engaged in a triangular trade with England and the West Indies in which American agricultural and forest products were traded to the islands for bills of exchange that were used to acquire English manufactured goods for colonial consumption. Ibid., 20; Oscar Theodore Barck, Jr., and Hugh Talmage Lefler, *Colonial America* (2nd ed.; New York: Macmillan Company, 1968), 377-78.

[9] Harry M. Tinkcom, Margaret B. Tinkcom, and Grant Miles Simon, *Historic Germantown: From the Founding to the Early Part of the Nineteenth Century, A Survey of the German Township* (Philadelphia: American Philosophical Society, 1955), 4-6, 27-31.

[10] By 1810 brick houses outnumbered frame houses three to one in the city, but in Southwark, on the city's southern border, there were twice as many frame houses as brick houses. Margaret B. Tinkcom, "Southwark, A River Community: Its Shape and Substance," *Proceedings of the American Philosophical Society* 114 (August 1970): 334.

[11] Hugh Morrison, *Early American Architecture: From the First Colonial Settlements to the National Period* (New York: Oxford University Press, 1952), 506, 509-10; George B. Tatum, *Penn's Great Town: 250 Years of Philadelphia Architecture Illustrated in Prints and Drawings* (Philadelphia: University of Pennsylvania Press, 1961), 25, 155; Roger W. Moss Jr., "Two Seventeenth-Century Swedish Churches in the Delaware River Valley," paper presented at twenty-eighth Annual Meeting of the Society of Architectural Historians, Boston, Mass., 23-28 April 1975.

[12] The casement window is one commonly used detail that could be considered medieval. Brick-pane construction (half-timber frame with brick nogging), a medieval form, was uncommon in Philadelphia, but is known to have existed on the rear ell of the Mears-Heaton House (PA-1070). The ell was built before 1765. Richard J. Webster, *Philadelphia Preserved: Catalog of the Historic American Buildings Survey* (Philadelphia: Temple University Press, 1976), 20.

[13] Tatum, *Penn's Great Town*, 21, 153, pl. 3. The Joshua Carpenter House was built between 1701 and 1722; a two-story gable-roof front addition was built in 1774 for John Dickinson, a prominent Philadelphia lawyer who attended the First and Second Continental Congresses. Scharf and Westcott, *History of Philadelphia*, 2:855, 899, 922; Philadelphia Contributionship Insurance Policy 1845 Survey, June 1774, Philadelphia Contributionship for the Insuring of Houses from Loss by Fire, Philadelphia, Pa.

[14] Among architectural historians the pent roof is a subject of more conjecture than consensus. Some historians argue that it was used to protect the wood, plaster, or chinking of the lower-level walls from the elements. Professor Gowans suggests that it was a medieval folk element that functioned in cities to protect pedestrians while satisfying the need for something traditional. One writer tries to strike a compromise by suggesting that it was used to protect log or half-timber walls and was simply carried over to masonry structures. The fact that Pennsylvania Germans also built pent roofs further muddies the water. The argument that Germans borrowed this detail from the English is countered by the assertion that the English borrowed it from the Germans; neither argument presents persuasive evidence. Professor Tatum's conclusion is that "in matters of this kind the simplest explanation often has the best chance of being the right one." Tatum, *Penn's Great Town*, 21; Alan Gowans, *Images of American Living: Four Centuries of Architecture and Furniture as Cultural Expression* (Philadelphia: J.B. Lippincott Company, 1964), 83-84; Thomas Jefferson Wertenbaker, *The Founding of American Civilization: The Middle Colonies* (New York: Charles Scribner's Sons, 1938), 306; Thomas Tileston Waterman, *The Dwellings of Colonial America* (Chapel Hill: University of North Carolina Press, 1950), 138-39; G. Edwin Brumbaugh, "Colonial Architecture of the Pennsylvania Germans": *Proceedings of the Pennsylvania German Society* (1933): 44; K. Edward Lay, "European Antecedents of Seventeenth and Eighteenth Century Germanic and Scots-Irish Architecture in America," *Pennsylvania Folklife* 32 (Autumn 1982): 18; Allen G. Noble, *Wood, Brick, and Stone: The North American Settlement Landscape*, 2 vols. (Amherst: University of Massachusetts Press, 1984), 1:46; Peter Smith, *Houses of the Welsh Countryside: A Study in Historical Geography* (London: Her Majesty's Stationery Office, 1975), 509.

[15] The Irish House is described in detail and related to Peter Kalm's 1750 description of Philadelphia houses, in Tinkcom, "Southwark," 331-33. For three eighteenth-century illustrations of London houses with pent roofs, see Joseph Burke and Colin Caldwell, *Hogarth: The Complete Engravings* (London: Thames and London, 1968), pls. 177, 178, 180. A detail of plate 177, *Morning* (a Covent Garden street scene), is illustrated in Gowans, *Images of American Living*, 83. Other than to note that London's domestic architecture "of the Restoration was borrowed from many sources, learned and vernacular," John Summerson in his study of eighteenth-century London does not discuss in detail the great mass of housing erected after

the city's calamitous fire of 1660. He does, however, point out two fire-conscious measures adopted in early-eighteenth-century London. One, in 1707, prohibited wooden cornices, which were striking features of Restoration London houses and eighteenth-century Philadelphia houses. London builders thereafter halfhid the roof behind a brick parapet and ran a brick or stone cornice across the front a few feet below the parapet's upper edge. The other law, enacted in 1709, required window frames to be recessed four inches, "leaving a naked 'reveal' of brickwork and incidentally giving a sense of solidity to the walls." John Summerson, *Georgian London* (London: Pleiades Books, 1945; rev. ed., Baltimore: Penguin Books, 1962), 36, 68.

[16] A. F. Kelsall, "The London House Plan in the Later 17th Century," *Journal of Post-Medieval Archaeology* 8 (1974): 80-85, 90-91; Summerson, *Georgian London,* 51, 66-67; William John Murtagh, "The Philadelphia Row House," *Journal of the Society of Architectural Historians* 16 (December 1957): 8-13. Murtagh has developed the standard classification of Philadelphia row house plans.

[17] Adolph B. Benson, ed., *The America of 1750: Peter Kalm's Travels in North America. The English Version of 1770 Revised from the Original Swedish with a Translation of New Material from Kalm's Diary Notes,* 2 vols. (New York: Wilson-Erickson, Inc., 1937), 1:99.

[18] The definitive work on the Powel House and its contemporaries is George B. Tatum, *Philadelphia Georgian: The City House of Samuel Powel and Some of Its Eighteenth-Century Neighbors* (Middletown, Conn.: Wesleyan University Press, 1976).

[19] George B. Tatum, "Thomas Carstairs (1759-1830)" in James C. Massey, ed., *Two Centuries of Philadelphia Architectural Drawings* (Philadelphia: Philadelphia Museum of Art, 1964), 15-16; Tatum, *Penn's Great Town,* 47, 164, pl. 33.

[20] Kenneth Ames, "Robert Mills and the Philadelphia Row House," *Journal of the Society of Architectural Historians* 27 (May 1968): 140-46; Robert Ennis, "Thomas Ustick Walter," paper presented to Philadelphia Chapter, Society of Architectural Historians, 13 December 1973.

[21] Webster, *Philadelphia Preserved,* 127, 295; Edwin Wolf 2nd, *Philadelphia: Portrait of an American City* (Harrisburg, Pa.: Stackpole Books, 1975), 328; George E. Thomas, "E. Allen Wilson, (active 1893-1936)," in James F. O'Gorman, Jeffrey A. Cohen, George E. Thomas, and G. Holmes Perkins, *Drawing toward Building: Philadelphia Architectural Graphics, 1732-1986* (Philadelphia: University of Pennsylvania Press for Pennsylvania Academy of the Fine Arts, 1986), 165; *Philadelphia Inquirer,* 19 June 1988, sec. E, 1, 6.

[22] Webster, *Philadelphia Preserved,* 156-57, 198-99, 255-56, 287, 310-13. An excellent illustrated history of Philadelphia industry after 1890 is Philip Scranton and Walter Licht, *Work Sights: Industrial Philadelphia, 1890-1950* (Philadelphia: Temple University Press, 1986). Many turn-of-the-century factories are illustrated with accompanying statistics in Moses King, *King's Views, Philadelphia* (New York: Moses King, 1900), 40-49. An excellent source for late-nineteenth-century mills is the Hexamer General Survey at the Free Library of Philadelphia.

[23] Edward W. Hocker, *Germantown, 1683-1933* (Philadelphia: By the author, 1933), 137-39, 163-73; Carroll L. V. Meeks, *The Railroad Station: An Architectural History* (New Haven: Yale

University Press, 1956), 88, 103-4; Jeffrey P. Roberts, "Railroads and the Downtown: Philadelphia, 1830-1900," in Cutler and Gillette, eds., *The Divided Metropolis*, 27-55; Margaret S. Marsh, "The Impact of the Market Street 'El' on Northern West Philadelphia: Environmental Change and Social Transformation, 1900-1930," in ibid., 169-92; Joseph M. Wilson, John A. Wilson, and Fred G. Thorn, *Catalog of Works Executed* (Philadelphia: J.B. Lippincott Company, 1885), 47-49; Joseph M. Wilson, "The Philadelphia and Reading Railroad Terminal and Station in Philadelphia," *American Society of Civil Engineers Transactions* 34 (August 1895): 115-84; James F. O'Gorman, *The Architecture of Frank Furness* (Philadelphia: Philadelphia Museum of Art, 1973), 57-58, 180-83; Webster, *Philadelphia Preserved*, 200, 291-92, 319.

[24] Other large late-seventeenth-century buildings whose builders understood Renaissance principles were the so-called Wren Building (1695-1702) at the College of William and Mary in Williamsburg, Virginia, Harvard College's Stoughton Hall (1699) in Cambridge, Massachusetts, and the first New York City Hall (1699). Only the Wren Building survives. Tatum, *Penn's Great Town*, 23, 153. A short history of Christ Church is Robert W. Shoemaker, "Christ Church, St. Peter's, and St. Paul's," in *Historic Philadelphia*, ed. Luther P. Eisenhart, vol. 43, part 1 of *Transactions of the American Philosophical Society*, 189.

[25] William H. Pierson, Jr., *American Buildings and Their Architects: The Colonial and Neoclassical Styles* (Garden City, N.Y.: Doubleday & Company, 1970), 135. The church is also discussed and praised as "the most ornate of Georgian churches in the colonies" in Morrison, *Early American Architecture*, 537-38, and as "a remarkable achievement" in Tatum, *Penn's Great Town*, 27-30, 33, 156.

[26] Pierson, *American Buildings and Their Architects: Colonial and Neoclassical Styles*, 108.

[27] For a complete history of the building, see Edward M. Riley, "The Independence Hall Group," in *Historic Philadelphia*, 7-42. For architectural assessments, see Tatum, *Penn's Great Town*, 32-33, 102-3, 137, 152, 160; Morrison, *Early American Architecture*, 532-37;

[28] Richard J. Betts, "The Woodlands," *Winterthur Portfolio* 14 (Autumn 1979): 229. The many aspects of Woodlands that were new to Americans are cited in Fiske Kimball, *Domestic Architecture of the American Colonies and of the Early Republic* (New York: Charles Scribner's Sons, 1922; reprint ed., New York: Dover Publications, 1966), 100, 154, 155, 163, 174, 203, 210, 211, 217, 226, 242, 252, 253. Woodlands is also evaluated in Pierson, *American Buildings and Their Architects: Colonial and Neoclassical Styles*, 219-21; Tatum, *Penn's Great Town*, 40-41, 51, 55.

[29] Tatum, *Penn's Great Town*, 59-60, 168; Pierson, *American Buildings and Their Architects: Colonial and Neoclassical Styles*, 348-57, 435; Talbot Hamlin, *Benjamin Henry Latrobe* (New York: Oxford University Press, 1955), 152-57, 344, 560. Hamlin calls it "the country's first Greek Revival structure" on page 153; Pierson explains why he disagrees on page 435.

[30] Hamlin, *Latrobe*, 151-52, 499-503; Tatum, *Penn's Great Town*, 65-66, 75, 89, 171, 177; Pierson, *American Buildings and Their Architects: Colonial and Neo-Classical Styles*, 434-36; Webster, *Philadelphia Preserved*, 238.

[31] Robert C. Smith, *John Notman and the Athenaeum Building* (Philadelphia: Athenaeum of Philadelphia, 1951), passim. The building's interior and parts of the Athenaeum's collection are illustrated and briefly discussed in Roger W. Moss Jr., "The Athenaeum of Philadelphia," *The Magazine Antiques* 114 (December 1978): 1264-79.

[32] Much has been written on City Hall. For a bibliography and a brief history and evaluation of the building, see Richard J. Webster, "Philadelphia City Hall (Public Buildings of the City of Philadelphia)," in Darrel L. Sewell, ed., *Philadelphia: Three Centuries of American Art* (Philadelphia: Philadelphia Museum of Art, 1976), 387-88.

[33] An exhibition of Furness's work at the Philadelphia Museum of Art in April and May, 1973, and James F. O'Gorman's accompanying monograph, *The Architecture of Frank Furness* (with a checklist by George E. Thomas and Hyman Myers of Furness's works and projects), have been major factors in the resurrection of Furness's reputation.

[34] Significant Philadelphia Romanesque Revival buildings constitute a short list, which would include Bethel African Methodist Church (PA-1318), 1889-90; First Baptist Church, 1897-1900; American Life Insurance Company Building (PA-1064), 1888; C. F. Rumpp & Sons, Inc., Factory (PA-1469), 1893; Curtis Publishing Company at 425 Arch Street; Union Trust Company at 713-19 Chestnut Street. Of this group only the churches survive.

[35] It is difficult to document the absence of New York architects from the pages of the *Builders' Guide*, but one significant example is the weekly's failure to note in 1893 that Henry Edwards-Ficken of New York was the architect for the new facade and extensive remodeling of Frances DeLancey Welsh's house on Spruce Street west of Rittenhouse Square. The London-born and European-trained Edwards-Ficken also designed the entrance and main hall of James Pinchot's Grey Towers (PA-1400) in Milford, Pike County, Pa. Philadelphia City Hall, Department of Licenses and Inspection, Building Permit 3850, 30 October 1893; *Grey Towers: Preliminary Historic Structure Report* (Albany, N.Y.: Preservation/Design Group, 1978), 11.

[36] Webster, *Philadelphia Preserved*, 132-33.

[37] For an excellent analysis of social class and architectural patronage, see George E. Thomas, "Architectural Patronage and Social Stratification in Philadelphia between 1840 and 1920," in Cutler and Gillette, eds., *The Divided Metropolis*, 85-123.

[38] Edward Teitelman, "Wilson Eyre, Jr., and the Arts and Crafts in Philadelphia," *Journal of the Society of Architectural Historians* 30 (October 1971): 245-46; George E. Thomas, "Wilson Eyre, Jr., FAIA (1858-1944)," in O'Gorman et al., *Drawing toward Building*, 163.

[39] Nathaniel Burt, *The Perennial Philadelphians: The Anatomy of an American Aristocracy* (Boston: Little, Brown and Company, 1963), 363. See *A Monograph of the Work of Mellor, Meigs & Howe* (New York: Architectural Book Publishing Co., 1923) for photos and drawings of some of the firms domestic commissions between 1914 and 1922 with commentary by such people as Arthur I. Meigs of the firm and Paul P. Cret, architect and University of Pennsylvania Professor of Architecture.

⁴⁰Much has been written about the PSFS Building. The most thorough discussion of the building is in William H. Jordy, *American Buildings and Their Architects: The Impact of European Modernism in the Mid-Twentieth Century* (Garden City, N.Y.: Doubleday and Company, 1970), 87-164. An excellent succinct analysis is Peter S. Reed, "Philadelphia Saving Fund Society Building," in O'Gorman et al., *Drawing toward Building*, 210-12. See also Harold B. Dickson, *A Hundred Pennsylvania Buildings* (State College, Pa.: Bald Eagle Press, 1954), pls. 92, 92A; Tatum, *Penn's Great Town*, 131-32. 203, pl. 136; Robert A. M. Stern, *George Howe: Toward a Modern American Architecture* (New Haven: Yale University Press, 1975),108-30

⁴¹Federal Writers' Project, *Philadelphia: A Guide to the Nation's Birthplace* (Philadelphia: William Penn Association, 1937), 525-27; Tatum, *Penn's Great Town*, 132-33, 203-4, pl. 137.

⁴²Construction in the city hit its low point in 1944, when only 2,945 building permits were issued, nearly all for repairs and minor alterations. This number was only two-thirds of the 4,672 building permits issued in 1933, the worst year of the Great Depression. The previous high had been reached in 1927 when the city's Department of Licenses and Inspection issued 11,006 building permits, a number not exceeded until the 1950s. Webster, *Philadelphia Preserved*, 357 (n. 65).

⁴³Vincent Scully, *Louis Kahn* (New York: George Braziller, 1962), 10-11, 28-31; Jordy, *American Buildings and Their Architects: The Impact of European Modernism*, 361-426; G. Holmes Perkins, "Louis I. Kahn, FAIA (1901-1974)" in O'Gorman et al., *Drawing toward Building*, 215-16.

⁴⁴*Progressive Architecture's* managing editor in 1961 suggested that Kahn's philosophy and design approach "heralds a new renaissance that might prove to be at least as important to the course of architectural history as the emergence of the Chicago School in the late nineteenth century." Fifteen years later, however, architectural editor and historian Robert Coombs claimed that "as a distinct geographical style, the Philadelphia School is a myth of destiny which did not manifest itself." In short, one cannot see Kahn's effects on Philadelphia in the sense that one can observe the effects of Adler and Sullivan or Burnham and Root on downtown Chicago. Coombs argues that Robert Venturi, through his students, had a greater effect on the city's architecture in the 1970s than did Kahn, Venturi's mentor. Jan C. Rowan, "Wanting to Be: The Philadelphia School," *Progressive Architecture* 42 (April 1961): 130-49; Robert Coombs, "Philadelphia's Phantom School: Philadelphia Architecture after Kahn," *Progressive Architecture*. 57 (April 1976). 58-63.

⁴⁵An insider's discussion of the influences on Robert Venturi and his firm, Venturi, Rauch and Scott Brown, is Denise Scott Brown, "A Worm's Eye View of Recent Architectural History," *Architectural Record* 172 (February 1984): 69-81. For an explanation of how his mother's house expresses his architectural philosophy, see Robert Venturi, *Complexity and Contradiction in Architecture* (New York: Museum of Modern Art in association with Graham Foundation for Advanced Studies in The Fine Arts, Chicago, 1966), 117-21. For brief assessments of the firm's work in general and the Vanna Venturi House in particular, see Vincent Scully, "Robert Venturi's Gentle Architecture," in Christopher Mead, ed., *The Architecture of Robert Venturi* (Albu-

querque: University of New Mexico Press, 1989), 8-33; Peter S. Reed, "Vanna Venturi House," in O'Gorman et al., *Drawing toward Building,* 227; David P. Handlin, *American Architecture* (London: Thames and Hudson, 1985), 265-67; Leland M. Roth, *A Concise History of American Architecture* (New York: Harper and Row, 1979), 311-13. Another disciple of Louis Kahn who enjoys an international reputation is Romaldo Giurgola of Mitchell/Giurgola. See Ehrman B. Mitchell and Romaldo Giurgola, *Mitchell/Giurgola, Architects* (New York: Rizzoli, 1983).

[46]Edmund N. Bacon discusses the historical sources of his city planning ideas in *Design of Cities* (New York: Viking Press, 1967); see 243-71 for "Putting the Ideas to Work—Philadelphia." For summaries of major redevelopment projects, see G. Holmes Perkins, "Independence Mall," "Market Street East," "Market Street East: Gallery I," and Peter S. Reed, "Penn Center Development, Philadelphia," in O'Gorman et al., *Drawing toward Building,* 214, 239, 243, 237. For the University City Science Center, see Leon S. Rosenthal, *A History of Philadelphia's University City* (Philadelphia: West Philadelphia Corporation, 1963), 73-80; *Philadelphia Inquirer,* 8 February 1976, sec. I, 9; 29 May 1976, sec. B, 1-2. For an interesting discussion of some of these projects while they were under way, see Tatum, *Penn's Great Town,* 137-39. The history of the Clark and Dilworth administrations is summarized in Joseph S. Clark Jr.. and Dennis Clark, "Rally and Relapse, 1946-1968" in Weigley, ed., *Philadelphia,* 650-61, 666-74, 692-96, 701-3. For a summary of the Philadelphia legacy of Vincent G. Kling, the architect who was responsible for Penn Center's master plan, most of its buildings, Kennedy and Dilworth plazas, the Municipal Services Building, Fidelity Mutual Building, and Centre Square Building, see Thomas Hine's articles in *Philadelphia Inquirer,* 9 June 1981, sec. D, 1, 3; 7 January 1987, sec. C, 1, 8. For the role of Reading Terminal in the Philadelphia Convention Center plans, see the editorial and Thomas Hine's article in *Philadelphia Inquirer,* 7 November 1984, sec. A, 26; 3 April 1988, sec. F, 1, 6.

[47]*Philadelphia Inquirer,* 6 April 1984, sec. A, 1, 12; 15 May 1984, sec. A, 1, 2; 14 May 1985, sec. A, 1, 6; 13 December 1986, sec. B, 3; 29 November 1987, sec. K, 1,2. For Thomas Hine's columns, which analyze and summarize plans, proposals, and arguments, see ibid., 5 April 1984, sec. C, 7; 8 April 1984, sec. K, 14; 26 April 1984, sec. C, 1, 8; 29 April 1984, sec. K, 17; 6 May 1984, sec. M, 18; 27 May 1984, sec. I, 10; 17 June 1984, sec. C, 1, 4; 30 December 1984, sec. H, 1, 14; 14 May 1985, sec. A, 6; 19 May 1985, sec. L, 14; 4 September 1984, sec. E, 1, 4; 23 January 1988, sec. I, 1, 6. For Paul Goldberger's positive critique, *New York Times,* 15 November 1987, sec. H, 41. For local columnists' commentaries, see *Philadelphia Inquirer,* 11 March 1984, sec. G, 7; 3 April 1984, sec. A, 9; 13 April 1984, sec. A, 15; 29 April 1984, sec. G, 7; 3 May 1984, sec. B, 1, 2; 5 May 1984, sec. A, 9; 9 May 1984, sec. A, 23; 23 May 1984, sec. B, 1; 24 May 1984, sec. A, 23; 13 June 1984, sec. B, 1; 14 June 1984, sec. A, 1; 15 June 1984, sec. A, 15; 19 June 1984, sec. A, 9; 13 May 1985, sec. A, 9; 24 June 1985, sec. A, 11; 6 December 1985, sec. A, 25. For representative letters to the editor, see ibid., 11 April 1984, sec. A, 18; 12 April 1984, sec. A, 26; 14 April 1984, sec. A, 8; 16 April 1984, sec. A, 14; 25 April 1984, sec. A, 12; 7 May 1984, sec. A, 10; 17 May 1984, sec. A, 22; 24 May 1984, sec. A, 22; 29 May 1984. sec. A, 10; 10 June 1984, sec. G, 6; 15 June 1984, sec. A, 14; 26 June 1984, sec. A, 8; 13 May 1985, sec. A, 8; 1 July 1985, sec. A, 8.

[48] Ibid., 24 November 1987, sec. B, 2; 29 December 1987, sec. B, 2; 17 January 1988, sec. I, 1, 6; 6 November 1988, sec. V, 1, 6; 15 January 1989, sec. J, 1, 6. Allen Freeman, "A Tale of Four New Towers and What They Tell of Trends," *Architecture* (May 1988): 125-31.

[49] Those seven skyscrapers are fifty-eight-story Two Liberty Place at Sixteenth and Chestnut Streets, Helmut Jahn of Chicago, architect; fifty-three-story Bell Atlantic Tower at Eighteenth and Arch Streets, Kling-Lindquist Partnership of Philadelphia, architect; fifty-four-story Mellon Bank Center at Eighteenth and Market Streets, Kohn Pederson Fox of New York, architect; thirty-four-story Two Logan Square on Eighteenth Street south of Logan Square, Kohn Pederson Fox, architect; twenty-nine-story Eleven Penn Center at Nineteenth and Market Streets; fifty-story 1919 Market Street at Nineteenth and Market Streets, WZMH of Toronto, architects; forty-story Commerce Square at Twenty-first and Market Streets, I.M. Pei and Partners of New York, architect. *City Sites: The Magazine of the Foundation for Architecture* 3 (Spring 1988): 1, 4; *Philadelphia Inquirer*, 2 December 1984, sec. B, 1, 10; 25 October 1987, sec. J, 1, 12; 11 September 1988, sec. F, 1; 6 November 1988, sec. V, 1, 6; 12 February 1989, sec. J, 1, 6.

[50] *Philadelphia Inquirer*, 3 June 1985, sec. A, 15; 28 June 1985, sec. W, 1.

[51] The Elliott Building, 235 Chestnut Street, is part of the Chestnut Street Area Study (PA-1402). It was a wholesale dry goods district in the last half of the nineteenth century. The Lee and Disston Houses are adjoining houses that were built in the early 1870s at 1437-39 North Fifteenth Street, at the corner of Jefferson Street. The houses have been renamed the Waller House in memory of the Reverend John Bernard Waller, pastor of National Temple Baptist Church. Its transformation into low-income housing was the work of Samuel Smith and Marie Nahikian of National Temple Non-Profit, who creatively financed the project through a Greater Philadelphia First Corporation grant, a low-interest Ford Foundation loan, and federal tax credits. Ibid., 5 October 1987, sec. D, 1, 14; 2 July 1988, sec. C, 10; 22 January 1989, sec. C, 1, 6.

[52] After vacating the arsenal in stages between 1976 and 1978, the federal government sold the eighty-six-acre complex to the city for one dollar. The city sought tenants who gradually transformed what some thought was a white elephant into an aggregation of warehouses, small manufactories, and laboratories. Lit Brothers, one of the city's great Market Street department stores for over half a century, closed in 1977, and appeared doomed until Mellon Bank in 1985 agreed to be its primary tenant. Two years and $90 million later, the rehabilitated building opened amid hoopla and front-page headlines as the Mellon Independence Center. The project not only preserved and restored the Lit Brothers Store's facades but also put to use the Doric paneling that John Haviland designed for an 1831 "restoration" of Independence Hall. The National Park Service removed the paneling in 1961, and it now lines a lobby in the Mellon Independence Center. The architectural firms in charge of the renovation and facade restoration were Burt Hill Kosar Rittelmann Associates and John Milner Associates, respectively. Their work received an award in 1988 from the Preservation Fund of Pennsylvania and in 1989 the National Trust for Historic Preservation recognized the architects and developer

(Independence Center Realty) with a Preservation Honor Award. For the architects' description of their renovation and restoration work, see *City Sites: Magazine of the Foundation for Architecture* 2 (February 1987), 2-3. For the National Trust award, see Jane Gillette, "The Year's Best," *Historic Preservation* (November/December 1989), 27. The information on Haviland's paneling is in "Mellon Gives New Life to Lits," *Preservation, Pennsylvania: The Preservation Fund of Pennsylvania, Inc.* 2 (Fall 1987): 1-2. For a journalistic history of the project's ups and downs, see *Philadelphia Inquirer,* 6 April 1977, sec. A., 1, 4; 27 April 1977, sec. D, 22; 22 May 1980, sec. B, 1, 2; 16 August 1981, sec. B, 1, 6; 12 January 1984, sec. A, 1, 17; 26 April 1984, sec. A, 1, 8; 18 July 1984, sec. B, 1; 19 July 1984, sec. B, 4; 24 August 1984, sec. B, 1, 6; 30 October 1985, sec. A, 1, 10; 4 October 1987, sec. G, 1, 16; 7 October 1987, sec. E, 1, 6.

Catalog

Philadelphia County

Abercrombie, Capt. James, House (Perelman Antique Toy Museum) (PA-1316), 268-70 S. Second St. 5 sheets (1959, 1960); 10 photos (1959, 1960, 1972). LC code: PA,51-PHILA,621.

Academy of Music. See American Academy of Music.

Academy of Notre Dame (PA-1492), 208 S. Nineteenth St., Rittenhouse Sq. 3 photos (1969). LC code: PA,51-PHILA,680.

American Academy of Music (Academy of Music) (PA-1491), 232-46 S. Broad St. 15 photos (1854, 1957, 1963, 1967). LC code: PA,51-PHILA,294. NHL.

American Fire Insurance Company Building (PA-1386), 308-10 Walnut St. 1 photo (1958); 1 data page (1984). LC code: PA,51-PHILA,316.

American Life Insurance Company Building (Manhattan Building) (PA-1064), 330-36 Walnut St. 9 photos (n.d., 1960, 1961); 10 data pages (1960). LC code: PA,51-PHILA,257.

American Philosophical Society (Philosophical Hall) (PA-1464), 104 S. Fifth St. 5 photos (1967). LC code: PA,51-PHILA,46. NHL.

Annan, William, House (PA-1539), 776 S. Front St. 1 photo (1957). LC code: PA,51-PHILA,444.

Arbour, William, House (PA-1051), 220 Spruce St. 1 sheet (1959); 3 photos (1957); 4 data pages (1959). LC code: PA,51-PHILA,250.

Arcade Building (Commercial Trust Building) (PA-1493), Fifteenth and Market Sts. 11 photos (ca. 1902, 1962-63, 1964); 9 data pages (1962). LC code: PA,51-PHILA,676.

501 Arch Street (House) (PA-1092). 1 photo (1959). LC code: PA,51-PHILA,465.

503-27 Arch Street (Houses) (PA-1387). 2 photos (1959). LC code: PA,51-PHILA,466.

620 Arch Street (House) (PA-1423). 1 photo (1965); 2 data pages (1965, 1984). LC code: PA,51-PHILA,468.

628-30 Arch Street (House) (PA-1424). 1 photo (1965); 2 data pages (1965, 1984). LC code: PA,51-PHILA,469.

Arch Street Friends Meetinghouse (PA-1388), 330 Arch St. 4 photos (1974). LC code: PA,51-PHILA,10. NR.

Arch Street Methodist Episcopal Church (PA-1494), Broad and Arch Sts. 1 photo (1974). LC code: PA,51-PHILA,312.

Arch Street Opera House (The Troc, Trocadero) (PA-1495), 1003-5 Arch St. 2 photos (1916, 1973). LC code: PA,51-PHILA,470. NR.

Arch Street Presbyterian Church. See West Arch Street Presbyterian Church.

Armat, Thomas, House (PA-1671), 5450 Germantown Ave. 2 photos (1957, 1960). LC code: PA,51-GERM,31.

Armory of the National Guard. See National Guard's Hall.

Arsenal on the Schuylkill. See Schuylkill Arsenal.

Art Gallery. See International Exhibition of 1876, Memorial Hall.

Ashmead, Albert, House (PA-1672), 5430 Germantown Ave. 1 photo (1957). LC code: PA,51-GERM,27.

Ashmead, William, House (PA-1673), 5434 Germantown Ave. 1 photo (1957). LC code: PA,51-GERM,28.

Askins-Jones House (PA-1541), 720-24 S. Front St. 3 photos (1961, 1967). LC code: PA,51-PHILA,439.

Athenaeum of Philadelphia. See The Philadelphia Athenaeum.

Atwater Kent Museum. See Franklin Institute.

Ayer, N.W., and Company Building (N.W. Ayer and Son, Incorporated, Building) (PA-1390), 204-12 S. Seventh St. 2 photos (1976). LC code: PA,51-PHILA,664.

Ayer, N.W., and Son, Incorporated, Building. See N.W. Ayer and Company Building.

Baird, Donald L., Company Warehouse (PA-1378), 327-29 S. Water St. 3 photos (1966). LC code: PA,51-PHILA,612.

Bake House and Oven (PA-1317), 423 S. Second St. 2 photos (1963). LC code: PA,51-PHILA,292.

Baltimore and Ohio Railroad Station (PA-1220), Twenty-fourth and Chestnut Sts. 3 sheets (1966, 1968); 18 photos (n.d., 1959). LC code: PA,51-PHILA,405.

Bank of Germantown. See Clarkson-Watson House.

Bank of North America (PA-1391), 305-7 Chestnut St. 4 photos (1959, 1972); 4 data pages (1984). LC code: PA,51-PHILA,383.

Bank of Pennsylvania (Philadelphia Bank, Philadelphia National Bank) (PA-1392), 421 Chestnut St. 4 photos (ca. 1910, 1972); 2 data pages (1984). LC code: PA,51-PHILA,376.

Bank Row (PA-1667), 407-31 Chestnut St. 2 photos (1959); 2 data pages (1985). LC code: PA,51-PHILA,374.

Barclay House. See Rhoads-Barclay House.

Barron, Commodore James, House (PA-1674), 5106 Germantown Ave. 2 photos (ca. 1900, 1957). LC code: PA,51-GERM,13.

Bartram, John, Hotel. See Hotel Walton.

Bartram, John, House (PA-1132), Fifty-fourth St. 8 sheets (1940); 11 photos (1938). LC code: PA,51-PHILA,38. NHL.

Baugh Warehouse. See Beck-Care Warehouse.

Baynton House. See Germantown Historical Society Area Study, 5208 Germantown Avenue.

111-13 Beck Street (Houses) (PA-1581). 1 photo (n.d.). LC code: PA,51-PHILA,337.

Beck Street Area Study (Court of Homes) (PA-1542), 203-15 Beck St. 2 photos (1961). LC code: PA,51-PHILA,338.

Beck-Care Warehouse (Baugh Warehouse) (PA-1188), 18-20 S. Delaware Ave. 5 sheets (1965, 1968); 4 photos (1958, 1965). LC code: PA,51-PHILA,392.

Beggarstown School (PA-1675), 6669 Germantown Ave. 1 photo (1972). LC code: PA,51-GERM,72. NR.

Bel Air (Belleaire, Singley House, Lasse Cock's Manor House) (PA-1124), League Island Park (Passyunk Twp.). 30 sheets (1940); 8 photos (1936). LC code: PA,51-PHILA,228.

Belfield. See Peale, Charles Willson, House.

Belleaire. See Bel Air.

Bellevue-Stratford Hotel (PA-1226), Broad and Walnut Sts. 34 photos (1976). LC code: PA,51-PHILA,344. NR.

Belmont Mansion (PA-1649), Belmont Mansion Dr. 5 photos (1926, 1931). LC code: PA,51-PHILA,304.

Bergdol House. See Kemble-Bergdol House.

Berry-Blair House (Reverend Samuel Blair House) (PA-1063), 415 Locust St. 2 photos (1958); 1 data page (1984). LC code: PA,51-PHILA,492.

Berry-Coxe House (PA-1062), 413 Locust St. 10 sheets (1954, 1962); 15 photos (1958, 1972); 7 data pages (1958, 1959). LC code: PA,51-PHILA,168.

Bethel African Methodist Episcopal Church (Mother Bethel African Methodist Episcopal Church) (PA-1318), 419 S. Sixth St. 2 photos (1973). LC code: PA,51-PHILA,288. NHL.

Bethel Christian Center. See Mariner's Bethel Church.

Billmeyer, Michael, House (PA-1677), 6505-7 Germantown Ave. 1 photo (1972). LC code: PA,51-GERM,67. NR.

Bilsland House See Sims, Joseph, House.

Binney, H., Esq., House (PA-1903), no address provided. 2 photos (1959). LC code: PA,51-PHILA,686.

Bird, Joseph, Houses (PA-1543), 813-15 S. Hancock St. 1 photo (n.d.). LC code: PA,51-PHILA,482.

Bishop-Sparks House (PA-1544), 948 S. Front St. 1 photo (1957). LC code: PA,51-PHILA,457.

Blackwell, Reverend Robert, House (St. Peter's Church House) (PA-1319), 313 Pine St. 1 photo (1972). LC code: PA,51-PHILA,322.

Blair House. See Berry-Blair House.

Blair, Reverend Samuel, House. See Berry-Blair House.

Blair, Samuel, Jr., House (PA-7-5), 6105 Germantown Ave. 7 sheets (1934); 4 photos (1934); 2 data pages (1936). LC code: PA,51-GERM,49.

Bleakley House. See Cannonball Farm.

Blight Warehouse (PA-1393), 101-3 S. Front St. 1 photo (1966). LC code: PA,51-PHILA,420.

Blockley Retreat Farm. See Busti, Paul, House.

Blue Bell Tavern (PA-131), Woodland Ave. near Cobbs Creek. 12 photos (1916, n.d.); 2 data pages (1937). LC code: PA,23-DARB.V,1.

Boat House Row (PA-1650), E. River Dr. 1 photo (1972); 2 data pages (1974). LC code: PA,51-PHILA,561. NHL.

Bonsall, John, House (PA-1394), 706 Locust St. 5 photos (1959, 1975). LC code: PA,51-PHILA,320.

Bourse Building. See Philadelphia Bourse.

Bridges, Robert, House. See Bridges-Latour House.

Bridges, Robert, House (PA-1320), 507 S. Front St. 1 photo (1958). LC code: PA,51-PHILA,428.

Bridges-Latour House (PA-1321), 509 S. Front St. 10 photos (1958, 1961, 1966); 1 data page (1984). LC code: PA,51-PHILA,429.

Bringhurst House (PA-1679), 5448 Germantown Ave. 15 photos (1957, 1960, 1982). LC code: PA,51-GERM,181.

British Buildings. See International Exhibition of 1876, St. George's House.

Broad Street Station. See Pennsylvania Railroad Station, Broad Street Station.

Brock, John and Sons, Warehouse (PA-1395), 242-44 N. Delaware Ave. 9 photos (1972, 1973, 1977). LC code: PA,51-PHILA,278.

Bromley, John and Sons, Building (Lehigh Mills) (PA-1744), 201-63 E. Lehigh Ave. 3 photos (1902, 1973). LC code: PA,51-PHILA,305.

Buchanan Company, Paper Dealers. See Megargee Brothers Paper Warehouse.

Bulletin Building (Penn Square Building) (PA-1496), 1315-25 Filbert St. 2 photos (1911, 1973); 1 data page (1984). LC code: PA,51-PHILA,410.

Burden, Joseph, House (PA-1949), 132 S. Fourth St. 3 photos (1959). LC code: PA,51-PHILA,645.

Burgin House. See 331 South Fifth Street.

Burholme (Ryers Mansion) (PA-186), Burholme Park at Cottman and Central Aves. 10 sheets (1930s); 2 photos (1972). LC code: PA,51-PHILA,273. NR.

Stables (PA-186A). 1 photo (1972). LC code: PA,51-PHILA,273A.

Burk, Alfred E., House (PA-1722), 1500 N. Broad St. 2 photos (1973). LC code: PA,51-PHILA,313.

Burnham, George, House (PA-1627), 3401 Powelton Ave. 2 photos (1973). LC code: PA,51-PHILA,279.

Burnside. See Hamilton-Hoffman House.

Bussey-Poulson House (PA-1323), 320 S. Front St. 1 sheet (1959); 3 photos (1959, 1972). LC code: PA,51-PHILA,144.

Busti, Paul, House (Kirkbride Mansion, Blockley Retreat Farm) (PA-1628), Forty-sixth St. and Haverford Ave. 8 photos (1958); 1 data page (1984). LC code: PA,51-PHILA,483.

Byrne-Cavenaugh Houses (PA-1545), 130-32 Queen St. 2 photos (1961, 1974). LC code: PA,51-PHILA,285.

Cadwalader House. See Norris-Cadwalader House.

Cannonball Farm (Bleakley House) (PA-134), Mud Island. 10 sheets (1940); 6 photos (1937, 1940); 1 data page (1937). LC code: PA,51-PHILA,222.

Care Warehouse. See Beck-Care Warehouse.

Carpenter, Joshua, House. See Carpenter's Mansion.

Carpenters' Company Hall (Carpenters' Hall) (PA-1398), 320 Chestnut St. and Carpenters' Ct. 3 sheets (1932); 10 photos (ca. 1898, 1939, 1975); 8 data pages (1811, 1912, 1984). LC code: PA,51-PHILA,229. NHL.

Front Store (PA-1398A). 3 sheets (1958); 5 photos (1957); 7 data pages (1954, 1983). LC code: PA,51-PHILA,229A.

New Hall (PA-1398B). 2 photos (1957); 1 data page (1960). LC code: PA,51-PHILA,229B.

Pemberton House (PA-1398C). 1 photo (1975). LC code: PA,51-PHILA,229C.

Rule Book (Carpentry Manual) (PA-1398D). 39 photos of 1786 publication. LC code: PA,51-PHILA,229D.

Carpenters' Hall. See Carpenters' Company Hall.

Carpenter's Mansion (Joshua Carpenter House) (PA-1397), 615-19 Chestnut St. 1 photo (n.d.). LC code: PA,51-PHILA,230.

Carpentry Manual. See Carpenter's Company Hall, Rule Book.

Cassatt House. See Rogers-Cassatt House.

Cast Iron Sidewalk (PA-1723), 1907 N. Seventh St. 5 photos (1972). LC code: PA,51-PHILA,291.

Cathedral of Saints Peter and Paul (PA-1497), Eighteenth and Race Sts. 3 photos (1928, 1973). LC code: PA,51-PHILA,552. NR.

Catherine Street (Courtyard) (PA-1128), bounded by Front, Catherine, Swanson, and Queen Sts. 1 photo (1967). LC code: PA,51-PHILA,368.

19-35 Catherine Street (Houses) (PA-5182). 1 photo (1967). LC code: PA,51-PHILA,357.

27 Catherine Street (Stoop) (PA-1928). 1 photo (1966). LC code: PA,51-PHILA,361.

29-31 Catherine Street (Alley) (PA-5181). 1 photo (1966). LC code: PA,51-PHILA,360.

30 Catherine Street (House) (PA-1573). 2 photos (1966). LC code: PA,51-PHILA,365.

33 1/2 Catherine Street (House) (PA-1069). 2 sheets (1962); 5 photos (1961); 1 data page (1984). LC code: PA,51-PHILA,359.

Cavenaugh Houses. See Byrne-Cavenaugh Houses.

Cedar Grove (PA-1651), Landsdowne Dr. 3 photos (ca. 1900, 1928, 1972). LC code: PA,51-PHILA,231.

Centennial Guard Box (PA-1652), Traffic Triangle, Benjamin Franklin Parkway. Vicinity. 1 photo (1973). LC code: PA,51-PHILA,289.

Centennial National Bank (PA-1095), Thirty-second and Market Sts. 3 sheets (1965); 1 photo (1961). LC code: PA,51-PHILA,525. NR.

Chalkley Hall (PA-110), Wheatsheaf La. and Sepviva St. 24 sheets (1937); 12 photos (1936, 1937); 9 data pages (1937, 1984). LC code: PA,51-PHILA,62.

Chamber of Commerce. See Commercial Exchange.

Chamounix Mansion (PA-1653), Chamounix Dr. 2 photos (1972). LC code: PA,51-PHILA,281. NR.

Chandler House. See Kid-Chandler and Kid-Physick Houses.

Cherry Hill Penitentiary. See Eastern State Penitentiary.

Chestnut Hill Academy. See Wissahickon Inn.

213-43 Chestnut Street. See Chestnut Street Area Study.

Chestnut Street Area Study (Commercial Buildings) (PA-1402), 213-43 Chestnut St. 3 photos (1972); 2 data pages (1976). LC code: PA,51-PHILA,373.

Chestnut Street Bridge (PA-1054), Schuylkill River, Chestnut St. vicinity. 5 photos (1957); 3 data pages (1957). LC code: PA,51-PHILA,253.

Chew Mansion. See Cliveden.

Chinatown YMCA (Chinese Cultural and Community Center) (PA-1498), 125 N. Tenth St. 5 photos (1974). LC code: PA,51-PHILA,315.

Chinese Cultural and Community Center. See Chinatown YMCA.

Christ Church (PA-1071), 22-26 N. Second St. 19 sheets (1933, 1959, 1971); 36 photos (1939, 1959, 1965, 1969). LC code: PA,51-PHILA,7. NHL.

Church of St. James the Less (PA-1725), 3200 W. Clearfield St. 3 photos (1972). LC code: PA,51-PHILA,318. NHL.

Church of St. Luke (Church of St. Luke and Epiphany) (PA-1499), 330 S. Thirteenth St. 3 photos (1974). LC code: PA,51-PHILA,300.

Church of St. Luke and Epiphany. See Church of St. Luke.

Church of St. Philip Neri (PA-1547), 220-28 Queen St. 3 photos (ca. 1880, 1974). LC code: PA,51-PHILA,550.

Church of St. Vincent De Paul (PA-1680), 101-07 E. Price St. 3 photos (ca. 1880, 1973). LC code: PA,51-PHILA,309.

Church of the Gesu (PA-1724), Eighteenth and Thompson Sts. 2 photos (1973). LC code: PA,51-PHILA,284.

Church of the Holy Trinity (Protestant Episcopal) (PA-1085), 200 S. Nineteenth St. 6 photos (1959); 5 data pages (1964). LC code: PA,51-PHILA,677.

Church of the Immaculate Conception (PA-1901), 1020 N. Front St. 1 photo (ca. 1880). LC code: PA,51-PHILA,419.

Church of the Redeemer (PA-1077), 101-7 Queen St. 8 photos (1961, 1962); 5 data pages (1962). LC code: PA,51-PHILA,263.

City Hall. See New Public Buildings, The.

Civil War Memorial. See Smith Memorial Arch.

Clarkson-Watson House (Bank of Germantown) (PA-1681), 5275-77 Germantown Ave. 1 photo (1973). LC code: PA,51-GERM,25. NR.

Cliffs, The (PA-185), Columbia Ave., Fairmount Park. 14 sheets (1930s); 4 photos (1931, 1932, 1972). LC code: PA,51-PHILA,274. NR.

Cliveden (The Chew Mansion) (PA-1184), 6401 Germantown Ave. 17 sheets (1972); 87 photos (1967, 1972); 9 data pages (1972, 1983). LC code: PA,51-GERM,64. NHL.

Clunie. See Mount Pleasant.

Clymers Alley (Clymers Court) (PA-1582), rear of 770 S. Front St. 1 photo (n.d.). LC code: PA,51-PHILA,441.

Clymers Court. See Clymers Alley.

Collins, Samuel, House (PA-1549), 783 S. Front St. 1 photo (1961). LC code: PA,51-PHILA,445.

Columbia Engine Company (PA-1629), 3420 Market St. 1 photo (ca. 1935). LC code: PA,51-PHILA,522.

Commercial Exchange (Chamber of Commerce) (PA-1406), 135 S. Second St. 4 photos (1868, 1875, 1972). LC code: PA,51-PHILA,314.

Commercial Trust Building. See Arcade Building.

Commercial Union Assurance Company Building (PA-1076), 416-20 Walnut St. 7 photos (1962, 1963); 6 data pages (1963). LC code: PA,51-PHILA,262.

Compton (Morris House) (PA-1682), Meadowbrook Ave. 12 photos (1964); 4 data pages (1964, 1984). LC code: PA,51-PHILA,527. NR.

Concord School (PA-12), 6309 Germantown Ave. 6 sheets (1934); 1 photo (1972); 4 data pages (1934). LC code: PA,51-GERM,59.

Congress Hall (Philadelphia County Courthouse; Independence Hall Complex, Congress Hall) (PA-1431), Sixth and Chestnut Sts. 35 sheets (1959); 24 photos (1959, 1963, 1964, 1975); 3 data pages (1985). LC code: PA,51-PHILA,6A.

Conner House. See Physick-Conner House.

Conynham-Hacker House See Germantown Historical Society Area Study, 5214 Germantown Avenue.

Cooper, Jacob, House (PA-1407), 118 Cuthbert St. 3 photos (1958). LC code: PA,51-PHILA,692.

Cope, Caleb, and Company Store (Goldberg's Army-Navy Store) (PA-1408), 429 Market St. 2 photos (n.d.). LC code: PA,51-PHILA,516.

Cope, Edward Drinker, Houses (PA-1500), 2100-2 Pine St. 4 photos (1984); 2 data pages (1984). LC code: PA,51-PHILA,539. NHL.

Cove Cornice House. See Stafford's Tavern-Paschall House.

Covered Bridge (PA-19), Thomas Mill Rd., spanning Wissahickon Creek. 1 sheet (1936); 2 photos (1972). LC code: PA,51-GERM,162.

Coxe House. See Berry-Coxe House.

Currie, Dr. William, House (PA-191), 271 S. Fifth St. 2 photos (1957); 2 data pages (1957). LC code: PA,51-PHILA,240.

Curtis, John, House (PA-1550), 785 S. Front St. 1 photo (1957). LC code: PA,51-PHILA,446.

Curtis Publishing Company Building (PA-1902), Sixth and Walnut Sts. 2 photos (ca. 1910). LC code: PA,51-PHILA,585.

Customs House. See Second Bank of the United States.

Davis-Lenox House (PA-1324), 217 Spruce St. 2 photos (1959, 1961). LC code: PA,51-PHILA,324.

Deimling Place. See Drinker's Court.

105 Delancey Street (Warehouse) (PA-1377). 1 photo (1961). LC code: PA,51-PHILA,464.

305 Delancey Street (House) (PA-1399). 2 photos (ca. 1950). LC code: PA,51-PHILA,386.

307 Delancey Street (House) (PA-1927). 1 photo (1972). LC code: PA,51-PHILA,387.

Delancey Street Area Study I (PA-1501), 1800-36 Delancey St. 8 photos (1974). LC code: PA,51-PHILA,389.

Delancey Street Area Study II (PA-1502), 2301-19 Delancey St. 3 photos (1973). LC code: PA,51-PHILA,390.

Deshler-Morris House (PA-1683), 5442 Germantown Ave. 5 photos (1950, 1960, 1973). LC code: PA,51-GERM,30. NR.

Detweiler House (PA-1684), 8226 Germantown Ave. 1 photo (1957). LC code: PA,51-GERM,187.

1601-35 Diamond Street. See Diamond Street Area Study

Diamond Street Area Study (1601-35 Diamond Street) (PA-1726). 2 photos (1973); 1 data page (1984). LC code: PA,51-PHILA,393.

Dilworth-Todd-Moylan House (Dolley Madison House) (PA-1409), 343 Walnut St. 14 sheets (1954, 1955, 1961); 1 photo (1966). LC code: PA,51-PHILA,593.

Rear Wing (PA-1409A), 149 S. Fourth St. ll sheets (1954). LC code: PA,51-PHILA,593A.

Dock Street Sewer (PA-1072), Dock and Third Sts. vicinity. 1 sheet (1962). LC code: PA,51-PHILA,407.

Dorfenille House (PA-1685), 5139 Germantown Ave. 1 photo (1957). LC code: PA,51-GERM,176.

Dowers-Okill House (PA-1410), 115 N. Water St. 4 photos (1957); 1 data page (1958, 1984). LC code: PA,51-PHILA,609.

Drexel and Company (PA-1503), 135-43 S. Fifteenth St. 1 photo (ca. 1925). LC code: PA,51-PHILA,311. NR.

Drexel Institute, Main Building (Drexel University) (PA-1630), Thirty-second and Chestnut Sts. 3 photos (ca. 1902, 1973). LC code: PA,51-PHILA,302.

Drexel University. See Drexel Institute, Main Building.

Drinker, John, House (Krider Gun Shop) (PA-1055), 133-35 Walnut St. 16 sheets (1953); 6 photos (n.d., 1953, 1959); 9 data pages (1963). LC code: PA,51-PHILA,186.

Drinker, John, House (PA-1325), 241 Pine St. 3 photos (1959, 1972); 1 data page (1957). LC code: PA,51-PHILA,317.

Drinker's Court (Deimling Place) (PA-1326), 236-38 Delancey St. 6 photos (1959, 1972). LC code: PA,51-PHILA,303. NR.

Duche House (PA-1552), 24 Catherine St. 6 photos (1966, 1967). LC code: PA,51-PHILA,362.

Duche-Walker House (PA-1553), 26 Catherine St. 4 photos (1966, 1967); 1 data page (1984). LC code: PA,51-PHILA,363.

Dunbar House. See Marks-Dunbar House.

Dunlap-Eyre House (PA-1504), 1003 Spruce St. 1 photo (1974). LC code: PA,51-PHILA,295. NR.

Eagle Hotel (PA-1727), 601-7 W. Girard Ave. 4 photos (1957); 1 data page (1958, 1984). LC code: PA,51-PHILA,355.

Eakins, Thomas, House (PA-1728), 1729 Mt. Vernon St. 1 photo (1967). LC code: PA,51-PHILA,528. NHL.

Eastburn Mariner's Bethel Church (Presbyterian) (Mariners' Bethel) (PA-1327), Front and Delancey Sts. 2 photos (1961); 2 data pages (1984). LC code: PA,51-PHILA,463.

Eastern State Penitentiary (Cherry Hill Penitentiary) (PA-1729), Fairmount, Corinthian, Brown, and Twenty-second Sts. 9 photos (1967); 1 data page (1984). LC code: PA,51-PHILA,354. NR.

Eckert-Tarrant House (PA-1554), 38 Catherine St. 4 photos (1966, 1967). LC code: PA,51-PHILA,366.

Eden, Beth, House. See Shunk School.

246 South Eighth Street (House) (PA-5206). 3 photos (1984); 5 data pages (1984). LC code: PA,51-PHILA,665.

248 South Eighth Street (House) (PA-5207). 3 photos (1984); 5 data pages (1984). LC code: PA,51-PHILA,666.

Elfreth, Jeremiah, House (PA-1413), 126 Elfreth's Alley. 6 photos (ca. 1910, 1959). LC code: PA,51-PHILA,272A.

Elfreth's Alley (Houses) (PA-1103), Elfreth's Alley (now Cherry St.) between Front and Seconds Sts. 19 sheets (1940); 10 photos (1965, 1972, 1976). LC code: PA,51-PHILA,272. NHL.

Elliott House. See Maxfield-Elliott House.

Elliot, John, House. See Marshall's Court Area Study, John Elliot House.

Elliot, John, House (PA-1555), 37 Queen St. 6 photos (1967). LC code: PA,51-PHILA,548.

Ellison, John B., and Sons, Building (PA-1414), 22-26 S. Sixth St. 2 photos (ca. 1890, 1961). LC code: PA,51-PHILA,290.

Elwell, Henry, House (PA-1556), 812 S. Front St. 1 photo (1957). LC code: PA,51-PHILA,449.

Episcopal Hospital. See Hospital of Protestant Episcopal Church in Philadelphia.

Estlack, Thomas, House (PA-1328), 413 Lombard St. 1 photo (1960). LC code: PA,51-PHILA,506.

Eyre House See Dunlap-Eyre House.

Fairmont Waterworks (PA-1654), Aquarium Dr., Fairmount Park. 8 photos (1973, 1979). LC code: PA,51-PHILA,328. HAER, NHL.

Far East Chinese Restaurant. See 907-9 Race Street (Commercial Buildings).

Farmers' and Mechanics' Bank (PA-1415), 427 Chestnut St. 4 photos (1972); 3 data pages (1984). LC code: PA,51-PHILA,377.

Federal Reserve Bank (Federal Reserve Bank of Philadelphia) (PA-1506), 921-39 Chestnut St. 6 photos (1951, 1975). LC code: PA,51-PHILA,301.

Federal Reserve Bank of Philadelphia. See Federal Reserve Bank.

Fell-Van Rensselaer House (Pennsylvania Athletic Club) (PA-1507), Eighteenth and Walnut Sts. 10 photos (1974). LC code: PA,51-PHILA,586.

Fielding, Mantle, House (PA-1687), 28 W. Walnut Ln. 1 photo (1973). LC code: PA,51-PHILA,286.

315-19 South Fifth Street (Townhouses) (PA-1322). 1 photo (1960); 1 data page (1984). LC code: PA,51-PHILA,652.

331 South Fifth Street (House). See Sink-Burgin House.

Finlow-Nichell House (PA-1558), 770 S. Front St. 3 photos (1961). LC code: PA,51-PHILA,442.

Fire Association Building (Irvin Building) (PA-1434), 401-3 Walnut St. 1 photo (1915). LC code: PA,51-PHILA,594.

Fireman's Hall. See Philadelphia Fire Department, Engine Company No. 8.

First Bank of the United States (Stephen Girard's Bank) (PA-1417), 120 S. Third St. 17 sheets (1958-60); 7 photos (1939, 1975). LC code: PA,51-PHILA,235. NHL.

First Baptist Church of Germantown (Polite Temple Baptist Church) (PA-1688), 36-42 E. Price St. 2 photos (1972). LC code: PA,51-PHILA,299.

First German Reformed Church (PA-1910), 322-30 Race St. 1 photo (1974). LC code: PA,51-PHILA,554.

First German Reformed Church Area Study (PA-1418), 129-51 N. Fourth St. 5 photos (1974); 1 data page (1984). LC code: PA,51-PHILA,643.

First National Bank (First Pennsylvania Banking and Trust Company) (PA-1011), 315 Chestnut St. 2 photos (1957); 4 data pages (1958). LC code: PA,51-PHILA,241.

First Pennsylvania Banking and Trust Company See First National Bank.

First Polish Baptist Church. See Mariners' Bethel Church.

First Presbyterian Church (Washington Square Presbyterian Church) (PA-1117), Seventh St. and Washington Sq. vicinity. 15 sheets (1940). LC code: PA,51-PHILA,211. LC code: PA,51-PHILA,124.

First Unitarian Church (PA-1508), 2121 Chestnut St. 4 photos (1955, 1973). LC code: PA,51-PHILA,296. NR.

Fitzgerald, Thomas, House (PA-1329), 437 Lombard St. 1 photo (1960). LC code: PA,51-PHILA,508.

11-23 Fitzwater Street (Houses). See Fitzwater Street Area Study I.

24-32 Fitzwater Street (Houses). See Fitzwater Street Area Study II.

Fitzwater Street Area Study I (PA-1559), 11-23 Fitzwater St. 3 photos (1961, 1967). LC code: PA,51-PHILA,411.

Fitzwater Street Area Study II (PA-1560), 24-32 Fitzwater St. 2 photos (1967). LC code: PA,51-PHILA,412.

Fleisher, Samuel S., Art Memorial (PA-1229), 711-21 Catherine St. 10 sheets (1980). LC code: PA,51-PHILA,369. NR.

Flickwer-Williamson Houses (PA-1561), 809-11 S. Hancock St. 1 photo (1961). LC code: PA,51-PHILA,481.

Folwell House (PA-1689), 5281 Germantown Ave. 1 photo (1957). LC code: PA,51-GERM,179.

Forrest House. See Gaul-Forrest House.

Fort Mifflin (PA-1225), Mud Island, Marine, and Penrose Ferry Rds. 9 sheets (1969-71); 73 photos (1777-1971); 128 data pages (1937, 1972). LC code: PA,51-PHILA,111. NHL.

Arsenal. See *Guard House.*

Artillery Shed (PA-1225B). 5 sheets (1970); 7 photos (1969); 5 data pages (1974, 1979). LC code: PA,51-PHILA,111B.

Commandant's House (Headquarters) (PA-1225C). 8 sheets (1970); 33 photos (1922, 1937, 1969, 1970); 11 data pages (1974, 1979). LC code: PA,51-PHILA,111C.

Commissary. See *Storehouse.*

Enlisted Men's Barracks. See *Soldier's Barracks.*

Frame Guard House (PA-1225J). 1 photo (1922). LC code: PA,51-PHILA,111J.

Guard House (PA-1225A). 2 sheets (1970); 6 photos (1915, 1937, 1969); 5 data pages (1974, 1979). LC code: PA,51-PHILA,111A.

Headquarters. See *Commandant's House.*

Hospital (Mess House) (PA-1225I). 6 sheets (1970); 4 photos (1937, 1969); 6 data pages (1974, 1979). LC code: PA,51-PHILA,111I.

Mess House. See *Hospital.*

Officers' Quarters (PA-1225F). 6 sheets (1969); 17 photos (1915, 1969, 1970); 7 data pages (1974, 1979). LC code: PA,51-PHILA,111F.

Powder Magazine (PA-1225G). 3 sheets (1970); 13 photos (1969); 8 data pages (1974, 1979). LC code: PA,51-PHILA,111G.

Smith's Shop (PA-1225H). 4 sheets (1969); 12 photos (1922, 1937, 1969); 5 data pages (1974, 1979). LC code: PA,51-PHILA,111H.

Soldiers' Barracks (Enlisted Men's Barracks) (PA-1225E). 5 sheets (1969); 16 photos (1915, 1937, 1969, 1970); 7 data pages (1979). LC code: PA,51-PHILA,111E.

Storehouse (Commissary) (PA-1225D). 2 sheets (1970); 5 photos (1937, 1969); 4 data pages (1974). LC code: PA,51-PHILA,111D.

Fountain of the Sea Horses (Italian Fountain) (PA-1656), Aquarium Lane. 2 photos (1928, 1972). LC code: PA,51-PHILA,287.

129-51 North Fourth Street (Houses). See First German Reformed Church Area Study.

Frankford Avenue (House) (House on Old Turnpike) (PA-1429). 2 photos (1936). LC code: PA,51-PHILA,236.

Frankford Town Hall (PA-1758), 4255 Frankford Ave. 1 photo (1959). LC code: PA,51-PHILA,293.

Franklin Hose Company, No. 28 (Harmony Engine Co. No. 6) (PA-1566), 730-32 S. Broad St. 2 photos (1963). LC code: PA,51-PHILA,349. NR.

Franklin Institute (Atwater Kent Museum) (PA-121), 15 S. Seventh St. 7 sheets (1936, 1937); 1 photo (1972); 2 data pages (1984). LC code: PA,51-PHILA,153. NR.

Franklin Row. See Sims, Joseph, House.

Franklin Sugar Refinery (Merchants Warehouse Company, Frazier Harrison and Company) (PA-1562), 701-15 S. Front St. 1 photo (1966); 1 data page (1984). LC code: PA,51-PHILA,438.

Free Quakers Meetinghouse (PA-1120), 500 Arch St. 20 sheets (1963, 1964); 11 photos (1961, 1976); 1 data page (1984). LC code: PA,51-PHILA,158. NR.

Friends Select School, Log Cabin (PA-143), Sixteenth and Race Sts. 2 photos (1940). LC code: PA,51-PHILA,227.

Friendship Engine Company, No. 15 (Friendship Hall, Hook and Ladder Company C) (PA-1759), 2200-04 E. Norris St. 1 photo (ca. 1935); 2 data pages (1963, 1984). LC code: PA,51-PHILA,533.

Friendship Hall. See Friendship Engine Company No. 15.

Fromberger, John, Houses (Germantown Insurance Company) (PA-1690), 5501 Germantown Ave. 1 photo (1973). LC code: PA,51-PHILA,298.

2-66 North Front Street (Commercial Buildings). See North Front Street Area Study.

North Front Street Area Study (2-66 North Front Street-Commercial Buildings) (PA-1448). 9 photos (ca. 1958, 1974). LC code: PA,51-PHILA,417.

312 South Front Street (House) (PA-1950). 2 photos (1961). LC code: PA,51-PHILA,422.

319 South Front Street (House) (PA-1337). 1 photo (1961). LC code: PA,51-PHILA,423.

321 South Front Street (House) (PA-1905). 1 photo (1961). LC code: PA,51-PHILA,424.

505 South Front Street (House). See Smith, Daniel Jr., House.

507 South Front Street (House). See Bridges, Robert, House.

510 South Front Street (House). See Wharton, Isaac, House.

600-858 South Front Street (Houses) (PA-1812), W side Front St. between South and Catherine Sts. 4 photos (1967). LC code: PA,51-PHILA,432.

603 South Front Street (House). See Hart-Patterson House.

606-8 South Front Street (Houses). See Fullerton, John, Houses.

626 South Front Street (House). See Spafford, William, House.

720-24 South Front Street (House). See Askins-Jones House.

734 South Front Street (House). See Moore, John, House.

783 South Front Street (House). See Collins, Samuel, House.

806-8 South Front Street (Houses) (PA-1594). 2 photos (1961). LC code: PA,51-PHILA,447.

836 South Front Street (House) (PA-1952). 1 photo (1961). LC code: PA,51-PHILA,450.

919 South Front Street (Doorway). See Wharton, John House.

Fullerton, John, Houses (PA-1563), 606-8 S. Front St. 1 photo (1961). LC code: PA,51-PHILA,435.

Garden, C.H., and Company, Building (PA-1419), 606 Market St. 2 photos (ca. 1868, 1962); 1 data page (1984). LC code: PA,51-PHILA,517.

Garrett-Buchanan Company, Paper Dealers. See Megargee Brothers Paper Warehouse.

Gaul-Forrest House (Heritage House) (PA-1730), 1326 N. Broad St. 1 photo (1973). LC code: PA,51-PHILA,323. NR.

General Wayne Hotel (PA-1691), 5060 Germantown Ave. 1 photo (1957); 1 data page (1985). LC code: PA,51-GERM,10.

Gentilhommiere. See Girard, Stephen, Country House.

George, Henry, House (PA-1509), 413 S. Tenth St. 9 sheets (1981); 1 photo (1974). LC code: PA,51-PHILA,310. NR.

Germantown Academy (Germantown Union School) (PA-7-4), 110 Schoolhouse La. 17 sheets (1934); 8 photos (1934, 1960); 2 data pages (1936). LC code: PA,51-GERM,33.

6000-2 Germantown Avenue (House) (PA-1698). 1 photo (1957). LC code: PA,51-PHILA,185.

6377 Germantown Avenue (House) (PA-1699). 4 photos (1961); 2 data pages (1961, 1984). LC code: PA,51-GERM,186.

6505-7 Germantown Avenue (House). See Billmeyer, Michael, House.

Germantown Cricket Club (Manheim Club) (PA-1693), 5140 Morris St. 2 photos (1972). LC code: PA,51-PHILA,104. NR.

Germantown Historic District. See Pastorius, Daniel, House.

Germantown Historical Society Area Study (PA-1694), 5208-5214-5218 Germantown Ave. 1 photo (1976). LC code: PA,51-GERM,177.

Baynton House (PA-1694A), 5208 Germantown Ave. 1 photo (1976). LC code: PA,51-GERM,178.

Conynham-Hacker House (PA-1694B), 5214 Germantown Ave. 1 photo (1976). LC code: PA,51-GERM,20. NR.

Howell House (PA-1694C), 5218 Germantown Ave. 2 photos (1976). LC code: PA,51-GERM,96. NR.

Germantown Insurance Company. See Fromberger, John, Houses.

Germantown Union School. See Germantown Academy.

Girard Avenue Bridge (PA-1657), Girard Ave, spanning Schuylkill River. 16 photos (ca. 1880, 1906, 1969, 1971). LC code: PA,51-PHILA,461.

Girard Bank. See Girard Trust Corn Exchange Bank.

Girard College, Founder's Hall (PA-1731), Girard Ave. and Corinthian St. 7 photos (1973). LC code: PA,51-PHILA,459A. NHL.

Girard, Stephen, Country House (Gentilhommiere) (PA-140), Shunk and Twenty-first Sts. 11 sheets (1940, 1962); 24 photos (1890s, 1901, 1940, 1962); 20 data pages (1962). LC code: PA,51-PHILA,226.

Utility Building (PA-1082). 3 sheets (1940, 1962); 5 photos (1962, 1965); 4 data pages (1962). LC code: PA,51-PHILA,226A.

Girard Row (Houses) (PA-1330), 326-34 Spruce St. 1 sheet (n.d.); 6 photos (1959). LC code: PA,51-PHILA,687.

Girard Trust Bank. See Girard Trust Corn Exchange Bank.

Girard Trust Corn Exchange Bank (Girard Bank) (PA-1510), 34-36 S. Broad St. 2 photos (1973). LC code: PA,51-PHILA,319.

Girard's, Stephen, Bank. See First Bank of the United States.

Gladstone Hotel (Greystone Apartments) (PA-1511), 328-38 S. Front St. 2 photos (1971); 1 data page (1984). LC code: PA,51-PHILA,425.

Glebe House (PA-139), Old River Rd. 14 sheets (1940); 2 photos (1940). LC code: PA,51-PHILA,225.

Glen Fern. See Livezey House.

Gloria Dei (Church) (Old Swedes Church) (PA-120), 929 S. Water St. 10 sheets (1936); 15 photos (1897, 1937, 1962); 2 data pages (1937). LC code: PA,51-PHILA,174. NHS.

Rectory (PA-120A). 2 photos (1962). LC code: PA,51-PHILA,174B.

Godley, Jesse, Warehouse (PA-1564), 19-27 Queen St. 4 photos (1961). LC code: PA,51-PHILA,544.

Godley's Stores. See Granite Street Vaults.

Goldberg's Army-Navy Store. See Cope, Caleb, and Company Store.

Gordon, George, Building (PA-1065), 300 Arch St. 4 sheets (1963); 5 photos (1959, 1962, 1963); 5 data pages (1961, 1963). LC code: PA,51-PHILA,258.

Granite Street Vaults (Godley's Stores) (PA-1420), 100-12 and 101-27 Granite St. 3 photos (1959); 1 data page (1984). LC code: PA,51-PHILA,543.

2201-5 Green Street (House). See Kemble-Bergdol House.

2213-15 Green Street (Houses) (PA-1906). 3 photos (1963, 1973). LC code: PA,51-PHILA,473.

2219 Green Street (House) (PA-1907). 1 photo (1963). LC code: PA,51-PHILA,474.

2221 Green Street (House) (PA-1908). 2 photos (1963). LC code: PA,51-PHILA,475.

2223 Green Street (House) (PA-1909). 4 photos (1963, 1973). LC code: PA,51-PHILA,476.

2225-27 Green Street (Houses) (PA-1911). 1 photo (1973). LC code: PA,51-PHILA,477.

2229-31 Green Street (Houses) (PA-1912). 1 photo (1973). LC code: PA,51-PHILA,478.

Green Street Area Study See 2201-5 Green Street; 2213-15 Green Street; 2219 Green Street; 2221 Green Street; 2225-27 Green Street; 2229-31 Green Street.

Green Tree Tavern See Pastorius, Daniel, House.

Greystone Apartments See Gladstone Hotel.

Griffith-Peale House (PA-1761), 8100 Frankford Ave. 3 photos (1959); 1 data page (1960, 1984). LC code: PA,51-PHILA,413.

Grumblethorpe (Wister's Big House) (PA-7-1), 5267 Germantown Ave. 10 sheets (1934); 6 photos (1934, 1972); 4 data pages (1936). LC code: PA,51-GERM,23. NR.

> *Tenant House* (PA-7-6). 9 sheets (1934); 4 photos (1934, 1972); 1 data page (1934). LC code: PA,51-GERM,24.

Hacker House. See Germantown Historical Society Area Study, 5214 Germantown Avenue.

Haines House. See Wyck.

Hall, John, House (PA-1331), 327 S. Third St. 1 sheet (1959); 5 photos (1959, 1972). LC code: PA,51-PHILA,638.

Hall-Wister House (PA-1332), 330 S. Third St. 3 photos (1959, 1972); 1 data page (1984). LC code: PA,51-PHILA,640A.

Hamilton, Andrew. House. See Woodlands.

Hamilton Village. See Woodlands.

Hamilton-Hoffman House (Burnside) (PA-1053), Coggs Creek Pkwy. 13 photos (1890, 1959); 8 data pages (1960). LC code: PA,51-PHILA,252.

Hansell, John, House (PA-1012), 153 N. Sixth St. 1 photo (1959); 4 data pages (1959). LC code: PA,51-PHILA,242.

Harmony Engine Company, No. 6. See Franklin Hose Company, No. 28.

Harper, Thomas, House, Wall Stencil (PA-5197), 421 S. Second St. 1 sheet (1973). LC code: PA,51-PHILA,624.

Harrison Building (PA-1088), 4 S. Fifteenth St. 15 photos (1895, 1900, 1962, 1964); 7 data pages (1962, 1964). LC code: PA,51-PHILA,268.

Harrison, Charles C., Building (PA-550), 1001-5 Market St. 7 photos (1979); 6 data pages (1979, 1980). LC code: PA,51-PHILA,520.

Harrison, Frazier, and Company. See Franklin Sugar Refinery.

Harrison House (PA-1458), Point No Point (Richmond Ave.). 2 photos (1936). LC code: PA,51-PHILA,232.

Harrison, Henry, Houses (PA-1421), 112-16 Cuthbert St. 1 sheet (1957-59); 4 photos (ca. 1959); 3 data pages (1984). LC code: PA,51-PHILA,691.

Hart, John, House (PA-1568), 601 S. Front St. 1 photo (1957). LC code: PA,51-PHILA,433.

Hart-Patterson House (PA-1569), 603 S. Front St. 1 photo (1961). LC code: PA,51-PHILA,434.

Hatfield House (PA-1658), Thirty-third St. and Girard Ave. 14 photos (1929, 1938, 1959); 2 data pages (1958, 1984). LC code: PA,51-PHILA,233. NR.

Heaton House. See Mears-Heaton House.

Hellings, Benjamin, House (PA-1570), 931 S. Front St. 1 photo (1957). LC code: PA,51-PHILA,455.

Hensel, Colladay, and Company Factory (PA-1422), 45-51 N. Seventh St. 2 photos (1965); 2 data pages (1965, 1984). LC code: PA,51-PHILA,308.

Heritage House. See Gaul-Forrest House.

Hill, David, House (PA-1333), 309 S. Third St. 7 photos (1959, 1972). LC code: PA,51-PHILA,283.

Hill-Physick House (Hill-Physick-Keith House) (PA-1334), 321 S. Fourth St. 5 photos (1959, 1972, 1976); 2 data pages (1964, 1984). LC code: PA,51-PHILA,36. NHL.

Hill-Physick-Keith House. See Hill-Physick House.

Hilyard, Eber, House (PA-1335), 427 Lombard St. 1 photo (1960). LC code: PA,51-PHILA,507.

Historical Society of Pennsylvania (Mantlepiece) (PA-1942), 1300 Locust St. 1 photo (ca. 1965). LC code: PA,51-PHILA,496.

Hockley, Thomas, House (PA-1512), 235 S. Twenty-first St. 1 photo (1973). LC code: PA,51-PHILA,282.

Hoffman House. See Hamilton-Hoffman House.

Holloway, Thomas, Houses (PA-1763), 125-31 Ellen St. 2 photos (ca. 1957). LC code: PA,51-PHILA,408.

Holy Redeemer Chinese Catholic Church and School (PA-1513), Vine St. and Ridge Ave. 2 photos (1973). LC code: PA,51-PHILA,557.

Holy Trinity Roman Catholic Church (German) (PA-1336), 601-9 Spruce St. 4 photos (ca. 1880, 1973). LC code: PA,51-PHILA,573.

Hood Cemetery, Entrance (Lower Burying Ground) (PA-1697), 4901 Germantown Ave. 2 photos (1973). LC code: PA,51-PHILA,325.

Hook and Ladder Company C. See Friendship Engine Company, No. 15.

Hope Engine Company, No. 17 (PA-1572), 733 S. Sixth St. 2 photos (1963); 2 data pages (1963, 1984). LC code: PA,51-PHILA,659.

Hope Hose Company, No. 6 and Fellowship Engine Company, No. 29 (PA-1351), Second St., between Pine and Lombard. 2 photos (1963). LC code: PA,51-PHILA,28.

Hopkinson House. See Williams-Hopkinson House.

Hospital of Protestant Episcopal Church in Philadelphia (Episcopal Hospital) (PA-1764), Front St. and Lehigh Ave. 14 photos (1860-62, 1869, 1873-75, ca. 1891, 1973). LC code: PA,51-PHILA,416.

Hotel Metropole. See Hotel Walton.

Hotel Walton (John Bartram Hotel, Hotel Metropole) (PA-1091), Broad and Locust Sts. 6 photos (1894, 1896, 1963); 11 data pages (1964). LC code: PA,51-PHILA,269.

House on Letitia Street. See Letitia Street House.

House on Old Turnpike. See Frankford Avenue (House).

Houston-Sauveur House (PA-1700), 8205 Seminole Ave. 2 photos (1972). LC code: PA,51-PHILA,565.

Howell and Brothers Building (PA-1428), 12-14 S. Sixth St. 1 photo (1961); 1 data page (1984). LC code: PA,51-PHILA, 657.

Howell House. See Germantown Historical Society Area Study, 5218 Germantown Avenue.

Huddell House. See Woolfall-Huddell House.

Hutchinson Building. See McClare-Hutchinison Building.

Independence Hall Complex, City Hall (Philadelphia City Hall, U.S. Supreme Court Building) (PA-1432), Chestnut and Fifth Sts. 2 sheets (1961); 6 photos (1918, 1959, 1975); 2 data pages (1985-86). LC code: PA,51-PHILA,6B. NHL.

Independence Hall Complex, Congress Hall. See Congress Hall.

Independence Hall Complex, Independence Hall (State House of Pennsylvania) (PA-1430), Chestnut St. 13 photos (1939, 1959, 1962, 1963). LC code: PA,51-PHILA,6. NHP.

Assembly Room (PA-1430B). 27 photos (1959, 1969, 1975).

First Floor Hall (PA-1430A). 41 photos (1959, 1969).

Garrett (PA-1430G). 6 photos (1959).

Second Floor (PA-1430D). 5 photos (1959).

Supreme Court Room (PA-1430C). 10 photos (1959).

Tower (PA-1430E). 18 photos (1959).

Tower Stairhall (PA-1430F). 31 photos (1959).

Independence National Historical Park (PA-1951), Walnut, Sixth, Chestnut, and Second Sts. 18 photos (1961, 1964). LC code: PA,51-PHILA,6D.

Independent Order of Odd Fellows (PA-1771), Third and Brown Sts. 4 photos (1961); 7 data pages (1963). LC code: PA,51-PHILA,353.

Institute of the Pennsylvania Hospital, Department for Males. See Pennsylvania Hospital for the Insane, Department for Males.

Insurance Patrol Building (PA-1433), 509 Arch St. 1 photo (1959); 2 data pages (1964, 1984). LC code: PA,51-PHILA,467.

International Exhibition of 1876, Memorial Hall (Art Gallery) (PA-1659), Belmont Ave. 4 photos (ca. 1875, 1876, 1972); 3 data pages (1984). LC code: PA,51-PHILA,265B.

International Exhibition of 1876, Ohio Building (Ohio House) (PA-1660), Belmont Ave. 5 photos (1876, 1972). LC code: PA,51-PHILA,265C.

International Exhibition of 1876, St. George's House (British Building) (PA- 1080), State's Dr. 7 photos (1875, 1876, 1961); 4 data pages (1964). LC code: PA,51-PHILA,265A.

Irish, Nathaniel, House (PA-1013), 704 S. Front St. 1 sheet (1959); 8 photos (1959, 1966, 1967); 8 data pages (1959). LC code: PA,51-PHILA,243. NR.

Irvin Building. See Fire Association Building.

Italian Fountain. See Fountain of the Sea Horses.

Italian Villa. See Lea, Henry Charles, House.

Iungerich Warehouse (PA-1403), 147 S. Front St. 1 photo (1966). LC code: PA,51-PHILA,421.

Ivy Lodge (PA-1701), 29 E. Penn St. 1 photo (1972). LC code: PA,51-PHILA,535. NR.

Jacoby, Wigard, House (PA-1702), 8327 Germantown Ave. 1 photo 1957); 1 data page (1957). LC code: PA,51-GERM,153.

Jayne Building (Dr. Jayne Granite Building) (PA-188), 242-44 Chestnut St. 16 sheets (1957); 15 photos (1951, 1957, 1958); 3 data pages (1957). LC code: PA,51-PHILA,237.

Jayne, Dr., Granite Building. See Jayne Building.

Jefferson Fire Insurance Company (PA-1435), 425 Walnut St. 2 photos (1915, 1959). LC code: PA,51-PHILA,597.

Jefferson, Joseph, House (PA-1340), 600 Spruce St. 1 photo (1958). LC code: PA,51-PHILA,572

Johnson House. See Murphy-Johnson House.

Johnson House (PA-7-7), 6306 Germantown Ave. 12 sheets (1934); 4 photos (1934); 3 data pages (1936). LC code: PA,51-GERM,55. NR.

Jones House. See 720-24 South Front Street.

Jordan-Stoddard House (PA-1341), 404 S. Fifth St. 1 photo (1960). LC code: PA,51-PHILA,656.

Justi, Henry D., House (PA-1632), Thirty-fourth and Baring Sts. 2 photos (1963). LC code: PA,51-PHILA,336.

Keen, James, House (PA-1587), 946 S. Front St. 1 photo (1957); 1 data page (1985). LC code: PA,51-PHILA,456.

Keith House. See Hill-Physick House.

Kemble-Bergdol House (PA-1732), 2201-5 Green St. 3 photos (1963, 1973). LC code: PA,51-PHILA,472. NR.

109 Kenilworth Street (House) (PA-1588). 2 photos (1961). LC code: PA,51-PHILA,486.

117 Kenilworth Street (House) (PA-1437). 1 photo (1961). LC code: PA,51-PHILA,487.

121-23 Kenilworth Street (Alley Door) (PA-1446). 1 photo (1961). LC code: PA,51-PHILA,488A.

Kensington National Bank (PA-1773), 2-8 W. Girard Ave. 2 photos (1974). LC code: PA,51-PHILA,460.

Kent, Atwater, Museum. See Franklin Institute.

Keyser, Jacob, House (PA-11), 6205 Germantown Ave. 7 sheets (1934); 2 data pages (1934). LC code: PA,51-GERM,52.

Kid-Chandler and Kid-Physick Houses (PA-1436), 323-25 Walnut St. 3 photos (1959, 1972); 1 data page (1984). LC code: PA,51-PHILA,591.

Kid-Chandler House (PA-1436A), 323 Walnut St. 49 photos (1958, 1959, 1961). LC code: PA,51-PHILA,591A.

Kid-Physick House (PA-1436B), 325 Walnut St. 20 photos (1958, 1959). LC code: PA,51-PHILA,591B.

Kirkbride Mansion. See Busti, Paul, House.

Kirkbride's Hospital. See Pennsylvania Hospital for Mental and Nervous Diseases.

Kosciuszko, General Thaddeus, House (PA-1342), 301 Pine St. 2 photos (1972). LC code: PA,51-PHILA,536.

Krider Gun Shop. See Drinker, John, House.

Lamb, Peter, House (PA-1590), 28 Catherine St. 1 photo (1966). LC code: PA,51-PHILA,364.

Land Title Bank and Trust Company (Land Title Building) (PA-1514), 100-18 S. Broad St. 2 photos (ca. 1902, 1973); 1 data page (1984). LC code: PA,51-PHILA,345.

Land Title Building. See Land Title Bank and Trust Company.

Lardner House. See Lynfield House.

Lasse Cock's Manor House. See Bel Air.

Latour Warehouse (PA-1056), 508 S. Water St. 8 sheets (1958); 9 photos (1958); 5 data pages (1959, 1960). LC code: PA,51-PHILA,254.

Laurel Hill (Randolph Rawle House) (PA-13), Fairmount Park. 10 sheets (1934); 1 photo (1938); 2 data pages (ca. 1938). LC code: PA,51-PHILA,12.

Laurel Hill Cemetery (PA-1811), 3822 Ridge Ave., Fairmont Park. 2 photos (1979). LC code: PA,51-PHILA,100. NR.

Gatehouse (PA-1811A). 2 photos (1972). LC code: PA,51-PHILA,100A.

Lea, Professor Henry Charles, House (Italian Villa) (PA-1633), 3903 Spruce St. 18 photos (1968). LC code: PA,51-PHILA,580.

123-25 League Street (Houses) (PA-1583). 1 photo (1961). LC code: PA,51-PHILA,490.

Lee, Robert M., House and Law Office (PA-1052), 109-11 N. Sixth St. 3 sheets (1959); 8 photos (1870, 1959); 11 data pages (1959, 1960). LC code: PA,51-PHILA,251.

Lehigh Mills. See Bromley, John, and Sons, Building.

Leidy, Dr. Joseph Jr., House (Poor Richard Club) (PA-1515), 1319 Locust St. 1 photo (1972). LC code: PA,51-PHILA,498. NR.

Leland Building (PA-1086), 37-39 S. Third St. 7 photos (1963, 1965); 7 data pages (1964). LC code: PA,51-PHILA,267.

Lemon Hill (PA-1010), Lemon Hill Dr., Fairmount Park. 2 sheets (1962); 4 photos (ca. 1940, 1962); 1 data page (1984). LC code: PA,51-PHILA,234.

Lenox House. See Davis-Lenox House.

Letitia Street House (PA-184), Lansdowne Dr., Fairmount Park. 4 sheets (1931); 3 photos (1932, 1938). LC code: PA,51-PHILA,45.

Lewis House. See Pancoast-Lewis-Wharton House.

Library Company of Philadelphia, Ridgway Branch (PA-1616), 900 S. Broad St. 24 photos (1962); 1 data page (1984). LC code: PA,51-PHILA,350.

Lippincott, Joshua B., House (PA-1516), 204 S. Nineteenth St. 8 photos (1969); 1 data page (1984). LC code: PA,51-PHILA,679.

Lit Brothers Store (PA-1438), 701-39 Market St. 3 photos (1972, 1973); 2 data pages (1984). LC code: PA,51-PHILA,519. NR.

Livezey House (Glen Fern) (PA-14), Livezey Ln. and Wissahickon Creek. 12 sheets (1935); 1 photo (1972). LC code: PA,51-GERM,91.

404-8 Locust Street (Houses) (PA-1915). 1 photo (1962). LC code: PA,51-PHILA,491.

1314-20 Locust Street (Buildings) (PA-1917). 1 photo (1964). LC code: PA,51-PHILA,497.

Log House. See Friends Select School, Log Cabin.

117 Lombard Street (House). See Palmer, John, House.

323 Lombard Street (House) (PA-1678). 2 photos (1960). LC code: PA,51-PHILA,502.

325 Lombard Street (House) (PA-1913). 1 photo (1960). LC code: PA,51-PHILA,503.

327-29 Lombard Street (Houses) (PA-1914). 1 photo (1960). LC code: PA,51-PHILA,504.

331-33 Lombard Street (Houses) (PA-1916). 1 photo (1960). LC code: PA,51-PHILA,505.

Loudoun (PA-1705), 4650 Germantown Ave. 2 photos (1972). LC code: PA,51-GERM,3.

Lukens House. See Port Royal.

Lyle-Newman Houses (PA-1592), 905-7 S. Front St. 1 photo (1957); 1 data page (1985). LC code: PA,51-PHILA,454.

Lynfield House (Lardner House) (PA-132), 4601 Rhawn St. 3 photos (1937); 1 data page (1937). LC code: PA,51-PHILA,221.

Mack, Connie, Stadium. See Shibe Park.

Mackley, Carl, Apartments (PA-1779), Castor Ave., Bristol, M, and Cayuga Sts. Photographic documentation underway 1990.

Madison House. See Stride-Madison House.

Madison, Dolley, House. See Dilworth-Todd-Moylan House.

Maloby, Thomas, House and Tavern (PA-1595), 700 S. Front St. 1 photo (1966). LC code: PA,51-PHILA,437.

Man Full of Trouble Tavern. See Stafford's Tavern-Paschall House.

Manhattan Building. See American Life Insurance Company Building.

Manheim Club. See Germantown Cricket Club.

Mariners' Bethel. See Eastburn Mariners' Bethel Church (Presbyterian).

Mariners' Bethel Church (First Polish Baptist Church, Bethel Christian Center) (PA-1596), 923 S. Front St. 1 photo (1961). LC code: PA,51-PHILA,306.

617-37 Market Street. See Market Street Area Study (Commercial Buildings).

Market Street Area Study (Commercial Buildings) (617-37 Market Street) (PA-1441). 5 photos (1965); 2 data pages (1984). LC code: PA,51-PHILA,518.

Market Street National Bank Building (One East Penn Square Building) (PA-1517), 1-21 Juniper St. 4 photos (1973). LC code: PA,51-PHILA,484.

Marks-Dunbar House (PA-1597), 849 S. Front St. 4 photos (1966). LC code: PA,51-PHILA,451.

Marshall, Joseph, Houses (PA-1598), 854-56 S. Front St. 1 photo (1957); 1 data page (1985). LC code: PA,51-PHILA,453.

Marshall-Morris House (PA-1599), 774 S. Front St. 1 photo (1957); 1 data page (1985). LC code: PA,51-PHILA,443.

Marshall's Court Area Study (403-11 Marshall's Court) (PA-1345). 3 photos (1958). LC code: PA,51-PHILA,523.

Elliot, John, House (PA-1345B), 407 Marshall's Ct. 6 photos (1958). LC code: PA,51-PHILA,525.

Shinn, Samuel, House (PA-1345A), 403 Marshall's Ct. 3 photos (1958). LC code: PA,51-PHILA,524.

Simpson, David, House (PA-1345C), 411 Marshall's Ct. 5 photos (1958). LC code: PA,51-PHILA,526.

Mason, James S., and Company Store (PA-1442), 138-40 N. Front St. 7 photos (1855, 1973); 1 data page (1985). LC code: PA,51-PHILA,418.

Massey and Janney Leather Warehouse (PA-1782), 355 N. Third St. 3 photos (1971); 1 data page (1985). LC code: PA,51-PHILA,628.

Mathurin House. See Williams-Mathurin House.

Maxfield-Elliott House (PA-1600), 35 Queen St. 5 photos (1967). LC code: PA,51-PHILA,547.

Maxwell, Ebenezer, House (PA-1098), 200 W. Tulpehocken St. 7 sheets (1966); 11 photos (1964); 9 data pages (1964, 1984). LC code: PA,51-GERM,190. NR.

McClare-Hutchinson Building (PA-1439), 20 S. Third St. 2 photos (1958, 1972). LC code: PA,51-PHILA,629.

McCraig, George, House (PA-1593), 810 S. Front St. 1 photo (1957). LC code: PA,51-PHILA,448.

McCrea, James, House (PA-1440), 108-10 Sansom St. 11 sheets (1984); 36 photos (1958, 1983); 11 data pages (1985). LC code: PA,51-PHILA,564.

McKean, Thomas Jr., House (PA-190), 269 S. Fifth St. 1 sheet (1957); 5 photos (1957); 4 data pages (1957). LC code: PA,51-PHILA,239.

McMullin, Robert, House (PA-1344), 411 Pine St. 8 photos (1965). LC code: PA,51-PHILA,537.

Mears-Heaton House (PA-1070), 240 Delancey St. 4 sheets (1954, 1962). LC code: PA,51-PHILA,385.

Mechanics' Bank (Norwegian Seamen's Church) (PA-1443), 22 S. Third St. 2 photos (1958); 1 data page (1984). LC code: PA,51-PHILA,630.

Megargee Brothers Paper Warehouse (Garrett Buchanan Company, Paper Dealers) (PA-1444), 18-20 S. Sixth St. 1 photo (1961). LC code: PA,51-PHILA,658.

Mehl House (PA-1706), 4821 Germantown Ave. 1 photo (1957); 1 data page (1985). LC code: PA,51-GERM,6.

Mellon, Thomas, House (PA-1346), 716 Spruce St. 1 photo (1959). LC code: PA,51-PHILA,574.

Mellor and Meigs Architectural Office (PA-1519), 205 S. Juniper St. 1 photo (1973); 2 data pages (1984). LC code: PA,51-PHILA,485.

Mennonite Meetinghouse (PA-15), 6119 Germantown Ave. 7 sheets (1934, 1935); 1 photo (1972); 2 data pages (1934). LC code: PA,51-GERM,51. NR.

Mercer, Thomas, Houses (PA-1601), 2-12 Christian St. 5 photos (1957, 1961). LC code: PA,51-PHILA,381.

Merchants' Exchange. See Philadelphia Exchange Company.

Merchants' Hotel (Washington Hotel) (PA-1445), 40-50 N. Fourth St. 12 photos (1857, 1962); 7 data pages (1963, 1966, 1984). LC code: PA,51-PHILA,642.

Merchants Warehouse Company. See Franklin Sugar Refinery.

Met, The. See Philadelphia Opera House.

Mikveh Israel Cemetery Gatehouse (PA-1602), 1114 Federal St. 2 photos (1963). LC code: PA,51-PHILA,409A.

Mitchell, Thomas, House (PA-1348), 276 S. Third St. 7 photos (1962). LC code: PA,51-PHILA,636.

Moffett, Robert, House (Moffett Urquhart House) (PA-1603), 35 Catherine St. 1 photo (1966). LC code: PA,51-PHILA,358.

Moffett-Urquhart House. See Moffett, Robert, House.

Monastery (PA-183), Kitchen's La. 23 sheets (1935); 2 photos (1972). LC code: PA,51-GERM,90. NR.

Moore, Clarence B., House (PA-1521), 1321 Locust St. 1 photo (1972). LC code: PA,51-PHILA,499. NR.

Moore, John, House (PA-1605), 734 S. Front St. 1 photo (1957); 1 data page (1985). LC code: PA,51-PHILA,440.

Morris Brewery Vaults (PA-5331), 210 Chancellor St. 1 data page (1987). LC code: PA,51-PHILA,331A.

Morris House. See Compton.

Morris House. See Deshler-Morris House.

Morris House. See Marshall-Morris House.

Morris House. See Reynolds-Morris House.

Mother Bethel African Methodist Episcopal Church. See Bethel African Methodist Episcopal Church.

Mount Moriah Cemetery Gatehouse (PA-1634), 6299 Kingsessing Ave. 4 photos (1975). LC code: PA,51-PHILA,489A.

Mount Pleasant (Clunie) (PA-1130), E. Fairmount Park. 31 sheets (1940); 24 photos (ca. 1897, 1938, 1939, 1960). LC code: PA,51-PHILA,15. NHL.

  Dependency (PA-1130A). 1 photo (1939). LC code: PA,51-PHILA,15A.

  Office (PA-1130B). 1 photo (n.d.). LC code: PA,51-PHILA,15B.

Mount Sinai Cemetery, Chapel (PA-1783), Bridge and Cottage Sts. 4 photos (1973). LC code: PA,51-PHILA,399A.

Moyamensing Prison. See Philadelphia County Prison.

Moylan House. See Dilworth-Todd-Moylan House.

Murphy-Johnson House (PA-1606), 42 Catherine St. 2 photos (1967). LC code: PA,51-PHILA,367.

Musical Fund Hall (Musical Fund Society Hall) (PA-1447), 808 Locust St. 1 photo (1976); 1 data page (1984). LC code: PA,51-PHILA,494. NHL.

Musical Fund Society Hall. See Musical Fund Hall.

Museum of Science and Art. See University of Pennsylvania, University Museum.

Mutual Fire Insurance Company Building (PA-1014), Germantown Ave. and School House La. 6 photos (1900, 1959); 6 data pages (1959). LC code: PA,51-PHILA,244.

National Bank of Northern Liberties (PA-1784), Third and Vine Sts. 3 photos (ca. 1880s, 1963). LC code: PA,51-PHILA,583.

National Guard's Hall (Armory of the National Guard) (PA-1015), 518-20 Race St. 8 photos (1959); 6 data pages (1959). LC code: PA,51-PHILA,245.

Navigator Statue. See Riggs and Brother, Navigator Statue.

Neave, Samuel, House and Store (PA-1349), 272-74 S. Second St. 10 sheets (1959, 1960); 19 photos (1959, 1960, 1972). LC code: PA,51-PHILA,622.

Nevel, Thomas, House (PA-1350), 338 S. Fourth St. 6 photos (1964, 1972). LC code: PA,51-PHILA,649.

New Century Club (PA-1522), 124 S. Twelfth St. 9 photos (1892, 1973); 1 data page (1984). LC code: PA,51-PHILA,675.

New Public Buildings, The (Philadelphia City Hall) (PA-1530), Penn Sq. 58 photos (ca. 1876, 1881, 1883, 1888, 1892, 1910, 1915, 1930, 1948, 1958, 1959, 1962, 1963, 1965, 1974, 1976, 1979, 1982); 22 data pages (1981). LC code: PA,51-PHILA,327.

New York Mutual Life Insurance Company Building (Victory Building) (PA-1523), 1001-5 Chestnut St. 3 photos (1902, 1975). LC code: PA,51-PHILA,379.

Newman House. See Lyle-Newman Houses.

Nichell House. See Finlow-Nichell House.

110 North Ninth Street (Restaurant and Apartment Building) (PA-1536). 2 photos (1963); 1 data page (1984). LC code: PA,51-PHILA,670.

39-43 Norfolk Street (Houses) (PA-1584). 1 photo (n.d.). LC code: PA,51-PHILA,532.

Norris-Cadwalader House (PA-1352), 240 S. Fourth St. 18 photos (ca. 1890, 1959, 1972). LC code: PA,51-PHILA,646.

Northern Liberty Hose Company Number 4 (The Snappers) (PA-1785), 714 New Market St. 1 photo (1963); 1 data page (1984). LC code: PA,51-PHILA,530.

Northern Saving Fund, Safe Deposit and Trust Company (Northern Trust Company) (PA-1733), 600 Spring Garden St. 5 sheets (1978); 13 photos (1974, 1979); 1 data page (1980). LC code: PA,51-PHILA-326. NR.

Northern Trust Company. See Northern Saving Fund, Safe Deposit and Trust Company.

Norwegian Seaman's Church. See Mechanics Bank.

Ohio House. See International Exhibition of 1876, Ohio State Building.

Okill House. See Dowers-Okill House.

Old Swedes Church. See Gloria Dei (Church).

One East Penn Square Building. See Market Street National Bank Building.

Ormiston House (PA-187), Reservoir Dr., Fairmount Park. 9 sheets (1935); 1 photo (1972). LC code: PA,51-PHILA,275.

Osbourne Houses. See Ely-Osbourne Houses and Stores.

Overbrook School for the Blind. See Pennsylvania Institution for the Instruction of the Blind.

Palmer, John, House (PA-1353), 117 Lombard St. 1 photo (1972); 1 data page of 1810 fire insurance survey. LC code: PA,51-PHILA,500.

Pancake, Philip, House (PA-1354), 333 S. Fifth St. 1 photo (1960). LC code: PA,51-PHILA,654.

Pancoast-Lewis-Wharton House (PA-1083), 336 Spruce St. 10 sheets (1932); 7 photos (1890, 1961, 1962); 10 data pages (1961). LC code: PA,51-PHILA,27.

Parry, Charles T., House (PA-1524), 1921 Arch St. 27 photos (ca. 1890, 1968); 2 data pages (1984). LC code: PA,51-PHILA,333.

Carriage House and Stable (PA-1524A). 1 photo (1968). LC code: PA,51-PHILA,333A.

Paschall House. See Stafford's Tavern-Paschall House.

Paschall, Jonathan, House (PA-1607), 36 Christian St. 2 photos (1966). LC code: PA,51-PHILA,383.

Pastorius, Daniel, House (Green Tree Tavern, Germantown Historic District) (PA-1695), 6023 Germantown Ave. 1 photo (1972). LC code: PA,51-GERM,45. NR.

Patterson House. See 603 South Front Street.

Peale House. See Griffith-Peale House.

Peale, Charles Willson, House (Belfield) (PA-1676), 5500 N. Twentieth St. 6 photos (1967). LC code: PA,51-GERM,191. NHL.

Pemberton House. See Carpenters' Company Hall.

Penn, John, House. See Solitude.

Penn Mutual Building. See Penn Mutual Life Insurance Company Building.

Penn Mutual Life Insurance Company Building (Penn Mutual Building) (PA-1451), Third and Dock Sts. 1 photo (1951); 1 data page (1984). LC code: PA,51-PHILA,406.

Penn Square Building. See Bulletin Building.

Pennsylvania Academy of the Fine Arts (PA-1525), Broad and Cherry Sts. 14 photos (n.d., 1965). LC code: PA,51-PHILA,340. NHL.

Pennsylvania Athletic Club. See Fell-Van Rensselaer House.

Pennsylvania Company for Insurances on Lives and Granting Annuities (PA-1452), 431 Chestnut St. 4 photos (1910, 1929, 1959); 3 data pages (1985). LC code: PA,51-PHILA,378.

Pennsylvania Company for Insurances on Lives and Granting Annuities (PA-1453), 304 Walnut St. 6 photos (1958, 1961); 2 data pages (1961, 1984). LC code: PA,51-PHILA,588.

Pennsylvania Fire Insurance Company (PA-1454), 508-10 Walnut St. 6 photos (1959, 1971, 1976); 2 data pages (1984). LC code: PA,51-PHILA,600.

Pennsylvania Hospital (PA-1123), Ninth and Pine Sts. 19 sheets (1940); 33 photos (1833, 1834, 1846, 1897, 1913, 1974, 1976); 1 data page (ca. 1976). LC code: PA,51-PHILA,39. NHL.

Pennsylvania Hospital for Mental and Nervous Diseases (Kirkbride's Hospital) (PA-1636), Forty-fourth and Market Sts. 10 photos (19th c., 1958); 2 data pages (ca. 1976). LC code: PA,51-PHILA,511.

Pennsylvania Hospital for the Insane, Department for Males (Institute of the Pennsylvania Hospital, Department for Males) (PA-1635), 111 N. Forty-ninth St. 1 photo (1973). LC code: PA,51-PHILA,512. NHL.

Pennsylvania Institution for the Deaf and Dumb (Philadelphia College of Art) (PA-1526), 320 S. Broad St. 5 photos (1973, 1974). LC code: PA,51-PHILA,348. NR.

Pennsylvania Institution for the Instruction of the Blind (Overbrook School for the Blind) (PA-1637), Sixty-fourth St. and Malvern Ave. 5 photos (1973). LC code: PA,51-PHILA,510.

Pennsylvania Museum and School of Industrial Art. See Philadelphia Museum of Art.

Pennsylvania Railroad Station, Broad Street Station (PA-1527), Broad and Market Sts. 7 photos (ca. 1893, ca. 1894, 1903, ca. 1910, ca. 1940). LC code: PA,51-PHILA,341.

Pennsylvania Railroad Station, Chestnut Hill Line (PA-1943), Chelton Ave. 1 photo (n.d.). LC code: PA,51-GERM,184.

Pennsylvania Railroad Station, Germantown Junction (PA-1941). 1 photo (n.d.). LC code: PA,51-GERM,183.

Pennypack Creek Bridge (PA-1786), 8300 Frankford Ave. 2 photos (1973). LC code: PA,51-PHILA,414.

Penrose House. See Stone-Penrose House.

Perelman Antique Toy Museum. See Abercrombie, Captain James, House.

Perseverance Hose Company, No. 5 (PA-1455), 316 Race St. 1 photo (ca. 1935). LC code: PA,52-PHILA,553.

Philadelphia and Reading Railroad, Terminal Station (Reading Terminal) (PA-1528), 1115-41 Market St. 11 photos (ca. 1890, ca. 1937, 1948, 1974). LC code: PA,51-PHILA,521. NHL.

Philadelphia Art Club (PA-1529), 220 S. Broad St. 4 photos (1972). LC code: PA,51-PHILA,329.

Philadelphia Athenaeum (PA-1389), 219 S. Sixth St. 1 sheet (1976); 3 photos (1972). LC code: PA,51-PHILA,116. NHL.

   Brick Privy (PA-1389A). 1 sheet (1962); 2 photos (1962). LC code: PA,51-PHILA,116A.

Philadelphia Bank. See Bank of Pennsylvania.

Philadelphia Bourse (Bourse Building) (PA-1456), 11-21 S. Fifth St. 7 photos (ca. 1925, 1973, 1974, 1976). LC code: PA,51-PHILA,651.

Philadelphia City Hall. See Independence Hall Complex, City Hall.

Philadelphia City Hall. See The New Public Buildings.

Philadelphia College of Art. See Pennsylvania Institution for the Deaf and Dumb.

Philadelphia Contributionship for the Insuring of Houses from Loss by Fire (PA-1457), 212 S. Fourth St. 7 photos (1835, 1958); 2 data pages (1984). LC code: PA,51-PHILA,141. NHL.

Philadelphia County Court House. See Congress Hall.

Philadelphia County Prison (Moyamensing Prison) (PA-1097), 1400 S. Tenth St. 10 photos (1965); 2 data pages (1984). LC code: PA,51-PHILA,672.

   Debtors' Wing (PA-1097A). 7 sheets (1965, 1966); 5 photos (1965); 2 data pages (1984). LC code: PA,51-PHILA,672A.

Philadelphia Exchange Company (Merchants' Exchange) (PA-1028), 143 S. Third St. 15 sheets (1954, 1961); 21 photos (1939, 1964, 1965, 1975). LC code: PA,51-PHILA,137.

Philadelphia Fire Department, Engine Company No. 8 (Fireman's Hall) (PA-1459), 149 N. Second St. 1 sheet (1974); 1 photo (1976). LC code: PA,51-PHILA,619.

Philadelphia Fire Department, Engine Company No. 21 (PA-1787), 826-28 New Market St. 1 photo (ca. 1875). LC code: PA,51-PHILA,531.

Philadelphia Fire Department, No. 3 and Patrol House. See Weccacoe Engine Company, Number 7.

Philadelphia, Germantown and Norristown Railroad, Germantown Depot (PA-1707), 5731-35 Germantown Ave. 1 photo (1972). LC code: PA,51-GERM,182.

Philadelphia Hose Company No. 1 (PA-1460), Seventh and Filbert Sts. 4 photos (ca. 1880, ca. 1935, 1965); 2 data pages (1965, 1984). LC code: PA,51-PHILA,660.

Philadelphia Masonic Temple (PA-1532), 1 N. Broad St. 39 photos (1867, ca. 1870, ca. 1900, 1963); 13 data pages (1967, 1971).

Philadelphia Museum of Art (Pennsylvania Museum and School of Industrial Art) (PA-1661), Benjamin Franklin Pkwy. 6 photos (1924, 1926, 1927, ca. 1928, 1966, 1972). LC code: PA,51-PHILA,335.

Philadelphia National Bank. See Bank of Pennsylvania.

Philadelphia Opera House (The Met) (PA-1734), 1400-18 Poplar St. 4 photos (ca. 1925, 1974). LC code: PA,51-PHILA,540.

Philadelphia Saving Fund Society (PA-1461), 306 Walnut St. 3 photos (ca. 1860, 1958). LC code: PA,51-PHILA,589.

Philadelphia Saving Fund Society (PA-1462), 700 Walnut St. 2 photos (1975). LC code: PA,51-PHILA,601.

Philadelphia Saving Fund Society (PSFS) (PA-1533), Twelfth and Market Sts. 33 photos (ca. 1929, 1985). LC code: PA,51-PHILA,584. NHL.

Philadelphia Trust, Safe Deposit and Insurance Company (PA-1181), 415 Chestnut St. 1 sheet (1965); 3 photos (ca. 1910, 1959). LC code: PA,51-PHILA,375.

Philadelphia, Wilmington and Baltimore Railroad, Freight Station (Semple Company Warehouse) (PA-1611), Fifteenth and Carpenter Sts. 10 photos (1914, 1917, 1969). LC code: PA,51-PHILA,356A.

Philadelphia Zoological Gardens, Bear Pits (PA-1662), W. Girard Ave. and Thirty-fourth St. 4 photos (1875, 1975). LC code: PA,51-PHILA,394B.

Philadelphia Zoological Gardens, Entrance Pavilions (PA-1663), W. Girard Ave. and Thirty-fourth St. 1 photo (1972). LC code: PA,51-PHILA,394A.

Philosophical Hall. See American Philosophical Society.

Physick House. See Hill-Physick House.

Physick House. See Kid-Chandler and Kid-Physick Houses.

Picklands, Thomas, House (PA-1357), 307 S. Third St. 4 photos (1959, 1972). LC code: PA,51-PHILA,637.

Piles, John, House (PA-1358), 328 S. Third St. 2 photos (1959, 1972). LC code: PA,51-PHILA,641.

524 Pine Street (House, Rainwater Conductor Head) (PA-5196). 1 sheet (1973). LC code: PA,51-PHILA,538.

Pine Street Church, Old. See Third Presbyterian Church.

Poe, Edgar Allan, House (PA-1735), rear of 530 N. Seventh St. 5 photos (1967). LC code: PA,51-PHILA,663A. NHL.

Polite Temple Baptist Church. See First Baptist Church of Germantown.

Poor Richard Club. See Leidy, Dr. Joseph, Jr., House.

Port Royal (Stiles-Lukens House) (PA-111), Tacony St. 7 sheets (1937); 5 photos (1900, 1937); 5 data pages (1937). LC code: PA,51-PHILA,5.

Portico Row. See Portico Square.

Portico Square (Portico Row) (PA-1534), 900-30 Spruce St. 4 photos (1975). LC code: PA,51-PHILA,576. NR.

Potts, Horace T., and Company Warehouse (PA-1789), 316-20 N. Third St. 7 sheets (ca. 1978); 3 photos (1963, 1974); 2 data pages (1980). LC code: PA,51-PHILA,627.

Potts, Joseph D., House (PA-1638), 3905 Spruce St. 10 photos (1959, 1961); 1 data page (1984). LC code: PA,51-PHILA,581.

Carriage House and Stable (PA-1638A). 1 photo (1961). LC code: PA,51-PHILA,581A.

Poulson House. See Bussey-Poulson House.

Powder Magazine (PA-124), Magazine La. 2 sheets (1936); 5 photos (1937); 2 data pages (1937). LC code: PA,51-PHILA,220.

Powel, Samuel, House (PA-1359), 244 S. Third St. 19 photos (1958, 1962, 1967, 1972); 1 data page (1984). LC code: PA,51-PHILA,25.

Preston Retreat (PA-1736), Twentieth and Hamilton Sts. 24 photos (1837, 1963); 6 data pages (1888, 1909, 1984). LC code: PA,51-PHILA,480.

Protestant Episcopal City Mission. See St. Paul's Protestant Episcopal Church.

Provident Life and Trust Company Bank (PA-1058), 409 Chestnut St. 2 sheets (1962); 19 photos (ca. 1885, 1959); 14 data pages (1960, 1985-86). LC code: PA,51-PHILA,256.

1880-90 Addition (PA-1058A). 1 photo (ca. 1910). LC code: PA,51-PHILA,256A.

PSFS. See Philadelphia Saving Fund Society.

Pullman House. See Rowley-Pullman House.

523-25 Quarry Street (Houses) (PA-1426). 1 photo (1959). LC code: PA,51-PHILA,524.

26-28 Queen Street (Houses) (PA-1613). 2 photos (1966, 1967). LC code: PA,51-PHILA,545.

31-33 Queen Street (Stoops) (PA-5194). 1 photo (1966). LC code: PA,51-PHILA,546.

907-09 Race Street (Commercial Buildings) (Far East Chinese Restaurant) (PA-1505). 2 photos (1973). LC code: PA,51-PHILA,297.

Ralston, Robert, House (PA-1016), 521 Arch St. 8 photos (1959); 3 data pages (1959). LC code: PA,51-PHILA,246.

Ralston School (PA-1614), 625 S. American St. 1 photo (ca. 1925); 1 data page (1974). LC code: PA,51-PHILA,334.

Rawle, Randolph, House See Laurel Hill.

Reading Terminal. See Philadelphia and Reading Railroad, Terminal Station.

Reed, Samuel and Joseph, Houses (PA-1615), 518-20 S. Front St. 4 photos (1958, 1961, 1967). LC code: PA,51-PHILA,431.

Reliance Insurance Company of Philadelphia (PA-1465), 429 Walnut St. 5 photos (ca. 1898, 1915, 1959); 1 data page (1984). LC code: PA,51-PHILA,598.

Reynolds-Morris House (PA-1107), 225 S. Eighth St. 9 sheets (1940); 5 photos (ca. 1897, 1972); 2 data pages (1984). LC code: PA,51-PHILA,40. NHL.

Rhoads-Barclay House (PA-1057), 217 Delancey St. 7 sheets (1961); 7 photos (1959, 1972, 1973); 6 data pages (1959, 1963). LC code: PA,51-PHILA,255.

Rich, Comly, House (PA-1794), 4276 Orchard St. 4 sheets (1977); 13 photos (1977). LC code: PA,51-PHILA,534.

Rich-Truman House (PA-1074), 320 Delancey St. 12 sheets (1962); 4 photos (1963); 8 data pages (1963). LC code: PA,51-PHILA,261.

Ridge Avenue Farmers' Market Company (PA-1737), 1810 Ridge Ave. 4 photos (1973). LC code: PA,51-PHILA,558. NR.

Ridgeland (PA-1664), Chamounix Dr., Fairmount Park. 8 photos (1959). LC code: PA,51-PHILA,395.

Riggs and Brother, Navigator Statue (Navigator Statue) (PA-1466), 310 Market St. 1 photo (ca. 1970); 1 data page (1966). LC code: PA,51-PHILA,513A.

Rittenhouse House (PA-16), Lincoln Dr. and Rittenhouse St. 7 sheets (1935); 3 photos (1925, 1972); 1 data page (1935). LC code: PA,51-GERM,78.

Robeson House. See Shoomac Park.

Robinson, William, House (PA-1361), 23 Clymer St. 1 photo (1966). LC code: PA,51-PHILA,689.

Rogers-Cassatt House (PA-1537), 202 S. Nineteenth St. 9 photos (1969); 1 data page (1984). LC code: PA,51-PHILA,678.

Roney, John, House (PA-1017), 117 N. Sixth St. 1 photo (1959); 3 data pages (1959). LC code: PA,51-PHILA,247.

Rowley-Pullman House (PA-1467), 238 S. Third St. 7 photos (1962, 1963, 1972). LC code: PA,51-PHILA,632.

Royal House (PA-1709), 5011 Germantown Ave. 1 photo (1957); 1 data page (1976). LC code: PA,51-GERM,175.

Royal Insurance Company Building (PA-1468), 212 S. Third St. 3 photos (1960). LC code: PA,51-PHILA,631.

Rumpp, C.E., and Sons, Inc., Factory (PA-1469), 114-30 N. Fifth St. 2 photos (ca. 1894, ca. 1959); 1 data page (1984). LC code: PA,51-PHILA,650.

Rush, Benjamin, Birthplace (PA-1796), Red Lion Rd. 4 photos (early twentieth century, 1959), 4 data pages (1959, 1984). LC code: PA,51-PHILA,556.

Springhouse (PA-1796A). 1 photo (1959). LC code: PA,51-PHILA,566A.

Rush, Benjamin, Homestead. See Rush, Benjamin, Birthplace.

Ryerss Mansion. See Burholme.

St. Agatha's Catholic Church (PA-1639), 3801 Spring Garden St. 3 photos (ca. 1885, 1973). LC code: PA,51-PHILA,568.

St. Andrew's Protestant Episcopal Church (St. George's Greek Orthodox Cathedral) (PA-1362), 250-54 S. Eighth St. 1 photo (1958); 1 data page (1984). LC code: PA,51-PHILA,667.

St. Augustine's Roman Catholic Church (PA-1471), Fourth and New Sts. 1 photo (1974); 2 data pages (1984). LC code: PA,51-PHILA,529. NR.

St. Charles Borromeo Roman Catholic Church (PA-1546), 900 S. Twentieth St. 3 photos (ca. 1885, n.d.). LC code: PA,51-PHILA,682.

St. Charles Hotel (PA-1472), 60-66 N. Third St. 3 photos (1962); 2 data pages (1984). LC code: PA,51-PHILA,626.

St. Clement's Protestant Episcopal Church (PA-1538), 128 N. Twentieth St. 7 photos (1974). LC code: PA,51-PHILA,681. NR.

St. Elizabeth Roman Catholic Church (PA-1940), 1845 N. Twenty-third St. 1 photo (ca. 1880). LC code: PA,51-PHILA,684.

St. Francis DeSales Roman Catholic Church (PA-1640), 4629-35 Springfield Ave. 4 photos (1973). LC code: PA,51-PHILA,567.

St. Francis Xavier's Church (Roman Catholic) (PA-1933), 2321 Green St. 1 photo (ca. 1880). LC code: PA,51-PHILA,479.

St. George's Greek Orthodox Cathedral. See St. Andrew's Protestant Episcopal Church.

St. George's House. See International Exhibition of 1876, St. George's House.

St. George's Methodist Episcopal Church (PA-1473), 235 N. Fourth St. 6 photos (1972). LC code: PA,51-PHILA,644.

St. James Roman Catholic Church (PA-1641), 3278 Chestnut St. 4 photos (ca. 1855, n.d., 1973). LC code: PA,51-PHILA,380.

202 St. James Street (House) (PA-1474). 2 photos (1959). LC code: PA,51-PHILA,562.

206 St. James Street (House) (PA-5195). 5 photos (1959). LC code: PA,51-PHILA,563.

St. John's Lutheran Church (PA-1935), 511-23 Race St. 4 photos (1924). LC code: PA,51-PHILA,555.

St. Mark's Church (Episcopal) (PA-1093), 1625 Locust St. 9 photos (1848, 1958); 10 data pages (1964). LC code: PA,51-PHILA,270. NHL.

St. Mary's, Old. See St. Mary's Roman Catholic Church.

St. Mary's Protestant Episcopal Church (PA-1642), 3916 Locust Walk. 3 photos (1973). LC code: PA,51-PHILA,509.

St. Mary's Roman Catholic Church (Old St. Mary's) (PA-1363), 244 S. Fourth St. 2 photos (ca. 1880, 1972). LC code: PA,51-PHILA,648.

Grave (PA-1363A). 1 photo (1958). LC code: PA,51-PHILA,648A.

St. Paul's Protestant Episcopal Church (Protestant Episcopal City Mission) (PA-1475), 225 S. Third St. 1 sheet (1973); 1 photo (1959). LC code: PA,51-PHILA,98.

St. Peter's Church House, Episcopal. See Blackwell, Reverend Robert, House.

St. Peter's Protestant Episcopal Church (PA-1118), Third and Pine Sts. 17 sheets (1940); 13 photos (1898, ca. 1920, 1976). LC code: PA,51-PHILA,108.

St. Stephen's Methodist Episcopal Church, Rectory (PA-1708), 5213 Germantown Ave. 1 photo (1957); 1 data page (1985). LC code: PA,51-GERM,19.

St. Stephen's Protestant Episcopal Church (PA-1576), 19 S. Tenth St. 2 photos (1972); 1 data page (1984). LC code: PA,51-PHILA,673. NR.

St. Timothy's Protestant Episcopal Church (PA-1710), 5720 Ridge Ave. 3 photos (1973). LC code: PA,51-PHILA,560.

Gateway (PA-1710A). 2 photos (1973). LC code: PA,51-PHILA,561.

St. Timothy's Working Men's Club and Institute (PA-1711), 5164 Ridge Ave. 2 photos (1973). LC code: PA,51-PHILA,559.

Sansom, William, House (Sansom's Row) (PA-1476), 707 Walnut St. 1 photo (1958). LC code: PA,51-PHILA,602.

Sansom's Row. See Sansom, William, House.

Sauveur House. See Houston-Sauveur House.

Schaeffer, Harriet, House (PA-1712), 433 W. Stafford St. 1 photo (1972). LC code: PA,51-PHILA,582.

Schenck Building (PA-1078), 535-37 Arch St. 3 photos (1875, 1958); 5 data pages (1963). LC code: PA,51-PHILA,264.

Schively, Henry, House (PA-1364), 329 S. Third St. 2 photos (1961). LC code: PA,51-PHILA,639.

Schuylkill Arsenal (Arsenal on the Schuylkill) (PA-1540), 2620 Gray's Ferry Ave. 2 data pages (1984). LC code: PA,51-PHILA,578.

Building No. 1 (U.S. Laboratory, Enlisted Men's Barracks, Luding Hall) (PA-1540A). 4 photos (1958); 1 data page (1984). LC code: PA,51-PHILA,578A.

Building No. 1A (Commandant's House, Executive Officers' Quarters) (PA-1540B). 6 photos (1958); 1 data page (1984). LC code: PA,51-PHILA,578B.

Building No. 2 (Mifflin Building) (PA-1540C). 2 photos (1958); 1 data page (1984). LC code: PA,51-PHILA,578C.

Building No. 2A (Surgeon's House) (PA-1540D). 2 photos (1958); 1 data page (1984). LC code: PA,51-PHILA,578D.

Building No. 6 (PA-1540E). 3 photos (1958); 1 data page (1984). LC code: PA,51-PHILA,578E.

Building No. 8 (Powder Magazine) (PA-1540F). 2 photos (1958); 1 data page (1984). LC code: PA,51-PHILA,578F.

Commandant's House. See *Building No. 1A.*

Enlisted Men's Barracks. See *Building No. 1.*

Executive Officer's Quarters See *Building No. 1A.*

Luding Hall. See *Building No. 1.*

Mifflin Building. See *Building No. 2.*

Powder Magazine. See *Building No. 8.*

Surgeon's House. See *Building No. 2A.*

U.S. Laboratory. See *Building No. 1.*

Schuylkill Hose, Hook and Ladder Company, No. 24 (PA-1577), 1227 Locust St. 1 photo (ca. 1934). LC code: PA,51-PHILA,496.

Scott-Wanamaker House (PA-1578), 2032 Walnut St. 11 photos (1972, 1973); 1 data page (1984). LC code: PA,51-PHILA,607.

Second Bank of the United States (Customs House) (PA-137), 420 Chestnut St. 19 sheets (1939); 43 photos (1939, 1959, 1965, 1976). LC code: PA,51-PHILA,223. NHL.

125-27 South Second Street (Commercial Buildings) (PA-1405). 1 sheet (n.d.). LC code: PA,51-PHILA,620.

252 South Second Street (House) (PA-1934). 1 photo (1959). LC code: PA,51-PHILA,188.

Sedgeley Guard House. See Sedgeley Porter's House.

Sedgeley Porter's House (Sedgeley Guard House) (PA-1665), Sedgeley Dr. and W. Girard Ave. 2 photos (1972). LC code: PA,51-PHILA,397A.

Semple Company Warehouse. See Philadelphia, Wilmington and Baltimore Railroad, Freight Station.

9 North Seventh Street (Commercial Building) (PA-1939). 1 photo (1965). LC code: PA,51-PHILA,661.

North Seventh Street Area Study (Commercial Buildings) (PA-1449), 21-33 N. Seventh St. 1 photo (1965). LC code: PA,51-PHILA,662.

Shaw House. See Toby-Shaw House.

Shibe Park (Stadium) (Connie Mack Stadium) (PA-1738), 2701 N. Twenty-first St. 12 photos (ca. 1909, 1963, 1970, 1973); 2 data pages (1984). LC code: PA,51-PHILA,683.

Shinn, Samuel, House. See Marshall's Court Area Study, Samuel Shinn House.

Shippen-Wistar House (PA-1365), 238 S. Fourth St. 3 photos (1959, 1963). LC code: PA,51-PHILA,647.

Shoomac Park (Robeson House) (PA-1067), Ridge Ave. and Wissahickon Dr. 6 sheets (1961); 7 photos (1956, 1961); 9 data pages (1961). LC code: PA,51-PHILA,259.

Siddons, William, House (PA-1618), 851 S. Front St. 1 photo (1957). LC code: PA,51-PHILA,452.

Simpson, David, House. See Marshall's Court Area Study, David Simpson House.

Sims, Joseph, House (Franklin Row, Sims-Bilsland House) (PA-1186), 228 S. Ninth St. 5 sheets (1965); 9 photos (ca. 1870, ca. 1920, 1962, 1965); 5 data pages (1962, 1984). LC code: PA,51-PHILA,671.

Sims-Bilsland House. See Sims, Joseph, House.

Singer, John, Warehouse (PA-1478), 319 1/2 Market St. 1 photo (1972); 1 data page (1984). LC code: PA,51-PHILA,515.

Singley House. See Bel Air.

Sink Burgin House (PA-1366), 331 S. Fifth St. 1 photo (1960). LC code: PA,51-PHILA,653.

Sisk Houses. See Stafford's Tavern-Paschall House.

Smith, Daniel Jr., House (PA-1367), 505 S. Front St. 1 photo (1961). LC code: PA,51-PHILA,427.

Smith Memorial Arch (Civil War Memorial) (PA-1666), Fairmont Park. 1 photo (1972). LC code: PA,51-PHILA,398A.

Snappers, The. See Northern Liberty Hose Company, No. 4.

Solitude (John Penn House) (PA-1127), Zoo Grounds, Fairmount Park. 9 sheets (1940); 22 photos (1897, 1939, 1961). LC code: PA,51-PHILA,30.

Somerton. See Strawberry Mansion.

Sons of Temperance Fountain (PA-1480), Independence Sq. 2 photos (ca. 1880, 1961); 1 data page (1984). LC code: PA,51-PHILA,265E.

Souder, Charles E., House (PA-1018), 514 Race St. 1 photo (1959); 3 photos (1959). LC code: PA,51-PHILA,248.

Southern Loan Company of Philadelphia (Tradesmen's National Bank of Philadelphia) (PA-1368), 300 S. Second St. 2 photos (1959, 1972). LC code: PA,51-PHILA,623.

Southwark Hose Company, No. 9 (PA-1369), 512 S. Third St. 1 photo (1961). LC code: PA,51-PHILA,641.

Sower House (Trinity Lutheran Church House) (PA-1717), 5300 Germantown Ave. 1 photo (1957); 1 data page (1985). LC code: PA,51-GERM,26.

Spafford, William, House (PA-1620), 626 S. Front St. 4 photos (1961, 1966, 1967). LC code: PA,51-PHILA,436.

Sparks Shot Tower (PA-1621), 129-31 Carpenter St. 2 photos (1973). LC code: PA,51-PHILA,195.

Spring Garden Institute (PA-1739), 523-25 N. Broad St. 2 photos (1971). LC code: PA,51-PHILA,351.

Spring Garden Insurance Company Building (PA-1481), 431 Walnut St. 2 photos (1915, 1957); 1 data page (1984). LC code: PA,51-PHILA,599.

200 Block Spruce Street (Houses) (PA-1713). 3 photos (1960). LC code: PA,51-PHILA,688.

700-14 Spruce Street (Houses) (PA-253). 4 sheets (1978); 28 photos (1977); 32 data pages (1977). LC code: PA,51-PHILA,321.

722-30 Spruce Street (Houses) (PA-1339). 5 photos (1958). LC code: PA,51-PHILA,575.

2009-45 Spruce Street. See Spruce Street Area Study.

Spruce Street Area Study (2009-45 Spruce Street) (PA-1579). 11 photos (1974). LC code: PA,51-PHILA,579.

Stable and Carriage House (PA-1401), rear of 422 Walnut St. 2 sheets (1958); 11 photos (1959). LC code: PA,51-PHILA,595A.

Stafford's Tavern-Paschall House (Man Full of Trouble Tavern, Cove Cornice House, Sisk Houses) (PA-128), Spruce and Mattis Sts. 4 sheets (1965, 1972); 6 photos (1958, 1961, 1972). LC code: PA,51-PHILA,276.

Stafford's Tavern (PA-128A). 5 sheets (1958); 7 photos (1958, 1959, 1961). LC code: PA,51-PHILA,276A.

Paschall House (PA-128B). 3 sheets (1958); 3 photos (1958, 1961). LC code: PA,51-PHILA,276B.

Stanfield House. See Woods, Capt. John, House.

State House of Pennsylvania. See Independence Hall Complex, Independence Hall.

Stenton (PA-1714), Courtland and Eighteenth Sts. 4 photos (1960). LC code: PA,51-PHILA,8. NHL.

Stetson, John B., Company (Stetson Hat Factory) (PA-1227), Germantown and Columbia Aves. 21 photos (1978); 18 data pages (1978, 1981). LC code: PA,51-PHILA,458.

Stetson Hat Factory. See Stetson, John B., Company.

Stewart, Thomas, House (PA-189), 410 Locust St. 7 sheets (1957); 2 photos (1957); 3 data pages (1957). LC code: PA,51-PHILA,238.

Stiles, William, House (PA-1371), 310 Cypress St. 8 photos (1962). LC code: PA,51-PHILA,462.

Stiles-Luken House. See Port Royal.

Stocker, John Clement, House (PA-1068), 402 S. Front St. 6 sheets (1960, 1961); 15 photos (1910, 1914, 1961); 11 data pages (1962). LC code: PA,51-PHILA-22.

Stoddard House. See Jordan-Stoddard House.

Stone-Penrose House (PA-1483), 700 Locust St. 3 photos (ca. 1975). LC code: PA,51-PHILA,493.

Strawberry Mansion (Summerville, Somerton) (PA-1668), Fairmount Park. 6 photos (1932, 1938, 1962, 1963). LC code: PA,51-PHILA,219.

Strawberry Mansion Bridge (PA-1669), Ford Rd. and E. River Dr., Fairmount Park. 3 photos (1908, 1972). LC code: PA,51-PHILA,404.

Stride-Madison House (PA-1073), 429 Spruce St. 6 sheets (1961); 10 photos (1914, 1961, 1962, 1965); 8 data pages (1964). LC code: PA,51-PHILA,260.

Sully, Thomas, House (PA-1372), 530 Spruce St. 6 photos (1968). LC code: PA,51-PHILA,571. NHL.

Summers-Worrell House (PA-1373), 505 Delancey St. 1 photo (1960). LC code: PA,51-PHILA,388.

Summerville. See Strawberry Mansion.

Swedes Church, Old. See Gloria Dei (Church).

Sweetbrier (PA-1670), Fairmount Park. 5 photos (1928, 1972). LC code: PA,51-PHILA,395.

Tabernacle Presbyterian Church (PA-1099), 3700 Chestnut St. 18 photos (1884, 1886, 1890, ca. 1930, 1963); 7 data pages (1965). LC code: PA,51-PHILA,271.

Tanner, Henry O., House (PA-1740), 2908 W. Diamond St. 4 photos (1930, ca. 1980); 1 data page (1984). LC code: PA,51-PHILA,391. NHL.

Tarrant House. See Eckert-Tarrant House.

Third Presbyterian Church (Old Pine Street Church) (PA-1374), 422 Pine St. 5 photos (1956, 1974). LC code: PA,51-PHILA,203.

17-63 North Third Street. See North Third Street Area Study.

North Third Street Area Study (17-63 North Third Street) (PA-1450). 6 photos (1974). LC code: PA,51-PHILA,625.

252 South Third Street (House) (PA-1945). 1 photo (1961). LC code: PA,51-PHILA,633.

266-76 South Third Street (Houses) (PA-1936). 1 photo (1961). LC code: PA,51-PHILA,635.

Toby-Shaw House (PA-1937), 12 Queen St. 1 photo (1966). LC code: PA,51-PHILA,542.

Todd House. See Dilworth-Todd-Moylan House.

Tradesmen's National Bank of Philadelphia See Southern Loan Company of Philadelphia.

Trinity Church, Oxford (Episcopal) (PA-17), 6900-02 Oxford Ave. 6 sheets (1934, 1935, 1936); 5 photos (ca. 1930, 1972); 4 data pages (1936). LC code: PA,51-PHILA,37.

Trinity Lutheran Church (PA-1716), 19 N. Queen La. 3 photos (1973). LC code: PA,51-GERM,189.

Trinity Lutheran Church House. See Sower House.

Troc, The. See Arch Street Opera House.

Trocadero. See Arch Street Opera House.

Truman House. See Rich-Truman House.

Tuttleman Brothers and Faggen Building (PA-1485), 56-60 N. Second St. 1 photo (1976). LC code: PA,51-PHILA,618.

Twelfth Street Meeting House (PA-1944), 20 S. Twelfth St. 9 sheets (1971); 48 photos (ca. 1892, 1902, 1971, 1972); 1 data page (1984). LC code: PA,51-PHILA,674.

Union League of Philadelphia (PA-1626), 140 S. Broad St. 2 photos (1864, 1972); 1 data page (1984). LC code: PA,51-PHILA,346. NR.

U.S. Bonded Warehouse (PA-1375), 415-19 S. Front St. 3 photos (1960). LC code: PA,51-PHILA,426.

U.S. Hose Company, No. 14 (PA-1804), 423 Buttonwood St. 1 photo (ca. 1935); 1 data page (1984). LC code: PA,51-PHILA,119.

U.S. Mint (PA-1741), Sixteenth and Garden Sts. 2 photos (1902, 1974). LC code: PA,51-PHILA,372.

U.S. Mint, Old (PA-1938), Chestnut and Juniper Sts. 2 photos (ca. 1888, 1902). LC code: PA,51-PHILA,371.

U.S. Naval Asylum, Biddle Hall (U.S. Naval Home, Biddle Hall) (PA-1622A), Gray's Ferry Ave. 23 photos (1826, 1836, 1843, 1844, 1964); 9 data pages (1965, 1984). LC code: PA,51-PHILA,577A. NHL.

Governor's Residence (PA-1622B). 5 photos (1964); 4 data pages (1965, 1984). LC code: PA,51-PHILA,577B.

Laning Hall, Building No. 2 (PA-1622D). 9 photos (1908, 1938, 1964); 3 data pages (1965, 1984). LC code: PA,51-PHILA,577D.

Stable Building (PA-1622E). 1 photo (1964). LC code: PA,51-PHILA,577E.

Surgeon's Residence (PA-1622C). 3 photos (1964); 4 data pages (1965, 1984). LC code: PA,51-PHILA,577C.

U.S. Naval Home. See U.S. Naval Asylum.

U.S. Supreme Court Building. See Independence Hall Complex, City Hall.

University of Pennsylvania, College Hall (PA-1643), Woodland Ave. 2 photos (1983); 1 data page (1984). LC code: PA,51-PHILA,566C. NR.

University of Pennsylvania, Furness Building (PA-1644), W. side Thirty-fourth St. 10 photos (1964). LC code: PA,51-PHILA,566D.

University of Pennsylvania, Mask and Wig Club. See Welsh Coach House and Stable.

University of Pennsylvania, Men's Dormitories (PA-1645), Spruce St. 5 photos (1973). LC code: PA,51-PHILA,566B.

University of Pennsylvania, University Museum (Museum of Science and Art) (PA-1646), 3620 South St. 4 photos (1973). LC code: PA,51-PHILA,566A.

Upper Ferry Bridge (PA-1946), Spring Garden St. 1 photo (n.d.). LC code: PA,51-PHILA,569.

Upsala (PA-1718), 6430 Germantown Ave. 3 photos (1973). LC code: PA,51-GERM,65. NR.

Urquhart House. See Moffitt, Robert, House.

Valley Green Inn (PA-1719), Wissahickon Dr. 11 sheets (1965); 1 photo (1972). LC code: PA,51-PHILA,83.

Van Rensselaer House. See Fell-Van Rensselaer House.

Vaults (PA-1486), Front and Walnut Sts. 1 data page (1985-87). LC code: PA,51-PHILA,415.

Vernon (PA-7-2), Germantown Ave., Vernon Park. 17 sheets (1934); 6 photos (1934, 1975); 3 data pages (1936). LC code: PA,51-GERM,38.

Victory Building. See New York Life Insurance Company Building.

Walker House See Duche-Walker House.

Waln, Isaac, House (PA-1376), 259 S. Third St. 6 photos (1960). LC code: PA,51-PHILA,634.

131 Walnut Street (Casement Window) (PA-1948). 2 sheets (n.d.). LC code: PA,51-PHILA,587.

329 Walnut Street (Mantlepiece) (PA-1947). 1 photo (ca. 1965). LC code: PA,51-PHILA,592.

423 Walnut Street (Railing) (PA-1715). 1 photo (1959). LC code: PA,51-PHILA,596.

Walnut Street Theater (PA-1487), 829-33 Walnut St. 16 photos (ca. 1830, 1865, 1880s, ca. 1890, ca. 1900, ca. 1905, ca. 1913, 1958, 1972). LC code: PA,51-PHILA,605. NHL.

Wanamaker House. See Scott-Wanamaker House.

Wanamaker, John, Store (PA-1692), Thirteenth and Chestnut Sts. 2 photos (1973, 1979). LC code: PA,51-PHILA,370.

Washington Hose Company, No. 10 (PA-1488), 35 N. Ninth St. 1 photo (ca. 1935). LC code: PA,51-PHILA,669.

Washington Hotel. See Merchants' Hotel.

Washington Square Area Study (PA-1489), Sixth, Seventh, Walnut, and Locust Sts. 9 photos (1842, 1914, 1957, 1962, 1965). LC code: PA,51-PHILA,603. NR.

Washington Square Presbyterian Church. See First Presbyterian Church.

113 North Water Street (House) (PA-1425). 2 photos (1957). LC code: PA,51-PHILA,608.

South Water Street (Houses) (PA-1953), S. Water and Fitzwater Sts. 1 photo (n.d.). LC code: PA,51-PHILA,610.

512-26 South Water Street (Houses) (South Water Street Area Study) (PA-1619). 3 photos (1957, ca. 1960). LC code: PA,51-PHILA,613.

532 South Water Street (House) (PA-1809). 1 photo (1958). LC code: PA,51-PHILA,614.

South Water Street Area Study (Houses). See 512-26 South Water Street (Houses).

South Water Street Area Study (Warehouses) (PA-1810), 100-50 S. Water St. 1 photo (1967). LC code: PA,51-PHILA,611.

Water Trough and Fountain (PA-1379), Ninth St. 2 photos (1974). LC code: PA,51-PHILA,668.

Watson House. See Clarkson-Watson House.

Wayne, General, Hotel See General Wayne Hotel.

Weccacoe Engine Company, No. 9 (Philadelphia Fire Department, No. 3 and Patrol House) (PA-1610), 117-21 Queen St. 3 photos (1893, 1896, 1973). LC code: PA,51-PHILA,549.

Welsh Coach House and Stable (University of Pennsylvania, Mask and Wig Club) (PA-1518), 310 S. Quince St. 1 photo (1975); 3 data pages (1984). LC code: PA,51-PHILA,551A.

West Arch Street Presbyterian Church (Arch Street Presbyterian Church) (PA-1696), 1726-32 Arch St. 8 photos (1974, 1976). LC code: PA,51-PHILA,280. NR.

Western Saving Fund Society of Philadelphia (PA-1703), 1000-8 Walnut St. 5 photos (ca. 1910, 1963); 1 data page (1984). LC code: PA,51-PHILA,606.

Wetherill, Joseph, House (PA-1380), 233 Delancey St. 4 photos (1959, 1972). LC code: PA,51-PHILA,330.

Wharton House. See Pancoast-Lewis-Wharton House.

Wharton, Isaac, House (PA-1381), 510 S. Front St. 1 photo (1958). LC code: PA,51-PHILA,430.

Wharton, John, House (PA-1624), 919 S. Front St. 1 photo (1961). LC code: PA,51-PHILA,690.

Wharton, Joseph, House (PA-1382), 119 Lombard St. 6 photos (1962, 1972); 1 data page (1984). LC code: PA,51-PHILA,501.

Wharton-Stewart House (PA-1185), 27 Christian St. 5 sheets (1968); 4 photos (ca. 1965, 1966). LC code: PA,51-PHILA,382.

White, Bishop William, House (PA-1490), 309 Walnut St. 1 photo (1974). LC code: PA,51-PHILA,590.

Widener, Peter A.B., House (PA-1742), 1200 N. Broad St. 2 photos (1973); 1 data page (1984). LC code: PA,51-PHILA,352.

Williams-Hopkinson House (PA-1084), 338 Spruce St. 13 sheets (1932, 1961); 10 photos (1914, 1959, 1961, 1962); 10 data pages (1961, 1964). LC code: PA,51-PHILA,266.

Williams-Mathurin House (PA-1383), 427 Spruce St. 9 photos (1961, 1962, 1972); 2 data pages (1964, 1984). LC code: PA,51-PHILA,570.

Williamson Houses. See Flickwer-Williamson Houses.

Winder, William H., Houses (PA-1384), 232-34 S. Third St. 4 photos (1962, 1972). LC code: PA,51-PHILA,9.

Winemore, Phillip, House (PA-1050), 220 Spruce St. 1 sheet (1959); 3 photos (1957); 5 data pages (1959). LC code: PA,51-PHILA,249.

Wissahickon Inn (Chestnut Hill Academy) (PA-1720), 500 W. Willow Grove Ave. 2 photos (1972). LC code: PA,51-PHILA,614. NR.

Wistar House. See Shippen-Wistar House.

Wister House. See Hall-Wister House.

Wister's Big House. See Grumblethorpe.

Wood, George, Houses (PA-1385), 335-37 S. Fifth St. 1 photo (1960). LC code: PA,51-PHILA,655.

Woodford (PA-1307), Fairmount Park. 31 photos (1897, 1932, 1938, 1960). LC code: PA,51-PHILA,13. NHL.

5901 Woodland Avenue (Cottage) (PA-138). 4 sheets (1940); 1 photo (1940). LC code: PA,51-PHILA,224.

Woodland Avenue Car Barn (PA-1956), Woodland Ave. and Forty-ninth St. 7 photos (1982); 1 data page (1982). LC code: PA,51-PHILA,616.

Woodland Terrace Area Study (Houses) (PA-1647), 501-19 and 500-20 Woodland Terrace. 8 photos (1973). LC code: PA,51-PHILA,617. NR.

Woodlands (Andrew Hamilton House, Hamilton Village) (PA-1125), Thirty-ninth St. and Woodland Ave. 18 sheets (1940); 6 photos (1938). LC code: PA,51-PHILA,29. NHL.

Woods, Capt. John, House (Stanfield House) (PA-1111), Front and Lombard Sts. 9 sheets (1932). LC code: PA,51-PHILA,277.

Woolfall-Huddell House (PA-1625), 9 Queen St. 2 photos (1966). LC code: PA,51-PHILA,541.

Workman Place (PA-133), 742-46 S. Front St. 7 photos (1937, 1961); 3 data pages (1937, 1984). LC code: PA,51-PHILA,42.

Worrell House. See Summers-Worrell House.

Wyck (Haines House) (PA-7-3), 6026 Germantown Ave. 22 sheets (1934); 8 photos (1934, 1972); 3 data pages (1936). LC code: PA,51-GERM,46. NR.

Wynnestay (PA-1648), Fifty-second St. and Woodbine Ave. 1 photo (1973). LC code: PA,51-PHILA,26.

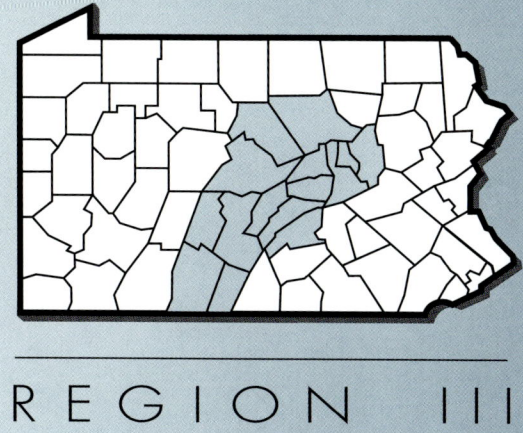

REGION III

Ridge and Valley

Essay by Richard J. Webster
Catalog entries by Deborah Stephens Burns

Bedford*
Blair
Centre
Clinton
Columbia
Fulton*
Huntingdon
Juniata*
Lycoming
Mifflin*
Montour*
Northumberland*
Perry*
Snyder
Union*

*no catalog entries

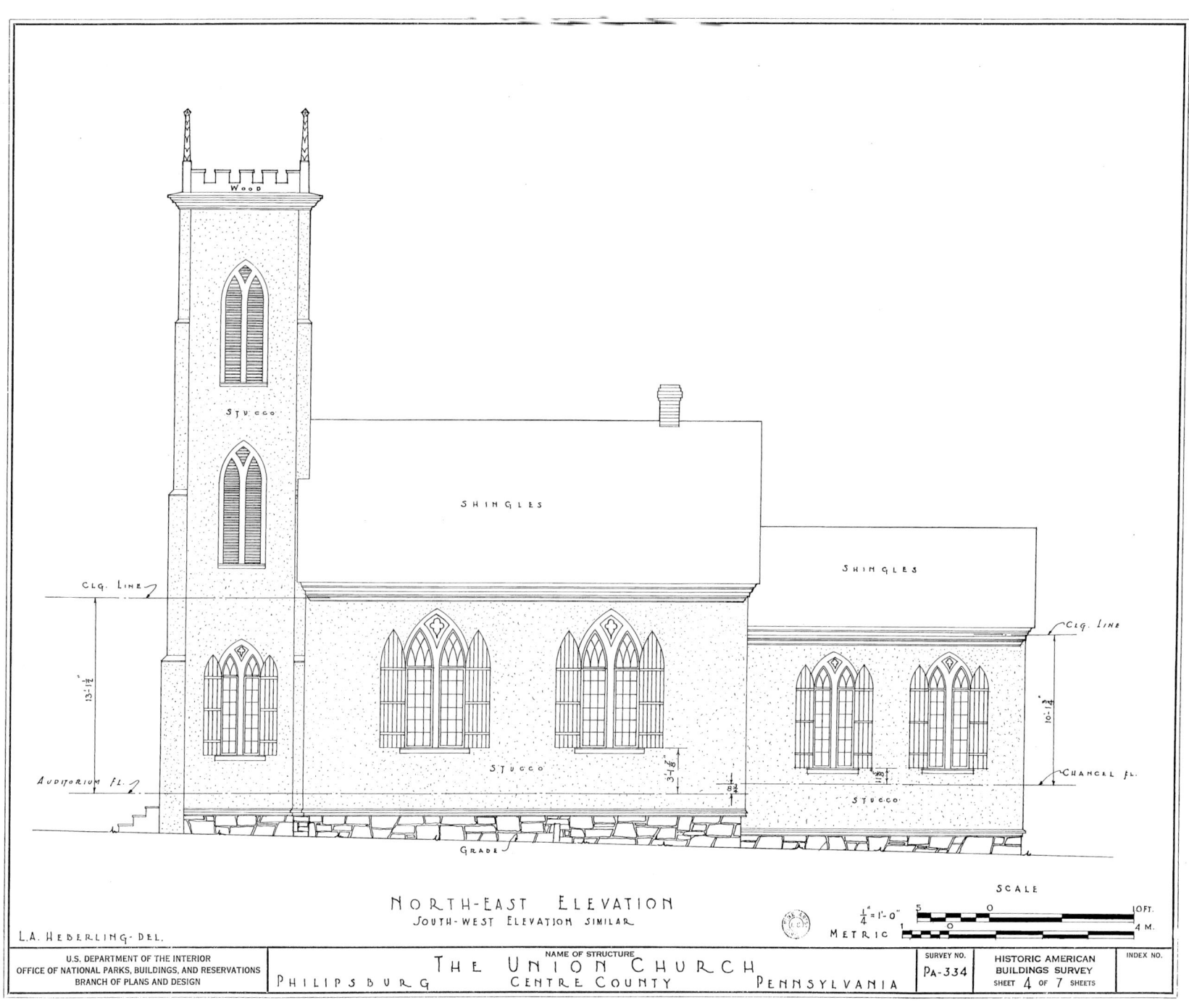

Union Church (PA-334) Philipsburg Borough, Centre County. Northeast elevation (L.A. Heberling, delineator, 1935) PA,14-PHILBU,2.

THE RIDGE AND VALLEY REGION is aptly named. It is dominated by parallel wooded ridges and cultivated valleys that sweep in southwest-northeast arcs across this fifteen-county area in the center of the state.[1] The topography, called the Folded Appalachians, was formed millions of years ago when a tremendous force pushed sedimentary rocks into vertical folds, forming sandstone ridges and limestone and shale valleys. Streams and rivers, in particular the Juniata and Susquehanna, found their way through geological faults in the ridges and meandered in many directions, but eventually more or less southeastwardly. Before 1740 these ridges stood as barriers to westward migration, but by the middle of the eighteenth century they were merely time- and energy-consuming hurdles as pioneers moved through the gaps and into the valleys. The region's distinctive geology, however, has had a permanent imprint on the built and political environment; roads, farms, and county boundaries all conform to the contours of the sandstone ridges.[2] HABS records for this region are sparse; only thirty sites had been recorded in the fifteen-county area the recording activity generated in the 1980s by the National Park Service's America's Industrial Heritage Project in Huntington and Blair Counties.

For the first half-century after Penn's arrival, the Ridge and Valley Region was undisputed Indian territory. By the 1740s, however, settlers had begun to maneuver through the passes of Blue Mountain into present-day Fulton, Huntingdon, Juniata, and Perry Counties. In the next two decades the more adventurous intruded into present-day Bedford County to the south and Centre County in the north, establishing the first American transmountain frontier well before the Revolution. Garrett Pendergrass, for example, arrived at the present site of Bedford in 1752, built a log house, and cleared forty to fifty acres before Indians drove him from his fields and burned his dwelling. He returned within two years, his security assured by the presence of Fort Bedford. Jacob

Stanford in Penns Valley (now Potter Township, Centre County), in the region's northern reaches, was not as fortunate. A group of Indians massacred him and his family in the spring of 1778. The Stanford family massacre was one of many British-incited Indian attacks during the American Revolution that temporarily turned back frontier settlers, but within a decade they returned in even greater numbers. Pennsylvanians' inexorable advance into the frontier was evident well before the end of the colonial period. A series of four Indian treaties between 1746 and 1768 removed imminent Indian threats from the region before the American Revolution and left the Pennsylvania tribes in possession of only the northwestern third of the province.[3]

Indian treaties and the French defeat in the French and Indian War spawned an inland migration that prompted Thomas and Richard Penn to lay out the town of Bedford in 1766 and make it the seat of Bedford County five years later. The next year, 1772, Northumberland County was created and Sunbury, its seat, was sited at the forks of the Susquehanna River. The opening of the region to settlement encouraged land speculation, especially on the part of prosperous Philadelphians. Often these land speculators contributed to frontier political tensions as they sided with the proprietors in their attempts to discourage "squatters" through more restrictive land disposal. Some speculators, rather than wait for civilization's arrival to increase the value of their land, took steps to enhance their investment while exercising such modest rights of ownership as naming their ventures. Dr. William Smith, provost of the College of Philadelphia (later the University of Pennsylvania), for example, laid out a town in 1767 on his extensive holdings along the Juniata River and named it Huntingdon, in honor of Selina Hastings, the Countess of Huntingdon, a prominent benefactor of the college.[4]

Agriculture has been the most common activity of the region but in most parts it has not been a prosperous undertaking. Because narrow, infertile shale valleys are more common in the region than fertile limestone valleys, most farmers have engaged in general agriculture with poor results. The region's median household income remains among the lowest in the state. The broad limestone valleys in the region's northwestern part, in particular the ninety-mile-long Nittany Valley and its extensions, are an exception to this pattern. They possess some of the state's richest land, and their dairy farms' productivity is nearly as high as that of the Great Valley.[5] The iron and coal mined in the region during the first half of the nineteenth century did not have a lasting impact on the local economy.

Southeastern Pennsylvania's three dominant ethnic groups—English, Scotch-Irish, and German—moved into the region's valleys after the 1740s, bringing with them their own building practices, some more syncretic than others. Once they made the journey into these valleys, psychological and physical conditions effected an isolation that, in turn, limited exposure to new building practices. Consequently the region's architecture reflects an interesting mixture of building methods and an understandable conservatism. The earliest buildings almost certainly were built of log or timber frame, their builders' ethnic backgrounds determining their construction details (such as corner notching or timber joining). Even when the ethnic background shares a common root, the physical results can be different, as two extant log houses in Potter Township, Centre County, illustrate. The 1809 Daniel Waggoner House is thoroughly Germanic, as indicated by its central chimney and asymmetrical fenestration. John Neff, on the other hand, a Lebanon County blacksmith of German ancestry, built his house about twenty years after the Waggoner House. The Neff House is a fusion of English and Germanic practices known as the Pennsylvania farmhouse, which is characterized by two front doors on a symmetrical facade.[6]

Of the log buildings that have survived in the region, HABS has recorded only two, the Revolutionary-era Quaker Meetinghouse (PA-212) in Catawissa, Columbia County, and Union Church (PA-334) in Philipsburg, Centre County. For Philipsburg's first twenty-three years, religious services were limited to circuit riders preaching in the tavern or people's homes. In 1820 the community subscribed $343 for a log building to serve as "a school, and a place of worship to be free for religious preachers of all denominations."[7] Townspeople soon called it the Union Church. Its log character, however, has not been detectable since 1842, when citizens (and Hardman Philips, a town founder who contributed handsomely to the building fund) decided to encase the church in roughcast stucco with Gothic-revival windows and a castellated bell tower.[8]

Geographical isolation also contributed to the region's conservative tastes, as suggested by the local longevity of Georgian forms. The region's prominent, affluent newcomers brought knowledge of the Georgian style with them, but it appears that few of the local inhabitants built Georgian houses before 1810, and there were often Georgian more in form than detail. Even when these Georgian dwellings had five-bay fronts with center-hall passages, they were often only one room deep and lacked such high-style details as frontispieces or modillion cornices.[9] Leading citizens, however,

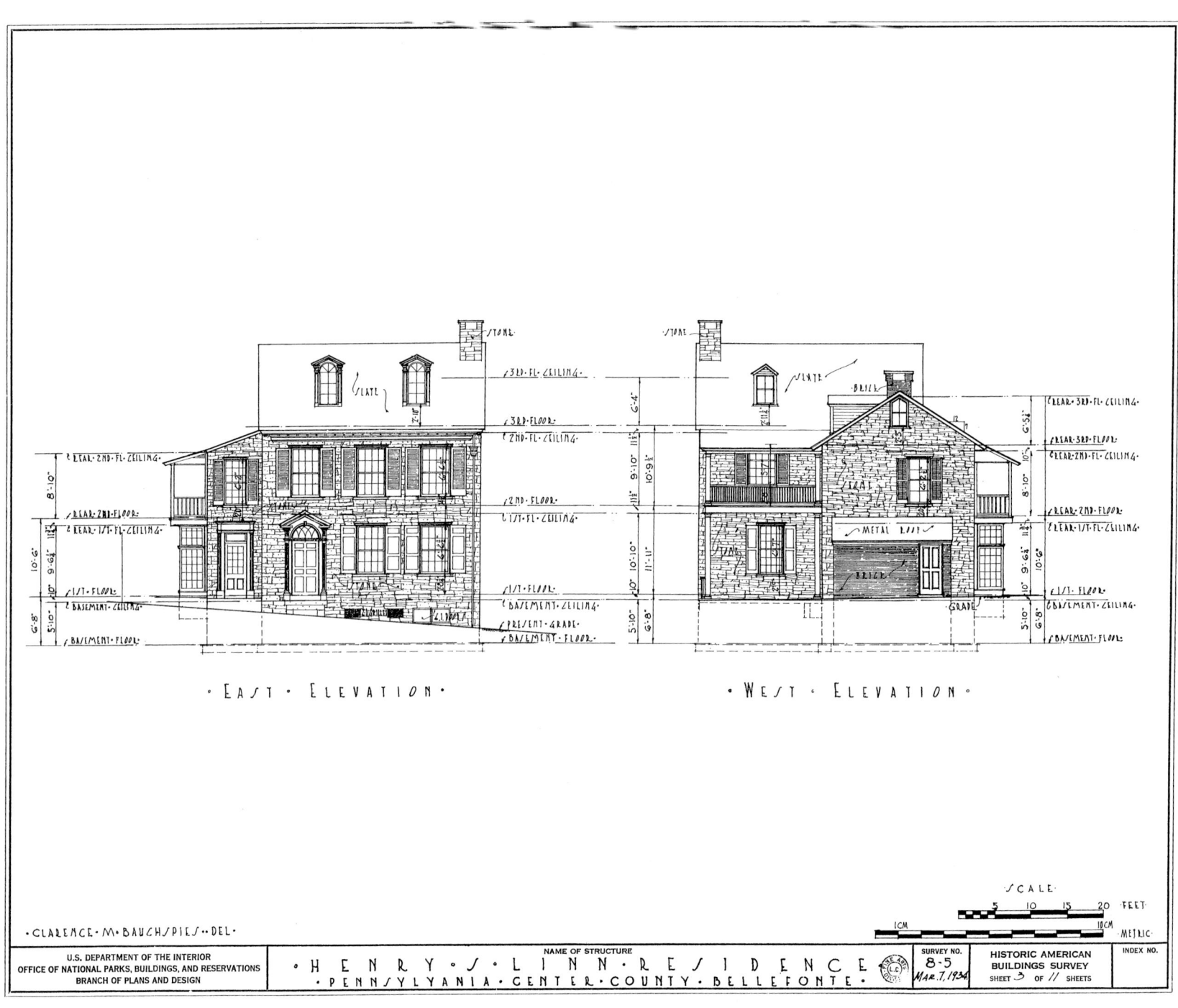

Benner-Walker House (Henry S. Linn House) (PA-8-5) Bellefonte Borough, Centre County.
East and west elevations (Clarence M. Bauchspies, delineator, 1934) PA,14-BELF,1.

such as General Philip Benner, owner of Centre County's first iron furnace, and Jonathan Hoge Walker, president judge of the fourth district, erected dwellings with up-to-date details as well as Georgian proportions. The 1810 Benner-Walker House (PA-8-5) in Bellefonte, Centre County, has a pedimented frontispiece with a fanlight and a denticulated cornice on its rubble three-bay facade and Federal-style chimney breasts in its library.[10] As in other outlying parts of the state, once established, Georgian forms proved practical. This was particularly the case with the double-pile central-passage plan, which remained popular through the first two-thirds of the nineteenth century, when local carpenters embellished the five-bay Georgian house with up-to-date Greek Revival or Italianate details.[11] On Judge Parson's House in Williamsport, Lycoming County, (PA-326) those details included flat lintels with rosettes, an Ionic distyle entrance porch, and a plain frieze with small rectangular windows below the cornice.[12] The region is not without high-style Greek Revival temple-form houses, such as Elias Baker's residence in Altoona, Blair County, but generally they were not the work of local builders but big-city architects, in this case Robert Carey Long Jr. of Baltimore.[13] This persistence of the Georgian form and plan as well as the expense of new construction were probably significant factors in homeowners' decisions to remodel Georgian houses rather than build new houses in historical styles. The resultant transmogrifications, such as the cross-gable and carpenter-Gothic windows of the Old Fort Tavern (PA-336) near Centre Hall, Centre County, probably were accepted in their time as modernizations.[14]

  As more settlers moved into the region in the early nineteenth century, and the legislature carved smaller new counties out of larger older ones, entrepreneurs laid out villages that they hoped would grow into towns. They usually established them near a stream that not only provided power for mills that transformed farm and forest products into marketable commodities, but often carried those goods to market as well. Invariably these communities are representative "Pennsylvania towns," with buildings clustered close to the streets and often in relation to the public square.[15] Bedford, with its brick courthouse, church, and residences arranged around the public square, is one of the better-preserved of these many towns, each of which has its own character. Among the exceptions to this pattern is Aaronsburg in Haines Township, Centre County. Aaron Levy, an Amsterdam-born merchant and land speculator in Northumberland, acquired 334 1/2 acres in Penns Valley in 1779 and seven years later laid out a grid plan with two especially broad intersecting streets: the one

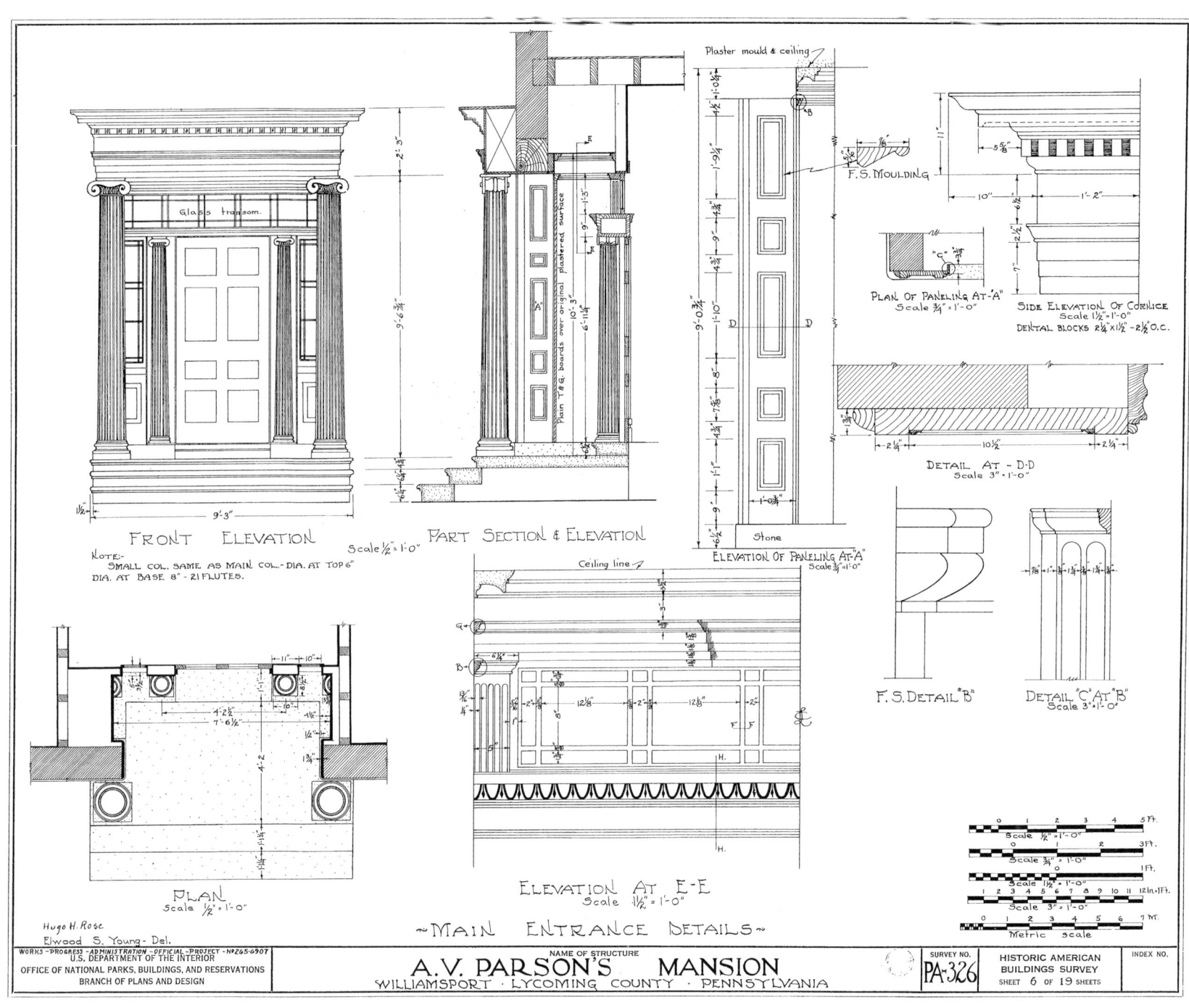

Judge A.V. Parson House (PA-326) Williamsport, Lycoming County. Main entrance details (Hugo H. Rose and Elwood S. Young, delineators, 1936) PA,41-WILPO,1.

hundred-foot-wide Rachel's Way (named for his wife) and the 160-foot-wide Aaron's Square. Levy defied convention by not locating his town close to a waterway. Instead he placed it near the center of the county (and the state) and at the expected intersection of roads to Fort Pitt (later Pittsburgh) and Sunbury (and via the Susquehanna River to Baltimore and Philadelphia). Levy apparently expected that his nascent town's geographically central location would make it a logical site for the county seat. He was wrong; Bellefonte won that honor. When the road intersection never materialized and the land-locked location assured no canal connections, Aaronsburg never grew beyond a quiet agrarian village, which it remains today.[16]

In the countryside, ironmaking emerged early as an important industry. By 1750 Pennsylvania had taken the lead among the British colonies in iron production, and at the outbreak of the Revolution Pennsylvania's furnaces alone were producing half the colonies' iron. Pennsylvania's colonial iron industry was centered in the Piedmont region, but at the close of the colonial era, attention shifted to the Juniata River Valley, whose hillsides possessed all the necessary resources for iron production: superior magnetite iron ore, limestone for fluxing out impurities, forests for charcoal fuel, and rapidly running streams to power the furnaces' bellows.[17]

Because of their relatively isolated sites, charcoal iron works developed "an almost feudal type of community,"[18] and became known as "plantations." In addition to the furnace, with its massive, tall stack, iron plantations included workers' dwellings, an office, a store, a barn, orchards, vegetable gardens, sometimes a gristmill, sawmill, and church, and always the architecturally most sophisticated building of all, the ironmaster's house. As skilled craftsmen and venturesome capitalists, successful ironmasters stood among an area's most important citizens, and their residences reflected their status.[19] Iron plantations like Hopewell Village (PA-5157) in Berks and Chester counties or Cornwall Furnace and its miners village in Lebanon County have not survived in the Ridge and Valley Region. One of the last of the region's ironworks villages, Curtin in Centre County, had been reduced to three workers' houses (PA-5355, 5356, 5357) in ruinous condition when HABS surveyed them in the mid-1980s. Many ironmasters' houses, however, have survived. The size and sophistication of these fieldstone houses varied according to the scale and success of their owners' operation. Only rarely, e.g., the Baker Mansion in Altoona, did any equal the sophistication of such Berks County examples as the 1777 Charming Forge ironmaster's stone house (PA-1022) or the brick 1840 Brooke Manor (PA-1075).

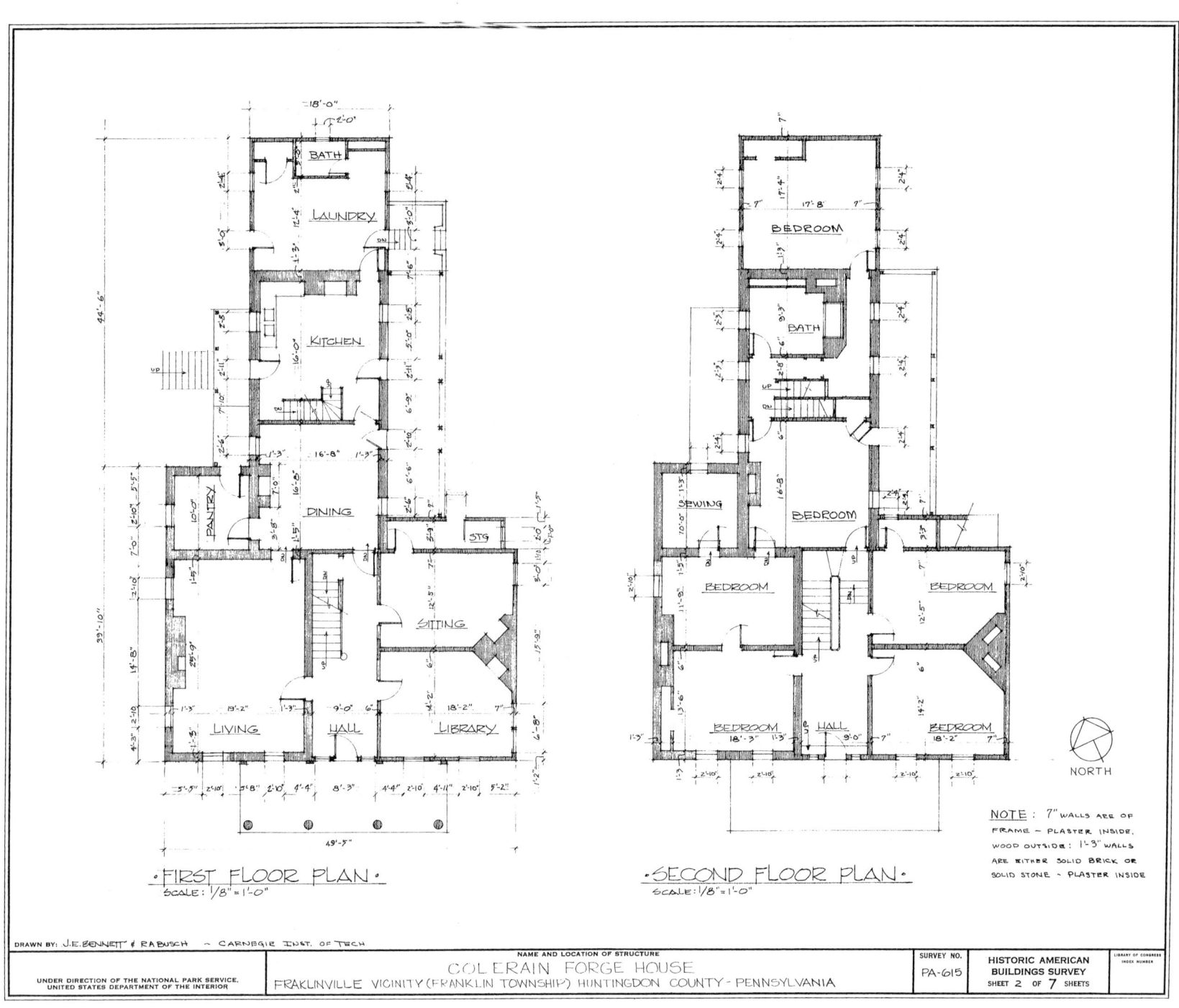

Colerain Forge House (PA-615) Franklinville vicinity (Franklin Township), Huntingdon County.
First and second floor plans (J.E. Bennett and R.A. Busch, delineators, 1968) PA,31-FRNK.V,1.

With its Georgian five-bay coursed-rubble front and central-hall plan, the 1834 Lyons House (PA-611) at Pennsylvania Furnace, Huntingdon County, is representative of the region's early-nineteenth-century examples. Also common was the expansion of a modest late-eighteenth-century ironmaster's house into a more imposing mansion. This was often accomplished by placing a new main block onto an end of the earlier dwelling, which then became a rear wing, as in the case of the Colerain Forge House (PA-615) in Franklin Township, Huntingdon County.[20] Another significant aspect of this house is its changing materials: stone for the initial 1787 part, frame for the 1830 front section, and brick for its lateral 1840 addition.[21]

Pennsylvanians exploited the region's forests not only for charcoal to fuel iron furnaces but also for timber, beginning particularly in the 1850s at the region's north end, in Clinton and Lycoming counties. Lumbermen cut the trees in the winter, mostly north of the region in the Allegheny Plateau, and rafted them on spring freshets to Lock Haven and Williamsport, where they collected the logs behind giant booms to be sawed during the summer and fall months. Because of its great lumber production, Williamsport during the last half of the nineteenth century was known as "Lumber City." In the early 1870s the city was producing over 300 million board feet of lumber. Although the Panic of 1873 drove production down in the mid-1870s, by 1880 it had risen to 200 million board feet, helping to make Pennsylvania for a time the nation's number one lumber producer. Unfortunately Williamsport's lumber industry declined shortly after the turn of the century, and its great steam-powered saw and planing mills are now gone. Its lumber barons' mansions, however, still stand along West Fourth Street. Although overshadowed by the northern reaches' tremendous lumber output, the region's southern mountains, especially in Bedford and Fulton counties, also produced a great deal of lumber in the second half of the nineteenth century.[22]

Efficient overland transportation was essential for the economic and cultural development of the region. Roads were so poor early in the nineteenth century that packhorses, rather than wagons, carried pig iron over the mountains to Pittsburgh's forges; such inefficient distribution cut deeply into ironmasters' profits. Roads gradually improved, but a more significant achievement was the 1834 inauguration of the State Works Main Line canal and railroad between Philadelphia and Pittsburgh. Two parts of this transportation system ran through the Ridge and Valley Region. The Juniata Division covered 127 miles from the Juniata River's mouth at the Susquehanna to Hollidaysburg, Blair County, which, as a major transfer and storage point, became one of the region's two largest towns by 1840. (The other town was Lewistown, Mifflin County, along the same canal.) To overcome the 584-foot rise in elevation along the Juniata Division, the canal's builders had to construct eighty-six locks. At Hollidaysburg engineers conquered the intimidating Allegheny Front by building the unique Allegheny Portage Railroad, a thirty-seven-mile railway of five inclined planes on each slope. A major engineering feat, its construction included not only the inclined planes and the steam-powered hoisting machinery but also a tunnel, and bridges, such as the skew-arch bridge (PA-1232) on the Allegheny and Juniata township line in Blair County. Within fifteen years of the Main Line's completion, the West Branch Canal had opened between Northumberland, Northumberland County, and Farrandsville, Clinton County, on the Susquehanna west of Lock Haven. A private canal extended from Farrandsville along Bald Eagle and Spring Creeks to Bellefonte. Railroads soon introduced even cheaper bulk transport. The Pennsylvania Railroad was running through the region by 1850, following the Juniata River. At first the railroad used the old portage railway, until in 1854 it finished the famous Horseshoe Curve west of Altoona, Blair County, and the long tunnel on the region's western edge, at Gallitzin, Cambria County. Within a few years after the Civil War nearly all significant points in the region enjoyed rail service.[23]

Railroads and canals inaugurated the region's golden age. The heyday of such towns as Hollidaysburg in Blair County, Lewisburg in Union County, and Catawissa in Columbia County was tied directly to the introduction of these transportation systems. As Peirce Lewis points out, however, for towns like Bellefonte this golden age was doomed even as it began. At the same time that canals and railroads were opening the region, the discovery of iron ore in the Mesabi Range, the completion of the Sault Sainte Marie Canal to Lake Superior, and the development of the Bessemer process would combine to destroy the region's iron industry by the beginning of the twentieth century. Railroad towns, on the other hand, such as Altoona, Blair County, with its extensive rail yards, and Berwick, Columbia County, with its railroad car works, continued to prosper well into the twentieth century.[24]

Canals and railroads not only moved iron, lumber, and wheat out of the region but also carried architects and design books into the region. Prosperity encouraged pride. Prosperous citizens and prospering towns sought monuments to their success, and ambitious architects eager to ply their trade were no more than a day or two

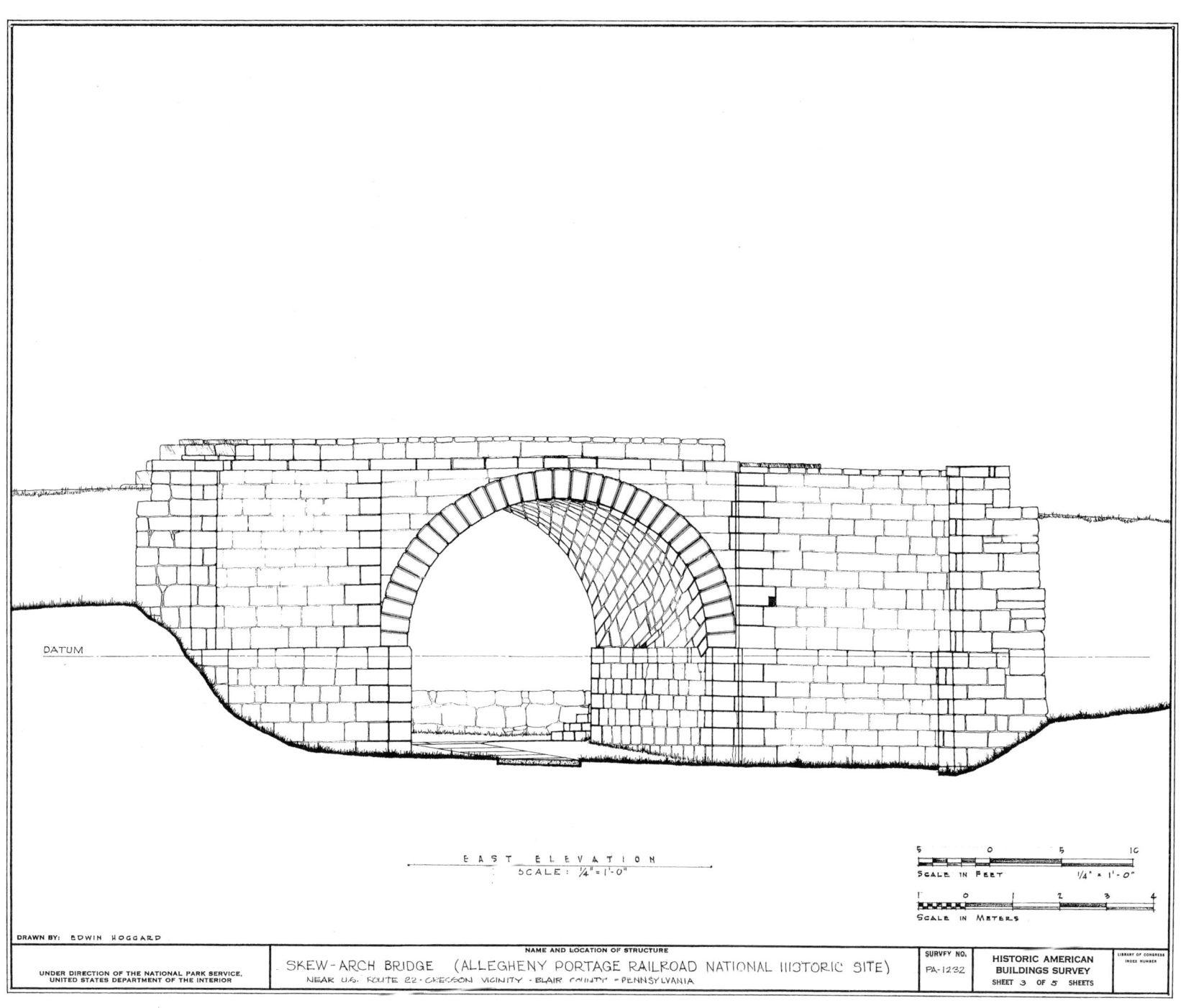

Allegheny Portage Railroad, Skew-Arch Bridge (PA-1232) Cresson vicinity, Allegheny-Juniata Townships, Blair County. East elevation (Edwin Hoggard, delineator, 1965) PA,7-CRES.V,1.

Region III: Ridge and Valley

away. Such mid-century Philadelphia architects as J. C. Hoxie and Samuel Sloan received innumerable commissions across the Pennsylvania countryside.[25] Sloan apparently visited some of the region's county seats. He received commissions for the courthouses in Williamsport, Lycoming County (1860-61), and Lock Haven, Clinton County (1867-69), and his work was so admired that a contractor copied the Williamsport building for the Northumberland County Courthouse in Sunbury.[26] Sloan probably cultivated prospective clients in his travels, which would help to explain why he was asked to design Great Island Presbyterian Church in Lock Haven (1863-69), the W. J. Elliot House in Williamsport (1860), and Eli Slifer's Delta Place (1860-61) in Lewisburg.[27] Sloan's imprint may have been even greater because of the many design books he authored, beginning with *The Model Architect* in 1852. Without written documentation, however, it is difficult to determine if he personally designed some buildings or if local carpenters copied their designs from Sloan's books.[28] On rare occasions a house's design was drawn from a design book. William M. Allison's House in Gregg Township, Centre County, duplicates in every detail a "Domestic Gothic Style" example illustrated in A. J. Bicknell's 1873 *Detail, Cottage, and Constructive Architecture*.[29] More important was the work of local builder-architects, such as Henry Hipple in Jersey Shore and Lock Haven. Such men may not have been especially innovative, but their designs exhibited a sound understanding of changing styles' massing and details.[30] By the end of the nineteenth century, improved transportation allowed local architects to move around within the region. Bellefonte, Centre County, for example, has late-nineteenth-century buildings designed by Williamsport and Danville (Montour County) architects as well as Philadelphia architects.[31]

Ironically, as improved communication and transportation systems were breaking down the region's cultural isolation by the end of the nineteenth century, its best architecture had already been built. As local economies declined after 1900 and population leveled out, old buildings began to decay and new construction became increasingly uncommon. After World War II, in desperate attempts to revitalize local economies, historic buildings were demolished and replaced with lesser structures or the lots were left empty, marking a net loss for the built environment.[32] Except for a few bright spots, State College being among the brightest, the short-term outlook for the region's built environment is dim.[33]

Notes

[1]Moving in two arcs from the southwest to the northeast parallel with the ridges and valleys, the ten eastern counties are Fulton, Huntingdon, Perry, Juniata, Mifflin, Snyder, Union, Northumberland, Montour, and Columbia, and the five western counties are Bedford, Blair, Centre, Clinton, and Lycoming. The county lines of the architectural-geographical region fit remarkably well within the topographically defined Ridge and Valley Region. Only the northwest quarter of Centre County and northern halves of Clinton and Lycoming Counties are outside of the geographical region. Raymond E. Murphy and Marion Murphy, *Pennsylvania: A Regional Geography* (Harrisburg: The Pennsylvania Book Service, 1937), 18.

[2]The Ridge and Valley geographical region continues northeastward beyond this fifteen-county area, narrowing as it exits Pennsylvania through Monroe County into New Jersey, and southwestward into Maryland and Virginia. For historical reasons, we have terminated the architectural Ridge and Valley region on its northwest edge at Columbia County, before it enters the anthracite region, which is treated in a separate essay. Ibid., 13-14, 27-32, 297-99; Ronald F. Abler, David J. Cuff, William J. Long, Edward K. Muller, and Wilbur Zelinsky, *The Atlas of Pennsylvania* (Philadelphia: Temple University Press, 1989), 19, 21-23, 50. For an explanation in layman's terms of the formation of Pennsylvania's geology, in particular the Folded Appalachians, see J. Ronald Mowery, "Geologic History of Pennsylvania," *Pennsylvania Heritage* 4 (September 1978): 7-12. Ibid., 13-14, 27-32.

[3]Nearly every county in the region suffered Indian attacks and massacres, especially during the French and Indian War. In present-day Snyder County in October 1755, for example, twenty-six settlers were killed, captured, or wounded; a few weeks later forty-seven families in present-day Fulton County were either killed or captured. The same uprising that led to the Stanford family's demise also brought a massacre to Lycoming County in June 1778. The final purchase of Indian land in 1784 effectively removed Indians from the state, and General Anthony Wayne's victory over the Indians at the Battle of Fallen Timers west of Lake Erie ten years later ended any threat of future Indian uprisings in Pennsylvania. Martha P. Birchenall, Sylvia Carson, and Gregory Ramsey, *Historic Buildings of Centre County, Pennsylvania: The Historic Registration Project of Centre County Library* (University Park, Pa.: Keystone Books, 1980), 6; Solon J. Buck and Elizabeth Hawthorn Buck, *The Planting of Civilization in Western Pennsylvania* (Pittsburgh: University of Pittsburgh Press, 1939), 137; Wayland F. Dunaway, A

History of Pennsylvania (second ed.; New York: Prentice-Hall, Inc., 1948), 156; Elsie S. Greathead, *The History of Fulton County, Pennsylvania* (McConnellsburg, Pa.: Fulton County News, 1936), 1-3, 13-17; Lois Mulkearn and Edwin V. Pugh, *A Traveler's Guide to Historic Western Pennsylvania* (Pittsburgh: University of Pittsburgh Press, 1954), 130; Sylvester K. Stevens, *Pennsylvania: Birthplace of a Nation* (New York: Random House, 1964), 54-55, 90.

[4]Mulkearn and Pugh, *Traveler's Guide*, 130; Stevens, *Pennsylvania*, 46, 364-65; A. H. Carstens, *Pennsylvania's Best*, (Cresco, Pa.: Pennsylvania Publications, 1960), 256.

[5]The Nittany Valley runs northeastward from Sinking Valley in northeastern Blair County, through northwestern Huntingdon County and the middle of Centre County, to southeastern Clinton County. Not only do many of the region's people farm, they farm on a full-time basis. In all but one of the region's counties, most of the farmers pursue agriculture as their principal occupation. (In Blair County, the one exception, between 40 and 49 percent of the farmers are full-time; in Mifflin County, on the other hand, more than 70 percent of the farmers list farming as their primary pursuit.) Nevertheless, outside of the Nittany Valley most farms remain low in value. Abler et al., *Atlas of Pennsylvania*, 182, 204, 206; Murphy and Murphy, *Pennsylvania*, 299-301, 311-14.

[6]The Pennsylvania farmhouse is characterized by a symmetrical facade with two front doors; it is discussed in the Pennsylvania essay. In the Neff House the stairway was centrally located with doorways leading to it from the rear of each room. Based on surviving examples, it seems that settlers in the Ridge and Valley Region preferred two-story log houses. In at least one case, in 1775, a Lewisburg resident built a three-story log house; a plank addition was built in 1810. Carstens, *Pennsylvania's Best*, p. 285. The two Centre County log houses are discussed and illustrated in Birchenall et al., *Historic Buildings of Centre County*, 14-15, 22-23. The Germanic log house is discussed in Robert C. Bucher, "The Continental Log House," *Pennsylvania Folklife* 12 (Summer 1962): 14-19.

[7]Quoted in Birchenall et al., *Historic Buildings of Centre County*, 174.

[8]In addition to erecting the bell tower, the congregation built a new rear wing, plastered the interior, added pews, and roughcast the exterior. At the time of the 1842 renovations, Hardman Philips wanted to make the building an Episcopal church, but townspeople insisted on keeping the church ecumenical. Ibid., 174-76.

[9]Single-pile houses (i.e., houses one-room deep) were common in the region during the first half of the nineteenth century. The scarcity of high-style details is also evident inside the region's early houses where mantelpieces and staircases lack the finely carved and turned embellishments found in eastern urban areas. There are no balusters, for example, on the stairs of the John Thompson House, a coursed-rubble double-pile house built circa 1814 in College Township, Centre County. Ibid., 46-47, 69, 72-75, 80-81, 84, 116-17, 164-65, 167, 178-80.

[10]Judge Walker directed the construction of this house for General Benner, who then rented it to the judge. For a century this house was home for a long list of local leaders, including high-ranking military officers, ironmasters, jurists, and political figures. Ruth Inez Kapp, *Belle-*

fonte, Its Founding and Development, from 1795 to 1835 (Bellefonte, Pa.: Mary Ellen McQuiston Endowment, 1937), 2-3; Dean E. Kennedy, "The Linn House, PA-8-5," HABS Report (Washington, D.C.: Library of Congress, 1936), 1-2.

[11]Ibid., 27, 31, 88-89, 108, 142-45, 171.

[12]The Parson House's facade, however, is not symmetrical; close examination shows that the eastern (right) half of the facade is wider than the western half. This is visible in the greater distances between the windows on the eastern end and is documented by HABS measured drawings. In addition to its Georgian proportions, the house's six-over-six sash windows, round-arched gable-end window, and chimney curtains are details more commonly associated with earlier neoclassical architecture than with the Greek Revival. The house was demolished circa 1940.

[13]In executing Long's 1844 plans a local builder made minor changes in the design, including an enlargement of the Ionic Order on the house's front portico. He finished the house in 1848. Harold B. Dickson, *A Hundred Pennsylvania Buildings* (State College: Bald Eagle Press, 1954), pl. 49.

[14]These "remuddlings" are still done today, as *The Old-House Journal* has reminded us. For three other late-nineteenth-century examples in Centre County, see Centre Hall, Oak Hall, and Harmony Forge Mansion in Birchenall et al., *Historic Buildings of Centre County*, 90-95, 164-65.

[15]Wilbur Zelinsky, "The Pennsylvania Town: An Overdue Geographical Account," *The Geographical Review* 67 (April 1977): 127-47. Zelinsky describes a host of characteristics of the Pennsylvania town, such as compactness, brick facades, duplex or semidetached houses, tree-lined streets, open space or squares, and a system of well-maintained alleys. For an excellent sampling of Centre County small towns and villages, illustrated with 1874 maps and contemporary photographs, see Birchenall et al., *Historic Buildings of Centre County*, 31-37, 50-61, 104-109, 120-34, 168-73.

[16]Born in Amsterdam in 1742, Levy immigrated to Philadelphia about 1760. He appears to have been among the first wave of settlers in Northumberland in 1769. On receiving news of the Wyoming massacre in July 1778, Levy and his wife Rachel fled to Lancaster, where they stayed for the duration of the Revolutionary War. After peace was restored, he and Rachel returned to Northumberland where he was deeply engaged in land speculation throughout the Ridge and Valley Region. In the mid-1790s, the Levys moved to Philadelphia. Sidney M. Fish, *Aaron Levy: Founder of Aaronsburg* (New York: American Jewish Historical Society, 1951), 1-13, 19-24, 31-35. The town is sensitively portrayed in text and photos in Birchenall et al., *Historic Buildings of Centre County*, 9-13.

[17]Arthur Cecil Bining, *Pennsylvania Iron Manufacture in the Eighteenth Century* (second ed.; Harrisburg: Pennsylvania Historical and Museum Commission, 1973), 50-52, 55; Sylvester K. Stevens, *Pennsylvania: Titan of Industry*, 3 vols. (New York: Lewis Historical Publishing Company, Inc., 1948) 1:57-61.

[18] Stevens, *Pennsylvania: Titan of Industry*, 1:66.

[19] Bining, *Pennsylvania Iron Manufacture*, 19-27.

[20] Other ironmasters' houses that evolved in a similar manner include the Logan Furnace Mansion in Spring Township, Centre County, in which the rubble two-story house of circa 1800 became the rear wing of a larger-scale coursed-rubble five-bay central-hall house in 1818. Also in Spring Township, Centre County, is the William Thomas House, a five-bay fieldstone house with a central-hall plan that was built in 1835 onto the end of the smaller-scale two-story random-rubble house that ironmaster William Lamb had built in 1785. Both are described and illustrated in Birchenall et al., *Historic Buildings of Centre County*, 116-20.

[21] According to Peirce Lewis, the more common chronological order for building materials in Bellefonte, if not the region, is stone, brick, and wood. Peirce F. Lewis, "Small Town in Pennsylvania," *Annals of the Association of American Geographers* 62 (June 1972): 327.

[22] Abler et al., *Atlas of Pennsylvania*, 95; Stevens, *Pennsylvania: Titan of Industry*, 270-73.

[23] William H. Shank, *The Amazing Pennsylvania Canals* (York, Pa.: American Canal and Transportation Center, 1981), 17-22, 25-33, 52-53; James M. Swank, *Progressive Pennsylvania: A Record of the Remarkable Industrial Development of the Keystone State* (Philadelphia: J.B. Lippincott Company, 1908), 139-48, 104-104, 144, 171; Murphy and Murphy, *Pennsylvania*, 128-29; Stevens, *Pennsylvania: Titan of Industry*, 58, 133. Fulton County never got a railroad. Plans for the South Penn Railroad reached the point of digging tunnels, but the railroad was never completed. Anne J. Lodge, "Fulton County: Where Country Is Still Country," *Pennsylvania Heritage* 10 (Summer 1984): 37.

[24] Craig A. Newton, "Columbia County Is Diversity," *Pennsylvania Heritage* 9 (Summer 1983): 2-8; Charles M. Snyder, "One Should Not Overlook Union County," *Pennsylvania Heritage* 4 (September 1978): 4; Lewis, "Small Town in Pennsylvania," 340-45; Mulkearn and Pugh, *Traveler's Guide*, 154, 157.

[25] Hoxie designed buildings across Pennsylvania, from Easton to Warren, including a Presbyterian church in Philipsburg, Centre County. Richard J. Webster, "Stephen D. Button: Italianate Stylist" (M.A. thesis, University of Delaware, 1963), 75-76.

[26] The Northumberland County Commissioners were so impressed with the Lycoming County Courthouse that they cited it as their model when they solicited bids in late 1864. D. S. Rissel, the builder of the Williamsport courthouse, won the contract because he already possessed the plans and specifications of the commissioners' model. He erected in Sunbury a mirror image of Sloan's courthouse in Williamsport, shifting the cupola from the left front tower to the right front tower. Understandably, Sloan sued and received a settlement. Lycoming County demolished its courthouse in 1969; its illegitimate twin in Sunbury still stands. Harold N. Cooledge, Jr., *Samuel Sloan: Architect of Philadelphia, 1815-1884* (Philadelphia: University of Pennsylvania Press, 1986), 79-81, 85, 208-9, 221.

[27] The Elliot House was demolished in the early twentieth century. Great Island Presbyterian Church and Eli Stifer's Delta Place survive. The church has been extensively remodeled, but Delta Place was restored in 1975-76 and is open as a historic house museum. Ibid., 85, 210, 213.

[28] Dean Wagner in Lock Haven attributes two houses, a church, a hotel, and a commercial building to Sloan between 1854 and 1863, but documentation establishing Sloan as the architect exists for only two Lock Haven buildings, the 1863 Great Island Presbyterian Church and the 1869 C. A. Mayer House. Unfortunately the church has been extensively altered and Mayer's towered Italian villa has been demolished. If local builders were indeed emulating Sloan's designs, his books were achieving at least two of their goals: improving taste and introducing new styles to the hinterland. In addition to his appropriately titled *The Model Architect,* which went through five editions between 1852 and 1873, Sloan wrote *City and Suburban Architecture* (two editions, 1859, 1867), *Sloan's Constructive Architecture* (three editions, 1859, 1866, 1873), and *Sloan's Homestead Architecture* (three editions, 1861, 1867, 1870). Dean R. Wagner, ed., *Historic Lock Haven: An Architectural Survey* (Lock Haven: Clinton County Historical Society, 1979), 36, 41, 45, 50, 67, 70, 88; Dell Upton, "Pattern Books and Professionalism: Aspects of the Transformation of Domestic Architecture in America, 1800-1860," *Winterthur Portfolio* 19 (Summer/Autumn 1984): 107-150; Cooledge, *Samuel Sloan,* 250-51.

[29] There are three minor deviations. Allison's house does not have the slightly pedimented window surrounds that appear in the Bicknell drawing, and the builder of Allison's house attenuated the front dormer and attic window. Bicknell's book was one of many architectural design books that were published throughout the nineteenth century. Because these books' purpose was to influence taste rather than to sell plans, it is rare to find a design executed in such detail as the Allison House. Plan books, on the other hand, were cheap catalogs of house plans for sale, and their sample illustrations were indeed executed. A. J. Bicknell, *Detail, Cottage, and Constructive Architecture: Containing 75 Large Lithographic Plates* (New York: A. J. Bicknell & Co., 1873; reprint ed., Watkins Glen, N.Y.: American Life Foundation, 1975), pl. 15; Birchenall et al., *Historic Buildings of Centre County,* 48-49. Upton, "Pattern Books and Professionalism," 107-8; James L. Garvin, "Mail-Order House Plans and American Victorian Architecture," *Winterthur Portfolio* 16 (Winter 1981): 309-334.

[30] Henry Hipple, Sr., was born into a family of builders in the Philadelphia area. In 1834 he moved to Jersey Shore and then to Lock Haven in 1861. Wagner, ed., *Historic Lock Haven,* 61.

[31] Among the works by late-nineteenth-century Philadelphia architects are the Bush Arcade (1887), by P. A. Walsh and William J. Nichols's cottage (1891), by Minerva Parker. Regional architects included C. S. Wetzel of Danville, who designed the W. F. Reynolds Bank Building in 1887, and Truman P. Reitmeyer from Williamsport, who extensively remodeled Governor Daniel H. Hastings's house in 1897. *Philadelphia Real Estate Record and Builders' Guide* 6 (25 March 1891): 192; Birchenall et al., *Historic Buildings of Centre County,* 129, 132-33.

[32] Nancy Shedd's 1976 study of the old section of Huntingdon cites the loss of forty-six buildings since 1911 in the four-block by three-block area. Parking lots, all but one of them "built"

since 1956, have replaced twenty-five of those forty-six buildings. Nancy S. Shedd, *An Architectural Study of the Ancient Borough of Huntingdon* (Huntingdon, Pa.: John S. Rodgers Company, 1976), 24. Bellefonte, which in the last three decades has lost people and trees as well as buildings, is discussed in Lewis, "Small Town in Pennsylvania," 323-51, see especially 343-48.

[33]Fifty years ago State College, with a population of less than 5,000 people, was smaller than neighboring Bellefonte. Today it is classified a metropolitan area. "The growth of State College, however, merely typifies a national trend in the late twentieth century, where money is attracted by a combination of brains, high-tech industry, and pleasant environmental surroundings. Colleges and universities possess such things quite naturally. . . ." (Abler et al., *Atlas of Pennsylvania*, 7.) Those conditions have helped small university towns like Lewisburg, home of Bucknell University, but it is more difficult for those towns whose colleges are small as in the cases of Juniata College in Huntingdon and Lycoming College in Williamsport. For a brief description of State College in the late 1930s, see Murphy and Murphy, *Pennsylvania*, 315.

Catalog

Blair County

Altoona

America's Industrial Heritage Project

As part of this NPS project, HABS documented three neighborhoods and two individual structures in 1989. The neighborhoods recorded were: Downtown and Ward 1; Ward 4; Llyswen. The individual structures recorded were: Dudley, Charles, House; Masonic Temple Building

Cresson Vicinity (Allegheny-Juniata Townships)

Allegheny Portage Railroad, Skew-Arch Bridge (PA-1232), N side of U.S. Rte. 22, 2.6 mi. E of Pa. 53, on Allegheny-Juniata Township line. Owned and operated by National Park Service as part of Allegheny Portage Railroad National Historic Site. Coursed ashlar, single skew arch with 19'-6" span and 16'-8" vertical clearance, 20'-11" opening with rusticated voussoirs and quoins flanked by segmental retaining walls, 16'-2" width of road. Built 1832-33. Built to carry traffic over Allegheny Portage Railroad, used until 1922. 5 sheets (1965, including plans, elevations, section). See Allegheny Portage Railroad, Staple Bend Tunnel (PA-1233), Cambria County, Geistown Vicinity, for site plan. LC code: PA,7-CRES.V,1. NHS.

Centre County

Bellefonte Borough

Benner-Walker House (Henry S. Linn House) (PA-8-5), 133 N. Allegheny St. Random rubble, 30'-6" (three-bay front) x 36'-3" with offset rear kitchen ell (21' x 33'-6"), two-and-a-half stories with basement, gable roof with dormers, pedimented doorway with fanlight flanked by pilasters on E (front) elevation; side hall plan. Main block built 1810 by Judge Jonathan Walker for General Philip Benner; 1841 front porch added (ca. 1924 porch removed and original doorway replaced); 1870 kitchen ell added; balustraded balcony at second floor level with glass bay below on ell added after 1870 (glass bay removed after 1934); porch added on W elevation of main block after 1870; 1907 brick wing added at rear of kitchen. Now a bank and apartment. 11 sheets (1934, including plans, elevations, section, details); 3 ext. photos (1934); 3 data pages (1936). LC code: PA,14-BELF,1. NR (Bellefonte Historic District).

Brockerhoff House (PA-333), NE corner of Spring and Bishop Sts. Brick, L-shaped, 46'-2" (five-bay front) x 36'-3" with rear ell (26'-3" x 30'-4"), two-and-a-half stories, gable roof with dormers, door with large fanlight and pediment supported by columns on S (front) elevation, tetrastyle porch with balustraded deck across E elevation, distyle entrance porch on W elevation, two-story porch on N elevation; central hall plan. Built 1833; demolished 1960; doorway moved to The State Museum, Harrisburg. 12 sheets (1935, including plans, elevations, details); 3 ext. photos (1935); 1 data page (1936). LC code: PA,14-BELF,3.

Harris, James, House (Willowbank) (PA-331), 308 Potter St. Random rubble, L-shaped, 81'-2" (seven-bay front) x 42'-4", two-and-a-half stories with basement, gable roof with dormers, entrance porches on S (front) and W elevations (W enclosed and S removed after 1935), two-story porch across N elevation (second story added after 1935), blind semi-elliptical door with louvered fanlight and side lights on ell (probably moved from original location in arched opening in N wall of original building; fine interior woodwork. Built 1795 (originally E five bays of S elevation, central hall plan); early addition of two-bay wing to W and ell to N; many original openings changed when altered for use as apartments after 1935. James Harris was cofounder of Bellefonte. 10 sheets (1934, including plans, elevations, section, details); 3 ext. photos (1935), 1 int. photo (1935); 1 data page (1936). LC code: PA,14-BELF,2.

Lin, Henry S., House. See Benner-Walker House.

Walker House. See Benner-Walker House.

Willowbank. See Harris, James, House.

Boalsburg (Harris Township)

Boalsburg Tavern (Duffy's Tavern) (PA-8-7), N side of E. Main St., E of intersection with N. Church St. Random rubble, uneven U-shaped, 56'-2" (seven-bay front) x 55'-2", two-and-a-half stories, gable roof with dormers, two entrances on S (front) elevation (tavern on W side, innkeeper's quarters on E side), two-story stone kitchen wing and one-and-a-half-story frame kitchen wing to rear of tavern, two-story brick kitchen wing to rear of innkeeper's quarters. Built 1819; innkeeper's quarters (E two bays) and three kitchen wings probably additions to original five-bay central hall plan structure; partially destroyed by fire 1934; repaired and used as restaurant. Stopping place on the stagecoach run. 8 sheets (1934, including plans, elevations, section, details); 6 ext. photos (1934), 1 int. photo (1934); 2 data pages (1936). LC code: PA,14-BOLBU,1. NR (Boalsburg Historic District).

Duffy's Tavern. See Boalsburg Tavern.

Centre Hall Vicinity (Potter Township)

Old Fort Tavern (PA-336), NE corner of State Rte. 45 and State Rte. 144, S of Centre Hall. Coursed rubble, L-shaped, 46'-9" (five-bay front) x 35'-2" with kitchen ell, two-and-a-half stories, gable roof, two entrances on S (front) elevation (innkeeper's quarters on W side and tavern on E side), triangular-topped window in front gable, porches on E and N elevations (N porch replaced with two-story addition after 1935); central hall plan. Built ca. 1785 (innkeeper's quarters, W two bays of S elevation, built before tavern section); shed added behind kitchen before 1935; porch added across S elevation after 1935; used as hotel and gas station in 1935; now American Legion Post. 10 sheets (1935, including plans, elevations, details); 3 ext. photos (1935); 1 data page (1936). LC code: PA,14-CENHA.V,1.

Curtin (Boggs Township)

Bathurst House (Ruins). See Curtin Village, Workers' Houses.

Curtin Village, Workers' Houses (PA-5356, 5355, 5357), on LR14010. Ruins of three frame and log workers' houses from Curtin Village, a self-contained community for the Eagle Iron Works founded by Roland Curtin in 1810 and remained in operation until 1922, last active ironworks in Centre County. Owned by the state, Curtin Village is restored and opened as a museum administered by the Roland Curtin Foundation. NR.

> *Bathurst House* (Ruins) (PA-5356). 7 ext. photos (1984), 1 ext. photo of outbuilding ruins (1984). LC code: PA,14-CURT,1.
>
> *Gingher House* (Ruins) (PA-5355). 6 ext. photos (1984). LC code: PA,14-CURT,2.
>
> *Schultz, Charles, House* (Ruins) (PA-5357). 6 ext. photos (1984). LC code: PA,14-CURT,3.

Gingher House (Ruins). See Curtin Village, Workers' Houses.

Schultz, Charles, House (Ruins). See Curtin Village, Workers' Houses.

Nittany Vicinity (Walker Township)

Schaeffer House (PA-8-6), S side of State Rte. 64, approx. 1 mi. SW of Nittany. Coursed rubble, L-shaped, 28'-1" (three-bay front) x 34'-2" with kitchen ell (18' x 26'-7"), two-and-a-half stories with basement, one-and-a-half-story ell, gable roofs, pedimented entrance porch on S elevation; side hall plan. Built 1820; one-story board and batten summer kitchen connected to rear porch. 6 sheets (1934, including plans, elevations, section, details); 4 ext. photos (1934), 1 int. photo (1934); 2 data pages (1936). LC code: PA,14-NIT,1.

Philipsburg Borough

Union Church (PA-334), NW side of E. Presqueisle St., SW of intersection with Seventh St. Log covered with roughcast stucco, 24'-9" x 30'-6" with entrance tower and rear wing, one story with three-story tower, gable roofs, crenelated entrance tower with finials and corner buttresses on SE elevation, pointed-arch windows and door. Built 1820 (originally a meetinghouse and schoolhouse); 1842 square tower and rear wing added, shape of windows changed, walls covered with roughcast stucco. 7 sheets (1935, including plans, elevations, details); 2 ext. photos (1935), 1 int. photo (1935); 1 data page (1936). LC code: PA,14-PHILBU,2. NR.

Philipsburg (Rush Township)

Halehurst. See Philips, Hardman, House.

Philips, Hardman, House (Halehurst) (PA-332), SE side of E. Presqueisle St., set back from road. Frame covered with stucco, irregular L-shaped, 72'-8" (seven-bay front), two-and-a-half stories, gambrel roof with dormers (originally gable roof), door with fanlight and side lights on NW (front) elevation, colonnaded porch with balustrade across NW elevation, two-story bays and porte-cochere on NE elevation, porch across rear, greenhouse on SE elevation, ell to SW with frame kitchen wing at rear, porch on ell connected to frame outbuilding. Built 1813; altered late nineteenth century. 10 sheets (1935, including plans, elevations, details); 2 ext. photos (1935); 1 data page (1936). LC code: PA,14-PHILBU,1. NR.

Rock Forge (Benner Township)

Benner House (PA-335), W side of Spring Creek, .5 mi. downstream from Fish Research Station, approx. 5 mi. SW of Bellefonte, now property of Rockview State Correctional Institution. Coursed rubble (S front elevation) and random rubble, L-shaped, 50'-10" (five-bay front) x 23'-10" (two bays) with 21' x 30'-2" ell, two-and-a-half stories, gable roof, doorway with pedimented porch on S elevation; central hall plan. Built 1812; ruinous 1935; demolished. 9 sheets (1935, including plans, elevations, details); 2 ext. photos (1935), 1 int. photo (1935). LC code: PA,14-ROLFO,1.

Clinton County

Lock Haven

Frank-Harvey House (PA-1304), 229 N. Jay St., SW corner of Jay and Bald Eagle Sts. Frame with clapboarding, L-shaped, 34'-4" (five-bay front) x 24' with kitchen ell to W 26'-7" x 20' (two bays), two-and-a-half stories with one-and-a-half story ell, gable roofs, recessed door with transom and side lights on W (front) elevation, Greek Revival details; central hall plan. Built ca. 1851; ell probably later addition; demolished 1975. 8 sheets (1975, including site plans, plans, elevations, section, details); 1 ext. photo (1975); 2 data pages (1975). LC code: PA,18-LOKHA,4.

Harvey House. See Frank-Harvey House.

McCormick, John F., House (PA-1305), 234 E. Church St., SW corner of Church and Jay Sts. Brick, originally L-shaped (U-shaped with additions), 28'-4" (three-bay front) x 53'-7", two-and-a-half stories, gable roof with parapets at gable ends, entrance with transom and side lights on N (front) elevation (changed to bay window), Greek Revival details; side hall plan. Built ca. 1842; John Stewart, builder; wings added to original ell and main block; remodeled as apartments; demolished 1975. 11 sheets (1975, including site plans, plans, elevations, section, details); 1 ext. photo (1975); 3 data pages (1975). LC code: PA,18-LOKHA,1.

Mussina, Lyons, House (PA-1306), 123 N. Jay St. Frame with rusticated wooden siding (E and W elevations) and vertical wooden siding (S elevation and ell), L-shaped, 40'-1" (three-bay front) x 45'-6" with rear kitchen ell, two-and-a-half stories, concave mansard roof with semicircular dormers, bracketed cornice, one and three-story bays on E (front) elevation, semicircular openings with label moldings, carved porch with scroll brackets, Second Empire details. Built ca. 1869; George Hipple, builder; two-story kitchen wing and one-story storage wing added to ell; remodeled as apartments; demolished 1975. 11 sheets (1975, including site plans, plans, elevations, section, details); 1 ext. photo (1975); 2 data pages (1975). LC code: PA,18-LOKHA,3.

Vosburg, Andrew, House (PA-1303), 302 E. Church St., SE corner of Church and Jay Sts. Brick, T-shaped, 40'-4" (five-bay front) x 32'-6", two-and-a-half stories with basement, gable roof with parapets at gable ends, entrance with Doric pilasters and entablature with recessed door with transom and side lights on N (front) elevation, two-and-a-half-story frame kitchen wing with two-story side porches on S elevation, Greek Revival details; central hall plan. Built 1852; Henry Hipple, builder; one-story frame and glass shop wing added 1920; demolished 1975. 10 sheets (1975, including site plans, plans, elevations, section, details); 1 ext. photo (1975); 3 data pages (1975). LC code: PA,18-LOKHA,2.

Columbia County

Berwick Vicinity

Methodist Episcopal Church (PA-213), N side of State Rte. 93, at intersection with RD #2, 1.7 mi. NW of Berwick. Coursed rubble, 40'-9" (four-bay front) x 29'-6" (two bays), one story, gable roof, two entrances on S elevation; partition originally divided interior into church and school (removed), pulpit platform on W wall (not original), vaulted ceiling (removed). Built 1808 (date stone added 1924); interior altered. 4 sheets (1936, including plan, elevations, section); 2 ext. photos (1936), 1 int. photo (1936); 3 data pages (1936). LC code: PA,19-BER.V,l.

Catawissa Borough

Quaker Meetinghouse (PA-212), S side of South St., between S. Third and S. Fourth Sts. Log, 30' x 27'-6", one story, gable roof; two rooms (men's side and women's side) with elevated platforms at N end. Built 1774-76. 4 sheets (1936, including plan, elevations, details); 1 ext. photo (1936), 1 photo of heating stove (1936); 3 data pages (1936). LC code: PA,19-CAT,l. NR.

Millville Borough

Friends Meetinghouse (PA-218), S side of Maine St. (State Rte. 254), E of intersection with Chestnut St. Brick, 60'-5" (six-bay front) x 40', one story, gable roof, two double doors and wooden porch on SW elevation; men's meeting room on NW side and women's meetingroom on SE side. Built 1846 (second meetinghouse on sight). 4 sheets(1936, including plan, elevations, details); 1 ext. photo (1936); 3 data pages (1936). LC code: PA,19-MILV, 1.

Huntingdon County

Alexandria Borough

America's Industrial Heritage Project

As part of this NPS project, HABS documented two nineteenth-century towns located on the Pennsylvania Main Line Canal, Alexandria and Saltsburg in Indiana County, with photographs and written data in 1988. Records being processed 1990.

The Alexandria structures recorded were: Alexandria High School (PA-5411); Alexandria Memorial Public Library (PA-5414); Alexandria Presbyterian Church (PA-5413); Alexandria, Town of (PA-5407); Baker, Soloman, House (PA-5404); Cameron, James, House (PA-5394); Charlton, Dr. James, House (PA-5398); Connor, Francis, House (PA-5403); Cresswell, John, House (PA-5400); Cross, Benjamin, House (PA-5395); German Reformed Church (PA-5412); Grafius, Israel, House (PA-5399); Houtz, Dr. Daniel, House (PA-5401); Houtz, Dr. Daniel, Office (PA-5402); McManus, Patrick, House (PA-5393); Pennsylvania Canal Lock Keeper's House (PA-5406); Pennsylvania Railroad Station (PA-5415); Porter, John, House (PA-5397); Stewart, Thomas, House (PA-5408); Stitt, Alexander, House (PA-5396); Thompson Carriage House (PA-5405); Walker, Evander P., Store (PA-5410); Willibrand, Henry, Brewery (PA-5409)

Franklinville Vicinity (Franklin Township)

Colerain Forge House (PA-615), set back on NE corner of State Rte. 45 and LR31106 (road to Huntingdon Furnace), approx. .5 mi. SW of Franklinville. Large irregular T-shaped house built in four stages: main block frame with clapboarding (E three bays) and brick (W two bays), approx. 49' (five-bay front) x 29'; rear stuccoed stone wing approx. 18' x 38' (four bays); frame wing with board and batten siding approx. 18' x 18' (two bays) to rear of stone wing; two-and-a-half stories, gable roofs with dormers, central doors with wide transoms and side lights flanked by pilasters on first and second stories of S (front) elevation, Doric tetrastyle porch on S elevation. Stone wing built 1787; frame section of main block added 1830; brick section of main block added 1840; rear frame wing added 1860-70. Original house probably built by Richard Ricketts in 1787; enlarged to present plan by Stewart family, owners of Colerain Forge. 7 sheets (1968, including site plan, plans, elevations, details). LC code: PA,31-FRNK.V,1.

McAlevys Fort Vicinity (Jackson Township)

McBurney Manor House and McAlevys Fort General Store (PA-5382), State Rte. 26 and 305. Robert McBurney acquired land in 1844 and built a brick house and bakeoven on the property. He later acquired adjacent 1840 McAlevys Fort General Store. 1 sheet (1988, site plan). LC code: PA,31-MAFO.V, 1-A,B.

McAlevys Fort General Store (PA-5382A). Brick, 24'-1" (three-bay front) x 36'-3", two stories, gable roof with gable end over entrance, semicircular window in gable end, door with transom, one-story porch across front elevation. Built 1840. 2 sheets (1988, including plans, elevations, section).

McBurney Manor House (PA-5382B). Brick, L-shaped, 38'-9" (five-bay front) x 64'-4", two-and-a-half stories with basement, gable roofs, paired chimneys, door with transom, carved porch with brackets and turned posts; central hall plan. Built ca. 1845; one-story rear addition on ell. 5 sheets (1988, including plans, elevations, section).

McBurney Manor House, Bakeoven (PA-5382C). Brick, 46'-5" x 12'-2", one story, gable roof, inside end chimney; central oven, smokehouse, storage, and outhouse. Built ca. 1845. 1 sheet (1988, including plan, elevations, section).

Pennsylvania Furnace (Franklin Township)

Lyons, John, House (Mansion House) (PA-611), W side of Pennsylvania Furnace Rd., .1 mi. N of State Rte. 45. Random rubble, L-shaped with enclosed stair tower in reentrant angle, 48'-6" (five-bay front) x 91', two-and-a-half stories with basement, truncated gable roof with truncated shed roof on ell, pedimented dormers, door with transom and side lights flanked by pilasters on E (front) elevation, porch supported by stone piers (added ca. 1910-24, replaced wrought-iron porch), cantilevered second-story porch on ell and stair tower; central hall plan. Built 1834 for John Lyons, an early nineteenth-century ironmaster. 9 sheets (1962, including plans, elevations, section, details). LC code: PA,31-PENFN,1.

Mansion House. See Lyons, John, House.

Robertsdale (Wood Township)

America's Industrial Heritage Project

As part of this NPS project, HABS documented the two Huntingdon County towns of Robertsdale (PA-5484) and Woodvale, both developed by the East Broad Top Coal and Iron Company, with photographs and written data in 1989. Records being processed 1990.

Woodvale (Wood Township)

America's Industrial Heritage Project

As part of this NPS project, HABS documented the two Huntingdon County towns of Woodvale (PA-5485) and

Robertsdale, both developed by the East Broad Top Coal and Iron Company, with photographs and written data in 1989. Records being processed 1990.

Lycoming County

Williamsport

Parson, Judge A.V., House (PA-326), 5 E. Fourth St. Brick, L-shaped, 45'-2" (five-bay front) x 40'-2", two-and-a-half stories with basement, gable roof, paired chimneys in parapets at gable ends, flat stone lintels with corner rosettes, Ionic distyle entrance porch on S elevation, recessed door with transom and side lights flanked by Ionic columns on S elevation, attic windows in cornice and basement windows with decorative grilles, porch on E elevation; central hall plan. Built 1840; two-story brick kitchen ell with porches added to N; one-story summer kitchen added to N of ell; demolished ca. 1940; decorative grilles in Lycoming County Historical Museum. 19 sheets (1936, including plans, elevations, sections, details); 11 ext. photos (ca. 1910, 1936), 5 int. photos (ca. 1910, 1936). LC code: PA,41-WILPO,1.

Updegraff, Thomas, House (PA-327), N side of Reach Rd., .25 mi. W of Arch St. Brick with frame ells, L-shaped, 53'-2" (five-bay front) x 60'-7" (including rear ells), two-and-a-half stories, gable roof, two entrances on S (front) elevation, entrance porch on N elevation, two-story frame dining ell (15'-11") with two-story porch added to N of brick section, one-and-a-half-story frame kitchen wing (22'-6") added to N of dining ell. Built 1736; porch with carved brackets and pediments added to S elevation; demolished ca. 1950. 8 sheets (1936, including plans, elevations, section, details). LC code: PA,41-WILPO,2.

Granary (PA-327A). Log, 22'-2" x 18', one-and-a-half stories, sloping site exposes coursed rubble basement with entrance on S (rear) elevation, gable roof, outdoor stairway to attic on E elevation. Built ca. 1836; used for storage 1936; demolished ca. 1950. 3 sheets (1936, including plans, elevations, details). LC code: PA,41-WILPO,2A.

Snyder County

Selinsgrove Borough

Old Academy. See Susquehanna Female College.

Susquehanna Female College (Old Academy) (PA-325), 204 N. Market St. Brick, 52'-6" (five-bay front) x 34'-5", three-and-a-half stories, hip roof with balustrade and square cupola, corner pilasters, double doors with pilasters on E (front) elevation, attic windows with guilloche-patterned grilles in cornice; brick wing (living quarters) added to N elevation of Seminary, 40'-10" (five-bay front) x 32'-1", two-and-a-half stories, gable roof, distyle entrance porch, attic windows in cornice, two-and-a-half-story brick kitchen wing (16'-10" x 24'-1") with porch added on W elevation; central hall plans. Built ca. 1845 (Seminary built first, living quarters added shortly after); frame sheds added on rear (removed after 1936); balustrade and cupola removed after 1936; frame shed added on kitchen wing after 1936; apartments 1936; apartments remodeled 1975. 19 sheets (1936, including plans, elevations, sections, details); 6 ext. photos (1936), 1 int. photo (1936); 3 data pages (1937). LC code: PA,55-SELI,1.

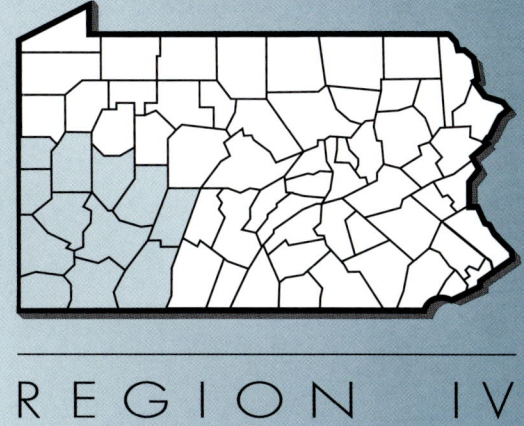

REGION IV

Southwestern

Essay by Richard J. Webster
Catalog entries by Deborah Stephens Burns

Allegheny
Armstrong*
Beaver
Butler
Cambria
Fayette
Greene
Indiana
Lawrence*
Somerset
Washington
Westmoreland

*no catalog entries

Joseph Dorsey House (PA-5176) West Brownsville vicinity (Centerville Township), Washington County. Main entrance on east elevation (Jack E. Boucher, photographer, 1963) PA,63-BROV.V,1-2.

SOUTHWESTERN Pennsylvania can be likened to a gigantic funnel in which the funnel's sloping sides are the high Allegheny Plateau draining its streams into the great spout, the Ohio River.[1] The Allegheny Plateau is an expanse of hills and narrow valleys that extends westward from the high escarpment of the Allegheny Front, the region's eastern boundary.[2] The Ohio River, called "the beautiful river" by local Indians,[3] is formed by the confluence of the Allegheny River, flowing from the oil country to the north, and the Monongahela River, running through the bituminous region to the south. The point of their merging, where Pittsburgh today stands, became the hub of an industrial sprawl that extends eastward to Johnstown, Cambria County, southward to Uniontown, Fayette County, and northward along Beaver River into the Youngstown, Ohio, area. Heavy industry, dominated by iron, steel, and coal, historically characterizes the twelve-county section of the Allegheny Plateau that is called Southwestern Pennsylvania for the purposes of this catalog.[4] The HABS collection for this region is quite extensive. Although Allegheny County buildings outnumber those in surrounding counties, the survey includes the region's representative building types and periods.

In large part because of the Ohio and its tributaries, Britain and France clashed in the only European conflict to have begun in America. Americans call it the French and Indian War; Europeans know it as the Seven Years' War. Tensions had been growing in the upper Ohio Valley for years before armed hostilities erupted in the summer of 1754 at Fort Necessity, near present-day Uniontown. British colonists from Pennsylvania and Virginia, seeking Indian trade, land speculation, and new farmlands, were moving toward the area at the same time that the French were trying to consolidate their North American empire. By the 1740s the French realized that, except for short portages around Niagara Falls and south of Lake Erie, they possessed a water route from Quebec to Louisiana—if they could secure the Forks of the Ohio. They did hold that strategic spot for about a decade, but in November 1758 they abandoned their outpost, Fort Duquesne, in the face of an advancing British force under the command of General John Forbes and Colonel Henry Bouquet.[5]

As an imperial cold war in the 1740s turned to combat in 1754, fort architecture became the region's first significant architectural type. The French got a head start, building a series of four small forts between Presque Isle (Erie) and the Forks of the Ohio in the early 1750s. At the outbreak of the French and Indian War, however, the British erected over two hundred defense bastions across Pennsylvania, mostly at gaps through the mountains.[6] They ranged from the small and simple Fort Necessity to the larger and more sophisticated Fort Ligonier.[7] The most elaborate British fort on the American frontier was Fort Pitt, a five-bastioned pentagonal-shaped dirt fort built between 1759 and 1761. It was much like other British forts, except for one major difference. Its walls were built of earth and sod, rather than horizontal logs; brick-faced stone masonry reinforced the two artillery-prone landside walls. Its site at the Point, where the Allegheny and Monongahela meet, made strategic sense even if it were vulnerable to spring floods, which badly damaged the fort's walls in January 1761 and again, less so, two years later. Some of this damage was never fully repaired, and with the French presence removed from North America in 1763, Fort Pitt's physical condition and strategic importance declined year by year and the British Army abandoned the facility in 1772. The only surviving element of this great fortress is the five-sided brick blockhouse, or redoubt (PA-430), which was finished in early 1764 outside the fort's walls in order to strengthen defenses.[8]

Settlement of southwestern Pennsylvania before 1790 moved slowly and erratically, primarily because of the mortal danger from Indians.[9] With Pontiac's defeat in 1763,[10] frontiersmen established the region's first permanent settlements, moving southwestward from what is today Westmoreland County to Fayette County in 1767 and Greene County in 1768. Yet, high land prices and instability from both the Revolutionary War and Indian threats inhibited settlement until the 1780s, and some areas deep in the mountains, such as present-day Cambria County, did not gain their first permanent community until 1790.[11]

In part because many of these early settlers were Virginians, the English dominated the region. Whether colonial- or English-born, settlers brought with them their own building traditions. The 1787 rubble Joseph Dorsey House (PA-5176), near

Fort Pitt Blockhouse (PA-430) Pittsburgh, Allegheny County. Front elevation (Jack E. Boucher, photographer, 1963) PA,2-PITBU,20-2.

West Brownsville, Washington County, for example, is very much like houses to be found in Ellicott City, Maryland, where Dorsey grew to maturity. Similarly, Presley Neville's 1785 frame house near Woodville, Allegheny County, reflects his Virginia roots, just as Isaac Manchester's brick country house, built in 1815 near West Middletown, Washington County, exhibits his New England origins in Newport, Rhode Island. Pennsylvania Germans also moved into the region, but because they remained a small minority, buildings with distinctively Germanic asymmetrical facades and central chimneys remain exceptions to the regional pattern.[12] Consequently the English not only played a leading role in establishing institutions but they probably also served "as a catalytic agency in the process of transforming the Scotch, the Irish, and the Germans into Americans and building a fairly homogeneous society in western Pennsylvania."[13]

Log buildings were once common elements on this frontier landscape. The region's first settlers evidently turned to log construction for their earliest dwellings and outbuildings, and succeeding generations built with logs well into the nineteenth century. In fact, log buildings were so numerous and stone so rare in some areas that one native vividly remembered his first childhood encounter in the 1770s with a stone building, an inn at Bedford: "I had no idea that there was any house in the world which was not built of logs; but here I looked round the house and could see no logs, and above I could see no joists; whether such a thing had been made by the hands of man, or had grown so of itself, I could not conjecture. I had not the courage to inquire anything about it."[14] Many of these log houses survive in southwestern Pennsylvania, as a 1970s survey of Washington County indicates.[15] Others, covered with weatherboards or stucco, may be standing unnoticed. As would be expected from the region's ethnic distribution cited above, few of these houses are overtly Germanic. Only one Washington County log house, in North Strabane Township, has the characteristic Germanic central chimney, and in this case two front doors as well, a common feature of nineteenth-century Pennsylvania German houses in the Great Valley.[16] HABS has recorded only two log houses in the region, but they are representative examples: the Robert Neal Cabin (PA-46), which the Pittsburgh History and Landmarks Foundation has restored in Pittsburgh's Schenley Park, and the Nixon Tavern (PA-8-3) near Fairchance, Fayette County, which was demolished in the 1950s.[17]

Settlers built stone houses when they had the means; many families, however, were unable to acquire such means for a generation or more. Because of log houses' greater perishability (from fire, decay, families' improved status, and changing nineteenth-century tastes), the region's stone houses today greatly outnumber log houses. Stone houses range from such small vernacular dwellings as the 1808 section of the James Miller House (PA-410) near Bethel Park, Allegheny County, to the outstanding Georgian double-pile mansion (PA-5475) that ironmaster Isaac Meason built in 1802 near Uniontown, Fayette County.[18] Between those extremes stand two Washington County houses more representative of the region: the aforementioned 1787 Joseph Dorsey House overlooking the Monongahela near West Brownsville and the John Roberts House (PA-1177) that was built between 1804 and 1815 next to a

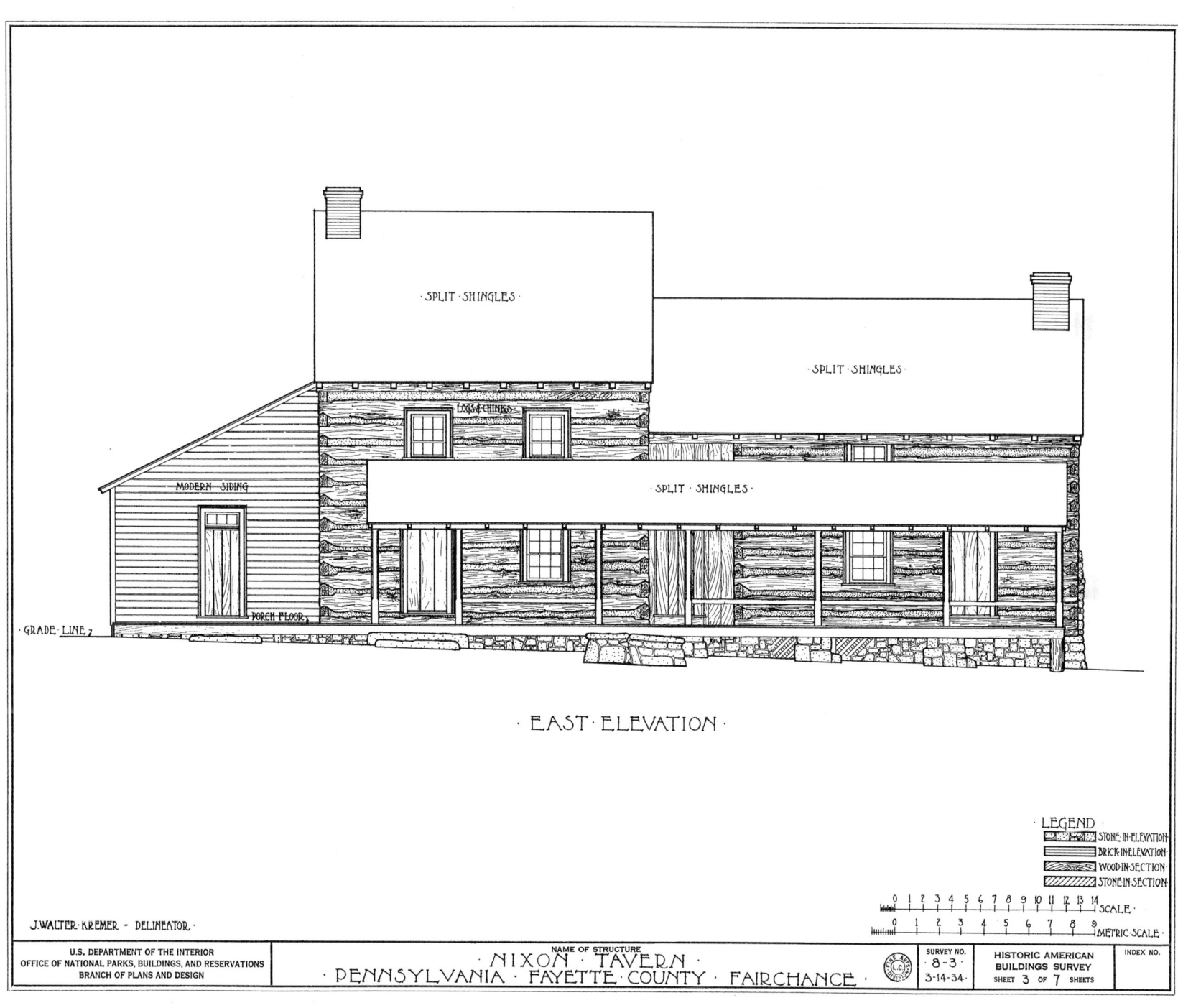

Nixon Tavern (Henry S. Linn House) (PA-8-3) Fairchance Vicinity (Georges Township), Fayette County. East elevation (J. Walter Kremer, delineator, 1934) PA,26-FACHA,1.

John Roberts House (PA-1177) Canonsburg Borough, Washington County. East elevation (Gary A. Wilson, delineator, 1967) PA,63-CANON,1.

log house in Canonsburg. Like most houses in the region, both have at least one blank end wall, gable-end chimneys, and gable roofs without dormers. (The shed dormers on the Roberts House are not original.)[19] While blank end walls are not uncommon on Georgian-period houses near the east coast, they are especially popular throughout southwestern Pennsylvania. Georgian or Federal-style frontispieces, however, which the Dorsey and Roberts Houses possess, are unusual, as is the cornice's extension across the Roberts House's gable. A Roberts House feature that seems to be restricted to the region is its long-short-long ashlar that simulates Flemish bond. It characterizes many Washington County early-nineteenth-century buildings.[20]

Many of these early houses, such as the Dorsey House, were oriented to waterways, but once the National Road was opened through the region's southwest corner between 1811 and 1820, subsequent buildings faced this important thoroughfare.[21] Generally considered the "greatest of all the turnpikes,"[22] the National Road was a major public works project. Although much of its eastern half wended along the path of the mid-eighteenth-century Braddock's Road, to construct a road thirty feet wide with no grade in excess of 5 percent elevation through the steep forests between Cumberland, Maryland, and Wheeling, (West) Virginia, and to cross a myriad of streams along the way required both patience and engineering feats. Bridges, such as the stone S-bridge near Claysville, Washington County, and the 1836 cast-iron bridge (the first iron bridge in America) over Dunlap's Creek in Brownsville, are surviving testaments to the engineers' and builders' skills.[23] The road had a significant impact on the area's economy before the advent of railroads at mid-century. It provided access to both western lands and eastern markets, allowing local ironmasters to ship their pig iron and farmers to herd their livestock to market. Before tolls were collected in the 1830s, livestock clogged the roadway. (Throughout the nineteenth century, livestock farming remained the major agricultural activity in the region's southwestern corner, stimulating related tanning and woolen manufacturing.)[24] In addition, the road's traffic created potential customers for road-related businesses. Taverns proliferated. The John Krepps Tavern near Centerville, Washington County, is but one of the approximately twenty-five taverns erected along the road in that county alone. These taverns not only provided overnight accommodations for travelers, wagoners, and drovers and their animals, they also served as neighborhood social and news-dispensing centers. In addition, general stores, livery stables, saddle and harness shops, and blacksmith shops sprang up to serve travelers' needs. Most of these businesses were concentrated in the major towns of Uniontown, Brownsville, and Washington, but, as evidenced by Mount Washington Tavern (PA-417), near Farmington, Fayette County, they appeared in smaller intervening towns as well.[25]

  Traffic volume was so great that even before the road's completion to Wheeling in 1820, it was beginning to deteriorate.[26] Facing increasingly exorbitant repair costs, the national government in the early 1830s relinquished the road to the states through which it ran. Pennsylvania accepted its portion of the road in 1832 on the condition that the national government repair the roads and bridges and appropriate funds for the erection of tollhouses, whose collections the state would use to maintain the road. Pennsylvania in the 1830s built six tollhouses with iron gates.[27] Two of these survive. HABS has recorded both: the brick Searights Tollhouse (PA-417) near

Mount Washington Tavern (PA-417) Farmington Vicinity (Wharton Township), Fayette County. General view (A.S. Burns, photographer, 1933) PA,26-UNITO.V,1-1.

Uniontown, Fayette County, and the ashlar Petersburg Tollhouse (PA-417) in Addison, Somerset County, each with a distinctive octagonal two-story tower that afforded a clear view of the road. Competition from the Pennsylvania and the Baltimore and Ohio railroads in the 1850s relegated the former National Road to local traffic until its twentieth-century rebirth as Route 40, which is now lined with characteristic twentieth-century roadside architecture.[28]

Handling even more traffic than the National Road was the Pennsylvania Road. The Pennsylvania Road followed the path of the Forbes Military Road, which had been cut through forests from Bedford to the Forks of the Ohio during the French and Indian War. From Bedford the road connected eastward with Chambersburg and York to give the Ohio Valley an important, albeit a difficult and inefficient, connection with Baltimore and Philadelphia in the first half of the nineteenth century.[29]

Searights Tollhouse, Fayette County. (Listed in catalog under National Trail PA-417, Somerset County) General view (A.S. Burns, photographer, 1933).

Exploiting its site at the Forks of the Ohio, Pittsburgh served not only as Gateway to the West but also Provider of the West, especially after 1817, when steamboats started carrying Pittsburgh's products inland. Frontier conditions forced Pittsburgh into an early industrial self-sufficiency, and industrialists moved increasingly into heavy manufacturing.[30] By 1860 Allegheny County was second to Philadelphia among Pennsylvania counties in the value of manufactures, and produced more than twice the value of the third-place county, Schuylkill.[31]

Allegheny County was only the center of an expanding circle of heavy industry that included bituminous coal mining throughout the region and iron foundries in Cambria County.[32] There, Johnstown, at the western end of the Main Line Canal's portage railroad, became a major warehousing and transshipment point by the mid-1830s. After the Pennsylvania Railroad replaced the canal in the 1850s, Johnstown's ironmasters, taking advantage of both the railroad and the high-quality iron ore nearby, emerged by 1870 as a major producer of iron rails. The once dominating role of the Cambria Iron Company and the Pennsylvania Railroad are evident yet today in the presence of the company's Gautier Division mill in downtown Johnstown and the grandeur of the classical revival railroad station (PA-5389), built in 1916 of reinforced concrete with brick walls and sandstone columns and trim.[33] By the end of the nineteenth century, Southwestern Pennsylvania's expansive steel mills and their massive production overwhelmed visitors; but also significant, although not as visually impressive, were such other local manufactories as Andrew Mellon's aluminum factories and George Westinghouse's air brake and electrical facilities.[34] This sprawling industrial network generated the wealth that underwrote both the region's architecture, art, and learning for at least a century, and, in the cases of the Carnegie libraries and the Frick and Mellon art collections, a large portion of the nation's culture as well.[35]

Housing for workers in the region's industries varied, but by the late nineteenth century the pattern in coal and mill towns was company-owned detached or semidetached wood-sided balloon-frame houses, the most cheaply built dwellings possible. Although row houses and tenements would have been even cheaper to erect, company officials, seeking less transient and presumably less troublesome married workers, knew that families preferred detached dwellings. Rows of these two-story gable-roof houses lined the streets, their front porches today often abutting sidewalks; small outbuildings and privies stood in the back. Generally a worker's living conditions varied directly with his family's tenure in America; the most recent immigrants endured the meanest housing as well as the hardest jobs. Cambria City's east European immigrants in 1887, for example, lived in company-owned houses "surrounded by huge piles of refuse from the furnaces," reported the state's Bureau of Industrial Statistics. "Outside privies built upon vaults, and prominently exposed to the view of the passerby, are located near the houses. The drainage is surface, there being no escape for slops and other waste matter."[36]

Social hierarchy in housing was obvious. In isolated coal towns, where superintendents had to remain near the mines, the manager's house stood apart, usually the town's largest and most ornamented residence. Foremen's houses generally were larger than miners' housing and included small amenities, such as closets and cellars.[37] By the end of the nineteenth century in small industrial cities like Johnstown, managers' and burghers' residences often stood near recreational facilities on the city's outskirts and up wind from the mills. Class-oriented advertisements aggressively promoted their salubrious sites. The affluent resident of Westmont, for example, on a hill above Johnstown, lived "far above the noise, smoke, and dust of the city [in] the pure country air and bright sunshine of that charming suburb," an 1898 advertisement boasted. "When he makes his descent into the thick, smoky fog of the valley his family is left in enjoyment of the morning sunshine, which will not reach the less fortunate town people for an hour or more...."[38]

As would be expected of a region remote from eastern style-setting centers, early-nineteenth-century architecture of Southwestern Pennsylvania suffered from a shortage of skilled craftsmen. In Pittsburgh, for example, the Shoenberger House (PA-43) was built in 1847, but its rounded bays gave it an outdated English Regency appearance, while about the same time William Croghan imported a Philadelphia ornament worker to decorate his new Greek Revival ballroom (PA-8-8).[39] Even after the Pittsburgh area was able to provide a livelihood for its own architects, local clients seem to have given big commissions to outsiders to a greater degree than in other cities, reserving residences for local architects.[40] When Pittsburgh's Trinity Episcopal Church, for example, decided in 1850 to build a "chapel of ease," the vestry turned to John Notman of Philadelphia, who had just established his reputation as a leading Gothic Revival church architect with his design for St. Mark's (PA-1093) in that city.[41] Local historian James Van Trump feels that Notman's design for Pittsburgh's St. Peter's Church (PA-48) lacks the sophistication of St. Mark's, and "in its starkness and simplicity, exemplifies forcibly the qualities of the pioneers who had established Pittsburgh."[42] Nevertheless, members of the congregation thought enough of the building to take it with them, stone by stone, when they moved to the city's Oakland section in 1901. In 1990, however, the congregation abandoned the church to demolition contractors.[43]

Hiring national architects for important buildings has given Pittsburgh some very good architecture, and none is better than the Allegheny County Courthouse and Jail (PA-610) by Henry Hobson Richardson, "the last great traditional architect."[44] The buildings' grandeur and design have impressed observers from the start. *Harper's Weekly* published Richardson's plans in early 1885 and commented extensively on the proposed lighting and ventilation systems and the buildings' "size, massiveness, and costliness."[45] Richardson's health was failing while he worked on this project and he did not live to see it completed, but he knew its importance and was

Pennsylvania Railroad Station (PA-5389) Johnstown, Cambria County. General view with freight building (Jet Lowe, photographer, 1988) PA,11-JOTO,13.

eager to stake his reputation on it, considering it one of his two best works.[46] Critics today tend to be more impressed by the jail, because it avoids overt historical references and derives effect from its massive rock-faced walls and boldlyarched openings.[47] Yet the complete complex, with its monumentality, expressive masonry, restrained ornament, and functional plan, stands as one of Victorian America's greatest buildings, and as one that influenced Southwestern Pennsylvania architecture for over a decade. Uniontown's 1892 rock-faced granite Fayette County Courthouse, for example, is a pale imitation of Richardson's monumental Allegheny County Courthouse, and Johnstown's city hall (PA-5387) is even paler, built of rock-faced buff-colored stone a decade later with a pyramidal-roofed cupola instead of a tower.[48] Local Richardsonian Romanesque examples also include dwellings, such as the brick and stone 1890-93 Charles Schwab House in North Braddock, Allegheny County, and churches, such as Pittsburgh's massive rock-faced ashlar Shadyside Presbyterian Church (PA-432), that was built in 1889-90 from the designs of Richardson's successors, Shepley, Rutan and Coolidge.[49]

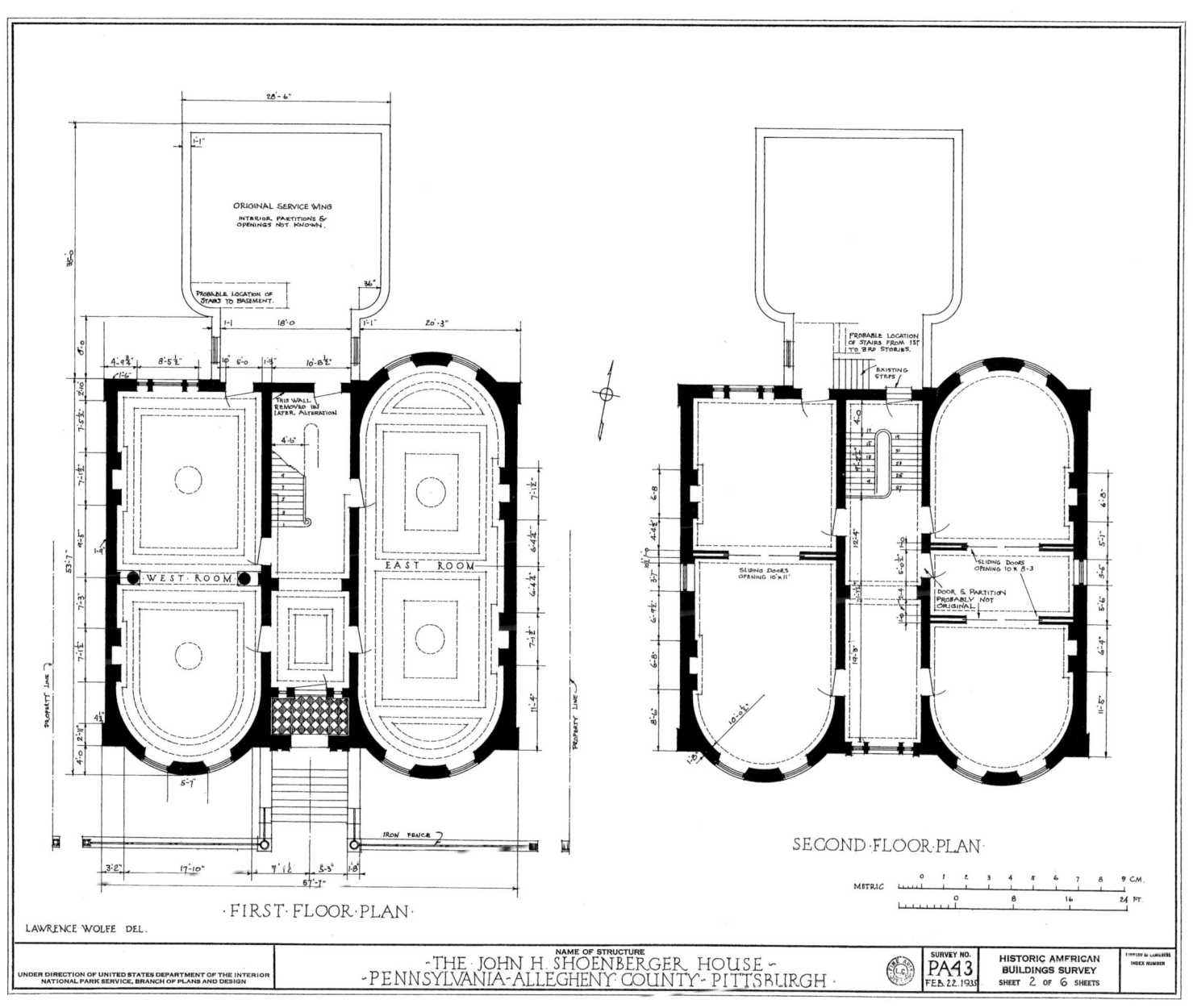

John H. Shoenberger House (PA-43) Pittsburgh, Allegheny County. First and second floor plans (Lawrence Wolfe, delineator, 1935) PA,2-PITBU,9.

William Croghan House (PA-8-8) Pittsburgh, Allegheny County. Entrance to ballroom (Charles M. Stotz, photographer, 1934) PA,2-PITBU,3-5.

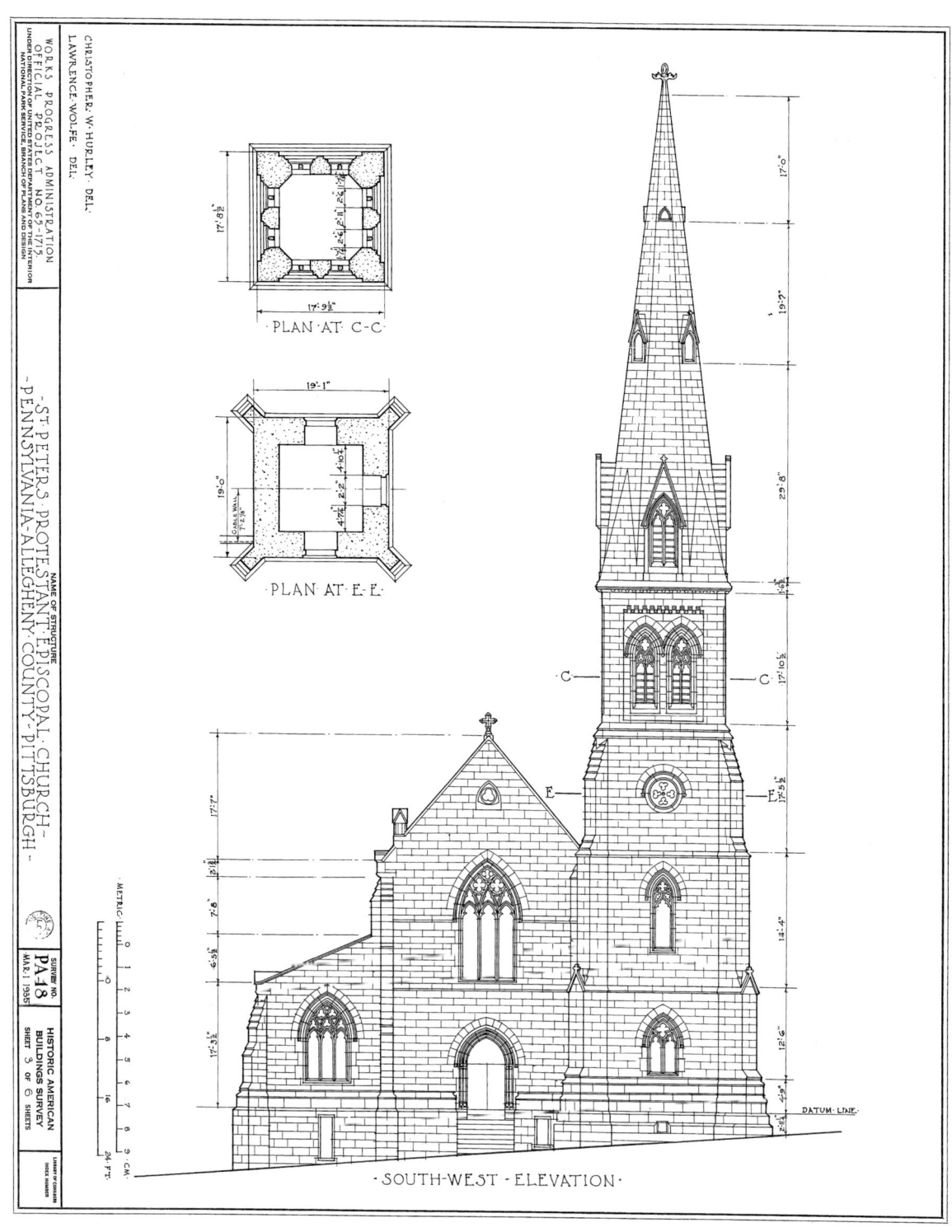

Saint Peter's Protestant Episcopal Church (PA-48) Pittsburgh, Allegheny County. Southwest elevation (Christopher W. Hurley and Lawrence Wolfe, delineators, 1935) PA,2-PITBU,14.

Allegheny County Courthouse and Jail (PA-610) Pittsburgh, Allegheny County. Courthouse, detail of dormers (Jack E. Boucher, photographer, 1963) PA,2-PITBU,29-5.

The ability of Pittsburgh's citizens and government to attract and compensate nationally known architects for major building projects testifies to the area's economic wealth and cultural leadership. Pittsburgh has served as the region's leading cultural and education center since at least 1819, when the Pittsburgh Academy became the Western University of Pennsylvania (now the University of Pittsburgh). In the 1890s that leadership became indisputable as generous philanthropists created and endowed a plethora of new institutions: the Phipps Conservatory in 1893, the

Johnstown City Hall (PA-5387) Johnstown, Cambria County. Front elevation (Jet Lowe, photographer, 1988) PA,11-JOTO,8.

Carnegie Museum and Library in 1895, the first Carnegie International Art Show and Pittsburgh Orchestra's first concert in 1896, and many others, including the Academy of Music, the New Grand Opera House, and an Academy of Science and Arts. Perhaps conscious that much of the city's greatness was built on the backs of poor and ill-housed workers, many of these benefactors also exhibited a social conscience. Mrs. Mary E. Schenley gave the city the 422-acre Schenley Park, which opened in 1893; the Civic Club formed in 1895 to work for public parks and playgrounds; in the same year Allegheny County funded the Allegheny Association for Improvement of the Poor; and the well-heeled Calvary Episcopal Church joined St. Mary's Catholic Church in various social projects.[50]

These civic leaders also expected to enjoy comfortable residences, some sumptuous enough to qualify as mansions. Alden and Harlow were especially popular architects for Pittsburgh's rich at the turn of the century. In the late 1880s, while practicing as Longfellow, Alden and Harlow and favoring the Richardsonian Romanesque, they kept offices in Boston and Pittsburgh. In 1896 Longfellow left the firm, and the architects shifted to Renaissance designs for wealthy Pittsburgh clients. Many of their greatest mansions have been demolished, but the 1898 Byers-Lyon House (PA-1158) in Pittsburgh has survived as offices for the Community College of Allegheny County. The architects designed a large double brick house for Alexander Byers, a pipe manufacturer, and his daughter and banker son-in-law, J. Denniston Lyon. They employed Flemish Renaissance gables and an arcaded courtyard with wrought-iron gates to help give the Byers-Lyon House mansion status.[51]

Frederick G. Scheibler Jr., on the other hand, worked on a smaller scale, building more-modest houses for more-modest clients. Scheibler was a Pittsburgher without exception. Born in the city in 1872, he attended Pittsburgh schools, learned architecture in the offices of Pittsburgh architects, and designed most of his works for Pittsburgh clients. He began his practice in 1898, working in the late Victorian styles of the time, but in 1905 he shifted to an arts and crafts style that allowed him to move toward modernism by casting aside historical academic styles. He did not, however, cast aside picturesqueness. Pittsburgh's Old Heidelberg Apartments (PA-431), which he designed in 1905, mark his movement in a new direction. Some themes of the apartment building are repeated in small single-family dwellings. The broad tiled roof and variable and asymmetrical fenestration of Old Heidelberg, for example, and the imitation thatch on the arched porch and rounded eaves of Eva Harter's 1923 house (PA-622) in Pittsburgh's Squirrel Hill illustrate Scheibler's skill in moving toward abstract modern forms while retaining a sense of Victorian charm.[52]

By the early twentieth century, Southwestern Pennsylvania architecture had become increasingly national. Just as local companies were absorbed by national corporations, leaving the region's economy vulnerable to national trends, local architects faced increased competition from large out-of-town firms and the region's architecture began to look like architecture everywhere else. National architectural offices designed more and more major buildings in downtown Pittsburgh. They range from D. H. Burnham and Company of Chicago, who did the twenty-story Frick Building in 1902, to Ralph Adams Cram, architect of the 1907 marble Early English Gothic Calvary Episcopal Church.[53]

Shadyside Presbyterian Church (PA-432) Pittsburgh, Allegheny County. South elevation (Jack E. Boucher, photographer, 1963) PA,2-PITBU,22-4.

Old Heidelberg Apartments and Cottages (PA-431) Pittsburgh, Allegheny County. West elevation (Jack E. Boucher, photographer, 1963) PA,2-PITBU,21-4.

By the 1930s architects of national reputation were designing local residences as well. Of these, Frank Lloyd Wright's Fallingwater (PA-5346) in Ohiopyle, Fayette County, is the most spectacular. Built for Pittsburgh department store magnate Edgar J. Kaufmann as a vacation retreat, Fallingwater remains one of the best-known residences in America.[54] Wright's exploitation of the house's natural setting and use of local stone make Fallingwater one of the best expressions of his organic architecture, but an anomaly in the region, where conservatism and tradition have governed most of its domestic building stock. Also avant garde when it was built in 1939 was the boldly Bauhaus residence for Robert and Cecilia Frank that Walter Gropius and Marcel Breuer designed on Woodland Road in Pittsburgh's Squirrel Hill.[55] The house is an uncompromising exercise in the International style and would have looked as appropriate—or inappropriate—anywhere in the western world.

Nevertheless, after World War II, that style and its variants dominated large-scale commercial architecture in the region. This was not the case for dwellings. Although such promoters of the new modernism as Walter Gropius and Marcel Breuer demonstrated the new style's possibilities in 1942 with the Aluminum City Houses in New Kensington, Westmoreland County,[56] local architects and developers chose not to emulate either the architects or their buildings for the great majority of dwellings built after the war. In the 1970s and 1980s, affluent clients retained such contemporary architectural greats as Robert Venturi, Denise Scott Brown, and Richard Meier to design their homes,[57] but the democratic tastes of the majority here, as elsewhere in the country, preferred standard tract housing with its weak allusions to colonial forms.

With the decline of steel and its related industries, hard times have visited southwestern Pennsylvania. As Pittsburgh shifts to a service economy, corporations commission new buildings, such as the 1984 steel-and-glass cathedral-like PPG Place,[58] and developers rehabilitate old ones. In the mill and mining towns, however, stores are being boarded up and abandoned houses are being demolished. Although fewer and fewer coal barges ply the Monongahela and the steel mills produce only a fraction of their former output, the historical pattern prevails. Pittsburgh, at the Forks of the Ohio, remains the region's economic and cultural center, and citizens in outlying counties try to emulate its example, while often living and working in buildings that evoke a vernacular spirit, even if that spirit is one of mobile homes and prefab houses.

Notes

[1] The funnel analogy is drawn from Raymond E. Murphy and Marion Murphy, *Pennsylvania: A Regional Geography* (Harrisburg, Pa.: Pennsylvania Book Service, 1937), 43; see also 33-37. For a brief explanation of the region's geologic origins, see J. Ronald Mowery, "Geologic History of Pennsylvania," *Pennsylvania Heritage* 4 (September 1978): 7-12.

[2] It is called a plateau because its layers of rock lie nearly flat one atop another, forming nearly uniform elevations for its hills. Those elevations, however, are quite high; in fact, Pennsylvania's highest point, Mount Davis, 3,213 feet above sea level, is in the Allegheny Plateau, in Somerset County. Murphy and Murphy, *Pennsylvania*, 36-37.

[3] George P. Donehoo, *A History of the Indian Villages and Place Names in Pennsylvania* (Harrisburg, Pa.: The Telegraph Press, 1928; reprint ed., Baltimore: Gateway Press, Inc., 1977), 132.

[4] Those twelve counties, extending southeastward in three bands from the region's northwest corner are Lawrence, Butler, Armstrong, Indiana, and Cambria in the northernmost band; and Beaver, Allegheny, Westmoreland, and Somerset in the middle band; Washington and Fayette in the southern band; with Greene County occupying the region's—and the state's—southwest corner.

[5] The Pennsylvania theater of the French and Indian War is well covered in Solon J. Buck and Elizabeth Hawthorn Buck, *The Planting of Civilization in Western Pennsylvania* (Pittsburgh: University of Pittsburgh Press, 1938), 41-114. The most thorough study of the war is in Lawrence Henry Gipson's fifteen-volume *The British Isles and the American Colonies*, 15 vols. (New York: Alfred A. Knopf, 1953-1970); see vol. 6, *The Years of Defeat, 1754-1757*, vol. 7, *The Victorious Years, 1758-1760*, vol. 8, *The Culmination, 1760-1763*. A very readable account, with a focus on the forts, is Walter O'Meara, *Guns at the Forks*, The American Forts Series (Englewood Cliffs, N. J.: Prentice-Hall, Inc., 1965). See also Howard H. Peckham, *The Colonial Wars, 1689-1762* (Chicago: University of Chicago Press, 1964), 120-212.

[6] Sylvester K. Stevens, *Pennsylvania: Birthplace of a Nation* (New York: Random House, 1964), 54.

[7] Both forts have been reconstructed and are discussed, Fort Ligonier in great detail, in an excellent volume by Charles Morse Stotz, *Outposts of the War for Empire. The French and Eng-*

lish in Western Pennsylvania: Their Armies, Their Forts, Their People, 1749-1764 (Pittsburgh: Historical Society of Western Pennsylvania, 1985), 21-24, 95-97, 146-89.

[8]The 1761 and 1763 floods were unusually high; they would not be surpassed until March 1936. Although the extant brick structure is nowadays called a blockhouse, the term originally referred to timber blockhouses that were built with timber "blocks." Ibid., 127-39.

[9]Buck and Buck, *Planting of Civilization in Western Pennsylvania*, 139-40. The first agricultural settlement in the region seems to have been a group of Germans who had been members of the Ephrata commune in Lancaster County. In 1750 or 1751 they settled for a few years at the mouth of Dunkard's Creek in what is now Greene County, before moving on to present-day West Virginia, where Indians massacred them in 1757.

[10]Pontiac, an Ottawa chief, organized a large number of tribes in a well-coordinated attack against the English in 1763, soon after the end of the French and Indian War. The attacks spread into the Cumberland Valley, and four frontier forts fell: Fort Burd was abandoned; Fort Venango was overrun and its inhabitants massacred; Fort Le Boeuf fell but its soldiers escaped; and Fort Presque Isle surrendered and its garrison was taken prisoner. Both Fort Ligonier and Fort Pitt were besieged. The uprising was repulsed in early August 1763, when troops under Colonel Henry Bouquet's command defeated the Indians in a two-day battle at Bushy Run, near the present Jeanette, Westmoreland County. Francis Parkman, *The Conspiracy of Pontiac and the Indian War after the Conquest of Canada*, 2 vols. (Boston, 1902; reprint ed., New York: AMS Press, Inc., 1969), 2:3-78.

[11]Buck and Buck, *Planting of Civilization in Western Pennsylvania*, 143-53.

[12]Charles Morse Stotz, *The Architectural Heritage of Early Western Pennsylvania: A Record of Building before 1860* (Pittsburgh: University of Pittsburgh Press, 1966), 43. See 52-59, 78-83 for illustrations of these three houses. The German Pietist settlement of Economy (PA-1176) in Beaver County was established too late (1824) and remained too isolated to have an influence on regional architecture.

[13]Buck and Buck, *Planting of Civilization in Western Pennsylvania*, 155. The Bucks based their estimations of the region's ethnic distribution on surnames in the 1790 census. Approximately 37 percent of the region's inhabitants were English, 7 percent were Welsh, 17 percent were Scottish, 19 percent were Irish, 12 percent were German, and 8 percent were from minor groups or were unassignable. "One of the surprising results" of the Bucks' statistical survey was the relatively small number of Scotch-Irish in the region compared with "the prevalent impression that they formed the main element in its population prior to the Civil War." (page 154) Because the Bucks included in their southwestern Pennsylvania region Bedford County, whose population was nearly one-third German, the German figures are higher than they would be in the catalog's twelve-county region which excludes Bedford County.

[14]Joseph Doddridge, *Notes on the Settlement and Indian Wars* (Pittsburgh: John S. Ritenour and Wm. T. Lindsey, 1912; reprint ed., Parsons, W.Va.: McClain Printing Company, 1960), 89. This personal account of growing up in western Pennsylvania was first published in 1824. The

1912 edition was an edited version of the original notes with addenda that was published in 1876.

[15] The survey included twenty-three houses, two springhouses, one smokehouse, and five barns. *Preserving Our Past: Landmark Architecture of Washington County, Pennsylvania* (Washington, Pa.: Washington County History and Landmarks Foundation, 1975), 10-40.

[16] The Washington County History and Landmarks Foundation illustrates two other houses with central chimneys, but one is a new chimney, replacing an earlier end chimney, and the other is a mid-nineteenth-century addition. It should be understood that central chimneys alone do not identify Germanic houses. More important in identifying a Germanic house is the house plan, which in Germanic houses often places the main fireplace near the center of the house. Pennsylvania German houses with two front doors, which Henry Glassie calls Pennsylvania farmhouses, are discussed in the comprehensive essay. The caption for the house in North Strabane Township in *Preserving Our Past* contends that two front doors sometimes indicated "that a house was used as a tavern or shop as well as a residence." That may be the case in towns, but in the countryside two front doors, especially in conjunction with a central chimney, more likely indicate that the house's builder was German. Ibid., 27; Robert C. Bucher, "The Continental Log House," *Pennsylvania Folklife* 12 (Summer 1962): 14-19; Henry Glassie, "Eighteenth-Century Cultural Process in Delaware Valley Folk Building," *Winterthur Portfolio* 7 (1972): 41-43.

[17] The Neal Cabin is a misnomer. Cabins were rude structures of round logs with clapboard roofing, wooden chimneys, and dirt floors, but the Neal Cabin has a window on two of its squared-log facades, plank floors, and a large random-rubble interior end chimney with two fireplaces. The Nixon Tavern (PA-8-3), near Fairchance, Fayette County, was built circa 1810, about five feet to the north of the main two-story house and connected to it with a roofed passageway. By erecting the tavern as a detached structure the builder avoided the difficult problem of joining logs. By comparison with the Neal Cabin, the Nixon Tavern was larger, contained a full second story with winding stairs, and had a better-constructed and finished chimney. Its later date may account for those differences. Stotz, *Architectural Heritage of Early Western Pennsylvania*, 34, 37; Walter C. Kidney, *Landmark Architecture: Pittsburgh and Allegheny County* (Pittsburgh: Pittsburgh History and Landmarks Foundation, 1985), 239.

[18] These two houses are illustrated in Stotz, *Architectural Heritage of Early Western Pennsylvania*, 60-67, 72. The Miller House is briefly discussed in Kidney, *Landmark Architecture*, 303.

[19] No one has done a statistical study of the frequency of blank end walls on early nineteenth-century regional houses, but a trip through the area or a perusal of the two books cited below leaves no doubt about the popularity of the blank end wall in the region. It may be traced to settlers from Virginia where the blank end wall is also common. Stotz, *Architectural Heritage of Early Western Pennsylvania*, 52-56, 70-71; *Preserving Our Past*, 43-45, 47, 50.

[20] Washington County buildings employing the long-short-long ashlar arrangement include the Jeremiah Jackson House in California, the 1807 Solomon Sivitz House in Amwell Township, the house on the John Hollcroft property in Union Township, and the Black House and

the 1824 Tucker United Methodist Church in Hanover Township. This masonry pattern is partially executed on other stone houses in the region, such as the Lemon House (PA-1236) in Cresson Township, Cambria County, and early nineteenth-century houses in Schellsburg, Bedford County, in the Ridge and Valley Region. Stotz, *Architectural Heritage of Early Western Pennsylvania*, 45-46, 144; *Preserving Our Past*, 50, 58, 61, 68, 72, 74; *The Lemon Family, the Lemon House* (Philadelphia: Eastern National Park and Monument Association, 1988), 9-11; George Swetnam and Helene Smith, *A Guidebook to Historic Western Pennsylvania* (Pittsburgh: University of Pittsburgh Press, 1976), 61.

[21] Congress passed legislation in March 1806 to build a road between Cumberland, Maryland, and Wheeling, West Virginia (then Virginia), on the Ohio River. Construction in Pennsylvania began in the spring of 1811 and moved slowly at first, but the pace picked up after the War of 1812 and the road was considered complete in December 1820. The success of this first link proved so successful that western interests pressured the federal government to extend the road to the Mississippi. It ended short of its target, however, in Vandalia, Illinois, during the mid-1850s, with some parts of the last stretch left incomplete. The road runs approximately eighty miles through Pennsylvania (six miles in Somerset County, thirty-four miles in Fayette County, and forty miles in Washington County) in a northwestwardly-southeastwardly direction between the Maryland border and Washington, Washington County, at which point the road shifts to a more nearly east-west direction. Denise L. Grantz, "National Road: Historic Resource Survey, Preliminary Research Report" (California, Pa: California University of Pennsylvania for Bureau for Historic Preservation, Pennsylvania Historical and Museum Commission, 1986), 2-3, 14.

[22] George Rogers Taylor, *The Transportation Revolution, 1815-1860, The Economic History of the United States*, vol. 4 (New York: Rinehart and Company, 1951), 22.

[23] Philip D. Jordan, *The National Road* (Indianapolis: Bobbs-Merrill Company, 1948; reprint ed., Gloucester, Mass.: Peter Smith, 1966), 53; Grantz, "National Road," 15. There were a number of S-bridges along the road. They "were erected, not because contractors were drunk or because they did not know their business, but because a bridge shaped like a letter S was easier to construct than one which was flung straight across a stream." Ibid., 85. The locally forged iron bridge is briefly described in Writers' Program of the Works Progress Administration in *Pennsylvania: A Guide to the Keystone State* (New York: Oxford University Press for the Pennsylvania Historical Commission and the University of Pennsylvania, 1940; reprint ed., St. Clair Shores, Mich.: Scholarly Press, 1976), 598. Another highly praised bridge is the massive, triple-arch stone bridge that was built in 1818 at Big Crossings in Somerfield, Somerset County. Archer Butler Hulbert, *The National Road: A Chapter of American Expansion* (Columbus: By the author, 1901), 117; Grantz, "National Road," 35, 57.

[24] Murphy and Murphy, *Pennsylvania*, 131, 155.

[25] During the road's heyday, between 1818 and 1852, over seventy taverns stood between West Brownsville and the (West) Virginia line. Grantz, "National Road," 26-27, 37. For descriptions of some of these early taverns, see Hulbert, *National Road*, 102-7.

[26] The extent of the road's traffic volume is indicated by some random statistics. In 1822, for example, Wheeling's six commission houses unloaded an average of a thousand wagons each, and in January and February 1843 a Somerset tavernkeeper reported feeding 2,300 head of cattle, an average of nearly forty a night. Grantz, "National Road," 17-20.

[27] The original six tollhouses (four brick, two stone) stood from east to west in Addison, Somerset County (the Petersburg tollhouse); near Farmington, Fayette County: near Uniontown, Fayette County (the Searights tollhouse); near Beallsville, Washington County, near Washington, and near West Alexander, Washington County. The state built an additional six toll gates with wood-frame houses in Washington and Fayette counties after 1852 to raise more funds for road repairs. The state ended the toll system on the old National Road in April 1905. Ibid., 18-19, 28-29; Hulbert, *National Road*, 60. For toll rates between 1831 and 1900 and annual toll incomes between 1831 and 1877, see Hulbert, *National Road*, 66-67, 73-74.

[28] The Pennsylvania Railroad reached Pittsburgh in late 1852 and the Baltimore and Ohio Railroad ran into Wheeling the next year. The National Road could not compete with this faster, cheaper means of bulk transportation. Mail coach service along the road to Wheeling ended in January 1853, and stagecoach operations ceased at about the same time. Grantz, "National Road,) 28-32; Stotz, *Architectural Heritage of Early Western Pennsylvania*, 173-74, 176; *Preserving Our Past*, 49-51; Thomas J. Schlereth, *U.S. 40: A Roadscape of the American Experience* (Indianapolis: Indiana Historical Society, 1985), 76-91.

[29] Murphy and Murphy, *Pennsylvania*, 104, 109; Writers' Program, *Pennsylvania*, 87.

[30] Early in the nineteenth century the boatbuilding, clothing, and metal industries were Pittsburgh's mainstay, but by mid-century coal-fueled rolling mills, foundries, steam-engine factories, and glass plants were more important. By the end of the Civil War, oil refining became another important industry, but the key enterprise remained iron manufacturing, fueled increasingly by coke from the beehive ovens in and around Connellsburg, Fayette County. Murphy and Murphy, *Pennsylvania*, 110-11, 133, 157-58.

[31] In 1860 Allegheny County was deeply in second place, hardly a contender for the top spot. Philadelphia's value of manufactures was more than five times that of Allegheny County. Sylvester K. Stevens, *Pennsylvania: Titan of Industry* (New York: Lewis Historical Publishing Company, Inc., 1948), 168-71, 174.

[32] By 1840 Brownsville had cotton, glass, and paper factories, a rolling mill, and a steam-engine maker, while nearby Connellsville had several iron foundries and plow factories. Although "by far the most numerous portion of the inhabitants [of Westmoreland County were] . . . engaged in agricultural pursuits" at the same time, the county already had four or five iron furnaces. Charles B. Trego, *A Geography of Pennsylvania: Containing an Account of the Historical, Geographical Features, Soil, Climate, Geology, Botany, Zoology, Population, Education, Government, Finances, Productions, Trade, Railroads, Canal, &c. of the State* (Philadelphia: Edward C. Biddle, 1843), 370; see also 205, 244; Murphy and Murphy, *Pennsylvania*, 132, 156.

[33] Cambria Iron Company began in 1853, but its local iron furnace roots reach back to the 1840s. By 1878 its complex spread over sixty acres, and its Gautier Division, which specialized in agricultural products, intruded into downtown Johnstown. In 1898 Cambria Iron Company became Cambria Steel Company, which Philadelphia's Midvale Steel and Ordnance Company purchased in 1916. Bethlehem Steel Corporation acquired the company in the 1920s. The hard times that hit the American steel industry in the 1970s were intensified in Johnstown by a flood in 1977. Yet the mills still operate, albeit with a fraction of the work force and production of the 1940s and 50s. Kenneth M. Murchison of New York designed Johnstown's Pennsylvania Railroad Station in 1914; it was built in 1915-16. Murchison, trained at the Ecole des Beaux Arts, also designed Baltimore's Union Station (1910) and Scranton's Delaware, Lackawanna and Western Station (1907). His stations are characterized by Beaux-Arts schemes and neoclassical designs. Kim E. Wallace, ed., *The Character of a Steel Mill City: Four Historical Neighborhoods of Johnstown, Pennsylvania* (Washington, D.C.: National Park Service, 1989), 11-14, 23-24; Terri Hartman, "Pennsylvania Railroad Station," HABS Report, PA-5389 (Washington, D.C.: Library of Congress, 1988), 1, 4-6.

[34] For a succinct but excellent discussion of the intertwining entrepreneurship, financing, and technology of the region's industry, see Thomas C. Cochran, *Pennsylvania: A History* (New York: W.W. Norton & Company, 1978), 136-61.

[35] Stevens, *Pennsylvania: Birthplace of a Nation*, 238, 326; Writers' Program, *Pennsylvania*, 307-9.

[36] Quoted in Wallace, ed., *The Character of a Steel Mill City*, 99. See also Margaret M. Mulrooney, *A Legacy of Coal: The Coal Company Towns of Southwestern Pennsylvania* (Washington, D.C.: National Park Service, 1989), 12-19, 23-29. The latter volume is an excellent summary of bituminous coal miners' housing in three coal towns: Colver, Cambria County; Star Junction, Fayette County; and Windber, Somerset County. It is abundantly illustrated with photographs and house plans. Both volumes are products of America's Industrial Heritage Project, and the results of surveys which the Historic American Buildings Survey and Historic American Engineering Record undertook in January 1988.

[37] Mulrooney, *A Legacy of Coal*, 16.

[38] Quoted in Wallace, ed., *The Character of a Steel Mill City*, 117. In 1889, after the famous flood, the Cambria Iron Company commissioned Miller and Yates, Philadelphia landscape architects, to design this suburb. The company built a racetrack, sponsored the Westmont Tennis Club, and donated the land for the Johnstown Country Club, all of which stood in Westmont before 1907, when houses replaced the racetrack. Ibid., 119-20.

[39] Mordecai Van Horn of Philadelphia decorated Croghan's Greek Revival ballroom, which Stotz considers "one of the most distinguished interiors of the style to be found in the United States." Stotz, *Architectural Heritage of Early Western Pennsylvania*, 110, 126-31; Kidney, *Landmark Architecture*, 31-32; Harold B. Dickson, *A Hundred Pennsylvania Buildings* (State College, Pa.: Bald Eagle Press, 1954), pl. 50.

[40] Kidney cites a long list of late-nineteenth- and twentieth-century Pittsburgh buildings by out-of-town architects and a short list of creative Pittsburgh architects. He suggests that southwestern Pennsylvania "has been too busy and distracted to develop a way of life in which good architecture, not exceptionally but as a normal occurrence, is produced." Kidney, *Landmark Architecture*, 14.

[41] A short history of the church and its construction is in James D. Van Trump, "Pittsburgh's St. Peters, by John Notman," *Journal of the Society of Architectural Historians* 15 (1956): 19-23. A contemporary description is transcribed in Constance M. Greiff, *John Notman, Architect* (Philadelphia: The Athenaeum of Philadelphia, 1979), 175-76. St. Peter's is compared with Philadelphia's St. Mark's in James D. Van Trump, *Life and Architecture in Pittsburgh* (Pittsburgh: Pittsburgh History and Landmarks Foundation, 1983), 193-200.

[42] Van Trump, *Life and Architecture in Pittsburgh*, 200. According to Van Trump, those pioneer qualities are "the forthrightness, the hearty quietude, the sobriety, the sturdy Protestantism, and the dislike of new doctrine and undue display."

[43] Kidney, *Landmark Architecture*, 223; *Preservation News* (Washington, D.C.), March 1990, 3.

[44] Henry-Russell Hitchcock, *The Architecture of H. H. Richardson and His Times* (rev. ed.; Cambridge, Mass.: MIT Press, 1966), 299. As one of the giants of American architecture, Richardson has been the subject of many studies. Hitchcock's book is the standard study of Richardson's life and work. The most complete and systematic compilation of Richardson's commissions is Jeffery Karl Ochsner, *H. H. Richardson: Complete Architectural Works* (Cambridge, Mass.: MIT Press, 1982). The earliest work on Richardson, and still useful, is Mariana Griswold Van Rensselaer, *Henry Hobson Richardson and His Works* (Boston: Houghton Mifflin and Company, 1888; reprint ed., New York: Dover Publications, Inc., 1969). A more recent work is the succinct and excellent study by James F. O'Gorman, *H. H. Richardson: Architectural Forms for an American Society* (Chicago: University of Chicago Press, 1987).

[45] Quoted in James D. Van Trump, *Majesty of the Law: The Courthouses of Allegheny County* (Pittsburgh: Pittsburgh History and Landmarks Foundation, 1988), 71. Van Trump discusses Pittsburgh's three courthouses, but focuses on the competition, construction, and subsequent history of Richardson's building. The book includes an essay by Walter C. Kidney on changes to the buildings since 1970. The buildings' monumental towers also functioned as key elements in the ventilating system. As Richardson explained to the county commissioners, "the supply of air is drawn from the top of the great tower by two fans in the basement. The air enters through openings about 250 feet above the street level, and is drawn through the turrets on the two front corners of the tower as far as the roof, where it passes into two flues . . . which carry it to the basement." (Ibid., 56.) There the air would be heated and cleaned and directed through ducts to the various rooms and exhausted through the two rear towers.

[46] Hitchcock, *The Architecture of H. H. Richardson*, 145. The other self-assessed great building was the Marshall Field Warehouse in Chicago, 1886-87.

[47] O'Gorman, *H. H. Richardson*, 52.

[48] E.M. Butz and William Kauffman were the architects of the Fayette County Courthouse, which was built in 1890-92 and still stands at 61 East Main Street, Uniontown. Charles Robinson of Altoona designed the Johnstown City Hall in 1900 with a steel frame. Project architect was Walter Myton, who, during the building's construction, opened his Johnstown architectural office, which prospered until his death in 1929. Completed in 1902, the building stands at the northeast corner of Main and Market Streets. Interview with Renee Logue, Office of Commissioners of Fayette County, Uniontown, 31 January 1990; Wallace, ed., *Character of a Steel Mill City*, 59-60; Terri Hartman, "Johnstown City Hall," HABS Report, PA-5387 (Washington, D.C.: Library of Congress, 1988), 1-3.

[49] The Schwab House is at 541 Jones Avenue in North Braddock. Other significant Richardsonian Romanesque buildings in Pittsburgh include Christ Methodist Church (now First United Methodist) (1891-93) at Aiken Avenue between Centre Avenue and Baum Boulevard, from the designs of Weary and Kramer; at 604 Fourth Avenue the Allegheny County Mortuary (1901-3, Frederick J. Osterling, architect) with rock-faced ashlar facades and wall dormers that imitate those of Richardson's courthouse; and the 1891 rock-faced ashlar Bellefield Presbyterian Church Rectory at Fifth and North Bellefield Avenues. Kidney, *Landmark Architecture*, 170, 231, 247, 259, 286-87; for his discussion of Richardson's influence on local buildings, see 57-59.

[50] Stevens, *Pennsylvania: Birthplace of a Nation*, 129, 238-39; Writers' Program, *Pennsylvania*, 307.

[51] Among Alden and Harlow's lost Pittsburgh mansions is steel magnate Alexander Rolland Peacock's Rowanlea. The brick and stone house was built in 1901; Peacock sold the house and its contents in 1921, and three years later a developer purchased the property and replaced the mansion with smaller dwellings. (Peacock died in New York in 1928, sixty-seven years of age.) Another is Edgehill, the swollen 1901 Renaissance-Colonial Revival mansion for Francis Lovejoy, former manager of the Carnegie Steel Company. Lovejoy never occupied the house. He took a bath in an Idaho mining venture, and in 1929, three years before his death at seventy-eight, the unfinished house was torn down. Kidney, *Landmark Architecture*, 183; Van Trump, *Life and Architecture in Pittsburgh*, 273-81.

[52] Van Trump, *Life and Architecture in Pittsburgh*. 283-90; Kidney, *Landmark Architecture*, 77, 270-71, 279; Dickson, *A Hundred Pennsylvania Buildings*, pl. 84.

[53] Dickson, *A Hundred Pennsylvania Buildings*, pls. 83, 85; Kidney, *Landmark Architecture*, 166, 253; Thomas S. Hines, *Burnham of Chicago: Architect and Planner* (New York: Oxford University Press, 1974), 298-300. Thomas C. Cochran briefly explains how the "great merger movement" at the turn of the twentieth century made the economies of the Philadelphia and Pittsburgh regions vulnerable to national trends in *Pennsylvania*, 161.

[54] Fallingwater is famous in part because its imaginative design and spectacular site have been captured in an oft-printed photograph, by which most Americans know it, and also because it has been the topic of numerous articles and books in both the popular and architectural press. Its history is presented by Donald Hoffmann, *Frank Lloyd Wright's Fallingwater: The House and*

Its History (New York: Dover Publications, Inc., 1978). A sympathetic work by the client's son (and a Wright student) is Edgar Kaufmann Jr., *Fallingwater: A Frank Lloyd Wright Country House* (New York: Abbeville Press, 1986).

[55] Kidney, *Landmark Architecture*, 113; Franklin Toker, *Pittsburgh: An Urban Portrait* (University Park, Pa.: Pennsylvania State University Press, 1986), 256-57.

[56] Walter Gropius and Marcel Breuer designed 250 Aluminum City houses in New Kensington, Westmoreland County, in 1942. Gropius and Breuer seem to have tried to soften their Bauhaus techniques by arranging the rows of housing informally along the contours of the landscape and finishing the south walls with vertical untreated cedar siding. Dickson, *A Hundred Pennsylvania Buildings*, pl. 96; Toker, *Pittsburgh*, 311.

[57] Even the affluent preferred traditional forms for their homes. As Kidney points out, the two houses by Venturi, Scott Brown and Meier in Pittsburgh's Squirrel Hill, "are untypical of the neighborhood." Kidney, *Landmark Architecture*, 121. Both houses are illustrated and briefly discussed in Toker, *Pittsburgh*, 257-58.

[58] For evaluations of PPG Place, see Donald Canty, "Historicist, Spired 'City of Glass,'" *Architecture* 73 (May 1984): 242-51; Darl Rastorfer, "Reflections on a Curtain Wall," *Architectural Record* 172 (October 1984): 193-99; Franklin K. B. S. Toker, "PJ and PPG: A Date with History," *Progressive Architecture* 60 (July 1979): 60-61.

Catalog

Allegheny County

Ben Avon Borough

Dalzell House (PA-605), 229 Dalzell Ave., SE corner of Dalzell and Church Aves. Brick, T-shaped, 40'-3" (three-bay front) x 46'-1", two-and-a-half stories, gable roofs with segmental dormers on wing, bracketed cornice, projecting entrance bay with arched openings, door with stained-glass fanlight, double windows with decorative moldings, bay windows, Italianate details; central hall plan. Built ca. 1868; remodeled 1942-48, G. Goodwin, architect, porches altered, kitchen wing replaced with two-story addition, planter wall added. 5 sheets (1964, including plans, elevations). LC code: PA,2-BENAV,1.

Bethel Park Vicinity (South Park Township)

Miller, James, House (Oliver Miller House, Stone Manse) (PA-410), S side of Stone Manse Dr., .1 mi. E of Corrigan Dr., in South Park. Museum owned by Allegheny County Department of Parks. Random rubble with quoins, built in three sections: W section 27'-3" (two bay front) x 20'-5", E section 20'-8" (two-bay front) x 20', N rear kitchen wing 16'-1" x 16'-9", two-and-a-half stories with one-story rear wing, gable roofs. Original house on property was two-story log house built ca. 1772 by Oliver Miller; E section added to log house 1808 by James Miller, Oliver's son; 1830 W section replaced log house; late nineteenth-century kitchen wing added on rear of 1830 section. House remained in Miller family until 1927 when acquired by county and opened as museum. 8 sheets (1936, including plans, elevations, details); 3 ext. photos (1936); 2 data pages (1936). LC code: PA,2-PITBU.V,1. NR.

Miller, Oliver, House. See Miller, James, House.

Stone Manse. See Miller, James, House.

Churchill Borough

Beulah Presbyterian Church (PA-602), NE corner of Beulah Rd. (State Rte. 130) and McCready Rd. Brick, 50' (three-bay front) x 60'-2" (four bays), one story with basement, gable roof, two double doors with transoms on S (front) elevation, fanlight in S gable end, flat lintels with corner blocks, Georgian details; one room, arched ceiling. Built 1837. Congregation founded in 1784. 8 sheets (1964, including site plan, plans, elevations, section). LC code: PA,2-CHURCHL,1. NR.

Dravosburg Vicinity (West Mifflin Township)

Rhodes Springhouse (PA-413), N side of Bettis Rd., E of Old Bettis Airport, approx. 1 mi. N of Dravosburg. Random rubble, 20' (two-bay front) x 15'-1", one story with loft on sloping site fully exposing cellar on SE elevation, gable roof overhangs on NE (front) elevation covering porch, partially open cellar passageway under porch; one room, corner fireplace. Built before 1850; A. S. Rhodes, probable builder. 3 sheets (1936, including plans, elevations, details); 4 ext. photos (1936); 1 data page (1936). LC code: PA,2-DRAVO.V,1.

Evergreen Hamlet (Ross Township)

Hampton-Kelly House. See Hampton, Wade, House.

Hampton, Wade, House (Hampton-Kelly House) (PA-606), N side of Evergreen Hamlet Rd., .1 mi. W of Babcock Blvd. Frame with board and batten siding, T-shaped, 46' (three-bay front) x 33' with kitchen wing to N, two stories with attic and basement, gable roof, bracketed cornice, porch with scroll brackets across S (front) elevation, door with transom and side lights, French windows on first story, Italianate details; central hall plan. Built 1852; attributed to J.W. Kerr, architect; kitchen and pantry added to N of original kitchen; porch added. One of five homes built in a private, chartered suburb of Pittsburgh. 10 sheets (1963, including site plan, plans, elevations, section, details). LC code: PA,2-EVGHM,1. NR.

Kelly House. See Hampton, Wade, House.

McKeesport

McConnell House. See Muse, John J., House.

Muse, John J., House (McConnell House) (PA-603), Muse's Ln. Brick, L-shaped, 46'-4" (five-bay front) x 40'-6", two-and-a-half stories with basement, gable roof, cornice with paired brackets, projecting entrance porch with carved wooden balustrade, door with side lights and transom, two-story porch on ell, rear kitchen wing; central hall plan. Built 1838; John J. Muse, builder. 7 sheets (1961, including plans, elevations). LC code: PA,2-MCKSPT,1.

Pittsburgh

Allegheny County Courthouse and Jail (PA-610), Courthouse 436 Grant St. with jail across street at 420 Ross St. Courthouse: rock-faced granite laid in alternating high and low courses, 301' x 209' with interior courtyard 145' x 70', five stories and attic with battered basement, steep gable and hip roofs with dormers, central entrance tower with turrets on W (front) elevation, slightly projecting corner pavilions, entrances (N and S elevations) flanked by turrets, four towers in courtyard, arched openings with massive voussoirs, connected to jail by enclosed bridge; Jail: coursed rock-faced granite, irregular plan with radial cell-block wings around central octagonal tower, tower at jail end of bridge, open interior yards, five stories with basement, hip, gable, and conical roofs, public entrance with machicolated feature, four-story arched windows with massive voussoirs face interior yards; Romanesque Revival style. Built 1884-88; Henry Hobson Richardson, architect; 1904 jail enlarged, F. J. Osterling, architect; 1923-24 arched entrances of N and S elevations partially filled; entrances in basement added 1928, Stanley L. Roush, architect. One of H. H. Richardson's finest monumental designs. 35 sheets (1963, including site plan, plans, elevations, sections, details); 10 ext. photos (1963), 1 int. photo (1963), 2 copy photos of ca. 1888 lithograph and ca. 1890 ext. photo; 1 data page (1984). LC code: PA,2-PITBU,29. NHL.

Arbuthnot Building. See Penn and Liberty Avenues (Commercial Buildings), Arbuthnot Building.

Baker Hall. See Carnegie Institute of Technology, Administration Building.

Beau Brummell Club (PA-625), 954 Liberty Ave. Club was located in first two stories of five-story masonry building, only club was documented, based on 1961 remodeling. Entrance facade of coursed rusticated ashlar, irregular L-shaped, four-bay facade, two stories with basement, bracketed cornice divides facade from upper stories of building; dining room with surrounding balcony. Remodeled 1961; George R. and George L. Simons, architects; Atna Builders. Burned 1963. 10 sheets possibly traced from architects' drawings (1967, including site plan, plans, elevation, sections). LC code: PA,2-PITBU,30.

Bedford, Dr. Nathaniel, Monument (PA-44), in Trinity Cathedral Churchyard, on NE side of Oliver Ave., between Wood and Smithfield Sts. Originally on ground of Dr. Bedford's home on S. 12th St. Sandstone monument, rectangular base with paneled sides, carved urn on top, 10'-2" high. Built ca. 1818; moved to present location when Bedford home was demolished 1909. Bedford was first physician of record to practice medicine in Pittsburgh, a surgeon at Fort Pitt. 1 sheet (1935, including elevation, details); 2 photos (1935); 3 data pages (1935). LC code: PA,2-PITBU,10. NR (Pittsburgh Central Downtown Historic District).

Bouquet's Redoubt. See Fort Pitt Blockhouse.

Brady Street Bridge (South Twenty-Second Street Bridge) (PA-614), spanning Monongahela River, connecting Brady and S. Twenty-Second Sts. Steel superstructure supported by four granite piers (two shore, two river) and abutments, central span with flanking spans with multiple-span approaches from end abutments (total span 2250', total length including end abutments 2530'), central span (520') of two-hinged arch-truss of Bonn type with modified Pratt bracing with riveted web members and eyebars for bottom chord, flanking spans (260' each) of similar construction with sloping top chord continuous with that of central span, N approach (837') consists of nine plate girder spans on lattice steel bents, S approach (350') consists of three fishbelly plate girder spans on lattice steel bents, decorative iron work. Built 1895-96; Schultz Bridge and Iron Company, contractors; 1909 piers rebuilt; demolished ca. 1978. First toll-free river bridge in Pittsburgh area. 14 sheets (1966, including site plan, plans, elevations, sections, details). LC code: PA,2-PITBU,31. HAER.

Brewer, Charles, House (PA-41), 1131 Western Ave. Brick, 48'-1" (five-bay front) x 39'-8", two-and-a-half stories with elevated coursed ashlar basement, gable roof with pedimented gable ends, identical pedimented Ionic porticos on N (front) and S elevations, Doric corner pilasters with entablature and denticulated cornice, belt course, door with fanlight and side lights flanked by pilasters, Greek Revival details; central hall plan. Built ca. 1830; two-story wing added to W elevation after 1860; apartments 1935; demolished. 11 sheets (1935, including plans, elevations, section, details); 1 ext. photo (1935), 2 int. photos (1935); 3 data pages (1935). LC code: PA,2-PITBU,7.

Brick Cornices. See Third Avenue.

Brunot House. See Hogg-Brunot House.

Byers Hall. See Byers-Lyon House.

Byers-Lyon House (Byers Hall) (PA-1158), 901 Ridge Ave. Brick with brownstone trim (quoins, belt courses, voussoirs over openings), large L-shaped double house (appears as single house) with entrance courtyard, three-and-a-half stories with basement, steeply pitched hip roof with large stepped dormers, massive chimneys, arcade supported by Doric columns with iron balustrade above facing entrance courtyard, elaborate wrought iron entrance gates to courtyard, Flemish Renaissance Revival details. Built 1898; Alden and Harlow, architects; now offices for Community College of Allegheny County. 8 ext. photos (1963). LC code: PA,2-PITBU,51. NR.

Carnegie Institute of Technology, Administration Building (Baker Hall) (PA-1172), on Carnegie-Mellon University Campus, N side of Frew St., W of Tech St. Brick with terra cotta trim, 91'-8" (five-bay front) x 54'-6" (three bays) with stairhall on rear elevation, three stories with basement, hip roof with cross-gable roof forming pediment over projecting pavilion of E (front) elevation and extending to W stairhall, central arch with recessed two-story glazed entrance on E elevation, recessed two-story panels divide bays, three-part windows with fanlights and transoms, Beaux-Arts details; central hall plan, Rafael Guastavino geometrical stair and tile vaulting system. Built 1912; part of original competition-winning campus design by Henry Hornbostel, architect, but altered in execution; connected to Porter Hall by later addition by Hornbostel. 14 sheets (1963-65, including site plan, plans, elevations, sections, details); 2 ext. photos (1963), 2 int. photos (1963). LC code: PA,2-PITBU,24B.

Carnegie Institute of Technology, Machinery Hall Tower (Hammerschlag Hall Tower) (PA-1174), on Carnegie-Mellon University Campus, N side of Frew St., behind Porter Hall. Brick with terra cotta trim, 65' square base with circular tower (35' diameter), 63' high, open arcaded tower with balustrade and decorative terra cotta panels at cornice, chimney flue through center of tower surrounded by arcade, cantilevered stairs around flue. Built 1912-13; Henry Hornbostel, architect. 6 sheets (1966, including site plan, plans, elevations, sections, details). LC code: PA,2-PITBU,24A.

Carnegie-Mellon University. See Carnegie Institute of Technology, Administration Building and Machinery Hall Tower.

Chatham College, Berry Hall. See Wilson House.

City-County Building (PA-5193), 414 Grant St. Granite-faced steel frame, approx. 183' x 300', eleven stories, three large entrance arches, Doric columns along upper stories, neoclassical massing with Beaux-Arts detailing; central gallery with bronze columns and 47' high vaulted ceiling, sculptured elevator doors, Rafael Guastavino tile vaults. Built 1915-17; Edward B. Lee, Palmer, Hornbostel and Jones, Associated Architects, but also attributed to Henry Hornbostel. 4 ext. photos (1981), 2 int. photos (1981); 3 data pages (1981). LC code: PA,2-PITBU,34.

Coltart, Joseph, House (PA-47), 3431 Forbes St., at intersection with Coltart St. Brick, 44'-2" (five-bay front) x 15' with symmetrical one-bay office wings, two-and-a-half stories with one-story wings, sloping site fully exposes basement on front elevation, gable roof with corner urns, hip roofs on wings, paired chimneys in parapets at gable ends, denticulated cornice, doors with side lights, Greek Revival details; central hall plan. Built ca. 1843; Joseph Coltart, possible designer; tetrastyle Ionic portico added on N elevation; vacant 1933; demolished ca. 1974. 4 sheets (1935, including plans, elevations, section); 1 ext. photo (1935); 2 data pages (1935). LC code: PA,2-PITBU,13.

Community College of Allegheny County, Byers Hall. See Byers-Lyon House.

Croghan, William, House (Schenley House, Picnic House) (PA-8-8), approx. .5 mi. S of Stanton Ave., near Stanton Heights Golf Course, in Stanton Heights. Large L-shaped house built in two sections, brick section 55'-3" (five-bay front) x 55'-2", random rubble E (rear) section (scored stucco on S elevation) 38'-4" x 67'-1" (four bays), two-story brick section and one-story stone section with elevated basement (scored stucco), hip roofs, Corinthian porch with fret design on frieze across N, W and S elevations, Greek Revival style; central hall plan, fine, elaborate Greek Revival interior with carved wooden and molded plaster decoration, ballroom decorated by Mordecai van Horne of Philadelphia. Stone section built ca. 1835; brick section built ca. 1840s; demolished ca. 1946, ballroom and oval vestibule acquired 1930s by University of Pittsburgh and installed in Cathedral of Learning. 14 sheets (1934, including plans, elevations, section, details); 3 ext. photos (1934), 7 int. photos (1934); 4 data pages (1936). LC code: PA,2-PITBU,3.

Emmanuel Protestant Episcopal Church (PA-426), SE corner of North and Allegheny Aves. Brick with rock-faced brownstone sills and imposts, 49'-4" (three-bay front) x 100' (including semicircular apse 49'-4" x 22'-4"), one story with lower courses battered, steep gable roof with steeply gabled dormers with pointed-arched openings, entrance arcade of three arches with series of brick archivolts with recessed double doors on N (front) elevation, recessed arched windows in groups of three with series of brick archivolts (Tiffany glass above entrance, stained glass in others), fine patterned brickwork (mouse-toothing, basketweave, soldier courses), corbeled cornice, Romanesque Revival style; central aisle, exposed wooden roof truss with laminated arched bottom chord. Built 1885-86; Henry Hobson Richardson, architect; Henry Schenk, builder; parish house added at SW corner 1887, Frank E. Alden, architect; marble and mosaic reredos in chancel added 1898 by Leake and Green. 6 sheets (1961, including plans, elevations, sections, details); 5 ext. photos (1963), 2 int. photos (1963); 4 data pages (1963). LC code: PA,2-PITBU,18. NR.

English-Oliver House (PA-425), 845 Ridge Ave. Coursed ashlar with quoins, rectangular with several projecting bays, 47'-9" (five-bay front) x 79'-1" with rear kitchen wing 47'-4" x 36'-10", two-and-a-half stories with two-story wing, hip roof with hip dormers, bracketed cornice, belt course with fret design, one-bay Ionic entrance porch on N (front) elevation, balustraded veranda, arched windows, Italianate style; elaborate carved and paneled interior woodwork, Tiffany windows. Built 1871 for Andrew H. English, publisher; extensively remodeled (Italianate features added) 1891 for Henry W. Oliver, industrialist, by Shepley, Rutan and Coolidge, architects; demolished 1969. 9 sheets (1961, including plans, elevations, sections); 3 ext. photos (1963), 4 int. photos (1963); 5 data pages (1963). LC code: PA,2-PITBU,17.

Fahnestock, Benjamin A., House (PA-45), 408 Penn Ave. Brick, L-shaped, three-bay front, three stories with basement, gable roof, entrance with fanlight and recessed double door flanked by Ionic columns on N (front) elevation, stone lintels with corner rosettes; side hall plan. Built 1835-40; interior remodeled; 1935 owned by Congress of Women's

Clubs; demolished 1950. 3 sheets (1935, including elevation, details); 1 ext. photo (1935); 2 data pages (1935). LC code: PA,2-PITBU,11.

Fort Pitt Blockhouse (Bouquet's Redoubt) (PA-430), in Point State Park (at the confluence of Allegheny and Monongahela Rivers). Museum. Brick with random rubble foundation (5' above grade), pentagonal (approx. 19' each side), two levels with loft, pyramidal roof, course of squared logs with gun ports on both levels, door with brick arch on SE elevation. Built 1764 under Colonel Henry Bouquet's command; 1785-1892 used as dwelling; 1875 brick residence built 4' to NW and several openings cut into walls of blockhouse; 1875-92 several sheds added; 1894 acquired by Allegheny County Chapter of Daughters of the American Revolution and restored. Oldest documented building in Pittsburgh area; built on west side of ramparts of Fort Pitt for defense against Indian attacks. 4 sheets (1963, including site plan, plan, elevation, section); 2 ext. photos (1963), 1 int. photo (1963); 3 data pages (1963). LC code: PA,2-PITBU,20. NHL.

Fulton Theater (Gayety Theatre) (PA-1180), SW corner of Fort Duquesne Blvd. and Barker Pl., entrance vestibule through adjoining Fulton Building at 101 Sixth St. Steel frame covered with brick (banded corners and first and fifth stories), 100'-2" x 161'-6", five-story front section with auditorium at rear, two-story wing connects theater to Fulton Building, gable roof with pedimented gable end, elaborate iron marquee at Sixth St. entrance. Built 1906; Dodge and Morrison, architects. Originally used as live theater, now as motion picture theater. 11 sheets (1967, including site plan, plans, elevations, sections, details). LC code: PA,2-PITBU,27.

Garden Theater (PA-1278), 10-14 W. North Ave. Glazed terra cotta (E front elevation) and brick, 59' (three-bay front) x 180', two-story front area with auditorium to rear, gable roof, bays defined by pilasters with entablature, pedimented central bay with parapet to either side, first story central bay is recessed open vestibule with ticket booth, store-fronts to either side of vestibule; textured polychrome plaster interior. Built 1914-15; Thomas H. Scott, architect; redecorated ca. 1927; marquee replaced 1958; ticket booth owned by Pittsburgh History & Landmarks Foundation. Continuously used as a movie theater. 1 sheet (1970 from original drawings by Scott 1914, including plan, elevation); 3 ext. photos (1972), 3 int. photos (1972); 14 data pages (1970, 1976, 1978). LC code: PA,2-PITBU,28.

Gayety Theater. See Fulton Theater.

Hamerschlag Hall Tower. See Carnegie Institute of Technology, Machinery Hall Tower.

Harper Building. See Penn and Liberty Avenues (Commercial Buildings), Harper Building.

Harter, Eva, House (PA-622), 2557 Beechwood Blvd. Coursed squared rubble (first story and basement) and stucco (second story), rectangular with projecting bays and porches, 46'-6" x 28', two stories with basement, hip roof with wooden shingles simulating thatched roof, curved roof with gabled dormer of wooden shingles over front porch, large end chimneys, leaded-glass windows, English Arts and Crafts Movement influence; garage of similar design. Built 1923; Frederick G. Scheibler Jr., architect. 10 sheets (1967, including plans, elevations, section, plans and elevations of garage). LC code: PA,2-PITBU,32.

Heathside Cottage (PA-623), 416 Catoma St. Brick, irregular plan, approx. 35' x 31', one-and-a-half stories with basement, intersecting hip and gable roofs with gabled dormers, decorative slate roof shingles, carved bargeboards with pendants and finials, porch across W (front) elevation, bay with pointed-arch windows, Gothic Revival style. Built ca. 1855-60; brick kitchen wing added on N elevation. 6 sheets (1968, including site plan, plans, elevations, sections, details). LC code: PA,2-PITBU,33, NR.

Heidelberg Apartments and Cottages. See Old Heidelberg Apartments and Cottages.

Hogg-Brunot House (PA-428), 216 E. Stockton Ave. Brick, L-shaped (half of double house), 25'-1" (three-bay front) x 48'-7" with rear wing 22'-5" x 61'-6", three-and-a-half-story main block and two-and-a-half-story wing with basement, gable roof, bracketed cornice, two-bay Corinthian entrance porch on S (front) elevation (porch extends across double house), door with transom framed by pilasters and entablature, stone lintels with corner blocks, Greek Revival details; side hall plan. Built ca. 1840-50; Salvation Army recreation center 1963; demolished. 3 sheets (1961, including plans, elevations, details); 2 ext. photos (1963), 2 int. photos (1963); 4 data pages (1963). LC code: PA,2-PITBU,19.

Karns, John, House (PA-424), 900 N. Canal St. Brick row house, L-shaped, 23'-6" (three-bay front) x 56', two-and-a-half stories with elevated scored stucco basement, gable roof with pedimented gable end, paired chimneys in parapet, two-bay bracketed Doric entrance porch on S (front) elevation (part of porch which extends across row houses), door with transom and side lights flanked by pilasters, Greek Revival details; side hall plan. Built ca. 1855; demolished. 4 sheets (1961, including plans, elevations); 2 ext. photos (1963); 3 data pages (1963). LC code: PA,2-PITBU,16.

King Building. See Penn and Liberty Avenues (Commercial Buildings), King Building.

Kingsbacher Building. See Penn and Liberty Avenues (Commercial Buildings), Kingsbacher Building.

Klages, Allen M., House (PA-621), 5525 Beverly Pl. Random rubble, irregular rectangle, approx. 38' (three wide bays) x 41'-8", two-and-a-half stories with basement, steep intersecting gable roofs with gabled dormers, projecting entrance bay, large stone arches over windows, numerous leaded-glass windows; interior leaded-glass windows and cabinets, tile fireplaces, carved mahogany woodwork, English Arts and Crafts Movement influence. Built 1923; Frederick G. Scheibler Jr. architect. 11 sheets (1968, including plans, elevations, details of int. elevations). LC code: PA,2-PITBU,35.

Landmarks Building. See Pittsburgh and Lake Erie Railroad Station.

Lipson Building. See Penn and Liberty Avenues (Commercial Buildings), Lipson Building.

Loyal Order of Moose Building. See Penn and Liberty Avenues (Commercial Buildings), Loyal Order of Moose Building.

Lyons House. See Byers-Lyons House.

McCormick Building. See Penn and Liberty Avenues (Commercial Buildings), McCormick Building.

Meade Street (Apartments) (PA-1096), 7211-25 Meade St. Two matching apartment buildings. Brick with stone trim, three stories, central three-story portico eliptical in plan, bowed windows, Classical Revival details. Built 1909; vacant and in poor condition when documented; to be rehabilitated for multifamily residential use. 4 ext. photos (1983); 5 data pages including reproductions of measured drawings (1983). LC code: PA,2-PITBU,50.

Miller, James, House. See Bethel Park Vicinity (South Park Township), Miller, James, House.

Mitchell, John M., House (PA-42), 524 Third Ave. Brick, L-shaped, 18'-4" (three-bay front) x 44'-3", two-and-a-half stories with basement, gable roof with pedimented dormer flanked by pilasters, denticulated cornice, door with transom and pilasters on N (front) elevation; side hall plan. Built between 1845 and 1860; demolished. 2 sheets (1935, including plans, elevation, section, details); 1 ext. photo (1935); 2 data pages (1935). LC code: PA,2-PITBU,8.

Moose Hall. See Penn and Liberty Avenues (Commercial Buildings), Loyal Order of Moose Building.

Morse School Annex (PA-5199), Sarah St., between Twenty-Fourth and Twenty-fifth Sts. Brick with framing system of steel and reinforced concrete, two stories with elevated basement, hip and gable roofs, decorated gable over entrance bays, Romanesque Revival details. Built 1905; demolished. 5 ext. photos (1982), 9 int. photos (1982); 17 data pages (1982). LC code: PA,2-PITBU,52A.

Neal, Robert, Cabin (Neill Log House) (PA-46), in Schenley Park, on N side of Serpentine Dr. Museum operated by Pittsburgh History & Landmarks Foundation. Log with heavy stone and clay chinking, 23'-7" (two-bay front) x 21'-2", one story with loft, gable roof, large random rubble chimney; one room. Built 1787-95; Robert Neal, builder; restored ca. 1970. One of the oldest extant domestic buildings in Pittsburgh. 2 sheets (1935, including plan, elevations, sections, details); 2 ext. photos (1935), 1 copy photo ca. 1900; 2 data pages (1935). LC code: PA,2-PITBU,12.

Neill Log House. See Neal, Robert, Cabin.

North Side Market (PA-601), SE corner of Federal and E. Ohio Sts. Brick, approx. 202' square, one-story section surrounds two-story central section with dome, barrel vaults intersecting at corners cover one-story section, hip roof with dome and cupola cover two-story section, slightly projecting brick piers divide bays, bracketed cornice, brick chevron pattern along cornice, various arched and circular windows, Italianate details; open interior, exposed iron roof trusses. Built ca. 1865; mezzanine rooms added 1934; demolished 1966. 10 sheets (1964, including plans, elevations, section, details). LC code: PA,2-PITBU,36.

North Side Post Office. See United States Allegheny Post Office.

Old Heidelberg Apartments and Cottages (PA-431), 401-23 S. Braddock Ave., SE corner Braddock Ave. and Waverly St. Stuccoed brick, main block 124' (eight-bay front) x 34'-6" with two E (rear) wings, three stories with basement, gable and hip roofs with eyebrow dormer, three-story porches on W elevation, varied fenestration, exposed steel I-beams for lintels; leaded-glass cabinets and doors, tile fireplaces, English Arts and Crafts Movement influence. Built 1905; Frederick G. Scheibler, architect; five additional dwelling units (cottages) built 1908 by Scheibler. 21 sheets (1962, including site plan, plans, elevations, sections, details); 3 ext. photos (1963), 2 int. photos (1963), 1 ext. copy photo from ca. 1906; 5 data pages (1963). LC code: PA,2-PITBU,21. NR.

Old Post Office Museum. See United States Allegheny Post Office.

Oliver House. See English-Oliver House.

Penn and Liberty Avenues (Commercial Buildings) (PA-5152), 600 and 700 blocks of Liberty Ave. and 600 block of Penn Ave. Commercial blocks representing the late nineteenth- and early twentieth-century character of the area. With good access to freight transportation, the commission merchant trade developed in the Penn-Liberty area in the 1860s. Produce commission houses dominated Penn and Liberty between Sixth and Eleventh Sts. These structures were modest in scale and design, usually three to four stories with shed porches across the facade to shelter loading areas (see King and Whitten Buildings). Larger mercantile warehouses developed by the end of the century (see Arbuthnot, Harper, McCormick, and Wallace and McAlister Buildings). By 1905 produce trading shifted from downtown and Penn-Liberty changed to a commercial, civic, and cultural area. With a trolley line on Liberty high-style theaters, offices, and dry goods stores developed on Penn and Liberty (see Kingsbacher, Lipson, and Loyal Order of Moose Buildings). Area deteriorated mid-twentieth century and presently is undergoing redevelopment. All structures documented were demolished 1984-85. 3 sheets (1984, including site plan, elevations); 5 ext. photos (1984, 1985), 4 copy photos of views from 1899 and 1906; 28 data pages including copies of maps and historical views (1985). LC code: PA,2-PITBU,40. See following entries for individual documentation.

Arbuthnot Building (Wurlitzer Building) (PA-5152D), 719-21 Liberty Ave. Brick walls and piers with steel beams, rock-faced ashlar facade, approx. 30' x 110', nine stories, flat roof, two-story storefront with recessed first floor and massive spanning lintel at second-floor level, facade composed of piers joined by arches at sixth and ninth stories, massive denticulated stone cornice, Richardsonian Romanesque style; clear-span interior. Built 1893; Charles Bickel, architect; interior and storefront altered; demolished 1985. Built by Arbuthnot-Stevenson Company, a well-known wholesale dry-goods firm established in 1843. 4 ext. photos (1984, 1985), 1 copy of 1893 photo; 28 data pages including copies of maps, historical views, 1985 photo, and sketch of floor plan (1985). LC code: PA,2-PITBU,46.

Harper Building (PA-5152E), 723-25 Liberty Ave. Brick walls and piers with steel beams, facade originally light brick with light brownstone trim (later painted), approx. 30' x 110', nine stories, flat roof, facade divided into three bays by brick piers on lower floors and narrow paired columns on upper floors, first-story storefront framed by limestone piers with Corinthian capitals; clear-span interior. Built 1892-93; Charles Bickel, architect; original Richardsonian Romanesque storefront replaced with limestone piers 1940, storefront further altered with brick and metal-framed window; original pressed metal cornice replaced with brick parapet; overhanging moldings at second and sixth floors removed; demolished 1985. Built as a mercantile warehouse by Lydia Harper as a tribute to her husband, John Arunah Harper, president of the Bank of Pittsburgh and a prominent financier, organizer, and philanthropist in late nineteenth century. Pittsburgh. 5 ext. photos (1984, 1985); 25 data pages including copies of maps, historical view, 1985 photo, and sketch of floor plan (1985). LC code: PA,2-PITBU,47.

King Building (PA-5152B), 639 Liberty Ave. Brick with brick over steel frame on facade, approx. 20' x 88', four stories, flat roof, three-part windows recessed at an angle to create illusion of bay windows, terra cotta cartouches, pressed metal cornice with dentils and end consoles; clear-span interior. Built ca. 1860-73 as Victorian-style commercial building; altered 1908, W.D. Beatty, contractor, facade reconstructed with classical details; interior and storefront altered; demolished 1984. One of first buildings in area constructed specifically to house produce commission merchants; redesigned when area changed to more fashionable retail district. 3 ext. photos (1984); 23 data pages including copies of maps, historical views, and sketch of floor plan (1985). LC code: PA,2-PITBU,44.

Kingsbacher Building (PA-5151), 637 Liberty Ave. Brick with terra cotta facade, approx. 20' x 180', three stories, flat roof, garlanded colonettes divide three window bays, arched windows with keystones, ornamental terra cotta blocks with name on frieze below cornice, Renaissance Revival style; clear-span interior. Built 1910; storefront remodeled 1962; demolished 1984. Housed Kingsbacher Brothers' jewelry store 1910-30; building replaced earlier three-story produce commission house when area changed from produce markets to retail enterprises. 2 sheets (1984, including site plan, elevations); 3 ext. photos (1984); 22 data pages including copies of maps and historical views (1985). LC code: PA,2-PITBU,43.

Lipson Building (PA-5152F), 636 Penn Ave. Brick walls with steel skeleton of girders and columns, terra cotta facade, approx. 20' x 60', six stories, flat roof, two-story base framed by piers with raised lozenges and cornice with lions' heads, terra cotta end piers with colonettes frame bays of upper stories, terra cotta cornice with arches springing from lions' heads; clear-span interior. Built 1905; Henry Lawrence Kreusler, contractor; original broad pivot-sash windows replaced with multipane casement windows; storefront altered; demolished 1984. Built as mercantile store and warehouse; leased to Jos. Lipson Co., fabric store, from 1933-84. 1 ext. photo (1984); 18 data pages including copies of maps, historical view, and sketch of floor plan (1985). LC code: PA,2-PITBU,48.

Loyal Order of Moose Building (Moose Hall) (PA-5149), 628-34 Penn Ave. Steel frame with brick curtain walls on masonry foundation, cladding of glazed terra cotta simulating stone courses on facade, 81'-4" x 118'-4", six stories, mansard roof with dormers at front with flat roof to rear, end bays flank three-story central colonnade, elaborate terra cotta ornamentation, Beaux Arts style; shops first floor, auditorium with elaborate plaster proscenium arch at stage and two-story supporting truss. Built 1914-15; U. J. Lincoln Peoples, architect; first-floor storefronts altered; seventh-story penthouse added behind mansard roof; demolished 1984; portions of facade removed and stored by Pittsburgh History & Landmarks Foundation. Built by Pittsburgh Lodge No. 46 and used by them until 1943. 13 sheets (1984, including site plan, plans, elevation, sections, details); 11 ext. photos (1984), 10 int. photos (1984); 26 data pages including copies of maps and historical view (1985). LC code: PA,2-PITBU,49.

McCormick Building (PA-5152A), 635 Liberty Ave. Brick with rock-faced ashlar on facade, approx. 20' x 110', four stories, flat roof, three-part windows with transoms, Richardsonian Romanesque style; clear-span interior. Built 1894; John P. Brennan, architect; original fifth story with gabled front removed after 1953 fire; first-story facade altered; demolished 1984. Part of row of buildings that housed produce commission merchants. 2 ext. photos (1984); 23 data pages including copies of maps, historical views, and sketch of floor plan (1985). LC code: PA,2-PITBU,42.

Wallace and McAlister Buildings (PA-5150), 631-33 Liberty Ave. Two buildings constructed 1894 joined by common facade 1913. Original buildings: brick with rock-faced ashlar facades, approx. 20' x 110', five stories, flat roofs, arched windows, Richardsonian Romanesque style; clear-span interiors. Wallace Building (631) built 1894, T. H. Scott, architect; McAlister Building (633) built 1894, John P. Brennan, architect. Buildings joined and refaced 1913: front walls rebuilt with steel columns and girders sheathed with terra cotta, Jacobean-Gothic Revival facade of simple geometric piers and spandrels with molded ornament of swags, garlands, and monkeys on pedestals, rectangular windows with transoms. First two stories further altered 1948; demolished 1984, several terra cotta ornaments preserved by Pittsburgh History & Landmarks Foundation. Built as produce commission houses, buildings refaced in Jacobean-Gothic Revival style reflecting area's transition into fashionable commercial center. 2 sheets (1984, including site plan, elevation); 3 ext. photos (1984); 36 data pages including copies of maps, historical views, and sketch of floor plan (1985). LC code: PA,2-PITBU,41.

Whitten Building (PA-5152C), 641 Liberty Ave. Brick with brick over steel frame on facade, approx. 20' x 88', four stories, flat roof, first-story terra cotta storefront with decorative shields and denticulated cornice, brick piers divide facade into three window bays, pressed metal cornice with modillions and end consoles; clear-span interior. Built ca. 1860-73 as Victorian-style commercial building; altered 1908, David T. Riffle, contractor, facade reconstructed with classical details; interior and storefront altered 1952; demolished 1984. One of first buildings in area constructed specifically to house produce commission merchants; redesigned when area changed to more fashionable retail district. 2 ext. photos (1984); 22 data pages including copies of maps, historical views, and sketch of floor plan (1985). LC code: PA,2-PITBU,45.

Pennsylvania Railroad Station, Rotunda (Union Railroad Station, Rotunda) (PA-1175), intersection of Liberty, Grant, and Eleventh Sts. Steel frame covered with terra cotta with granite base, large central dome with four domed corner pavilions connected by broad elliptical horseshoe-shaped arches, approx. 130' square, Beaux Arts Classical details; open interior, four decorative pendentives, coffered dome with skylight. Built 1901-02; D.H. Burnham and Company, architects; adjoins twelve-story station on N elevation; deteriorating, restoration planned. 6 sheets (1963, including site plan, plans, elevations, sections, details); 4 ext. photos (1963), 2 int. photos (1963), 1 copy of undated photo of demolished train shed; 1 data page (1983). LC code: PA,2-PITBU,37. NR.

Open Concourse and Concourse Roof Extension (PA-1175B). Decorative steel trusses supported on columns, roof of iron with terra cotta tile, concrete, and built-up roof material, open concourse side later filled with wood-framed windows, open interior space. Open concourse added on E elevation of station to serve as connecting area between waiting room and track platforms, concourse roof extension added to S of open concourse to connect it to former barrel-vaulted train shed. Built 1892-1902; D. H. Burnham and Company, architects; concourse roof extension demolished and windows removed from open concourse. 2 ext. photos (1982), 2 int. photos (1982); 6 data pages including copies of photos (1987). LC code: PA,2-PITBU,37C.

South Baggage Passage and Canopy (PA-1175A). Steel frame canopy with glass light set in roof. Appendage on S elevation of station next to baggage room which provided covered access from rotunda (taxi stand) to open concourse. Built 1892-1902; D. H. Burnham and Company, architects. 1 ext. photo (1982), 3 int. photos (1982); 8 data pages including copies of photos (1987). LC code: PA,2-PITBU,37B.

Picnic House. See Croghan, William, House.

Pittsburgh and Lake Erie Railroad Station (Landmarks Building) (PA-1231), W side of Smithfield St., N of Carson St. Steel frame covered with coursed ashlar tooled, rock-faced, and rusticated (basement, first and second floors) and brick (office block), terra cotta trim, nine by nine bays, seven stories, terra cotta panels and string courses and entablature with floral and geometric patterns, modillioned cornice, false pediment with relief of locomotive; two-story waiting room decorated by Crossman and Sturdy of Chicago, barrel vault of stained glass (painted over until 1978), large stained-glass fanlight at W end of vault, Corinthian columns and pilasters painted to imitate marble, stained-glass Palladian windows and arched windows, carved woodwork. Built 1898-1901; William George Burns, architect; renovated and now used as restaurant. 2 int. photos (1964); 1 data page (1983). LC code: PA,2-PITBU,55. NR.

Pittsburgh Club. See Shoenberger, John H., House.

Point Bridge (PA-604), spanning Monongahela River, W. Carson St. to Point of Pittsburgh. Coursed ashlar abutments and two river piers supporting steel arched cantilevered trusses with cantilevered side spans, central deck suspended from arched trusses, 1200' overall length, 430' span for river traffic, 30' roadway, unadorned steel-plate portals. Built 1925-27 (replaced original suspension bridge); Stanley L. Roush, architect; George S. Richardson, engineer in charge of design; demolished 1970. 6 sheets (1966, including site plan, plans, elevations, details). LC code: PA,2-PITBU,38. HAER.

St. Peter's Protestant Episcopal Church (PA-48), NE corner of Forbes and Craft Aves., originally located at NW corner of Diamond (presently Forbes Ave.) and Grant Sts. Coursed ashlar, approx. 65' x 114' (including projecting altar end), two-story nave, one-story side aisles, clerestory windows, gable roof, four-stage corner tower (approx. 19' square, 141' high) with spire on S (front) elevation, corner and wall buttresses, lancet windows with tracery, compound pointed-arch entrance, Gothic Revival style; basilica plan, hammer-beam trusses over nave, pointed-arch side aisles defined by pointed-arch arcade on clustered columns. Built 1851-52; John Notman, architect; John Eassieman, builder; moved to present location with slight alterations 1901; Vrydaugh and Wolfe, architects for rebuilding; demolished 1989-90. 6 sheets (measured 1901, drawn 1935, including plans, elevations, sections); 1 ext. photo (1935); 2 data pages (1935). LC code: PA,2-PITBU,14.

Schenley House. See Croghan, William, House.

Shadyside Presbyterian Church (PA-432), NE corner of Amberson Ave. and Westminster Pl. Random rock-faced ashlar, cruciform plan of large central rectangular tower (100' high) with lower transepts on each side (narthex, transepts, and chancel), steep pyramidal roof with kick at eaves line with pyramidal ventilator dormers on tower, steep gable roofs on wings, massive arched openings with rock-faced ashlar voussoirs and carved archivolts supported by colonettes, band of arched clerestory windows around tower, rose window over entrance on W (front) elevation, arcaded walkways, Richardsonian Romanesque style; interior of tower open with vaulted wings. Built 1889-90; Shepley, Rutan and Coolidge, architects; 1892 Shepley, Rutan and Coolidge built chapel connected to church by walkway; 1920 stained glass installed; 1937-38 Wilson Eyre and McIlvaine added offices and remodeled interior (added apse at E end and choir gallery in W wing); 1952 Hoffman and Crumpton remodeled chapel and added offices and parish hall; limestone Romanesque style addition on W ca. 1983. 7 ext. photos (1963), 3 int. photos (1963), 1 ext. copy photo from ca. 1906; 5 data pages (1963). LC code: PA,2-PITBU,22. NR.

Shoenberger, John H., House (Pittsburgh Club) (PA-43), 425 Penn Ave. Stuccoed brick, 57'-7" (five-bay front) x 53'-7" with passageway connecting house to rear service wing, two-and-a-half stories with basement, low gable roof with parapet, semicircular bays on S (front) elevation, door with transom and slightly pedimented cornice with scroll brackets, cornice with scroll brackets over windows, attic windows with cast-iron grilles in frieze, denticulated cornice, Greek Revival details; central hall plan, elaborate plaster ceiling decorations. Built 1847; used by the Pittsburgh Club after 1884; demolished 1950. 6 sheets (1935, including plans, elevations, section, details); 1 ext. photo (1935); 2 data pages (1935). LC code: PA,2-PITBU,9.

Singer, John F., House. See Wilkinsburg Borough, Singer, John F., House.

Snider Buildings (PA-5200), 2400, 2402, 2402 1/2 Sarah St. Brick, two-and-a-half stories, mansard roofs with patterned slate shingles and dormers face street, sloping roof behind parapet. Built ca. 1860-71; originally commercial properties later converted to apartments; rear additions; demolished. 8 ext. photos (1982); 14 data pages including sketch of floor plan (1982). LC code: PA,2-PITBU,54.

South Twenty-Second Street Bridge. See Brady Street Bridge.

Third Avenue (Brick Cornices) (PA-49), 101 Grant St., 442 Third Ave., 132 Second Ave., 334 Liberty Ave., 124 Fancourt St., NW corner of Fancourt St., and Penn Ave. Various brick cornices built between 1840 and 1860; all demolished. 2 sheets (1935); 1 data page (1935). LC code: PA,2-PITBU,15.

Union Railroad Station, Rotunda, Open Concourse and Concourse Roof Extension, and South Baggage Passage and Canopy. See Pennsylvania Railroad Station.

United States Allegheny Arsenal (PA-8-1), bounded by Fortieth St., Penn Ave., Thirty-ninth St., and Allegheny River. Designs for the arsenal complex were drawn by Benjamin H. Latrobe in 1814, but there were many departures from the original plans when construction began in 1815. The arsenal was extensive at one time, especially during the Civil War, but declined around 1868 and closed in 1900. Portion given to city 1907; remainder sold at public auction 1926; buildings used for various purposes; only three structures remain. 2 sheets (1934, including site plans, plaque details); 2 data pages (1936). LC code: PA,2-PITBU,6. See following entries for individual structures.

Armory (PA-8-1-F), NW end of complex, between Thirty-ninth and Fortieth Sts. Coursed ashlar, 60'-5" (three-bay front) x 40'-4", two stories with basement, hip roof, stepped stone cornice, stone lintels with corner blocks, Greek Revival details. Built 1814-20. 3 sheets (1934, including plans, elevations, section, details); 2 ext. photos (1934). LC code: PA,2-PITBU,6F.

Barracks (PA-8-1-C), NE side of Thirty-ninth St., NW of Butler St. Brick, 125' (nine-bay front) x 25', two stories with basement, gable roof, open arcade across NE (front) elevation with enclosed stairwell at each end and corridor above arcade, separate entrance to each room behind arcade. Built 1814-20. Similar to *Noncommissioned Officers' Quarters*. 4 sheets (1934, including plans, elevations, sections, details); 6 ext. photos (1934). LC code: PA,2-PITBU,6C.

Boiler House (PA-8-1-G), NW end of complex, between Thirty-ninth and Fortieth Sts. Brick, 48'-7" (five-bay front) x 48'-2", one story, hip roof with louvered monitor, brick pilasters separate bays, wide entablature, arched entrance on SW (front) elevation, Greek Revival details. Built 1814-20; poor condition 1934. 2 sheets (1934, including plan, elevations, section, details); 1 ext. photo (1934). LC code: PA,2-PITBU,6G.

Carriage Shop (PA-8-1-L), NW end of complex, SW side of Fortieth St. Brick, three by eight bays, two stories, hip roof with two gabled monitors, brick pilasters separate bays, wide entablature, double doors with fanlight on SW (front) elevation (fanlight removed prior to 1934), Greek Revival details. Built 1814-20; originally U-shaped connected with *Machine Shop*. 1 ext. photo (1934). LC code: PA,2-PITBU,6L.

Commandant's Quarters (PA-8-1-A), SW side of Fortieth St., NW of Butler St. Coursed ashlar (SE front elevation) and coursed rubble with quoins, 45' (five-bay front) x 40', two stories and attic with basement, hip roof with small hipped monitor, four large corbeled chimneys, denticulated cornice, belt course, porch across SE and SW elevations, Greek Revival details. Built 1814-20; later brick wing connected to NW by recessed passageway; demolished. Similar to *Officers' Quarters*. 8 sheets (1934, including plans, elevations, section, details); 4 ext. photos (1934). LC code: PA,2-PITBU,6A.

Entrance Gates (PA-8-1-J), NE side of Thirty-ninth St., NW of Butler St. Roadway gate and walkway gate, posts of coursed rough-faced ashlar with chiseled margins with pyramidal caps, two iron gates across roadway, iron gate missing from walkway, random ashlar wall extends from each post (part of wall which encloses arsenal complex). Built 1814-20. 1 sheet (1934, including plans, elevations, details); 4 ext. photos (1934). LC code: PA,2-PITBU,6J.

Guardhouse (PA-8-1-K), SE side of Butler St., between Thirty-ninth and Fortieth Sts. Brick with stone quoins (stuccoed later), groin vaulted passageway with room above flanked by one-story symmetrical wings, 53' x 17'-4" (over-all dimensions), crenelated octagonal towers at corners of central section, stone crenelation on top of central section and wings, stone voussoirs around entry arch, iron entrance gate, three-part pointed-arch windows, coursed ashlar wall connected to wings (part of wall which encloses arsenal complex), Gothic Revival details. Built mid-nineteenth century. 2 sheets (1934, including plans, elevations, section, details); 2 ext. photos (1934). LC code: PA,2-PITBU,6K.

Machine Shop (PA-8-1-H), NW end of complex, SW side of Fortieth St. Brick, 48'-9" (three-bay front) x 75'-11" (seven bays), two stories, hip roof, brick pilasters separate bays, wide entablature, double doors with fanlight on SW (front) elevation (fanlight removed prior to 1934), Greek Revival details. Built 1814-20; originally U-shaped connected with *Carriage Shop*; poor condition 1934. 2 sheets (1934, including plan, elevations, section, details); 2 ext. photos (1934). LC code: PA,2-PITBU,6H.

Noncommissioned Officers' Quarters (PA-8-1-D), NE side of Thirty-ninth St., NW of Butler St. Brick, 82' (six-bay front) x 25', two stories with basement, gable roof, blind arcade on NE (front) elevation, door with transom and wide side lights on SW elevation. Built 1814-20; two-story brick wing added to NW elevation; one-story brick wing added to NW elevation of earlier wing. Similar to *Barracks*. 7 sheets (1934, including plans, elevations, section, details); 3 int. photos (1934). LC code: PA,2-PITBU,6D.

Officers' Quarters (PA-8-1-B), NE side of Thirty-ninth St., NW of Butler St. Coursed ashlar (SE front and SW elevations) and coursed rubble with quoins, 45' (five-bay front) x 40', two stories and attic with basement, hip roof, denticulated cornice, belt course, pedimented distyle entrance porch, Greek Revival details. Built 1814-20; later brick wing connected to NW by recessed passageway. Similar to *Commandant's Quarters*. 4 sheets (1934, including plans, details); 4 ext. photos (1934), 1 int. photo (1934). LC code: PA,2-PITBU,6B.

Storehouse (PA-8-1-E), NW end of complex, between Thirty-ninth and Fortieth Sts. Brick, 43'-4" (three-bay front) x 217'-1" (sixteen bays), two-and-a-half stories, gable roof, bays defined by blind arcade on first story, double doors with large fanlights in each arch, stone belt courses. Built 1814-20. 4 sheets (1934, including plans, elevations, section, details); 2 ext. photos (1934). LC code: PA,2-PITBU,6E.

United States Allegheny Post Office (North Side Post Office, Old Post Office Museum) (PA-1178), 1 Landmark Square. Coursed granite, 74' (five bays) x 91' (five bays), one story and setback second story with circular dome, partially exposed basement, flat roofs with balustrades, N and S elevations with projecting pedimented entrance pavilion with arcaded openings flanked by Corinthian pilasters, E and W elevations with arcaded entrance and projecting pedimented terminal pavilions with Corinthian pilasters, rectangular drum with arcaded windows and pilasters with small dome at each corner and central dome (44'-8" diameter) with circular lantern (drum to lantern 56' high), Second Renaissance Revival style; central rotunda, coffered dome. Built 1894-97; William M. Aiken, supervising architect of the Treasury Department; Frank E. Rutan, resident architect; remodeled 1971, second-story mezzanine added; operated by Pittsburgh History & Landmarks Foundation. 13 sheets (1967, including site plan, plans, elevations, sections, details). LC code: PA,2-PITBU,25. NR.

U.S. Bureau of Mines, Experiment Station (PA-1166), 4800 Forbes Ave. 1 sheet (n.d., showing elevation of cornice at main entrance). LC code: PA,2-PITBU,39. NR.

Washington Crossing Bridge (PA-1179), spanning Allegheny River at Fortieth St. Fifteen spans of steel plate-girders on concrete piers (river piers faced with coursed ashlar), 2622.31' overall length, river spans consist of three arched steel plate-girders (323', 353', and 232' respectively) with deck supported on open spandrels, roadway 38' wide. Built 1923-24; Benno Janssen, architect; Charles S. Davis, associate engineer. 14 sheets (1967, including site plan, plans, elevations, sections, details). LC code: PA,2-PITBU,26.

Western Avenue (House) (PA-1247), 815-17 Western Ave. Brick, double house (each side with three-bay front), two-and-a-half stories with battered basement, gable roof, large inside end chimneys with diaper design, recessed doors in center two bays, convex outer two bays on each side with polygonal dormers above, brick belt courses and water table, mouse-toothing in gable ends, second-story iron porch; side hall plans. Built late nineteenth century; two-and-a-half-story brick wing added. 2 ext. photos (1963); 1 data page (1983). LC code: PA,2-PITBU,56.

Whitten Building. See Penn and Liberty Avenues (Commercial Buildings), Whitten Building.

Wilson House (Chatham College, Berry Hall) (PA-1250), 106 Woodland Rd. Brick, five-bay front, three stories, hip roof, elaborate chimneys, slightly projecting pedimented pavilion, entrance porch with balustrade supported by clustered Doric columns, door with broken scroll pediment and side light, wide entablature with denticulated cornice, stone belt course, flat stone lintels with corner blocks, two-story semicircular bay, porch with balustrade supported by clustered Doric columns on side, Georgian Revival style. Built 1893; John Bissell, architect; now dormitory. 1 ext. photo (1963); 1 data page (1983). LC code: PA,2-PITBU,57.

Wurlitzer Building. See Penn and Liberty Avenues (Commercial Buildings), Arbuthnot Building.

Sewickley Heights Borough

Fairacres (B. F. Jones House) (PA-607), Blackburn Rd. Steel frame faced with limestone with quoins, rectangular with projecting entrance pavilion at E end and enclosed veranda at W end, approx. 62' x 158' with offset service wing (28' x 76') at NE corner, three-story main section, two-story entrance pavilion, veranda, and wing, low hip roof with balustrades, denticulated cornice, belt courses, circular and polygonal bays, French windows with fanlights on veranda, Second Renaissance Revival style; one hundred and two rooms. Built 1915; Hiss and Weekes, architects; demolished 1964. 9 sheets (1967, including plans, elevations, details). LC code: PA,2-SEWICH,1.

Jones, B.F., House. See Fairacres.

Sharpsburg Vicinity (O'Hara Township)

Ferry House (PA-616), 403 Dorseyville Rd. Brick, T-shaped (central section with projecting symmetrical side wings, recessed porches between projections of wings), 56'-8" (six-bay front) x 36'-3", one story, hip roof, central corbeled chimney, front porch with Doric columns, pedimented front door with fanlight flanked by pilasters. Built early nineteenth century. 3 sheets (1967, including plan, elevations, details). LC code: PA,2-SHARP.V,1.

South Park

Miller House. See Bethel Park Vicinity (South Park Township), Miller, James, House.

Swissvale Borough

Trevanion Avenue (House) (PA-626), S side of Trevanion Ave., across from Milton Ave. Stucco on structural clay tile (first story) and clapboarded (second story), 31'-6" x 29'-6" (house with recessed garage to N), two stories with basement, gambrel roof on house, gable roof with overhang on garage, pent roof over E entrance (extension of garage roof), leaded-glass in windows and door; side hall plan, tile fireplaces, leaded-glass cabinets, English Arts and Crafts Movement influence. Built 1922; Frederick G. Scheibler Jr., architect. 4 sheets (1967, including plans, elevations, details). LC code: PA,2-SWISV,1.

Wilkinsburg Borough

Singer, John F. House (PA-433), 1318 Singer Pl. Coursed ashlar with quoins, irregular rectangular plan, 59'-7" x 74'-8", two-and-a-half stories with basement, steep intersecting gable roofs with slight flare at eaves line, gabled dormers, elaborately carved bargeboards with pendants, bracketed cornice, pointed-arch and flat hood moldings over openings, bracketed hoods with bargeboards over some openings, carved wooden porches, Victorian Gothic style; central hall plan, elaborate woodwork and plasterwork. Built 1869; apartments 1963. 6 sheets (1962, including plans, elevations); 4 ext. photos (1963), 6 int. photos (1963), 1 copy photo of early sketch; 5 data pages (1963). LC code: PA,2-PITBU,23.NR.

Beaver County

Ambridge Borough

Economy (PA-1176). A group of German Pietists, headed by George Rapp (1757-1847), immigrated to America to escape persecution and organized the Harmony society in 1805. The group established Economy as their third communistic settlement in 1824 (Harmony, Pa. 1804-15, Harmony, Ind. 1815-25). Covering 3,000 acres, the town was a grid plan of wide streets with simple, functional buildings and open spaces including a community garden. Frederick Reichert Rapp designed the buildings and planned the community. Economically successful with their agricultural, commercial, and industrial activities, economy was self-sufficient and prospered through the 1860s. Declining slowly, the society was dissolved in 1905. The state acquired 1.5 blocks of Economy in 1916 (bounded by Ohio River Blvd., Church, Thirteenth, and Fifteenth Sts.), this area, including seventeen original buildings, was restored and opened as Old Economy Village operated by the Pennsylvania Historical and Museum Commission. 5 sheets (1967, including town plan in 1840 and 1966, plan of central area, details of Garden Grotto). LC code: PA,4-AMB,1. NHL.

Feast Hall (PA-612), W side of Church St., at Fourteenth St. Museum, part of Old Economy Village. Brick, 54' (three-bay front) x 120' (ten bays), two stories with double attic and basement, clipped gambrel roof with flared eaves, hipped dormers (louvered ventilator attic dormers), denticulated cornice, pedimented door with fanlight and pilasters on E (front) elevation, espaliers on E, W, and S elevations; central hall plan, auditorium (second story) with pilasters and vaulted ceiling. Built 1828; Frederick Reichert Rapp, designer; restored. Auditorium used for gatherings and three annual feasts, building also housed the Harmonist Museum, adult school, and printing press. 11 sheets (1965, including site plan, plans, elevations, details). LC code: PA,4-AMB, 1A.

Meetinghouse (St. John's Lutheran Church) (PA-627), E side of Church St., between Thirteenth and Fourteenth Sts. Brick, 55'-4" flared eaves, bracketed cornice, four-story entrance tower with coved cornice and balustrade on W (front) elevation, octagonal belfry with louvered openings and four one-handed clock faces, octagonal cupola; basket-handle arched ceiling. Built 1828-31; Frederick Reichert Rapp, designer. 6 sheets (1967, including plan, elevations, sections, details). LC code: PA,4-AMB,1B.

Tailor Shop and Wine Cellar (PA-613), W side of Church St., across from Fourteenth St. Museum, part of Old Economy Village. Brick, approx. 59' (seven-bay front) x 36' (four bays), two stories with double attic and basement, gable roof with flared eaves, door with transom on S and N elevations, enclosed entrance to wine cellar, espaliers on S and W elevations; central hall plan, stone vaulted wine cellar. Built 1826-27; Frederick Reichert Rapp, designer; restored. Housed shops for tailor, shoemaker, hatmaker, and barber, with wine cellar. 9 sheets (1966, including site plan, plans, elevations, sections). LC code: PA,4-AMB,1C.

St. John's Lutheran Church. See Economy Meetinghouse.

Monaca Borough

George Washington School (PA-1356), SE corner Eleventh St. and Pennsylvania Ave. Brick veneer with structural steel columns and concrete floors, 167' x 60', two stories, flat roof, projecting vertical panels form decorative entrance bays on E (front) elevation, doorways framed by concrete trim, multipane steel encased windows, decorative brickwork, Art Deco style. Built 1931; Bradley and Stetson, architects; later used as warehouse; demolished 1986 to clear site for town plaza. 6 ext. photos (1986), 4 int. photos (1986); 20 data pages including sketch of floor plans, drawing of proposed town plaza, site development plan, copy of area map, and copy of 1965 photo (1986).

Butler County

Harmony Vicinity

Stauffer-Bame House and Stauffer, David, Farmbuildings. See Zelienople Vicinity (Lancaster Township), Stauffer, David, Farm.

Zelienople Vicinity (Lancaster Township)

Bame House. See Stauffer, David, Farm.

Stauffer-Bame House. See Stauffer, David Farm.

Stauffer, David, Farm, House (Stauffer-Bame House) (PA-414), N side of Lower Scott Ridge Rd., 1.4 mi. W of U.S. Rte. 19 (Perry Hwy.), approx. 3.5 mi. N of Zelienople. Irregular coursed ashlar, 40'-2" (five-bay front) x 30'-1" (two bays), two and a half stories with basement, gable roof, door with transom and door at second-story level on Sw (front) elevation, pedimented porch on NE elevation attached to frame passageway which connects house with woodshed and carriage shelter; central hall plan. Built 1839 (painted date in gable end); one-story porch across SW elevation replaced original two-story porch before 1936. Documented outbuildings include stone bank barn, frame stock barn, pigery, and wagon shed. 24 sheets (1937, including plans, elevations, sections, details); 10 ext. photos (n.d., 1936); 2 data pages (1937); records include house and outbuildings. LC code: PA,10-HARM.V,1.

Cambria County

Colver (Cambria Township)

America's Industrial Heritage Project. As part of this NPS project, HABS/HAER documented three 19th and 20th c. coal company towns, Colver, Star Junction in Fayette County, and Windber in Somerset County, with photographs and written data in 1988. Records being processed 1990.

Cresson Vicinity (Cresson Townships)

Lemon, Samuel, House (PA-1236), W side of Gallitzin Rd. (LR07068), N of intersection with U.S. Rte. 22, 2.1 mi. E of State Rte. 53. Owned and operated by National Park Service as part of Allegheny Portage Railroad National Historic Site. Coursed rubble, L-shaped, 52'-6" (five-bay front) x 43'-6" with wing to W 22'-1" (three-bay front) x 29', two and a half stories with basement, gable roofs, arched doorway with cut voussoirs and fanlight, fanlight with cut voussoirs in gable end; central hall plan. Built ca. 1832 (wing added later); partially underground garage added (removed 1973). Used to house travelers on the Allegheny Portage Railroad. 12 sheets (1965, 1971, including plans, elevations, section, details). See Allegheny Portage Railroad, Staple Bend Tunnel (PA-1233) for site plan. LC code: PA, 11-CRES.V,1. NHS.

Geistown Vicinity (Conemaugh Township)

Allegheny Portage Railroad, Staple Bend Tunnel (PA-1233), E bank of Little Conemaugh River, NW of U.S. Rte. 219, N of Johnstown-Cambria County Airport. In boundaries of Allegheny Portage Railroad National Historic Site, the tunnel is owned by Bethlehem Steel Corporation and managed under a cooperative agreement between the National Park Service and Bethlehem Steel. Tunnel is 900' long (600' solid rock, 150' stone vaulted at each end), maximum width of portal opening 19'-11", approx. height of portal opening 16', W portal of coursed ashlar with rusticated arch flanked by paired pilasters with wide entablature, E portal with rusticated arch (repaired with secondary concrete arch). Built 1833; entrances filled with concrete block and steel doors. First railroad tunnel in United States. 2 sheets (1965, including site plan, plan, elevations). LC code: PA,11-GEITO.V,1. NHS.

Johnstown

America's Industrial Heritage Project. As part of this NPS project, HABS documented four neighborhoods and six individual structures in 1988. Records being processed 1990.

The neighborhoods recorded were:
   Cambria City
   Central Park; Minersville
   Westmont

The individual structures recorded were:
   Johnstown City Hall (PA-5387)
   Johnstown Public Library (PA-5386)
   Mayer, L.H., Building (PA-5385)
   Penn Traffic Building (PA-5388)
   Pennsylvania Railroad Station (PA-5389)
   U.S. Post Office (PA-5390)

Fayette County

National Trail. See Somerset County, National Trail.

Brownsville Borough

Bowman's Castle (Nemacolin Castle) (PA-429), Front and Second Sts. Museum. Brick, irregular plan with projecting bays and octagonal tower, 102'-5" x 59'- 9", two-and-a-half stories with basement, three-story crenelated tower, gable roofs with dormers, bracketed cornice, brick corner pilasters, lattice-work porch on E elevation, two-story crenelated arcaded porch (partially enclosed 1890s) on W elevation; fine interior woodwork and plaster ornament. Board and batten outbuildings. Built ca. 1789 as log house by Jacob Bowman, an early settler of Brownsville; several nineteenth-century additions; restored after 1963 by Brownsville Historical Society. 7 sheets (1961, including plans, elevations, sections); 6 ext. photos (1963), 5 int. photos (1963); 1 data page (1984). LC code: PA,26-BROVI,1. NR.

> *Barn* (PA-429A). Coursed rubble (lower stable level) and frame with board and batten siding (upper level), two levels, cross gable roof with brackets, circular vent with radiating louvers, arched louvered windows. Built nineteenth century. 1 ext. photo (1963). LC code: PA,26-BROVI,1A.
>
> *Outbuildings* (PA-429B). Several frame outbuildings with board and batten siding, one story, hip and gable roofs, wooden trim along eaves. Built nineteenth century. 1 ext. photo (1963). LC code: PA,26-BROVI,1B.

Nemacolin Castle. See Bowman's Castle.

Chalkhill Vicinity (Stewart Township)

Hagan, Isaac N. House (PA-5347), S side of SR2010, .4 mi. E of SR1055, .8 mi. W of SR2019, just below peak of Kentuck Knob, off Ohiopyle Rd., NE of U.S. Rte. 40. Native sandstone and red cypress, stone walls with bands of windows above, one story grows out of hillside to a V-shaped point, hipped roof with deep overhangs with hexagonal openings, large central chimney, windows with geometric cutouts, terraces, designed of hexagonal modules; interior materials similar to exterior, stone walls and floors, built-in furniture. Built 1954; Frank Lloyd Wright, architect. Burned and rebuilt using HABS photos. 22 ext. photos (1985), 17 int. photos (1985).

Connellsville

America's Industrial Heritage Project. As part of this NPS project, HABS documented the Carnegie Free Library (PA-5476) with photographs and written data in 1989. Records being processed 1990.

Fairchance Vicinity (Georges Township)

Nixon Tavern (PA-8-3), SE corner of Elm and Main Sts., just across borough boundary. Log partially covered with wooden siding, tavern (29'-10" x 21'-11") connected by passageway (later enclosed) to house (22'-11" x 28'-6") with storage shed (14'-3" x 28'-6") attached to S elevation, one-and-a-half-story tavern with two-story house and one-story shed, gable roofs, porch across E elevation. House built ca. 1810; tavern built a short distance from house connected by extended roof; lean-to added ca. 1835; demolished ca. 1950s. 7 sheets (1934, including site plan, plans, elevations, sections, details); 7 ext. photos (1934); 3 data pages (1936). LC code: PA,26-FACHA,1.

Fairhope Vicinity (Washington Township)

Cook, Colonel Edward, House (PA-412), W side of LR64137, 1.1 mi. NE of State Rte. 201 and Fairhope. Coursed rubble stuccoed on SE (front) elevation (stucco later removed), 36' (four-bay front) x 29', two-and-a-half stories with basement, gable roof, denticulated cornice; corner fireplaces. Built 1772-76; Jesse Cunningham, builder; one-story random rubble kitchen wing (22' x 24'-10") added on NE elevation before 1798; frame shed and three porches added; minor structural renovation 1952; addition built on N elevation. Frame and stone outbuildings. One of the oldest extant houses in area, built for Colonel Cook, an early settler and a leading figure in early Pennsylvania history. 9 sheets (1936, including site plan, plans, elevations, details); 3 ext. photos (1936); 3 data pages (1936). LC code: PA,26-FACI.V,1. NR.

Farmington Vicinity (Wharton Township)

Mount Washington Tavern (Fort Necessity Museum) (PA-417), S side of U.S. Rte. 40 (National Trail), 1.4 mi. NW of Farmington, in Fort Necessity National Battlefield. Museum administered by the National Park Service. Brick, five by two bays, two-and-a-half stories, gable roof with paired chimneys in parapets at gable ends, double door with semielliptical fanlight and side lights on front elevation. Built ca. 1818; Nathaniel Ewing; builder; became a National Battlefield Site in 1931. Built to serve travelers on the National Road. Overlooks site of Fort Necessity where the opening battle of the French and Indian War was fought in 1754. 1 ext. photo (1933). LC code: PA,26- UNITO.V,1. NR (Fort Necessity National Battlefield).

Fayette City Vicinity

Cook, Colonel, House. See Fairhope Vicinity (Washington Township), Cook, Colonel Edward, House.

Hopwood. (North Union Township)

Hayden, Benjamin, House (PA-8-4), E side of U.S. Rte. 40 (National Trail), across from Church St. Coursed ashlar front elevation with coursed and random rubble sides, clapboarded rear shed and offset coursed and random rubble kitchen wing, 36' (five-bay front) x 18' with rear shed (36' x 9'-10") and kitchen wing (16' x 18'-2"), one-and-a-half-story house with one-story wings, gable roofs, inside end chimneys, two doors on W (front) elevation. House built ca. 1822; kitchen built and shed (originally porch) enclosed ca. 1850. 5 sheets (1934, including site plan, plans, elevations, section, details); 6 ext. photos (1934); 3 data pages (1936). LC code: PA,26-HOP,1.

Mount Braddock (North Union Township)

America' Industrial Heritage Project.. As part of this NPS project, HABS documented the Isaac Meason House (PA-5475) with photographs in 1989. Records being processed 1990.

New Geneva Vicinity (Springhill Township)

Painter House (PA-5201), .25 mi. W of State Rte. 116, overlooking Monogahela River, on property of Friendship Hill National Historic Site. Frame with stucco and decorative half timbering, rectangular with two rear wings, two and a half stories, gable roof with dormers, Tudor Revival style. Built ca. 1900 as summer home for Charles Albert Painter, Pittsburgh industrialist and businessman, on original estate of Albert Gallatin, late eighteenth- and early nineteenth-century financial and political figure; demolished. 11 sheets (1981, including site plans, plans, photos of elevations, photos and drawings of details). LC code: PA,26-NEGEN.V,1.

Ohiopyle (Stewart Township)

Fallingwater (Edgar J. Kaufmann House) (PA-5346), off State Rte. 381 on Bear Run. Museum operated by Western Pennsylvania Conservancy. Native sandstone walls, piers and chimney core with cantilevered reinforced concrete trays forming floors, balconies and canopy slabs; three stories built over waterfall with hanging stairs to stream, flat roof, metal window and door sash; irregular open plan, interior finishes similar to exterior with floors finished in flagstone, black walnut plywood woodwork, furniture designed for house (mostly built-in). Built 1935-36 as a summer home for Edgar J. Kaufmann of Pittsburgh; Frank Lloyd Wright, architect. Guest wing and servants' quarters of similar design built 1938-39 on hill above house. House given to Western Pennsylvania Conservancy in 1969. Designed as part of the natural landscape, Fallingwater is one of the finest, most original and most well-known houses in America. 62 ext. photos (1985), 46 int. photos (1985). NHL.

Kaufmann, Edgar J., House. See Fallingwater.

Penn-Craft (Luzerne Township)

America's Industrial Heritage Project. As part of this NPS project, HABS documented two Depression-era planned communities, Penn-Craft and Norvelt in Westmoreland County, with photographs and written data in 1989. Records being processed 1990.

Star Junction (Perry Township)

America's Industrial Heritage Project. As part of this NPS project, HABS/HAER documented three nineteenth- and twentieth-century coal company towns, Star Junction; Colver, Cambria County; Windber, Somerset County—photographs and written data in 1988. Records being processed 1990.

Uniontown Vicinity

Mount Washington Tavern. See Farmington Vicinity (Wharton Township), Mount Washington Tavern.

Searights Tollhouse. See Somerset County, National Trail.

Uniontown Vicinity (North Union Township)

America's Industrial Heritage Project.. As part of this NPS project, HABS documented Levi Springer House (PA-5482) measured drawings in 1989. Records being processed 1990.

Uniontown Vicinity (South Union Township)

America's Industrial Heritage Project.. As part of this NPS project, HABS documented the Thomas Gaddis House (Fort Gaddis) (PA-5474) with photographs and written data in 1989. Records being processed 1990.

Greene County

Brock (Wayne Township)

Valley Methodist Manse (PA-619), N side of T355, just W of Rudolf Run. Frame with clapboarding, L-shaped, 30'-2" (three-bay front) x 20'-3" with kitchen ell (15' x 15'), one-and-a-half stories with one-story ell, gable roofs, corner pilasters, pedimented door with fanlight and pilasters on S (front) elevation; central hall plan. Built mid-nineteenth century; only remnants left 1967. 4 sheets (1967, conjectural drawings, including site plan, plans, elevations). LC code: PA,30-BROC,1.

Ruff Creek Vicinity (Washington Township)

Grimes Covered Bridge (PA-618), spans Ruff Creek, on T546 near merge with State Rte. 221, approx. 1 mi. E of town of Ruff Creek. King-post truss supported on coursed ashlar abutments, single span 34'-6", overall length 44', 11'-9" wide roadway, covered with vertical wooden siding, gable roof. Built ca. 1900. 5 sheets (ca. 1964, including site plan, elevations, sections, isometric section). LC code: PA,30-RUFCR.V,1. NR.

Indiana County

Saltsburg Borough

America's Industrial Heritage Project. As part of this NPS project, HABS documented two nineteenth-century towns located on the Pennsylvania Main Line Canal, Saltsburg and Alexandria in Huntingdon County, with photographs and written data in 1988. Records being processed 1990.

The Saltsburg structures recorded were:
    Andre, Andrew, House (PA-5423)
    First National Bank of Saltsburg (PA-5431)
    Martin, John, House (PA-5422)
    McFarland, Dr. John, House (PA-5425)
    McGlaughlin, James, House (PA-5429)
    McIlwaine, William, House (PA-5424)
    Moore, Samuel, House and Store (PA-5421)
    Murray, Dr. Thomas, House (PA-5417)
    Pennsylvania Railroad Station (PA-5437)
    105 Point Street (House) (PA-5419)
    Robinson, James, House (PA-5427)
    Robinson, Thomas and John, House (PA-5428)
    Robinson, William C., House (PA-5418)
    Rombach, Mathias, House (PA-5430)
    St. Matthew's Catholic Church (PA-5436)
    Saltsburg Academy (PA-5433)
    Saltsburg, Town of (PA-5438)
    Shupe, P.D., Hardware Store (PA-5432)
    Sons of Zebedee Evangelical Lutheran Church (PA-5435)
    Stewart, William, House (PA-5416)
    Taylor, R.J., House (PA-5420)
    United Presbyterian Church (PA-5434)
    Wray House (PA-5426)

Somerset County

National Trail (PA-417). The National Trail (now U.S. Rte. 40) was the artery to western migration, entering Pennsylvania from Maryland in Somerset County and extending through Fayette and Washington Counties into West Virginia and westward. Congress authorized construction of the National Road in 1803 and the Pennsylvania section was completed by 1818. A photographic survey was made of structures along the road in 1933 and organized as a single entry in the collection; but locations for individual structures were not provided. Photos include: A) Bridge, 2 photos; B) Bridge, 2 photos; C) Culvert built 1826, 2 photos; D) Culvert detail, 1 photo; E) Culvert detail and milestone, 1 photo; F) Milepost, 1 photo; G) Tollhouse with plaque showing toll rates, 3 photos; H) Tollhouse, 2 photos; J) House, 1 photo. Bridge A is the S Bridge, Washington Vicinity, Washington County, owned by the county and listed on the NR. G Tollhouse is the Searights Tollhouse, Uniontown Vicinity, Fayette County, restored and operated as a museum by the Pennsylvania Historical and Museum Commission and listed on the NR. H Tollhouse is the Petersburg Tollhouse, Addison, Somerset County, owned by the Great Crossings Chapter of the DAR and listed on the NR.

Addison

Tollhouse (PA-5177). See Somerset County, National Trail.

Rockwood Borough

Laurel Hill. See Shaulis, W.L., House.

Shaulis, W.L., House (Laurel Hill) (PA-416), near Rockwood Post Office. Frame with clapboarding, five by two bays, two stories with attic, sloping site exposes basement at rear, gable roof, one-story frame shed on front elevation, porch across rear elevation. Built early nineteenth century; poor condition 1938. 4 ext. photos (1938). LC code: PA,56-ROCHO.V,1.

Winber Borough

America's Industrial Heritage Project. As part of this NPS project, HABS/HAER documented three nineteenth- and twentieth-century coal company towns, Windber, Colver in Cambria County, and Star Junction in Fayette County, with photographs and written data in 1988. Records being processed 1990.

Washington County

National Trail. See Somerset County, National Trail.

Brownsville Vicinity

Krepps, John, Tavern (Malden Inn). See Centerville Vicinity (Centerville Township), Krepps, John, Tavern.

Canonsburg Borough

Gowern Building (PA-5368), 35-43 N. Jefferson Ave. Brick, 67' (nine-bay front) x 42', two stories, flat roof, corbeled brick parapet, four storefronts across facade; first floor commercial space, second floor apartments. Built 1903 (date stone) by William J. Gowern, prominent local businessman; two rear wings (16' x 25') added to rear elevation; scheduled for demolition. 3 ext. photos (1988), 3 int. photos (1988); 12 data pages (1988).

Roberts, John, House (PA-1177), 225 N. Central Ave. Stone and brick, L-shaped house built in three sections, coursed ashlar section 13' (three-bay front) x 14'-3", brick section 9'-3" (two-bay front) x 11' to N, random rubble kitchen wing 9' x 14'-5" to W, two-and-a-half stories with basement, gable roofs with pedimented gable end, decorative cornice with star motif, pedimented entrance flanked by pilasters with recessed door with fanlight on E (front) elevation, Georgian details; corner fireplaces. Originally two-story log house built ca. 1804; random rubble section (added first) and coursed ashlar section (built shortly after) built between 1804 and 1815; brick section replaced log house ca. 1840s; one-story frame kitchen wing added to W; dormers added; acquired by Washington and Jefferson College after 1816 until 1930s; then used as residence. 11 sheets (1967, including site plan, plans, elevations, section, details). LC code: PA,63-CANON,1. NR.

Carroll Township

Taylor Run-Yorty Run Schoolhouse. See Wickerham Manor Vicinity (Carroll Township), Taylor Run-Yorty Run Schoolhouse.

Centerville Vicinity (Centerville Township)

Krepps, John, Tavern (Malden Inn) (PA-417), N side of U.S. Rte. 40, (National Trail), 2.5 mi. E of Centerville. Coursed ashlar S (front) elevation and random rubble, 56'-2" (six-bay front) x 32', two-and-a-half stories with basement, gable roof, paired chimneys in parapets at gable ends. W section built 1822, E section built 1830 (date stone "Liberty Kreppsville 1830"); John Krepps, builder; two parallel two-story random rubble wings added on N elevation (originally one-story, frame second story added ca. 1910, frame changed to stone 1938); tetrastyle Doric porch added on S elevation ca. 1910 (removed 1938); extensive interior alterations. Early tavern on the National Trail. 6 ext. photos (ca. 1933, 1963), 1 int. photo (1963); 4 data pages (1963). LC code: PA,63-BROVI.V,1. NR.

Malden Inn. See Krepps, John, Tavern.

Charleroi Borough

First Christian Church (PA-5358), 553 Fallowfield Ave. Brick with stone trim, 58' x 94', one level with basement, gabled and hipped roofs, three-story entrance towers with arched doorways, front gable with rose window, arched stained-glass windows with label molds, corbeled brick trim, Romanesque Revival style. Built 1901; R. L. Barnhart, architects; 1977 converted to community center; demolished. 7 ext. photos (1986), 11 int. photos (1986); 8 data pages including site map and floor plans (1987).

Finleyville Vicinity (Union Township)

James Chapel Methodist Church (PA-600), N side of Gill Hall Rd. (LR62087), 1.5 mi. E of Finleyville. Random ashlar with quoins, 45'-7" (four bay front) x 40'-10" (two bays), one story, gable roof, deep eaves, two doors on front elevation. Built 1817; Robert James, builder; original doors removed and door cut in side; slightly pedimented door and window frames added 1876; frame cupola added; cinder block school wing added to rear 1956. 4 sheets (1967, show building in original condition, including site plan, plan, elevations). LC code: PA,63-FINV,1.

Meadow Lands Vicinity (North Strabane Township)

Miller Barn. See Wylie-Miller Barn.

Wylie-Miller Barn (PA-427), W side of U.S. Rte. 19, .6 mi. NE of Meadow Lands Race Track. Frame with vertical tongue and groove siding, octagonal, 25' each side, sloping site exposes two levels, polygonal roof with octagonal louvered cupola, two levels of louvered windows on second story, slightly pedimented architraves over windows. Built 1888; John Vester, architect; McPeak Brothers, builders; poor condition 1963. 6 sheets (1962, including plans, elevations, section); 4 ext. photos (1963), 2 int. photos (1963); 3 data pages (1963). LC code: PA,63-WASH.V,1.

Washington

Washington and Jefferson College, Administration Building (PA-8-2), on Washington and Jefferson College Campus, NW corner of S. Lincoln and E. Wheeling Sts. Random rubble section with slightly projecting symmetrical brick wings, 120' (eleven-bay front) x 40'-3", two-and-a-half stories with basement, gable roofs, projecting pedimented Doric portico on W (front) elevation of central section, entrance porches on E elevations of wings. Central section built 1793; wings and portico added 1816. Chartered in 1787 as Washington Academy, later merged with Jefferson Academy. 7 sheets (1934, including plans, elevations, sections, details); 3 ext. photos (1934); 2 data pages (1936). LC code: PA,63-WASH,3. NR.

Washington Vicinity

S Bridge on National Trail. See Somerset County, National Trail.

Wylie-Miller Barn. See Meadow Lands Vicinity (North Strabane Township), Wylie-Miller Barn.

West Brownsville Vicinity (Centerville Township)

Dorsey, Joseph, House (PA-5176), 113 Cherry Ave., approx. 1 mi. W of West Brownsville. Random rubble with quoins, approx. 35' square (four-bay front), two-and-a-half stories, gable roof, denticulated cornice, large inside end chimney, door with fanlight framed by fluted pilasters and denticulated pediment on SE (front) elevation, door with transom and gabled hood on NW elevation (hood added 19th c.); side hall plan, fine original interior woodwork. Built 1787; few changes; one-story brick wing added ca. 1830. Good example of a well preserved eighteenth-century house. Destroyed by fire winter 1993-94. 3 ext. photos (1963); 1 data page (1983). LC code: PA,63-BROWV.V,1. NR.

House, Now Malden Inn. See Centerville Vicinity (Centerville Township), Krepps, John, Tavern.

Wickerham Manor Vicinity (Carroll Township)

Taylor Run-Yorty Run Schoolhouse (PA-1157), State Rte. 481 (LR62175) and Taylor Run Rd. (LR62161), W of Wickerham Manor. Coursed rubble, 20'-2" (three-bay front) x 24'-5", two stories, gable roof, inside end chimneys. Built ca. 1837 as public schoolhouse; converted to dwelling by 1866; two-story frame wing with porch added on S elevation early twentieth century; roof replaced ca. 1960; demolished. 2 sheets (1985, including site plans, plans, elevations, section); 5 ext. photos (1985), 9 int. photos (1985); 16 data pages (1985). LC code: PA,63-CARTO,1.

Westmoreland County

Fellsburg (Rostraver Township)

Fellsburg Methodist Episcopal Church (PA-608), NW corner of Webster Rd. (LR64118) and State Rte. 201. Random rubble, 40'5" (three-bay front) x 50'-2", two stories, gable roof, two double paneled doors on S (front) elevation; open interior with balcony on three sides. Built 1834; replaced original log church built by Benjamin Fell in 1792; acquired for Rostraver Township Municipal Building 1976. 12 sheets (ca. 1965, including site plan, plans, elevations, section, details). LC code: PA,65-FELB,1.

Greensburg

Green, General, Hotel. See Rappe Hotel.

Greensburger Hotel. See Rappe Hotel.

Rappe Hotel (Greensburger Hotel, General Green Hotel) (PA-5192), 40 E. Pennsylvania Ave. Brick, seven by seven bays, eight stories, mansard roof, large dormers with broken scroll pediments, several decorative cornices, lintels with keystone motif. Built 1903; John Sakal, architect; store fronts altered; demolished. 11 ext. photos (1983), 4 int. photos (1983); 5 data pages (1983). LC code: PA,65-GREEB,1.

Laughlintown Vicinity (Ligonier Township)

Penguin Court. See Scaife, Alan M., House.

Scaife, Alan M., House (Penguin Court) (PA-620), approx. 1 mi. E of T505 on private road, .7 mi. S of U.S. Rte. 30 and Laughlintown. Reinforced concrete and brick faced with stone, large irregular plan with numerous projecting wings, total length including attached garage 226', two-and-a-half stories with basement, gable roofs, elaborate chimneys, wall buttresses, pointed-arch openings, oriel window and penguin antefix above W (front) elevation, Tudor Revival style. Built 1938; Alfred Hopkins, architect; large estate with numerous terraces and vast grounds including wildlife preserve (Scaife raised penguins), Annette H. Flanders, landscape architect; demolished 1966. 12 sheets (ca. 1966, including site plan, plans, elevations, details). LC code: PA,65-LAULT.V,1.

Milligantown (Upper Burrell Township)

Milligan, Samuel, Mill (PA-411), S side of Shaffer Dr., on N bank of Little Pucketos Creek, approx. .5 mi. N of State Rte. 780. Frame with clapboarding with coursed rubble lower level, 28' square, sloping site exposes three levels (gear, grinding and separating levels), gable roof, wooden overshot water wheel with frame wheel house on E elevation of gear level; much original machinery remained 1936. Built 1825-26; Samuel Milligan, builder; lean-to added; clapboarding covered with modern siding prior to 1936; wheel house demolished before 1936; demolished after 1950. 9 sheets (1936, including plans, elevations, sections, details of machinery); 1 ext. photo (1936), 1 photo of water wheel (1936); 2 data pages (1936). LC code: PA,65-MILTO,1.

New Alexandria Borough

America's Industrial Heritage Project. As part of this NPS project, HABS documented Alter's Halfway House (PA-5477) with photographs in 1989. Records being processed 1990.

New Kensington Vicinity

Milligan, Samuel, Mill. See Milligantown (Upper Burrell Township), Milligan, Samuel, Mill.

Norvelt (Mount Pleasant Township)

America's Industrial Heritage Project. As part of this NPS project, HABS documented two Depression-era planned communities, Norvelt and Penn-Craft in Fayette County, with photographs and written data in 1989. Records being processed 1990.

West Newton Borough

Plumer, John C., House (PA-617), 131 S. Water St. Frame with clapboarding, 25' (three-bay front) x 24'-3" with 32' (four-bay front) x 24'-3" brick addition, two-and-a-half stories with basement, gable roofs, door with transom, one-story frame shed added to rear; central hall plan. Built 1816; shed added soon after; brick addition built 1840; owned by West Newton Historical Society. Oldest extant house in West Newton. 6 sheets (1967, including plans, elevation). LC code: PA,65-NEWTW,1. NR.

West Newton Vicinity

Bells Mill Covered Bridge (PA-415), spans Sewickley Creek, connects LR64180 and T970, approx. 1.5 mi. W of Yukon. Burr arch truss supported on coursed rubble abutments, single span 90', over-all length 106'-6", 13' roadway, covered with clapboards, gable roof, pedimented openings flanked by pilasters. Built 1850 (date stone); Daniel McCain, builder. 2 sheets (1936, including elevations, sections, details); 2 ext. photos (1936); 1 data page (1936). LC code: PA,65-NEWTW,1. NR.

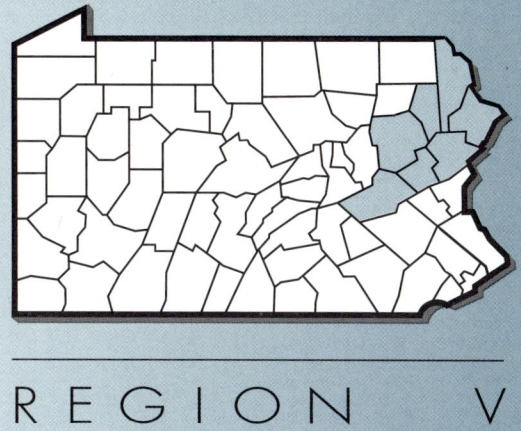

REGION V

Anthracite and Poconos

Essay by Richard J. Webster
Catalog entries by Deborah Stephens Burns

Carbon
Lackawanna
Luzerne
Monroe
Pike
Schuylkill
Wayne

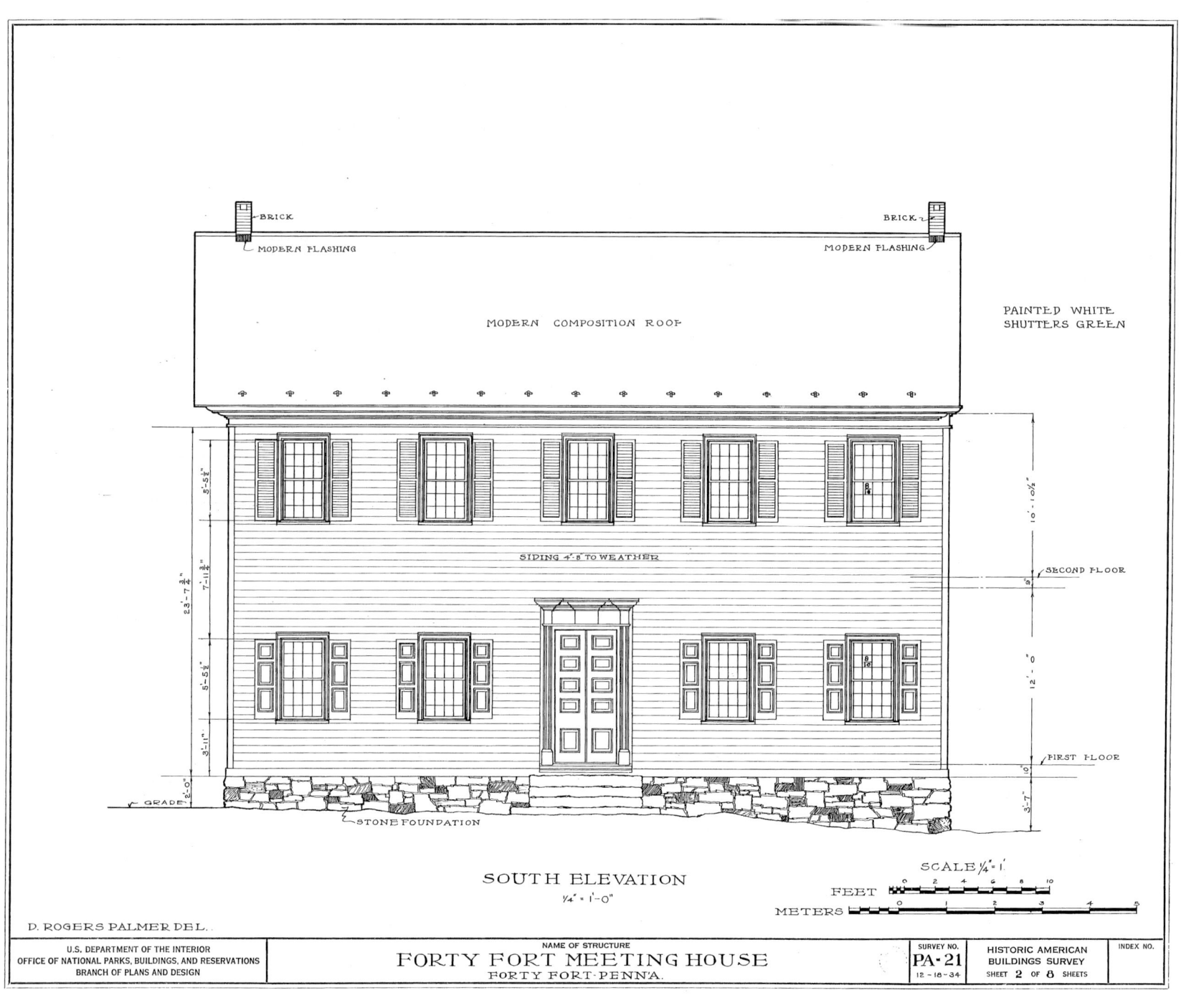

Forty Fort Meetinghouse (PA-21) Forty Fort Borough, Luzerne County. South elevation (D. Rogers Palmer, delineator, 1934) PA,40-FOFO,1.

THE ANTHRACITE AND POCONOS REGION is a combination of two adjoining geographical regions, the former characterized today by its declining anthracite coal industry and the latter by its hunting, fishing, and vacation resorts. The Anthracite Region is a northeastern extension of the Ridge and Valley Region of the folded Appalachians, but it is unique for its great anthracite coal deposits. Although the Susquehanna River helped to determine the region's early settlement patterns in the eighteenth century, the Lehigh and Schuylkill Rivers, flowing southeastwardly into the Delaware River, played major roles in transporting the valuable anthracite to market in the nineteenth century. Two major cities, Scranton and Wilkes-Barre, developed in the region and have combined with many smaller trading centers and clusters of houses in coal "patches" to make the region's narrow valleys some of the state's most densely populated areas.[1] Until after World War II these communities had been held together for a century by the common thread of anthracite mining and a tangled web of railroads that seemed to be "reaching out, scrambling, for the coal business which [was] their life's blood."[2]

For the purposes of this catalog, the Anthracite Region includes four counties (Carbon, Lackawanna, Luzerne, and Schuylkill) in which most of the region's four coal fields lie. The Northern Field, or Wyoming Basin, is an elongated basin approximately fifty miles long and up to six miles wide that extends from Forest City, in Susquehanna County's southeast corner, southwestward to below Nanticoke, Luzerne County. It has been the source of most of the region's coal and is the site of its two largest cities, Scranton and Wilkes-Barre. The Middle Field consists of two separate sections. The eastern part, a grouping of nine parallel troughs, lies mostly in southern Luzerne County, where Hazleton, unique among the region's urban centers for its high elevation, is its major city. The western part begins near Mahanoy City,

Schuylkill County, and ends approximately thirty miles to the west beyond Shamokin, Northumberland County. The largest anthracite area is the Southern Field, which spreads seventy miles from Jim Thorpe, Carbon County, to Dauphin and Lykens in Dauphin County, at the two ends of the field's "fishtail." Pottsville, Schuylkill County, the field's dominant trading center, stands about midway along the field's length.[3]

As part of the Allegheny Plateau, the Poconos Region is characterized by a nearly level, forested highland with shallow valleys. It is bordered on the east by the Delaware River, on the south by the escarpment of Pohopoco Mountain, and on the west by the Lehigh River and Moosic Mountain. Its northern edge has no pronounced topographical feature; the wooded hills simply give way to cleared agricultural lands. Because of its forested elevation, glacier-formed lakes and waterfalls, and proximity to the densely populated New York and Philadelphia metropolitan areas, the Poconos Region in the twentieth century has increasingly become a resort area. Three counties—Wayne, Pike, and Monroe—stretch along the Delaware River southward from the New York border to form the region.[4]

Most of the buildings recorded by HABS in the Anthracite Region and Poconos were built before 1840. This provides valuable historical documentation of the region's early period of timber-frame architecture, but except for a small recent recording project in Jim Thorpe, it fails to include any buildings from the Anthracite Region's great period of growth, the hundred years beginning in the 1830s when coal was king. Today the kingdom of coal is in decline; that era is past. Perhaps a future HABS project will expand on what has been recorded in Jim Thorpe and will include additional representative buildings from the century of coal, such as operators' mansions, miners' houses, mining structures, and commercial buildings, before they are demolished or remodeled beyond recognition, or collapse from decay.

During most of the eighteenth century this mountainous region was so remote that few Pennsylvanians ventured into it. That remoteness, however, and the consequent sparseness of its population helped to make the region attractive to Connecticut's leaders. Under its royal charter of 1662, Connecticut claimed the northern third of Pennsylvania, but did not exercise its asserted rights until 1762 when, operating through the Susquehanna Company, a joint-stock company, Connecticut people began moving into the Wyoming Valley in the vicinity of present-day

Wilkes-Barre. The first Connecticut settlement ended abruptly when Indians killed about twenty farmers in their fields. Shortly thereafter another Connecticut venture, the Delaware Company, acquired a large tract from the Indians in what is now Wayne County, between the Delaware River and the Susquehanna Company claim. The Penns countered by firming up their Indian land purchases in the 1768 Fort Stanwix Treaty and securing an order from the king to end Connecticut migration into their lands, but to no avail.

Between 1769 and 1783 hostilities between Pennsylvania and Connecticut settlers erupted three times in what are called the Yankee-Pennamite Wars. The first two conflicts were not between the provincial governments but between the Penn family and the Susquehanna Company. The Yankees had the advantage of receiving unofficial encouragement from the Connecticut government while the Penns had to contend with an Assembly that was at best indifferent to the Penn family's land disputes far removed from the province's settled areas. In early 1769 the first Yankee-Pennamite War broke out when forty Connecticut Yankees erected a blockhouse called Forty Fort on the west side of the Susquehanna and immediately confronted Pennsylvanians already there. Over the next two years a series of small forts merely changed hands, but in 1771 the outnumbered Pennsylvanians retreated. By 1774, with nearly two thousand Yankees living in the valley, Connecticut incorporated it as Westmoreland Township and settlements expanded as far south as Muncy, Northumberland County. This expansion sparked the second Yankee-Pennamite War, in 1775, in which a Pennsylvania force destroyed Muncy but was turned back when it marched on the Wyoming Valley.

The Revolutionary War redirected hostilities, and in the summer of 1778 a Loyalist and Native American force from New York invaded the valley and annihilated settlements in the gruesomely thorough Wyoming Massacre. After the Revolution, in December 1782, a special commission established by Congress found in favor of Pennsylvania, but because conflicting land claims were not resolved, the third Yankee-Pennamite War erupted with yet more bloodshed, until in 1787 Pennsylvania recognized the claims of the Connecticut settlers. Finally, in 1800, Connecticut renounced all claims on Pennsylvania territory.[5]

Pennsylvania won the land, but Connecticut left its mark upon it. Throughout the Yankee-Pennamite Wars, Connecticut setttlers outnumbered Pennsylvanians, and when peace was restored they had the greater impact on the built environment. As early as 1770, Yankees had laid out Wilkes-Barre as a New England town, with its public square serving as the town green.[6] By 1812 a union church, county courthouse, county records office, market, and academy were located on this public space, the first such urban complex in northeastern Pennsylvania. Joseph Hitchcock, a New Haven native, designed the square's two most imposing buildings, the Georgian courthouse, built 1801-1804, and Old Ship Zion Church, a steepled New England meetinghouse begun in 1800.[7]

A similar Congregational meetinghouse (PA-21), built in 1807-1808, also by Hitchcock, still stands in Forty Fort, Luzerne County, only a few miles up the Susquehanna from Wilkes-Barre. Exterior embellishments on this timber-frame weatherboarded New England meetinghouse are restricted to a simple casing about its entrance, a lunette (now closed) in one gable, and a plain fascia and cornice return across the gable to form a pediment for the lunette. Its fenestration accurately suggests its interior organization. The great distance between the two tiers of plain sash windows indicates the presence of a balcony on three sides of the interior, while an arched window in the middle of the north facade marks the pulpit's location. Placing the entrance and pulpit on the building's short axis, in contrast to the traditional long-axial plan, was a self-conscious counter-Catholic decision that dates from the earliest Puritan meetinghouses. Forty Fort Meetinghouse stands as a remarkably strong cultural statement of a determined band of Congregationalists.[8]

Weatherboarded timber-frame construction was widely practiced throughout this region both by Yankees, who brought the tradition with them, and by Pennsylvania Germans, who quickly adopted it. Nathan Denison, an early Yankee leader, patterned his new house (PA-25) in Forty Fort in 1790 after the one he had left behind in New England. With its ample proportions, timber frame, weatherboard walls, and central chimney, it is similar to innumerable examples throughout New England.[9] Thirty-five years later a Pennsylvania German congregation in nearby Hanover Green, Luzerne County, sheathed its timber-frame meetinghouse (PA-26) with weatherboards and built a central entrance to a galleried meeting room beneath an arched ceiling. It was not greatly different from the Forty Fort Meetinghouse. This tradition of weatherboarded exteriors persisted well into the middle of the nineteenth century in many of the region's Greek Revival buildings. Although the Dutch Reformed congregation in Dingman's Ferry, Pike County, embellished its church

Nathan Denison House (PA-25) Forty Fort Borough, Luzerne County. East and south elevations (John Jennings, photographer, 1934) PA,40-FOFO,3-1.

Hanover Green Meetinghouse (PA-26) Hanover Green (Hanover Township), Luzerne County. Interior (John Jennings, photographer, 1934) PA,40-HANO,1-4.

Dutch Reformed Church (PA-1273) Dingmans Ferry (Delaware Township), Pike County. West and south elevations (George Eisenman, photographer, 1970) PA,52-DING,3-2.

(PA-1273) with a Doric tetrastyle portico in 1850, it used conventional weatherboards on the walls. Similarly the builder of the 1840 Silkman House (PA-217) in Scranton, Lackawanna County, even though he finished the front with flush horizontal siding, applied weatherboarding on the other three sides and lateral wings.

Agriculture dominated the early economy of the region until the 1820s,[10] when the beginnings of the anthracite coal industry marked a radical divergence

Silkman House (PA-217) Scranton, Lackawanna County. Northeast view (Stanley Jones, photographer, 1936) PA,35-SCRAN,1-2.

between the Anthracite Region and the Poconos. The latter remained agrarian; coal drove the economy of the former for over a century. As early as the 1760s, Wyoming Valley settlers uncovered "stone coal," as anthracite was then known. Because the fuel was difficult to ignite and burn and was located in remote mountains, a half century passed before it became economically viable. In 1807 specially designed boats called arks carried the first shipment down the Susquehanna to Columbia, Lancaster

County. Later other shipments went to Baltimore, and by 1820 similar vessels were operating on the Lehigh and Delaware Rivers. River travel, however, was treacherous; nearly one-third of the arks were lost in the early trips down the Susquehanna.[11]

By the mid-1820s, as improved coal grates were being patented, further stimulating the anthracite market, Pennsylvania's energetic canal building program provided the cheap transportation that made the anthracite boom possible.[12] The Schuylkill Canal between Philadelphia and Pottsville opened in 1825 and soon became the nation's busiest coal-carrying canal.[13] Coal companies also built their own canals, often faster and better than did the state. The Lehigh Coal and Navigation Company, for example, hired Canvass White, a veteran engineer from the great Erie Canal project, to engineer its canal from Mauch Chunk (now Jim Thorpe), Carbon County to Easton, Northampton County. White began digging in the summer of 1827 and, using his patented waterproof limestone concrete, completed the combined slackwater and canal system within two years. Meanwhile the state's connecting sixty-mile-long Delaware Canal from Easton to Philadelphia, authorized in 1827, was not finished until 1832.[14] During the 1830s the company extended the Lehigh Canal northward to White Haven, Luzerne County, and in 1838 connected it via the Lehigh and Susquehanna Railroad to the North Branch Division of the Pennsylvania Canal at Nanticoke, south of Wilkes-Barre.[15]

In the northern reaches of the region, the Delaware and Hudson Canal Company contracted with Benjamin White, chief engineer of the Erie Canal, to survey and build a canal between the Hudson River and the coal country. White began construction in 1825, the year the Erie Canal opened, and in October 1829 completed the work between Eddyville, New York, near Kingston on the Hudson, and Honesdale, Wayne County. A sixteen-mile inclined-plane railroad carried the system on to Carbondale, Lackawanna County.[16] The canal's operations grew steadily, peaking in 1872. Almost from the canal's beginning, the rope-ferry slackwater crossing of the Delaware River at the mouth of the Lackawaxen River caused a traffic bottleneck and legal and physical conflicts with river raftsmen. In 1846 the canal company resolved these problems by commissioning John A. Roebling to construct suspension aqueducts over these rivers. Roebling finished the work in the spring of 1849.[17] The aqueducts proved remarkably effective, making the canal so efficient that it cut rates by a half and thereby competed successfully with railroads until the last quarter of the nineteenth century.[18] Construction of these canals demonstrates two patterns that were established in the region at the outset of the anthracite boom: big-company domination of the local economy and the central role of transportation.[19]

In the wake of the canals came the railroads, which could scale the ridges more easily and remained less vulnerable to winter freezes and spring freshets. The earliest coal roads were gravity railroads connecting mines and canals,[20] but by the 1840s two major steam railways were running on lines roughly parallel to the canals. By early 1842 the Philadelphia and Reading Railroad, operating between Philadelphia and Pottsville, was serving nearly all of the same towns as the Schuylkill Canal. Within five years its overall tonnage, composed mostly of anthracite, exceeded that of the Erie Canal. Similarly the Lehigh Valley Railroad posed serious competition for the Lehigh Canal. In 1855 the railroad reached Mauch Chunk from Phillipsburg, New Jersey, opposite Easton on the Delaware River, and soon afterwards entered Wilkes-Barre. By 1868 the railroad was carrying more than twice the freight of the canal. Scranton got its rail connection to New York in 1853, when the Delaware, Lackawanna and Western Railroad opened.[21]

Coal and transportation spawned boomtowns. The population of Carbondale, the Northern Field's first coal town and the Delaware and Hudson Canal system's eastern terminus, virtually exploded, increasing by fifty times in the five years between 1828 and 1833. Speculators, coal operatives, and miners repeated this process throughout the century. Nanticoke, for example, mushroomed from three thousand inhabitants in 1880 to eight thousand only three years later.[22] Wilkes-Barre and Scranton, however, quickly emerged as the region's metropolitan giants. The competition between Wilkes-Barre and Scranton has not been one that normally arises between neighboring communities. In the nineteenth century it was an intense fight for regional economic and political hegemony. Wilkes-Barre exercised its considerable political power to retain its dominance, and succeeded for a quarter century in preventing the Scranton area from leaving Luzerne County. It would not be until 1878 that the legislature would approve the formation of Lackawanna County, the last county formed in Pennsylvania; Scranton became its seat. Wilkes-Barre was the older and more conservative of the two cities. Its nineteenth-century leadership was overwhelmingly English in background and came from the Wyoming Valley, while Scranton's leaders more easily accepted outsiders—in fact had to, if the city were to grow. Wilkes-Barre became a coal city from the beginnings of the coal boom, but because Scranton's first significant industry was iron manufacturing, it developed after the Civil War a more diversified industrial economy with manufacturing plants of all types and sizes. Yet while Scranton was dominating Lackawanna Valley coal towns by 1880, New York was dominating Scranton. Dreaming of national power and looking at national markets, New York entrepreneurs only invested in major industries, which in Scranton were the Lackawanna Iron and Steel Company and the Delaware, Lackawanna and Western Railroad. Starved for capital, these companies welcomed the New York investors who would eventually take them over and in 1901 move the iron and steel company to Buffalo.[23]

Anthracite coal is associated with deep mines. Strip mining is possible when coal seams are close to the surface, but that is unusual in the anthracite region. Although an increasingly large percentage of the relatively small quantity of the anthracite available comes from strip mines, as recently as the early 1930s stripping accounted for only 11 percent of the region's coal production. Because of the anthracite coal beds' tight folds, steep tilts, and frequent faults, most of the region's coal before World War II was extracted from shaft mines. The architecture of a late-nineteenth- or early-twentieth-century anthracite mine was grim and functional. Most of what remains today stands as abandoned and decaying reminders of a once-powerful and lucrative industry. At the mine shaft's opening is the headframe with its great hoisting wheels and other multistory apparatus and cables. Nearby is the hoisting shed, which houses the hoisting machinery, and the boiler house that generated the power for the hoists and other machinery. The most striking structure is the breaker, a gigantic building that looms over the denuded landscape. Once of timber frame, most surviving breakers are built of steel or concrete, with many glass panes. In the breaker the coal was crushed and sorted by size, and impurities such as slate were removed and conveyed to great culm (waste) piles while the coal was dumped in rail cars.[24]

Not far from every pit head stand the simple houses of former miners or their descendants. In the coal "patches" (small clusters of houses near a small mine), they are usually simple weatherboarded balloon-frame dwellings built by the coal company, in larger towns they often are built of brick. Typically they are laid out in rows—some sink into the ground from the subsidence of the mines below.[25] "They are cleaner now, for poverty and decline have at least brought purer air. Yet many of the older homes in the older patch towns have been indelibly colored by grimy coal dust, smoke, and soot."[26]

Residents of these houses included mining families from a variety of ethnic groups: descendants of the region's early English, Scottish, Irish, and Welsh miners as well as Poles, Ukrainians, Italians, Czechs, Slovaks, Serbians, Hungarians, Lithuanians, and other nationalities who flowed into the region after 1880.[27] This jumble of late-nineteenth-century immigrants "spoke a babel of incomprehensible languages. To the native-born Americans they seemed a race apart, entirely strange, and wherever they went they encountered suspicion and undisguised discrimination."[28] Understandably clannish, these immigrants and their offspring lived in a society where leaders made virtually no effort to bridge ethnic gulfs.[29] Living in their separate communities, they radically changed the character of such towns as Mount Carmel, Northumberland County, and Shenandoah, Schuylkill County. Nanticoke, for example, became the most Polish town in the state.[30] The labor of these people, and the "black diamonds" they dug from the earth, paid for the region's high-style architecture.

New York and Philadelphia architects designed the best of the coal region's architecture. Because of Scranton's early ties to New York, first along the Delaware and Hudson Canal and after 1856 along the Delaware, Lackawanna and Western Railroad, New York architects designed many of Scranton's buildings, ranging from James C. Cady's 1885 stone Second Presbyterian Church to the Indiana limestone depot that the Delaware, Lackawanna and Western Railroad built from the 1907 Beaux-Arts designs of Kenneth M. Murchison. Wilkes-Barre, on the other hand, tended to have stronger ties to Philadelphia along the Lehigh Canal and the Lehigh and Susquehanna Railroad, but by 1867 the Lehigh Valley Railroad had connected the city with New York as well. By the middle of the nineteenth century, architects from both cities were designing public buildings in Wilkes-Barre. Joseph C. Wells of New York and John McArthur of Philadelphia, for example, designed the third Luzerne County Courthouse (1856) and the Luzerne County Prison (1867), respectively. This practice of employing out-of-town architects continued in Scranton, when, three years after the state formed Lackawanna County in 1878, I. G. Perry of Binghamton, New York, designed the new courthouse.[31]

As Scranton and Wilkes-Barre grew in size, they attracted architects who developed extensive local practices and political influence, and by the end of the nineteenth century this convention of hiring out-of-town architects for public projects was not sitting well with the local architects. In 1899 they and their friends forced the commissioners of Luzerne County to cancel their courthouse design contract with Elijah E. Myers, a nationally known architect of public buildings, who understandably sued the commissioners. The county held another competition, and again chose an out-of-town architect, Frederick J. Osterling of Pittsburgh. Angered, most of Wilkes-Barre's architects joined in seeking an injunction against the commissioners' decision on the grounds that Osterling's estimate was deliberately and unreasonably low. Although it was shown that two commissioners had seen Osterling's design before the competition, the architects' argument lost in court, but it was borne out in fact. When the predicted cost overruns occurred, the commissioners dismissed Osterling and appointed one of his leading opponents, Fred McCormick of Wilkes-Barre, who at the time was in a partnership with Harry Livingston French. In 1909 McCormick finished what became known as the Million-Dollar Courthouse. A large part of the courthouse's expense lay in its marble interior and murals by such great muralists as Edwin Howland Blashfield, Kenyon Cox, Will H. Low, and William T. Smedley.[32]

Some out-of-town architects garnered local commissions because of their design specialties. Because Philadelphia architects Edwin F. Durang and Charles M. Burns were known for their Catholic and Episcopal church designs respectively, Durang numbered Wilkes-Barre's St. Mary's Catholic Church (1870-72), Scranton's Church of St. Vincent de Paul (1883-84, later called Saints Peter and Paul Cathedral), and Nanticoke's St. Francis's School (1884) among his local works, and Burns received commissions for two Episcopal churches in Wilkes-Barre, St. Clement's (1870's) and St. Stephen's (1899). Similarly A. C. Wagner of Philadelphia, a brewery architect, designed Wilkes-Barre's Stegmaier Brewery in 1894, and Albert H. Kipp, an architect with New York's Cooperative Building Plan Association, was the logical choice in 1886 for designing a speculative row in Wilkes-Barre.[33]

In a region populated with a wide assortment of European immigrants, some architects apparently won commissions for their ethnicity as much as for their design skills. German-born William Schickel of New York, for example, designed Wilkes-Barre's St. Nicholas German Catholic Church in 1883 and returned a decade later to design an addition to the Mallinckrodt Convent. Ethnic loyalty appears to have continued well into the twentieth century. Joseph Fronczak of Buffalo beat out many local architects in 1936 to win the competition for Wilkes-Barre's Polish Union Building, perhaps in part because he had an association with the Polish Union.[34]

In some towns a local patron personally selected architects who would alter a community's appearance, as Asa Packer did in Mauch Chunk (now Jim Thorpe).

Asa Packer Mansion (PA-5330) Jim Thorpe Borough, Carbon County. Section (Timothy Buehner, Patrick Koby, Sandra Moore, and Eric Zehrung, delineators, 1986) PA,13-JIMTH,7.

Packer was one of the coal region's great entrepreneurs, and unquestionably Mauch Chunk's most prominent citizen during the mid-nineteenth century. Befitting his role as the town's leading industrial baron, he built his eclectic mansion (PA-5330) in 1852 on a prominent height overlooking this coal and transportation center, where he engaged in public service and philanthropy as well as business. A major benefactor of St. Mark's Episcopal congregation, he was responsible in 1867 for selecting Richard Upjohn of New York, America's leading Gothic stylist at the time, to design the new church (PA-5457).[35] The Packer family's more favored architect, however, was Addison Hutton of Philadelphia, whom Asa Packer employed to design his son's Mauch Chunk house and the library for Lehigh University, which he had founded in Bethlehem, Northampton County.[36] His family followed his example, and after Packer's death his widow had Hutton design the St. Mark's parish house in 1881 as a memorial to her late husband. In 1882 his son, Judge Harry Packer, commissioned Hutton to design the Lehigh Valley Railroad office in Mauch Chunk and surely used his considerable influence to see that Hutton also designed St. Mark's Sunday school and the town's opera house.[37] Other Mauch Chunk citizens, however, did not emulate the Packer family's taste in architects. When the executors of Milton Dimmick's will chose an architect for the Dimmick Memorial Library (PA-5459) in 1889, they turned to T. Roney Williamson of Philadelphia, not Addison Hutton.[38] Williamson also worked in Pottsville.[39] It is not clear how urban architects of modest skills, such as Williamson, made themselves known in Pennsylvania's outlying towns. They evidently advertised in newspapers but probably also cultivated friendships and business, lodge, and religious relationships. It is an aspect of architectural history that needs more study.

Boom times in the region stimulated enough new construction to provide steady work for builder-architects in large towns outside the cities of Scranton and Wilkes-Barre. Many of those who were locally born, such as David Schooley in Pittston (active in the 1860s) and George Hoover in Honesdale (active between approximately 1850 and 1870), started as carpenters and never fully completed the transition to professional architect, whereby they were able to live solely from their design commissions. As the 1854 John Torrey House (PA-229) in Honesdale, Wayne County, indicates, however, these builder-architects, aided by architectural design books, could produce bold, up-to-date designs. At a time when the Italianate style was still new, the builder (possibly George Hoover) applied to the blockish building

Dimmick Memorial Library (PA-5459) Jim Thorpe Borough, Carbon County. Front elevation (Jet Lowe, photographer, 1979) PA,-13-JIMTH,3.

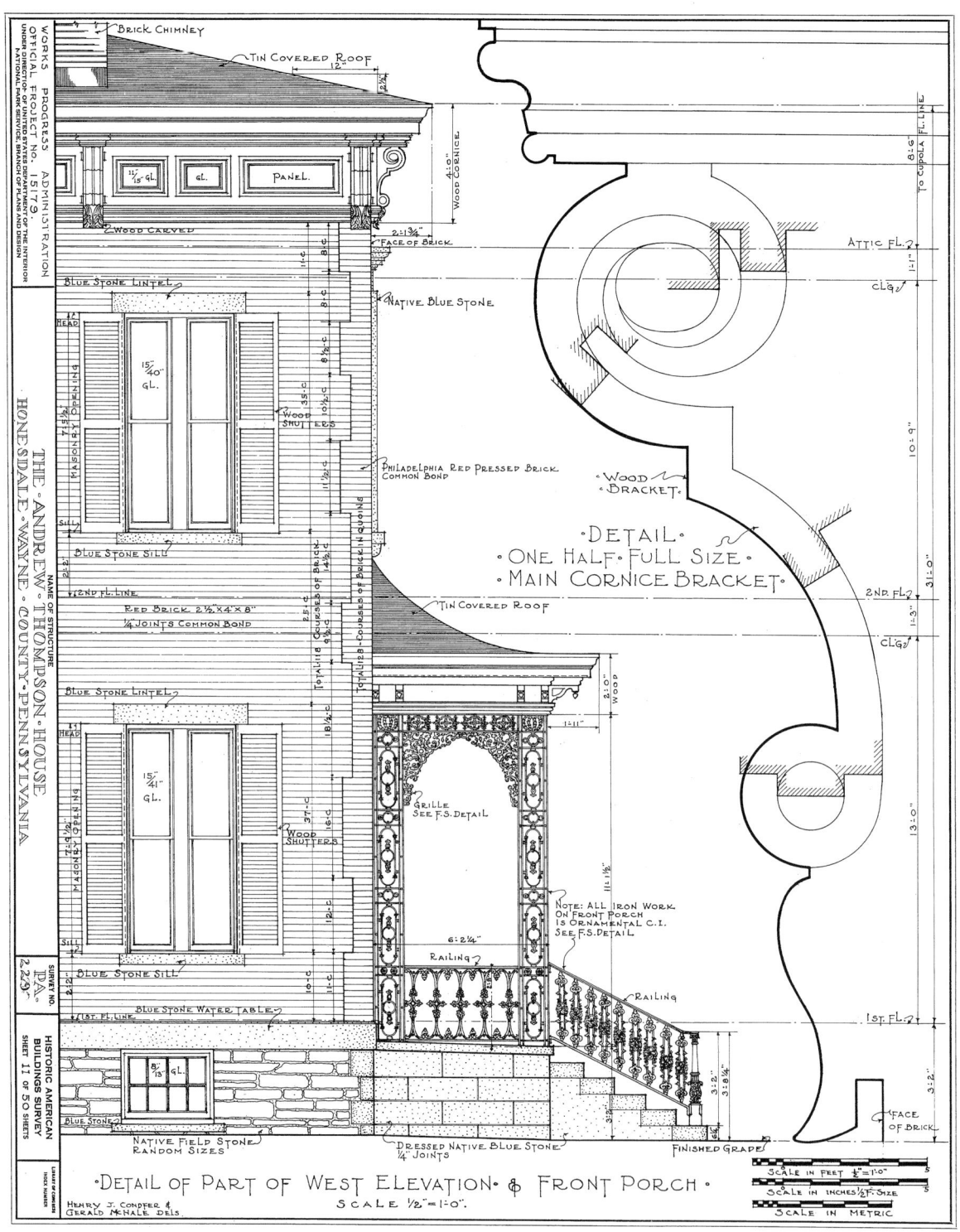

John Torrey House (Andrew Thompson House) (PA-229) Honesdale Borough, Wayne County. Detail of west elevation showing porch and bracket details (Henry J. Condfer and Gerald McHale, delineators, 1938) PA,64-HOND,1.

such picturesque details as a paneled frieze with attic windows and a square cupola to set the house apart from older buildings in the community. Joel Amsden made his living in Scranton as an engineer with the Lackawanna Iron and Coal Company and the Delaware, Lackawanna, and Western Railroad, but he demonstrated shortly after arriving in town his ability to design buildings in an array of historical styles. He certainly helped to establish his credentials as an architect in 1857 by designing an Italian villa for the city's founder, George W. Scranton.[40] At that point the town of Scranton had been a post office address for only six years, but the city was growing rapidly. Amsden died in 1868 but through his sons Frank and Frederick he established a small architectural dynasty in Scranton that, like the city's economy, flourished throughout the second half of the nineteenth century.[41]

Many of the region's successful and accomplished nineteenth-century architects began their careers in large cities and settled briefly in Scranton and Wilkes-Barre before seeking opportunities elsewhere. This was particularly the case in Wilkes-Barre, where after the Civil War, four professional architects set up practices, but only one stayed more than six years. The most important of these was Bruce Price. After his training in the Baltimore offices of Niernsee and Neilson and a tour of England, in 1874 Price moved to Wilkes-Barre, his wife's hometown. His Wilkes-Barre work of this period reflects a strong preference for the High Victorian Gothic Style that he apparently acquired during his English trip. When economic depression hit the coal region in 1876 Price moved to New York, where he developed a national reputation. Isaac Price, apparently no relation to Bruce, arrived in Wilkes-Barre in 1867 after having trained under P. B. Wight in New York. He helped to establish the Second Empire Style in the area before leaving in 1873, about the same time that Willis G. Hale arrived from Philadelphia. After a three-year stay in which he tried—unsuccessfully—to become an opera singer, Hale returned to his city of origin. Only Albert H. Kipp of New York stayed. He moved to Wilkes-Barre in 1886 to supervise the aforementioned Wilkes-Barre row house project and was still there twenty years later.[42]

Scranton also had transient architects. Between 1850 and 1920, approximately eighty-five men listed themselves as architects in city directories, some for only one year.[43] The two men with the longest tenures in the post-Civil War era were H. R. Noll and Cornelius Brinkerhoff, both of whom started their careers as carpenters. Noll advertised himself as an architect for eight years (1867-1875) before apparently leaving the area. During his last three or four years in Scranton, he teamed up with

Brinkerhoff, who spent the 1870s in Scranton after earlier working in New York and Philadelphia architectural offices. In the 1880s, however, three young architects established practices in Scranton that lasted until their deaths in the early twentieth century. Edwin L. Walter, a former carpenter who learned architecture in the offices of the Amsden brothers during the 1870s, struck out on his own in 1880. He worked until 1903 and included the city's only municipal building (1888-93) among his many local works. Frederick Lord Brown, a Cornell University architectural graduate, came to Scranton in 1883 after working as an architect for the United States Department of the Treasury in Washington, D.C., and practiced architecture in the city until 1920. John A. Duckworth studied architecture in Toronto, his birthplace. After working in New York, Chicago, and San Francisco, he opened his Scranton office in 1884, beginning a twenty-eight-year practice in which he designed over six hundred buildings in northeastern Pennsylvania. By contrast, Wilkes-Barre had difficulty retaining professionally trained architects until the 1890s; in 1892 Fred McCormick and Henry Livingston French established a partnership that lasted for three decades.[44]

By comparison with the Anthracite Region, nineteenth-century progress bypassed the Pocono Mountains Region. Both regions endured productive but destructive exploitation of the land, but since the exploitation in the Poconos consisted of timbering, the land recovered when the forests grew back. Because of the rugged terrain and the sparse population, the built environment changed slowly and mostly in valleys and along the Delaware River. Initial settlers came in small numbers from New York near the beginning of the eighteenth century, but by the end of that century the migration was from southeastern Pennsylvania and Connecticut. Farmers dominated the region, but because of the high elevation, hilly terrain, and poor soil, both their numbers and yields were small throughout the eighteenth and nineteenth centuries. Beginning in the 1760s, and for the next century and a quarter, they supplemented their incomes with logging during the winter months. They had cut most of the highly sought white pine by the second quarter of the nineteenth century, but an abundance of hemlock, spruce, beech, and oak kept timbering a significant regional enterprise until after the Civil War, when it began its decline.[45]

The region's natural beauty attracted travelers as early as the 1820s, in particular to the Delaware Water Gap, where the Kittatinny House was built in 1829. In 1843 geographer Charles B. Trego rhapsodized on Wayne County's streams: "Their crystal waters sleep calmly embosomed in the dark woods, and find but rarely a solitary traveller upon their banks to gaze upon their serene and quiet beauty. These deep and secluded retreats, seldom visited except by the hunter or fisherman, offer an exquisite treat to the admirers of natural scenery."[46] About this same time (1848), the owners of the Halfway House, a log-frame house that had been built in 1836 in Henryville, Monroe County, on the road between Easton, Northampton County, and the Lackawanna Valley, responded to the growing number of fishermen visiting nearby Brodhead Creek, "an angler's mecca," by enlarging the building and giving it its present name, Henryville House. By the 1860s the resort industry was firmly rooted in the Poconos Region. Express trains in the 1870s boosted business, making Stroudsburg and the Delaware Water Gap area sufficiently crowded that attention shifted to other sites, such as Bushkill, Pike County, and Mount Pocono, Monroe County. The latter site grew into a large resort area in the 1880s. By this time modest frame boarding houses and large hotels perched on hillsides along the river and creeks, affording guests scenic views and serving them family-style dinners featuring local produce and dairy products.[47] Some, such as the Peters House Hotel (PA-1138) in Bushkill, Pike County, were built on the site of earlier taverns, and their owners added to the building as business expanded. By this time the state was taking steps to encourage the area's resort industry. In 1879 the state Fish Commission started stocking local streams with brook trout, and a decade later introduced the European brown trout to them. In 1897 the commission began stocking Saylor Lake with lake trout, about the same time that the Game Commission responded to the decline in hunting by establishing regulations designed to help wild game make a comeback. After the turn of the century, entrepreneurs erected large resort hotels and recreational complexes, laying out the region's first golf course in 1904 at Buck Hill Falls. The Poconos' cool summers have helped to make golf an increasingly popular local recreation, but winter sports also started to come into vogue before World War I. Since World War II increased affluence, paid vacation time, and improved highways have contributed to an exponential growth of the region's resort industry.[48]

    Year-round nineteenth-century inhabitants in the region lived in modest vernacular houses. Log houses were constructed, but only a very few survive. Stone and timber-frame seem to have been more popular, especially for nineteenth-century farmhouses. Generally smaller than farmhouses in the state's more prosperous agricultural areas, such as the Great Valley and Piedmont, these nineteenth-century houses invariably had two-and-a-half stories, gable roofs (often with cornice returns), and rear

Peters House Hotel (PA-1138) Bushkill (Lehman Township), Pike County. South and west elevations (George Eisenman, photographer, 1970) PA,52-BUSH,1-1.

wings.[49] By comparison, eighteenth-century dwellings could be quite humble. Because the rubble Jacobus Van Gorden House (PA-5180) near Egypt Mills, Pike County, was built into a bank, the ground level served as food storage and kitchen, leaving only the upper floor with its single fireplace for habitation. The attic was unfinished.[50] Although eighteenth-century houses on the opposite side of the Delaware, in New Jersey, resemble seventeenth-century Dutch houses along New York's Hudson River Val-

Jacobus Van Gorden House (PA-5180) Egypt Mills vicinity (Lehman Township), Pike County. Northeast and northwest elevations (George Eisenman, photographer, 1970) PA,52-EGYMI.V,2-2.

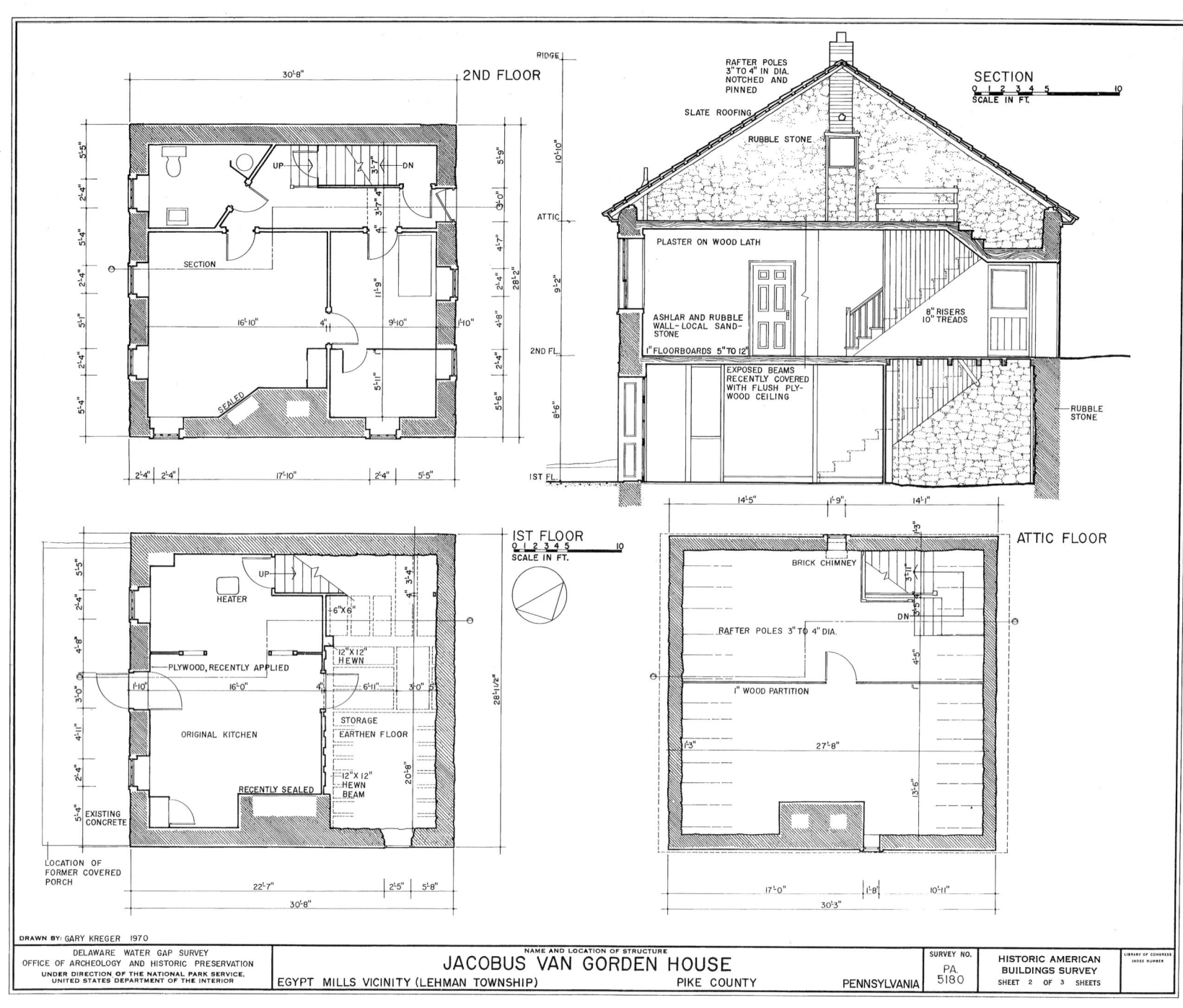

Jacobus Van Gorden House (PA-5180) Egypt Mills vicinity (Lehman Township), Pike County. Plans and section (Gary Kreger, delineator, 1970) PA,52-EGYMI.V,2.

ley, extant examples on the Pennsylvania side of the Delaware do not. The Van Gorden House, for example, was built about 1770 with rubble masonry walls that are common along the upper Delaware, but its construction is not Dutch.[51]

By the nineteenth century, people of means enjoyed stylish residences in spite of their locations in remote villages. The 1811 David Wilmot House (PA-225) in Bethany, Wayne County, for example, is modest in size but its entrance is finished with a gouged Federal-style frontispiece. Immodest but clearly stylish is Grey Towers (PA-1400), the country house that Richard Morris Hunt designed for James Pinchot in 1886, when he returned to his hometown, having made a fortune in New York City. A re-creation of a medieval French chateau, Grey Towers stands on a hill overlooking Milford, Pike County, affording its owner a position not unlike that of a lord surveying his fiefdom.[52] Grey Towers is very good architecture, but with its great size, sophisticated design, and complex site plan it is not representative of the region's dwellings.

While the Poconos Region changed gradually, retaining its rural character and expanding its resort industry, the Anthracite Region suffered cataclysmic changes. Anthracite production increased steadily for nearly a century, reaching its peak of over 99.6 million tons in 1917. By the 1980s only 6 million tons were being mined annually, with more than half of that quantity from strip mines. Since World War II, emigration, high unemployment, and low incomes (the lowest per capita income in the state) have characterized the region.[53] Because of the Anthracite Region's economic downturn, there has been little significant architecture here since 1930. Scranton's Masonic Temple and Scottish Rite Cathedral stands as that city's architectural last hurrah of the coal era. An exercise in the stripped Gothic Revival style of the period, the four- and five-story Masonic Temple was designed by the firm of Raymond H. Hood, Godley, and Fouilhoux, architects of New York's Rockefeller Center. The Masonic order insisted on the best materials, Indiana limestone on the exterior walls, travertine marble for the lobby walls, and specially designed and woven rugs and draperies for the public spaces. The building formally opened in May 1930 (three years and six weeks after ground was broken), as the nation was falling into the Great Depression.[54] No building of such significance has been built in the region since.[55] The coal region has survived its hard times, and a more diversified economy is developing. With the aid of federal redevelopment and tax programs, parts of the region's two largest cities, Scranton and Wilkes-Barre, were rehabilitated and rebuilt in the 1970s and 80s, but much remains to be done there and in the surrounding towns.

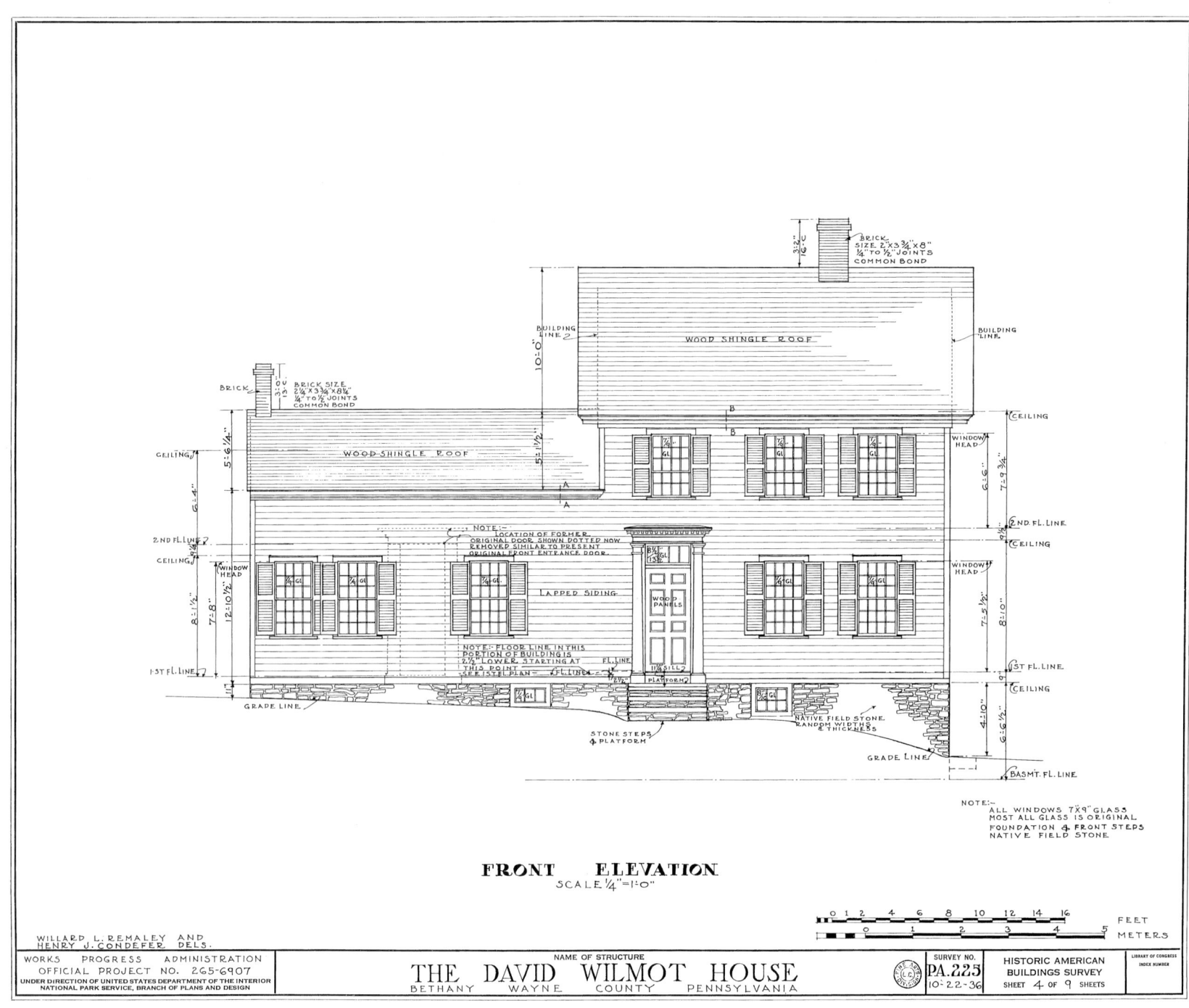

David Wilmot House (PA-225) Bethany Borough, Wayne County. Front elevation (Willard L. Remaley and Henry J. Condefer, delineators, 1936) PA,64-BETH,1.

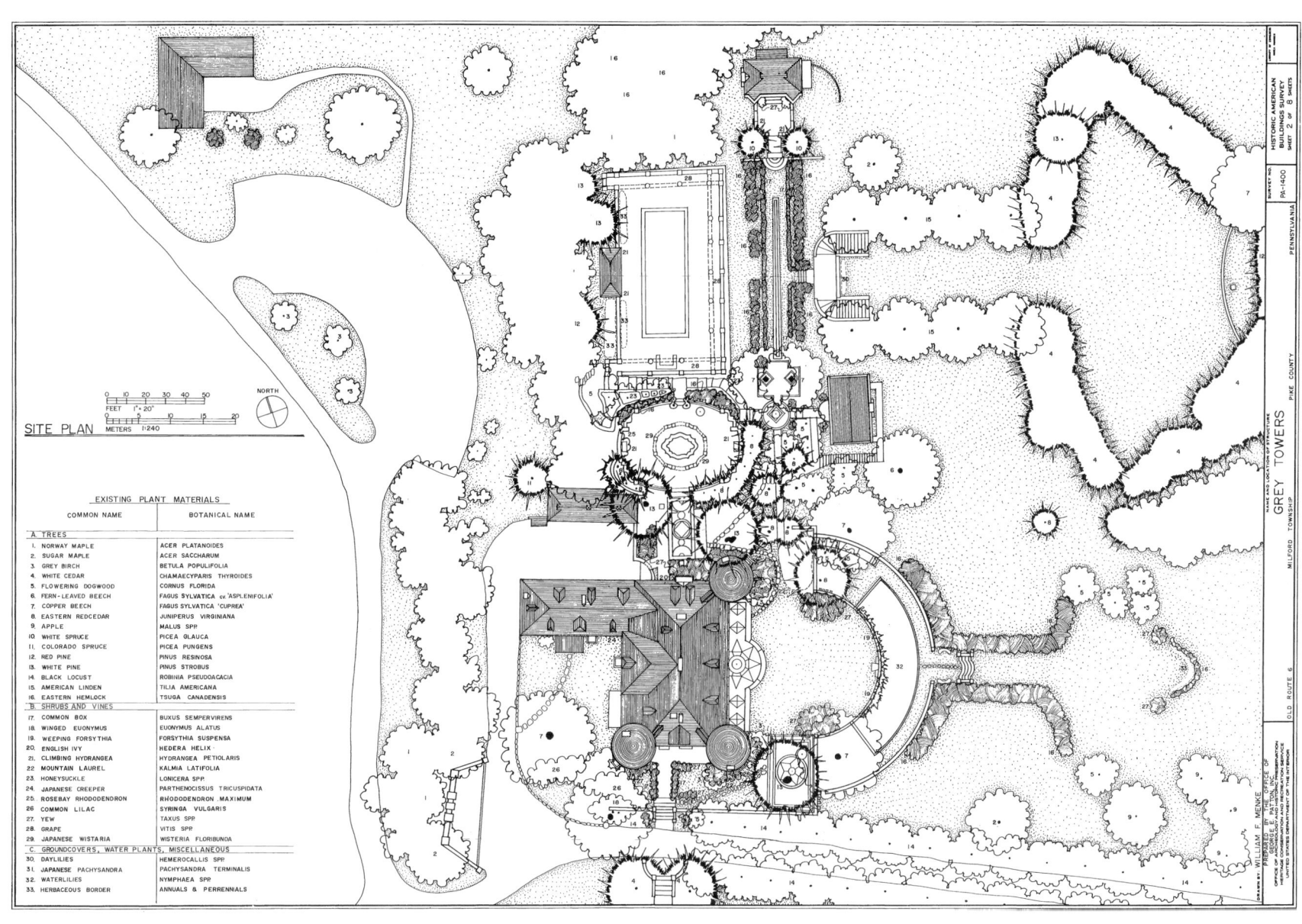

Grey Towers (PA-1400) Milford vicinity, Pike County. Landscape plan (William F. Menke, delineator, after 1933) PA,52-MIVF.V,4.,

Region V: Anthracite and Poconos • 499

Notes

[1] The region's 1930 population density of about 1,500 persons per square mile (when the state's average was 214.8) has declined but remains high relative to most of the state. In 1980, for example, Lackawanna County had a population density between 400 and 800 persons per square mile, placing it among the state's eleven most densely populated counties. (The four most densely populated counties are Philadelphia, Delaware, Allegheny, and Montgomery.) The region's population density figures are misleading, however, because the population is squeezed into the valleys, leaving the ridges virtually uninhabited. Raymond E. Murphy and Marion Murphy, *Pennsylvania: A Regional Geography* (Harrisburg: The Pennsylvania Book Service, 1937), 325-27, 337; Ronald F. Abler, David J. Cuff, Edward K. Muller, William J. Young, and Wilbur Zelinsky, *The Atlas of Pennsylvania* (Philadelphia: Temple University Press, 1989), 86, 120.

[2] Murphy and Murphy, *Pennsylvania*, 327. For a discussion of the meaning of the region's landscape to its people in relation to its economy, see Benn Marsh, "Continuity and Decline in the Anthracite Towns of Pennsylvania," *Annals of the Association of American Geographers* 77 (September 1987): 337-52.

[3] Murphy and Murphy, *Pennsylvania*, 342-56; Abler et al., *Atlas of Pennsylvania*, 39, 104-5.

[4] Murphy and Murphy, *Pennsylvania*, 38-39, 362-67.

[5] For a good summary of the Yankee-Pennamite Wars see Wayland F. Dunaway, *A History of Pennsylvania* (New York: Prentice-Hall, Inc., 1948), 131-37. The most thorough discussion of the conflict is in Julian P. Boyd, ed., *The Susquehanna Company Papers*, 6 vols. (Ithaca, N.Y.: Cornell University Press, 1930), Robert J. Taylor, ed., *The Susquehanna Company Papers*, 5 vols. (Ithaca, N.Y.: Cornell University Press, 1969-1971); see in particular, vols. 1, 2, and 7. Another Tory-Indian attack in the region, in addition to the famous Wyoming Massacre, was the Battle of Minisink, near the present site of Lackawaxen, Pike County. About 175 settlers attacked a party of three hundred Indians and Tories under Chief Joseph Brant in July 1779 after the latter had burned Minisink, now Port Jervis, New York. Only twenty of the local settlers survived. Writers' Program of the Works Projects Administration, *Pennsylvania: A Guide to the Keystone State* (New York: Oxford University Press for the Pennsylvania Historical Commission and the University of Pennsylvania, 1940; reprint ed., St. Clair Shores, Mich.: Scholarly Press, 1976), 357.

[6] Wilkes-Barre was laid out by John Durkee, a Connecticut veteran of the French and Indian War, and was named for two members of the British Parliament, John Wilkes and Colonel Isaac Barre, who were popular among American colonists for championing individual rights. Public Square was intersected from its corners by Main Street, running northeast-southwest, and Market Street, running southeast-northwest. Thus four triangles were formed on which public buildings were erected. The conception and early development of Public Square was different from that of Philadelphia's Centre Square. William Penn evidently expected the Centre Square would be an important center in his city, and built a large Quaker meetinghouse on it. Population, however, concentrated along the Delaware River, where the jobs were, and in a few years the meetinghouse was dismantled. The city did not build a government building on the square until 1871, when Philadelphia City Hall (PA-1530) was begun in the middle of the square. Writers' Program, *Pennsylvania*, 335; Oscar Jewell Harvey and Ernest Gray Smith, *A History of Wilkes-Barre, Luzerne County, Pennsylvania* 6 vols. (Wilkes-Barre: By the authors, 1909-1930), 3:1759. For Connecticut colonial town plans, see Anthony N.B. Garvan, *Architecture and Town Planning in Colonial Connecticut* (New Haven: Yale University Press, 1955).

[7] Both buildings were timber frame. The church was finished with weatherboards. The courthouse was sheathed with one-inch boards grooved to resemble stone; the grooves were painted white and the rest of the building red. The courthouse stood in the square's southern triangle, the church in the western triangle. Some historians have noted that the courthouse resembled Philadelphia's Carpenters' Hall (PA-1398), but, in fact, it was based on a public building in Fredericktown, Maryland. The stone jail was built in the eastern triangle, 1802-1808, and the initial academy building was the 1788 log courthouse, which was moved when the new courthouse was begun in 1801. Harvey and Smith, *History of Wilkes-Barre*, 3:1628-29, 1735-36, 1754-57, 1759; Vito J. Sgromo and Michael Lewis, *Wilkes-Barre Architecture: 1860 to 1960* (Wilkes-Barre: Wyoming Historical and Geological Society, 1983), 3.

[8] A window, in particular an arched window, in the middle of a facade behind the pulpit has been a common feature in New England meetinghouses at least since 1681, when a pair of narrow round-arched windows were placed behind the pulpit of the Old-Ship Meetinghouse in Hingham, Massachusetts. See Leland M. Roth, *A Concise History of American Architecture* (New York: Harper and Row, Publishers, 1979), 18. Initially the meetinghouse served as a union church, the Congregationalists allowing the Methodists and Presbyterians to use the building for services. Harvey and Smith, *History of Wilkes-Barre*, 3:1746. The Forty Fort Meetinghouse is discussed in Harold B. Dickson, *A Hundred Pennsylvania Buildings* (State College: Bald Eagle Press, 1954), pl. 36. The most definitive work on early New England meetinghouses is Marian Card Donnelly, *The New England Meeting Houses of the Seventeenth Century* (Middletown: Wesleyan University Press, 1968). See page 105 for an illustration of the 1773 Sandown, N.H., Meetinghouse, which is very similar to the Forty Fort example.

[9] The outstanding study of early houses in Massachusetts is Abbott Lowell Cummings, *The Framed Houses of Massachusetts Bay, 1625-1725* (Cambridge: The Belknap Press of Harvard University Press, 1979). For Connecticut houses see J. Frederick Kelly, *The Early Domestic Architecture of Connecticut* (New Haven: Yale University Press, 1924).

[10]Sylvester K. Stevens, *Pennsylvania: Titan of Industry* (New York: Lewis Historical Publishing Company, Inc., 1948), 167.

[11]Donald L. Miller and Richard E. Sharpless, *The Kingdom of Coal: Work, Enterprise, and Ethnic Communities in the Mine Fields* (Philadelphia: University of Pennsylvania Press, 1985), 6-25.

[12] The demand for coal had been building since before the American Revolution. Because of the depletion of forests in southeastern Pennsylvania, Philadelphians began using soft coal as early as the 1770s and were consuming more than a thousand tons a year by the 1790s. Since most of it was imported from Great Britain, the prospects of using domestic coal were very attractive. Once Pennsylvania's anthracite was shown to be a viable fuel, iron grates for open fires were promoted with a combination of scientific evidence and shrill advertising and remained the popular means of burning coal until the Civil War period, when freestanding airtight stoves, available since the 1830s, became more common. Miller and Sharpless, *The Kingdom of Coal*, 8, 24-25; Frederick M. Binder, "Anthracite Enters the American Home," *Pennsylvania Magazine of History and Biography* 82 (January 1958): 82-99.

[13]Miller and Sharpless, *The Kingdom of Coal*, 34-36.

[14]Josiah White of Philadelphia formed the Lehigh Coal Company and the Lehigh Navigation Company in 1818; the companies consolidated two years later and were incorporated as the Lehigh Coal and Navigation Company in February 1822. The Lehigh Canal ran forty-six miles from Mauch Chunk to Easton, navigating a 354.7-foot drop in elevation. Canvass White, who was locally acclaimed for the use of his patented waterproof limestone concrete on the Lehigh Canal, was later employed to repair the state-built Delaware Canal, which had leaked so badly before White's arrival that it ran dry. These two linking canals proved so profitable that they were two of only four Pennsylvania canals to survive into the twentieth century; both closed in 1931. There were also connections with New York City via the Morris Canal at Phillipsburg, New Jersey, beginning in 1831 and the Delaware and Raritan Canal at Lambertville and Bordentown, New Jersey, in 1834. John P. Miller, *The Lehigh Canal: A Thumb Nail History, 1829-1931* (Allentown,: By the author, 1979), 14-19, 26; James M. Swank, *Progressive Pennsylvania: A Record of the Remarkable Industrial Development of the Keystone State* (Philadelphia: J.B. Lippincott Company, 1908), 147-48. William H. Shank, *The Amazing Pennsylvania Canals* (York: American Canal and Transportation Center, 1981), 60-64, 69.

[15]The Upper Grand Section of the Lehigh Canal extended above White Haven to Port Jenkins, and consisted of 5.5 miles of canal and 20.5 miles of slackwater navigation. In March 1863 a flood destroyed much of this upper canal and the company replaced it with a railroad. Miller, *The Lehigh Canal*, 20-21, 24; Miller and Sharpless, *The Kingdom of Coal*, 30-31, 34-38.

[16]Along its first four miles west of Honesdale, the inclined-plane, or gravity, railroad climbed 950 feet to the summit of Moosic Mountain. The railroad opened in the summer of 1829 and was altered in the early 1840s and again in 1866. The tonnage of coal it carried dropped drastically during the 1890s, and the company closed the road in January 1899 and shifted to a standard gauge locomotive track with direct connections with the Erie Railroad in Honesdale.

The company had closed the canal a few months earlier, in November 1898. Shank, *The Amazing Pennsylvania Canals*, pp. 55-58. The most detailed history of the canal is Manville B. Wakefield's thoroughly illustrated *Canal Boats to Tidewater: The Story of the Delaware & Hudson Canal* (South Fallsburg, N.Y.: Steingart Associates, 1965); for the canal's construction, see pp. 4-8; for the gravity railroad, see pp. 13-31. Also helpful is Edwin D. LeRoy, *The Delaware and Hudson Canal: A History* (Honesdale, Pa.: Wayne County Historical Society, [1950]).

[17] Besides the fact that Roebling's suspension scheme was considerably cheaper to build and provided more clearance than a masonry bridge, the three piers supporting the four spans of the Delaware aqueduct reduced the chances of damage from floods and ice jams that plagued that part of the Delaware River. In 1849-51 Roebling built two other suspension aqueducts for the canal. Both were in New York, one over the Neversink River at Cuddebackville and the other over Rondout Creek at High Falls, near Eddyville. Robert M. Vogel, *Roebling's Delaware & Hudson Canal Aqueducts*, Smithsonian Studies in History and Technology, no. 10 (Washington: Smithsonian Institution Press, 1971), 9-11, 17, 23-25.

[18] Of the four aqueducts, only the one over the Delaware River found adaptive use—as a highway toll bridge. It is still in use. Vogel, *Roebling's Delaware and Hudson Canal Aqueducts*, 2, 25; Shank, *The Amazing Pennsylvania Canals*, 56.

[19] Miller and Sharpless, *The Kingdom of Coal*, 37.

[20] Two of the earliest of these gravity roads were the 1827 Mauch Chunk Railroad, which connected with the Lehigh Canal, and the aforementioned railroad over Moosic Mountain from Carbondale, Lackawanna County, to Honesdale and the Delaware and Hudson Canal. This road made history in August 1829 when the English-built *Stourbridge Lion* became the first locomotive to run on rails in the United States. Stevens, *Pennsylvania: Titan of Industry*, 132.

[21] The Lehigh Valley Railroad was chartered in 1846 as the Delaware, Lehigh, Schuylkill, and Susquehanna Railroad; it changed its name in 1853 after Asa Packer and his friends and family acquired majority control of its stock. The Delaware, Lackawanna, and Western Railroad was the consolidation of two railroads promoted by George W. and Selden Scranton: Liggett's Gap Railroad and Delaware and Cobb's Gap Railroad. Swank, *Progressive Pennsylvania*, 167-70, 172; Dunaway, *History of Pennsylvania*, 598-99; Jules I. Bogen, *The Anthracite Railroads: A Study in American Railroad Enterprise* (New York: Ronald Press Company, 1927), 27; Miller and Sharpless, *The Kingdom of Coal*, 71-72; Writers' Program, *Pennsylvania*, 323.

[22] Rowland Berthoff, "The Social Order of the Anthracite Region, 1825-1902," *Pennsylvania Magazine of History and Biography* 89 (July 1965): 262.

[23] Burton W. Folsom, Jr., *Urban Capitalists: Entrepreneurs and City Growth in Pennsylvania's Lackawanna and Lehigh Regions: 1800-1920* (Baltimore: Johns Hopkins University Press, 1981), 38-41, 68-83.

[24] Also essential at every mine were the ventilating shaft and fan and a timber yard for storing timbers used to shore up the shafts as the mines expanded. Murphy and Murphy, *Pennsylvania*, 328-33; Abler et al., *Atlas of Pennsylvania*, 39.

[25] Murphy and Murphy, *Pennsylvania*, 339.

[26] Miller and Sharpless, *The Kingdom of Coal*, xix. Many of these coal patches can be found along the roads of the region, but one, the remains of Eckley, has been preserved and opened to the public by the Pennsylvania Historical and Museum Commission, another indication that the age of coal is history. Eckley Miners' Village was a privately owned company patch near Hazleton, Luzerne County, until 1971. Retired miners and miners' widows still live there.

[27] Murphy and Murphy, *Pennsylvania*, 339-40; Miller and Sharpless, *The Kingdom of Coal*, 172. Professors Miller and Sharpless have written particularly sensitive and informative chapters on both Irish and so-called Slavic immigrants' lives in the coal region; see chapters 5 and 6.

[28] Miller and Sharpless, *The Kingdom of Coal*, 172.

[29] Despite the now legendary Molly Maquire episode of alleged Irish violence against British and American miners and superintendents in the 1860s and early 1870s, intergroup conflict seems to have been infrequent. Ethnic separation, on the other hand, in both work places and neighborhoods was the rule. Public school officials did not perceive Americanization of their charges as one of their responsibilities until after the beginning of the twentieth century. Berthoff, "The Social Order of the Anthracite Region," 266-71.

[30] Miller and Sharpless, *The Kingdom of Coal*, 181-82.

[31] Sgromo and Lewis, *Wilkes-Barre Architecture*, 3, 8; Joseph H. Young, "Early Architects and Architecture of Scranton, Pennsylvania" *Charette* 46 (April 1966): 10; Writers' Program, *Pennsylvania*, 324.

[32] Osterling was accustomed to controversy. He aroused the Pittsburgh elite when he proposed adding two stories to the Allegheny County Courthouse (PA-610) in the early 1900s, and in 1917 he alienated Henry Clay Frick over construction of the Union Arcade in Pittsburgh. Sgromo and Lewis, *Wilkes-Barre Architecture*, 18; Martin Aurand, "Frederick J. Osterling and a Tale of Two Buildings," *Pennsylvania Heritage* 15 (Spring 1989): 16-21; Writers' Program, *Pennsylvania*, 337-38.

[33] Sgromo and Lewis, *Wilkes-Barre Architecture*, 4-5, 14; Young, "Early Architects and Architecture of Scranton," 9.

[34] Sgromo and Lewis, *Wilkes-Barre Architecture*, 12, 27.

[35] Asa Packer led a stereotypical rags-to-riches life. A representative nineteenth-century entrepreneur, he enjoyed a successful combination of good timing, vision, ambition, and risk-taking. He was a young carpenter seeking opportunities when he arrived in Mauch Chunk in 1833 soon after the Lehigh Canal opened. He moved quickly from being a boat hand to being a boat operator and soon an owner of boatyards in Mauch Chunk and Pottsville. He also purchased coal lands, and in 1851 risked everything in his takeover of the Lehigh Valley Railroad. Defying the odds and predictions of financial and railroad leaders, Packer completed construction of the railroad and became a multi-millionaire. He later turned to politics, serving two terms in the United States House of Representatives, having his name entered in

nomination for President at the 1868 Democratic National Convention, and running unsuccessfully for governor in 1869. A good summary of his career is in Miller and Sharpless, *The Kingdom of Coal*, 68-72. See also Milton C. Stuart, *Asa Packer, 1805-1879: Captain of Industry; Educator; Citizen* (Princeton: Princeton University Press, 1938); *Dictionary of American Biography*, s.v. "Packer, Asa," by Lawrence H. Gipson. The Packer family's dominant role within the church is indicated by the mechanical connection in 1883 of the church chimes (for which Asa Packer was the major contributor) to the Packers' Lehigh Valley Railroad offices' clock. St. Mark's is discussed in Dickson, *A Hundred Pennsylvania Buildings*, pl. 64. For buildings cited, see Hans G. Egli, *Guide/History to Jim Thorpe* (Jim Thorpe: By the author, 1977), 12-13, 35-36; Donna J. Carney, *Jim Thorpe, Pennsylvania: "An Image Preserved"* (Phillipsburg, N.J.: Harmony Press, c. 1982), 26-27.

[36]In the fall of 1864 Packer asked William Bacon Stevens, bishop of the Episcopal Diocese of Pennsylvania, to draw up a plan for a university that he intended to establish with a half-million-dollar endowment. The school, Lehigh University, opened in September 1866. Besides Packer, the initial board of trustees included ironmaster John Fritz; Garret B. Linderman, superintendent of the Bethlehem Iron Works; Robert H. Sayre, superintendent and engineer of the Lehigh Valley Railroad; and Eckley B. Coxe, a benefactor of Philadelphia's University Museum (PA-1646) and a major coal operator after whom Eckley, Pennsylvania, was named. Stuart, *Asa Packer*, 21-22; Elizabeth Biddle Yarnall, *Addison Hutton: Quaker Architect, 1834-1916* (Philadelphia: Art Alliance Press, 1974), 53.

[37]Egli, *Guide to Jim Thorpe*, 12-13, 26, 35-36.

[38]*Philadelphia Real Estate Record and Builders Guide* 4 (24 April 1889): 186. Williamson designed the alterations to the Mauch Chunk Presbyterian Church at the same time. Since he was very active in the Presbyterian Church, it is not clear whether he received this commission because of his religious affiliations or because he was in town at the right time. *Philadelphia Real Estate Record and Builders' Guide* 4 (4 June 1889): 258. I am indebted to Professor Harry G. Schalck, West Chester University, for the information and sources on Williamson.

[39]Williamson was responsible for alterations to Guy C. Farquahar's house in 1890 and the plans for the McQuail House in 1891. *Philadelphia Real Estate Record and Builders Guide* 5 (3 December 1890): 752, 6 (18 March 1891): 162.

[40]Joel Amsden was born in Hartland, Vermont in 1812. After graduating from Norwich University with a degree in civil engineering, he worked on various canal and railroad projects. He was working for an Easton iron works, when on a New York business trip he met George W. Scranton, who hired him for the Scrantons & Platt iron works. One of his first assignments was laying out the town of Scranton. Young, "Early Architects and Architecture of Scranton," 8.

[41]There were five houses in the future site of Scranton (then called Slocum Hollow), when George W. Scranton and his brother Selden arrived in 1840 to build the iron forge that over the years grew into the Lackawanna Iron and Steel Company. When a post office was established there in 1851 the town was called Scrantonia; less than a year later the name of the

post office and town was simplified to Scranton. Young, "Early Architects and Architecture of Scranton," 8-12; Dorothy Allen, "Faded Images: Former Buildings and Forgotten Men," *Lackawanna Historical Society Bulletin* 19 (February 1987): n.p.; Writers' Program, *Pennsylvania*, 323.

[42] Sgromo and Lewis, *Wilkes-Barre Architecture*, 6-7, 9-10, 14, 17.

[43] Many of those self-proclaimed architects probably made their livings as civil and mining engineers, carpenters, and masons. Young, "Early Architects and Architecture of Scranton," 9.

[44] Besides McCormick and French, two other notable turn-of-the-century Wilkes-Barre firms are Welsh, Sturdevant, and Poggi, which practiced between 1905 and 1918, and the Olds and Puckey partnership, which began approximately 1897 and apparently ended with Frederick L. Olds' death in 1912. Two important Scranton architects of this period are Edward Herbert Davis and Edward Langley. Davis graduated from the Washington (D.C.) School of Fine Arts, and after working for seven years in Washington, D.C., and Wilkes-Barre, he opened his office in Scranton in 1892 and worked by himself until 1919, when he formed a partnership with George M. D. Lewis. Langley was born in Toronto in 1873, the son of an architect. He learned the profession from his cousin and in 1902 left New York for Scranton, where he practiced architecture until his death in 1936. Young, *Early Architects*, 9-12; Sgromo and Lewis, *Wilkes-Barre Architecture*, 18-21.

[45] Charles B. Trego noted that by 1843 most of Wayne County's white pine "has long since been destroyed" and Pike County's was "becoming scarce." Charles B. Trego, *A Geography of Pennsylvania: Containing an Account of the Historical, Geographical Features, Soil, Climate, Geology, Botany, Zoology, Population, Education, Government, Finances, Productions, Trade, Railroads, Canal, &c. of the State* (Philadelphia: Edward C. Biddle, 1843), 299-300, 340, 367; Dennis N. Bertland, Patricia M. Valence, and Russell J. Woodling, *The Minisink: A Chronicle of One of America's First and Last Frontiers* (Stroudsburg, Pa.: Four-County Task Force on the Tocks Island Dam Project, 1975), 48, 126-29, 150-51; Murphy and Murphy, *Pennsylvania*, 126-27, 148.

[46] Trego, *Geography of Pennsylvania*, 367.

[47] John C. Appel, Joan B. Groff, Joel Keller, Vertie Knapp, Thomas H. Knepp, Reg Nauman, Edna Ponder, *History of Monroe County, Pennsylvania: 1725-1976* (East Stroudsburg: Pocono Hospital Auxiliary, 1976), 51, 98-99; Bertland et al., *The Minisink*, 150-51; Murphy and Murphy, *Pennsylvania*, 148.

[48] Appel et al, *History of Monroe County*, 129, 189-90; Murphy and Murphy, *Pennsylvania*, 365-67; Abler et al., *Atlas of Pennsylvania*, 158, 225.

[49] Bertland et al., *The Minisink*, 83-105, 107-8. Although no statistical survey has been conducted, the most common type of barn in the Poconos appears to be the Pennsylvania bank barn that is discussed in the Great Valley and Piedmont essay. In the eighteenth century most barns were evidently log; 1798 glass tax returns in Northampton County, which then included much of the Poconos Region, indicate that over 60 per cent of the barns were log.

[50] Bertland, *The Minisink*, 100-101.

[51] The Van Gorden House's first floor framing, for example, does not span clear as do nearby (and earlier) New Jersey Dutch houses. Instead the upper floor rests on joists that are mortised into girders. Also, the windows and doors have timber lintels rather than the segmental arches of Dutch practice. Wesley L. Shank, "Eighteenth-Century Architecture of the Upper Delaware River Valley of New Jersey and Pennsylvania," *Journal of the Society of Architectural Historians* 31 (May 1972): 137-38, 141-43.

[52] Some people see Grey Towers as a premier private resort, but the Pinchot family's relationship with the town and townspeople was less that of summer vacationers than that of the community's leading family and local benefactor. That image is reinforced by the moat that James Pinchot's son Gifford constructed along the side of the house that overlooks the town. Chester H. Aldrich of Delano and Aldrich in New York designed the ivy-draped ashlar wall in 1927; it was slated for completion in 1929 and is known to have existed by 1931. *Grey Towers: Preliminary Historic Structure Report* (Albany, N.Y.: Preservation/Design Group for U.S. Department of Agriculture, Forest Service, 1978), 10; *Grey Towers, Milford, Pa.: Final Historic Structure Report, Landscape Report, and Management Plan* (West Chester, Pa.: John Milner Associates for U.S. Department of Agriculture, Forest Service, 1980), 83-84. Hunt's importance as an architect is assessed in Paul R. Baker, *Richard Morris Hunt* (Cambridge: MIT Press, 1980).

[53] Stevens, *Pennsylvania: Titan of Industry*, 356; Miller and Sharpless, *The Kingdom of Coal*, 323.

[54] In addition to its many masonic functions, the Masonic Temple has served much as a grand community center. Its meeting and reception rooms accommodate many local organization and private parties, and its 1,800-capacity auditorium is the site of Broadway shows. It stands at 420 North Washington Avenue. *Masonic Temple and Scottish Rite Cathedral Association Mortgage Burning Celebration, November 28, 1964* (Scranton, Pa.: Masonic Temple and Scottish Rite Cathedral Association, 1964), n.p.; Writers' Program, *Pennsylvania*, 325.

[55] Recent buildings of note include the Rite-Aid Building in Scranton (1984 by Leung, Hemmler, Camayd, architects) and in Wilkes-Barre the addition to Wilkes College's Stark Learning Center (1973 by Lacy, Atherton, and Davis, architects). Resort hotels have dominated the postwar architecture in the Poconos. No postwar building in either area, however, rivals the Scranton Masonic Temple for monumentality.

Catalog

Carbon County

Jim Thorpe Borough

Courthouse Square (PA-5473). Two views showing Hoover Building on Courthouse Square and view on Broadway towards Courthouse Square (1979. NR (Old Mauch Chunk Historic District).

Dimmick Memorial Library (PA-5459). Brick with stone foundation and trim, two stories, gable and polygonal roofs, front gable with small-paned windows, wide entablature with library name, Tudor Revival details. Built 1889 (date in gable end); T. Roney Williamson, architect. 1 ext. photo (1979). NR (Old Mauch Chunk Historic District).

Packer, Asa, Mansion (PA-5330), Packer Rd. Museum owned by borough. Brick, rectangular with projecting wings, approx. 48' (five-bay front) x 40', three stories with two-story winds, hip and gable roofs, bracketed cornice, central octagonal belvedere, stone window frames of ogee arches with label molds, wooden veranda with ogee arches; central-stair plan, elaborately carved woodwork, original furnishings and decorative features remain; combination of Gothic, Tudor, and Italianate details. Built 1852; probably designed by owner Asa Packer (apprenticed as a carpenter) based on designs published by architect Samuel Sloan. Home of Asa Packer (1805-1879), wealthy industrialist, politician, and philanthropist; built Lehigh Valley Railroad and founded Lehigh University. One of the best preserved mid-nineteenth-century houses in country. 15 sheets (1986, including plans, elevations, details). NR (Also in Old Mauch Chunk Historic District).

Saint Mark's Episcopal Church (PA-5457), Race and Susquehanna Sts. Coursed and rusticated ashlar with contrasting stone trim, Latin-cross shaped, multiple levels built into rock shelf, square crenelated bell tower (135' high) with octagonal stair tower, three flights of covered stairs form entrance, rose window, pointed-arch windows with tracery, Louis Tiffany stained glass, late Gothic Revival style; lavish interior features, stone reredos built 1880 replicating one at Windsor Castle Chapel in England, 1912 Otis elevator. Built 1867-69; Richard Upjohn, architect; stone annex added 1887; stone office wing added 1890, Addison Hutton, architect. Elaborate Upjohn church built on an unusual site, financed largely by the Asa Packer family. 2 ext. photos (1979). NHL (Also in NR Old Mauch Chunk Historic District).

Stone Row (Houses) (PA-5458), 25-55 Race St. row of sixteen stone houses, three-and-a-half stories, gable roofs with dormers, decorative wooden trim over openings. Built 1848 by Asa Packer for employees working on the Lehigh Valley Railroad. 2 ext. photos (1979); 1 data page (1979). NR (Old Mauch Chunk Historic District).

Palmerton Borough

Marshall Hill (PA-5455), NE of junction of Rte. 248 and Aquashicola Creek. House built on hill in 1881 by Elisha G. Marshall, former Union Army general. 3 views with house in background (1979); 1 data page (1979).

Parryville Borough

Carbon Iron Company Stables (PA-5456), Lehigh Gap Rd. Random rubble, one-and-a-half stories, gable roof, arched openings. Built 1855 by Carbon Iron Company to house draft animals. 1 ext. photo (1979); 1 data page (1979).

Weissport Vicinity

Weider's Crossing Stone House (PA-5454), one of two remaining houses at Weider's Crossing. Random rubble, two-and-a-half stories with basement, gable roof, porch across front elevation. Built nineteenth century 1 ext. photo (1979).

Lackawanna County

Carbondale

Miners and Mechanics Bank Building (PA-5153), 13 N. Main St. Coursed ashlar (two street facades) and brick faced on concrete block, 60'-10" (three-bay front) x 91'-8" (five bays), two stories, flat roof with brick parapet faced with stone balustrade, two-story Ionic columns and Doric pilasters, plain frieze with denticulated cornice, three art windows divided by bronze spandrels, central entrance with cornice supported on consoles. Built 1915; functioned as bank until 1931; demolished. 4 sheets (1977, including site plan, plan, elevations); 5 ext. photos (1977), 6 int. photos (1977); 4 data pages (1980). LC code: PA, 35-CARB,1.

Clarks Green

Stone, Lemuel, House. See Waverly Vicinity (Abington Township), Stone, Lemuel, House.

Clarks Summit Borough

Clark, William, House (PA-231), 123 N. Abington Rd. (State Rte. 407). Frame with clapboarding, 43'-9" (five-bay front) x 33"-7" (four bays), two-and-a-half stories with basement, gable roof with pedimented gable ends, pilasters and denticulated cornice, doors with semielliptical fanlights and side lights with Palladian windows; central hall plan. Built 1811; tetrastyle porch added across middle three bays of SE (front) elevation; one-story kitchen wing added to rear ca. 1860; interior remodeled. 16 sheets (1936, including plans, elevations, details); 5 ext. photos (1936), 3 int. photos (1936); 4 data pages (1936). LC code: PA, 35-CLAR, 1.

Scranton

Silkman House (PA-217), 2006 N. Main St. Frame with flush horizontal wooden siding on N (front) elevation and clapboarding on sides and rear, rectangular with setback wing on each side and rear wing, main block 24'-3" (three-bay front) x 44'-5", side wings 6'-3" (one bay fronts), rear wing 19'-11" x 13', two-and-a-half stories with one-story side wings, gable roof with pedimented gable end and flat roofs on side wings, two-story porch on rear wing, Greek Revival style; side hall plan. Built 1840; two-story bay window added; Scranton Public Library since 1936. 12 sheets (1936, including plans, elevations, details); 3 ext. photos (1936); 3 data pages (1936). LC code: PA, 35-SCRAN, 1. NR.

United States Post Office (PA-1251), N. Washington and Linden Sts. Coursed ashlar (rusticated first story), rectangular with one-bay projecting terminal pavilions, seven-bay front, two-and-a-half stories, mansard roofs, elaborate dormers, central octagonal clock tower with belfry, Second Empire style. Built 1894; James H. Windrim, supervising architect of the Treasury Department; demolished 1930 and replaced with larger post office and court building. 1 copy photo of drawing (1890). LC code: PA, 35-SCRAN, 2.

Waverly (Abington Township)

Main Street (School) (One Room School) (PA-214), E side of Main St. (State Rte. 407), opposite Cole St. Frame with flush horizontal wooden siding on NW (front) elevation and clapboarding on rear and sides, 24'-6" (three-bay front) x 32'-7" (two bays), one story, gable roof, pedimented gable end with semielliptical wooden fan, pilasters on facade, arched windows and door with fanlight, Greek Revival style. Built ca. 1830; remodeled as residence. One of the first schools in Lackawanna County. 6 sheets (1936, including plan, elevations, details); 2 ext. photos (1936); 2 data pages (1936). LC Code: PA, 35-WAV, 1.

One Room School. See Main Street (School).

Waverly Vicinity (Abington Township)

Oakford House. See Stone, Lemuel, House.

Stone, Lemuel, House (Stone-Oakford House) (PA-220), NE side of Glenburn Rd., .1 mi. SE of Oakford Rd., S of Waverly. Frame with clapboarding, 54'-9" (six-bay front) x 20'-6" (two bays), two-and-a-half stories with basement, gable roof, door with fanlight framed by pilasters and entablature on SW (front) elevation; central hall plan. Built 1822; addition to NE not recorded; extensive interior alterations; now Glen Oak Country Club. 8 sheets (1936, including plans, elevations, details); 2 ext. photos (1936), 1 int. photo (1936); 3 data pages (1936). LC code: PA,35-WAV,2.

Stone-Oakford House. See Stone, Lemuel, House.

Luzerne County

Exeter

Coray House. See Upper Exeter Vicinity (Exeter Township), Sutton, Samuel, House.

Coray Water Mill. See Upper Exeter Vicinity (Exeter Township), Coray, Elisha Atherton, Mill.

Forty Fort Borough

Corey, David, House (Tripp House) (PA-236), 1086 Wyoming Ave. (U.S. Rte. 11). Frame with clapboarding, L-shaped with rear kitchen wing, 34'-4" (three-bay front) x 50'-2" with rear wing (17'-4" x 20'-4"), two-and-a-half stories with one-story wing, gable roofs, cornice returns, door flanked by Ionic columns with transom and side lights on S (front) elevation, wooden porch with carved supports; porch on kitchen; side hall plan. Built 1832; David Corey, builder; demolished. 18 sheets (1938, including plans, elevations, details); 3 ext. photos (1938), 3 int. photos (1938); 7 data pages (1938). LC code: PA,40-FOFO,6.

Culver, William, House (PA-240), 278 River St. Frame with clapboarding, 35'-10" (three-bay front) x 24'-6" (two bays), two-and-a-half stories, gable roof, cornice returns, pedimented doorway with fanlight and pilasters on W (front) elevation; central hall plan. Built 1820; porch with central pediment added across W elevation 1884; two-and-a-half-story ell and two porches added to E elevation 1914. 8 sheets (1939, including plans, elevations, details); 2 ext. photos (1939), 1 int. photo (1939); 3 data pages (1939). LC code: PA,40-FOFO,7.

Denison, Nathan, House (PA-25), 35 Denison St. Museum owned by Pennsylvania Historical and Museum Commission. Frame with clapboarding, irregular U-shaped with numerous additions, original house 35'-9" (three-bay front) x 28'-5", two-and-a-half stories, gable roof, cornice returns, large central chimney, central door with transom and side lights on S (front) elevation; original large kitchen fireplace and hand hewn paneling. Built 1790; mid-nineteenth-century additions (overall dimensions with additions approx. 45' x 69'), extensive two-and-a-half-story L-shaped wing on N elevation, small one-story wing on E elevation, bracketed porch across S and W elevations (removed after 1935), numerous porches and sheds; acquired by state and restored. Built by Colonel Nathan Denison, a Revolutionary War soldier, based on his eighteenth-century New England house. 6 sheets (1934-35, including plans, elevations, details); 2 ext. photos (1934), 3 int. photos (1935); 2 data pages (1936). LC code: PA,40-FOFO,3. NR.

Elm Lawn. See Shoemaker House.

Forty Fort Meetinghouse (PA-21), E side of River St., just S of U.S. Rte. 11 (Wyoming Ave.). Frame with clapboarding, 50'-5" (five-bay front) x 40'-5" (three bays), two stories, gable roof with pedimented W gable end, double paneled door framed by pilasters and entablature on S (front) elevation, central arched window (behind pulpit) on N elevation; interior gallery with turned supports. Built 1806-08; Joseph Hitchcock, designer and builder; restored 1923 by the Pennsylvania Society of Colonial Dames of America. 8 sheets (1934, including plan, elevations, section, details); 2 ext. photos (1934), 2 int. photos (1934); 2 data pages (1936). LC code: PA,40-FOFO,1. NR.

Perkins House (PA-232), location not determined. Frame with clapboarding, two attached four-bay sections, one-and-a-half stories, gable roof with gabled dormers, roof overhangs to form porch on one section, door with side lights and porch on other section. Built 1782; David Perkins, builder; demolished. David Perkins's father, John, was one of the original Connecticut settlers to come to area. 1 copy photo (n.d.). LC code: PA,40-FOFO,8.

Real, Benjamin, House (PA-233), 318 River St. Frame with clapboarding (front elevation changed to shiplap siding before 1938) and board and batten siding (kitchen lean-to), 22'-3" (two-bay front) x 16'-10" with lean-to on E elevation (22'-3" x 10'-10"), one-and-a-half stories with one-story lean-to, gable roof, latticed entrance porch on W (front) elevation (latter addition). Built 1804; demolished 1939. 5 sheets (1938-39, including plans, elevations, section, details); 1 ext. photo (1938), 1 copy photo (n.d.); 3 data pages (1939). LC code: PA,40-FOFO,5.

Shoemaker House (Elm Lawn) (PA-22), 1577 Wyoming Ave. (U.S. Rte. 11). Brick covered with clapboarding, T-shaped, 46'-4" (five-bay front) x 67'-10" (including rear kitchen wing), two-and-a-half stories with exposed basement on rear, gable roof with dormers and paired chimneys, door with fanlight and side lights with Palladian window above on NW (front) elevation, three-bay porch with paired columns on NW elevation, one- and two-story porches on kitchen wing; central hall plan, fine interior woodwork. Built 1820; Peter Allabach, builder; built for Elijah Shoemaker Jr. 6 sheets (1934-35, including plans, elevations, details); 3 ext. photos (1934), 5 int. photos (1934); 4 data pages (1936). LC code: PA,40-FOFO,2.

Snowden, Father, House (PA-223), 991 Wyoming Ave. (U.S. Rte. 11). Frame with clapboarding, L-shaped, 40'-4" (four-bay front) x 32'-3" with rear kitchen ell (11'-3" x 9'-10"), one-and-a-half stories with one-story ell, gable roof with pedimented dormers, door with transom and side lights framed by pilasters and wide entablature on W (front) elevation, entrance porch with paired columns (replaced with bracketed porch before 1937), Greek Revival style; central hall plan, simple mantels with plain pilasters and entablatures. Built 1839; frame shed added on ell; poor condition 1937; demolished. Built by Reverend Ebenezer Hazard Snowden, a clergyman of Forty Fort. 15 sheets (1937, including plans, elevations, section, details); 3 ext. photos (1937), 1 copy photo (n.d.), 3 int. photos (1937); 4 data pages (1937). LC code: PA,40- FOFO,4.

Tripp House. See Corey, David, House.

Hanover Green (Hanover Township)

Hanover Green Meetinghouse (PA-26), 639 Main Rd. Frame with clapboarding, 40'-4" (five-bay front) x 30'-4" (three bays), two stories with basement, gable roof, double paneled doors with plain entablatures on E (front) and N elevations; interior gallery with fine paneling, arched ceiling. Built 1825; built by Pennsylvania-German settlers. 8 sheets (1935, including plans, elevations, section, details); 2 ext. photos (1934), 3 int. photos (1935); 2 data pages (1936). LC code: PA,40-HANO,1.

Kingston Borough

Exchange Hotel (Helme Tavern) (PA-235), 238 Wyoming Ave. (U.S. Rte. 11). Frame with clapboarding, U-shaped, 43'-11" (five-bay front) x 36' with two wings to rear, two-and-a-half stories, gable roof with dormers, entrance with fanlight framed by pilasters and entablature and second entrance with transom on SE (front) elevation, two-story rear kitchen wing and one-story rear shed; central hall plan, fine mantels. Built 1804-07; John Ebert began constructing the Exchange Hotel in 1804 but was unable to complete building, James Wheeler completed structure 1807; store fronts added ca. 1929; used continuously as hotel and tavern; demolished. A popular local meeting place. 16 sheets (1938, including plans, elevations, details); 2 ext. photos (1938), 6 int. photos (1938); 5 data pages (1938). LC code: PA,40-KING,1.

Helme Tavern. See Exchange Hotel.

Myers, Lawrence, House (PA-245), 90 Main St. Frame with clapboarding, L-shaped, 42'-3" (five-bay front) x 18'-2" (one bay) with rear kitchen ell (19'-9" x 10'-3"), two-and-a-half stories with basement, gable roof, cornice returns, door with fanlight framed by pilasters and entablature on N (front) elevation, one-story kitchen ell with latticed porch. Built ca. 1800. 8 sheets (1940, including plans, elevations, details); 2 ext. photos (1940); 3 data pages (1940). LC code: PA,40-KING,2.

Nanticoke

Mill, Peter, House (Samantha J. Mill House) (PA-24), 493 E. Main St. Frame with clapboarding, 35'-4" (five-bay front) x 17'-8" with rear kitchen wing and store room, two-and-a-half stories with one-and-a-half-story kitchen wing and one-story store room, gable roofs, door with transom and side lights on N (front) elevation, bracketed porch across N elevation (originally on three sides), porch on kitchen; central hall plan, large cooking fireplace with original crane in kitchen. Built early nineteenth century; Peter Mill, builder. 6 sheets (1935, including plans, elevations, details); 5 ext. photos (l934), 3 int. photos (1934); 4 data pages (1936). LC code: PA,40-NANT,l.

Mill, Samantha J., House. See Mill, Peter, House.

Nanticoke Vicinity

Hanover Green Meetinghouse. See Hanover Green (Hanover Township), Hanover Green Meetinghouse.

Harvey House. See West Nanticoke (Plymouth Township), Harvey House.

Plymouth Borough

Gaylord, Henderson, House (PA-28), 135 W. Main St. (U.S. Rte. 11). Frame with flush horizontal siding and clapboarding, irregular L-shaped, three-bay main section with flanking one-bay wings with several rear wings (overall dimensions 46'-5" x 73'-2"), two-and-a-half-story main section with one-story side wings and one- and two-story rear wings, gable roof with pedimented gable end on main section, pilasters and door with fanlight and side lights on SE (front) elevation, Greek Revival style. Built ca. 1850; several porches added. Gaylord family were among first settlers of the Wyoming Valley; Henderson Gaylord was one of the earliest coal dealers in the area. 8 sheets (1935, including plans, elevations, details); 3 ext. photos (1935), 1 int. photo (1935); 1 data page (1936). LC code: PA,40-PLYM,1.

Wright, Colonel H. B., House See Wright, Joseph, House.

Wright, Joseph, House (Colonel H. B. Wright House) (PA-224), 843-45 W. Main St. (U.S. Rte. 11). Frame with clapboarding, L-shaped, 44'-2" (two three-bay facades with central entrances) x 16'-9", two-and-a-half stories, gable roof, central chimney, two doors framed by pilasters and entablatures on S (front) elevation, entrance porch with paired columns at W entrance, one-and-a-half-story kitchen ell at NE corner, one-story bedroom wing at NW corner. Built 1807; demolished 1938. Built by Joseph Wright; his oldest son, Hendrick Bradley Wright, was a lawyer, writer, and active in politics. 9 sheets (1937, including plans, elevations, details); 4 ext. photos (1937), 1 copy photo (n.d.), 1 copy photo of H.B. Wright (n.d.); 4 data pages (1937). LC code: PA,40-PLYM,2.

Upper Exeter Vicinity (Exeter Township)

Coray, Elisha Atherton, House. See Sutton, Samuel, House.

Coray, Elisha Atherton, Mill (PA-216), W bank of Sutton Creek, .2 mi. S of State Rte. 92. Frame with clapboarding, 40'-4" (three-bay front) x 54'-6", one-and-a-half stories (NW front elevation) sloping to three-and-a-half stories (SE elevation) towards creek, low gambrel roof, cornice returns, loading doors on four levels of SE elevation; wooden gear wheels. Built 1846; E. A. Coray, builder; poor condition 1936; demolished 1938. Third mill on site; 1776 James Sutton and James Hadsall built first mill, destroyed by Indians 1778; ca. 1780 son Samuel Sutton built second mill, destroyed in flood 1786; third mill built by Coray. Samuel Sutton House (PA-27) located across street from mill. 11 sheets (1936, including plans, elevations, section, details); 2 ext. photos (1936), 3 int. photos (1936), 1 photo of iron scale (1936); 4 data pages (1936). LC code: PA,40-EXT.V,1.

Sutton, Samuel, House (Elisha Atherton Coray House) (PA-27), W side of road, W of Sutton Creek, .2 mi. S of State Rte. 92. Frame with clapboarding, L-shaped with setback wing, 28'-2" (three-bay front) x 39'-5" with wing extended 28'-7", two stories with one-story wing, intersecting gable roofs on main block with gable roof on wing, door with fanlight framed by pilasters and entablature on E (front) elevation, recessed porch on wing; side hall plan. Built ca. 1840 by Samuel Sutton. James Sutton built mill on

Sutton Creek 1776 (destroyed 1778); son Samuel built second mill on site ca. 1780 and house across road ca. 1840; property sold to Elisha Atherton Coray 1846 who built third mill on site (PA-216). 6 sheets (1935, including plans, elevations, details); 3 ext. photos (1935); 1 data page (1936). LC code: PA,40-EXT,1.

Wapwallopen Vicinity (Conyngham Township)

Union Reformed and Lutheran Church (PA-219), E side of State Rte. 239, just S of Ruckle Hill Rd., approx. 1 mi. NE of Wapwallopen. Operated by Wapwallopen Historical Society. Frame with clapboarding, 36'-3" (three-bay front) x 32'-3" (three bays), two stories, gable roof, bracketed cornice, door with transom and pilasters with carved church vessels above and finely carved entablature on S (front) elevation, carved trim on other entrances, rose window in W gable end; balcony on three sides with finely carved railing with octagonal supports, arched ceiling with central medallion. Built 1833 by Reformed and Lutheran adherents; poor condition and vacant 1936; restored 1956. 8 sheets (1936, including plans, elevations, section, details); 3 ext. photos (1936), 3 int. photos (1936), 1 photo of land warrant (1936); 4 data pages (1936). LC code: PA,40-WAP,1.

West Nanticoke (Plymouth Township)

Harvey House (PA-237), 72-74 McDonald St. Frame with clapboarding, 52'-6" (two three-bay sections) x 32'-4", two-and-a-half stories with basement, gable roof with pedimented gable ends, door with fanlight framed by pilasters and entablature with carved decoration, recessed entrance porch with Doric columns on S (front) elevation, recessed porch and shed-roof porch (later addition) on N elevation. E three bays built 1832 (date on leader head); W three bays added soon after; Jameson Harvey, builder; 1871 sold to Susquehanna Coal Company used as tenant house; ca. 1930 divided into two sections; poor condition 1938. Jameson Harvey began mining coal on property by hand and later on a larger scale, he was one of the original coal operators in area. 17 sheets (1938, including plans, elevations, details); 4 ext. photos (1938), 3 int. photos (1938); 7 data pages (1938). LC code: PA,40-NANTW,1.

Wilkes-Barre

Bowman, Samuel, House (PA-241), 220 N. Main St. Frame with flush horizontal siding (E front elevation) and clapboarding, 47' (five-bay front) x 49' with one-bay setback wing on S side, two-and-a-half stories with basement, hip roof, bracketed cornice, large corbeled chimneys, projecting pedimented two-story porch with fluted columns on central bay of E (front) elevation with flanking one-story sections, doors with pilasters, pediment on N elevation (porch removed); central hall plan. Built 1810-11; original rear porch removed; two-story addition on W elevation. Captain Samuel Bowman was one of the minutemen on Lexington Commons 1775. 15 sheets (1939, including plans, elevations, details); 2 ext. photos (1939), 2 int. photos (1939); 2 data pages (1940). LC code: PA,40-WILB,3.

Butler House (PA-239), originally located at River and Northampton Sts., moved to 313 S. River St. 1868. Frame with clapboarding, L-shaped, 24'-6" (three-bay front) x 47'-7" (including rear ell), two-and-a-half stories, gable roofs, door with transom and entrance porch with paired columns on SE (front) elevation (porch not original), porch with enclosed pantry on ell; side hall plan. Built 1793-94 incorporating part of 1773 log house previously on site; Lord Butler, builder; built as five-bay house, changed to three bays when moved; one-story addition on ell. Colonel Zebulon Butler, leader of the first Connecticut settlers to move to area in 1769 and director of the Susquehanna Company, built log house 1773; Butler's oldest son, Lord, built frame house on same site incorporating parts of log house 1793. Oldest extant house in Wilkes-Barre. 11 sheets (1939, including plans, elevations, section, details); 1 ext. photo (1939), 1 copy photo (n.d.), 2 int. photos (1939); 5 data pages (1939). LC code: PA,40-WILB,2.

McLean, Alexander, House (PA-242), originally located at 156 Carey Ave., moved to rear of original lot 1928, present location 17-19 Alexander St. Frame with flush horizontal siding (NW front elevation) and clapboarding, 49'-7" (five-bay front) x 35'-4" with rear kitchen ell, two-and-a-half stories with basement, gable roof with pedimented dormers, two-story fluted Ionic pilasters with connecting semielliptical arches across front elevation, door with transom and side lights framed by pilasters and entablature, window with side lights and carved semielliptical panel above door; central hall plan. Built 1841; original three-bay front porch removed; moved and converted to a double dwelling 1928. 11 sheets (1939, shown in original condition, including plans, elevations, details); 3 ext. photos (1939, details), 1 copy photo (1928, during move), 1 int. photo (1939); 3 data pages (1940). LC code: PA,40-WILB,4.

Pickering, Timothy, House (PA-230), 130 S. Main St. Frame with clapboarding, approx. 42' (five-bay front) x 34', two-and-a-half stories, gable roof, entrance porch with paired columns on N (front) elevation, one-story kitchen wing on S elevation, one-story store room on W elevation, terrace across S elevation; central hall plan, fine interior woodwork especially mantels. Built 1787; demolished 1931; some interior woodwork (mantels, doors, staircase, wall paneling) preserved and in storage. Colonel Timothy Pickering served in George Washington's Cabinet. 7 sheets (1936, drawings made from measurements taken of the sections removed from the razed structure, including plans, details of interior woodwork); 1 copy photo of ext. (ca. 1930), 7 copy photos of int. (ca. 1930), 1 photo of mantel (1936, after removal); 5 data pages (1936). LC code: PA,40-WILB,1.

Wyoming Borough

Crawford House (PA-234), 482 Wyoming Ave. (U.S. Rte. 11). Frame with clapboarding, 26'-3" (three-bay front) x 36'-4" main section with flanking setback two-bay wings (E wing 14'-1" x 12'-3", W wing 14'-1" x 15'-4"), two-and-a-half-story main section with one-and-a-half-story wings (W wing roof raised to allow for second story windows on N elevation), gable roofs with wide entablatures and cornice returns, projecting pedimented Ionic portico on N (front) elevation, Ionic porches on wings, door with transom and side lights, Greek Revival style; side hall plan. Built 1851; W wing altered; sheds added on wings; demolished. Built by Dr. John Barclay Crawford, a physician. 17 sheets (1937-38, including plans, elevations, details, sheet on privy); 8 ext. photos (1938); 4 data pages (1938). LC code: PA,40-WYOM,4.

Swetland House (PA-23), 885 Wyoming Ave. (U.S. Rte. 11). Museum owned by Wyoming Historical and Geological Society. Frame with clapboarding, L-shaped built in four sections, overall dimensions 54'-3" (six-bay front) x 88'-4", two-and-a-half stories with one-and-a-half-story rear kitchen wing, gable roofs, denticulated cornice with paired brackets, two doors with fanlights on S (front) elevation, three-bay porch with Doric columns on S elevation. Original two-room house with central chimney (now rear kitchen wing) built 1797; separate two-story house with one room on each floor (W three bays of front section) built ca. 1803; side hall plan section (E three bays of front section) added to 1803 section 1809; fourth section added to rear of 1803 section connecting two houses 1813; 1850 cornice and porch added and windows altered. Original house built by Luke Swetland, among the first settlers of area from Connecticut; son Belding built second section; grandson William, opened Swetland Store (PA-211) across street 1815, completed house. 7 sheets (1935, including plans, elevations, details); 3 ext. photos (1934), 3 int. photos (1935); 2 data pages (1936). LC code: PA,40-WYOM,1. NR.

Swetland Store (PA-211), 828 Wyoming Ave. (U.S. Rte. 11). Frame with clapboarding, L-shaped, 66'-5" x 58'-5", one-and-a-half stories with fully exposed basement (exposed when street level was lowered 8'), gable roofs, double doors and display windows framed by pilasters and entablature on N (front) elevation (originally at street level), elevated porch across S elevation; original vault and display cases with columns. Built ca. 1815; William Swetland, builder; doors and windows added when street level changed; unoccupied 1936. Swetland was one of the first merchants in area, store opened July 4, 1815. Across street from Swetland House (PA-23). 9 sheets (1936, including plans, elevations, details); 2 ext. photos (1936), 1 photo of original wooden hand truck and lantern (1936); 5 data pages (1936). LC code: PA,40-WYOM,3.

Wyoming Institute (PA-29), end of Institute St., .1 mi. NW of U.S. Rte. 11 (Wyoming Ave.). Brick, 40'-4" (three-bay front) x 50'-6" (four bays), two stories, gable roof with pedimented gable end with date stone, open brick and frame cupola with Ionic columns and dome at E gable end, door with transom and side lights and entrance porch on E (front) elevation. Built 1849 (date stone); Mr. Fell, architect; one-story setback brick wings added on N and S elevations 1925. Built by the Luzerne Presbytery as a nonsectarian coeducational school; Wyoming Presbyterian Church used building as Sunday school. 2 sheets (1935, wings not shown, including plans, elevations); 2 ext. photos (1935); 1 data page (1936). LC code: PA,40-WYOM,2.

Monroe County

Bushkill Vicinity (Middle Smithfield Township)

Clark-Heller Mill (PA-1159), W side of U.S. Rte. 209, .1 mi. SW of Sand Hill Creek, .7 mi. SW of LR51001 and Bushkill, in Delaware Water Gap National Recreation Area. Frame with clapboarding, approx. 30' (three irregular bays) x 42', two-and-a-half stories with elevated random rubble basement, gable roof, roof extends over hoist on E (front) elevation, loading doors on three levels of E elevation. Built early nineteenth century; grist mill built by Simon Heller and William Clark; demolished. 2 ext. photos (1971); 3 data pages (1971). LC code: PA,45-BUSH.V,1.

Heller Mill. See Clark-Heller Mill.

Delaware Water Gap Borough

Delaware Water Gap Railroad Station (Delaware-Lackawanna-Western Railroad) (PA-1168), between U.S. Rte. 80 and Delaware River, off Alt. U.S. Rte. 611. Brick with battered water table and stone trim, rectangular, central passenger station with sheltered waiting area at N end and freight station at S end separated from passenger station by wide passageway, one-and-a-half-story freight station and two-story passenger station, continuous hip roof interrupted by higher hip roof over passenger station, large carved brackets support wide roof overhang, projecting ornamental rafters, roof of sheltered waiting area supported by chamfered columns with large carved brackets on battered brick piers, decorative half-timbering on second story of passenger station, attached semicircular newsstand covered with decorative half-timbering, bay window on E (track side) elevation.

Built 1904. 3 ext. photos (1968); 1 data page (1980). LC code: PA,45-DELWA,1.

Saylorsburg Vicinity (Ross Township)

Ross Common Manor (PA-177), S side of old State Rte. 115, approx. 3 mi. S of Saylorsburg. Random rubble, five by two bays, two-and-a-half stories, gable roof with dormers, one-and-a-half-story stone kitchen wing to rear with sheds on either side. Kitchen wing is original structure on site built ca. 1809; manor built ca. 1810; kitchen connected to manor ca. 1890; restored 1970s. Home of Judge John Ross, then an inn on the stagecoach run. 1 ext. photo (ca. 1925, rear elevation only). LC code: PA,48-WIGAP.V,1. NR.

Shawnee on Delaware Vicinity (Middle Smithfield Township)

Camp Ministerium. See Turn, John, Farm.

Cold Springs Farm. See Dewitt Farm.

Dewitt farm, House (Cold Spring Farm) (PA-1165), SE side of River Rd. (LR45012), 1.4 mi. S of U.S. Rte. 209, approx. 6 mi. NE of Shawnee on Delaware, in Delaware Water Gap National Recreation Area. Frame with clapboarding, irregular L-shaped, 26'-2" (three-bay front) x 18'-3" with 27'-11" wing added on SW (rear) elevation, two-and-a-half stories, one-story shed on each side of wing, gable roofs with diamond pattern on NE slope, cornice returns, central door with transom and porch on NE elevation, recessed porch on wing. Built ca. 1800; 1935 minor alterations; demolished after 1970. 3 sheets (1968, including site plan, plans, elevation, section); 1 ext. photo (1968), 1 copy photo of ext. (n.d.), 1 int. photo (1968); 13 data pages (1968, 1970). LC code: PA,45-SHAWD.V,1.

Barn (PA-1165A). Frame with wooden siding and metal siding (SW elevation), 44'-6" x 30'-5", bank barn, two levels, gable roof, frame forebay. Built nineteenth century; demolished. 7 sheets (1968, including site plan, plans, elevations, section, isometric of framing, construction details); 2 ext. photos (1968), 2 int. photos (1968). LC code: PA,45-SHAWD.V,1A.

Springhouse (PA-1165B). Random rubble, 21'-10" x 14'-6", one story, gable roof with louvered ventilator cupola; single room. Built early nineteenth century; 1948 partially destroyed and rebuilt; owned by U.S. Army Corps of Engineers. Water from springhouse supplied pond on S side; adjacent frame structure housed churn driven by undershot water wheel and iron gears powered by water from pond, only foundations and gears remain. 3 sheets (1969, including site plans, plan, elevations, section); 3 ext. photos (1968, 1969), 1 int. photo (1969), 1 photo of gears (1969), 1 copy photo of frame wheelhouse (n.d.). LC code: PA,45-SHAWD.V,1B. NR.

Woodshed (PA-1165C). Frame with vertical wooden siding, 24'-3" x 14'-1", one story, gable roof, SE (front) elevation partially open. Built early nineteenth century; demolished. 2 sheets (1971, including site plan, plan, elevations, section); 1 ext. photo (1971). LC code: PA,45-SHAWD.V,1C.

Farrington House. See Michael, Samuel, House.

Michael Barn (PA-1259), S side of River Rd. (LR45012), .8 mi. NE of township line, approx. 4 mi. NE of Shawnee on Delaware, in Delaware Water Gap National Recreation Area. Frame with clapboarding (clapboarding replaced original vertical siding ca. 1920), 60'-6" x 40'-7", bank barn, two levels, gable roof, frame forebay supported on rubble end walls (concrete block wall built to enclose area under forebay); mortised and tenoned and pegged frame (common construction of early nineteenth century), some original hardware. Built early nineteenth century; small concrete block shed added on SE corner; burned ca. 1972. Built and long owned by Michael family; possibly built by John George Michael who acquired the land in 1794, or by his sons. Typical early barn of area. 15 sheets (1971, including site plan, plans, elevations, sections, isometrics of framing, construction and hardware details); 2 ext. photos (1971), 1 int. photo (1971); 8 data pages (1971). LC code: PA,45-SHAWD.V,2A.

Michael, George, House (Theune House) (PA-1160), S side of River Rd. (LR45012), approx. .5 mi. NE of township line, approx. 4 mi. NE of Shawnee on Delaware, in Delaware Water Gap National Recreation Area. Random rubble (later stuccoed), two-and-a-half stories, gable roof, distyle Doric entrance porch on N (front) elevation; central hall plan. Probably built first half of nineteenth century (possibly before 1833); extensive alterations; two-story clapboarded ell added on S elevation and two-story bay window added on W elevation 1929; burned ca. 1972. Extant small stone springhouse (ca. 1840) across road. John George Michael acquired the land in 1794; his son, George, probably built a frame house at this site and then replaced it with stone house. 1 ext. photo (1968); 7 data pages (1971). LC code: PA,45-SHAWD.V,2.

Michael, Samuel, House (Farrington House) (PA-1170), N side of River Rd. (LR45012), 4.5 mi. NE of Shawnee on Delaware, 1.1 mi. NE of township line, in Delaware Water Gap National Recreation Area. Brick (stuccoed 20th c.), L-shaped, approx. 39' (five-bay front) x 20' (two bays) with rear ell (approx. 18' x 20'), two-and-a-half stories with one-story ell, gable roof with cornice returns, pedimented lintels. Built mid-nineteenth century: porch with turned posts and carved brackets added across S elevation late nineteenth century (late 1930s replaced with simple screened porch); clapboarded second story added on ell early twentieth century; small clapboarded laundry wing added on W elevation of ell late 1930s; burned after 1971. Outbuildings. Built by Samuel Michael, grandson of John George Michael who acquired the land in 1794. 1 ext. photo (1968), 5 copy photos (ca. 1930s); 8 data pages (1971). LC code: PA,45-SHAWD.V,3.

Barn (PA-1170C). Frame with vertical siding, two levels, gable roof with gabled monitor. Built mid-nineteenth century; demolished. 1 copy photo (n.d.). LC code: PA,45-SHAWD.V,3B.

Schoolhouse (PA-1170B), on S side of River Rd. (LR45012), across from Samuel Michael Farm. Frame with clapboarding, one-and-a-half stories, gable roof. Built mid-nineteenth century; demolished. 1 copy photo (n.d.). LC code: PA,45-SHAWD.V,4.

Smokehouse (PA-1170A). Brick, approx. 9' x 5', one story built into hill, gable roof. Built ca. 1840. 1 ext. photo (1968). LC code: PA,45-SHAWD.V,3A.

Theune House. See Michael, George, House.

Turn, John, Farm (Camp Ministerium) (PA-1274), E side of River Rd. (LR45012), 1.8 mi. S of U.S. Rte. 209, approx. 6 mi. NE of Shawnee on Delaware, in Delaware Water Gap National Recreation Area. Considered a model farm at one time. Remained in Turn family until 1945, then sold to Evangelical Lutheran Ministerium and converted to a camp; only three outbuildings remain, owned by U.S. Army Corps of Engineers. 1 copy photo of farm complex (ca. 1910); 9 data pages (1970). LC code: PA,45-SHAWD.V,7. NR.

House (PA-1274A). Frame with clapboarding, four-bay front, two-and-a-half stories, gable roof, porch across W (front) elevation. Built 1832 (possibly earlier); John Turn, builder (a carpenter by trade); two frame wings added (S and E elevations); demolished 1977. 1 ext. photo (1970), 1 int. photo (1970). LC code: PA,45-SHAWD.V,7A.

Barn (PA-1274B). Frame with clapboarding, large bank barn, three levels, gambrel roof with central louvered ventilator. Original barn built 1833 by John Turn, demolished; second barn built ca. 1912 by Victor H. Dimmick; second barn greatly enlarged and altered mid-twentieth century, only portion of 1912 framing remains; remodeled as camp dining hall after 1945; demolished after 1970. 1 ext. photo (1970), 1 int. photo (1970). LC code: PA,45-SHAWD.V,7B.

Lime Kiln (PA-1274C), W side of River Rd. Random rubble lime kiln built into hillside, approx. 16' square, 14'-5" high, openings in SE (front) elevation and top (top is level with road to quarry), masonry above front opening supported by three iron railroad rails, six iron tie rods run through masonry. Built late nineteenth century. Smaller random rubble lime kiln on farm, ruinous condition. 3 sheets (1970, including site plan, plans, elevations, section, details); 1 photo (1970), 1 photo of smaller kiln (1970). LC code: PA,45-SHAWD.V,7C.

Smokehouse (PA-1274D). Random rubble, 10'-2" square, one story, gable roof, single outer door on SW elevation with double inner doors. Built nineteenth century; concrete poured around foundation. 2 sheets (1970, including site plan, plan, elevations, section, details); 1 ext. photo (1970). LC code: PA,45- SHAWD.V,7D.

Weave House (PA-1274E). Frame with clapboarding, 20'-6" x 16'-6", one-and-a-half stories, sloping site fully exposes basement on SE (rear) elevation (stone walls 18" thick), SE basement wall partially open, gable roof, large inside end chimney on SW elevation with large fireplace in basement; lower level used as washhouse, upper level used as weave house. Built nineteenth century; greatly altered, present superstructure built late nineteenth century, but some early framing remains. 3 sheets (1970, including site plan, plans, elevations, section, detail); 2 ext. photos (1970), 1 int. photo (1970). LC code: PA,45-SHAWD.V,7E.

Zion Evangelical Lutheran Church (PA-1136), N side of River Rd. (LR45012), .9 mi. NE of township line, approx. 4 mi. NE of Shawnee on Delaware, in Delaware Water Gap National Recreation Area. Brick, rectangular with rectangular apse, 33'-2" (three-bay front) x 50'-1" (three bays and apse), one story, gable roof with entablature and cornice returns, double paneled doors on W (front) elevation, large double hung windows, Greek Revival details; narthex and nave with balcony at W end. Built 1851 (date stone); brick chimney and small frame shed added on E elevation. 7 sheets (1967, including site plan, plan, elevations, sections); 2 ext. photos (1967), 2 int. photos (1967); 5 data pages (1967, 1970). LC code: PA,45-SHAWD.V,10. NR.

Shawnee on Delaware Vicinity (Smithfield Township)

Kautz House. See Walter-Kautz Farm.

River Schoolhouse (Stone Schoolhouse) (PA-1167), N side of River Rd. (LR45012), .6 mi. SW of township line, 2.8 mi. NE of Shawnee on Delaware, in Delaware Water Gap National Recreation Area. Random rubble, 26' (three-bay front) x 36' (three bays), one-and-a-half stories, gable roof, three wooden roof trusses with vertical iron tie rods exposed in attic, SW (original front) entrance with gabled hood, large windows with slightly arched frames; one room. Built 1888; converted to residence 1927; entrance changed and porch added to SE elevation; concrete block chimney added (replaced original central brick chimney); interior partitions added; demolished after 1970. 4 sheets (1968, including site plan, plan, elevations, section); 1 ext. photo (1968), 1 copy photo (ca. 1900); 7 data pages (1968, 1970). LC code: PA,45-SHAWD.V,5.

Robacker House. See Weaver, Valentine, House.

Rouch House. See Treible, Peter, House.

Stone Schoolhouse. See River Schoolhouse.

Treible, Peter, House (Rouch House) (PA-1161), N side of River Rd. (LR45012), just SW of township line, approx. 3.5 mi. NE of Shawnee on Delaware, in Delaware Water Gap National Recreation Area. Random rubble, 32'-1" (four-bay front) x 24'-4", two-and-a-half stories on sloping site exposing basement on SE (front) elevation, gable roof, recessed door with paneled reveal framed by pilasters and entablature; original interior woodwork and hardware. Built 1832 (date stone); Peter Treible, builder; two-and-a-half-story clapboarded wing added to NE elevation late nineteenth century; porch elevated on stone wall added across SE elevation (space under porch later enclosed); restored by Rouch family 1960-66; demolished. House served as post office and tavern during nineteenth century 13 sheets (1968, including site plan, plans, elevations, sections, details); 5 ext. photos (1968), 3 int. photos (1968), 1 copy photo of ext. (ca. 1900), 1 photo of storerooms built into hill behind house (1968); 9 data pages (1968, 1970). LC code: PA,45-SHAWD.V,6.

Walter Kautz Farm (PA-1169), N side of River Rd. (LR45012), 1.2 mi. SW of township line, 2.3 mi. NE of Shawnee on Delaware, in Delaware Water Gap National Recreation Area. Good example of typical area farm. 3 general views of farm (1968), 1 copy photo of cutting ice on Delaware River; 15 data pages (1967-71). LC code: PA,45-SHAWD.V,8.

House (PA-1169A). Random rubble with quoins, three by two bays, two-and-a-half stories with basement, gable roof with cornice returns; two-room plan. Built ca. 1828; alterations 1867 (date stone); bracketed porch across S (front) elevation; two-story frame and stone kitchen wing added to NE corner in several stages; demolished after 1971. Probably built by George Walter, in the Walter family until 1884; in the Kautz family most of the twentieth century. 2 ext. photos (1968). LC code: PA,45-SHAWD.V,8A.

Barn (PA-1169B), S side of River Rd. Frame, 48'-6" x 30'-2", bank barn, two levels, gable roof, frame forebay, frame pig barn (15'-1" x 25'-8") added at NE corner, original hand wrought hardware. Built ca. 1877; forebay and pig barn added; burned 1970. 13 sheets (1969, including site plan, plans, elevations, sections, hardware and construction details); 8 ext. photos (1968, 1969), 7 int. photos (1968, 1969, including construction details). LC code: PA,45-SHAWD.V,8B.

Corn Crib-Wagon Shed (PA-1169C), S side of River Rd. Frame with clapboarding, approx. 20"-3" x 36'-2", two levels with loft on sloping site, gable roof, lower level open at E and W ends (sheltered wagon storage) with random rubble wall on S elevation and corn crib of vertical wooden slats on N elevation, upper level wagon shed with double sliding doors approached by ramp on S elevation; upper level floor open over corn crib for loading. Built ca. 1880; demolished. Unusual combination of two typical farm structures. 7 sheets (1968, including site plan, plans, elevations, section, isometric of framing, details); 3 ext. photos (1968). LC code: PA,45-SHAWD.V,8C.

Icehouse (PA-1169D), N side of River Rd. Random rubble (lower level) and frame with shiplap siding (upper level), approx. 12' square, one story with loft, gable roof, doors in S (front) elevation of stone section and one in each gable end. Built ca. 1880; demolished. Used to store ice cut in the Delaware River. 3 sheets (1968, including site plan, plan, elevations, section, isometric of framing); 1 ext. photo (1968). LC code: PA,45- SHAWD.V,8D.

Washhouse-Woodshed (PA-1169E), N side of River Rd. Frame with novelty siding, approx. 20' x 10', two stories, gable roof, woodshed in SW corner of first floor with wide opening on S (front) elevation, washhouse on SE corner of first floor, workshop on second floor reached by a bridge from hill on N elevation. Built ca. 1894; demolished. 1 ext. photo (1968). LC code: PA,45-SHAWD.V,8E.

Weaver, Valentine, House (Robacker House) (PA-1164), N side of River Rd. (LR45012), 1 mi. SW of township line, 2.5 mi. NE of Shawnee on Delaware, in Delaware Water Gap National Recreation Area. Random rubble with quoins, L-shaped, 33'-4" (three-bay front) x 46'-4", two-and-a-half stories with one-and-a-half-story wing, gable roofs, cornice returns, recessed door with transom and side lights, slightly pedimented lintels over windows, porches on S (front) elevation (not original) and E elevation of ell; central hall plan. Built 1867; large exterior stone chimney added on W elevation mid-twentieth century; demolished after 1970. Built by Valentine Weaver as an inn but never used as inn, ell was intended as tap room and large rooms had folding partitions. Frame outbuilding and foundations of schoolhouse on property. 12 sheets (1968, including site plan, plans, elevations, sections, details); 4 ext. photos (1968), 1 photo of outbuilding and school foundations (1968); 10 data pages (1968, 1970). LC code: PA,45-SHAWD.V,9.

Pike County

Bushkill (Lehman Township)

Bushkill Hotel. See Peters House Hotel.

Bushkill Mill (Peters Mill) (PA-1137), NW corner of U.S. Rte. 209 and T301, just N of Bushkill Creek, in Delaware Water Gap National Recreation Area. Frame with clapboarding (present siding covers original vertical wooden siding), 30'-5" (three-bay front) x 43'-6" (three bays), two stories with basement, gable roof, roof ridge projects over hoist and loading doors on E (front) elevation, scalloped barge boards, contains much original machinery. Built ca. 1790; substantially altered at various times; barge boards ninteenth century addition; demolished. Owned by Peters family for over one hundred years. 9 sheets (1967, including site plan, plans, elevations, sections); 3 ext. photos (1967), 4 int. photos (1967), 4 detail photos of machinery (1967), 1 ext. copy photo (ca. 1905), 1 copy photo of aerial view drawing (before 1955, also shows Peters House Hotel PA-1138), 1 copy photo of painting (1940); 8 data pages (1967, 1970). LC code: PA,52-BUSH,2.

Peters House Hotel (Bushkill Hotel) (PA-1138), E side of U.S. Rte. 209, across from T301, just N of Bushkill Creek, in Delaware Water Gap National Recreation Area. Frame with clapboarding, two rectangular sections connected at corners, three-and-a-half stories, gable roofs, large projecting two-story bay with third-story veranda on W (front) elevation, numerous one- and two-story porches. Original section was two stories of S section built 1861 by Charles R. Peters; sons Harry and Edwin enlarged structure in several stages and built hotel annex across street between 1867 and 1900; demolished 1972. There was an inn on this site as early as 1813 when John Heller sold property with log house used as inn to Henry Peters, father of Charles R.; in Peters family until 1947; functioned as hotel until demolition. 1 ext. photo (1970); 5 data pages (1971). See Bushkill Mill (PA-1137) for copy photo of aerial view drawing showing mill and hotel. LC code: PA,52-BUSH,1. NR.

Peters Mill. See Bushkill Mill.

Dingmans Ferry (Delaware Township)

Delaware House Hotel (PA-1162), W side of U.S. Rte. 209, .2 mi. S of State Rte. 739, in Delaware Water Gap National Recreation Area. Frame with clapboarding (replaced with asbestos shingles twentieth century), three-bay center section with flanking three-bay wings, three-story center section with two-story wings, gable roofs (center section originally had mansard roof), gabled hoods over three entrances of E (front) elevation (twentieth-century additions). Built 1866 by John Lattimore; addition 1897 (possibly S wing); original porches on E elevation of three sections altered and then removed; openings altered; demolished ca. 1972. Hotel was center of township activities for a century. 1 ext. photo (1970); 1 data page (1980). LC code: PA,52-DING,2.

Dutch Reformed Church (PA-1273), E side of U.S. Rte. 209, .2 mi. N of State Rte. 739, in Delaware Water Gap National Recreation Area. Frame with clapboarding, approx. 33' (three-bay front) x 51', two stories, gable roof, pedimented Doric portico across front elevation, Greek Revival details. Built 1850 (date stone), plans begun 1837, after revisions built 1850; shed addition to rear; ca. 1960 converted to residence, windows and interior altered. 2 ext. photos (1970); 5 data pages (1971). LC code: PA,52-DING,3. NR.

St. John the Evangelist Episcopal Church (PA-1254), S side of State Rte. 739, .2 mi. E of U.S. Rte. 209, in Delaware Water Gap National Recreation Area. Frame with board and batten siding, T-shaped, approx. 22'-3" x 50'-2", one story, steep gable roof and open belfry with shingled spire on nave, enclosed entrance bay with double lancet door on N (front) elevation, intersecting gable roofs on chancel and flanking sacristies, deep eaves, lancet windows with diamond panes, Carpenter Gothic details; exposed scissors truss in nave and chancel. Built 1887 (date stone); organ alcove added ca. 1960; plywood geodesic dome attached to S elevation ca. 1960; demolished. Good example of Carpenter Gothic church. 6 sheets (1970, including site plans, plan, elevations, sections, details); 3 ext. photos (1970), 1 int. photo (1970); 6 data pages (1970). LC code: PA,52-DING,4.

Egypt Mills Vicinity (Lehman Township)

Eshback House. See Nyce, William, House.

Eshback Tenant House. See Van Gorden, Jacobus, House.

Nyce, William, House (Eshback House) (PA-1163), W side of U.S. Rte. 209, 1.5 mi. N of Egypt Mills, in Delaware Water Gap National Recreation Area. Frame with clapboarding, five-bay main section with two-bay setback wing on N elevation, two-and-a-half stories, gable roof, door with fanlight and side lights on E (front) elevation; central hall plan, reeded and gouged carved mantels. Built late eighteenth century; porches added. Built by William Nyce, remained in family until 1940s; burned. Used as early stage stop. See Jacobus Van Gorden House (PA-1258), adjacent house now part of estate. 2 ext. photos (1970); 1 data page (1980). LC code: PA,52-EGYMI.V,1. NR.

Van Gorden, Jacobus, House (Eshback Tenant House) (PA-5180), W side of U.S. Rte 209, 1.5 mi. N of Egypt Mills, in Delaware Water Gap National Recreation Area. Random rubble (later stucco partially gone), 28'-2" (three-bay front) x 30'-8", one-and-a-half stories on sloping site fully exposing basement, gable roof, entrances at both levels. Built ca. 1770s; porch on SE elevation added late nineteenth century and removed early twentieth century; used as tenant house; exterior rehabilitated. Built by Jacobus Van Gorden and remained in family until 1876; purchased by George Nyce 1909 and joined with adjacent Nyce estate (PA-1163). One of the oldest houses in Pike County. 3 sheets (1970, including site plan, plans, elevations, section); 3 ext. photos (1970), 2 int. photos (1970); 7 data pages (1970). LC code: PA,52-EGYMI.V,2. NR.

Lackawaxen (Lackawaxen Township)

Grey, Zane, House (PA-5371), Roebling Rd., at confluence of the Lackawaxen and Delaware Rivers. Frame with clapboarding, original four-square house with two additions, 65'-3" x 30'-5", two-and-a-half stories, hip roofs with cross-gables and dormers, porch on front and rear elevations (roofs with spindles and brackets removed); painted friezes in study and library depict Native American figures. Original four-square house built 1906; study addition to N 1915; addition to rear of study 1916. Part of Grey family complex consisting of three dwellings and several outbuildings. Built for Romer and Rebecca Grey; purchased by Zane Grey from his brother 1914; used as inn 1945-73; currently operated as museum of Zane Grey memorabilia. Zane Grey (1872-1939) was a well-known author of western novels and noted fisherman. 9 sheets (1988, including site plan, plans, elevations, sections, details); 7 ext. photos (1988), 11 int. photos (1988); 29 data pages (1989). NR.

Milford Borough

Milford Jail (PA-221), N corner of Broad St. (U.S. Rte 6-209) and High St. Coursed squared rubble, L-shaped, 48'-3" (five-bay front) x 51'-2", two-and-a-half stories with one-story ell, gable roof, hexagonal louvered cupola; S side is sheriff's living quarters, N side is jail. Built 1814; Daniel Dimmick, builder; coal shed and enclosed porch added to rear; still used as county jail. Built as courthouse (second oldest courthouse in Pennsylvania); converted to jail 1871. 7 sheets (1936, including plans, elevations, details); 3 ext. photos (1936), 1 int. photo (1936); 3 data pages (1936). LC code: PA,52-MILF,1.

Milford Vicinity (Dingman Township)

Callahan House. See Helm, Jacob, House.

Helm, Jacob, House (Callahan House) (PA-1275), W side of U.S. Rte. 209, just S of Sawkill Creek and Milford Borough boundary, in Delaware Water Gap National Recreation Area. Frame with clapboarding, approx. 54' (six-bay front) x 18', one-and-a-half stories with basement, gable roof, porch on N (front) elevation, small gabled bay on W elevation probably connected house with summer kitchen; central hall plan. Possibly built late eighteenth century (E three bays built first, W three bays added soon after); probably built by Jacob Helm; altered several times during ninteenth and twentieth century; frame shed and concrete block chimney added mid-twentieth century. Possibly used as early tavern. 2 ext. photos (1971); 8 data pages (1971). LC code: PA,52-MILF.V,1. NR.

Milford Vicinity (Milford Township)

Grey Towers (PA-1400), old Rte. 6, approx. .5 mi. W of Milford. Stone with brick window surrounds, L-shaped with three circular towers, three stories with attic and basement, hip roofs with dormers, Chateauesque features. Outbuildings and extensive plantings. Built 1885-86 as summer home of James Wallace Pinchot; based on design by Richard Morris Hunt, modified probably by Pinchot; extensive interior changes 1917-24, 1930-31, 1964; 1963 became property of Department of Agriculture to house Pinchot Institute for Conservation Studies. Pinchot's son, Gifford, was a well-known conservationist, first chief of the Bureau of Forestry and twice governor of Pennsylvania; his other son, Amos R.E., was founder of the American Civil Liberties Union. 8 sheets (ca. 1983, including site plans, planting plan, plans, elevations, sections). LC code: PA,52-MILF,2. NHL.

Gate House (PA-1400A). Stuccoed stone with quoins, two by three bays, one-and-a-half stories, hip roof with dormers, enclosed porch on S elevation. Built ca. 1886. 2 sheets (ca. 1983, including plans, elevations, section). LC code: PA,52-MILF,2A.

Bait Box (PA-1400B). One-story frame structure with octagonal enclosure of coursed ashlar walls. Built 1925-26; Chester H. Aldrich of Delano and Aldrich, architect. 1 sheet (ca. 1983, including plan, elevations, section). LC code: PA,52-MILF,2B.

Letter Box (PA-1400C). Random rubble, rectangular, one story with interior gallery, gable roof with parapets, concave entrance with convex entrance porch. Built 1925-27; Chester H. Aldrich of Delano and Aldrich, architect; interior altered 1964. 1 sheet (ca. 1983, including plan, elevations, section). LC code: PA,52-MILF,2C.

Milford Vicinity (Westfall Township)

Peirce, Charles S., House (PA-5198), U.S. Rte 209, approx. 2 mi. N of Milford, in Delaware Water Gap National Recreation Area. 1 reduced copy photo of measured drawing (1978) showing evolution of 1888 frame house as numerous additions and alterations occurred. LC code: PA,52-MILF.V,2.

Schuylkill County

Pottsville

Capitol Theatre (PA-5202), 218-20 N. Centre St. Brick with cast stone (front elevation) and terra cotta block, L-shaped, three stories with basement (theatre on first floor, apartments on second and third), Spanish Colonial Revival style; ornate sculptured plaster interior in Moorish style. Built 1927; demolished. One of the first theaters specially built for sound movies; one of the largest movie theaters in state. 3 ext. photos (1982), 3 copy photos of int. on opening night (1927); 3 data pages (1982). LC code: PA,54-POTTS,1.

Wayne County

Bethany Borough

Wilmot, David, House (PA-225), E side of Wayne St. (State Rte. 670), at Sugar St. Frame with clapboarding, 24'-2" (three-bay front) x 31'-2", two-and-a-half stories, gable roof, door with transom flanked by pilasters and entablature on W (front) elevation; side hall plan. Built ca. 1811; John Gustin, builder; one-and-a-half-story clapboarded side wing (24'-3" x 32'-3") with saltbox roof added to N elevation; door on wing changed to window (originally two front entrances). David Wilmot was born in the house in 1814; he was a noted lawyer and member of Congress, known for his Wilmot Proviso (1846) which proposed prohibiting slavery in new territories. 9 sheets (1936, including plans, elevations, details); 3 ext. photos (1936), 2 int. photos (1936); 5 data pages (1936). LC code: PA,64-BETH,1. NR.

Honesdale Borough

Farnham House. See Park Street and West Side Avenue (House).

Italian Villa Style House. See Park Street and West Side Avenue (House).

Park Street and West Side Avenue (House) (Italian Villa Style House, Farnham House) (PA-5175), NE corner of Park St. and West Side Ave. Frame with clapboarding, four by two bays, two stories, hip roof, overhanging eaves with plain brackets, ornamental cast-iron porch across front elevation; Italianate style. Built ca. 1850; one-story wing to side; owned by Norman C. Farnham 1930s. 1 ext. photo (1936). LC code: PA,64-HOND,2.

Thompson, Andrew, House. See Torrey, John, House.

Torrey, John, House (Andrew Thompson House) (PA-229), NW corner of Park and West Sts. Brick, T-shaped, 51'-1" (three-bay front) x 42'-1" (three bays) with rear kitchen wing (31'-4" x 41'-1"), two-and-a-half stories, hip roof with gable roof on wing, central square cupola, bracketed cornice, paneled frieze with attic windows, double doors with transom and side lights on S (front) elevation, porch with ornamental cast-iron railings, brick pantry on kitchen wing, Italianate style; central hall plan, fine interior woodwork. Outbuildings: brick office and frame washhouse. Built 1854 by John Torrey, a prominent local businessman; several additions and alterations; demolished. 50 sheets (1938, including plans, elevations, sections, details); 10 ext. photos (1937), 5 int. photos (1937), 1 ext. photo of office (1937), 2 ext. photos of washhouse (1937); 7 data pages (1937). LC code: PA,64-HOND,1.

Whites Valley (Mount Pleasant Township)

Octagonal Schoolhouse. See Schoolhouse.

Schoolhouse (Octagon Schoolhouse) (PA-228), 5 mi. SE of Pleasant Mount. Random rubble, octagonal, 12'-2" sides, one story, shingled polygonal roof, central brick chimney suspended below ceiling, flat brick arches over openings; one room. Built 1840; classes discontinued 1928; restored 1931 by Wayne Chapter of Daughters of the American Revolution (bronze tablet placed on door 1931). 5 sheets (1936, including plans, elevations, section, details); 1 ext. photo (1936), 1 int. photo (1936); 3 data pages (1936). LC code: PA,64-WHIVA,1.

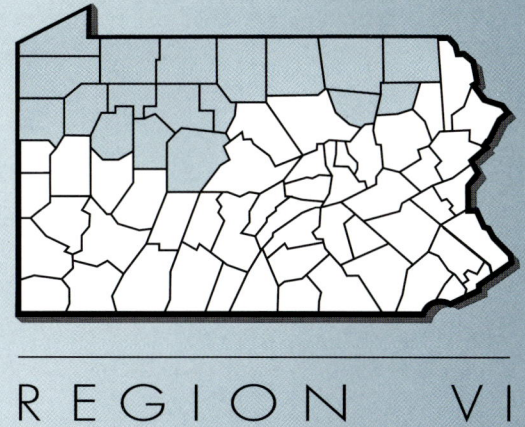

REGION VI

Allegheny Plateau

Essay by Richard J. Webster
Catalog entries by Deborah Stephens Burns

Bradford
Cameron*
Clarion*
Clearfield*
Crawford
Elk*
Erie
Forest*
Jefferson
McKean
Mercer
Potter
Sullivan
Susquehanna
Tioga*
Venango
Warren
Wyoming

*no catalog entries

Log Barn (PA-5127) Coudersport Borough, Potter County. Northwest elevation (William J. Bulger, photographer, 1936) PA,53-___,1B-1

THE ALLEGHENY PLATEAU REGION covers approximately two-thirds of the Commonwealth, extending north and west of the Ridge and Valley and Anthracite Regions to the four-mile-wide coastal zone along Lake Erie. It encompasses eighteen counties.[1] The region was once a high flat area, as indicated by the nearly uniform heights of its many hills, but over millions of years numerous streams cut through the flat-lying sedimentary rock to develop a tree-like pattern of deep valleys.[2] In spite of this common topography, prehistoric transformations have produced four distinct areas within the region. The "land-of-milk-and-honey" is the Northeastern Glaciated Section, which includes Susquehanna, Bradford, and Wyoming Counties and the eastern half of Tioga County. Here short summers and the fair soils of the rolling glaciated hills support dairy farms with their fields of hay, oats, and buckwheat, which, in turn, help to support a prosperous beekeeping industry. Dairy farms also dominate at the opposite end of the northern tier, in the Northwestern Glaciated Section of Erie, Crawford, and Mercer Counties and the northwestern third of Warren County, while deposits of oil, bituminous coal, and natural gas lie beneath the forests of the Allegheny High Plateaus.[3] The fourth area is the Allegheny "Mountains." This finger of heavily forested high elevation extends northeastwardly from the Maryland border to Sullivan and Clearfield Counties and the southern half of Cameron County.[4] HABS holdings for this sparsely populated region are strongly skewed toward Greek Revival architecture. Except for a few commercial buildings in the city of Erie and five log structures, vernacular buildings and those from the region's industrial era are excluded.

    Hostile Indians along the frontier helped to retard settlement in the Allegheny Plateau's western parts, but so did the region's remoteness and scarcity of good farmland. Except for a few small settlements along the Susquehanna River and one in Meadville, Crawford County, the region remained virgin territory as late as 1790, and some parts were still unsettled thirty years later. Even after the 1795 Treaty of Greenville removed any potential Indian menace far to the west of Pennsylvania, only small numbers of pioneers moved into the region. Most settlers avoided it and moved along the Ohio River or the Great Lakes into the Northwest Territory. After the Land Act of 1792 drastically reduced land prices and removed the maximum on purchases, land companies acquired much of the region's territory. Most of these companies were headquartered in Philadelphia, including foreign groups, such as the French-owned Ceres Land Company and the Holland Land Company, an association of Amsterdam investors, which by the end of the decade owned 1.5 million acres of northern Pennsylvania.[5] Because Pennsylvania failed to maintain a consistent land policy, however, speculators rarely profited and few pioneers moved into the area.[6]

Those who first ventured into these mountains often endured difficult times in rudimentary dwellings. Frontier conditions were invariably harsh but in few areas were they as harsh as in the Allegheny High Plateau. A widely-traveled land agent wrote the Holland Land Company representative in 1805 that the situation west of the Allegheny River "offers a picture of wretchedness I have never seen equalled in America."[7] One Potter County pioneer remembered his troubled early years there: "I sold one yoke of my oxen in the fall, the other yoke I wintered on browse; but in the spring one ox died, and the other I sold to procure food for my family, and was now destitute of a team, and had nothing but my own hands to depend upon to clear my lands and raise provisions. We wore out all our shoes the first year. We had no way to get more—no money, nothing to sell, and but little to eat—and were in dreadful distress for the want of the necessaries of life. I was obliged to work and travel in the woods barefooted. . . . When I finished planting we had nothing to eat but leeks, cow-cabbage, and milk. We lived on leeks and cow-cabbage as long as they kept green—about six weeks."[8] The northern Susquehanna area, the former Tioga Circuit, was notorious among early Methodist circuit riders. William Colbert, who rode this circuit in the 1790s, recalled being served frozen turnips for breakfast one morning, and other times faced even worse food—it was simply inedible. After four months in this region in 1793, Colbert found it "one of the most disagreeable places for travel I ever was in, among a refractory sort of people. I lived hard, labored hard, but I fear did little good."[9] Three years later Englishman Timothy Weld Jr., found conditions no better during his voyage down the Susquehanna River. North of Tioga Point, in the present Athens-Sayre area, he did not eat with one family because they barely had enough for themselves. At the only other houses within two or three miles, the woman had only corn meal, and another family downstream had to roast potatoes for breakfast.[10]

Log houses were once common in the region. Because virtually no research has been conducted on log buildings here, it can only be conjectured that the Blair Cabin (PA-510) in Girard Township, Erie County, represents the region's more common type of log house. Built about 1818, it had one story and a loft, no basement, V-notching, an exterior end chimney, and doors attached with wooden pins. As log construction continued into the twentieth century, the quality of workmanship evidently declined. The builder of the 1900 log barn (PA-5127) near Coudersport, Potter County, for example, used the most primitive log-building technique.[11] He employed logs in their natural round shape and joined them with simple saddle notches, requiring the logs to extend beyond the corners in a rustic manner. Because of this simple construction in combination with vertical gable boards and large wooden roof shingles, the twentieth-century barn appears more rustic and primitive than log houses a hundred years older.

Settlers entered the Allegheny Plateau from each end, leaving the high elevations in the north central section the last to be populated. In the eastern end they moved into the region from both north and south, down from the Finger Lakes district of central New York and up the Susquehanna River from the Wyoming Valley. Most of those taking the latter route were Connecticut people, following the footsteps of those who had taken lands farther south under Connecticut's claim to western lands.[12] Actively sought by land companies, New Englanders and children of New Englanders were also among those migrating from the north. Settlers also entered the western end of the region from both north and south, up the Allegheny River from the Pittsburgh area and from western New York, especially after Erie developed as a lakeport in the early nineteenth century. Once established, northern tier towns tended to communicate northward with such small New York cities as Binghamton, Elmira, and Olean, and via the Finger Lakes to the Erie Canal towns and eastward into New England.[13] Largely because of these settlement patterns, geographers place most of the region within the New England Extended Cultural Region, which includes nearly all of New York. The same general pattern persists yet today, in spite of U.S. Route 6 that runs east and west across the region's northern edge and other highways that lead south as well as north. Inhabitants' speech, for example, is linguistically akin to that of upstate New York and New England, and in the region's eastern end New York professional sports teams have stronger followings than Philadelphia teams.[14]

New England Yankees probably did not constitute a majority of the region's inhabitants, but they left a strong cultural imprint on its built environment.[15] Mid-nineteenth-century observers commented on the northern tier's New England character, attributing the "attention to education" and the private academies in Harford and Montrose, Susquehanna County; Athens and Towanda, Bradford County; and Wellsboro, Tioga County, to the presence of New Englanders.[16] Their influence is clearly seen in the region's early dwellings. The 1806 hewn-log house (PA-227) of Connecticut-born Jonathan Terry stands near the Susquehanna River, in Terrytown, Bradford County, approximately forty miles north of the Wyoming Valley, which Terry left in 1786.[17] The house's proportions (with a height one-half and a depth three-fourths of its length), central chimney, and chink log construction make it an architectural rarity, a Yankee log house. Although log construction was not part of the New England building tradition, most frontiersmen possessed the skills—hewing logs and cutting half-dovetail joints—necessary for building Terry's house.[18] The house's plan is remarkably similar to the two-room and added lean-to plan of seventeenth-century New England timber-frame dwellings[19] New Englanders in the eighteenth century continued to build houses with this plan, incorporating the lean-to portion into the house's volume as part of the house's two stories. Terry's closed-string staircase in the squarish entry "porch" turns as it rises against the stone chimney stack, and five first-floor rooms are arranged more or less symmetrically around the two large, central back-to-back fireplaces.

Similarly Sylvanus Mulford's 1818 house (PA-215) in Montrose, Susquehanna County, is a small New England saltbox house in "a New England country village."[20] The Mulford House's weatherboarded timber frame, central chimney, and "saltbox" shape, in which the side elevations slope from a two-story front to a one-story rear, are like those of many similar New England houses.[21] Mulford was not from New England but from eastern Long Island, which was settled by New England Puritans[22] and where in the colonial period English villages stood—"neat, clustered, white under the elm trees, every line and shadow of house and barn and village common bespeaking their New England ancestry."[23] Although the house's enclosed pas-

Captain Jonathan Terry Cabin (PA-227) Terrytown (Terry Township), Bradford County. South elevation (Stanley Jones, photographer, 1936) PA,8-TERTO,1-2.

sage to the rear barn suggests the well-known New England practice of connecting farm buildings, New Englanders did not begin building their farmsteads in this distinctively regional manner until the 1830s, at least a decade after the Mulford House's completion.[24] Consequently the barn was probably attached to the house a generation after the house was completed. However, the woodshed of the Westgate-Brunner House (PA-519) in Riceville, Crawford County—at the western end of the northern tier—appears to have been attached to the house's kitchen and pantry wing since the house's construction between 1839 and 1847. Benjamin Boles Westgate, the house's builder and first occupant, migrated from Rhode Island in the late 1830s and may have brought the idea of attached buildings with him. His story-and-a-half weatherboarded timber-frame dwelling is a good example of a Cape Cod house with Greek Revival frontispieces.[25]

Congregational churches, eighteenth-century expressions of seventeenth-century Puritanism, represent another form of New England influence. Abundant in New England and virtually nonexistent south of the old Connecticut claim, they were among the first churches erected in the Allegheny Plateau's northern tier. The 1828 Wysox Presbyterian Church (PA-222), near the Susquehanna River in Bradford County, was initially a Congregational church. Isaac Foster, a native of Massachusetts and agent for a land company operating under the Connecticut-based Susquehanna Company, arrived in the area in 1785. Six years later, he and Reverend Jabez Culver from Connecticut were instrumental in establishing the congregation as Pennsylvania's first organized church of Anglo-Americans north of Wilkes-Barre. In 1828 the congregation erected the present brick church.[26] With its Flemish-bond front, round-arch windows set within blind-arches, and the belfry rising from the roof's peak, it resembles Federal-style Congregational churches in the Connecticut River Valley.[27] Two years after the present church's construction, the Congregationalists united with local Presbyterians, and ever since the building has been known—and used—as the Wysox Presbyterian Church.[28] Before the Civil War, Congregational churches stood in many towns and valleys across the northern tier, from Harford in the east to Riceville in the west.[29]

Methodists were the region's other dominant early-nineteenth-century denomination, and remain numerous today.[30] Methodist circuit-riding preachers ventured along the upper Susquehanna in the 1790s, first preaching in 1792 in such Bradford County communities as Towanda, Burlington, and Sheshequin, and building a log church in West Burlington Township as early as 1796.[31] By 1822, the West Burlington Township congregation replaced its log meetinghouse with a small two-story weatherboarded, timber-frame church. An elevated octagonal paneled pulpit, set within a semicircular alcove and behind an elliptical wooden railing, dominates the plain interior of side aisles, pews, and balconies. The two arched entrances (with fanlights) and the partition down the center of the pews indicate the congregation's early separation by gender, not unlike that of Quakers. The building's austerity, however, reflects a class consciousness and determined independence rather than the humility on which the Quaker plain style was based. Methodist church leaders insisted that their "churches be built plain and decent, and with free seats; but no more expensive than is absolutely unavoidable; otherwise the necessity of raising money will make rich men necessary to us." If that should occur, the church fathers

Wysox Presbyterian Church (PA-222) Wysox (Wysox Township), Bradford County. Southeast elevation (Stanley Jones, photographer, 1936) PA,8-WYSO,1-1.

warned, the denomination would become "dependent on them, yea, and governed by them. And then farewell to Methodist discipline, if not doctrine too."[32]

Because education has been an important aspect of New England culture ever since the opening of Harvard College in 1636, it was reasonable for transplanted Yankees to establish colleges as well as churches. In June 1815 Roger Alden, former representative of the Holland Land Company and brigade major in the Connecticut Line, chaired a meeting of prominent gentlemen in Meadville, Crawford County. In the best interests of their "fellow creatures, and influenced . . . by a desire for promoting the glory of God,"[33] they founded Allegheny College. They named Alden's cousin, the Reverend Timothy Alden president, even though he would not be inaugurated for another two years. Timothy Alden was of the sturdiest Yankee stock. Born in Yarmouth, Massachusetts, and a descendant of John Alden and Priscilla Mullins, whom Longfellow made famous in *The Courtship of Myles Standish*, he was a Harvard graduate as had been his father and grandfather before him. Alden not only raised funds and designed the curriculum but also designed the college's first building, the three-story brick Bentley Hall (PA-525).[34] In July 1820 Alden presided at the laying of the cornerstone, under which was deposited, among other items, a piece of Plymouth Rock. For New Englanders this was tantamount to a relic from the true cross! Fund-raising proved difficult and fifteen years passed before the building was completed.[35] Bentley Hall reflects both Alden's status as a novice architect and his New England origins. The layered pilasters with their thin stone caps, for example, serve no visual structural function; those at the ends stop short of the cornice and the two center ones float below the central pediment. At the same time, Alden handles other details, from the wings' overly attenuated Doric columns and thin entablatures to the two upper-story Palladian windows, in a characteristically New England manner.[36]

The aforementioned flow of ideas and people from New York and New England during the early nineteenth century helps to account for the popularity of the Greek Revival style in the region. The concentration of Greek Revival style buildings here, often in towns with classical names, is greater than in any other part of Pennsylvania. No one has conducted a statistical study to establish that the Allegheny Plateau Region possesses Pennsylvania's greatest concentration of Greek Revival buildings, but a tour through the area makes the claim readily apparent. Greek Revival houses remain predominant in the older sections of some Bradford County villages, such as Monroeton and West Burlington. Place names and their

Allegheny College, Bentley Hall (PA-525) Meadville, Crawford County. Front elevation (William J. Bulger, photographer, 1937) PA,20-MEDVI,2A-1.

namesakes are even more obvious. In Bradford County alone there are Athens, Rome, Troy, and Macedonia.

America's Greek Revival expressed the young nation's self-conscious republican spirit and achieved a national following unequaled in any other country. A variant of the neoclassicism that came into vogue after the American Revolution, Greek Revival swept the nation beginning in the 1820s.[37] It served as a cultural emulsifier, an instrument of Americanization that helped to bring immigrants into the cultural mainstream but did not destroy their own distinctive identities. Jacob Weiderich, a German weaver, for example, immigrated to Pennsylvania in 1830 and soon purchased a farm in Roulette, Potter County. Within a decade he moved into his new dwelling (PA-5129), a Greek Revival house that exhibits New England, not German, influences.[38] The new Greek style was communicated by books, both foreign archaeological works that were especially popular among high-style architects, and builders' handbooks that local carpenters consulted. Rather than reducing regional differences, this proliferation of books and manuals actually contributed to subtle regional characteristics, especially those that developed in New England and New York and came together in Pennsylvania's northern tier.

New England remained conservative in its architectural tastes, especially in its older settlements, and grafted the Federal style's delicate attenuation onto Greek forms. Builders in the New England countryside relied on Asher Benjamin's books so much that his volumes are credited with having standardized in that part of the country a late colonial neoclassicism that strongly influenced architecture there as late as the Civil War. Benjamin was slow to illustrate Greek Revival details in his books, and when he did, those details were relatively heavy and simple.[39] New Englanders built a variety of Greek Revival houses, but the form they preferred had its pedimented end facing the street, often with thin corner pilasters supporting a broad cornice.[40] Understandably, many houses like this were built in northern Pennsylvania. The Terry House (PA-555) in Pittsfield, Warren County, is one of the better examples. A more popular variant is Dr. Horace Coleman's House (PA-557) in Liberty Township, McKean County, with its side wing. In this case the wing's facade is flush with the main facade. Equally common is the recessed side wing, as in the case of the Bell House (PA-564) in Mercer, Mercer County. In all cases, however, the side wings also were ornamented with pilasters and broad entablatures. The Coleman House's gable-end lunette is a Federal-style carry-over that was not uncommon in western Massachusetts and Connecticut Greek Revival houses.

New Yorkers, on the other hand, embraced the new style more positively. Whereas Benjamin's design books set the neoclassical taste in New England, Minard Lafever's did the same in New York and in other parts of the country. Trained as a carpenter in New York's Finger Lakes region, Lafever was sensitive to the needs of carpenters and those trying to move from the building trades to the architectural profession. His books display contrasts of simple planes, inventive Greek Revival forms,

Dr. Horace Coleman House (PA-557) Port Allegheny vicinity (Liberty Township), McKean County. Northeast elevation (William J. Bulger, photographer, 1936) PA,42-PORAL.V,1-2.

and delicate details, which demonstrate that he was "perhaps the greatest designer of architectural decoration of his time in America."[41] New Yorkers in new upstate towns were especially fond of monumental houses whose two-story main blocks had central pedimented porticoes and flanking one-story wings.[42] A well-documented Pennsylvania northern tier example is the Timothy Ives House (PA-528) in Coudersport, the Potter County seat. Ives was a Connecticut native who lived in New York state and

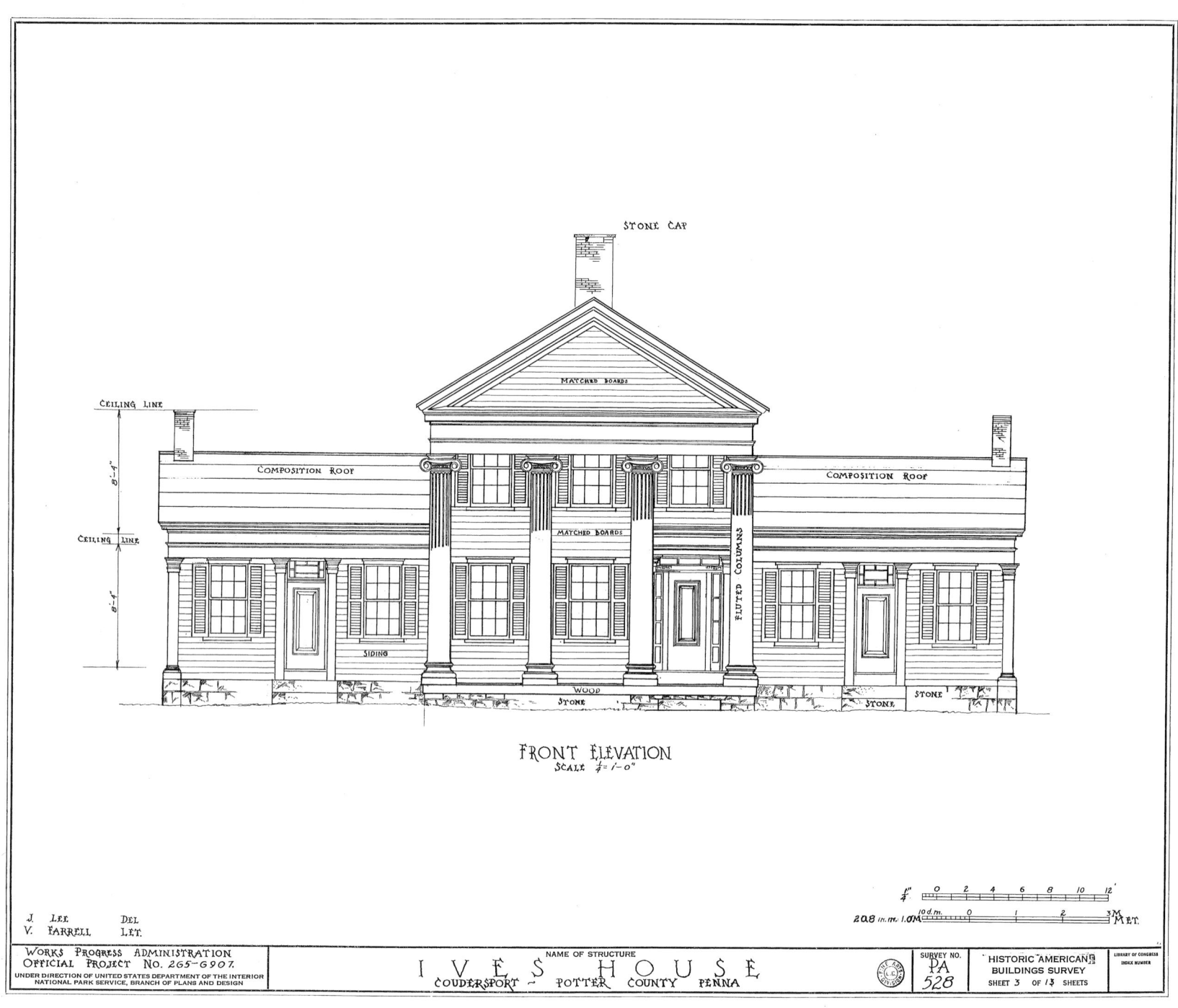

Timothy Ives House (PA-528) Coudersport Borough, Potter County. Front elevation (J. Lee and V. Farrell, delineators, 1936) PA,53-COUD,1.

Tioga County, Pennsylvania, before moving to Coudersport in 1826. He served at various times as county treasurer, judge, and state representative, and was an owner of the county's first newspaper and a founding trustee of the local academy.[43] Evidently Ives's son-in-law, N. L. Dike, built the timber frame for the house, and in April 1843 Ives contracted with two Cuba, New York, carpenters to enclose it "in a neat substantial manner and after the style agreeable to the directions of the first party [Ives] as the work is progressing."[44] Ives supplied all materials, including "the sash with the lights set therein," and apparently drawings as well, serving as his own architect, almost certainly with the aid of handbooks.[45] Unfortunately, the Ives House has been disassembled, but other equally important houses of this type, such as the 1840 Taylor-Jones House in Harford, Susquehanna County, still stand in the region.[46]

A smaller form of Greek Revival houses also popular in upstate New York and this region is characterized by a squarish main block flanked by wings with small porticoes. This type of house usually had two stories, a flat roof, and small rectangular frieze windows with iron grilles that relieved the heavy planarity of the frieze.[47] In 1840 Stephen Collins Foster, the noted antebellum composer of popular songs, supposedly lived briefly in such a house in Towanda, Bradford County. Built for George Wansey between 1828 and 1840,[48] the brick house's central three-bay block has a one-story Ionic portico at its side entrance and is flanked by smaller identical three-bay wings with one-story Ionic porticoes at their entrances.

More common in the region, however, are the less sophisticated weatherboarded frame houses designed and built by local carpenters emulating New England models. The Flint House (PA-576), near New Richmond, Crawford County, for example, suggests the appropriate temple form with its gable end facing the road, and is graced with minimal Greek Revival details: a simply framed frontispiece of pilasters and plain entablature, corner pilasters, and a plain frieze with cornice returns. In order to retain appropriate classical proportions on the small-scaled building and still fit second-story windows into the front, the carpenter could not carry the cornice across the gable end to form a pediment, but had to interrupt it by using cornice returns. Although the frontispiece was centered on the facade, it was centered on a four-bay first story to give the facade an inappropriate asymmetry. "Perhaps the climax of this carpenter Greek Revival was reached in the H. E. Hendryx house"[49] (PA-520) in Riceville, Crawford County. The carpenter concentrated nearly all of his carpentry and design skills on the entry, applying his inverted jig-sawn anthemion to the

Flint House (PA-576) New Richmond vicinity (Richmond Township), Crawford County. Front elevation (William J. Bulger, photographer, 1937) PA,20-NEWRI.V,1-1.

pilasters of the frontispiece, to the house's front corners, and to the panel above the frontispiece's entablature. He enriched the entry by adding carved guttae below the frieze and egg-and-dart molding around each of the door's six panels.

    Canals and railroads that extended into the region carried the ideas, carpenters' manuals, and architectural drawings that made these Greek Revival buildings possible. Because of the region's elevation and remoteness, newer transportation systems entered the area over a twenty-year period and later than in the state's southern parts. Railroads did not penetrate Susquehanna County until the late 1840s; the

Beaver and Erie Canal connected the Ohio River and Lake Erie as late as 1844,[50] a time when the railroad was already supplanting the canal in less remote parts of the state. The North Branch Canal of the Pennsylvania canal system was not completed between Pittston, Luzerne County, and the New York state line until 1856. It had leakage problems from the beginning and never did become economically viable. Eventually Asa Packer acquired the canal and in 1869 extended his Lehigh Valley Railroad along the canal's right-of-way to Waverly, New York.[51] Between the Susquehanna River and Lake Erie, however, there was no coherent transportation system, unless the Allegheny River steamboats would be considered such. That absence of transportation inhibited economic development. When Timothy Ives built his porticoed mansion in Coudersport, for example, he paid his carpenters only 35 percent of the contracted fee in cash; the remainder was paid in goods which he carried to his Coudersport store by wagon from New York state.[52]

This reliance on wagons contributed to a distribution nightmare when the oil boom erupted in the region's western parts during the Civil War. The oil industry initially developed in the Titusville, Crawford County, vicinity after Edwin L. Drake drilled the first oil well in August 1859 south of the town in Venango County.[53] At this time the closest railroad, the Sunbury and Erie (renamed the Philadelphia and Erie by 1861), was approximately twenty-five miles away, with stations at three locations: Union City, Erie County; Corry, Erie County; and Garland, Warren County. Hauling barrels of oil to those rail depots proved extremely arduous and very expensive. Teams of horses struggled over roads dismissed locally as "wholly unclassable, almost impassable, scarcely jackassable."[54] It was easier to ship by water to Pittsburgh, even though freezing made it impossible during winter months, and even in the summer it was tricky, especially along the route's first stage, the narrow, shallow Oil Creek.[55] In providing a transportation solution, railroad and pipeline companies after the Civil War set off a transportation competition nearly as intense as that within the oil industry itself.[56] The Pennsylvania oil boom hit its peak in the 1890s; after 1900 Texas and Oklahoma became the nation's oil drilling center.[57]

HABS has recorded only two buildings of the oil boom era, the Edwin Drake House (PA-5108) in Titusville, Crawford County, and the old hotel (PA-585) in Tidioute, Warren County. Drake eventually made a respectable profit from his drilling venture, but about 1858, when he is believed to have built his house, he was a wildcatter with limited funding.[58] Thus his dwelling is quite modest, a traditional two-

Edwin Drake House (PA-5108) Titusville, Crawford County. East elevation (William J. Bulger, photographer, 1937) PA,20-TITVI,1-1.

story frame Georgian house with a Greek Revival frontispiece. The hotel, on the other hand, was finished with more Greek Revival elements: pedimented gable ends, a Doric portico, and pedimented lintels. In oil boomtowns like Pithole, similar hotels were thrown up in a single day,[59] suggesting use of balloon frames, but in the case of Tidioute's hotel, it is not known whether it had a balloon frame or traditional timber framing.

Oil was not the only natural resource to be extracted from the region's hills. In such western counties as Clarion and Venango, the mining of iron ore was a significant industry during the 1840s and 1850s, and because of their great stands of pine and hemlock, lumbering was a major nineteenth-century activity throughout the region. Shortly after the turn of the twentieth century, lumber companies had deforested enough hillsides to end that enterprise in most counties. As lumber land declined, bituminous coal mining filled the void in Clarion and Clearfield Counties and the Blossburg area of Tioga County.[60] By their nature, these extractive industries encouraged relatively short boom and bust cycles, which exaggerated the nineteenth-century pattern of picturesque mansions for the successful entrepreneurs and hastily erected frame commercial buildings and rude houses and shacks for the masses. The shacks are gone and multistory brick and iron-front stores have replaced the early frame commercial buildings, but many of the mansions still line the streets in such towns as Tunkhannock and Franklin. They give each town its unique character and serve as reminders of earlier prosperity. During the 1980s HABS recorded some of these doomed houses, such as the 1897 Arbuckle House (PA-31) in Erie and the 1887 Henry-Windsor House (PA-5205) in Warren. Constructed of different materials (stone for the Erie house and brick for the Warren house) and embellished with a complex of roofs, gables, and turrets, they were two different expressions of the picturesque Queen Anne style. A more exuberant example of this fin-de-siecle style, the 1899 Roueche House, still stands on Meadville's Park Avenue. Unfortunately the region's generally poor economic condition during most of the twentieth century has prevented continuation of such high-quality architecture; when old buildings fall they rarely are replaced with buildings of equal quality.

Notes

[1] The Allegheny Plateau is part of the Appalachian Plateaus that stretch from New York state to Alabama. For purposes of this catalog the southwestern portion of Pennsylvania's Allegheny Plateau is separated into its own region, called southwestern Pennsylvania. The eighteen counties in this essay's Allegheny Plateau Region are from east to west in the northernmost tier: Susquehanna, Bradford, Tioga, Potter, McKean, Warren, Erie; in the middle tier: Wyoming, Sullivan, Cameron, Elk, Forest, Venango, Crawford; and in the southernmost tier: Clearfield, Jefferson, Clarion, and Mercer. Raymond E. Murphy and Marion Murphy, *Pennsylvania: A Regional Geography* (Harrisburg: Pennsylvania Book Service, 1937), 33-39. For a short description of the region's geological development, see J. Ronald Mowery, "Geologic History of Pennsylvania," *Pennsylvania Heritage* 4 (September 1978): 7-12.

[2] Geographers call this tree-like pattern dendritic. In the northeastern and northwestern parts of the region, glaciers thousands of feet thick deranged these steams and formed lakes and waterfalls. When the glaciers receded, the Susquehanna River became the primary channel for carrying the meltaway. Mowery, "Geological History of Pennsylvania," 12.

[3] The Allegheny High Plateaus include both the forest region of Potter, Cameron, Elk, Clearfield, and Jefferson Counties and the oil region of McKean, Venango, Clarion, Forest, and Elk Counties, and two-thirds of Warren County. Murphy and Murphy, *Pennsylvania*, 371-422.

[4] Murphy and Murphy, *Pennsylvania*, 18, 35-37.

[5] For a clear explanation of Pennsylvania's post-colonial land policies, the different kinds of land distribution, and the Land Act of 1792 in particular, see Philip S. Klein and Ari Hoogenboom, *A History of Pennsylvania* (New York: McGraw-Hill Company, 1973), 163-67. These foreign land companies left their marks in the region's place names. Dutch bankers who dealt with the Ceres Land Company, for example, were the namesakes for two northern tier county seats. Coudersport, Potter County, was named for John Coudere, head of the banking firm, Coudere, Brants, Changuion of Amsterdam, and Smethport, McKean County, was named for the Dutch bankers Raymond and Theodore de Smeth. Ronald F. Abler, David J. Cuff, Edward K. Muller, William J. Young, and Wilbur Zelinsky, *The Atlas of Pennsylvania* (Philadelphia: Temple University Press, 1989), 83; Victor L. Beebe, *History of Potter County, Pennsylvania* (Coudersport: Potter County Historical Society, 1934), 20, 22.

[6] Solon J. Buck and Elizabeth Hawthorn Buck, *The Planting of Civilization in Western Pennsylvania* (Pittsburgh: University of Pittsburgh Press, 1939), 204-17.

[7] Quoted in Paul Demund Evans, *The Holland Land Company* (Buffalo: Buffalo Historical Society, 1924), 161. Evans explains that "the most potent cause for the backwardness of the settlement was the lamentable controversy over titles." (163) Because of protracted disputes between land companies and pioneers who ignored companies' claims, settlers were reluctant to invest much effort in improving land until titles were established. At the same time more industrious people would not come to an area where property rights were uncertain.

[8] Quoted in Beebe, *History of Potter County*, 35-36. The pioneer was John Peet, who moved to Potter County from Elizabeth, New Jersey, in May 1811. His hard times were partly self-inflicted. He supposedly would not kill animals; he (or his sons) would catch fish in a basket but not with a hook and line. Nevertheless, people with more conventional eating practices also had difficult times along this early-nineteenth-century frontier. For examples, see the stories of Benjamin Burt in Potter County in 1811 and Joshua Raynsford in Susquehanna County in 1802 and 1803. Beebe, *History of Potter County*, 33; Emily C. Blackman, *History of Susquehanna County, Pennsylvania* (Philadelphia: Claxton, Remsen & Haffelfinger, 1873), 292.

[9] Quoted in Frederick E. Maser, *Methodism in Central Pennsylvania, 1771-1969* (Lebanon: Central Pennsylvania Annual Conference, The United Methodist Church, 1971), 39. Inhabitants' coolness toward Colbert and his preaching certainly contributed to his dejection. After he preached in Wyalusing, Bradford County, for example, and suggested a public contribution, the listeners said nothing and gave nothing. Their behavior may have resulted from their New England Calvinist beliefs as much as from their penury. Pennsylvania Methodist and Presbyterian preachers occasionally clashed verbally well into the nineteenth century. Maser, *Methodism*, 40, 114-16.

[10] Isaac Weld Jr., *Travels through the States of North America, and the Provinces of Upper and Lower Canada during the Years 1795, 1796, and 1797*, 2 vols., 3rd ed. (London: John Stockdale, 1800), 334-60.

[11] Terry B. Jordan, *American Log Buildings: An Old World Heritage* (Chapel Hill: University of North Carolina Press, 1985), 15. It was not uncommon for residents of the region to erect log buildings at the turn of the twentieth century. Samuel Bouse in Asylum Township, Bradford County, for example, built a log house for himself and his wife Ella to live in about 1900 while he was constructing his weatherboarded balloon-frame Queen Anne house from mail-order plans. Interview with Bessie Bouse Webster, Asylum Township, Bradford County, 7 September 1989.

[12] For a discussion of Connecticut's claims on Pennsylvania lands and the resultant Yankee-Pennamite wars, see the essay on the Anthracite and Poconos Region.

[13] Settlement patterns can be roughly traced by noting the dates that people established homes in the region's future county seats. In the eastern part, the first settler arrived in Towanda, Bradford County, circa 1786, and in Wellsboro, Tioga County, in 1799, about the same time

that the first settlers moved to Meadville, Crawford County (1788) and Mercer, Mercer County (1796). Pioneers first arrived in future county seats of the central counties as much as thirty-five years later. First settlers moved to Emporium, Cameron County, in 1811, to Smethport, McKean County, and Ridgway, Elk County, in 1822, and to Coudersport, Potter County, in 1825. Another example of the ties between Pennsylvania's northern tier and New York's southern tier is the similarity of their dairy industries; Pennsylvania's dairy region is essentially a southern extension of New York's dairy region. C. F. Heverly, *History of the Towandas, 1776-1886* (Towanda, Pa.: Reporter-Journal Printing Company, 1886), 3; Writers' Program of the Work Projects Administration, *Pennsylvania: A Guide to the Keystone State* (New York: Oxford University Press, 1940), 365; Lois Mulkearn and Edwin V. Pugh, *A Traveler's Guide to Historic Western Pennsylvania* (Pittsburgh: University of Pittsburgh Press, 1954), 181, 192, 200, 279, 286; Stewart H. Holbrook, *The Yankee Exodus: An Account of Migration from New England* (New York: Macmillan Company, 1950), 15-19; Murphy and Murphy, *Pennsylvania*, 371.

[14]Abler et al., *Atlas of Pennsylvania*, 147, 154, 160.

[15]Buck and Buck, *Planting of Civilization in Western Pennsylvania*, 213-14.

[16]Charles B. Trego, *A Geography of Pennsylvania: Containing an Account of the Historical, Geographical Features, Soil, Climate, Geology, Botany, Zoology, Population, Education, Government, Finances, Productions, Trade, Railroads, Canal, &c. of the State* (Philadelphia: Edward C. Biddle, 1843), 194, 354-55.

[17]After living a year in Wyalusing on the opposite side of the river, Captain Jonathan Terry founded Terrytown in 1787. Like so many frontier community founders, Terry was more than a farmer. On his six-hundred-acre farm he erected a gristmill, sawmill, tannery, and distillery, and operated the area's first ferry across the Susquehanna. He also served as a justice of peace for nine years, between 1812 and 1821. Bettie Toal Morrissey, "Log Cabin, Terrytown, Bradford County, Pennsylvania, PA-227," HABS Report (Washington, D.C.: Library of Congress, 1936), 1.

[18]Half-dovetail notching, rare in southeastern Pennsylvania, is a common midland American type. Jordan, *American Log Buildings*, 19, 91. See also Fred Kniffen and Henry Glassie, "Building in Wood: A Time-Place Perspective," *Geographical Review* 56 (January 1966): 55-56; Fred Kniffen, "On Corner-Timbering," *Pioneer America* 1 (January 1969): 3.

[19]In plan and massing the Terry House most closely resembles two weatherboarded timber-frame Connecticut houses: the 1750 Warham Williams House (CT-53) in Northford and the 1761 Trumbull House in North Haven. J. Frederick Kelly, *Early Domestic Architecture of Connecticut* (New Haven: Yale University Press, 1924; reprint ed., New York: Dover Publications, 1963), 7-8, 14, pl. 3; Hugh Morrison, *Early American Architecture: From the First Colonial Settlements to the National Period* (New York: Oxford University Press, 1952), 20-22, 40-41.

[20]Charles Trego's 1843 visual assessment of Montrose still holds true: "The houses are generally built of wood; mostly painted white and presenting a neat appearance; the whole, as has been frequently remarked, much resembles a New England country village." Amy Oakley

echoed Trego's description a century later, observing that Montrose "distinctly reflects, with long-established houses and village green, its inheritance from Connecticut settlers." Trego, *Geography of Pennsylvania*, 352; Amy Oakley, *Our Pennsylvania: Keys to the Keystone State* (Indianapolis: Bobbs-Merrill Company, 1950), 221.

[21] See Kelly, *Early Domestic Architecture of Connecticut*, 8-13, 48-56, pls. 2, 3, 5, 8, 12; Abbott Lowell Cummings, *The Framed Houses of Massachusetts Bay, 1625-1725* (Cambridge: Belknap Press of Harvard University Press, 1979), 31; Abbott Lowell Cummings, *Architecture in Early New England* (Sturbridge, Mass.: Old Sturbridge Village, 1958), n.p.; Mary Mix Foley, *The American House* (New York: Harper & Row, 1980), 22-23.

[22] Mulford was thirty-two when he arrived in Montrose from East Hampton, Long Island, and set up business as a merchant. He built his house in 1818, the year he married Fanny Jessup of Southampton, Long Island. Both he and his wife were members of old eastern Long Island families. John and William Mulford were among the first East Hampton settlers from the Lynn, Massachusetts, vicinity in 1648, and John Jessup was among Southampton founders from Lynn and Ipswich, Massachusetts, in 1640. (Both Long Island towns were under Connecticut's jurisdiction until 1674, when New York extended its authority to that end of the island.) The Mulfords continued their New England ties even after their move to Pennsylvania. Three of Sylvanus Mulford's sons attended Yale; another three sons stayed in Montrose and ran the family business. Blackman, *History of Susquehanna County*, 321, 323; Benjamin F. Thompson, *History of Long Island: From Its Discovery and Settlement to the Present Time*, 3rd ed., 3 vols. (New York: Robert H. Dodd, 1918; reprint ed., Port Washington, N.Y.: Ira J. Friedman, 1962), 2:85-91, 143-57.

[23] Morrison, *Early American Architecture*, 120.

[24] Thomas C. Hubka, *Big House, Little House, Back House, Barn: The Connected Farm Buildings of New England* (Hanover, N.H.: University Press of New England, 1984), 20-21, 28-30.

[25] The Westgate-Brunner House fits the stereotype of early-nineteenth-century Cape Cod double houses in almost every respect, including the location of the living room to the right of the front and a bedroom to the left, the arrangement of gable-end windows (two large ground-floor windows and a large window in the peak flanked by small windows), and the ten-foot height of its front to allow more headroom on the second floor. It is similar in appearance to the late-eighteenth-century Cook House in North Truro, Massachusetts, which also has a long wing. When recorded in 1936, however, the Westgate-Brunner House did not have the characteristic central fireplace and chimney, but had a chimney on the roof ridge near each gable end and one on the kitchen wing's roof ridge for the brick oven or fireplace. Ernest Allen Connally, "The Cape Cod House: An Introductory Study," *Journal of the Society of Architectural Historians* 19 (May 1960): 47-56; Annie Scott Baxter, "Westgate-Brunner House, Riceville, Crawford County, Pennsylvania, PA-519," HABS Report (Washington, D.C.: Library of Congress, 1936), 1.

[26] Victor Charles Detty, *History of the Presbyterian Church of Wysox, Pennsylvania, 1791-1936* (Wysox: By the author, 1937), 16, 22, 76.

[27] The Wysox church is somewhat similar to the 1824 brick First Church of Deerfield, Massachusetts (MA-639), except that the Wysox church does not have its side rectangular windows set within arched recesses and its steeple is less imposing. *Historic Buildings of Massachusetts: Photographs from the Historic American Buildings Survey* (New York: Charles Scribner's Sons, 1976), 38; J.P. Spang III, "Brick Architecture in Deerfield, Massachusetts, 1797-1825," *The Magazine Antiques* 106 (October 1974): 632.

[28] Presbyterians and Congregationalists in 1801 formed the Plan of Union, which lasted fifty-one years. Dissension appeared long before the union's end. The scarcity of Congregational churches in northern Pennsylvania lends mute testimony to the nineteenth-century wag's observation that "Presbyterians milked Congregationalist cows, only to make Presbyterian butter and cheese." Martin E. Marty, *Pilgrims in Their Own Land: 500 Years of Religion in America* (Boston: Little, Brown and Company, 1984), 342; Detty, *History of the Presbyterian Church of Wysox*, 76.

[29] The First Congregational Society of Harford was organized in 1800; its 1821-22 church building is still used by the congregation. The First Congregational Church of Riceville (PA-514) was organized in 1858; its 1859 church building, constructed through the generosity of a transplanted Rhode Islander and a Connecticut native, was demolished in 1962. *Looking Back: Souvenir Book of Susquehanna County Sesquicentennial Celebration, 1810-1960* (Montrose: Susquehanna County Sesquicentennial Committee, 1960), n.p.; Annie Scott Baxter, "First Congregation Church, Riceville, Crawford County, Pennsylvania, PA-514," *HABS Report* (Washington, D.C.: Library of Congress, 1936), 1.

[30] In 1926, Methodism was the dominant denomination in Bradford, Wyoming, Tioga, Warren, Forest, and Clarion Counties, and the secondary denomination in Susquehanna, Potter, McKean, Erie, Crawford, Mercer, Venango, and Cameron Counties. As recently as 1980 Methodists remained numerous throughout the region, claiming no less than 5 percent and as much as 25 percent of the church membership in the region's counties. Roman Catholicism, however, was the most dominant faith by 1980, claiming 54 percent of the church membership in Elk County, 33 percent in Erie County, 30 percent in Jefferson County, 26 percent in Mercer and Sullivan Counties, and between 15 and 25 percent in seven other counties. Abler, et al., *Atlas of Pennsylvania*, 91, 142.

[31] Maser, *Methodism in Central Pennsylvania*, 41.

[32] *The Doctrines and Discipline of the Methodist Episcopal Church*, 21st ed. (New York: N. Bangs and T. Mason for the Methodist Episcopal Church, 1821), 158.

[33] This short excerpt from the preamble to the founders' meeting of 20 June 1815 is quoted in Ernest Ashton Smith, *Allegheny—A Century of Education: 1815-1915* (Meadville, Pa.: Allegheny College History Company, 1916), 15.

[34] The trustees named Allegheny College's first building for Reverend William Bentley, D.D., of Salem, Massachusetts. Bentley, a friend of Alden and a trustee of the college, had willed his extensive library to this new, unbuilt college. The college received an even larger bequest of

three tons of books in 1821 from Massachusetts Judge James Winthrop, a charter trustee of the college and a descendant of Massachusetts' first governor. Ernest Ashton Smith, *Allegheny*, 33-34, 43-47. Bentley Hall is illustrated in Charles Morse Stotz, *The Architectural Heritage of Early Western Pennsylvania: A Record of Building before 1860* (Pittsburgh: University of Pittsburgh, 1966), 21, 215, 218-21; Harold B. Dickson, *A Hundred Pennsylvania Buildings* (State College: Bald Eagle Press, 1954), pl. 41.

[35] In the meantime, Alden held classes at various sites: his home, the log courthouse, the county jail, and a log cabin on the outskirts of town. Smith, *Allegheny*, 49.

[36] Talbot Hamlin, *Greek Revival Architecture in the United States: Being an Account of Important Trends in American Architecture and American Life Prior to the War between the States* (New York: Oxford University Pres,, 1944), 173-74.

[37] For a thorough discussion of the four phases of American neoclassicism, including the Greek Revival, see William H. Pierson, Jr., *American Buildings and Their Architects: The Colonial and Neoclassical Styles* (Garden City: Doubleday & Company, 1970), 205-460.

[38] In the spring of 1830, Weiderich and his wife sailed from Havre, France, with three other families, including two of his sisters and their husbands. They arrived in Philadelphia in June of that year. Many Germans settled in the valley between Coudersport and Roulette. Beebe, *History of Potter County*, 86-87.

[39] Asher Benjamin's genius (and contribution to nineteenth-century architecture) was his recognition of the distinctiveness of American architecture and design, and writing books to meet the distinctive needs of American builders. A balanced assessment and demonstration of Benjamin's contributions, including an annotated bibliography of writings about him, is Jack Quinan, "Asher Benjamin and American Architecture," *Journal of the Society of Architectural Historians* 38 (October 1979): 244-56. Asher Benjamin illustrated the Greek orders in *The American Builder's Companion*, 6th ed. (Boston: R.P. & C. Williams, 1827; reprint ed., New York: Dover Publications, 1969). He later illustrated Greek Revival frontispieces and profiles of Greek Revival trim in three other books: *The Practical House Carpenter*, which went through fourteen printings between 1830 and 1857; *Practice of Architecture*, which had eight printings between 1833 and 1851; and *The Builder's Guide or, Complete System of Architecture* (1839), which was renamed *The Architect or, Complete Builder's Guide* in the third edition and reissued four more times to 1854. The last work illustrates more lavish Greek Revival designs, including churches. Hamlin, *Greek Revival Architecture*, 95, 163-64 (n. 8-11), 169-70.

[40] Hamlin, *Greek Revival Architecture*, 163-79, 258.

[41] Hamlin, *Greek Revival Architecture*, 165. Lafever's three best-known books are *The Young Builder's General Instructor* (1829), *The Modern Builder's Guide* (1833), and *The Beauties of Modern Architecture* (1835). His sensitivity and restraint of design progressed in each work. Hamlin, *Greek Revival Architecture*, 165. The standard study of his career is Jacob Landy, *The Architecture of Minard Lafever* (New York: Columbia University Press, 1970).

[42] Talbot Hamlin, *Greek Revival Architecture*, 266-70.

[43] Robert Currin, president, Potter County Historical Society, to Richard J. Webster, 6 September 1989; Beebe, *History of Potter County*, 51, 78, 81-84, 97-98.

[44] The building contract is quoted in full in Stotz, *Architectural Heritage of Early Western Pennsylvania*, 21-22. The contract directs the carpenters "to enclose a certain frame put up for a dwelling house in the village of Coudersport and known by the name of the Dike frame." Beebe, in *History of Potter County*, 81, notes that "it is a matter of dispute" whether Ives or his son-in-law, N. L. Dike, was responsible for building the house.

[45] Stotz, *Architectural Heritage of Early Western Pennsylvania*, 22. Although Timothy Ives and Almon Woodcock in 1834 received the contract to build the Potter County courthouse, there is no indication that the men served as more than contractors. The courthouse was a very simple two-story rubble gable-roof building with no architectural embellishments. A circa 1867 photograph of the 1834 and 1852 courthouses serves as the frontispiece in Beebe, *History of Potter County*. The Ives House is discussed in Dickson, *A Hundred Pennsylvania Buildings*, pl. 51.

[46] The Ives House was bequeathed to the Potter County school board in 1959, which within a year sold it to Mr. and Mrs. Kenneth Wingo. They disassembled the house with the intention of rebuilding it in Brookland, north of Coudersport, but that has yet to be done. It probably is no coincidence that Coudersport and Harford are nearly equidistant from the New York state line (Coudersport approximately 17 miles, Harford approximately 15 miles). Joab Tayler, prominent farmer and deacon of the Harford Congregational Church, built the Taylor-Jones House; Henry M. Jones, farmer and storekeeper, acquired it in 1865. Robert Currin, president, Potter County Historical Society, to Richard J. Webster, 6 September 1989; Rhamanthus M. Stocker, Centennial History of Susquehanna County, Pennsylvania (Philadelphia: R.T. Peck & Co., 1887), 716, 722; Harford Township, Susquehanna County, Pennsylvania, 1790-1940 (Montrose, Pa.: Harford Sesquicentennial Committee, 1940), 90.

[47] Hamlin, *Greek Revival Architecture*, 269.

[48] In the early 1840s, William B. Foster Jr., Stephen's older brother, was state engineer of Public Works, and was stationed at Towanda, supervising construction of the North Branch Canal. He brought Stephen to the area to attend Towanda Academy in spring 1840 and then the more prestigious Athens Academy for the 1840-41 academic year. It was while attending Athens Academy that Foster wrote his first composition, *The Tioga Waltz*. Wansey was "an Englishman of culture and considerable landed estate." He apparently rented a room in the house at 100 River Street or possibly the whole house to William Foster (and his younger brother). In 1850 Wansey sold the house to Ephraim W. Baird, a prominent local attorney, and moved to Genesee Falls, New York. Although from the street the house appears to have a flat roof, it in fact has a low hipped roof. There is no agreement that Stephen Foster lived in the Wansey-Baird House; some Towandians claim that he boarded at a house still standing at Poplar Street and Western Avenue or one nearby at 227 Poplar Street. There is no dispute, however, about the former Towanda Academy, which is now a residence at the northeast corner of State and North Fourth Streets. Jessie Welles Murray, "Stephen C. Foster's School Days at the Athens Academy," *Foster Hall Bulletin* no. 11 (February 1935): 1-6; Deed books 7-347,

32-318, Recorder of Deeds, Bradford County Courthouse, Towanda, Pa.; Heverly, *History of the Towandas*, 147, 158, 304, 313, 335, 340; Carl Carmer, *The Susquehanna* (New York: Rinehart & Co., 1955), 380-84; Interview with Thomas L. Jennings, Wysox, Pa., 27 September 1989.

[49] Hamlin, *Greek Revival Architecture*, 275-76.

[50] The Erie Railroad built sprawling rail shops and a combined passenger station and hotel in Susquehanna, Susquehanna County, approximately four miles east of its famous Starucca Viaduct, which was completed in 1848. The Erie, however, did little more than dip into Susquehanna County to cross the viaduct and then returned to New York state. Delaware, Lackawanna, and Western Railroad, on the other hand, ran the county's north-south width, opening the stretch between Great Bend and Scranton in 1851. Jules I. Bogen, *The Anthracite Railroads: A Study in American Railroad Enterprise* (New York: Ronald Press Company, 1927), 82-83; William H. Shank, *The Amazing Pennsylvania Canals*, 3rd ed. (York, Pa.: American Canal and Transportation Center, 1977), 57-58; Edward Hungerford, *Men of Erie: A Story of Human Effort* (New York: Random House, 1946), 103-4.

[51] It took twenty years, 1836-1856, to build the last stage of the North Branch Canal between Pittston, Luzerne County, and the New York state line. When finished, it stretched 167 miles along the Susquehanna River from Northumberland to near Elmira, New York, where it connected with a private junction canal that tied it to the New York system. Shank, *The Amazing Pennsylvania Canals*, 51-52; Bogen, *The Anthracite Railroads*, 118.

[52] In such distant places as Potter County, the barter system was not uncommon before the Civil War, when often there was no cash in the county's treasury. Stotz, *Architectural Heritage of Early Western Pennsylvania*, 22; Beebe, *History of Potter County*, 78, 95.

[53] In view of the Appalachian Plateau's early history, it should be no surprise that Connecticut entrepreneurs stood in the vanguard of Pennsylvania's oil exploration. The well that Edwin L. Drake, a Connecticut native, drilled in Venango County near Titusville was financed by the Pennsylvania Rock Oil Company of Connecticut, which in 1858 formed the Seneca Oil Company of Connecticut to raise the oil. Harold F. Williamson and Arnold R. Daum, *The American Petroleum Industry: The Age of Illumination, 1859-1899* (Evanston: Northwestern University Press, 1959), 68-85.

[54] In the early 1860s it cost more to ship oil from Oil Creek to the rail depot than from the depot to New York City. Spilled oil made the dirt roads a slippery, caustic muck that burned the horses so badly that they had no hair below their necks. Klein and Hoogenboom, *A History of Pennsylvania*, 276.

[55] The second stage of the water route was the Allegheny River, navigated by steamboats towing barges. They could operate, however, only when water levels were normal. Nevertheless, boats gathering around Oil City's twenty-one landings in 1864 clogged the town's riverfront. Charles D. Martens, *The Oil City: A History* (Oil City, Pa.: First Seneca Bank and Trust Company, 1971), 33; Williamson and Daum, *The American Petroleum Industry*, 165-69.

[56] Williamson and Daum, *The American Petroleum Industry*, 170-88, 194-201.

[57] Sylvester K. Stevens, *Pennsylvania: Birthplace of a Nation* (New York: Random House, 1964), 216.

[58] The oil company's finances were so limited that they hired Drake in part because, as a former railroad conductor, he could get a rail pass to Titusville. When Drake struck oil in August 1859, the financially strapped company had already mailed him directions to abandon the venture, but he had not received them. Drake was overwhelmed by events following his initial strike. He left the oil region in 1863 to become a New York oil stockbroker, but by 1866 he had lost everything. He spent his last years in poverty and obscurity in South Bethlehem, Pennsylvania, surviving on a small state pension that friends had arranged. He died an invalid in 1880. Paul H. Giddens, *The Birth of the Oil Industry* (New York: Macmillan Company, 1938), 49, 58-59, 66-68.

[59] A newspaper at the time, 1865, referred to a sixty-person capacity hotel as a balloon, which increases the suspicion that it was a balloon-frame building. William Culp Darrah, *Pithole, the Vanished City: A Story of the Early Days of the Petroleum Industry* (Gettysburg: By the author, 1972), 32.

[60] Sylvester K. Stevens, *Pennsylvania: Titan of Industry* (New York: Lewis Historical Publishing Company, 1948), 143, 167, 169, 215, 217; George A. Scott, "Clearfield County: Land of Natural Resources," *Pennsylvania Heritage* 7 (Winter 1981): 4-7; Robert W. Unger, "Tioga County: A Last Frontier," *Pennsylvania Heritage* 7 (Summer 1981): 4-6; Terry L. Hess, "McKean County: Where Gold Is Green," *Pennsylvania Heritage* 9 (Winter 1983): 4-6; Carolee K. Michener and Michael J. O'Malley III, "The Last Frontier: Venango County," *Pennsylvania Heritage* 10 (Spring 1984): 34-37; Samuel A. Farmerie, "The Call of the Clarion," *Pennsylvania Heritage* 11 (Spring 1985): 33-37; Alex Badenoch, "Forest County: What Better Name?" *Pennsylvania Heritage* 12 (Summer 1986): 34-37; Michael J. O'Malley III, "Cameron County: Where Legends Are Legion," *Pennsylvania Heritage* 13 (Summer 1987): 31; Robert K. Currin, "Potter County: At the Edge of the Forest," *Pennsylvania Heritage* 15 (Spring 1989): 24-28.

Catalog

Bradford County

Athens Vicinity (Athens Township)

Franklin, Colonel John, House (PA-226), off Orange Hill Rd., just E of Riverside Dr. (Athens-Sheshequin Rd.), approx. 1 mi. SE of Athens. Frame with clapboarding, L-shaped, three-bay front, two-and-a-half stories with basement, gable roof, corner pilasters, plain entablature, pedimented entrance porch on W (front) elevation, door with side lights, one-and-a-half-story frame ell to E; central hall plan. Built 1796-98; burned ca. 1940; gravesite (located near homesite) bought by relative of Franklin's 1953 and restored as Colonel Franklin Memorial Park 1959, memorial road-marker on Riverside Dr. Franklin was an early settler and military and civil leader of the area. 3 ext. photos (1937), 1 photo of Franklin's grave (1937), 1 photo of Franklin's portrait (1937); 9 data pages (1937). LC code: PA,8-____,1.

Terrytown (Terry Township)

Log Cabin. See Terry, Captain Jonathan, Cabin.

Terry, Captain Jonathan, Cabin (Terry-Welles Cabin) (PA-227), E side of State Rte. 187, .6 mi. N of Terrytown Center, across Susquehanna River from Wyalusing. Log, 36'-1" (three-bay front) x 26' (two bays), two-and-a-half stories with basement, gable roof, large central chimney. Built 1806; shed added on rear; restored 1929, 1964. Captain Jonathan Terry was the first permanent settler in township. 15 sheets (1936, including plans, elevations, section, details); 5 ext. photos (1936), 2 int. photos (1936); 5 data pages (1936). LC code: PA,8-TERTO,1.

Terry-Welles Cabin. See Terry, Captain Jonathan, Cabin.

Welles Cabin. See Terry, Captain Jonathan, Cabin.

Wysox (Wysox Township)

Old Brick Church. See Wysox Presbyterian Church.

Wysox Presbyterian Church (Old Brick Church) (PA-222), N side of State Rte. 187, .3 mi. NE of intersection with U.S. Rte. 6. Brick, 42'-4" (three-bay front) x 54'-4", one-story church with balconies on three sides with two-story vestry on SE elevation (schoolroom on second story), gable roof, frame tower with octagonal belfry and dome over vestry, denticulated cornice, double doors with fanlight on SE (front) elevation, large arched windows set in recessed brick arches, Federal details; interior coved ceiling. Built 1828; attributed to Joseph Marie Piollet; one-story brick addition on NW 1960. Built as a Congregational Church 1828, became Presbyterian 1830. 17 sheets (1937, including plans, elevations, sections, details); 3 ext. photos (1936), 5 int. photos (1936); 5 data pages (1937). LC code: PA,8-WYSO,1.

Crawford County

Conneautville Borough

Conneautville Baptist Church. See Trinity Protestant Episcopal Church.

Trinity Protestant Episcopal Church (Conneautville Baptist Church) (PA-609), 1301 Water St. Frame with board and batten siding, 28'-3" (three-bay front) x 44'-2" (four bays) with rear choir and sanctuary wing 27'-9" x 14'-3", one story with basement, gable roofs with cross on church and wing, bracketed cornice, projecting pedimented entrance bay, pointed-arch windows and doors with label moldings, Carpenter Gothic details. Built 1870; P.B. Carpenter, architect and builder; became Baptist Church 1954. 8 sheets (1961, including plan, elevations, sections, details). LC code: PA,20-CONT.V,1.

East Titusville Vicinity (Oil Creek Township)

Chase House (PA-1237), N side of Old Enterprise-Titusville Rd., .1 mi. N of bridge over Pine Creek, .5 mi. NE of East Titusville. Frame with clapboarding, five by two bays, two stories, gable roof with pedimented gable ends, corbeled inside end chimneys, denticulated cornice, two-story pilasters on facade, wide entablature, entrance with fanlight and side lights, porches on front and rear elevations, Greek Revival details. Built mid-nineteenth century. 1 ext. photo (1937). LC code: PA,20-TITVE.V,1.

Hydetown Borough

Ridgway, Charles, House (PA-5130), W side of Main St., S of Thompson Run Bridge; originally located near Austin Bridge over Oil Creek on road to Gresham. Frame with clapboarding, six-bay front, two-and-a-half stories, gable roof, cornice returns and plain entablature, corner pilasters, two doors flanked by pilasters on N (front) elevation, porch across front (removed ca. 1970), Greek Revival details, one and two-story wings to S. Built 1830; moved late nineteenth century. 3 ext. photos (1937). LC code: PA,20-HYD,21.

Ridgway, Titus, House (PA-543), E side of Main St., .3 mi. S of Thompson Run Bridge. Frame with clapboarding, two-story main block (three-bay front) with one-story side wing to E, gable roofs, cornice returns and plain entablature, corner pilasters, door with transom and side lights framed by pilasters and entablature on S (front) elevation, recessed porch on S wing, Greek Revival style; side hall plan. Built ca. 1850. 1 ext. photo (1936). LC code: PA,20-HYD,1.

Meadville

Allegheny College, Bentley Hall (PA-525), on Allegheny College campus (Park Ave. and Baldwin St.). Brick, three-story main block approx. 60' (five-bay front) x 45' with symmetrical two-story side wings approx. 30' (three-bay fronts) x 40', hip roofs, octagonal cupola, denticulated cornice, pedimented central bay with entrance flanked by fanlight and side lights and Palladian windows above, brick pilasters, tetrastyle Doric porticos across wings, flat stone lintels with keystones, Federal and Greek Revival details. Built 1820-24; Reverend Timothy Alden (founder and first president of college), architect; few exterior changes, interior alterations. Bentley Hall was the original building of Allegheny College, housed classrooms, extensive library, and living quarters; now administrative offices. 1 ext. photo (1937). LC code: PA,20-MEDVI,2A. NR.

Baldwin, Henty, House. See Baldwin-Reynolds House.

Baldwin-Reynolds House (Henry Baldwin House) (PA-548), 639 Terrace St. Museum operated by Crawford County Historical Society. Brick, five-bay front, two-and-a-half stories with basement, mansard roof with segmental dormers, two-story porch surrounds most of structure. Built 1840-43. Henry Baldwin was a U.S. Congressman and Supreme Court Justice. William Reynolds, Baldwin's nephew, served as first mayor of Meadville. 1 ext. photo (1937). LC code: PA,20-MEDVI,3. NR.

Independent Congregational Church (PA-524), 346 Chestnut St. Brick, approx. 40' (three-bay front) x 65' (four bays), one story with raised basement, gable roof, modillioned cornice, pedimented Doric portico and brick pilasters on N (front) elevation, Greek Revival style; balcony with Doric columns. Built 1830; General G.W. Cullum, architect, he also designed Fort Sumter; presently Unitarian Church. 1 ext. photo (1936). LC code: PA,20-MEDVI,1. NR.

Reynolds House. See Baldwin-Reynolds House.

Meadville Vicinity

Sterrett Cabin. See Erie County, Sterrettania (McKean Township), Sterrett Cabin, original location.

Meadville Vicinity (Cosewago Township)

Thomas, Albert, Summer House (PA-563), E side of State Rte. 98. Frame with clapboarding, two-story main block (three-bay front) with one-and-a-half-story side wing to N (three bays), gable roofs with gabled dormers, door flanked by side lights and pilasters with entablature on W (front) elevation, porch on wing; Greek Revival style; side hall plan. Built early nineteenth century. 1 ext. photo (1937). LC code: PA,20-MEDVI.V,1.

New Richmond Vicinity (Richmond Township)

Flint House (PA-576), N side of State Rte. 77, .3 mi. E of State Rte. 408. Frame with clapboarding, four irregular bays by two bays, one-and-a-half stories, gable roof, cornice returns and plain entablature, corner pilasters, pilasters and entablature frame front door; Greek Revival style. Built early nineteenth century; garage added to side (removed after 1937); covered with aluminum siding after 1937. 1 ext. photo (1937). LC code: PA,20-NEWRI.V,1.

Riceville (Bloomfield Township)

Bruner House. See Westgate-Bruner House.

First Congregational Church (PA-514), S side of State Rte. 77, .7 mi. W of State Rte. 8. Frame with clapboarding, 38' (three-bay front) x 50'-4" (three bays), one story with basement, gable roof with pedimented gable end, cupola with Doric columns over entrance, Ionic pilasters on N (front) elevation, plain entablature, double doors framed by Ionic pilasters with wide entablature on N elevation, slightly pedimented lintels, Greek Revival style; cove ceiling. Built 1859; Dowd of Meadville, architect; remodeled 1875 (windows changed); demolished 1962. 4 sheets (1936, including plans, elevations, section, details); 2 ext. photos (1936); 3 data pages (1936). LC code: PA,20-RICVI,1.

Grist Mill (PA-532), N side of Oil Creek, N of State Rte. 77, approx. .5 mi. W of State Rte. 8. Frame with clapboarding, three by three bays, two-and-a-half stories, sloping site exposes basement on S elevation (towards creek), gable roof with gabled monitor, cornice returns and plain entablature, covered platform on front elevation; Greek Revival details. Built 1857; Jesse Smith and J. W. Gray, builders; demolished ca. 1950. 2 ext. photos (1936); 2 data pages (1936). LC code: PA,20-RICVI,4.

Hendryx House (PA-520), N side of State Rte. 77, .4 mi. W of State Rte. 8. Frame with clapboarding, one-and-a-half-story main block 16'-7" (three-bay front) x 24'-8" with one-story side wing to E 16'-4" (three-bay front) x 16'-4", gable roofs, cornice returns and plain entablature, corner pilasters with anthemion motifs, pilasters and entablature with anthemion motifs surround S (front) entrance, Greek Revival style. Built ca. 1852 (possibly earlier); Dowd of Meadville, architect; kitchen wing with porch supported by pierced wooden posts added to N; woodshed and enclosed stair well added to kitchen ell. 11 sheets (1936, including plans, elevations, details); 3 ext. photos (1936); 3 data pages (1936). LC code: PA,20-RICVI,3.

Westgate-Bruner House (PA-519), S side of State Rte. 77, .4 mi. W of State Rte. 8. Frame with clapboarding, 40'-6" (two three-bay fronts) x 22'-4", one-and-a-half stories, gable roof, two doors framed by pilasters and entablature on N (front) elevation, one-story rear kitchen wing with meathouse and porches (pump on S porch), covered passageway connects kitchen to woodshed, Greek Revival details. Built ca. 1839 (before 1847); Benjamin Boles Westgate, builder; demolished ca. 1970. 3 sheets (1936, including plan, elevations, details); 2 ext. photos (1936), 1 int. photo (1936); 3 data pages (1936). LC code: PA,20-RICVI,2.

Saegertown Borough

Saeger, Edward, House (PA-523), SE corner of Main St. (U.S. Rte. 6-19) and Erie St. Frame with clapboarding, three by four bays, two-and-a-half stories, gable roof with pedimented gable end, two-story porch on front elevation extends to recessed second story porch on side elevations, Greek Revival details. Built 1843. 1 ext. photo (1936). LC code: PA,20-SAGTO,1. NR.

Titusville

Drake, Edwin, House (PA-5108), address not determined. Frame with wooden shingles, five-bay front, two stories, gable roof, door with transom and side lights flanked by pilasters on E (front) elevation, porch on E elevation; Greek Revival details. Built ca. 1858. Drake was a pioneer petroleum industrialist; he drilled the first commercial oil well in 1859. 1 ext. photo (1937). LC code: PA,20-TITVI,1.

Titusville Vicinity (Oil Creek Township)

Kelly, William, House (PA-5115), Perry St., just N of city limits. Frame with clapboarding, six by two bays, two stories, gable roof, cornice returns, pent roof across front elevation projects to form hoods over two entrances, one-story wing to side, Greek Revival details. Built mid-nineteenth century William Kelly was a teacher and early settler of the area. 1 ext. photo (1937). LC code: PA,20-TITVI,2.

Townville Borough

Stevens House (PA-5126), address not determined. Frame with clapboarding, one-and-a-half-story main block (three-bay front) with symmetrical one-story side wings (two-bay fronts), gable roofs, cornice returns on main block, pedimented gable ends on wings, plain entablature, porches with square columns on wings, Greek Revival style. Built ca. 1846. 2 ext. photos (1936). LC code: PA,20-TOWNVI,1.

Woodcock Borough

McPheeter House (PA-546), NE corner of State Rte. 86 and Center St. Brick, five by two bays, two-and-a-half stories with basement, gable roof, cornice returns, door with transom and side lights flanked by pilasters, flat stone lintels over openings, clapboarded wing to rear, Federal details. Built ca. 1828. 1 ext. photo (1937). LC code: PA,20-WOOD,1.

Woodcock Methodist Church (PA-5135), on Cherry Ln., one block E of State Rte. 86 and N of Center St. Brick, one bay (presently central entrance, originally three doors) by three bays, one story, gable roof, cupola over entrance, pointed-arch entrance with fanlight on E (front) elevation (later addition), pointed-arch windows (later addition). Built 1839; original porch on E elevation removed. Congregation organized 1809. 1 ext. photo (1937). LC code: PA,20-WOOD,2.

Erie County

Corry Borough

Hatch School (Wright School) (PA-515), NE corner of Wright and E. Congress Sts. Brick, rectangular with projecting S (front) entrance pavilion and recessed side entrances, nine-bay front, two-and-a-half stories, hip roof with cross-gable forming pediments over entrances, elaborate cornice, decorative corner piers, arched windows and arcaded front entrance. Built 1870; A. V. Powell and Leo Helme, architects; remodeled 1936, changed to one story with flat roof; now wing of Wright Elementary School. 4 ext photos (1936, before remodeling); 3 data pages (1936). LC code: PA,25-COR,1.

Wright School. See Hatch School.

Edinboro Borough

First Constitutional Presbyterian Church (PA-5114), location not provided. Frame with clapboarding, three-bay front, one story, gable roof with pedimented gable end, square belfry with hexagonal spire, pilasters on facade, wide entablature, Greek Revival style. Built mid-nineteenth century; one-story clapboarded wing with pedimented entrance added to W elevation; demolished. 1 ext. photo (1936). LC code: PA,25-EDBO,2.

Hencke House. See Vunk, Francis C., House.

Vunk, Francis C., House (Hencke House) (PA-5113), N side of Market St. (U.S. Rte 6N), W of Edinboro Rd. (State Rte. 99). Frame with clapboarding, three by three bays, two-and-a-half stories, gable roof with gable end over entrance, cornice returns, wide entablature, recessed entrance framed with pilasters and entablature on S (front) elevation, door with transom and side lights, Greek Revival style. Built mid-nineteenth century; two one-story additions; poor condition. 2 ext. photos (1936, 1937). LC code: PA,25-EDBO,1.

Erie

Arbuckle House (Carey-Murphy House) (PA-311), 140 E. Fifth St. Brick, approx. 32' x 42', two-and-a-half stories, hip roof with gabled dormers, corner turret, porch across front elevation, Queen Anne style. Built 1897; frame addition; demolished. 12 ext. photos (1980), 1 photo of carriage house (1980); 3 data pages (1982). LC code: PA,25-ERI,10.

Blass House. See Cunningham-Blass House.

Carey-Murphy House. See Arbuckle House.

Colt, George P., House (PA-5359), 628 1/2 E. Sixth St. Brick, rectangular with projecting bays and tower, approx. 70' x 35', two-and-a-half stories with four-story tower, mansard roof with gabled dormers, bracketed cornice, windows with stone moldings and brick arches with keystones, carved wooden panels above windows, Second Empire style. Built 1870-72; converted to rental housing 1908 and surrounded by housing development since 1917; vacant and in poor condition. Built for prominent Erie banker, George P. Colt; Colt family early settlers of Erie. 7 ext. photos (1987), 1 int. photo (1987), 2 copy photos of site plans from 1900 and 1917 atlas; 7 data pages including site plan (1987). LC code: PA,25-ERI,14.

Crittenton, Florence, Home. See Sterrett, James M., House.

Cunningham-Blass House (Hughes Log House) (PA-5117), 136 E. Third St. Log with clapboarding, four-bay front, two stories, gable roof, transom over S entrance. Probably built 1806; log covered with aluminum siding. Possibly the oldest extant house in central Erie; family of Hugh Cunningham lived here for over sixty years; by tradition house was also an early post office. 1 ext. photo (1936). LC code: PA,25-ERI,7.

Dickson's Tavern (Perry Memorial Building) (PA-52), 201 French St. Museum owned by city. Frame with clapboarding, 28'-5" (three-bay front) x 36'-4" (four bays), two stories with exposed basement, gable roof with pedimented gable end over entrance; series of tunnels and rooms under basement (reputedly part of the Underground Railroad during pre-Civil War times); two-story clapboarded wing on S elevation. Built ca. 1812; wing early addition; porch added on E elevation; acquired by city 1924, several later wings removed and tavern restored by city beginning in 1963. Built by innkeeper John Dickson; designated by city as a memorial to Commodore Perry. 13 sheets (1935, including plans, elevations, details); 4 ext. photos (1934, 1936), 7 int. photos (1934, 1936); 7 data pages (1936, 1938). LC code: PA,25-ERI,l.

Empire Store (Gage Hotel) (PA-5142), 50l-05 State St. Brick, approx. 56' (nine-bay front) x 70', four stories, flat roof with parapet, bracketed cornice, pedimented entrance and window lintels. Built as two separate structures 1848-49 and 1852-53; joined late 1860s; demolished. 14 ext. photos (1980), 14 int. photos (1980), 2 copy photos (ca. 1850, 1876); 9 data pages (1980). LC code: PA,25-ERI,9.

Erie Club Building. See Reed Mansion.

Erie County Historical Society. See United States Bank of Pennsylvania, Erie Branch, Cashier's House.

Frank's Hotel. See Reed, C.M., Block.

Gage Hotel. See Empire Store.

Hughes Log House. See Cunningham-Blass House.

Land Lighthouse (PA-517), NW side of Front St., between Dunn Blvd. and Lighthouse St., in Land Lighthouse Park. Coursed ashlar (Berea sandstone) lined with brick, tapering cylinder (approx. 19' at base, 14' at top), 49'-4" high topped with cornice, cast-iron interior steps; wing on S elevation, coursed ashlar, 16'-3" x 8'-9", one story, gable roof, central door with date stone above, connected to tower by double steel doors. Built 1867 (date stone); owned by city and restored. Site of the first lighthouse to be built on the Great Lakes by the government in 1818, the second on this site was built in 1858, the present light operated until 1886. 2 sheets (1936, including plan, elevation, sections, details); 3 ext. photos (1936); 4 data pages (1936). LC code: PA,25-ERI,5. NR.

Murphy House. See Arbuckle House.

Old Customhouse. See United States Bank of Pennsylvania, Erie Branch.

Perry Memorial Building. See Dickson's Tavern.

Presque Isle Lighthouse (PA-624), lake side of Peninsula Dr., 1.3 mi. NE of intersection with Fisher Dr., in Presque

Isle State Park. Lighthouse: brick, one-story square base (11'-10") with five-story slightly setback square tower (10'-l0") topped with decagonal lantern surrounded by railing, arched windows at each level (paired windows around third level watchroom). Lightkeeper's house: connected to light tower, brick, rectangular with projecting central bay, 32' (four-bay front) x 28', kitchen wing to W, one-and-a-half stories with one-story wing, gable roofs with cross gable over projecting central bay, entrance porch on E elevation. Built 1872 (date stone). 6 sheets (1962, including plans, elevations, section). LC code: PA,25-ERI,8. NR.

Reed, C.M., Block (Frank's Hotel) (PA-1957), 22-26 E. Fifth St. Brick, approx. 120' (eighteen-bay front) x 60' (nine bays), two stories, flat roof, interesting brick patterns. Built 1860; John Hill, architect; first floor substantially altered ca. 1930; adapted as hotel 1940; demolished. 4 ext. photos (n.d.); 3 data pages (1982). LC code: PA,25-ERI,13.

Reed Mansion (Erie Club Building) (PA-57), 524 Peach St. Stuccoed brick (stucco later removed), rectangular with numerous bays and wings, 68'-5" (seven-bay front) x 71'-10", two-and-a-half stories with elevated basement, flat roof with central temple-like monitor (46' x 22'), pedimented Ionic portico across middle three bays of E (front) elevation, pilasters with wide entablature, denticulated cornice, Greek Revival style; elaborate interior with Greek Revival, Gothic Revival and Rococo rooms. Built 1849; E. F. Barger, architect; small additions on W elevation. Built by General Charles M. Reed, a prominent Erie businessman; purchased by Erie Club 1904. 3 ext. photos (1935), 14 int. photos (1935); 3 data pages (1936). LC code: PA,25-ERI,4. NR.

Sterrett, James M., House (Florence Crittenton Home) (PA-178), 501-03 Holland St. Brick, 42' (five-bay front) x 64', two-and-a-half stories with basement, cross gable roof, bracketed cornice, hood over entrance, Italianate details. Built 1842; David Kennedy, architect; Italianate details added 1850s; addition to rear 1920s; demolished. 9 ext photos (1982), 8 int. photos (1982); 4 data pages (1982). LC code: PA,25-ERI,11.

Teel-Whitman House (Benjamin Whitman House) (PA-542), SW corner of Ninth and Peach Sts. Frame with clapboarding, L-shaped, five by two bays, two stories, gable roof, bracketed cornice, low pedimented lintels, two-story clapboarded wing with oriel window on rear elevation. Built mid-nineteenth century; demolished. 1 ext. photo (1936). LC code: PA,25-ERI,6.

Tracy Building (PA-5154), 523-27 French St. Brick, nine-bay front, three-and-a-half stories, mansard roof with decorative slate, cast-iron store fronts, corbeled brick cornice. Built 1872; demolished. 12 ext. photos (1981), 8 int. photos (1981); 5 data pages (1981, 1982). LC code: PA,25-ERI,12.

United States Bank of Pennsylvania, Erie Branch (Old Customhouse) (PA-53), 409 State St. Museum administered by the Pennsylvania Historical and Museum Commission. Marble (W facade) and stuccoed brick (scored on E elevation), marble secured by hand-forged dowels, 49'-1" (five-bay front) x 70'-2", two stories on podium with marble steps, gable roof, pedimented hexastyle Doric portico with full entablature on W (front) elevation, Greek Revival style. Built 1839 (date stone); William Kelly, architect. Built for Erie Branch of the United States Bank of Pennsylvania; then Customhouse 1849-88; later home of the Strong Vincent Post of the Grand Army of the Republic until 1932; Erie County Historical Society 1923-74; restored 1969-74; museum since 1975. One of the best examples of Greek Revival architecture in the state. 13 sheets (1935, including plans, elevations, details); 1 ext. photo (1935), 4 int. photos (1935, 1936); 3 data pages (1936). LC code: PA,25-ERI,2. NR.

United States Bank of Pennsylvania, Erie Branch, Cashier's House (Erie County Historical Society, Woodruff House) (PA-56), 417 State St. Museum administered by the Pennsylvania Historical and Museum Commission. Stuccoed brick, irregular L-shaped, 30'-2" (three-bay front) x 125'-5", three stories with basement, flat roof with parapet, plain entablature, recessed door framed by pilasters and wide entablature on W (front) elevation, Greek Revival style; side hall plan, ornate Egyptian Revival interior. Built 1837-39; William Kelly, architect; one-story addition on N elevation of ell (later removed). Built by Erie Branch of the United States Bank of Pennsylvania (PA-53) as a residence for the cashier of the bank; used at various time for school, residence, and commercial purposes; last occupant was Erie Drug Company; acquired by state 1963; restored 1969-70 and 1973-74; Erie County Historical Society since 1974. Unusual combination of Greek and Egyptian Revival styles. 6 sheets (1935, including plans, elevation, sections, details); 1 ext. photo (1934); 3 data pages (1936). LC code: PA,25-ERI,3. NR.

Whitman, Benjamin, House. See Teel-Whitman House.

Woodruff House. See United States Bank of Pennsylvania, Erie Branch, Cashier's House.

Erie Vicinity (Waterford Township)

Strong, Levi, House (PA-559), E side of U.S. Rte. 19 (Perry Hwy.), S of State Rte. 86. Frame with clapboarding, three-bay center section with symmetrical side wings (two bays each), two-story center section, one-story wings, gable roof with gable end over facade, cornice returns, wide entablature, corner pilasters, recessed door with side lights framed by pilasters and entablature on W (front) elevation, Greek Revival style; side hall plan. Built mid-nineteenth century. 1 ext. photo (1936). LC code: PA,25-ERI.V,l.

Girard Borough

Hutchinson House (PA-59), 155 E. Main St., NW corner of E. Main St. and Penn Ave. Brick, L-shaped, 44'-2" (five-bay front) x 52'-11", two-and-a-half stories, gable roof with parapets at ends, modillioned cornice, elaborate central entrance with semielliptical fanlight and side lights flanked by pilasters on S (front) elevation, stone lintels, Federal style; central hall plan. Built ca. 1830 by Judge Myron Hutchinson; rear ell enlarged; porch added on ell. 7 sheets (1936, including plans, elevations, details); 2 ext. photos (1935), 1 int. photo (1935); 3 data pages (1936). LC code: PA,25-GIRA,l.

Girard Vicinity (Girard Township)

Blair Cabin (PA-510), SE side of S. Creek Rd. (Blair Rd.), NE of State Rd., approx. 3.5 mi. SE of Girard. Squared logs, 26'-8" x 20'-5", one-and-a-half stories, gable roof, one-story frame wing on S elevation. Built ca. 1818; probably built by James Blair, early settler of area; ruinous 1936; very little remains. One of the oldest log houses in Erie County. 2 sheets (1936, including plan, elevations, section, details); 3 ext. photos (1936), 1 int. photo (1936); 3 data pages (1936). LC code: PA,25-GIRA,2.

Thompson, Denman, House (PA-58), NW side of S. Creek Rd. (Blair Rd.), near intersection with Orr Rd., approx. 3.5 mi. SE of Girard. Frame with clapboarding, 21'-6" (three-bay front) x 16'-7", one-and-a-half stories, gable roof; one room. Built ca. 1832; probably built by Capt. Rufus Thompson; front section of house moved approx 50' NW of original location by Lyman Luther Foster ca. 1864 when he built larger front section on original kitchen wing; poor condition 1936; demolished. Birthplace of Denman Thompson, successful actor and playwright. 1 sheet (1936, including plans, elevations, details); 2 ext. photos (1936); 3 data pages (1936); documentation covers original front section of house. LC code: PA,25-GIRA.V,l.

Harborcreek (Harborcreek Township)

Davidson House (PA-5110), N side of U.S. Rte. 20. Frame with clapboarding, three-bay center section with one-bay symmetrical wings, two-story center section with one-story wings, gable roof with gable end over facade on center section, hip roofs on wings, pilasters and wide entablature, three-part window with scroll above entrance, tetrastyle porch across N (front) elevation, one-story clapboarded rear ell, Greek Revival style. Built mid-nineteenth century; demolished. 1 ext. photo (1937). LC code: PA,25-HARB,l.

Dodge, John, House (PA-5121), N side of U.S. Rte. 20, W of Bartlett Rd. Brick, three by two bays, two stories, hip roof with square cupola, cornice with paired brackets, stone lintels, porch on N elevation, Italianate details. Built 1854 by Dodge family. 1 ext. photo (1937). LC code: PA,25-HARB,2.

Moorheadville (Harborcreek Township)

Backus House (PA-5120), N side of U.S. Rte. 20, just E of Moorheadville Rd. Frame with clapboarding, main section (five-bay front) with offset rear wing, two-story center section (three bays) with one-story end bays, gable roof with gable end over facade, shed roofs on end bays, wide entablature, tetrastyle porch on N (front) elevation, Greek Revival details. Built nineteenth century; altered. 1 ext. photo (1937). LC code: PA,25-MOOR,2.

Moorhead, J.Y., House (PA-51), SW corner of U.S. Rte. 20 and Moorheadville Rd. Brick, 48'-2" (five-bay front) x 38'-2", two-and-a-half stories, gable roof, paired chimneys in parapets at gable ends, denticulated cornice, recessed door with side lights on N (front) elevation, stone lintels, Federal style; central hall plan. Built ca. 1810; two-story kitchen wing (18' x 26') added to S elevation; Doric porches added on N and E elevations twentieth century. Built by James Moorhead, early settler of area; house used as tavern. One of the oldest houses in Erie County. 11 sheets (1935, including plans, elevations, details); 3 ext. photos (1934), 4 int. photos (1934); 4 data pages (1936). LC code: PA,25-MOOR,l.

North East Borough

First Baptist Church (PA-513), 43 S. Lake St. Frame with clapboarding, 35'-7" (three-bay front) x 56'-7", one story, gable roof with pedimented gable end, octagonal louvered belfry with spire, Doric pilasters and wide entablature, projecting enclosed pedimented entrance on E (front) elevation, large windows with colored leaded glass, Greek Revival style. Built 1859; two-story offset rear school wing added 1870; sanctuary added 1956. 3 sheets (1936, including plan, elevations, details); 3 ext. photos (1935, 1937), 1 int. photo (1935); 3 data pages (1936). LC code: PA,25-NORE,2.

North East Vicinity (North East Township)

Butt, A.W., Octagonal Barn (Octagonal Barn) (PA-574), 11441 East Middle Rd., approx. 1 mi. E of North East. Brick, octagonal, approx. 80' diameter, one story with exposed basement, polygonal roof with octagonal cupola, double entrance with semicircular transom, small round windows. Built 1879 by A.W. Butt (date stone). 1 ext. photo (1937). LC code: PA,25-NORE,3.

Octagonal Barn. See Butt, A.W., Octagonal Barn.

Phillips House. See Silliman-Phillips House.

Silliman-Phillips House (PA-512), 11578 Buffalo Rd. (U.S. Rte. 20), approx. 1 mi. E of North East. Brick, five by two bays, two-and-a-half stories, gable roof with wide overhang (overhang not original), tetrastyle porch across facade (not original); central hall plan. Built 1813; rear addition. Built by James Silliman, settled in area ca. 1800, to replace log cabin. One of the earliest brick houses in county outside city of Erie. 1 ext. photo (1936); 3 data pages (1936). LC code: PA,25-NORE,l.

North Springfield Vicinity (Springfield Township)

Dickson Stevenson House (PA-55), N side of State Rte. 5 (Lake Rd.), just W of township line. Frame with clapboarding, T-shaped, 41'-4" (five-bay front) x 34'-5" (two bays), rear kitchen wing 22'-4" x 34'-5" (four bays), two-and-a-half stories, one-story wing, gable roof with pedimented gable ends, wide entablature with paneled frieze and denticulated cornice, recessed entrance with semielliptical fanlight and side lights flanked by Ionic pilasters on S (front) elevation, porch on wing, Federal and Greek Revival details; central hall plan. Rear wing built 1824; main section built 1844; destroyed by fire. 9 sheets (1936, including plans, elevations, details); 3 ext. photos (1935, 1936), 2 int. photos (1935); 3 data pages (1936). LC code: PA,25-SPRIFN,l.

Stevenson House. See Dickson-Stevenson House.

Sterrettania (McKean Township)

Sterrett Cabin (PA-511), NW side of State Rte. 832 (Sterrettania Rd., Conneaut Rd.). Squared logs, 30'-9" (three irregular bays) x 26'-9", two-and-a-half stories, gable roof; three rooms on each floor. Built 1817; one-story frame wing added on E elevation 1819; later beveled siding replaced with metal siding; porch added on S elevation twentieth century; moved 1960s to S side of Ryan Rd., E of State Rte. 86, N of Meadville, Meadville Vicinity, Crawford County, restored. Built by David Sterrett on site of 1807 log cabin, first structure in Sterrettania, built by his father, Robert; remains of 1807 house were visible in basement. 8 sheets (1936, including plans, elevations, section, details); 5 int. photos (1936); 3 data pages (1936). LC code: PA,25-STER,l.

Summit (Summit Township)

Summit Stone School (PA-5122), S side of Town Hall Rd., .7 mi. E of U.S. Rte. 19 (Perry Hwy.). Coursed rubble, rectangular, one by three bays, one story, gable roof, open square bell tower with pyramidal roof. Built 1822; demolished. 1 ext. photo (1937). LC code: PA,25-SUM,1.

Union City Borough

Humphrey-Rockwell House (PA-5124), 38 E. High St. Frame with clapboarding, three-bay main section with three-bay setback side wing, two stories with basement, low hip roofs, two-story Doric portico and pilasters on main section, wide entablature, slightly pedimented lintels over windows, porch on wing, two-story frame wing on rear elevation, Greek Revival style. Built ca. 1840 by Dr. Jonas Humphrey. 1 ext. photo (1936). LC code: PA,25-UNCI,1.

Rockwell House. See Humphrey-Rockwell House.

Waterford Borough

Barton's, Dr., Office (Doctor's Office) (PA-5134), overlooking West Park. Frame with clapboarding, main block (three-bay front) with setback side wing (one bay), one story, gable roofs with pedimented gable ends, tetrastyle portico, small one-story rear wing, Greek Revival style. Built mid-nineteenth century; demolished. 1 ext. photo (1937). LC code: PA,25-WAFO,7.

Brotherton House (PA-5102), E side of Cherry St., between First and Second Sts. Frame with clapboarding, three-bay front, two stories, gable roof, central chimney, two-story side wing with porch, two-story rear ell. Built mid-nineteenth century; covered with aluminum siding. 1 ext. photo (1937). LC code: PA,25-WAFO,6.

Doctor's Office. See Barton's, Dr., Office.

Eagle Hotel (PA-521), 32 High St. Irregular coursed ashlar with quoins, L-shaped, approx. 50' (five-bay front) x 40' (four bays) with rear kitchen ell 20' x 36' (four bays), two-and-a-half stories, gable roof with dormers, stepped gable ends with paired chimneys, door with semielliptical fanlight and side lights on E (front) elevation, stone lintels with keystones over windows, wooden eagle over door (originally on a pole near the road, removed from door after 1936); central hall plan. Built 1826 (date stone); E. Evans, master builder; built for Thomas King; used as hotel until 1977 when purchased by Fort LeBoeuf Historical Society. Good example of early public house in western Pennsylvania. 1 ext. photo (1936). LC code: PA,25-WAFO,2. NR.

Judson, Amos, House (PA-522), SE corner of First and High Sts. Frame with clapboarding, L-shaped, main block (three-bay front) with two wings to one side, two stories, gable roof with pedimented gable end over entrance, denticulated cornice, Doric pilasters and wide entablature, pedimented distyle entrance porch on W (front) elevation, flat reeded lintels, Greek Revival style; one-and-a-half-story frame dining room wing (four bays) on S elevation; two-story frame kitchen wing (three bays) built on S elevation of dining wing. Original house is one-and-a-half-story frame wing built 1810 by Amos Judson; two-story main section built 1820; Judson opened one of the first stores in Waterford in the far south wing, this wing has been removed; restored by Pennsylvania Historical and Museum Commission. 1 ext. photo (1936). LC code: PA,25-WAFO,3.

Saint Peter's Episcopal Church (PA-544), NE corner of Cherry and E. Third Sts. Brick, three-bay front, one story, gable roof, projecting brick entrance tower with setback stone belfry, corner buttresses with pinnacles, tracery in belfry openings, large pointed-arch windows with leaded glass, Gothic Revival details. Built 1832; remodeled 1871-72. 1 ext. photo (1937). LC code: PA,25-WAFO,5.

Waterford Academy (Waterford High School) (PA-54), E side of Cherry St., between Third and Fourth Sts. Coursed ashlar, 50'-4" (four-bay front) x 34'-5", two-and-a-half stories, gable roof with front pediment, octagonal cupola, doorway with inset semicircular panel inscribed with academy name flanked by side lights and pilasters on W (front) elevation, Federal and Greek Revival details. Built 1822 (date in pediment); three-story brick dormitory wing added to N 1859; brick laboratory wing added to E; gymnasium added to S; 1899 academy transferred to borough and used as high school; demolished. 8 sheets (1935, including plans, elevations, details); 2 ext. photos (1935), 1 int. photo (1935); 2 data pages (1936). LC code: PA,25-WAFO,1.

Waterford High School. See Waterford Academy.

Waterford Vicinity (Waterford Township)

Waterford Covered Bridge (PA-535), on Wattsburg Rd., over LeBoeuf Creek, just W of Penn Central RR tracks, SE of Waterford. Town lattice truss bridge, coursed sandstone abutments supporting frame structure with iron tie rods, 87'-6" long (65'-6" span), 18'-8" wide, 19' high, gable roof. Built ca. 1880-1890; Richard Cross, designer. One of few extant covered bridges in western Pennsylvania. 1 sheet (1936, including elevation, section, construction details); 1 ext. photo (1936), 1 photo of construction details (1936); 3 data pages (1936). LC code: PA,25-WAFO,4. NR.

Wattsburg Borough

Bestor-Towne House (Chaffee House) (PA-590), Main St. Frame with clapboarding, six-bay front, one-and-a-half stories (small windows under portico), hip roof, Ionic pilasters and wide entablature with pierced wooden cornice, tetrastyle Ionic portico, porch on side with pierced woodwork and finials, Greek Revival style. Built mid-nineteenth century; demolished. 1 ext. photo (1936). LC code: PA,25-WATBU,1.

Chaffee House. See Bestor-Towne House.

Double, Howard, House. See Harwood, W.W., House.

Harwood, W.W., House (Howard Double House) (PA-5116), SW corner of Main St. and Jamestown Rd. Frame with clapboarding, main block (four-bay front) with symmetrical side wings (two bays each), two stories with one-story wings, gable roof on main block, hip roofs on wings project to form front porches, wide entablature. Built mid-nineteenth century; demolished. 1 ext. photo (1936). LC code: PA,25-WATBU,2.

Towne House. See Bestor-Towne House.

Jefferson County

Brockway Vicinity (Snyder Township)

Leffler, Ross, Training School Complex (PA-5361), State Rte. 1010, approx. 5 mi. NW of Brockway. Two buildings used by the Pennsylvania Game Commission as a conservation officer training school, the first of its kind in the country. School closed 1986; buildings demolished. 2 ext. photos of complex (1987); 2 data pages including site plan (1987). LC code: PA,33-BROWA.V,1.

Classroom Building (PA-5361B). Stuccoed reinforced concrete and clay tile, 49' x 24' with projecting stairwell (4' x 16'-6"), two stories, gable roof; classroom and library on first floor, dormitory above. Built 1941; designed by Clarence Weaver, chief construction engineer of Game Commission; constructed by members of the third training class; demolished. 4 ext. photos (1987), 3 int. photos (1987); 8 data pages including floor plans (1987).

Main Building (PA-5361A). Stuccoed reinforced clay tile, 45' x 54'-6", two stories, modified hipped roof, frame enclosed porches on three sides; public spaces on first floor, dormitory on second. Built 1909-10 as a hunting lodge and summer home for Pittsburgh attorney, Meredith A. Marshall, originally T-shaped with open porches on three sides and enclosed porch on rear; 1929-32 alterations to convert to school; 1935 increased space by enclosing first-floor porches and extending second-floor enclosed porch around building; demolished. 4 ext. photos (1987), 8 int. photos (1987), 1 copy photo of ext. before alterations (n.d.); 9 data pages including floor plans (1987).

McKean County

Betula Vicinity (Norwich Township)

Shattuck, Richard, Lodge (PA-5106), S side of Sackett Hollow Rd., .4 mi. E of State Rte. 46, approx. 1 mi. N of Betula. Frame with clapboarding, four-bay front, one-and-a-half stories with attic, gable roof, door framed by pilasters and plain entablature. Built ca. 1830; covered with asphalt shingles after 1936. 2 ext. photos (1936), 3 int. photos (1936). LC code: PA,42-BETU,1.

Bullis Mills Vicinity (Ceres Township)

Chevalier, Henry, House (PA-5104), E side of King's Run Rd., 3.5 mi. S of Bullis Mills Rd., 7 mi. SE of Bullis Mills. Frame with clapboarding, 33'-4" (four-bay front) x 23'-9", one-and-a-half stories, gable roof with dormer, pilasters at corners and flanking entrance on E (front) elevation, low pedimented doorway with transom on E elevation; paneled ceiling and wainscoting. Built 1836-37; demolished. 5 sheets (1936, including plans, elevations, details); 1 ext. photo (1936); 3 data pages (1936). LC code: PA,42-CER.V,1.

Ceres Vicinity

Chevalier House. See Bullis Mills Vicinity (Ceres Township), Chevalier, Henry House.

Crosby Vicinity (Norwich Township)

Marsh, Robert, House (PA-5105), E side of State Rte. 46 (Bucktail Trail), .5 mi. N of Crosby, 4.5 mi. S of Smethport. Irregular coursed ashlar, 40'-2" (four-bay front) x 28' (two bays), one-and-a-half stories, gable roof. Built 1853; wooden porch with scroll brackets added on W (front) elevation (replaced with wooden pedimented porch after 1936); frame woodshed added on E elevation. 6 sheets (1936, including plans, elevations, details); 1 ext. photo (1936); 3 data pages (1936). LC code: PA,42-CROSB.V,1.

Eldred Borough

Chrisman House (PA-551), 230 N. Main St. (State Rte. 446). Frame with clapboarding, three by two bays, two stories with basement, hip roof, central corbeled chimney, deep eaves, wooden porch with scroll brackets added across front elevation, crenelated diminutive wooden parapet on porch repeated around lower slope of roof, connected to small frame outbuilding. Built ca. 1840; outbuilding demolished after 1936; ca. 1950s house enlarged (more than doubled in size) and substantially altered (covered with aluminum siding and form stone), original building almost unrecognizable; now a funeral home. 1 ext. photo (1936). LC code: PA,42-ELD,1.

Eldred Vicinity (Eldred Township)

Lamphier, Benjamin H., House (PA-552), W side of W. Eldred Rd., 1.5 mi. S of State Rte. 346. Frame with clapboarding, L-shaped, seven-bay front, two stories with basement, gable roof, wide entablature, small second-story windows in frieze on N (rear) elevation, two entrances on S elevation, Greek Revival details, one-and-a-half-story frame kitchen wing and small frame woodshed on N elevation; small detached random rubble smokehouse. Built 1837-40 (E side of main block built first, then W side, then kitchen and woodshed, but all built within three years); Benjamin H. Lamphier, builder. 4 ext. photos (1936); 5 data pages (1937). LC code: PA,42-ELDW,1.

Port Allegheny Vicinity (Liberty Township)

Coleman, Dr. Horace, House (PA-557), S of U.S. Rte. 6, between road and Allegheny River, 2.5 mi. E of Port Allegheny. Frame with clapboarding, three-bay front, two-and-a-half stories, gable roof with pedimented gable end, semicircular window in gable end, corner pilasters with wide entablature, doorway with side lights framed by pilasters and entablature, Greek Revival style; wing to side (used as tap room), frame with clapboarding, three-bay front, one-and-a-half stories, gable roof, deep eaves, corner pilasters; one-story frame wing to rear. Built early nineteenth century (ca. 1812 when Dr. Coleman was married); destroyed by fire from lightning 1940. Used as home and halfway house (hotel) between Coudersport and Smethport. 3 ext. photos (1936), 2 int. photos (1936). LC code: PA,42-PORAL.V,1.

Smethport Borough

Backus House (PA-533), originally located at NW corner of State Rte. 59 and State St., across from Courthouse; moved after 1936 to SE corner of Green and State Sts. Frame with clapboarding, T-shaped, main block 44'-4" (five-bay front) x 19'-7" (two bays) with 24'-9" 50'-9" wing to rear, two-and-a-half stories, gable roof with pedimented gable ends, corner pilasters, doorway with semielliptical fanlight and side lights with tracery flanked by Ionic pilasters on N (front) elevation; central hall plan. Built 1825-40; attributed to Solomon Sartwell, architect; porches added; exterior covered with asbestos shingles after 1936; rear wing altered after 1936. 6 sheets (1937, including plans, elevations, details); 3 ext. photos (1936), 4 int. photos (1936); 1 data page (1937). LC code: PA,42-SMETH,1.

Medbury House (PA-5103), 604 E. Main St. Frame with clapboarding, L-shaped, main block 24'-6" (three-bay front) x 44'-4" with setback wing to E (26' x 15'-3"), one-and-a-half-story main block and one-story wing, gable roofs, corner pilasters, wide entablature with small second-story windows in frieze, door with side lights framed by pilasters and entablature on S (front) elevation, Greek Revival style; side hall plan. Built mid-nineteenth century. 7 sheets (1937, including plans, elevations, section, details); 2 ext. photos (1936), 1 int. photo (1936). LC code: PA,42-SMETH,2.

West Eldred

Lamphier House. See Eldred Vicinity (Eldred Township), Lamphier, Benjamin H., House.

Mercer County

Greenville Borough

Goodwin House (PA-567), 36 S. Mercer St. Frame with flush horizontal wooden siding (W front elevation) and clapboarding, three-bay front, two-and-a-half stories, gable roof, denticulated cornice, pedimented Doric portico on W elevation with louvered fan in pediment, door flanked by side lights with pilasters and entablature, bay window on N elevation, two-story setback ell with porch on S elevation, Greek Revival style; side hall plan. Built early nineteenth century. 2 ext. photos (1936), 1 int. photo (1936). LC code: PA,43-GRENV,1.

Penn High School (PA-547), Penn Ave. at Main St. Brick with concrete and terra cotta trim, irregularly shaped, 205' x 189', flat roof, ornate entrances on three sides, Jacobean Revival details. Built 1917-19; Thayer and Thayer, architects; remodeled 1960 and 1963; demolished 1979. 21 copy photos of 1917 drawings; 8 ext. photos (1979), 4 int. photos 1979); 2 data pages (1979). LC code: PA,43-GRENV,3.

Stewart, Vance, House (PA-568), 115 Columbia Ave. Frame with flush horizontal wooden siding (E front elevation) and clapboarding, three by four bays, two-and-a-half stories with basement, gable roof, pedimented Doric portico with louvered fan in pediment, plain entablature, pilasters and entablature frame recessed door with side lights and columns, bay window on N elevation, portico with three chamfered columns on W elevation, Greek Revival style; side hall plan. Built mid-nineteenth century. 3 ext. photos (1936), 1 int. photo (1936). LC code: PA,43-GRENV,2.

Mercer Borough

Bell House (PA-564), 200 N. Pitt St. Frame with clapboarding, main block (three by two bays) with setback wing to N (two-bay front), two stories, gable roofs, pedimented gable end on main block, corner pilasters with entablature with recessed door with side lights on W (front) elevation, porch with scroll brackets on W elevation of wing, Greek Revival style; side hall plan. Built mid-nineteenth century (before 1856). 2 ext. photos (1936). LC code: PA,43-MERC,5.

Garrett Cenotaph (PA-534), in original Mercer Cemetery, at SW corner of North and N. Erie Sts. Sandstone, rectangular base 6'-2" x 5'-4" and 4'-11" high set on platform, tapering pyramid 4' x 4' at base and 8'-9" high set on base, corner pilasters with entablature on base, simple carving near apex of pyramid, inscriptions in script. Built ca. 1835. 1 ext. photo (1936); 3 data pages (1936). LC code: PA,43-MERC,1.

Jail (Old Stone Jail) (PA-560), 107 Venango St. Irregular coursed ashlar, five-bay front, two-and-a-half stories, cross gable roof, pedimented gable end with double window on N (front) elevation, arched door on N elevation, porch on W elevation. Built 1819; Thomas Templeton, builder; used until present jail was completed 1869; remodeled for hotel 1870. 1 ext. photo (1936). LC code: PA,43-MERC,2.

Magoffin House (PA-565), 119 S. Pitt St. Museum operated by Mercer County Historical Society. Frame with clapboarding, five-bay front, two stories with attic and basement, gable roof, double doors with semielliptical fanlight and side lights on W (front) elevation. Built 1821; two-story wing added to E elevation. 2 ext. photos (1936). LC code: PA,43-MERC,6.

Magoffin, Dr. Beriah, House (PA-561), 116 Venango St. Frame with flush horizontal siding (front elevation) and clapboarding, three by three bays, two stories, gable roof, pedimented Doric portico on front elevation, lintels with scroll brackets over openings, two-story frame wing to rear, Greek Revival style; side hall plan. Built early nineteenth century; demolished. 2 ext. photos (1936), 1 int. photo (1936). LC code: PA,43-MERC,3.

Old Stone Jail. See Jail.

Robinson W.J., House (PA-562), 208 N. Pitt St. Random ashlar, five-bay front, two stories, gable roof, door with fanlight set in recessed arched opening on W (front) elevation, flat stone arches over windows. Built 1810. 1 ext. photo (1936). LC code: PA,43-MERC,4.

Mercer Vicinity

Johnson House. See Springfield Falls (Springfield Township), Johnston's Tavern.

Sheakleyville Borough

Scriven's House (PA-558), W side of Main St. (U.S. Rte. 19). Frame with clapboarding, four by two bays, two-and-a-half stories with basement, gable roof, deep eaves, door with transom and side lights framed by pilasters and entablature on E (front) elevation, one-story clapboarded wing. Built mid-nineteenth century. 2 ext. photos (1937), 2 int. photos (1937). LC code: PA,43-SHEAK,2.

Scriven's Store (PA-537), W side of Main St. (U.S. Rte. 19). Frame with flush horizontal wooden siding (front elevation) and clapboarding, 25'-4" (four-bay front) x 44'-5", two stories with attic and basement, gable roof with pedimented gable end, store front with three large windows and double door, Doric pilasters supporting entablature separate openings on E (front) elevation, double doors on second story of W elevation (ramp missing), Greek Revival style. Built ca. 1852; William Moyer, probable builder; originally a carriage and blacksmith shop. 5 sheets (1936, including plans, elevations, section, details); 2 ext. photos (1937); 4 data pages (1937). LC code: PA,43-SHEAK,1.

Springfield Falls (Springfield Township)

Johnson House. See Johnston's Tavern.

Johnston's Tavern (Johnson House) (PA-581), E side of U.S. Rte. 19, 1 mi. N of State Rte. 208. Museum operated by Pennsylvania Historical and Museum Commission. Coursed rubble, five-bay front, two-and-a-half stories, gable roof, door flanked by side lights with stone arch above with date on keystone on E (front) elevation (fanlight replaced after 1936 during restoration). Built 1831 by Arthur Johnston; housed post office 1836-45; restored by Charles M. Stotz, architect. A main stage stop on the Pittsburgh-Erie Turnpike. 1 ext. photo (1936). LC code: PA,43-MERC.V,1. NR.

Potter County

Coudersport Borough

Barn, Log (PA-5127), S side of U.S. Rte. 6, .2 mi. E of State Rte. 872. Log, 48'-8" x 29'-10", one level, gambrel roof. Built 1900; Charles Bailey, builder; poor condition 1936; demolished 1961. 2 sheets (1936, including elevations, section, details); 2 ext. photos (1936); 3 data pages (1936). LC code: PA,53-COUD,l.

Butterworth, Appleton, House (Lillibridge House) (PA-5107), 304 N. Main St. Frame with clapboarding, main block (three-bay front) with setback side wing (three-bay front), two stories with basement with one-story wing, gable roofs, cornice returns, corner pilasters, plain entablature, pilasters with entablature frame entrance with recessed door flanked by side lights and pilasters, porch on wing, Greek Revival style; side hall plan. Built 1849; Appleton Butterworth, builder; demolished. 3 ext. photos (1936). LC code: PA,53-COUD,3.

Coudersport Jail (PA-5132), 102 E. Second St. Coursed rock-faced ashlar with dressed stone quoins, five-bay front, two stories, hip roof, cupola with louvered openings and hip roof with bracketed cornice, arched dressed stone window heads and door frame, courts on each side of jail surrounded by stone walls, Italianate details. Built 1870; L. R. Decker, builder; demolished. 1 ext. photo (1937). LC code: PA,53-COUD,4.

Independent Order of Odd Fellows Building. See Presbyterian Church.

Ives, Timothy, House (PA-528), NW corner of Third and East Sts. Frame with clapboarding and flush horizontal siding on S (front) elevation of main block, main block 23'-6" (three-bay front) x 58'-3" (including rear kitchen wing and woodshed) with symmetrical setback side wings 18'-4" (three-bay fronts), two-story main block and one-story wings, gable roofs, pedimented Ionic portico, cornice returns, corner pilasters, plain entablature, door with transom and side lights framed by pilasters and entablature on main block, doors with transoms flanked by pilasters on wings, Greek Revival style; side hall plan. Built 1843; Timothy Ives Jr., architect; John Crosier and George Snyder, builders; dismantled ca. 1960 and placed in storage, never reconstructed. Ives was county treasurer and a representative in the General Assembly. 13 sheets (1936, including plans, elevations, details); 4 ext. photos (1936); 5 data pages (1936). LC code: PA,53-COUD,1.

Lillibridge House. See Butterworth, Appleton, House.

Presbyterian Church (Independent Order of Odd Fellows Building) (PA-529), 310 N. Main St. Frame with clapboarding, three by four bays, one story, gable roof, cornice returns, corner pilasters, plain entablature, double doors framed by pilasters and entablature, Greek Revival style. Built 1848-52; moved from Fifth and West Sts. to Main St. 1869; two-tier square tower with pilasters and spire added 1869 (removed 1930s); additions on rear; sold to Women's Temperance Union early 1900s; sold to Methodist Church as recreation center 1915; deeded to Independent Order of Odd Fellows 1939; later converted to apartments. First church built in Potter County. 1 ext. photo (1936). LC code: PA,53-COUD,2. NR (Coudersport Historic District).

Roulette (Roulette Township)

Weiderich, Jacob, House (PA-5129), NE corner of Main St. (old State Rte. 101) and Fishing Creek Rd (LR52009). Frame with clapboarding, main block (three-bay front) with setback side wing (six bays), two stories and attic with basement with one-and-a-half-story wing, gable roofs, cornice returns, corner pilasters, wide entablature, recessed doorway with distyle entrance porch on main block, recessed porch on wing, Greek Revival style; side hall plan. Built 1840. 1 ext. photo (1936). LC code: PA,53-ROUL,1.

Sullivan County

Colley

Ricketts House. See Ganoga Lake (Colley Township), Ricketts House.

Ganoga Lake (Colley Township)

Ricketts House (PA-210), W side of Lakeview Dr., 1.2 mi. NW of State Rte. 487, approx. 5 mi. N of Red Rock. Random ashlar, L-shaped, 60'-4" (five-bay front) x 35'-8" (two bays) with rear ell 24'-2" (two bays) x 40'-6" (four bays), two-and-a-half stories with basement, gable roof, porch with paired columns and balustrade across W (front) elevation, door with semielliptical fanlight and side lights, open terrace on E elevation connected with two-story porch on S elevation of ell; central hall plan. Built 1852; segmental dormers added and two rear windows enlarged 1912; setback kitchen wing (48'-3") added on N elevation 1913; restored 1970s. 5 sheets (1935, including plans, elevations, details); 3 ext. photos (1935); 5 data pages (1936). LC code: PA,57-COL,1. NR.

Susquehanna County

Montrose Borough

Lyons, John, House. See Mulford, Sylvanus, House.

Mulford, Sylvanus, House (John Lyons House) (PA-215), 65 Church St. (State Rte. 706). Frame with clapboarding, 40'-5" (five-bay front) x 52'-7", one-and-a-half stories, gable roof with longer rear slope, double doors with semielliptical fanlights and pilasters on S (front) elevation, tetrastyle porch on S elevation connected with open terrace with balustrade on W elevation (terrace removed after 1936), passage to barn on N elevation; interior inaccessible for measurement. Built 1818; distyle porch added on E elevation (removed after 1936). 6 sheets (1936, including plan, elevations, details); 2 ext. photos (1936); 6 data pages (1936). LC code: PA,58-MONT,1. NR.

Venango County

Cherrytree (Cherrytree Township)

Cherrytree Presbyterian Church (PA-530), E side of State Rte. 8, .5 mi. N of Cherrytree. Frame with clapboarding, 42'-2" (three-bay front) x 50'-1" (four bays), one story, gable roof with pedimented gable end, belfry on S end of ridge (altar end), Palladian window on S elevation, double doors framed by pilasters and entablature; cove ceiling. Built 1837; Elijah Stewart, head of congregation, supervised construction; chapel for cemetery 1937; belfry destroyed by lightning. 5 sheets (1936, including plan, elevations, section, details); 2 ext. photos (1936), 2 int. photos (1936); 5 data pages (1937). LC code: PA,61-CHERT,1.

School. See Toonerville (Cherrytree Township), Cherrytree Public School.

Franklin

Ridgway Log House (PA-578), U.S. Rte. 322 (Liberty St.), below 9th St. Log, three by two bays, two-and-a-half stories, gable roof, frame shed added on rear. Built early nineteenth century; probably built by John Ridgway; Broad Arrow Society Headquarters 1936. One of the oldest houses in the city. 1 ext. photo (1936). LC code: PA,61-FRANK,1.

Pleasantville Borough

Allegheny Baptist Church. See Free Methodist Church.

Free Methodist Church (Allegheny Baptist Church) (PA-531), W side of State Rte. 27, .3 mi. N of intersection of State Rtes. 27, 227 and 36. Frame with clapboarding, 35'-6" (three-bay front) x 50'-6" (four bays), one story, gable roof with pedimented gable end, rectangular belfry, Doric corner pilasters, plain entablature, entrance framed by Doric pilasters and entablature on S (front) elevation, Greek Revival style. Built 1847-49; Manly Colton Beebe, designer. 4 sheets (1936, including plan, elevations, details); 2 ext. photos (l936); 4 data pages (1937). LC code: PA,61-PLEAV,2. NR.

Quinn House (PA-518), State Rte. 27, .2 mi. N of intersection of State Rtes. 27, 227 and 36. Frame with clapboarding, main section 16'-6" (three-bay front) x 27' with symmetrical side wings (16'-1" x 21'-10"), one-and-a-half stories with one-story wings, gable roofs, cornice returns, corner pilasters, plain entablature, central entrance framed by pilasters and entablature, recessed entrance porches on wings, Greek Revival style. Built 1843-46; Manly Colton Beebe, designer; Aaron Benedict, builder; kitchen wing added to rear of N wing. 2 sheets (1936, including plan, elevation); 3 ext. photos (1936), 2 int. photos (1936); 4 data pages (1936). LC code: PA,61-PLEAV,1.

Toonerville (Cherrytree Township)

Cherrytree Public School (PA-539), address not provided. Museum. Frame with clapboarding, three by five bays, two stories, gable roof with pedimented gable end, frame cupola on ridge, Doric pilasters on facade, plain entablature, central door framed by pilasters and entablature, Greek Revival style. Built 1855. 1 ext. photo (1936). LC code: PA,61-CHERT,2.

Warren County

Garland (Pittsfield Township)

Mill (PA-540), E side of Brokenstraw Creek, on S side of State Rte. 27. 1 int. view (1937) of water mill, showing grind stone and feeding hopper; in use 1937; demolished. LC code: PA,62-GARL,1.

Irvine (Brokenstraw Township)

Irvine Estate, Irvine House (PA-525), on W bank of Allegheny River, .2 mi. E of Dunn's Eddy Rd., .9 mi. S of

Irvine. Random rock-faced ashlar with quoins, main block 20'-7" (three-bay front) x 33' with symmetrical side wings 9'-7" (one-bay fronts) x 33', two stories with one-story wings, hip roofs, rusticated flat arch with keystone over E (front) entrance, N wing (woodshed) partially open, S wing with recessed porch. Built ca. 1840; Dr. W. A. Irvine, architect; James M. Halliday, builder; demolished. 14 sheets (1936, including plans, elevations, details); 1 ext. photo (1936); 6 data pages (1937). LC code: PA,62-IRV,2A.

House by the Pines (PA-522), E side of Dunn's Eddy Rd., 1.2 mi. S of Irvine. Coursed rock-faced ashlar on E (front) elevation with random rubble side elevations with smooth ashlar quoins, three-bay front, two stories, hip roof, smooth ashlar lintels over openings. Built ca. 1840; Dr. W. A. Irvine, architect; James M. Halliday, builder; restored. 1 ext. photo (1936); 1 data page (1937). LC code: PA,62-IRV,2F.

Miller's House (PA-526), W bank of Brokenstraw Creek, .2 mi. S of Main St. (old U.S. Rte. 6). Random rock-faced ashlar with quoins, 20'-4" (three-bay front) x 30'-6", two stories with basement, hip roof; two rooms. Built ca. 1840; Dr. W. A. Irvine, architect; James M. Halliday, builder. 7 sheets (1936, including plans, elevations, details); 2 ext. photos (1936); 3 data pages (1937). LC code: PA,62-IRV,2B.

Tenant House (PA-527), .1 mi. S of Main St. (old U.S. Rte. 6), .1 mi. E of Brokenstraw Creek. Random rock-faced ashlar on N (front) elevation and random rubble on side and rear elevations with quoins, main block (three-bay front) with symmetrical side wings (one-bay fronts), 42'-8" x 35'-3" (main block and wings), two-story main block with one-story wings, hip roof with shed-roof wings. Built ca. 1840; Dr. W. A. Irvine, architect; James M. Halliday, builder; demolished (now site of Forestry Lab). 9 sheets (1936, including plans, elevations, details); 1 ext. photo (1936); 4 data pages (1937). LC code: PA,62-IRV,2C.

Irvine Presbyterian Church (PA-516), S side of Main Street (old U.S. Rte. 6), .2 mi. W of Dunn's Eddy Rd. Coursed rock-faced ashlar on N (front) elevation and random rock-faced ashlar on side elevations with rusticated quoins, 25'-2" (three-bay front) x 35'-2" (three bays), one story, gable roof, recessed double doors framed with rusticated stones with keystone on N (front) elevation, rusticated arches with keystones over windows flanked by fluted pilasters, louvered fanlight with rusticated arch in N gable end; vaulted ceiling. Built 1839; James M. Halliday, architect. Severe form with simple classical lines. 7 sheets (1936, including plan, elevations, details); 4 ext. photos (1937), 1 int. photo (1937); 4 data pages (1936). LC code: PA,62-IRV,1. NR.

Pittsfield (Pittsfield Township)

Acock House (PA-554), NW corner of State Rte. 27 and Church St. Frame with clapboarding, main block (three-bay front) with setback side wing to E (three-bay front), two stories with one-story wing, hip roofs, paired brackets under cornice, segmental lintels over windows, arched entrance with columns and label molding on S (front) elevation, porch on wing with pierced wooden posts and ogee curves, Italianate main block with unusual details; side hall plan. Built mid-nineteenth century. 1 ext. photo (1936). LC code: PA,62-PITFI,1.

Hotel (Old Hotel) (PA-553), NW corner of State Rte. 27 and Ross St. Frame with clapboarding, six by three bays, two-and-a-half stories, gable roof, cornice returns, plain entablature, main door on S (front) elevation flanked by side lights and pilasters, secondary door on S elevation flanked by pilasters, porch on S elevation. Built 1853; James L. Acocks, builder. 1 ext. photo (1936). LC code: PA,62-PITFI,3.

Old Hotel. See Hotel.

Presbyterian Church (United Methodist Church) (PA-5133), SE corner of Prospect and Church Sts. Frame with clapboarding, three by three bays, one story, gable roof with pedimented gable end, belfry over front entrance, pilasters on facade, plain entablature, central entrance framed by pilasters and entablature, Greek Revival style. Built 1854. 1 ext. photo (1937). LC code: PA,62-PITFI,2.

Rhodes House (PA-556), address not provided. Frame with clapboarding, five-bay first story with recessed two-bay second story, hip roof on first story, gable roof with pedimented gable end on second story, pilasters on facade, Greek Revival details. Built mid-nineteenth century; frame shed added; demolished. 1 ext. photo (1936). LC code: PA,62-PITFI,4.

Terry House (PA-555), S side of State Rte. 27, 1/2 block W of Church St. Frame with clapboarding, three by three bays, two stories, gable roof with pedimented gable end, corner pilasters, plain entablature, one-story clapboarded rear wing, Greek Revival style. Built mid-nineteenth century; one-story porch added. 1 ext. photo (1936). LC code: PA,62-PITFI,5.

United Methodist Church. See Presbyterian Church.

Tidioute Borough

Main Street (Hotel) (Old Hotel, Ryan House) (PA-585), 76 Main St. Frame with clapboarding, seven irregular bays by five bays, three-and-a-half stories with basement, gable roof with pedimented gable end, Doric portico across facade (second-story porch with iron railing supported by portico), doors with side lights and pedimented lintels, slightly pedimented lintels over windows, Greek Revival details. Built 1861; W. P. Shaw, builder; enlarged 1894; demolished. 1 ext. photo (1936). LC code: PA 62-TIDI,1.

Old Hotel. See Main Street (Hotel).

Ryan House. See Main Street (Hotel).

Warren Borough

Henry-Windsor House (Newmaker House) (PA-5205), 203 Market St. Random ashlar and brick, rectangular with projecting bays, approx. 50' x 60', three stories with attic and basement, steep gable roofs and hip roof, front gable with clapboarding and shingles, Queen Anne style. Built 1887; stone porte-cochere replaced original two-story porch ca. 1930; remodeled as apartments; demolished. 8 ext. photos (1984), 5 int. photos (1984); 2 data pages (1984). LC code: PA,62-WAR,1.

Newmaker House. See Henry-Windsor House.

Windsor House. See Henry-Windsor House.

Young Men's Christian Association (YMCA) (PA-5352), 310 Liberty St. Brick with rusticated stuccoed basement and stuccoed third floor, original interior wood framing replaced with steel beams and columns, 100' (seven-bay front) x 38', three stories on elevated basement, flat roof with parapets at end walls, central entrance bay with arched parapet, diamond motif under windows. Built 1912-14; Louis E. Jallade, architect; one-story concrete block annex (56' x 95') and gymnasium (73' x 93') added to rear prior to 1946; fire 1946 resulting in major renovations; one-story steel-framed natatorium (45' x 96') added to rear 1961-63; 1981 YMCA moved to new quarters, vacant, to be demolished. 4 ext. photos (1986), 3 ext. copy photos (ca. 1912, ca. 1915, ca. 1967), 5 int. copy photos (ca. 1935, ca. 1945, ca. 1967); 12 data pages including floor plans (1986). LC code: PA,62-WAR,2.

Wyoming County

North Mehoopany (Mehoopany Township)

Kintner Mill (PA-238), W of State Rte. 87, .1 mi. S of SR4013, N of junction with Little Mehoopany Creek. Random rubble (first story) and frame with flush horizontal siding, 33' (three-bay front) x 48' (four bays), three-and-a-half stories, gable roof, four loading doors on four levels of S elevation. Built 1842; Paul Bishop Jennings, builder; three-story frame storage shed added late nineteenth century; gabled frame monitor added late nineteenth century; one-story frame shed added; several additions and alterations since 1930s, clapboarding added, two-story concrete block garage added on W elevation, one-story frame wing added on E elevation. 11 sheets (1938, including plans, elevations, section, details); 2 ext. photos (1938); 5 data pages (1938). LC code: PA,66-MEHOPN,1.

Appendix 1

Historic American Buildings Survey Inventory Forms

Historic American Buildings Survey Inventory Forms (HABSI) are single-page forms on which basic data for a structure can be recorded. The information includes name, location, date of construction, architect, a short description of features and significance, and often a location map and small photograph. The HABSI forms were devised in the 1950s, but discontinued when their purpose as a nationwide inventory of historic sites was filled by the formation of the National Register of Historic Places in 1966. Though not considered a formal part of the HABS collection, they are available for research and reproduction at the Library of Congress.

Following is a list of the HABSI forms available for Pennsylvania. The list is arranged alphabetically by county, town, and then building name. Often structures recorded with a HABSI form are also represented in the formal HABS collection; these are noted with an asterisk. If the HABSI form uses a name different from the name used elsewhere in the catalog, the HABSI name is included parenthetically to aid the researcher in locating the form at the Library of Congress.

Allegheny County

Ben Avon Borough
Dalzell House*

Churchill Borough
Beulah Presbyterian Church*

Evergreen Hamlet (Ross Township)
Wade Hampton House (Hampton-Kelly House)*
Wisteria Cottage

Mckeesport
John J. Muse House*

Pittsburgh
Allegheny County Courthouse and Jail*
Beau Brummell Club*
Brady Street Bridge*
Felix R. Brunot House
Carnegie Institute of Technology, Administration Building*
Carnegie Institute of Technology, Machinery Hall Tower*
Chestnut and Canal Streets (house)
Emmanuel Protestant Episcopal Church*
English-Oliver House (Oliver-Rae House)*
Fort Pitt Blockhouse (Block House, Formerly Redoubt)*
Fulton Theater*
Eva Harter House*
Heathside Cottage*
Allen M. Klages House*
North Side Market*
Old Heidelberg Apartments and Cottages*
Pennsylvania Railroad Station Rotunda (Union Station Cab Stand)*
Point Bridge*
United States Allegheny Post Office (Old Allegheny U.S. Post Office)*
Washington Crossing Bridge*

Sewickley Heights Borough
Fairacres (B. F. Jones Mansion)*

Sharpsburg Vicinity (O'Hara Township)
Ferry House*

Swissvale Borough
Trevanion Avenue (house)*

Wilkinsburg Borough
John F. Singer House*

Beaver County

Ambridge Borough
Economy (2 HABSIs on Grotto and Great House Garden and Town Plan)*
Economy Feast Hall*
Economy Meetinghouse (St. John's Lutheran Church)*

Berks County

Limekiln Vicinity (Oley Township)
Bertolet-Herbein Cabin (Snyder Farm)*
George DeBenneville House*

Oley Vicinity (Oley Township)
Bertolett Homestead
Abraham Bertolett House
Bertolett Sawmill
Blacksmith Shop
John DeTurk House*

Stonersville Vicinity (Exeter Township)
Exeter Friends Meetinghouse*

Yellow House Vicinity (Oley Township)
Henry Fisher House*

Bucks County

Holicong
Old Congress

New Hope Vicinity
Ferndon

Washington Crossing
Thompson-Neeley House* (Additional documentation on barn only)

Chester County

Birmingham (Birmingham Township)
Birmingham Friends Meetinghouse*

Chester Springs
D. A. Metz House

Crawford County

Conneautville Borough
Trinity Protestant Episcopal Church (Conneautville Baptist Church)*

Erie County

Erie
Presque Isle Lighthouse*

Fayette County

Brownsville Borough
Bowman's Castle*

Franklin County

Richmond Furnace
Mount Pleasant Iron Works

Greene County

Waynesburg
Short Span Covered Bridge

Huntingdon County

Franklinville Vicinity (Franklin Township)
Colerain Forge House*

Pennsylvania Furnace (Franklin Township)
John Lyons House (listed as Mansion House at Pennsylvania Furnace, Centre County)*

Lancaster County

Lancaster
Lutheran Church of the Holy Trinity*

Marietta Vicinity (East Donegal-Rapho Townships)
Johnson's Mill Covered Bridge*

Willow Street Vicinity (West Lampeter Township)
Hans Herr House*

Lebanon County

Millbach
Illick House

Newmanstown Vicinity (Millcreek Township)
Heinrich Zeller House (Fort Zeller)*

Montgomery County

Gladwyne
The Old Guard House Inn

Philadelphia County

101-05 Arch Street (Commercial Building)
Thomas Armat House, 5450 Germantown Ave.*
Ashmead House, 5430 Germantown Ave.*
Ashmead House, 5434 Germantown Ave.*
Barron House, 5106 Germantown Ave.*
Bechtel House, 5226 Germantown Ave.
Bringhurst House, 5448 Germantown Ave.*
John Brock and Sons Warehouse, 242-44 N. Delaware Ave.*
Cast Iron Sidewalk, 1907 N. Seventh St.*
Chestnut Street Area Study (Commercial Buildings), 213-43 Chestnut St.*
Commercial Exchange, 135 S. Second St.*
112-16 Cuthbert Street (Houses), 3 HABSI forms
202 Delancey Street (house)
236 Delancey Street (house)
1800-36 Delancey Street (Houses)*
2301-23 Delancey Street (Houses)*
Detweiler House, 8226 Germantown Ave.*
Dorfenille House, 5139 Germantown Ave.*
Theobald Endt House, 5222-24 Germantown Ave.*
Folwell House, 5281 Germantown Ave.*
320 South Fourth Street (house)
Framberger House, Market Sq. and Church Ln.
505 South Front Street (house)*
507 South Front Street (house)*
509 South Front Street (house)
510 South Front Street (house)*
518 South Front Street (house)
520 South Front Street (house)
521 South Front Street (house)
523 South Front Street (house)
524 South Front Street (house)
525 South Front Street (house)
601 South Front Street (house)
602 South Front Street (house)*
603 South Front Street (house)*
606 South Front Street (house)*
608 South Front Street (house)*
618 South Front Street (house)*
626 South Front Street (house)*
700 South Front Street (tavern)*
702 South Front Street (house)*
704 South Front Street (house)*
706 South Front Street (house)*
722 South Front Street (house)*
724 South Front Street (house)*
734 South Front Street (house)*
768 South Front Street (house)*
770 South Front Street (house)*
774 South Front Street (house)*
776 South Front Street (house)*
783 South Front Street (house)*
785 South Front Street (house)
806 South Front Street (house)*
808 South Front Street (house)*
810 South Front Street (house)*
812 South Front Street (house)*
830 South Front Street (house)*
832 South Front Street (house)*
834 South Front Street (house)*
836 South Front Street (house)*
849 South Front Street (house)
851 South Front Street (house)
852 South Front Street (house)*
854 South Front Street (house)*
856 South Front Street (house)*
905 South Front Street (house)
907 South Front Street (house)
919 South Front Street (house)*
921 South Front Street (house)
931 South Front Street (house)
946 South Front Street (house)
948 South Front Street (house)
General Wayne Hotel, 5060 Germantown Ave.*
George House, 6099 Drexel Rd.
6000 Germantown Ave. (house)*
Germantown Historical Society Area Study (Conyngham-Hacker House), 5214 Germantown Ave.*
Germantown Historical Society Area Study (Howell House), 5218 Germantown Ave.*
Thomas Hockley House, 235 S. Twenty-first St.*
Wigard Jacoby House, 8327 Germantown Ave.*
Dirck Jansen House, 6112 Germantown Ave.
Kensington National Bank, 2-8 W. Girard Ave.*
Keyser House, 5918-26 Germantown Ave.
Loudoun, 4650 Germantown Ave.*
Mehl House, 4821 Germantown Ave.*
Naglee House, 4518 Germantown Ave.
Ottinger House, 4825 Germantown Ave.
Philadelphia Art Club, 220 S. Broad St.*
Joseph D. Potts House, 3905 Spruce St.*
Provident Life and Trust Company Bank, 409 Chestnut St.*
Ridge Avenue Farmers' Market Company, 1810 Ridge Ave.*
Riggs and Brother, Navigator Statue (Navigator Statue), 310 Market St.*
Royal House, 5011 Germantown Ave.*
St. Stephen's Methodist Episcopal Church, Rectory, 5213 Germantown Ave.*

Scott-Wanamaker House (John Wanamaker House), 2032 Walnut St.*
John Singer Warehouse, 319 1/2 Market St.*
Sower House (Trinity Lutheran Church House), 5300 Germantown Ave.*
Spring Garden Institute, 523-25 N. Broad St.*
2009-45 Spruce Street (Houses)*
Stone-Meredith-Penrose House, 700 S. Washington Sq.*
307 South Third Street (house)
309 South Third Street (house)
324 South Third Street (house)
327 South Third Street (house)
University of Pennsylvania, Furness Building (Library), W side Thirty-fourth St.*
Valley Green Inn, Wissahickon Dr.*
508 South Water Street (house)
516 South Water Street (house)*
518 South Water Street (house)*
520 South Water Street (house)*
522 South Water Street (house)*
524 South Water Street (house)*
526 South Water Street (house)*
532 South Water Street (house)*

Schuylkill County

Pottsville
Schuylkill County Prison
Schuylkill County Prison Extension

Washington County

Canonsburg
John Roberts House*

Centerville Vicinity (Centerville Township)
John Krepps Tavern (Malden Inn)*

Finleyville Vicinity (Union Township)
James Chapel Methodist Church*

Meadow Lands Vicinity (North Strabane Township)
Wylie-Miller Barn*

Westmoreland County

Fellsburg (Rostraver Township)
Fellsburg Methodist Episcopal Church*

Laughlintown Vicinity (Ligonier Township)
Alan M. Scaife House (Penguin Court)*

West Newton Borough
John C. Plumer House*

Appendix 2

Photogrametric Plates

The Historic American Buildings Survey and the Historic American Engineering Record have photogrammetric stereopairs for some Philadelphia structures.

Stereopairs are glass plate photographs taken from different camera positions which, when viewed, form a stereo model that can be measured in three dimensions. Dimensional drawings can then be prepared without labor-intensive hand measuring, an especially useful technique for large or complex structures.

The stereopairs are archived at the Library of Congress and can be reproduced with special permission. Film copy negatives have been produced for all HABS/HAER stereopairs and are included in the formal collection.

Historic American Buildings Survey
Bank of Pennsylvania (PA-1392)
    2 4"x6" glass plate negatives
Bank Row (PA-1667)
    4 4"x6" glass plate negatives
Congress Hall (PA-1431)
    8 4"x6" glass plate diapositives
    12 4"x6" glass plate negatives
Independence Hall photogrammetric work is currently underway.
Independence Hall Complex, City Hall (PA-1432)
    4 5"x7" glass plate diapositives
    44 5"x7" glass plate negatives
Pennsylvania Company for Insurances on Lives and Granting Annuities (PA-1452)
    4 4"x6" glass plate negatives
Provident Life and Trust Company Bank (PA-1058)
    8 4"x6" glass plate diapositives
    8 4"x6" glass plate negatives

Historic American Engineering Record
Falls Bridge (PA-35)
    4 prints mounted on 5"x7" cards in pairs
    6 5"x7" glass plate negatives
Pennsylvania Railroad, Brick Viaduct (PA-38)
    2 5"x7" glass plate negatives
Pennsylvania Railroad, Mantua Junction Viaduct (PA-37)
    10 prints mounted on 5"x7" cards in pairs
    6 5"x7" glass plate negatives
Philadelphia and Reading Railroad, Wissahickon Creek Viaduct (PA-36)
    8 prints mounted on 5"x7" cards in pairs
    1 print mounted on 5"x7" card
    7 5"x7" glass plate negatives
Philadelphia and Reading Railroad, Schuylkill River Viaduct (PA-39)
    6 prints mounted on 5"x7" cards in pairs
    9 5"x7" glass plate negatives

Appendix 3

Historic American Engineering Record in Pennsylvania

The Historic American Engineering Record (HAER) was founded in 1969 to meet the problem of rapidly disappearing engineering and industrial sites. HAER was established to prepare archival documentation on important historic structures around the nation. Founded and implemented by a tripartite agreement similar to that which established HABS in 1933, HAER is operated as a part of the National Park Service in cooperation with the Library of Congress and the American Society of Civil Engineers. Its goal is to prepare original measured drawings, photogrammetric stereopairs, professional photographs and photocopies, historical reports, technical analyses, and in some cases motion pictures of historic structures with engineering, industrial, or technological importance. The HAER collection is available for research and reproduction at the Library of Congress, Prints and Photographs Division, and, for those records not yet transmitted, at the HAER office at the National Park Service.

Following is a list of HAER sites in Pennsylvania. The list is arranged alphabetically by county, town, and then by the name of the documented structure. Each entry includes the historic name of the structure, the secondary name if given, the HAER number, and an itemization of documentary materials—number of sheets of measured drawings, photographs, and data pages. If a structure has also been documented by HABS, this fact is noted at the end of the entry by the letters HABS.

Adams County

East Berlin Vicinity
Kuhn's Fording Bridge (PA-68). 12 photos; 14 data pages. LC code: PA,1-EBER.V,1.

Allegheny County

Clairton
United States Steel Corporation: Clairton Works (PA-49). 2 photos. LC code: PA,2-CLAIR,1.
  Blast Furnace Blowing Engine Building (PA-49A). 6 photos; 2 data pages. LC code: PA,2-CLAIR,1A.
  14-Inch Mill Engines No. 1 and No. 2 (PA-49B). 2 photos; 2 data pages. LC code: PA,2-CLAIR,1B.
  22-Inch Mill Engine (PA-49C). 1 photo; 1 data page. LC code: PA,2- CLAIR,1C.

Duquesne
USX Duquesne Works, Carnegie Steel Company (PA-115). 62 photos; 3 data pages.

Pittsburgh
Brady Street Bridge (South Twenty-Second Street Bridge) (PA-3). 28 photos; 40 data pages. LC code: PA,2-PITBU,31. HABS.
Hays Army Ammunition Plant (PA-77). 46 data pages. LC code: PA,2-PITBU,61.
Jones and Laughlin Steel Corporation: Morgan Billet Mill Engine (PA-48). 8 photos. LC code: PA,2-PITBU,62A.
North Side Point Bridge (Manchester Bridge) (PA-4). 24 photos; 1 data page. LC code: PA,2-PITBU,59.
Pittsburgh and Steubenville Extension Railroad Tunnel (PA-70). 8 photos; 6 data pages. LC code: PA,2-PITBU,60.
Point Bridge (PA-5). 6 photos. LC code: PA,2-PITBU,38. HABS.
Smithfield Street Bridge (PA-2). 28 photos; 42 data pages. LC code: PA,2-PITBU,58.
South Twenty-second Street Bridge. *See* Brady Street Bridge.

Pittsburgh Vicinity
Davis Island Dam and Lock Number 1 (PA-65). 4 photos; 35 data pages. LC code: PA,2-PITBU.V,2.
West End-North Avenue Bridge (PA-96). 50 photos; 18 data pages.

Sewickley
Sewickley Bridge (PA-33). 32 photos; 88 data pages. LC code: PA,2-SEW,1.

Beaver County

Shippingport
Shippingport Atomic Power Station (PA-81). 177 photos; 30 data pages. LC code: PA,4-SHIP,1.

Berks County

Bernville
Heister Mill. See Pleasant Valley Roller Mill.
Pleasant Valley Roller Mill (Heister Mill) (PA-59). 16 photos; 17 data pages. LC code: PA,6,BERN.V,4.

Bernville Vicinity
Conrad's Warehouse (Union Canal Warehouse) (PA-57). 3 sheets; 6 photos; 5 data pages. LC code: PA,6-BERN.V,6.
Gruber Wagon Works (PA-14). 11 sheets; 215 photos; 29 data pages. LC code: PA,6-BERN.V,8.
Lamm's Mill (PA-58). 2 photos; 1 data page. LC code: PA,6-BERN.V,10.
Speicher Bridge (PA-60). 3 sheets; 14 photos; 10 data pages. LC code: PA,6-BERN.V,9.
Union Canal Locks (PA-66). 32 photos; 10 data pages. LC code: PA,6-BERN.V,7.
Union Canal Warehouse. *See* Conrad's Warehouse.

Hay Creek
Hay Creek Forge (PA-62). 2 photos; 1 data page.

Reading
Philadelphia and Reading Railroad: Pedestrian Suspension Bridge (Swinging Bridge) (PA-120). 3 photos.
Reading Depot (PA-121). 5 photos; 1 data page.
Reading Depot Bridge (PA-117). 3 photos.
Skew Arch Bridge (PA-116). 3 photos. HABS.
Swinging Bridge. See Pedestrian Suspension Bridge.
Walnut Street Bridge (PA-119). 2 photos.

Reading Vicinity
Philadelphia and Reading Railroad: Peacock's Lock Viaduct (PA-118). 4 photos.

Bradford County

Sayre
Lehigh Valley Railroad: Sayre Repair Shops (PA-33). 9 photos. LC code: PA,8-SAYRE,2.
Sayre Station (PA-32). 5 photos. LC code: PA,8-SAYRE,1.

Bucks County

Doylestown Vicinity
Moravian Pottery and Tile Works (Henry Chapman Mercer Tile Works) (PA-107). 68 photos. HABS.

Point Pleasant Vicinity
Pennsylvania Canal: Delaware Division (PA-103). 13 data pages.

Riegelsville
Delaware River Bridge (PA-31). 5 photos. LC code: PA,9-RIEG,1.

Carbon County

Jim Thorpe
Central Railroad of New Jersey: Jim Thorpe Station (PA-170). 1 photo. LC code: PA,13-JIMTH,1.
Lehigh Coal and Navigation Building (PA-169). 3 photos; 1 data page.

Lehighton
Baer Silk Mill (PA-167). 3 photos; 1 data page.

Lower Towamensing
Lehigh Canal:
  Aquashicola Creek Aqueduct (PA-178). 1 photo; 1 data page.
  Lock 20 (Lehigh Gap Lock) (PA-162). 2 photos; 1 data page. LC code: PA,13-TOWLO,1A.

Packerton
Lehigh Valley Railroad: Packerton Shops (PA-168). 1 photo; 1 data page.

Palmerton
New Jersey Zinc Company: Palmerton Plant (PA-163). 1 photo; 1 data page. LC code: PA,13-PALM,1.Parryville
Parryville Mill (Souder's Supply Store) (PA-164). 1 photo; 1 data page.

Weissport
Rickert's Coal and Freight Company (PA-166). 1 photo; 1 data page.

Weissport Vicinity
Lehigh Canal: Lock 10 (PA-165). 1 photo; 1 data page.

Chester County

St. Peters Vicinity
Mount Pleasant Grist Mill (PA-104). 25 sheets.

Columbia County

Bloomsburg
East Bloomsburg Bridge (PA-100). 41 photos; 13 data pages. LC code: PA,19-BLOOM,1.

Catawissa Vicinity
Catawissa Bridge (PA-90). 58 photos; 5 data pages. LC code: PA,19-CAT,2.

Crawford County

Cambridge Springs
Erie Railway: Cambridge Springs Station (PA-26). 2 photos. LC code: PA,20-CAMSP,1.

Cambridge Springs Vicinity
Erie Railway:
  Diverging French Creek Bridges (PA-27). 5 photos. LC code: PA,20-CAMSP.V,1.
  Parallel French Creek Bridges (PA-28). 4 photos. LC code: PA,20-CAMSP.V,2.

Cochranton
Erie Railway: Cochranton Passenger and Freight Station (PA-29). 4 photos. LC code: PA,20-COCH,1.

Meadville
Atlantic and Great Western Railroad:
  Meadville Blacksmith Shop (PA-11B). 4 sheets; 12 photos. LC code: PA,20-MEDVI,4B.
  Meadville Machine and Erecting Shop (PA-11A). 2 sheets; 12 photos. LC code: PA,20-MEDVI,4A.
  Meadville Repair Shops (PA-11). 4 photos. LC code: PA,20-MEDVI,4.
  Meadville Storehouse (PA-11C). 4 sheets; 6 photos. LC code: PA,20-MEDVI,4C.
  Erie Railway: Meadville Roundhouse (PA-13). 5 photos. LC code: PA,20-MEDVI,4D.
  Meadville Station (PA-12). 2 photos. LC code: PA,20-MEDVI,5.
  Mead Avenue Bridge (PA-19). 9 photos. LC code: PA,20-MEDVI,6.

Meadville Vicinity
Erie Railway: Buchanan Junction Interlocking Tower PA-20). 6 photos. LC code: PA,20-MEDVI.V,2A.

Dauphin County

Harrisburg
Pennsylvania Railroad: Harrisburg Station and Trainshed (PA-85). 16 sheets; 58 photos; 3 data pages. LC code: PA,22-HARBU,23.

Erie County

Corry Vicinity
Pennsylvania Railroad: Erie Railroad Bridge (PA-34). 3 photos. LC code: PA,25-COR.V,1.

Union City
Bridge Street Bridge (PA-91). 24 photos; 26 data pages. LC code: PA,25-UNCI,2.
Erie Railway: Crossing Gate Tower (PA-47). 1 photo. LC code: PA,25-UNCI,5A.
Union City Freight Station (PA-46). 2 photos. LC code: PA,25-UNCI,4.
Union City Station (PA-45). 4 photos. LC code: PA,25-UNCI,3.

Fayette County

Brownsville
Dunlap's Creek Bridge (PA-72). 6 photos; 2 data pages. LC code: PA,26-BROVI,2.

Franklin County

Chambersburg
Letterkenny Army Depot (PA-79). 55 data pages. LC code: PA,28-CHAMB,5.

Huntingdon County

Orbisonia Vicinity
East Broadtop Railroad (PA-127). 150 photos.

Lackawanna County

Scranton
Scranton Army Ammunition Plant (PA-76). 60 data pages. LC code: PA,35-SCRAN,3.

Lancaster County

Christiana Borough
Christiana Borough Bridge (PA-88). 1 sheet; 47 photos; 22 data pages. LC code: PA,36-CHRIS,1.

Lehigh County

Allentown
Central Railroad of New Jersey: Allentown Station (PA-150). 2 photos; 1 data page. LC code: PA,39-ALLEN,4.
Germania Brewery (Neuweiler Brewery) (PA-152). 6 photos; 1 data page. LC code: PA,39-ALLEN,5.
Hamilton Street Dam (PA-89). 27 photos; 6 data pages. LC code: PA,39-ALLEN,3A.
Lehigh Canal: Lock 40 (PA-149). 1 photo; 1 data page. LC code: PA,39-ALLEN,3B.
Neuweiler Brewery. *See* Germania Brewery.

Allentown Vicinity
Stahl Pottery (Powder Valley Pottery) (PA-124). 35 data pages.

Bethlehem
Ashbury Graphite Mill. See Pettinos Brothers Graphite Manufacturing Mill.
Central Railroad of New Jersey: Bethlehem Station (PA-145). 2 photos; 1 data page. LC code: PA,39-BETH,1. HABS.
Pettinos Brothers Graphite Manufacturing Mill (Ashbury Graphite Mill) (PA-147). 1 photo; 1 data page. LC code: PA,39-BETH,2.
Saquoit Silk Mill (Rossmaessler Mill) (PA-148). 2 photos; 1 data page.

Catasauqua
Lehigh Crane Iron Works (Thomas Iron Works) (PA-154). 3 photos; 1 data page. LC code: PA,39-CATS,1.

Coplay
Coplay Cement Company (PA-156). 1 photo; 1 data page. LC code: PA,39-COP,1.

Emmaus
Tank Farm Road Bridge (PA-123). 7 photos.

Lynnville Vicinity
Betz's Mill (PA-64). 9 sheets. LC code: PA,39-LYNVI.V,1.

Slatington
Barn (PA-177). 1 photo.
Kern's Mill. (Slatington Roller Mill) (PA-161). 1 photo; 1 data page.

Wanamakers
Ontelaunee Creek Bridge (PA-122). 6 photos.

Whitehall
Whitehall Cement Company (PA-157). 1 photo. LC code: PA,39-WHITO,1.

Luzerne County

Wilkes-Barre
Dorrance Colliery Fan Complex (PA-61). 7 sheets; 24 photos. LC code: PA,40-WILB,5.
South Street Bridge (PA-105). 42 photos; 8 data pages.

Lycoming County

Muncy Vicinity
Reading-Halls Station Bridge (PA-55). 5 sheets; 30 photos; 41 data pages.

Williamsport
Memorial Avenue Bridge (PA-102). 42 photos; 21 data pages.

McKean County

Mount Jewett
Erie Railway: Bradford Division, Bridge 27.66 (Kinzua Viaduct) (PA-7). 27 photos. LC code: PA,42-MOJEW.V,1.

Mount Jewett Vicinity
Erie Railway: Mount Jewett Station (PA-21). 6 photos. LC code: PA,42-MOJEW,1.

Mercer County

Greenville
College Avenue Bridge (PA-83). 21 photos; 31 data pages. LC code: PA,43-GRENV,4.

Monroe County

Tobyhanna
Tobyhanna Army Depot (PA-78). 33 data pages. LC code: PA,45-TOBY,1.

Montgomery County

Franconia
Allentown Road Bridge (PA-112). 18 photos; 8 data pages.

Norristown
West Marshall Street Bridge PA-54). 10 photos; 8 data pages. LC code: PA,46-NOR,1.

Valley Forge
Valley Forge Observation Tower (Mount Joy Observation Tower) (PA-114). 10 photos; 6 data pages.

Montour County

Washingtonville Vicinity
Washington Bridge (PA-98). 12 photos; 5 data pages. LC code: PA,47-WASH.V,1.

Northampton County

Bethlehem
Bethlehem Union Station (PA-146). 1 photo; 1 data page. LC code: PA,48-BETH,15.
Lehigh Canal: Monacacy Creek Aqueduct (PA-144). 1 photo; 1 data page. LC code: PA,48-BETH,17A.
Luckenbach Flour Mill (PA-50). 5 sheets; 24 photos; 24 data pages. LC code: PA,48-BETH,10.

Easton
Lehigh Canal:
   Easton Dam (PA-133). 3 photos; 1 data page.
   Outlet Lock (PA-136). 1 photo; 1 data page.
Lehigh Valley Railroad: Easton Car Shops (PA-137B). 3 photos; 1 data page.
   Easton Station (PA-137A). 1 photo; 1 data page.
   Easton Steam Laundry and Dining Car (PA-137C). 2 photos; 1 data page.

Freemansburg
Canal Manager's House (PA-142). 2 photos.
Freemansburg-Steel City Bridge (PA-141). 1 photo; 1 data page.
Lehigh Canal: Freemansburg (PA-176). 4 photos. LC code: PA,48-FREEM,1.
Lock 44 (PA-140). 1 photo; 1 data page.

Glendon
Glendon Iron Company (PA-138). 1 photo; 1 data page.
Lehigh Canal: Guard Lock 8 and Lockhouse (PA-139). 2 photos; 1 data page.

Hellertown
Old Mill Road Bridge (County Bridge No. 16) (PA-93). 11 photos.

Laury's Station Vicinity
Lehigh Canal:
   Guard Lock 5 (PA-158). 3 photos; 1 data page.
   Slate Dam (PA-171). 1 photo.

North Catasauqua
Lehigh Canal: Hockendauqua Dam (PA-153). 1 photo; 1 data page. LC code: PA,48-CATSN,1A.

Northampton
Northampton Brewery (PA-155). 1 photo; 1 data page. LC code: PA,48-NORTH,1.

Treichlers
Mauser Mill Company (White Star Mills) (PA-159). 2 photos; 1 data page. LC code: PA,48-TREIC,1.

Walnutport
Lehigh Canal: Lock 23 (Kelchner's Lock) (PA-160). 1 photo; 1 data page. LC code: PA,48-WALNPO,1A.

Philadelphia County

Philadelphia
Callowhill Street Bridge (Spring Garden Street Bridge, Fairmount Bridge) (PA-86). 10 photos; 1 data page.
Fairmount Waterworks (PA-51). 36 sheets; 162 photos; 198 data pages. LC code: PA,51-PHILA,328. HABS.
Fairmount Waterworks Rehabilitation Project (PA-51). 16 sheets.
Falls Bridge (PA-35). 12 photos; 2 data pages. LC code: PA,51-PHILA,701.
Frankford Arsenal (PA-74). 6 photos; 1 data page. LC code: PA,51-PHILA,693.
Keyser Brothers Iron Works (PA-40). 16 photos. LC code: PA,51-GERM,192.
Northeast Railroad Corridor (PA-71). 32 photos. LC code: PA,51-PHILA,694.
Pennsylvania Railroad: Brick Viaduct (PA-38). 2 photos; 2 data pages. LC code: PA,51-PHILA,696.
Mantua Junction Viaduct (PA-37). 7 photos; 3 data pages. LC code: PA,51-PHILA,695.
Philadelphia and Reading Railroad: Schuylkill River Viaduct (Reading Railroad: Schuylkill River Viaduct) (PA-39). 7 photos; 3 data pages. LC code: PA,51-PHILA,697.
Wissahickon Creek Viaduct (Reading Railroad: Wissahickon Creek Viaduct) (PA-36). 8 photos; 3 data pages. LC code: PA,51-PHILA,698.
Philadelphia Gas Works: Point Breeze Meter House (PA-41). 6 sheets; 17 data pages. LC code: PA,51-PHILA,699A.
Reading Railroad: Schuylkill River Viaduct. See Philadelphia and Reading Railroad: Schuylkill River Viaduct.
Wissahickon Creek Viaduct. See Philadelphia and Reading Railroad: Wissahickon Creek Viaduct.
Shur's Lane Mill (PA-73). 1 photo; 1 data page. LC code: PA,51-PHILA,700.
Spring Garden Street Bridge. See Callowhill Street Bridge.

Pike County

Dingman's Ferry
Dingmans Ferry Bridge (Delaware River Bridge) (PA-15). 6 sheets; 3 photos. LC code: PA,52-DING,1.

Lackawaxen
Delaware and Hudson Canal: Delaware Aqueduct (PA-1). 8 sheets; 56 photos; 12 data pages. LC code: PA,52-LACK,1.
Erie Railway: Delaware Division, Bridge 110.54 (PA-24). 19 photos. LC code: PA,52-LACK,2.

Milford Vicinity
Erie Railway: Pond Eddy Side Hill Cut and Fill (PA-30). 3 photos. LC code: PA,52-MILF.V,3.

Millrift
Erie Railway: Delaware River Bridge (PA-23). 1 photo. LC code: PA,52-MILRI,1.

Shohola
Erie Railway : Shohola Creek Bridge (PA-43). 8 photos. LC code: PA,52-SHOH,1.
Shohola Station (PA-42). 7 photos. LC code: PA,52-SHOH,2.

Shohola Vicinity
Erie Railway: Shohola Side Hill Cut and Revetment (PA-44). 3 photos. LC code: PA,52-SHOH.V,1.

Schuylkill County

Schuylkill Haven Borough
Schuylkill Canal: Bausman's Lock Number 12 (PA-69). 6 photos; 4 data pages. LC code: PA,54-SCHUYH,1A.

Snyder County

Beaver Springs Vicinity
Gross Covered Bridge (Klinepeter's Covered Bridge) (PA-67). 22 photos; 1 data page. LC code: PA,55-BEAVS.V,1.
Klinepeter's Covered Bridge. See Gross Covered Bridge.

Susquehanna County

Lanesboro
Erie Railway:
   Delaware Division, Bridge 189.46 (Starrucca Viaduct) (PA-6). 3 sheets; 16 photos. LC code: PA,58-LANBO,1.
   Delaware Division, Bridge 190.13 (PA-16). 6 photos. LC code: PA,58-LANBO,2.
   Delaware Division, Culvert 190.21 (PA-17). 1 photo. LC code: PA,58-LANBO,3.
Starrucca Viaduct. See Erie Railway: Delaware Division, Bridge 189.46.

Lanesboro Vicinity
Erie Railway: Cascade Bridge Site (PA-18). 2 photos. LC code: PA,58-LANBO.V,1.

Susquehanna
Erie Railway:
   Susquehanna Blacksmith Shop (PA-10C). 3 photos. LC code: PA,58-SUSQ,1C.
   Susquehanna Boiler Shop (PA-10D). 3 photos. LC code: PA,58-SUSQ,1D.
   Susquehanna Boiler Shop, 1900 (PA-10E). 2 photos. LC code: PA,58-SUSQ,1E.
   Susquehanna Carpenter Shop (PA-10B). 3 photos. LC code: PA,58-SUSQ,1B.
   Susquehanna Freight Station (PA-9). 1 photo. LC code: PA,58-SUSQ,2.
   Susquehanna Machine and Erection Shop (Long Shop) (PA-10A). 3 sheets; 4 photos. LC code: PA,58-SUSQ,1A.
   Susquehanna Repair Shops Office Building (PA-10F). 4 photos. LC code: PA,58-SUSQ,1F.
   Susquehanna Repair Shops (PA-10). 2 sheets; 4 photos. LC code: PA,58-SUSQ,1.
   Susquehanna Station and Hotel (Starracca House) (PA-8) 7 sheets; 22 photos. LC code: PA,58-SUSQ,3.
   Susquehanna Transfer Table (PA-10G). 3 photos. LC code: PA,58-SUSQ,1G.

Union County

Lewisburg
St. Anthony Street Bridge (PA-99). 24 photos; 18 data pages. LC code: PA,60-LEWB,1.

Venango County

Emlenton
Emlenton Bridge (PA-101). 39 photos; 19 data pages. LC code: PA,61-EML,1.

Oil City
Erie Railway: Meadville Division, Bridge 33.14 (PA-63). 1 photo. LC code: PA,61-OICI,1.
Pennsylvania Railroad: Allegheny River Bridge (PA-22). 5 photos. LC code: PA,61-OICI,2.

Wayne County

Hawley
Erie Railway: Hawley Coaling Station (PA-25). 5 photos. LC code: PA,64-HAW,1.

Honesdale
Honesdale Coal Pockets (PA-82). 11 photos; 8 data pages. LC code: PA,64-HOND,3.

Westmoreland County

Smithton
Smithton Bridge (PA-97). 24 photos; 5 data pages. LC code: PA,65-SMIT,1.

Wyoming County

Nicholson
Erie-Lackawanna Railroad: Tunkhannock Viaduct (PA-87). 10 photos; 1 data page. LC code: PA,66-NICH,1.

York County

New Cumberland
New Cumberland Army Depot (PA-80). 44 data pages. LC code: PA,67-NECUM,1.

York
American Chain and Cable Company Factory (PA-52). 18 photos; 10 data pages. LC code: PA,67-YORK,16.

Bibliography

The following bibliography lists a selection of publications dealing primarily with Pennsylvania architecture. Few sources attempt to cover the full range of architecture in the state. Most concentrate on a specific area, period, or building type. Since early Pennsylvania structures were so influential to the development of American architecture as a whole, standard architectural history texts usually cite many Pennsylvania examples.

Included here is a brief section on Historic American Buildings Survey publications. Numerous books and articles have been published about and by HABS, but only a few basic sources are listed here. A comprehensive bibliography of sources written about the history and recording activities of HABS, as well as items published by HABS about its collection and recording standards, is currently being produced by the Survey and will be available shortly.

Philadelphia sources, listed separately, are limited to a selection of primary works on the city's architecture. More complete bibliographical information may be found in the Philadelphia essay notes in this publication, compiled by Richard J. Webster, and in the 1976 HABS Philadelphia catalog, *Philadelphia Preserved*, also by Webster.

The Pennsylvania section concentrates on sources that cover the state's architecture as a whole, regional architecture, building types, construction techniques, ethnic building origins and designs, and specific time periods. General, regional, and local histories are not included, although many contain valuable information on buildings. Monographs on architects and works on individual structures are beyond the scope of this list. General books on American architecture or specific architectural styles are not included unless they contain numerous Pennsylvania examples and important references to the influence of Pennsylvania architecture.

For additional sources refer to the essay notes in this book and to the bibliographies which appear in many of the publications listed.

Historic American Buildings Survey Publications

Burns, John A., ed. *Recording Historic Structures*. Washington, D.C.: The HABS/HAER, NPS (National Park Service), Department of the Interior, American Institute of Architects Press, 1989. Handbook for the production of architectural and engineering documentation according to HABS/HAER standards. Includes articles on various recording methods authored by HABS/HAER staff members. Replaces the now out of print manual, *Recording Historic Buildings*, by Harley J. McKee.

DeLony, Eric, Ellen Boone, and Alice Keyes. *HAER Checklist 1969-1985: A Listing of Sites, Structures, and Objects Documented by the Historic American Engineering Record*. Washington, D.C.: HABS/HAER, NPS, Department of the Interior, 1985. A listing of the HAER collection since the 1976 catalog.

Historic American Buildings Survey. *Catalog of Completed Records, December 15, 1933 to July 15, 1934*. Washington, D.C.: HABS, NPS, Branch of Plans and Designs, Department of the Interior, 1934. An informal catalog listing over 1,000 sites documented by HABS nationwide during its first year. Catalog accompanied an exhibition of HABS records.

_____. *Catalog of Completed Records, December 15, 1933 to December 31, 1935*. Washington, D.C.: HABS, NPS, Branch of Planning and Design, Department of the Interior, 1936.

_____. *Catalog of the Measured Drawings and Photographs of the Survey in the Library of Congress, January 1, 1938*. Washington, D.C.: HABS, NPS, Department of the Interior, GPO, 1938. Catalog compiled by John P. O'Neill of HABS, with an introduction by Leicester B. Holland of the Library of Congress. First HABS national catalog produced for wide distribution.

_____. *Catalog of the Measured Drawings and Photographs of the Survey in the Library of Congress, March 1, 1941*. Washington, D.C.: HABS, NPS, Department of the Interior, GPO, 1941. The comprehensive catalog of structures recorded by HABS during the various economic recovery programs of the 1930s. There are over six thousand entries. Catalog edited by Frederick D. Nichols.

_____. *Catalog Supplement, Catalog of the Measured Drawings and Photographs of the Survey in the Library of Congress, Comprising Additions Since March 1, 1941*. Washington, D.C.: HABS, NPS, Department of the Interior, GPO, 1959. A supplement to the 1941 catalog, lists only additional structures recorded. Catalog compiled by Worth Bailey.

McKee, Harley J. *Recording Historic Buildings*. Washington, D.C.: HABS, NPS, Department of the Interior, GPO, 1970. A standard text on documenting historic structures based on techniques developed by HABS. Out of print and recently replaced by the HABS/HAER publication *Recording Historic Structures*, edited by John A. Burns.

Peatross, C. Ford, ed. and Alicia Stamm, compiler of checklist. *Historic America: Buildings, Structures, and Sites Recorded by the Historic American Buildings Survey and the Historic American Engineering Record*. Washington, D.C.: Library of Congress, GPO, 1983. A series of excellent articles published for the fiftieth anniversary of HABS. It includes a checklist of all structures recorded by HABS, the first nationwide catalog since 1941.

Sackheim, Donald E. *Historic American Engineering Record Catalog*. Washington, D.C.: HAER, NPS, Department of the Interior, GPO, 1976. A comprehensive catalog of HAER sites recorded nationwide through 1976.

Smith, Carol C. *Fifty Years of the Historic American Buildings Survey*. Alexandria, Va.: Historic American Buildings Survey Foundation, 1983. A good general essay on the history of HABS with an introduction by former chief of HABS, James C. Massey.

Philadelphia

American Institute of Architects, Philadelphia Chapter. *Philadelphia Architecture*. New York: Reinhold, 1961.

Brownlee, David B. *The Benjamin Franklin Parkway and the Philadelphia Museum of Art*. Philadelphia: Philadelphia Museum of Art, 1989.

Eberlein, Harold Donaldson and Cortlandt Van Dyke Hubbard. *Portrait of a Colonial City: Philadelphia, 1670-1838*. Philadelphia: J. B. Lippincott, 1939.

Eisenhart, Luther P., ed. *Historic Philadelphia: From the Founding until the Early Nineteenth Century*. Transactions of the American Philosophical Society, vol. 43, part 1, 1953. A series of articles on significant early Philadelphia buildings.

Group for Environmental Education. *Philadelphia Architecture: A Guide to the City*. Edited by John Andrew Gallery. Cambridge: The MIT Press, 1984.

Massey, James C., ed. *Two Centuries of Philadelphia Architectural Drawings*. Philadelphia: Society of Architectural Historians and The Philadelphia Museum of Art, 1964. An exhibition catalog edited by the former chief of HABS.

Murtagh, William J. "The Philadelphia Row House." *Journal of the Society of Architectural Historians* 16 (1957): 8-13. This article developed the standard classification of Philadelphia row house plans.

O'Gorman, James F. "A New York Architect Visits Philadelphia in 1822." *Pennsylvania Magazine of History and Biography* 117 (July 1993): 153-176. Two sketchbooks of John McComb Jr., record Philadelphia's transition to Greek Revival architecture.

O'Gorman, James F., Jeffrey A. Cohen, George E. Thomas, and G. Holmes Perkins. *Drawing Towards Building: Philadelphia Architectural Graphics, 1732-1986*. Philadelphia: University of Pennsylvania Press for Pennsylvania Academy of the Fine Arts, 1986.

Peterson, Charles E. "HABS-In and Out of Philadelphia." In *Philadelphia Preserved,* by Richard J. Webster. Philadelphia: Temple University Press, 1976. An excellent essay on HABS and its personnel authored by the founder of the Survey.

Sewell, Darrel L., ed. *Philadelphia: Three Centuries of American Art*. Philadelphia: Philadelphia Museum of Art, 1976. Publication covering architecture, art, and decorative arts in Philadelphia, authored by numerous experts in each area. Good account of important buildings and their architects, including bibliographical citations. Accompanied a bicentennial exhibition.

Tatman, Sandra L. and Roger W. Moss. *Biographical Dictionary of Philadelphia Architects: 1700-1930*. Boston: G.K. Hall and Co., 1985. A comprehensive list of Philadelphia architects compiled for The Athenaeum of Philadelphia.

Tatum, George B. "Documenting a City: Philadelphia." In *Historic America: Buildings, Structures, and Sites Recorded by the Historic American Buildings Survey and the Historic American Engineering Record*. Edited by C. Ford Peatross. Washington, D.C.: Library of Congress, GPO, 1983.

_____. *Penn's Great Town: 250 Years of Philadelphia Architecture Illustrated in Prints and Drawings*. Philadelphia: University of Pennsylvania Press, 1961. A standard source for the city's high-style architecture.

_____. *Philadelphia Georgian*. Middletown, Ct.: Wesleyan University Press, 1976. An excellent source on Georgian style in Philadelphia. Primarily about the Powel House, with excellent photographs by Cortlandt V. D. Hubbard.

Teitelman, Edward and Richard W. Longstreth. *Architecture in Philadelphia: A Guide*. Cambridge: The MIT Press, 1974.

Tinkcom, Harry M., Margaret B. Tinkcom, and Grant Miles Simon. *Historic Germantown*. Philadelphia: American Philosophical Society, 1955.

Webster, Richard J. *Philadelphia Preserved: Catalog of the Historic American Buildings Survey*. Philadelphia: Temple University Press, 1976. Informative essays, including a fine history of HABS by Charles E. Peterson, and catalog entries on over six hundred structures in Philadelphia recorded by HABS. A companion to this HABS Pennsylvania Catalog.

White, Theo B., ed. *Philadelphia Architecture in the Nineteenth Century*. Philadelphia: University of Pennsylvania Press, 1953. A seminal, but now dated, work focusing attention on the city's nineteenth-century architecture. Published for the Philadelphia Art Alliance.

Pennsylvania Architecture References

Alexander, Edwin P. *On the Main Line: The Pennsylvania Railroad in the 19th Century.* New York: Bramhall House, 1971. A study of the railroad between Philadelphia and Pittsburgh, including information on stations.

Allen, George H. "Some European Origins of Early Pennsylvania Architecture." *American Journal of Archaeology* 40 (1936). A paper submitted to the Archaeological Institute of America.

Archambault, A. Margaretta, ed. *A Guide Book of Art, Architecture and Historic Interests in Pennsylvania.* Philadelphia: John C. Winston Co., 1924. A general county by county survey.

Ball, Bernice. *Barns of Chester County, Pennsylvania.* West Chester: Chester County Day Committee of the Women's Auxiliary, Chester County Hospital, 1974.

Bennett, Lola. *The Company Towns of the Rockhill Iron and Coal Company: Robertsday and Woodvale, Pennsylvania.* Washington, D.C.: HABS/HAER and America's Industrial Heritage Project, 1990. Heavily-illustrated study of two coal company towns on the eastern slope of Huntingdon County's Broad Top Mountain; based on a 1989 HABS/HAER recording project.

Bergengren, Charles. "The Cycle of Transformations in Schaefferstown, Pennsylvania, Houses." In *Perspectives in Vernacular Architecture, IV,* Thomas Carter and Bernard L. Herman, eds. Columbia: University of Missouri Press, 1991.

Bircenall, Martha P., Sylvia Carson and Gregory Ramsey. *Historic Buildings of Centre County, Pennsylvania.* University Park: Pennsylvania State University Press, 1980. A survey prepared for the Historic Registration Project of the Centre County Library.

Bounds, A. Pierce. "Pennsylvania Firehouses: The Evolution of Design." *Pennsylvania Heritage* 10 (1984): 24-28.

Brumbaugh, G. Edwin. "Architecture in Pennsylvania." *Pennsylvania History* 17 (1950): 103-105.

_____. "Colonial Architecture of the Pennsylvania Germans." *Proceedings of the Pennsylvania German Society* 41, part 2 (1933). Authored by a well-known Pennsylvania restoration architect, article covers interior and exterior features as well as construction techniques.

_____. "Medieval Construction at Ephrata." *Antiques* 46 (July 1944): 18-20. Mainly on restoration work at Ephrata.

Bucher, Robert C. "The Continental Log House." *Pennsylvania Folklife* 12 (1962): 14-19.

_____. "The Cultural Backgrounds of Our Pennsylvania Homesteads." *Bulletin of the Historical Society of Montgomery County, Pennsylvania* 15 (1966): 22-26.

_____. "Steep Roofs and Red Tiles." *Pennsylvania Folklife* 12 (1961): 19-26.

_____. "The Swiss Bank House in Pennsylvania." *Pennsylvania Folklife* 18 (1968-69): 2-11.

Butko, Brian A. "Larger than Life along the Lincoln Highway." *Pennsylvania Heritage* 21 (Summer 1995): 20-29. A survey of brazen and bizarre examples of roadside architecture.

Butler, David M. "Quaker Meeting Houses in America and England: Impressions and Comparison." *Quaker History* 79 (Fall 1990): 93-104.

Byrne, Jacob Hill. "Typical Old Lancaster Buildings and Architecture." *Journal of the Lancaster County Historical Society* 26 (1922): 138-43.

Cashman, William M. "Buildings, Builders and Activity in Warren in the Early Part of the Twentieth Century." *Stepping Stones* 19 (1975): 572-580.

Clouse, Jerry and Kate Kauffman. "Watt's Folly." *Pennsylvania Heritage* 15 (1989): 12-17. Article on Frederick Watts, who propagated the bank barn while head of the Bureau of Agriculture during President Grant's administration.

Comings, Marion. "Pioneer Architecture of Western Pennsylvania." *Carnegie Magazine* 11 (1938): 305-08.

Cook, Anne H. and Ann L. Snider. "If Only the Walls Could Talk: The Story of the Federal Barn." *Pennsylvania Heritage* 9 (1983): 23-26.

Cooper, Patricia Irvin. "Some Misconceptions in American Log-Building Studies." *Material Culture* 23 (Summer 1991): 43-62. Gives credit to Swedes and Finns for introducing log-building traditions that, with later features from Swiss and Germans, flowed out of the Delaware Valley into the Chesapeake to become part of the southern plain's cultural landscape.

Cope, Gilbert and Henry Graham Ashmead. *Historic Homes and Institutions and Genealogical and Personal Memoirs of Chester and Delaware Counties, Pennsylvania*. New York: Lewis Publishing Co., 1904.

Craft, John L. "Ephrata Cloister, an Eighteenth-Century Religious Commune." *Antiques* 118 (October 1980).

Cummings, Hubertus. "Pennsylvania's State Houses and Capitols." *Pennsylvania History* 20 (1953): 409-16.

Del Sordo, Stephen G. "Eighteenth-Century Grist Mills: Some Chester County, Pennsylvania Examples." In *Perspectives in Vernacular Architecture*. Annapolis: Vernacular Architecture Forum, 1982.

Dickson, Harold E. *A Hundred Pennsylvania Buildings*. State College: Bald Eagle Press, 1954. A fine sampling of significant Pennsylvania buildings with illustrations and brief text.

Dieffenbach, Victor C. "Building A Pennsylvania Barn." *Pennsylvania Folklife* 12 (1961): 20-24.

Domer, Dennis. "Genesis Theories of the German-American Two-Door House." *Material Culture* 26 (Spring 1994): 1-35. A new theory to help explain German-Americans' affection for the two-door house from Pennsylvania to Kansas.

Dornbusch, Charles H. and John K. Heyl. *Pennsylvania German Barns*. Pennsylvania German Folklore Society, vol. 21, 1956. Allentown: Schlechter's, 1958. A standard text which classifies different types of Pennsylvania German barns. Charles Dornbusch donated his barn photographs to the HABS collection.

Eberlein, Harold Dickson and Horace Mather Lippincott. *The Colonial Homes of Philadelphia and Its Neighborhood*. Philadelphia: J. B. Lippincott, 1912.

Embury, Aymar II. "Pennsylvania Farmhouses: Examples of Rural Dwellings of a Hundred Years Ago." *The Architectural Record* 30 (November 1911): 475-485.

Ensminger, Robert F. "A Comparative Study of Pennsylvania and Wisconsin Forebay Barns." *Pennsylvania Folklife* 32 (1983): 99-114.

Ensminger, Robert F. *The Pennsylvania Barn: Its Origin, Evolution, and Distribution in North America*. Baltimore: Johns Hopkins University Press, 1992. The definitive work on the Pennsylvania barn: all one wants to know about Pennsylvania barns and much one never thought to ask.

_____. "A Search for the Origin of the Pennsylvania Barn." *Pennsylvania Folklife* 30 (1980-81): 50-71.

Eshelman, John E. "Society of Friends and Their Meeting Houses in Berks County." *Berks County Historical Society Review* 1 (1936): 34-40.

_____. "The Society of Friends and Their Meeting Houses in Berks County." *Historical Review of Berks County* 19 (1954), p. 104.

Federal Writers' Project. *Pennsylvania: A Guide to the Keystone State*. American Guide Series. New York: Oxford University Press, 1940. Contains a section on architecture and includes many good photographs of historic buildings.

Fegley, H. Winslow. *Among Some of the Older Mills in Eastern Pennsylvania*. Norristown: Pennsylvania German Society, 1930.

Fitzsimons, Gray, ed. *Blair County and Cambria County, Pennsylvania: An Inventory of Historic Engineering and Industrial Sites*. Washington, D.C.: HABS/HAER and America's Industrial Heritage Project, NPS, Department of the Interior, 1990. Publication based on a HAER recording project in 1987 that includes iron furnaces, Pennsylvania Railroad's Altoona Works, and Cambria Iron Works in Johnstown.

Friesen, Steve. "Home Is Where the Hearth Is." *Pennsylvania Folklife* 40 (Spring 1991): 98-115, 118. Examines use of the raised hearth in early Pennsylvania German houses.

_____. *A Modest Mennonite Home*. Intercourse: Good Books, 1990. Relates the history of the Hans Herr House (PA-371) in Lancaster County from construction to restoration.

Garfinkel, Susan. "Letting in the 'World': (Re)interpretive Tensions in the Quaker Meeting House." In *Gender, Class, and Shelter: Perspectives in Vernacular Architecture, V*, Elizabeth Collins Cromley and Carter L. Hudgins, eds. Knoxville: University of Tennessee Press, 1995.

Gibson, Jane Mork. "The Fairmount Waterworks." *Bulletin, Philadelphia Museum of Art* 84 (Summer 1988): 2-48.

Glass, Joseph W. *The Pennsylvania Culture Region: A View from the Barn*. Ann Arbor: UMI Research Press, 1986. A scholarly and quantified study of Pennsylvania barns.

Glassie, Henry. "A Central Chimney Continental Log House." *Pennsylvania Folklife* 18 (1968-69): 32-39.

_____. "The Double Crib Barn in South Central Pennsylvania." *Pioneer America* 2 (1970).

_____. "Eighteenth-Century Cultural Process in Delaware Valley Folk Building." *Winterthur Portfolio* 7 (1972): 29-58.

_____. *Pattern in the Material Folk Culture of the Eastern United States*. Philadelphia: University of Pennsylvania Press, 1968. The standard text for students of folklife covering many forms of material culture including buildings. Pennsylvania farmhouses and outbuildings are discussed and illustrated, including sketches of floor plans. Includes an extensive bibliography.

_____. "The Pennsylvania Barn." *Pennsylvania Folklife* 15 (1965-66): 8-19 and 15 (1966): 12-25.

Gollin, Gillian Lindt. *Moravians in Two Worlds: A Study of Changing Communities*. New York: Columbia University Press, 1967.

Goode, Ned. "An Album of Chester County Farmhouses." *Pennsylvania Folklife* 13 (1962): 19-24. Goode was the photographer for the HABS Chester County project which documented 100 structures in the 1950s.

Gowans, Alan. *Images of American Living: Four Centuries of Architecture and Furniture as Cultural Expression*. New York and Philadelphia: J. B. Lippincott, 1964. Includes many Pennsylvania examples.

Hamlin, Talbot. *Greek Revival Architecture in America*. New York: Oxford University Press, 1944. A classic book on Greek Revival style, it includes sections on Philadelphia and Pennsylvania. The examples of Greek Revival houses in the Northern Tier Region are well covered. The book also includes an annotated bibliography.

Hanna, Susan E. "The Farmhouse Styles of Lawrence County." *Pennsylvania Heritage* 4 (1978): 10-12.

Harpster, John W. "Eighteenth Century Inns and Taverns of Western Pennsylvania." *Western Pennsylvania Historical Magazine* 19 (1936): 5-16.

Heald, Sarah H., ed. *Fayette County, Pennsylvania: An Inventory of Historic Engineeering and Industrial Sites*. Washington, D.C.: HABS/HAER and America's Industrial Heritage Project, 1990. A descriptive work based on a 1989 HABS/HAER recording project.

Hoagland, Alison K. and Mulrooney, Margaret M. *Norvelt and Penn-Craft, Pennsylvania: Subsistence-Homestead Communities of the 1930s*. Washington, D.C.: HABS/HAER and America's Industrial Heritage Project, 1991. A study of Norvelt, Westmoreland County, and Penn-Craft, Fayette County, planned communities built by the U.S. Division of Subsistence Homesteads and American Friends Service Committee (AFSC) respectively. Abundantly illustrated with Farm Service Administration, AFSC, and HABS photographs.

Historic Preservation Trust of Lancaster County. *Lancaster County Architecture, 1700-1850*. Lancaster, Pa.: Historic Preservation Trust of Lancaster County, 1992. Essentially a picture book (with a ten-page introduction), but one with high-quality photos and correctly dated captions.

Horst, Melvin and Elmer L. Smith. *Covered Bridges of Pennsylvania Dutchland*. Akron, Pa.: Applied Arts, 1960.

Hurivitz, Elizabeth Adams. "Decorative Elements in the Domestic Architecture of Eastern Pennsylvania." *Dutchman* 7 (1955): 6-29.

Israel, Cora M. "Historic Churches of Pennsylvania." *American Monthly Magazine* 41 (July 1912): 10-16.

Jordan, Albert F. "Some Early Moravian Builders in America." *Pennsylvania Folklife* 24 (1974): 2-17.

Jordan, Terry G. *American Log Buildings: An Old World Heritage*. Chapel Hill: University of North Carolina Press, 1985. A definitive work on log construction in America and the most recent book on its origins in this country.

_____. "Moravian, Schwenkfelder and American Log Construction." *Pennsylvania Folklife* 33 (1984): 98-124.

_____. "Some Neglected Swiss Literature on the Forebay Bank Barn." *Pennsylvania Folklife* 37 (1987-88): 75-80.

_____. Kaups, Matti and Richard M. Lieffort. "New Evidence on the European Origin of Pennsylvania V Notching." *Pennsylvania Folklife* 36 (1986): 20-30.

Kauffman, Henry J. "Church Architecture in Lancaster County." *Dutchman* 6 (1955): 16-27.

_____. "Domestic Architecture in Lancaster County." *Pennsylvania Folklife* 31 (1982): 104-108.

_____. "Moravian Architecture in Bethlehem." *Dutchman* 6 (1955): 12-19.

_____. "Pennsylvania Barns." *Farm Quarterly* 9 (1954), p. 58.

_____. "The Summer House." *Dutchman* 8 (1956): 2-7.

Kennedy, Dean. "Century Old Farmhouses, Oley Valley, Berks County, Pennsylvania." *Pencil Points* 13 (1932): 540-54. Kennedy served as a HABS deputy district officer in the 1930s. HABS had a later recording project in this area.

Keyser, Alan G. and William P. Stein. "The Pennsylvania German Tri-level Ground Barn." *Der Reggeboge* 9 (1975): 1-25.

Kidney, Walter C. *Landmark Architecture: Pittsburgh and Allegheny County*. Pittsburgh: Pittsburgh History & Landmarks Foundation, 1985. A historical essay and a well-illustrated guide to significant pre-1940 architecture in Allegheny County.

_____. *Pittsburgh's Landmark Architecture: The Historic Buildings of Pittsburgh and Allegheny County*. Pittsburgh History and Landmarks Foundation, 1997.

_____. *Allegheny Cemetery: A Romantic Landscape in Pittsburgh*. Pittsburgh: Pittsburgh History and Landmarks Foundation, 1991.

Kimball, Fiske. *Domestic Architecture of the American Colonies and of the Early Republic*. New York: Charles Scribners Sons, 1922, reprinted New York: Dover, 1966. Scholarly work of great detail; a classic reference for American architecture with many Pennsylvania examples.

Kniffen, Fred. "Folk Housing: Key to Diffusion." *Annals of the Association of American Geographers* 55 (1965): 549-577. Southeastern Pennsylvania is seen as the starting place for the spread of vernacular architecture southward and westward.

_____ and Henry Glassie. "Building in Wood in the Eastern United States: A Time-Place Perspective." *The Geographical Review* 56 (1966): 40-66.

Kocher, Alfred Lawrence. "The Early Architecture of Lancaster County, Pennsylvania." *Lancaster County Historical Society Papers* 24 (1920): 91-106.

_____. "Early Architecture of Pennsylvania–In Fourteen Parts." *Architectural Record*: part 1 48: 513-40; part 2 49: 31-47; part 3 49: 135-55; part 4 49: 233-48; part 5 49: 310-30; part 6 49: 409-22; part 7 49: 519-35; part 8 50: 27-43; part 9 50: 147-57; part 10 50: 214-26; part 11 50: 398-406; part 12 51: 507-20; part 13 52: 121-32; part 14 52: 434-44 (December 1920-November 1922). Kocher, an architect, prepared this excellent series of articles, well illustrated with photographs and drawings. An early work of importance.

Koegler, Karen. "Building in Stone in Southwestern Pennsylvania: Patterns and Process." In *Gender, Class, and Shelter: Perspectives in Vernacular Architecture*, V, Elizabeth Collins Cromley and Carter L. Hudgins, eds. Knoxville: University of Tennessee Press, 1995.

Landis, D. B. "Lancaster Houses of 150 Years Ago." *Lancaster County Historical Society Papers* 26 (1922): 136-37.

Landis, H. K. "Early Kitchens of the Pennsylvania Germans." *Pennsylvania German Society Proceedings*, vol. 47, part 3, 1939.

Lanier, Gabrielle. "Samuel Wilson's Working World: Builders and Buildings in Chester County, Pennsylvania, 1780-1827." In *Perspectives in Vernacular Architecture, IV*, Thomas Carter and Bernard L. Herman, eds. Columbia: University of Missouri Press, 1991.

Lawton, Arthur J. "The Ground Rules of Folk Architecture." *Pennsylvania Folklife* 23 (1973): 13-19.

_____. "The Pre-Metric Foot and Its Uses in Pennsylvania German Architecture." *Pennsylvania Folklife* 19 (1969): 37-45.

Lay, K. Edward. "European Antecedents of Seventeenth and Eighteenth Century Germanic and Scots-Irish Architecture in America." *Pennsylvania Folklife* 32 (1982): 2-43.

Leach, Sara Amy, ed. *Two Historic Pennsylvania Canal Towns: Alexandria and Saltsburg.* Washington, D.C.: HABS/HAER and America's Industrial Heritage Project, NPS, Department of the Interior, 1989. A publication based on data prepared during a 1988 HABS/HAER recording project of two towns located on the Pennsylvania Main Line Canal.

Lestz, Gerald S. *Historic Heart of Lancaster.* Lancaster: John Baer's Sons, 1962. Street by street guidebook.

Lewis, Peirce F. "Common Houses, Cultural Spoor." *Landscape* 19 (1975): 1-22. Traces common American house types from east coast areas since the colonial period.

Lewis, Virginia E. "Reflections of Changing Taste in Pittsburgh Architecture." *Carnegie Magazine* 31 (1957): 27-32.

Lippold, John W. "Early Lancaster Architecture." *Journal of Lancaster County Historical Society* 75 (1972): 145-178.

Long, Amos Jr. "Bank (Multi-Level) Structures in Rural Pennsylvania." *Pennsylvania Folklife* 20 (1970-71): 31-39.

_____. *The Pennsylvania German Family Farm.* Vol. 6. Breinigsville, Pa.: Pennsylvania German Folklore Society, 1972. Discusses farm buildings with separate sections on different outbuildings. Long also has a series of articles on individual farm outbuildings that was published in Pennsylvania Folklife during the 1960s.

Lord, Arthur C. "Architectural Characteristics of Houses in Lancaster County, 1798." *Journal of Lancaster County Historical Society* 85 (1981): 132-151.

_____. "Barns of Lancaster County, 1798." *Journal of Lancaster County Historical Society* 77 (1973): 26-40.

Marsh, John L. "Styled for Worship: The Country Churches of Northwestern Pennsylvania." *Pennsylvania Heritage* 19 (Winter 1993): 32-37.

Martin, Park H. "City of Bridges." *Carnegie Magazine* 23 (1949): 154-58. Covers bridges in Pittsburgh from 1818-1949.

Master Detail Series. "The Pennsylvania Farm House." *Architectural Forum* 60 (May 1923): 369-84.

Maurer, J. A. and H. K. Schuchard, "Moravian Buildings in Bethlehem." Archaeology 3 (1950): 226-32.

McFall, Nancy J. "Preserving York's Architectural Heritage." *Pennsylvania Folklife* 16 (1967): 20-23.

McInerney, Suzanne. "A Capitol Idea! A Brief and Bumpy History of Pennsylvania's Capitols." *Pennsylvania Heritage* 20 (Winter 1994): 24-31.

Merritt, Olive. "Recessed Porches of Southeastern Pennsylvania." *Historical Review of Berks County* 45 (1980), p. 100.

Miller, Annie Clark. "Old Houses and Estates in Pittsburgh." *Western Pennsylvania Historical Magazine* 9 (1926): 129-68.

Miller, E. Willard and Ruby M. Miller. *Pennsylvania–Natural Resources and Economic Development: A Bibliography*. Monticello, Ill: Vance Bibliographies, 1985. Not a complete bibliography, but contains over one hundred entries dealing with Pennsylvania architecture, organized by area and building type

Milner, John D. "Germanic Architecture in the New World." *Journal of the Society of Architectural Historians* 34 (1975): 296-301. Authored by a well-known Pennsylvania restoration architect and former employee of HABS.

Milspaw, Yvonne J. "Ordinary Architecture of the Pennsylvania Germans: The Turnpike Houses." *Pennsylvania Folklife* 33 (1983): 30-35.

Monroe County Planning Commission. *Monroe County–Historic Legacy*. Stroudsburg, Pa.: Monroe County Planning Commission, 1980.

Montgomery, Richard S. "Houses of the Oley Valley." *Dutchman* 6 (1954): 16-26. HABS had a recording project in the Oley Valley shortly after this article was published.

Morrison, Hugh. *Early American Architecture from the First Colonial Settlements to the National Period*. New York: Oxford University Press, 1952. A comprehensive survey of early American architecture using many Pennsylvania examples from Independence Hall to bank barns.

Mulrooney, Margaret M. *A Legacy of Coal: The Coal Company Towns of Southwestern Pennsylvania*. Washington, D.C.: HABS/HAER and America's Industrial Heritage Project, NPS, Department of the Interior, 1989. Publication based on a HABS/HAER recording project centered in three coal company towns: Star Junction in Fayette County, Windber in Somerset County, and Colver in Cambria County.

Murtagh, William J. "Half-Timbering in American Architecture." *Pennsylvania Folklife* 9 (1957-58).

_____. *Moravian Architecture and Town Planning: Bethlehem, Pennsylvania and Other Eighteenth-Century American Settlements*. Chapel Hill: University of North Carolina Press, 1967. A comprehensive book on the subject.

Nelson, Lee H. "The Colossus of Philadelphia." In *Material Culture of the Wooden Age*. Brooke Hindle, ed. Tarrytown: Sleepy Hollow Press, 1981. Contains information on the history of covered bridges in Pennsylvania.

Nelson, Vernon H. and Lothar Madeheim. "The Moravian Settlements of Pennsylvania in 1757; The Nicholas Garrison Views." *Pennsylvania Folklife* 19 (1969): 2-13.

Noble, Allen G. *Wood, Brick, and Stone: The North American Settlement Landscape*. 2 vols. Amherst: University of Massachusetts Press, 1984. A compendium by a cultural geographer of regional house types and their environments, diffusion, and modifications.

_____, and Brian Coffey. "Barns and Silo Types in Pennsylvania." *Pennsylvania Geographer* 12 (1974): 19-29.

Paxson, Henry D. "Log Houses of Bucks County." *Bucks County Historical Society Papers* 4 (1917): 204-9.

Pendleton, Philip E. *Oley Valley Heritage: The Colonial Years: 1700-1775*. Birdsboro: Pennsylvania German Society, 1994. Excellent study of three Berks County townships (Amity, Exeter, and Oley) rich in architecture.

Pennsylvania Department of Transportation, and Pennsylvania Historical and Museum Commission. *Historic Highway Bridges in Pennsylvania*. Harrisburg: Pennsylvania Historical and Museum Commission, 1986.

Pennsylvania Historical and Museum Commission. *Historic Structures Report for Old Economy Village*, prepared by Clio Group Inc. and Marianna Thomas, Architects, 1989-1990, Vols. 1-10).

Pennsylvania Historical and Museum Commission. *Pennsylvania's Landmarks*. Harrisburg: Pennsylvania Historical and Museum Commission/Applied Arts Publishers, 1987.

_____, and Preservation Technology Project/Pennsylvania State University. *Repair and Preservation Maintenance for Historic and Older Homes*. Harrisburg: Pennsylvania Historical and Museum Commission, 1982.

Pennsylvania Planning Commission. *Northumberland County Preservation Plan*. Sunbury: Pennsylvania Planning Commission, 1978.

Peterson, Charles E. *Building Early America*. Radnor: Chilton Book Company, 1976. Series of articles on building construction and preservation published for the Carpenters' Company of Philadelphia.

―――. "Eight-Sided Schoolhouses, 1800-1840." *Journal of the Society of Architectural Historians* 12 (1953): 21-22. Covers those of southeastern Pennsylvania.

Pillsbury, Richard. "The Construction Materials of the Rural Folk Housing of the Pennsylvania Culture Region." *Pioneer America* 8 (1976): 98-106.

―――. "Patterns in the Folk and Vernacular House Forms of the Pennsylvania Cultural Region." *Pioneer America* 9 (1977): 12-31. Examines the I House form in Bucks, Montgomery, and Chester Counties.

Pinkowski, Edward. *Washington's Officers Slept Here: Historic Homes of Valley Forge and Its Neighborhood*. Philadelphia: Sunshine Press, 1953. Covers thirty-four buildings existing in 1777.

Price, B. Llewellyn. "Early Stonework of Eastern Pennsylvania." *House Beautiful* 67 (January 1930), p. 58.

Puig, Francis J. "The Porches of Quaker Meeting Houses in Chester and Delaware Counties." *Pennsylvania Folklife* 24 (1974-75): 21-30.

Putnam, Mary and Chase Putnam, eds. *Historic Buildings in Warren County*. 3 vols. Warren, Pa., 1971-74.

Raymond, Eleanor. *Early Domestic Architecture of Pennsylvania*. New York: William Helburn, 1931; reprinted Princeton: Pyne Press, 1973. An early work recognizing the significance of small dwellings and utilitarian structures, filled with excellent photographs and drawings.

Reinberger, Mark. "Graeme Park and the Three-Cell Plan: A Lost Type in Colonial Architecture." In *Perspectives in Vernacular Architecture, IV*, Thomas Carter and Bernard L. Herman, eds. Columbia: University of Missouri Press, 1991.

Riccardi, Saro John. "Pennsylvania Dutch Folk Art and Architecture." *New York Public Library Bulletin* 46 (1942): 471-83. An annotated bibliography.

Rice, William S. "Early Pennsylvania Arts." *School Arts Magazine* 32 (1933), 395. Includes some architectural line drawings.

Richman, Irwin. *Pennsylvania Architecture*. University Park: Pennsylvania Historical Association, 1969. An illustrated statewide survey.

Rivinus, Willis M. *Old Stone Work in Bucks County*. Doylestown: Bucks County Historical Society, 1972.

Roos, Frank J. Jr. *Bibliography of Early American Architecture: Writings on Architecture Constructed Before 1860 in Eastern and Central United States*. Urbana: University of Illinois Press, 1968. Very important reference book. The Pennsylvania section includes general references and references for specific counties and towns.

Schalck, Harry G. "West Chester Buildings." In *175th Anniversary of West Chester*, Ray Doyle, ed. West Chester, Pa.: Biehn Printing, 1974.

Schiffer, Margaret B. "Chester County Log Houses." *Chester County History* 1 (1975): 19-28.

―――. *Survey of Chester County, Pennsylvania Architecture: 17th, 18th and 19th Centuries*. Exton, Pa,: Schiffer Publishing, 1976. Mostly illustrated with HABS photographs.

Schmertz, Robert W. "Architecture in Pittsburgh Dating 1900." *Carnegie Magazine* 23 (1949): 78-82.

Schuyler, Montgomery. "Architecture of American Colleges Part 5: University of Pennsylvania, Girard, Haverford, Lehigh, and Bryn Mawr." *Architectural Record* 28 (September 1910): 183-212.

Sgromo, Vito J. and Michael Lewis. *Wilkes-Barre Architecture, 1860 to 1960*. Wilkes-Barre: Wyoming Historical and Geological Society and Northeastern Pennsylvania Chapter, American Institute of Architects, 1983.

Shedd, Nancy S. *An Architectural Study of the Ancient Borough of Huntingdon*. Huntingdon: J.S. Rodgers Co., 1976.

Shedd, Nancy S. *Huntingdon County, Pennsylvania: An Inventory of Historic Engineering and Industrial Sites*, Sarah H. Heald, ed. Washington, D.C.: HABS/HAER and America's Industrial Heritage Project, NPS, Department of the Interior, 1991. Descriptive and historical information on nearly eighty structures, ranging from furnaces and bridges to churches and company stores.

Shoemaker, Alfred. "Church and Meetinghouse, Stables and Sheds." *Pennsylvania Folklife* 11 (1960): 22-23.

_____, ed. *The Pennsylvania Barn*. Kutztown: The Pennsylvania Folklife Society, 1955. Series of articles, written by different authors, on Pennsylvania barns.

Shurtleff, Harold. *The Log Cabin Myth: A Study of the Early Dwellings of the English Colonists in North America*. Cambridge: Harvard University Press, 1939. Classic work on log structures.

Siskind, Aaron and William Morgan. *Bucks County: Photographs of Early Architecture*. New York: Horizon Press, 1974. Published for the Bucks County Historical Society. Little text, but many fine photographs.

Snyder, John J. *Handbook of Lancaster County Architecture: Styles and Terms*. Lancaster: Historic Preservation Society of Lancaster County, 1979.

_____. *Lancaster Architecture, 1719-1927: A Guide to Publicly Accessible Buildings in Lancaster County*. Lancaster, Pa.: Historical Preservation Trust of Lancaster County, 1979.

_____. "Pennsylvania's Architectural Heritage: Statehouses and Capitols." *Pennsylvania Heritage* 7 (1981): 21-27.

Snyder, Karl H. *Moravian Architecture of Bethlehem, Pennsylvania*. White Pine Series of Architectural Monographs, vol. 13, no. 4, 1927.

Spitulnik, Karen. "The Inn Crowd: The American Inn, 1730-1830." *Pennsylvania Folklife* 22 (1972-73): 25-41.

Stair, J. William. "Brick-End Barns." *Dutchman* 6 (1954): 14-33. Well-illustrated article on Pennsylvania barns, with numerous examples of decorative brick vents.

Stotz, Charles Morse. *The Early Architecture of Western Pennsylvania*. New York and Pittsburgh: William Helburn for the Buhl Foundation, 1936. Reprinted as *The Architectural Heritage of Early Western Pennsylvania*. Pittsburgh: University of Pittsburgh Press, 1966. Based on the Western Pennsylvania Architectural Survey of 1932-35, this is a classic study with numerous photographs and drawings similar to HABS documentation. An early regional survey which greatly influenced HABS and others in the field of architectural documentation. Stotz was one of the original HABS district officers, and many of those associated with this survey went on to complete the HABS documentation in the 1930s in western Pennsylvania.

Swank, Scott T. "The Germanic Fragment" and "The Architectural Landscape." In *Arts of the Pennsylvania Germans*, Catherine E. Hutchins, ed. New York: W.W. Norton for the Henry Francis DuPont Winterthur Museum, 1983.

Swetnam, George and Helene Smith. *A Guidebook to Historic Western Pennsylvania*. Pittsburgh: University of Pittsburgh Press, 1976. A county by county guidebook. Contains a bibliography divided by counties.

Szylvian, Kristin M. "Bauhaus on Trial: Aluminum City Terrace and Federal Defense Housing Policy during World War II." *Planning Perspectives* 9 (1994): 229-254.

Toker, Franklin. *Pittsburgh: A Urban Portrait*. Pittsburgh: University of Pittsburgh Press, 1986. A well-illustrated, informative guide to the city and both its stylish and industrial suburbs.

Trindell, Roger T. "Building in Brick in Early America." *The Geographical Review* 58 (1968).

University of Pittsburgh. "Reflections of Changing Taste in Pittsburgh Architecture." Henry Clay Frick Fine Arts Department Honors Seminar. *Carnegie Magazine* 31 (1957): 27-32.

Upper Allen Heritage Committee. *Early Architecture in Upper Allen Township*. Mechanicsburg, Pa.: Centre Square Press, 1976.

Upton, Dell. "Traditional Timber Framing." In *Material Culture of the Wooden Age*, Brooke Hindle, ed. Tarrytown: Sleepy Hollow Press, 1981. A good summary of continental framing techniques compared with other carpentry forms.

Valley Forge Historical Society. "The Quarters of General Washington's Staff." *Picket Post* 43 (1954): 6-23. Includes discussion on twenty-three buildings existing in 1777.

Van Stone, James W. "Fortified Houses in Western Pennsylvania." *Pennsylvania Archaeology* 20 (1950): 19-24.

Van Trump, James D. *An Architectural Tour of Pittsburgh*. Pittsburgh: Pittsburgh History & Landmarks Foundation, 1965.

_____. "The Gothic Revival in Pittsburgh: A Medievalistic Excursion." *Carnegie Magazine* 48 (1974): 57-69.

_____. "The Lamp of Demos: Some Pittsburgh Public School Buildings of the Past." *Charette* 42 (March 1962): 17-20.

_____. *Life and Architecture in Pittsburgh*. Pittsburgh: Pittsburgh History & Landmarks Foundation, 1983. A collection of previously published articles and unpublished radio transcripts by Van Trump, a recognized authority on Pittsburgh architecture, consolidated in one publication.

_____. "From Log Cabin to Cathedral: The Pittsburgh Church Building 1787-1960." *Charette* 41 (September 1961): 2-13.

_____. *Majesty of the Law: The Courthouses of Allegheny County*. Pittsburgh: Pittsburgh History & Landmarks Foundation, 1988. Information on Pittsburgh's three courthouses, focusing on H. H. Richardson's structure.

_____. "The Palace, the Loft and the Tower—Some Notes on the Development of the Urban Hotel in Pittsburgh." *Charette* 42 (October 1962): 12-17.

_____. *Railroad Stations of Pennsylvania: Their Architecture and History 1800-1964*. Pittsburgh, 1964.

_____. "Revived Romanesque in Pittsburgh." *Carnegie Magazine* 48 (1974): 108-113.

_____. "The Romanesque Revival in Pittsburgh." *Journal of the Society of Architectural Historians* 16 (1957): 23-29.

_____ and Arthur P. Ziegler. *Landmark Architecture of Allegheny County, Pennsylvania*. Pittsburgh: Pittsburgh History & Landmarks Foundation, 1967. A standard work on the area organized by location, with short text describing each building and many illustrations. Includes a bibliography.

Wagner, Dean R., ed. *Historic Lock Haven: An Architectural Survey*. Lock Haven, Pa.: Clinton County Historical Society, 1979.

Wall, Carol, ed. *Bibliography of Pennsylvania History: A Supplement*. Harrisburg: Pennsylvania Historical and Museum Commission, 1976. Published as a supplement to Wilkinson's bibliography from 1957, it covers books published between 1953 and 1967.

Wallace, Kim E., ed. *The Character of a Steel Mill City: Four Historic Neighborhoods of Johnstown, Pennsylvania*. Washington, D.C.: HABS/HAER and America's Industrial Heritage Project, NPS, Department of the Interior, 1989. Based on the 1988 HABS/HAER recording project in Johnstown. Includes overall history of city and four neighborhoods, with written data for six individual structures.

Wallace, Kim E., comp. *Railroad City: Four Historic Neighborhoods in Altoona, Pennsylvania*. Washington, D.C.: HABS/HAER and America's Industrial Heritage Project, NPS, Department of the Interior, 1990. Publication based on a HABS/HAER recording project in 1988 and 1989.

Ware, Donna M. and James Vaseff. *Lehigh Canal: An HCRS Project Report*. Washington, D.C.: Heritage Conservation and Recreation Service, Department of the Interior, 1981. Publication based on a Historic American Engineering Record rehabilitation study of the Lehigh Canal.

Washington County History and Landmarks Foundation. *Preserving Our Past: Landmark Architecture of Washington County, Pennsylvania*. Washington, Pa.: Washington County History and Landmarks Foundation, 1975. A pictorial review of county architecture before 1900, with a general history and historical notes regarding each building illustrated.

Waterman, Thomas Tileston. *The Dwellings of Colonial America*. Chapel Hill: University of North Carolina Press, 1950. A classic book on the subject, citing many Pennsylvania examples.

Weaver, William Woys. "Pennsylvania German Architecture: Bibliography in European Backgrounds." *Pennsylvania Folklife* 24 (1975): 36-40.

Weslager, Clinton Alfred. *The Log Cabin in America*. New Brunswick, N.J.: Rutgers University Press, 1969.

———. "Log Houses in Pennsylvania During the Seventeenth Century." *Pennsylvania History* 22 (1955): 256-66.

Wilkinson, Norman B. *Bibliography of Pennsylvania History*. Harrisburg: Pennsylvania Historical and Museum Commission, 1957. Covers books published up to 1952. A supplement by Carol Wall published in 1976 continues the bibliography through 1967.

Woerner, H. Ray. "The Taverns of Early Lancaster and the Later-day Hotels." *Journal of Lancaster County Historical Society* 73 (1969): 37-89.

Young, Joseph A. "Early Architects and Architecture of Scranton." *Charette* 46 (1966): 8-12.

Zacher, Susan M. *Covered Bridges of Pennsylvania: A Guide*. Harrisburg: Pennsylvania Historical and Museum Commission, 1993.

Zelinsky, Wilbur. "The Pennsylvania Town: An Overdue Geographical Account." *The Geographical Review* 67 (1977).

Index

Aaronsburg, 399, 401
Abbey, Edwin Austin, 138
Abercrombie, Capt. James, House, 363
Academy of Music, 116, 363
Academy of Music, Pittsburgh, 437
Academy of Notre Dame, 363
Academy of Notre Dame de Namur, 302
Academy of Science and Arts, 437
Acock House, 566
Acocks, James L., builder, 566
Adam, Robert, architect, 84, 89
Adamesque-Federal, 84, 87, 89-90, 302
Adams County, 6, 7, 59, 105, 210, 234-40, 575; Courthouse, 234; Historical Society, 235
Addison, 428, 469
African Americans, 259, 365, 555
African Methodist Episcopal Churches, 259, 365
Aiken, William M., 462
air-conditioning, 146
Alburtis, 212, 312, 313
Alcoa Buildings, 151, 153
Alden, Frank E., 454
Alden, Roger, 532
Alden, Rev. Timothy, 91, 532, 552
Alden and Harlow, architects, 437, 453
Aldrich, Chester H., architect, 130-31, 521
Alexandria, 12, 416; German Reformed Church, 416; High School, 416; Memorial Public Library, 416; Presbyterian Church, 416
Allabach, Peter, builder, 511
Allegheny Arsenal, U.S., 6, 461
Allegheny Baptist Church, 565
Allegheny Cemetery Gatehouse, 110
Allegheny City, 111, 116
Allegheny College, 90, 532, 552; Bentley Hall, 90, 532, 533, 552
Allegheny County, 6, 8, 60, 112, 113, 116, 138, 139, 140, 421, 423, 424, 429, 432, 433, 434, 435, 439, 440, 451-63; Community College of, 438, 453; Courthouse and Jail, 8, 124-27, 153, 431-32, 436, 452, 569, 575; Department of Parks, 451
Allegheny International Corporation, 11
Allegheny Portage Railroad, 404, 413, 429, 465; Skew Arch Bridge, 405, 413; Staple Bend Tunnel, 465
Allegheny River, 462
Allegheny River Bridge, 580
Allen House, 278
Allentown, 209, 220, 313, 315, 577-78
Allentown Road Bridge, 578
Allison, William, 289
Allison, William M., House, 406
Allison Hill houses, 289
Alter's Halfway House, 472
Althouse Tavern, 245
Altoona, 399, 401, 404, 413
Aluminum City Houses, 441
Alverthorpe, 117, 118, 318; Park, 318
Ambler, 215, 316
Ambridge, 55, 56, 57, 464, 570
America's Industrial Heritage Project, 11, 155, 395, 413, 416, 417, 465, 466, 467, 468, 469, 472
American Academy of Music. *See* Academy of Music
American Chain and Cable Company Factory, 580
American Federation of Hosiery Workers, 147, 349
American Fire Insurance Company Building, 363
American Institute of Architects, viii, 3, 4, 11, 133, 145-46
American Legion Post, 414
American Life Insurance Company Building, 363
American Philosophical Society, 363
American Renaissance, 133
American Revolution, 209, 243, 263, 271, 301, 303, 335, 344, 396, 397, 401, 477, 510, 513. *See also* Continental Army; Continental Congress; Daughters of the American Revolution; *and names of participants and battles*
Amish, 27

Index • 595

Amsden, Frank, architect, 491, 492
Amsden, Frederick, architect, 491, 492
Amsden, Joel, architect, 491
Anabaptists, 27
Anchor Hotel, 326
Andalusia, 258
Anderson, Bart, ix
Andorra Inn Barn, 317
Andre, Andrew, House, 468
Ankrim, Samuel, Shop, 207, 208, 278
Annan, William, House, 363
Anselma, 265
anthracite mining, 220, 475-76, 480-86; 497
apartment buildings, 143, 146-47, 148, 152, 255, 347, 352, 373, 378, 380, 381, 438, 456, 457, 569
Aquetong, 259
Arbour, William, House, 363
Arbuckle House, 541, 554
Arbuthnot-Stevenson Company Building, 457
Arcade Building, 363
Arch Street Friends Meeting, 62, 363
Arch Street houses, 363
Arch Street Methodist Episcopal Church, 363
Arch Street Opera House, 363
Arch Street Presbyterian Church, 114, 391
architects, 6, 7, 11, 13, 14, 20, 32, 62, 87, 94, 97, 101, 104, 105, 110, 115, 120, 128, 131, 133, 139, 141, 143, 147, 148, 150, 151, 153, 155, 224, 339, 344, 346, 349, 399, 404, 406, 436, 438, 485, 486, 492; English, 347. *See also names of individual architects and architectural firms*
architectural design books, 111, 120, 139, 141, 344, 404, 488, 534. *See also English design books*
Ardmore, 150
Armat, Thomas, House, 363, 571
Arnold, Thomas, 40
Arnold-Temple House, 40, 277
Art Deco, 143-44, 146, 464
Art Nouveau, 143, 144
Artible, Salomay, carpenter, 321
Arts and Crafts movement, 141, 143, 347, 455, 456, 457, 463
Ashbridge House, 272
Ashbury Graphite Mill, 578
Ashmead, Albert, House, 364, 571
Ashmead, William, House, 364, 571
Ashwood, 301
Askins-Jones House, 364
Athenaeum of Philadelphia, 11, 115-16, 344, 345, 382
Athens, 528, 551
Atlantic and Great Western Railroad, 577
Atna Builders, 452

Atwater Kent Museum, 371
Augustus Lutheran Church, 57
Avondale, 36, 265
Ayer, N.W. and Son, Inc., Building, 364

Bachman, Michael, 310
Bachman-Landis-Kauffman House, 310
Backus House, 557, 561
Bacon, Edmund N., 349
Bacton, 265, 296
Baer, Reuben, House, 117
Bailey, Charles, builder, 563
Bair, Mary A., House, 266
Baird, Donald L., Co. Warehouse, 364
Baker, Elias, Mansion, 399, 401
Baker, Louis Carter, Jr., architect, 316
Baker, Solomon, House, 416
bakeries, 83, 284
Bala Cynwyd, 316
Bald Eagle Creek, 404
Baldwin, Henry, House, 552
Baldwin, Robert, 268
Baldwin Locomotive Works, 340
Baldwin-Reynolds House, 552
Baldwin-Sharpless House, 272
Baltimore, 399, 401
Baltimore and Ohio Railroad, Philadelphia Station, 364
balloon-frame construction, 131, 225, 430, 484, 540
Bank of Chester County, 283
Bank of Germantown, 367
Bank of North America, 364
Bank of Pennsylvania, 92, 344, 364, 573
Bank of the United States, 87; First, 370; Second, 92-94, 95, 344, 387
Bank Row, Philadelphia, 364, 573
banks, 81, 92-94, 95, 97, 99, 133, 136, 137, 139, 144-45, 146, 283, 285, 344, 346, 347, 363, 364, 366, 367, 370, 373, 377, 378, 379, 380, 383, 384, 387, 388, 391, 468, 509, 556, 571, 573
Baptist Church of West Chester, 115, 283
Baptist Churches, 101, 114, 115, 274, 283, 370, 378, 551-52, 558, 565
Barber, George F., 128
Barclay, Thomas, House, 263
Barger, E. F., 97, 556
Barnhard, R. L., architect, 470
barns, 11, 209-19, 235, 237, 238, 239, 242, 243, 244, 245, 246, 247, 248. 249, 251, 254, 255, 257, 259, 260, 261, 262, 263, 264, 265, 268, 270, 271, 273, 274, 275, 276, 281, 283, 286, 287, 303, 304, 306, 307, 308, 309, 310, 311, 312, 313, 314, 315, 316, 317, 318, 319, 320, 321, 325, 326, 327, 330, 466, 470, 515, 517, 518, 516,

524; bank, 218, 316, 516, 517, 518, 529; log, 524, 527, 563; octagonal, 558; Pennsylvania, 209, 212-17, 300. *See also* hex signs
Barnes-Brinton House, 35, 43, 267
Baroque, 40, 62, 114, 131; English, 341
Barren Hill, 317
Barron, Commodore James, House, 364, 571
Barton's, Dr., Office, 559
Bartram, Israel, 288
Bartram, John: House, 364; Hotel, 375
Bartram's Covered Bridge, 288
Bateman, Thomas, 285
Battle of Brandywine, 266, 275, 276, 281, 295, 296, 305
Battle of Germantown, 321
Battle of Gettysburg, 7, 235, 236, 237, 238, 239, 240
Baugh Warehouse, 364
Bauhaus, 147, 148, 150, 441
Baumstown, 241, 245
Baus, Alfred B., Barn, 318
Bausman, 303
Bausman's Lock Number 12, 580
Bayer Silk Mill, 576
Baynton House, 373
Bear Run, 148
Beard, John Michael, Tavern, 330
Beau Brummell Club, 452, 569
Beaux-Arts style, 133, 138-39, 140, 146, 255, 349, 453, 454, 458, 459, 485
Beaver and Erie Canal, 539
Beaver County, 55, 56, 64, 570, 576
Beaver River, 421
Beaver Springs, 580
Bechtel House, 571
Beck Street: Area Study, 364; Houses, 364
Beck-Care Warehouse, 364
Bedford, 97, 122, 395, 396, 399, 428
Bedford, Dr. Nathaniel, Monument, 452
Bedford County, 97, 395, 396, 403
Beebe, Manly Colton, architect, 565
Beehive, The, 287
Beggarstown School, 364
Beissel, Conrad, 52, 304, 305
Bel Air (Belleaire), 364
Bel Orme (house), 299
Belfast, 322
Bell House, 322, 534, 562
Belle School, 273
Bellefonte, 91, 398, 399, 401, 404, 406, 413, 414, 415
Bellevue-Stratford Hotel, 364
Bells Mill Covered Bridge, 472

Belmont Mansion, 364
Ben Avon, 451, 569
Bender, Theodore, House, 235
Benedict, Aaron, builder, 565
Benjamin, Asher, 534
Benner, Gen. Philip, 399, 413
Benner House, 415
Benner-Walker House, 91, 398, 399, 413
Bensalem African Methodist Episcopal Church, 259
Bentley Hall. *See* Allegheny College
Berger Farm, 247
Berks County, 7, 8, 10, 43, 44, 45, 47, 50, 62, 66, 67, 76, 78, 211, 214, 218, 219, 241-58, 274, 401, 576; Historic Preservation Trust of, 242, 246, 253, 570
Bermudian, 234
Bernville, 241, 576
Berry-Blair House, 364
Berry-Coxe House, 365
Bertolet-Herbein Cabin, 43, 44, 245, 569
Bertolett, Abraham, House, 570
Bertolett Homestead, 570
Bertolett Sawmill, 570
Bertolette, E. F., architect, 283
Berwick, 404, 416; Methodist Episcopal Church, 416
Berwyn, 266
Bestor-Towne House, 560
Beth Sholom Synagogue, 150
Bethany, 497, 498
Bethel African Methodist Episcopal Church, 365
Bethel Christian Center, 378
Bethel Park, 424, 451
Bethesda Baptist Church, 274
Bethlehem, 8, 51-52, 53, 57, 91, 220, 313, 322-25, 488, 578; Union Station, 578. *See also* Moravian Community (Bethlehem)
Bethlehem Steel Corporation, 465
Betts, Richard J., 87
Betula, 560
Betz's Mill, 578
Beulah Presbyterian Church, 451, 569
Bickel, Charles, architect, 457, 458
Bicknell, A. J., 406
Biddle, Nicholas, 95; House, 258
Biddle, Owen, architect, 62
Biddle Hall, 389
Billmeyer, Charles, 328; House, 117, 121, 328
Billmeyer, Michael, House, 365
Binney, H., Esq., House, 365
Birchrunville, 266, 296
Bird, Mark, 243
Bird, Joseph, Houses, 365

Bird, William, House, 241
Bird-in-Hand, 303
Birdsboro, 241; Furnace, 241
Birmingham, 61, 266-67; Friends Meetinghouse, 61-62, 206, 570; Octagonal Schoolhouse, 266; Society of Friends, 266
Bishop-Sparks House, 365
Bissell, E. Perot, 3
Bissell, John, architect, 463
bituminous mining, 417, 541
Black Horse Tavern, 236
blacksmith shops, 256, 277
Blackwell, Rev. Robert, House, 365
Blair, J. C., 127
Blair, Rev. Samuel, House, 354
Blair, Samuel, Jr., House, 365
Blair, James, Cabin, 527, 557
Blair County, 12, 395, 399, 404, 405, 413
Blashfield, Edwin Howland, 486
Blight Warehouse, 365
Blocher House, 236
Blockley Retreat Farm, 366
Bloomsburg, 577
Blossburg, 541
Blue Bell, 317; Tavern, 365
Blue Marsh Lake, 10
Boalsburg, 414; Tavern, 414
Boat House Row, 365
Bohemia, 43, 322
Bolingbroke, 299
Bolton, Rev. John, 285
Bonsall House, 297
Bonsall, John, House, 365
Bones, William and Rebecca, House, 27
Boone, Daniel, 245, 257; birthplace, 241, 245
Borchers, Perry, x
Bordley, John Beale, 214
Boston, 140; Prison Discipline Society, 107
Bottomley, William Lawrence, architect, 131-33
Boucher, Jack E., 14
Bouquet, Col. Henry, 455; Redoubt, 455
Bourse Building, 383
Bowman, Jacob, 466
Bowman, John Gabbert, 144
Bowman, Samuel, House, 513
Bowman's Castle, 466, 570
Boyertown, 257; Road House, 244
Braddock's Road, 427
Bradford County, 113, 528, 529, 530, 531, 532, 537, 551, 576; Jail, 108
Bradford Friends Meetinghouse, 277

Bradley and Stetson, architects, 464
Brady Street Bridge, 453, 569, 575
Brand Stable, 303
Brandywine Battlefield State Park, 290. *See also* Battle of Brandywine
Brandywine Bridge, 270
Brandywine Creek, 51, 270, 271, 286
Branson, William, House, 276
Brennan, John P., architect, 458, 459
Breuer, Marcel, architect. 147, 441
Brewer, Charles, House, 453
breweries, 380, 417, 486, 577, 579
Brick House, 301
Bricker, Leonard, (Fox) Outdoor Bake Oven, 236
Bricker, Peter, Farm, 304
Brickersville, 304
Bridesburg, 352
Bridge Street Bridge, 577
Bridges, Latour, House, 365
Bridges, Robert, House, 365
bridges, 240, 255, 270, 276, 367, 368, 373, 382, 389, 390, 405, 413, 427, 453, 460, 462, 470, 472, 569, 573, 575, 576, 577, 578, 579, 580, 581. *See also* covered bridges
Bridgewater, 259
Bringhurst House, 365, 571
Brinkerhoff, Cornelius, architect, 491-92
Brinton, John, Barn, 276
Brinton, Sibyla, (Serpentine) House, 113, 221, 223, 283
Brinton, William, House, 40, 41, 42, 43, 297
Bristol, 220
Britain, 59, 205, 376
British, 28, 41, 206; Army, 271, 422
Broad Arrow Society, 565
Broad Street Market House, 223-24, 292
Broad Street Station (Philadelphia), 342
Broad Street Subway, 341
Brock, 468
Brock, John and Sons, Warehouse, 365, 571
Brockerhoff House, 413
Brockway, 560
Bromley, John and Sons, Building, 365
Brooke, David, 299
Brooke, Nathan, 299
Brooke family, 241; Manor, 241, 401
Brooks, John B., architect, 255
Broomall, 295
Brotherton House, 559
Brown, Denise Scott, architect, 441
Brown, Frederick Lord, architect, 492
Brown House, 257

Brownstone (village), 306
Brownsville, Berks Co., 219, 242, 249
Brownsville, Fayette Co., 102, 427, 466, 570, 577; Historical Society, 466
Brownsville, Washington Co., 469
Brumbaugh, G. Edwin, architect, 262, 280, 297
Brunot, Felix, House, 569
Bryan (Brien) House, 236
Bryn Athyn, 139
Bryn Mawr, 317
Buchanan, James, 91; family, 309. *See also* Wheatland
Bucher, Robert C., 51
Buck, Adam R., Barn, 304
Buck Hill Falls, 493
Buckingham, 259
Buckingham House, London, 66
Bucks County, 5, 96, 207, 220, 248, 258-65, 326, 570, 576; Department of Parks and Recreation, 261; Historical Society, 260, 261
Buckwalter, John, House, 276
Budd's Row, 38
Buffalo, N.Y., 120
Bull, Thomas, House, 267
Bull family, 267
Bulletin Building, 365
Bullis Mills, 561
Bulltown, 267
Burd, Col. James, House, 294
Burden, Joseph, House, 365
Burgee, John, architect, 152
Burholme, 365
Burk, Alfred E., House, 366
Burlington, 530
Burnham, Daniel H., 134-36; and Company, architects, 346, 438, 459
Burnham, George, House, 366
Burns, Charles M., architect, 486
Burns, John A., architect, 16
Burns, William George, 460
Burnside, 374
Burr, Theodore, 327
Burr arch truss, 240, 310, 327, 472
Bushkill, 493, 494, 515, 519: Hotel, 519; Mill, 519
Bushman House, 236
Bushong's Mill Covered Bridge, 310
Bussey-Poulson House, 366
Busti, Paul, House, 366
Butler, Lord, 513
Butler, Col. Zebulon, 513
Butler County, 6, 55, 464
Butler House, 513

Butt, A. W., Octagonal Barn, 558
Butterworth, Appleton, House, 563
Button, S. D., architect, 110, 114
Byers, Alexander, 438
Byers-Lyon House, 438, 453
Byrne-Cavenaugh Houses, 366
Byzantine style, 114

Cady, James C., architect, 485
Calder, Alexander Milne, sculptor, 346
Callahan House, 521
Callowhill Street Bridge, 579
Calvary Episcopal Church, Pittsburgh, 438
Cameron, James, House, 416
Cambria City, 430, 465
Cambria County, 12, 91, 404, 421, 422, 429, 432, 437, 465
Cambria Iron Co., 430
Cambridge Springs, 577
canals, 12, 220, 221, 247, 313, 326, 403, 404, 416, 417, 429, 468, 482, 483, 485, 539, 576, 577, 579, 580. *See also* Allegheny Portage Railroad; Pennsylvania Canal; Union Canal
Cannonball Farm, 366
Canonsburg, 426, 469, 572
Cape Cod house, 529
Capitol Theatre, 521
Carbon County, 482, 487, 489, 508, 576
Carbon County Courthouse Square, 508; Hoover Building, 508
Carbon Iron Company Stables, 508
Carbondale, 482, 483, 509
Carey-Murphy House, 554
Carlisle, 90, 208
Carnegie, Andrew, 136
Carnegie Building, 136
Carnegie Free Library: Connellsville, 466
Carnegie Institute of Technology, 8; Administration Building, 453, 569; Machinery Hall Tower, 453, 569
Carnegie Museum and Library, Pittsburgh, 437
Carnegie Steel Company, 575
Carpenter, Joshua, Mansion, 335, 366
Carpenter, P. B., architect and builder, 552
Carpenter, Samuel, House, 341
Carpenter Gothic, 113, 279, 297, 399, 520, 552
Carpenters' (Company) Hall, 69, 366
Carstairs, Thomas, architect, 336
Carter, Scott, and Willis, builders, 281
Cascade Bridge, 580
Cashier's House, 97
cast iron sidewalk, 366, 570
Catalogue Building, 282
Catasauqua, 313, 578

Catasauqua Lake, 313
Catawissa, 62, 397, 404, 416; Bridge, 577
Catherine Street Courtyard, 366
Cedar Grove, 366
Cedar Hollow Railroad Station, 222, 224, 279
Cedarcroft, 275
Celli, Thomas, 153
cemeteries and cemetery gatehouses, 110, 300-1, 305, 375, 377, 379, 380, 562
Center Chimney House, 268
Center Square, 317
Center Valley, 313
Centerport, 242
Centerville, 427, 470, 572
Centennial Exhibition, 1876, 133, 134; Catalogue Building, 282; Memorial Hall, 133, 134, 376; Ohio Building, 376; St. George's House, 376
Centennial Guard Box, 366
Centennial National Bank, 366
Central Moravian Church. See Moravian Community (Bethlehem)
Central Railroad of New Jersey, Allentown Station, 577; Bethlehem Station, 313, 578; Jim Thorpe Station, 576
Centre County, 6, 91, 394, 395, 396, 397, 398, 399, 401, 406, 413-15; first iron furnace, 399
Centre Hall, 399; American Legion Post, 414
Ceres, 561
Chad, John, House, 295
Chadds Ford, 33, 35, 36, 267, 295; Historical Society, 267, 295
Chaffee House, 560
Chalkhill, 150, 466
Chalkley Hall, 75, 366
Chamber of Commerce, Philadelphia, 368
Chambers, Joseph, 209; House, 328, 329
Chambersburg, 209, 303, 428, 577
Chamounix Mansion, 367
Chandler, Theophilus Parsons, architect, 300, 302
Chanock and Senderowitz, architects, 313
Charleroi, 470
Charles Evans Cemetery Gatehouse, 110
Charlestown, 268; Village House, 268
Charlton, Dr. James, House, 416
Charming Forge Iron Master's House, 257, 401
Chase House, 552
Chatham, 268
Chatham College, Berry Hall, 463
Cherry Hill Penitentiary, 369
Chesapeake area, 41, 43
Chester, 27
Chester County, 7, 8, 30, 32, 35, 36, 40, 41, 42, 51, 61, 71, 73, 83, 86, 96, 98, 113, 115, 204, 206, 207, 208, 209, 217, 221, 222, 223, 224, 243, 265-89, 401, 570, 576; Courthouse, 283, 285; National Bank of, 283; Prison, 284; Historical Society, 8, 265, 283, 285, 287, 296, 297, 577; Horticultural Hall, 224, 225, 283; Hotel, 284; Survey, 8
Chester Creek, 36
Chester Springs, 269, 570; Hotel, 268
Chester Valley Railroad, 222, 279
Chestnut Hill, 333, 347, 349; Academy, 391
Chestnut Street, Philadelphia, Area Study, 367, 571
Chestnut Street Bridge, 367
Chevalier, Henry, House, 561
Chew, Benjamin, 75; Mansion, 367
Chicago, 134, 459; Commercial Style, 136
Chinatown YMCA (Chinese Cultural and Community Center), 367
Chislett, John, architect, 110
Chrisman House, 561
Christ Church, 62, 63, 64, 72, 122, 341-43, 367
Christ Evangelical Lutheran Church, Gettysburg, 234
Christ Lutheran Church, York, 328
Christiana Borough Bridge, 577
Chrome, 269; Hotel, 269
Chuckswood, 301
Church of England, 62, 102, 122
Church of the New Jerusalem, Cathedral, 139
Church of St. James the Less, 104
Church Street Market House, 224
churches, 57, 58, 59, 61, 62, 63, 64, 65, 66, 67, 68, 101-105, 106, 114, 115, 139, 234, 240, 242, 256, 259, 271, 274, 278, 280, 281, 283, 284, 285, 294, 295, 300, 304, 307, 320, 322, 327-28, 363, 365, 366, 367, 369, 370, 373, 375, 378, 379, 385, 386, 389, 391, 394, 415, 416, 431, 432, 435, 437, 439, 451, 454, 460, 468, 470, 471, 478, 479, 480, 485, 486, 488, 508, 510, 511, 513, 515, 517, 519, 520, 530-32, 551-52, 553, 554, 558, 559, 564, 565, 566, 569, 570, 571, 572
Churchill, 451, 569
Churchtown, 304
Cider Press at Hesses' Mill, 304
Cinruss Building, 325
Civil War, 461; Memorial, 387
Civil Works Administration, 2, 3, 4
Clairton, 575
Clarion County, 541
Clark, Mayor Joseph S., Jr., 349
Clark, Tom, Barn, 276
Clark, William, 515
Clark, William, House, 509
Clark-Heller Mill, 515
Clarks Green, 509
Clarks Summit, 509

Classical Revival, 92, 114, 116, 117, 136, 456, 225, 283, 459
classicism, 133, 136, 153
Claysville, 427
Clearfield County, 541
Cliffs, The, 75, 367
Clifton Heights, 28, 29, 296
Clinton County, 403, 404, 406, 415-16
Cliveden, 75, 367
Clonmell, 71, 269
Clunie, 380
Clymer, George, House, 263
Clymers Alley (Clymers Court), 367
Coatesville, 270
Cobean Farm, 236
Cocalico, 304
Cochranton, 577
Coleman, Dr. Horace, House, 534, 535, 561
Colerain Forge, 417; House, 402, 403, 417, 570
College Avenue Bridge (Greenville), 578
colleges. *See* universities and colleges
Colliday, William and Abraham, architects and builders, 64
Collins, Joseph, House, 40, 41, 43, 286
Collins, Samuel, House, 367
Colonial Berks Real Estate Company, 255
Colonial Dames of America, Pennsylvania Society, 510
Colonial Revival, 139, 140, 141, 143, 224, 347
Colt, George P., House, 555
Coltart, Joseph, House, 454
Columbia and Philadelphia Railroad, 220
Columbia County, 62, 397, 404, 416, 576-77
Columbia Engine Company, 367
Colver, 12, 465, 468
Combs House, 313
commercial buildings, 127, 255, 294, 318, 325, 326, 329, 351, 352, 364, 365, 368, 371, 372, 373, 376, 377, 378, 379, 382, 383, 384, 387, 388, 389, 390, 391, 457-59, 460, 469, 525; Victorian, 458, 459. *See also* industrial, office buildings and warehouses; *building names*
Commercial Exchange, 368, 571
Commercial Trust Building, 363
Commercial Union Assurance Co. Building, 368
Community Development Block Grant Program, 11
Compton (Morris House), 368
Concord School, 368
Concordville, 32, 296
condominiums, 148
Conestoga Creek, 306, 307, 309, 310
Conewago Creek, 48, 240, 327
Conewago Presbyterian Church, 240
Confederate States of America, 235, 236, 239, 240

Congregational churches, 478, 510, 530, 551, 553
Congregationalists, 478
Congress Hall, 368, 573
Conneautville, 551, 570; Baptist Church, 551-52, 570
Connecticut settlement, 476-78, 492, 511, 513, 527, 528, 530, 532, 534
Connellsville, 466
Connie Mack Stadium, 387
Connor, Francis, House, 416
Conrad, John, House, 77, 248
Conrad, Joseph, Farm, 248
Conrad's Warehouse, 576
Conshohocken, 317
Continental Army, 309, 321, 324
Continental Congress, 309, 328, 329, 330; First, 69
Conynham-Hacker House, 373
Cook, Col. Edward, House, 466
Cookes, Johannes, House, 328
Cooper, Jacob, House, 368
Cooper, James Fenimore, 94, 100
Cope, Caleb, and Company Store, 368
Cope, Edward Drinker, House, 368
Cope's Bridge, 270
Copesville, 71, 73, 270
Coplay Cement Company, 578
Coray, Elisha Atherton, Mill, 512
Corey, David, House, 510
Cornwall Furnace, 401
Corry, 554, 577
Costagini, L., 328
Cotton Mill, 304
Coudersport, 525, 527, 535, 536, 539; Historic District, 564; Jail, 563; Methodist Church, 564; Presbyterian Church, 101, 564
Court of Homes. *See* Beck Street Area Study
Cove Cornice House, 388
Coventry Forge, 271; Inn, 271
Coventryville, 271
covered bridges, 240, 256, 288, 303, 310, 327, 368, 468, 472, 560, 570, 580
Cox, Kenyon, 486
Craig, John, House, 258
Cram, Ralph Adams, architect, 139, 438
Cramond, William, House, 344
Crawford, Dr. John Barclay, House, 514
Crawford County, 6, 91, 100, 101, 529, 532, 538, 539, 540, 551-54, 570, 577; Historical Society, 552
Cresson, 405, 413, 465
Creswell, John, House, 416
Cret, Paul Philippe, architect, 133, 302
Cricket Slope Farm Barn, 243

Crittenton, Florence, Home, 556
Crogan House, 144
Croghan, William, 431; House, 434, 454
Crosby, 561
Crosier, John, 564
Cross, Benjamin, House, 416
Cross, Richard, bridge designer, 560
Cross Keys Tavern, 269
Crossing Gate Tower, 577
Crossman and Sturdy, 459
Croyden, 260
Crum Creek, 302
Cubist movement, 144
Cullum, Gen. George W., architect, 101, 552
Culp House, 234
Culver, Eber, architect, 120
Culver, Rev. Jabez, 530
Culver, William, House, 510
Cumberland County, 90, 289
Cunis, John, architect, 322
Cunningham, Hugh, 555
Cunningham, Jesse, builder, 466
Cunningham Blacksmith Shop, 277
Cunningham-Blass House
Curley Hill, 260
Currie, Dr. William, House, 368
Curtin, Roland, 414; Foundation, 414
Curtin Village, Workers' Houses, 401, 414
Curtis, John, House, 368
Curtis Publishing Company Building, 368
Customs House, 387
Czechs, 485

Dallastown, 327, 330
Dalzel House, 451, 569
Danville, 406
Darby, 297
Darby Creek, 296, 299
Darlington, Thomas, House, 267
Daughters of the American Revolution, 325, 455, 469, 522
Dauphin County, 6, 57, 58, 80, 81, 220, 289-95, 577
Davidsburg, 327
Davidson House, 557
Davis, Charles S., 462
Davis, James, carpenter, 69
Davis Island Dam and Lock Number 1, 575
Davis-Lenox House, 368
DeBenneville, George, House, 246, 570
Decker, L. R., builder, 564
Declaration of Independence, 263, 325

Deery family, 82, 268
DeHaven, John, 294
Delancy Street (Philadelphia), 339, 368
Delano and Aldrich, architects, 130, 521
Delaware Aqueduct, 579
Delaware and Hudson Canal, 482, 483, 485, 579
Delaware Canal, 482
Delaware Company, 477
Delaware County, 5, 7, 28, 29, 30, 32, 33, 36, 37, 38, 40, 42, 91, 150, 206, 295-303
Delaware Division Canal, 220
Delaware House Hotel, 519
Delaware, Lackawanna and Western Railroad, 483, 484, 485, 491, 515
Delaware River, 96, 128, 205, 258, 264, 297, 333, 334, 335, 340, 350, 475, 482, 483, 497
Delaware River Bridge, 576, 579
Delaware Water Gap, 492, 493, 515; Railroad Station, 515
Delaware Water Gap National Recreation Area, 10, 326, 515-21; Survey, 10
Delta Place, 406
Denison, Nathan, 478; House, 479, 510
Denon, Vivant, 108
Denton's Bridge, 276
department stores, 133-34, 135, 136, 146, 351, 352, 378, 390
Deppen, Dr. Daniel, 251
Derr, Cyrus G., architect, 255
Deshler-Morris House, 368
Detters Mill, 327; Covered Bridge, 327
DeTurk, John, House, 48, 50-51, 253, 570; Farm, 253
Detweiler House, 571
Devault, 271
Dewitt Farm House, 515
Diamond Rock Schoolhouse, 279
Diamond Street (Philadelphia), 339, 340, 368
Dickens, Charles, 94, 106-107
Dickinson College, 90
Dickson-Stevenson House, 92, 558
Dickson's, John, Tavern, 555
Dietz House, 330
Dike, N. L., 537
Dilks, A. W., architect, 270
Dilworth, Mayor Richardson, 349
Dilworth Plaza, 349
Dilworth-Todd-Moylan House, 368
Dilworthtown, 42, 297
Dimmick, Daniel, builder, 520
Dimmick, Milton, 488; Memorial Library, 488, 489, 508
Dimmick, Victor H., 517
Dingmans Ferry, 480, 519, 579

Dingmans Ferry Bridge, 579
Direct Hotel, 329
Dock Street Sewer, 369
Dodge, John, House, 557
Dodge and Morrison, architects, 455
Dorfenille House, 369, 571
Dorfer, Abraham, Barn, 314
Dornbusch, Charles H., architect, 11, 217
Dorrance Colliery Fan Complex, 578
Dorsey, Joseph, House, 420, 422, 424, 426, 471
Douglassville, 66, 67, 242
Dowd of Meadville, architects, 553
Dowers-Okill House, 369
Downing, Andrew Jackson, 110, 116
Downing House, 273
Downingtown, 270, 271, 272, 273
Doylestown, 260-62, 369, 576
Drake, Edwin L., 539; House, 539, 540, 553
Dravosburg, 451
Drexel University, 350; Main Building, 369
Drinker, John, House, 369
Drinker's Court, 369
Drumore, 304
Duche House, 369
Duche-Walker House, 369
Duckworth, John A., architect, 492
Dudley, Charles, House, 413
Duffy's Tavern, 414
Duhring, Okie, and Ziegler, architects, 141
Dundore, Jacob, 218
Dundore, John, 218, 252
Dundore, John Adam, 218
Dundore, Lydia, house, 253
Dundore Farm, 218, 219, 249-50, 252
Dunkers, 304
Dunlap-Eyre House, 369
Dunlaps Creek, 427; Bridge, 577
Duquesne, 575-76
Durang, Edwin F., architect 486
Durchganigenhaus, 51, 52
Durham, Walter, architect, 301
Dutch (Netherland), 27, 333, 399; Quakers, 335
Dutch Reformed Church, Dingmans Ferry, 478, 480, 519

Eagle Hotel, 369, 559
Eagle Iron Works, 414
Eagle School, 282
Eakins, Thomas, 124, 297; House, 369
Eassieman, John, builder, 460
East Berlin, 575

East Bloomsburg Bridge, 576
East Broad Top Coal and Iron Company, 417
East Broadtop Railroad, 577
East Greenville, 318
East Texas, Lehigh Co., 314, 315
East Titusville, 552
Eastburn Mariners' Bethel Church (Presbyterian), 369
Eastern State Penitentiary, 105-107, 369
Eastlake trim, 329
Easton, 208, 220, 325, 482, 483, 579; Car Shops, 579; Station, 579
Easton Steam Laundry and Dining Car, 579
Ebbs, William, 96, 285; House, 285
Ebert, John, 511
Eckert-Terrant House, 369
eclecticism, 120, 122, 124, 127, 133
Economy (borough), 55, 57, 464, 569; Feast Hall, 56, 464, 570; Meetinghouse, 464, 570; Tailor Shop and Wine Cellar, 464
Eddyville, N.Y., 482
Edge, Jacob, 272
Edgell, George, 143
Edgemont, 262
Edinboro, 554
Edinburgh, Scotland, 75
Ege, George, House, 76-77, 84, 87, 256
Egypt Mills, 494, 495, 520
Egyptian Revival, 108, 151, 556
Eichelberger, Martin, 34, 329
Eisenhower, Dwight D., Farms, 237
Eisenhower, Mamie Dowd, 237
Elder, John, House, 292
Eldred, 561
Elfreth, Jeremiah, House, 369
Elfreth's Alley, 336; Houses, 369
Elkins Park, 150
Ellicott, Andrew, 308
Elliot, W. J., House, 406
Elliott, John, House, 369, 378
Elliott Building, 352
Ellison, John B., and Sons, Building, 369
Elm Lawn, 511
Elwell, Henry, House, 369
Emanuel Evangelical Lutheran Church, Brickersville, 304
Emlenton Bridge, 580
Emmanuel Episcopal Church, 454, 569
Emmaus, 314, 578
Empire Store, 555
Endt, Theobald, House, 571
England, 36, 40, 41, 69, 77, 102, 113, 141, 143. *See also* Britain
English, 27, 30, 32, 40, 43, 51, 67, 87, 110, 128, 241, 397, 422-23, 483, 485, 530. *See also* British

English design, 43, 84, 114, 116, 122, 124, 206, 301, 330, 335, 341-43, 347, 397; books, 70, 72, 87, 105, 143, 344
English (Andrew H.)-Oliver (Henry W.) House, 454, 569
English Quaker house, 270, 275, 287, 288, 297. See also Friends, Religious Society of; Quakers
English Regency, 431
English traditions, 59, 72, 75
Ephrata, 304; Cloister, ix, 6, 27, 51, 52-55, 304-306
Episcopal Churches, 36, 62, 64, 72, 101, 102, 104, 114, 122, 271, 285, 292, 300, 313, 335, 341-43, 365, 367, 385, 386, 389, 431, 452, 454, 460, 486, 488, 508, 520, 552, 559
Episcopal Hospital, Philadelphia, 375
Episcopalians, 102, 114, 486. See also Church of England
Erie, 94, 97, 98, 99, 120, 154, 422, 527, 541, 554-57. See also Presque Isle
Erie Club Building, 556
Erie County, 6, 92, 93, 98, 99, 101, 539, 554-60, 570, 577; Historical Society, 556
Erie Railway, 577, 578, 579, 580
Eshback: House 520; Tenant House, 520
Essington, 297
Estlack, Thomas, House, 370
Europe, 145, 347; central, 143; northern, 205; modernism, 349
Evangelical Lutheran Ministerium, 517
Evans, Clark Wright, architect, 140
Evans, David, Jr., architect, 89
Evans, David, Sr., carpenter, 89
Evans, E., builder, 559
Evergreen, 452, 569
Everhart, William, Building, 284
Ewing, Nathaniel, builder, 467
Exchange Hotel, 511
Exeter, 510; Friends Meetinghouse, 62, 256, 570
Exposition des Arts Decoratifs et Industriels, Paris, 143-44
Eyre, Wilson, Jr., architect, 141-43, 299, 347

Fahnestock, Benjamin A., House, 454
Fairacres, 139, 453, 569
Fairchance, Fayette Co., 424, 425, 466
Fairfield, 234; Inn, 234
Fairhope, 466
Fairmount Bridge, 579
Fairmount Park, 72, 75, 110, 344, 377, 380, 381, 387, 391
Fairmount Waterworks, 370, 579
Fairview Village, 318
Fallingwater, 148-50, 441, 467
Fallowfield Octagonal House, 282
Falls Bridge, 573, 579
Fallsington, 262
Far East Chinese Restaurant, 384

Farmar, Edward, Mill, 321
Farmar, Jasper, 321
Farmers' and Mechanics' Bank, 370
Farmington, 428, 467
Farmsville, 306
Farnham, Norman C., 522
Farnham House, 522
Farrandsville, 404
Farrington House, 516
Fayette City, 467
Fayette County, 6, 12, 77, 80, 102, 148, 149, 150, 421, 422, 424, 425, 428, 429, 441, 466, 469, 570, 577; Courthouse, 432
Federal Emergency Relief Act, 2, 5
Federal Reserve Bank of Philadelphia, 133, 370
Federal Revival, 136
Federal style, 90, 91, 92, 259, 267, 274, 275, 287, 308, 322, 344, 399, 426, 497, 530, 534, 551, 552, 554, 557, 558, 559. See also Adamesque
Fell, Mr., architect, 515
Fell, Benjamin, builder, 471
Fell-Van Rensselaer House, 370
Fellsburg, 471; Methodist Episcopal Church, 471, 572
Ferndon, 570
Fielding, Mantle, architect, House, 370
Finady, W. A., Barn, 264
Finleyville, 470, 572
Finlow-Nichell House, 370
Finns, 27, 28, 333
Fire Association Building, 370
firehouses, 367, 371, 374, 375, 381, 383, 387, 388, 389, 390, 391
First Baptist Church: Germantown, 370; North East, 101, 558; Philadelphia, 114
First Christian Church, Charleroi, 470
First Congregational Church, Riceville, 553
First Constitutional Presbyterian Church, 554
First German Reformed Church, Philadelphia, 370
First National Bank: Philadelphia, 370; Saltsburg, 468
First Pennsylvania Banking and Trust Company, 370
First Polish Baptist Church, 378
First Presbyterian Church: Philadelphia, 87, 101, 370; West Chester, 284; York, 114, 328
First Unitarian Church, Philadelphia, 370
Fish Research Station, 415
Fisher, Henry, House, 76-77, 87, 258, 570
Fisher, Joshua Francis, 318
Fisher, Rev. Samuel R., Stable, 303
Fishing Creek, 304
Fitzgerald, Thomas, House, 370
Fitzwater Street (Philadelphia), 370
Flanders, Annette H., landscape architect, 471

Fleisher, Samuel S., Art Memorial, 370
Flickwer-Williamson Houses, 370
Flint House, 537, 538, 553
Flintlock (house), 297
Floradale, 234
Flurküchenhaus, 43, 45, 51, 55, 57, 207, 219
Fogelsville, 315
Folwell House, 371, 571
Fonthill, 261
Forbes Military Road, 428
Fort Bedford, 395
Fort Gaddis, 468
Fort Hunter 80, 81, 289
Fort Leboeuf Historical Society, 559
Fort Ligonier, 422
Fort Mifflin, 371
Fort Necessity, 422; National Battlefield Museum, 467
Fort Pitt, 401, 422, 452; Blockhouse, 423, 455, 569
Fort Stanwix Treaty, 477
Fort Washington, 141
Fort Zeller, 49, 312, 570
Forty Fort, 474, 477, 479, 510, 511; Congregational Meetinghouse, 474, 478, 510
Foster, Isaac, 530
Foster, Lyman Luther, 557
Foster, Stephen Collins, 537
Fountain of the Sea Horses, 371
fountains, 285, 371, 386, 387, 391
Framberger House, 571
France, 57; architecture, 109, 122, 128, 521; See also French Huguenot
Franconia, 578
Frank, Robert Cecilia, 441
Frank-Harvey House, 415
Frankford, 61, 339, 341; Arsenal, 352, 579; Elevated, 341; Hose Company, 371; Town Hall, 371
Frankford Avenue House, 371
Franklin, 541, 565
Franklin, Col. John: House, 551; Memorial Park, 551
Franklin County, 303, 570, 577
Franklin Institute, 371
Franklin Row, 339, 387
Franklin Sugar Refinery, 371
Franklinville, 402, 417, 570
Frank's Hotel, 556
Frazier Harrison and Company, 371
Free Quakers Meetinghouse, 371
Freemansburg, 579
Freemansburg-Steel City Bridge, 579
French, Harry Livingston, architect, 486, 492

French and Indian War, 48, 396, 421-22, 428, 467
French Huguenot, 245, 246, 253, 312
Frick, Henry Clay, 136
Frick Building, 136, 438
Friedensburg, 243; farm buildings, 243
Friends Meetinghouses, 59, 61-62, 206, 255, 256-57, 262, 266, 277, 281, 298, 299, 319, 334, 363, 371, 397, 416, 570
Friends, Religious Society of. *See* Quakers, English, Welsh and Dutch
Friends Select School, Log Cabin, 371
Friendship Engine Company, No. 15, 371
Friendship Hall, 371
Friendship Hill National Historic Site, 467
Fromberger, John, Houses, 372
Fronczak, Joseph, architect, 486
Fullerton, John, Houses, 372
Fulton County, 3, 395, 403
Fulton Building and Theater, 455, 569
Furness, Frank, architect, 124, 302, 316, 346
Furness, Horace Howard, 302, 303; Estate, 302
Furness, Evans and Co., architects, 302, 339
Futurist movement, 144

Gabelsville, 243
Gaddis, Thomas, House, 469
Gage, George F., 128
Gage Hotel, 555
Gallatin, Albert, 467
Gallitzin, 404
Gambrel Roof House (Meetinghouse), 262
Ganoga Lake, 564
Gap, 306
Garden, C. H., and Company, Building, 372
Garden Theater, 455
Garland, 539; Mill, 565
Garnier, Charles, architect, 136
Garrett, Aaron, 289
Garrett and Jones, stonemasons, 285
Garrett-Buchanan Company, 379
Garrett Cenotaph, 562
Garvan, Beatrice, 69
Gates, Gen. Horatio, House, 328, 329
Gaul-Forrest House, 372
Gaybrook, 299
Gayety Theatre, 455
Gaylord, Henderson, House, 512
Gemeinhaus. *See* Moravian Community (Bethlehem)
General Green Hotel, 471
General Wayne Hotel, 372, 571
Gengembre, Charles Antoine Colomb, architect, 116

Gentilhommiere, 373
George, Henry, House, 372, 571
Georgian style, 62, 64, 66, 67, 69, 70, 72, 75, 76, 77, 80, 82, 84, 91, 92, 113, 120, 139, 141, 209, 221, 236, 245, 256, 257, 258, 263, 267, 276, 279, 280, 294, 318, 321, 328, 341-43, 397, 399, 424, 426, 426, 469, 540; American, 55; English, 330; Revival, 463
Germania Brewery, 577
Germanic architecture, 52, 55, 57, 59, 77, 258, 294, 304, 311, 322, 327, 328, 329, 397, 424
Germanic houses: bank, 48-51; Virginia, 48. *See also* Pennsylvania Germanic houses
Germans, 27, 28, 30, 34, 206, 217, 297, 375, 397, 416, 464, 486, 534. *See also* names of religious groupings
Germantown, 27, 72, 75, 110, 254, 333, 335, 339, 340; Academy, 372; Battle of, 321; Cricket Club, 140, 373; Historical Society Area Study, 373, 570; Insurance Company, 371; Union School, 372
Germany, 147, 246
Gesu, Church of the, 367
Gettysburg, 209, 210, 234, 235, 236, 239. *See also* Battle of Gettysburg
Gettysburg Battlefield Memorial Association, 238
Gettysburg College, 95, 224, 235
Gettysburg National Military Park, 7, 234-35, 236, 237, 238, 239
Gibbs, James, 62
Gilded Age, 124
Gilpin, Gideon, 296
Gilpin, Isaac G., 296
Gilpin, Joseph, 296; House, 32, 33, 295
Girard, 92, 93, 557
Girard, Stephen, 95; Bank, 370; Country House, 373
Girard College, Founder's Hall, 95, 96, 373
Girard Row (houses), 373
Girard Trust Corn Exchange Bank (Girard Bank), 139, 373
Gladstone Hotel, 373
Gladwyne, 570
Glass, Joseph W., 214
Glassie, Henry, 30, 59, 82
Glebe House, 373
Glen Fern, 378
Glen Oak Country Club, 510
Glendon, 325, 579; Hotel, 325; Iron Company, 579
Glenloch, 221, 222, 273
Glenmoore, 273
Gloria Dei Church, 36, 335, 373
Godfrey, Lincoln, House, 301
Godley, Jesse, Warehouse, Stores, 373
Goldberg's Army-Navy Store, 368
Goldberger, Paul, 153
Golden Plough Tavern, 30, 31, 34, 209, 328, 329

Good News Building, 268
Goodwin, G., architect, 451
Goodwin House, 562
Gordon, George, Building, 373
Gothic style, 113, 139, 144, 323, 328, 406, 488, 508. *See also* Carpenter Gothic
Gothic Revival, 101-105, 108, 110-15, 120, 221, 222, 258, 283, 285, 303, 344, 397, 431, 455, 460, 462, 497, 508, 556; Early English, 438; High Victorian, 122, 124, 240, 273, 285, 339, 346, 491; Jacobean, 459; Victorian, 317, 463
Goundie, John Sebastian, 91, 323; House, 323
government buildings, 67, 69, 108, 116, 138, 234, 283, 285, 294, 307, 308, 330, 368, 382, 387, 406, 415, 432, 452, 453, 461-62 465, 492, 520, 556, 562
Gowans, Alan, 40
Gowern, William J., Building, 469
Graeme, Dr. Thomas, 318
Graeme Park, 318
Grafius, Israel, House, 416
Graham, Anderson, Probst and White, architects, 144
Granary, 418
Grand Army of the Republic, Strong Vincent Post, 556
Granite Street Vaults, 373
Gray, J. W., 553
Great Conewago Presbyterian Church, 59, 240
Great Depression, 2, 5, 6, 13, 133, 144, 462, 472, 497
Great Island Presbyterian Church, 406
Greek Revival, 6, 12, 91, 92, 94, 95, 96, 97, 98, 100, 110-11, 115, 120, 124, 144, 224, 234, 235, 241, 258, 283, 284, 285, 286, 298, 328, 344, 399, 415, 416, 431, 453, 454, 456, 460, 461, 462, 478, 509, 511, 512, 514, 517, 519, 525, 529, 532-38, 540, 552, 553, 554, 556, 557, 558, 559, 560, 561, 562, 563, 564, 565, 566, 567
Green Lawn, 273
Green Street (Philadelphia), 373-74
Greene, Gen. Nathanael, 321
Greene County, 422, 468, 570
Greensburg, 471
Greensburger Hotel, 471
Greenville, 562, 578
Grey, Rebecca and Romer, 520
Grey, Zane, House, 520
Grey Towers, 128-33, 499, 521
Greystone Apartments, 373
Griesemer Mill, 256; Covered Bridge, 256
Griffith, William R., House, 292
Griffith-Peale House, 374
Grimes Covered Bridge, 468
Gropius, Walter, architect, 147, 441
Gross Covered Bridge, 580
Grubb, C. B., 97

Grubbs Mill, 274
Gruber, Franklin, 250
Gruber, Jacob, House, 250
Gruber House (tavern), 250
Gruber Wagon Works, 250, 251, 576
Grumblethorpe, 374
Guastavino, Rafael, 453
Guckes (Gugges). *See* Cookes, Johannes
Guggenheim Museum, 150
Guild House, 152
Guinston Presbyterian Church, 57, 327
Gulf Building, 144
Gunkle, Michael, Spring Mill, 266
Gustin, John, builder, 521
Guth, Lorentz, 313

Ha Penny Farm, 245
Haag-Haak Log House, 241
Hadsall, James, 512
Hagan, Isaac N., House, 466
Hagen, I. N., House, 150
Hagley Museum, 276
Haines House, 392
Hale, Willis G., architect, 491
Halehurst, 415
half-timber construction, 30, 34, 52, 57, 207, 252, 307, 312, 329
Halfway House, 493
Hall, Albin, mason, 287
Hall, John, House, 374
Hall-Wister House, 374
Hallam, 327
Halley House, 275
Halliday, James M., builder, 566
Hammerschlag Hall Tower, 453
Hamilton, Andrew, 66; House, 392
Hamilton, William, 87, 344
Hamilton Disston Houses, 352
Hamilton Street Dam, 577
Hamilton Village, 392
Hamilton-Hoffman House, 374
Hamorton, 274
Hampton, Wade, (Hampton-Kelly) House, 452, 569
Hand, Gen. Edward, House, 309
Hanover Green, 478, 511; Meetinghouse, 479, 511
Hansell, John, House, 374
Harborcreek, 557
Harford, 528, 537
Harmony, 55, 464
Harmony Engine Co., No. 6, 371, 374
Harmony Grove, 327

Harmony Society, 55, 57, 464. *See also* Economy; Old Economy
Harper, Lydia and John Arunah, Building, 457
Harper, Thomas, House, wall stencil, 374
Harris, James, House, 414
Harrisburg, 11, 108, 114, 153, 220, 223, 289-94, 344, 413, 577
Harrison, Charles C., Building, 374
Harrison, Henry, Houses, 374
Harrison and Abramowitz, architect, 151
Harrison Building, 374
Harrison House, 374
Hart, John, House, 374
Hart-Patterson House, 374
Harter, Eva, House, 143, 438, 455, 569
Hartley, Robert, 237
Hartley, William, House, 122
Harvey, Jameson, 513
Harvey, Job, House, 82, 268
Harvey, William, 51; House, 267
Harvey House, 260, 415, 513
Harwood, W. W., House, 560
Hatch School, 554
Hatfield House, 374
Hause family: Store, 277; Smokehouse, 217, 277
Haviland, John, architect, 105, 106, 107, 108, 151
Haverford, 297; Friends Meetinghouse, 61, 29
Haverford College, 267
Haverford Township Historical Society, 298
Havertown, 297, 298
Hawley Coaling Station, 580
Hawthorne, Mrs. Nathaniel, 102
Hay Creek Forge, 576
Hayden, Benjamin, House, 467
Hayes Army Ammunition Plant, 575
Heathside Cottage, 111, 112, 455, 569
Heck-Stamm-Unger Farm, 251
Heidlersburg, 240
Heister Mill, 576
Heller, Simon, Mill, 512-13
Heller, John, 519
Hellertown, 325, 326, 579
Hellings, Benjamin, House, 374
Helm, Jacob, House, 521
Helme, Leo, architect, 554
Helme Tavern, 511
Hencke House, 554
Hendryx, Henry E., House, 100, 537, 553
Henry, Howard, 141
Henry, William, Jr., and Son, 322
Henry Gun Factory, 322
Henry-Windsor House, 541, 567

Henryville, 493; House, 493
Hensel, Colladay, and Company Factory, 374
Herbein, Peter, 246
Herdic, Peter, House, 120
Heritage House, 372
Hermit's House, 330
Herr, Christian, 45-46, 311
Herr, Hans, 45, 311; House, 45, 46, 48, 311, 570
Hesses' Mill, 304
hex signs, 247, 312, 313, 314, 315, 320, 326
Hibernian Furnace, 241
Hibberd family, 288
Hibbs, Hannah M., House, 262
Hickman, (Mrs.) John, Fountain, 285
Hickman House, 278
High Hollow, 347
Highspire, 294
Hill, David, House, 375
Hill, James G., architect, 294
Hill-Physick-(Keith) House, 84, 85, 375
Hills, Stephen, architect, 87, 136, 292, 294, 307
Hillside, 299
Hillsover, 302
Hilyard, Eber, House, 375
Hinkletown, 306
Hipple, George, builder, 416
Hipple, Henry, builder, 406, 416
Hirte, Tobias, 325
Hiss and Weekes, architects, 463
Historic America, 17
Historic American Buildings Survey, vii-ix, 1-20, 155, 205, 207, 333, 395, 397, 401, 413, 416, 465, 466, 468, 469, 472, 476, 525, 539, 541; Inventory, 15, 20, 569-72
Historic American Engineering Record, 9, 19, 20, 251, 465, 468, 469, 573, 575-80
Historic Bethlehem, Inc., 8, 323, 324
Historic Yellow Springs, Inc., 269
Historic York, Inc., 328, 330
Hitchcock, Joseph, architect, 478, 510
Hock, C., Farmhouse, 244
Hockendauqua Dam, 579
Hockley, Thomas, House, 375, 571
Hoffman, H. & S., Barn, 320
Hoffman and Crumpton, architects, 460
Hoffman Barn, 262
Hogg-Brunot House, 455
Holicong, 570
Holland, Leicester, viii, 3
Holland Land Company, 526, 532
Hollenback Cemetery Gatehouses, 110

Hollidaysburg, 404
Hollinger, C. H., Barn, 310
Holloway, Thomas, Houses, 375
Holme, Thomas, 334
Holy Redeemer Chinese Catholic Church and School, 375
Holy Trinity Episcopal Church: Philadelphia, 114, 367; West Chester, 285
Holy Trinity Lutheran Church: Lancaster, 307; Philadelphia, 64, 66
Holy Trinity Roman Catholic Church (German), 375
Honesdale, 482, 488, 490, 522, 580
Honeybrook, 274
Hood, Raymond H., Godley, and Fouilhoux, architects, 497
Hood Cemetery, 375; Entrance, 110
Hoof, Jac. C., architect, 255
Hook and Ladder Company C, Philadelphia, 371
Hoopes, Daniel and Jane, House, 282
Hoopes, Joshua H., 282
Hoopes Currying Shop, 272
Hoopes family, 287
Hoover, George, architect, 488
Hope Engine Company, No. 17, 375
Hope Hose Company, No. 6 and Fellowship Engine Company, No. 29, 375
Hope Lodge, 321
Hopewell Academy, 84, 86, 274
Hopewell: Furnace, 241, 243; Village National Historic Site, 7, 243-44, 274-75, 401
Hopkins, Alfred, architect, 471
Hopkins, Harry, 2
Hopper, Margaret, Log House, 265
Hornbostel, Henry, architect, 453, 454
Horseshoe Curve, 404
Horsham, 318
hospitals, 89, 90, 297, 375, 382
hotels and inns, 241, 250, 255, 257, 268, 269, 284, 318, 319, 324, 325, 326, 328, 329, 330, 364, 369, 372, 373, 375, 379, 385, 390, 391, 470, 471, 493, 494, 511, 519, 539-40, 555, 556, 559, 566, 567, 571, 572, 580. *See also individual names*
Hottenstein Farm, 249
House by the Pines, 566
Houston-Sauveur House, 375
Houtz, Dr. Daniel, House and Office, 416
Howard Avenue House, 34
Howard Double House, 560
Howe, George, architect, 146, 150, 347, 349
Howell and Brothers Building, 375
Howell House, 373
Hoxie, Joseph C., architect, 114, 352, 406
Hughes Log House, 555
Hummelbaugh, Jacob, Farm, 237

Humphrey, Dr. Jonas, 559
Humphrey-Rockwell House, 559
Hunt, Richard Morris, architect, 128, 130, 346, 497, 521
Hunt-Pollock Mill, 271
Hunter, James, 302
Hunter, Samuel, 235
Hunter House, 256
Hunter-Bair House, 266
Hunterstown, 59, 240
Huntingdon, 30, 127, 128, 396
Huntingdon and Broad Top Railroad, 128
Huntingdon County, 3, 11, 12, 30, 395, 402, 403, 416-18, 468, 570, 577
Huntingtown Presbyterian Church, 237
Huston, Joseph M., architect, 136, 138
Hutchinson, Judge Myron, House, 92, 93, 557
Hutton, Addison, architect, 221, 273, 286, 488, 508
Hydetown, 97, 552

Illick House, 570
Illigs Mill, 311
Immaculate Conception Catholic Church, 367
Independence Hall, 66, 67, 151, 341-43, 344, 349, 573; Complex, 151, 368, 375, 573
Independence Mall, 350
Independence National Historical Park, 6, 350, 376
Independent Congregational Church (Unitarian), 101, 552
Indian Springs, 240
Indiana County, 12, 416, 468
Indians. *See* Native Americans
industrial, office buildings and warehouses, 127, 150, 225, 250, 251, 322, 323, 324, 333, 351, 364, 365, 368, 373, 376, 377, 379, 384, 385, 387, 388, 389, 572
inns. *See* hotels and inns
Insurance Patrol Building, 376
International Exhibition of 1876. *See* Centennial Exhibition
International Style, 145, 146, 147, 150, 151, 152, 225, 347, 349, 441
Irish, 59, 485
Irish, Nathaniel, House, 38, 335, 337, 376
iron, architectural, 120, 124, 366, 556
iron mines, 220, 541
Iron Springs, 240
iron and steel industry, 240, 241, 243-44, 257, 267, 271, 274-75, 289, 399, 401, 402, 403, 414, 417, 465, 471, 483, 484, 491, 570, 575, 576, 578. *See also names of companies and furnaces*
Ironville, 307
Irvin Building, 370
Irvine 565; Estate, House, 565; Miller's House, 566; Presbyterian Church, 566; Tenant House, 566

Irvine, Dr. W. A., architect, 566
Isabella Furnace, 289
Italian Fountain, 371
Italian Villa, 377
Italianate style, 113-14, 115-22, 124, 139, 223, 241, 275, 320, 344, 399, 451, 452, 454, 488, 508, 522, 556; High Victorian, 328
Iungerich Warehouse, 376
Ives, Timothy, Jr., architect, 539; House, 535, 536, 564
Ivy House, 274
Ivy Lodge, 376

Jackson, Andrew, 94
Jackson, Joseph, House, 287
Jacksonwald, 244
Jacobean Revival, 562
Jacobs, John, House, 265, 296
Jacobsburg Historical Society, 322
Jacobsburg State Park, 322
Jacoby, Wigard, House, 376, 571
Jahn, Helmut, architect, 153, 350
Jallade, Louis E., architect, 567
James, Robert, builder, 470
James Chapel Methodist Church, 470, 572
Jansen, Dirck, House, 571
Janssen, Benno, architect, 462
Jarman family, 301
Jayne, Horace, House, 303
Jayne (Dr. Jayne Granite) Building, 376
Jefferson, Joseph, House, 376
Jefferson County, 560
Jefferson Fire Insurance Company, 376
Jenkins, William, 91, 309
Jenkintown, 117, 118, 318
Jenks, Thomas, Hall, 263
Jenks, Thomas, Jr., 263
Jennings, Paul Bishop, builder, 567
Jerman-Walker Springhouse, 279
Jersey Shore, 406
Jim Thorpe, Pa., 13, 476, 482, 483, 486-88, 489, 508, 576; Opera House, 488
Johnson, Philip, architect, 152
Johnson, S. C., Administration Building, 150
Johnson House, Philadelphia, 376
Johnson's Mill Covered Bridge, 310, 570
Johnston, William, architect, 110
Johnston's, Arthur, Tavern (Johnson House), 563
Johnstown, 12, 154, 421, 429-30, 431, 432, 465; City Hall, 432, 437, 465; Post Office Building, 465; Public Library, 465
Jones, B. F., architect, 139; House, 463
Jones, John, 277

Jones, Mouns, House, 242
Jones and Laughlin Steel Corporation, 575
Jones Farmhouse, 303
Jones House, 320
Jordan, Terry, 28
Jordan-Stoddard House, 376
Judson, Amos, House, 92, 559
Juniata County, 395
Juniata Division (Pennsylvania Canal), 403
Juniata River, 396, 403; Valley, 401
Justi, Henry D., House, 376

Kaighn, Robert, architect, 339
Kalm, Peter, 336
Kahn, Louis I., architect, 151-52, 349
Kaolin, 275
Kapsch, Robert J., 9
Karns, John, House, 456
Kauffman, Hiram G., 310
Kaufman, David, house, 254
Kaufman, Jacob, House, 253; Barn, 211
Kaufman Farm, 211, 254
Kaufmann, Edgar J., 148-49, 441; House, 467
Kaufmann, Edgar J., Jr., l49
Kearsley, John, architect, 62
Keim, Johannes, House, 246
Keim Stone Cabin, 45, 47, 207
Keith, Sir William, 318
Kelly, William, architect, 94, 97, 556
Kelly, William, House, 554
Kemble-Bergdol House, 376
Kenilworth Street Houses, 376
Kennett Square, 275
Kennedy, David, architect, 556
Kennedy Mansion, 117, 119, 320
Kennedy Plaza, 349
Kensington, 334, 339, 340; National Bank, 377, 571
Kent, Atwater, 267, 371
Kern's Mill, 578
Kerr, J. W., architect, 452
Keyser, Jacob, House, 377, 571
Keyser Brothers Ironworks, 579
Kid-Chandler and Kid-Physick Houses, 377
Kimberton, 275
Kimball, Fiske, viii
King, Martin Luther, Jr., Park, 328
King, Thomas, 559
King Building, 458
King of Prussia, 318-19; Inn, 318
king-post truss, 303, 468

Kingsbacher Brothers Jewelry Store Building, 458
Kingseessing, 110
Kingston, 511
Kintner Mill, 567
Kintnersville, 248, 262
Kinzua Viaduct, 578
Kipp, Albert H., architect, 486, 491
Kirk, John, mason, 318
Kirkbride Mansion, 366
Kirkbride's Hospital, 382
Kittatinny House, 492
Klages, Allen M., House, 143, 456, 569
Klauder, Charles Z., 144
Kleinfeltersville, 311
Kleiser House, 327
Klinepeter's Covered Bridge, 580
Knabb, Abraham, House, 245
Knabb, John, 245
Knabb-Bieber Mill, 245
Knauertown, 276
Kniffen, 30
Knor, Jacob, carpenter, 75
Knoxville, Tenn., 128
Konig-Speicher Farm, 247
Koppers Building, 144
Kosciuszko, Gen. Thaddeus, House, 377
Krepps, John, 470; Tavern, 427, 470, 572
Kreusler, Henry Lawrence, contractor, 458
Kreuzhaus, 45, 51, 57
Krider Gun Shop, 369
Kuhn's Fording Bridge, 575
Kutztown, 245

Lab, William, 260
Lackawanna County, 480, 481, 482, 483, 485, 509-10, 577
Lackawanna Iron and Steel Company, 484, 491
Lackawaxen, 520, 579
Lackawaxen River, 482
Lafayette, Marquis de, 130, 308, 319; Headquarters, 295
Lafever, Minard, 534
La Grange, 130. *See also* Lafayette
Lake Luxembourg, 263
Lakeside, 265
Lamb, Peter, House, 377
Lamm's Mill, 576
Lamphier, Benjamin H., House, 561
Lancaster, 34, 66, 84, 87, 89, 91, 97, 108, 117, 207, 208, 220, 250, 307-309, 570; Municipal Building, 308; Old City Hall, Heritage Center, 67, 68, 307

Lancaster County, 6, 7, 27, 45, 46, 51, 54, 66, 68, 87, 89, 91, 97, 207, 213, 303-11, 570, 577; Historic Preservation Trust of, 308
Lancaster Mennonite Conference Historical Society, 311
Land Lighthouse, 555
Land Title Bank and Trust Co. Building, 136, 137, 346, 377
Landenberg, 276
Landingford Plantation, 301
Landis, Christian and Fanny, Barn, 309
Landis, Henry, Barn, 309
Landis, John, 310
Landis Valley, 309
Landisville, 310
Landmarks Building, 459
Lanesboro, 580
Langhorne, 262
Lanrick Manor, 265
Lardner House, 378
Larry's Station
La Scala (Milan), 116
Lashee, Christiana, 327
Lasse Cock's Manor House, 364
Latour Warehouse, 377
Latrobe, Benjamin Henry, architect, 6, 90, 92, 258, 336, 344, 461
Lattimore, John, 519
Lauer-Gerhard Farm, 242
Laughlintown, 471, 572
Laurel, 327
Laurel Hill, 377, 469
Laurel Hill Cemetery, 377; Gatehouse, 110
Lawrence Cabin (log), 298
Lawrence Park, 298
Lazaretto (hospital), 297
Lea, Prof. Henry Charles, House, 377
League Street Houses, 377
Leake and Green, architects, 454
Leaman Rifle Works Covered Bridge, 310
Lebanon, 220
Lebanon County, 45, 46, 49, 51, 122, 248, 311-12, 397, 401, 570
LeBrun, Napoleon, architect, 116
Lee, A. and S., Barn, 254
Lee, Edward B., architect, 138
Lee, Edward B., Palmer, Hornbostel and Jones, Associated Architects, 138, 454
Lee, Robert M., House and Law Office, 377
Lee, Samuel, 257
Leffler, Ross, Training School Complex, 560
Lehigh and Susquehanna Railroad, 482, 485
Lehigh Canal, 220, 313, 326, 482, 483, 485, 576, 577, 578, 579
Lehigh Coal and Navigation Company, 482, 576
Lehigh County, 212, 312-16, 577-78

Lehigh Crane Iron Works, 577
Lehigh River, 475
Lehigh University, 488, 508
Lehigh Valley Railroad, 483, 485, 488, 508, 539, 576, 579
Lehighton, 576
Leidy, Dr. Joseph, Jr., House, 141, 142, 377
Leinbach, Thomas and Elisabeth, Barn, 243
Leiper, Thomas, House, 91, 302
Leister, Lydia, House, 237
Leithsville, 216, 326
Leland Building, 377
Lemon, Samuel, House, 91, 465
Lemon Hill (house), 84
Lenape, 276
L'Enfant, Pierre C., 308
Lenhartsville, 245, 248
Lenox-Keene House, 259
Lescaze, William, architect, 146, 347
Lester House, 323
Letitia Street House, 38, 39, 377
Letterkenny Army Depot, 577
LeVan, Jacob, Mill, 245
Levittown, 262
Levy, Aaron, 399
Lewis, John, 270
Lewisburg, 404, 406, 580
Lewistown, 404
Liberty Bell Pavilion, 151
Liberty Place, 153, 350
libraries, 150, 272, 377, 466, 488, 489, 508, 509
Library Company of Philadelphia, Ridgway Branch, 377
Library Hall, Philadelphia, 89. See also American Philosophical Society
Library of Congress, 1, 3, 4, 5, 15, 17, 18, 19, 20, 155
lighthouses, 555-56
Lillibridge House, 563
lime kilns, 257
Limekiln, 44, 245, 246, 570; barn, 245
Limeport, 315
Lincoln, Abraham, 257
Lindenshade, 302
Linglestown, 294
Linn, Henry S., House, 413
Lippincott, Joshua B., House, 377
Lippincott, Mather, architect, 266
Lipson, Jos., Co. Building, 458
Lit Brothers Store, 351, 352, 378
Lititz, 213, 310
Little Chickies Creek, 310
Little Conestoga Creek, 303

Little Lehigh Creek, 314
Littlestown, 240
Livezey House, 378
Lloyd, Harrison, House, 274, 275
Lobachsville, 47
Loch Aerie, 222, 273
Lock Haven, 403, 406, 415
Lockwood, William E., 221; House, 273
log structures, 5, 28, 29, 30, 31, 38, 43, 44, 48, 60, 62, 77, 206, 207, 217, 218, 237, 238, 239, 241, 245, 248, 249, 251, 262, 265, 274, 296, 298, 323, 327, 329, 330, 371, 397, 415, 418, 424, 426, 456, 466, 493, 513, 524, 525, 527, 528, 530, 551, 555, 557, 558, 563, 565
Logan, James, 70
Lombard Street Houses, 378
Lombard style, 114
London, England, 34, 64, 66; churches, 62; house plan, 38, 335-36; Restoration, 335
Long, Jacob E., Barn, 309
Long, Robert Carey, Jr., architect, 399
Longfellow, Alden and Harlow, architects, 438
Lotman, George, mason, 64
Loudoun, 378, 571
Low, Will H., 486
Lower Burying Ground, 375
Lower Merion Friends Meetinghouse, 319
Lower Silesia, 30
Lower Swedish Log Cabin, 29, 296
Lower Towamensing, 576
Lowman, George, stonemason, 294
Loyal Order of Moose Building, 458
Lucas House, 274
Luckenbach Flour Mill, 578
Luckenbach Grist Mill, 323
Luden, William H., 225
Ludwigs Corner, 276
Lukens Stone Barn, 317
lumbering, 541
Lundale Farm, House, 280
Lutheran Church of the Holy Trinity, 570
Lutheran Churches, 57, 64, 66, 105, 234, 240, 294, 304, 307, 320, 328, 385, 389, 464, 468, 513, 517, 570
Lutheran Theological Seminary, Main Building, 235
Lutherans, 27, 57, 294, 307, 328, 513.
Luzerne County, 5, 105, 106, 474, 478, 479, 482, 483, 510-15, 539; Courthouse, 69, 478, 485-86; Prison, 485
Luzerne Presbytery, 515
Lycoming County, 3, 399, 400, 406, 418, 578; Courthouse, 116; Historical Museum, 417

Lyle-Newman Houses, 378
Lynfield House, 378
Lynnville, 578
Lyon, J. Denniston, 438
Lyon, William, House, 97
Lyon Valley, 315
Lyons, John, Mansion House, 417
Lyons House, 403, 570

Mack, Abraham, Barn, 318
Mackey, Capt. James, House, 294
Mackley, Carl, Houses (apartments), 147, 347, 378
Maclay, William, House, 293
Macpherson, John, 72
Macungie, 312, 314, 315
Mader, Louis, 280
Madison, Dolley, House, 368
Magoffin, Dr. Beriah, House, 563
Magoffin House, 562
Maiden Creek, 247
mail order plans, 128, 140
Malden Inn, 470
Mallinckrodt Convent, 486
Maloby, Thomas, House and Tavern, 378
Man Full of Trouble Tavern, 388
Manatawny Creek, 48, 253, 254, 256
Manayunk, 333, 340
Manchester, Isaac, 423
Manchester Bridge, 575
Manhattan Building, 363
Manheim, 310
Mansion House Hotel, 284
Mantua Junction Viaduct, 579
Marietta, 310, 570
Mariners' Bethel Church, 369, 378
market houses, 222-24, 292, 384, 457, 569, 571. *See also individual names*
Market Square Presbyterian Church, 114
Market Street Area Study, 378
Market Street East Project, 350
Market Street National Bank Building, 144, 145, 378
Marks-Dunbar House, 378
Marlborough Plank House, 273
Marple-Newtown Historical Society, 298
Marsh, 277
Marsh, Robert, House, 561
Marshall, Elisha G., Hill (house), 508
Marshall, Humphry, House, 82-84, 277
Marshall, Meredith A., 560
Marshall Field Warehouse, Chicago, 127

Marshall-Morris House, 378
Marshall's Court Area Study, 378
Marshallton, 277; Blacksmith Shop, 277; Friends Meetinghouse, 277
Martin, Fred, architect, 260
Martin, John, House, 468
Martin, Sydney, viii
Martin, Stewart and Noble, architects, 150
Martin's Corner, 278; Corner House, 278
Mason, James S., and Company Store, 379
Masonic Temple and Scottish Rite Cathedral, Scranton, 497
Masonic Temple Building, Altoona, 413
Massachusetts, 530, 532, 534
Massey, James C., architect, 7, 9, 16
Massey, Mordecai, 38
Massey, Thomas, 36-38; House, 43, 298
Massey and Janney Leather Warehouse, 379
Mather, Isaac, Mill, 321
Matlack, George, House, 287
Matlack, Isaiah, 285
Matlack-Townsend House, 285
Mauch Chunk. See Jim Thorpe; Old Mauch Chunk Historic District
Maul Barn, 254
Mauser Mill Company, 579
Mausoleum at Halicarnassus, 144
Maxfield-Elliott House, 379
Maxwell, Ebenezer, House, 379
Mayer, L. H., Building, 465
Mayfield (house), 96, 97, 98, 285
McAlevys Fort General Store, 11, 417
McAlister Building. See Wallace and McAlister Buildings
McAllister, Archibald, House, 80, 289
McArthur, John, contractor, 344
McArthur, John, Jr., architect, 122, 485
McBurney, Robert, Manor, 11, 417
McCain, Daniel, builder, 472
McClare-Hutchinson Building, 379
McClean, Moses, House, 238
McConnell House, 452
McCormick, Fred, architect, 486, 492
McCormick, John F., House, 415
McCormick Building, 458
McCraig, George, House, 379
McCrea, James, House, 379
McFarland, Dr. John, House, 468
McGlaughlin, James, House, 468
McIlwaine, William, House, 468
McKean, Thomas, Jr., House, 379
McKean County, 6, 534, 535, 560-62, 578

McKee, Harley J., 16
McKeesport, 452, 569
McKim, Mead and White, architects, 139, 140
McLean, Alexander, House, 513
McManus, Patrick, House, 416
McMellen, Elias, builder, 303, 310
McMullin, Robert, House, 379
McPeak Brothers, builders, 470
McPheeter House, 554
McPherson Barn, 238
Mead, Gen. George Gordon, Headquarters, 238
Mead Street (apartments), 456
Meadow Lands, 470, 572
Meadville, 91, 101, 532, 533, 541, 553, 577
Mears-Heaton House, 34, 379
Meason, Isaac, House, cover, 77-80, 84, 87, 424, 467
Mechanics Bank, 94, 379
Mechanicsville, 310
Medbury House, 562
Media, 299
medieval, 34, 36, 40, 43, 55, 70, 102, 104, 105, 111, 114, 115, 124, 153, 206, 335; French chateau, 497; German, 327, 329
Megargee Brothers Paper Warehouse, 379
Mehl House, 379, 571
Meier, Richard, architect, 441
Mellon, Andrew, 430
Mellon, Thomas, House, 379
Mellor, Meigs and Howe, architects, 143, 146, 259, 347
Memorial Avenue Bridge, 578
Memorial Hall, Philadelphia, 133, 134
Mendenhall, Aaron, 272
Mendenhall, James, 272
Mendenhall House, 32, 296
Mendenhall-Valentine-Edge House, 272
Mennonite Meetinghouse, 379
Mennonites, 27, 310, 311; Dutch, 335; Swiss, 311. See also Anabaptists
Mercer, 534, 562-63; Cemetery, 562; Jail, 562
Mercer, Henry Chapman, 138, 260, 261; House, 261
Mercer, Thomas, Houses, 379
Mercer County, 6, 534, 562, 578; Historical Society, 562
Mercer Museum, 260, 261
Merchants' Exchange, 382
Merchants' Hotel, 379
Merchants Warehouse Company, 371
Mercur, Mahlon, House, 113
Merion Friends Meetinghouse, 319
Methodist Churches, 101, 278, 363, 385, 386, 416, 471, 470, 554, 564, 565, 566
Methodists, 530.

Metropolitan Museum of Art, 75
Metz, D.A., House, 370
Mewhorter, Thomas, House, 313
Michael, George, House, 516
Michael, John George, 516
Michael, Samuel, House, 516
Michael (family) Barn, 516
Middletown, 294
Mifflin County, 3, 404
Mikveh Israel Cemetery Gatehouse, 110, 379
Milan, Italy, 116
Milford, 128, 129, 132, 497, 499, 520-21, 579; Jail, 52
Mill, Peter, House, 512
Mill, Samantha J., House, 512
Mill Creek, 46
Mill Tract Farm, 257
Millbach, 45, 311, 312, 570
Miller, Charles P., landscape architect, 273
Miller, Jacob and Elizabeth, Barn, 308
Miller, James, House, 424, 451
Miller, John, 234
Miller, Oliver, House, 451
Miller, Peter, 305
Miller, William, House, 36, 43, 234, 265
Miller-Pusey Mill, 276
Miller's Farm, 248
Miller's House, 263
Milligan, Samuel, Mill, 471
Milligantown, 471
Millrift, 579
Mills, Robert, architect, 339
mills and millers, 223, 245, 256, 266, 269, 271, 272, 274, 275, 276,
   281, 288, 303, 304, 305, 311, 321, 323, 327, 471, 510, 512-13,
   515, 519, 553, 561, 565, 566, 567, 570, 576, 577, 578, 579
Milltown, 278; Plank House, 278
Millville Friends Meetinghouse, 62, 416
Milner, John, Associates, architects, 288
Miners and Mechanics Bank Building, 509
Minersville, 465
Minick, Ralph, architect, 283
Mission Style, 261
Mitchell, John M., House, 456
Mitchell, Thomas, House, 379
Mitchell/Giurgola, architects, 151
Moffett, Robert, House, 379
Moffett-Urquhart House, 379
Monaca, 464
Monocacy Creek, 322, 323, 324
Monocacy Creek Aqueduct, 578
Monastery, 379
Monongahela River, 424, 453, 460
Monroe County, 10, 493, 515-19, 578
Monroeton, 532
Montgomery, William, House, 87, 89, 307
Montgomery County, 5, 27, 57, 117, 118, 119, 139, 141, 150, 215,
   314, 316-21, 570, 578
Montour County, 406, 578
Montrose, 528
Moon-Williamson House, 262
Moore, Clarence B., House, 37
Moore, John, House, 380
Moore, Nathaniel, 287
Moore, Samuel, House and Store, 468
Moore, Tory William, 280
Moore, William: House (Moore Hall), 75, 280; Barn, 260
Moorhead, J. Y., House, 558
Moorhead, James, 558
Moorhead House, 252
Moorheadville, 557
Moorish style, 124, 308, 521
Moravia, 43, 57, 322
Moravian buildings, 8, 51-52, 57
Moravian Church, 52, 245, 325
Moravian Churches, 322, 464
Moravian College, 8, 324
Moravian Community (Bethlehem), 322-25; Bell House, 323, 324;
   Central Church, 322; Gemeinhaus, 322, 323; Single Brethren's
   House, 324; Single Sisters' House, 324; Widows' House, 325. *See
   also* Moravian Industrial Area *and names of individual sites*
Moravian Industrial Area, Eighteenth-Century, 323-325. *See also*
   Moravian Community (Bethlehem) *and names of individual sites*
Moravian Museum, 323
Moravian Pottery and Tile Works, 261, 576
Moravian Seminary for Girls, 322, 324
Moravians, 91, 253, 322, 323, 324, 325
Morgan, Samuel, builder, 302
Morgan Billet Mill Engine, 575
Morgan Farmhouse, 299
Morris, Samuel, House, 321
Morris Brewery Vaults, 380
Morris Canal, 220
Morris House (Compton), 368
Morriseianna, 268
Morrisville, 262
Morse School Annex, 456
Morton Homestead, 30
Mortonsen, Morton, House, 299
Moselem Springs, 247
Mother Bethel African Methodist Episcopal Church. See Bethel
   African Methodist Episcopal Church

Mount Braddock, 80, 467
Mount Carmel, 485
Mount Jewett, 578; Station, 578
Mount Joy Observation Tower (Valley Forge), 578
Mount Minsi Farm, 326
Mount Moriah Cemetery Gatehouse, 110, 380
Mount Pleasant, Berks Co., 78, 79, 214, 219, 247-53
Mount Pleasant (house), 72-75, 267, 380
Mount Pleasant Gristmill, 576
Mount Pleasant Ironworks, 570
Mount Pocono, 493
Mount Rocky, 207, 208, 278; Methodist Church, 278
Mount Sinai Cemetery Chapel, 380
Mount Washington Tavern, 427, 428, 467
Mountain View Dairy Farm, Barn, 216, 326
Moyamensing Prison, 382
Moyer, William, builder, 563
Mueller House, 45, 311
Muhlenberg, Heinrich Melchoir, 320
Mulford, Sylvanus, House, 528-29, 564
Muncy, 477, 578
Munsch House, 326
Murchison, Kenneth M., 485
Murphy-Johnson House, 380
Murray, Dr. Thomas, House, 468
Muse, John J., House, 452, 569
museums, 115, 124, 125, 260, 261, 311, 345, 371, 380, 381, 382, 383, 390, 437
Musical Fund Society Hall, 380
Musser, Michael, House, 84, 308
Musser-Reigart House, 308
Mussina, Lyons, House, 415
Mutual Fire Insurance Company Building, 255, 380
Myers, Elijah E., architect, 486
Myers, Lawrence, House, 511
Myerstown, 248
mysticism, 52-55

Nagle, Peter, Jr., 257
Naglee House, 571
Nanticoke, 483, 485, 486, 512
Nantmell Hall, 300
Narberth, 319
National Archives, 3
National Farm School, 261
National Guard Hall (armory), 380
National Historic Landmark, 19
National Historic Preservation Act of 1966, 9; Amendments of 1980, 10, 16
National Industrial Recovery Act, 5

National Landmarks Program, 9
National Museum of American History. *See* Smithsonian Institution
National Park Service, 1, 2, 4, 5, 6, 7, 8, 9, 13, 17, 18, 237, 243, 320, 321, 395, 413, 416, 465, 468
National Register of Historic Places, 9, 10, 12, 19, 155
National Road, 426-28, 469; tollhouses, 427-28, 469
National Trail, 469
Native Americans, 312, 396, 421, 422, 477, 512, 520
Navigator Statue, 384
Naylor House, 263
Nazareth, 326
Neal, Robert, Cabin (Neill Log House), 59, 60, 424, 456
Neave, Samuel, House and Store, 380
Neff, John, House, 397
Nemacolin Castle, 466
Neoclassical Revival, 139, 346
neoclassicism, 84, 87, 92, 138, 454, 533, 534
Neshaminy, 263
Neuweiler Brewery, 577
Nevel, Thomas, House, 380
Neville, Presley, 423
New Alexandria, 472
New Berlinville, 253
New Britain, 263
New Century Club, 380
New Cumberland Army Depot, 581
New England, 423, 478, 527-30, 532-37
New Geneva, 467
New Grand Opera House, 437
New Half-Way House Tavern, 268
New Harmony, Ind., 55
New Hope, 264, 570
New Jersey, 10
New Jersey Zinc Company, 576
New Kensington, 147, 441, 472
New Richmond, 537, 538, 553
New Smithfield, 316
New Sweden, 30
New Tripoli, 315
New York City, 108, 117, 120, 128, 130, 138, 140-41, 144, 146, 150, 151, 152, 153
New York Mutual Life Insurance Company Building, 380
New York State, 527, 532, 534-37
Newmaker House, 567
Newmanstown, 49, 312, 570
Newtown, 263
Newtown Square, 278
Newville, 289
Niantic, 319-20

Index • 615

Nicholson, 580
Niernsee and Neilson, architects, 491
Nitre Hall Mills, Powder Magazine, 298
Nittany, 415
Nittany Valley, 396
Nixon Tavern, 424, 425, 466
Noble, Robert W., architect, 150-51
Noll, H. R., architect, 491
Nolts Point Mill Covered Bridge, 310
Norkfolk Street Houses, 380
Norris-Cadwalader House, 380
Norristown, 220, 578
Norriton, 57
North Braddock, 432
North Branch Canal, 539
North Catasaqua, 579
North East, 101, 558
North Front Street: Area Study, 372; commercial buildings, 372; houses, 371, 372
North Mehoopany, 567
North Ninth Street Restaurant and Apartment Building, 380
North Philadelphia, 341, 352
North Seventh Street, 387; Area Study, Commercial Building, 387
North Side: Market, 457, 569; Post Office, 462; Point Bridge, 575
North Sixth Street Houses, 293
North Springfield, 558
North Third Street: Area Study, 389; House, 389
North Water Street House, 390
Northampton, 326, 579; Brewery, 579
Northampton County, 5, 10, 51, 53, 91, 216, 322-26, 482, 488, 578-79
Northbrook, 278
Northern Liberties, 339, 340; National Bank of, 380
Northern Liberty Hose Company, No. 4, 381
Northern Saving Fund, Safe Deposit and Trust Company, 380
Northern Trust Company, 381
Northumberland, 139, 399; National Bank, 139
Northumberland County, 396, 404, 477, 485; Courthouse, 406
Norvelt, 472
Norwegian Seamen's Church, 379
Norwood, 299
Notman, John, architect, 102, 104, 110, 114, 115, 117, 318, 344, 431, 460
Nunnemacher, Daniel, House, 313
Nutt, Samuel, House, 271
Nutting, Wallace, 141
Nyce, George, 520
Nyce, William, House, 520

Oakley, Thornton, 302
Oakley, Violet, 138
Obolds-Billman Hotel, 250
Octagon House, 252
Octagon Schoolhouse, 522
Octagonal Barn, 558
Odd Fellows Cemetery Gate, 110
Odd Fellows Hall, 109, 376
office buildings. See industrial, office buildings, and warehouses
Office of Archeology and Historic Preservation, 9
O'Gorman, James, 127
Ohio Building, 376
Ohiopyle, 149, 441, 467
Oil City, 580
oil industry 539-41
Okie, R. Brognard, 271, 299
Old Academy, 418
Old Conestoga Wagon Trail, 272
Old Congress, 570
Old Customhouse, 556
Old Dry Road Farm, Inc., 219
Old Economy, 55, 464. See also Economy; Harmony Society
Old Fort Tavern, 399, 414
Old Guard House Inn, 570
Old Heidelberg Apartments, 143, 438, 440, 457, 569
Old Mauch Chunk Historic District, 508
Old Mill Road Bridge, 579
Old Philadelphia Development Corporation, 350
Old Post Office Museum, 462
Old Ship Zion Church, Wilkes-Barre, 478
Old Stone Jail, Mercer, 562
Old Superintendent's Quarters, 320
Old Swede's House, 242
Old Swedes Church, 373
Old Trappe Church, 320
Old West, Dickinson College, 90
Olde York Inn, 330
Olds, Frederick L., 127-28
Oley Twp., Berks Co., 43, 48, 50, 76, 211, 243, 245, 253, 254, 258, 570
Oley Valley, 8, 253, 254, 256
Oliver, Henry W., 136, 454. See also English-Oliver House
Oliver Building, 136
One East Penn Square Building, 378
One Liberty Place, 153, 350. See also Liberty Place
O'Neill, John P., architect, 3, 5
Ontelaunee Creek Bridge, 578
Opperman's Corner, 265
Orbisonia, 577
Oregon, Pa., 310

Ormiston House, 381
Orthodox Churches, 101, 385
Osborne, Richard, bridge designer, 255
Osterling, Frederick J., 452, 486
Ottinger House, 571
Ottsville, 264
Overbrook School for the Blind, 382
Owen, Robert, 55

PPG Place, 441
Packer, Asa, 539; Mansion, 13, 486-88, 508
Packer, Judge Harry, 488
Packerton, 576
Page, George B., architect, 302
Page Brothers, architects, 339
Paine, Thomas, 328
Painter, Charles Albert, 467
Painter, Uriah, 284
Palatinate, 27, 43
Palladio, Andrea, 69
Palliser, Charles, architect, 139
Palliser, George, architect, 128, 139
Palmer, John, House, 381
Palmer, Hornbostel and Jones, architects, 138
Palmerton, 508, 576
Pancake, Philip, House, 381
Pancoast-Lewis-Wharton House, 381
Pantheon, 139
Paoli, 73, 221, 224, 279
Paris, 122, 144; Opera House, 136
Parke, David, House, 279
Parke, John, House, 279
Parke House, 32, 34, 272
Parkesburg, 279-80
Parry, Charles T., House, 381
Parryville, 508
Parryville Mill, 576
Parson, Judge A. V., House, 399, 400, 418
Parsons, Elijah, House, 117
Parsons, William, 325
Parsons-Taylor House, 325
Paschall, Jonathan, House, 381
Pastorius, Daniel, House, 381
Patio Club Building, 325
Patterson Farm, 265
Patterson House, 238
Payne, George F., Company, contractors, 136
Paxson Barn, 264
Paxtang, 57, 58, 295
Paxton Presbyterian Church, 57, 58, 295

Peale, Charles Willson, House, 381
Pei, I. M., architect, 339
Pekruhn, John, 8
Pencoyd Farm, House, 316
Pendergrass, Garrett, 395
Penguin Court, 471
Penn, John, House, 387
Penn, Richard, 396
Penn, Thomas, 396
Penn, William, 1, 27, 31, 70, 301, 319, 321, 396; family, 207-208, 251, 325, 333, 334, 335, 341, 477
Penn and Liberty Avenue Commercial Buildings, 457
Penn Center, 349
Penn-Craft, 467
Penn High School, Mercer, 562
Penn Mutual Life Insurance Company Building, 151, 381
Penn Square Building, 365
Penn Traffic Building, 465
Penn Wick, 275
Pennock, Joseph, House, 269
Pennock, William, House, 301
Penn's Landing, 350
Penns Valley, 396, 399
Pennsburg, 27
Pennsylvania Academy of the Fine Arts, 124, 125, 381
Pennsylvania Athletic Club, 370
Pennsylvania Bar Association, 293
Pennsylvania Canal, 12, 403, 416, 429, 468, 482, 576; Lock Keeper's House, Alexandria, 417. *See also* Allegheny Portage Railroad *and names of canal divisions*
Pennsylvania Capitol, 87, 136, 138, 153, 293
Pennsylvania College. *See* Gettysburg College
Pennsylvania, Commonwealth of, 305, 307, 318, 321
Pennsylvania Company for Insurances on Lives and Granting Annuities, 381, 573
Pennsylvania Dutch Folk Culture Society, 248
Pennsylvania farmhouse, 77, 141, 299, 347, 397
Pennsylvania Fire Insurance Company, 381
Pennsylvania Furnace, 403, 417, 570
Pennsylvania Game Commission, 289, 560
Pennsylvania-German architecture, 8
Pennsylvania-German Barn Recording Project, 11
Pennsylvania-German farms, 10, 206, 217-18, 242, 246, 247, 248, 249, 250, 253, 254
Pennsylvania Germanic houses, 32, 43, 45, 48-52, 77, 209, 219, 246, 247, 248, 249, 250, 251, 252, 254, 312, 424. *See also* Germanic architecture; Germanic houses
Pennsylvania Germans, 43, 45, 77, 478, 511
Pennsylvania Hall, Gettysburg College, 95, 224, 235

Pennsylvania Historical and Museum Commission, 13, 18, 155, 241, 245, 250, 264, 304, 318, 321, 464, 469, 510, 556, 559, 563. *See also* State Museum of Pennsylvania *and names of historic sites*
Pennsylvania, Historical Society of, mantlepiece, 375
Pennsylvania Hospital, 89, 90, 382
Pennsylvania Hospital for Mental and Nervous Diseases, 382
Pennsylvania Hospital for the Insane, 382
Pennsylvania Institution for the Deaf and Dumb, 382
Pennsylvania Institution for the Instruction of the Blind, 382
Pennsylvania Land Office, 308
Pennsylvania Museum and School of Industrial Art, 383
Pennsylvania Railroad, 138, 220, 221, 282, 293, 317, 404, 429-30, 573, 579; Alexandria Station, 417; Broad Street Station, 341, 342, 349, 382; Brick Viaduct, 573; Bryn Mawr Station, 317; Chestnut Hill Line Station, 382; Germantown Junction Station, 382; Harrisburg Station, 575; Johnstown Station, 432, 465; Mantua Junction Viaduct, 573; Pittsburgh (Union) Station, Rotunda, 459, 569; Saltsburg Station, 468; West Chester Station, 285; Wissahickon Creek Viaduct, 573
Pennsylvania Road, 428
Pennsylvania State Archives, 18
Pennsylvania State University, 11, 17, 18
Pennsylvania System (penal reform), 106
Pennypack Creek Bridge, 382
Peoples, U. J. Lincoln, architect, 458
Pequea Creek, 45
Perelman Antique Toy Museum, 363
Perkin's Run, 289
Perkins, David, 511
Perkins, John, 511
Perkins House, 510
Perry, I. G., architect, 485
Perry, Roland Hinton, sculptor, 136
Perry County, 395
Perry Memorial Building, 555
Peters, Charles R., 519
Peters, Edwin, 519
Peters, George, House, 234
Peters, Harry, 519
Peters, Henry, 519
Peters, John, House, 234
Peter's Corner, 264
Peters House Hotel, 493, 494
Petersburg Tollhouse, 428, 469
Peterson, Charles E., architect, vii-ix, 2, 6, 9, 11
Pettinos Brothers Graphite Manufacturing Mill, 578
petroleum industry, 539-41, 554
Philadelphia, 2, 3, 5, 6, 9, 19, 11, 34, 36, 38, 39, 40, 43, 61, 62, 63, 64, 65, 69, 72, 73, 74, 75, 84, 85, 87, 88, 89, 90, 92, 94, 95, 96, 97, 101, 102, 103, 104, 105, 107, 108, 109, 110, 114, 115, 117, 120, 123, 124, 125, 133, 134, 135, 136, 137, 138, 139, 140, 141, 142, 143, 144, 145, 146, 148, 150, 151, 152, 153, 207, 208, 220, 221, 332-90, 401, 403, 406, 429, 431, 454, 482, 483, 485, 488, 571, 579; Center Square, 334; Dilworth Plaza, 349; Kennedy Plaza, 349; Penn Center, 349; Reyburn Plaza, 349; Washington Square, 339
Philadelphia and Reading Railroad. *See* Reading Railroad
Philadelphia Art Club, 382, 571
Philadelphia Athenaeum, *See* Athenaeum
Philadelphia Bourse Building, 382
Philadelphia City Hall, 122, 123, 128, 146, 153, 154, 344, 349, 350, 375, 380
Philadelphia City Planning Commission, 349, 350
Philadelphia, College of, 396. *See also* University of Pennsylvania
Philadelphia College of Art, 382
Philadelphia Contributionship for the Insuring of Houses from Loss by Fire, 382
Philadelphia Convention Center, 341
Philadelphia County, 27, 61, 363-92; Courthouse, 368; Prison, 108, 382
Philadelphia Exchange Company, 382
Philadelphia Fire Department, 383, 391. *See also names of individual companies*
Philadelphia Free Library, 18; Mercantile Library, 150
Philadelphia Functionalism, 145
Philadelphia Gasworks, 579
Philadelphia, Germantown and Norristown Railway, 340; Germantown Depot, 383
Philadelphia Historical Commission, 350
Philadelphia Masonic Temple, 383
Philadelphia Municipal Services Building, 349
Philadelphia Museum of Art, 311, 383
Philadelphia (National) Bank, 364
Philadelphia Navy Yard, 339
Philadelphia Opera House, 383
Philadelphia Redevelopment Authority, 350
Philadelphia Saving Fund Society: 383; Building, 145-46, 347, 348
Philadelphia Trust, Safe Deposit and Insurance Company, 383
Philadelphia, Wilmington and Baltimore Railroad, Freight Station, 383
Philadelphia Zoological Gardens: Bear Pits, 383; Entrance Pavilions, 383
Philips, Hardman, 397; House, 415
Philipsburg, 3, 94, 397, 415
Phillipsburg, N.J., 483
Philosophical Hall, 363. *See also* Library Hall
Phipps Conservatory, 436
Phoenixville, 220, 280
photogrammetric plates, xi, 573
Pickering, Timothy, House, x, 514

Picklands, Thomas, House, 383
Picnic House, 454
Pierce, Charles S., House, 521
Pierce, Lukens, House, 282
Pierce, Nicholas, architect, 235
Pietism, 55, 304
Pietists, German, 335, 464
Pike County, 10, 128, 129, 132, 478, 480, 493, 494, 495-96, 497, 499, 519-21, 579; Courthouse, 520
Pikeville, 254
Piles, John, House, 383
Pim, Richard, Hexagonal School, 282
Pinchot, Amos R. E., 521
Pinchot, Cornelia Bryce, 130-33
Pinchot, Gifford, 130, 131, 133, 521
Pinchot, James W., 128, 130, 497, 521
Pine Street House, 383
Pine Street Presbyterian Church, Philadelphia, 64, 389
Piollet, Joseph Marie, architect, 551
Pithole, 540
Pitner House, 263
Pittenturf, J. M., and Brothers, builders, 240
Pittsburgh, 3, 8, 11, 59, 60, 96, 104, 108, 110, 111, 112, 116, 124-25, 126, 136, 138-39, 140, 143, 144, 150, 151, 152, 153, 154, 285, 401, 403, 423, 424, 429, 431, 433, 434, 435, 436-41, 452-63, 527, 569, 576; City-County Building, 140, 453
Pittsburgh and Lake Erie Railroad Station, 459
Pittsburgh and Steubenville Extension Railroad Tunnel, 575
Pittsburgh Civic Club, 437
Pittsburgh Club, 460
Pittsburgh History and Landmarks Foundation, 424, 455, 456, 458, 459, 462
Pittsburgh Plate Glass Corporation, 152
Pittsfield, 534, 566; Old Hotel, 566; Presbyterian Church, 566; United Methodist Church, 566
Pittston, 488, 539
Plank, George, 239
Pleasant Valley, 264
Pleasant Valley Roller Mill (Bernville), 576
Pleasanton, Gen. Alfred, 237, 238
Pleasantville, 254, 565; Free Methodist Church, 101, 565
Plumer, John C., House, 472, 572
Plumsock (house), 288
Plymouth, 512
Plymouth, Mass., 36
Pocopson Creek, 276
Poe, Edgar Allan, House, 383
Point Bridge, 460, 569, 575
Point Pleasant, 576
Polite Temple Baptist Church, 370

Pont Reading House, 298
Poor Richard Club, 382
Poppeliers, John C., 9
Port Allegheny, 535, 561
Port Kennedy, 117, 119, 320
Port Royal (house), 75, 383
Porter, John, House, 417
Porteus, James, builder, 341
Portico Row, 383
Portico Square, 339, 383
Portland, 326
postmodernism, 152, 153, 349
Potter County, 101, 524, 527, 534, 536, 563-64
Potts, Horace T., and Company Warehouse, 384
Potts, Isaac, 82; House, 320, 321
Potts, Joseph D., House, 384, 571
Potts family, 289
Pottstown, 220, 320
Pottsville, 220, 280, 482, 483, 488, 521, 572
powder magazines, 298, 384
Powder Valley Pottery, 578
Powel House, 69, 332, 336
Powell, A. V., architect, 554
Powell, Samuel, House, 332, 384
PPG Place, 153
precast concrete, 151
Presbyterian Church, 57, 59, 114, 328, 530
Presbyterian Churches, 57, 59, 64, 87, 101, 114, 140, 240, 284, 295, 327, 328, 369, 370, 389, 391, 406, 416, 432, 451, 460, 468, 485, 515, 530, 546, 551, 554, 564
Presque Isle, 422; Lighthouse, 555, 570; State Park, 555
Preston Retreat, 384
Price, Bruce, architect, 491
Price, Isaac, architect, 491
Price, John, 321
Price, William L., architect, 141
Price and Walton, 284
Pricetown, 254
Primitive Hall (house), 70, 71, 269
Printz, Gov. Johan, 242
prisons, 105-9, 284, 369, 382, 415, 572
Progress, 295
Prospect Hill Cemetery, 329
Prospect Park, 30
Providence Quaker Meetinghouse, 299
Provident Life and Trust Company Bank, 384, 571, 573
public housing, 147; Schuylkill Falls, 148
Public Works Administration, 4, 147, 349
Pugh, James, Springhouse, 280
Pughtown, 280

Pugin, Augustus Welby Northmore, 102
Puritans, New England, 528, 530
Pusey, Caleb, House, 36, 37, 276, 301
Pusey, Joshua, 268
Pusey, William, House, 268
Pyle, Walter, C., Barn, 275
Pyle House, 289

Quaker meetinghouses. See Friends meetinghouses *and individual names*
Quaker-plan house, 31, 206. See also English Quaker house
Quakers, 27, 32, 59, 61, 70, 206, 241, 266, 267, 273, 282, 289, 296, 530. *See also* Dutch; English; Welsh
Quarry Street Houses, 384
Queen Anne style, 72, 128, 141, 266, 294, 541, 555
Querean House, 252
Quinn House, 565

Race Street Commercial Buildings, 384
Racine, Wisc., 150
Radnor, 299, 300; Historical Society, 7
railroad stations, 222, 223, 279, 282, 285, 313, 317, 342, 349, 364, 365, 382, 383, 432, 459-60, 468, 515, 569, 577, 578. See also *railroad names and individual stations*
railroads, 128, 220, 222, 279, 282, 313, 317, 340, 364, 383, 403, 404, 482, 483, 484, 495, 488, 508, 515, 539, 577, 579, 580, 581. *See also* Pennsylvania Railroad; Reading Railroad
Ralston, Robert, House, 384
Ralston School, 384
Rapp, Frederick Reichert, 464
Rapp, George, 55
Rappe Hotel, 471
Re, Victor, contractor, 237
Read, Thomas Buchanan, 209
Reading, 108, 110, 208, 220, 225, 255, 576; Friends Meetinghouse, 255
Reading-Halls Station Bridge, 578
Reading News Building, 255
Reading Railroad, 138, 220, 255, 280, 310, 483, 576; Terminal, 341, 343, 350, 382, 576; Schuylkill River Viaduct, 573
Real, Benjamin, House, 511
Reber Barn, 242
Reber Farm House, 247
Redeemer, Church of the, 367
Reed, Charles M., House, 97, 120, 556; Block, 556
Reed, Samuel and Joseph, Houses, 98, 384
Rees, Edward, 319
Rees, William, 318
Reese, Joseph, House, 297
Reformed Church, 2, 57, 245, 513

Reformed Churches, 105, 370, 416, 478, 513, 519
Reifsnyder Farm, 242
Reifsnyder House, 251
Reigart, Adam, 308
reinforced concrete, 148, 151
Reliance Insurance Company of Philadelphia, 384
Renaissance, 40, 42, 70, 72, 94, 110, 113, 115, 120, 124, 127, 134, 139, 335, 336, 341, 438; Flemish Revival, 453; French, 128, 130; Italian Revival, 110, 115; Revival, 136, 138, 139, 153, 285, 308, 458; Second Revival, 346, 462, 463
Rensselaer Lee Houses, 352
restaurants, 370
Reyburn Plaza, 349
Reynolds, William, 552
Reynolds-Morris House, 69, 384
Rhoads-Barclay House, 384
Rhode Island, 529
Rhodes, A. S., Springhouse, 451
Rhodes House, 566
Rialto Theater, 313
Riceville, 100, 529, 537, 553
Rich, Colmly, House, 384
Rich-Truman House, 384
Richards Medical Research Building, 151
Richardson, George S., engineer, 460
Richardson, Henry H., architect, 8, 124-25, 127-28, 346, 431-32, 452, 454
Richmond Furnace, 570
Rickert's Coal and Freight Company, 576
Ricketts, Richard, 417
Ricketts House, 564
Ridge Avenue Farmers' Market Company, 571
Ridgeland, 384
Ridgway, Charles, House, 552
Ridgway, John, Log House, 565
Ridgway, Titus, House, 97, 100, 552
Riegelsville, 576
Riem, George, 251
Riem-Schmidt-Deppen Farm, House, 251
Riggs and Brother, Navigator Statue, 384, 571
Rittenhouse House, 385
Ritter and Shay, architects, 144
River Schoolhouse, 517
Roberts, John, House, 424, 426, 469, 572
Roberts, Owen, 267
Roberts Estate, 316
Roberts' Plantation, 267
Robertsdale, 417-18
Robesonia, 76
Robinson, James, House, 468

Index • **620**

Robinson, Thomas and John, House, 468
Robinson, W. J., House, 563
Robinson, William, House, 385
Robinson, William C., House, 468
Rock Ford, 309
Rockview State Correctional Institution, 415
Rockwood, 469
Rocky Hill, 280
Rococo style, 120, 556
Roebling, John A., 482
Roeder, S. and R. G., Barn, 315
Rogers, Philip, House, 275
Rogers, William and Mary, 287; House, 287
Rogers-Cassatt House, 385
Rogers-Hoopes House, 287
Roman, 114, 336
Roman Catholic Churches, 102, 105, 114, 136, 366, 367, 375, 386, 486
Roman Catholics, 102, 115, 251, 486
Roman Revival, 92
Romanesque, 110, 114, 125, 127, 222; Revival, 224, 452, 454, 456; Richardsonian, 346, 432, 438, 452, 457, 458, 459, 460
Romans, John, Barn, 281
Romansville, 281; Friends Meetinghouse Sheds, 281
Rombach, Mathias, House, 468
Roney, John, House, 385
Rose, George Washington, Farm, 238; Barn, 238
Rose Valley artist colony, 141
Rosicrucianism, 55
Ross, Judge John, 515
Ross Common Manor, 515
Rossmaessler Mill, 578
Rostraver Township Municipal Building, 471
Rouech House, 541
Rouch House, 518
Roulette, 534, 564
Rouse, Willard, III, 350
Rouse Urban Housing, Inc., 339
Roush, Stanley L., architect, 452, 460
Rowley-Pullman House, 385
Royal House, 385, 571
Royal Insurance Company Building, 385
Ruff Creek, 468
Rumpp, C. E., and Sons, Inc., Factory, 385
Runge, Gustav, architect, 116
Rush, Benjamin, 217; Birthplace, 385
Rush, William, 307
Rutan, Frank E., 462
Rutherford Stone House and Springhouse, 295
Ryan House, 567
Ryers Mansion, 365

S-bridge, 427
Saegertown, 553
St. Agatha's Catholic Church, 385
St. Andrew-by-the-Wardrobe Church, London, 62
St. Andrew's Episcopal Church, 101, 385
St. Anthony Street Bridge, 580
St. Augustine's Catholic Church, 385
St. Charles Borromeo Catholic Church, 385
St. Charles Hotel, 385
St. Clement's Episcopal Church: Philadelphia, 385; Wilkes-Barre, 486
St. David's Episcopal Church, 300
Saint Davids, 300
St. Elizabeth Catholic Church, 385
St. Francis DeSales Catholic Church, 385
St. Francis School, Nanticoke, 486
St. Francis Xavier's Catholic Church, 385
St. Gabriel's Church, Douglassville, 66, 67, 242
St. George's Greek Orthodox Cathedral, 101, 385
St. George's House, 376
St. George's Methodist Episcopal Church, 385
St. James Catholic Church, 385
St. James Street Houses, 385
St. James the Less Episcopal Church, 102, 104, 367
St. John the Evangelist Episcopal Church, 520
St. John's Lutheran Church: Adams County, 105, 240; Ambridge, 464; Philadelphia, 385
St. Luke and the Epiphany Episcopal Church, 367
St. Mark's Episcopal Church, Philadelphia, 102, 104, 386, 431
St. Mark's Episcopal Church, Jim Thorpe, 488, 508; Parish House, 488
St. Martin's Church, Radnor, 300; Parish Hall, 299
St. Martin-in-the-Fields Church, London, 62
St. Mary's Catholic Church: Philadelphia, 386; Wilkes-Barre, 486
St. Mary's Episcopal Church, 386
St. Matthew's Church: Saint Matthews Corner, 281; Saltsburg, 468
Saint Matthews Corner, 281
St. Michael's Church: Strasburg, 66; Long Stanton, Cambridgeshire, 102
St. Nicholas German Catholic Church, Wilkes-Barre, 486
St. Paul's Episcopal Church, 386
St. Peters, 577
St. Peter in the Great Valley Episcopal Church, Devault, 271
St. Peter's Church, Pittsburgh, 431
St. Peter's Episcopal Church: Philadelphia, 64, 65, 72, 365, 386; House, 386; Pittsburgh, 435, 460; Waterford, 559
St. Peter's Roman Catholic Church, Brownsville, 102, 105
Saint Peters, Chester Co., 281
St. Peter's Basilica, 136
St. Peter's Kierch, Middletown, 294

St. Peters, Berks Co., 256
SS. Peter and Paul Cathedral: Philadelphia, 114, 366; Scranton, 486
St. Philip Neri Church, 367
St. Stephen's Episcopal Cathedral, Dean's House, 292
St. Stephen's Episcopal Church, Philadelphia, 64, 72, 103, 365, 366; House, 386; Wilkes-Barre, 486
St. Stephen's Methodist Episcopal Church, Rectory, 386, 571
St. Timothy's Episcopal Church, 386
St. Timothy's Working Men's Club and Institute, 386
St. Vincent De Paul Church, Philadelphia, 367
St. Vincent De Paul Church, Scranton. See SS. Peter and Paul Cathedral, Scranton
Sakal, John, architect, 471
Saltsburg, 12, 416, 468; Academy, 468; 105 Point Street house, 468; Town of, 468
Salunga, 307
Salvation Army center, 456
Sanderson, Joseph, 138
Sansom, William, House and Row, 336, 338, 386
Saquoit Mill, 578
Sartwell, Solomon, architect, 562
Savage, William D., architect, 284
sawmills, 469
Saxony, 30
Saylorsburg, 515
Sayre, 576
Scaife, Alan M., House, 471, 572
Schaeffer, Alexander, House, 51
Schaeffer, Harriet, House, 386
Schaeffer House, 415
Schaefferstown, 51, 122, 312
Scheibler, Frederick G., Jr., architect, 143, 438, 455, 456, 457, 463
Schenck, Martin, 325
Schenck Building, 386
Schenk, Henry, builder, 454
Schenley, Mary E., 437
Schenley House, 454
Schenley Park, 424, 437
Schickel, William, architect, 486
Schively, Henry, House, 386
Schlatter, Rev. Michael, 245
Schmidt, Philip, 251
Schneider, David, House, 245
Schner-Ellicott House, 308
Schnitz House, 323
Schober, Andrew, 325
schools, 84, 86, 263, 264, 266, 273, 274, 279, 282, 286, 302, 322, 324, 363, 364, 368, 371, 372, 375, 382, 384, 391, 418, 456, 458, 464, 468, 471, 486, 509, 514-15, 516, 517, 522, 554, 559, 560, 562, 565

Schooley, David, architect, 488
Schriner, John H., Barn, 213, 310
Schultz Bridge and Iron Company, 453
Schulze, Carl, 52, 325
Schuylkill Arsenal, 386
Schuylkill Canal, 220, 482, 483, 580
Schuylkill County, 429, 485, 521, 572, 580; prison, 572
Schuylkill Falls, 147
Schuylkill Haven, 580
Schuylkill Hose, Hook and Ladder Company, No. 24, 387
Schuylkill River, 208, 321, 333, 475
Schuylkill River Viaduct, 579
Schuylkill Valley Survey, 8
Schwab, Charles, House, 432
Schwarzmann, Hermann, architect, 133
Schweinitz, Lewis David von, 323
Schwenkfelders, 27, 30, 57
Sconnelltown, 281; House, 281
Scotch-Irish, 27, 30, 59, 240, 327, 397
Scott, Thomas H., 455, 459
Scotland, 72, 75, 341; town halls, 69
Scott-Wanamaker House, 386, 572
Scranton, 154, 475, 480, 481, 483-84, 485, 486, 491-92, 497, 509, 577; Municipal Building 492; Post Office, 509; Public Library, 509
Scranton, George W., 491
Scranton Army Ammunition Plant, 577
Scriven's House, 563; Store, 563
Searights Tollhouse, 427, 429, 469
Second Empire style, 122-24, 286, 321, 346, 416, 491, 509, 555
Second Presbyterian Church, Scranton, 485
Sedgeley, 344
Sedgeley Porter's (Guard) House, 387
Sehner, Gottlieb, 308
Selinsgrove, 418
Sellers, Lester H., 299
Semple Company Warehouse, 383
Seventh Day German Baptists, 27, 304
Sewickley Bridge, 576
Sewickley Heights, 139, 463, 569
Shadyside Presbyterian Church, 432, 439, 460
Shappell and Crothers, architects, 260
Sharitz Road House, 273
Sharp, William A., Building, 255
Sharples, Philip, House, 286
Sharpless, Isaac, 267
Sharpless House, 266
Sharpsburg, 463; Ferry House, 463, 569
Shattuck, Richard, Lodge, 560
Shaulis, W. L., House, 469

Shaw, George B., architect, 299
Shaw, W. P., builder, 567
Shawnee on Delaware, 515-19
Sheakleyville, 563
Shedd, Nancy, 31
Shenandoah, 485
Shenandoah Valley, 48
Shepley, Rutan and Coolidge, architects, 432, 454, 460
Sheshequin, 530
Shibe Park, 387
Shimerville, 316
Shippen-Wistar House, 387
Shippingport Atomic Power Station, 576
Shoemaker, Elijah Jr., House, 511
Shoemaker, L. D., 141
Shoenberger, John H., House, 431, 433, 460
Shohola, 579; Station, 579
Shohola Creek Bridge, 579
Shoomac Park, 387
Shoppell, Robert W., 128
Short Span Covered Bridge, 570
Shultz, Martin, House, 327
Shupe, P. D., Hardware Store, 468
Shur's Lane Mill, 579
Sickles, Gen. Daniel, 239
Siddons, William, House, 387
Silesia, 57
Silkman House, 480, 481, 509
Silliman, James, 558
Silliman-Phillips House, 558
Simons, George R. and George L., architects, 452
Sims, Joseph, House, 339, 387
Sims-Bilsland House, 387
Singer, John, Warehouse, 387, 572
Singer, John F., House, 111-13, 463, 569
Singmaster, John Adam, Barn, 315
Sink Burgin House, 387
Sisk Houses, 388
Six-Sided School, 282
Skew Arch Bridge, 255, 405, 413, 576
Skidmore, Owings, and Merrill, architects, 150
skyscrapers, 136, 144, 151, 153, 154, 441
Slate Dam, 579
Slate Roof House, 341
Slateford House, 326
Slatington, 316, 578; Roller Mill, 578
Slifer, Eli, 406
Sloan, Samuel, architect, 115, 116, 117, 221, 283, 406, 508
Slyder, W. J., House, 238
Smedley, William T., 486

Smethport, 561
Smith, Judge Charles, House, 308
Smith, Jesse, 553
Smith, John C., architect, 294
Smith, Robert, builder, 69, 72
Smith, Dr. William, 396
Smith (Civil War) Memorial Arch, 387
Smithfield Street Bridge, 575
Smithsonian Institution, viii, 4, 269
Smithton Bridge, 580
Snider Buildings, 460
Snowden, Father (Rev. Ebenezer Hazard), House, 511
Snyder, George, builder, 564
Snyder County, 418, 580
Snyder's Fording Covered Bridge, 240
Society Hill, 64, 69, 350; Towers, 339
Solebury, 264
Solitude, 387
Somerset, 138; City-County Building, 138
Somerset County, 6, 12, 428, 468, 469; Courthouse, 138
Somerton, 388
Sons of Temperance Fountain, 386
Sons of Zebedee Evangelical Lutheran Church, 468
Souder, Charles E., House, 388
Souder's Supply Store, 576
South Bernville Hotel, 241
South Philadelphia, 110, 341
South Street Bridge (Wilkes-Barre), 578
South Water Street: Area Study, 391; Houses and Warehouses, 390, 391
Southeast National Bank, 283
Southern Loan Company of Philadelphia, 388
Southwark, 334, 339; Hose Company, No. 9, 388
Sower House, 388, 572
Spackman Corner Chimney House, 267
Spafford, William, House, 388
Spahr, Frederick and Michael, 327
Spang House, 256
Spangler, Henry, Farm, 239; Barn, 239
Spangsville, 256
Spanish Colonial Revival, 521
Sparks Shot Tower, 388
Speicher Bridge, 576
Spring Creek, 404
Spring Garden Institute, 388, 572
Spring Garden Insurance Company Building, 388
Spring Garden Street Bridge, 579
Springer, Levi, House, 468
Springfield Falls, 563
Springtown, 264

Spruce Street: Area Study, 388; Houses, 388
Square Shadows, 150
stadiums, 387
Stafford's Tavern-Paschall House, 388
Stahl Pottery, 578
Stamm, Eliza, House, 77, 78, 79, 252
Stamm Farm, 214, 251
Stamm, Isaac, House, 207, 252
Stamm, Werner, Farm, 251
Stanfield House, 392
Stanford, Jacob, 396
Stapler, John, House, 265
Star Junction, 12, 468
Starracca House, 580
Starrucca Viaduct, 580
State College, 127
State Museum of Pennsylvania, 75, 280
State Store Building, Reading, 255
State Works Main Line canal and railroad, 403, 404
Staudt, Elias, 241
Stauffer, David, Farm, House, 465
Stauffer-Bame House, 465
steel-frame construction, 133, 134, 136, 139, 144, 145, 150, 152, 459
Stegmaier Brewery, 486
Steinsburg, 315
Stenton, 70-72, 73, 388
Sterrett, David, Cabin, 558
Sterrett, David, House, 289
Sterrett, James, M., House, 556
Sterrett, Robert, 558
Sterrettania, 558
Stetson, John B., (Hat) Company, 388
Stevens, Thaddeus: Furnace, 240; Viaduct, 240
Stevens House, 97, 100, 554
Stewart, Elijah, 565
Stewart, John, architect and builder, 115, 283, 415
Stewart, Thomas, House, 388, 417
Stewart, Vance, House, 562
Stewart, William, House, 468
Stewart family, 417
Stiegel House, 312
Stiles, William, House, 388
Stiles-Lukens House, 383
Stitt, Alexander, House, 417
Stocker, John Clement, House, 388
Stoltzfus House, 270
Stolzfus Stone Barn, 254
Stone, Lemuel, House, 510
Stone Farmhouse, 253

Stone Manse, 451
Stone-Oakford House, 510
Stone-Penrose House, 388, 572
Stone Schoolhouse, 517
Stoner House, 278
Stoneroads Mill Covered Bridge, 303
Stonersville, 62, 256, 570
Stonorov, Oskar, architect, 146, 147, 349
Stoopville, 264
stores, 11, 255, 277, 280, 284, 352, 368, 370, 378, 379, 380, 389, 417, 432, 468, 514, 530, 555, 563. *See also* department stores
Stotz, Charles M., architect, viii, 3, 563
Stoudt, George, House, 252
Strafford, 282; Railroad Station, 282
Strasburg, 66, 311
Strawberry Mansion, 388; Bridge, 389
Strickland, William, architect, 64, 66, 92-94, 101, 110, 284, 344
Stricklerstown, 311
Stride-Madison House, 389
Strode's Grist Mill, 281
Strong, Levi, House
Stuart and Revett's *Antiquities of Athens*, 283
Sullivan County, 564
Sully, Thomas, 258; House, 389
Summers-Worrell House, 389
Summerseat, 263; School, 263
Summerville, 388
Summit, 559; Stone School, 559
Sun Inn, 324
Sunbury, 396, 406
Suntop Homes, 150
Suplee, 274
Surrey, England, 64
Susquehanna, 580
Susquehanna Coal Company, 513
Susquehanna Company, 476-77, 513, 530
Susquehanna County, 528, 537, 538, 564, 580
Susquehanna Female College, 418
Susquehanna Memorial Gardens, 330
Susquehanna River, 220, 396, 401, 403, 404, 475, 477, 527, 528
Sutton, James, 512
Sutton, Samuel, House, 512
Swarthmore, 301
Swartzville, 311
Swedenborgians. *See* Church of the New Jerusalem
Swedes, 27, 28, 30, 31, 32, 242, 262, 296, 298, 333, 335, 336
Swedish cabins, 298
Sweetbrier, 389
Swetland, Belding, 514
Swetland, Luke, House, 514

Swetland, William, Store, 514
Swinging Bridge, 576
Swiss, 45, 347
Swissvale, 463, 569
Switzerland, 43, 57, 212; trained in, 146
synagogues, 110, 150

Tabernacle Presbyterian Church, 389
Tanguy, 282
Tank Farm Road Bridge, 578
Tannenberg, David, 307
Tanner, Henry O., House, 389
tanneries, 324
Tannery, Moravian, 323, 324
Taft, William Howard, 134
"Tapeworm Railroad," 240
Tatum, George, 150
taverns, 31, 34, 209, 236, 245, 250, 268-69, 329, 330, 365, 378, 381, 388, 414, 424, 427, 428, 466, 467, 511, 555, 563, 572
Taylor, Abiah, II, 70
Taylor, Abiah, House, 43, 270
Taylor, Anthony, House, 270
Taylor, Bayard, House, 275
Taylor, George, 325
Taylor, James Knox, architect, 308
Taylor, Lowndes, Barn, 287
Taylor, Phoebe, 36
Taylor, R. J., House, 468
Taylor, Thomas, 270
Taylor-Jones House, 537
Taylor-Parke House, 70, 71, 270
Taylor Run-Yorty Run Schoolhouse, 471
Teel-Whitman House, 556
Telegram Building, 294
Temple-Webster-Stoner House, 277
Templeton, Thomas, builder, 562
Templin House, 27
Terry, Jonathan, 528; Cabin, 529, 551
Terry House, 534, 567
Terry-Wells Cabin, 551
Terrytown, 528, 529, 551
Thayer and Thayer, architects, 562
theaters, 313, 363, 383, 390, 437, 455, 521, 569
theosophy, 55
Theune House, 516
Third Presbyterian (Pine Street) Church, 64, 389
Thomas, Albert, Summer House, 553
Thomas Iron Works, 577
Thomas Mill, 288
Thompson, Andrew, House, 522

Thompson, Daniel, 319
Thompson, Denman, House, 557
Thompson, Capt. Rufus, 557
Thompson Building, 270
Thompson Carriage House, 417
Thompson-Neeley-Pedcock Barn, 264, 570
Thorndale, 282
Thornton, William, architect, 89
Tidioute, 539, 567; Main Street, Old Hotel, 539-40, 567; Young Men's Christian Association, 567
Tiffany, Louis, 508; windows, 454
Tinian (house), 294
Tioga County, 3, 528, 537
Titusville, 539, 540, 553-54
Toby-Shaw House, 389
Tobyhanna Army Depot, 578
Tocks Island Reservoir, 10
Todd, Dr. William A., House, 272
tollhouses, 427-28, 429, 469
Toonerville, 565
Torrey, John, House, 488, 490, 522
Towanda, 108, 113, 117, 528, 530, 537
Towerville, 282
Town truss, 560
Townsend, David, House, 285
Townsend, Samuel, 270, 280
Townville, 97, 100, 554
Tracy Building, 556
Tradesmen's National Bank of Philadelphia, 388
Trappe, 57, 320
Trautwine, John C. 95, 235
Treible, Peter, House, 518
Treichlers, 326, 579; Cafe, 326
Trinity Cathedral Churchyard, Pittsburgh, 452
Trinity Church, Pittsburgh, 104, 431
Trinity (Oxford) Episcopal Church, Philadelphia, 389
Trinity Episcopal Church, Conneautville, 552, 570
Trinity Lutheran Church, Philadelphia, 389; House, 388
Tripartite Agreement, 4
Trocadero (The Troc), 363
Trostle Barn, 210, 239
Trowbridge and Livingston, architects, 144
Trumbauer, Horace, architect, 260
Tudor, 110, 344, 508; Revival, 302, 467, 471, 508
Tulpehocken Creek, 218; Survey, 10
Tunkhannock Viaduct, 580
tunnels, 465, 575
Turn, John, Farm, 517
Turner, Richard, 36
Tuttleman Brothers and Faggen Building, 389

Twelfth Street Meeting House, 389
Tyson, Charles J., 234

U.S. Bonded Warehouse, 389
U.S. Hose Company, No. 14, 389
Ulm, Germany, 55
Underground Railroad, 555
Union Army, 237, 238, 239
Union Canal, 218, 220, 241, 247, 249, 251, 576
Union Church, 394, 397
Union City, 539, 559, 577; Freight Station, 577; Station, 577
Union County, 3, 404, 580
Union League of Philadelphia, 389
Union Reformed and Lutheran Church, Wapwallopen, 105, 106, 513
Uniontown, 77, 424, 427-28, 468, 469
Unitarian Church, Meadville, 101, 552
Unitarian Churches, 101, 370, 552
Unitarians, 101, 370, 552. *See also names of individual churches*
United Brethren Church, 309
United Presbyterian Church, Saltsburg, 468
United States Army Corp of Engineers, 10, 516, 517
United States Bank of Pennsylvania, 94, 97
United States Bank of Pennsylvania, Erie Branch, 99, 556; Cashier's House, 99, 556
United States Bureau of Mines, Experiment Station, 462
United States Department of Agriculture, 521
United States Department of the Interior, 9
United States Mint, 389
United States Naval Asylum (Home), Biddle Hall, 389
United States Post Office, Allegheny, 462, 569; Scranton, 509
United States Post Office and Courthouse: Harrisburg, 294; Lancaster, 308
United States Steel Corporation, 575
universities and colleges, 7, 8, 90, 91, 94, 95, 96, 144, 151, 224, 235, 260, 267, 286, 324, 349, 350, 369, 373, 382, 390-91, 396, 418, 436, 438, 453, 454, 469, 470, 488, 532, 533, 552, 569, 572
University City Science Center, 350
University of Pennsylvania, 7, 8, 151, 349, 350, 390, 396, 572; Alfred Newton Richards Medical Research Building, 349; Goddard Laboratories, 349; Mask and Wig Club, 390, 391
University of Pittsburgh, 144, 436, 454; Cathedral of Learning, 144, 454
Up-and-Down Sawmill, 269
Updegraff, Thomas, House, 418
Upjohn, Richard, architect, 488, 508
Upland, 36, 37, 301
Upper Ferry Bridge, 390
Upper Swedish Log Cabin, 296
Upper Octoraro Presbyterian Church Session House, 280

Upsala, 390
Urban, C. Emlen, architect, 308
USX Duquesne Works, 575

Valentine, Robert, 272
Valentine, Robert, Jr., 272
Valentine-Edge Mill, 272
Valley Forge, 281, 321, 578; Centennial and Memorial Association of, 321; National Historical Park, 82, 319, 320, 321; Observation Tower, 578; Washington's Headquarters, 82, 320, 321
Valley Green Inn, 390, 572
Valley Inn, 330
Valley Methodist Manse, 468
Van Gordon, Jacobus, House, 494, 495-96, 497, 520
Van Horne, Mordecai, decorator, 454
Van Rensselaer, Mariana Griswold, 127
Van Trump, James, 136, 431
Vanor, 300
Vaults, 390
Vaux-Wetherill Stone Barn, 321
Venango County, 6, 101, 541, 565, 580
ventilation, 125
Venturi, Robert, architect, 152, 349, 441
Venturi, Vanna, House, 152
vernacular, 141, 347; industrial, 124
Vernon, 390
Vester, John, architect, 470
Victorian, 12, 346, 438, 458, 459. *See also names of architectural styles*
Vierendeel truss, 151
Villa Maria Convent, 286
Villa Rotunda, 69
Villanova, 301-302
Virginians, 422-23
Vogdes, Jacob, House, 288
Vrydaugh and Wolfe, architects, 460
Vunk, Francis C., House, 554

Waggoner, Daniel, House, 397
Wales, 41
Wallace and McAlister Buildings, 458
Wallingford, 91, 302
Walker, Evander P., Store, 417
Walker, Judge Jonathan Hoge, 399, 413
Walker House, 266
Walker Springhouse, 279
Waln, Isaac, House, 390
Walnut Street Bridge, 576
Walnut Street Theater, 390
Walnutport, 326, 579

Walter, Edwin L., architect, 492
Walter, George, 518
Walter, Thomas U., architect, 95, 96, 101, 108-10, 111, 258, 259, 283, 284, 285, 286, 339
Walter Kautz Farm, 518
Walters, Hugh, architect, 269
Wanamaker, John, 133; Store Building, 134, 135, 136, 146, 390
Wanamakers, 578
Wansey, George, 537
Wapwallopen, 105, 106, 513; Historical Society, 513
warehouses. *See* industrial, office buildings, and warehouses
Warminster, 263
Warner, James H., architect, 294
Warren, 541, 567
Warren County, 6, 534, 539, 565-67
Warrenpoint (house), 276
Warwick Furnace, 267
Washington, 427, 469, 470
Washington, George, 264, 269, 308, 319, 514. *See also* Valley Forge
Washington, George, School, 464
Washington and Jefferson College, 469; Administration Building, 470
Washington Bridge, 578
Washington County, 420, 423, 426, 427, 469, 470, 572
Washington Crossing, 264, 570; State Park, 264
Washington Crossing Bridge, Pittsburgh, 462, 569
Washington Hose Company, No. 10, 390
Washington Square Area Study, 390
Washington Square Presbyterian Church, 370
Washingtonville, 578
Waterford, 92, 559, 560; Academy (High School), 559
Waterford Covered Bridge, 560
Waterworks, Moravian, 323, 324
Watson, John Fanning, 38
Wattsburg, 560
Waverly, 509
Wawaset, 283
Wayne, 303; Railroad Station, 282
Wayne, Anthony, 279
Wayne, Gen. Anthony, 72, 279, 300, 319
Wayne, General Anthony, Inn, 319
Wayne, Isaac, 72, 279
Wayne County, 482, 488, 490, 492, 497, 498, 521-22, 580
Wayne family, 279
Waynesborough (house), 72, 73, 75, 279
Waynesburg, 570
Weaver, Clarence, engineer, 560
Webster, Richard J., 2, 19
Weccacoe Engine Company, No. 9, 391
Weiderich, Jacob, 534; House, 564

Weider's Crossing Stone House, 509
Weigley, William, House, 122
Weikert House, 239
Weissport, 509, 576
Wells, Joseph C., architect, 485
Wellsboro, 528
Welsh, 27, 30, 300, 485; Quakers, 206
Welsh Coach House and Stable, 391
Wenner, Howard W., Barn, 314
Wertenbaker, Thomas J., 35, 61
Wertz, Peter, 327
Wertz-Lashee House, 48, 327
West Arch Street Presbyterian Church, 114, 391
West Branch Canal, 404
West Brownsville, 420, 423, 424
West Chester, 30, 41, 82, 83, 96, 98, 113, 115, 220, 221, 223, 224, 283-87; State Normal School, State College, University, 286
West Chester Baptist Church, 115
West Chester Young Ladies Seminary, 286
West End-North Avenue Bridge, 575
West Grove, 287
West Marshall Street Bridge (Norristown), 578
West Middletown, 423
West Nanticoke, 513
West Newton, 472, 572
West Philadelphia, 87, 339, 341, 350
Western Pennsylvania Conservancy, 150, 467
Western Saving Fund Society of Philadelphia, 391
Westboro, 264
Westgate, Benjamin Boles, builder, 529, 553
Westgate-Brunner House, 529, 553
Westinghouse, George, 430
Westmont, 431, 465
Westmoreland County, 6, 147, 422, 441, 471, 572, 580
Westtown, 204, 287
Wetherill, John, 321
Wetherill, Joseph, House, 391
Wetherill, Samuel, 321
Wetherills Corner, 321
Wharton, Isaac, House, 391
Wharton, John, House, 391
Wharton, Joseph, House, 391
Wharton-Stewart House, 391
Wheatland, 91, 309
Wheeler, James, 511
White, Benjamin, engineer, 482
White, Canvass, engineer, 482
White, Bishop William, House, 87, 391
White Hall of Bristol College, 260
White Haven, 482

White Star Mills, 579
Whitehall Cement Company, 578
Whitehall Railroad Station, 317
Whitehorse, 288
Whitemarsh, 321
Whites Valley, 522
Whitman, Benjamin, House, 556
Whitten Building, 459
Wickerham Manor, 471
Widener, Peter A. B., House, 391
Wight, P. B., architect, 491
Wilkes-Barre, 69, 141, 475, 477, 478, 483, 485-86, 491, 497, 513, 530, 578
Wilkinsburg, 113, 463, 570
William Penn Tavern, 250
Williams, Joseph, Barn, 271
Williams-Hopkinson House, 391
Williamson, T. Roney, architect, 283, 284, 285, 488, 508
Williamsport, 116, 120, 154, 399, 400, 403, 578
Willibrand, Henry, Brewery, 417
Willis, William, mason, House, 36, 329-30
Willistown, 288
Willow Dale Farmhouse, 295
Willow Street, 46, 311, 570
Willowbank, 414
Wills, James J., Farm, 235
Wilmington, Del., 30
Wilmot, David, House, 497, 498, 521
Wilson, Adam, builder, 77-80
Wilson, E. Allen, 339
Wilson, James, 234
Wilson, Joseph M., architect, 317
Wilson House, 463
Wilson Springhouse, 279
Windber, 12, 468
Winder, William, 97; Houses, 391
Windrim, James H., architect, 308, 509
Windsor House, 567
Winemiller, Henry, builder, 235
Winemore, Phillip, House, 391
Winterthur Museum, 75
Wissahickon Creek, 321; Covered Bridge, 368; Viaduct, 579
Wissahickon Inn, 391
Wissahickon schist, 143, 335
Wister, Owen, 138
Wisteria Cottage, 569
Wister's Big House, 374
Wolff Barn, 330
Wollerton, Charles, House, 274
Womelsdorf, 257

Women's Christian Temperance Union, 564
Wood, Ferdinand, contractor, 288
Wood George, Houses, 391
Woodcock, 554; Methodist Church, 554
Woodford (house), 75, 391
Woodland Avenue: Cottage, 392; Car Barn, 392
Woodland Terrace, Philadelphia, 117; Area Study (houses), 392
Woodlands, 87, 88, 89, 392
Woodruff House, 99
Woods, Capt. John, House, 392
Woodstock (house), 301
Woodvale, 417
Woodville, 423
Woodward, Richard, House, 42, 43, 204, 206, 287
Woolfall-Huddell House, 392
Workman Place, 392
Works Projects Administration, 5
World War I, 341
World War II, 5, 341, 347
World's Columbian Exposition, 134
Wray House, 468
Wright, Frank Lloyd, 144, 148-50, 441, 466, 467
Wright, Col. H. B., House, 512
Wright, Joseph, House, 512
Wright School, 554
Wurlitzer Building, 457
Wyck, 392
Wyebrooke, 289
Wyeth, John Jr., 295
Wylie-Miller Barn, 470, 572
Wynnestay, 392
Wyoming County, 567, 580
Wyoming Institute, 514
Wyoming Massacre, 477
Wyoming, Pa., 514
Wyoming Presbyterian Church, 515
Wyoming Valley, 476, 481, 483, 512, 527, 528
Wysox, 551; Presbyterian Chuch, 530, 531, 551

Yale University, 349
Yankee-Pennamite Wars, 477
Yardley, 265
Yarnall, David, 280
Yarnall, Francis, 288
Yarnall and Cooper, builders, 286
Yarnall-Garrett House, 288
Yarnall-Hibberd House, 288
Yellow House, 257-58, 570; Hotel, 257
Yellow Springs Tavern, 268
Yoder, Jacob, House, 246

York, 30, 31, 34, 36, 114, 117, 121, 208, 328-29, 428, 581; Friends Meetinghouse, 62
York County, 7, 30, 31, 48, 67, 121, 327-30, 580; Courthouse, 330; Historical Society of, 329
Young Men's Christian Association: Philadelphia Chinatown, 367; Tidioute, 567
Yukon, 472

Zelienople, 465
Zeller, Heinrich, House, 45, 46-48, 49, 312, 570
Zinzendorf, Count Nicholas von, 245
Zion Evangelical Lutheran Church, Shawnee on Delaware, 517
Zion Lutheran Church, Philadelphia, 64
zoos, 383